HUGH JOHNSON'S

MODERN ENCYCLOPEDIA OF

Wine

— *4th Edition* —

Simon & Schuster

Hugh Johnson's Modern Encyclopedia of Wine, 4th Edition
Hugh Johnson

 SIMON & SCHUSTER
Rockerfeller Center
1230 Avenue of the Americas
New York, NY 10020

SIMON & SCHUSTER and colophon are
registered trademarks of Simon & Schuster, Inc.

The author and publisher would be grateful for any information
that will assist them in keeping future editions up to date. Although
all reasonable care has been taken in the preparation of this book,
neither the publisher nor the author can accept liability for any
consequences arising from the use thereof or from the information
contained therein.

Manufactured in Spain.

10 9 8 7 6 5 4 3 2 1

Library of Congress Cataloging-in-Publication Data is available.

ISBN 0-684-84589-X

CONTENTS

INTRODUCTION

For all its air of seamless and senior tradition, its classifications and regulations, nothing ever stands still in the world of wine. It is its constant fascination that every vintage is different, and then keeps changing in barrel or bottle with every year of maturity – and not by any means at a predictable pace. It has all the excitement of a moving target.

But much more is on the move than just the vintage quality and maturity. The ownership of vineyards and estates, laws and regulations, winemakers and vineyard managers are all in constant flux, and with them the quality of what they produce.

There is one constant in all this: the *terroir*, the soil – but more than that; the whole natural environment – in which the vines grow and the wine is made and cellared. *Terroir* is the ultimate factor in deciding both character and quality. Less often considered is the market. All abuzz the industry may be, but today wine-drinkers, their tastes, perceptions and demands have a major role in the ever-changing scene which must be added to all the other factors.

All these are potent reasons why a *Wine Companion* published in 1997 is a changed animal from its 1991 edition – let alone its first one in 1983. Then I compared recent changes with those that led the 19th-century writer Cyrus Redding to coin the term Modern Wine. To Redding the word 'modern' distinguished the wines of his time from those of the Ancients. His 'modern' methods are now old-fashioned. They created most of the wines now referred to as 'classics', but history has moved on again. Modern wine to us is the creation of the technology evolving in the last years of the 20th century – though perhaps the word technology is too brutal; the way the great winemakers proceed today could almost be described as scientific philosophy.

This modern world began with such radical discoveries as the effects of different temperatures on fermentation. (We should remember that the nature of fermentation itself was only discovered, by Pasteur, in the 1860s.) The ability to slow down fermentation by refrigeration was the first great breakthrough. Without it the New World of wine, essentially those regions whose Mediterranean climates had limited their potential in the past, would never have challenged the Old.

Their challenge, though, from the mid-1960s on, has made the Old World look again at its entrenched ideas, has made it modify, adapt and discard old dogma, to the point where the simple concept of Old World and new has only a geographical meaning. Old World and New, in fact, have met in what is becoming the global wine village.

Such neighbourliness carries its dangers. The first is the inclination to make the same sort of wine as everyone else – the principal trend of the 1980s, happily growing less fashionable in the '90s. Its most obvious manifestation was the near universal planting of Cabernet and Chardonnay. A more insidious one was the fashion of using oak, not as it was originally intended, for conditioning the wine ready for bottling, but actually to flavour it like a dash of ketchup. A generation grew up under the delusion that Chardonnay actually tastes of oak – while in reality if it does it is either badly made or not ready to drink.

This book is a portrait of this world of modern wine: its methods, its plant of vineyards and cellars, and above all its practitioners. It is designed to be a practical companion in choices that become more varied and challenging all the time. Like any portrait, it tries to capture the reality of a single moment. The moment is past as soon as the shutter has clicked. The closer the focus and the greater the detail the more there is to change and grow out of date. Yet the detailed record of a single season in wine's long history is as close to reality as it is possible to get. This edition has been revised and updated to reflect the reality of 1997.

To be a practical companion I have tried to give the essential information about each wine country and wine region you are likely to encounter or which is worth making an effort to know. I have shunned a catalogue of the legislation that surrounds the wine business increasingly each year. It casts little light and does nothing to add to the pleasure of our subject – which is, after all, either a pleasure or a failure.

The essentials, it seems to me, are the names and as far as possible (which is not very far) descriptions of the world's worthwhile wines, who makes them, how much there is of them, how well they keep, and where they fit into our lives – which are too short, alas, to do justice to anything like all of them. You will also find answers to the recurring questions about grape varieties, production methods and the ways of the wine trade. You will not find a historical survey or a technical treatise; just enough information, I hope, to indicate essential differences and the trends of change in winemaking today.

The heart of the book is arranged by countries on the same system as my annual *Pocket Wine*, with the Index as the alphabetical alternative to find a name you cannot immediately place in a national or regional context. The *Companion* is updated far less frequently than its annual pocket-sized stablemate, leaving to its more ephemeral editions the questions of current vintages, their quality and maturity. Both will be much clearer if you possess the current (fourth) edition of *The World Atlas of Wine*, in which the regions are graphically displayed.

Each section gives the essential background information about the wines in question, then lists with succinct details the principal producers. In a few well-trodden areas the lists make themselves. In most others a complete catalogue would be as unhelpful as it would be unmanageable. My method then has been to consult first my own experience, then the advice of friends, local brokers and officials whom I have reason to respect. I have corresponded with as many producers as possible, asking them specific questions about their properties or firms, their methods, products and philosophies. Often, unfortunately, the exigencies of space have forced me to leave out good producers I would have liked to include. In most countries I have also employed intermediaries to research, interview and pass me their findings. I have tasted as many of the wines described as I could (which is why some specific tasting notes go back ten years or more).

The enjoyment of wine is a very personal thing. Yet if you love it, and spend your life among other wine lovers, you will find a remarkable consensus about which wines have the power to really thrill and satisfy us. Prejudice and narrow-mindedness have no place; preferences are what it is all about. I have not tried to hide mine among the fabulous variety described in this book.

MODERN WINE

At its simplest, wine is made by crushing grapes and allowing the yeast naturally present on the skins to convert the sugar in their juice to alcohol. This is the process of fermentation. No more human intervention is needed than to separate the juice from the skins by pressing. Crushed and fermented like this, white grapes make white wine and red grapes red.

The art of the winemaker can be equally simply expressed. It is to choose good grapes, to carry out the crushing, fermenting and pressing with scrupulous care and hygiene, and to prepare the wine for drinking by cleaning it of yeasts and all foreign bodies. For some sorts of wine this entails ageing it as well; for others the quicker it gets to market the better.

These are the eternal verities of wine and winemaking, well understood for hundreds of years. They can be carried to perfection with no modern scientific knowledge or equipment whatever – with luck. Great wines came to be made in the places where nature, on balance, was kindest. Given a ripe crop of grapes in a healthy state, the element that determined success more than any other was the temperature of the cellar during and after the fermentation. France (but not the south), Germany, the Alps, Hungary, had these conditions. The Mediterranean and places with a similar climate did not.

If there is one innovation that has made the most difference between old and modern winemaking it is refrigeration. Refrigeration and air conditioning have added the whole zone of Mediterranean climate to the world of potentially fine wine.

But technology has advanced on a broad front. Every aspect of grape-growing and wine-making is now under a degree of control undreamed of before. These controls are now common practice in almost all the bigger and newer plants where wine is made. Its scientific basis is widely understood even in traditional areas and among small properties.

One California professor confesses that winemakers now have more possible controls than they know how to use. In leading-edge California white-winemaking is so clinically perfected that one of the main problems is deciding what sort of wine you want to make.

On the other hand, as Professor Peynaud of Bordeaux University has said, 'The ultimate goal of modern oenology is to avoid having to treat the wine at all.'

The following pages summarize some of the more important modern techniques and currently held views on the many factors that affect the qualities of wine. They follow the processes of grape-growing and winemaking more or less sequentially so that they can be read as an account or referred to as a glossary. Some processes apply to white wine only, some to red, some to both. The stages of making wine are shown diagramatically on pages 30–32.

THE VINE

A wine grower in the Clos de Vougeot has no choice about what grapes to plant. It has been a sea of Pinot Noir for centuries. Nothing else is permitted. A wine grower in the Médoc has an important choice to make: half a dozen varieties within the family of the Cabernets are allowed. The emphasis he places on the harsher or the smoother varieties is the basis of his house style.

A wine grower in the New World is free as the air. His own taste and his view of the market are his only guide. This choice, and the debates it has started, has made all wine lovers far more grape-conscious than ever before. Not only are more wines named by their grape varieties, but this very fact has made the clear ascendancy of some varieties over others public knowledge.

What is a variety? It is a selection from among the infinity of forms a plant takes by natural mutation. In the basic economy of viticulture a wine grower looks first for fruitfulness, hardiness and resistance to disease in his plants. Then he looks for the ability to ripen its fruit before the end of the warm autumn weather. Lastly he looks for flavour and character.

There has been plenty of time since the discovery of wine to try out and develop different varieties. In the botanical genus *Vitis*, the vine, there are more than 20 species. The wine vine is only one, a wild woodland plant of Europe and eastern Asia, *Vitis vinifera*. It was scrambling through the treetops of France long before the idea of crushing and fermenting its grapes was imported, via Greece, from the Near East.

Nobody knows the precise origins of any of the varieties of vine that were developed locally in France, Italy, Spain, along the Danube and in the rest of wine-growing Europe. But the assumption is that they started as selections by trial from local vine varieties, possibly inter-breeding with imported ones of special quality. In Germany, for instance, the Romans made the brilliant discovery of a variety with habits perfectly adapted to the cool northern climate: the Riesling, or its ancestor. Selections, adaptations or descendants from it have become all the other grapes in the German style.

There are now 4,000 or more named varieties of wine grape on earth. Perhaps 40 have really recognizable flavour and character. Of these a bare dozen have moved into international circulation, and the dozen can be narrowed again to those that have personalities so definite (and so good) that they form the basis of a whole international category of wine. They are the principal red and white grapes of Bordeaux, the same of Burgundy, the Riesling of Germany, the Gewürztraminer of Alsace, the Syrah of the Rhône and the grandfather of them all, the Muscat.

Today there is an increasing temptation to plant the champion grapes everywhere. It is a difficult argument between quality and that most precious attribute of wine – variety.

CLASSIC GRAPES

Riesling

(Johannisberg Riesling, Rhine Riesling, White Riesling). The classic grape of Germany disputes with Chardonnay the title of the world's best white grape. The Riesling produces wines of crisp fruity acidity and transparent clarity of flavour. Even its smell is refreshing. In Germany it ranges from pale green, fragile and sharp on the Mosel to golden, exotically luscious wines, especially in the Rheinpfalz, It is remarkably versatile in warmer climates; perhaps at its most typical in Alsace, becoming more buxom in California and Australia where it ages to its unique mature bouquet of lemons and petrol more rapidly.

Chardonnay

The white burgundy grape makes fatter, more winey and potent-feeling wine than Riesling, less aromatic when young, maturing to a rich and broad, sometimes buttery, sometimes smoky or musky smell or flavour. The finesse of Blanc de Blancs champagne, the mineral smell of Chablis, the nuttiness of Meursault, the ripe fruit smells of Napa Valley wines show its versatility. It is adapting superbly to Australia, Oregon, New Zealand, northern Italy.

Cabernet Sauvignon

The Médoc grape. Most recognizable and most versatile of red grapes, apparently able to make first-class wine in any warm soil in just about any wine-growing region of the world. Small, dark, rather late-ripening berries give intense colour, strong blackcurrant and sometimes herby aroma and much tannin, which makes it the slowest wine to mature. It needs age in oak and bottle and is best of all blended with Merlot etc, as in Bordeaux.

Pinot Noir

Gerwürztraminer

Pinot Noir

The red burgundy and champagne grape. So far apparently less adaptable to foreign vineyards, where the fine Burgundian balance is hard to achieve. Sweeter, less tannic, richer-textured than Cabernet and therefore enjoyable far younger. Rarely blended except in Champagne. It has proved successful in Oregon, California and New Zealand.

Syrah or Shiraz

Widespread and the great grape of the Rhône, blended in Châteauneuf-du-Pape. Makes tannic, peppery dark wine which can mature superbly. Very important as Shiraz in Australia. Increasingly grown in the Midi, both for AC wines and *vins de pays* and in South Africa and California.

Gewürztraminer

The beginner's grape for its forthright spicy smell and flavour. Once almost unique to Alsace; now spreading rapidly.

Sauvignon Blanc

The name derives from *sauvage*, wild, which could well describe its grassy or gooseberry flavour. Widespread in Bordeaux, where it is blended with Sémillon for both sweet and dry wines, but most characteristic in Sancerre. A successful transplant to the New World, New Zealand in particular. It can be light and aromatic, or heavier like Chardonnay.

Muscat

(Muscat Blanc à Petits Grains, Moscato Canelli)

The finest of the ancient tribe of Muscats is the small white used for sweet *vins doux naturels* from the south of France and for Asti Spumante. Most dry Muscats of Alsace come from a more regular yielding variety, Muscat d'Ottonel.

PRINCIPAL GRAPE VARIETIES IN EUROPE

FRANCE

All eight classic grapes are grown to perfection in France. The Muscat, Riesling and Gewürztraminer are long-established imports, but the remaining five, the reds and whites of Burgundy, the Rhône and Bordeaux, appear to be natives of France, representing an eastern and a western tradition; that of the Alps and that of the Atlantic. (They meet on the Loire).

Nobody can say with any confidence how many other grapes make up this great tradition: a single variety may have four or five different names in different areas quite close together – or indeed the grape may be a local strain and not quite the same variety. These local characters range from such common plants as the red Carignan of the Midi, to the delicate white Viognier, once restricted to the Rhône but now being more widely used for *vins de pays*, and such rare ones as the white Tresallier (limited to one tiny zone in the upper reaches of the Loire).

Shiraz

Red grape varieties

Abouriou grown in the Côtes du Marmandais in the southwest of France.
Aleatico red Muscat variety of Corsica, makes a wine of the same name.
Alicante synonym of Grenache.
Alicante-Bouschet prolific variety of southern table-wine vineyards.
Aramon high-yielding southern table-wine variety.
Aspiran an old variety of the Languedoc.
Auxerrois synonym of Malbec in Cahors.
Bouchet synonym of Cabernet Franc in St-Emilion.
Braquet main variety of Bellet, near Nice.
Brocol synonym of Fer in Gaillac.

Cabernet Franc high-quality cousin of Cabernet Sauvignon used in Bordeaux (esp. St-Emilion) and in the Loire.
CABERNET SAUVIGNON see p. 10.
Carignan leading bulk-wine producer of the Midi; harmless but dull. Greatly improved by carbonic maceration.
Carmenère old Bordeaux variety.
César tannic traditional variety of Irancy (Yonne).
Cinsaut (or **Cinsault**) prominent southern Rhône variety, that is used in Châteauneuf-du-Pape, etc, and the Midi.
Cot synonym of Malbec in the Loire.
Duras local Gaillac variety.
Fer (or **Ferservadou**) used in several wines of the southwest, notably Marcillac.
Fuelle Noir (or **Folle Noire**) Bellet variety.
Gamay Beaujolais grape: juicy, light and fragrant. Also grown in the Loire esp. Touraine, and in central France.
Grenache powerful but pale red used in Châteauneuf-du-Pape for rosés (eg Tavel) and dessert wines in Roussillon.
Grolleau (or **Groslot**) common Loire red used in, for example, Anjou Rosé.
Jurançon Noir Gaillac (Tarn) grape – not used in Jurançon.
Malbec important variety now fading from the best Bordeaux but central to Cahors.
Mataro synonym of Mourvèdre.
Merlot essential element in fine Bordeaux; the dominant grape of Pomerol.
Meunier (or **Pinot Meunier**) inferior 'dusty-leaved' version of Pinot Noir 'tolerated' in Champagne.
Mondeuse chief red of Savoie.
Mourvèdre key variety of Bandol in Provence – one of the improving *cépages améliorateurs* of the Midi.
Negrette variety peculiar to Frontonnais.
Nielluccio Corsican var. Possibly related to Sangiovese.
Noirien synonym of Pinot Noir.
Petit Verdot high-quality subsidiary grape of Bordeaux.
Pineau d'Aunis local to the Loire Valley, esp. Anjou.
PINOT NOIR see p. 10.
Portugais Bleu once widespread in the south of France, now declining in importance.
Poulsard Jura variety.
Pressac St-Emilion synonym for Malbec.
Sciacerello Corsican variety.
SYRAH see p. 10.
Tannat tannic variety of the southwest, esp. Madiran.
Tempranillo Spanish (Rioja) variety grown in the Midi.
Trousseau majority grape in Jura reds but inferior to Poulsard.

White grape varieties

Aligoté secondary Burgundy grape of high acidity. Wines for drinking young.
Altesse Savoie variety. Wines are sold as 'Roussette'.
Arruffiac Béarnais variety (Pacherenc du Vic Bilh)
Auvergnat (or **Auvernat**) Loire term for the Pinot family.
Baroque used in Béarn for Tursan.
Beaunois synonym of Chardonnay at Chablis.
Beurot synonym in Burgundy of Pinot Gris.

Chardonnay

Blanc Fumé synonym of Sauvignon Blanc at Pouilly-sur-Loire.

Blanquette synonym of Mauzac.

Bourboulenc Midi (Minervois, La Clape) variety, also goes into (red) Châteauneuf-du-Pape .

Camaralet Jurançon variety

CHARDONNAY see p. 10.

Chasselas neutral variety used in Savoie, Pouilly-sur-Loire and Alsace.

Clairette common neutral-flavoured Midi grape, also makes sparkling Rhône Clairette de Die.

Colombard minor Bordelais grape most common in the Côtes de Gascogne. Also distilled for Cognac and Armagnac.

Courbu Jurançon variety (alias Sarrat).

Folle Blanche formerly the chief Cognac grape, also grown in Bordeaux and Brittany.

Frontignan synonym of Ugni Blanc in Blaye, Bordeaux.

Gamay Blanc synonym of Chardonnay in the Jura.

GEWÜRZTRAMINER see p. 10.

Gros Manseng one of the main grapes of Jurançon.

Gros Plant synonym of Folle Blanche in the western Loire.

Jacquère the grape of Apremont and Chignin in Savoie.

Jurançon Blanc minor Cognac variety (not in Jurançon)

Klevner name used for Pinot Blanc in Alsace.

Len-de-l'el (Loin de l'Oeil) variety used in Gaillac.

Maccabeu (or **Maccabeo**) Catalan variety used in Roussillon for dessert 'VDN'. Malvoisie synonym of Bourboulenc in the Languedoc, of Torbato in Roussillon and Vermintino in Corsica.

Marsanne with Roussanne the white grape of Hermitage (northern Rhône).

Mauzac used in Blanquette de Limoux and Gaillac.

Morillon synonym of Chardonnay.

Muscadelle minor, slightly Muscat-flavoured variety used in Sauternes.

Muscadet gives its name to the wine of the western Loire. Also called Melon de Bourgogne.

MUSCAT see. p. 10.

Ondenc Gaillac variety.

Petit Manseng southwestern variety used in Jurançon etc.

Petite Sainte Marie synonym of Chardonnay in Savoie.

Picpoul synonym of Folle Blanche in Armagnac, the southern Rhône and the Midi (Picpoul de Pinet).

Pineau de la Loire synonym in the Loire of Chenin Blanc (not a Pinot).

Pinot Blanc closely related to Pinot Noir, grown in Burgundy, Champagne and Alsace.

Pinot Gris (Tokay d'Alsace) a mutation of the Pinot Noir, widespread in Alsace.

Piquepoul *see* Picpoul.

RIESLING see p. 10.

Rolle Italian Vermentino in Provence.

Romorantin grown only at Cheverny on the Loire; makes dry, often sharp wine.

Roussanne (with Marsanne) makes white Hermitage.

Roussette synonym of Altesse in Savoie.

Sacy minor variety of Champagne and the Yonne.

St-Emilion synonym of Ugni Blanc in Cognac.

SAUVIGNON BLANC see p. 10.

Savagnin the 'yellow wine' grape of Château-Châlon (Jura); related to Gewürztraminer.

Sylvaner the workhorse light-wine grape of Alsace.

Traminer see Gewürztraminer.

Tresallier variety of the extreme upper Loire (St-Pourçain-sur-Sioule) now fading.

Ugni Blanc common Midi grape; Italy's Trebbiano; 'St-Emilion' in Cognac.

Vermentino Italian grape known in Provence as Rolle; possibly the Malvoisie of Corsica.

Viognier rare aromatic grape of Condrieu in the northern Rhône. Also fashionable in the Midi, especially as a varietal *vin de pays*.

ITALY

Italy's grape catalogue is probably the longest of all. With wine-growing so universal a factor of Italian life, uninterrupted for millennia before the phylloxera, local selection has blurred the origins and relationships of many varieties beyond recall. Is the fish caught off Tunisia and called by an Arab name the same as a similar one caught in the Adriatic and called by a name peculiar to the Romagna? Italian grapes are scarcely less slippery a subject.

In general their selection has been on the grounds of productivity and good health, along with adaptability to the soil and reliable ripening, rather than great qualities of flavour of ability to age. The mass of Italian grapes are therefore sound rather than inspiring; their flavours muted or neutral. The only international classic to (maybe) come from Italy is the (Gewürz) Traminer, from the South Tyrol.

But once you start to list the exceptions, the Italian grapes with personality and potentially excellent quality, it does seem strange that more of them have not yet made a real name for themselves in the world. The Nebbiolo, the Barbera, the Teroldego, the Brunello, the Montepulciano, the Aglianico are reds with much to offer. There are fewer first-class whites, but Cortese, Greco, Tocai, Verdicchio and Vernaccia all make original contributions, and the Moscato of Piedmont, while not exclusively Italian, is a very Italian interpretation of the most ancient of grapes.

More and more is being heard of Cabernet, Merlot, Pinot Bianco and even Chardonnay and Rhine Riesling. The northeast is now almost as international in its ampelography as any of the wine areas of the New World. The appearance of Cabernet and Chardonnay in Chianti in recent years is an important sign of changes in the wind.

The central question over the future of Italian wine is how far she will defend her traditions (which is the purpose of the DOC legislation) in sticking to her indigenous grapes, and how far she will bow to the international trend – as she is tending to do in winemaking techniques.

The world is beginning to appreciate just what variety Italy has to offer. She will do well to develop her native flavours to the full. They include as wide a range as the wines of any country – France included.

There is no general rule on the mention of grape varieties on labels: local custom dictates whether the wine is labelled by place, grape or a name unrelated to either. With the current increase in variety consciousness, it seems likely that producers will make more of the grape varieties in future – at least on wines destined for export.

Red grape varieties

Aglianico source of full-bodied Taurasi in Campania and Aglianico del Vulture in Basilicata.
Aleatico Muscat-flavoured grape used for dark dessert wines in Latium, Apulia and elsewhere.
Barbera dark, acidic Piedmont variety widely grown in the northwest.
Bombino Nero used in Apulia's Castel del Monte rosato.
Bonarda minor variety widespread in Lombardy and Piedmont.
Brachetto makes pleasant, fizzy Piedmont wines.
Brunello di Montalcino a noble strain of Tuscany's Sangiovese.
Cabernet (especially **Franc**) widespread in the NE: increasing elsewhere.
Calabrese source of Sicilian DOC Cerasuolo light reds.
Cannonau leading dark var. of Sardinia for DOC wines.
Carignano (French Carignan), prominent in Sardinia.
Cesanese good Latium red.
Chiavennasca Nebbiolo in Valtellina, N. Lombardy.
Corvina Veronese main grape of Valpolicella, Recioto.
Croatina much used in Lombardy's Oltropo Pavese.
Dolcetto low-acid Piedmont var., source of several DOCs.
Freisa Piedmont variety, makes sweet, often fizzy wines.
Gaglioppo source of most Calabrian reds, incl. Ciro.
Grignolino makes light, pleasant wines around Asti in Piedmont.
Guarnaccia red variety of Campania, esp. Ischia.
Lagrein grown in Alto Adige for faintly bitter reds and dark rosés.
Lambrusco prolific source of Emilia's effervescent wines.

Malbec seen occasionally in Apulia and Venezia.
Malvasia Nera makes sweet, fragrant, sometimes sparkling DOC reds in Piedmont; also a fine dessert wine in Apulia.
Marzemino dark grape grown in Trentino and Lombardy.
Merlot Bordeaux native widely grown in Italy, esp. in the NE.
Monica makes Sardinian DOC reds.
Montepulciano dominant dark variety of Abruzzi; Molise.
Nebbiolo the great grape of Piedmont, the base of Barolo, Barbaresco, Gattinara, etc. Its wine varies from smoothly fruity to biting black, ageing superbly.
Negroamaro potent Apulian variety of the Salento peninsula.
Nerello Mascalese Sicilian grape, for Etna reds and rosés.
Petit Rouge used in some Valle d'Aosta reds.
Piedirosso (or **Per'e Palummo**) features in Campania reds.
Pinot Nero Burgundy's Pinot Noir (see p. 10), grown in much of NE Italy.
Primitivo Apulian grape, said to be Zinfandel.
Raboso worthy Veneto native.
Refosco source of dry, full-bodied Friuli DOC reds. Known as Mondeuse in France.
Rossese fine Ligurian variety, makes DOC at Dolceacqua.
Sangiovese mainstay of Chianti and one of Italy's most widely planted vines.
Schiava widespread in Alto Adige.
Spanna synonym for Nebbiolo.
Teroldego unique to Trentino, makes Teroldego Rotaliano.
Tocai Rosso (or **Tocai Nero**) makes DOC red in Veneto's Colli Berici.
Uva di Troia main grape of several DOC wines in N. Apulia.
Vespolina often blended with Nebbiolo in E. Piedmont.

Nebbiolo

White grape varieties

Albana Romagna grape, makes dry and semi-sweet wines.
Arneis Piedmont variety that is enjoying a revival.
Biancolella native of Ischia.
Blanc de Valdigne source in Valle d'Aosta of Blanc de Morgex, Blanc de la Salle.

Bombino Bianco main grape of Apulia's San Severo
bianco; in Bruzzi, known as Trebbiano d'Abruzzo.
Bosco in Liguria, the main ingredient of Cinqueterre.
Catarratto widely grown in W. Sicily; used in Marsala,
Bianco d'Alcamo etc.
CHARDONNAY grown in Trentino-Alto Adige, Veneto and
Friuli and now used for *vino da tavola* in Tuscany, Umbria,
Piedmont and elsewhere.
Cortese used in S. Piedmont's finest whites: found also in
Lombardy's Oltropo Pavese.
Fiano in Campania makes Fiano di Avellino.
Forastera partners Biancolella in Ischia bianco.
Garganega main grape of Soave.
Grechetto variety of Umbria, important in Orvieto.
Greco Campania's best white.
Grillo figures, usually with Catarratto, in Marsala.
Inzolia used in Sicilian whites, e.g. Marsala and Corvo
bianco.
Malvasia common for both dry and sweet wines, esp. in
Latium (for Frascati etc.)
MOSCATO (see p. 10) widespread in sparkling wines (eg Asti
Spumante) and dessert wines (eg. the Moscatos of Sicily).
Müller-Thurgau increasing in Friuli, Trentino-Alto Adige.
Nuragus ancient Sardinian grape.
Picolit Friuli source of Italy's most expensive dessert wines.
Pigato grown only in SW Liguria; makes good table wines.
Pinot Bianco Burgundy's Pinot Blanc, grown all over N.
Italy. Weissburgunder in Alto Adige.
Prosecco prominent in Veneto, mainly for sparkling wines.
Rheinriesling see Riesling Renano.
Riesling Italico not a true Riesling, probably native to NE
Italy. Used in DOCs.
RIESLING RENANO Rhine Riesling, superior to Riesling Italico.
SAUVIGNON BLANC grown in parts of the northeast
for DOC varietals.
Tocai Friulano used for DOC whites in Lombardy and
Veneto as well as in its native Friuli.
Traminer native of Alto Adige.
Trebbiano d'Abruzzo see Bombino Bianco.
Verdeca Apulian grape used in southern DOC whites.
Verdicchio main light grape of the Marches.
Verduzzo Friulian variety used also in the Veneto for both
dry and dessert wines.
Vermentino source of DOC white in Sardinia and good
table wines in Liguria.
Vernaccia di Oristano in Sardinia makes a sherry-like
dessert wine.
Vernaccia di San Gimignano ancient Tuscany variety,
wine of the same name.

GERMANY

The international reputation of German wine for a unique
effect of flowery elegance is based on one grape alone: the
Riesling. But the widespread use of the Riesling as we know
it is probably no more than two or three hundred years old.
Germany has several old varieties of local importance which

Riesling

continue to hold their own. More significantly, her vine
breeders have been struggling for a century to produce a
new vine that offers Riesling quality without its inherent disadvantage – ripening so late in the autumn that every vintage
is a cliffhanger. The centenary of the first important Riesling
cross (with Silvaner) was celebrated in 1982. The past 100
years have seen its fruit, the Müller-Thurgau, become
Germany's most popular grape, with 24,400 acres planted.
(Riesling is second, with 22,800 acres).

Yet none of the new varieties, not even Müller-Thurgau,
has supplanted Riesling in the best and warmest vineyards.
None has achieved more than either a sketch or a caricature
of its brilliant balance and finesse. Nor have any survived
such ultimate tests of hardiness as January 1979, when the
temperature dropped by 40 degrees, to –20˚F (–29˚C) in 24
hours. Thousands of vines were killed. Riesling survived.

Over 80% of the German vineyard is white. Of the 18%
that is red, Spätburgunder (Pinot Noir) is marginally more
widely planted than the inferior Portugieser, and more than
twice as common as Trollinger.

Grape varieties

Bacchus a new early-ripening cross of (Silvaner x Riesling)
x Müller-Thurgau. Spicy but rather soft wines, best as
Ausleses, frequently used as Süssreserve.
Ehrenfelser (Riesling x Silvaner). A good new cross,
between Müller-Thurgau and Riesling in quality.
Elbling once the chief grape of the Mosel, now only grown
high upriver. Neutral and acidic but clean and good in
sparkling wine.
Faber Weissburgunder x Müller-Thurgau, with a certain fol-
lowing in Rheinhessen and the Nahe.
GEWÜRZTRAMINER see p.10.
Gutedel south Baden name for the Chasselas, or Swiss
Fendant. Light, refreshing but short-lived wine.
Huxelrebe (Gutedel x Courtiller musqué). A prolific new
variety, very aromatic, with good sugar and acidity. Popular
in Rheinhessen.

Morio-Muskat It is hard to believe that this early-ripening cross of Silvaner and Weissburgunder has no Muscat blood. The wine it makes in Rheinpfalz and Rheinhessen is good but often too blatant and best blended with something more neutral (e.g. Müller-Thurgau).

Optima (Silvaner x Riesling x Müller-Thurgau). An improvement on Bacchus, particularly in Rheinpfalz. Delicately spicy.

Ortega (Müller-Thurgau x Siegerrebe). Very early ripening, aromatic and spicy with good balance. On trial on the Mosel and in Franken.

Perle (Gewürztraminer x Müller-Thurgau). A very aromatic new cross under trial in Franken.

Reichensteiner Müller-Thurgau x (Madeleine Angevine x Calabreser Fröhlich). A Euro-cross, slightly better for both sugar and acid than Müller-Thurgau.

Riesling see p. 10.

Scheurebe the second cross (Silvaner x Riesling) to become celebrated, now well established (Rheinhessen, Rheinpfalz) for highly aromatic, often unsubtle wine. At its best when made sweet.

Silvaner a late ripener like the Riesling, also badly affected by drought in light or thin soils, steadily giving ground to Müller-Thurgau and others. Scarcely noble, but at its best (in Franken and Rheinhessen) the true yeoman: blunt, trustworthy, with unsuspected depths.

Weissburgunder (Pinot Blanc) makes good fresh full-bodied wine in Baden.

SPAIN AND PORTUGAL

Spain and Portugal have been net exporters, rather than importers, of grape varieties. A few of the international varieties have been planted, but they have certainly not yet taken hold in a way that radically alters the wine, whereas

Cabernet Sauvignon

their grapes exported to the world include the Palomino (to California, South Africa and Australia), the Verdelho (to Australia) and, probably, the Carignan, much the most widespread red grape of the South of France.

Traditionally, there are few 'varietals' in Spain and Portugal, although, as elsewhere, this is starting to change. Most wines contain proportions of at least three grapes, balanced for their qualities. The most notable exceptions are the four varietals of Madeira: Sercial, Verdelho, Bual and Malmsey.

Red grape varieties

Agua Santa early-ripening red of Bairrada, giving stronger wine than the Baga.

Alvarelhao Dão variety, also grown for port.

Azal red grape with high tartaric acid, used for *vinho verde*.

Bastardo a rather pale and low-acid but aromatic and well-balanced grape used for port and in Dão.

Baga dark, tannic, potentially noble grape of Bairrada. Gives berry-fruit flavours.

Borraçal red *vinho verde* grape providing high malic acidity.

Cabernet Sauvignon (see p. 10) increasingly being planted in Spain, eg in Penedès for Torres' Mas la Plana, in Navarra by Sarria, at Vega Sicilia in Ribera del Duero and by Riscal in Rioja along with many others.

Cariñena Carignan in France, originated in Cariñena (Aragnón) but now more grown in Catalonia.

Castelão a minor Bairrada red, soft and neutral.

Cencibel synonym in La Mancha and Valdepeñas for Tempranillo.

Garnacha Tinta used in Rioja Baja for powerful, if pale Riojas, also Penedès, and Navarra where it dominates. Synonym French Grenache Noir.

Graciano the most 'elegant' and aromatic of Rioja grapes, gives quick-maturing wine.

Jaen a constituent of red Dão.

Mazuelo a Riojan red grape, possibly a synonym for Cariñena.

Mencia used in Léon and Galicia for light reds.

Monastrell a widely grown red of good colour and texture, especially in Penedès, the Levante and Valdepeñas.

Mourisco Semente minor grape of port and N of Portugal.

Pinot Noir (see p. 10) Torres grows Pinot for his red Santa Digna. Also found in Navarra.

Ramisco the tannic, blue-black secret of Colares. Needs v. long ageing.

Samsó Penedès variety.

Souzão deeply coloured and excellent port grape.

Tempranillo fine, aromatic and early ripening and basis for Rioja. Grown throught Spain under a variety of synonyms.

Tinto Aragonés a form of Garnacha Tinta; one of the grapes of Vega Sicilia.

Tinta Pinheira minor Bairrada varity; pale, low acid but alcoholic.

Tintorera one of the Valdepeñas grapes.

Touriga Naçional deep-coloured, big-yielding port variety, also used in Dão.

Ull de Llebre Penedès synonym for Tempranillo.

Vinhão *Vinho verde* red grown for its relatively high alcohol.

White grape varieties

Airen see Lairén.

Albariño the best Galician variety for clean, dry, often *pétillant* whites, also grown in Portugal for *vinho verde*.

Albillo used, with red grapes, in Vega Sicilia.

Arinto used for lemony white Dão and Bairrada and to make the rare, dry Bucelas and sweet Carcavelos.

Barcelos recommended white Dão variety.

Bical fragrant and fine Bairrada white, complementary to the sharper Arinto.

Bual sweet Madeira grape, with luscious flavours, also used in Carcavelos and Alentejo.

CHARDONNAY (see p. 10) becoming more established in Spain with wines from Penedès, Somontano and elsewhere. Also the occasional Portuguese example.

Gouveio minor white-port variety.

Lairén (alias Airen) the main white grape of Valdepeñas and La Mancha.

Listàn synonym of Palomino.

Macabeo synonym in Catalonia of Viura. For sparkling wines.

Malvasía important white grape in port, Rioja, Navarra, Catalonia and the Canary Islands.

Maria Gomes the principal white grape of Bairrada.

Moscatel widespread sweet wine grape.

Pansa grown in Alella. Synonym of Xarel-lo of Penedès.

Parellada used in Penedès for delicately fruity whites and sparklers.

Pedro Ximénez grown for blending in Jerez, Málaga, and the principal in Montilla: dried, it adds intense sweetness and colour.

Traminer used (with Moscatel) by Torres for Viña Esmeralda.

Verdelho white Dão variety, better known in Madeira.

Viura the principal grape of white Rioja, also Navarra. Alias Macabeo.

Xarel-lo Catalan grape, important in Penedès.

Zalema main variety in *vino generoso* of Huelva, being replaced by Palomino.

SOUTHEAST & CENTRAL EUROPE

The grape varieties of southeast Europe and the countries fringing the Black Sea are as old as those of the west. The Romans colonized the Danube at the same time as the Rhine. Under the Austro-Hungarian Empire the only wines to reach international fame were those of Hungary, led by Tokay. The local grapes, therefore, evolved slowly on their own course making their own sort of spicy, often sweetish whites and dry tannic reds.

The eastern fringes of the Alps in Slovenia, Austria and north into Bohemia (Czech Republic) are essentially white wine country, dominated by their local low-key namesake of the Riesling (variously known as Italian, Welsch, Olasz or Laski) and Austria by its sappy, vigorous Grüner Veltliner. Hungary is most prolific in native white grapes of strength and style, led by the Furmint of Tokay. Its red, the Kadarka, is widespread in the Balkans, more recently joined by the Pinot Noir and Gamay. Warmer climates near the Adriatic and Black Seas have favoured reds and sweet whites. The last two decades or so, however, have seen an invasion of classics from the west.

Ezerjó white variety making fine wine at Mór, in Hungary. Also a bulk producer from the Serbian border region with Hungary and Romania. Makes one of the best dry whites of Hungary.

Furmint the classic white grape of Tokay. Known as Sipon in Slovenia.

Hárslevelü second main variety for making Tokay. Full and aromatic.

Kadarka the common red grape of Hungary but widespread throughout the region, producing stiff spicy red, built for ageing. Known as Gamza in Bulgaria.

Kékfrankos (Austrian Blaufränkisch) more reliable than Kadarka and hence being planted as a substitute, esp. in Hungary.

Kéknyelü white low-yielding variety of Hungary's vineyards north of Lake Balaton making concentrated golden-green wines.

Kraski Teran the Refosco of Italy, makes crisp tangy red in Slovenia.

Léanyka delicate dry white esp. from Eger in the north of Hungary.

Lunel (or **Yellow**) **Muscat**. Sargamuskotály in Hungarian. One of the four grape varieties permitted for use in Tokay.

Mavrud makes Bulgaria's best red, dark and plummy, can last 20 years.

Mézesfehér Hungarian white grape ('little honey') but less grown now.

Misket indigenous to Bulgaria, both red and white often used to make a fatter blend

Muscat Ottonel the East European Muscat, a speciality of Romania.

Olaszrizling Hungarian name for Riesling Italico. Widely planted. Grasevina in Slovenia and Croatia.

Oremus cross between Furmint and Bouvier, authorized for use in Tokay since 1994.

Plovdina dark-skinned red grape, native to Macedonia.

Prokupac red grape of Serbia blended to make Zupsko Crno, and much used to make rosé.

Rebula (or **Ribolla**) an Italian export which makes slightly creamy yellow wine in Slovenia.

Rkatziteli Russian variety for strong white wines, preferred sweet by local market. Also used in NE Bulgaria.

Saperavi variety indigenous to Georgia, giving intense, peppery wines akin to Syrah.

Smederevka chief white of Serbia and Kosovo for fresh dry whites.

Szürkebarát a form of Pinot Gris grown in the Badacsonyi region of Hungary for rich, not necessarily sweet, wine.

Vranac makes vigorous reds in Montenegro.

Zilavka white variety with faint apricot flavour, e.g. from southern Serbia.

Zweigelt red grape making deep-coloured pleasantly scented spicy wine, esp. in Austria.

IN THE VINEYARD

Grape Varieties

The choice of grape varieties is the most fundamental decision of all. See pages 10–16.

Source of Grapes

There are arguments both for and against growing your own grapes. Those in favour are that you have total control over the management of the vineyard and thus decide the quality of the grapes. The argument against is that an independent winemaker can pick and choose among the best grapes of specialist growers in different areas.

In France and throughout most of Europe almost all quality wine (except for most champagne) is 'home-grown'. In California and Australia the debate is more open. Wine makers who buy their grapes (almost always from the same suppliers) include some of the very best.

Virus-free Vines

Certain authorities (notably at the University of California) are convinced that the only way to achieve a healthy vineyard is to 'clean' the vine stocks in it of all virus infections. It was not appreciated until recently that the beautiful red colouring of vine leaves in autumn is generally a symptom of a virus-infected plant.

Plants can now be propagated free of virus infection by growing them very fast in a hot greenhouse, then using the growing tips as mini-cuttings (or micro-cuttings, growing minute pieces of the plant tissue in a nutrient jelly). The virus is always one pace behind the new growth, which is thus 'clean' and will have all its natural vigour.

It must be said that virus elimination is not a substitute for selection of the best vines for propagation. The Office International du Vin officially declared in 1980 that 'it is a fantasy to try to establish a vineyard free of all virus diseases' and recommended its members to 'select clones resistant to dangerous virus diseases and which will still be capable, after infection, of producing a satisfactory crop both as to quality and quantity' (see Cloning).

Cloning

Close observation of a vine will show that some branches are inherently more vigorous, bear more fruit, ripen earlier or have other desirable characteristics. These branches (and their buds) are 'mutations', genetically slightly different from the parent plant. The longer a variety has been in cultivation the more 'degenerate' and thus genetically unstable it will be, and the more mutations it will have. The Pinot family is extremely ancient and notoriously mutable.

A recent technique is to select such a branch and propagate exclusively from its cuttings. A whole vineyard can then be planted with what is in effect one identical individual plant – known as a clone. There is thus not one single Pinot Noir variety in Burgundy but scores of clones selected for different attributes. Growers who plant highly productive clones will never achieve the best-quality wine. Those who choose a shy-bearing, small-berried clone for colour and flavour must reckon on smaller crops.

One advantage of a single-clone vineyard is that all its grapes will ripen together. A disadvantage is that one problem, pest or disease will affect them all equally. Common sense seems to indicate that the traditional method of selecting cuttings from as many different healthy vines as possible (known as 'mass selection') rather than one individual, carries a better chance of long-term success.

The Choice of Rootstocks

The great majority of modern vineyards are of a selected variety of European vine grafted on to a selected American rootstock which has inbuilt resistance to the vine-killing pest phylloxera. Compatible rootstocks have been chosen and/or bred and virus-freed to be ideal for specific types of soil. Some are recommended for acid to neutral soils (such as most in California) while others flourish on the limey or alkaline soils common to most of Europe's best vineyards.

Grafting

The grafting of a 'scion' of the chosen vine variety on to an appropriate rootstock is either done at the nursery before planting ('bench grafting') or onto an already-planted rootstock in the vineyard ('field grafting'). In California recently it has become common practice for growers to change their mind after a vine has been in production for several years, deciding that they want (say) less Zinfandel and more Chardonnay. In this case they simply saw off the Zinfandel vine at rootstock level, just above the ground, and 'T-bud' graft a Chardonnay scion in its place. Within two years they will have white wine instead of red. Not only do growers lose less production but take advantage of the well-established root system of the mature vines.

Grafted vines dovetailed into established rootstock.

Hybrid Vines

After the phylloxera epidemic encountered in Europe a century ago a number of France's leading biologists started breeding hybrid vines by marrying the European classics to phylloxera-resistant American species. Once the technique of grafting the French originals on to American roots was well established the French establishment rejected these '*producteurs directes*', or 'PDs' (so-called because they produced 'directly' via their own roots). Good, hardy and productive as many of them are they are banned from all French appellation areas for fear of altering their precious identity. Their American parenthood, however, has made them highly suitable for use in the eastern United States, where hardiness is a perpetual problem (see page 477). These hybrid vines were also once popular in New Zealand and some of the better ones are quite extensively planted in England.

New Crossings of European Vines

Germany is the centre of a breeding programme which is quite distinct from 'hybrid' vines. Its object is to find within the genetic pool of varieties of *Vitis vinifera* a combination of desirable qualities which could supplant, in particular, the Riesling, Germany's finest vine but one that ripens relatively late, thus carrying a high risk element at vintage time. So far no cross has even remotely challenged the Riesling for flavour or hardiness – though many have for productivity, strongly aromatic juice and early ripening. The Müller-Thurgau was the first and is still the best-known example.

The University of California also has a *vinifera* breeding programme which has produced some useful additions, particularly among high-yielding grapes for hot areas which are capable of retaining good aromas and acidity. The best-known examples resulting from this programme include Ruby Cabernet (Cabernet Sauvignon/Carignan), Carnelian and Centurion (Cabernet Sauvignon/Grenache), Carmine (Cabernet Sauvignon/Merlot), Emerald Riesling (Riesling/Muscadelle) and Flora (Gewürztraminer/Sémillon), all produced by Dr. Harold Olmo at Davis.

South Africa has produced the Pinotage, said to be a cross between Pinot Noir and Cinsaut (though unfortunately with few of the qualities of the former). With over 3,000 named varieties already in circulation to choose from there seems to be a limited point in breeding for the sake of breeding.

Soil

Soil is always given pride of place in French discussions of wine quality. It is considered from two aspects: its chemical and its physical properties. Current thinking is that the latter is much the more important. Most soils contain all the chemical elements the vine needs.

The physical factors that affect quality are texture, porosity, drainage, depth and even colour. In cool climates anything that tends to make the soil warm (i.e. absorb and

Pinotage, a crossing of Pinot Noir and Cinsaut.

store heat from the sun) is good. Stones on the surface store heat and radiate it at night. Darker soil absorbs more radiation. In Germany vine rows are oriented to expose the soil to maximum sunlight.

Dry soil warms up faster. Another important advantage of good deep drainage (eg on Médoc gravel) is the fact that it makes the vine root deep to find moisture. Deep roots are in a stable environment: a sudden downpour just before harvest will not instantly inflate the grapes with water. On the other hand experiments at Davis, California, recently have shown that where the soil is cooler than the above-ground parts of the vine the effect can be good for the grape pigments and give deep-coloured red wine. (Château Pétrus on the iron-rich clay of Pomerol would seem to bear this out. St-Estèphe also has more clay and its wines often more colour than the rest of the Médoc.)

In California clay also seems to produce stable white wines that resist oxidation and therefore have a greater ability to mature. But in California over-rapid ripening often leads to wines that are low in acid and easily oxidized. The cool of clay may simply be slowing the ripening process: the very opposite of the effect required in, say, Germany.

A reasonable conclusion would be that the best soil is the soil that results in the grapes coming steadily to maturity: warm in cool areas, reasonably cool in hot areas. It should be deep enough for the roots to have constant access to moisture, since a vine under acute stress of drought closes the pores of its leaves. Photosynthesis stops and the grapes cannot develop or ripen.

Expert opinion seems to be that if the soils of the great vineyards (eg Bordeaux first-growths) have more available nutrients and minerals (especially potassium) it is because over the years their owners have invested more in them. The closest scrutiny of the Côte d'Or has not revealed chemical differences between the soils of the different crus which would account for their acknowledged differences of flavour.

Steep, rocky terraces in the Douro Valley, Portugal. Creating such terraces is a huge engineering feat and involves blasting the slate-based soil and building it up into supporting walls.

Sites, Slopes and Microclimates

It is conventional wisdom that wine from slopes is better. The words *côtes* and *coteaux*, meaning slopes, constantly recur in France. The obvious reasons are the increased solar radiation on a surface tipped towards the sun, meaning warmer soil, and the improved cold-air drainage, reducing the risk of frost. A south slope (in the northern hemisphere) is almost always the ideal, but local conditions can modify this. In areas with autumn morning fog a westerly slope is preferable, since the sun does not normally burn through the fog until the afternoon. The best slopes of the Rheingau are examples. But in Burgundy and Alsace easterly slopes have the advantage of sun all morning to warm the ground, which stores the heat while the angle of the sun decreases during the afternoon. Alsace also benefits from a particularly sunny local climate caused by the 'rain shadow' of the Vosges mountains to its west.

Many of the best Old World vineyards (eg in Germany, the Rhône Valley, the Douro Valley) were terraced on steep slopes to combine the advantages of slope with some depth of soil. Being inaccessible to machinery, terraces are largely being abolished. In Germany huge earth-moving projects have rebuilt whole hills to allow tractors to operate. The Douro Valley is being remodelled with wide sloping terraces instead of the old narrow flat ones. Experiments with 'vertical' planting on the steep Douro slopes – doing away with terraces altogether – have been inconclusive. Heavy rains can wash soil nutrients to the bottom of the slope.

A flat valley floor (as in the Napa Valley) is the most risky place to plant vines because cold air drains to it on spring nights when the vines have tender shoots (*see* Frost protection, below).

It is noteworthy that in Burgundy the Grands Crus vineyards have a lower incidence of frost damage than the Premiers Crus – presumably because growers have observed the cold spots and lavished their attentions on the safer ones. The same distinction is even true of the incidence of hail.

The term microclimate refers to the immediate surroundings of the vine. The slightest difference can become important in the long period between bud break and harvest. In the Rheingau wind is considered a principal enemy since it can blow out accumulated warmth from the rows – which are therefore planted across the prevailing summer southwest wind.

Another microclimatic factor is the shade and possible build-up of humidity under a dense canopy of leaves (*see* Training and trellising). Yet another is the greater incidence of frost over soil covered with herbage than over bare earth, which makes it worth cultivating the vine rows in spring.

Frost Protection

A dormant *vinifera* vine in winter can survive temperatures down to −28°C (−18°F). In regions where lower temperatures regularly occur it is common practice to bury the lower half of the vines by earthing-up in late autumn. A vine is most vulnerable to frost in spring when its new growth is green and sappy. The only old means of protection (still widely practised) was to light stoves (or 'smudge pots') in the vineyards on clear spring nights. It was often a forlorn hope. An improvement introduced in frost-prone areas of California, for example, was a giant fan to keep the air in the vineyard moving and prevent cold air accumulating, but it has proved ineffectual without heaters as well.

Dangerous as it looks, a layer of ice actually prevents tender vine shoots from being damaged by sub-zero temperatures.

Helicopters are also an efficient if expensive way of circulating freezing air to prevent frost damage. Then there is the sprinkler, which simply rains heavily on the almost-freezing vine. The water freezes on contact with the young shoots and forms a protective layer of ice, which acts as insulation against frosts on spring nights. Such sprinklers can be an excellent investment, doubling as a method of irrigation during dry, hot summers.

Training and Trellising

Most vineyards used to consist of innumerable individual bushes, 'head' or 'Gobelet'-pruned back to a few buds from the short trunk after each harvest. With a few famous exceptions (among them the Mosel, parts of the Rhône, Beaujolais) most modern vineyards are 'cordoned' – that is, with the vines trained on to one or more wires parallel to the ground, supported at intervals by stakes.

The need to use mechanical harvesters has encouraged the use of higher trellising systems, often designed to spread the foliage at the top by means of a crossbar supporting two parallel wires four feet apart. The first such trellis was developed in Austria in the 1930s by Lenz Moser.

High trellises are not suitable for cool areas such as Germany, where heat radiation from the ground is essential for ripening. On the other hand they have been used immemorially in northern Portugal to produce deliberately acidic wine. Widespread 'curtains' of foliage, or 'double curtains' where the vine is made to branch on to two high supporting wires, have several advantages in warm areas. They expose a larger leaf surface for photosynthesis, at the same time shading the bunches of grapes from direct sunlight. In fertile soils which can support vigorous growth the so-called 'lyre' system, spreading the vine top into two mounds of foliage, is very successful, if not for top-quality wine, at least for good quantities of ripe grapes.

Canopy Management

Generally viticulturists, especially in newer wine regions, have become much more aware of the concept of canopy management. They appreciate how it is possible to manipulate the vine, to give the ripening grapes more or less direct exposure to sunlight and control the amount of vegetation so that humidity within the canopy does not cause disease. Any number of ingenious trellising methods are being developed (especially by the New Zealand guru of the canopy, Dr. Richard Smart), not only the 'double curtain' and 'lyre' system, but also Scott Henry and Sylvoz, all with the same intent of obtaining the best fruit.

Pruning Methods

Pruning methods have been adapted to new methods of vine training. By far the most significant new development is mechanical pruning, which dispenses with the highly skilled but laborious handwork in the depths of winter by simply treating the vine row as a hedge. Aesthetically appalling as it is,

results (initially in Australia) show that a system of small circular saws straddling the vine and cutting all wood extending beyond a certain narrow compass is just as satisfactory as the practised eye and hand. Some follow-up hand pruning may be necessary, but the same method has been used in commercial apple orchards for some years with no harmful effects, and is certain to become more common in vineyards. Experience in California, for example, has shown that mechanical pruning costs as little as 15 percent of the cost of hand pruning.

Growth Regulators

For many years it has been customary to trim excessively long leafy shoots from the tops and sides of vines in summer. A new development is the growth-regulating spray, a chemical which slowly releases ethylene gas, can be sprayed on the foliage when it has reached an ideal point of development. It inhibits further leaf growth, preventing the canopy from becoming too dense and making the plant's reserves of carbohydrates available to the fruit, instead of allowing it to waste them on useless long shoots. It apparently also encourages ripening and makes it easier for a mechanical harvester to detach the grapes from their stems.

Excessive vigour is a particular problem in New Zealand, where growers attempt to combat it with various trellising and pruning methods. Good vineyard management also helps, such as planting cover crops, such as chicory, which has a deep tap root, so that it will take up excess water.

Systematic Sprays

The traditional protection against fungus diseases such as mildew in the vineyard is 'Bordeaux mixture', a bright blue copper-sulphate solution sprayed on from a long-legged tractor (but washed off again by the next rain). New 'systematic' sprays are chemicals that are absorbed into the sap-stream of the plants and destroy their fungus (or insect) victim from inside the leaf or grape when the parasite attacks. Unfortunately fungus diseases and such pests as red-spider mites can rapidly develop resistance to specific chemicals, making it necessary for manufacturers to vary the formula (at great expense). The best-known systemic fungicide, benomyl, is now of limited use for this reason.

Organic Cultivation

Wine can be grown by organic methods, just as can any other crop. This cuts out artificial fertilizers and insecticides and other sprays. Three years must pass since the vineyard was last artificially fertilized before the wine can be called 'organic'. Some sprays can be used – old-fashioned copper sulphate is one. And of course the organic logic must be followed through into the winery. Even more exacting than organic is biodynamic viticulture, which follows principles laid down by Rudolf Steiner. There is a complete viticultural calendar which advises on the most appropriate time to treat the vines, all based on the phases of the moon.

FROM GRAPES TO WINE

Controlling Yield

Higher quantity means lower quality. Acceptance of this golden rule is built into the appellation regulations of France, Italy and most other wine-producing nations. In France the highest-quality areas limit the *rendement,* or yield, to 35 hectolitres a hectare (about two tons an acre) or even less. *vins de pays* are allowed to produce up to 80 hectolitres or even more. In Italy the limits are expressed in a similar way, as so many quintals (100 kg) of grapes a hectare, with a limit on the amount of juice that may be extracted from each quintal.

The New World as yet has no regulations in this regard – which, in view of its laissez-faire philosophy, is not surprising. However, conscientious growers are keenly aware of the detrimental effect of too high a yield and many, if their crop looks like being excessive, will, come mid-summer, carry out a green harvest. This entails the removal of part of the potential crop so that the vine concentrates its energy on ripening what is left. Others may suggest that this upsets the natural balance of the vine and ideally the crop should be regulated by intelligent pruning.

What is surprising, however, is that Germany permits such enormous crops. In 1900 the average yield there was 25 hectolitres a hectare; 100 hectolitres a hectare is now normal in Germany. Modern German winemaking deliberately concentrates on lightness and transparency of flavour. It lays all the emphasis on 'balance' between sweetness and fruity acidity. As a result most of its wines lack concentration and the ability to improve from more than a few years in bottle. Today it is more realistic to rewrite the golden rule to read 'higher quantity means lighter, more rapidly maturing wine' – the style which is most in demand.

A recent rebellion by top German growers has seen voluntary restraint on yields, bringing Germany or at least its conscientious producers once more into line with the other quality wine zones. Even so, 55–60 hl/ha is considered 'low' in the Mosel-Saar-Ruwer.

Irrigation

Irrigation used to be considered utterly incompatible with quality wine. But such important regions as Argentina, Chile, Washington State and large parts of Australia could not grow grapes at all without it. No one can deny the quality of their best wines. Once again it is a question of understanding the metabolism of the vine and using intelligence and moderation.

Mechanical Harvesting

A machine for picking grapes, saving the stiff backs (and high wages) of the tens of thousands who turn out to the harvest each year, only became a reality in the 1960s (in

Mechanical harvesting New World style. Harvesting at night is often preferable, when the vineyard temperature is cooler.

New York State, picking Concord grapes). By the 1980s, machines harvested a third of all America's wine grapes and the percentage is now higher still. The mechanical harvester is an inevitable advance. In France it has gained wide acceptance in big vineyards, though some quality areas still resist, especially where steep terrain makes the use of a machine impractical.

The machine works by straddling the vine row and violently shaking the trunks, while slapping at the extremities of the vine with flexible paddles or striker bars. The grapes fall on to a conveyor belt, which carries them from near ground level to a chute above the vine tops. Here they pass in front of a fan which blows away any loose leaves and are shot into a hopper towed by a tractor in the next alley between the vines. In many cases the hopper leads straight to a crusher and the crusher to a closed tank, so that the grapes leave the vineyard already crushed, sheltered from sunlight and insects and dosed with sulphur dioxide to prevent oxidation.

The harvester has many advantages. It can operate at night, when the grapes are cool. It needs only two operators. Whereas a traditional team may have to start while some grapes are still unripe, and finish when some are overripe, the machine works fast enough to pick a whole vineyard at ideal maturity. The harvesting rate in California is up to 150 tons (or up to about 40 acres) a day.

Disadvantages include the need for especially robust trellising, the loss of perhaps 10% of the crop and the slight risk of including leaves in the crush. In addition, skin contact is inevitable and for this reason machines are not permitted in Champagne, or in Beaujolais where whole bunches are essential to the vinification process. However, mechanical harvesters are becoming more refined.

Botrytis Infection

The benevolent aspect of the fungus mould *Boyrytis cinerea* as the 'noble rot' which produces great sweet wines receives so much publicity that its malevolent appearance in the vineyard at the wrong time can be forgotten. In some regions (particularly in Germany) its prevalence has made it the most serious and widespread disease the grower has to deal with. The more fertile the vineyard and luxuriant the vine, the more likely it is to strike at the unripe or (most vulnerable) semi-ripe grapes and rot the bunch. It starts by attacking grapes punctured by insects or 'grape worm': controlling the bugs is therefore the most effective protection. Only when the sugar content in the grapes has reached about 70° Oechsle or 17° Brix (enough to make wine of about 9° natural alcohol) does evil rot become noble rot. For a description of noble rot *see* page 69 (Château d'Yquem).

The occurrence and exploitation of noble rot in the vineyards of California has been one of the most noteworthy innovations of recent years. California has coined the inelegant word 'botrytized' (with the stress on the 'bot') to mean infected with *Botrytis cinerea* – of the noble variety.

In stark contrast to the mechanical harvest, botrytized grapes may need to be handpicked individually.

Sugar and Acid Levels

The crucial decision of when to pick the grapes depends on the measurement of their sugar and acid contents. As they ripen sugar content increases and acid decreases. For each type of wine there is an ideal moment when the ratio is just right.

Ripening starts at the moment called *véraison,* when the grape, which has been growing slowly by cell division, still hard and bright green, begins to grow rapidly by the enlargement of each cell. This is when red grapes begin to change colour.

Sugar content is usually measured with a handheld 'refractometer'. A drop of juice is held between two prisms. Light passing through it bends at a different angle according to its sugar content: the angle is read off on a scale calibrated as degrees Brix, Oechsle or Baumé, the American, German and French systems respectively for measuring ripeness.

In warm weather sugar content may increase by up to 0.4° Brix a day, while acidity drops by as much as 0.15°. 'Ripe' grapes vary between about 18° and 26° Brix (i.e. with a potential alcohol level of 9.3 to 14% by volume). Different levels of acidity are considered ideal for different styles of wine. In Germany acid levels as high as 0.9% would be commendable for a wine of 11.3% potential alcohol (90° Oechsle). In France or California the recommended acid level for grapes with the same sugar content would be approximately 0.7% for white wine and slightly lower for red. One risk in hotter regions is rapidly rising sugar levels which induce growers to pick before the whole grape is fully mature, resulting in harsh 'green' tannic flavours.

The third variable taken into account is the pH of the juice. This is a measure of the strength, rather than volume, of its acidity. The lower the figure, the sharper the juice. Normal pH in wine is in the range 2.8 to 3.8. Low pH readings are desirable for stability and (in red wines) good colour.

A leading California winemaker, Walter Schug, uses the pH reading as his signal to pick. 'A sharp rise in pH, usually upon reaching 3.25 or over, means that the fruit should be picked regardless of the degree Brix.'

MAKING WINE

Handling the Fruit

A good winemaker will not accept grapes that have been badly damaged on the way from the vineyard, or with a high proportion of mouldy bunches or what the Californians call MOG (matter other than grapes, eg leaves, stones and soil). For winemaking at the highest standard the bunches are picked over by hand – '*triage*' – and rotten grapes thrown out. Where large quantities are involved a degree of imperfection has to be accepted.

Several regions of Europe specify the size and design of container that must be used for bringing in the grapes. The object here is to prevent the weight of large quantities from

crushing the grapes at the bottom before they reach the cellar. The huge 'gondolas' often used for transporting grapes in California, often under a hot sun, have the distinct drawback that many of the grapes at the bottom will be broken, and macerating in juice, long before they even reach the carefully controlled hygienic conditions of the winery.

SO2

The first step in all winemaking procedures is the addition of a small dose of sulphur dioxide to the crushed grapes, or must. Nothing has supplanted this universal and age-old antiseptic of the winemaker in protecting the must from premature or wild fermentation, and both must and wine from oxidation, though some advanced winemakers use very little and strive to use none – putting instead physical barriers (eg inert gases) between the juice or wine and the oxygen in the atmosphere.

The amount of SO_2 allowed is regulated by law. Wine with too much has a sharp brimstone smell and leaves a burning feeling in the throat – a common occurrence in the past, particularly in semi-sweet wines where the sulphur was used to prevent refermentation in the bottle. Sterile filters have now eliminated the need for this and the consumer should be unaware that wine's old preservative is still used at all. Some people may suffer ill-effects from SO_2 in wine or anything else: thus the US regulation that labels should state 'contains sulfites'.

Grapes being delivered to a Napa Valley winery. Speed is all, to get the crop out of the heat and away from insects.

White Wine: immediate pressing or 'skin-contact'

Light, fresh and fruity white wines are made by pressing the grapes as soon as possible after picking. The aim is to prevent the juice from picking up any flavours or 'extract' from the skin. The grapes are gently crushed (*foulé*) just hard enough to break their skins. This 'pomace' is then loaded directly into the press. In wineries looking for maximum freshness, the juice or even the grapes may be chilled.

Many bigger wineries now use a 'dejuicer' between the crusher and the press. This may consist of a mesh screen, sometimes in the form of a conveyor belt, through which the 'free' juice falls. A dejuicer reduces the number of times the press has to be laboriously filled and emptied, but it increases the chance of oxidation of the juice. One dejuicer that avoids oxidation is a stainless steel tank with a central cylinder formed of a mesh screen. The crushed pomace is loaded into the space around this cylinder and CO_2 is

An Archimedean screw is used to move the grapes swiftly into the cool, hygenic conditions of the winery.

pumped under pressure into the headspace. The free juice is gently forced to drain out via the central cylinder, leaving relatively little pomace to be pressed. Up to 70% can be free-run juice, leaving only 30% to be extracted by pressing.

Fuller, more robust wines with more flavour, and tannins to preserve them while they age, are made by holding the skins in contact with the juice in a tank for up to 24 hours after crushing. This maceration (at low temperature, before fermentation starts) extracts some of the elements that are present in the skins but not the juice. The pomace is then dejuiced and pressed as usual. Few winemakers go further and ferment white wines with their skins, like red wines – the resulting wine would be too 'heavy' for today's taste.

White Wine: stems or no stems

White grapes are usually pressed with their stems, unless they are machine-harvested. The reason is that unfermented grape flesh and juice is full of pectins and sugar, slippery and sticky. The stems make the operation of the press easier, particularly when it comes to breaking up the 'cake', to press a second time. The press should not be used at a high enough pressure to squeeze any bitter juice out of stems or pips.

Types of Press

There is a wide choice of types of press, ranging from the old-fashioned vertical model, in which a plate is forced down on to the pomace contained in a cylindrical cage of vertical slots, to the mass-production continuous 'Coq' press. The first is the most labour-intensive but still produces the clearest juice; the second is very cheap and easy to run but cannot make better than medium-grade wine. Most good wineries choose either a Vaslin horizontal basket press, which works on a principle similar to the old vertical press, squeezing the pomace by means of plates which are brought together by a central screw, or a Willmes 'bladder' or 'membrane' press. A bladder press contains a long rubber balloon which when inflated squeezes the pomace against the surrounding fine grille. Both are 'batch' presses, meaning that they have to be filled and emptied anew for each batch of pomace, whereas the continuous press spews forth an unending stream of juice below and 'cake' at the far end.

White Wine – cold fermentation

The most revolutionary invention in modern winemaking is controlled-temperature fermentation, particularly for white wines, which in warm climates used to be flat, low in acid and lack-lustre. What used to be achieved naturally by using small barrels in the cold cellars of Europe is now practised industrially in California, Australia and elsewhere by chilling the contents of often colossal stainless steel vats. Most of such vats are double-skinned or 'jacketed' with a layer of glycol or ammonia as the cooling agent between the skins. Another cooling technique is to dribble cold water continuously down the outside surface. A second-best method is to circulate the wine through a heat exchanger (or a coil submerged in cold water) outside the vat.

Each winemaker has his own idea about the ideal temperature for fermentation. Long, cool fermentation is reputedly good for fruity flavours, though when practised to extremes on certain grapes, particularly nonaromatic sorts, it seems to leave its mark on the wine as a 'pear-drop' or acetaldehyde smell. A number of modern Italian white wines, and even occasionally red ones, are spoilt by over-enthusiastic refrigeration. In Germany, to the contrary, very cold fermentation has gone out of fashion. The normal temperatures for white-wine fermentation in California are between 8° and 15°C (46°–59°F). In France 18°C (64°F) is considered cold. If the temperature is forced down too far the fermentation will 'stick' and the yeasts cease to function. It can be difficult to start again and the wine will almost certainly suffer in the process.

A completely different approach is used to make 'big', richer, smoother and more heavy-bodied wines from Chardonnay and sometimes Sauvignon Blanc. They are fermented at between 15° and 20°C (59°–68°F), or in barrels even as high as 25°C (77°F). California Chardonnay in this style is made in exactly the same way as white burgundy.

White Wine – clarifying the juice

Modern presses are more efficient than old models but often produce juice with a higher proportion of suspended solids (pieces of grape skins, flesh, pips or dirt). Fermentation of white wine with these solids tends to produce bitterness, so the juice must be cleaned first. This can be done by holding it for a day or more in a 'settling' tank, at a cool temperature, allowing particles to sink to the bottom, by filtering through a powerful 'vacuum' filter, or (fastest) by use of a centrifuge pump, which uses centrifugal force to throw out all foreign bodies. Over-centrifuged wine can be stripped of desirable as well as undesirable constituents: great care is needed.

White Wine – adjusting acidity

Either de- or re-acidification of white-wine must may be necessary, depending on the ripeness of the crop. Overacid juice is de-acidified by adding calcium carbonate (chalk) to remove tartaric acid, or a substance called Acidex, which removes malic acid as well by 'double-salt precipitation'. In Germany the addition of sugar and (up to 15%) water to wines of Qualitätswein level and below naturally lowers the proportion of acidity. In France chaptalization with dry sugar (permitted in the centre and north) has the same effect to a lesser degree. In the south of France, however, only concentrated must, not sugar, is allowed for raising the alcoholic degree: it naturally raises the acid level at the same time.

In California and other warm countries where the usual problem is too little acid it is permitted to add one of the acids that naturally occur in grapes – malic, citric and tartaric. Tartaric is preferred since it has no detectable flavour and also helps towards tartrate stability (*see* Cold stabilization). But it is more expensive.

Controlling the fermentation temperatures is massively simplified by investing in stainless-steel tanks.

Tanks and Vats

The unquestioned grandeur and nobility of traditional fermenting vats of oak (or sometimes chestnut, acacia or redwood) is accompanied by many disadvantages. Most important are the problems of disinfecting them and keeping them watertight between vintages.

Early in the 20th century concrete began to replace them in newer and bigger wineries. It is strong, permanent and easy to clean. Moreover it can be made in any shape to fit odd corners and save space. Like wood, however, it is a bad conductor of heat. The only way to cool wine in a concrete vat is to pump it out through a cooling plant.

In modern wineries stainless steel is king. It is strong, inert, simple to clean and to cool (it conducts heat perfectly). Moreover it is versatile: the same tank can be used for fermentation and, later in the year, for storage, ageing or blending. Its high initial cost is thus quite quickly recouped.

To make good wine a winery must have ample capacity.

It often happens that in an abundant vintage there is a shortage of space. Grapes cannot be stored so the only answer is to cut short the fermenting time of the early batches. With red wines this will mean shorter maceration on the skins and thus lighter wine. Well-designed modern wineries not only have plenty of tank space, they have tanks in a variety of sizes to avoid leaving small lots of wine in half-full containers or being obliged to mix them.

Yeasts

There are yeasts naturally present in every vineyard which will cause fermentation if they are allowed to. Some consider them part of the stamp, or personality, of their property and believe they help to give their wine its individuality. Many modern wineries, wanting to keep total control, take care to remove the natural yeast (by filtering or centrifuging), or at least to render it helpless with a strong dose of SO_2. Some even 'flash-pasteurize' the juice by heating it to 55°C (131°F) to kill off bacteria and inhibit the wild yeasts. They they proceed to inoculate the must with a cultured yeast of their choice which is known to multiply actively at the temperature they choose for fermentation. Some of the most popular yeasts in California go by the promising names of 'Montrachet', 'Champagne' and 'Steinberg'.

The secret is to start the fermentation with a generous amount of active yeast; once the whole vat is fermenting such problems as oxidation can temporarily be forgotten. The activity of yeast increases rapidly with rising temperature. For each additional degree Celsius, yeast transforms 10% more sugar into alcohol in a given time. The ceiling to this frantic activity occurs at about 30° to 35°C (86°–95°F) when the yeasts are overcome by heat. A 'run-away' fermentation can 'stick' at this temperature, just as most yeasts will not function below about 10°C (50°F).

Specialized use of *flor* yeast for producing sherry is now greatly advanced. New ways have been found to produce the sherry effect much faster and more certainly than with the naturally occurring layer of *flor* floating on the wine.

White Wines – malolactic fermentation

Secondary or malolactic fermentation (*see* Red wine – malolactic fermentation) is less common with white wine then with red. It is sometimes encouraged, to reduce excess acidity in wines from cool climates (eg Chablis and other parts of Burgundy, the Loire, Switzerland, but less commonly in Germany). Its complex biological nature may help to add complexity to flavours. In warmer regions where acidity tends to be low, such as California and Australia, malolactic fermentation in white wines is generally avoided.

White Wines – residual sugar

A completed natural fermentation makes a totally dry wine, all its sugar converted to alcohol. The only exceptions are wines made of grapes so sweet that either the alcohol level or the sugar, or both, prevents the yeasts from functioning.

To make light sweet wines, either the fermentation has to be artificially interrupted or sweet juice has to be blended with dry wine. The former was the old way. It needed a strong dose of SO_2 to stop the fermentation, and more in the bottle to prevent it starting again. The invention of filters fine enough to remove all yeasts, and means of bottling in conditions of complete sterility, now solve the sulphur problem. But winemakers today generally prefer the second method: blending with 'sweet reserve'. This is the standard procedure for producing the sweet and semi-sweet wines of Germany up to Auslese level and is increasingly used elsewhere.

The method used is to sterilize a portion of the juice instead of fermenting it. (It can be stored in a deepfreeze as a block of ice.) The majority of the wine is made in the normal way, fermented until no sugar is left. The 'sweet reserve' (in German *Süssreserve*) is then added to taste and the blend bottled under sterile conditions. The addition of unfermented juice naturally lowers the alcohol content of the wine.

Some of the best winemakers prefer to maintain a small degree of unfermented ('residual') sugar in certain wines (California Rieslings and Gewürztraminers, for example) by cooling the vat to stop fermentation at the appropriate moment, then using a centrifuge and/or fine filtering to remove the yeasts and sterilize the wine.

White Wine – after fermentation

After white wine has fermented it must be clarified. The traditional method was to allow it to settle and then rack it off its lees (largely of dead yeast cells). When Muscadet is bottled *sur lie* this is exactly what is happening. Modern wineries, however, tend to use a centrifuge or a filter for this clarification, too, if necessary with the additional precaution of fining with a powdery clay (from Wyoming) called bentonite, which removes excess proteins, potential causes of later trouble in the form of cloudy wine. Bentonite fining is also sometimes used on the must before fermentation.

White wines not intended for ageing (i.e. most light commercial wines) then need only to be stabilized and filtered before they can be bottled and distributed. Those intended for ageing are usually transferred into barrel for clarification, so that they enjoy the same benefits of barrel-ageing as red wines. They may be left for several months on the fine lees, which may be regularly stirred up, in a process called *bâtonnage*, so that the wine benefits from the effects of yeast autolysis, whereby the lees, including dead yeast, impart extra complexity to the flavour of the wine.

White Wine – cold stabilization

The tartaric acid which is a vital ingredient in the balance and flavour of all wines has an unfortunate habit of forming crystals in combination with either potassium (quite big sugary grains) or calcium (finer and whiter powdery crystals). In former times wine was kept for several years in cool cellars and these crystals formed a hard deposit on the walls of their casks, known in Germany as 'Weinstein' – 'wine stone'. With faster modern methods, most wineries consider it essential to prevent the crystals forming after the wine is bottled – which they will unless something is done about it. The crystals have no flavour at all and are totally natural and harmless, there are ignorant and querulous customers who will send back a bottle with any sign of deposit.

Unfortunately it is a costly business to remove the risk of tartrate crystals. The simplest way is to chill the wine to just above freezing point in a tank for several days. The process is accelerated by 'seeding' with added tartrate crystals to act as nuclei for more crystals to form. More efficient ways of achieving this strictly unnecessary object will keep research chemists busy for years to come.

Red Wine – stems or no stems

Each red-winemaker has his own view about whether the grape stems should be included, wholly or in part – and it changes with the vintage. In Beaujolais and the Rhône the stems are always included, in Burgundy usually a proportion, in Bordeaux few or none, in Chinon on the Loire the stems are left on the vine. Opinions are equally divided in other countries, but in California stems are usually excluded.

The argument for leaving the stems out is that they add astringency, lower the alcohol content, reduce the colour and take up valuable space in vat. The argument for keeping some of them in is that they help the process of fermentation by aerating the mass, they lower the acidity and they make pressing easier. In any case, the stems must be ripe, or they will add 'green' flavours to the wine.

Red Wine – pumping over

When a vat of red wine ferments the skins float to the surface, buoyed up by bubbles of carbon dioxide, which attach themselves to solid matter. The 'cap' (French, '*chapeau*', Spanish '*sombrero*') that they form contains all the essential colouring matter – and is prone to overheat and be attacked by bacteria. It is therefore essential to keep mixing the cap back into the liquid below. There are several methods.

In Bordeaux the cap is often pushed under by men with long poles. In Burgundy, with smaller vats, it is trodden under ('*pigeage*') by men, formerly naked, who jump into the vat. Another widespread method is to fit a grille below the filling level which holds the cap immersed (*chapeau immergé*). Mechanical 'plungers' attached to a crankshaft are also used. But the most widespread method now used is 'pumping over', taking wine by a hose from the bottom of the vat and spraying it over the cap, usually several times a day.

Several ingenious alternatives have been invented. The 'Rototank' is a closed horizontal cylinder which slowly rotates, continually mixing the liquids and solids inside. An automatic system developed in Portugal, where the traditional way of extracting the colour was night-long stomping by all the village lads to the sound of accordions, involves an ingenious gusher device activated by the build-up of carbon dioxide pressure in a sealed tank.

Red Wine – pressing

By the time fermentation is finished, or nearly finished and merely simmering slightly, most (up to 85%) of the red wine is separated from the solid matter and will run freely from the vat. This 'free run' or *vin de goutte* is siphoned out of the vat into either barrels or another tank. The remaining 'marc' is pressed.

Red wine is pressed in the same types of presses as white, but after fermentation the pulp and skins have partly disintegrated and offer less resistance.

Relatively gentle pressure will release very good quality vin de presse, which is richer in desirable extracts and flavours than the vin de goutte. It may need such treatment as fining to reduce astringency and remove solids, but in most cases it will be a positive addition and make better wine for longer keeping. Wine from a second, more vigorous, pressing will almost always be too astringent and be sold separately, or used in a cheap blend.

The Value of Barrels

The development of winemaking in the New World, with its more questioning approach, has drawn attention to what has long been known, but taken for granted, in France and elsewhere: that new barrels have a profound effect on the flavour of wine stored in them – and even more on wine fermented in them. California Chardonnays fermented in the same French oak as white burgundy can have an uncanny resemblance to its flavour.

Barrels were invented (probably by the Romans) of necessity as the most durable and transportable of containers, supplanting the amphora and the goatskin in regions that could afford them. They have developed to their standard sizes and shapes over centuries of experience. The 200-odd-litre barrels of Bordeaux, Burgundy and Rioja are the most that one man can easily roll or two men carry – but they also happen to present the largest surface area of wood to wine of any practicable size.

The advantages of this contact lie partly in the very slow transfer of oxygen through the planks of the barrel, but mainly through the tannin and other substances that the wine dissolves from the wood itself. The most easily identified (by taste or smell) of these is vanillin, which has the flavour of vanilla. Oak tannin is useful in augmenting, and slightly varying the tannins naturally present in wine as preservatives. Other scents and flavours are harder to define, but can be well enough expressed as the 'smell of a carpenter's shop'.

Which wines benefit from this addition of extraneous flavours? Only those with strong characters and constitutions of their own. It would be disastrous to a fragile Mosel or a Beaujolais Nouveau. The 'bigger' the wine and the longer it is to be matured, the more oak it can take.

New barrels are extremely expensive. US$1,000 is a typical 1997 price. The full impact of their oak flavour diminishes rapidly after the first two or three years' use, but there is a lively trade in secondhand barrels, particularly those that have contained great wines. Barrels can also be renewed to full pungency by shaving the wine-leached interior down to fresh wood.

A cheap but effective way of adding oak flavour to wine is to use oak chips. These are still strictly forbidden in France, and indeed considered shocking, but chips are widely accepted in the New World for cheaper wines. They vary in size from sawdust granules to matchsticks and must be properly seasoned to avoid any harsh flavours. Vignerons need to calculate how much they need by weight, according to the volume of the wine and the desired degree of oakiness, and the chips are added to the wine in a muslim bag. Properly used, they are very effective in flavouring both Chardonnay and red wine for those who like the extraneous flavour of oak (I don't).

A quite different role is played by the huge permanent oak barrels, *foudres* or *demi-muids* in French, *Fuders* or *Stücks* in German, which are common in southern France, Germany, Italy, Spain and eastern Europe. Their oak flavour has been minimized or neutralized by constant impregnation with wine, and often by a thick layer of tartrate crystals. Their value seems to lie in offering an ideal environment, with very gradual oxidation, for the maturing and slow stabilizing of wine. Before the advent of sterile bottling, an oak vat was simply the safest place for a grower to store wine – sometimes for years, topped up with fresh wine as necessary.

In California cooperage has become something of a fetish. Comparative tastings are held between the same wine aged in oak from different French forests; even from the same forest but different barrel makers. The names of Demptos and Nadalie of Bordeaux, of Taransaud and Séguin-Moreau of Cognac and François Frères and the Tonnelleries de Bourgogne of Burgundy are more familiar in the Napa Valley than in France. Current opinion seems to be that Limousin oak, which is faster growing with wider rings, imparts coarser flavours to wine, whereas the much tighter-grained oaks of the forests of the Massif Central, Tronçais, Allier and Nevers, and from the Vosges, provide much more refined flavours, for both red and white wines. American white-oak uncharred Bourbon barrels are also used. They offer less flavour and tannin (but a higher tannin/flavour ratio) – good for Cabernet and Zinfandel, less so for white wines. American oak is significantly cheaper than French oak, which has encouraged some French coopers, such as Demptos and Séguin-Moreau to establish cooperages in California, where they use French methods to treat American oak, with some success.

Baltic, Balkan and other oaks are also used and much has been written about their relative merits. Since there is no visual difference and a cooper's shop contains oak from many sources, one may well be sceptical about such fine distinctions in any case. Other factors such as the thickness of the staves, whether they have split or sawn, air dried or kiln dried, steamed or 'toasted', with varying degrees of toasting, even whether the barrel is washed in hot water or cold can all start arguments among the initiated. Consequently some people place more emphasis on the type of oak, while others attach more importance to the individual cooper.

Red Wine – carbonic maceration

The technique of fermenting uncrushed grapes known as *macération carbonique* has been developed in France since 1935 by Professor Michel Flanzy and others. The method is described on page 150. It began to make a real impact in the early 1970s in dramatically improving the quality of the better Midi wines. It is now well established in France as the best way to produce fruity, 'supple', richly coloured reds for drinking young, but its acceptance has been surprisingly slow in other countries. It is particularly surprising that California has paid so little attention to it. Low acidity tends to make pure maceration wines short lived, which is inappropriate for the finest growths. But a proportion can be a valuable element in a blend with a tannic and/or acidic red.

Fining

The ancient technique of pouring whipped egg-whites, gelatin, isinglass (fish glue), blood or other coagulants into wine is still widely used both on must and finished wine, despite modern filters and centrifuges. Its object is to clean the liquid of the finest suspended solids, which are too light to sink. The 'fining', poured on to the surface, slowly sinks like a superfine screen, carrying any solids to the bottom. Certain finings such as bentonite (*see* White wine – after fermentation) are specific to certain undesirable constituents. 'Blue' fining (potassium ferrocyanide) removes excess iron from the wine.

Racking

Once the gross lees, or sediment, in a barrel or vat have sunk to the bottom, the wine is 'racked' off them simply by pouring the clear liquid from a tap above the level of the solids. In wines that are kept over a length of time in barrels, racking is repeated every few months as more solids are precipitated. If the wine is judged to need more oxygen, racking is done via an open basin; if not, it is done by a hose linking one barrel directly to another.

Red Wine – malolactic fermentation

Growers have always been aware of a fresh activity in their barrels of new wine in the spring following the vintage. Folklore put it down to a 'natural sympathy' between the wine and the rising sap in the vineyards. It seemed to be a further fermentation, but it happened in wine that had no sugar left to ferment.

The science of microbiology has found the answer. It is a form of fermentation carried on by bacteria, not yeasts, which are feeding on malic (apple) acid in the wine and converting it to lactic (milk) acid, giving off carbon dioxide bubbles in the process. It has several results: a lowering of the quantity and of its sharpness (lactic acid is milder to taste than malic); increase of stability, and a less quantifiable smoothing and complicating of the wine's flavour. For almost all red wines, therefore, it is highly desirable, and winemakers take steps to make sure that it takes place.

In most cases a gentle raising of the temperature in the cellar to about 20°C (68°F) is sufficient. Sometimes it is necessary to import the right bacteria and with improved technology it is now possible to seed the malolactic fermentation artificially. Sometimes (this is considered very desirable) the malolactic fermentation can be encouraged to happen concurrently with the first (alcoholic) fermentation.

Blending for Complexity

Champagne, red and white Bordeaux, Rhône reds, Chianti, Rioja, port, are examples of wines made of a mixture of grapes. Burgundy, Barolo, sherry, German and Alsace wines are examples of one-grape wines. American varietal-consciousness has tended to put a premium on the simplistic idea that '100% is best'. But recent research has shown that even among wines of humble quality a mixture of two is often better than the lesser of the two and generally better than either. This is taken to prove that 'complexity' is in itself a desirable quality in wine; that one variety can 'season' another as butter and salt do eggs.

There is a general trend in California, therefore, towards Bordeaux-style blending of Merlot with Cabernet and Semillon with Sauvignon Blanc. On the other hand no other grape has been shown to improve Pinot Noir, Chardonnay or Riesling. Added complexity in their already delicious flavours either comes with the help of barrel-ageing, in Riesling with 'noble-rot', or simply with years in bottle.

Filtration

The Seitz Company of Bad Kreuznach, Germany, has been the pioneer in the developing of ever finer and finer filters capable of removing almost everything, even the flavour, from wine if they are not used with discretion. Most filters consist of a series of 'pads' alternating with plates, through which the wine is forced under pressure. The degree of filtration depends on the pore size of the pads. At 0.65 microns they remove yeast, at 0.45 bacteria as well. To avoid having to change them frequently, wine is nearly always clarified by such other means as fining or centrifuging before filtration.

Some winemakers make a point of labelling their wine 'unfiltered'. They believe that it is worth running the risk of slight sediment for the sake of extra flavour. So do I.

Pasteurization

Louis Pasteur, the great French chemist of the late 19th century who discovered the relationship of oxygen to wine, and hence the cause of vinegar, gave his name to the process of sterilization by heating to kill off harmful organisms. In wine this means any yeast and bacteria that might start re-fermenting.

A temperature of 60°C (140°F) for about 30 minutes is needed – although an alternative preferred today (for

bulk wine only) is 'flash' pasteurization at a much higher temperature, 85°C (185°F), for a much shorter time (up to one minute). Normally pasteurization is only used on cheap wines not intended to mature further, although there is evidence that it does not permanently inhibit further development. Modern sterile handling and filtration is steadily phasing out pasteurization from modern wineries.

Ageing

There are two separate and distinct ways in which wine can age: 'oxidative' ageing in contact with oxygen and 'reductive' ageing when the oxygen supply is cut off. Barrel-ageing is oxidative; it encourages numerous complex reactions between the acids, sugars, tannins, pigments and multifarious polysyllabic constituents of wine.

Bottle-ageing is reductive. Once the wine is bottled the only oxygen available is the limited amount dissolved in the liquid or trapped between the liquid and the cork. (No oxygen enters through a cork.) In wines with a high carbon dioxide content (eg champagne) there is not even this much oxygen. Life-forms depending on oxygen are therefore very limited in their scope for activity. 'Reductive' means that the oxygen is reduced – eventually to zero. In these conditions different complex reactions between the same constituents occur at a much slower rate. The ultimate quality and complexity in most wines is only arrived at by a combination of these two forms of ageing, though the proportions of each can vary widely. Many white wines are bottled very young but improve enormously in bottle. Champagne and vintage port are matured almost entirely in bottle. Fine red wines may spend up to three years in barrel and then perhaps two or three times as long in bottle. Tawny port and sherry are matured entirely in barrel and are not normally intended for any further bottle-age.

Bottling

The question of where and by whom wine should be bottled has been much debated, but since the introduction in France of the mobile bottling unit in the 1960s it has become the rule, rather than the exception, for producers even on a small scale to bottle their own wine. The unit is simply a lorry equipped as a modern semi-automatic bottling plant. Its arrival meant that the evocative words *mis en bouteille au château* or *au domaine*, widely supposed (especially in America) to be a guarantee of authenticity and even quality, could be used by all the little properties that used to rely on merchants to bottle for them. The change rubbed both ways: some merchants' names were a guarantee of well-chosen, well-handled wine; others were not.

Modern automatic bottling lines, particularly for fragile semi-sweet wines such as Germany's, can be like a cross between an operating theatre and a space shuttle, with airlock doors for total antiseptic sterility. The wine is often 'sparged', or flushed out with CO_2 or an inert gas such as nitrogen, to remove any oxygen. The bottle is first filled with nitrogen and the wine filled into it through a long nozzle (a

'Mosel cock') to the bottom, pushing out the gas as the level rises. Another common device with standard wines is 'hot-bottling': heating the wine to about 54°C (130°F) at the point of filling the bottle. All this is to avoid any chance of refermentation. For naturally stabilized wines that have spent a long time in barrel, such precautions should not be needed.

Carbon Dioxide for 'spritz'

Many light white, rosé and occasionally red wines benefit from being bottled with a degree of carbon dioxide dissolved in them – just enough for a few faint bubbles to appear at the brim or the bottom of the glass. In many wines this is a natural occurrence. In others it is an easy and effective way of giving a slight prickle of refreshing sharpness to wines that would otherwise be dull, soft and/or neutral.

Cooperatives

Arguably the most important development for the majority of winemakers in Europe has been the rise of the cooperative movement. By pooling resources and qualifying for generous government grants and loans, the peasant wine-farmers of the past are now nearly all grape growers who deliver their whole harvest to a well-equipped central winery. Most are now extremely up-to-date with vats and presses far better than the district would otherwise have, and a qualified oenologist to make the wine. A few are outright leaders in their regions: nobody else can afford such heavy investment in modern plant. Nearly all use premiums to encourage farmers to produce riper, healthier, cleaner grapes and charge fines for rot, leaves and soil in the crop.

'Flying Winemakers'

The trend for what are now called flying winemakers first began among the coops of the south of France which have greatly benefited from an input of New World technology and knowhow, particularly concerning hygiene and temperature control. The concept and the term were invented by the pioneering English wine merchant Tony Laithwaite. It is now by no means uncommon to find a New Zealand winemaker in Chile or South Africa and many of the young graduates of the Roseworthy College in Australia begin their winemaking experience by clocking up as many vintages as possible on both sides of the world. Central and Eastern Europe in particular has benefited from their input. Often the graduates are employed by established flying winemakers (among them Kym Milne, Jacques Lurton and Hugh Ryman) to produce a specific wine for a specific customer, more often than not for a British supermarket.

Sparkling Wines

The *méthode champenoise* (or classic method as we must now call it since the Champenois have properly claimed the term as belonging to their region) is not susceptible to many short cuts or labour-saving devices, although machines have been devised for most of the laborious hand work involved. The latest and most notable is an automatic 'riddling rack' to replace the unremitting chore of shaking and turning each bottle regularly. The massive framework, which vibrates and tips automatically at intervals, is known in France as a Gyropalette, in the US simply as a VLM – Very Large Machine.

Other methods of making sparkling wine, none of which achieves the same degree of dissolved gas as the classic method, include refermenting the wine in a bottle, then decanting it into a tank under CO_2 pressure, filtering out the sediment (still under pressure) and rebottling it. These wines may be labelled 'fermented in the bottle', but not 'fermented in *this* bottle' – or 'classic method'. The *cuve close* or Charmat process avoids the first bottling by inducing the secondary fermentation in a tank, then filtering and bottling. This is the most common method for cheaper sparkling wines. Very cheap ones are sometimes simply 'carbonated' by pumping CO_2 into still wine. It does not stay there long.

Chemical Analysis

Whoever coined the phrase 'a chemical symphony' described wine perfectly. (There are, of course, string quartets too.) Good wine gets its infinitely intriguing flavour from the interweaving of innumerable organic and inorganic substances in amounts so small that they have hitherto been untraceable. But this is no longer the case. A gas chromatograph is an instrument capable of identifying and measuring up to 250 different substances in wine so far. It (and similar instruments) can produce a graphic chemical profile. University of California researchers are playing the fascinating computer game of trying to match the sensory (eg smell and taste) perception of teams of tasters with the drawings of the chromatograph to discover which substance is responsible for which taste – the idea presumably being that once we know, vineyards and grapes will become obsolete.

At a more humdrum level it is normal to do simple laboratory checks on about 20 constituents, from alcohol and acidity to sugar and sulphur, before giving any wine a clean bill of health.

The Critical Audience

A catalogue of the influences and advances in modern wine would be one-sided without a mention of the consumer. At least as striking as the technological changes of the past 25 years has been the snowballing interest in wine as a topic as well as a drink. It began in England, spread rapidly to America, Holland, Germany, Scandinavia, and in the past few years has even stirred the great bastions of conservatism and complacency: France, Italy and Spain, the major wine-producing nations.

Books and articles about wine, comparative tastings, newsletters and reviews have turned the spotlight on the individual winemaker. The motivation is there not just to sell, but to excel. The spirit of rivalry and the friendly confrontation between producer and consumer may be the most important driving force of all. We are all the beneficiaries.

HOW WINE IS MADE

Wine is simply fermented grape juice. The basic stages in making white and red wines are shown on pages 31 and 32; variations on the main theme are explained here.

Dry White Wines

Plain dry wine of no special character, fully fermented, not intended to be aged. Usually made with non-aromatic grapes, especially in Italy, southern France, Spain, California. Outstanding examples are Muscadet and Soave. Wine-making is standard, with increasing emphasis on freshness by excluding oxygen and fermenting cool.

Fresh, fruity, dry to semi-sweet wines for drinking young, made from aromatic grape varieties: Riesling, Sauvignon Blanc, Gewürztraminer, Muscat Blanc, for example. Extreme emphasis on picking at the right moment, clean juice, cool fermentation and early bottling.

Dry but full-bodied and smooth whites usually made with a degree of 'skin contact', fermented at higher temperatures, sometimes in barrels. Bottled after a minimum of nine months and intended for further ageing. Chardonnay from Burgundy is the classic example, which the New World aspires to emulate. Sauvignon Blanc is occasionally used in this way.

Sweet White Wines

Fresh, fruity, light in alcohol, semi-sweet to sweet in the German style. Now made by fermenting to dryness and 'back-blending' with unfermented juice.

The same style but made by stopping fermentation while some sugar remains. Usually has higher alcohol and more winey, less obviously grapey flavour. Most French, Spanish, Italian and many New World medium-sweet wines are in this category.

Botrytis (noble rot) wines with balance of either low alcohol with very high sugar (German style) or very high alcohol and fairly high sugar (Sauternes style) Hungary's Tokay Aszú lies in the middle, balancing high sugar and moderate alcohol with high acidity.

Very sweet wines made from extremely ripe or partially raisined grapes, where the sugars are concentrated. Italian *vin santo* is the classic example.

Rose Wines

Pale rosé from red grapes pressed immediately to extract juice with very little colour, sometimes called *vin gris* (literally 'grey wine') or Blanc de Noirs in the case of sparkling wines.

Rosé with more colour made from red grapes crushed and *'saigné* or bled so that the juice is run off the skins after a short red-wine type maceration or vatting, then pressed and fermented like white wine. The more common method used for Tavel rosé, Anjou rosé, Italian Chiaretto and *vin d'une nuit.*

Champagne rosé is made in two ways: the 'maceration process' is when skins of black grapes are left in contact with the juice during the initial fermentation, producing a delicate, pale pink wine. The wine then undergoes a second fermentation in the bottle to produce the sparkle. The second method is to blend still red and still white wines together after the initial fermentation. The second fermentation follows once the wine has been bottled.

Red Wines

Light, fruity wines made with minimum tannin by short maceration period. Should be drunk early as the extract, pigments and tannin necessary for maturation are absent. Can be made with aromatic grapes but are more commonly made of simple fruity or neutral grapes.

Softer, richer, more savoury and deep-coloured wines (but still low in tannin) made by carbonic maceration or interior fermentation of the grapes before pressing. Heating the must is another method of producing colour and smoothness.

Full-blooded reds for maturing (known as *vins de garde*) made by long contact of the skins with the juice to extract pigments, tannins, phenols, etc. All great red wines are made this way.

Fortified Wines

Vin doux naturel is naturally very sweet wine fermented to about 15° alcohol, when further fermentation is stopped (muté) by adding spirits.

Port follows the *vin doux naturel* procedure, but fermentation is stopped earlier, at 4–6°, by a larger dose of spirits: a quarter of the volume.

Sherry is naturally strong white wine fully fermented to dryness. Then a small quantity of spirits is added to stabilize it while it matures in contact with air.

Madeira is white wine with naturally high acidity stopped with alcohol before fermentation has stopped of its own accord. Then it is baked in 'stoves' (*estufas*) before being aged in barrels or big glass jars.

Sparkling Wines

White (or sometimes red) wines made to ferment a second time by the addition of yeast and sugar. The gas from the second fermentation dissolves in the wine. In the classic champagne method the second fermentation takes place in the bottle in which the wine is sold, involving complicated and laborious processing (see page 164), which inevitably makes it expensive.

Only wines from the designated Champagne region can now be identified as produced by the *méthode champenoise*. Wines from elsewhere, however good, can only be described as being made by the 'classic method' or, in French, *méthode traditionnelle*. Cheaper methods are:

The transfer process The wine is transferred, via a filter, under pressure to another bottle.

Cuve close The second fermentation takes place in a tank; the wine is then filtered under pressure and bottled.

Carbonization Carbon dioxide is pumped into still wine (although the bubbles are scarcely long-lived).

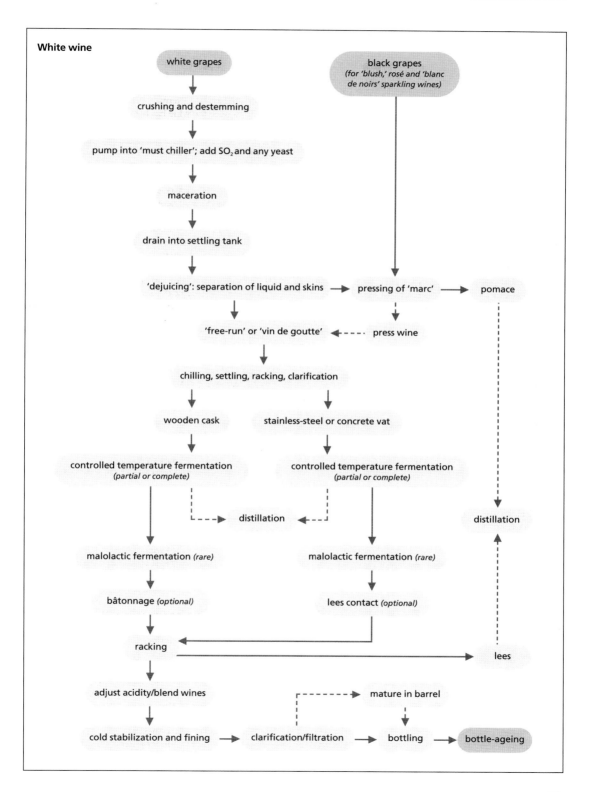

White wine

white grapes

black grapes
(for 'blush,' rosé and 'blanc de noirs' sparkling wines)

crushing and destemming

pump into 'must chiller'; add SO_2 and any yeast

maceration

drain into settling tank

'dejuicing': separation of liquid and skins → pressing of 'marc' → pomace

'free-run' or 'vin de goutte' ◄--- press wine

chilling, settling, racking, clarification

wooden cask

stainless-steel or concrete vat

controlled temperature fermentation
(partial or complete)

controlled temperature fermentation
(partial or complete)

distillation

malolactic fermentation *(rare)*

malolactic fermentation *(rare)*

bâtonnage *(optional)*

lees contact *(optional)*

distillation

racking

lees

adjust acidity/blend wines

mature in barrel

cold stabilization and fining → clarification/filtration → bottling → bottle-ageing

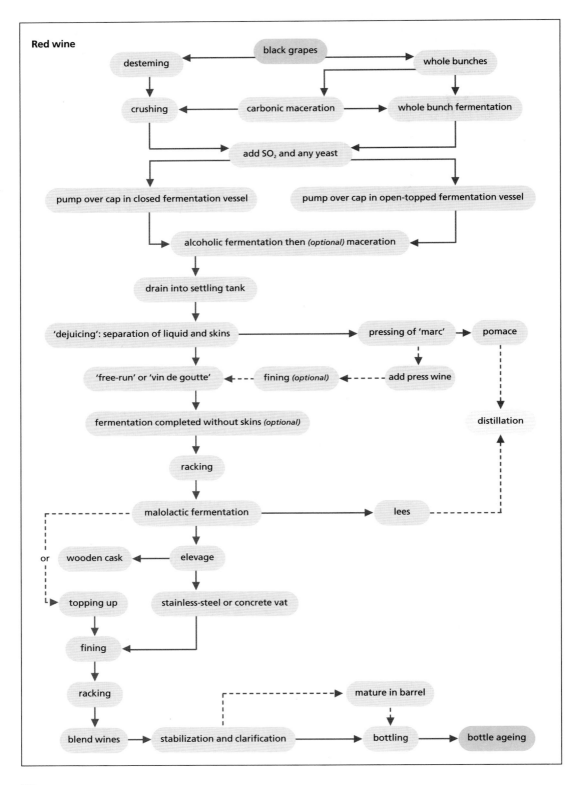

Red wine

- black grapes
- desteming
- whole bunches
- crushing
- carbonic maceration
- whole bunch fermentation
- add SO$_2$ and any yeast
- pump over cap in closed fermentation vessel
- pump over cap in open-topped fermentation vessel
- alcoholic fermentation then *(optional)* maceration
- drain into settling tank
- 'dejuicing': separation of liquid and skins
- pressing of 'marc'
- pomace
- 'free-run' or 'vin de goutte'
- fining *(optional)*
- add press wine
- fermentation completed without skins *(optional)*
- distillation
- racking
- malolactic fermentation
- lees
- or
- wooden cask
- elevage
- topping up
- stainless-steel or concrete vat
- fining
- racking
- mature in barrel
- blend wines
- stabilization and clarification
- bottling
- bottle ageing

Wines, Vineyards and Winemakers of the World

FRANCE

Calais
Lille

Le Havre
Caen

Reims
CHAMPAGNE

Paris
Strasbourg
ALSACE

Seine
Marne

Brest

LOIRE
Loire
Chablis
Saône

Tours
Loire
Pouilly-
Fumé

Nantes
Anjou-
Saumur
Sancerre
Dijon

Muscadet
Touraine
Côte de Nuits
BURGUNDY
JURA

Cher
Côte Chalonnaise
Geneva

Côte de Beaune
Mâconnais

La Rochelle
Bugey

Beaujolais
Lyon
SAVOIE

BORDEAUX
Côte Rôtie

Médoc
Dordogne
Condrieu
RHONE
Grenoble

Pomerol
Bergerac
St-Joseph

Bordeaux
St-Emilion
Cornas
Crozes Hermitage

Graves
Hermitage

Entre-Deux-Mers
Cahors

Sauternes
Garonne
Rhône

Côtes du
Marmandais
SOUTHWEST
Tarn
Côtes du
Rhône-Villages
Châteauneuf-du-Pape
Beaumes-de-Venise

Buzet
Gaillac

Tursan
Côtes de
St-Mont
Côtes du Frontonnais
LANGUEDOC
PROVENCE
Nice

Madiran
Toulouse
St-Chinian
Montpellier
Bandol

Biarritz
Jurançon
Minervois
Marseille

Corbières

Fitou
Rivesaltes

Roussillon
Perpignan

Banyuls

Bastia
CORSICA

Ajaccio

Nobody argues with the primacy of France as the country that set the international standards by which wine is judged. Germany's Rieslings, Spain's sherry and Portugal's port are the only non-French wines accepted as universal models to be imitated and emulated. This is not to invalidate Chianti or Barolo or Rioja; but they remain vernacular styles. Bordeaux, burgundy, champagne and certain Loire, Rhône and Alsace wines are targets that winemakers everywhere aim at – in the first instance by planting their grapes.

A form of natural selection gave France these ideas of what wine can be. Her first vineyards were planted in the Midi in the 6th or 7th centuries BC. The Romans established what are now all the highest-quality areas – Burgundy, Bordeaux, Champagne, the Rhône and Loire valleys and Alsace. They chose them because they were promising-looking slopes near centres of population with reasonable transport facilities; ideally by water, but failing water by a main trade route with good going for heavy wagons. They planted them, after trying Italian vines, with selections of native woodland vines of Gaul and her neighbours Spain, the Rhineland and the Alps. We can be fairly certain that their descendants are the vines grown today.

The soils are the same; the climate and the conditions of cellarage have not changed very much. With allowances for different techniques and tastes, we can speculate that French wines have honed their identities over almost 2,000 years. Identity and fame once established, there is the inevitable problem of fraud. For every person who knows what a given wine ought to taste like there are a hundred who are ready to pay for something they will be unable to identify.

The problem is age-old. Many laws have been passed (and taxes raised) to regulate how wine is made, how much, when, where, by whom, of what grapes, and under what name and at what price it can be sold. At the start of the 20th century the problem was acute, since phylloxera had left Europe with a serious shortage. In France the need for a national system of control was clear, and in 1932 the Institut National des Appellations d'Origine was founded to regulate the entire quality wine industry. The Office National Interprofessionnel des Vins de Table was also founded to keep order among the peasantry making *vins ordinaires* without the dignity of an *appellation d'origine*.

These distinctions are now central to the whole wine system in Europe. In EU terms every wine is either a Vin de Qualité Produit dans Une Région Determinée (VQPRD) or a *vin de table* – an absurd choice of category, incidentally: almost all wines are made to be drunk at table, and it is perfectly fair to say that Château Lafite is a table wine. The French system itself has become more elaborate. Apart from *vin de consommation courante*, where the price only depends on the alcoholic degree, there are three classification categories for all the wines of France:

Appellation (d'Origine) Contrôlée (AC or AOC)

A more or less strict control of origin, grape varieties and methods used, alcoholic strength and quantity produced. Most AC wines are limited to a basic production in the region of 40 hectolitres a hectare (445 cases of wine an acre) but a complicated system of annual reassessment usually allows more, and sometimes very considerably more.

The nature of appellation control varies. In Bordeaux the most specific and restricted appellation is a whole village, within which individual properties ('châteaux') are given wide liberties to plant where and what (within the regional tradition) they like. In the best sites of Burgundy each field has its own appellation. The appellation Champagne covers a whole region and its method of working. Each region is a particular case with its own logic.

The ceiling on production, or Plafond Limite de Classement (PLC), is always lower for Grands Crus (in regions that have them) than for humbler appellations. The differences used to provide manoeuvring space for notorious fiddles. But now stricter controls try to ensure that each appellation is treated entirely separately in the grower's and merchant's cellar.

The AC system was not instituted originally to provide quality control, only guarantees of origin and authenticity. Quality control by compulsory tasting has now been introduced at least in theory. In practice as much as 97% of wines submitted for tasting are nodded through: relations between growers and inspectors are far too close for the good of the system. The result? An AC is a sure indicator of origin, but it is only the producer's name that even indicates, let alone guarantees, quality.

Vins Délimités de Qualité Supérieure (VDQS)

The second rank of appellations was instituted in 1945 for regions with worthwhile identities and traditions producing 'minor' wines. It has similar systems of control, and in practice became a sort of training ground for true AOCs. Without further recruits it will gradually disappear.

Vins de Pays

Vins de pays are now in reality the dynamic second tier after AC. The notion of 'country wines' was crystallized in the 1970s, organized like ACs on several levels of precision; the regional being the broadest, *vins de pays de zone* the most precise, usually with the highest standards.

There are four regional *vins de pays*: Jardin de la France for the Loire Valley, Comté Tolosan for the Southwest, Comtés Rhodaniens for the Rhône region and Vins de Pays d'Oc for the whole of the Midi. Thirty-nine *départements* give their names to *vins de pays* grown within their borders and (up to a point) their viticultural traditions. No fewer than 100 defined districts, with a great concentration in the Midi, produce *vins de pays de zone*. This is the logical breeding ground for new ideas, whether based on grape variety or distinctive *terroir*. Those that succeed in producing attractive quality and consistent identity, and perhaps eventually go on to matriculate as ACs, will inevitably combine both grape variety (or varieties) and *terroir* in their definition. In the end, there is no other way to define and delimit what is distinctive about any wine.

BORDEAUX

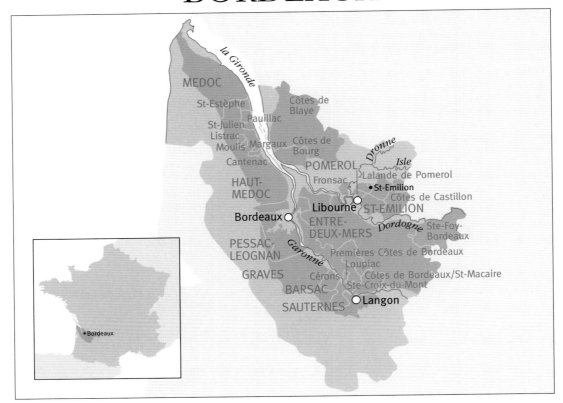

Four factors make Bordeaux the most important vineyard region of all: its quality, size, variety and unity. The last two are not contradictory but complementary. They are the reason we keep coming back for more: the range of styles and types of Bordeaux is sufficiently wide for everybody; no two are ever identical, and yet there is an unmistakable identity among all of them, a clean-cut, appetizing, easily digestible and stimulating quality that only Bordeaux offers.

The Bordeaux character comes from the strains of grapes and the maritime climate rather than the soil (which varies from gravel to limestone to clay). And of course it comes from traditions of making, handling and enjoying wine in a certain way, an amalgam of the tastes of the French and their northern neighbours, the British, Belgians, Dutch, Germans and Scandinavians, who have paid the piper since the Middle Ages.

In 1994/95 half of the total white-wine production of Bordeaux and a fifth of its red was exported. But the proportion among the best growths (Pauillac, Graves and Margaux, for example) rose to two-thirds or even three-quarters. Over six times as much red wine is made as white, and red is worth five times as much as white on the export market.

Bordeaux supplies four basic styles of wine: light everyday red, fine red, dry white and sweet, sticky, 'liquorous' white. There is not a great deal to be said about the first except that there is a vast supply, up to 2,500,000 hectolitres (330 million bottles) a year, varying from the excitingly tasty to the merely passable or occasionally poor and watery. It may be offered under a brand name or as the production of a Petit Château.

There is a degree of overlap between this everyday red and 'fine' red, where the former excels itself or the latter lets the side down, but the fine red is really a distinct product, a more concentrated wine made for keeping and matured in oak. This is where the distinctions between different soils and situations produce remarkable differences of flavour and keeping qualities, more or less accurately reflected in the system of appellations and of classifications within the appellations. The total quantity available in this category is even more impressive for this class of wine: approaching one bottle for every two of the everyday red.

The dry whites belong, in the main, alongside the light reds. A very few rise to the level of fine white burgundy but this is an area where Bordeaux has recently made exciting progress. Modern techniques are finding great character in Bordeaux's traditional white grapes, and fermenting in oak is adding to their stature. There is less than half as much made as there is of comparable red. The sweet whites are a drop in the ocean, only about one bottle in 40, but a precious speciality capable of superlative quality, and much appreciated in Bordeaux even at a humble level as an aperitif.

Every Bordeaux vintage is subject to the most fickle of climates. Overriding all other considerations is the unpredictable seaside weather. A great vintage will give even the commonest wines an uncommon vitality, but conversely the category of fine wines can be sadly depleted by a really bad one, and the sweet whites can be eliminated altogether.

This shifting pattern of vintages against the already complex background of appellations and properties, and the long life span of the good wines, makes the appreciation of Bordeaux a mesmerically fascinating pursuit which never ends.

BORDEAUX IN ROUND FIGURES

Over the 30 years from 1963 to 1993 the total area of *appellation contrôlée* vineyards in Bordeaux dwindled for a while, then recently began to increase. In 1993 it

reached 284,000 acres. A mere 4% of the entire Gironde vineyard is now non-appellation. Red wine currently accounts for 82% of Bordeaux's production, an average between 1990 and 1995 of 4.5 million hectolitres, while white wine has dropped dramatically as a proportion of this total – from 60% in the 1950s to 18% in the mid-1990s. When new plantings come onstream, the proportion of red wine will increase to about 90%.

Meanwhile the number of individual properties continues steadily to decrease. In 1950 the total was 60,327 and in 1994, it was just 13,957; a drop of 77%. The average size of holding, though, edges up; from 3 acres in 1950 to 20 acres in 1996.

With this concentration of ownership, efficiency has improved. Vintages of the 1950s (admittedly including a disastrous frost in 1956) produced an average crop of 30 hectolitres; the decade 1985 to 1994 an average of 52 hectolitres.

The production figures below, comparing 1995, a bountiful harvest, with 1991, a crop devastated by spring frosts, show how much the weather can still affect the outcome.

PRODUCTION: RED WINES (HECTOLITRES)

	1995	1991
Bordeaux (basic red appellation;the wine need only attain 10° alcohol)	2,269,229	873,306
Bordeaux Supérieur (as above with an alcohol degree of 10.5 or more)	518,974	306,849
The 'Côtes' (Blaye, Bourg, Castillon, Francs and the Premières Côtes de Bordeaux; outlying areas of generally higher quality and individuality)	857,363	372,600
St-Emilion	294,770	82,960
Pomerol	40,882	8,086
St-Emilion area – total	700,94	189,629
Bas Médoc	300,656	103,807
Haut-Médoc	247,075	78,628
Graves	113,299	49,002
St-Estèphe	70,982	40,113
Margaux	68,816	24,917
Pauillac	59,874	28,792
St-Julien	44,694	16,805
Moulis & Listrac	75,078	24,475
Pessac-Léognan	52,080	14,838
Médoc and Graves area – total	1,032,554	381,377

PRODUCTION: WHITE WINES (HECTOLITRES)

	1995	1991
Bordeaux (basic)	647,813	226,470
Entre-Deux-Mers	139,428	67,165
Graves and Pessac-Léognan	58,577	20,550
Total dry whites	905,529	366,626
Sauternes	31,392	14,197
Barsac	15,602	6,644
Total sweet white	138,925	62,555

Export figures fluctuate from year to year but in 1994–95 the main customers were:

Germany	299,000 hl	3.3m cases	77% red
UK	294,000 hl	3.2m cases	69% red
Benelux	227,000 hl	2.5m cases	52% red
Denmark	189,000 hl	2.1m cases	89% red
USA	110,000 hl	1.2m cases	75% red
Switzerland	86,000 h	946,000 cases	80% red
Japan	64,000 hl	704,000 cases	61% red
Canada	60,000 hl	660,000 cases	61% red

During the same period, and in terms of the average price paid for a bottle of Bordeaux, the leading export markets, in descending order, were:

USA, Switzerland, Japan, UK and Denmark, Germany, Benelux, Canada

CLASSIFICATIONS

The appellations of Bordeaux are themselves a sort of preliminary classification of its wines by quality, on the basis that the more narrowly they are defined the higher the general level of the district. This is as far as overall grading has ever (officially) gone. More precise classifications are all local to one area without cross-referencing.

The most effective way of comparing the standing of châteaux within different areas is by price – the method used for the first and most famous of all classifications, that done for the Médoc for the Paris Exhibition of 1855.

In 1855 the criterion was the price each wine fetched, averaged over a long period, up to 100 years, but taking into account its recent standing and the current condition of the property. The list is still so widely used that it is essential for reference even 142 years later. A few châteaux have fallen by the wayside; the majority have profited by their notoriety to expand their vineyards, swallowing lesser neighbours. It is certain that the original classification located most of the best land in the Médoc and gave credit to the proprietors who had planted it. What they subsequently did with it has proved to be less important than the innate superiority of the gravel banks they chose to plant.

The Concept of a Château

The unit of classification in Bordeaux is not the land itself (as in Burgundy) but the property on the land – the estate or 'château'. The château is either a first- or a fourth-growth or a Cru Bourgeois. A proprietor can buy land from a neighbour of greater or lesser standing and add it to his own and (given that it is suitable land) it will take his rank. Vineyards can go up or down the scale according to who owns them.

An example. Château Gloria is an estate of high quality in St-Julien, formed since World War II by buying parcels of land from neighbouring Crus Classés. When the land changed hands it was 'classed', but because the buyer had no classed château the vines were demoted to Cru Bourgeois.

Conversely, many classed growths have added to their holdings by buying neighbouring Cru Bourgeois vines. When the Rothschilds of Château Lafite bought the adjacent Château Duhart-Milon they could theoretically have made all its wine as Lafite.

The justification for this apparent injustice is that a château is considered more as a 'marque' than a plot of ground. Its identity and continuity depend so much on the repeated choices the owner has to make, of precisely when and how to perform every operation from planting to bottling, that he has to be trusted with the final decision of what the château wine consists of. A recent sign of how seriously owners take their responsibilities is the proliferation of 'second labels' for batches of wine that fail to meet self-imposed standards.

This is the Médoc method. St-Emilion is different. Some of its châteaux, the Premiers Grands Crus, have a semi-permanent classification renewable (in theory) after ten years – and last reviewed in 1996. Others, the Grands Crus, have to submit each vintage for tasting.

Only the Médoc and the single Château Haut-Brion in Graves were classified in 1855. The list divides them into five classes, but stresses that the order within each class is not to be considered significant. Only one official change has been made since: the promotion in 1973 of Château Mouton-Rothschild from second- to first-growth.

Crus Bourgeois and Petits Châteaux

Whether an unclassed château has any official rank or not is not simple either. It depends partly on whether the owner is a loner or a joiner, since membership of the Syndicat de Crus Bourgeois, the next ranking authority, is purely voluntary. The list of members of the Syndicate of Crus Bourgeois of the Médoc, revised in September 1996, includes 321 properties of which 108 are Médoc AOC, 109 Haut-Médoc (24 from St-Seurin de Cadourne), 16 Moulis AOC, 24 Listrac AOC, 34 St-Estèphe AOC, 10 Pauillac AOC, 6 St-Julien AOC and 14 Margaux AOC. The confusing concepts of Cru Grand Bourgeois and Cru Grand Bourgeois Exceptionnel no longer exist – perhaps one of the better minor rulings of the EU – although the terms are still seen on labels.

The terms Cru Artisan and Cru Paysan are sometimes used for properties below Cru Bourgeois in size and/or quality. In 1989 the Syndicat des Crus Artisans was formed for properties of under 17 acres. It has 236 members. The wine trade tends to lump them all together as Petits Châteaux – a relative term, since no doubt Rothschilds consider Crus Bourgeois in these terms.

A great number of the thousands that used to exist are now allied to the caves coopératives, but more and more are sought out by wine merchants and given the dignity of their own labels. Many, indeed, lose their identity in the anonymity of the cooperative and then miraculously find it again later. There is no object in listing their endless names, however evocative, but to the claret lover with an open mind they are always worth exploring, offering some of the best bargains in France. In good vintages, drunk at no more than three or four years old, they can be both delicious and reasonable in price.

THE BORDEAUX CLASSIFICATION OF 1855
First-Growths (Premiers Crus)
Château Lafite-Rothschild, Pauillac
Château Latour, Pauillac
Château Margaux, Margaux
Château Haut-Brion, Pessac, Graves
Château Mouton-Rothschild, Pauillac
   (elevated to First-Growth in 1973)

Second-Growths (Deuxièmes Crus)
Château Rausan-Ségla, Margaux
Château Rauzan-Gassies, Margaux
Château Léoville-Las-Cases, St-Julien
Château Léoville-Poyferré, St-Julien
Château Léoville-Barton, St-Julien
Château Durfort-Vivens, Margaux
Château Lascombes, Margaux

Château Gruaud-Larose, St-Julien
Château Brane-Cantenac, Cantenac-Margaux
Château Pichon-Longueville-Baron, Pauillac
Château Pichon-Lalande, Pauillac
Château Ducru-Beaucaillou, St-Julien
Château Cos d'Estournel, St-Estèphe
Château Montrose, St-Estèphe

Third-Growths (Troisièmes Crus)
Château Giscours, Labarde-Margaux
Château Kirwan, Cantenac-Margaux
Château d'Issan, Cantenac-Margaux
Château Lagrange, St-Julien
Château Langoa-Barton, St-Julien
Château Malescot-St-Exupéry, Margaux
Château Cantenac-Brown, Cantenac-Margaux
Château Palmer, Cantenac-Margaux
Château La Lagune, Ludon
Château Desmirail, Margaux
Château Calon-Ségur, St-Estèphe
Château Ferrière, Margaux
Château d'Alesme, Margaux
Château Boyd-Cantenac, Cantenac-Margaux

Fourth-Growths (Quatrièmes Crus)
Château St-Pierre (Bontemps et Sevaistre) St-Julien
Château Branaire-Ducru, St-Julien
Château Talbot, St-Julien

Château Duhart-Milon-Rothschild, Pauillac
Château Pouget, Cantenac-Margaux
Château La Tour-Carnet, St-Laurent
Château Lafon-Rochet, St-Estèphe
Château Beychevelle, St-Julien
Château Prieuré-Lichine, Cantenac-Margaux
Château Marquis-de-Terme, Margaux

Fifth-Growths (Cinquièmes Crus)
Château Pontet-Canet, Pauillac
Château Batailley, Pauillac
Château Grand-Puy-Lacoste, Pauillac
Château Grand-Puy-Ducasse, Pauillac
Château Haut-Batailley, Pauillac
Château Lynch-Bages, Pauillac
Château Lynch-Moussas, Pauillac
Château Dauzac, Labarde-Margaux
Château d'Armailacq, Pauillac (formerly known as Mouton d'Armailhacq and Mouton Baronne-Philippe)
Château du Tertre, Arsac-Margaux
Château Haut-Bages-Libéral, Pauillac
Château Pédesclaux, Pauillac
Château Belgrave, St-Laurent
Château de Camensac, St-Laurent
Château Cos Labory, St-Estèphe
Château Clerc-Milon-Rothschild, Pauillac
Château Croizet-Bages, Pauillac
Château Cantemerle, Macau

THE BORDEAUX MARKET 1995 – 140 YEARS ON

A new official classification of all Bordeaux châteaux is unlikely to be agreed. There are too many vested interests and rivalries at stake. But the Bordeaux market, the 'place', run by Bordeaux brokers still operates based on merchant and consumer demand and châteaux come out each year with an opening price that is tested in the market place as the wine is traded in subsequent years.

Opening prices rise and fall with the world economy, and the quality and size of the vintage. The prolific but weak 1992s were sold cheaply. 1995, a good year after four less good vintages, began high. 1990 and 1986 were good

vintages that immediately followed another good vintage. 1989 and 1985 had both started high and 1990 and 1986 started lower but have more than caught up since. Small properties with less to sell often try to aim higher than larger ones; witness the starting prices of small Pomerol estates, such as La Conseillante, whose wines are much in tune with modern international taste.

The figures in the chart below show a selection of opening trade prices in francs per bottle at time of release in the Spring after the vintage, beside the price in Bordeaux in Autumn 1996 when stocks of vintage wine were low and prices high.

Vintage:	1995	1992	1990	1986
Château	Opening/Autumn 96 price (FF)	Opening/Autumn 96 price (FF)	Opening/Autumn 96 price (FF)	Opening/Autumn 96 price (FF)
Latour, Pauillac	240/585	140/265	205/1925	180/600
La Conseillante, Pomerol	190/290	105/157	160/700	125/295
Pichon-Lalande, Pauillac	126/310	65/97	100/300	95/430
Cos d'Estournel, St-Estèphe	116/225	58/105	100/285	82/363
Pape Clément, Pessac	98/158	55/99	80/210	70/198
Canon, St-Emilion	95/145	60/95	100/197	90/247
Léoville Barton, St-Julien	95/175	48/80	65/240	57/244
Lagrange, St-Julien	73/95	42/64	57/132	47/181
La Lagune, Haut-Médoc	62/80	40/70	55/176	54/173
Chasse-Spleen, Haut-Médoc	59/78	39/67	50/176	40} no longer
Potensac, Médoc	35/44	21/46	29/77	24} available

The Red Grapes of Bordeaux

The particulars given in the following pages of each of the principal Bordeaux châteaux include the proportions of the different grape varieties in their vineyards, as far as they are known.

The classic Bordeaux red-wine varieties are all related, probably descended from the ancient *biturica,* whose name is still preserved as Vidure (a synonym for Cabernet Sauvignon in the Graves). Over the centuries, four principal varieties have been selected for a combination of fertility, disease resistance, flavour and adaptability to the Bordeaux soils.

Cabernet Sauvignon is dominant in the Médoc. It is the most highly flavoured, with small berries making dark, tannic wine that demands ageing, but then has both depth and 'cut' of flavour. It flowers well and evenly and ripens a modest crop relatively late, resisting rot better than softer and thinner-skinned varieties. Being a late ripener it needs warm soil. Gravel suits it well, but the colder clay of Pomerol makes it unsatisfactory.

Its close cousin, the **Cabernet Franc**, is a bigger, juicier grape. Before the introduction of Cabernet Sauvignon in the 18th century it was the mainstay of Bordeaux and is still widely planted, particularly in Pomerol and St-Emilion, where it is known as the Bouchet. Cabernet Franc wines have delicious soft-fruit flavours (which are also vividly seen in Chinon and Bourgueil, wines made from this grape on the Loire) but less tannin and 'depth'. Less regular flowering and a thinner skin are also drawbacks, at least in the Médoc.

More important today is the **Merlot**, a precocious grape that buds, flowers and ripens early, making it more vulnerable in spring but ready to pick sooner, with an extra degree of alcohol in its higher sugar. Unfortunately, at harvest time its tight bunches need only a little rain to start them rotting.

Merlot wine has good colour and an equally spicy but softer flavour than Cabernet Sauvignon, making wine that matures sooner. In the Médoc a judicious proportion – rarely above 40 percent – is used; rather more in the Graves; more again in St-Emilion, and in Pomerol up to 95 percent. This is the grape that gives Château Petrus its opulent texture and flavour.

A fourth red grape that is still used in small amounts in the Médoc is the **Petit Verdot**, another Cabernet cousin that ripens late with good flavour and ageing qualities, but flowers irregularly and has other quirks. A little in the vineyard is nonetheless a source of added complexity and 'backbone' in the wine.

A fifth, found more in St-Emilion and largely in the minor areas, is the **Malbec** (alias Pressac), a big, juicy, early-ripening grape which has serious flowering problems (*coulure*). It is grown in the Gironde more for quantity than quality. Paradoxically, under its synonym Auxerrois (or Cot) it is the grape of the historically famous 'black wines' of Cahors.

In the long run, a château proprietor 'designs' his wine by the choice and proportions of varieties he plants.

The White Grapes of Bordeaux

The classic white-wine vineyard in Bordeaux is a mixture of two principal varieties and one or two subsidiary ones as variable in proportions as the red.

Sauvignon Blanc and **Sémillon** make up at least 90 percent of the best vineyards, Sauvignon for its distinct flavour and good acidity, Sémillon for its susceptibility to 'noble rot'. Thus the sweet wine vineyards of Sauternes tend to have more Sémillon, and often a small plot of the more highly flavoured **Muscadelle**.

Unfortunately Sauvignon Blanc has flowering problems in Bordeaux which makes it an irregular producer; to keep a constant proportion of its grapes means having a disproportionate number of vines. A variant known as Sauvignon Gris is also interesting. Recently some excellent fresh dry white has been made entirely of Sémillon. Other white grapes include Ugni Blanc, Folle Blanche, Colombard and Riesling.

THE WINE TRADE IN BORDEAUX

Since Roman times, when a *negotiator britannicus* was reported buying wine in Burdigala, Bordeaux's overseas trade has been one of the mainstays of the life of the city. In the Middle Ages the chief customer was England. From the 17th century it became the Dutch, and later the Germans, then the English again and latterly the Americans. In the 1980s the Japanese joined in. The north of France, and above all Belgium, now absorb the biggest share, much of it by direct sales.

For two centuries up to the 1960s the trade was largely in the hands of a group of négociants, nearly all of foreign origin, with their offices and cellars on the Quai des Chartrons, on the river just north of the centre of the city. The oldest firm still in business is the Dutch Beyermann, founded in 1620. The 'Chartronnais' families, including Cruse, Calvet, Barton & Guestier, Johnston and Eschenauer, were household names and their power was considerable.

Most of these firms have been taken over or their names absorbed, their importance diminished with the growth of direct sales from the châteaux, of bottling at the châteaux and above all with the sheer cost of holding stock. New ways of selling new kinds of brand name wines to fewer but more powerful retailers have created a new class of trade. Most of them have also moved out of Bordeaux to more accessible warehouses. Ten shippers now account for 52 percent of the Bordeaux trade. The following 22 are among the most influential.

Castel Frères

Principal: Pierre Castel. Offices in Blanquefort. 10% is export. The shipper with the largest turnover but 45% of whose business is *vin de consommation courante* – base-level, everyday wine, Castelvin. Castel have huge properties in Arcins, Haut Médoc, where they bought the growers' cooperative and two big châteaux in the Lower Médoc and Côtes de Bourg.

Grands Vins de Gironde

Principal: Pierre-Michel Alzac. A group formed by Rémy Cointreau in 1991 from de Luze, de Rivoyre, Diprovin and Chantecaille and bits of the defunct SDVF, with a fine wine arm La Grande Cave. Its offices are at Carbon Blanc. Export 30%.

CVBG (Consortium Vinicole de Bordeaux et de Gironde)

Principal: Jean-Marie Chadronnier. Including Dourthe and Kressmann, this major player on the Bordeaux scene is part of the Grands Terroirs Associés group owned by the Dutch drinks firm Bols. Offices and cellars at Parempuyre in the Médoc. CVBG owns Château Belgrave and Château La Garde.

Ginestet

Principal: Jacques Merlaut. A complicated company with a great history and under Monsieur Merlaut a recent record of aggressive expansion. 95% of the business is Bordeaux with 30% export. Châteaux Chasse-Spleen, Haut Bages Liberal, Ferrière and La Gurgue are all in the same ownership.

Baron Philippe de Rothschild SA

Managed for Philippine de Rothschild by Xavier de Eizaguirre who in 1996 succeeded Philippe Cottin, one of the wisest heads in Bordeaux. The company, based in the Médoc, commercializes Bordeaux's best-known brand Mouton Cadet and the Baron Philippe range as well as first-growth Mouton Rothschild, Château d'Armailacq, Clerc Milon and Aile d'Argent.

Duclot

Principal: Jean-François Moueix, brother of Christian Moueix of the powerful family firm in Libourne, has a group of companies specializing in top-quality Bordeaux, sold largely to private customers. The smart Bordeaux wine shops, Badie and L'Intendant are also in the same ownership.

Etablissements Cordier

Principal: François du Chaxel. The Cordier family sold to a big financial group in 1984. The firm owns Châteaux Lafaurie-Peyraguey, Meyney, Clos des Jacobins etc. and distributes Gruaud Larose and Cantemerle.

Yvon Mau

Principal: Jean-Francois Mau. Commercially astute policy of brands and châteaux exclusivities has brought success with major retailers. 40% export. A significant part of the business is *vin de table* in bottle and bulk.

Joanne

The three Castéja brothers, Pierre-Antoine, Olivier and Eric, successfully specialize in *crus classés* and château-bottled wines. The firm is based at Fargues St-Hilaire. 50% export.

André Quancard

Principal: Joel Quancard: A house with a good reputation especially for *bourgeois* growths and *petits châteaux*. 11% export.

Barton et Guestier

Principal: Etienne Brault. Part of Seagrams. Offices in Blanquefort. 87% export. Only a third of the business is now Bordeaux and the connection with the original firm, founded in 1725 by an Irishman whose descendants still own Château Langoa-Barton, is only in the name.

Sovex Grands Châteaux

Principal: Justin Onclin. Tightly run company at Carbon Blanc dealing in 100% AC Bordeaux with 64% export. Strong in Belgium.

Bouey et Fils

Principal: Serge Bouey. Family company established in 1959 at Ambarés specializing in the home market.

Borie Manoux

Principal: Emile Castéja. Largest supplier of Bordeaux to hotels, restaurants and specialist retailers on the home market. Export 58%. Owners of 'Beau Rivage' 2nd largest Bordeaux brand; controls over 600 acres of vines in the major appellations: Château Batailley, Château Haut Bages Monpelou; Château Beau Site; Château Trottevieille; Château Bergat; Domaine de L'Eglise.

Calvet SA

Owned by Allied Domecq. Principal: Gilles de Courcel. Founded in 1870 but originally from the Rhône and still with connections there and in Burgundy. 57% is export of many appellations. The range has been revitalized by a team of young winemakers.

William Pitters

Principal: Bernard Magrez. An enterprising merchandizing house in Bordeaux.

Dulong Frères et Fils

A family company exporting an increasing quantity of table wine as well as AC Bordeaux in bottle and bulk.

Mahler-Besse

Principal: Franck Mahler-Besse. A family firm in Bordeaux, Holland, Belgium, Spain and Portugal with the majority holding in Château Palmer and a formidable stock of old vintages.

Mestrezat et Domaines SA

Principal: Jean-Pierre Angliviel de la Beaumelle. Merchants in Bordeaux dealing exclusively in bottled Bordeaux wine from *petitis châteaux* to first growths. Part of the Paribas group owning 750 acres of vineyards, which include Châteaux Grand Puy Ducasse, Rayne Vigneau, Lamothe Bergeron, etc.

Cheval Quancard

Principal: Marcel Quancard. Based in La Grave d'Ambarés (Entre-Deux-Mers). Owns Ch. Terrefort Quancard (among others) and brands, Le Chai des Bordes red and Canter white.

Sichel

Principal: Peter Sichel. Incorporates Edmond Coste. 89% export: Bordeaux and Midi wines. Part owner of Château Palmer, Peter Sichel and his family own Château d'Angludet and a winery at Verdelais in the Premières Côtes to make fruity modern claret and 'Sirius' a brand of excellent barrel-fermented white and oak-aged red Bordeaux.

Nathaniel Johnston et Fils

Bordeaux family firm, founded 1734. Denis and Archibald Johnston are ninth generation. 50% export mostly fine wines. Exclusivities include Bahans, the 2nd wine of Haut Brion.

Madame Jean Descaves

One of the characters of Bordeaux with the biggest stock of rare old top wine at ever-increasing prices.

Dubos

Principal: 'Wum'-Kai-Nielsen. Specialists in selling top wines. Owned by Laurent Perrier.

MEDOC

The Médoc is the whole of the wedge of land north of Bordeaux between the Atlantic and the wide estuary of the Gironde, the united rivers Garonne and Dordogne. Its vineyards all lie within a mile or two of its eastern estuarine shore on a series of low hills, or rather plateaux, of more or less stony soil separated by creeks, their bottom land filled with alluvial silt.

Dutch engineers in the 17th century cut these *jalles* to drain the new vineyards. Their role is vital in keeping the water table down in land which, despite its gravel content, can be very heavy clay six to nine feet down where the vine roots go.

The proportion of *graves* (big gravel or small shingle) in the soil is highest in the Graves region, upstream of Bordeaux, and gradually declines as you go downstream along the Médoc. But such deposits are always uneven, and the soil and subsoil both have varying proportions of sand, gravel and clay. The downstream limit of the Haut-Médoc is where the clay content really begins to dominate the gravel, north of St-Estèphe.

The planting of the *croupes*, the gravel plateaux, took place in a century of great prosperity for Bordeaux under its *Parlement*, whose noble members' names are remembered

in many of the estates they planted between 1650 and 1750. The Médoc was the Napa Valley of the time and the Pichons, Rauzans, Ségurs and Léovilles the periwigged Krugs, Martinis, de la Tours and Beringers.

The style and weight of wine these grandees developed have no precise parallel anywhere else. In some marvellous way the leanness of the soil, the vigour of the vines, the softness of the air and even the pearly seaside light seem to be implicated. Of course, it is a coincidence (besides being a terrible pun) that 'clarity' is so close to 'claret' – but it does sound right for the colour, smell, texture, weight and savour of the Médoc.

The centuries have only confirmed what the original investors apparently instinctively knew: that the riverside gravel banks produce the finest wine. The names that started first have always stayed ahead. The notion of 'first-growths' is as old as the estates themselves.

Today the Médoc is divided into eight appellations: five of them limited to one commune (St-Estèphe, Pauillac, Moulis, Listrac and St-Julien), one (Margaux) to a group of five small communes, one (Haut-Médoc) a portmanteau for parts of equal merit outside the first six, and the last, Médoc, for the northern tip of the promontory.

MARGAUX

The Margaux appellation covers a much wider area than the village: vineyards in the Margaux commune (1,022 acres), plus neighbouring communes Cantenac (1,291), Labarde (210), Arsac (775) and Soussans (839) – a total of 4,137 acres, rather more than Pauillac or St-Estèphe, with more Crus Classés than any other, and far more high-ranking ones.

Margaux is a big sleepy village, with a little *Maison du Vin* to direct tourists. Wine from Margaux itself comes from the lightest, most gravelly land in the Médoc and is considered potentially the finest, most fragrant of all. That of Cantenac in theory has slightly more body and that of Soussans, on marginally heavier, lower-lying land going north, less class. The châteaux of Margaux tend to huddle together in the village, with their land much divided into parcels scattered around the parish. Postcode: 33460 Margaux.

Premier Cru

Château Margaux

1er Cru Classé 1855. Owner: SCA Château Margaux. AOC: Margaux. 193 acres red, 30 acres white; 32,000 cases. Grape var. red: Cab.Sauv. 75%, Merlot 20%, Petit Verdot and Cab.Fr. 5%; White: Sauv.Bl. 100%.

With Château Lafite, the most stylish and obviously aristocratic of the first-growths both in its wine and its lordly premises. The wine is never blunt or beefy, even in great years; at its best it is as fluidly muscular as a racehorse and as sweetly perfumed as any claret – the very taste and smell of elegance.

Like Lafite, Margaux emerged in the late 1970s from 15-odd years of unworthy vintages. The late M. André Mentzelopoulos, whose daughter Corinne directs the estate today, bought the property (for 60 million francs) in 1977, invested huge sums in a total overhaul of château, vineyards and plant. His ambition for perfection showed immediately with the excellent 1978. Professor Peynaud advised the sweeping changes that put Château Margaux back at the very top.

The château is a porticoed mansion of the First Empire, unique in the Médoc; the *chais* and cellars, pillared and lofty, are in keeping. Magnificent avenues of plane trees lead through the estate. Some of the lowest riverside land is planted with white (Sauvignon) grapes to make a light, fittingly polished dry wine, Pavillon Blanc. The second label for red is Pavillon Rouge.

Margaux Crus Classés

Châteaux Boyd-Cantenac

3ème Cru Classé 1855. Owner: P. Guillemet. AOC: Margaux. 44 acres. 8,000 cases. Grape var: Cab.Sauv. 67%, Cab.Fr. 7%, Merlot 20%, Petit Verdot 6%.

The strange name, like that of Cantenac-Brown, came from a 19th-century English owner. A small property not widely seen nor much acclaimed but full of stalwart old-fashioned virtues, long lasting and highly flavoured in such excellent years as 1970, '82, '86, '89 and '90.

Château Brane-Cantenac

2ème Cru Classé 1855. Owner: Lucien Lurton. AOC: Margaux. 210 acres. 12,500 cases. Grape var: Cab.Sauv. 70%, Cab.Fr. 10%, Merlot 20%.

One of the most respected names of the Margaux second-growths; a very big and well-run property on a distinct pale gravel plateau. The wine is generally enjoyable and 'supple' at a fairly early stage but lasts well, although some critics faulted it during the '70s for coarseness and for developing too fast. Good vintages of the '80s hold their own among the good second-growths. The second labels are Ch. Notton and Baron de Brane.

Château Cantenac-Brown

3ème Cru Classé 1855. Owner: AXA Millésimes. Administrator: Jean-Michel Cazes. AOC: Margaux. 100 acres. 12,000 cases. Grape var: Cab.Sauv. 65%, Cab.Fr. 10%, Merlot 25%.

A great prim pile of a building like an English public school on the road south from Margaux. Conservative wines capable of terrific flavour. It went through a bad patch, until a change of owner (1987) invested heavily in both vineyards and cellar. Still a way to go and most Cantenac is finally a coarser wine than classic Margaux. The second label is Canuet.

Château Dauzac

5ème Cru Classé 1855. Owner: MAIF. AOC: Margaux. 98 acres. 22,000 cases. Grape var: Cab.Sauv. 58%, Cab.Fr. 5%, Merlot 37%.

A new owner (insurance company) brought in André Lurton of La Louvière to advise in 1992 and built a new cellar in 1994. Has been reliably smooth if uninspiring but should improve. Second wine is La Bastide Dauzac.

Château Desmirail

3ème Cru Classé 1855. Owner: Denis Lurton. AOC: Margaux. 69 acres. 5,000 cases. Grape var: Cab.Sauv. 79%, Cab.Fr. 5%, Merlot 15%, Petit Verdot 1%.

A third-growth that disappeared for many years into the vineyards and vats of Ch'x Palmer and Brane-Cantenac. Now established in its own right. So far delicate, fragrant wines to drink young. Second label: Château de Fontarney.

Château Durfort-Vivens

2ème Cru Classé 1855. Owner: Gonzague Lurton. AOC: Margaux. 74 acres plus 5,000 cases. Grape var: Cab.Sauv. 70%, Cab.Fr.15%, Merlot 15%.

The name of Durfort, suggesting hardness and strength, used to sum up the character of this almost all-Cabernet wine – which seemed to want keeping for ever. The new generation in 1992 increased the Merlot. The wine usually has more structure than Brane Cantenac – of the same stable but with less charm.

Château Ferrière

3ème Cru Classé 1855. Owner: Claire Villars. AOC: Margaux. 19 acres. 4,000 cases. Grape var: Cab.Sauv. 75%, Merlot 20%, Petit Verdot 5%.

Until 1992, this was part of Lascombes. Now it is in the same capable hands as Chasse Spleen. Exciting quality in '94 and '95.

Château Giscours

3ème Cru Classé 1855. Owner: G.F.A. du Château Giscours. AOC: Margaux (at Labarde). 200 acres. 44,000 cases. Grape var: Cab.Sauv. 75%, Cab.Fr. 2%, Merlot 22%, Petit Verdot 1%.

One of the great success stories of the 1970s when it made an outstanding '70 and much better '75 than most. The eighties were decidedly shakey. The vast Victorian property has been virtually remade since the 1950s by the Tari family, including making a 20-acre lake to alter the microclimate: by creating turbulence between the vines and the neighbouring woodland it helps to ward off spring frosts. The wines are tannic, robustly fruity, often dry but full of the pent-up energy that marks first-class claret – not the suavely delicate style of Margaux.

Château d'Issan

3ème Cru Classé 1855. Owners: the Cruse family. AOC: Margaux. 74 acres. 12,500 cases. Grape var: Cab.Sauv. 70%, Merlot 30%.

One of the (few) magic spots of the Médoc: a moated 17th-century mansion down among the poplars where the slope of the vineyard meets the riverside meadows. Issan is never a 'big' wine, but old vintages have been wonderfully, smoothly persistent. Some recent ones appear rather too light to last as well, though '82, '83, '85 and '88 are excellent.

Château Kirwan

3ème Cru Classé 1855. Owner: insurance group Gan is major share holder. AOC: Margaux. 86 acres. 17,000 cases. Grape var: Cab.Sauv. 40%, Cab.Fr. 20%, Merlot 30%, Petit Verdot 10%.

The third-growth neighbour to Brane-Cantenac. Kirwan seems to have had few friends among the critics, although it is carefully run and at its best (1961, '70, '75, '79) is as long-lived and classic as any of the Margaux second-growths, making elegant, feminine claret. Michel Rolland has consulted here since 1992 and its wine has gained fruit, weight and oak.

Château Lascombes

2ème Cru Classé 1855. Owner: Bass Charrington. AOC: Margaux. 232 acres. 35,000–40,000 cases. Grape var: Cab.Sauv. 65%, Cab.Fr. 3%, Merlot 30%, Petit Verdot 2%.

A superb great property (one of the biggest in the Médoc) restored by the energy of Alexis Lichine in the 1950s to making delectable, smooth and flavoury claret. Since his days it has rarely made truly second-growth standard wine, though the top vintages of the later '80s are excellent. The second label is Château Ségonnes.

Château Malescot-St-Exupéry

3ème Cru Classé 1855. Owner: Roger Zuger. AOC: Margaux. 58 acres. 14,000 cases. Grape var: Cab.Sauv. 50%, Cab.Fr. 10%, Merlot 35%, Petit Verdot 5%.

A handsome house in the main street of Margaux with vineyards scattered north of the town. For many years it was run in tandem with what was then Marquis d'Alesme-Becker, but since 1979 has taken flight on its own, showing signs of becoming even finer – with fruity flavour hidden by the tannic hardness of youth.

Château d'Alesme

3ème Cru Classé 1855. Owner: Jean-Claude Zuger. AOC: Margaux. 42 acres. 9,500 cases. Grape var: Cab.Sauv. 30% and Cab.Fr. 15%, Merlot 45%, Petit Verdot 10%.

A small vineyard in Soussans, owned and run by the brother of the owner of Château Malescot (q.v.). Château d'Alesme wines are known for their old-fashioned toughness, the flavour of the heavier soil of Soussans, giving them long life. The winemaking is modern, but the Zuger zeal is perennial.

Château Marquis de Terme

4ème Cru Classé 1855. Owner: Ph. Sénéclauze. AOC: Margaux. 86 acres. 14,000 cases. Grape var: Cab.Sauv. 55%, Cab.Fr. 3%, Merlot 35%, Petit Verdot 7%.

A respected old name which is not seen often enough in commerce; the greater part is sold direct to French consumers. It is made notably tannic for very long life, although since 1985 a more delicate touch has given it more immediate charm.

Château Palmer

3ème Cru Classé 1855. Owner: Société Civile du Château Palmer. AOC: Margaux. 106 acres. 18,000 cases. Grape var: Cab.Sauv. 55%, Merlot 40%, Petit Verdot 5%.

A possible candidate for promotion to first-growth, whose best vintages (1961, '66, '70, '78, '79, '83, '86, '88, '90) set the running for the whole Médoc. They combine finesse with most voluptuous ripeness, the result of a superb situation on the gravel rise just above Château Margaux and old-fashioned long fermentation with not too many new barrels, but, probably most of all, the very skilful selection by the three owners, French, Dutch and English, whose flags fly along the romantic roof-line of the château.

Château Pouget

4ème Cru Classé 1855. Owner: Pierre Guillemet. AOC: Margaux. 25 acres. 4,500 cases. Grape var: Cab.Sauv. 66%, Merlot 30%, Cab.Fr. 4%.

The same property as, and in practice an alternative label for, Boyd-Cantenac.

Château Prieuré-Lichine

4ème Cru Classé 1855. Owner: Sacha Lichine. AOC: Margaux. 175 acres. 38,000 cases. Grape var: Cab.Sauv. 54%, Cab.Fr. 2%, Merlot 39%, Petit Verdot 5%.

The personal achievement of the late Alexis Lichine, now upheld by his son, who assembled a wide scattering of little plots around Margaux in the 1950s and created one of the

Enjoying claret

There are four important variables among the red wines of Bordeaux. The most important is the vintage, the next the class or quality of the wine, the third its age and the fourth the region.

Ripe vintages upgrade all qualities and districts, intensify their characters, make them slower to mature and give them a longer life span. The Bordeaux habit is to drink young wines rather cooler than mature ones, and Médocs cooler than St-Emilions and Pomerols. Wines still in the firmness of their youth are served with such strongly flavoured or rich dishes as game or duck (and especially young St-Emilion with Dordogne lampreys cooked in red wine). Mature wines are served with plain roasts of lamb or beef and very old wines with all kinds of white meat or fowl.

It is worth noting that lamb is the almost inevitable choice at banquets in the Médoc.

Enjoying Sauternes

Sauternes and the other sweet white wines of Bordeaux (Barsac, Ste-Croix du Mont) are served locally with such rich first courses as foie gras or smooth pâtés, melon, fish or sweetbreads in creamy sauces, or to bring out the sweetness in lobster. They are popular as apéritifs and also survive the onslaught of a salty Roquefort much better than red wines. They go excellently with simple fruit tarts, or fruit, or alone after a meal. 'Very cool, but not iced', is the regular formula for describing the right temperature.

Enjoying dry white Bordeaux

Dry white Bordeaux is served in the region with almost any fish dish, especially with oysters (which are often served iced, accompanied by hot and peppery little sausages – an exciting combination). It cuts the richness of pâtés and terrines, but is generally not served as an apéritif without food.

most reliable and satisfying modern Margaux, harmonious and even rich at times, needing 10 years to show its real class. Libourne oenologist Michel Rolland now advises here. The second label is Ch. de Clairefont.

Château Rausan-Ségla

2ème Cru Classé 1855. Owner: Chanel inc. AOC: Margaux. 112 acres: 20,000 cases. Grape var: Cab.Sauv. 65%, Cab.Fr. 2%, Merlot 33%.

The larger of the two parts of the estate that used to be second only to Ch. Margaux, but far behind since the '50s. At its best ('61, '75, '83, '86, '90) exceedingly fragrant in the Margaux manner, but for many years not the echoing symphony a second-growth should be. 1983 was the beginning of a major revival with vintages like '85, '86, '88 and '90 setting a new standard which the new owners (since 1994) and management are taking even further. The second label is Ségla.

Château Rauzan-Gassies

2eme Cru Classé 1855. Owners: Mme Paul Quié & J.-M. Quié. AOC: Margaux. 69 acres. 13,000 cases. Grape var: Cab.Sauv. 65%, Cab.Fr. 10%, Merlot 25%.

Consistently disappointing over the last two decades. Its 1970 was fading at only 10 years old. A new generation took over in the late 1970s; wines of the '80s are full of flavour, if not finesse. The owners seem to like it as it is.

Château du Tertre

5ème Cru Classé 1855. Owners: the Capbern-Gasqueton family. AOC: Margaux. 124 acres. 20,000 cases. Grape var: Cab.Sauv. 85%, Cab.Fr. 5%, Merlot 10%.

This backwoods vineyard at Arsac, taken in hand by the owner of Calon-Ségur in 1961, despite an excellent '70 and encouraging vintages in the 1980s has not really delivered its promise. The percentage of Cabernet is high.

OTHER CHATEAUX

Château d'Angludet Cantenac. Owners: M & Mme Peter Sichel. 79 acres; 16,000 cases. Home of the English partner of Ch. Palmer and, like it, badly undervalued in the official classification. Firm, foursquare wines which take time to show their unquestionable class.

Château Bel-Air-Marquis d'Aligre Margaux. Owner: Pierre Boyer. 42 acres; 4,500 cases plus. Despite its grand name, one of the more basic and backward Margaux. It usually rewards patience. Old vines.

Château Deyrem-Valentin Soussans. Owner: Jean Soye. 29 acres; 6,000 cases. Elegant, mid-weight Margaux, sometimes rather stretched.

Château La Gurgue Margaux. Owner: Société Civile du Château La Gurgue. 24 acres; 5,000 cases. A formerly run-down château in the centre of Margaux. Since 1978 under the same energetic direction as Ch. Chasse-Spleen. Full, fruity style.

Château Haut Breton Larigaudière Soussans. 92 acres; 7,000 cases. A tiny property better known as one of the few good restaurants in the Médoc.

Domaine de l'Ile Margaux Margaux. Owner: Mme L D Sichère. 33 acres; 3,000 cases. On an island on the river and therefore outside the Margaux appellation, but a fascinating place and rather good wine.

Château Labégorce Margaux. Owner: M. Perrodo. 76 acres; 16,000 cases. Potential frontrunner, grand mansion and all, considered unofficially a Cru Exceptionnel. At present wines have less than real Margaux elegance.

Château Labégorce-Zédé Soussans. Owner: Luc Thienpont. 66 acres; 17,000 cases plus. Among the best minor Margaux, in the same Flemish family as Vieux-Château-Certan. One of nature's Crus Exceptionnels. Second label: Domaine Zédé.

Château Marsac-Séguineau Soussans. Owner: Société Civile du Château. 25 acres; 4,400 cases. Part of the same group as Ch. Grand-Puy-Ducasse (Pauillac).

Château Martinens Grand Bourgeois, Cantenac-Margaux. Owners: Mme Dulos and J. P. Seynat-Dulos. 74 acres; 10,000 cases. A good property which is getting better, re-equipped in 1989. The 18th-century château was built, I am told, by three English sisters, the Whites (of Limerick fame).

Château Monbrison Arsac. Owner: Laurent van de Heyden. 47 acres. 11,000 cases. Jan Luc van der Heyden, who died too young, made a reputation for this property in the '80s with wines of breadth and finesse. His brother maintains this tradition. Second label: Château Cordet.

Château Paveil de Luze Grand Bourgeois, Soussans. Owner: Baron Geoffrey de Luze. 66 acres plus; 15,000 cases. A gentlemanly estate with smooth, well-mannered wine to match. The small vineyard has been enlarged.

Château Pontac-Lynch Cantenac. Owner: Marie-Christine Boudon 25 acres; 6,000 cases. A little place chiefly remarkable for bearing two of Bordeaux's most illustrious names.

Château Siran Labarde. Owner: W.A. Miailhe. 56 acres; 14,000 cases. Fine estate run by a fanatic, making most attractive wine and out to win classed-growth status (which 40% of his vineyard had, before changes in ownership). M. Miailhe has commissioned a historical map to put the cat among the pigeons by proving that many classed-growths have less of '1855' land than Siran. Heliport and antinuclear cellar seem to point to a man who means business.

Château La Tour-de-Mons Soussans. Owner: Bertrand Clauzel. 74 acres; 18,000 cases. Romantic, old-fashioned property long owned by the family who sold Ch. Cantemerle in 1981. Generally considered a natural Cru Exceptionnel with round, well-structured wines (40% Merlot).

MOULIS AND LISTRAC

Moulis and Listrac are two communes of the central Haut-Médoc whose appellations (each has its own) are deemed more stalwart than glamorous. Between Margaux and St-Julien the main gravel banks lie farther back from the river with heavier soil. No château here was classified in 1855 but a dozen Crus Bourgeois make admirable wine of the more austere kind. The best soil is on a great dune of gravel stretching from Grand Poujeaux in Moulis (where Châteaux Chasse-Spleen and Maucaillou are both regularly among the best value in the Haut-Médoc) inland through Listrac.

The total area of vines is 1,420 acres in Moulis, 1,600 in Listrac. Both saw rapid expansion in the heady atmosphere of the 1980s. The leaner years of the early '90s were a tough testing ground for these inland Médoc châteaux where Cabernet ripens later than in vineyards closer to the Gironde. Closer to the river the villages of Arcins, Lamarque and Cussac have only the appellation Haut-Médoc (q.v.). Postcode: 33480 Castelnau de Médoc.

MOULIS AND LISTRAC CHATEAUX

Château La Bécade Cru Bourgeois, Listrac. Owner: Altus Finances. 56 acres; 13,000 cases.

Château Bellegrave Mele Listrac. Owner: Roger Mele. Small high-grade property making full-flavoured wine with advice from Pichon-Lalande.

Château Biston-Brillette Moulis. Owner: Michel Barbarin. 51 acres; 10,000 cases.

Château Brillette Cru Bourgeois, Moulis. Owners: the Berthault family. 88 acres; 20,000 cases. A sound reputation among the good bourgeois wines of Moulis, on the next plateau to the various Poujeaux.

Château Cap Léon Veyrin Cru Bourgeois, Listrac. Owner: Alain Meyre. 56 acres; 13,000 cases.

Château Chasse-Spleen Grand Bourgeois Exceptionnel, Moulis. Dir: Claire Villars. 180 acres; 36,000 cases. Regularly compared with Crus Classés for style and durability. Expertly made with classic methods.

Château Clarke Cru Bourgeois, Listrac. Owner: Baron Edmond de Rothschild. 126 acres; 45,000 cases. A Rothschild project with every advantage. *See* also Ch. Malmaison and Ch. Peyre-Lebade.

Château La Closerie du Grand-Poujeaux Cru Bourgeois, Moulis. Owner: Mme Bacquey. 12 acres; 2,500 cases. Small but one of the best.

Château Ducluzeau Cru Bourgeois, Listrac. Owner: Jean-Eugène Borie. Tiny but admirable 90% Merlot wine made by the owner of Ducru Beaucaillou. 11 acres, 2,000 cases.

Château Duplessis-Fabre Cru Bourgeois, Moulis. Owner: Ch. Maucaillou. 42 acres; 6,500 cases. Owned by Dourthe since 1989.

Château Duplessis-Hauchecorne Grand Bourgeois, Moulis. Owner: Marie-Laure Lurton. 44 acres; 4,000 cases. Lighter, more easy-going wine than most in this parish.

Château Dutruch Grand Poujeaux Cru Bourgeois Exceptionnel, Moulis. Owner: François Cordonnier. 56 acres plus; 13,000 cases. Old family property, now one of the leaders of the parish. Tannic wine for long maturing.

Château Fonréaud Cru Bourgeois, Listrac. Owner: Jean Chanfreau. 84 acres; 20,000 cases. Well known with its sister-château Lestage for pleasant, rather light wines.

Château Fourcas-Dupré Grand Bourgeois Exceptionnel, Listrac. Director: Patrice Pagès. 107 acres; 20,000 cases. (Part of the vineyard is in Moulis.) One of the best in an area of excellent Crus 25,000 Bourgeois. Second label is Ch. Bellevue-Laffont.

Château Fourcas-Hosten Grand Bourgeois Exceptionnel, Listrac. Dirs: Bertrand de Rivoyre and Patrice Pagès. 107 acres; 25,000 cases. The outstanding property of Listrac today; perfectionist wine-making. 40% Merlot suits the relatively heavy soil, making stylish, concentrated wine to lay down.

Château Fourcas Loubaney Cru Bourgeois. Owner: Altus Finance. Classy wine. 61 acres. 12,500 cases. Second label Château Moulin de Laborde.

Château Gressier Grand-Poujeaux Cru Bourgeois Supérieur, Moulis. Owner: Bertrand Marcellus. 44 acres; 11,000 cases. Neighbour to Chasse-Spleen. Repays cellaring.

Château Lafon Grand Bourgeois, Listrac. Owner: J.-P. Théron. 28 acres; 6,500 cases.

Château Lestage Cru Bourgeois, Listrac. Owners: the Chanfreau family. 106 acres; 24,000 cases. *See* Ch. Fonréaud.

Château Malmaison Cru Bourgeois, Moulis. Owner: Baronne Nadine de Rothschild. 59 acres. 13,000 cases.

Château Maucaillou Moulis. Owners: the Dourthe family. 190 acres; 44,000 cases. Important property of at least Grand Bourgeois standing, with vineyards partly in Listrac and Lamarque. Good deep wine, tannic but fruity.

Château Mayne-Lalande Cru Bourgeois. Owner: Bernard Lartigue. 32 acres. 8,000 cases.

Château Mauvesin Moulis. Owner: Société Viticole de France. 148 acres; 30,000 cases. A big estate and, like nearby Ch. Clarke, a sign of the growing importance of the Moulis-Listrac area.

Château Moulin à Vent Grand Bourgeois, Moulis. Owner: Dominique Hessel. 59 acres; 12,000 cases. Run with energy and competence.

Château Peyre-Lebade Cru Bourgeois, Listrac. Owner: Baron Benjamin de Rothschild. 138 acres. 30,000 cases. Once home of the painter Odilon Redon. Neighbour to Ch. Clarke.

Château Pomeys Moulis. Owner: Jean-François Barennes. 20 acres; 3,000 cases.

Château Poujeaux Grand Bourgeois Exceptionnel, Moulis. Owners: François & Philippe Theil. 123 acres; 30,000 cases. The principal property of the Poujeaux plateau. Vies with Chasse-Spleen as the leading wine of its commune. Recent vintages increasingly fine. Second label: La Salle de Poujeaux.

Château Ruat-Petit-Poujeaux Moulis. Owner: Pierre Goffre-Viaud. 37 acres; 7,000 cases.

Château Saransot-Dupré Listrac. Owner: Yves Raymond. 29 acres; 7,000 cases full Merlot-based wine. Also 5 acres of Bordeaux Blanc.

Château Sémeillan Mazeau Cru Bourgeois, Listrac. Owner: H. Mazeau. 42 acres; 8,000 cases.

Cave Coopérative Grand Listrac Listrac. 400 acres; 75,000 cases. One of the biggest Médoc coops. Good reputation.

ST-JULIEN

St-Julien, with a high proportion of Crus Classés, is the smallest of the top-level Médoc appellations. It has only 2,237 acres, but 80% of this is classed second-, third-, or fourth-growth (no first and no fifth, and very little Cru Bourgeois). Its prominent gravel plateau by the river announces itself as one of the prime sites of Bordeaux.

St-Julien harmonizes force and fragrance with singular suavity to make the benchmark for all red Bordeaux, if not the pinnacle. Farther inland, towards the next village, St-Laurent, the wine is less finely tuned.

The two villages of St-Julien and Beychevelle are scarcely enough to make you slow your car. Postcode: 39320 St-Julien.

St-Julien Crus Classés

Château Beychevelle

4ème Cru Classé 1855. Owner: pension fund GMF. President: Jean-Louis Petriat. AOC: St-Julien. 220 acres. 50,000 cases. Grape var: Cab.Sauv. 60%, Merlot 28%, Cab.Fr. 8%, Petit Verdot 4%.

A regal château built in the 17th century with riverside vineyards and dazzling roadside flowerbeds on the hill running up to St-Julien from the south. Its silky, supple, aristocratic wine is the one I most associate with the better

class of English country house. Blandings must have bulged with it. Beychevelle can be difficult when young but finds a blue-blooded elegance after 10 years or so. The 1964, '66, '67, '70, '71 and '75 are all good examples. Ownership changes (in 1983) and subsequent significant investment heralded a return to consistency: both 1982 and '83 were good wines; the '85 is excellent. The curious boat on the label commemorates its admiral founder, to whose rank passing boats on the Gironde used to *baisse les voiles* – hence, they say, the name. The second label is Amiral de Beychevelle.

Château Branaire-Ducru

4ème Cru Classé 1855. Owner: Groupe privé. AOC: St-Julien. 128 acres. 25,000 cases. Grape var: Cab.Sauv. 70%, Cab.Fr. 5%, Merlot 22%, Petit Verdot 3%.

Vineyards in several parts of the commune; the château opposite Beychevelle. Model St-Julien, relying more on flavour than force; notably fragrant and attractive wine with a track-record of reliability. New owners in 1988 have beefed up the wine and added sterner tannins. The second label is Château Dulac.

Château Ducru-Beaucaillou

2ème Cru Classé 1855. Owner: Jean-Eugène Borie. AOC: St-Julien. 123 acres. 19,000 cases. Grape var: Cab.Sauv. 65%, Cab.Fr. 5%, Merlot 25%, Petit Verdot 5%.

Riverside neighbour of Ch. Beychevelle with a château almost rivalling it in grandeur, if not in beauty, built over its barrel cellars. One of the few great châteaux permanently lived in by the owner, who also owns Ch'x Grand-Puy-Lacoste and Haut-Batailley in Pauillac. Always among the top Médocs the firm but seductive flavour of the best St-Juliens. The Cru Bourgeois Lalande-Borie (q.v.) is also made here.

Château Gruaud-Larose

2ème Cru Classé 1855. Owner: Alcatel Alsthom group. AOC: St-Julien. 207 acres. 40,000 cases. Grape var: Cab.Sauv. 64%, Cab.Fr. 9%, Merlot 24%, Petit Verdot 3%.

Second-growth with a magnificent vineyard on the south slope of St-Julien, for many years the pride of the merchant house Cordier and still under the same management, led by Georges Pauly. Consistently one of the fruitiest, smoothest, easiest to enjoy of the great Bordeaux, although as long-lived as most. The new owners (1993) have completely renovated *cuvier* and *chais* and have installed drainage vital to the vineyard. Second wine: Sarget de Gruaud-Larose.

Château Lagrange

3ème Cru Classé 1855. Owner: Suntory. AOC: St-Julien 279 acres. 65,000 cases. Grape var: Cab.Sauv. 66%, Merlot 27%, Petit Verdot 7%.

A magnificent wooded estate inland from St-Julien. The Japanese owners took over in 1983 and started to expand and re-equip. Now in tip-top condition and much expanded to become the largest St-Julien producer. The second label is Les Fiefs-de-Lagrange.

Château Langoa-Barton

3ème Cru Classé 1855. Owners: the Barton family. AOC: St-Julien. 41 acres. 7,000 cases. Grape var: Cab.Sauv. 74%, Cab.Fr. 6%, Merlot 20%.

The noble sister château of Léoville-Barton and home of the Bartons. Similar excellent wine, although by repute always a short head behind the Léoville. Second wine: Lady Langoa.

Château Léoville-Barton

2ème Cru Classé 1855. Owners: the Barton family. AOC: St-Julien 111 acres. 20,000 cases. Grape var: Cab.Sauv. 72%, Cab.Fr. 8%, Merlot 20%.

The southern and smallest third of the Léoville estate, owned by the Irish Barton family since 1821. One of the finest and most typical St-Juliens, often richer than Léoville Las Cases, made with very conservative methods in old oak vats at the splendid 18th-century Château Langoa, built over its barrel cellars. Major investments recently are raising standards even higher – while prices have remained remarkably steady. The cornerstone of many a great claret cellar.

Château Léoville Las Cases

2ème Cru Classé 1855. Owner: Société Civile du Château Léoville Las Cases. Dir: Michel Delon. AOC: St-Julien. 235 acres. 40,000 cases. Grape var: Cab.Sauv. 65%, Cab.Fr. 12%, Merlot 20%, Petit Verdot 3%.

The largest third of the ancient Léoville estate on the boundary of Pauillac, adjacent to Ch. Latour. Still owned by descendants of the Léoville family; now run by Michel Delon, son of Paul Delon, one of the Médoc's best

Commanderie du Bontemps de Médoc et des Graves

The Médoc unites with the Graves in its ceremonial and promotional body, the Commanderie du Bontemps de Médoc et des Graves. In its modern manifestation it dates from 1950, when a group of energetic château proprietors, on the initiative of the regional deputy, M. Emile Liquard, donned splendid red velvet robes and started to 'enthronize' dignitaries and celebrities, wine merchants and journalists at a series of protracted and very jolly banquets held in the chais of the bigger châteaux.

The Commanderie claims descent from an organization of the Knights-Templar of the Order of Malta at St-Laurent in the Médoc in 1154 – a somewhat tenuous link. Its three annual banquets are the festivals of Saint Vincent (the patron saint of wine) in January, the Fête de la Fleur (when the vines flower) in June and the Ban des Vendanges, the official proclamation of the opening of the vintage, in September. Male recruits to the Commanderie are usually entitled Commandeur d'Honneur, and female Gourmettes – a pun meaning both a woman gourmet and the little silver chain used for hanging a cork around the neck of a decanter.

A selection of wine blended for its use is marketed as Cuvée de la Commanderie.

winemakers. A top-flight second-growth and a favourite of the critics, consistently producing connoisseur's claret, extremely high-flavoured and dry for a St-Julien, needing long maturing and leaning towards austerity. The stone gateway of the vineyard is a landmark but the chais are in the centre of St-Julien beside the château, which belongs to Léoville-Poyferré. Severe selection means that the grand vin often represents less than half the total made. The second wine is Clos du Marquis. See also Château Potensac (Médoc).

Château Léoville-Poyferré

2ème Cru Classé 1855. Owners: the Cuvelier family. AOC: St-Julien 190 acres. 40,000 cases. Grape var: Cab.Sauv. 65%, Merlot 25%, Petit Verdot 8%, Cab.Fr. 2%.

The central portion of the Léoville estate, including the château. Potentially as great a wine as Léoville Las Cases, although not the same critical success in the last 20 years. A new director, one of the Cuvelier family, is set on rivalling his neighbour with oenologist Michel Rolland's help. The second wine takes the name of a Cru Bourgeois, Ch. Moulin-Riche.

Château St-Pierre (-Sevaistre)

4ème Cru Classé 1855. Owner: Domaines Martin. AOC: St-Julien. 42 acres. 8,000 cases. Grape var: Cab.Sauv. 70%, Cab.Fr. 10%, Merlot 20%.

The smallest and least-known St-Julien classed growth but superbly situated. The property was bought in 1982 by Henri Martin of Château Gloria who raised it to new heights, and now run by his son-in-law Jean-Louis Triaud. No glamour, but fruity, deep-coloured wine from old vines at a reasonable price.

Château Talbot

4ème Cru Classé 1855. Owners: the Cordier family. AOC: St-Julien. 250 acres. 54,000 cases. Grape var: Cab.Sauv. 66%, Cab.Fr. 3%, Merlot 24%, Petit Verdot 5%, Malbec 2%.

One of the biggest and most productive Bordeaux vineyards, just inland from the Léovilles, sister château to Gruaud-Larose and home of its owner. Marshal Talbot was the last English commander of Aquitaine. Like Gruaud-Larose, a rich, fruity, smooth wine but without quite the same plumpness or structure. A small quantity of dry white 'Caillou Blanc' is produced on 15 acres. The second label is Connétable Talbot.

OTHER CHATEAUX
Château La Bridane Cru Bourgeois, St-Julien. Owner: P. Saintout. 38 acres. 3,500 cases.

Château du Glana Grand Bourgeois Exceptionnel, St-Julien. Owner: Gabriel Meffre. 111 acres. 20,000 cases. Oddly unrenowned as one of St-Julien's only two big unclassed growths. The owner is a wine merchant with several properties who has built a giant chais more like a warehouse just north of St-Julien. His splendidly sited vineyards produce respectable wine.

Château Gloria St-Julien. Owner: Mme Triaud. 110 acres. 20,000 cases: The classic example of the unranked château of exceptional quality, the creation of the illustrious mayor of St-Julien (and Grand Maître of the Commanderie du Bontemps, the ceremonial order of the Médoc). The late Henri-Martin assembled the vineyard in the 1940s with parcels of land from neighbouring Crus Classés, particularly Ch. St Pierre. The wine is rich and long-lasting with less oak flavour than most fine Médocs, being matured in 7,000-litre casks instead of 225-litre *barriques*. Ch. Haut-Beychevelle-Gloria and Ch. Peymartin are names for selections made for certain markets.

Château Lalande Borie St-Julien. Owner: J. E. Borie. 45 acres. 8,000 cases. A vineyard created from part of the old Lagrange in 1970 by the owner of Ch. Ducru-Beaucaillou, where the wine is made. In effect, a baby brother of Ducru.

Château Moulin de la Rose St-Julien. Owner: G. Delon. 10 acres. 2,000 cases.

Château Terrey-Gros-Caillou and Château Hortevie St-Julien. Owners: Mme Fort and M. Pradère. 46 acres. 10,000 cases. A union of two small properties producing very creditable St-Julien.

PAUILLAC

Pauillac is the only town in the vineyard area of the Médoc, and a pretty quiet one at that. Within the last generation it has been enlivened (if that is the word) by a huge Shell oil refinery subsequently closed (1986) and now dismantled on the river immediately north and a marina (although the word sounds more animated than the fact) along its tree-lined quay. Disappointingly there is no old hotel, no restaurant haunted by wine growers. Only the *Maison du Vin* (worth a visit) on the quay gives a hint of its world renown. That, and the famous names on signs everywhere you look in the open steppe of the vineyards.

The wine of Pauillac epitomizes the qualities of all red Bordeaux. It is the virile aesthete; a hypnotizing concurrence of force and finesse. It can lean to an extreme either way (Latour and Lafite representing the poles) but at its best strikes such a perfect balance that no evening is long enough to do it justice. There are 2,840 acres of vineyards with more Crus Classés than any other commune except Margaux, surprisingly weighted towards fifth-growths – some of which are worth better than that. Postcode: 33250 Pauillac.

Pauillac Premiers Crus

Château Lafite-Rothschild

1er Cru Classé 1855. Owners: the Rothschild family.
AOC: Pauillac. 250 acres. 21,000 cases. Grape var: Cab.Sauv. 70%, Cab.Fr. 10%, Merlot 20%.
See The Making of a Great Claret, page 52.

Château Latour

1er Cru Classé 1855. Owner: Pinault-Printemps group. AOC: Pauillac. 150 acres. 17,000 cases. Grape var: Cab.Sauv. 78%, Cab.Fr. 4%, Merlot 17%, Petit Verdot 1%.
Château Latour is in every way complementary to Château Lafite. They make their wines on different soils in different ways; the quality of each is set in relief by the very different qualities of the other. Lafite is a tenor; Latour a bass. Lafite is a lyric; Latour an epic. Lafite is a dance; Latour a parade.

Lafite lies on Pauillac's northern boundary with St-Estèphe, Latour on the southern, St-Julien, limit of the commune four miles away on the last low hill of river-deposited gravel before the flood plain and the stream that divides the two parishes. The ancient vineyard, taking its name from a riverside fortress of the Middle Ages, surrounds the modest mansion, its famous domed stone tower and the big square stable-like block of its *chais*. Two other small patches of vineyard lie half a mile inland near Ch. Batailley.

For nearly three centuries the estate was in the same family (and up to 1760 connected with Lafite). Its modern history began in 1963, when the de Beaumonts sold the majority share to an English group headed by the banker Lord Cowdray and including the wine merchants Harveys of Bristol. They set in hand a total modernization, starting with temperature-controlled stainless steel fermenting vats in place of the ancient oak. Combined English and French talent has since rationalized and perfected every inch of the property, setting such standards that Latour has, rather unfairly, become almost more famous for the quality of its lesser vintages than for the splendour of such years as 1961, '66, '70, '75, '78, '82, '83, '86, '88, '89, '90 and '95. Its consistency and deep, resonant style extends into its second label, Les Forts de Latour, which fetches a price comparable to a second-growth château. Les Forts comes partly from vats of less than the Grand Vin standard, but mainly from two small vineyards (35 acres) formerly Latour, farther inland towards Batailley. These were replanted in 1966 and their wine first used in the blend in the early 1970s. There is also a third wine, modestly labelled Pauillac, which by no means disgraces its big brothers.

In 1989 Allied-Lyons Ltd (owners of Harvey's of Bristol) bought the Cowdray-Pearson share, valuing the property at around US $100 million and making it the world's most expensive vineyard. The 30-year English occupation ended when Allied-Lyons subsequently sold Latour in 1994 to the French entrepreneur François Pinault, for 680 million francs, ten times the price Mentzenopoulos had paid for Margaux in 1977.

Château Mouton-Rothschild

1er Cru Classé 1973. Owner: Baron Philippe de Rothschild S.A. AOC: Pauillac. 185 acres. 27,500 cases. Grape var: Cab.Sauv. 80%, Cab.Fr. 10%, Merlot 8%, Petit Verdot 2%.
Mouton is geographically neighbour to Lafite, but gastro-nomically closer to Latour. Its hallmark is a deep concentration of the flavour of Cabernet Sauvignon, often described as resembling blackcurrants, held as though

between the poles of a magnet in the tension of its tannin – a balancing act that can go on for decades, increasing in fascination and grace all the time. In 1976 I noted of the 1949 Mouton: 'Deep unfaded red; huge, almost California-style nose; resin and spice; still taut with tannin, but overwhelming in its succulence and sweetness. In every way magnificent.'

More than any other château, Mouton-Rothschild is identified with one man, the late Baron Philippe de Rothschild, who came to take it over as a neglected property of his (the English) branch of the Rothschild family in 1922 and died in 1989. This remarkable man of many talents (poet, dramatist, racing-driver among them) determined to raise Mouton from being first in the 1855 list of second-growths to parity with Lafite. It took him 51 years of effort, argument, publicity, and above all perfectionist winemaking. He gained official promotion in 1973, the only change ever made to the 1855 classification.

Baron Philippe and his American wife Pauline created a completely new house in the stone stable block and collected in the same building the world's greatest museum of works of art relating to wine, displayed with unique flair (and open to the public by appointment). He was succeeded in 1989 by his daughter Philippine.

The baron's love of the arts (and knack for publicity) led him to commission a different famous artist to design the top panel of the Mouton label every year from 1945 on. Of these vintages the most famous are the 1949 (the owner's favourite), '53, '59, '61, '66, '70, '75, '82, '85, '86, '88, '89, '90 and '95.

The baron's empire expanded over the years to include Châteaux d'Armailacq and Clerc-Milon, and La Baronnie, his company that produces and markets Mouton-Cadet, the best-selling branded Bordeaux. Mouton itself had no second label until 1994; wine not up to Grand Vin standard being blended (along with much else) into Mouton-Cadet, which maintains a consistently high level of value for money. In 1994 Le Petit Mouton de Château Mouton Rothschild became the second wine. Since 1991 a small quantity of intense dry white, Aile d'Argent, has been made. It has yet to prove itself.

Pauillac Crus Classés

Château d'Armailacq

5ème Cru Classé 1855. Owner: Baron Philippe de Rothschild S.A. AOC: Pauillac. 123 acres plus; 19,000 cases. Grape var: Cab.Sauv. 50%, Cab.Fr. 23%, Merlot 25%, Petit Verdot 2%.

Originally Mouton-d'Armailhacq, bought in 1933 by Baron Philippe de Rothschild and renamed in 1956, the name, altered again from Baron to Baronne for the Baroness Pauline (d. 1976) in 1974, has returned to square one (minus Mouton) in 1989. The vineyard is south of Mouton, next to Pontet-Canet, on lighter, even sandy soil which with a higher proportion of both Cabernet Franc and Merlot gives a rather lighter, quicker-maturing wine, but a star nonetheless, made to the customary Mouton standards.

Château Batailley

5ème Cru Classé 1855. Owner: Emile Castéja. AOC: Pauillac. 148 acres. 20,000 cases. Grape var: Cab.Sauv. 70%, Cab.Fr. 5%, Merlot 25%.

The name of the estate, another of those divided into easily confusable parts, comes from an Anglo-French disagreement in the 15th century. Charles II's favourite wine merchant was called Joseph Batailhé – I like to think he was a son of this soil, the wooded inland part of Pauillac. Batailley is the larger property and retains the lovely little mid-19th-century château in its 'English' park. Its wine is tannic, muscle-bound for years, never exactly graceful but eventually balancing its austerity with sweetness: old (20-year) bottles keep great nerve and vigour. These are the Pauillacs that approach St-Estèphe in style. The wine is usually excellent value.

Château Clerc-Milon

5ème Cru Classé 1855. Owner: Baron Philippe de Rothschild S.A. AOC: Pauillac. 74 acres. 13,000 cases. Grape var: Cab.Sauv. 70%, Cab.Fr. 10%, Merlot 20%.

An obscure little estate known as Clerc-Milon-Mondon until 1970, when it was bought by Baron Philippe de Rothschild. The vineyard (there is no château) is promisingly positioned close to Château Lafite, Château Mouton-Rothschild. Typical Rothschild perfectionism, energy and money have made a series of good vintages, starting with a remarkably fine 1970. '86, '89 and '90 are particular successes.

Château Croizet-Bages

5ème Cru Classé 1855. Owners: Mme L. Quié and J. M. Quié. AOC: Pauillac. 64 acres. 15,000 cases. Grape var: Cab.Sauv. 40%, Cab.Fr. 15%, Merlot 45%.

A property known for round and sound, not exactly glamorous Pauillac, belonging to the owners of Ch. Rauzan-Gassies, Margaux. No château, but vineyards on the Bages plateau between Lynch-Bages and Grand-Puy-Lacoste. Compared with the firmness and vigour of the Lynch-Bages of the same year, the 1961 at 20 years old was rather old-ladyish, sweet but fragile. Recent vintages have been light even in top years.

Château Duhart-Milon-Rothschild

4ème Cru Classé 1855. Owners: the Rothschild family. AOC: Pauillac. 150 acres. 17,000 cases. Grape var: Cab.Sauv. 70%, Cab.Fr. 5%, Merlot 20%, Petit Verdot 5%.

The little sister (or baby brother) of Ch. Lafite, on the next hillock inland, known as Carruades, bought by the Rothschilds in 1964 and since then completely replanted and enlarged. Its track record was for hard wine of no great subtlety, but the resolve (seen at Lafite recently) to make the best possible extends to Duhart-Milon. As the young vines age this is becoming a great château again, making long-living claret. The second label is Moulin de Duhart.

Château Grand-Puy-Ducasse

5ème Cru Classé 1855. Owner: Société Civile de Grand-Puy-Ducasse. AOC: Pauillac. 98 acres. 14,000 cases. Grape var: Cab.Sauv. 62%, Merlot 37%, Petit Verdot 1%.

Three widely separated plots of vineyard, one next to Grand-Puy-Lacoste, one by Pontet-Canet, the third nearer Batailley, and *chais* and château on the Pauillac waterfront. Much replanted and renovated by the same company that owns Ch. Chasse-Spleen (Moulis) since 1971 but already known for big, well-built and long-lived wine (e.g. 1961, '64, '66, '67, '70). '86 and '89 were stars of the '80s and good value but the '90s have been less sure-footed. Artigues-Arnaud is a second label.

Château Grand-Puy-Lacoste

5ème Cru Classé 1855. Owners: the Borie family. AOC: Pauillac. 123 acres. 16,000 cases. Grape var: Cab.Sauv. 75%, Merlot 25%.

For a long time, in the words of the 'Bordeaux bible', *'très supérieur à son classement'*. Sold in 1978 by the Médoc's greatest gastronome, Raymond Dupin, to one of its most dedicated proprietors, Jean-Eugène Borie (of Ducru-Beaucaillou, Haut-Batailley, etc.), whose son Xavier lives at the château and runs it. A rather remote but attractive property with an extraordinary romantic garden, a thousand miles from the Médoc in spirit, on the next 'hill' inland from the Bages plateau. The wine has tremendous 'attack', colour, structure and sheer class. The second label is Lacoste-Borie.

Château Haut-Bages Libéral

5ème Cru Classé 1855. Owner: Claire Villars. AOC: Pauillac. 66 acres. 13,000 cases. Grape var: Cab.Sauv. 80%, Merlot 20%.

A vineyard bordering Ch. Latour to the north. The owner, who also runs Chasse-Spleen, has invested heavily. A property making much better wine than its rather limited reputation suggests, with every sign of realizing its high ambitions. The second label is Chapelle de Bages.

Château Haut-Batailley

5ème Cru Classé 1855. Dirs: Jean-Eugène and François-Xavier Borie. AOC: Pauillac. 52 acres. 10,000 cases. Grape var: Cab.Sauv. 65%, Cab.Fr. 10%, Merlot 25%. Price (1989): 57 francs a bottle.

Another triumph of the men whose gifts have established Ducru-Beaucaillou among the leaders. They make similar but rather less rustic and more gentlemanly wine than their Batailley neighbour. For sheer tastiness there are few wines you can choose with more confidence. The second label of Haut-Batailley is La Tour l'Aspic.

Château Lynch-Bages

5ème Cru Classé 1855. Owners: the Cazes family. AOC: Pauillac. 210 acres. 35,000 cases. Grape var: Cab.Sauv. 75%, Cab.Fr. 10%, Merlot 15%.

An important estate fondly known to its many English friends as 'lunch-bags'; a perennial favourite for sweet and meaty, strongly Cabernet-flavoured wine, epitomizing Pauillac at its most hearty. The Bages plateau, south of the town, has relatively 'strong' soil over clay subsoil. The best vintages ('82, '85, '86, '88, '89 and '90) are very long-lived; the '61 is perhaps now at its peak. The director, Jean-Michel Cazes, Pauillac's leading insurance broker and son of its very popular mayor, rebuilt the crumbling château and the

former cavernous, gloomy *chais* in the '80s and raised the name of his property to new heights. He is also director of the AXA wine estates (*see* Pichon-Longueville-Baron). His other property is Les Ormes-de-Pez in St-Estèphe. In addition he is director of Ch. Pichon-Baron. The second label is Haut-Bages-Averous. There is also a tiny supply of soft, fruity Semillon white.

Château Lynch-Moussas

5ème Cru Classé 1855. Owner: Emile Castéja. AOC: Pauillac. 74 acres. 11,000 cases. Grape var: Cab.Sauv. 75%, Merlot 25%.

Stablemate since 1969 of its neighbour Ch. Batailley. M. Castéja has replanted and totally renovated the château and chais. So far it has shown no serious sign of catching up with Lynch-Bages but as the young vines age, vintages of the '90s show more depth of flavour.

Château Pédesclaux

5ème Cru Classé 1855. Owner: Bernard Jugla. AOC: Pauillac. 49 acres. 12,000 cases. Grape var: Cab.Sauv. 65%, Cab.Fr. 5%, Merlot 25%.

The least renowned classed growth of Pauillac, scattered around the commune like Grand-Puy-Ducasse, and enthusiastically making suave wines much to the taste of its principal customers, the Belgians. M. Jugla (*see also* Château Colombier Monpelou) uses the names of two of his Crus Bourgeois, Grand Duroc Milon and Belle Rose, as second labels.

Château Pichon-Longueville au Baron de Pichon-Longueville

2ème Cru Classé 1855. Owner: AXA Millésimes. AOC: Pauillac. 125 acres. 20,000 cases. Grape var: Cab.Sauv. 75%, Merlot 24%, Petit Verdot 1%.

The following entry gives the background to the unwieldy name. New owners (the insurance company AXA) since 1987 set lustily about competing with the Comtesse across the road, which for years had made much better wine. With J-M. Cazes (*see* Ch. Lynch-Bages) as director, and a seemingly bottomless purse, an aggressive building programme has transformed the place. The wine is now an earnest contender (a stunning and powerful '90) with its neighbour; perhaps more full-bloodedly Pauillac in style with its preponderance of Cabernet. Second wine is Les Tourelles de Longueville.

Château Pichon-Longueville, Comtesse de Lalande

2ème Cru Classé 1855. Dir: Mme de Lencquesaing. AOC: Pauillac. 185 acres. 40,000 cases. Grape var: Cab.Sauv. 45%, Cab.Fr. 12%, Merlot 35%, Petit Verdot 8%.

Two châteaux share the splendid 225-acre Pauillac estate that was planted in the 17th century by the same pioneer who planted the Rauzan estate in Margaux. The châteaux were long owned by his descendants, the various sons and daughters of the Barons de Pichon-Longueville. Two thirds of the estate eventually fell to a daughter who was Comtesse de Lalande – hence the lengthy name, which is often shortened to Pichon Lalande or Pichon Comtesse. The family of the present owners bought it in 1925.

Château Lafite-Rothschild

The Making of a Great Claret

This is the place to study the author's control of his superlatives. Wine for intelligent millionaires has been made by this estate for well over 200 years, and when a random selection of 36 vintages, going back to 1799, was drunk and compared in recent times the company was awed by the consistency of the performance. Underlying the differences in quality, style and maturity of the vintages, there was an uncanny resemblance between wines made even a century and a half apart.

It is easy to doubt, because it is difficult to understand the concept of a Bordeaux 'cru'. As an amalgam of soil and situation with tradition and professionalism, its stability depends heavily on the human factor. Sometimes even Homer nods. Lafite had its bad patch in the 1960s and early 1970s. Since 1976 it has once again epitomized the traditional Bordeaux château at its best.

As a mansion, Lafite is impeccably chic rather than grand; a substantial but unclassical 18th-century villa, elevated on a terrace above the most businesslike and best vegetable garden in the Médoc, and sheltered from the north by a titanic cedar of Lebanon. There are no great rooms; the red drawing room, the pale blue dining-room and the dark green library are comfortably cluttered and personal in the style of 100 years ago. The Rothschild family of the Paris bank bought the estate in 1868. It has been the apple of their corporate eye ever since. In 1974 the 34-year-old Baron Eric de Rothschild took over responsibility from his uncle Elie, who had been in charge since 1946.

Grandeur starts in the *cuvier*, the vat house, and the vast low barns of the *chais*, where the barrels make marvellous perspectives of dwindling hoops seemingly for ever. In 1989 a unique and spectacular new circular *chai*, dug out of the vineyards and supported by columns to test Samson, was inaugurated. History is most evident in the shadowy moss-encrusted bottle cellars, where the collection stretches back to 1797 – the first Bordeaux ever to be château-bottled, still in its original bin.

Quality starts with the soil: deep gravel dunes over limestone. It depends on the age of the vines: at Lafite an average of 40 years. It depends even more on restricting their production: the figure of 40–45 hectolitres is achieved by modest manuring and stern pruning.

Vintage in the Médoc starts at any time between early September and late October, depending on the season, when the grapes reach an optimum ripeness, judged above all by the sugar content (although allowance may have to be made for the threat of rainy weather or an attack of rot). In a big vineyard (Lafite has 250 acres) it is impossible to pick every grape at precisely the ideal moment. Picking teams begin with the Merlot, which ripens first, and move as quickly as they can. Lafite employs some 250 people to shorten the harvest as far as possible.

The vital work of selection starts in the vineyard, with bunches that are unevenly ripe or infected with rot being left on the ground. It continues at the *cuvier*, where the grapes arriving in *douilles*, which hold enough for one barrel of wine, are inspected before being tipped in the *égrappoir-fouloir*, a simple mill that first strips the grapes off the stalks, then half crushes them. (A subtle difference here; most estates use a *fouloir-égrappoir* that crushes and destems at the same time: perfectionists remove the stalks first. By controlling the speed of the rollers it is possible to prevent green grapes being crushed at all.)

The crushed grapes, each variety separately, are pumped into splendid upright oak vats, gleaming with varnish on the outside, each holding between 15,750 and 20,250 litres. If the natural sugar in the grapes would produce less than 11.5 per cent of alcohol in the wine, enough pure sugar is added to make up the difference. In mild weather the juice and pulp start to ferment spontaneously within a day. In cold weather the whole *cuvier* is heated.

The temperature of fermentation is controlled to rise no higher than 30°C (85°F) – enough to extract the maximum colour from the skins; not enough to inhibit the yeasts and stop a steady fermentation. If it threatens to go higher, the must wine is pumped from the bottom of the vat to the top through a serpentine cooling system. Pumping it over the floating 'cap' of skins also helps to extract their colour.

Fermentation may take anything from one week to three depending on the yeasts, the ripeness of the grapes and the weather. The wine may be left on the skins for up to a total of 21 days if necessary to leach the maximum colour and flavour from them. By this time, with luck, the malolactic fermentation will be under way or even finished. The juice is now run off into new 225-litre *barriques* made at the château of oak from the forest of Tronçais in the Bourbonnais, north of the Massif Central. The remaining 'marc' of skins and pips is pressed in a hydraulic press. Some of the 'press' wine, exaggeratedly tannic, can be blended in if necessary. At Lafite the proportion varies between 10 percent and none at all.

The *barriques*, up to 1,100 of them in a plentiful year, stand in rows in the *chai*, loosely bunged at the top while the malolactic fermentation finishes. Early in the new year the proprietor, his manager, the *maître de chai* and the consultant oenologist, Professor Boissenot, taste the inky, biting new wine to make the essential selection: which barrels are good enough for the château's Grand Vin, which are fit for the second wine, Carruades de Lafite, and which will be rejected as mere Pauillac. This is the moment for the '*assemblage*' of the wines of the

four different varieties, up to now still separate. The barrels are emptied into vats to be blended, the barrels washed and slightly sulphured and the assembled wine put back.

For a further year they stand with loose bungs, being topped up weekly to make good any 'ullage', or loss by evaporation. During this year they will be 'racked' into clean casks two or three times and 'fined' with beaten egg whites. The white froth poured on to the top coagulates and sinks, taking any floating particles with it to the bottom. When the year is up the bungs are tapped tight with a mallet and the casks turned '*bondes de côte*' – with their bungs to the side. From now on the only way to sample them is through a tiny spiggot hole plugged with wood at the end of the cask.

At Lafite the wine is kept in cask for a further 9–12 months, until the second summer or autumn after the vintage, then it is given a final racking, six casks at a time, into a vat which feeds the bottling machine. If it were bottled straight from individual casks there would be too much variation.

Complicated as it is to relate, there is no simpler or more natural way of making wine. The factors that distinguish first-growth winemaking from more modest enterprises are the time it takes, the number of manoeuvres and the rigorous selection.

In recent years Rothschild enterprise has been at work to use the technical (as well as financial) strength of Lafite in new fields both near and far. The neighbouring Château Duhart-Milon has been bought and renovated; Château Rieussec in Sauternes and leading Pomerol Château L'Evangile acquired; and joint ventures started in both Chile (1988), California (1989) and Portugal (1992).

The mansion (recently restored, with splendid new underground *chais*) lies in the vineyards of Ch. Latour, but most of its vineyard is across the road, on gravelly soil with clay below, surrounded by the vines of the other Pichon château and parts of the vineyards of Ch'x Latour, Ducru-Beaucaillou and Léoville Las Cases. The southern portion of the vineyard is actually in St-Julien. With its relatively generous proportion of Merlot the wine lacks the concentrated vigour of Ch. Latour but adds a persuasive perfumed smoothness which makes it one of the most fashionable second-growths.

Big investment since the 1960s and new administration and expert advice since 1978 are now making fabulously good wine of the kind everyone wants – stylish Pauillac of the St-Julien persuasion; not so rigid with tannin and extract that it takes decades to mature. Each vintage since 1975 is among the best of its year with spectacular successes in '81, '82, '83, '84, '85 '86, '89, '94 and '95. The second label is Réserve de la Comtesse.

Château Pontet-Canet

5ème Cru Classé 1855. Owner: Guy Tesseron. AOC: Pauillac. 192 acres. 38,000 cases. Grape var: Cab.Sauv. 62%, Cab.Fr. 6%, Merlot 32%.

Sheer size has helped Pontet-Canet to become one of Bordeaux's most familiar names. That, and over a century of ownership by the shippers Cruse & Fils Frères. Its situation near Mouton promises top quality; the 1929 was considered better than the Mouton of that great year. But 1961 was the last great vintage Pontet-Canet has made, and that, like all its wines of that epoch, was very variable from bottle to bottle. The Cruse family did not believe in château bottling. In 1975 the estate was sold to M. Tesseron of Cognac (and Château Lafon-Rochet, St-Estèphe), son-in-law of Emmanuel Cruse. The 1980s saw steady improvement, though greatness still seems elusive, '94 and '95 are the most promising wines here for years. The double-decker *cuvier, chais* and bottle cellars are on an enormous scale even by Médoc standards. The second label, Les Hauts de Pontet (13,000 cases produced annually), was introduced in 1982.

OTHER CHATEAUX

Chateau La Bécasse Owner: Georges Fonteneau. Tiny but admirable estate making 2,500 cases of deep-flavoured Pauillac.

Château Belle Rose Cru Bourgeois. The second wine of Château Pédesclaux.

Carruades de Lafite New name for Moulin de Carruades.

Château Colombier Monpelou Grand Cru Bourgeois. Owner: Bernard Jugla. 61 acres. 18,000 cases. Usually attractive stablemate of the Cru Classé Château Pédesclaux.

Chateau Cordeillan Bages Owner: J. M. Cazes. A mere 1,000 cases from the château hotel vineyard.

Château La Fleur Milon Grand Cru Bourgeois. Owner: André Gimenez. 30 acres. 7,400 cases.

Château Fonbadet Owner: Pierre Peyronie. 41 acres. 7,500 cases. A good growth in the category considering itself 'exceptionnel'. Part of the vineyard is now Ch. Plantey (q.v.). M. Peyronie also owns Ch'x La Tour du Roc Milon, Haut-Pauillac, Padarnac and Montgrand Milon, all in Pauillac.

Les Forts de Latour *See* Ch. Latour. The first of the 'second' wines of the Médoc, and still the best.

Château Gaudin Owner: Pierre Bibian. 24 acres. 6,500 cases.

Château Grand Duroc Milon Cru Bourgeois. A second label of Ch Pédesclaux.

Château Haut-Bages Monpelou Cru Bourgeois. Owners: Hérit. Borie-Manoux (Emile Castéja). 87 acres. 8,300 cases. Part of the former vineyard of Ch. Duhart-Milon, now in the same hands as Ch Batailley and effectively its second wine.

Château Haut-Padarnac Cru Bourgeois. Owner: Bernard Jugla. Another wine from the Ch. Pédesclaux estate.

Moulin des Carruades The second wine of Carruades, so Lafite's third wine.

Château Pibran Cru Bourgeois. Owner: AXA. 25 acres. 4,000 cases. Classy wine under J M Cazes' direction.

Château Plantey Owner: Gabriel Meffre. 74 acres. Formerly part of Ch. Fonbadet, M. Meffre, a merchant, also owns Ch. du Glana (St-Julien).

La Tour l'Aspic Owner: Jean-Eugène Borie. Second label of Ch. Haut-Batailley.

Château La Tour Pibran Owner: Jacques Gounel. 20 acres. 3,400 cases.

Château La Tour du Roc Milon Owner: Pierre Peyronie. 12 acres. 2,000 cases. *See* Ch. Fonbadet.

Cave Coopérative La Rose Pauillac Growers' cooperative with an average production of 46,000 cases a year of well-made Pauillac. Labels include Château La Rose.

ST-ESTEPHE

St-Estèphe is more pleasantly rural than Pauillac; a scattering of six hamlets with some steepish slopes and (at Marbuzet) wooded parks. It has 3,330 acres of vineyards, mainly Crus Bourgeois, on heavier soil planted with, as a rule, a higher proportion of Merlot to Cabernet than the communes to the south. Typical St-Estèphe keeps a strong colour for a long time, is slow to show its virtues, has less perfume and a coarser, more hearty flavour than Pauillac, with less of the tingling vitality that marks the very best Médocs. With a few brilliant exceptions the St-Estèphes are the foot soldiers of this aristocratic army. Postcode: 33250 Pauillac.

St-Estèphe Crus Classés

Château Calon-Ségur

3ème Cru Classé 1855. Dir: Mme Capbern-Gasqueton. AOC: St-Estèphe. 143 acres. 20,000 cases. Grape var: Cab.Sauv. 65%, Cab.Fr. 15%, Merlot 20%.

The northernmost classed growth of the Médoc, named after the 18th-century Comte de Ségur who also owned Lafite and Latour but whose 'heart was at Calon' – and is remembered by a red one on the label. The wine sometimes has more flesh than excitement, but is impressively full of flavour as befits its class. The walled vineyard surrounds the fine château. Other Capbern-Gasqueton properties are Ch'x du Tertre (Margaux) and d'Agassac (qq.v.).

Château Cos d'Estournel

2ème Cru Classé 1855. Owner: Domaines Prats. Director: Bruno Prats. AOC: St-Estèphe. 158 acres. 25,000 cases. Grape var: Cab.Sauv. 60%, Cab.Fr. 2%, Merlot 38%.

Superbly sited vineyard sloping south towards Ch. Lafite. No house but a bizarre chinoiserie *chai*. The most (perhaps the only) glamorous St-Estèphe, one of the top second-growths with both the flesh and the bone of great claret and a fine record for consistency. The director, Bruno Prats, uses modern methods to make wine with old-fashioned virtues, including very long life. 15–20 years is a good age to drink it. The second label is Ch. (de) Marbuzet. The 's' of Cos is sounded, like most final consonants in southwest France.

Château Cos Labory

5ème Cru Classé 1855. Owner: Mme Cécile Audoy. AOC: St-Estèphe. 44 acres. 10,000 cases. Grape var: Cab.Sauv. 50%, Cab.Fr. 10%, Merlot 35%, Petit Verdot 5%.

A business-like little classed growth next door to Cos d'Estournel, but only geographically. The rather scattered vineyards with a high proportion of Merlot vines make a blunt, honest St-Estèphe, relatively soft and fruity for drinking in four or five years.

Château Lafon-Rochet

4ème Cru Classé 1855. Owner: Guy Tesseron. AOC: St-Estèphe. 74 acres. 22,000 cases. Grape var: Cab.Sauv. 54%, Merlot 40%, Cab.Fr. 6%.

A single block of vineyard sloping south towards the back of Ch. Lafite on the south bank of St-Estèphe. The château was rebuilt in the 1960s by the cognac merchant Guy Tesseron, who spares no expense to make good wine and has steadily improved the property making further changes recently. He makes full-bodied, warm, satisfying wine which is worth keeping for smoothness, but does not seem to find great finesse. A very good '82. Numéro 2 is the second label.

Château Montrose

2ème Cru Classé 1855. Owner: Jean-Louis Charmolüe. AOC: St-Estèphe. 168 acres. 30,000 cases. Grape var: Cab.Sauv. 65%, Cab.Fr. 10%, Merlot 25%.

Isolated, seemingly remote property overlooking the Gironde north of St-Estèphe with a style of its own; traditionally one of the 'firmest' of all Bordeaux, hard and forbidding for a long time, notably powerful in flavour even when mature. The deep colour and flavour of the wine probably come from the clay subsoil under reddish, iron-rich gravel. Being right on the river also helps the grapes to early ripeness. Wines of the period 1978–85 let the standard drop, being much softer and 'easier'; a superb '90. Since the late '80s the tone has again been sterner, tempting some to call Montrose the 'Latour of St-Estèphe'. The second label is La Dame de Montrose.

OTHER CHATEAUX

Château Andron-Blanquet Grand Bourgeois Exceptionnel. Owner: Mme Cécile Audoy. 39 acres. 11,000 cases. Made at Cos Labory (q.v.). Second label: Château St-Roch (Bourgeois).

Château Beau Site Grand Bourgeois Exceptionnel. Owners: the Castéja-Borie family *see* Ch. Batailley, Pauillac). 79 acres. 20,000 cases. A fine situation in the hamlet of St-Corbin. Distributed by Borie-Manoux.

Château Le Boscq Cru Bourgeois. Owner: CVBG. 37 acres. 10,000 cases. With Dourthe investment a good wine is getting better still.

Château Capbern-Gasqueton Grand Bourgeois Exceptionnel. Owners: the Capbern-Gasqueton family. 85 acres. 10,000 cases. Ch'x Grand-Village-Capbern, La Rose-Capbern, Moulin-de-Calon all refer to the same property. Distributors: Dourthe Frères.

Château Chambert-Marbuzet see Ch. Haut-Marbuzet.

Château Coutelin-Merville Cru Bourgeois. Owner: Bernard Estager. 47 acres. 12,000 cases.

Château Le Crock Grand Bourgeois Supérieur. Owners: Cuvelier & Fils. 82 acres. 17,000 cases. A classical mansion in a fine park, home of the owners of Léoville-Poyferré (Cru Classé, St-Julien). Second label: St-Estèphe La Croix.

Château Haut-Marbuzet Grand Bourgeois Exceptionnel. Owners: H. Duboscq & Fils. 123 acres. 25,000 cases. Today the outstanding Cru Bourgeois of St-Estèphe, and regularly one of the best buys of the Médoc; sold directly to private clients: oaky, fleshy, luxurious and instantly appealing. Ch. Chambert-Marbuzet and Ch. MacCarthy are Crus Bourgeois with the same owners. Second label: Ch. Tour de Marbuzet.

Château Houissant Owners: Jean Ardouin & Fils. 66 acres. 16,000 cases. Also called Leyssac.

Château Laffitte-Carcasset Owner: Vicomte de Padirac. 83 acres. 19,000 cases. Ch. Brame Les Tours is on the same estate.

Chateau Lilian Ladouys Big investments were made to buy land for this château and the '89 and '90 were very good, but the future is uncertain.

Château MacCarthy *See* Haut-Marbuzet.

Château (de) Marbuzet Grand Bourgeois Exceptionnel. The second label of Cos d'Estournel (q.v.). A guarantee in itself.

Château Meyney
Grand Bourgeois Exceptionnel. Owner: Cordier (the négociants; *see also* Ch. Gruaud-Larose, St-Julien). 125 acres. 28,000 cases. One of the best-sited and best made of the many reliable Crus Bourgeois in St-Estèphe. Second label: Prieur de Meyney.

Château Morin Cru Bourgeois. Owners: the Sidaine family. 24 acres. 6,000 cases.

Château Les-Ormes-de-Pez Grand Bourgeois. Owner: Jean-Michel Cazes *see* Ch. Lynch-Bages, Pauillac). 80 acres. 15,000 cases. Extremely popular and highly regarded property.

Château de Pez Owner: Louis Roederer. 60 acres. 15,500 cases. One of the best Cru Bourgeois in St-Estèphe. Noble, very long-lived wine of classed-growth standard. At 20 years the 1970 was magnificent. Recent lack of direction likely to be corrected by Champagne Roederer who bought the property in 1995.

Château Phélan-Ségur Grand Bourgeois Exceptionnel. Owner: Xavier Gardinier. 163 acres. 40,000 cases. Important property including also Ch'x Fonpetite and La Croix. Recently totally rebuilt and full of ambition. To watch. Frank Phélan is second label.

Chateau Ségur de Cabanac Owner: Guy Delon. Only 3,000 cases of excellent quality.

Château Tronquoy-Lalande Grand Bourgeois. Owner: Mme Castéja. 40 acres. 9,000 cases. Well distributed by Dourthe Frères.

OTHER GROWTHS
Château Haut Beauséjour 44 acres. 11,000 cases (also Ch. Picard).

Château Beau-Site-Haut-Vignoble 37 acres. 8,000 cases.

Château Canteloup 20 acres. 5,000 cases (also Ch. La Commanderie; property of G. Meffre, *see* Ch. Glana, St-Julien).

Château Lartigue 17 acres. 3,000 cases.

Château St-Estèphe 51 acres. 14,000 cases.

Château La Tour de Pez 56 acres. 13,000 cases.

Château La Tour-des-Termes 74 acres. 16,000 cases.

Marquis de St-Estèphe Coop for 135 growers with 419 acres.

HAUT-MEDOC

Haut-Médoc is the catch-all appellation for the fringes of the area that includes the most famous communes. It varies in quality from equal to some of the best in the very south, where Château La Lagune in Ludon and Château Cantemerle are out on a limb, to a level only notionally higher than the best of the lower, northerly end of the Médoc. Some of this land lies along the river in the middle of the appellation, in the low-lying communes of Arcins, Lamarque and Cussac – which also, it must be said, have some very good gravel. Some lies back inland along the edge of the pine forest.

With a total of 10,127 acres, the Haut-Médoc appellation is only an indication, not a guarantee, of high quality.

Haut-Médoc Crus Classés

Château Belgrave

5ème Cru Classé 1855. Owner: CVBG – Dourthe-Kressmann. AOC: Haut-Médoc. 136 acres. 20,000 cases. Grape var: Cab.Sauv. 40%, Cab.Fr. 20%, Merlot 35%, Petit Verdot 5%.
A lost property until 1980, now ultra-modernized with the advice of first Professor Emile Peynaud and now Michel Rolland.

Château de Camensac

5ème Cru Classé 1855. Owners: the Forner family. AOC: Haut-Médoc. 185 acres. 29,000 cases. Grape var: Cab.Sauv. 60%, Merlot 40%.
Neighbour of Ch'x Belgrave, La Tour-Carnet and Lagrange in the St-Laurent group, inland from St-Julien and out of the serious running for many years. Largely replanted since 1965 by M. Forner, the former owner of the neighbouring huge Cru Bourgeois Larose-Trintaudon. The result is good, full bodied, forthright wine with plenty of vigour, needing much longer maturing than the 'easy' Cru Bourgeois.

Château Cantemerle

5ème Cru Classé 1855. Owner: SMABTP group. 165 acres. 40,000 cases. Grape var: Cab.Sauv. 35%, Cab.Fr. 23%, Merlot 40%, Petit Verdot 2%.
The next château north from La Lagune, hidden behind a wooded 'park' of mysterious beauty with canals reflecting graceful white bridges and immense trees. The tree beside

the house on the pretty engraved label is a plane that now dominates the house completely – a monster.

The old-fashioned estate, with dwindling vineyards (now half their former size) and totally traditional methods, was sold in 1981 to a syndicate led by Cordier, who have more than doubled production and modernized it. The old peculiarities included de-stalking the grapes by rubbing the bunches through a wooden grille, fermentation at a high temperature and the use of well-aged barrels for as long as two and a half years. The result, with light soil and a good deal of Merlot, was wine of incredible charm yet formidable stability. Vintages of the '50s and '60s were marvellous; those of the '70s not quite so good, but quality was regained with '82 and '83 and now stands high, as in all Cordier properties and will get better as the younger wines mature.

Second wine: Baron Villeneuve de Cantemerle.

Visiting châteaux

Visitors to the Médoc will have no difficulty in finding châteaux willing to show them how they make their wine, and to let them taste it from the barrel. One simple way of arranging a château visit is to call at one of the little offices called Maison du Vin. The principal one is in the heart of Bordeaux near the Grand Théâtre. Margaux, Pauillac, St-Estèphe and several other villages have local ones. They will suggest an itinerary and if necessary make contacts. An even simpler method, but only really practicable for those who speak some French, is to stop at any of the many châteaux that advertise *dégustation* (tasting) and *vente directe* – direct sales – on roadside signs. They include some important châteaux as well as many modest ones. At any reasonable time (i.e. not during the harvest or any period of frantic activity, and not at lunch time, from noon to two o'clock) you can expect a more or less friendly welcome from the *maître de chai*, the cellar master.

In big châteaux he is a man of considerable dignity and responsibility, whatever he is wearing. He has seen many visitors pass and will make up his own mind, rightly or wrongly, about how much to show you. He will expect moderate praise for the chilly, tannic and (to the non-expert) almost untastable sample he draws from the barrel and hands you in a glass. Unless an obvious receptacle (often a tub of sawdust) is provided you may – indeed must – spit it out on the floor. I tend to wander off ruminating to the doorway and spit into the outside world. It gives me a chance to compose my thoughts – and recover from my grimace.

Clearly the idea of vente directe is that you should buy a bottle or two, but you need not feel obliged. The maître de chai of a modest château would often just as soon accept a pourboire.

Advanced students will have to judge for themselves how far into detailed discussion of techniques, weather conditions and earlier vintages the maître de chai is prepared to go. It is not unknown for young and even not-so-young bottles to be opened in the enthusiasm of explanation. But it is scarcely reasonable to expect such treatment.

Château La Lagune

3ème Cru Classé 1855. Owner: Jean-Michel Ducellier. AOC: Haut-Médoc. 173 acres. 38,000 cases. Grape var: Cab.Sauv. 60%, Cab.Fr. 10%, Merlot 20%, Petit Verdot 10%.

The nearest important Médoc château to Bordeaux and a charming 18th-century villa. The vineyard had almost disappeared in the 1950s, when it was totally replanted and equipped with the latest steel vats and pipes. In 1961 the owners of Ayala champagne bought it and have been making better and better wine as the vines have rooted deeper in the light, sandy gravel. Sweetness, spiciness, fleshiness and concentration are all qualities found in it by critics. In poor vintages it can almost caricature itself with a rather jammy effect; in great ones it is now on a par with such second-growths as Léoville Las Cases and Ducru-Beaucaillou. Like a first-growth, La Lagune uses new barrels for all the wine every year.

Château La Tour Carnet

4ème Cru Classé 1855. Owner: Guy François Pelegrin. AOC: Haut-Médoc. 99 acres. 20,000 cases. Grape var: Cab.Sauv. 53%, Cab.Fr. 10%, Merlot 33%, Petit Verdot 4%.

A moated medieval castle in the relatively rolling, wooded back country of St-Laurent, restored in the 1960s and still perhaps suffering from the youth of its vines. The wine is light in colour and pretty in style, maturing quickly. Enjoyable, but scarcely a fourth-growth if Cantemerle is a fifth.

OTHER CHATEAUX

Château d'Agassac Grand Bourgeois Exceptionnel, Ludon. Dir: P. Capbern-Gasqueton. 83 acres plus; 10,000 cases. The Médoc's most romantic château, medieval, moated and deep in the woods. The owner (also of Ch'x Calon-Ségur and du Tertre) is making increasingly good wine. The Cru Classé La Lagune is nearby.

Château d'Arche Ludon. Owner: Mähler-Besse. 25 acres. 5,500 cases. A good wine.

Château d'Arcins Arcins. Owner: Castel. 240 acres. 38,000 cases. The two biggest Arcins properties have recently been restored by the important wine-merchant family of Castel, famous for their Castelvin brand. Their huge new stone-clad warehouse seems to fill the village. Their presence here is bound to make the neglected name of Arcins familiar. Its wine should be of Cussac standard, which can be high.

Château d'Arnauld Arcins. Owner: Theil-Roggy. 66 acres. 11,000 cases. (*See* Ch. Poujeaux, Moulis.) A very good wine (50% Merlot).

Château Balac Cru Bourgeois, St-Laurent. Owner: Luc Touchais. 37 acres. 8,300 cases. The Touchais family are better known for their Anjou wines.

Château Barreyres Arcins. Owner: Castel. 270 acres. 38,000 cases. An imposing property near the river, now linked with Ch. d'Arcins (q.v.).

Château Beaumont Grand Bourgeois, Cussac. Owner: GMF/MAIF. 260 acres plus; 66,000 cases plus. Grand château in the woods north of Poujeaux, in the same hands as Beychevelle, making stylish, good-value claret. Second label: Moulin d'Arvigny.

Chateau Bel Air Cussac. Owner: Triaud. Commercial claret from Domaines Martin. 20,000 cases.

Château Bel-Orme-Tronquoy-de-Lalande Grand Bourgeois, St-Seurin. Owner: Mme L. Quié and J.-M. Quié. 64 acres. 13,000 cases. Well-sited property of the family that owns Ch'x Rauzan-Gassies and Croizet-Bages. Potential to do better. Easily confused with Château Tronquoy-Lalande, St-Estèphe.

Château Bonneau-Livran Cru Bourgeois, St-Seurin. Owner: M Gautreau of Sociando-Mallet bought the property in 1990. 12 acres. 3,300 cases.

Château Le Bourdieu Vertheuil. Owners: the Richard family. 134 acres. 34,000 cases plus. Vertheuil lies just inland from St-Estèphe on similar clayey gravel. This big property (which includes the château with the promising name of Victoria) can make good St-Estèphe-style wine.

Château du Breuil Cru Bourgeois, Cissac. Owner: Ch. Cissac. 57 acres. 13,000 cases. On the edge of the parish just behind the Carruades plateau of Pauillac and Ch. Duhart-Milon. Stylish wines.

Chateau Cambon la Pelouse Macau. Owner: David Faure. Large estate between Cantemerle and Giscours farmed by the Carrere family.

Château Caronne-Ste-Gemme Grand Bourgeois Exceptionnel, St-Laurent. Owner: J. and F. Nony-Borie. 111 acres. 20,000 cases. A substantial property whose label is a mass of medals, but all of long ago. Well made, somewhat lean wine, capable of charm with time. Rounder since 1995.

Château Charmail, St-Seurin. Owner: Olivier Sèze. 54 acres. 14,000 cases. Full, fruity claret. A wine to watch.

Château Cissac Grand Bourgeois Exceptionnel, Cissac. Owner: Louis Vialard, 123 acres. 26,000 cases. A pillar of the bourgeoisie; reliable, robust, mainstream Médoc at its best after 10 years or so. M. Vialard is a man of authority and style. Second label: Reflets de Cissac.

Château Citran Grand Bourgeois Exceptionnel, Avensan. Owner: Touko-Hans. 220 acres. 47,000 cases. A pace-setting Cru Exceptionnel with a wide following and a long record of good vintages. Round, full wine (42% Merlot) with ageing potential, benefiting from Japanese investment since 1987.

Château Coufran Grand Bourgeois, St-Seurin. Director: Jean Miailhe. 185 acres. 45,000 cases. The northernmost

The châteaux – how the list was compiled

'The only complete list of wine growers in any serious part of France is the telephone directory.' The remark was made to me in Burgundy but it is equally true for much of Bordeaux. Everybody is a wine-grower. So who do you put in and who do you leave out?

The answer is a long sifting process, starting with published lists of classified properties at various levels of importance, going through members of syndicates, reviewing wine lists, books and articles, re-reading tasting notes and finally, most of all, relying on people on the spot – merchants, mayors of villages, brokers who specialize in one corner of the country. I am acutely aware of the subjectivity of everything short of the telephone book – but this is the nature of the subject matter. Some growers have reputations exceeding their worth; others are worthy workers and reliable suppliers but have never known how, or felt the need, to build a reputation. In some areas where vineyards are very small I have simply had to employ the guillotine – which has been abolished for its original purpose. Otherwise I would not have dared. (See index pages 562–63.)

estate of the Haut-Médoc, it is unusual in being 85% Merlot to make softer, more 'fleshy' wine than its neighbouring sister – Ch. Verdignan (q.v.). Miailhe is president and spokesman for the league of Crus Bourgeois.

Château Dillon Blanquefort. Owner: Ecole d'Agriculture. 86 acres. 20,000 cases. The local agricultural college. Some good wines, including dry white Ch. Linas.

Château Fonpiqueyre Cru Bourgeois, St-Sauveur. Included in Ch. Liversan. 6,700 cases.

Château Fontesteau Grand Bourgeois, St-Sauveur. Owners: MM. Fouin and Barron. 49 acres. 11,000 cases. Good conservative wine in the classic Médoc style for maturing.

Château Le Fournas-Bernadette St-Sauveur. Owners: Bernadotte and Proche-Pontet. 74 acres. 13,000 cases.

Chateau Gironville Macau. Owner: M.M. Fouin and Mercier. First vintage 1990 promised well.

Château Grandis St-Seurin-de-Cadourne. Owner: M. Vergez. 22 acres. 3,800 cases.

Château Grand Moulin Grand Bourgeois, St-Seurin. Owner: R. Gonzalvez. 44 acres. 11,000 cases. Also appears under the name Ch La Mothe.

Château Hanteillan Grand Bourgeois, Cissac. Owner: SARL du Château Hanteillan. 205 acres. 50,000 cases. Old property lavishly restored and replanted since 1973, and incorporating part of Larrivaux. Now run with dedication by Catherine Blasco.

Château Hourtin-Ducasse Cru Bourgeois, St-Sauveur. Owner: Maurice Marengo. 61 acres. 13,000 cases. An elegant wine.

Château Lamarque Grand Bourgeois, Lamarque. Director: Roger Gromand. 116 acres. 25,000 cases. The finest remaining medieval fortress in the Médoc, in the village where the ferry leaves for Blaye. Developed by the present owners up to Cru Exceptionnel standards, proving the potential of the central Médoc. Cap de Haut is second label.

Château Lamothe Bergeron Cru Bourgeois, Cussac. Owner: Les Grands Vignobles. 163 acres. 19,000 cases. The same owners as Ch. Grand-Puy-Ducasse.

Château Lamothe-Cissac Grand Bourgeois, Cissac. Owner: G. Fabre. 82 acres. 18,000 cases. Up-to-date property related (by marriage) to Ch. Cissac.

Château Landat Cru Bourgeois, Cissac. Owner: G. Fabre (see Lamothe-Cissac). 61 acres. 10,000 cases.

Château Lanessan Cussac. Owners: the Bouteiller family. 160 acres. 32,000 cases. Includes Ch. Lachesnaye and Ste-Gemme. An extravagant Victorian mansion and park with a popular carriage museum. The best-known estate in Cussac with the standards of a Cru Exceptionnel, if not a Cru Classé. Polished rather than exciting wine. Ages well.

Château Larose-Trintaudon Grand Bourgeois, St-Laurent. Owner: Assurances Générales de France. President: J. Papon. 425 acres. 83,000 cases. The biggest estate in the Médoc, planted since 1965, built up by the Forner family, owners of the admirable Rioja Marqués de Cáceres (and the neighbouring Cru Classé Ch. de Camensac). Modern methods include mechanical harvesting. Quantity does not seem to impede steady, enjoyable quality. The Forners sold the estate in 1986 and continued to manage it until 1989.

Château Larrivaux Cissac. 62 acres. 11,000 cases.

Château Lartigue de Brochon Cru Bourgeois, St-Seurin. Owner: J. Gautreau. 30 acres. 4,000 cases. M. Gautreau is also proprietor of the admirable Ch. Sociando-Mallet.

Château Lestage Simon Cru Bourgeois, St-Seurin. Owner: C. Simon. 74 acres. 18,000 cases. Concentrated and fruity.

Château Lieujean St-Sauveur. Owner: Fournier-Karsenty. 123 acres. 28,000 cases.

Château Liversan Cru Bourgeois, St-Sauveur. Owner: Prince Guy de Polignac. 124 acres. 22,000 cases. Charming property including Ch. Fonpiqueyre. Conscientious wine-making backed by new investment.

Chateau Magnol Blanquefort. Owner: Barton et Guestier. 7,200 cases.

Château Malescasse Lamarque. Owner: Alcatel Alsthom. 91 acres. 20,000 cases plus. Replanted in the 1970s. Promises good wine as the vines mature. New corporate owners in '92 making further investments. Very good in '82, '85, '86.

Château de Malleret Grand Bourgeois, Le Pian. Owner: Comte Bertrand du Vivier. 163 acres. 38,000 cases.

Château Le Meynieu Grand Bourgeois, Vertheuil. Owner: J. Pédro. 34 acres. 6,500 cases. A recent addition to the number of serious and competent bourgeois châteaux.

Château du Moulin Rouge Cru Bourgeois, Cussac. Owner: Guy Pelon. 37 acres. 9,000 cases.

Châteaux Peyrabon Grand Bourgeois, St-Sauveur. Owner: Jacques Babeau. 130 acres. 20,000 cases.

Château Clément Pichon Parempuyre. Owner: C. Fayat. 60 acres. 8,000 cases. Dourthe Frères distributes. Bland up-front style.

Château Plantey de la Croix Cru Bourgeois, St-Seurin. Second label of Ch. Verdignan.

Château Pontoise-Cabarrus Grand Bourgeois, St-Seurin. Owner: M Tereygeol. 76 acres. 16,500 cases. A serious, well-run property.

Château Puy Castéra Cru Bourgeois, Cissac. Owner: M.M. Marès. 62 acres. 17,000 cases. A recent creation, apparently in good hands.

Château Ramage La Batisse Cru Bourgeois, St-Sauveur. Owner: Société Civile. 98 acres. 24,000 cases. A vineyard created since 1961. Now one of the bigger Cru Bourgeois with modern methods but traditional oak-aged style, winning medals for quality.

Château du Retout Cussac. Owner: R. Kopp. 74 acres. 18,000 cases.

Château Reysson Grand Bourgeois, Vertheuil. Owner: Sankraku. 165 acres. 15,000 cases. Japanese owners since '87.

Château de la Rose Maréchal Cru Bourgeois, St-Seurin. A second label of Ch Coufran.

Chateau Saint Ahon Blanquefort. Owner: Bernard de Colbert. 16,000 cases.

Château de St-Paul St-Seurin. Owner: M. Bouchet. 47 acres. 10,000 cases.

Château Ségur Grand Bourgeois, Parempuyre (alias Ch. Ségur-Fillon). Owner: Société Civile. 88 acres. 24,000 cases. Early-maturing claret from vines on good, deep gravel in the extreme south of the Médoc. Popular in Holland.

59

Château Sénéjac Le Pian. Owner: Charles de Guigné. 64 acres. 14,000 cases plus. Old family property. Seriously good in '89 and '90 but shakier since.

Château Senilhac St-Seurin. Owner: M Grassin. 50 acres. 11,000 cases.

Château Sociando-Mallet Grand Bourgeois, St-Seurin. Owner: J. Gautreau. 123 acres. 25,000 cases. A star of the bourgeoisie. Recent vintages, needing long maturation, have outshone many *crus classés*. Second wine: Demoiselle de Sociando-Mallet.

Château Soudars Cru Bourgeois, St-Seurin. Owner: Eric Miailhe (son of Jean, Ch. Coufran). 54 acres. 13,000 cases.

Château du Taillan Grand Bourgeois, Le Taillan. Owner: Mme Henri-François Cruse. 52 acres. 10,000 cases. Pleasant red, 40% Merlot, from a charming estate north of Bordeaux. La Dame Blanche is the estate's white wine.

Château Tour du Haut Moulin Grand Bourgeois, Cussac. Owner: Laurent Poitou. 76 acres. 17,000 cases. Full-flavoured wine (45% Merlot) with a wide following. Until his retirement in 1982, M. Poitou managed several other estates for Les Grands Vignobles.

Château La Tour du Mirail Cru Bourgeois, Cissac. Owners: Hélène and Danielle Vialard (*see* Ch. Cissac). 44 acres. 9,000 cases.

Château Tour du Roc Cru Bourgeois, Arcins. Owner: Philippe Robert. 30 acres. 6,000 cases.

Château La Tour St-Joseph Cru Bourgeois, Cissac. Owners: M. and C. Quancard. 24 acres. 5,000 cases.

Château Tourteran St-Sauveur. 49 acres. 12,000 cases. Same owner as Ch. Ramage La Batisse.

Château Verdignan Grand Bourgeois, St-Seurin. Owner: Jean Miailhe. 150 acres. 36,000 cases. In contrast to its sister-château Coufran, Verdignan has the classic Médoc proportion of Cabernet and needs keeping two or three years longer.

Château Villegeorge Avensan. Owner: Marie-Laure Lurton. 37 acres. 2,500 cases. A minor property of the owner of Ch. Brane-Cantenac and many others. Deep, rich-flavoured wine from a 60% Merlot vineyard. Fine '90.

Caves Coopératives 'Cru La Paroisse St-Seurin de Cadourne' St-Seurin de Cadourne. 222 acres. 36,000 cases. The coop of the next parish north from St-Estèphe.

Fort Médoc Cussac 148 acres. 95,000 cases. Sound cooperative cellar at the impressive riverside fort built by Vauban to command the Gironde.

APPELLATION MEDOC

The lower Médoc (in the sense of being farther down the Gironde) was formerly called Bas-Médoc, which made it clear that it was this area and not the whole peninsula under discussion. The soil and therefore the wines are considered inferior here. The last of the big-calibre gravel has been deposited by glaciers higher up between Graves and St-Estèphe. Although the ground continues to heave gently the humps become more scattered and their soil much heavier with a high proportion of pale, cold clay, suited to Merlot rather than Cabernet (although patches of sandier soil persist here and there).

The wine has distinctly less finesse and perfume, but good body and 'structure' with some of the tannic 'cut' that makes all Médocs such good wines at table. Good vintages last well in bottle without developing the sweet complexities of the Haut-Médoc at its best.

The last decade has seen a great revival of interest in this productive area. Half a dozen big properties have made the running and now offer a good deal, if not a bargain. The 1996 basic price was about 16 francs a bottle compared with 19 francs for the appellation Haut-Médoc. The best properties fetch about double this, whereas in the Haut-Médoc the range runs up to about three times the base price.

In 1972 there were 4,535 acres in production in the appellation Médoc. By 1994 this figure had more than doubled – to 11,362 acres. The legally permitted yield here is slightly higher than in the Haut-Médoc: 45 hl/ha compared with 43.

Much the most important commune is Bégadan, with several of the most prominent estates and a very big growers' coop-erative. Nearly a third of the whole appellation comes from the one parish. Next in order of production come St-Yzans, Prignac, Ordonnac, Blaignan, St-Christoly and St-Germain.

The principal producers are given here in alphabetical order, followed by the names of their communes. The central town for the whole area is Lesparre.

Postcode for all the communes mentioned is 33340 Lesparre Médoc.

LOWER MEDOC CHATEAUX

Château Bellevue Cru Bourgeois, Valeyrac. 56 acres. 14,500 cases.

Château Blaignan Cru Bourgeois. Owner: Mestrezat. 185 acres. 37,500 cases of red.

Château Le Boscq Cru Bourgeois, St-Christoly. Owner: C. Lapalu (*see also* Ch. Patache d'Aux).

Château Bournac Owner: P. Secret. 32 acres. 8,000 cases of solid, fruity red.

Château Carcannieux Cru Bourgeois, Queyrac. Dir: M. Paul. 90 acres. 18,000 cases.

Château La Cardonne Grand Bourgeois, Blaignan. Owner: Charloux. 172 acres. 30,000 cases. A Rothschild development since 1973, which provided a great boost to the lower Médoc with its prestige and predictably well-made wine. However, the property changed hands again in 1990.

Château Ramafort is another property in the group. Cardus and Malaire are second labels.

Château du Castéra Cru Bourgeois, St-Germain. 123 acres. 22,000 cases. A lovely old place with a drawbridge, relic of more exciting times (it was besieged by the English during the 14th century) belonging to German owners, Dengos. Stainless steel in use since 1981.

Château La Clare Cru Bourgeois, Bégadan. Owner: Paul de Rozières. 49 acres. 10,000 cases.

Château La France Cru Bourgeois, Blaignan. Owner: M. Querre. 54 acres. 13,000 cases.

Château Gallais-Bellevue *See* Ch. Potensac, Ordonnac.

Château Les Grands Chênes Cru Bourgeois. St. Christoly. 17 acres. 4,400 cases. An excellent performer with Cuvée Prestige.

Château Greysac Bégadan. Owner: Dom. Codem. 148 acres. 28,000 cases. Big, efficient property making sound wine, which is well-known in the USA. Greysac is approachable young but capable of ageing. The second label is Domaine de By.

Chateau Grivière Cru Bourgois. Prignac. 10,000 cases. Part of the Rothschild empire complete with concentrator and stainless steel.

Château Haut-Canteloup Grand Bourgeois, St-Christoly. 88 acres. 23,000 cases.

Château Hauterive St-Germain d'Esteuil. Owner: M. Lafage. 217 acres. 55,000 cases plus Brie Caillou as other label.

Château Hourbanon Cru Bourgeois, Prignac. Owner: Mme Delayat. 30 acres. 6,500 cases.

Cru Lassalle *See* Château Potensac, Ordonnac.

Château Laujac Bégadan. Owners: the Cruse family. 66 acres. 10,000 cases. A home of the famous family of shippers, hence well known abroad long before most of the other châteaux in the district.

Château La Valière Cru Bourgeois, St-Christoly. Owners: Cailloux family. 38 acres. 7,500 cases.

Château Liversan *See* Patache d'Aux.

Château Livran St-Germain (also includes La Rose Garomey). Owner: Robert Godfrin. 123 acres. 27,000 cases. A lovely old country house with old vines (55% planted in Merlot). As M. Godfrin puts it: 'We have the pleasures we deserve.'

Château Loudenne Grand Bourgeois, St-Yzans. Owner: Gilbeys. Director Charles Eve MW. 123 acres. 27,000 cases. The showplace of the area; a low, pale pink château on a hill of gravelly clay overlooking the river. Loudenne has been in English hands for over a century. Great care in winemaking produces well-balanced and long-lived red and one of Bordeaux's best dry whites. Seat of a wine *Ecole*.

Château Monthil Cru Bourgeois, Bégadan. Owner: Codem. 74 acres. 27,000 cases. Second label: Château des Bertins (*see* Greysac).

Château Les Ormes Sorbet Cru Bourgeois, Couquèques. Owner: Jean Boivert. 52 acres. 12,000 cases. A conscientious wine maker to be watched. Richly, highly-oaked wines.

Château de Panigon Cru Bourgeois, Civrac. Owner: J. K. and J. R. Leveilley. 123 acres. 26,000 cases.

Château Patache d'Aux Grand Bourgeois, Bégadan. Owner: Claude Lapalu. 105 acres. 26,000 cases. Popular full-flavoured Médoc with wide distribution, now linked with the aristocratic Château Liversan.

Château Potensac Grand Bourgeois, Ordonnac (includes Ch. Gallais-Bellevue, Cru Lasalle and Ch. Goudy La Cardonne). Owner: Mme Paul Delon. 128 acres. 26,000 cases. A very successful enterprise of the owners of Ch. Léoville Las Cases. Well-made, fruity, enjoyable claret (by whatever name) with a stylish flavour of oak – no doubt barrels retired from Léoville.

Château Sestignan Cru Bourgeois. Owner: B. de Rozières. 48 acres. 12,200 cases.

Château St-Bonnet Cru Bourgeois, St-Christoly. 125 acres. 32,000 cases.

Château Sigognac Grand Bourgeois, Yzans. Owner: Mme Bonny 110 acres. 25,000 cases. A good light wine.

Château La Tour-Blanche Cru Bourgeois, St-Christoly. Owner: D. Hessel (*see also* Ch. Moulin à Vent, Moulis). 62 acres. 11,000 cases.

Château La Tour de By Grand Bourgeois, Bégadan (includes Ch'x La Roque de By, Moulin de la Roque, Caillou de By). Director: Marc Pagés. 180 acres. 46,000 cases. Extremely successful estate with a high reputation for enjoyable and durable, if not literally fine, wine.

Château La Tour Haut-Caussan Cru Bourgeois, Blaignan (alias Ch. Pontet). Owner: M. Courrian. 39 acres. 10,000 cases. Fine off-vintages give this property one of the best records in the Médoc.

Château des Tourelles Cru Bourgeois, Blaignan. Owner: F. Miquau. 74 acres. 18,000 cases.

Château La Tour Prignac Prignac. Owner: Philippe Castel. 345 acres. 44,000 cases. Vast new enterprise of the Castelvin family, whose Haut Médoc headquarters is at Arcins (*see* Ch. d'Arcins).

Château La Tour St-Bonnet Cru Bourgeois, St-Christoly. Owner: P. Lafon. 100 acres. 17,000 cases plus. One of the pioneers of the lower Médoc renaissance. Good value traditional Médoc, tannic when young. Good '95.

Château Vieux Robin Cru Bourgeois, Bégadan. Owner: Maryse Roba. 42 acres. 10,000 cases. Also Vieux Robin Bois de Lunier matured in new oak.

Vieux-Château Landon Cru Bourgeois, Bégadan. Owner: Philippe Gillet. 98 acres. 17,500 cases. An energetic proprietor with ambitions. Sound, lively wine.

CAVES COOPÉRATIVES

Bégadan The largest cooperative in the area, sourcing grapes from about 1,400 acres. Labels include Château Bégadanais.

Prignac About 700 acres.

Les Vieux Colombiers Part of Uni-Médoc which markets the wine of four Médoc groups.

St-Yzans About 500 acres. As an example of the quality of this cooperative's production, the 1970 was excellent at 12 years old.

GRAVES

Wine was first made at Bordeaux in what is now the city and the suburbs immediately across the river and to the south. Graves was the name given to the whole of the left (city) bank of the Garonne for as far as 40 miles upstream, beyond the little town of Langon, and back away from the river into the pine forests of the Landes – an area not much different in size from the wine-growing Médoc, but more cut up with woodland and farms and containing few extensive vineyards or big châteaux.

Graves' distinguishing feature (hence its name) is its open, gravelly soil, the relic of Pyrenean glaciers in the Ice Ages. In fact, the soil varies within the region just as much as that of the Médoc. Sand is common. Pale clay and red clay are both present. But as in the Médoc, it is pretty certain that by now most of the potentially good vineyard land is being put to good use. In all there are some 12,844 acres of vineyards.

But Graves is too diffuse to grasp easily. It would be helpful (and accurate) if the authorities established an appellation Haut-Graves to distinguish the few communes of the northern section where all the Crus Classés are situated. Instead they have established the AC Pessac-Léognan for a rather wider area. An enclave in the south of the region has quite different styles – of landscape, ownership and wine. This is Sauternes.

Although Graves is divided between two-thirds red wine and one-third white, the great majority of the top-quality wine is red. The words commonly used to explain how red Graves differs from Médoc all make it sound less fine: 'earthy', 'soft', 'maturing sooner' sound more homely than inspiring. The late Maurice Healey got it in one when he said that Médoc and Graves were like glossy and matt prints of the same photograph. The matt picture can be equally beautiful, but less crisp and sharp-edged, with less glittering colours.

White Graves at its best is a rare experience – and an expensive one. Very few estates even aim for the unique combination of fullness and drive that comes to white Graves with time. The best is equal in quality to the great white burgundies. Opinion is divided even on the grapes to make it with. Some favour all Sémillon, some all Sauvignon and some a mixture, in various proportions. Some make it in stainless steel and bottle it in the early spring. Others (including the best) make it and mature it, at least briefly, in new oak barrels. The tendency among the lesser growths making dry wine has been to pick too early for full ripeness. Sauvignon Blanc in any case ripens unevenly here. The best makers now concentrate on full ripeness and complete fermentation to give clean, dry wine with plenty of flavour.

The communes of what might be called 'Haut-Graves' are as follows, starting in the north on the doorstep of Bordeaux: Pessac and Talence (in the suburbs); Gradignan and Villenave-d'Ornon (with very little wine today); Léognan, the most extensive, with six classed growths; Cadaujac and Martillac. Up to 1987 all shared the single appellation Graves. In that year the new AC Pessac-Léognan was created, to include 55 châteaux and domaines in 10 communes; a total of 3,210 acres of vines. South of this district, but increasingly important for similar wine, is Portets. Cérons, on the threshold of Barsac and Sauternes, makes both sweet and dry white wine, the dry now gaining in quality and popularity. Red has been steadily increasing at the expense of white.

The châteaux of Graves were classified in 1953 and 1959 in a blunt yes-or-no fashion which gives little guidance. Château Haut-Brion having been included in the Médoc classification 100 years earlier, 12 other châteaux were designated Crus Classés for their red wine, in alphabetical order. In 1959, six of them and two additional châteaux were designated Crus Classés for white wine. There is no other official ranking in Graves so all the rest can call themselves Crus Bourgeois.

Graves Premier Cru

Château Haut-Brion

1er Cru Classé 1855. Pessac. Owner: Domaine Clarence Dillon. AOC: Pessac-Léognan. 106 acres. 16,000 cases. Grape var: Cab.Sauv. 45%, Cab.Franc 18%, Merlot 37%.

The first wine château to be known by name, late in the 17th century, and although now surrounded by the suburbs of Bordeaux still one of the best of all, regularly earning its official place beside the four first-growths of the Médoc.

The situation of the 16th-century manor house of the Pontacs is no longer particularly impressive, but its 30-foot deep gravel soil gives deep-flavoured wine that holds a remarkable balance of fruity and earthy flavours for decades. Mouton has resonance, Margaux has coloratura; Haut-Brion just has harmony – between strength and finesse, firmness and sweetness. I shall never forget the taste of an Impériale of the 1899 – the most spell-binding claret I have ever drunk.

The present owners, the family of an American banker, Clarence Dillon, bought the estate in a near-derelict condition in 1935. In 1983 they added the next-door Château La Mission-Haut-Brion (q.v.). The present president is Dillon's granddaughter. Haut-Brion was the first of the first-growths to install stainless steel vats for the quite quick and relatively warm fermentation which is its policy. Rather than select the 'best' strain of each vine, M.

Delmas, the administrator, believes in diversity. He reckons to have nearly 400 different clones in the vineyard. This, and the fairly high proportion of Cabernet Franc, contribute complexity and harmony. As for age, Haut-Brion demands it. The good vintages of the 1970s – '71, '75, '78, '79 – are only now reaching their peak; the apogee of the 1980s is still some time away. '89 Haut-Brion is already a legend A tiny quantity of very good white Graves (37:63 Sauvignon:Sémillon) is also made and sold at an extravagant price.

The second wine of Haut-Brion, Bahans-Haut-Brion, was unusual in being a non-vintage blend until 1983.

Graves Crus Classés

Château Bouscaut

Cru Classé de Graves (red and white), Cadaujac. Owner: Société Anonyme du Château Bouscaut. (Sophie and Louis Lurton.) AOC: Pessac-Léognan. 111 acres. 22,000 cases red, 3,000 cases white. Grape var. red: Merlot 55%, Cab.Sauv. 35%, Cab.Fr. 5%; white: Sém. 70%, Sauv. 30%.

A handsome 18th-century house with rather low-lying vineyards, which was bought from its American owners in 1979 by Lucien of the ubiquitous Lurton family. The style is rather understated and there may be a tendency to overproduce but both the '83 and '90 are delicious and more recent vintages made by the new generation look good.

Bordeaux glossary

Barrique the standard Bordeaux barrel for ageing and sometimes shipping the wine; holds 225 litres.

Cépage, encépagement grape variety; choice of grape varieties in a vineyard.

Chai, maître de chai the storage place for wine in barrels, in the Médoc usually a barn above ground or slightly sunk in the earth for coolness; in St-Emilion frequently a cellar. The cellar master in charge of all wine-making operations.

Chef de culture in larger properties, the outdoors equivalent of the maître de chai; the foreman of the vineyard.

Collage fining; clarification of the wine, usually with beaten egg white.

Cru 'growth' – any wine-making property, as in Cru Classé, **Cru Bourgeois**, etc.

Cuve, cuvier, cuvaison vat, vat-house, vatting (i.e. time the wine spends fermenting in the vat).

Engrais (chimique, organique) fertilizer (chemical, organic).

Fouloir-égrappoir (foulage, éraflage) rotary machine for tearing the grapes off their stalks and crushing them.

Foulage is crushing, éraflage removing the stalks.

Gérant general manager of a property, the man in charge.

Grand Vin not a recognized or regulated term, but generally used to mean the first or selected wines of a property, in contrast to the second or other wines.

Millésime the vintage year (e.g. 1982).

Monopole a contract between a grower and shipper for the monopoly in handling his wine.

Négociant a merchant or 'shipper'.

Oenologue oenologist or technical wine-making consultant.

Porte-greffe root-stock of phylloxera-resistant vine on to which the desired variety is grafted.

Propriétaire owner.

Récolte harvest.

Régisseur manager or bailiff of an estate.

Rendement (à l'hectare) crop (measured in hectolitres per hectare).

Taille pruning.

Tonneau the measure in which Bordeaux is still bought and sold from the château (900 litres, or four barriques or 100 dozen bottles) although such big barrels are no longer in use.

Viticulteur a wine grower.

Château Carbonnieux

Cru Classé Graves (red and white), Léognan. Owner: Société des Grandes Graves. Dir: Antony Perrin. AOC: Pessac-Léognan. 192 acres. 13,000 cases white, 12,000 cases red. Grape var. red: Cab.Sauv. up to 65%, Merlot 30%, Cab.Fr. 7%, Malbec 2%, Petit Verdot 1%; white: Sauv. 60%, Sém. 34%, Musc. 1%.

An old embattled monastery built around a courtyard, restored and run by a family who left Algeria in the 1950s. Bigger and hence better known than most Graves properties, particularly for its white wine, one of the flag-carriers for white Graves. The white is aged briefly in new oak *barriques*, then bottled young, thus keeping freshness while getting some of the proper oak flavour. Quality took a marked step forward during the late '80s. Three or four years in bottle are needed to perfect it. The red faces more competition but is well-made typical Graves, dry and persistent.

Château Le Sartre (good white) is also in the family. La Tour Léognan is the second wine.

Domaine de Chevalier

Cru Classé de Graves (red and white), Léognan. Owner: Société Civile. Dirs: Olivier Bernard. AOC: Pessac-Léognan. 76 acres. 16,000 cases. Grape var: Cab.Sauv. 65%, Cab.Fr. 5%, Merlot 30%, white: Sauv. 70%, Sém. 30%

A strange place to find a vineyard, in the middle of a wood. Total rebuilding revolutionized a sombre old place in the 1980s. The soil and the style of the red wine are similar to the nearby Haut-Bailly (q.v.); starting stern, maturing dense and savoury. 1961, '64 and '66 were all magnificent and the 1980s have been very fine. The château often succeeds when others fail, for example in '84 and '91.

The white wine is second only to Laville Haut-Brion in quality, designed for astonishingly long life. It is made with the care of a great Sauternes, fermented and matured in barrels. To drink it before 5 years is a waste, and the flavours of a 15-year-old bottle can be breathtaking. In 1996 Olivier Barnard joined with three like-minded neighbours, Châteaux de Fieuzal, Smith-Haut-Lafite and Landiras to promote 'Les Grands Blancs de Bordeaux'.

Château Couhins

Cru Classé de Graves (white), Villenave-d'Ornon. Owner: Institut National de la Recherche Agronomique (INRA). 34 acres. 5,500 cases red. 1,700 cases white. Sauv. 80%, Sém. 20%.

The Institut National de la Recherche Agronomique bought the land in 1968 for viticultural research.

Château Couhins-Lurton

Cru Classé de Graves, Pessac-Léognan. A 14-acre fraction of Ch. Couhins run by André Lurton, making 3,000 cases of 100% Sauvignon white.

In 1970 André Lurton bought 6 hectares of this classed-growth which he had farmed since 1967. The wine, unusually, is pure Sauvignon, fermented and aged in oak. It rewards keeping five to ten years. The Lurtons bought the château and original cellar in 1992.

Château de Fieuzal

Cru Classé de Graves (red), Léognan. Owner: Banques Populaires. Dir: Gérard Gribelin. AOC: Pessac-Léognan. 108 acres. 14,200 cases. Grape var. red: Cab.Sauv. 60%, Merlot 25%, Petit Verdot and Cab.Fr.10%; white: Sauv. 50%, Sém. 50%.

One of the smallest classed Graves châteaux, capable of tuning the masculine, tannic, earthy style of the region to fine harmony and in recent years a regular top performer. The production (2,500 cases) of white is not technically 'classé' although it is better than some that are. A 'Grand Blanc de Bordeaux' (*see* Domaine de Chevalier).

Château Haut-Bailly

Cru Classé de Graves (red), Léognan. Owner: SCI Sanders. Dir: Jean Sanders. AOC: Pessac-Léognan. 70 acres. 16,000 cases. Grape var: Cab.Sauv. 65%, Cab.Fr. 10%, Merlot 25%.

A modest-looking place with a farmyard air, the property of a Belgian family, generally considered one of the top five châteaux of (red) Graves. It makes no white wine. One quarter of the vineyard is a mixed plantation of very old vines. Relatively shallow stony soil over hard clay is an unusual site for a great vineyard and the result can be problems during drought.

The great years (1966, '70, '78, '79, '81, '86, '88, '89) I can best describe as nourishing, like long-simmered stock, deep, earthy and round. I love them. Second label: La Parde de Haut Bailly.

Château Laville-Haut-Brion

Cru Classé de Graves (white), Talence. Owner: Domaine Clarence Dillon. AOC: Pessac-Léognan. 9 acres. 1,000 cases. Grape var: Sém.70% Sauv. 30%.

The white wine of La Mission-Haut-Brion, first made in 1928 on a patch where former owner M. Woltner decided the soil was too heavy for his red. Bordeaux's best dry white wine. Drunk young its quality may go unnoticed – and its price will certainly seem excessive. The wine is fermented in oak *barriques* and bottled from them the following spring. Its qualities – apart from an increasingly haunting flavour as the years go by – are concentration and the same sort of rich-yet-dry character as Ygrec, the dry wine of Ch. d'Yquem, but with more grace. '88, '89 and '94 stand out.

Château Malartic-Lagravière

Cru Classé de Graves (red and white), Léognan. Owner: Laurent Perrier. AOC: Pessac-Léognan. 46 acres. 8,300 cases red, 1,800 cases white. Grape var. red: Cab.Sauv. 50%, Cab.Fr. 25%, Merlot 25%, white: Sauv. 85%, Sém.15%.

A generally underrated château of notable quality for both red and white wine. A square stone house in a typical Graves landscape, patched with woods and gently tilted vineyards. The red is a firm, austere, dark-coloured *vin de garde*, finishing fine rather than fleshy, though since 1994 the style appears rounder. The white (unusual in being mostly Sauvignon) is dazzling when young but becomes even better – and more typical of Graves – with five or ten years in bottle. The property was bought by Champagne Laurent Perrier in 1990.

Professor Emile Peynaud

No single man has had such a direct influence over the style and standards of wine-making in Bordeaux over 40 years up to 1990 as Emile Peynaud. A former director of the Station Oenologique of the University of Bordeaux, he is France's most celebrated consultant oenologist, with an astonishing list of clients among the châteaux and the growers' cooperatives of Bordeaux. His great book *Le Goût du Vin* is an exposition of his philosophy of wine. To his clients his preliminary advice has sometimes been brutal: he has declined to advise a château unless the owner is prepared to be more selective in choosing his 'Grand Vin', and to sell substandard vats under a second label – or in bulk.

Professor Peynaud has looked for better balance and keeping qualities with less harshness in claret by encouraging harvesting of the grapes as ripe as possible, then adding to the 'free-run' wine at least some of the more tannic pressed wine to give a firm tannic structure. But above all he emphasizes selection at every stage. His clients include, or have included: Châteaux Lafite, Margaux, Cheval Blanc, Rauzan-Gassies, Brane-Cantenac, Giscours, Boyd-Cantenac, Malescot, Prieuré-Lichine, Léoville Las Cases, Léoville-Poyferré, Ducru-Beaucaillou, Lagrange, Beychevelle, Branaire-Ducru, Pichon-Lalande, Duhart-Milon, Batailley, Haut-Batailley, Grand-Puy-Lacoste, La Lagune, Pape-Clément, La Mission-Haut-Brion, Malarctic-Lagravière, Haut-Bailly, Pavie …

Château La Mission-Haut-Brion

Cru Classé de Graves (red). Talence. Owner: Domaine Clarence Dillon. AOC: Pessac-Léognan. 49 acres. 7,500 cases. Grape var: Cab.Sauv. 48%, Cab.Franc 7%, Merlot 45%.

The immediate neighbour and former rival to Haut-Brion, equally in the Bordeaux suburbs of Pessac and Talence with the Paris–Madrid railway running in a cutting (good for the drainage) through the vineyard. Owned since 1983 by the proprietors of Haut-Brion. The claim is that the urban surroundings give the advantage of one degree centigrade (1.8˚F) higher temperature than the open country, and also a large harvesting force at short notice.

The wines show the effect of warm and dry conditions: concentration and force. Beside Haut-Brion, which is no weakling, they can appear almost butch. Michael Broadbent makes use of the words iron, earth, beef and pepper in his notes on various vintages. After due time (often 20 years) they combine warmth with sweetness in organ-like tones that make it a 'super second' in quality. Laville-Haut-Brion, is discussed separately.

Château Olivier

Cru Classé de Graves (red and white), Léognan. Owner: J-J de Bethmann. AOC: Pessac-Léognan. 108 acres. 14,500 cases red, 6,000 white. Grape var. red: Cab.Sauv. 51%, Cab Franc 8%, Merlot 41%, white: Sém. 48%, Sauv. 44%, Musc. 8%.

A moated fortress with vineyards operated for the owner until 1981 by the shippers Eschenauer & Co, but now under the control of the family again. Its red wine has never enjoyed the fame of its white, which is of the modern school of easy-come, easy-go Graves; a good, light meal-opener. A new broom in '89 is upgrading quality.

Château Pape-Clément

Cru Classé de Graves (red and white), Pessac. Owners: the Montagne family. AOC: Pessac-Léognan. 74 acres. 13,000 cases.

Grape var. red: Cab.Sauv. 60%, Merlot 40%; white: Sém. 45%, Sauv. 45%; Musc. 10%.

One-time property of Bertrand de Goth, the 14th-century Bishop of Bordeaux who, as Clement V, brought the papacy to Avignon, in fact the Pape du Châteauneuf. The vineyard is in scattered plots and one large block at the extreme edge of Pessac, where it is quasi-rural and the gravel soil finer but no less deep. There is no Cabernet Franc in the vineyard but a high proportion of Merlot. New barrels are used for 70% of the crop. Since the arrival of Bernard Pujol in 1985, the property has moved up a gear with a series of seductively scented reds and, recently, a tiny quantity of white.

Château Smith-Haut-Lafitte

Cru Classé de Graves (red), Martillac. Owner: Florence and Daniel Cathiard. AOC: Pessac-Léognan. 135 acres. 19,900 cases red, 4,800 white. Grape var. red: Cab.Sauv. 55%, Cab.Franc 10%, Merlot 35%; white: Sauv.Bl. 100%.

With cash from their sportswear business and considerable flair and enthusiasm, the Cathiards have, since 1990, transformed the reputation of their famous old estate with modernization of vineyard, cellar and château. The white (not a classed-growth) is one of the best of the region and the red improves steadily under the influence of a Mouton-trained winemaker. A 'Grand Blanc de Bordeaux' (*see* Domaine Chevalier).

Château La Tour-Haut-Brion

Cru Classé de Graves (red), Talence. Owner: Domaine Clarence Dillon. AOC: Pessac-Léognan. 12 acres. 8,000 cases. Grape var: Cab.Sauv. 42%, Cab.Fr. 35%, Merlot 23%.

Formerly the second label of Ch. La Mission Haut-Brion, but now run as a separate vineyard. Up to '93 it used to be more powerful and tannic than Haut Brion's Bahans Haut Brion, but Monsieur Delmas has made recent vintages more elegant with the proportion of Cabernet Franc increased.

Château La Tour Martillac

Cru Classé de Graves (red and white), Martillac. Owner: Jean Kressman. AOC: Pessac-Léognan. 50 acres red, 15 acres white; 10,000 cases red, 2,000 white. Grape var. red: Cab.Sauv. 60%, Merlot 30%, Malbec and Cab.Franc 5%; white: Sém. 55%, Sauv. 40%, Muscadelle 5%.

The home of the retired shipper Jean Kressman, a remote little property once in the Montesquieu family (who owned the magnificent moated La Brède nearby). The owner is an enthusiast who patiently cultivates old vines for quality. The white wine, now made in small quantities, is classic Graves, best with bottle-age; the red is a good example of the robust, savoury style of the region.

OTHER CHATEAUX

Château d'Archambeau Illats. Owner: M Dubourdieu. 10,000 cases good fruity dry white. Since 1985. 7,500 cases of fragrant barrel-aged reds.

Château d'Arricaud Landiras. Owner: A. J. Bouyx. 56 acres. 5,000 cases white: Sém. 65%, Sauv. 30%, Musc. 5%; 6,000 cases red: Cab.Sauv. 45%, Merlot 55%. Substantial property overlooking the Garonne valley from the south of Barsac.

Château Baret Villenave-d'Ornon. Owners: the Ballande family. 33 acres. 6,500 cases white, 4,000 cases red. Property in the heart of 'Haut-Graves', formerly high among Graves' second growths. Run by Philippe Castéja of Borie Manoux.

Château Brown. Pessac-Léognan. Owner: Bernard Barthe. Revived by new owners in 1994. To watch.

Château Cantegril Pujols. 3,000 cases of good red from Ch. Doisy Daëne-owner Pierre Dubourdieu, and delicious Sauternes, especially '90.

Château de Cardaillan Toulenne. Owner: Comtesse de Bournazel. Fragrant red of Château de Malle, Sauternes. 5,000 cases.

Château Les Carmes Haut-Brion Pessac. Owner: H. Chantecaille. 9 acres. 2,000 cases red: Cab.Sauv. 10%, Cab. Franc 40%, Merlot 50%. A miniature neighbour of Haut-Brion with a new lease of life since Didier Furt took over in 1986. Good Cru Bourgeois standards.

Château Cazebonne St-Pierre-de-Mons. Owner: Marc Bridet. 15 acres red; 2,700 cases. 20 acres white; 2,300 cases.

Château de Chantegrive Podensac. Owners: Henri and Françoise Lévêque. 61 acres. 13,000 cases red: Cab.Sauv. 45%, Cab Franc 10%, Merlot 45%. 69 acres. 12,000 cases white: Sém. 58%, Sauv. 32%, Musc. 10%. A substantial property, using modern methods. The family farm several other properties, Château Moulin de Marc, Domaine du Bourdieu. Reliable wines.

Château Cheret-Pitres Portets. Owner: J. Boulanger. 30 acres. 5,300 cases red: Merlot 50%, Cab. Sauv. 50%.

Château Chicane Toulenne. Owner: François Gauthier. 15 acres. 3,000 cases red: nearly two thirds Cab.Sauv. The nephew of Pierre Coste, the Langon merchant, puts the emphasis on ripe fruit. Stylish reds. Grapey whites.

Château de Courbon Toulenne. Owner: Philippe Sanders (see Ch. Haut-Bailly). 20 acres. 2,500 cases white: Sauv. 50%, Sém. 50%.

Château de Cruzeau St-Médard-d'Eyrans. Owner: André Lurton, 101 acres. 17,000 cases red. 22 acres. 3,500 cases white: Sauv. 85%, Sém. 15%. A Lurton property bought and replanted in 1973. St-Médard, on the southern fringe of 'Haut-Graves', has deep, pebbly soil which should mean good wine.

Château Doms Portets. Dir: M. Duvigneau and L. Parage. 41 acres. 3,500 cases white, 6,000 cases red. Second label: Clos du Monastère.

Château Ferrande Castres. 74 acres. 16,000 cases red: Cab.Sauv. 33%, Merlot 33%, Cab.Franc 33%. 22 acres. 5,000 cases white: Sauv. 60%, Sém. 35%. Musc. 5%. The principal property of Castres, just north of Portets. Drink young. Ch. Lognac is the second label.

Clos Floridène Bequey. Owners: M. et Mme. Dubourdieu. 29 acres. 1,700 cases: Sém. 50%, Sauv. Blanc 30%, Musc. 20%. Original, full and richly characterful white made by Denis Dubourdieu who has done for Bordeaux whites what Emile Peynaud did for reds. Keeps for five years.

Château de France Léognan. Owner: Bernard Thomassin. 66 acres. 16,000 cases red: Merlot 40%, Cab.Sauv. 55%, Cab.Franc 5%. 1,000 cases white. A minor property among some of the best of the district modernized and enlarged since 1971. The second wine is Ch. Coquillas (Supérieur).

Domaine de Gaillat Langon. Owners: the Coste family. 27 acres. 5,500 cases red.

Château La Garde Martillac. Owner: Dourthe. 111 acres. 20,000 cases red: Cab.Sauv. 65%, Merlot 35%. 12 acres. 2,500 cases white: Sauv. 100%. The red in good vintages is robust and meaty. The white is grapey and oaky.

Château du Grand Abord Portets. Owner: M. Dugoua. 44 acres. 8,300 cases red, 2,000 cases white. Also sold as Bel Air and Lagarde.

Domaine La Grave Portets. Owner: Peter Vinding-Diers. 17 acres. 2,000 cases red: Merlot 60%, Cab.Sauv. 40%; 900 cases white: Sém. 100%. Exceptional small estate with old vines plus the inspired winemaking of Peter Vinding-Diers (see also Ch. Landiras).

Château Haut Bergey Pessac-Léognan. Owner: Mme Garcin-Cathiard. 8,000 cases of red and a tiny amount of white. The new owner (since 1991) has big plans. *See* Smith-Haut-Lafite.

Château Haut Gardère Pessac-Léognan. Owners: the Lesineau family. Reborn in 1979, this once famous estate's wines look highly promising.

Château Haut-Nouchet Pessac-Léognan. Owner: Louis Lurton. Where to look for good value white Graves of the better sort, with bottle age.

Château Jean-Gervais Portets. Owners: M. F. Counilh & Fils. 93 acres. 12,000 cases red; 7,000 cases white.

Château de Landiras Landiras. A medieval château on the edge of Landiras, replanted in the 1980s and managed by the innovative Peter Vinding-Diers. Very stylish whites: 80% Sem., 20% Sauv., considered in the same class as Château Fieuzal, Smith-Haut-Lafitte etc. *See* also Domaine de Chevalier.

Château Larrivet-Haut-Brion Léognan. Owner: SA Andros. 86 acres. 17,000 cases red: Cab.Sauv. 55%, Merlot 45%. 1,000 cases white. One of the better second-rank Graves, although a long way from Haut-Brion in every sense. New owners have considerably expanded the vineyards.

Château La Louvière Léognan. Owner: André Lurton. 86 acres. 18,000 cases red: Cab.Sauv. 64%, Merlot 30%, Cab.Franc 3%. 37 acres. 5,500 cases white: Sauv. 85%, Sém.15%. The show place of M. Lurton's considerable estates, a noble 18th-century house where he makes avant-garde dry white of Loire-like freshness and typically masculine, earthy red of Cru Classé standard. Château Coucheroy is also vinified here.

Château Magence St-Pierre-de-Mons. Owner: Dominique Guillot de Suduiraut. 34 acres. 7,500 cases white: Sém. 36%, Sauv. 64%. 22 acres. 10,000 cases red: Cab.Sauv. 43%, Cab.Franc 23%, Merlot 34%. Prominent over the last two decades as one of the most modern properties; a leader in fresh, dry white wine and fruity red for drinking young. The owner is president of a group of like-minded proprietors.

Château Millet Portets. Owners: Henri & Thierry de la Mette. 54 acres. 9,000 cases. The most imposing château in Portets.

Château Montalivet Pujols-sur-Ciron. Dir: Pierre Coste (*see* Château Chicane). 26 acres. 7,500 cases red. 9 acres. 2,500 cases white.

Château Pique-Caillou Owner: Alphonse Denis. 49 acres. 10,000 cases: 40% Cab.Sauv., 20% Cab.Franc, 40% Merlot. The only cru in Merignac, near the airport. Can be seductive.

Château Piron St-Morillon. Owner: P. Boyreau. 49 acres. 6,000 cases white; 2,000 cases red. An old family property in the hinterland of Graves on gravel slopes with a chalk content that favours white wine.

Château de Portets Portets. Owner: Jean-Pierre Théron. 93 acres. 12,000 cases red: 50% Cab.Sauv. 50% Merlot; 2,000 cases white: Sém. 70%, Sauv. 30%. The reputation of Portets is growing, particularly for red wine. A good workmanlike example.

Château Rahoul Portets. Owner: Alain Thienot. 71 acres. 10,000 cases red: Merlot 60%, Cab.Sauv. 40%; 1,000 cases white: Sém. 100%. Estate with a reputation for stylish wood-aged reds and crisp whites. The leader in the commune. Second label: La Garance.

Château Respide St-Pierre-de-Mons and Langon. Owner: Pierre Bonnet & Fils. 98 acres in St-Pierre; 8,000 cases white and 98 acres of red, on the sandy soil of Langon, have been known longer than most in this up-and-coming area. A 20-year-old bottle of white Respide at the old Café de Bordeaux was nearly great, soft but sappy Graves.

Château de Rochemorin Martillac. Owner: André Lurton. 165 acres. 25,000 cases red. 42 acres. 9,000 cases white: Sauv.Bl. 90%, Sém. 10%. A major old estate abandoned in the 1930s, replanted since 1973 by M. Lurton. Modern, fruity reds. Dry aromatic whites.

Château Le Sartre Léognan. Owner: GFA. Manager: Antony Perrin. 5,000 cases red, 1,500 cases white. (*See* Ch. Carbonnieux.)

Château La Tour Léognan Léognan. Owner: Soc. Civile. Manager: Antony Perrin. The second label of Château Carbonnieux.

Château La Tour-Bicheau Portets. Owners: Y. Daubas & Fils. 50-acre property among the good red producers of Portets. About 10,000 cases.

Château Tourteau-Chollet Arbannats. Owner: Société Civile. 74-acre property owned by the Mestrezat-Preller group. Red and white wines.

Château Le Tuquet Beautiran. Owner: Paul Ragon. 34 acres. 8,000 cases white; 88 acres. 17,000 cases red. Beautiran's principal property on main Bordeaux to Langon road.

Château La Vieille France Portets. Owner: Michel Dugoua. 46 acres. 10,000 cases red. 10 acres. 2,500 cases white. A sound and enterprising proprietor who also owns Ch. Grand-Abord.

Vieux Château Gaubert Portets. Owner: Dominique Haverlan. Up and coming estate. 6,000 cases of lovely balanced red and 2,000 cases of rich lees-matured white.

SAUTERNES

Towards the south of the Bordeaux region, red winemaking dwindles to insignificance compared with white. A slightly warmer and drier climate and very limey soil are ideal for white grapes; the wine naturally has what the French call great '*sève*' – sap – a combination of body and vitality.

The best of the region is the relatively hilly enclave of Sauternes, an appellation that applies to five villages just south of a little tributary of the Gironde called the Ciron. On the other side of the Ciron, on flatter land, lies Barsac, which also has the right to the appellation. The Ciron is said to be responsible for misty autumn conditions that give rise to the famous 'noble rot', and the possibility of *vin liquoreux*. For the last 150 years Sauternes has specialized in this extraordinarily concentrated golden dessert wine. Between 1982 and 1990 the tide of fortune turned strongly in its favour with a string of excellent years but this was cruelly balanced by a number of bad years in the 1990s.

Unlike most of the Graves region, Sauternes has big estates in the manner of the Médoc. Historically its position on the inland route up the Garonne gave it military importance. Later, its fine climate and its good wine made it a desirable spot to replace castles with mansions. A score of these were already famous for their 'sappy' white wine when the 1855 classification was made for the Paris Exhibition. They were classified in three ranks, with Château d'Yquem alone in the first, nine classed as Premiers Crus and another nine as Deuxièmes Crus – which is, broadly speaking, still a fair classification, except that divisions of property have increased the Premiers Crus to 11 and the Deuxièmes to 12. They are surrounded by a host of unofficial Crus Bourgeois, some of a comparable quality. The combined vineyard area of the six communes is 5,434 acres. There is no *cave coopérative*.

The laborious procedure for making great Sauternes is described on on the opposite page. With sweet wines out of fashion in the '60s and '70s, it became unrealistic for most proprietors, who could not afford the labour needed to pick single grapes at a time, or the new barrels, or the years of waiting. But fashion, and apparently climate, have both changed so radically recently that Sauternes is entering a new golden age.

The ultimate short cut, used by many of the humbler growers, is simply to wait for fully ripe grapes (hoping that at least a few are 'nobly rotten'), pick them all together, add sugar to bring the potential alcohol up to about 18 percent, then stop the fermentation with sulphur dioxide when the fermentation has produced 13 or 14 degrees, leaving the wine sweet. It is a bastard approach to winemaking, with predictably mediocre results. The wine has none of the classic Sauternes flavour and should, in fairness, be called something else.

What is the classic flavour? It depends on the vintage. In some it is forceful, hot and treacly. In others it is rich and stiff with flavour, but almost literally sappy and not very sweet. In the best, with all the grapes 'nobly rotten', it is thick with sugar yet gentle, creamy, nutty, honeyed. Barsacs tend to be a little less rich than Sauternes, but can produce their own spellbinding equilibrium of the rich and the brisk. Bottles can be better than ever after as much as 40 or 50 years.

Yields of Sauternes vary worryingly according to the weather. Some years hardly any sweet wine is made, or a whole crop is declassified to another label. An average harvest even in a good year might give 18 hl/ha (80 dozen an acre) when a St-Julien classed-growth for example will make about 230 dozen an acre with much less trouble.

The postal address for the whole of Sauternes is 33210 Langon.

Premier Cru Supérieur

Château d'Yquem

1er Cru Supérieur 1855. Owner: Comte Alexandre de Lur Saluces. AOC: Sauternes. 260 acres. 6,500 cases (plus an additional 2,000 cases of dry white Bordeaux). Grape var: Sém. 80%, Sauv. 20%.

Indisputably the greatest sweet wine of France, but also recognized as the best white wine of Bordeaux long before the fashion for sweet wine was initiated in the 19th century. The extreme pains that go into its making are described in detail on the opposite page.

Château d'Yquem also makes 'Y' (which is pronounced Ygrec), its rare dry wine, made from half Sauvignon, half Semillon. It has some of the concentration of Yquem, and the same alcohol content, but only a trace of sweetness for balance. Yquem's owner the Comte Alexandre de Lur Saluces also owns the exceptional Cru Bourgeois Château de Fargues.

Sauternes Premiers Crus

Château Climens

1er Cru Classé 1855. Owner: Lucien Lurton. AOC: Barsac. 74 acres. 6,000 cases. Grape var: Sém. 98%, Sauv. 2%.

Barsac's sweetest and richest wine, made by the old methods with a crop nearly as derisory as that at Yquem, giving it almost caramel concentration as it ages, yet with a touch of elegance typical of Barsac. The property changed hands in 1971 (a superb vintage). Since then it has only enhanced its reputation with such wines as the '83, '86, '88 and '90. The locals pronounce the final 'ns' emphatically, with a sort of honking effect. The second label is Les Cyprès de Climens.

Château Coutet

1er Cru Classé 1855. Owner: Marcel Baly. AOC: Barsac. 95 acres. 5,500 cases. Grape var: Sém. 75%, Sauv. 23%, Muscadelle 2%.

With Ch. Climens, the leading growth of Barsac, using traditional barrel fermentation to make exceptionally fine

Château d'Yquem

The Making of a Great Sauternes

Wine has few legends more imposing than the hilltop fortress of Yquem and its golden nectar. Only France could produce such a monument to aristocratic craftsmanship. The Lur Saluces family of Yquem has made quality its dynastic vocation for 200 years.

In 1785 Josephine Sauvage d'Yquem, whose family has already held the estate for 200 years, married the Comte de Lur Saluces. Two years later Thomas Jefferson paid a famous visit to the château and rated the wines so highly that he ordered a consignment for America. But if you want to taste the wine that impressed him you must seek out the rare 'Y', the dry wine of the château, because the modern concept of Sauternes as a *vin liquoreux*, an intensely sweet, concentrated and unctuous dessert wine, was only gradually introduced from the late 18th century onwards. Legend says that the German proprietor of Château La Tour-Blanche, Monsieur Focke, experimented with the method used to make the great sweet wines of the Rhine. 1847 is the first Yquem vintage recorded as being entirely *liquoreux*.

Today, the painstaking care at Yquem is difficult to exaggerate. A description of its methods is a description of the ideal – to which other châteaux only approximate to a greater or lesser degree.

The principle must first be understood. Under certain autumnal conditions of misty mornings and sunny afternoons, one of the forms of mould common in vineyards reverses its role; instead of ruining the grapes, it is entirely beneficial. Given a healthy, ripe and undamaged crop without other fungus infections, it begins to feed on the sugar and the tartaric acid in each grape, probing with roots so fine that they penetrate the microscopic pores of the grape-skin. The grapes rapidly shrivel, turning first grey with fungus spores, then warm violet-brown, their skins mere pulp. By this time they have lost more than half their weight, but less than half their sugar. Their juice is concentrated, extremely sweet and rich in glycerine. If conditions are perfect (as they were in 1967 and 1989) the process is sudden and complete; not a grape in the bunch is recognizable. They are a repulsive sight.

Unfortunately in most years the process is gradual; the berries rot patchily – even one by one. At Yquem the pickers, in four gangs 40 strong, move through the vines at a snail's pace gathering the grapes, if necessary, one at a time, then going back over the same vines again and again, up to ten, once up to eleven, times. The final crop amounts to about one glass of wine per vine.

In the *cuvier* the grapes are slightly sulphured, put through a gentle wooden *fouloir* (crusher), then immediately pressed in old-fashioned vertical presses three times, the 'cake' being cut up with shovels and thrown into a strange mill to remove the stalks between pressings. The whole day's picking – up to 40 barrels – is assembled together in one vat, then poured straight into new oak barriques, filling them three quarters full, to ferment. The day's crop, the '*journée*', is the critical unit to be

tasted again and again to see whether it has the qualities of the Grand Vin. If it does not have those qualities it will be sold to the trade as anonymous Sauternes. There is no court of appeal, no second wine, at Yquem.

The *chai* is heated to 20°C (68°F) to encourage a steady fermentation, which lasts between two and six weeks. When it reaches between 13 and 14 degrees of alcohol a miraculous natural control, an antibiotic produced by the botrytis, stops the yeasts working, leaving up to 120 grammes of sugar to a litre (12 percent of the wine). Without this antibiotic the alcohol would reach 17 degrees, throwing the wine right out of balance. The sums are critical here. Twenty percent total sugar (`potential alcohol') in the juice is ideal. With 25 per cent, the fermentation would stop at nine or ten degrees – as in Trockenbeerenauslese. (The extreme example is Tokay Essencia, with so much sugar that the potential alcohol content is 35 degrees but fermentation never starts at all.)

Château d'Yquem is kept for no less than three and a half years in cask, racked every three months and never bunged tight – which means twice-weekly topping up over the whole period, and a loss by evaporation of 20 percent. The wine is so thick that it never 'falls bright', or clears itself fully by gravity. The sediment, at the same density as the liquid, remains in suspension. So it must be 'fined' – but never with egg whites, says Alexandre de Lur Saluces; one of the eggs might be bad.

The Comte Alexandre de Lur Saluces, the present proprietor, is nephew of the famous Marquis Bertrand, whose last vintage before his death was the great 1967.

and stylish wine (although strangely failing in the great '67 vintage). The old manor house dates back to the English rule of Aquitaine. In the best years ('71,'75, '81, '83, '86, '88 and '89) a selection of the richest wine is labelled Cuvée Madame but not in '90 when the harvest was of uniformly high quality. Chartreuse de Coutet is the second wine.

Château Guiraud

1er Cru Classé 1855. Owner: Frank Narby. Dir: Xavier Planty. AOC: Sauternes. 200 acres, plus 37 acres of red grapes (Bordeaux Supérieur); 10,000 cases max. Grape var: Sém. 65%, Sauv. 35%.
The southern neighbour of Yquem employing Yquem-like methods, picking individual grapes and fermenting in new barrels (45% in 1990). Vintages of the 1980s had mixed success, with power sometimes outweighing finesse, but Guiraud is now hitting its stride. The '90 is superb. Excess Sauvignon is used to make a dry white called 'G'.

Château Clos Haut-Peyraguey

1er Cru Classé 1855, Bommes. Owner: Jacques Pauly. AOC: Sauternes, 37 acres. 3,000 cases. Grape var: Sém. 83%, Sauv. 15%, Muscadelle 2%.
Formerly the upper part of the same estate as Ch. Laufaurie-Peyraguey, separated in 1879 and in the Pauly family since 1914. A modest estate making relatively light but fine wine with care. The Cru Bourgeois Ch. Haut-Bommes has the same owner and has effectively become the second wine.

Château Lafaurie-Peyraguey

1er Cru Classé 1855, Bommes. Owner: Cordier family. AOC: Sauternes. 93 acres. 5,800 cases. Grape var: Sém. 90%, Sauv. 8%, Musc. 2%.
A fortress to challenge Yquem – militarily, that is – with a fine reputation for beautifully, structured, long-lived Sauternes, particularly since 1979. 1983 was the first of a run of great wines.

Château Rabaud-Promis

1er Cru Classé 1855, Bommes. Owner: GFA Rabaud-Promis. Administrator: Mme Michèle Dejean. AOC: Sauternes. 79 acres. 3,750 cases. Grape var: Sém. 80%, Sauv. 18%, Musc. 2%.
The larger part of the formerly important Rabaud estate, making rich wine, fat without being heavy. Since 1986 a reliably good property to follow.

Château Rayne-Vigneau

1er Cru Classé 1855, Bommes. Owner: Société Civile. Dir: Patrick Eymery. AOC: Sauternes. 167 acres. 9,000 cases. Grape var: Sém. 80%, Sauv. 20%.
A big estate now detached from its château but celebrated in history for its soil being – literally – full of precious stones. The fortunate Vicomte de Roton (a Pontac, whose descendants still have the château) found himself picking up sapphires, topaz, amethysts and opals by the thousand. (The rest of the soil is gravel.) Modern methods produce rich and good, but not the most ambitious, Sauternes and a little Rayne-Vigneau Sec. The second label is Clos L'Abeille.

Château Rieussec

1er Cru Classé 1855, Fargues. Owner: Domaines Rothschild. AOC: Sauternes. 179 acres. up to 8,300 cases. Grape var: Sém. 89%, Sauv. 8%, Muscadelle 3%.
Yquem's eastern neighbour, perched even higher on the same line of hills, with a strange gazebo a little too like a gun emplacement to be considered ornamental. Rieussec, traditionally aromatic, elegant yet powerful, changed significantly in the '70s under its previous owner, when it became darker and richer with honeyed botrytis character. The '62 has been a favourite of mine for years. 1971, '75' '79 and '88 are all first class. A dry white, inspired by Yquem's 'Y', is called 'R'. The Lafite-Rothschilds, who bought the property in 1985, have not yet clearly established a style, but '89 and '90 are predictably fine and ambitions are high. The second property is Clos Labère.

Château Sigalas Rabaud

1er Cru Classé 1855, Bommes. Owner: Marquis de Lambert des Granges. AOC: Sauternes. 34 acres: 2,000 cases. Grape var: Sém. 85%, Sauv. 15%.
One third of the former Rabaud estate, descended for over a century in the Sigalas family. The wine was mainly made and aged in tanks until 1988 to avoid oak flavours and concentrate on richness and finesse, which it has in abundance. Now half-aged in oak, the wine is still bottled relatively early to keep freshness and fruit. It is marketed by Cordier who took a share in this property in 1994.

Château Suduiraut

1er Cru Classé 1855, Preignac. Owner: AXA. AOC: Sauternes. 153 acres. 12,000 cases. Grape var: Sém. 80%, Sauv. 20%.
A château of great splendour with parkland of great, if neglected, beauty and the next vineyard to Yquem, going north. One of the most respected names, despite a period of relative neglect in the early 1970s. Manager Pierre Pascaud, is forthright and determined. Suduiraut at its best ('67, '76, '82, '88 and '90) is plump and unctuous, truly *liquoreux*; the poor man's Yquem. Other vintages (e.g. '83) can be oddly disappointing. Second wine since '93: Castelnau de Suduiraut. A *crème de tête* of 500 dozen was made in '82 and '89.

Château La Tour Blanche

1er Cru Classé 1855, Bommes. Owner: Ministère de l'Agriculture, Dir: Jean Pierre Jausserand. AOC: Sauternes. 83 acres. 5,000 cases. Grape var: Sém. 77%, Sauv. 20%, Musc. 3%.
Probably the first estate on which sweet Sauternes was made and placed first after Yquem in the 1855 classification. Bequeathed to the French state in 1912 by M. Osiris (an umbrella tycoon), whose name still appears on the label. The vineyard slopes steeply westwards towards the River Ciron. Winemaking has, since 1983, been run dynamically and to the great benefit of quality by M. Jausserand. Since 1989 the entire crop has been fermented in new oak – before 1983 it was all in steel tank. There is also a college of viticulture here, but clearly separated from the wine estate. Second label is Mademoiselle de Saint Marc. A small quantity of white Bordeaux, Osiris, is also made.

Sauternes Deuxièmes Crus

Château d'Arche

2ème Cru Classé 1855. Owners: the Bastit-St-Martin family. Dir: Jean Perromat. AOC: Sauternes. 70 acres. 2,900 cases. Grape var: Sém. 90%, Sauv. 10%.

Respectable rather than inspired Sauternes, at its best ('83 and '90) typically luscious. A part of Ch. Lamothe also belongs to the Bastit-St-Martins.

Château Broustet

2ème Cru Classé 1855. Owner: Didier Laulan. AOC: Barsac. 39 acres. 3,000 cases. Grape var: Sém. 68%, Sauv. 25%, Muscadelle 7%.

Remembered as the property of the cooper who standardized the now-universal Bordeaux *barrique*. His descendants (who also ran the great Ch. Canon, St-Emilion) make an adequate but scarcely distinguished wine, rich but not *liquoreux*. A new owner since 1994 may well make changes. Their second label is Ch. de Ségur.

Château Caillou

2ème Cru Classé 1855. Owners: J.B. and M.J. Bravo. AOC: Barsac. 32 acres. up to 3,300 cases. Grape var: Sém. 90%, Sauv. 10%.

A businesslike property on the higher ground of 'Haut' Barsac, near Ch. Climens. There is a small production of superior Private Cuvée in top years. With the owner's other Barsac property, Ch. Haut Mayne, it also produces a dry white, Domaine Sarraute, which I have found to be rather clumsy.

Château Doisy-Daëne

2ème Cru Classé 1855. Owner: Pierre Dubourdieu. AOC: Barsac. 39 acres. 5,000 cases. Grape var: Sém. 90%, Sauv. 10%.

In the forefront of modern wine-making with sophisticated use of steel and new oak to make fresh, lively sweet wines of real class and a trend-setting dry one, a model for growers who want to restore the old prestige of Graves. The same estate contains Ch. Cantegril (39 acres), making both sweet white and a good red. A Sauvignon-dominated dry white is also produced under the label Grand Vin Sec de Doisy-Daëne.

Château Doisy-Dubroca

2ème Cru Classé 1855. Owner: Lucien Lurton. AOC: Barsac. 9 acres. 750 cases. Grape var: Sém. 100%.

A small property linked for a century to the neighbouring Ch. Climens and now made with the same traditional techniques of intense care (and Professor Peynaud's advice).

Château Doisy-Védrines

2ème Cru Classé 1855. Owner: Pierre Castéja. AOC: Sauternes. 66 acres. 3,000 cases. Grape var: Sém. 80%, Sauv. 20%.

I always assumed from its quality that this was a first rather than a second-classed growth. It is one of the rich Barsacs, fermented in barrels and built for long life. It is much liked in the UK.

Château Filhot

2ème Cru Classé 1855. Owner: Comte Henri de Vaucelles. AOC: Sauternes. 130 acres. 12,500 cases. Grape var: Sém. 60%, Sauv. 35% , Muscadelle 5%.

A palace, or nearly, built by the Lur Saluces family in the early 19th century on the edge of the woods south of Sauternes. The big vineyard on sandy soil produces distinctively light wines by classical Sauternes standards. They are all the more appetizing and savoury for it; excellent for rich fish dishes and such shellfish as lobster, crawfish and crab cooked with cream. The 1975 had a slightly salty tang that I found delicious.

Château Lamothe

2ème Cru Classé 1855. Owner: Jean Despujols. AOC: Sauternes. 18 acres. 1,800 cases. Grape var: Sém. 85%, Sauv. 10%, Muscadelle 5%.

Minor Sauternes bottled within a year for early drinking.

Château Lamothe Guignard

2ème Cru Classé 1855. Owners: the Guignard family. AOC Sauternes. 42 acres. 4,000 cases. Grape var: Sém. 90%, Sauv. 5%, Muscadelle 5%.

The Guignards, a winemaking family from the Graves, bought this part of the vineyard from the proprietor of Château d'Arche in 1981 and have been making excellent spicily fruity, luscious Sauternes at a fair price since. A rising star.

Château de Malle

2ème Cru Classé 1855, Preignac. Owner: Comtesse Pierre de Bournazel. AOC: Sauternes (and Graves). 67 acres Sauternes, 61 acres Graves; 4,000 cases Sauternes. Grape var. white: Sém. 70%, Sauv. 25%, Muscadelle 5%; red: Cab.Sauv. 80%, Merlot 20%.

The most beautiful house and garden in Sauternes – possibly in Bordeaux – and much appreciated by tourists. Built for the owner's family (related to the Lur Saluces) about 1600. 'Italian' gardens were added 100 years later. The vineyard is in Sauternes and Graves and produces roughly equal quantities of sweet white and red. The two Graves reds (made by carbonic maceration) are Ch'x de Cardaillan or Tours de Malle and Chevalier de Malle (Bordeaux Supérieurs). The vineyard, on light sandy soil, was entirely replanted in 1956. The late owner was a trained oenologist who 'designed' his wine, using both stainless steel and new oak to produce fruitiness with undertones – excellent Sauternes in '88, '89 and '90. The second wine is Château de Sainte Hélène.

Château de Myrat

2ème Cru Classé 1855, Barsac. Owner: M. Pontac. AOC Barsac. 54 acres. Grape var. Sém. 88%, Sauv. 8%, Musc. 4%.

The father of the present owner uprooted all the vines in 1976. 22 acres were replanted in time to produce the first vintage in 1990 but the first entitled to the Sauternes appellation was '91 which, after the frost amounted to only 500 cases.

Château Nairac

2ème Cru Classé 1855, Barsac. Owner: Mme Nicole Tari-Heeter. AOC: Sauternes. 22 acres. 1,400 cases. Grape var: Sém. 90%. Sauv. 7%, Muscadelle 3%.

A young American, Tom Heeter, made this formerly run-down estate one of the leaders of the district, with wines of the racy, less sticky Barsac style that bear keeping 10 years or more. Professor Peynaud was called in for his invaluable advice. The wine is now made by Nicolas Tari-Heeter. The dignified mansion lies on the low ground near the village of Barsac and the Garonne.

Château Romer du Hayot

2ème Cru Classé 1855. Owner: André du Hayot. AOC: Sauternes. 37 acres. 4,000 cases. Grape var: Sém. 70%, Sauv. 20%, Musc. 10%. The château was demolished for the new autoroute and the wine is made at the owner's Cru Bourgeois Ch. Guiteronde in Barsac. A modern Sauternes, aged for two years in tanks.

Château Suau

2ème Cru Classé 1855. Owner: M. Roger Biarnès. AOC: Barsac. 20 acres. 2,000 cases. Grape var: Sém. 80%, Sauv. 10%, Muscadelle 10%.

The relic of a more important property, near the Garonne on heavier soil than the best growths. The wine, made at the owner's home, is Château de Navarro, Illats, Graves, together with Sauternes Cru Bourgeois and Domaine du Coy.

OTHER CHATEAUX

Château Bastor-Lamontagne Cru Bourgeois, Preignac. Owner: Crédit Foncier de France. 123 acres. 10,000 cases. A substantial and well-kept property with a history of good vintages to substantiate its claim to be 'as good as a second-growth'.

Château Cantegril Cru Bourgeois, Barsac. Owners: Messieurs Dubourdieu and Masencal. 50 acres. 4,500 cases. Part of the former Ch. de Myrat vineyard, beautifully kept but rather unambitious until 1988. The '90 is fabulous. Made by Pierre Dubourdieu.

Cru Barrejats Barsac. Owner: Dr Mireille Daret. 6 acres. 500 cases. Tiny high-quality estate between Climens and Caillou which went live in 1990.

Château Gilette Owner: Christian Médeville. 8.6 acres. 400–900 cases. A unique producer of long-aged Sauternes of great splendour: e.g. '49, '55, '59, '61, '62, not bottled until its idealistic owner considers it ready to drink – at 25 years or so. Monsieur Médeville also makes the more conventional Château les Justices.

Château de Fargues Cru Bourgeois, Fargues. Owner: Comte Alexandre de Lur Saluces. 30acres; 1,000 cases. Grape var: Sém. 80%, Sauv. 20%. A proud castle in ruins, with a diminutive vineyard but the perfectionist standards of Yquem. Lighter wine, but impeccable and sometimes brilliant (e.g. '67, '75, '80, '86).

Château Haut Bergeron Preignac. Owners: the Lamothe family. 54 acres. 5,000 cases.

Château Liot Cru Bourgeois, Barsac. Owner: J. David. 49 acres. 4,500 cases. Grape var: Sém. 85%, Musc. 5%, Sauv. 10%. Large property on the best slopes in Barsac. The general level is 'good commercial', sometimes over-sulphured.

Château du Mayne Cru Bourgeois, Barsac. Owner: Jean Sanders. 20 acres. 1,500 cases. Grape var: Sém. 70%, Sauv. 30%. A pretty cream house among ancient vines (many 80 years old) cultivated for small amounts of very good wine. The same owner as Ch. Haut-Bailly (Graves).

Château de Ménota Cru Bourgeois, Barsac. Owner: N. Labat. 40 acres. 7,500 cases.

Château Pernaud Cru Bourgeois, Barsac. Owner: M Jacolin. 38 acres. 3,300 cases. An old property down by the Ciron, replanted and now run by the dynamic manager of Ch. Suduiraut. Worth watching.

Château Piada Cru Bourgeois, Barsac. Owner: Jean Lalande. 22 acres. 2,500 cases. Grape var: Sém. 98%. One of the better-known lesser Barsacs. Clos du Roy is a second label.

Château Piot-David Barsac. Owner: M David. 17 acres. 1,600 cases. 80% Sém.. Old vines and fairly high yields. Good standard. Fair prices.

Château Raymond-Lafon Cru Bourgeois, Sauternes. Owner: Pierre Meslier. 37 acres. 2,000 cases. Grape var: Sém. 80%, Sauv. 20%. Owned by the ex-manager of Ch. d'Yquem, neighbour to the great château, made with similar care and regularly first-class (e.g. '75, '78, '88 and '89). Second wine is Lafon-Laroze.

Château de Rolland Cru Bourgeois, Barsac. Owners: Jean and Pierre Guignard. 32 acres. 3,300 cases. An attractive little hotel and restaurant (the only one in Barsac) with worthwhile wine of its own.

Château Roumieu Cru Bourgeois, Barsac. Owner: Mme Craveia-Goyaud. 3,750 cases. 89% Sém. A 50-acre vineyard next to Ch. Climens. The wines I have tasted have been respectable.

Ch. Roumieu-Lacoste Cru Bourgeois, Barsac. Owner: Hervé Dubourdieu. 27 acres. 3,000 cases. The nephew of the owner of the excellent Doisy-Daëne makes good wine here.

Château Saint Amand Preignac. Owners: the Ricard family. 49 acres. 4,000 cases. Admirable quality in the style of Barsac. Sold by Sichel as La Chartreuse.

Château Simon Cru Bourgeois, Barsac. Owner: J. Dufour. 40 acres. 4,500 cases. A well-run property, in the same hands as the little Ch. Grand-Magne (Barsac).

ST-EMILION

As a town, every wine lover's idea of heaven; as an appellation, much the biggest for high-quality wine in France, producing not much less than the whole of the Côte d'Or of Burgundy. Nowhere is the civic and even the spiritual life of a little city so deeply imbued with the passion for making good wine.

St-Emilion, curled into its sheltered corner of the hill, cannot expand. Where other such towns have spread their nondescript streets over the countryside, around St-Emilion there are priceless vineyards, most of its very best, lapping up to its walls, which prevent any sprawl. It burrows into its yielding limestone to find building blocks and store its wine – even to solemnize its rites. Its old church is a vast vaulted cave, now used for the meeting of the Jurade, St-Emilion's ceremonial organization (see below).

The vineyards envelop several distinct soils and aspects while maintaining a certain common character. St-Emilion wines are a degree stronger than Médocs, with less tannin. Accessible, solid tastiness is their stamp, maturing to warm, gratifying sweetness. They are less of a puzzle than Médocs when young and mature faster, but are no less capable of asking unsolvable questions as they age.

The best St-Emilions come from the relatively steep *côtes*, the hillside vineyards and the cap of the escarpment around the town, and from an isolated patch of gravel soil on the plateau two miles northwest, almost in Pomerol. The *côtes* wines are the more smiling, in degrees from enigmatic to beaming; the wines of the *graves* more earnest and searching. Michael Broadbent defines the difference as 'open' (*côtes*) and 'firm' (*graves*).

But they can easily be confused with one another, with Médocs, with Graves and even with burgundy. And some of the same qualities are found in vineyards on substantially different soils, both down in the sandy (*sables*) region in the Dordogne Valley below St-Emilion town itself and in the five 'satellite' villages to the north and east.

The classification of St-Emilion follows a pattern of its own. It was settled in 1954 and is the only one planned to be regularly revised; even, for the third category, to be revised every year.

There are now, since the 1985 vintage, two appellations, simple AOC St-Emilion and AOC St-Emilion Grand Cru. The Crus Classés come in two classes: Premier Grand Cru Classé and Grand Cru Classé. The top class is divided into two: 'A' and 'B'. The current classification names two châteaux (Cheval Blanc and Ausone) as Premiers Grands Crus Classés 'A' and eleven as 'B'. The Bs are the approximate equivalent in value to Médoc second- and third-growths. Then come 55 Grands Crus Classés, elected for (about) ten years. They were revised in 1969, in 1986 and again in 1996.

The St-Emilion Grand Cru, for which proprietors have to reapply every year by submitting their wines for tasting belongs to the AOC.

Obviously St-Emilion is not an area of big estates. The average size of holding is about 20 acres, the biggest not much more than 100 and many as small as five or six, making a mere few hundred cases. In fact 'Grand Cru' in St-Emilion, unqualified, is the same broad category as Crus Bourgeois in the Médoc.

Postcode: 33330 St-Emilion.

St-Emilion Premiers Grands Crus

Château Ausone

1er Grand Cru Classé. Owners: the Dubois-Challon and Vauthier families. AOC: St-Emilion. 17 acres. 2,250 cases. Grape var: Merlot 50%, Cab.Fr. 50%.

If you were looking for the most obviously promising vineyard site in the whole Bordeaux area this would be first choice. No wonder its name is associated with the Roman poet Ausonius (connoisseur also of the Moselle). It slopes south and east from the rim of the St-Emilion escarpment, whose limestone cap has been quarried for building and provides perfect cool, commodious cellars. The soil is pale alkaline clay, in a shallow layer over permeable limestone (which vine roots love). The château is a dainty building perched above and among the vines, where an old white mare shambles around doing the cultivating, hull-down in the green leaves.

Ausone went through a long eclipse when its wine was good, but not good enough. Its neighbours seemed to dim their lamps at the same time. Matters were put right from 1975 by a new manager, Pascal Delbeck, and each good

The Jurade de St-Emilion

The ceremonial and promotional organization of St-Emilion is probably the oldest in France. The Jurade de St-Emilion was formally instituted by King John of England and France in 1199 as the body of elders to govern the little city and its district – a dignity granted to few regions at the time. Nobody seriously pretends that the modern institution is a linear descendant, but its impressive processions to Mass in the great parish church and to its own candle-lit solemnities in the cloisters cut out of the solid limestone in the centre of the town, are full of dignity as well as good humour.

The Jurade also played an important role in the control of quality and administration of the various categories of châteaux. Its annual tastings give a boost to St-Emilion quality in a similar way to the tastevinage undertaken by the Chevaliers de Tastevin in Burgundy. On a memorable autumn weekend in 1981 the Jurade visited the great medieval city of York, arriving by river in a state barge, to process to the Minster for a service conducted by the Archbishop, and to dine in the splendour of Castle Howard. They do these things with style.

vintage now takes its proper place among the first-growths. 1976, '78 and '79 were all confirmed excellent and '82, '83, '89 and '90 continue the high standards. 1995, the first vintage made by M Vauthier with Michel Rolland's advice, shows a new, rich, seductive, less individual Ausone. Time will tell which works best.

Winemaking here is exactly the same in principle as in the Médoc. New barrels are used for the whole, pathetically small crop. (I was present by chance at a cellar tasting of Ausone from barrels washed before filling with steam, hot water and cold water. The differences were astonishing. Hot water won.) The wine is bottled slightly sooner than Médoc first-growths and its whole evolution to drinkability is slightly quicker, yet its potential lifespan, judging by very rare old bottles, is no shorter. The final result is the pure magic of claret, sweet lively harmony with unfathomable depths.

Château Cheval Blanc

1er Grand Cru Classé. Owner: Société Civile du Cheval Blanc. Administrator: Pierre Lurton. AOC: St-Emilion. 89 acres. 13,500 cases. Grape var: Cab.Fr. 60%, Merlot 37%, Malbec 2%, Cab. Sauv. 1%.

Although it shares the first place in St-Emilion with Ausone, the soil and situation (and tradition) of Cheval Blanc are totally different. It lies back on the plateau near the boundary of Pomerol on much deeper soil, an irregular mixture of gravel, sand and clay with clay subsoil. The main grape is Cabernet Franc (known in these parts as Bouchet). There is no white horse here, and the château is an unfanciful cream-painted residence that for some reason always reminds me of Virginia. The new *chais* are a more imposing building. The same family have owned the property since its 19th-century beginning.

Cheval Blanc is the Mouton of St-Emilion: the blockbuster. The 1947 is a legend, a wine of heroic style and proportions, with the combined qualities of claret, port, sculpture and Hermès or Gucci – or is this lèse-majesté? The '61 is only just ready; a tough piece of beef that needed to marinate for years. Not all vintages are so awe-inspiring: but 1975, '82, '83, '89, '90 and '95 are in the grandest tradition. The second wine is Le Petit Cheval (which was the only wine released in frost struck '91).

Château l'Angélus

1er Grand Cru Classé 1996. Owners: the Boüard de Laforest family. 61 acres. 12,500 cases. Grape var: Merlot 50%, Cab.Fr. 45%, Cab.Sauv. 5%.

On the slope below Ch. Beauséjour where the soil is heavy. The owners' passionate pursuit of excellence caused Angelus' promotion in 1996 after a series of high-grade vintages in the second half of the '80s and the more difficult early '90s.

Château Beau-Séjour Bécot

1er Grand Cru Classé. Owners: Gérard and Dominique Bécot. AOC: St-Emilion. 41 acres. 6,500 cases. Grape var: Cab.Sauv. 6%, Cab.Fr. 24%, Merlot 70%.

Two thirds of an estate that was divided in 1869 (the smaller part got the house). The vineyard slopes west from the crest behind Ch. Ausone. Michel Bécot, helped by his two sons, Gérard and Dominique, since 1969 has modernized the property with a complete new *cuvier* and restored its dimmed reputation to that of a leader in the tight circle of the St-Emilion *côtes*, making the sort of rich wine for the medium term (say 10 years) that makes St-Emilion so popular. Demoted in the 1985 classification because M. Bécot had extended the property by buying two other vineyards, but now rightly reinstated in 1996. Second label is La Tournelle des Moines.

Château Beauséjour

1er Grand Cru Classé. Owners: Duffau-Lagarosse heirs. Dir: Jean-Michel Dubos. AOC: St-Emilion. 17 acres. 3,000 cases. Grape var: Merlot 55%, Cab.Fr. 30%, Cab.Sauv. 15%.

The smaller part of Beauséjour but with the charming house and garden. Run in the traditional small family château style; full-bodied, well extracted but tending to be short of finesse, though the '90 has a sensational reputation.

Château Belair

1er Grand Cru Classé 1985. Owner: Mme J. Dubois-Challon. AOC: St-Emilion. 32.5 acres. 5,000 cases. Grape var: Merlot 60%, Cab.Fr. 35%.

The bigger but junior brother of Château Ausone with the same owner and manager. Part of the same sloping vineyard, plus a patch on the flat top of the hill behind. It has its own quarry caves, which once caused a serious landslip of the vines, and, like many St-Emilion châteaux, its own chapel (full of lumber). The wine is now excellent (e.g. the '89 and '95), close to Ausone but perhaps, to split hairs, a shade clumsier (or less deft). Ten years is a good age for it.

Château Canon

1er Grand Cru Classé. Owner: Chanel group. AOC: St-Emilion. 44 acres. 7,500 cases. Grape var: Merlot 55%, Cab.Fr. 45%.

My instinct is to spell the name with two 'n's: a great bronze gun-barrel (rather than a genteel cleric) expresses the style of Canon nicely. If it were only bigger this would be one of the most famous Bordeaux; generous, masculine, not too aggressive young, but magnificent with 20 years in bottle. Recent vintages put it among the very top St-Emilions. The Fournier family sold to the Wertheimers of Chanel, also owners of Rausan-Ségla in 1996.

Château Figeac

1er Grand Cru Classé. Owner: Thierry Manoncourt. AOC: St-Emilion. 96 acres. 17,500 cases. Grape var: Cab.Sauv. 35%, Cab.Fr. 35%, Merlot 30%.

Ch. Figeac has the aristocratic air of a Médoc Cru Classé and once had an estate on the grand Médoc scale, including what is now Ch. Cheval Blanc, and two others which still bear the name of Figeac. The house could be called a mansion and the park has a seigneurial feeling absent in most of the Libournais. The owner even has the features of an old-school aristocrat. The present vineyard, still among the biggest in St-Emilion, has stonier ground and a higher proportion of Cabernet Sauvignon than the others – which may account for its different style from Cheval Blanc. Figeac is more welcoming, less dense and compact; closer to a Médoc (again) in its structure of sweet flesh around a firm spine. It is big but not strapping, maturing relatively early and beautifully sweet in maturity – always individual. The 1970 was deceptively easy drinking even at 5 years old. 1982, '85, '86, '89 and '90 have been notably successful. The grapes are picked late for maximum ripeness so run the risk that the weather will turn.

The second wine is La Grange Neuve de Figeac, which was launched in 1983. It was formerly a wine drunk only by the de Manoncourt family, production having started in 1954.

Clos Fourtet

1er Grand Cru Classé. Owners: Lurton Brothers. AOC: St-Emilion. 45 acres. 7,500 cases. Grape var: Merlot 70%, Cab.Fr. 20%, Cab.Sauv. 10%.

The first Cru Classé that visitors stumble on as they walk out of the lovely old walled town into the vineyards. A modest-looking place, but with a warren of limestone cellars. (The old quarry-cellars are said to run for miles under the plateau, one château's cellars connecting with another. Paradise for an oenospelaeologist-burglar.) Old vintages of Clos Fourtet were tough going for many years. The 1966 was still immature in 1982. More recently (with Professor Peynaud's advice) the wine has been made a bit kindlier, but without reaching the peaks of quality or price. The '95 promises well. Lucien Lurton is the proprietor of Ch. Climens (Sauternes), who also owns Ch. Brane-Cantenac (Margaux).

Château La Gaffelière

1er Grand Cru Classé. Owner: Comte Léo de Malet-Roquefort. AOC: St-Emilion. 54 acres. 10,500 cases. Grape var: Merlot 65%, Cab.Fr. 30%, Cab.Sauv. 5%.

The tall Gothic building at the foot of the hill up to St-Emilion, with vineyards at the foot of Ausone and Pavie. Three centuries in the de Malet-Roquefort family, a history of noble vintages which aged well and gracefully ('55 was a favourite). Recent experience has been less consistent but the '79 is rich and well balanced, both '82 and '83 are fine wines. The ubiquitous Michel Rolland began advising here in 1995 so the wine is likely to become more in line with today's preference for up-front fruit.

Château Magdelaine

1er Grand Cru Classé. Owner: Etablissements Jean-Pierre Moueix. AOC: St-Emilion. 26 acres. 5,200 cases. Grape var: Merlot 90%, Cab.Fr. 10%.

Impeccably conducted little property next to Ch. Belair, with a vineyard on the plateau and another on the south slope. The wine is made by Christian Moueix and Jean-Claude Berrouet, the brilliant resident oenologist of the house of J. P. Moueix at Libourne. Its high proportion of Merlot makes it almost a Pomerol, but less plummy, with

the 'meat' of St-Emilion and great finesse. There can scarcely be a more reliable or fascinating St-Emilion to watch vintage by vintage.

Château Pavie

1er Grand Cru Classé. Owner: Consorts Valette. Administrator: Jean-Paul Valette. AOC: St-Emilion. 89 acres plus; 15,000 cases. Grape var: Merlot 55%, Cab.Fr. 25%, Cab.Sauv. 20%.

A priceless site, the whole south-by-west slope of the central St-Emilion côtes; the biggest vineyard on the hill with the advantage of both top and bottom as well; some good should come out of almost every vintage. The spacious cellars are dug under the top part of the vineyard, whose vine roots can be seen rejoicing in their fragrant humidity. The house lies in the middle of the vines. Pavie was formerly known for warm, round claret of medium weight, more delicious than deeply serious: 'supple' is the technical term. Recent vintages have displayed a firmer hand. The Valettes also own Ch. Pavie-Decesse on the not-quite-so-good slopes next door.

Château Trottevieille

1er Grand Cru Classé. Owner: Philippe Castéja. AOC: St-Emilion. 25 acres. 3,500 cases. Grape var: Merlot 50%, Cab.Fr. 45%, Cab.Sauv. 5%.

Detached from the solid block of Crus Classés along the côtes, on the plateau east of the town, on richer-looking but still shallow clay with pebbles over limestone. The owners are the Médocain Castéja family of Ch. Batailley (Pauillac). Full-flavoured wine with plenty of character and better since '85 as a result of stricter selection in vineyard and cellar.

St-Emilion Grands Crus Classés

Château L'Arrosée

Owner: François Rodhain. 24 acres. 4,100 cases. Grape var: Merlot 50%, Cab.Sauv. 35%, Cab.Fr. 15%.

At the bottom of the côtes near the town. The name l'Arrosée means 'watered' (by springs). The wine itself, on the contrary, is extremely concentrated and serious; regularly one of the stars of St-Emilion. Opulent and seductive.

Château Balestard La Tonnelle

Owner: Jacques Capdemourlin. 26 acres. 5,000 cases. Grape var: Merlot 65%, Cab.Fr. 20%, Cab.Sauv. 10%, Malbec 5%.

The Capdemourlin family has owned this property since the 15th-century, when the poet Villon described its wine as 'ce divin nectar'. I have been more prosaically satisfied with this full-bodied, meaty wine. A new cellar was built in 1995.

Château Bellevue

Owners: the daughters of Louis Horeau. 15 acres. 3,500 cases. Merlot 67%, Cab.Sauv. and Franc 33%.

Well named for its situation high on the west slope of the côtes. I have not tasted the wine.

75

Château Bergat

Owners: the Castéja family. Adm.: Philippe Castéja
(see Ch. Batailley, Pauillac). 9 acres. 1,500 cases. Grape var:
Merlot 50% , Cab.Fr. 40%, Cab.Sauv. 10%.
Tiny vineyard in the sheltered gully east of the town linked
by ownership with Ch. Trottevieille.

Château Berliquet

Owners: Vicomte & Vicomtesse de Lesquen. 9 acres. 4,200 cases.
Grape var: Merlot 67%, Cab.Fr. 25%, Cab.Sauv. 8%.
Old estate modernized in the 1970s, promoted in 1985, and
made and marketed by the St-Emilion cooperative.

Chateau Cadet-Bon

Owner: SA Loriene. 16 acres. 2,500 cases. Grape var: Merlot
70%, Cab.Fr. 20%, Cab.Sauv. 10%.
A change of owner and robust wines gained this small *cru*
promotion in 1996.

Château Cadet-Piola

Owners: the Jabiol family. 17 acres. 3,000 cases. Grape var:
Merlot 51%, Cab.Sauv. 28%, Cab.Fr. 18%, Malbec 3%.
Memorable for the only Bordeaux label to portray (and very
prettily) the female bosom. But a sturdy, even masculine,
wine.

Château Canon-La-Gaffelière

Owner: Count zu Neipperg. 48 acres. 14,800 cases. Grape var:
Merlot 55%, Cab.Fr. 40%, Cab.Sauv. 5%.
German-owned property on sandy soil by the railway under
the *côtes*. Total renovation in 1985 has brought some
startlingly good wines. A property to watch.

Château Cap-de-Mourlin

Owner: Jacques Capdemourlin (see Ch. Balestard). 35 acres.
6,000 cases. Grape var: Merlot 60%, Cab.Fr. 25%, Cab.Sauv.
12%, Malbec 3%.
Situated one mile north of St-Emilion town on clay soil. For
several years until 1982 this estate was divided, but is now
one again, and is making strikingly high-flavoured wine.

Château Chauvin

Owners: Marie-France Février and Béatrice Ondet. 32 acres. 6,000
cases. Grape var: Merlot 70%, Cab.Fr. 20%, Cab.Sauv. 10%.
Inconsistent property being given a face lift with Michel
Rolland's help.

Château La Clotte

Owners: Héritiers Chailleau. 8 acres. 1,200 cases. Grape var:
Merlot 70%, Cab.Fr. 30%.
Beautifully situated in the fold of the hill east of the town.
Drink this wine at the owner's restaurant, Logis de la Cadène.

Château La Clusière

Owner: Consorts Valette. 7 acres. 1,000 cases. Grape var: Merlot
70%, Cab.Fr. 30%.
Part of the vineyard of Ch. Pavie (q.v.) not quite up to
Premier Grand Cru standard.

Château Corbin

Owner: Domaines Giraud. 32 acres. 7,000 cases. Grape var:
Merlot 70%, Cab.Fr. 24%, Cab Sauv. 6%.
Corbin is the northern hamlet of *graves* St-Emilion, near
the Pomerol boundary and sloping gently northeast.
Some flesh, some tannin but, on balance, not very
distinctive wine.

Château Corbin-Michotte

Owner: Jean Noël Boidron. 15 acres. 3,000 cases. Grape var:
Merlot 65%, Cab.Fr. 30%, Cab.Sauv. 5%.
See the previous entry; but this seems to me more delicate
and 'supple'.

Chateau La Couspaude

Owner: Vignobles Aubert. 17 acres. 3,000 cases. Grape varieties:
Merlot 70%, Cab.Fr. 20%, Cab.Sauv. 10%.
Re-established in the classification in 1996. Now that the
wine is château-bottled, this well-placed property is taking
a new lease of life under Michel Rolland's direction. One
to watch.

Château Couvent-des-Jacobins

Owner: Mme Joinaud-Borde. 22 acres. 4,400 cases. Grape var:
Merlot 65%, Cab.Fr. 30%,Cab.Sauv. 5%.
Excellent *côtes* vineyard right under the town walls to the
east, with venerable cellars in the town centre. Well-
structured, ripe and juicy wine.

Château Curé-Bon

Owner: Société Loriene. 11 acres. 1,500 cases. Grape var: Merlot
80%, Cab.Fr. 20%.
Bon was the priest who owned this little patch among
the great *côtes* vineyards of Canon, Belair, etc. This is
concentrated and powerful wine, jammy but tannic – most
impressive.

Château Dassault

Owner: SARL Château Dassault. 56 acres. 13,300 cases. Grape
var: Merlot 65%, Cab.Fr. 30%, Cab.Sauv. 5%.
One of the biggest *graves* vineyards, northeast of the
town. Steady rather than distinguished; mainstream St-
Emilion.

Château La Dominique

Owner: Clément Fayat. Administrator: Etienne Prion. 55 acres.
10,000 cases. Grape var: Merlot 75%, Cab.Fr. 15%, Cab.Sauv.
5%, Malbec 5%.
Neighbour to Cheval Blanc reflecting its privileged position
in an almost unbroken sequence of concentrated, fleshy,
fine wines, with the Michel Rolland touch.

Château Faurie-de-Souchard

Owners: the Jabiol family. 28 acres. 6,000 cases. Grape var:
Merlot 65%, Cab.Fr. 20%, Cab.Sauv. 9%.
Confusingly the neighbour of Petit-Faurie-de-Soutard. Same
owners as of Ch. Cadet-Piola and Ch. Cadet-Peychez; now
tightening its grip.

Château Fonplégade

Owner: Armand Moueix. 44 acres. 10,000 cases. Grape var: Merlot 60%, Cab.Fr. 40%.

One of the grander châteaux, on the *côtes* among the very best, yet never one of the great names. Delicious meaty wine that seems persistently underrated.

Château Fonroque

Owners: Ets J-P. Moueix. 40 acres. 8,000 cases. Grape var: Merlot 90%, Cab.Fr. 10%.

A relatively modest member of the impeccable Moueix stable. Fonroque is dark, firm wine of definite character that ages well.

Château Franc-Mayne

Owner: M Georgy Fourroy. 18 acres. 3,000 cases. Grape var: Merlot 70%, Cab.Fr. 15%, Cab.Sauv. 15%.

A serious little property on the western *côtes*, acquired in 1989 by the insurance group AXA, resold in 1996.

Château Grand Mayne

Owner: Jean-Pierre Nony. 47 acres. 9,500 cases. Grape var: Merlot 72%, Cab.Fr. 23%.

A well-placed property realizing its considerable potential for rich-tasting, serious claret.

Chateau Grandes Murailles

Owners: the Malen heirs. 5 acres. 1,000 cases. Grape var: Merlot 70%, Cab. Fr. 30%.

Wines from a tiny plot below the ruined wall of the 13th-century Dominican church, a well-known local landmark outside the town.

Château Grand-Pontet

Owners: the Bécot and Pourquet families. 35 acres. 6,000 cases. Grape var: Merlot 75%, Cab.Fr. 15%, Cab.Sauv. 10%.

Next to Beau-Séjour Becot and like it revitalized since 1985. Showy wine.

Château Guadet-St-Julien

Owner: Robert Lignac. 15 acres. 2,000 cases. Grape var: Merlot 75%, Cab.Fr. 25%.

Vineyard just out of town to the north; cellars in the Rue Guadet. A property to follow.

Château Haut-Corbin

Owner: Soc Haut-Corbin. 16 acres. 4,300 cases. Grape var: Merlot 70%, Cab.Sauv. 20%, Cab.Fr. 10%.

The least of the Corbins up near the Pomerol border.

Château Haut-Sarpe

Owner: Joseph Janoueix. 28 acres. 5,600 cases. Grape var: Merlot 70%, Cab.Fr. 30%.

The Janoueix family are merchants in Libourne with six small properties in Pomerol. Haut-Sarpe straddles the border of St-Christophe des Bardes, east of St-Emilion, and is one of several good properties making firm, earthy wine.

Château Clos des Jacobins

Owner: Ets. Cordier. 20 acres. 4,800 cases. Grape var: Merlot 55%, Cab.Fr. 40%, Cab.Sauv. 5%.

The house of Cordier makes characteristically attractive wine here; in the centre of the commune where *côtes* begins to shade to *graves*. This is an excellent example of the 'open' *côtes* style.

Château Laniote

Owner: M. de La Filolie. 12 acres. 2,700 cases. Grape var: Merlot 70%, Cab.Sauv. 20%, Cab.Fr. 10%.

One of the many little properties so appreciated in Belgium that they are unknown elsewhere. The cave in the hillside where Saint Emilion himself lived in the 7th century is on the property.

Château Larcis-Ducasse

Owner: Mme H. Gratiot-Alphandery. 24 acres. 5,000 cases. Grape var: Merlot 65%, Cab.Fr. and Cab.Sauv. 35%.

The best vineyard of St-Laurent-des-Combes, splendidly sited on the *côtes* just east of Château Pavie (q.v.). A good bet, but much less elegant than its Premier Grand Cru neighbour.

Château Larmande

Owner: Groupe d'Assurance la Mondiale. 61 acres. 12,500 cases. Grape var. Merlot 65%, Cab.Fr. and Cab.Sauv. 35%.

A series of lovely wines in the 1980s ('83, '85, '86 and '88) made this property's reputation, which was then enhanced by new ownership in 1991.

Château Laroque

Owners: the Beaumartin family. 143 acres. 33,000 cases. Grape var: Merlot 80%, Cab.Fr.15%, Cab.Sauv. 5%.

This is the largest property on the St-Emilion côtes in St-Christophe.

Château Laroze

Owner: Georges Meslin. 62 acres. 13,000 cases. Grape var: Merlot 59%, Cab.Fr. 38%, Cab.Sauv. 3%.

Lying low on the western *côtes* on sandy soil. Not one of the outstanding vineyards, but modern and well managed, and capable of very good wine for four to five years' maturing.

Château Matras

Owner: Véronique Gaboriaud-Bernard. 24 acres. 5,000 cases. Grape var: Cab.Fr. 50%, Merlot 40%, Cab.Sauv. 10%.

Beautifully sited château at the foot of the western *côtes* next to Ch. L'Angélus. Recent replanting suggests much-needed new ideas.

Château Moulin du Cadet

Owner: Ets J-P. Moueix. 12 acres. 1,800 cases. Grape var: Merlot 90%, Cab.Fr. 10%.

Impeccably made wine typical of the Moueix establishment. A combination of clay soil and a *côtes* situation gives solidity and sweetness.

Château Lamarzelle

Owner: Edmond Carrère. 32 acres. 5,800 cases. Grape var: Merlot 80%, Cab.Fr. 20%.
Promoted in 1985, a property in the same ownership as Ch. Grand Barrail Lamarzelle Figeac.

Clos de L'Oratoire

Owner: Count zu Neipperg. 25 acres. 5,000 cases. Grape var: Merlot 75%, Cab.Fr. 25%.
A *côtes* property that has grown recently, it is now making solid, unassuming wines in mainstream St-Emilion style.

Château Pavie-Decesse

Owners: the Valette family. 22 acres. 4,500 cases. Grape var: Merlot 65%, Cab.Fr. 20%, Cab.Sauv 15%.
The junior partner of Ch. Pavie, from the flatter land at the top of the *côtes*. The wine is considered a shade harder, less supple and 'giving' than Pavie but can (e.g. in '85) be as fine.

Château Pavie-Macquin

Owners: the Corre-Macquin family. 37 acres. 6,400 cases. Grape var: Merlot 70%, Cab.Fr. 30%.
Organically farmed vineyard and fine winemaking by Nicolas Thienpont of the Vieux Château Certan family. Worth watching.

Château Petit-Faurie-de-Soutard

Owner: Mme Françoise Capdemourlin. 20 acres. 3,500 cases. Grape var: Merlot 60%, Cab.Fr. 30%, Cab.Sauv. 10%.
Neighbour of the Cap-de-Mourlin, now managed by Jacques C. Readily confused with next-door Faurie-de-Souchard. Technically *côtes* wines, but like Ch. Soutard (of which it was once a part) harder to penetrate.

Château Le Prieuré

Owner: SCE Baronne Guichard. 12 acres. 1,500 cases. Grape var: Merlot 70%, Cab.Fr. 30%.
On the eastern *côtes* in an ideal situation but apparently ticking over at present.

Château Ripeau

Owner: Mme Françoise de Wilde. 38 acres. 8,000 cases. Grape var: Merlot 60%, Cab.Fr. 30%, Cab.Sauv. 10%.
A well-known *graves* château in the past, considered on a par with Château La Dominique. Less prominent recently, but heading for a revival.

Château St-Georges (Côte-Pavie)

Owner: Jacques Masson. 13 acres. 2,500 cases. Grape var: Merlot 80%, Cab.Sauv. and Franc 20%.
An enviable spot between Pavie and Ch. La Gaffelière. Worth seeking out.

Château La Serre

Owner: Bernard d'Arfeuille. 17 acres. 3,500 cases. Grape var: Merlot 80%, Cab.Fr. 20%.
Just outside the town on the *côtes* to the east. Despite its surprising proportion of Merlot, this lacked charm in the 1980s but things seem to be looking up.

Château Soutard

Owners: the des Ligneris family. 55 acres. 10,000 cases. Grape var: Merlot 60%, Cab.Fr. 40%.
An important property on a rocky outcrop north-by-east of the town. Can be well-made, warm and powerful wine. The great vintages are long-keeping classics. Second label: Clos de la Tonnelle.

Château Tertre-Daugay

Owner: Léo de Malet-Roquefort. 39 acres. 5,000 cases. Grape var: Merlot 60%, Cab.Fr. 40%.
A spectacularly well-sited château on the final promontory of the *côtes* west of Ch. Ausone, in disarray for some years, but since 1978 in the same hands as Ch. La Gaffelière and replanting. Recent vintages have shown the true class of the property. 15 acres of young vines produce Roquefort, a St-Emilion Grand Cru.

Château La Tour Figeac

Owner: Soc. Civile. 34 acres. 6,000 cases. Grape var: Merlot 60%, Cab.Fr. 40%.
Formerly part of Ch. Figeac, now owned and run by a German with the help of an American cellar-master. This is a very worthy wine.

Château La Tour-du-Pin-Figeac (Giraud Belivier)

Owner: GFA Giraud Belivier. 24 acres. 5,500 cases.
A predominantly Merlot vineyard north of Figeac, beside Cheval Blanc, but not above average in quality.

Château La Tour-du-Pin-Figeac

Owner: Héritiers Marcel Moueix. 21 acres. 4,000 cases. Grape var: Merlot 60%, Cab.Fr. 30%, Malbec and Cab.Sauv. 10%.
Powerful, pungent wines from a privileged situation among the great plateau vineyards.

Château Troplong-Mondot

Owner: Christine Valette. 72 acres. 11,000 cases. Grape var: Merlot 80%, Cab.Sauv. and Cab.Fr. 10%, Malbec 10%.
A famous vineyard on the crest of the *côtes* east of the town, above Ch Pavie. Reliably good in the '80s and, since '88, powerfully concentrated oaky wines. Enthusiastic following.

Château Villemaurine

Owner: GFV-UFG. 20 acres. 4,000 cases. Grape var: Merlot 70%, Cab.Sauv. 30%.
At the gates of the town, a *côtes* vineyard with more Cabernet Sauvignon than most, consequently less easy wine but worth waiting for. There are splendid cellars.

Château Yon-Figeac

Owner: Dom. du Libournais. 62 acres. 13,000 cases. Grape var: Merlot 80%, Cab.Fr. 20%.
A former part of the Figeac domaine in the *graves*; one of the better reputed of its class.

GRANDS CRUS

The quality of such a number of châteaux obviously varies very widely. Those marked with an asterisk are known to me to have particularly high and consistent standards.

Château Barde-Haut St-Christophe des Bardes. Owner: Jean-Claude Gasparoux. 41 acres. 7,500 cases.

Château Bellefont-Belcier* St-Laurent des Combes. 30 acres. 6,000 cases.

Château Bellegrave Vignonet. Owner: Xavier Dangin. 26 acres. 6,250 cases.

Château Bigaroux St-Sulpice de Faleyrens. Owner: GFA Mestre-Guilhem. 37 acres. 7,500 cases.

Château Bonnet d'Armens St-Pey d'Armens. Owner: M. Bonnet. 61 acres. 11,000 cases.

Château Calvaire St-Etienne de Lisse. Owner: Domaine Dumas. 37 acres. 6,000 cases.

Château Cantenac St-Emilion. Owners: the Brunot family. 37 acres. 7,500 cases.

Château Capet-Guillier St-Hippolyte. Owners: the Galinot Family. 37 acres. 8,300 cases.

Château Cardinal Villemaurine* St-Emilion. Owner: J-F. Carrille. 24 acres. 5,000 cases.

Château Carteau-Côtes-Daugay* St-Emilion. Owner: J. Bertrand. 31 acres. 7,000 cases.

Château du Cauze St-Christophe des Bardes. Owner: Bruno Laporte. 49 acres. 12,000 cases.

Château Le Chatelet St-Emilion. Owner: SC Berjat. 12 acres. 2,400 cases.

Château Cormeil-Figeac* St-Emilion. Owners: Héritiers R. & L. Moreaud. 24 acres. 5,600 cases.

Château Cote de Baleau St. Emilion. Owner: SC Grandes Murailles. 42 acres. 7,500 cases.

Château Bernateau St-Etienne de Lisse. Owner: Régis Lavau. 64 acres. 8,300 cases.

Château Coutet St-Emilion. Owners: the Beaulieu family. 29 acres. 6,000 cases.

Château Croque-Michotte St-Emilion. Owner: Geoffrion. 34 acres. 6,500 cases.

Château La Fagnouse St-Etienne de Lisse. Owner: Mme Coutant. 27 acres. 6,800 cases.

Château de Ferrand* St-Hippolyte. Owner: Baron Bich. 74 acres. 17,500 cases.

Château La Fleur* St-Emilion. Owner: Lily Lacoste. 16 acres. 3,000 cases.

Château Fombrauge* St-Christophe des Bardes. Owner: Hans Just. 123 acres. 25,000 cases.

Château Fonrazade St-Emilion. Owner: Guy Balotte. 32 acres. 6,500 cases.

Château Fourney St-Pey d'Armens. Owner: Vignobles Rollet. 51 acres. 11,500 cases.

Château Franc Bigaroux St-Sulpice de Faleyrens. Owner: Yves Blanc. 19 acres. 5,000 cases.

Château Franc-Grâce-Dieu St-Emilion. Owner: Germain Siloret. 20 acres. 3,800 cases.

Château Gaillard St-Hippolyte. Owner: Jean-Jacques Nouvel. 49 acres. 12,500 cases.

Château Gaubert St-Christophe des Bardes. Owner: Honoré Menager. 34 acres. 6,500 cases.

University research

The standard of winemaking and the understanding of problems that beset both grapes and wine have been immeasurably enhanced over the last century, but especially the last 40 years, by the Station Oenologique of the University of Bordeaux. A succession of famous directors has included Professor Ulysse Gayon, a pupil of Louis Pasteur, who introduced the science of microbiology to wine-making. His grandson, Jean Ribereau-Gayon, succeeded him and was in turn succeeded in guiding the wine makers of Bordeaux along scientific lines by his pupil, Emile Peynaud, and his own son, Pascal Ribereau-Gayon. Meanwhile the more recent white winemaking revolution is led by Denis Durbourdieu.

Château La Grâce Dieu St-Emilion. Owner: SC Pauty. 34 acres. 6,000 cases.

Château La Grâce-Dieu-Les-Menuts St-Emilion. Owner: Xans Pilotte. 32 acres. 6,500 cases.

Château Grand Barrail Lamarzelle Figeac St-Emilion. Owner: Carrere Edmond. 47 acres. 8,400 cases.

Château Grand Corbin. St-Emilion. Owner: Giraud. 33 acres. 7,600 cases.

Château Grand-Corbin-Despagne St-Emilion. Owner: Despagne. 65 acres. 12,500 cases.

Château Gueyrot St-Emilion. Owner: Tour de Fayet Frères. 21 acres. 4,000 cases.

Château Guillemin La Gaffelière St-Emilion. Owner: Yves Fomperier. 41 acres. 8,500 cases.

Château Guinot St-Etienne de Lisse. Owner: Hubert Tauziac. 35 acres. 8,600 cases.

Château Haut Brisson* Vignonet. Owner: Yves Blanc. 27 acres. 5,500 cases.

Château Haut-Lavallade St-Christophe des Bardes. Owner: Jean Pierre Chagneau. 25 acres. 5,500 cases.

Château Haut Mazerat. St-Emilion. Owner: Christian Gouteyron. 15 acres. 3,000 cases.

Château Haut Ségottes St-Emilion. Owner: Danielle André. 22 acres. 5,000 cases.

Château L'Hermitage St-Emilion. Owner: de Mazerat. 9 acres. 2,000 cases.

Château Jacques Blanc St-Etienne de Lisse. Owner: Pierre Chouet. 47 acres. 10,000 cases.

Château Jean-Voisin St-Emilion. Owner: Soc. Chassagnoux. 35 acres. 7,800 cases.

Château Le Jurat St-Emilion. Owner: SC Haut Corbin. 17 acres. 3,500 cases.

Château Lapelletrie St-Christophe des Bardes. Owners: the Jean family. 30 acres. 6,000 cases.

Château Lapeyre St-Etienne de Lisse. Owner: Hubert Tauziac. 18 acres. 4,000 cases.

Château Laroque* St-Christophe des Bardes. Owner: Société Civile. 111 acres. 20,000 cases.

Château Lassègue St-Hippolyte. Owner: J. P. Freylon. 57 acres. 13,000 cases.

Château Lescours St-Sulpice de Faleyrens. Owner: Soc. du Château. 54 acres. 10,000 cases.

Château Haut Mazerat St-Emilion. Owners: Gouteyron & Fils. 14 acres. 3,300 cases.

Clos des Menuts St-Emilion. Owner: Pierre Rivière. 60 acres. 11,500 cases.

Château Milon St-Christophe des Bardes. Owner: Christian Bouyer. 49 acres. 8,500 cases.

Château Monbousquet* St-Sulpice de Faleyrens. Owners: the Querre family. 74 acres. 17,000 cases.

Château Montlabert St-Emilion. Owner: Société Civile. 32 acres. 7,800 cases.

Château Moulin Bellegrave Vignonet. Owner: Max Perier. 37 acres. 5,000 cases.

Château Moulin Saint Georges St-Emilion. Owner: Alain Vauthier. 3,500 cases.

Château Palais Cardinal La Fuie St-Sulpice de Faleyrens. Owner: Gérard Frétier. 34 acres. 7,300 cases.

Château Panet St-Christophe des Bardes. Owner: Jean-Claude Carles. 34 acres. 7,800 cases.

Château Patris St-Emilion. Owner: Michel Querre. 30 acres. 6,000 cases.

Château Peyreau St-Emilion. Owner: Comte de Neipperg. 32 acres. 4,700 cases.

Château de Peyrelongue St-Emilion. Owner: M Bouquey. 29 acres. 6,000 cases.

Château Pindefleurs* St-Emilion. Owner: Micheline Dior. 19 acres. 3,800 cases.

Château Pipeau St-Laurent des Combes. Owners: Richard Mestreguilhem & Fils. 86 acres. 15,500 cases.

Château Pontet-Clauzure St-Emilion. Owner: Société Civile. 25 acres. 5,500 cases.

Château Franc Pourret St-Emilion. Owner: François Ouzoulias. 13 acres. 2,500 cases.

Château de Pressac St-Etienne de Lisse. Owner: Jacques Pouey. 81 acres. 13,500 cases.

Château Puy-Blanquet* St-Etienne de Lisse. Owner: R. Jacquet. 57 acres. 10,000 cases.

Château Puyblanquet Carille St-Christophe des Bardes. Owner: Jean-François Carrille. 29 acres. 7,500 cases.

Château de Cantin St-Christophe des Bardes. Owner: Société Civile. 74 acres. 20,000 cases.

Château du Rocher St-Etienne de Lisse. Owner: Baron de Montfort. 37 acres. 7,000 cases.

Château de Rol St-Emilion. Owner: Jean Sautereau. 17 acres. 3,000 cases.

Château La-Rose-Côtes Rol St-Emilion. Owner: Yves Mirande. 21 acres. 3,500 cases.

Château La Rose Pourret St-Emilion. Owner: Bernard Warion. 19 acres. 4,300 cases.

Château Rozier St-Laurent des Combes. Owner: Jean-Bernard Saby. 43 acres. 8,500 cases.

Château La Sablière St-Emilion. Owner: Robert Avezou. 22 acres. 5,300 cases.

Château St-Christophe St-Christophe des Bardes. Owner: M. Richard. 27 acres. 5,400 cases.

Château de St-Pey St-Pey d'Armens. Owner: Maurice Musset. 44 acres. 10,000 cases.

Château Tour des Combes St-Laurent des Combes. Owner: Jean Darribéhaude. 30 acres. 8,600 cases.

Château Trapaud St-Etienne de Lisse. Owner: André Larribière. 30 acres. 7,500 cases.

Clos Trimoulet St-Emilion. Owner: Appollot. 22 acres. 5,000 cases.

Château Val d'Or Vignonet. Owner: Roger Bardet. 56 acres. 11,500 cases.

Château Grand Corbin Manuel St-Emilion. Owner: Pierre Manuel. 17 acres. 3,300 cases.

Château Vieux Rivallon St-Emilion. Owner: Charles Bouquey. 34 acres. 2,550 cases.

Château Vieux Sarpe* St-Christophe des Bardes. Owner: J.-F. Janoueix. 16 acres. 4,000 cases.

MERCHANTS IN LIBOURNE

Most of the thriving trade of St-Emilion, Pomerol and their neighbours is handled by a group of négociants clustered on the Quai du Priourat, by the rustic riverside of the Dordogne. A peculiarity of Libourne business is the number of independent salesmen known as *Les Corréziens* (they hail from the Corrèze, up-country along the Dordogne and scarcely a land of opportunity). *Les Corréziens* spend a winter season in the north of France and Belgium collecting private orders, which they pass to the Quai du Priourat. Other houses are based in St-Emilion and the villages around.

Principal Libourne négociants in approximate order of importance are:

SA Grands Vins d'Aquitaine Ste Foy la Grande.

Maison d'Arfeuille Libourne.
Merchants and proprietors.

Maison Audy Libourne.

Ets Chassagnoux et Fils Libourne

Grands vins J P Estager Libourne

Maison Aubert Frères La Couspaude, St. Emilion

Maison Grenouilleau Ste-Foy-La-Grande.

Maison Horeau-Beylot Libourne.
A family firm of proprietors and shippers founded in 1740.

Maison Joseph Janoueix Libourne.

Maison Lebègue Libourne.
Dealers in a wide range of wines in bottle and bulk.

Maison SA Milhade Galgon.
Merchants based in the Fronsac area.

Etablissements Jean-Pierre Moueix Libourne.
Founder: Jean-Pierre Moueix. His son Christian is also a celebrated figure. The family firm that makes the running in Libourne, owning or managing a score of the best châteaux (see the individual château entries). Duclot in Bordeaux is related.

Armand Moueix Pomerol.
Merchants and proprietors based at Château Taillefer, Pomerol.

SA Promocom St Emilion.

Maison Michel Querre Libourne.

Ets Pierre Rivière et fils St-Emilion.

Maison René Vedrenne Libourne.

THE 'SATELLITES' OF ST-EMILION

Apart from the five saintly villages (St-Emilion, St-Laurent, St-Christophe, St-Etienne and St-Hippolyte) that are considered part of the appellation St-Emilion, four more to the north and east are granted the privilege of adding St-Emilion to their names. They are known as the satellites. They lie just north of the little river Barbanne, which forms the northern boundary of glory and renown. Their citizens argue that the formation of the valley gives two of them, St-Georges and Montagne, a better situation than some of St-Emilion. Be that as it may, those two, plus Puisseguin and Lussac, are honoured. Proprietors in St-Georges may call their wine Montagne-St-Emilion if they wish. St-Georges has a splendid château that gives it pride in its own name. Their wine is indeed like St-Emilion and can be made almost equally meaty and long lived. More growers, however, prefer using a good deal of Merlot and making softer (still strong) wine that can be delicious in two or three years. Postcode: 33570 Lussac.

PUISSEGUIN-ST-EMILION CHATEAUX

Château Bel-Air Owner: Robert Adoue. 37 acres. 10,000 cases.
Chateau Durand-Laplagne Owner: J Besson. 34 acres. 8,500 cases.
Château Guibeau La Fourvieille Owner: Henri Bourlon. 101 acres. 23,000 cases.
Château des Laurets Owner: GFA du Domaine des Laurets et de Malengin. 88 acres. 20,000 cases.
Château de Puisseguin Owner: Jean Robin. 47 acres. 8,500 cases.
Château Soleil Owner: Jean Soleil. 35 acres. 9,000 cases.
Château Teyssier Owner: Société Civile. 40 acres. 9,000 cases.

LUSSAC-ST-EMILION CHATEAUX

Château de Barbe Blanche Owner: A. Bouvier. 69 acres. 15,500 cases.
Château Bel-Air Owner: J.-N. Roi. 50 acres. 12,500 cases
Chateau du Courlat Owner: Pierre Bourotte. 34 acres. 9,000 cases.
Château Tour de Grenet Owner: M. Brunot. 72 acres. 16,500 cases.
Château La Tour de Ségur 33 acres. 7,000 cases red, 1,000 white.

MONTAGNE-ST-EMILION CHATEAUX

Château Calon Owner: Jean-Noël Boidron. 59 acres. 13,500 cases.
Château Faizeau Owner: Lebreton and Raynaud. 24 acres. 5,000 cases.
Château Haut Gillet Owner: Sophie Castandet. 9 acres. 2,500 cases.
Château Maison Blanche Owner: M Despange-Rapin. 79 acres. 15,000 cases.
Chateau de Maison Neuve Owner: Michel Coudroy. 96 acres. 26,000 cases.
Château Montaiguillon Owner: M. Amart. 69 acres. 17,000 cases.
Château Roudier Owner: Jacques Capdemourlin. 74 acres. 15,000 cases.
Château Teyssier Owner: Durand Teyssier. 24 acres. 6,500 cases.
Vieux Château Rocher Corbin Owner: M. Durand. 223 acres. 5,000 cases.
Vieux-Château-St-André (Corbin) Owner: Jean-Claude Berrouet. 14 acres. 3,000 cases.

ST-GEORGES–ST-EMILION CHATEAUX

Château Saint-André Corbin Owner: Carre and du Priourat. 47 acres. 8,000 cases.
Château St-Georges Owner: M G Desbois. 123 acres. 25,000 cases.
Château Tour du Pas St-Georges. Owner: J Dubois-Challon. 37 acres. 8,300 cases.

Bordeaux trade measures

For official and statistical purposes, all French wine production is measured in hectolitres, but each region has its traditional measures for maturing and selling its wine. In Bordeaux the measure is the *tonneau*, a notional container since such big barrels are no longer made. A *tonneau* consists of 4 *barriques* – the barrels used at the châteaux, and still sometimes for shipping. A *barrique bordelaise* must by law contain 225 litres, which makes 25 cases of a dozen 75 cl. bottles each. The *tonneau* is therefore a simple and memorable measure: 100 cases of wine.

POMEROL

If there are doubters (and there are) about the differences that different soils make to wine, they should study Pomerol. In this little area, flanked by the huge spread of St-Emilion, like a market-garden to Libourne on the north bank of the Dordogne, there are wines as potent and majestic as any in France cheek by jowl with wines of wispy, fleeting fruitiness and charm – and dull ones, too.

The soil grades from shingly sand around the town of Libourne through increasingly heavy stages to a climactic plateau where the clay subsoil is very near the surface. A yard down, the clay is near-solid and packed with nuggets of iron. This, at the giddy height of 50 feet above its surroundings, is in every sense the summit of Pomerol.

Despite its (recent) international reknown, Pomerol will always be an abstruse, recherché corner of the wine world. Its whole vineyard area is no larger than St-Julien, the smallest of the great communes of the Médoc. Perhaps half of this (as against two-thirds of St-Julien) is of truly distinctive, classed-growth standard.

The size of the properties is correspondingly small. There are 136 members of the growers' syndicate, sharing 1,880 acres: 10 acres each on average. The biggest estate is 120 acres. Many growers have a mere acre or two – sufficient for 200 or 300 of the annual total of about 358,000 cases entitled to the appellation. There is no cooperative: small growers tend to make their wine and sell it direct to consumers all over France, and particularly to Belgium.

It is only 100 years since the name of Pomerol was first heard outside its immediate area, yet tradition has already provided it with a clear identity. Its best soil is clay; therefore cold. The early-ripening Merlot does better than the later Cabernet, and of the Cabernets the Franc (alias Bouchet) rather than the Sauvignon. The mellow, brambly Merlot and the lively, raspberryish Bouchet pick up the iron from the clay, are matured in fragrant oak – and *voilà*, you have a greatly over-simplified recipe for Pomerol. Where does it get its singular texture of velvet, its chewy flesh, its smell of ripe plums and even cream, and even honey? Wherever, it was more than an edict from the bureaucracy that fixes appellations.

Authorities put Pomerol between St-Emilion and the Médoc in style. To me it is closer to St-Emilion; broader, more savoury and with less 'nerve' than Médocs of similar value, maturing in five years as much as Médocs do in ten – hence tending to overlay them at tastings, as California wines do French. Great Pomerols, however, show no sign of being short lived.

No official classification of Pomerol has ever been made. Professor Roger published a personal one in 1960, in *The Wines of Bordeaux*, dividing 63 châteaux into four ranks, with Château Pétrus on its own, Yquem-like, at the head. I have taken the advice of the most influential voice in the district, the merchants and proprietors Etablissements Jean-Pierre Moueix of Libourne, in listing some 40 properties as the best in the district. Below these I list only others with more than the average (10 acres) of vineyard.

Postcode: 33500 Libourne.

Pomerol First-Growth

Château Pétrus

Owner: S.C. Ch. Pétrus. AOC: Pomerol. 27 acres. 3,700 cases. Grape var: Merlot 95%, Cab.Fr. 5%.
See Pétrus, Pomerol's First-Growth, page 85.

Pomerol Leading Châteaux

Château Beauregard

Pomerol. Owner: Credit Foncier de France. 32 acres. 5,000 cases. Grape var: Merlot 60%, Cab.Fr. 30%, Cab Sauv. 10%.
In contrast to most of the modest 'châteaux' of Pomerol, the 17th-century Château Beauregard is so desirable that Mrs Daniel Guggenheim had it copied stone for stone on Long Island. Richer and fruitier than before under new ownership (1991). Second label is Benjamin de Beauregard.

Château Le Bon-Pasteur

Pomerol. Owner: Michel Rolland. 17 acres. 4,200 cases. Grape var: Merlot 90%, Cab.Fr. 10%.
M. Rolland not only makes his own richly sensuous Pomerol, but is a valuable consultant partly responsible for a new era of more luscious Pomerols and, more recently, Médocs too.

Château Bourgneuf-Vayron

Pomerol. Owners: Charles and Xavier Vayron. 22 acres. 4,400 cases. Grape var: Merlot 90%, Cab.Fr. 10%.
In the heart of Pomerol, lying between Trotanoy and Latour. Potent, plummy wine; not the most stylish.

Château La Cabanne

Pomerol. Owner: Jean-Pierre Estager. 25 acres. 5,000 cases. Grape var: Merlot 92%, Cab.Fr. 8%.
The name means 'the hut' or the 'shanty', which seems excessively modest for an estate situated in the heart of Pomerol with Trotanoy as a neighbour. The soil is middling between gravel and clay; the wine is not remarkable. Recently modernized. Haut Maillet is a sister château.

Château Certan de May

Pomerol. Owner: Mme Barreau-Badar. 12 acres. 2,000 cases. Grape var: Merlot 70%, Cab.Fr. 25%, Cab.Sauv. 5%.
Formerly called Ch. Certan. Perfectly sited next to Vieux Château Certan and Pétrus; but verging more towards Pétrus in richness and concentration. One of the top Pomerols today.

Château Certan-Giraud

Pomerol. Owner: Domaines Giraud. 18 acres. 4,300 cases. Grape var: Merlot 80%, Cab.Fr. 20%.

Ch. Certan-Giraud includes the former Ch. Certan-Marzelle. Geographically close to the last, but much easier-going in style; soft and creamy. It is also sold under the label of Clos du Roy.

Château Clinet

Pomerol. Owner: Georges Audy. 22 acres. 4,400 cases. Grape var: Merlot 75%, Cab.Sauv. 15%, Cab.Fr. 10%.
Formerly a lean, almost Médoc-style wine, but recently much fatter. The '88 is outstandingly rich.

Clos du Clocher

Pomerol. Owner: Jean Audy. 14 acres. 2,600 cases. Grape var: Merlot 80%, Cab.Fr. 20%.
Central vineyard next to the Certans making well-balanced, middle-weight wine with plenty of flavour.

Château La Conseillante

Pomerol. Owner: Héritiers Louis Nicolas. 29 acres. 5,000 cases. Grape var: Merlot 65%, Cab Franc 30%, Malbec 5%.
The splendid silver-on-white label is designed around an 'N' for the family that has owned the château for more than a century. Coincidentally, London's Café Royal has the same motif for the same reason. La Conseillante lies between Pétrus and Cheval Blanc, but makes a more delicate, as it were high-pitched wine. Sometimes as fine and fragrant as any Pomerol but less plummy and fat. Fermentation is now in stainless steel. Recent vintages are first class.

Château La Croix

Pomerol. Owner: Société Civile J. Janoueix. 24 acres. 5,000 cases. Grape var: Merlot 60%, Cab.Sauv. 20%, Cab.Fr. 20%.
Includes Ch. La Croix-St-Georges. Another 6 acres is La Croix-Toulifaut. These crosses are in the south of the commune on relatively light soil with a high iron content, not to be confused with Croix de Gay on the northern edge. Sturdy, generous wine not noted for great finesse but repaying bottle age.

Château La Croix de Gay

Pomerol. Owner: Noël Raynaud. 29 acres. 6,000 cases. Grape var: Merlot 80%, Cab.Sauv. 10%, Cab.Fr. 10%.
A well-run, second-rank vineyard on the gravelly clay sloping north down to the River Barbanne. As in so many Pomerol properties, its wines are being made with more care for a more demanding market. There is (since 1982) a 100% Merlot *cuvée prestige* Fleur du Gay which is the best part (about 1,200 to 1,500 cases) of the crop.

Clos L'Eglise

Pomerol. Owners: Michel and François Moreau. 14.5 acres. 2,800 cases. Grape var: Merlot 57%, Cab.Fr. 43%.
A superb little vineyard located on the north rim of the plateau, bought in the 1970s by the owners of the bigger but less distinguished Château Plince on the outskirts of Libourne. Old Clos l'Eglise vintages were backward, long-lived wines.

Château L'Eglise-Clinet

Pomerol. Owner: Denis Durantou. 13.5 acres. 1,700 cases. Grape var: Merlot 80%, Cab.Fr. 20%.
For long generally rated above Clinet; a stouter production with tannin and even brawn. Recently reaching far higher: luscious deep wines of top class. Second label: La Petite Eglise.

Château L'Enclos

Pomerol. Owner: Société Civile du Château L'Enclos. Administrators: Mme Marc and M. Weydert. 23 acres. 4,400 cases. Grape var: Merlot 80%, Cab.Fr. 19%, Malbec 1%.
With Clos René, one of the most respected châteaux of the western half of Pomerol, with the sort of deeply fruity and rewarding wine that impresses you young but needs at least 7 or 8 years in bottle to do it justice.

Château L'Evangile

Pomerol. Owners: Dom. Barons de Rothschild and Héritiers P. Ducasse. 36 acres. 4,500 cases. Grape var: Merlot 65%, Cab.Fr. 35%.
In the top ten of Pomerol for both quality and size. At its best (e.g. 1990) a voluptuous, concentrated wine for a long life, but accused of being facile in lesser vintages. The (Lafite) Rothschilds bought a majority share in 1990. Its situation between Pétrus and Cheval Blanc is propitious, to say the least.

Château Feytit-Clinet

Pomerol. Owners: the Domergue family. 16 acres. 3,000 cases. Grape var: Merlot 85%, Cab.Fr. 15%.
I have had some wonderful old wines from this little château, across the road from the illustrious Latour à Pomerol. Under Moueix management since the mid-1970s. Largely replanted in 1975 and 1976, so the new vines are beginning to deliver the goods.

Château La Fleur Gazin

Pomerol. Owner: Mme Delfour Borderie. 19 acres. 3,900 cases. Grape var: Merlot 80%, Cab.Fr. 20%.
Northern neighbour of Ch. Gazin, makes elegant, smooth, well-bred wine. I found myself noting the 'noble flavour' of the '79.

Château La Fleur-Pétrus

Pomerol. Owner: Ets Jean-Pierre Moueix. 32 acres. 5,000 cases. Grape var: Merlot 90%, Cab.Fr. 10%.
The third best Moueix Pomerol – which is high praise indeed. The vineyard is more gravelly than Pétrus and Trotanoy, the wine less fat and fleshy with more obvious tannin at first, poised, taut, asking to be aged. Enlarged in 1985 to take in part of its neighbour, Le Gay, planted with very old vines.

Château Le Gay

Pomerol. Owner: Mlle Marie Robin. 17 acres. 1,500 cases. Grape var: Merlot 80%, Cab.Fr. 20%.
See Château Lafleur.

Château Gazin

Pomerol. Owner: GFA Ch. Gazin. 59 acres. 8,000 cases. Grape var: Merlot 85%, Cab.Fr. 10%, Cab.Sauv. 5%.

One of the biggest Pomerol properties, despite selling a section to its neighbour, Château Pétrus, in 1970. The record was uneven; at best a fittingly fruity, concentrated wine but usually a shade full. 1989 seemed to mark a turning point in an excellent long-term wine and the nineties have been excitingly good. Second label is Château l'Hospitalet.

Château Gombaude-Guillot

Pomerol. Owners: the Laval family. 17 acres. 2,800 cases.

A well-regarded property (listed by Prof. Roger as a 'first-growth') right in the centre near the church.

Château la Grave (Trigant de Boisset)

Pomerol. Owner: Christian Moueix. 20 acres. 4,000 cases. Grape var: Merlot 85%, Cab.Fr. 15%.

Not the most full-bodied Pomerol, but particularly well balanced and stylish with tannin to encourage long development. The pretty château near the *route nationale* to Lalande and Perigueux was restored in the 1970s by the man who runs Ch. Pétrus. The soil here is *graves*, not clay – hence finesse rather than flesh.

Château Guillot

Pomerol. Owner: GFA Luquot. 11.5 acres. 2,300 cases. Merlot 70%, Cab.Fr. 30%.

Usually less marked by new oak than its neighbour and near names (e.g. Gombaude Guillot) but richly fruity in years like '85, '89 and '90.

Château Lafleur

Pomerol. Owner: Mlle Marie Robin. 12 acres. 1,800 cases. Grape var: Merlot 50%, Cab.Fr. 50%.

The two adjacent properties of Mlle Robin are united in the statistics, but distinct in quality. Lafleur (next to La Fleur Pétrus) is a model of balance, body with finesse and considerable style. Le Gay (17 acres, across the road to the north) is a shade plainer and perhaps less potent, always needing a good 8 years' ageing. Both are nursed by their elderly owner like children and must be among the most consistently good Pomerols. Second wine is Les Pensées de Lafleur.

Château Lafleur du Roy

Pomerol. Owner: Yvon Dubost. 7 acres. 1,700 cases. Grape var: Merlot 80%, Cab.Fr. 10%, Cab.Sauv. 10%.

Little property on the outskirts of Libourne, near Ch. Plince. A minor wine with a good name.

Château Lagrange

Pomerol. Owner: Ets Jean-Pierre Moueix. 20 acres. 4,000 cases. Grape var: Merlot 95%, Cab.Fr. 5%.

Another Moueix property in the Pétrus group on the plateau. Less spectacularly flavoury than some of its neighbours, but has been good recently.

Château Latour à Pomerol

Pomerol. Owner: Mme Lacoste-Loubat. 19 acres. 3,900 cases. Grape var: Merlot 90%, Cab.Fr. 10%.

The property is run by the house of Moueix for one of the family who own a share of Pétrus (and used to run the best restaurant in Libourne). They regard it as their number four Pomerol, with a fuller, fruitier style than La Fleur Pétrus: more fat, less sinew – words can be very misleading. Paradoxically, it is a *graves* wine, from westwards of the fat band of clay.

Château Moulinet

Pomerol. Owner: Société Civile. Dir: Armand Moueix. 45 acres. 10,000 cases. Grape var: Merlot 60%, Cab. Sauv 30%, Cab.Fr. 10%.

An isolated estate on the northern edge of Pomerol where both the soil and the wine are lighter; the wine is stylish notwithstanding. A very good '79.

Château Nenin

Pomerol. Owner: François Despujol. 61 acres. 10,000 cases. Grape var: Merlot 70%, Cab.Fr. 20%, Cab.Sauv. 10%.

One of the biggest properties, lying between the great Châteaux Trotanoy and La Pointe, but raising two cheers rather than three from most critics. On an upsurge, though, since 1985.

Château Petit-Village

Pomerol. Owner: AXA Millésimes. 27 acres. 3,900 cases. Grape var: Merlot 80%, Cab.Sauv. 10%, Cab.Fr. 10%.

Uppermost Pomerol from the Cheval-Blanc zone. Sold in 1989 by the owner of Cos d'Estournel to the insurance group that also bought Ch. Pichon-Baron. A long-respected property with plenty of money behind it.

Château Le Pin

Pomerol. Owner: the Thienpont family. 4.5 acres. 900 cases. Grape var: Merlot 100%.

The Thienponts bought this tiny property on top of the Pomerol plateau next to Certan de May in 1979. Their aim was to make a wine to rival Pétrus. They have achieved superb results, with the '82 being perhaps the top wine of the vintage and recent vintages selling (mainly in Asia) for prices to make you blanch.

Château Plince

Pomerol. Owners: the Moreau family. 20 acres. 3,500 cases. Grape var: Merlot 68%, Cab.Fr. 24%, Cab.Sauv. 8%.

The same owner as at Clos L'Eglise produce a more 'supple', fruity wine on sandier soil.

Château La Pointe

Pomerol. Owner: Bernard d'Arfeuille. 56 acres. 11,500 cases. Grape var: Merlot 75%, Cab.Fr. 25%.

Sister château of La Serre in St-Emilion, and big enough to be widely known. The vineyard is on the doorstep of Libourne, in gravel and sand over the famous iron-bearing clay. Its full potential should be realized by consultant oenologist, Michel Rolland, who started in 1985.

Château Pétrus

Pomerol's First-Growth

As Château Yquem is to Sauternes, so Château Pétrus is to Pomerol; the perfect model of the region and its aspirations. Like its region, Pétrus is a miniature; there are 4,000 cases in a good year, and often less. Among first-growths it is unique in that it has never been officially classified, and that its emergence as a wine worth as much or more than any other red Bordeaux only started in 1945. The Loubat family were the promoters of its quality and status. Since 1961 it has been owned jointly by Madame Loubat's niece, Madame Lacoste, and Jean-Pierre Moueix.

The house of Moueix, directed by Jean-Pierre with his son Christian, holds centre stage in Pomerol. Its modest offices and vast *chais* on the Libourne waterfront have a position of prestige without an exact equivalent anywhere in France. The resident oenologist, Jean-Claude Berrouet, has technical control of a score of the best properties both in St-Emilion and Pomerol.

Pétrus is the flagship. Outwardly it is a modest little place. The *cuvier* is a cramped space between batteries of narrow concrete vats. The *chais*, recently rebuilt, are more spacious, but by no means grand.

The magic lies in the soil. No golf course or wicket is more meticulously tended. When one section of ancient vines (the average age is 40 years) was being replaced I was astonished to see the shallow topsoil bulldozed aside from the whole two-acre patch and the subsoil being carefully graded to an almost imperceptible slope to give a shade more drainage. It was a remarkable opportunity to see how uninviting this famous clay is.

The principle of winemaking at Pétrus is perfect ripeness, then ruthless selection. If the October sun is kind, the Merlot is left to cook in it. It is never picked before lunch, to avoid diluting the juice with dew. The crop is small, the new wine so dark and concentrated that fresh-sawn oak, for all its powerful smell, seems to make no impression on it. At a year old the wine smells of blackcurrant. At two a note of tobacco edges in. But any such exact reference is a misleading simplification. Why Pétrus (or any great wine) commands attention is by its almost architectural sense of structure; of counterpoised weights and matched stresses. How can there be such tannin and yet such tenderness?

Because Pétrus is fat, fleshy, not rigorous and penetrating like a Médoc but dense in texture like a Napa Cabernet, it appears to be 'ready' in ten years or less. Cigar smokers probably should (and anyway do) drink it while it is in full vigour. To my mind it takes longer to become claret. In a sense the great vintages never do.

Clos René

Pomerol. Owner: Pierre Lasserre. 30 acres. 6,000 cases. Grape var: Merlot 70%, Cab.Fr. 20%, Malbec 10%.

Unpretentious and on the unfashionable (western) side of the commune, yet unmistakably serious Pomerol. The style of wine became lusher in the '80s. Very fine wines. Moulinet Lasserre is a second label.

Château Rouget

Pomerol. Owners: the Labruyère family. 39 acres. 6,700 cases. Grape var: Merlot 85%, Cab.Fr. 15%.

I cast envious eyes on Ch. Rouget each time I pass; it has the prettiest situation in Pomerol in a grove of trees leading down to the river Barbanne. Ideas here are conservative: the wine tough by modern standards and needs 7–8 years. Although the recent installation of new stainless steel tanks and considerable modernisation may change this.

Château de Sales

Pomerol. Owner: GFA du Château de Sales – the Lambert family. Dir: Bruno de Lambert. 116 acres. 22,500 cases. Grape var: Merlot 70%, Cab.Fr. 15%, Cab.Sauv. 15%.

The only noble château of Pomerol, remote down long avenues to the northwest, then rather disconcertingly having the railway line running right through the garden. The big vineyard is beautifully run and the wine increasingly well made, yet without the concentration and sheer personality of the great Pomerols. The second labels are Château Chantalouette and du Delias.

Château du Tailhas

Pomerol. Owners: Société Civile P. Nebout & Fils. 26 acres. 5,000 cases. Grape var: Merlot 70%, Cab.Fr. 15%, Cab.Sauv. 15%.

The southernmost Pomerol vineyard, a stone's throw from the edge of the sandy riverside area of St-Emilion. It still has Pomerol's iron-rich clay subsoil, hence its dense, if somewhat rustic, character – which is very popular in Belgium.

Château Taillefer

Pomerol. Owner: Bernard Moueix. 28 acres. 5,800 cases. Grape var: Merlot 70%, Cab.Fr. 30%.

Owned by the Moueix family since 1923 and forms the centre of the Armand Moueix enterprise.

Château Trotanoy

Pomerol. Owner: Ets Jean-Pierre Moueix. 20 acres. 3,000 cases. Grape var: Merlot 90%, Cab.Fr. 10%.

Generally allowed to be the runner-up to Ch. Pétrus, made by the same hands to the same Rolls-Royce standards. The little vineyard is on the western slope (such as it is) of the central plateau. The vines are old, the yield low, the darkly concentrated wine matured in new *barriques* (which lend it a near-Médoc smell in youth). For 10 years or more the best vintages have a thick, almost California-Cabernet texture in your mouth. Tannin and iron show through the velvet glove. The 1982, '79, '76 and '71, '89 and '90 are considered the best recent vintages.

Vieux Château Certan

Pomerol. Owner: Héritiers Georges Thienpont. 33 acres. 5,000 cases. Grape var: Merlot 60%, Cab.Fr. 30%, Cab.Sauv. 10%.

The first great name of Pomerol, though overtaken at a canter by Pétrus in the last 30 or 40 years. The style is quite different; drier and less fleshy but balanced in a Médoc or Graves manner. At early tastings substance can seem to be lacking, to emerge triumphantly later. The 1945 was unforgettable in 1980. The handsome old château lies halfway between Pétrus and Cheval Blanc. Its Belgian owners take intense pride in its unique personality. '85 and '86 are recent triumphs.

Château La Violette

Pomerol. Owner: Vignobles S. Dumas. 11 acres. 2,000 cases. Grape var: Merlot 80%, Cab Fr 20%.

A little neighbour of the big Château Nenin (q.v.), as modest as its name, and not known for consistency.

Château Vray-Croix-de-Gay

Pomerol. Owner: La Baronne Guichard. 9 acres. 1,800 cases. Grape var: Merlot 80%, Cab.Fr. 15%, Cab.Sauv. 5%.

The name means 'the real Croix-de-Gay', implying that the neighbours pinched the name. Jockeying for position seems appropriate here on the northern rim of the precious plateau. Good Pomerol, but I have no record of very notable bottles.

OTHER CHATEAUX

Château Bel-Air Owners: Sudrat & Fils. 32 acres. 6,000 cases.

Château Bonalgue Owner: P Bourotte. 16.5 acres. 2,500 cases.

Château de Bourgueneuf Owner: M. Meyer. 11 acres. 2,400 cases.

Château Le Caillou Owner: L. Giraud. 17 acres. 2,500 cases.

Château Cloquet Owner: M. Vigier. 15 acres. 1,300 cases.

Château La Commanderie Owner: Societé du Château La Commanderie. 14 acres. 3,600 cases.

Château La Croix du Casse Owner: M Arcante. 22 acres. 5,300 cases.

Domaine de l'Eglise Owner: P. Castéja. 17 acres. 3,500 cases.

Château Ferrand Owner: Soc. Civ. du Ch. Ferrand. 27 acres. 5,000 cases.

Château Franc-Mallet Owner: G. Arpin. 13.8 acres. 3,200 cases.

Château de Grange-Neuve Owner: Yves Gros. 17 acres. 3,300 cases.

Château Grate-Cap Owner: A. Janoueix. 23 acres. 5,000 cases.

Château Haut-Maillet Owner: J-P Estager. 12 acres. 2,500 cases.

Château Mazeyres Owner: 45 acres. 9,400 cases.

Clos Mazeyres Owners: Laymarie & Fils. 23 acres. 5,000 cases.

Château La Patache Owner: GFA de la Diligence. 8 acres. 1,000 cases.

LALANDE-DE-POMEROL

The northern boundary of Pomerol is the little River Barbanne. The two communes on its other bank, Lalande and Néac, share the right to the name Lalande-de-Pomerol for red wine which at its best is certainly of junior Pomerol class. Traditionally, they have grown more of the Malbec (or Pressac), a difficult grape which is now going out of fashion. But the gravel-over-clay in parts is good and two châteaux, Bel-Air and Tournefeuille, have high reputations. Altogether there are 2,700 acres of vines; 840 more than Pomerol. Some 210 growers (without a cooperative) make an average total of 600,000 cases. The price is generally a shade higher than for a plain St-Emilion, half as much as Pomerol.

Postcode: 33500 Libourne.

LALANDE-DE-POMEROL CHATEAUX

Château des Annereaux Lalande-de-Pomerol. Owner: MM. Milhade. 44 acres. 9,000 cases.

Château de Bel-Air Lalande-de-Pomerol. Owner: Jean-Pierre Musset. 37 acres. 7,500 cases.

Château Belles Graves Néac. Owner: Hermine Theallet. 34 acres. 7,000 cases.

Château Bertineau St-Vincent. Néac. Owner: M. Rolland. 10 acres. 2,000 cases.

Château La Croix de Bellevue Lalande-de-Pomerol. Owner: Armand Moueix. 19 acres. 4,000 cases.

Château La Croix St André Néac. Owner: M. Carayon. 40 acres. 8,300 cases.

Château La Fleur St-Georges. Néac. 41 acres. 8,300 cases.

Château Grand Ormeau. Lalande-de-Pomerol. Owner: Jean-Claude Beton. 28 acres. 6,300 cases.

Château Haut-Chaigneau Lalande-de-Pomerol. Owner: M. & Mme. André Chatonnet. 51 acres. 10,000 cases.

Château Les Hauts-Conseillants Lalande-de-Pomerol. Owner: Pierre Bourotte. 22 acres. 4,500 cases.

Château des Moines Owner: M W Darnajou. 41 acres. 7,000 cases.

Clos des Moines Lalande-de-Pomerol. Owner: Jean-Bernard Martin. 37 acres. 9,000 cases.

Château Moncet Néac. Owners: Baron L-G. and E. de Jerphanion. 46 acres. 8,000 cases.

Château Sergant Lalande-de-Pomerol. Owner: Jean Milhade. 44 acres. 8,500 cases.

Château Les Templiers Néac. Owner: Servant-Dumas. 17 acres. 4,000 cases.

Clos des Templiers Lalande-de-Pomerol. Owner: M Meyer. 27 acres. 6,000 cases.

Château Tournefeuille Néac. Owners: the Sautarel family. 39 acres. 8,900 cases.

BORDEAUX'S MINOR REGIONS

The vast extent of the Gironde vineyards begins to sink in when you look at the number and size of growers' cooperative cellars dotted over the *département*. Most of the areas covered by this section are cooperative-dominated. Most communes have one or two well-established châteaux – old manor houses, whose wine has long been made in the manner of a not-very-ambitious family business.

In many cases the small grower has sold his vineyard to the bigger grower as an alternative to joining the coop. A number of well-run larger châteaux are thereby adding to their acreage, revising their methods and starting to specialize in either red or white instead of dabbling in both. Several now offer a proportion of their best vats as a top

cuvée – aged in oak and at a higher price than their basic wine. In some cases they have switched from third-rate sweet wines to second-rate (occasionally even first-rate) dry ones. Unquestionably a new understanding of winemaking techniques, coupled with a far more enterprising, diligent and demanding generation of wine-buyers and -drinkers, is transforming the outlying regions of Bordeaux, as it is the whole of southwest France and even the Midi.

They cover a wide spectrum of styles and qualities, which are discussed in the head-note to each area. In each area I list the châteaux, their proprietors and production, which I have tasted or which have been recommended to me by local brokers and friends.

FRONSAC AND CANON-FRONSAC

The town of Libourne lies on the Dordogne at the mouth of its little northern tributary, the Isle. It has Pomerol as its back garden, St-Emilion as its eastern neighbour, and only a mile to the west another, surprisingly different, little wine area.

Fronsac is a village on the Dordogne at the foot of a jumble of steep bumps and hollows, a miniature range of hills (up to 300 feet) where vines and woods make pictures as pretty as any in Bordeaux. Several of the châteaux were obviously built as country villas rather than as plain farms. Under it all there is limestone. The vines are nearly all red, the usual Bordeaux varieties, traditionally

with more stress on the soft and juicy Malbec than elsewhere. Having plenty of colour and alcohol, Fronsac wine has been much used in the past as *vin médecin* for weaklings from more famous places.

Historically Fronsac took precedence over Pomerol. During the 18th century its wines were even drunk at court. But circumstances gave Pomerol the advantage it has so profitably exploited, and it is only over the past 20 years that Fronsac has begun to climb back – and only in the past 10 years that real investment has been able to change its image.

Now the Libourne house of J. P. Moueix owns three châteaux and offers excellent generic Fronsac, while the important and well-publicized estate of Ch. La Rivière offers large quantities of good wine.

There are 2,800 acres of vineyards. Over two-thirds of the hills (the lower parts) are AOC Fronsac; the rest, where the soil is thinner with more lime, is AOC Canon-Fronsac. Its wines can be delectable, full of vigour and spice, hard enough to resemble Graves or St-Emilion more than Pomerol, and worth a good five years' ageing. Postcode 33126 Fronsac.

CANON-FRONSAC CHATEAUX

Château Canon Canon-Fronsac. Owner: Christian Moueix. 3 acres. 700 cases.

Château Canon-de-Brem Canon-Fronsac. Owner: Ets J.-P. Moueix. 10 acres. 2,400 cases.

Château Canon-Moueix Canon-Fronsac. Owner: Ets J. P. Moueix. 10 acres. 2,000 cases.

Château Cassagne-Haut-Canon St-Michel de Fronsac. Owner: Jean-Jacques Dubois. 32 acres. 6,500 cases.

Château Charlemagne Canon-Fronsac. Owner: J.-P Moueix (previously Château Bodet). 34 acres. 5,000 cases.

Château Coustolle Fronsac. Owner: Alain Roux. 49 acres. 10,000 cases.

Château Dalem Saillans, Fronsac. Owner: Michel Rullier. 36 acres. 7,500 cases.

Château Junayme Fronsac. Owner: Héritiers de Coninck. 38 acres. 10,000 cases.

Château Mausse St-Michel-de-Fronsac. Owner: Guy Janoueix. 25 acres. 5,000 cases.

Château Mazeris St-Michel-de-Fronsac. Owner: M. de Cournuaud. 37 acres. 7,500 cases.

Château Mazeris-Bellevue St-Michel-de-Fronsac. Owner: Jacques Bussier. 27 acres. 5,000 cases.

Château Moulin-Pey-Labrie Fronsac. Owner: M. Hubau 16 acres. 2,600 cases.

Château Toumalin Fronsac. Owner: M. d'Arfeuille. 19 acres. 4,000 cases.

Château Les Trois Croix Canon-Fronsac. Owners: the Leon family. 34 acres. 8,000 cases

Château La Valade Canon Fronsac. Owner: Bernard Roux. 38 acres. 9,000 cases.

Château La Vieille Cure Saillons. 44 acres. 8,900 cases.

Château Vray-Canon-Boyer St-Michel-de-Fronsac. Owner: R. de Coninck (Horeau-Beylaut). 20 acres. 2,200 cases.

FRONSAC CHATEAUX

Château de Carles Saillans, Fronsac. Owner: Antoine Chastenet de Castaing. 49 acres. 5,800 cases.

Château de La Dauphine Fronsac. Owner: Ets J.-P. Moueix. 20 acres. 4,000 cases.

Château Fontenil Saillans. Owner: Michel Rolland. 17 acres. 3,500 cases.

Château Mayne-Vieil Galgon, Fronsac. Owners: the Sèze family. 64 acres. 16,000 cases.

Château Moulin Haut-Laroque and Chateau Cardeneau Saillans. Owner: Jean Noël Hervé. 37 acres. 6,700 cases.

Château La Rivière La Rivière, Fronsac. Owner: Jean Leprince. 107 acres. 22,000 cases.

Château Villars Saillans, Fronsac. Owner: J. C. Gaudrie. 61 acres. 11,500 cases.

COTES DE CASTILLON AND COTES DE FRANCS

Two areas adjoining the St-Emilion satellites to the east, still within the general appellation area of Bordeaux, were granted their own independent *appellations d'origine contrôlée* in 1989. The larger is the Côtes de Castillon in the hills to the north of the Dordogne valley overlooking Castillon-la-Bataille, where the French defeated the English forces in 1452 and ended English rule in Aquitaine. Ten communes are affected, with a total of some 6,910 acres of vines.

To its north, the Côtes de Francs is about one quarter of its size, taking in parts of the communes of Francs, Les Salles, St-Cibard and Tayac; tranquil and remote country long known as a good producer of Bordeaux Supérieur, but only now recognized on its distinctive merits.

Côtes de Castillon and Côtes de Francs wines in general are like lightweight St-Emilions. But they should not be dismissed out of hand. Several châteaux are beginning to show real ambition and are making wine to mature five years or more.

COTES DE CASTILLON CHATEAUX

Château de Belcier Les Salles. Owner: MACIF. 128 acres. 32,000 cases.

Château Beauséjour. St-Magne-de-Castillon Owner: MM. Verger. 51 acres. 13,000 cases.

Château La Clavière-Laithwaite Owner: Tony Laithwaite.

Château Cap de Faugères Ste-Colombe. Owner: M Guisez. 62 acres. 14,500 cases.

Château Fonds Ronds St-Genes-de-Castillon. Owner: Fomperier. 5 acres. 1,300 cases.

Château Haut Tuquet St-Magne-de-Castillon. Owner: Lafaye. 41 acres. 10,000 cases.

Château Lartigue Belvès-de-Castillon. Owner: Veuve Larroque. 25 acres. 3,500 cases.

Château Moulin Rouge St-Magne-de-Castillon. Owner: M. Bassilieaux. 96 acres. 22,000 cases.

Château de Pitray Gardegan. Owner: Mme la Comtesse Pierre-Edouard de Boigne. 74 acres. 16,700 cases.

Château Robin Belvès-de-Castillon. Owner: Sté Lurkcroft. 31 acres. 5,300 cases.

Château Rocher-Bellevue St-Magne-de-Castillon. Owner: Rocher Cap de Rive. 35 acres. 9,400 cases.

COTES DE FRANCS CHATEAUX

Château Les Charmes-Godard Francs. Owners: the Thienpont family. 9 acres. 2,200 cases.

Château de Francs Francs. 61 acres. 10,300 cases.

Château Laclaverie St-Cibard. Owner: Nicolas Thienpont. 22 acres. 5,000 cases.

Château La Prade St-Cibard. Owner: Patrick Valette. 11 acres. 2,800 cases.

Château Puygueraud St-Cibard. Owners: the Thienpont family. 54 acres. 13,000 cases.

COTES DE BOURG

The right bank of the Gironde was a thriving vineyard long before the Médoc across the water was planted. Bourg, lying to the north of the Dordogne where it joins the Garonne (the two form the Gironde), is like another and bigger Fronsac: hills rising steeply from the water to 200 feet or more, but unlike the hills of Fronsac almost solidly vine covered.

The Côtes de Bourg makes as much wine as the lower Médoc – and so does its immediate neighbour to the north, the Côtes de Blaye. Bourg specializes in red wine of a very respectable standard, made largely of Merlot and Cabernet Franc, round and full-bodied and ready to drink at four or five years – but certainly not in a hurry. The châteaux that line the river bank have to all appearances a perfect situation. Farther back from the water is largely cooperative country with an increasing proportion of white wine of no special note.

Postcode: 33710 Bourg sur Gironde.

COTES DE BOURG CHATEAUX

Château de Barbe Villeneuve. Owners: the Richard family. 158 acres. 38,000 cases.

Château La Barde Tauriac. Owner: Alain Darricarrère. 38 acres. 6,600 cases.

Château du Bousquet Bourg. Owner: Castel Frères. 153 acres. 36,000 cases.

Château Brûlesécaille Tauriac. Owners: Jacques and Martine Rodet. 48 acres. 10,000 cases.

Château La Croix Millorit Bayon. Owner: M. Jaubert. 54 acres. 10,000 cases.

Château Falfas Bayon. Owner: Riveaux Beychade. 41 acres. 9,500 cases.

Château Guerry Tauriac. Owner: de Rivoyre. 53 acres. 13,000 cases.

Château Grand-Jour Prignac-et-Marcamps. Owner: SC Grand Jour. 98 acres. 25,000 cases red.

Château de La Grave Bourg. Owner: Robert Bassereau. 99 acres. 21,000 cases red.

Château Guionne and Château Beauguérit Lansac. Owner: Richard Porcher. 43 acres. 14,000 cases.

Château Haut Macô Tauriac. Owners: Bernard and Jean Mallet. 91 acres. 20,000 cases.

Château Lalibarde Bourg. Owner: Roland Dumas. 84 acres. 22,000 cases red.

Château de Mendoce Villeneuve. Owner: Philippe Darricarrère. 34 acres. 6,000 cases.

Château Mercier St-Trojan. Owner: M. Chety. 53 acres. 12,800 cases.

Château le Roc des Cambes Bourg. Owner: M. Mitjaville. 23 acres. 4,700 cases.

Château Tayac Bayon. Owner: Pierre Saturny. 72 acres. 16,000 cases.

Cave de Tauriac 1,110 acres. 27,700 cases.

Château Les Tours Séguy St-Ciers. Owner: Mme Beylot. 27 acres. 7,000 cases.

PREMIERES COTES DE BLAYE

Two miles of water, the widening Gironde, separates Blaye from the heart of the Médoc. Blaye is the northernmost vineyard of the 'right bank'; the last place, going up this coast, where good red wine is made. North of this is white-wine country; the fringes of Cognac. Blaye already makes about one third white wine, a rather nondescript, full-bodied, sometimes semi-sweet style which no doubt could be improved.

Premières Côtes de Blaye is the appellation reserved for the better vineyards, nearly all red, whose wine is to all intents like that of Bourg – although generally considered not quite as good or full-bodied. Cooperatives handle about two-thirds of production. Nonetheless the following châteaux are worth noting.

Postcode: 33390 Blaye.

PREMIERES COTES DE BLAYE CHATEAUX

Château Barbé Cars. Owner: Xavier Carreau. 74 acres. 15,000 cases red, 3,500 cases white.

Châteaux Bertinerie, Cubnezais, and Chateau Haut Bertinerie Owner: GFA Bantegnies. 108 acres. 19,000 cases red, 7,000 cases white.

Château Chante Alouette Plassac. Owner: Georges Lorteaud. 59 acres. 13,000 cases.

Château Charron St-Martin-Lacaussade. Owner: Vignobles Germain. 62 acres. 13,000 cases red and 2,500 cases white.

Château L'Escadre Cars. Owners: Georges Carreau & Fils. 79 acres. 13,000 cases.

Château La Graulet and Château Grand Barrail Cars. Owner: Denis Lafon

Château Haut Sociondo. Cars. Owner: Filles Martinaud. 39 acres. 10,000 cases.

Château Les Jonqueyres. St-Paul. Owner: Pascal Montaut. 19 acres. 3,900 cases.

Château Le Menaudat St-Androny. Owner: Mme. Edouard Cruse. 37 acres. 10,000 cases.

Château Mondésir Gazin Plassac. Owner: M Plasquet. 27 acres. 6,000 cases.

Château Perenne St-Genés-de-Blaye. 145 acres. 38,000 cases. A good wine.

Château Peyraud Cars. Owner: Guy Rey. 19 acres. 5,000 cases.

Château La Rivalerie St-Paul-de-Blaye. Owner: M. Gillibert. (Reg. Mme Bernabé.) 82 acres. 17,000 cases red, 850 white.

Château Segonzac St-Genés. Owner: Marmet-Champion. 74 acres. 20,000 cases.

Château La Tonnelle. Blaye. Owner: M. Rouchi. 46 acres. 13,000 cases.

Châteaux Virou and La Croix du Montil St-Girons. Owner: Mme François Monier. 153 acres. 41,000 cases red.

PREMIERES COTES DE BORDEAUX

A long, narrow strip of the east bank of the Garonne facing Graves enjoys the doubtful prestige of this appellation. Its hinterland is Entre-Deux-Mers. At their northern end they were some of Bordeaux's Roman and medieval vineyards – now buried under houses. At their southern end, at Cadillac and into Ste-Croix-du-Mont, they are known for sweet wines, at their best up to Sauternes standards.

Along the way the mix is about two thirds red and one third white, the white recently made much drier and fresher than formerly. (Château Reynon is perhaps the best example.) Red Premières Côtes is potentially much better than plain Bordeaux Supérieur from less well-placed vineyards. and this is beginning to be recognized. Lack of incentive is a real problem. Nonetheless there are those who do, and some very grand and prosperous names appear among the owners who are improving this area.

A notable pioneer in the region is Peter Sichel, who has a New World-style winery at Verdelais where he vinifies the grapes he buys in the district to make very fruity and attractive claret for drinking young. Oddly, the practice of buying grapes, common elsewhere, is almost unknown in Bordeaux except in the cooperative, profit-sharing system.

LEADING CHATEAUX OF THE PREMIERES COTES

Château Birot Béguey. Owner: Jacques Boireau. 84 acres. 5,000 cases red, 15,000 white.

Château de Bouteilley Yvrac. Owner: Jean Guillot. 50 acres.

Château Brethous Camblanes. Owner: François Verdier. 32 acres. 7,000 cases red.

Château Cayla Rions. Owner: Patrick Doche. 35 acres. 6,700 cases.

Château Carsin. Rions. Owner: Juan Berglund. 86 acres. 5,500 cases red, 11,500 cases white.

Château Duplessy Cénac. Owner: SC Ch. Duplessy. 29 acres. 6,000 cases.

Château Fayau. Cadillac. Owner: Jean Médeville. 88 acres. 12,000 cases red, 4,000 white. Perhaps the outstanding property.

Château du Grand Moueys Capian. Owner: SCA du Ch Grand Moueys. 175 acres. 30,000 cases red, 10,000 white.

Chateau de Haux Haux. Owner: MM. Jorgensen. 71 acres. 13,000 cases red, 4,500 cases white.

Château du Juge Haux. Owner: Jean Médeville. 69 acres. 9,000 cases red, 3,300 white.

Château Lafitte-Mengin Camblanes. 49 acres. 11,500 cases red.

Château Le Gardéra (red) and Château Tanesse (red+white) Langoiran. Owner: Ets. Cordier. 185 acres. 33,000 cases red, 12,000 white.

Chateau Lagarosse Tabanac. Owner: G. Laurencin. 76 acres. 16,000 cases red, 2,200 cases white.

Château Lamothe de Haux Haux. Owner: Fabrice Néel. 98 acres. 21,000 cases red, 11,000 white.

Château Laroche Baurech. Owner: Julien Palau. 50 acres. 8,000 cases red, 1,000 white.

Chateau Lezongars. Villenave de Rions. Owner: SC Chateau Lezongars. 111 acres. 21,000 cases.

Chateau de Marsan Lestiac sur Garonne. Owner: Paul Gonfirer. 155 acres. 26,000 cases red, 75,000 cases white.

Chateau Montjouan Bouliac. Owner: Mme Le Barazer. 17 acres. 4,400 cases.

Château du Peyrat Capian. Owner: Société Civile. 240 acres. 44,000 cases red, 17,000 white.

Chateau de Pic Le Tourne. Owner: Francois Masson Regnault. 75 acres. 18,000 cases.

Chateau Plaisance. Capian. Owner: M. Bayle. 59 acres. 12,000 cases.

Chateau Plassan Tabanac. 86 acres. 9,000 cases red, 6,000 cases white.

Chateau Puy Bardens. Cambes. Owner: Lamiable. 41 acres. 10,000 cases.

Château Reynon Béguey. Owners: Denis and Pierre Dubourdieu-David. 86 acres. 9,500 cases red and 11,000 cases excellent white.

ENTRE-DEUX-MERS

The two 'seas' in question are the rivers Dordogne and Garonne, whose converging courses more or less define the limits of this big wedge-shaped region; the most diffuse and territorially the most important (with 74,000 acres under vines in 125 communes) in Bordeaux. Three-quarters of production is red, sold as Bordeaux or Bordeaux Supérieur. The appellation Entre-Deux-Mers is now reserved for dry white wine only.

The south of the region is relaxed patchwork countryside with as much woodland and pasture as vineyard. The north is almost a monoculture of the vine. Its biggest cooperative, at Rauzan, makes 1.4 million cases a year. The cooperatives make a third of the production of Bordeaux dry white.

Entre-Deux-Mers is the one wine Bordeaux has succeeded in redesigning in modern marketing terms. The region was bogged down with cheap sweet wine nobody wanted any more. Some bright spark thought of the catch-phrase '*Entre deux huitres, Entre-Deux-Mers*' ('Between two oysters,' etc...) and a rosy future opened up for dry white: the Muscadet of the southwest.

I have yet to taste an Entre-Deux-Mers of the sort of quality that would win medals in California – but the world needs its staples too. It varies from the briskly appetizing to the thoroughly boring, but in ways that are hard to predict. A good cooperative is just as likely to produce a clean and bracing example as a property with a long name. A handful of private growers like Francis Courselle of Thieuley and Jean-Louis Despagne of La Tour Mirambeau sets a standard that others emulate. La Gamage has been a consistently good cooperative wine, as have merchant brands like Dourthe No1.

Within the appellation an area limited to the southern communes with theoretically superior wine can use the appellation 'Haut-Benauge' in addition to 'Entre-Deux-Mers' or 'Bordeaux'.

ENTRE-DEUX-MERS CHATEAUX

Château Bauduc Créon. Owner: David Thomas. 50 acres. 7,500 red. 7,000 white.

Château Bel Air Perponcher Naujan et Postiac. Owner: J-L Despagne. 80 acres. 10,000 cases red, 11,000 cases white.

Château la Blanquerie Merignac. Owner: M. Rougier. 76 acres. 15,000 cases red, 5,500 white. Good organic wines.

Château Bonnet Grézillac. Owner: André Lurton. 280 acres. 44,000 cases red and 26,000 cases white.

Château de Camarsac Camarsac. Owner: Lucien Lurton. 148 acres. 33,000 cases.

Domaine Challon Baigneaux. Owner: Mme Dubois Challon. 29 acres. 5,500 cases oak fermented white.

Domaine de Courteillac Ruch. Owner: S Asséo. 41 acres. 6,000 cases red.

Château Fonchereau Montussan. Owner: Mme Georges Vinot-Postry. 69 acres. 15,000 cases red.

Château La France Beychac-et-Caillau. Owner: France Assurances. 148 acres. 35,000 cases red, 7,000 white.

Château Grand Monteil Salleboeuf. Owners: the Techenet family. 280 acres. 65,000 cases red, 8,500 cases white.

Château Guibon Daignac. Owner: André Lurton. 74 acres. 11,000 cases white.

Château Launay Soussac. Owner: M. Greffier. 150 acres. 10,000 cases red, 25,000 cases white.

Château Marjosse Tizac de Curton. Owner: Pierre Lurton. 14 acres. 3,200 cases.

Château Martinon Gornac. Owner: M. Trolliet. 108 acres. 10,000 cases red, 15,000 white.

Château Queyret-Pouillac Sainte Antoine de Queyret. Owner: M. Charland. 150 acres. 27,000 cases red, 8,000 cases white.

Château Raymond & Ch. Ramonet Owner: de Montesquieu. 28,000 cases red, 5,000 white.

Château Reynier Grézillac. Owner: Dominique Lurton. 185 acres. 35,000 cases red and 9,000 cases white.

Château Thieuley La Sauve. Owner: Francis Courselle. 115 acres. 4,500 cases red, 20,000 cases white. The outstanding producer of the region.

Château Tour de Mirambeau Naujan et Postiac. Owner: J-L Despagne. 270 acres. 19,000 cases red, 54,000 cases white.

Château de Toutigeac Targon. Owner: René Mazeau. 370 acres. 70,000 cases.

STE-CROIX-DU-MONT AND LOUPIAC

The southern end of the Premières Côtes de Bordeaux faces Barsac and Sauternes across the Garonne. From Cadillac southwards the speciality is sweet white wine, growing more 'liquorous' the nearer it gets to Sauternes. Ste-Croix-du-Mont gazes across at the hills of Sauternes from its higher river bank and often shares the same autumnal conditions that lead to noble rot and sticky wines. Without quite the same perfection of soil or pride of tradition it cannot afford the enormous investment in labour needed to make the greatest wines, but it succeeds remarkably often in producing wine at least as good as run-of-the-mill Sauternes, and often better.

To my surprise, I have been given Ste-Croix-du-Mont in the German Palatinate by a grower famous for his Beerenausleses, who told me he thought it compared well with his wines. (I must admit the Riesling said more to me.)

The only differences in the regulations between Sauternes and these right-bank wines is the quantity allowed. The same grapes and alcohol content are required but the grower is allowed 40 hl/ha as against only 25 for Sauternes. This is not to say that perfectionist growers make their full quota. They also make dry wines of potentially fine quality and a little light red sold as Bordeaux. There are 1,170 acres of vines with 100 growers making about 180,000 cases a year. It sells for a mere half of the Sauternes price.

Loupiac is not quite so well placed and makes slightly less liquorous wines on 915 acres. About 70 properties make Loupiac, though only 50 bottle their own production (66,000 cases or double that in a good year). Growers make dry white and red too. Postcode: 33410 Cadillac.

STE-CROIX-DU-MONT CHATEAUX

Château Lagrave Owner: M. Tinon. 4,000 cases white.

Château Loubens Owner: M. de Sèze. 3,000 cases white.

Château des Mailles Owner: Daniel Larrieu-Derrieu. 37 acres. 3,300 cases white.

Domaine de Morange Château L'Oustau-Vieil. Owner: M. Sessacq. 4,500 cases white.

Château La Rame Owner: F. Armand. 5,000 cases white.

LOUPIAC CHATEAUX

Château du Cros Owner: Michel Boyer. 2,500 to 6,000 cases white.

Clos Jean Owner: Lionel Bord. 8,000 cases white.

Château Loupiac-Gaudet Owner: Marc Ducau. up to 8,300 cases white.

Château de Ricaud Owner: Alain Thienot. 2,500 cases white plus a good red.

GRAVES DE VAYRE AND STE-FOY-BORDEAUX

Within the same block of vineyard two smaller zones have separate appellations defined with Gallic precision, one on the basis of its soil and potential for something out of the rut, the other, I suspect, for political reasons.

Graves de Vayres, across the river from Libourne, has more gravel than its surroundings. Unfortunately its name invites comparison with Graves, which it cannot sustain. The whites are made sweeter than Entre-Deux-Mers. The quickly maturing reds have been compared in a charitable moment to minor Pomerols.

The other appellation, Ste-Foy-Bordeaux, looks like a natural part of the Bergerac region cobbled on to Bordeaux. Its wines are not notably different from the wines of Bergerac, and its history is identical. For centuries the Dutch came for the two commodities most in demand in the Low Countries and the Baltic: sweet wine and wine for distilling.

COTES-DE-BORDEAUX-ST-MACAIRE

Ten villages beyond Ste-Croix-du-Mont rejoice in this appellation for their 45,000 cases of semi-sweet wine, a trickle of which finds its way to Belgium. Red sold as Bordeaux or Bordeaux Supérieur is much more important. Postcode: 33490 St-Macaire.

CERONS

The appellation Cérons applies to the three Graves villages (Podensac and Illats are the other two) that abut on to Barsac on the north and have a natural tendency to make sweet wines. Their wines are classified according to their natural degree of alcohol as either Graves or Graves Supérieures (at 11 or 12 degrees and naturally dry), or at half a degree more as Cérons, which inclines to be *moëlleux*, the grey area which is sweet but not *liquoreux*. Occasionally it attains *liquoreux* stickiness. All depends on the autumn and the vinification, which used sulphur as its crutch and left much to be desired. Modern methods can mean much cleaner and better wine, as the growing reputations of some of the properties indicate.

Production of Cérons has declined from 166,000 cases in 1970 to about 28,000 in 1996. Only 26 producers make Cérons (many more make Graves or red Bordeaux), but sweet or dry it only fetches a moderate price. France consumes nearly all of it; the only export is a tiny amount to Belgium and Germany. Postcode: 33720 Podensac.

Bordeaux wine prices

In the first edition of this book, individual prices were quoted for the majority of the *crus classés*. These were the amounts asked at the château for the 1980 vintage in the middle of 1982, when that vintage was entering the market. Since 1982, prices of *crus classés* have fluctuated considerably with the health of the world economy as much as with the quality of the vintage. Initial prices were high for the '85, '89 and '95 vintages, low for the '92. This has made sensible price comparison hard. The question is: what price, when, and to whom? Consumers are buying wine *en primeur* to a far greater extent than formerly, and fashionable wines become scarce. Proprietors have been competing to out-do each other. Some châteaux are releasing only enough wine to set a price – only a few *tonneaux* – and holding back much of their stock in the hope that the market will rise. Prices of humble appellations, where quantities and choice are so much larger, are relatively stable. Good wines should, and often can, command a premium. In 1996 Bordeaux rouge might vary between about FF8 and FF22 a bottle, Médoc between FF14 and FF35. As in any market there are bargains and bad buys and wines for different tastes.

All this makes comparison between properties, the intended purpose of the prices in the first edition, still more difficult.

CERONS CHATEAUX

Château d'Archambeau Illats. Owner: J-Philippe Dubourdieu. 5,000 cases red; 8,500 white.
Château de Cérons Cérons. Owner: Jean Perromat. 3,000 cases.
Château de Chantegrive Podensac (*see* Graves).
Grand Enclos du Château de Cérons Cérons. Owner: Olivier Lataste. 1,000 cases Cérons.

BORDEAUX AND BORDEAUX SUPERIEUR

The basic appellations underlying all the more specific and grander names of Bordeaux are available to anyone using the approved grape varieties, achieving a certain degree of alcohol and limiting the harvest to a statutory maximum (which varies from year to year).

The standing definitions for red wines: Bordeaux must have 10 degrees at a maximum of 55 hectolitres a hectare. Bordeaux Supérieur needs 10.5 degrees at a maximum of 40 hectolitres a hectare – hence more concentration and flavour.

For white wines: Bordeaux must have 10.5 degrees at 65 hectolitres a hectare. Bordeaux Supérieur needs 11.5 degrees at 40 hectolitres a hectare.

CUBZAC

The districts that regularly carry the simple appellation, having no other, include St-André-de-Cubzac and the nearby Cubzac-Les-Ponts, and Guitres and Coutras. Cubzac is where the great iron bridge built by Eiffel (of the tower) crosses the Dordogne on the way from Bordeaux to Paris. It lies between the hills of Fronsac and those of Bourg, on flat land which can nonetheless make respectable wine. Postcode: 33240 St-André-de-Cubzac.

CUBZAC CHÂTEAUX

Château Timberlay St-André-de-Cubzac. Owner: R. Giraud. 320 acres. 55,000 cases red, 11,000 cases white.
Château du Bouilh St-André-de-Cubzac. Owner: Patrice Comte de Feuilhade de Chauvin. 118 acres. 22,000 cases.
Château de Terrefort-Quancard Cubzac-Les-Ponts. Owners: the Quancard family. 150 acres. 37,000 cases red.

GUITRES AND COUTRAS

Guitres and Coutras are very much on the fringe, to the north of Cubzac where wine-growing used to be directed towards Cognac. One property in the area uses a typically Pomerol mix with 75% Merlot on clay soil with encouraging results. Postcode: 33230 Coutras.
Château Méaume Maransin. Owner: Alan Johnson-Hill. 70 acres. 15,000 cases red.

BURGUNDY

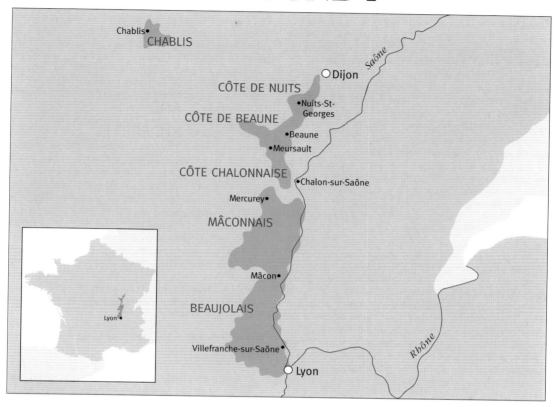

Burgundy has the best-situated shop window in France, if not in Europe. The powerful, the influential, the enterprising and the curious have been filing by for two millennia along the central highway of France, from Paris to Lyon and the south, from the Rhine and the Low Countries to Italy. Every prince, merchant, soldier or scholar has seen the Côte d'Or, rested at Beaune or Dijon, tasted and been told tall tales about the fabulous wine of this narrow, scrubby hillside.

Whether any other hillside could do what the Côte d'Or can is a fascinating speculation – without an answer. What it does is to provide scraps of land and scattered episodes of weather that bring two grape varieties to a perfection not found anywhere else. In certain sites and in certain years only, the Pinot Noir and Chardonnay achieve flavours valued as highly as any flavour on earth.

So specific are the sites and the conditions needed that the odds are stacked quite strongly against them. It is an uncertain way to make a living. So Burgundy has organized itself into a system that makes allowances – for crop failures, for human errors, for frailties of all kinds. Its legislation is a delicate structure that tries to keep the Burgundian one jump ahead of his clients without them tumbling to the fact.

The Burgundy of wine falls into five distinct parts. What is

true of the Côte d'Or is equally true of Chablis, its northern outpost, but much less so of the region of Mercurey and the regions of Mâcon and Beaujolais to the south. The chapters on these areas summarize the local issues and conditions.

There is no simple or straight answer to the conundrum of Burgundy. The essential information is presented here in the form of geographical lists of the vineyards, their appellations and official ranking, and alphabetical lists of selected growers and merchants, showing who owns what and giving some idea of his standing.

THE CLASSIFICATION OF BURGUNDY

Bordeaux has a random series of local classifications of quality. Burgundy has a central system by which every vineyard in the Côte d'Or and Chablis (although not in Beaujolais and the Mâconnais) is precisely ranked by its appellation. Starting at the top, there are some 30 Grands Crus which have their own individual appellations. They do not (except in Chablis) use the names of their communes. They are simply and grandly Le Corton, Le Musigny, Le Montrachet. In the 19th century the villages that were the proud possessors of this land added the Grand Cru name to their own, so that Aloxe became Aloxe-Corton; Chambolle, Chambolle-Musigny; Puligny and Chassagne both added Montrachet to their names. Hence the apparent anomaly that the shorter name in general means the better wine.

In parentheses it must be said that the decisions about which sites are Grands Crus are old and in some cases unfair. They were taken on observations of performance over many years. Their soil is ideal. They are generally the places that suffer least from spring frost, summer hail and autumn rot. But they can be well or badly farmed. There are certainly some of the next rank, Premier Cru, which reach or exceed the level of several Grands Crus. The rank of Premier Cru is given with much deliberation over detail to certain plots of land in the best non-Grand Cru vineyards of all the best communes. For several years a review was in progress that entails nitpicking over minute parcels of vines. It was only finally completed in 1984. The upshot is, for example, that in the Pommard vineyard (or *climat*) of Les Petits Epenots plots 2 to 8 and 13 to 29 are classed as Premier Cru, while plots 9 to 12 are not. I give this instance not to confuse the issue but to show how extremely seriously the authorities take the matter.

The biggest and best Premiers Crus have reputations of their own, particularly in the Côte de Beaune (where Le Corton is the only red Grand Cru). Such vineyards as Volnay Caillerets and Pommard Rugiens can be expected to produce fabulously good wine under good conditions. In such cases the producer proudly uses the name of the vineyard. The law allows the vineyard name to be printed on the label in characters the same size as the commune name. There are smaller Premiers Crus, however, without the means to acquire a great reputation, whose wine is often just sold as, for example Volnay Premier Cru. Often a grower's holdings in some vineyards are so small that he is obliged to mix the grapes of several holdings in order to have a vatful to ferment. This wine will have to settle for an unspecific name.

The Grands Crus and Premiers Crus form an almost unbroken band of vineyards occupying most of the east-facing Côte d'Or slope, perfectly exposed to the morning sun. The villages with their evocative names – Gevrey-Chambertin, Aloxe-Corton, Pommard – generally sit at the foot of the slope, encompassing in their parish boundaries both the best (upper) land and some, less good or even distinctly inferior, either on the flat at the bottom or in angles of the hills that face the 'wrong' way. This also is classed. The best of it, but not up to Premier Cru standard, is entitled to use the name of the village and the vineyard. In practice not many vineyards below Premier Cru rank are cited on labels. The law in this case demands that a vineyard name be printed in characters only half the size of the commune name. The *appellation contrôlée* here applies to the village name, not the vineyard. In the descriptions of properties that follow, I refer to these as 'Village' wines.

Inferior land within a village is not even allowed the village name. It falls under the rubric of *appellations régionales*: the most specific name it can have is Bourgogne (when it is made from the classic grapes, red and white, of the region), Bourgogne Passe-tout-grain, Bourgogne Aligoté or Bourgogne Grand Ordinaire. These terms are explained on page 96.

Grapes and Wine

Burgundy is easier wine to taste than Bordeaux, but harder to judge and understand. The Pinot Noir, which gives all the good reds of the Côte d'Or, has a singular and memorable smell and taste, sometimes described as 'peppermint', sometimes as 'floral' or 'fleshy'; certainly beyond the reach of my vocabulary.

Singular as it is, it varies in 'pitch' more than most grapes from one site to another and one vintage to another. In unripe years it smells mean, pinched and watery (German red wines give a good idea of the effect). At the other extreme it roasts to a raisiny character (many California Pinot Noirs are out of key in this way).

The ideal young red burgundy has the ripe-grape smell with neither of these defects, recognizably but lightly overlain with the smell of oak. And it tastes very much as it smells; a little too astringent for total pleasure but with none of the wither-wringing, impenetrable tannin of a great young Bordeaux. Good burgundy tastes good from birth.

The object of keeping it in barrels is to add the flavour of oak and some tannin and to allow the wine to stabilize naturally. The object of maturing it in bottle is to achieve softness of texture and a complex alliance of flavours that arise from the grape, yet seem to have little to do with it. Fine old red burgundy arrives at an intense, regal red with a note of orange (the decorator's 'burgundy' is that of young wine). It caresses the mouth with a velvet touch which loses nothing of vigour by being soft. And it smells and tastes of a moment of spring or autumn just beyond the grasp of your memory.

Strange to say, white burgundy can have a distinct resemblance to red – not exactly in smell or taste but in its texture and 'weight' and the way that it evolves.

Chardonnay wine is not markedly perfumed when it is new: just brisk and, if anything, appley. The traditional burgundy method of fermenting it in small barrels adds the smell of oak immediately. Thereafter, the way it develops in barrel and bottle depends very much on which district it comes from, and on the acid/alcohol ratio of the particular vintage. An ideally balanced vintage such as 1989, '90 or '92 keeps a tension between the increasingly rich flavours of maturity and a central steeliness, year after year. A sharp, barely ripe vintage such as '87 or '93 leans too far towards the steel – and not very springy steel at that. A very ripe vintage such as '76 produced many wines that were too fat and lacked 'cut'. All in all, however, the success rate of white burgundy vintages is very much higher than that of red.

How Burgundy is Made

Red burgundy is normally made in an open-topped cylindrical wooden *cuve* filled to about two-thirds of its capacity with grapes crushed in a mill (*fouloir/égrappoir*) which removes some or all of the stalks. Every grower has his own theory of how much or little of the stems should be included, depending on the ripeness of the grapes (and of their stalks), the colour and concentration of the vintage, and whether he wants to make a tannic *vin de garde* or a softer wine to mature more quickly. Ultra-conservative growers still tend to include all the stalks. Among the arguments in favour are that it makes the pressing easier – to the contrary that it robs the wine of colour and can add bitter tannin. Avant-garde growers today often use 'cold maceration' – keeping the skins in the juice at a low temperature that prevents fermentation for a few days to encourage fruity flavours.

To start the pulpy mass fermenting it is sometimes necessary to add a measure of actively fermenting wine from another vat, with a teeming yeast population – known as a *pied de cuve*. In cold weather it may also be necessary to break up the cap and redistribute it evenly across the vat. The ancient way to get things moving was for all (male) hands to strip naked and jump in, lending their body heat to encourage the yeast. In an account of the Côte d'Or in 1862 by Agoston Haraszthy, reporting to the government of California, 'Five days is generally sufficient for the fermenting of wine in this part, unless it is cold weather, when the overseer sends his men in a couple of times more in their costume *à l'Adam* to create the necessary warmth.' He adds that 'This, in my eyes, rather dirty procedure could be avoided by throwing in heated stones or using pipes filled with steam or hot water.' And indeed it is. Pinot Noir needs a warm fermentation to extract all the colour and flavour from the skins.

The operation of *pigeage*, or mixing the floating cap of skins with the fermenting juice, is still sometimes performed in small cellars by the vigneron or his sons, scrupulously hosed down, in bathing shorts, but more up-to-date establishments either pump the juice from the bottom of the vat over the '*chapeau*' ('*remontage*') or use a grille which prevents the cap from floating to the top ('*chapeau immergé*'). I am told by practitioners that it is the positively physical rubbing of the '*marc*' by *pigeage* that is important. It liberates elements that *remontage* or *chapeau immergé* cannot possibly obtain.

Individual ideas on the right duration of this '*macération*' of the skins in the *cuve* vary from a very few days to up to almost three weeks, by those who are determined to get deep-dyed wine with maximum 'extract' – hence flavour. The 'free-run' wine is then drawn off and the *marc* pressed in presses of every shape and form. The wine of the first pressing is usually added to the free-run juice and the ensemble filled into barrels, old or new according to the means and motives of the proprietor, to settle down and undergo its quiet secondary, malolactic, fermentation as soon as may be. The malolactic fermentation is often encouraged by raising the temperature of the cellar. Once they have finished this infantile fretting they are moved ('racked bright') into clean barrels.

Fine red burgundies are usually kept in barrel for up to two years – not quite as long as the best Bordeaux. Unlike Bordeaux, they are racked from one barrel to another as little as possible to avoid contact with the air. They are simply topped up and left alone until it is time for bottling. Two months before bottling they may need to be 'fined' to remove the very faintest haze. Some cellars use filters to clarify the wine, but other producers avoid this.

Making White Burgundy

The procedure for making all dry white wines, white burgundy included, is virtually standardized today (see pages 32–33). The object is maximum freshness, achieved by minimum contact with the air. Careful, clean and cool handling of the grapes is followed by a quick pressing and slow, cool fermentation.

In big modern plants in Chablis, and the best of the big cooperative cellars of the Mâconnais, this clinical procedure is carried out and the flavours of the resulting wines owe everything to grape and soil. Chablis, having more acidity and a more distinctive flavour, can benefit from maturing in a steel or concrete vat and then in bottle for a considerable time. The simpler, rounder taste of Mâcon wines has little to gain by keeping.

But the classic white burgundies of the Côte d'Or are another matter. They are fermented in small oak barrels, filled to allow a little airspace on top. The finest and most concentrated wines are given new barrels for at least half of the crop every year. The pungent, almost acrid smell of new oak is part of the personality of the wine from the start.

The majority of growers, those with good but not the finest land, settle for barrels that have been used several times before, perhaps replacing a few each year. In this case the oak has less of the obvious carpenter's-shop effect on the wine; the barrel is simply the ideal size and shape of container for maintaining fermentation at an even, low temperature, cooled by the humid ambience of the cellar. A greater volume of wine would generate too much heat as fermentation progresses.

Fermentation over, the wine stays in the barrel, on its yeasty sediment, until it becomes clear, which may take a good six months. It is then racked into clean barrels and kept until the maker judges it is ripe for bottling. What he is doing is allowing a gentle and controlled oxidation of the wine to introduce nuances and breadth of flavour that would otherwise not develop. It is then ready for drinking – unless the buyer wants to continue the ageing process in the bottle. To me the possibility of this 'reductive' ageing is the whole point of buying the great white burgundies. No other white wines reward patience so well.

Adding Sugar

It is regular practice in Burgundy, as it is in most of France, to add sugar to the must, the unfermented grape juice. The long experience of growers has shown that slightly more than the natural degree of sugar produces a better fermentation and a more satisfactory final wine. It is not purely the extra one or two degrees of alcohol but the evolution and final balance of the wine that is affected (they say).

All 'chaptalization' is strictly controlled by law. Until 1979 there was a statutory allowance for each Burgundy appellation. Since 1979, each year has been treated *ad hoc*, the minimum natural degree and the maximum degree after chaptalization being decided in view of the vintage as a whole. Nobody in any appellation may add more than 2 degrees alcohol to any wine by adding sugar. (There is a temptation to add the maximum: sugar not only increases the total volume of wine, it makes it easier to sell. The extra alcohol makes it taste more impressive and 'flattering' in its youth when buyers come to the cellar to taste.)

In 1987 the regulations in Burgundy stipulated that to use the humblest appellation for red wine, Bourgogne, the wine must have a natural alcoholic degree of 10. The maximum degree allowable, after chaptalization, was 13 degrees. So a 10-degree wine was permitted to be raised to 12 degrees, 10.5 to 12.5, and 11 and upwards to 13.

The equivalent figures for white wine are always 0.5 degree higher: e.g. Bourgogne Blanc must be naturally 10.5 degrees and may be pushed up to 13.5 degrees.

As the dignity of the appellation increases, so does the degree. The minimum and maximum figures set for 1988 in higher appellations were as follows:

Appellation communale or 'Village'; e.g. Aloxe-Corton:				
red	minimum	10.5°	maximum	13.5°
white	minimum	11°	maximum	14°
Premier Cru, e.g. Aloxe-Corton Les Fournières:				
red	minimum	11°	maximum	14°
white	minimum	11.5°	maximum	14.5°
Grand Cru, e.g. Corton:				
red	minimum	11.5°	maximum	14.5°
white	minimum	12°	maximum	14.5°

The best producers, using their judgement, usually chaptalize between 0.5 and 1.5 degrees – rarely to the maximum, but rarely not at all (except for white wines, which in good vintages often reach 13° naturally).

General Appellations

There are four appellations that are available to growers in the whole of Burgundy with certain provisos:

Bourgogne

Red, white or rosé wines. The whites must be Chardonnay and/or Pinot Blanc. The reds must be Pinot Noir, Pinot Liebault or Pinot Beurot, except in the Yonne, where the César and the Tressot are traditional and are admitted, and the *crus* of Beaujolais, whose Gamay may be sold as 'Bourgogne'. No other Beaujolais wine or other Gamay is allowed.

The maximum crop is 55 hectolitres per hectare for red and rosé, 60 for white. Minimum strength: 10 degrees for red and rosé, 10.5 degrees for white. It is worth ageing Bourgogne Rouge at least two years. Bourgogne AC made by top growers in the major villages from vines grown just outside the village boundaries represent the best-value wine. In Burgundy the name of the producer is everything.

Bourgogne Passe-tout-grain

Red or rosé wines from any area made of two-thirds Gamay and at least one-third Pinot Noir fermented together. Maximum crop 55 hectolitres per hectare. Minimum strength 9.5 degrees. Bourgogne Passe-tout-grain can be delicious after at least one year's ageing, and is not heady as Beaujolais.

Bourgogne Aligoté

White wine of Aligoté grapes, with or without a mixture of Chardonnay, from anywhere in Burgundy. Maximum crop 60 hectolitres per hectare. Minimum strength 9.5 degrees. One commune, Bouzeron in the Côte Châlonnaise, has gained its own appellation for Aligoté; the permitted maximum crop is 45 hectolitres per hectare. Aligoté often makes a sharp wine with considerable local character when young. The classic base for a *vin blanc cassis*, or Kir.

Bourgogne Grand Ordinaire (or Bourgogne Ordinaire)

Red, white or rosé from any of the permitted Burgundy grape varieties. Maximum crop is 55 hectolitres per hectare for red and rosé, 60 for white. Minimum strength 9 degrees for red and rosé, 9.5 degrees for white. This appellation is now not often used.

BURGUNDY IN ROUND FIGURES

'Greater Burgundy', the region including not only the Côte d'Or but Beaujolais, the Mâconnais, Mercurey and the Yonne (Chablis), now produces 15 percent of all *appellation contrôlée* wines.

In the past 35 years the area under vines has increased by nearly one half from 66,700 acres to 98,800 acres. The increase has been uniform in all districts except the Yonne, where the Chablis vineyards have expanded by more than 160 percent. At the same time vineyards producing the non-appellation *'vins de consommation courante'* have decreased sharply.

The trend in Burgundy, as in Bordeaux and elsewhere in France, has been towards more specialization and fewer but bigger holdings of vines. For example, in the Côte d'Or in 1955, 16,500 farmers had vineyards amounting to less than 2.5 acres. The figure today is less than 2,000. In contrast the number of *'exploitations'* of between 12.5 and 25 acres has more than doubled, of those between 25 and 50 almost trebled, and of those of 50 acres and upwards quadrupled. Similar trends, if anything more marked, apply to the other areas of Burgundy. Today approximately 18,000 growers own almost 100,000 acres and produce a total of over a two and a half million hectolitres (the equivalent of over 28 million cases).

The average annual production for the five years 1991–95 is summarized below for the principal brackets of Burgundy appellations.

White wines	hl	cases
Côte d'Or Grands Crus	3,500	38,850
Côte d'Or other ('Village') wines	47,000	521,700
Chablis	200,000	2,220,000
Côte Chalonnaise	23,000	255,300
Mâcon 'Crus' (e.g. Pouilly Fuissé)	80,000	888,000
Mâcon Blanc (other)	190,000	2,109,000
Beaujolais	8,000	88,800
Regional appellations (simple Bourgogne, etc.)	165,000	1,831,500
Total production of white wines	**716,500**	**7,953,150**

Red wines	hl	cases
Côte d'Or Grands Crus	12,000	133,200
Côte d'Or other ('Village') wines	171,000	1,898,100
Côte Chalonnaise	37,000	410,700
Mâcon	51,000	566,100
Beaujolais and Beaujolais-Villages	964,000	10,700,400
Beaujolais 'Crus' (e.g. Fleurie)	351,000	3,896,100
Regional appellations (simple Bourgogne, etc.)	254,000	2,819,400
Total production of red wines	**1,240,000**	**20,424,000**
Total production, red and white	**2,556,500**	**28,377,150**

The principal markets for Burgundy, by volume, in 1996 were :

	Total (%)	% white wine	% red wine
France	44.0	34.0	57.0
UK	11.5	15.5	6.5
Germany	10.0	15.0	4.5
Benelux	9.0	10.5	8.0
USA	8.0	10.5	4.5
Switzerland	4.5	0.5	8.5
Other	13.0	14.0	11.0

CHABLIS

Chablis and the few other scattered vineyards of the Yonne département are a tiny remnant of what was once the biggest vineyard area in France. It was the 100,000 acres of the Yonne, centred around the city of Auxerre, that supplied the population of Paris with its daily wine before the building of the railways brought them unbeatable competition from the Midi. Whether one is to draw any conclusion from the fact that its best vineyard was called La Migraine is hard to say.

Any vineyard so far north is a high-risk enterprise. When falling sales were followed by the phylloxera disaster, Auxerre turned to other forms of agriculture. Chablis dwindled but held on, encouraged by the merchants of Beaune, who provided its chief outlet. When it was first delineated as an appellation in the 1930s there was not much more than 1,000 acres, but they included the hillside of the seven Grands Crus. Nobody could ignore the quality of their wine. I remember a 45-year-old half-bottle of Les Clos 1923 as being one of the best white wines I ever drank.

It was the merchants of Beaune who made Chablis famous. In the simple old days when Beaune, being a nice easy name to remember, meant red burgundy, Chablis meant white. The name was picked up and echoed around the wine-growing world as a synonym for dry white wine. In California it still is.

But the real thing remained a rarity. Year after year, spring frosts devastated the Chablis vineyards and discouraged replanting. Only in the 1960s did new methods of frost control turn the scales. The introduction of sprinkler systems to replace stoves among the vines on cold spring nights made Chablis profitable. Advances in chemical weed and rot control made it very attractive to invest in a name that was already world famous. Within a decade the acreage doubled, with each acre yielding far more wine more reliably than ever before. It continues to grow. Today there are over 8,800 acres, and an average crop is around a quarter to one-third of all white burgundy.

Inevitably the old guard strongly resists the granting of the appellation to so much new land. However, as in the rest of Burgundy, the Grands and Premiers Crus are more or less sacrosanct: it is in Chablis 'simple' or 'Village', with no vineyard name, that there is room for more expansion.

Unqualified 'Village' Chablis, as it is generally made today, competes in the marketplace with Mâcon-Villages. In style it is lighter, sharper, drier and cleaner, with more of a 'lift' in your mouth. A good example is distinctly fruity with a quality that only Chardonnay gives. A poor one is simply neutral and more or less sharp. A small amount of wine from inferior plots is only allowed the appellation Petit Chablis. Many say it should not be called Chablis at all.

Premier Cru and Grand Cru Chablis are different wines; there are distinct steps upward in body, flavour and individuality. Some people find the best Premiers Crus the most satisfyingly typical, with plenty of flavour and a distinctive 'cut' of acidity. The Grands Crus add a richness and strength which round them out; occasionally too much so. To be seen at their best the Grands Crus need at least three and sometimes up to ten years ageing in bottle. Those made in barrels (the minority) keep longest and best.

The scent and flavour that develop are the quintessence of an elusive character you can miss if you only ever drink Chablis young. I can only define it as combining the fragrances of apples and hay with a taste of boiled sweets and underlying mineral note that seems to have been mined from the bowels of the earth.

The price of Chablis has not kept pace with its value. Grand Cru Chablis is happily in much better supply than Bâtard-Montrachet, otherwise it could well fetch as high a price. Premier Cru Chablis from a good grower is the best value in white burgundy.

Leading Chablis Growers

René and Vincent Dauvissat
8 rue Emile Zola, 89800 Chablis.
René Dauvissat's great-grandfather was a cooper, so it is no surprise that his cellars, unlike most in Chablis today, are still full of barrels. He ages the wine from his 22 acres for about

12 months in wood in the old style. His best wines are the Grands Crus Les Clos and Les Preuses – 7 acres in all. His remaining acres are all Premier Cru.

Jean-Paul Droin

Rue Montmain, 89800 Chablis.
Droin's great-grandfather presented his wines to Napoléon III when he visited Auxerre in 1866. His cellars have not changed overmuch. But he keeps the wines from his 17 acres of Premiers Crus (mainly Vaillons) in barrels for 6 months, the Grands Crus for 12, whereas his great-grand-father would have kept them for several years. The Grands Crus are Vaudésir, Les Clos, Valmur and Grenouilles – 9 acres in all. They are some of the finest Chablis made today.

Maison Joseph Drouhin

7 rue d'Enfer, 21200 Beaune.
The famous Beaune négociant has since 1979 added 89 acres of Chablis to his domaine and makes immaculate, beautifully tender and aristocratic wine from the Grands Crus Vaudésir, Les Clos, Preuses and vividly typical Premier Cru from his holdings in Vaillons, Côte de Lechet, Mont de Milieu, etc.

Jean Durup

4 Grande rue, Maligny, 89800 Chablis.
The large and growing estate of Jean Durup, President of the lobby that favours expanding the appellation Chablis. He has 370 acres, of which 81 are in Premiers Crus (principally Fourchaume and Vau de Vey). An impeccable modern winery whose wines appear under the names Domaine de l'Eglantière and Château de Maligny. 55% is exported.

William Fèvre

Dom. de la Maladière. 14 rue Jules Rathier, 89800 Chablis.
The largest owner of Grands Crus and a traditionalist in his winemaking – one of the very few in Chablis to ferment his wine in new oak. His 40 acres of Grands Crus include 10 of Les Clos, 15 of Bougros and 7 of Les Preuses, with 3 each of Valmur and Vaudésir and 1.5 of Grenouilles. He has a similar amount of Premiers Crus, split into seven vineyards – the biggest are 6.5 acres in Vaulorent and 6 in Montmains-Forêt. He also owns 49 acres of Chablis 'simple'. William Fèvre was head the Syndicat de Défense de l'Appellation Chablis, the body in favour of restricting the appellation to well-proven sites. He is also a négociant, using the Jean-Paul Filippi label.

Domaine Alain Geoffroy

4 rue de l'Equerre, 89800 Chablis.
A third of the 86-acre domaine is Premier Cru, mainly Beauroy (17.2 acres), with 7.4 acres of Vau Ligneau and 3.7 of Fourchaume.

Corinne & Jean-Pierre Grossot

4 rte du Mont-de-Milieu, 89800 Fleys.
Enthusiastic growers with 40 acres, 27 in straight Chablis the rest in Premiers Crus Fourchaume, Fourneaux, Vaucoupin, Mont de Milieu and Côte de Troesmes. Vinification is mostly in stainless steel although some oak is used for the better wines.

Lamblin & Fils

Maligny, 89800 Chablis.
A négociant and grower, whose 26 acres account for only 10% of his wine: the rest is bought as grapes or juice from others. 'Domaine' wines include small parcels of Grands Crus Valmur (2 acres) and Les Clos (2.5 acres), and 12 acres of Premiers Crus. Chablis is 70% of his business; the rest is white Bourgogne Blanc, Aligoté, white table wine and sparkling. The Lamblin style is light and fresh; the wines are for drinking young and not for ageing. Other labels include Jacques Arnouls, Jacques de la Ferté, Paul Javry and Bernard Miele.

Domaine Laroche

L'Obédiencerie, 22 rue Louis Bro, 89800 Chablis.
Michel Laroche is the fifth-generation owner of an estate of nearly 240 acres. There are 15 acres of Chablis Grand Cru, including 11 acres of Les Blanchots, and 72 of Premier Cru. Modern equipment makes Chablis in an austere, vigorous style, though some new oak is used for the Grands and Premiers Crus. Their Grands Crus should be kept for between three and six years. The name Laroche also appears on a wide range of non-domaine wines, including a good brand of simple Chablis, St Martin. They also blend good non-regional Chardonay and have now embarked on a range of Midi wines.

Long-Depaquit

45 rue Auxerroise, 89800 Chablis.
A first-class old-established family company which is now merged with the négociants Bichot of Beaune but still run autonomously. Of their 100-odd acres 47 are Chablis 'simple', 30 Premiers Crus and 20 Grands Crus, including 6.4 of Vaudésir. Their most famous property is the 6-acre Moutonne vineyard, a part of the Grands Crus Vaudésir and Les Preuses, whose history goes back to the Abbey of Pontigny and its monks, who apparently skipped like young sheep under its inspiration. Long-Depaquit wines are very thoughtfully and professionally made with modern methods, but not for instant drinking.

Domaine des Malandes

63 rue Auxerroise, 89800 Chablis.
A 17.3-acre domaine with 2.2 acres in Grand Cru Vaudésir, and 7.5 acres of Premiers Crus including Fourchaume (3 acres) and Montmains (3 acres).

Louis Michel & Fils

11 boulevard de Ferrières, 89800 Chablis.
The son and grandson of small growers who has tripled his acreage by dedicated winemaking. He now has 33 acres of Premiers Crus (some in Montmains and Montée de Tonnerre) and 6 acres of Grands Crus (Vaudésir 3; Grenouilles and Les Clos 1.3 each). Monsieur Michel believes in letting the wine make itself as far as possible. He uses no barrels, but by modest yields and careful handling makes concentrated wines that repay years of bottle-age. 80% of his wine is exported.

J. Moreau & Fils

Route d'Auxerre, 89800 Chablis.

The largest proprietor in Chablis, and now a big business in non-Chablis white wines from the north of France, which are all skilfully made and marketed. Total sales amount to some 375,000 cases a year. The Moreaus have been in making wine since 1814 and have built up an estate of 175 acres. 125 acres of this is the Domaine de Biéville, appellation Chablis 'simple', and 25 is Premier Cru Vaillons. Of their 25 acres of Grands Crus, 17 are Les Clos and include the Clos des Hospices, which produces their best wine, and which was bought by the Moreau family from the local hospital in 1850. All the wine is made to be drunk young and fruity – very fruity in the case of Les Clos.

Jean-Marie Raveneau

Rue de Chichée, 89800 Chablis.

An 18-acre domaine in Grands Crus (Blanchots, Valmur, Les Clos) and Premiers Crus, considered by some to be the best in Chablis. The wines, aged in barrels for at least one year, and made famous by Jean-Marie's father, sell mainly to restaurants in France.

A. Regnard & Fils

28 boulevard du Docteur Tacussel, 89800 Chablis.

A family firm of négociants, founded in 1860, handling wine of all qualities. Patrick de Ladoucette, a leading producer of Pouilly-Fumé in the Loire (Ch. de Nozet), now has a large holding. The Regnard specialities include Premier Cru Fourchaume and Grands Crus Vaudésir and Valmur. As well as Chablis they sell Aligoté and Sauvignon de St-Bris. Other labels used are Michel Rémon and Albert Pic. They now own 25 acres of vineyard, as well as buying in from over 370 acres.

Simonnet-Febvre & Fils

9 avenue d'Oberwesel, 89800 Chablis.

A small domaine of 9 acres but a well-known négociant going back five generations. The present head is Jean-Pierre Simonnet. The company makes wine from bought-in juice as well as its own, particularly from the Premiers Crus Mont de Milieu, Montée de Tonnerre, Fourchaume and Vaillons. Their best wine is the Grand Cru Preuses. Other wines they offer are Aligoté, Irancy, Sauvignon de St-Bris, and Crémant de Bourgogne. Other labels are Jean-Claude Simonnet, André Vannier, Georges Martin, Jean Deligny, Alexandre Goulard and Gilles Blanchard. 60% is exported.

Robert Vocoret

Rue d'Avallon, 89800 Chablis.

A century-old family domaine of 76 acres, 10 in Grands Crus (Les Clos, Valmur, Blanchots), 33 in Premiers Crus and 33 in Chablis 'simple'. Vocoret is one of the very few Chablis growers left who ferment as well as age their wine in barrels. The result is wine with less of the immediately appealing 'fruit' but a firm grip that rewards keeping.

Cave Coopérative La Chablisienne

89800 Chablis.

A quarter of all Chablis comes from this growers' cooperative, founded in 1923 and now handling the grapes from 1,225 acres, of which 827 are Chablis 'simple', 237 Premiers Crus, 123 Petit Chablis and 37 Grands Crus. Of the Grands Crus vineyards, 17 acres of Grenouilles and 12.5 acres of Preuses are significant holdings. Fourchaume, with 86 acres, is much their most important Premier Cru. Their methods are modern and their wine well made, clean and honest; with some experimentation with oak. Most of the wine is exported, under about 50 different labels, usually the names of grower-members. 'La Chablisienne' is sometimes seen.

OTHER CHABLIS PRODUCERS

Other leading Chablis producers include: Adhémar Boudin, Jean-Claude Bessin, Jean Collet, Bernard Legland, Gilbert Picq et Fils, Louis Pinson, Denis Race, Olivier Savary, Marcel Servin, Domaine Gérard Tremblay and Domaine de Vauroux.

The vineyards of Chablis

Chablis comes in four grades: Chablis AC (also known as 'simple' or 'village'), Petit Chablis, Premier Cru and Grand Cru. In 1996 the superior Premier Cru covered 1,730 acres. Vineyard names (listed here) are sometimes used in conjunction with Premier Cru names. In the same year the Grands Crus occupied 222 acres. In Chablis new vines are being planted at a rate of 500 acres a year by the turn of the century the total area under vine could be as great as 10,000 acres.

Premiers Crus

Premier Cru Chablis may be sold either with the names of individual vineyards or those of groups of fields. The latter is generally the case, so in practice only a relatively small number of names are in use. In alphabetical order, together with the names of the vineyards that have the right to use the name in question (since 1986): Les Beauregards (Côte de Cuissy); Beauroy (Troesmes, Côte de Savant); Berdiot; Chaume de Talvat; Fourchaume (Vaupulent, Côte de Fontenay, l'Homme Mort, Vaulorent); Les Fourneaux (Morein, Côte des Prés-Girots); Côte de Jouan; Les Landes et Verjuts; Côte de Léchet; Mont de Milieu; Montée de Tonnerre (Chapelot, Pied d'Aloup, Côte de Bréchain), Montmains (Forêts, Butteaux); Vaillons (Chatains, Sécher, Beugnons, Les Lys, Mélinots, Roncières, les Epinottes); Côtes de Vaubarousse; Vaucoupin; Vau de Vey (Vaux Ragons); Vau Ligneau; and Vosgros (Vaugiraut).

Grands Crus

Blanchot (31 acres); Bougros (31 acres); Les Clos (67 acres); Grenouilles (22 acres); Preuses (28 acres); Valmur (33 acres); and Vaudésir (36 acres). La Moutonne is a vineyard of 5.75 acres in Vaudésir and Les Preuses.

THE COTE D'OR

The heart of Burgundy is the 30-mile line of hills running south from Marsannay on the southern outskirts of Dijon, inclining westwards as it goes and presenting a broadening band of southeast-facing slopes until it stops at Santenay. The eight villages of the northern sector, ending at Prémaux, are the Côte de Nuits. The 20 villages running south from Aloxe-Corton are the Côte de Beaune.

The Côte de Nuits is almost exclusively devoted to red wine – almost all Pinot Noir. On these steep, sharp slopes the most potently flavoured, concentrated, eventually smooth and perfumed wines are made.

The villages are listed here from north to south. Each is briefly described with an appreciation of its wine and a list of its Grands Crus (if any) and Premiers Crus, their acreages and the vineyard acreage of the whole commune.

The figures given are those arrived at in 1984 after a long process of official deliberation. The first edition of this Companion gave an average price for each of the majority of the appellations. Fluid market conditions at present make this information impossible to obtain and, more importantly, the price in bottle can vary enormously from grower to grower even when 'bulk' prices are stable. The growers listed under each village entry are those whose particulars will (in the majority of cases) be found in the list of Côte d'Or growers, beginning on page 112. It is by no means an exhaustive list – only the telephone directory is that. The details of growers' holdings, in almost every case supplied by themselves, give a vivid picture of the infinitely complex structure of the world's most highly prized vineyards.

MARSANNAY-LA-CÔTE

Formerly known only for its excellent Rosé de Marsannay, this village now has, uniquely in Burgundy, an appellation for all three colours. The whites mostly lack interest, the rosés are deliciously perfumed and elegant, the reds on the light side but extremely pretty. Marsannay also covers the few remaining vineyards (e.g. Clos du Roy) of Chenove which is now a light industrial and commercial suburb of Dijon. Marsannay covers 262 acres but has no designated premier cru vineyards.

GROWERS

Domaine Bart	Bruno Clair
Bernard Coillot	Fougeray de Beauclair
Domaine Collotte	Château de Marsannay

FIXIN

The Premiers Crus are splendidly situated and capable of wines as good as those of Gevrey-Chambertin. Even the 'village' wines are stout-hearted and long-lived. Between Fixin and Gevrey-Chambertin the village of Brochon has no appellation of its own. Its better vineyards are included in Gevrey-Chambertin. The lesser ones are plain Côte de Nuits-Villages.

PREMIERS CRUS

Arvelets (8)	Queue de Hareng
Clos du Chapitre (11.8)	(Brochon)
Cheusots (4.5)	Appellation Communale:
Hervelets (9.5)	246 acres.
Meix-Bas (5)	Appellations Régionales:
Perrière (12)	486 acres.

GROWERS

Domaine Bart	Pierre Gelin
Clemencey Frères	Philippe Joliet
	Domaine de la Perrière

GEVREY-CHAMBERTIN

There is a very wide range of quality in the production of Gevrey – the biggest of any of the townships of the Côte d'Or. Some of its flat vineyards beyond the valley road are of middling quality only. But there is no questioning the potential of its constellation of Grands Crus. Chambertin and the Clos de Bèze are acknowledged to lead them; an extra charge of fiery concentration gives them the edge. The seven others must always keep the 'Chambertin' after their names; Clos de Bèze may put it before, or indeed simply label itself Chambertin. They are all stern, essentially male (since everything in France has a gender) wines that I cannot imagine even Astérix himself tossing back in bumpers. Obélix, perhaps. French critics claim for Chambertin the delicacy of Musigny allied to the strength of a Corton, the velvet of a Romanée and the perfume of the Clos Vougeot. I have certainly tasted fabulous complexity, but delicacy is not the word I would choose. Great age is probably the key. Two of the Premiers Crus of Gevrey on the hill behind the village, Les Verroilles and Clos St-Jacques, are widely thought to be on the same level of quality as the bevy of hyphenated Chambertins.

GRANDS CRUS

Chambertin (31.9)	Griotte-Chambertin (6.7)
Chambertin	Latricières-Chambertin (18)
Clos de Bèze (38)	Mazis-Chambertin (22.4)
Chapelle-Chambertin (13.6)	Ruchottes-Chambertin (8.2)
Charmes- (or Mazoyères-)	
Chambertin (76)	

PREMIERS CRUS

Total area:	Champitonnois (also called
210 acres	Petite Chapelle) (10)
Bel Air (6.5)	Champonnets (8)
La Boissière*	Clos du Chapitre (2.5)
Cazetiers (25)	Cherbaudes (5)
Champeaux (16.5)	Closeau (1.3)
	Combe-aux-Moines (11.78)

Combottes (11.3)
Corbeaux (7.5)
Craipillot (6.8)
Ergot (3)
Etournelles (5)
Fonteny (9)
Gémeaux*
Goulots (4.5)
Issarts (1.5)
Lavaux (23.5)
Perrière (6)
Poissenot (5.5)

GROWERS

Pierre Amiot et Fils
Denis Bachelet
Domaine Bart
Thomas Bassot
Adrien Belland
Maison Albert Bichot
J.-C. Boisset
Bouchard Père & Fils
Alain Burguet
Camus Père & Fils
Bruno Clair
Damoy
Maison Joseph Drouhin
Dujac
Frédéric Esmonin
Michel Esmonin
Maison J. Faiveley
Dominique Gallois
Pierre Gelin
Antonin Guyon
Harmand-Geoffroy

Clos Prieur-Haut (5)
La Romanée*
Clos St-Jacques (16.5)
Les Verroilles (15)
*No acreage specified
in the latest official
documents.
Appellation Communale:
892 acres.
Appellations Régionales
in the commune:
234 acres.

Philippe Leclerc
René Leclerc
Georges Lignier & Fils
Hubert Lignier
Henri Magninen
J.P. Marchand
Maume
Denis Morlet
Thierry Morlet
Moillard-Grivot
Georges Mugneret
Naigeon-Chauveau
J.M. Ponsot
Henri Rebourseau
P.L. Rossignol
Joseph Roty
Armand Rousseau
Thomas-Moillard
Tortochot
Louis Trapet
Dom des Varoilles
Vienot

MOREY ST-DENIS

The least known of the villages of the Côte de Nuits despite having four Grands Crus to its name and part of a fifth. Clos de la Roche is capable of making wine with the martial tread of a Chambertin; Clos St-Denis marginally less so; Clos de Tart (at least as its sole owner interprets it) is considerably lighter. All the wines of Morey are worth study, for authenticity and a chance of a bargain.

GRANDS CRUS

Bonnes Mares (a small part) (4)
Clos des Lambrays (22)

Clos de la Roche (41.75)
Clos St-Denis (16.35)
Clos de Tart (18.5)

PREMIERS CRUS

Total area 106 acres:
Bouchots
Maison Brûlée (2.5)
Calouères

Clos de la Bussière (7.5)
Chabiots
Chaffots (2.5)
Charmes (2.5)

Charrières (5)
Chénevery (7.5)
Façonnières (2.5)
Fremières
Froichots
Genevrières (7.5)
Gruenchers (7.5)
Meix-Rentiers
Les Millandes

Monts-Luisants
Riotte
Ruchots
Clos Sorbés
Les Sorbés
Appellation Communale:
158 acres.
Appellations Régionales:
305 acres.

GROWERS

Pierre Amiot et Fils
Bertagna
Bruno Clair
Dujac
R. Groffier
Georges Lignier & Fils

Hubert Lignier
Mommessin
Perrot-Minot
Ponsot
Ropiteau
Armand Rousseau

CHAMBOLLE-MUSIGNY

The lilt of the name is perfectly appropriate for the wines of this parish – as is the apparent evocation of the muse. It is hard to restrain oneself from competing in similes with the much-quoted sages of Burgundy, but Gaston Roupnel seems to have it precisely right. Musigny, he says, 'has the scent of dewy garden … of the rose and the violet at dawn.' Le Musigny is my favourite red burgundy, closely followed by Premiers Crus Les Amoureuses and Les Charmes and the other Grand Cru, Les Bonnes Mares. A contributory reason is that some particularly good winemakers own this land.

GRANDS CRUS

Bonnes Mares (33.5)
(see also Morey St-Denis)

Musigny (26)

PREMIERS CRUS

Total area 148 acres:
Amoureuses
Aux Beaux Bruns
Borniques (2.5)
Carrières
Chabiots
Charmes (12.5)
Châtelots (5)
Combes d'Orveaux
Combottes (5)
Aux Combottes (5)
Cras (10)
Derrière la Grange (10)

Echanges
Fousselottes (10)
Fuées
Grands Murs
Groseilles
Gruenchers
Niorts
Plantes (5)
Sentiers (10)
Appellation Communale:
315 acres
Appellations Régionales:
83.5 acres

GROWERS

Pierre Amiot et Fils
Barthod-Noëllat
Bouchard Père & Fils
Château de Chambolle-
  Musigny
Georges Clerget

Maison Joseph Drouhin
Drouhin-Laroze
Dufouleur Frères
Dujac
Faiveley
Jean Grivot

Antonin Guyon
Maison Leroy
Georges Lignier et Fils
Hubert Lignier
Domaine Machard de
 Gramont
Georges Mugneret
Patrice Rion
Maison G. Roumier
Domaine
 des Varoilles
Comte de Vogüé

VOUGEOT

The great vineyard of the Clos (de) Vougeot has the most resounding reputation in Burgundy. 125 acres within a single wall built by the 14th-century monks of Cîteaux add a certain presence. The land at the top of the slope, next to Musigny and Grands Echézeaux, is equal to the best in Burgundy, but with its present fragmented ownership it is rare to meet a bottle that answers this description. Or perhaps I do not try often enough. Classical references always stress its perfume. My impression is of a more meaty, extremely satisfying but less exotic wine than those of its great neighbours.

GRAND CRU Clos de Vougeot (125)

PREMIERS CRUS RED
Cras   Petit Vougeot

PREMIER CRU WHITE
Total area 7.4 acres: Appellation Communale:
Vigne Blanche or   17 acres
Clos Blanc de Vougeot   Appellations Régionales:
 (4.5)   10.5 acres

GROWERS
Pierre André
Bertagna
Champy Père & Cie
Georges Clerget
Maison Joseph Drouhin
Dufouleur Frères
René Engel
Faiveley
Jean Grivot
The Gros family
Hudelot-Noëllat
Lamarche
Maison Leroy
Machard de Gramont
Denis Mortet
Georges Mugneret
Charles Noëllat
Maison Pierre Ponnelle
Jacques Prieur
G. Roumier
Thomas-Mollard
Domaine des
 Varoilles
Vienot

FLAGEY-ECHEZEAUX

Exists as a village but not as an appellation, despite the fact that it has two Grands Crus in the parish. They are effectively treated as being in Vosne-Romanée, having the right to 'declassify' their wine under the Vosne name. In reality Grands Echézeaux is at Grand Cru level – an ideal site adjacent to the best part of the Clos Vougeot. Its wines can have all the flair and the persuasive depths of the greatest burgundy. But the huge 75-acre Les Echézeaux would be more realistically classified as one or several Premiers Crus.

Its lack of any readily spotted identity joined with its apparently unmanageable name means that it sells for a reasonable price. There is a lightness of touch, a gentle sweetness and airy fragrance about a good Echézeaux which make it less of a challenge than the biggest burgundies.

VOSNE-ROMANEE

If Chambertin has the dignity, the name of Romanée has the glamour. Only the very rich and their guests have ever even tasted La Romanée-Conti. The Domaine de la Romanée-Conti, sole owner of that vineyard and the next greatest, La Tâche, casts its exotic aura equally over Richebourg, Romanée-St-Vivant and Grands Echézeaux, where it also owns or manages property. The Domaine's wines are marked with a character that seems to be their own, rather than that of Vosne-Romanée as a whole. Out of the torrent of words that has poured around Vosne and its sacred ground over the centuries I would pick three: 'fire', 'velvet' and 'balance'.

In the excitement of the Grands Crus, the Premiers Crus of Vosne-Romanée can be unwisely overlooked.

GRANDS CRUS
Total area 163.5 acres
Echézeaux (93)
Grande Rue (2.5)
Grands Echézeaux (22.5)
Richebourg (21)
La Romanée (2)
Romanée-Conti (4.5)
Romanée-
 St-Vivant (23)
La Tâche (15)
Chaumes (17.5)
Croix Rameau

PREMIERS CRUS
Total area 146 acres (30.5
are in Flagey-Echézeaux)
Beaux Monts
Cros Parentoux
Orveaux
Gaudichots (14.5)
Malconsorts (14)
Petits Monts (9)
Clos de Réas (5)
Orveaux
Raignots (4.5)
Rouges du Dessus Suchots
 (33.5)
Appellation Communale:
260 acres of which 33 are in
Flagey-Echézeaux
Appellations Régionales:
198 acres.

GROWERS
Maison Albert Bichot
Bruno Clair
Georges Clerget
René Engel
Jean Grivot
Anne Gros
Jean Gros
H. Jayer
J. Jayer
Lamarche
Machard de Gramont
Méo-Camuzet
Moillard
Mongeard-Mugneret
Mugneret-Gibourg
Mugneret-Gouachon
Charles Noëllat
Daniel Rion
Domaine de la
 Romanée-Conti
Thomas-Moillard
Charles Viénot

ROMANEE-CONTI

A Great Burgundy Estate

All the conundrums of wine come to a head at this extraordinary property. It has been accepted for at least three centuries that wine of inimitable style and fascination comes from one four-and-a-half-acre patch of hill, and different wine, marginally but consistently less fascinating, from the sites around it. Romanée-Conti sounds like a supersuccessful public relations exercise. In some ways it is even organized as one. But there is no trick.

On such a small scale, and with millionaires eager for every drop, it is possible to practise total perfectionism. Without the soil and the site the opportunity would not be there: without the laborious pursuit of perfection it would be lost. A great vineyard like this is largely man-made. The practice in the days of the 18th-century Prince de Conti, who gave it his name, was to bring fresh loam up from the pastures of the Saône Valley in wagonloads to give new life to the soil. Ironically, today the authorities would forbid so much as a bucketful from outside the appellation. Does this condemn the great vineyard to a gradual decline?

The co-proprietors of the Domaine today are the Leroy and de Villaine families. (M. Aubert de Villaine, whose home is at Bouzeron, near Chagny, makes particularly good Aligoté.) Their policy is to delay picking until the grapes are consummately ripe, running the gauntlet of the autumn storms and the risk of rot, simply rejecting all the grapes that have succumbed. The proportion of stems put in the vat depends on the season. Fermentation is exceptionally long: from three weeks to even a full month. All the wine is matured in new barrels every year. There is a minimum of racking and filtration. It is indeed the grapes that do it.

As the prices of the Domaine's wines are so spectacularly high, one expects to find them not only exceptional in character but in perfect condition. They are essentially wines for very long bottle-ageing. What is surprising is that they often show signs of instablity. It is almost the hallmark of `D.R.C.' wines that they are instantly recognizable by their exotic opulence, yet rarely identical from bottle to bottle. Too often bottles are in frankly poor condition.

The same elusive quality applies to the wine in your glass. Of a bottle of La Tâche 1962, which has been one of the very best burgundies for years (at least in my view), I noted in 1982: 'Overwhelming high-toned smell of violets to start with, changing within 20 minutes to a more deep and fruity bouquet which seemed at first like oranges, then more like blackcurrants. The flavour was best about half an hour after opening – exotically rich and warm – then seemed to become a bit too alcoholic and lose some of its softness. Very exciting wine – not least for the speed and range of its metamorphoses.'

M. de Villaine conducts the distribution of Romanée-Conti in the USA, which buys 50 percent of the crop, and in Britain, which buys 10 percent (*see also* Maison Leroy, page 121).

The precise holdings, and average production figures, of the Domaine are as follows:

La Romanée-Conti, 4.45 acres, 6,000 bottles;
La Tâche, 14.8 acres, 20,000 bottles.
Richebourg, 8.6 acres, 12,000 bottles.
Grands-Echézeaux, 7.4 acres, 12,000 bottles.
Echézeaux, 11.5 acres, 16,000 bottles.
Romanée-St-Vivant is rented *'en fermage'* from the Domaine Marey-Monge, whose name appears on the label.
Le Montrachet, 1.66 acres, 3,000 bottles.

NUITS-ST-GEORGES

As a town, Nuits-St-Georges does not bear comparison with the alluring city of Beaune; its walls have long gone and it has no great public monuments. But it is the trading centre of the Côte de Nuits, the seat of a dozen négociants, its endless silent cellars maturing countless big-bellied *pièces*. In another way, too, it echoes Beaune: its long hill of vines produces highly prized and famous wine without a single peak. If Nuits had a Grand Cru it would be Les St-Georges, and possibly Les Vaucrains, Les Cailles and Les Porrets on the slope above and beside it. But none of these vineyards has convinced the world that its wine alone rises consistently above the Premier Cru level.

Compared with the wines of Beaune, which they sometimes are, those of Nuits-St-Georges are tougher, less fruity and giving in their youth, and often for many years. It is hard to understand why they should be the popular favourite of Anglo-Saxon countries, as they are, since ten years is often needed to turn toughness to warmth of flavour. The best Nuits has marvellous reserves of elusive character that demand leisurely investigation.

Prémeaux, the village to the south (whose name recalls the spring waters which are its other product) is part of the appellation Nuits-St-Georges and itself has a run of Premiers Crus of equal merit, squeezed on to a steep and narrow slope between the road and the woods.

PREMIERS CRUS

Total area 353 acres:
De l'Arlot
Aux Argillats (4.5)
Les Argillères, Prémeaux (11)
Clos Arlots, Prémeaux (16.5)
Boudots (15)
Bousselots (10.5)
Cailles (8.5)
Chaboeufs (7.5)
Chaignots (14.5)
Chaines-Carteaux (6)
Champs Perdrix (1.8)
Corvées, Prémeaux (19)
Cras (7.5)
Crots (10)
Damodes (21)
Didiers, Prémeaux (6)
Les Forêts, Prémeaux (17.5)
Les Grandes Vignes, Prémeaux (5)
Clos de la Maréchale, Prémeaux (25)
Murgers (12.5)
Aux Perdrix, Prémeaux (8.5)
Perrières (7.5)
Perrière-Noblot (0.75)
Poirets (17.5)
Poulettes (5)
Procès (5)
Pruliers (17.5)
Richemone (5.5)
Roncière (5)
Rue de Chaux (5)
Les St-Georges (18.5)
Thorey (12.5)
Vallerots (2)
Vaucrains (15)
Vignes Rondes (9.5)
Appellation Communale: 42 acres.
Appellations Régionales: 735 acres.

GROWERS

Dom. de l'Arlot
J.-C. Boisset
F. Chauvenet
Robert Chevillon
Robert Dubois & Fils
Dufouleur Frères
Faiveley
Henri Gouges
Jean Grivot
Jean Gros
Dom de la Juvinière
Chantal Lescure
Lupé-Cholet et Cie
Machard de Gramont
A. Michelot
Missery
Moillard
Mugneret-Gibourg
Georges Mugneret
Hospices de Nuits-St-Georges
Dom de la Poulette
Henri et Gilles Remoriquet
Daniel Rion
Thomas-Moillard
Charles Viénot

COTE DE NUITS-VILLAGES

This appellation is a consolation prize for the parishes at either end of the main Côtes: Prissey, Comblanchien and Corgoloin next to Prémeaux on the road south, and Fixin, Brochon and Marsannay on the Dijon road beyond Gevrey-Chambertin. Fixin and Marsannay have appellations of their own. For the others this is the highest aspiration. Stone quarries are more in evidence than vineyards on the road to Beaune. The marble from the hill here is some of France's best. Only one important vineyard stands out as a Premier Cru *manqué*; the Clos des Langres, property of La Reine Pédauque, the extreme southern tip of the Côte de Nuits.

LADOIX-SERRIGNY

The Côte de Beaune starts with its most famous landmark, the oval dome (if you can have such a thing) of the hill of Corton. The dome wears a beret of woods but its south, east and west flanks are all vines, forming parts of three different parishes: in order of approach from the north Ladoix-Serrigny, Aloxe-Corton and – tucked round the corner out of sight – Pernand-Vergelesses. The best vineyards of all three are those on the mid- and upper slopes of the hill, which share the appellation Corton Grand Cru (the only red Grand Cru of the Côte de Beaune) and in parts, for white wine, Corton-Charlemagne.

Ladoix-Serrigny has the smallest part of 'Corton', and not the best, in its vineyards of Rognet-Corton and Les Vergennes, names which are not used but subsumed in the general title of Corton, as all the Grand Cru territory can be. Similarly the 'Village' wines of Ladoix, which few people have ever heard of, often take advantage of the appellation Côte de Beaune-Villages.

GRANDS CRUS

Total area 55 acres:
Corton-Charlemagne white wines only:
Basses Mourettes (2.5)
Hautes Mourettes (4.5)
Le Rognet-Corton (7.85)

Corton red and white:
Les Carrières (1)
Les Grandes Lolières (7.5)

Les Moutottes (2)
Le Rognet et Corton (20.75)
La Toppe au Vert (0.25)
Les Vergennes (8.5)
Parts of Ladoix-Serrigny may be sold under the appellation Aloxe-Corton, the rest may be sold as Côte de Beaune-Villages.
Total area 845 acres.

PREMIERS CRUS

Total area 56.5 acres:
Basses Mourettes (2)
Bois Roussot (4.5)
Le Clou d'Orge (4)
La Corvée (17.5)
Hautes Mourettes (1.5)
Les Joyeuses (2)

Les Lolières
La Micaude (4)
Appellation Communale
Ladoix-Serrigny: 298 acres.
Appellations Régionales
421 acres.

GROWERS

Bouchard Père & Fils   Domaine de Serrigny

ALOXE-CORTON

The major part of the Grands Crus Corton and Corton-Charlemagne dominates this parish, but still leaves a substantial amount of lower land with the appellation Aloxe-Corton, both Premier Cru and 'Village'. It is important to remember that Corton *tout-court* is always a superior appellation to Aloxe-Corton. Louis Latour is the most celebrated grower of Corton.

It is almost impossible (and in any case not really essential) to grasp the legalities of the Grands Crus here. 'Corton' embraces a dozen different adjacent vineyards, the top of which is actually called Le Corton. The others may be labelled either Corton, or, for example, Corton-Clos du Roi, Corton-Bressandes. On such a big hillside there is inevitably a wide range of style and quality. Bressandes, lowest of the Grands Crus, is considered to produce richer wine (from richer soil) than Clos du Roi above it ... and so on.

Corton-Charlemagne is a white Grand Cru from some of the same vineyards as red Corton – those on the south slope and the top ones where the soil is paler and more impregnated with lime. Perversely enough there is also a appellation for white Grand Cru Corton (although this is rarely seen).

True to their national inclinations, the French rate (red) Corton the best wine of the hill, comparing it for sheer force of personality with Chambertin, whereas the British speak of Corton-Charlemagne in the same breath as Le Montrachet. I have certainly been surprised to see French authors mildly liken it to Meursault. It expresses great driving vigour of a kind closer to Montrachet, though with more spice, even earth, and correspondingly less of the simple magic of ripe fruit. It is in the nature of Corton-Charlemagne to hide its qualities and show only its power, as red wines do, for as many as seven or eight years. Red Corton needs keeping as long as the Grands Crus of the Côte de Nuits.

The dominant name among Corton growers, both red and white, is that of Louis Latour, whose press-house and cellars are cut into the foot of the hill itself and who gives the name of his château, Grancy, to a selection of Corton of even greater than usual power.

GRANDS CRUS

Total area 120.5 acres
Corton red wines only:
Le Charlemagne (41.85)
Le Corton (28.85)
Les Languettes (17.85)
Les Pougets (24.25)
Les Renardes (7)

Corton-Charlemagne for white wines only (in same parcels as reds above):
Le Charlemagne (41.85)
Le Corton (28.85)
Les Languettes (17.85)
Les Pougets (24.25)

Corton for red and white wines (i.e., *not* Corton-Charlemagne) (177.5 acres):
Les Bressandes (43)
Les Maréchaudes (11)
Les Perrières (23.5)
Les Renardes (28)
Le Clos du Roi (26.5)

Parts (smaller than 10 acres) of Les Chaumes and Voirosses, Les Combes, Les Fiètres, Les Grèves, Les Meix, Les Meix Lallemand, Les Pauland, Le Village and La Vigne au Saint in Aloxe-Corton.

PREMIERS CRUS

Appellation Aloxe-Corton
Premiers Crus, 72 acres:
Les Chaillots (11.5)
Les Fournières (13.75)
Les Guérets (6.5)
Les Valozières (16)
Les Vercots (10.5)
Maréchaudes, Les Meix,

Basses Moutottes, Les Paulands, La Toppe au Vert, Les Grandes Lolières, Les Petites Lolières
Appellation Communale: 222 acres
Appellations Régionales: 13.25 acres.

GROWERS

Arnoux
Pierre André
Adrien Belland
Bonneau du Martray
Bouchard Père & Fils
Maurice Chapuis
Jean-François Coche-Dury
Daudet-Corcelle
Maison Doudet-Naudin
Maison Joseph Drouhin

Dubreuil-Fontaine
Faiveley
Girard-Vollot
Goud de Beaupuis
Antonin Guyon
Maison Louis Jadot
Dom de la Juvinière
Louis Latour
Lequin Roussot
Lucien Jacob

Leroy
Machard de Gramont
Prince Florent de Mérode
Moillard
Maison Pierre Ponnelle
Rapet Père et Fils
Daniel Senard

Domaine
  de Serrigny
Thomas-Moillard
Tollot-Beaut & Fils
Tollot-Voarick
Charles Viénot
Michel Voarick

PERNAND-VERGELESSES

The Grand Cru of Pernand-Vergelesses is Corton-Charlemagne; there is no red Corton on the western slope of the hill (the only western slope in the whole of the Côte d'Or). But its Premiers Crus are in a completely different situation, directly facing Corton-Charlemagne across the narrow valley that leads to this hidden village. The Premiers Crus are red; they continue the best vineyards of neighbouring Savigny, and in a sense those of Beaune.

GRAND CRU

Total area 42.5 acres:
Charlemagne (white only)
and Corton (red only) are

both in same parcel:
En Charlemagne (42.5)

PREMIERS CRUS

Total area 138 acres:
Basses Vergelesses (45)
Caradeux (35)
Creux de la Net (7.5)
Fichots (27.5)
Ile des Hautes
  Vergelesses (23)

Total area 828 acres:
Appellation Communale
Pernand-Vergelesses:
338 acres
Appellations Régionales:
350 acres.

GROWERS

Bonneau du Martray
Chanson Père & Fils
Daudet-Corcelle
Maison Doudet-Naudin
Jacques Germain
Girard-Vollot
Antonin Guyon

Domaine
  Laleure Piot
Maison Louis Latour
Lucien Jacob Leroy
Rapet Père & Fils
Tollot-Voarick
Michel Voarick

SAVIGNY-LES-BEAUNE

Savigny, like Pernand-Vergelesses, stops the head of a little valley cut back into the Côte and grows vines on both sides of it. On the Pernand side they face south, on the Beaune side northeast. The best are at the extremities of the parish, where both incline most to the east; respectively Les Vergelesses and Lavières, and La Dominode and Marconnets. The valley is drained by the little River Rhoin. Savigny has a substantial château, a great number of good growers, and best of all a tendency to more moderate prices than its neighbours. Its wines are in every way classic, apt to age, yet never ultra-chic. They need a good vintage to bring them up to their full strength – but whose do not?

PREMIERS CRUS

Total area approx.
    530 acres:
Basses Vergelesses (4.5)
Bataillere (42.5)
  (also called Aux
  Vergelesses)
Charnières (5)
Clous (38)
Fourneaux
Gravains (16.5)
Guettes (53.5)
Jarrons (37.5)

Hauts Marconnets (23)
Lavières (45)
Bas Marconnets (23)
Narbantons (25)
Petits Godeaux (19)
Peuillets (53)
Redrescut (2.5)
Serpentières
Talmattes

Appellations
  Régionales: 148 acres.

GROWERS

Pierre André
G.A.E.C. Simon Bize
Bouchard Père & Fils
Capron-Charcousset
Chandon de Briailles
Chanson Père & Fils
Bruno Clair
Daudet-Corcelle
Doudet-Naudin
P. Dubreuil-Fontaine
  Père& Fils
Girard-Vollot

Goud de Beaupuis
Antonin Guyon
de la Juvinière
Lucien Jacob
Leroy
Machard de Gramont
Ch. de Meursault
Jean-Marc Pavelot Père
Pierre Seguin
Tollot-Beaut & Fils
Tollot-Voarick
Henri de Villamont

BEAUNE

Beaune offers more temptation than any town to turn a wine encyclopedia into a guide book. It begs to be visited. Walking its wobbly streets between its soothing cellars is one of the great joys. The oldest, biggest, grandest and most of the best négociants have their warrens here. They also own the greater part of its wide spread of vineyards. Do not look to Beaune for the most stately or the most flighty wines. 'Franc de goût' is the classic description, which is almost impossible to translate. 'Franc' signifies straight, candid, open, real, downright, forthright and upright. Not dull, though. Young Beaune is already good to drink; as it ages it softens and broadens its bouquet.

If there is a pecking order among the Premiers Crus the following are near the top of it: Les Grèves, Fèves, Cras, Champimonts and Clos des Mouches (which also produces a rare and excellent white wine). But nobody would claim to be able to distinguish them all, and more depends on the maker than the site. For this reason the various 'monopoles' of the négociants are usually worth their premium. Their names are prefixed with the word 'Clos'. The three biggest landowners are Bouchard Père & Fils, Chanson and the Hospices de Beaune.

PREMIERS CRUS

Total area 795 acres:
Aigrots (37)
Avaux (33.5)

Bas Teurons (17.9)
Belissand
Blanches Fleurs (23)

Boucherottes (22)
Bressandes (44)
Cent Vignes (58)
Champs
    Pimont (41)
Chouacheux (12.5)
Coucherias (57)
Cras (12.5)
A l'Ecu (7.5)
Epenottes (35)
Fèves (10.5)
En Genèt (12.5)
Grèves (79.5)
Sur les Grèves (10)
Marconnets (25.2)
Mignotte (5)
Montée Rouge (41)
Montrevenots (20)
Clos des
    Mouches (61.4)

Clos de la Mousse (8)
En l'Orme (5)
Perrières (8)
Pertuisots (14)
Reversées (13)
Clos du Roi (34)
Seurey (3)
Sizies (21)
Teurons (38)
Tiélandry (4)
Toussaints (15)
Tuvilains
Vignes Franches (25)
Appellation Communale:
    316 acres
Appellations Régionales:
    370 acres
(The acreages in Beaune
are not officially
confirmed.)

GROWERS

Robert Ampeau & Fils
Arnoux
Besancenot-
    Mathouillet
Billard-Gonnet
Jean-Marc Boillot
Bouchard Aîné & Fils
Bouchard Père & Fils
Pierre Bourré
Louis Carillon & Fils
Chanson Père & Fils
Coron Père & Fils
Daudet-Corcelle
Maison Doudet-Naudin
Maison Joseph Drouhin
Michel Gaunoux
Jacques Germain
Goud de Beaupuis
Hospices de Beaune
Maison Louis Jadot
Michel Lafarge

Maison Louis Latour
Lycée Viticole
Machard de Gramont
Mazilly Père & Fils
Ch. de Meursault
Moillard
Jean Monnier & Fils
René Monnier
Albert Morot
André Mussy
Patriarche
    Père & Fils
Jacques Prieur
Rapet Père & Fils
Guy Roulot & Fils
Daniel Senard
René Thévenin-
    Monthelie & Fils
Thomas-Moillard
Tollot-Beaut & Fils
Tollot-Voarick

CHOREY-LES-BEAUNE

The little appellation of Chorey-lès-Beaune slips off the map down into the plain. Its wine is generally commercialized as Côte de Beaune-Villages.

Best growers: Tollot Beaut and Jacques Germain.

COTE DE BEAUNE

This appellation was instituted, as it seems, to discover who was dozing during the complexities of Côte de Beaune-Villages (*see* page 111). It applies only to wine from Beaune

(which has no reason to use it) or from another 22 acres adjoining, which appear to be just as deserving. La Grande Châtelaine, the Clos de Topes and Clos de Monsnières are the only vineyards I know that use it, for an admirable white as well as red.

Best grower: J. M. Allexant.

POMMARD

In the war of words that continually tries to distinguish one village from another, the wines of Pommard seem to have been labelled *'loyaux et marchands'*, which translates as 'loyal and commercial'. The suggestion is not of poetic flights. Pommard makes solid, close-grained wines of strong colour, aggressive at first, bending little even with age. Les Rugiens with its iron-red soil is the vineyard with most of these qualities, considered the best of the village. Les Epenots, on the edge of Beaune, gives rather easier wine. But there are some proud and decidedly loyal growers in the parish.

PREMIERS CRUS

Total area 309 acres:
Argillières (10)
Arvelets (20)
Bertins (8.5)
Clos Blanc (11)
Boucherottes (4.5)
Chanière (25)
Chanlins Bas (17.5)
Chaponnières (8)
Les Charmots (7)
Combes Dessus (7)
Chanlins Bas (11)
Clos de la
    Commaraine (10)
Croix Noires (3)
Les Charmots (24)
Derrière St-Jean (0.5)
Fremiers (12.5)

Grand Epenots (25)
Les Jarolières (8)
Clos Micot (7)
Petits Epenots (51)
Pézerolles (14.5)
Platière (6)
Poutures (11)
Refène (6)
Rugiens-Bas (15)
Rugiens-Hauts (14)
Saussiles (9)
Clos de Verger (6)

Appellation Communale:
522 acres.
Appellations Régionales:
823 acres.

GROWERS

Robert Ampeau & Fils
Comte Armand
Marquis-d'Angerville
Billard-Gonnet
Jean-Marc Boillot
Pierre Boillot
Bouchard Père & Fils
Y. Clerget
de Courcel
F. Gaunoux
Michel Gaunoux
Goud de Beaupuis
Bernard et Louis Glantenay
Lequin Roussot
Maison Leroy
Machard de Gramont

Mazilly Père & Fils
Ch. de Meursault
Michelot-Buisson
Jean Monnier & Fils
René Monnier
Monthelie-Douhairet
de Montille
André Mussy
Parent
Jean Pascal & Fils
Ch. de Pommard
Henri Potinet
Dom. de la Pousse d'Or
Ropiteau-Mignon
Serrigny
Joseph Voillot

VOLNAY

Corton and Volnay are the extremes of style of the Côte de Beaune. The first regal, robust, deep-coloured and destined to dominate; the second tender, 'lacy', a lighter red with a soft-fruit scent, all harmony and delight. The dictum goes that Volnay is the Chambolle-Musigny of the Côte de Beaune. Personally I find it exact: each is my favourite from its area. To shift the ground a little, Château Latour answers to Corton; Lafite lovers will want Volnay.

The lovely little village hangs higher in the hills than its neighbours, its 284 acres of Premiers Crus on the mid-slopes below. The long ramp of vines that leads down to Meursault contains Les Caillerets, in now-obsolete terms the *tête de cuvée;* something between a Premier Cru and a Grand Cru. Champans, beside it under the village, reaches the same class. There is no clear division between Volnay and its southern neighbours, Meursault in the valley and Monthelie on the hill. The same style of wine, even the same vineyard names continue. Meursault is allowed to use the name of Volnay for red wine grown in its part of Caillerets, Santenots, Pitures and Cras (as long as it uses Pinot Noir). To taste them beside the white Premiers Crus of Meursault is to discover that red and white wine are by no means chalk and cheese.

PREMIERS CRUS

Angles	Lurets (5)
Bousse d'Or (5)	Mitans (10)
Brouillards (14)	En l'Ormeau (11)
En Caillerets (7)	Pitures Dessus (9)
Cailleret Dessus (28)	Pointes d'Angles (3)
Carelle sous la Chapelle (9.5)	Robardele (7.5)
Carelle Dessous (3.5)	Ronceret (5)
Champans (28)	Santenots (20)
Chanlins (7)	Taille Pied (22)
Clos des Chênes (38)	En Verseuil (1.5)
Chevret (15)	Le Village (16)
Clos des Ducs (6)	Appellation Communale:
Frémiets (18.25)	527 acres.

GROWERS

Robert Ampeau & Fils	Comte Lafon
Marquis d'Angerville	Joseph, Thierry &
Jean-Marc Boillot	Pascale Matrot
Pierre Boillot	Ch. de Meursault
Bouchard	René Monnier
Père & Fils	Monthelie-Douhairet
Y. Clerget	Dom de Montille
Jean-François	André Mussy
Coche-Dury	Jean Pascal & Fils
Jacques Gagnard-	Henri Potinet-Ampeau
Delagrange	Domaine de la
F. Gaunoux	Pousse d'Or
Bernard &	Jacques Prieur
Louis Glantenay	Ropiteau-Mignon
Antonin Guyon	
Michel Lafarge	

MONTHELIE

Just as Corton-Charlemagne goes on round the corner into Pernand-Vergelesses, so the best Volnay vineyard flows into the lesser-known Monthélie. It changes its name to Les Champs-Fulliot. The centre of interest in the village of Monthélie is its château, the property of its most distinguished grower, Robert de Suremain.

PREMIERS CRUS

Total area: 77 acres:	Riottes (1.85)
Cas Rougeot (1.5)	Taupine (4)
Champs Fulliot (20)	Vignes Rondes (7)
Duresses (16.5)	Total area 305 acres:
Château Gaillard (1.2)	Appellation Communale:
Clos Gauthey (4.5)	267 acres
Sur La Velle (15)	Appellations Régionales:
Meix-Bataille (6.5)	103.5 acres

GROWERS

Jean-François Coche-Dury	Ropiteau-Mignon
Monthelie-Douhairet	Robert de Suremain
Jean-Philippe Fichet	René Thévenin-Monthelie
Paul Garandet	& Fils
Comte Lafon	

MEURSAULT

If Meursault has convinced itself that it is a town, it fails to convince visitors looking for amenities – still less action. Its streets are a bewildering forest of hoardings to cajole the tourist into the cellars that are its whole *raison d'être*. Levels of commercialism vary. In one property half-hidden with invitations to enter I was told, and curtly, that I could not taste unless I was going to buy. There seemed to be no answer to my mild protest that I could not tell if I was going to buy until I had tasted.

There is a mass of Meursault, and it is mixed. Its model is a drink that makes me thirsty even to think of it; a meeting of softness and succulence with thirst-quenching clarity and 'cut'. A 'Village' Meursault will be mild; the higher up the ladder you go the more authority and 'cut' the wine will have. I am thinking of a '78 Premier Cru Charmes from Joseph Matrot, which at three years old was almost painful to hold in your mouth: this is the authority and concentration of a first-class wine of a great vintage. With age comes rounding out, the onset of flavours people have described with words like oatmeal and hazelnuts and butter; things that are rich but bland.

The white wine vineyards of Meursault are those that continue unbroken into Puligny-Montrachet to the south, and the best those that are nearest to the parish line: Les Perrières, Les Charmes, Les Genevrières. The hamlet of Blagny, higher on the same hill, also contains Meursault Premiers Crus of the top quality: Sous le Dos d'Ane and La Pièce sous le Bois – names that seem to express a rustic crudity which is far from being the case. Village wines from high on the hill (Les Tillets, Les Narvaux) are excellent. Like Blagny they are slow to develop.

The best red wines of Meursault sell as Volnay-Santenots.

PREMIERS CRUS

Total area 397 acres:
Red and white: 215 acres;
white only: 272 acres;
red only (Volnay):
128 acres.
Divided as follows
Red and white:
Bouchères (10.5)
Caillerets (2.5)
Charmes Dessous (41.6)
Charmes Dessus (32.25)
Clos des Perrières (74)
Chaumes de Narvaux (0.3)
Cras (8.75)
Genevrières Dessous
and Genevrières
Dessus (39.5)
Gouttes d'Or (13)
Jeunelotte (13)

Perrières Dessous and
Perrières Dessus (34)
La Pièce sous le Bois (28)
Pitures (26)
Porusots (10.75)
Porusot Dessus (17.5)
Santenots Blancs (7.5)
Santenots du Milieu (20)
Sous le Dos d'Ane (7.5)
Red (Volnay) only:
Les Plures (26)
Les Santenots Blancs (7)
Les Santenots Dessous (19)
Les Santenots du
Milieu (20)
Total acreage: 1,257 acres.
Appellation Communale
Meursault: 735 acres
Appellations Régionales
103.5 acres

GROWERS

Robert Ampeau & Fils
Comte Armand
Marquis-d'Angerville
Pierre Boillot
Bouchard Père & Fils
Michel Bouzereau
Yves Boyer-Martenot
Jean-François Coche-Dury
Darnat
Jean-Philippe Fichet
F. Gaunoux Fils
Antonin Guyon
Charles et Remi Jobard
François Jobard
Jean Joliot & Fils
Michel Lafarge
Comte Lafon
Leflaive
Maison Leroy

Domaine du Duc de
Magenta
René Manuel
Joseph, Thierry &
Pascale Matrot
Mazilly Père & Fils
Ch. de Meursault
Michelot-Buisson
Jean Monnier & Fils
René Monnier
Monthelie-Douhairet
Henri Potinet-Ampeau
Jacques Prieur
Ropiteau Frères
Guy Roulot & Fils
Etienne Sauzet
René Thévenin-Monthelie
& Fils
Joseph Voillot

BLAGNY

Blagny has no appellation of its own, but possesses excellent vineyards in both Meursault and Puligny-Montrachet. Total area 134 acres.

PULIGNY-MONTRACHET
PREMIERS CRUS

51 acres:
La Garenne (24.5)

Hameau de Blagny (10.5)
Sous le Puits (16.75)
Appellation Communale
Blagny: 19.5 acres

MEURSAULT PREMIERS CRUS

58 acres:
La Jeunelotte (12.5)
La Pièce sous le Bois (29)
Sous Blagny (5.5)

Sous le Dos d'Ane (12.5)
Appellation Communale
Blagny: 4.5 acres

GROWERS

Robert Ampeau
& Fils
Leflaive

Joseph, Thierry & Pascale
Matrot
Jean Pascal & Fils

AUXEY-DURESSES

The village above and behind Meursault where a valley at right angles to the Côte provides a south slope at the correct mid-point of the hill for a limited patch of Premier Cru vineyard, mostly planted in Pinot Noir. Among other growers, the Duc de Magenta produces white wine like very crisp Meursault which I find more exciting than Auxey red. Much of the red, I gather, is sold as Côte de Beaune-Villages. The village also shelters the fabulous stocks of Mme Bize-Leroy, the *Gardienne des Grands Millésimes' (see* Maison Leroy).

PREMIERS CRUS

78 acres:
Bas des Duresses (20)
Bréterins
Duresses (20)
Ecusseaux (8)
Grands Champs (10)

Reugne (8)
Climat or Clos du Val (23)
Total acreage: 1,235 acres.
Appellation Communale
Auxey-Duresses: 341 acres.
Appellations Régionales
815 acres.

GROWERS

Robert Ampeau & Fils
Jean-François Coche-Dury
Maison Leroy
Dom du Duc de Magenta

Henri Potinet-Ampeau
Guy Roulot & Fils
Roland Thévenin

ST-ROMAIN

A pretty little village lurking in the second wave of hills, behind Auxey-Duresses, and only promoted to Côte de Beaune-Villages status in 1967. It has no Premier Cru land, being too high on the hills, and makes more and better white wine than red.

Best grower: Alain Gros.

PULIGNY-MONTRACHET

Puligny and Chassagne appear at first sight like Siamese twins linked by their shared Grand Cru, Le Montrachet. But the impression is a false one. Puligny is a dedicated white-wine parish. Chassagne, despite the Montrachet of its name, used to earn most of its living from red.

There is no magic by which white wine from Meursault Charmes must taste different from the Puligny Premier Cru Les Combettes, which meets it at the boundary. I can only repeat that I would expect the Puligny-Montrachet to have a slightly more lively taste of fruit, a bit more bite and perhaps a floweriness which is not a Meursault characteristic. Sheaves of old tasting notes tend to contradict each other, so my description is pure Impressionism – all that airy metaphor in dabs of paint representing orchards does seem to have something to do with the taste I cannot describe.

What is more tangible is the superiority of the Premiers Crus. Those of Combettes and Champ Canet at the Meursault end of Puligny, and the part of Blagny that lies in this parish with the appellation Blagny Premier Cru, can be expected to be closer to Meursault in style. A slightly higher premium is normally put on the ones that border the Grands Crus: Le Cailleret and Les Pucelles.

Two of the Grands Crus that are the white-wine climax of Burgundy lie entirely within Puligny-Montrachet; Chevalier-Montrachet, the strip of hill above Montrachet, and Bienvenues-Bâtard-Montrachet, half the shallower slope below. The accepted appreciation of 'Chevalier' is that it has the fine flavour of Montrachet but in less concentrated form (concentration being the hallmark of this grandest of all white wines). The critics do not normally distinguish between Bienvenues and Bâtard (to shorten their unwieldy names). Any such generalization is inevitably overturned by the next tasting of a different vintage or a different grower's wine.

As for Puligny-Montrachet 'Village' without frills – it is still expensive. Is it worth more than Meursault? Probably not, as there is more excitement to be had from the better 'village' wines of Meursault. The Puligny-Montrachet is likely to be slightly the more expensive of the two, about the same as a *grand cru* Chablis or 'Reserve' quality California Chardonnay.

GRANDS CRUS

Total area 56.5 acres:	Bienvenues-Bâtard-
Bâtard-	Montrachet (9)
Montrachet (15)	Chevalier- Montrachet (18)
	Montrachet (10)

PREMIERS CRUS

Total area 247 acres:	Hameau de Blagny (11)
Cailleret (9.75)	Pucelles (16.5)
Chalumeaux (14.25)	Referts (34)
Champ Canet (8)	Sous le Puits (16.75)
Clavoillon (13.5)	Appellation Communale
Combettes (16.5)	Puligny-Montrachet:
Folatières (43)	272 acres.
Garenne (28)	Appellations Régionales:
	606 acres.

GROWERS

Robert Ampeau & Fils	Louis Carillon & Fils
Adrien Belland	Chartron & Trebuchet
Jean-Marc Boillot	Gérard Chavy
Bouchard Père & Fils	Philippe Chavy

Maison Joseph Drouhin	René Monnier
Maison Louis Jadot	Jean Pascal & Fils
Domaine Leflaive	Paul Pernot
Olivier Leflaive Frères	Jacques Prieur
Maison Leroy	Domaine de la
Lycée Viticole	Romanée-Conti
Dom du Duc de Magenta	Etienne Sauzet
Jean Monnier & Fils	Roland Thévenin

CHASSAGNE-MONTRACHET

Almost half of the Grands Crus Le Montrachet and Bâtard-Montrachet and the whole of Criots-Bâtard-Montrachet occupy the hill corner that ends the parish to the north. Unfortunately, the steep south-facing slope that runs at right angles to them, along the road to St-Aubin in the hills, has not enough soil for vines. If this were the Douro there would be terraces. Between here and the village there is some Premier Cru land, but the famous wines begin again where the Côte picks up its momentum and its tilt in the Clos St-Jean above the little township. Caillerets, Ruchottes and Morgeot are names seen on expensive and memorable white bottles. Clos St-Jean, La Boudriotte ... in fact all the rest stress red.

Any association of ideas that suggests that red Chassagne should be a light wine is quite wrong. Far from being a gentle fade-out from Volnay, Chassagne returns to the meat and muscle of Corton or the Côte de Nuits. The best example I know of the brilliant duality of this land is the Duc de Magenta's Clos de la Chapelle, part of the Premier Cru Abbaye de Morgeot, which is half red and half white, and (at least in the early 1970s) was brilliant on both counts. Red Chassagne, moreover, sells at the price of the lesser-known villages – much cheaper than the grand names of the Côte de Nuits and every bit as satisfying.

GRANDS CRUS

Total area 28 acres	Criots-Bâtard-Montrachet (4)
(all white):	Montrachet (10)
Bâtard-Montrachet (14)	

PREMIERS CRUS

Total area 395 acres (red	Chenevottes (28)
and white, but En Cailleret	Grandes
produces red only;	Ruchottes (7.5)
Cailleret, also known	Macherelles (10)
as Chassagne, produces	Maltroie (23)
white only)	Morgeot (9.75)
Abbaye de Morgeot	Romanée
Boudriotte (45)	Clos St-Jean (36)
Brussonnes (45)	Vergers (23)
Cailleret (15)	Appellation Communale
En Cailleret (15)	Chassagne-Montrachet:
Champs Gain (71)	442 acres.

GROWERS

Amiot-Bonfils	Père & Fils
Bachelet-Ramonet	Adrien Belland
	Louis Carillon & Fils

Fernand Coffinet	Ch. de la Maltroye
Jacques Gagnard-	Albert Morey
Delagrange	& Fils
J.N. Gagnard	Jacques Prieur
Domaine Leflaive	A. Ramonet
Lequin-Roussot	Ramonet-Prudhon
Dom. du Duc de Magenta	Etienne Sauzet

Le Montrachet

All critics agree that the best Montrachet is the best white burgundy. In it all the properties that make the mouth water in memory and anticipation are brought to a resounding climax. The first quality that proclaims it at a tasting with its neighbours is a concentration of flavour. I have wondered how much this is due to its singular site and its soil and how much to the regulations (and common sense) that keep its crop to a minimum. There is little doubt that other good vineyards could pack more punch if their keepers kept them more meanly pruned and fertilized, picked late and used only the best bunches. Such economics only work for a vineyard whose wine is as good as sold before it is made, at almost any price. The principal owners of Le Montrachet are the Marquis de Laguiche (whose wine is handled by Drouhin of Beaune), Baron Thénard of Givry, Bouchard Père & Fils, Fleurot-Larose of Santenay, Roland Thévenin and the Domaine de la Romanée-Conti. The Comte Lafon and Domaine Leflaive produce excellent wines.

ST-AUBIN

St-Aubin is a twin to St-Romain, a village tucked into the first valley behind the Côte but with a slight advantage of situation that gives it some Premiers Crus, which are mainly exploited for red wine. The village of Gamay (the presumed source of the grape that makes Beaujolais but it is a taint to the Côte d'Or) contributes about half the land in this appellation. Both Raoul Clerget and Hubert Lamy make a speciality of it, but the greater part is simply sold as Côte de Beaune-Villages. There are some good whites in a sub-Puligny style.

SANTENAY

It is a conceit, I know, but I have always found the names of the villages of Burgundy to be a useful clue to the nature of their wines. Chambertin has a drum-roll sound, Chambolle-Musigny a lyrical note, Pommard sounds precisely right for its tough red wine and so does Volnay for its more silky produce. Santenay sounds like good health. (Funnily enough it has a far-from-fashionable spa for the treatment of rheumatism and gout.)

Healthiness seems just the right sort of image to attach to the wines of Santenay. They are rather plain, even-flavoured with no great perfume or thrills but good solid drinking. At their best, in Les Gravières, La Comme and Le Clos de Tavannes, they are in the same class as Chassagne-Montrachet, weighty and long-lived. Other parts of the parish with stonier, more limey soil have paler reds and a little white wine. Best growers: Lequin-Roussot, Morey, Domaine de la Pousse d'Or.

PREMIERS CRUS

Total area 306 acres	Gravières (72.5)
(red and white)	Maladière (33)
Beauregard (82)	Passe Temps (31)
Beaurepaire (42.5)	Clos des Tavannes (66)
Comme (80)	Appellation Communale:
Clos Foubard	628 acres

GROWERS

Domaine Bart	René Monnier
Adrien Belland	Domaine de
Fleurot-Larose	la Pousse d'Or
Lequin-Roussot	Prieur-Brunet
Mestre Père & Fils	

MARANGES

This new (1989) appellation covers the three rather forlorn little villages which share the vineyard Les Maranges, along the hill just west of Santenay and to their regret just over the *département* line of the Côte d'Or, in the outer darkness of Saône-et-Loire. Their names are Sampigny, Dézize and Cheilly – but Côte de Beaune-Villages is more likely to appear on their labels. The wines are well structured with deep colour, generally quite tannic. They age well and make splendid drinking when 8 years old, as the local clientele buying direct have proved time and again. In an average year some 130,000 cases make use of this appellation.

CHEILLY-LES-MARANGES PREMIERS CRUS (RED AND WHITE)
Boutières, Maranges and Plantes de Maranges (together 108 acres)

DEZIZE-LES-MARANGES PREMIER CRU (RED AND WHITE)
Maranges (150)

SAMPIGNY-LES-MARANGES PREMIERS CRUS (RED AND WHITE)
Clos des Rois (36)
Maranges (35)

GROWERS

Bernard Bachelet et Fils	Y. & C. Contat-Grange
Paul Chevrot	

COTE DE BEAUNE-VILLAGES

All the villages of the Côte de Beaune, with the exception of Beaune, Pommard, Volnay and Aloxe-Corton, have this as a fallback appellation in red wine (only).

GROWERS AND MERCHANTS

The almost literally priceless land of the Côte d'Or is broken up into innumerable small units of ownership, variously expressed as ares (a hundredth of a hectare) and centiares (a hundredth of an are) or as *ouvrées* (an old measure which is one twenty-fourth of a hectare, or about a tenth of an acre). These little plots come about by the French system of inheritance, by the size of the capital needed to buy more, and by the dread of local disasters, which make it inadvisable to put all your eggs in one basket.

They mean that a grower who has, say, 20 acres may well have them in 30 different places – often just a few rows of vines separated from his others in the same vineyard.

The precious land is also divided by ancient custom into a jigsaw of *'climats'*, or fields, sometimes with natural and obvious boundaries, sometimes apparently at random. Each *'climat'* is a known local character with a meaning and value to the farmers that is hard for an outsider to grasp.

Overlay the one pattern on the other and you have the fragmentation of ownership which bedevils buyers of burgundy. Whereas in Bordeaux a château is a consistent unit doing one or at most two things on a reasonably large scale, a Burgundy domaine is often a man and his family coping with a dozen or more different wines with different needs and problems. If he is a good husbandman of vines his talent does not necessarily extend to the craftsmanship of the cellar – or vice versa. For any number of reasons, inconsistency is almost inevitable.

There are major exceptions in the form of bigger vineyards with richer owners. But the concept of the little man trying to do everything is fundamental. It explains the importance of the négociants or 'shippers', whose traditional role is to buy the grower's grapes or newly made wine, mature it and blend it with others of the same vineyard or village or district to make marketable quantities of something consistent.

It takes little imagination to see that an unscrupulous merchant could get away with almost anything under these conditions. Consumers have probably always, since Roman times, had grounds for complaint. The old and profitable game of 'stretching' the limited supplies with imports from the south is now made very much harder by the application of the strict appellation laws. But there is still plenty of room for manoeuvre in the area of quality. There are governemnt inspectors, but nobody pretends there is comprehensive and effective inspection.

When most consumers hear that merchants are venal their reaction is to look for authenticity from the growers, direct. Bottling at the domaine has been presented as the answer. It brings us back, though, to the basic question: who is more competent and more conscientious? Ownership of a corner of a fine and famous field does not carry with it a technical degree in winemaking or *'élevage'* – the 'bringing up' of wine in the cellar – or bottling.

It can be a depressing experience to taste a set of broker's samples submitted to a négociant from good vineyards, even after a good vintage. A considerable proportion of the wines are likely to be either over-sugared or in poor condition, or both.

The greatest change of the past 15 years in Burgundy, though, has been the growing competence of a younger generation of growers, well-schooled and innovative, who are making often small lots of far better wine than Burgundy has probably ever seen.

Domaine Pierre Amiot & Fils

21220 Morey St-Denis.
A traditionalist grower with small plots totalling 26 acres in Grands Crus Clos de la Roche and Clos St-Denis as well as Gevrey-Chambertin Les Combottes and Chambolle-Musigny.

Robert Ampeau & Fils

6 rue du Cromin 21190 Meursault.
Outstanding 25-acre domaine respected particularly for its white wines. The best known are from Meursault Perrières, Charmes and La Pièce sous le Bois (partly in Blagny), 11 acres in all, and 2 acres in Puligny Combettes; wines with a good 10-year life span. Unusually M. Ampeau only sells wines well bottle-aged in his own cellars. Reds include 1 acre of Beaune Clos du Roi, 4 of Savigny Premier Cru (Lavières and Fourneaux) and 4 of Pommard. 'It is always difficult,' says M. Ampeau, 'to talk objectively about your own wine.'

Pierre André

Château de Corton-André, 21420 Aloxe-Corton.
Négociants and growers on the largest scale. Pierre André founded La Reine Pédauque. His 'château' at Corton is the centre for the 95-acre estate, which includes parts of Clos Vougeot (2.6 acres), Corton (Clos du Roi, Combes and Charlemagne), and Savigny Premier Cru Clos des Guettes (7.5 acres). Also produces Bourgogne Réserve Pierre André, Mâcon-Villages and Supérieur 'Domaine du Prieuré de Jocelyn'; Fleurie 'Domaine de la Treille', Beaujolais-Villages, Coteaux du Tricastin from the Rhône, etc. Sales are largely to restaurants and private clients in France, with 35% exports.

Domaine Marquis d'Angerville

Volnay, 21190 Meursault.
The impeccable domaine of a totally dedicated nobleman: 28 acres of Volnay Premier Cru, 1 of Pommard and 2.5 of Meursault Santenots – a rare appellation and a singularly succulent white. The monopole Clos des Ducs is an unusual steep and chalky 5.9-acre vineyard whose wine is noticeably alcoholic, tends to be pale and to my mind misses the velvet of the best Volnay, but can age magnificently. I prefer the domaine's more sumptuous Champans (from 10 acres). All its wines are beautifully made. The greater part is exported.

Domaine de l'Arlot

Prémeaux, 21700 Nuits-St-Georges.
Formerly the property of négociants Jules Belin, the domaine is now owned by the insurance group AXA. The director in Burgundy, Jean-Pierre de Smet, worked for many years at

Domaine Dujac (q.v.). The 39-acre domaine comprises three 'monopoles' – Nuits-St-Georges Premiers Crus 'Clos de l'Arlot' (red and white) and 'Clos des Forêts St Georges', and Côte de Nuits-Villages 'Clos du Chapeau'.

Domaine du Comte Armand

Place de l'Eglise, 21630 Pommard.
New life was breathed into this domaine which owns the monopoly of the excellent Pommard Premier Cru vineyard, Clos des Epeneaux, when the young Québecois Pascal Marchand was put in charge in 1985. These are deeply coloured intense wines which require significant ageing. Since 1995 the domaine has added vineyards in Auxey Duresses (red and white), Volnay and Meursault through share-cropping agreements.

Domaine Denis Bachelet

21220 Gevrey-Chambertin.
One man's tiny (7-acre) enterprise in Gevrey-Chambertin, Premier Cru Les Corbeaux and Charmes-Chambertin. But brilliantly stylish wines.

Domaine Bart

24 rue de Mazy, 21160 Marsannay-La-Côte.
André Bart has handed his property to his children, Odile and Martin, and it is now known as Domaine Bart. The domaine has 43 acres, including 20 at Marsannay, 3.5 at Fixin, 4 at Santenay and 2 in the Grands Crus Bonnes Mares and Clos de Bèze. Rosé de Marsannay, and Marsannay Blanc and Fixin Premier Cru Les Hervelets are the specialities.

Domaine Adrien Belland

21590 Santenay.
In 1954 Adrien Belland's father divided his domaine between his four sons, and the present domaine of 30 acres includes parcels of one Chambertin Grand Cru, three Corton Grands Crus, three Santenay Premiers Crus and one Chassagne-Montrachet Premier Cru.

Domaine Bertagna

Rue du Vieux Château, 21640 Vougeot.
Owners of some of the limited area of Vougeot Premier Cru outside the Clos Vougeot, including the 'monopole' Clos de la Perrière (5 acres), the hill just below Le Musigny. I have found this wine much better than many other growers' Clos Vougeot. Bertagna have a total of 70 acres, with 1 in Clos St-Denis and 5 in Chambertin.

Domaine Besancenot

21200 Beaune.
A 27-acre domaine with high standards created by a Beaune citizen of great repute and scholarship, M. Besancenot, whose advice I gratefully acknowledge. He died, alas, in 1981. 17 acres are in Beaune Premiers Crus (Bressandes, Clos du Roi, Toussaints, etc.), of which half is a parcel of Cent-Vignes with venerable vines, some 50 years old, which can give one of the best wines of Beaune. A part of the domaine which is rented includes a little Aloxe-Corton

Premier Cru and 2.5 acres of Pernand-Vergelesses, where there are some vines of Pinot Blanc.

Maison Albert Bichot

6 bis, boulevard Jacques Copeau, 21200 Beaune.
The biggest exporter of burgundy, with 85% of its 100-million-franc turnover in exports. The firm was founded in Beaune in 1831 and in 1927 opened an office in Bordeaux (where it owns the firm of Chantecaille). As a négociant Bichot also trades under the names of several of the companies it has taken over: Paul Bouchard, Charles Drapier, Rémy Gauthier, Bouchot-Ludot, Léon Rigault, Maurice Dard, etc. As a grower, Bichot owns two domaines: Clos Frantin in the Côte d'Or and Long-Depaquit in Chablis. The Domaine du Clos Frantin, based at Vosne-Romanée, has 32 acres, scattered through Gevrey-Chambertin, Richebourg, Clos de Vougeot, Grands-Echézeaux, Echézeaux, Vosne-Romanée Les Malconsorts, Nuits-St-Georges and Corton Charlemagne. See also Lupé-Cholet. Their own wines are first-rate; as négociants they sell all sorts.

Domaine Billard-Gonnet

21630 Pommard.
12.5 acres of the 24.7-acre domaine are scattered between seven Pommard Premiers Crus including 3.7 acres in Le Clos de Verger. There is also a small parcel of Beaune Premier Cru Clos des Mouches (blanc).

Simon Bize & Fils

21420 Savigny-lès-Beaune.
A domaine of 35 acres entirely in Savigny, with 12.5 acres in the Premiers Crus Vergelesses (5.4 acres), Guettes, Talmettes, Fournaux and Marconnets. Father and son go to the length of buying new barrels for a third of their wine, which might be taken as a model of the lively, crisp style of Savigny. Vergelesses is their speciality. They also make 1,600 cases of a Bourgogne Blanc.

Domaine Jean Boillot et Fils

Volnay, 21190 Meursault.
A total of 53 acres makes this a major domaine in Volnay (10 acres), Puligny-Montrachet (10 acres, including the 'monopole' Clos de la Mouchère) and Pommard Premier Cru (5.5 acres).

Jean-Marc Boillot

21630 Pommard.
Jean-Marc's inheritance comes partly through his paternal grandfather, Henri and partly from his maternal grandfather, the late Etienne Sauzet (q.v.). He is equally at home making richly oaked white wines from various vineyards mostly in Puligny Montrachet, or clearly defined reds from Volnay and Pommard.

Domaine Lucien Boillot & Fils

21220 Gevrey-Chambertin.
Two more grandchildren of Henri Boillot, Louis and Pierre, run this flourishing domaine in Gevrey, Nuits, Pommard, Volnay and Fixin. Excellent quality.

Pierre Boillot

21190 Meursault.

A 15.6-acre domaine that includes 1.3 acres of Meursault-Charmes Premier Cru, where the vines are 60 years old, and half an acre of Meursault Goutte d'Or Premier Cru, as well as very tasty and powerful Pommard and Volnay Santenots.

Jean-Claude Boisset

21701 Nuits-St-Georges.

A recent (in Burgundian terms – 1961) foundation which has since swallowed up many long-established names, including Charles Viénot, Bouchard Aîné, Pierre Ponnelle, Jaffelin, Louis Violland and recently the Cellier des Samsons in the Beaujolais. The company also owns just under 100 acres of land. In general Boisset has been more praised for commercial skills and marketing acumen than for attaining peaks of quality with its wines.

Domaine Bonneau du Martray

Pernand-Vergelesses, 21420 Savigny-lès-Beaune.

One of the biggest producers of the inimitable Corton-Charlemagne, with a solid block of 22 acres making some 4,000 cases a year, and an adjacent 5 acres giving red Corton Grand Cru. The famous Cuvée François de Salins, the costliest wine of the Hospices de Beaune, comes from the same prime hill-corner site. The domaine's wine is made in an unpretentious cellar in Pernand, using a modern press but otherwise strictly traditional methods, including new barrels for fermentation.

Quality has always been fine but a new generation in the cellars and in charge – Jean-Charles Le Bault de la Morinière having succeeded his father – has raised standards even higher. New cellars have been built to hold more bottles, in order to put the *grands crus* on the market at 7–10 years according to vintage. The Corton-Charlemagne behaves more like a red, ageing majestically. Three-star restaurants, alas, offer it at 3 years old when it should be 10. Ninety percent is exported – I hope to people with cellars.

Bouchard Aîné & Fils

36 rue Ste-Marguerite, 21203 Beaune.

The smaller Bouchard, although almost as old as the giant. A domaine with 57 acres of (all red) vines in Mercurey (Le Clos la Marche and La Vigne du Chapitre) and Beaune, which also makes (in Beaune) the wines of the Domaine Marion at Fixin (Clos du Chapitre, La Mazière and a little Chambertin-Clos de Bèze). Their wines are generally considered correct rather than exciting. Bouchard Aîné is one of the firms now in the hands of Jean-Claude Boisset (q.v.).

Bouchard Père & Fils

Au Château, 21202 Beaune.

The biggest domaine in Burgundy and one of the best négociants, run by Bouchards from father to son since 1731 until the company was sold to Henriot (of champagne fame) in 1995. Joseph Henriot immediately set in train a series of measures to raise the standing of the wines, including the declassification of some *grand cru* stocks such as Le

Montrachet which he thought not up to scratch – a move typical of the complex character of a man who is at once an agile businessman and a passionate guardian of quality.

Bouchard's biggest holdings are in Beaune, where their 43 acres of *premiers crus* include the 'monopoles' of the famous 10-acre Grèves Vigne de l'Enfant Jésus, the 8-acre Clos de la Mousse and the 5-acre Clos St-Landry. Other large plots are 10 acres of Marconnets and about 6 each of Cent Vignes and Teurons. Wine from smaller parcels is made and sold as Beaune du Château Premier Cru. Beyond Beaune their principal parcels are 17 acres in Corton (some 9 of red Corton and 8 of Corton-Charlemagne), 10 in Savigny Les Lavières, 13.5 in Volnay (of which 10 is Caillerets), a little Pommard, and important plots of 2.5 acres in Le Montrachet and 5 – the biggest part – in Chevalier-Montrachet. Among their more notable wines are Volnay Caillerets labelled as 'Ancienne Cuvée Carnot', untypically foursquare and long-lived Volnay from very old vines. They also have exclusive distribution rights over the Grand Cru La Romanée, an excellent Premier Cru Nuits-St-Georges, 'Clos St-Marc', and two-thirds of the production of Bourgogne Aligoté Bouzeron (appellation status since 1979).

Pierre Bourée Fils

21220 Gevrey-Chambertin.

Pierre Bourée is a négociant-grower. Most (5.2 acres) of the 9.8-acre domaine is in Clos de la Justice. Between 60 and 90% of production is exported. Also known as Vallet Frères.

Lionel J. Bruck

6 quai Dumorey, 21700 Nuits-St-Georges.

A flourishing merchant house which has contracts with growers totalling 110 acres in the Côte d'Or, including the 15-acre Domaine du Château de Vosne-Romanée, a parcel of Corton Clos du Roi and 17 acres of the Savigny Premier Cru Les Guettes. The same firm uses the name F. Hasenklever. Now part of the Jean-Claude Boisset stable (q.v.).

Domaine Alain Burguet

21220 Gevrey-Chambertin.

A small domaine of Village vines that has grown from 5 acres to 15 since beginning in 1974. The average age of the vines is 50 years. The *'cuvée vieilles vignes'* is considered better than some Premiers Crus in the village.

Louis Carillon & Fils

Puligny-Montrachet, 21190 Meursault.

A proud family domaine of 29 acres, going back 350 years, now run by Louis with his sons (while the generations before and after are also in evidence). They include a little patch of Bienvenues-Bâtard-Montrachet, 6 acres of Puligny Premier Cru and 12 of Puligny 'Village', with smaller parcels of Chassagne and Mercurey.

Some of the crop is sold in barrels to négociants, the rest in bottles to clients, who consider the name Carillon close behind the great domaines of Leflaive and Sauzet – or even alongside them in the 1990s. Carillon's Bienvenues-Batard-Montrachet 1986 is particularly respected.

Yves Chaley

Curtil-Vergy, 21220 Gevrey-Chambertin.

Yves Chaley is a skilful grower, making the lighter wines of the Hautes Côtes de Nuits. He has 32 acres of Pinot Noir and Chardonnay, and smaller parcels of Aligoté and Gamay. The red is vatted for 12 days in stainless steel and aged 18 months in oak barrels. Five years is a good age for it. There is also a fruity white, bottled after a year, which is for immediate drinking.

Château de Chambolle-Musigny

21700 Chambolle-Musigny.

The property of the Mugnier family, taken in hand by Frédéric Mugnier in 1984. His wines from Bonnes Mares, Musigny and Chambolle-Musigny Premiers Crus (Amoureuses and Les Fuées) are some of the finest of the commune, and steadily improving.

Maison Champy

5 rue du Grenier à Sel, 21200 Beaune.

Probably Beaune's oldest négociant house, founded in 1720, was sold in 1990: Louis Jadot (q.v) took the vineyards while the negociant operation was resurrected by Henri and Pierre Meurgey who have started out with some impressive wines, mostly red.

Domaine Chandon de Briailles

1 rue Soeur Goby, 21420 Savigny-lès-Beaune.

An important 32-acre property, largely in the best red-wine vineyards of Savigny (Les Lavières) and the neighbouring Ile des Vergelesses in Pernand, now run by mother and daughter to a very high standard. Also considerable owners in Corton with 7.5 acres in Bressandes, 2.5 in Clos du Roi and a little Corton Blanc.

Chanson Père & Fils

10 rue Paul Chanson, 21201 Beaune.

Négociants and growers (founded 1750) with a fine domaine of 110 acres, 60 of them in Beaune Premiers Crus, 10 in Savigny and 19 in Pernand-Vergelesses (which include 6 acres of Chardonnay). Their best wines are perhaps their Beaune Clos des Fèves (9.3 acres), Teurons (13 acres) and Bressandes (5.2 acres), but they have parts of all the best Beaune 'climats' and make excellent Savigny Premier Cru La Dominode.

The taste of the company is for wine aged in wood until it appears to be devoid of fruit and colour, but it will mature, as the Chansons assure us, 'sans surprise'. It is an old-fashioned way of producing stable wines for long keeping.

Maurice Chapuis

21420 Aloxe-Corton.

Maurice, son of Louis (who retired in 1985) farms 22 acres, of which he owns 2.5 and rents the rest. They include 9.5 acres of Corton-Charlemagne, producing 250 cases a year. Nearly 8 acres of Corton produce 700 cases of red. This, together with over 10 acres of Aloxe-Corton and 2 acres of Aloxe-Corton Premier Cru, accounts for more than half of their total

production. White wine is fermented in barrels; red in open vats to be *vins de garde*. His 1976 Corton was outstanding, as are the '83 and '88.

Chartron & Trebuchet

Puligny-Montrachet, 21190 Meursault.

The marriage of the Chartron domaine and the négociant Trebuchet, much talked about for oaky wines very much to some clients' taste. Could do better.

F. Chauvenet

6 rue de Chaux, 21700 Nuits-St-Georges.

One of the larger merchant houses, founded in 1853, and now owned by Jean-Claude Boisset (q.v.). It has the biggest share of the Burgundy direct-sales business in France and Belgium. Other names include Chevillot (selection of the Hôtel de la Poste at Beaune) and a 50% share (with the Max family) in the brand Louis Max.

Robert Chevillon

68 rue Félix Tisserand, 21700 Nuits-St-Georges.

A typical, family-run 32-acre estate, part owned and part rented. Outstanding winemaking, produces splendid Premier Cru Nuits-St-Georges from (especially) Les Cailles, Les St-Georges, Les Vaucrains, etc. His cousins, Georges and Michel Chevillon, also make fine Nuits-St-Georges.

Bruno Clair

21160 Marsannay-la-Côte.

When Domaine Clair Daü was divided in 1985, Bruno Clair received 43.6 acres, and he now sells very good wines under his own name in conjunction with his neighbour, André Geoffroy, who contributes an unusual Fixin Blanc, Clos Moreau. He has just under an acre of Chambertin Clos de Bèze Grand Cru, and 8.5 acres of Premiers Crus in Givry, Gevrey-Chambertin and Savigny-lès-Beaune (the excellent Les Dominodes). There are also 14.5 acres of Marsannay rouge, 7 acres of Marsannay rosé and small parcels of Marsannay blanc, Vosne-Romanée and Morey St-Denis, rouge and blanc.

Domaine Y. Clerget

Volnay, 21190 Meursault.

A domaine of 13 acres with an incredibly long history: the Clergets made wine in Volnay in 1268, the time of the Crusades. The pride of the house is their resounding Pommard Rugiens. Other parcels are in the Premier Cru Carelle sous la Chapelle and Volnay Caillerets and Meursault 'Village'. Yvon Clerget only bottles good vintages. 90% is exported to countries including Australia and Great Britain.

Georges Clerget

21640 Vougeot.

Owner of 7.5 acres and farmer of another 2.5: a very small domaine divided with equal (1.25-acre) plots in Chambolle-Musigny Premier Cru Charmes, Chambolle 'Village', Vougeot Premier Cru, Morey St-Denis and Vosne-Romanée. The rented parts are 2.5 acres in Echézeaux and a bare third of an acre in Bonnes Mares. The 'Charmes' is M. Clerget's own favourite; he does not like his wines too 'hard'. He removes three-quarters of the stems and ferments for 8–10 days.

Raoul Clerget

St-Aubin, 21190 Meursault.
For sheer antiquity the Clergets have no competitors. They are growers in a moderate (42-acre) way and négociants in quite a big one with a range of high standard Côte d'Or wines, Beaujolais, table wines, and one of Burgundy's best Cassis. St-Aubin (red and white) is a speciality. 1979 was the first vintage of their own replanted St-Aubin Domaine de Pimont (27 acres). Maurice Chenu now owns this house.

Jean-François Coche-Dury

21190 Meursault.
Jean-François is the third generation to own this 21-acre domaine that includes a small parcel of Meursault-Perrières. He has an almost fanatical following for his powerful and oaky, yet wonderfully balanced white wines – even his Bourgogne Blanc. His Volnay and Auxey-Duresses reds are less well-known.

Domaine de Courcel

21630 Pommard.
The Courcels have made Pommard here for 400 years. Their 20-acre domaine includes the 12-acre 'Grand Clos des Epenots' within the Premier Cru Epenots, and 2.5 acres of Rugiens. The vats, vertical press and cellars are strictly traditional. I opened a 16-year-old bottle of 1966 Courcel Rugiens to find out where I should be pitching my enthusiasm. Pommard is not normally my favourite burgundy. This wine was astonishingly dark and pure 'burgundy' red. The smell and taste were stubborn and inaccessible on first opening. After two hours in a decanter it began to give off a seductive creamy smell of nuts and damsons, which developed into what Michael Broadbent describes as fish-glue – in any case the smell of very fine old burgundy. Yet curiously the flavour remained austere and straight backed. Good but not great.

Domaine Pierre Damoy

20 rue des Forges, 21190 Meursault.
The biggest single share of Chambertin and Clos de Bèze (14 acres) belongs to the Damoy family. (Their other interests include the Château du Moulin à Vent in Beaujolais and Château La Tour de By in the Médoc.) Apart from 170 cases of Chambertin and 1,800 of Clos de Bèze of high quality, the Damoys make 900 of Chapelle-Chambertin and 600 of a Gevrey-Chambertin 'Monopole' Clos du Tamisot. The wines, though, were indifferent until a change of generation in 1993.

Domaine Darnat

20 rue des Forges, 21190 Meursault.
The owner of the tiny 'Clos Richemont', and a small parcel of the Premier Cru Goutte d'Or. Darnat also has another acre of Meursault 'Village' and a little Bourgogne Blanc.

Foreign investment and the support of wine enthusiasts have resulted in improvements to the estate.

Domaine Delagrange-Bachelet

Chassagne-Montrachet, 21190 Meursault.
One of the best-known domaines in Chassagne. 25 acres which include 1.25 acres each of Bâtard- and Criots-Bâtard-Montrachet, 2.5 of Premier Cru Caillerets, 5 of Morgeot (red and white) and small plots of Volnay and Pommard Premiers Crus. Edmond Delagrange-Bachelet died in 1996 at a great age. The vineyards now belong to his daughters and grand-daughters (Domaines Gagnard Delagrange, Blain-Gagnard and Fontaine-Gagnard).

Maison Doudet-Naudin

1 rue Henri Cyrot, 21420 Savigny-lès-Beaune.
A house associated with 'old-fashioned', very dark-coloured, concentrated, almost 'jammy' wines which have had a great following in Britain in the past. Berry Bros. & Rudd of St. James's bottled many of them. But they last, and 20-year-old bottles can be richly velvety and full of character. Lately the style has been lighter, more in tune with today's taste for fresh grapey flavours. Their 12-acre domaine is in Savigny (Les Guettes, red, and Le Redrescut, a not-very-graceful white), in Beaune Clos du Roy, Corton Charlemagne, Corton Maréchaudes and Pernand-Vergelesses. Other names are Albert Brenot and Georges Germain.

Maison Joseph Drouhin

7 rue d'Enfer, 21000 Beaune.
A leading négociant (founded in 1880) with one of the biggest domaines in Burgundy, augmented by 89 acres in Chablis. Now a total of 151 acres comprises Chablis, Chablis Grand Cru, Chablis Premier Cru, Chorey-lès-Beaune, Beaune Premier Cru, Beaune Clos des Mouches, Corton Charlemagne, Corton Bressandes, Volnay Clos des Chênes, Clos de Vougeot, Chambolle-Musigny Premier Cru, Griotte-Chambertin, Chambertin Clos de Bèze, Chambolle Musigny Amoureuses, Echézeaux, Grands-Echézeaux, Musigny and Bonnes Mares. The head of the house is Robert Drouhin, though ownership is now partly Japanese.

The whole gamut of Drouhin wines is made very conscientiously, rising to the appropriate peaks and never falling below fine quality in the Grands Crus. The speciality of the house is the excellent Beaune Clos des Mouches: long-lived, full-bodied wine, both red and white. After a serious fire in 1972 things did not go well for a while, but from 1976 on standards are first class. Red wines are fermented in oak at a fairly high temperature with at least half of their stems, and macerated for up to 2 weeks. New barrels are used for half the red and a quarter of the white. The best vintages (e.g. '85 red, '88 red and white, '85 white) are designed for long maturing. Drouhin also has sole rights on the superb Montrachet of the Marquis de Laguiche. As a négociant, he handles a wide range of well-chosen wines from all over Burgundy of which 75% is exported. Drouhin was the first Burgundian to plant Pinot Noir in the USA – in the Willamette Valley, Oregon.

Robert Dubois & Fils

Prémeaux-Prissey, 21700 Nuits-St-Georges.

An up-to-date family estate with 44 acres, of which 10 in Nuits include 2.5 in the Premiers Crus Les Porêts and Clos des Argillières. They use 'thermovinification', heating the must to get plenty of colour, followed by the usual methods. Forty percent of their production is exported.

Domaine P. Dubreuil-Fontaine Père & Fils

Pernand-Vergelesses, 21420 Savigny-lès-Beaune.

Bernard Dubreuil, the present manager, is the grandson of the founder of this 52-acre domaine, with 6 acres of Grand Cru Corton (principally Bressandes) and 2 of Corton-Charlemagne, as well as 9 of Savigny-Vergelesses Premier Cru and 13 of Pernand (red and white). They own the whole of the 2.5-acre Clos Berthet in the village of Pernand. His father Pierre has been mayor of Pernand for years and does the honours of the village for visitors with a perfect range of the wines of this privileged corner. His Grands Crus need keeping for a good 10 years.

Dufouleur Frères

1 rue de Dijon, 21701 Nuits-St-Georges.

An old family firm of négociants (four brothers and their father) with a small domaine in Nuits-St-Georges, Clos Vougeot and Musigny plus vineyards at Mercurey in the Côte Chalonnaise. Their wines are powerful and full of flavour.

Domaine Dugat

21220 Gevrey Chambertin.

Maurice and Claude Dugat have a tiny domaine in Gevrey Chambertin making wines of the highest class in the picturesque Cellier des Dîmes. Their cousin Bernard Dugat also makes very good wine under his own label.

Domaine Dujac

Morey St-Denis, 21220 Gevrey-Chambertin.

Jacques Seysses is the 'Jac' of the name. He is a qualified oenologist and is widely regarded as the most serious wine-maker in Morey St-Denis, with natural, patient (necessarily expensive) methods: fermenting stems and all for as long as possible, using new barrels, never filtering. The result is freshness with depth, as red burgundy should be. Clos de la Roche, where he has 4.8 acres, is his own favourite of his 27-acre domaine, which includes nearly 4 acres of Clos St-Denis, 8 of Morey 'Village', 3 of Gevrey-Chambertin Premier Cru 'Combottes', as well as small parcels of Charmes-Chambertin, Chambolle-Musigny Premier Cru, Echézeaux and of Bonnes Mares. Domaine Dujac wines are listed by most of France's three-star restaurants and have been served at the Elysée. Some 90 percent is exported.

Domaine René Engel

3, Place de la Mairie, 21700 Vosne-Romanée.

René Engel is a well-known name in Burgundy as raconteur as well as vigneron. *Propos sur l'Art de Bien Boire* was his philosophy in print. René's grandson Philippe is now in charge and has made great improvements. The domaine of 17 acres includes 3.4 acres on the upper slope of the Clos Vougeot and plots in Grands-Echézeaux, Echézeaux and Vosne-Romanée (both Premier Cru and 'Village'). The wines are fine, masculine, powerful characters.

Maison J. Faiveley

21700 Nuits-St-Georges.

The Faiveleys, an unbroken family succession since 1825, have the biggest domaine in Burgundy: 270 acres. 160 acres are in Mercurey, where their 13-acre 'monopole' Clos des Myglands is their best-known wine. Another 12 acres are in the neighbouring Rully. In Nuits their 74-acre holding includes the entire Clos de la Maréchale, a 24-acre Premier Cru 'monopole' in Prémeaux and 4 acres of the Premier Cru Les Porêts. 21 acres in Gevrey-Chambertin includes 3 each of the Grands Crus Mazis, Latricières and Clos de Bèze and 8.5 of Premiers Crus. They own 3 acres of Clos Vougeot, 2 of Echézeaux, 1.25 of Chambolle-Musigny, including a parcel of Le Musigny, and in the Côte de Beaune they have a 7-acre 'monopole' Corton Clos des Cortons Faiveley at Ladoix and a little Corton Blanc. In addition the Faiveleys have a further 20 acres of Bourgogne Rouge scattered about, and in those communes where they own no vines they buy in grapes and make the wine themselves at Nuits-St-Georges.

As if all this were not activity enough, Guy Faiveley, father of the present president of the company, François, has been the most active and entertaining protagonist of the Chevaliers de Tastevin for many years.

Faiveley wines are solidly structured, built-to-last burgundies at all levels. In Corton, Clos de Bèze etc, they reach the summit.

Domaine Fleurot-Larose

21590 Santenay.

This domaine of 42 acres also has vineyards at Pouilly-sur-Loire. Its main holding comprises 16 acres of Chassagne-Montrachet Premier Cru Abbaye de Morgeot (red and white) and 12.5 of Santenay Premier Cru, but it also owns three-quarters of an acre of Le Montrachet and half as much Bâtard-Montrachet.

Domaine Gagnard-Delagrange

Chassagne-Montrachet, 21190 Meursault.

A seventh-generation family of growers whose 13-acre domaine includes a small parcel of Le Montrachet, 5 of Chassagne-Montrachet Premier Cru (Morgeot and La Boudriotte), half an acre of Bâtard-Montrachet and 2 acres of red Chassagne. In addition, they have 1 acre of Volnay Champans (their top red). Jacques Gagnard's daughters' domaines, Blain-Gagnard and Fontaine-Gagnard, are also worth seeking out.

Domaine F. Gaunoux

21190 Meursault.

François Gaunoux is President of the Comité de Viticulture de la Côte d'Or and brother of Michel Gaunoux of Pommard. His 28-acre domaine, established in 1955, has 11 acres in

Meursault (5 in the Premiers Crus Perrières and Goutte d'Or), 3 in Volnay Clos des Chênes, 2 each in the Premiers Crus Beaune Clos des Mouches and Pommard (Rugiens and Epenots). Also 7 more of Pommard 'Village'. M. Gaunoux's own favourites are his Beaune and Volnay.

Domaine Michel Gaunoux

Rue Notre Dame, 21630 Pommard.

Brother of François of Meursault, considered by Hubrecht Duijker to contest the crown of best grower in Pommard with Jacques Parent (q.v.). Gaunoux has 17 acres, about 8 of them in Pommard Premier Cru with the biggest part in Epenots and the best (nearly 2 acres) in Rugiens. There are also nearly 1.5 acres of Corton Renardes and 5 acres of Beaune including the Premier Cru Boucherottes.

The wine is made with a fairly cool, slow fermentation which seems to extract all the lasting power of Pommard, staying firm and robust for a good decade. Most is sold direct to fine French restaurants; only 20 percent is exported.

Domaine Pierre Gelin

2 rue du Chapitre, Fixin, 21220 Gevrey-Chambertin.

The leading domaine in Fixin was run until recently by Stephen Gelin (son of Pierre) and André Molin. The latter has retired and his son has taken his share of the vineyards to start on his own. Which of Gelin and Molin will make the better wines now?

Domaine Jacques Germain

Château de Chorey-lès-Beaune, 21200 Beaune.

François Germain's turreted medieval Château de Chorey, below the *côtes* north of Beaune, has 10 acres of red in Chorey, 15 in Beaune Premier Cru and 7 (white) Pernand-Vergelesses. His Beaune includes Teurons (5 acres), Cent Vignes, Vignes Franches, Cras and Boucherottes. Total production is about 6,000 cases. Germain's philosophy is gentle and natural winemaking from old vines. The grapes are fermented with stems and aged in new barrels for some time before racking, letting fermentation finish slowly and naturally. The result is real finesse in full-bodied wines needing age.

Jean Germain

9 rue de la Barre, 21190 Meursault.

A committed cellar-craftsman and négociant who sets very high standards in the small quantities (about 1,000 cases in total) of white burgundies from his own small property in Meursault (La Barre, Meix Chavaux), Puligny-Montrachet and St-Romain. He also makes the wine of the little Domaine Darnat in Meursault, whose Clos Richemont is outstanding. 'Maison Jean Germain' is run in conjunction with Tim Marshall of Nuits-St-Georges and Joseph de Bucy.

Domaine Girard-Vollot & Fils

21420 Savigny-lès-Beaune.

A domaine of 42 acres with sites in three Savigny-lès-Beaune Premiers Crus vineyards – 1.7 acres each in Rouvrettes and Les Peuillets and 11 acres in Narbantons.

There are also 12 acres of Pernand-Vergelesses Premier Cru. These are solid, rustic wines which can age well.

Maison Camille Giroud

3 rue Pierre Joigneaux, 21200 Beaune.

An extraordinary house founded in Beaune in 1865 and currently run by the founder's daughter-in-law and her sons, using methods which hark back to 1900 wherever possible. The wines are sturdy, long lived and frequently impressive. Much of the stock is only released when the wine is ready to drink – hence a 1979 Pouilly Fuissé on offer in 1996.

Soc. des Domaines Bernard & Louis Glantenay

Rue de Vaut, 21190 Volnay.

The 18-acre domaine of the mayor of Volnay and his brother; largely Volnay 'Village' (5 acres) and Premier Cru (6 acres), with a little Pommard 'Village', 3 acres of Premier Cru, 1 acre of Puligny-Montrachet and just under an acre each of Bourgogne Passe-tout-grain and Aligoté. A wholly traditional establishment selling partly in cask to the négociants but increasingly bottling at the domaine.

Domaine Goud de Beaupuis

Château des Moutots, 21200 Chorey-lès-Beaune.

A family domaine founded in 1787 with 25 acres, principally red wines in the Premiers Crus of Pommard (Epenots), Beaune (Grèves, Vignes Franches, Theurons), Savigny (Vergelesses) and Aloxe-Corton. Also some white Aligoté. Sales are largely to restaurants in France.

Domaine Henri Gouges

7 rue du Moulin, 21700 Nuits-St-Georges.

In many minds and for many years the top grower of Nuits; a complete specialist with almost all his 36 acres in the Premiers Crus, including the whole 8 acres of the Clos des Porrets. His other main plots are in Les St-Georges (2.5 acres), Les Pruliers (4.2) and Les Vaucrains (2.5). Gouges' reds reach *grand cru* class: powerful, slow to develop and long in the finish.

Jean Grivot

Vosne-Romanée, 21700 Nuits-St-Georges.

Etienne Grivot (son of Jean) is a deeply dedicated grower with a number of small parcels of exceptionally good land – 31 acres in all. He has 4.5 acres of Clos Vougeot and nearly 10 of Vosne-Romanée, including 2.3 in the excellent Premier Cru Beaumonts and bits of Suchots and Brûlées, which are sandwiched between the Grands Crus Richebourg and Echézeaux. 5 acres of Nuits Premiers Crus and 1.5 of Chambolle-Musigny give a wide range of top-class wines. Grivot believes in dense planting for small crops. He likes ripe wines without acidity or 'brutality' but with bouquet.

Domaine Robert Groffier

Morey St-Denis, 21220 Gevrey-Chambertin

An excellent little domaine in the best sites of Bonnes Mares, Clos de Bèze, and above all the owner's favourite

Chambolle-Musignys, Les Amoureuses and Les Sentiers. Robert Groffier captures the elegance of Musigny.

Domaine Jean Gros

Vosne-Romanée, 21700 Nuits-St-Georges.

Jean Gros is patriarch of a distinguished Vosne-Romanée family. His son Michel makes the wines here and under his own label. Another son, Bernard, is responsible for Dom. Gros Frère et Soeur, while daughter Anne-Françoise (Dom. A.-F. Gros) and niece Anne (Dom. Anne et François Gros) make excellent wines, especially the Clos Vougeot 'Le Grand Maupertuis' and Richebourg from Anne Gros.

Domaine Antonin Guyon

21420 Savigny-lès-Beaune.

A very substantial domaine of 116 acres, half of it at Meuilley in the Hautes Côtes de Nuits, where vineyards abandoned after the phylloxera have been replanted in the last 20 years. Otherwise the biggest holdings are 5.3 acres of Corton Grand Cru, 5.5 acres in Pernand-Vergelesses Premier Cru and 8.5 in Chambolle-Musigny; 6 each in Gevrey-Chambertin 'Village' and Aloxe-Corton Premier Cru, 5.5 in Savigny and 2 each of Meursault-Charmes and Volnay Clos des Chênes. Also a tiny parcel of Charmes-Chambertin. Altogether a remarkable spread of good sites, considering which it is strange that the name is not better known. Being a recent creation the firm uses modern methods (e.g. keeping white wines under a blanket of inert nitrogen to preserve freshness). Their Cortons are their particular pride.

Domaine Hudelot-Noëllat

21640 Vougeot.

Well-reputed 25-acre estate in Clos Vougeot, Richebourg, Romanée-St-Vivant, Chambolle-Musigny and Nuits. The owner is Alain Hudelot, who believes in tenacious wines.

Jaboulet-Vercherre

5 rue Colbert, 21200 Beaune.

A family firm of négocants originally from the Rhône, with notable wines from their own 30-acre domaine. The 10-acre Premier Cru Clos de la Commaraine around the old château of the same name in Pommard is their particular pride. They also have some excellent Grand Cru Corton-Bressandes, Beaune Clos de l'Ecu, 'monopoles' Premier Cru Volnay Caillerets, Puligny-Montrachet Les Folatières and Santenay Clos Rousseau. Their wines are made at a modern plant visible from the autoroute.

Maison Louis Jadot

5 rue Samuel Legay, 21200 Beaune.

The American concern Kobrand now own this firm based in the medieval Couvent des Jacobins since the early 19th century, when they were growers on the slopes of Beaune. The Domaine Louis Jadot now covers almost 100 acres, including their original holding, the 6-acre Clos des Ursules in Les Vignes Franches, and the part of Clair-Daü which was bought when the property was split up in 1985. In Beaune they also own part of the Premier Cru Theurons. Clos des

Coucherous, Les Chouacheux, Les Bressandes, and 6 acres of Boucherottes on the edge of Pommard, with Pommard-like sturdy wine. In Corton they have holdings of Pougets (Grand Cru) and Corton-Charlemagne. In Puligny-Montrachet they own parcels of Les Folatières and Chevalier-Montrachet (a plot they call Les Demoiselles, after the spinster sisters Adèle and Julie Voillot who sold it to them in 1846). Since 1985 they have purchased the grapes of Domaine du Duc de Magenta (q.v.), although the wine is sold under that label. Their brilliant white wines are probably their greatest pride: especially their Corton-Charlemagne or Chevalier-Montrachet. But Jadot reds are equally reliable: their domaine wines lead a first-class list of classic burgundies. This is a shining example of a grower-cum-négociant.

Maison Jaffelin

Caves du Chapitre, 2 rue Paradis, 21200 Beaune.

An old company of négociants, originally distillers, occupying the magnificent 13th-century cellar of the canons of Notre Dame in the centre of Beaune. The company was bought by Joseph Drouhin (q.v.) in 1969 and subsequently sold to Jean-Claude Boisset (q.v.). Jaffelin wines are long-macerated, pungent with oak, intense and long-lived.

Domaine François Jobard

21190 Meursault.

Everybody in Meursault has great respect for the quiet, lean, wiry François Jobard than whom no grower is more meticulous. Superb Meursault from such vineyards as Poruzots, Charmes and Genevrières. Domaine Charles and Rémi Jobard is also becoming a good source.

Domaine Jean Joliot & Fils

Nantoux, 21190 Meursault.

Nantoux is a village in the hills only 3 miles west of Pommard, the northernmost of the Hautes Côtes de Beaune. Jean Joliot has 27 acres in the Hautes Côtes, where he makes some 1,000 cases of good red wine, which is austere for burgundy but highly popular with private clients, half of them abroad. On the Côte d'Or he has a parcel of Beaune Premier Cru Boucherottes, 3 acres of Pommard, and 5 acres of Meursault and a little Aligoté. He also makes about 250 cases of Crémant de Bourgogne.

Domaine de la Juvinière

Clos de Langres, Corgoloin, 21700 Nuits-St-Georges.

The Clos de Langres is the southernmost limit of the Côte de Nuits on the way to Beaune, a walled vineyard still equipped with the ancient *pressoir* of the Bishop of Langres. The domaine centred here is the property of La Reine Pédauque, négociants in Beaune. Apart from the 8-acre Clos, the substantial 60-acre estate has 10 in Savigny, 13 in Corton and Aloxe-Corton, 2.7 of Clos Vougeot and 1.5 of Corton-Charlemagne. Their wines tend to be written off as commercial and lacking individuality, but those visiting Beaune may try them for themselves in the domaine's hospitable exhibition cellars.

Maison Labouré-Roi

21700 Nuits-St-Georges.

A négociant emerging as one of the most consistent and reliable wines at quite modest prices. His specialities are domaine wines from René Manuel in Meursault and Chantal Lescure in Nuits. Also surprisingly good Chablis Premier Cru.

Domaine Michel Lafarge

Volnay, 21190 Meursault.

An old family estate which survived the doldrums of Burgundy in the mid-1930s by the initiative of Michel Lafarge's grandfather, who bottled his wine and attacked the Paris market with it in person. There are still bottles of 1904 in the cellar.

Of the 23 acres, 10.5 are in Volnay (4.5 Premier Cru), 2.5 in Meursault, 1 in Beaune Grèves and the rest in rather good Bourgogne vineyards (including Passe-tout-grain and Aligoté). Painstaking vinification, throwing out rotten grapes, fermenting for 10-plus days and using about one third new barrels produce lovely clean and elegant wines.

Domaine des Comtes Lafon

Clos de la Barre, 21190 Meursault.

One of the rare producers to excel with both red and white wines. René Lafon made great wines, albeit irregular at times, until 1982 while pursuing other careers. Dominique Lafon took over as full-time winemaker, producing sublime Meursault from the Premier Cru Charmes, Genevrières and Perrières vineyards plus their own 'back garden', Clos de la Barre, and a tiny amount of the Grand Cru Le Montrachet. His reds were all from Volnay: Champans, Clos des Chênes and especially a large holding of Santenots-du-Milieu, to which some Monthelie has been added.

Domaine Laleure Piot

Pernand-Vergelesses, 21420 Savigny-lès-Beaune.

A 20-acre domaine producing reputable Pernand-Vergelesses, particularly 1,000 cases of white, with some Grand Cru Corton Bressandes and Premier Cru Vergelesses from Savigny and Pernand.

Domaine Henri Lamarche

Vosne-Romanée, 21700 Nuit-St-Georges.

A fourth-generation little family domaine with the good fortune to own the 'monopole' of La Grande Rue, a narrow strip of 3.5 acres running up the hill between Romanée-Conti and La Tâche, the two greatest Grands Crus. A bottle of the 1961 at 21 years old was a miracle of subtle sensuality; understated beside La Tâche, but in its quieter way among the great bottles of my experience. The rest of the 30-acre property includes 2.5 acres of Clos de Vougeot, and parcels of Grands-Echézeaux and the Vosne-Romanée Premiers Crus Malconsorts and Suchots.

Domaine Lamy

Chassagne-Montrachet, 21190 Meursault.

The domaine was founded in 1968 by René Lamy, who was *régisseur* for the Duc de Magenta from 1968–73, and his brother. Their 42 acres are in St Aubin, Santenay, Blagny and Chassagne-Montrachet including 5 acres of red Premiers Crus and 2.5 of white.

Maison Louis Latour

18 rue des Tonneliers, 21204 Beaune.

One of Burgundy's names to conjure with, founded in the 18th century and since 1867 owned and directed, father-to-son, by Latours called Louis. The centre of their domaine is the 'Château' de Grancey at Aloxe-Corton, one of the first large-scale, purpose-built 'wineries' in France: three storeys above ground, two below. The domaine totals 116 acres, of which some 103 are in Corton and Aloxe-Corton, including 25 of Corton-Charlemagne, 47 of red Corton Grand Cru, a 6-acre 'monopole' of Grand Cru Clos de la Vigne au Saint and 11 of Premier Cru Les Chaillots. Some 12 acres in Beaune Premier Cru include 7 of Vignes Franches. There are 2 acres of Chambertin and similar parcels of Romanée-St-Vivant and Pernand-Vergelesses Ile des Vergelesses. Latour has a famous 1.3 acres of Chevalier-Montrachet Les Demoiselles.

Latour is most celebrated for his white wines, above all Corton-Charlemagne, which he almost literally put on the map at the end of the 19th century. They are powerful and must be kept. I was surprised to learn that he pasteurizes his reds, which in theory should mean there is no point in keeping them – which is certainly not the case.

Domaine wines account for one quarter of their turnover. Their selections of other wines, particularly whites, are reliable. Montagny is a speciality to look out for, and they have introduced a Chardonnay Vin de Pays de l'Ardèche which is remarkable in character and volume. Ninety percent of the firm's business is in export.

Domaine Philippe Leclerc

21220 Gevrey Chambertin.

Dynamic wines are made chez Philippe Leclerc, brother of René (q.v.). But you need to like a significant amount of new wood, garish labels and preferably leather trousers, motorbikes and heavy metal as well if you want to make the most of this producer.

Domaine René Leclerc

21220 Gevrey-Chambertin.

The larger share of a family property concentrated in Gevrey-Chambertin Premiers Crus. René's brother Philippe (q.v.) has the smaller. Both are good conscientious producers.

Domaine Leflaive

Puligny-Montrachet, 21190 Meursault.

The grand old man of Puligny Montrachet, Vincent Leflaive, established a fabulous reputation for his Puligny Montrachet from such vineyards as Clavoillons, Combettes and Pucelles plus Grands Crus Batard-, Bienvenue-Batard- and Chevalier-Montrachet. The jewel in the crown, Le Montrachet, has now been added. Perhaps in Vincent's later days quality slipped a little but his daughter, Anne-Claude, assisted by a revitalized team and some dynamic experiments with biodynamic methods, is rapidly restoring the image of this great domaine.

Oliver Leflaive Frères

Puligny-Montrachet, 21190 Meursault.

Nephew of Vincent Leflaive, now the most highly-regarded négociant in the area, thanks to winemaker Franck Grux, with brilliant Pulignys and excellent St Romain, Auxey-Duresses etc: model wines from the Côte de Beaune.

Domaine Lequin-Roussot

21590 Santenay.

A well-known domaine founded by the Lequins in 1734. Each generation, according to brothers René and Louis, has added its stone to the edifice. They now have 33 acres, of which 23 are in Santenay (7 Premier Cru). In Chassagne they have 1.5 acres of red Premier Cru Morgeot and 14 of white Premier Cru Morgeot; also three-quarters of an acre of Bâtard-Montrachet producing 600 bottles a year. The rest of the domaine is in small parcels in Corton (Les Languettes), Pommard and Nuits. The policy is to destem the bunches and aim for big but not hard wines, then to sell them as they mature.

In 1993 the domaine was divided between René and Louis. It remains to be seen whether different styles evolve.

Maison Leroy

Auxey-Duresses, 21190 Meursault.

A company known to the world almost as much for the personality (and reputed wealth) of its owner, Mme Lalou Bize-Leroy, as for its wines. She is both grower and négociant as well as co-proprietor of the Domaine de la Romanée-Conti (of which she inherited half from her father). She is also a well-known mountaineer and a formidable wine taster.

Mme Leroy's total of 10.5 acres is small but choice, including white vines in Meursault and Auxey-Duresses and small parcels of red in Chambertin, Musigny, Clos de Vougeot, Pommard and Auxey-Duresses. In 1988 she absorbed the distinguished Domaine Noëllat which added 35 acres, including Clos Vougeot (4 acres), Richebourg and Romanée-St-Vivant (3.5 acres), plus Nuits and Savigny. In 1989 Mme Leroy added 6 acres in Gevrey-Chambertin, including part of Le Chambertin. The style of the house is very firmly aimed at *vins de garde*. The reds are unstemmed and stay in the vat for 3 weeks, are racked only once, fined with egg whites and never filtered. Strength comes from fully ripe grapes – never more than 1 degree of chaptalization. At 10 years the wines taste young; at 20 in full bloom. Other growers' wines passing through Mme Leroy's hands seem to acquire (or are chosen for) the same qualities. They need patience, and they cost a fortune. The self-styled *'Gardienne des Grands Millésimes'* has a stock of 2.5 m. bottles.

Domaine Georges Lignier & Fils

21220 Gevrey-Chambertin.

A 34-acre patchwork of 60 sites spread over nearly 4 miles from north to south. The best parcels are in Grands Crus Clos St-Denis, Clos de la Roche and Bonnes Mares, and Premiers Crus Morey St-Denis and Gevrey Chambertin. Half the wine is sold to négociants. The Lignier label goes on the best.

Hubert Lignier

21220 Gevrey-Chambertin.

The great-grandfather of the present owner began working in 1860 on what is now the domaine, working his way up to become the *maître-chai*. The family took over the property in 1890. There are now 18.5 acres. The most important sites are 1.9 acres of Clos de la Roche, and small holdings in Chambolle-Musigny and Gevrey-Chambertin Premiers Crus.

Lupé-Cholet

17 ave. Général de Gaulle, 21700 Nuits-St-Georges.

Two amusingly aristocratic sisters, the Comtesses Inès and Liliane de Mayol de Lupé, run this old family business, best known for its Nuits Premier Cru 'Château Gris', a 6.6-acre parcel of Les Crots above the town which has produced some memorable *vins de garde*. Their elegant house in Nuits also has the 5.6-acre Clos de Lupé (appellation Bourgogne) beyond the garden. Some years ago the company merged with Bichot of Beaune.

Lycée Agricole et Viticole

21200 Beaune.

The young farmers' college (47 acres) of Beaune, founded in 1884, includes 4 small parcels of Beaune Premiers Crus, as well as 2.5 acres of white Puligny-Montrachet. They make some 2,500 cases of first-rate, long-lived wine, of which 20% is exported.

Domaine Machard de Gramont

6 rue Gassendi, 21700 Nuits-St-Georges.

A 47-acre domaine created over the last 25 years by two brothers with amazing energy and professionalism. Much of their best land was abandoned *'friches'*, the stony edges of good vineyards, until they planted it. Unfortunately, a family problem reduced their holdings from 75 acres in 1983. Their biggest plots now are in Nuits (6.5 acres of Premier Cru, especially Hauts-Pruliers, 7.5 of 'Village'), Pommard (10 acres of the excellent Clos Blanc, a 'Village' site of Premier Cru quality), and Savigny-lès-Beaune (5 acres, mostly Premier Cru Les Guettes). They also have 2.5 acres of Beaune Premier Cru Epenottes and small parcels in Chambolle-Musigny and Aloxe-Corton (very tasty, this). They ferment at a high temperature (35°C/95°F) with most of the stems, age in barrels in cellars and rack their wine as little as possible. Their policy is only to bottle selections from good vintages and old vines, and to sell the rest in bulk. The brothers are modest about their achievement, but they make some of the best red burgundy of its class today.

Domaine du Duc de Magenta

Abbaye de Morgeot, Chassagne-Montrachet, 21190 Meursault.

The descendant of the French victor of the battle of Magenta (1859, with Piedmont against the Austrians) owns 30 acres, of which 11 – half red and half white – are the Clos de la Chapelle of former Cistercians of the Abbaye de Morgeot, a dependency of Cluny. 5 acres are the Premier Cru 'Clos de la Garenne' in Puligny, 8 (red and white) in

Auxey-Duresses and 2 in Meursault 'Meix Chavaux'. In the past, his wines were firm, vigorous and full of character, keeping well. His red 'Morgeot' has been outstanding. The 1969 in 1982 had a beautiful flavour of cherries and almonds. Then followed some vintages which were less impressive. Since 1985 all the Domaine's wines have been made by Maison Louis Jadot (q.v.), though some vineyards have been rented to Domaine du Comte Armand (q.v.) since 1995.

Domaine Henri Magnien

21220 Gevrey-Chambertin.
A 300-year old family domaine of 7.4 acres. It includes a parcel of Ruchottes-Chambertin Grand Cru and 4 Gevrey-Chambertin Premiers Crus, of which Estournelles is the biggest. Well-oaked, stylish wines.

Château de la Maltroye

Chassagne-Montrachet, 21190 Meursault.
The source of some outstanding white Chassagne under the 'monopole' label of the château. In addition, the 32-acre estate has a small piece of Bâtard-Montrachet as well as red-wine vineyards in Chassagne Clos St-Jean and Santenay La Comme.

Domaine Jean-Philippe Marchand

21220 Gevrey-Chambertin.
A family property in Gevrey (including a little Charmes-Chambertin) and Morey St-Denis. These are rather tannic but sufficiently rich wines. Also a small négociant business.

Domaine Tim Marshall

47c rue Henri Challand, 21700 Nuits-St-Georges.
A small property of 4 acres in the Nuits Premiers Crus Les Perrières and Les Argillats, and Volnay, the work of a Yorkshireman who has carved out a unique place for himself as a broker, guide, philosopher and friend to Anglo-Saxons (and Burgundians too) in Burgundy.

Domaine Joseph, Thierry et Pascale Matrot

21190 Meursault.
A 44-acre domaine now run by Thierry Matrot. It has 4 acres in the Puligny Premiers Crus Combettes and Chalumeaux, 4 in Meursault Charmes and Perrières and a further 4 of white in the Meursault section of Blagny. There are also 3.5 acres of red Volnay-Santenots and an unusual red Blagny, the 6-acre La Pièce sous le Bois, which makes a vivid, somewhat harsh wine, as a change from the gentler Volnay. I have found Matrot's Meursault (particularly his Charmes) beautifully made.

Prosper Maufoux

21590 Santenay.
One of the most respected of family firms in the traditional business of buying, 'bringing-up' and selling burgundy from small growers, which was sold in 1994 to its American importer Robert Fairchild. The present principal, Pierre Maufoux, is the grandson of the founder. Maufoux red wines are reliably *vins de garde*; on occasions I have found even his 'Village' wines to have been in pefect condition at 20 years and his Premiers and Grands Crus exceptional.

Maufoux has a share in the Domaine St-Michel (q.v.), which also supplies him with Pouilly Fumé. I have found his Chablis Mont de Milieu and Vaudésir reliable, typical and good value; his Santenay Blanc, Meursault Charmes and (particularly) Puligny-Montrachet Les Folatières first class. This house is the answer to anyone who thinks that all good burgundy is domaine bottled. Marcel Amance is another trade name.

Crémant – a new term of quality

Three high-quality French white-wine regions successfully established a new appellation for their best-quality sparkling wine. The term 'crémant', originally used in Champagne for wines produced at about half the full sparkling-wine pressure, thus gently fizzing instead of frothing in the glass, has been borrowed (with the consent of Champagne) as a controlled term for these full-sparklers of high quality. A new term was needed because the old one, 'mousseux', had acquired a pejorative ring: any old fizz made by industrial methods could (and can) use it. Burgundy and the Loire in 1975, and Alsace in 1976, joined in agreeing that crémant had to be made with champagne-type controls. Specifically, they concern the grape varieties used, the size of the crop, the way it is delivered to the press-house with the bunches undamaged and the pressure that should be applied (with a limit of two thirds of the weight of the grapes being extracted as juice). Thereafter, the champagne-method rules apply, with the minimum time in bottle with the yeast being specified as 9 months in Burgundy and Alsace and 12 in the Loire. (An influential lobby wants to increase the 9 months to 12 but so far its efforts have been resisted.)

The result of these controls is a category of sparkling wine of excellent quality, though so far in very small supply. Heavy initial investment deters cellars from upgrading from mousseux to crémant. But in 1996 total crémant production was 5 m. bottles: confirmation that the term crémant, in its new meaning, is well understood.

Among concerns producing Crémant de Bourgogne are:
Bouchard Aîné, Beaune
R. Chevillard, La Rochepot
Caves de Bailly, St-Bris-le-Vineux
Caves Delorme-Meulien, Rully
Cave de Lugny-St-Gengoux, Lugny
Cave de Viré, Viré
Labouré-Gontard, Nuits-St-Georges
Moingeon-Gueneau Frères, Nuits-St-Georges
Henri Mugnier, Charnay-lès-Mâcon
Parigot-Richard, Savigny-lès-Beaune
Picamelot, Rully
SICA du Vignoble Auxerrois, Bailly, St-Bris-le-Vineux
Simmonet-Febvre, Chablis
Veuve Ambal, Rully
Vitteau Alberti, Rully

Domaine Maume

21220 Gevrey-Chambertin.

Bernard Maume is a professor of biochemistry at Dijon University as well as being proprietor of this 9.8-acre domaine. He is assisted by his son, Bertrand, who has a degree in oenology and has worked in an Australian winery. He believes in macerating the skins at low temperatures before fermentation to accentuate the fruit flavour. The largest and best parcel is 1.5 acres of Mazis-Chambertin Grand Cru. There is also a small site of Charmes-Chambertin Grand Cru and 3 Gevrey-Chambertin Premiers Crus. 80– 90% of the 11,600 case production is exported.

Maizilly Père & Fils

Meloisey, 21190 Meursault.

Growers in the Côte de Beaune since 1600, largely in the Hautes Côtes (8.5 acres) with 3.4 acres of Pommard, 2 of Meursault and 1 of Beaune Premier Cru. Sound, strong wines aimed for body more than finesse.

Domaine Méo-Camuzet

21700 Vosne-Romanée.

A long-established grower in Vosne, Nuits, Clos de Vougeot, Corton and Le Richebourg which emerged in the '80s as one of the highest class, with rich but well-structured wines. The domaine is now run by Jean-Nicolas who makes outstanding wines under the inspired guidance of Henry Jayer.

Domaine Prince Florent de Mérode

21550 Ladoix-Serrigny.

A domaine of high standing in Corton and Pommard. Of the 28 acres, some 9 are in Corton Grand Cru and the same in the 'monopole' Pommard Clos de la Platière.

Mestre Père & Fils

Place du Jet d'Eau, 21590 Santenay.

One of Santenay's bigger domaines (44 acres), in the fifth generation, with 17.5 acres of Premiers Crus in all the best vineyards, and smaller holdings in Aloxe-Corton (including a small portion of Corton Grand Cru), Chassagne-Montrachet, and Ladoix (Appellation Côte de Beaune). Careful wine-making, but surprisingly only 20% is bottled at the domaine. The Swiss (who love Santenay) buy the greater part in cask.

Marc de Bourgogne and Cassis

The pulpy residue of skins, pips and stalks left in the press after the juice has been run off is often distilled to produce a spirit known as marc. The clear spirit is matured in oak to give it colour and, with luck, a little finesse.

Most marc is made by growers for private consumption. Some of the larger houses, such as Bouchard Père & Fils and Louis Latour, make carefully aged commercial versions. Cassis is an alcoholic blackcurrant liqueur which serves to soften the sharpness of white wine – in Burgundy usually Aligoté – in a proportion of 1 of cassis to 3 or 4 of wine. The resulting drink is often called Kir after a brand of cassis which was developed by Canon Félix Kir, one-time mayor of Dijon.

Château de Meursault

21190 Meursault.

An 89-acre domaine with the signature of the Comte de Moucheron, the former owner, bought in 1973 by the négociants Patriarche of Beaune and turned into a showplace for visitors, with a permanent help-yourself tasting in the spectacular medieval cellars. The vineyards include substantial parcels of the Meursault Premiers Crus Charmes and Perrières – sold as Château de Meursault – and the former gardens of the château, replanted with vines as the 'Clos du Château'. Red vineyards include part of the Premiers Crus of Volnay (Clos des Chênes), Pommard (Clos des Epenots), Beaune (Fèves, Grèves, Cent Vignes, Clos du Roi) and Savigny. The total production averages 17,000 cases. My impression is that the whole range, but particularly the Meursaults, are extremely well made – and expensive.

Domaine Alain Michelot

21700 Nuits-St-Georges.

A 21-acre property, mostly in Nuits, created by the last two generations of the Michelots. His Premiers Crus (especially Richemone and Vaucrains) are Nuits-St-Georges at its best; solid and searching.

Maison P. Misserey

21702 Nuits-St-Georges.

The Misserey family's vines are all in Nuits-St-Georges Premiers Crus: five parcels making a total of 4.4 acres. Maison Misserey also has long-term contracts with domaines in the Côte de Nuits and Côte de Beaune, and vinifies more than 26 different appellations of Premier Cru and Grand Cru status. Jules Belin is now owned by Misserey.

Maison Moillard, Domaine Thomas-Moillard and Domaine Moillard-Grivot

21700 Nuits-St-Georges.

A family firm in the fifth generation (the name is now Thomas) with a 64-acre domaine, but also making wine from purchased grapes from a much larger area and playing the traditional role of négociants with stocks of no less than 8 million bottles – certainly the biggest in Nuits. They are known for the efficiency and modernity of their techniques, and still respected for their domaine wines, which are made 'supple' and round for relatively early drinking. The domaine includes little parcels of 8 different Nuits Premiers Crus (Clos de Thorey and Clos des Grandes Vignes are 'monopoles'), Chambertin and Clos de Bèze, Bonnes Mares, Clos Vougeot, Romanée St-Vivant and Vosne-Romanée Beaux Monts and Malconsorts, Corton Clos du Roi and Corton-Charlemagne.

Domaine Mommessin

La Grange St-Pierre, B.P. 504, 71009 Mâcon.

The famous Beaujolais growers have owned the whole of the 18.5-acre Grand Cru Clos de Tart in Morey St-Denis since 1932. They adopt the unusual technique of keeping the 'cap' of skins immersed throughout the fermentation period. The wine is fine although still on the light side, rather surprisingly for a Grand Cru, and neighbour to Bonnes Mares.

Mongeard-Mugneret

21670 Vosne-Romanée.

A 50-acre estate making very fine and long-lived Vosne Les Suchots, Echézeaux, Grands-Echézeaux, Vougeot, etc. Jean Mongeard has just retired after 50 years at the helm.

Domaine Jean Monnier & Fils

20 rue du 11 Novembre, 21190 Meursault.

Members of the Monnier family have been wine-growers in Meursault since 1720. Their 41-acre domaine comprises 15 acres of Meursault (including Charmes and Genevrières), 2.5 acres of Puligny-Montrachet, 2.5 acres of Beaune, 10 acres of Pommard, 10 acres of Bourgogne Rouge and 1.75 acres of Bourgogne Aligoté, which includes their 'monopole' Clos de Cîteaux in Les Epenots.

Domaine René Monnier

6 rue Docteur Rolland, 21190 Meursault.

The Monnier family has built up one of the biggest private domaines in the Côte de Beaune – 45 acres – over 150 years. The biggest plots are in Meursault Chevalières and the Premier Cru Charmes, Beaune Cent Vignes and Toussaints and Puligny Folatières. Other plots are in Pommard, Volnay and Santenay. The reds are fermented for as long as possible at a high temperature (for plenty of colour) and aged in one third of new barrels a year. The whites are balanced between half new oak and half stainless steel, aimed at wine with plenty of flavour not needing long ageing. Well known in three-star restaurants.

Domaine Monthelie-Douhairet

Monthélie, 21190 Meursault.

Nonagenarian Mlle Armande Douhairet, the domaine's current proprietor, is a figure of living history in Burgundy. The estate of 15 acres includes 2.5 acres of Premiers Crus Pommard, Volnay and Monthélie Rouge, some juicy Meursault and just under an acre of Monthélie Blanc.

Domaine Hubert de Montille

Volnay, 21190 Meursault.

The 17-acre property of a Dijon lawyer, scattered among the Premiers Crus of Volnay (Champans, Taillepieds, Mitans) and Pommard (Epenots, Rugiens, Pézerolles). Both the Pommard and Volnay are richly coloured, flavoursome and age well.

Albert Morey & Fils

Chassagne-Montrachet, 21190 Meursault.

An old family domaine of some 30 acres, largely in Chassagne and almost equally divided between white and red wines. 'The French drink the red', according to M. Morey. His best-known white wine is the Premier Cru Les Embrasées (2.5 acres), though his 2 acres of Caillerets, 1 each of Morgeot and Les Champs-Gains and a tiny plot in Bâtard-Montrachet are all excellent. He also owns 2 acres of Santenay for red and rents 2 of Beaune Grèves. Cousins Bernard and Jean-Marc Morey are also reputed growers in Chassagne-Montrachet, Santenay and Beaune.

Albert Morot

Château de la Creusotte, 21200 Beaune.

13 acres of Beaune Premiers Crus in Teurons, Grèves, Cent Vignes, Toussaints, Bressandes and Marconnets. 4.5 acres of Savigny-Vergelesses 'Clos la Bataillère'. Mlle Françoise-Guigone Choppin has responsibility for making the wines. A fine property through which to discover the characters of top-level Beaune Premiers Crus.

Domaine Denis Mortet

21220 Gevrey Chambertin.

A rising star, as evidenced by his superlative 1993s, made from a clutch of single vineyard Gevrey Chambertins and a tiny holding of Grand Cru. Denis Mortet makes fine, deep-coloured wines with impressive definition. They should age very well but are attractive even when young.

Domaine Georges Mugneret/Mugneret-Gibourg

Vosne-Romanée, 21700 Nuits-St-Georges.

There are seven growers called Mugneret in Vosne. This 21-acre domaine, run by the widow and daughter of the late Dr Georges, includes less than an acre each of Grand Cru Clos de Vougeot and Ruchottes-Chambertin. They have 3 acres of Nuits Premier Cru; the rest is Chambolle-Musigny Premier Cru. The yield is low and the wine serious.

Domaine Mugneret-Gouachon

Prémeaux-Prissey, 21700 Nuits-St-Georges.

Bernard Mugneret runs his father's property in Vosne-Romanée and his father-in-law's in Nuits – a total of 26 acres, of which 8.5 are his 'monopole' Premier Cru Les Perdrix in Prémeaux. He has 3 acres each of Echézeaux and Vosne-Romanée and over 8, producing 750 cases, of Bourgogne Rouge. Les Perdrix is a splendid wine regularly bought and shipped to the USA since 1959 by the late Frank Schoonmaker and his successors.

Jacques-Frédéric Mugnier

Château de Chambolle Musigny, 21200 Chambolle Musigny.

A 10-acre estate with first-class delicate Chambolle Musigny. The domaine includes some Premier Cru (les Amoureuses) as well as 2.75 acres of Musigny and less than an acre of Bonnes-Mares.

Domaine André Mussy

21630 Pommard.

Very much a family concern – the present proprietor, André Mussy, is twelfth generation, and he is assisted by his son-in-law and his nephew. The domaine of 14.8 acres includes 1.8 acres of Pommard Epenots Grand Cru, and the same of Pommard Premier Cru, 2.47 acres of Beaune-Epenottes Premier Cru and 3.7 of Beaune-Montremenots Premier Cru. Some 75% of the wine is exported.

Maison Naigeon-Chauveau

21220 Gevrey-Chambertin.
Good-quality négociant house under the same direction (J-P Naigeon) as Domaine de Varoilles (q.v.).

Hospices de Nuits-St-Georges

Rue Henri Challand, 21700 Nuits-St-Georges.
The lesser-known and smaller Nuits counterpart of the great Hospices de Beaune, founded in 1634 and now endowed with 31 acres. They include 14 of Nuits Premier Cru and 5.5 of Nuits 'Village'. The rest is Bourgogne and Bourgogne Grand Ordinaire, which is sold in bulk. The best *cuvées* are sold by auction in March. The Cuvée des Soeurs Hospitalières is Nuits (Village) Les Fleurières; the Cuvée Les Sires de Vergy is Les St-Georges; the Cuvées Fagon, Duret and Cabet are Les Didiers. All are serious *vins de garde*.

Domaine Parent

21630 Pommard.
A 30-acre domaine founded in 1750, best known for its Pommard, Epenots, Chanlins, Fremiers and Chaponniers, but also with vineyards in Corton, Volnay, Beaune, Ladoix and Monthélie.

Patriarche Père & Fils

Couvent des Visitandines, 21200 Beaune.
Possibly the biggest firm in Burgundy (it claims to have the biggest cellars) with a history going back to 1780. Patriarche has a paradoxical image: on one hand proprietor of the excellent Ch. de Meursault and Beaune Premiers Crus totalling 100 acres, regularly the biggest buyer at the Hospices de Beaune auctions until 1995. and a house of great prestige; on the other a brand which the snob in me would describe as definitely down-market. Perhaps it is the dismal design of their labels. Their greatest success must be Kriter Brut de Brut, created in the early 1960s as a high-quality, non-appellation sparkling wine. The Kriter factory on the road south of Beaune boasts a vast celebratory fountain. Appellation wines account for 60 percent of turnover. Brand names include Père Patriarche, Cuvée Jean Baptiste, Noëmie Vernaux.

Jean-Marc Pavelot

21420 Savigny-lès-Beaune.
The Pavelots have been growers in Savigny since 1640. Their domaine comprises 38 acres, a little under half of it in the Premier Cru vineyards of the slopes. Their wines are made in modern conditions. They bottle the best, notably Savigny 'Dominode' and 'Guettes', and sell the rest in cask to négociants.

Domaine de la Perrière

Fixin, 21220 Gevrey-Chambertin.
An unusually simple property making only one wine: the famous Fixin Clos de la Perrière, established by the Cistercian monks of Citeaux in the 12th century. The original manor, its cellars and their great press, 700 years old, are still here. The 13 acres produce some 2,000 cases of bold, uncompromising wine, made by long fermentation (up to three weeks) in covered vats with most of the stems included. Then long barrel-ageing and no filtration – very much what the monks must have done. The wine has been compared with Chambertin for power, if not for finesse.

Château de Pommard

21630 Pommard.
The château is very much in evidence from the main road, with a label and a sales approach which might lead one to think it is strictly for tourists. In fact it is extremely serious; with 50 acres said to be the biggest single vineyard with one proprietor in Burgundy, and acknowledged to make excellent wine from a high proportion of old vines. Despite being a 'Village' wine, it is made like a good Premier Cru. The owner, Jean-Louis Laplanche, uses new barrels every year, keeps the wine 2 years in wood and does not filter. The tourists are important too: a major portion of his sales is direct to private clients, 40% is exported, 25% within Europe.

Maison Pierre Ponnelle

Abbaye St-Martin, 53 avenue de l'Aigue, 21200 Beaune.
One of the smaller négociants, now owned by Jean-Claude Boisset, evidently thriving, with new premises outside Beaune and a new shop in the town. The present director, Bruno Ponnelle, is the great-grandson of the founder. Their domaine is only 12 acres, but includes parcels of Musigny, Bonnes Mares, Charmes-Chambertin, Clos Vougeot, Corton Clos du Roi and Beaune Grèves. Their wine list is remarkable in quality and diversity and in the old stocks they offer. In my experience Ponnelle wines are true to type and very long-lived: a 1950 Clos Vougeot (not a famous year) was in good condition thirty years on.

Domaine Jean-Marie Ponsot

Morey St-Denis, 21220 Gevrey-Chambertin.
An 25-acre domaine over a century old, all in Morey St-Denis except for a small parcel of Latricières-Chambertin. Half of the total is in the splendid Clos de la Roche, making concentrated, long-lived wine difficult to distinguish from Chambertin. White Premier Cru Morey 'Monts Luisants' is Ponsot's other speciality; one of the few whites of the Côte de Nuits, grown on high trellising 'Swiss-style' on the steep upper slopes.

Poulet Père & Fils

12 rue Chaumergy, 21200 Beaune.
A firm of négociants with a long history, known for sturdy wines rather than finesse. It is now owned by Chauvenet.

Domaine de la Pousse d'Or

Volnay, 21190 Meursault.
A 32-acre domaine entirely in the Premiers Crus of Volnay, Pommard and Santenay. Its reputation is as high as any in the Côte de Beaune. Almost every three-star restaurant offers its wines. The domaine has three monopoles in Volnay: Clos de la Bousse [*sic*] d'Or, Clos des Soixante Ouvrées and Clos d'Audignac. The first and last are typically gentle, sociable Volnays, delicacy and elegance that reaches its peak in the

'Bousse d'Or'; the '60 Ouvrées', however, is a prime piece of Caillerets, more forceful wine demanding maturity. (An *ouvrée* is one twenty-fourth of a hectare: 60 = 2.5 ha = just over 6 acres.) Another parcel of Caillerets of the same size produces lighter wines. Two similar plots in Santenay's best Premiers Crus (Tavannes and Gravières) and 2.5 acres of Pommard Jarollières complete the domaine. Director Gérard Potel ferments his wine for 12–14 days, looking, he says, 'for long life but finesse, with subtle and delicate perfumes. Ideally wine with the maximum freshness and maximum *nervosité.'* Few Côte de Beaunes mature longer than his.

Domaine Jacques Prieur

Rue des Santenots, 21190 Meursault.

One of Burgundy's most remarkable properties, including parts of both Chambertin and Montrachet, with all its 40 acres in great vineyards. Its architect was Jacques Prieur, one of the prime movers of the Chevaliers de Tastevin, whose grandson Martin now runs it. In 1988, 50% of the shares were acquired by Financiers des Grands Vignobles de Bourgogne, represented by Sté Antonin Rodet (*see* under Mercurey). The vines include 2.4 acres in Chambertin and Clos de Bèze, 2 in Musigny, 3 in Clos Vougeot, 4.5 in Beaune (Clos de la Féguine), 6 in the Volnay Premiers Crus Santenots, Clos des Santenots and Champans, 8 in Meursault Clos de Mazeray (red and white), 4.5 in Puligny Les Combettes and Chevalier-

Montrachet and 1.4 (making 2,000 bottles) of Le Montrachet. All the wines (some 5,000– 8,000 cases a year) are made in Meursault in modern conditions. The domaine had a fading reputation for both red and white wines which Antonin Rodet has started to restore.

Domaine Ramonet

Chassagne-Montrachet, 21190 Meursault.

A distinguished old name in Chassagne. Half of the 34-acre domaine is white, including Bâtard-, Bienvenues-Bâtard-Montrachet and Le Montrachet, racy Chassagne Premier Cru Les Ruchottes, and Chassagne 'Village'. Their red wines are less famous but remarkably fine: Clos de la Boudriotte, Clos St-Jean and red Chassagne 'Village' are as good as any red wines of the southern Côte de Beaune. The grand old man, Pierre Ramonet, died in 1995 and his grandsons Noël and Jean-Claude now make the wine

Rapet Père & Fils

Pernand-Vergelesses, 21420 Savigny-lès-Beaune.

A highly reputed 40-acre domaine including parcels of Corton-Charlemagne and (red) Corton Grand Cru, Pernand-Vergelesses Premier Cru and Bourgogne (red and white). The enigmatic Monsieur Rapet's motto is *'Le moins on en dit, le mieux on se porte'* – in other words, 'My wine speaks for itself.' Not 5-star quality, but good value.

The Hospices de Beaune

The Hospices de Beaune has a unique role as a symbol of the continuity, the wealth and the general benevolence of Burgundy. It was founded as a hospital for the sick, poor and aged of Beaune in 1443 by the Chancellor to the Duke of Burgundy, Nicolas Rolin, and his wife Guigone de Salins. They endowed it with land in the Côte de Beaune for its income; a practice that

has been followed ever since by rich growers, merchants and other citizens. The Hospices now owns about 106 acres of vineyards and much more farmland.

The wine from its scattered vineyard plots is made in *cuvées*, not necessarily consisting of the wine of a single *climat* but designed to be practicable to make and agreeable to drink. Each *cuvée* is named after an important benefactor of the Hospices. There are 32 *cuvées*, all but one in the Côte de Beaune.

The wine is sold, *cuvée* by *cuvée* and cask by cask, at a public auction on the third Sunday of November in the market hall across the road from the Hospices. The profits are spent on running the hospital, which now has every sort of modern equipment. Its original wards, chapel and works of art are open to the public.

Buyers include merchants, restaurants, individuals and syndicates from all over the world, who are attracted by the idea of supporting this ancient charity, and the publicity that accompanies it. The wine-making of the Hospices has been much criticized recently, and it is certainly not easy to judge the wines so soon after the harvest, when buyers have to make their choice. Both excellent and second-rate bottles are produced, but the cachet of a Hospices label means a great deal.

The third weekend in November is the most important date in the Burgundy calendar, known as *Les Trois Glorieuses* from the three feasts which make it a stiff endurance test. On Saturday the 'Chevaliers de Tastevin' hold a gala dinner at the Clos de Vougeot. On Sunday after the auction the dinner is at the Hospices and Monday lunch is a wine-growers' feast known as the *Paulée* at Meursault: this last a gigantic bottle party.

La Reine Pédauque

21200 Beaune.

A well-known commercial house owned by Pierre André. They own 125 acres including the 10-acre Clos des Longres, 5 acres in Corton-Renardes and 5 of Corton Charlemagne.

Remoissenet Père & Fils

21200 Beaune.

A small domaine of 6 acres in Beaune Premier Cru (where Grèves and Toussaints make their own best wines) but an important broker and négociant who supplies burgundies to the French firm of Nicolas and the Bristol one of Avery's. Through the latter I have had many good bottles, particularly of white wines.

Henri et Gilles Remoriquet

25 rue de Charmois, 21700 Nuits-St-Georges.

The Remoriquets are an established family of growers in Nuits with 3.7 acres in Premiers Crus Les St-Georges, Rue de Chaux, Les Bousselots and Les Damodes and 7 Nuits 'Villages', including 2 acres in Les Allots, a good 'climat' on the road to Vosne-Romanée, which is domaine-bottled and the house speciality. M. Remoriquet was a pioneer of the Hautes Côtes de Nuits with an acre at Chaux, 2 miles west on top of the hill.

Domaine Armelle et Bernard Rion

Vosne-Romanée, 21700 Nuits St Georges.

A domaine with an emerging reputation. 30 acres in Vosne-Romanée, Nuits, Chambolle-Musigny and Clos Vougeot. Wines tending to firmness, made to last. Bernard Rion also makes delicious Chambolle Musigny under his own label, Domaine Patrice and Michèle Rion.

Domaine Daniel Rion et Fils

Prémeaux, 21700 Nuits-St-Georges.

Patrice Rion, cousin of Bernard, has been known longer for his luscious yet elegant wines from Clos Vougeot, Vosne-Romanée and several Premiers Crus of Nuits.

Domaine de la Romanée-Conti

Vosne Romanée, 21700 Nuits-St-Georges.
See Romanée-Conti – A Great Burgundy Estate, page 103.

Ropiteau Frères

21190 Meursault.

The firm are négociants handling the output of their own Domaine Ropiteau-Mignon and other wines. The domaine is the biggest in Meursault with 12 acres of Premiers Crus in Genevrières, Perrières and 4 other 'climats', and 32 in the 'Village' vineyards. A further 4 acres apiece of Premier Cru Puligny and Monthelie make them strong in fine white wines. Their red holdings are small parcels in Volnay, Monthelie, Pommard, Beaune (Grèves), Clos Vougeot, Echézeaux and Chambolle-Musigny. The top Ropiteau whites are ideal white burgundy, balancing oak and grape flavours and needing time to develop. Now owned by Jean-Claude Boisset (q.v.).

Domaine Philippe Rossignol

21220 Gevrey-Chambertin.

Another young man's tiny domaine achieving finer quality with new ideas than many bigger, more traditional, ones.

Joseph Roty

21220 Gevrey-Chambertin.

A small but impeccable grower in Charmes-Chambertin, Gevrey Premier Cru and Villages. Even his Bourgogne Rouge is a noble wine.

Emmanuel Rouget

21700 Flagey-Echézeaux.

The nephew and inheritor of Henry Jayer's legendary estate, including Grand Cru Echézeaux, Vosne Romanée Premiers Crus Les Meaumonts, Cros Parantoux, and Nuits-St-Georges. Splendid wines (especially the Cros Parantoux) made under the guiding hand of Henry Jayer.

Domaine Guy Roulot

1 rue Charles Giraud, 21190 Meursault.

A family domaine of 31 acres, 16 in Meursault (including Perrières, Tessons, Luchets, Les Meix Chavaux and Charmes), 3.7 in Auxey-Duresses red, with a quantity of Monthelie, Passe-tout-grain, Bourgogne Chardonnay and Pinot. The property also has a still making Fine de Bourgogne (brandy) and Marc de Bourgogne. For both whites and reds they use the unusual phrase 'garde garantie 10 ans'. Serious, well-judged wines. Excellent wines made by Jean-Marc Roulot, especially his Meursault Tessons, Le Clos de Mon Plaisir.

Domaine G. Roumier

Chambolle-Musigny, 21220 Gevrey-Chambertin.

Christophe Roumier has taken over the family property, started in 1924, with 35 acres; 18 in Chambolle-Musigny, 6 in Morey St-Denis, 6 of very old vines in Bonnes Mares, 2.5 in Clos de Vougeot and about 1 each in Le Musigny and Les Amoureuses. The family's wines are classics of depth and harmony. They even include a little Corton-Charlemagne.

Domaine Armand Rousseau

21220 Gevrey-Chambertin.

The most respected grower of Chambertin. The founder's son, Charles Rousseau, now owns 19 acres, including 4 of Chambertin, 2 of Clos de Bèze, and parcels in Mazis and Charmes-Chambertin as well as in the Clos de la Roche in Morey and (his particular pride) 5.5 acres of Gevrey Clos St-Jacques on the hill above the village. His wine is vatted for 2 weeks. No one makes bigger, more gutsy burgundies. His '85s are a triumph.

Domaine Roux Père & Fils

St-Aubin, 21190 Meursault.

A competent proprietor whose 50 acres in St-Aubin, Meursault, Santenay Premiers Crus, Chassagne- and Puligny-Montrachet can be relied on for the true taste of their respective villages. He is also known for good Passe-tout-grain. The family are also négociants.

Domaine St-Michel

21590 Santenay.

This estate is jointly run by Michel Gutrin and the Santenay négociant Pierre Maufoux (q.v.). They own 74 acres, mainly located in Santenay 'Village', Premier Cru Comme and Clos Rousseau, as well as in Puligny-Montrachet for white wines. Also a 20-acre vineyard at Pouilly-sur-Loire. The Bourgogne Rouge St-Michel is good value. Most sales are to private clients in France.

Domaine Etienne Sauzet

Puligny-Montrachet, 21190 Meursault.

Etienne Sauzet (who died in 1975) was the third of the five generations to have built up a reputation for richly flavoured white burgundies. Many critics consider the domaine second only to Leflaive. The house style is to keep the wines on their lees for a year to develop flavour and 'fat'. The main holding is 12.5 acres in Puligny Premiers Crus, with about 4 each of Combettes (their best-known wine) and Champ-Canet. They have a further 8 acres in Puligny, 2 in Chassagne and small parcels of Bâtard- and Bienvenues-Bâtard-Montrachet.

Maison Séguin-Manuel

Rue Paul Maldant, 21420 Savigny-lès-Beaune.

The date of foundation, 1720, gives this property a claim to being the oldest merchant in Burgundy. The small (10-acre) domaine is in Savigny; most of the business is in other appellations, including Beaujolais, Côtes du Rhône, spirits and Oeil de Perdrix sparkling rosé.

Domaine Daniel Senard

21420 Aloxe-Corton.

Farms 20 acres of his own land, 13 of them in the Grands Crus of Corton, Clos du Roi and Bressandes, and the entire 5-acre 'Clos Meix'; 6 in (red) Aloxe-Corton and small parcels of Beaune Les Coucherias and Chorey-lès-Beaune. The eighth generation of Senards operate in 14th-century cellars (and a tower). Exceptionally long-lived and well-balanced reds are made by controlling fermentation temperatures. Exports are 85% of sales. Guy Accad has been the consultant oenologist here since 1988.

Domaine de Serrigny

21550 Ladoix-Serrigny.

Of the 28 acres, 9.4 are in Corton Grands Crus (Clos du Roi, Bressandes, Renardes and Maréchaudes), 1.6 in Aloxe-Corton Premier Cru and nearly an acre in Ladoix Premier Cru.

Robert de Suremain

Château de Monthelie, 21190 Meursault.

A small, old-fashioned but famous estate whose 13 acres of old vines in Monthelie produce a red wine comparable with good Volnays. He also has vineyards in Rully producing both red and white wines.

Domaine Thénard

71640 Givry.

see Société Civile du Domaine Thénard, Côte Chalonnaise.

Thévenot Le Brun & Fils

Marey-lès-Fussey, 21700 Nuits-St-Georges.

Maurice Thévenot's father purchased an abandoned monastic walled vineyard, the Clos du Vignon, in the Hautes Côtes de Nuits in 1933. Maurice and his sons replanted the property in 1967 and they now have 64 acres making some of the best wine of the Hautes Côtes from Pinot Noir (30 acres), which is mixed with Gamay for his Passe-tout-grain, and Aligoté, which is bottled without racking to be drunk very young and faintly fizzy.

Domaine Tollot-Beaut & Fils

Chorey-lès-Beaune, 21200 Beaune.

A family property since 1880 with impeccable standards, which is sometimes cited as a model for Burgundy. Of a total of 50 acres, a little under half is at Chorey and the remainder divided among the Premiers Crus of Beaune (Grèves and Clos du Roi, 4.2 acres), Savigny and Aloxe-Corton, with some 400 cases a year of Corton-Bressandes, 250 of Le Corton and 125 of Corton-Charlemagne (white). No secrets here, but careful traditional winemaking, plunging the 'cap' twice daily and controlling the temperature. The special pride of the house is in the Corton-Bressandes and Beaune Clos du Roi.

Domaine Tortochot

21220 Gevrey-Chambertin.

A 27-acre family property. They own parcels of between 1 and 2 acres in the Grands Crus Charmes- and Mazis-Chambertin, a similar piece of Lavaux St-Jacques on the hill above the village and considered worthy of Grand Cru standing, some good land in Morey St-Denis and a half acre in Clos Vougeot.

Domaine Trapet et Fils

53 route de Beaune, 21220 Gevrey-Chambertin.

Jean Trapet and his son Jean-Louis now own half of the original Louis Trapet domaine which was divided in 1990. The pride of the house is still its Chambertin, made in the traditional way and showing great delicacy and finesse.

Domaine des Varoilles

11 rue de l'Ancien Hôpital, 21220 Gevrey-Chambertin.

A 30-acre domaine with one of the highest reputations in Burgundy for serious *vins de garde* that really must be matured. It takes its name from its 15-acre Clos des Varoilles, planted on the south-facing hill above Gevrey by monks from Langres during the 12th and 13th centuries. The Clos du Couvent, Clos du Meix des Ouches and La Romanée are other 'monopoles' in Gevrey, besides 2 acres of Charmes- and Mazoyères-Chambertin, 1.3 of Bonnes Mares and 6.5 of Clos de Vougeot. The director, Jean-Pierre Naigeon, makes some of Burgundy's firmest, best-structured wines, selecting from old vines and constantly mixing in the skins during fermentation. He quotes the gourmet-critic Gaston Roupnel on Varoilles wines: 'Only age can tame its almost savage force … and give it at last the scents of violets and spring.' Amen.

Domaine Charles Vienot

Prémeaux Prissey 21700 Nuits-St-Georges.
This 9.8-acre property (now part of the J.-C. Boisset stable) is scattered between eleven different parcels in a number of communes, including Nuits-St-Georges (two Premiers Crus), Gevrey-Chambertin (one Premier Cru), Corton and Clos de Vougeot.

Henri de Villamont

Rue du Docteur Guyot, 21420 Savigny-lès-Beaune.
Négociants and growers founded by the huge Swiss firm of Schenk in 1964, when they bought the 15-acre Domaine Marthenot at Savigny and the 10-acre Domaine Modot in Chambolle-Musigny and Grands-Echézeaux. In 1969 they purchased the business of Arthur Barolet in Beaune. The name Barolet figures largely in their annals since they found and marketed the extraordinary hoard of fine old burgundies of the late Dr Barolet in 1968. Seventy percent is exported.

Domaine Michel Voarick

21420 Aloxe-Corton.
A 22-acre family 'exploitation' which includes farming the famous 6-acre Corton Cuvée Dr Peste for the Hospices de Beaune. Voarick owns 5 acres of Corton Grand Cru (Clos du Roi, Bressandes, Languettes, Renardes) and 3 of Corton-Charlemagne, besides 6 acres in Pernand-Vergelesses and 7 in Aloxe-Corton. He produces a total of some 3,850 cases of red wine and 500 of white. Old-fashioned methods include fermenting stalks-and-all in oak *cuves* to make *vins de garde*.

Domaine Comte Georges de Vogüé

Chambolle-Musigny, 21220 Gevrey-Chambertin.
Considered by some to be the finest domaine in Burgundy, descended by inheritance since 1450. The name de Vogüé appears in 1766. Splendid vaulted cellars under the 15th-century house hold the production of 30 acres, of which 15 are in Le Musigny, 6.5 in Bonnes Mares, 1.5 in the Premier Cru Les Amoureuses and 5 in the appellation Chambolle-Musigny. Some 3,000 Chardonnay vines in Musigny produce an average 100 cases a year of a unique Musigny Blanc. After a flat patch in the 1970s and early '80s the wines are once again superlative. The name Vieilles Vignes is given to the best wine, which is burgundy at its grandest and yet most subtle – beyond description. Seventy-five percent is exported.

Cave Coopérative des Grands Vins Rosés

21 rue de Mazy, 21160 Marsannay-La-Côte.
One of the few growers' cooperatives of the Côte d'Or, founded in 1929 and now counting 19 members whose properties vary between 2 and 35 acres. The wines are Bourgogne Rouge and their speciality, Rosé de Marsannay, which is largely sold to passing tourists in summer.

André Ziltener Père & Fils

Chambolle-Musigny, 21220 Gevrey-Chambertin.
Swiss-owned merchant and proprietor of a domaine that includes a Château de Chambolle-Musigny (there are two) and a restaurant in the village. Ziltener offers a full range of good sturdy examples of both red and white burgundies, including a well-oaked Chablis.

THE COTE CHALONNAISE

Santenay brings the Côte d'Or to a close at its southern end. There is scarcely time for lunch at the luxurious Lameloise at Chagny before the wine scout has to be alert again for the five villages that make up the Côte Chalonnaise. In fact, Chalon-sur-Saône has little to do with the district today and the tendency is to refer to the Région de Mercurey, the biggest and best known of the wine parishes. But in antiquity Chalon was one of the great wine ports of the Empire. It was the point where wine coming or going north to or from Paris or the Moselle had to be transshipped from river to road – 25,000 amphoras were found in one dredging operation in the Saône at Chalon.

A new appellation, Bourgogne Côte Chalonnaise, was introduced in 1990 which distinguishes the wines of the Côte Chalonnaise from the rather large and undefined appellation of Bourgogne itself. The Côte from Chagny southwards is less distinct and consistent than from Santenay northwards. So is its wine. Rising demand and prices have only recently made wine-growing profitable rather than marginal, and encouraged replanting of land abandoned after phylloxera, or whose owners were killed during World War I. Of the 9,000 acres included in the Côte Chalonnaise appellation, less than 2,000 are currently planted, over 90 percent with Pinot Noir; the remainder with Chardonnay. Although its best wines are up to minor Côte de Beaune standards, it is difficult to pin them down with a regional character. They vary remarkably from village to village.

Mercurey and Givry are dedicated 90 percent to red wine, which should be firm and tasty Pinot Noir at least on a level with, say, a good Côte de Beaune-Villages; if anything harder and leaner, with Givry, traditionally the bigger, demanding longer keeping.

Rully is split equally between red wine and white. Here the white at its best is marvellously brisk with a touch of real class. The red, at least as most growers make it today, can be rather thin compared with Mercurey. High acidity in Rully whites makes them ideal for sparkling wines.

Montagny is entirely a white-wine appellation, with the peculiarity that almost all its wines of 11.5 degrees alcohol or more are entitled to be labelled Premier Cru – which seems scarcely fair to the carefully limited Premier Crus of the other villages. Montagny whites tend to have a little more body and less finesse than those of Rully. The one most often seen abroad, a selection by the Beaune négociant Louis Latour, is quite a fat dry wine.

The fifth appellation of the Côte Chalonnaise is the only specific one of the Aligoté grape in Burgundy. The village of Bouzeron, between Rully and Chagny, has made a speciality of a normally plain, sharp café wine. In 1979 it was granted the appellation Bourgogne Aligoté de Bouzeron.

Besides these specific appellations the Région de Mercurey makes a considerable quantity of honourable Bourgogne Rouge, most of which is sold in bulk. But a few growers in Bouzeron and St-Désert bottle it. Like all red burgundy, it should be kept a minimum of two years in bottle.

The other regional speciality is Crémant de Bourgogne, sparkling wine whose quality will amaze those who think that champagne is first and the rest nowhere. (*See* the box on page 122.) Three sizeable producers account for most of the *crémant* production. They are Delorme at Rully, R. Chevillard at La Rochepot on the road to Paris, and Parigot-Richard at Savigny-lès-Beaune.

THE REGION IN ROUND FIGURES

Appellation	Average annual production		
Mercurey	20,000 hl	222,000 cases	(mainly red)
Givry	4,000 hl	44,000 cases	(mainly red)
Rully	8,000 hl	88,800 cases	(white)
	7,000 hl	77,700 cases	(red)
Montagny	3,000 hl	33,300 cases	(white)

Leading Côte Chalonnaise Producers

Chateau de Chamirey *see* Antonin Rodet

Emile Chandesais

Château St-Nicolas, 71150 Fontaines.
A négociant, based in the Côte Chalonnaise, with a reputation for wines from the Région de Mercurey. From their own 27 acres of vineyards they produce 7,000 cases of Bourgogne AC and Rully Les St-Jacques.

Domaine Chanzy-Daniel

Domaine L'Hermitage, Bouzeron, 71150 Chagny.
One of the two considerable domaines in Bouzeron where they have some 27 acres, 30 in Rully and 6 in Mercurey. Over half of the Bouzeron vineyard is planted in Aligoté, which is considered Burgundy's best. M. Chanzy's Bourgogne (i.e. Pinot Noir and Chardonnay) vineyards in Bouzeron are called Clos de la Fortune. His biggest production is of Rully Rouge (2,500 cases from 19 acres). His Premier Cru Mercurey vineyards are called Clos du Roy. He insists that red burgundy must be kept 3–4 years in bottle to show its personality.

Jean-François Delorme

Domaine de la Renarde, Rully, 71150 Chagny.
The most remarkable enterprise in the region; a 163-acre estate built from scratch in 30 years, largely by reclaiming vineyards abandoned long ago and turned to scrub. Delorme is equally well known as one of Burgundy's best sparkling-wine specialists, for which the very clean, slightly austere whites of Rully are excellent. 64 acres of the domaine in Rully are Chardonnay; 57 are Pinot Noir. Varot is the 44-acre vineyard that gives his best white, notable for freshness and finesse. Its austerity brings it closer in character to Chablis than, say, a Mâcon white. Domaine de la Renarde red is also delicate, 'nervous' and without surplus flesh. A comparison with his Mercurey (12 acres) shows the Mercurey to be plumper and to have more substance. He also has 11 acres of Givry, 4.2 of Bouzeron Aligoté and 12 at La Rochepot. 37,500 cases of Crémant de Bourgogne are made from Pinot Noir and Chardonnay in an impressive new cellar; a real alternative to champagne – a *cuvée* that is tasty without being coarse; delicate without being timid.

Michel Derain

St-Désert, 71390 Buxy.
A small-scale producer of 'serious' Bourgogne Rouge and Givry Blanc from 14 acres.

Du Gardin

71640 Givry.
The 15-acre 'monopole' Clos Saloman in Givry has been owned by the Du Gardin family for over 300 years. Very sound wine.

Michel Goubard

Basseville, St-Désert, 71390 Buxy.
An example of how good Bourgogne Rouge without a specific appellation can be in this part of the Côtes. Michel Goubard also bottles approximately 7,250 cases of Côte Chalonnaise.

Paul & Henri Jacqueson

Rully, 71150, Chagny.
Father and son together take great pride in this small domaine of 17 acres making wine in the old way. The reds are trodden by foot, stems and all, fermented for up to 22 days and raised in new barrels every year. 5 acres of Rully Premier Cru are called 'Les Clous' (red) and 'Grésigny' (white). The other wines are (red) Mercurey and Rully, and some Aligoté and Passe-tout-grain. Their label is seen in some very smart restaurants.

Domaine Michel Juillot

71640 Mercurey.
One of the best Mercurey makers, regularly carrying off gold medals for the red Clos des Barraults from his 69 acres (of which 11.8 are Chardonnay). He destems all his grapes, ferments in open vats and buys one third of his barrels new each year. He also owns vines in Aloxe-Corton and Montagny.

Paul and Yves de Launay

Clos du Château de Montaigu, Mercurey, 71640 Givry.
A traditional small property with vines around the ruins of the Château de Montaigu, producing Mercurey red as well as some Aligoté.

Jean Maréchal

71640 Mercurey.

Maréchals have made Mercurey for 300 years. 17 of their 22 acres are in the Premiers Crus, almost all red. The aim is to produce long-lived wines, especially his 'Cuvée Prestige'.

Armand Monassier

Domaine du Prieuré, Rully, 71150 Chagny.

The property of a Paris restaurateur (Chez Les Anges, one-star, Boulevard Latour-Maubourg), born in Rully, who since 1958 has assembled a total of 18 acres, 11 of Rully Rouge (5 are Premier Cru) and 5 of Rully Blanc (half Premier Cru). With a little red Mercurey, he also makes Crémant de Bourgogne, Passe-tout-grain, *marc* and *fine*.

E. and X. Noël-Bouton

Domaine de la Folie, Rully, 71150 Chagny.

A substantial property with 1,000 years of history, in the parish of Chagny but in the appellation of Rully. The 44 acres are in one block around the house, with Chardonnay in a majority, producing some 3,300 cases a year of Rully Blanc Clos St-Jacques; Pinot Noir making 2,500 cases of Rully Rouge Clos de Bellecroix; and a smaller patch of Aligoté. Xavier Noël-Bouton buys as much as 40% of his barrels new each year to make aromatic wines with the potential to develop. A leader of the commune.

Domaine Maurice Protheau & Fils

Mercurey, 71640 Givry.

A major domaine of 110 acres, including 15.5 in Clos L'Evéque, 11 in La Fauconnière and 10 in the Clos des Corvées. Négociants François Protheau, now Swiss owned, market the wines.

Domaine Ragot

Poncey, 71640 Givry.

A small domaine in its fourth generation with a dignified château, with 10 acres of Givry Rouge and 5 of Givry Blanc out of a total of 18. The proportion of white is unusually high for Givry and the keeping qualities of the wine are remarkable – particularly in years of high acidity. Ripe vintages, says M. Ragot, are best drunk sooner. His red and white are both regular gold-medal winners.

Antonin Rodet

Mercurey, 71640 Givry.

An important négociant as well as proprietor in Mercurey. The fourth generation of the Rodet family is represented by the Marquis de Jouennes d'Herville, whose name appears on the domaine's label, Château de Chamirey. The 66-acre vineyard consists of nearly the whole of the Mercurey Premier Cru Clos du Roi and produces some 8,500 cases of red and 1,500 of white. To many, the red Château de Chamirey is the archetypal Mercurey.

Antonin Rodet deals in wines from all parts of Burgundy, taking special pride in its Bourgogne Rodet, Mercurey, Meursault and Gevrey-Chambertin. Laurent-Perrier now has a stake in the company.

Domaine Saier

Mercurey, 71640 Givry.

Purchasers, in 1979, of the 22-acre Grand Cru Clos des Lambrays in Morey St-Denis. 7.4 acres of the 62-acre domaine are in Mercurey Premier Cru Les Champs Martin. There are 27 more acres of red Mercurey and 7.4 of white.

Domaine Château de la Saule

Montagny-lès-Buxy, 71390 Buxy.

A 32-acre property almost entirely devoted to fresh, vigorous, white Montagny. The grapes are pressed as fast as possible after picking, the juice fined and fermented in oak barrels, to be bottled the following June. Freshness is the aim, but 'big' vintages have been known to improve for 8–10 years.

Hugues de Suremain

Mercurey, 71640 Givry.

A leading proprietor whose own 30 acres are known for concentrated and age-worthy wines.

Société Civile du Domaine Thénard

71640 Givry.

Much the grandest estate of Givry, with 50 acres in the village (almost all red Premiers Crus) but better known to the world as the owner of the second-biggest single plot of Le Montrachet, 4.5 acres, as well as 2 acres each of Corton Clos du Roi, Iles des Vergelesses and 1.4 of Grands-Echézeaux. The property has been in the family for 200 years. All the wine is made in the atmospheric oak-beamed *cuverie* and cellars at Givry. Three Givry Premiers Crus, all robust *vins de garde*, are sold under their vineyard names: Boischevaux, Cellier aux Moines and Clos St-Pierre.

A. and P. de Villaine

Bouzeron, 71150 Chagny.

A grower better known as co-proprietor of the Domaine de la Romanée-Conti, but equally proud to have helped bring Bouzeron from obscurity to having its own appellation in 5 years (1973–78) of impeccable winemaking. M. Aubert de Villaine treats Aligoté as a noble grape, using half barrels (for finesse) and half tanks (for fruit). His Bourgogne Rouge is similarly made, with selective pickings, long fermentation with the stems, and no rackings. His 25 acres of Aligoté produce about 4,350 cases a year. 8 acres of Chardonnay are called Bourgogne Blanc Les Clous and 13.5 acres of Pinot Noir are called by their vineyard names, La Digoine and La Fortune. Bourgogne Rosé is made in suitable years. Since 1994 white Rully and red Mercury have been added to the list.

Caves des Vignerons de Buxy

Les Vignes de la Croix, St-Gengoux Le Nuit, 71390 Buxy.

Important and very modern growers' coop for Buxy and Montagny, founded in 1931 but re-equipped recently. Its members own 580 acres of vines, less than half with generic appellations (Bourgogne Rouge, Passe-tout-grain, Aligoté and Bourgogne Grand Ordinaire are its main productions.) The remainder include white Montagny, with some Premier Cru, Rully, red Côte Chalonnaise, and Crémant de Bourgogne.

MACON

Say 'Mâcon' to most wine drinkers today and their knee-jerk response will be 'blanc'. The region is riding high on the reliability and uncomplicated pleasantness of its Chardonnay whites. They have the advantage of being recognizably white burgundy but half the price of Côte d'Or wines, and marvellously easy to choose – since most of them are made by skilful cooperatives and marketed by their efficient central Union des Coopératives Vinicoles de Bourgogne de Saône-et-Loire.

The Mâconnais is a widespread and disjointed region, taking its name from the important commercial city on the Saône just outside its limits to the east. It has little of the monoculture of Beaujolais; its mixed farming land is more attractive, and in places geologically spectacular. Pouilly-Fuissé is its only appellation with *grand vin* aspirations.

Most Mâcon wine used to be red, made of Gamay but grown on heavy chalky soil which prevents it from ripening to Beaujolais softness and vitality. Mâcon Rouge was indeed merely *vin ordinaire* with an appellation until Beaujolais methods of fermentation were introduced. Recently there have been some much better wines up to Beaujolais-Villages standards.

Pinot Noir from the Mâconnais can aspire no higher than the appellation Bourgogne Rouge or (mixed with Gamay) Passe-tout-grain.

Chardonnay now occupies two-thirds of the vineyards, including (in the more northerly communes in particular) a strain of Chardonnay known as the 'Musqué' for its decidedly richer, melony-musky flavour. Used to excess it can produce a blowzy, unsubtle wine. In due proportion it adds a hint of richness to otherwise rather straight dry white; undoubtedly an element in the popularity of Mâcon-Villages or with the name of a particular village.

Pouilly-Fuissé rises higher in the quality league, for local reasons of soil and situation – but not as high as its price infers. The four villages in the appellation area have been prominent over the centuries, partly for their proximity to Mâcon, partly as a tourist attraction for the mighty limestone bluffs that dominate them and the prehistoric traces that litter the district, partly for the chalky clay and sunny slopes that make their wine at least as good as any south Burgundy white.

Pierre Bréjoux describes it as 'masculine and long-lived', but variable according to the precise location of the vineyard in a country that is all bumps and dips. Such variations are not easy to follow where there are very few domaines of more than a few acres. The best I have tasted have been full-bodied and dry but rather half-hearted in flavour compared with, say, Meursault or a good Chablis. The growers' cooperative of Chaintré is much the biggest source of Pouilly-Fuissé.

The fact that wines of more or less equal value are produced in the surrounding area has given rise to two other appellations. The smaller Pouilly-Vinzelles (which includes Pouilly-Loché) has somehow failed to catch the public's eye. The much larger St-Véran, which scoops in eight villages, including the northern fringe of the Beaujolais country, was added in 1971 and now offers extremely good value.

THE APPELLATIONS OF MACON

The Mâconnais has seven appellations of its own and shares the right to five more with the rest of Burgundy. Its own appellations are:

FOR WHITE WINES

Mâcon Blanc. Chardonnay wine from delimited areas with a minimum 10 degrees of natural alcohol. This wine can also be labelled Pinot Chardonnay de Mâcon.

Mâcon Supérieur. The same with one more degree of alcohol.

Mâcon-Villages (or Mâcon- followed by the name of one of 43 villages in the eastern half of the region). The best known of these are Clessé, Prissé, Lugny, Viré and Chardonnay – the latter being the village with the credit for finding the noblest white grape of France. The minimum degree is 11, as for Mâcon Supérieur.

St-Véran. The same as for Mâcon-Villages but from eight of the southernmost communes, overlapping into Beaujolais at St-Amour. The eight are Chânes, Chasselas, Davayé, Leynes, Prissé, St-Amour, St-Vérand [sic] and part of Solutré, which is not in the appellation Pouilly-Fuissé. Davayé and Prissé lie to the north and are based on classic Burgundian limestone which gives the wines weight and concentration, the rest are to the south of Pouilly-Fuissé on the granitic sand of the Beaujolais which is much less suited to white wine production. They but offer lighter, thinner wines, which can also be sold as Beaujolais Blanc, Mâcon-Villages or Bourgogne Blanc if the customer prefers one of these names. If a particular vineyard is named on the label the minimum degree is 12, with the implication that the wine is better and more concentrated.

Pouilly-Fuissé. Chardonnay wine of 11 degrees from specified parts of the villages of Pouilly, Fuissé, Solutré, Vergisson and Chaintré. If a vineyard name is used it must have 12 degrees.

Pouilly Loché. May be sold as itself or labelled as Pouilly Vinzelles.

Pouilly-Vinzelles. The same rules as for Pouilly-Fuissé, but for wine from the two villages of Vinzelles and Loché to the east – marginally less good but more than marginally cheaper.

FOR RED WINES

Mâcon Rouge. Gamay red wine of at least 9 degrees. It can also be made pink and offered as Mâcon Rosé.

Mâcon Supérieur. The same with an extra degree of alcohol and from certain specified zones. It can also be labelled as Mâcon- (followed by a village name), but *not* Mâcon-Villages.

GENERAL APPELLATIONS

Aligoté. As in the rest of Burgundy.

Bourgogne. For Chardonnay whites and Pinot Noir reds.

Bourgogne Grand Ordinaire. For whites.

Crémant de Bourgogne. As in the rest of Burgundy.

Passe-tout-grain. For Gamay and Pinot Noir (2:1) reds.

Leading Mâcon Producers

The great bulk of Mâcon, both white and red, is produced by the 18 growers' cooperatives of the area. The best known are those of Chaintré (for Pouilly-Fuissé), Lugny (for Mâcon-Lugny and Mâcon Rouge Supérieur), Prissé (Mâcon-Prissé and St-Véran) and Viré (Mâcon-Viré).

All except those marked with an asterisk are distributed by the Union des Coopératives Vinicoles de Bourgogne de Saône-et-Loire, Charnay-lès-Mâcon, 71008 Mâcon, which also offers a good Crémant de Bourgogne under various labels, among them Prince de Chardonne.

The following are the few individual producers with more than a local reputation. The average holding is about 10 acres, producing 2,000– 3,000 cases a year.

POUILLY-FUISSE

Château de Beauregard Fuissé, owner Georges Burrier

Clos de Bourg Fuissé, owner Maurice Luquet

Joseph Corsin Fuissé

Roger Duboeuf Chaintré

Michel Forest

Château de Fuissé owner Jean-Jacques Vincent.
   The outstanding grower of the area.

Claude-Guérin Vergisson

Gérard Valette

POUILLY-VINZELLES

Gérard Valette

Jean Mathias Chaintré

ST-VERAN

Lycée Agricole Davayé

Georges Chagny Leynes

André Chavet Davayé

Domaine des Deux Roches

R. Duperron Leynes

MACON-CLESSE

Jean Thevenet Quintaine-Clessé, Lugny

MACON-VIRE

A. Bonhomme

Clos du Chapitre Viré, owner Jacques Depagneux

Château de Viré Viré, owner Hubert Desbois

In addition very good wines are offered by several of the négociants well known for their Beaujolais; notably Georges Duboeuf, Thorin and Piat, and by Louis Latour, Robert Drouhin and Louis Jadot of Beaune.

MACON LA ROCHE VINEUSE

Olivier Merlin

CAVES COOPERATIVES

Production figures are for AOC wines only. Most of these coops also make a limited amount of *vin de table*, which is mostly sold in bulk.

Aze* 71260 Lugny. 511 acres; 125 members; 110,000 cases.

Bissey-sous-Cruchaud 71390 Buxy. 121 acres; 80 members; 27,900 cases.

Buxy* 71390 Buxy. 1,200 acres; 203,600 cases.

Chaintré 71570 La Chapelle de Guinchay. 487 acres; 187 members; 117,300 cases.

Chardonnay* 71700 Tournus. 538 acres; 113 members; 119,000 cases.

Charnay-lès-Mâcon 71000 Mâcon. 160 acres; 73 members; 33,000 cases.

Genouilly 71460 St-Gengoux Le National. 151 acres; 185 members; 22,800 cases.

Igé* 71960 Pierreclos. 593 acres; 102 members; 166,000 cases.

Lugny* 71260 Lugny. 2,359 acres; 505 members; 678,000 cases.

Mancey 71240 Sennecey-Le-Grand. 1,010 acres; 180 members; 59,000 cases.

Prissé 71960 Pierreclos. 882 acres; 234 members; 245,000 cases.

Sennecé-lès-Mâcon* 71000 Mâcon. 91 acres; 84 members; 20,300 cases.

Sologny 71960 Pierreclos. 459 acres; 145 members; 107,000 cases.

Verzé 71960 Pierreclos. 2,067 acres; 91 members; 122,000 cases.

'La Vigne Blanche' Clessé, 71260 Lugny. 293 acres; 83 members; 73,000 cases.

Vinzelles 71145 Vinzelles. 311 acres; 133 members; 76,000 cases.

Viré* 71260 Lugny. 692 acres; 245 members; 200,000 cases.

BEAUJOLAIS

The Beaujolais region is no more complex than its lighthearted wine. Thirteen appellations take care of the whole 55,000 acres and the almost 15 million cases of wine they make every year. They could really be reduced to half a dozen without greatly grieving anyone but the gastronomes of Lyon. What is needed is a grasp of the essential grades of quality and a good address list – which need not be long.

The great majority of Beaujolais is made either by a growers' cooperative or by tiny properties. Two thousand five hundred Beaujolais-makers have between two and ten acres – enough to make, say, up to 3,000 cases each. Another 1,400 have between 10 and 18 acres – which will keep their clients supplied, but scarcely make a reputation.

The details given here are therefore a guide to the major sources of Beaujolais, the merchants and cooperatives of the region, and a very short selection of some standard-setting properties.

HOW BEAUJOLAIS IS MADE

The secret of the fresh grape fruitiness of Beaujolais lies in the way the Gamay grape– a variety of modest pretentions to quality – is handled and fermented. Winemaking in the Beaujolais combines the classic method of making burgundy with *macération carbonique* – the activity of enzymes inside an uncrushed grape which, provided it is surrounded by carbon dioxide, causes an internal fermentation and the extraction of colour and flavour from the inner skin.

The trick is to fill the fermentation vat with grapes in their whole bunches, on their stalks, as little crushed and damaged as possible. In a modern Beaujolais *cuverie* a common way is to load the vat with a belt-elevator carrying the bunches to an opening in the top. The weight of the upper grapes crushes the lower ones, which start a normal fermentation with their natural yeasts. The carbon dioxide given off by this process (helped along with gas from a bottle, if necessary) blankets off the air from the uncrushed upper layers. Here the grapes quietly feed on themselves, many of them splitting in the process.

After six or seven days of spontaneous fermentation, the vat is about one-third full of juice, known as 'free-run'. This is run off, and the solid matter pressed to extract the remaining juice and the two products blended together. In normal red-winemaking the *vin de presse* is in a minority (and may not be used at all). In the Beaujolais method it accounts for between two-thirds and three-quarters of the total, and the resulting wines tend to be softer, less astringent, than those fermented traditionally.

At this stage the juice still has unfermented sugar in it. Fermentation has to finish before the juice is stable enough to be called wine. The law says that this will happen by the third Thursday in November, although in years when the harvest is late some fairly brutal methods of stabilization are needed to 'finish' the wine in time.

The world's perception of Beaujolais today is very different from what it was 20 or so years ago. Beyond its own region and Paris, where it was *the* café wine, Beaujolais used to be traded as a cut-price burgundy, imitating the weight of the Pinot Noirs of the Côte d'Or; by dint of picking as ripe as possible and adding plenty of sugar, achieving strength without grace. I have always been mystified by mid-19th-century figures showing Beaujolais *crus* with 15 degrees of alcohol (while Médocs had 9 or 10 degrees). Very few red wines need anything like that strength, and least of all Gamay, which lacks the flavour to countenance it. The Gamay of Beaujolais has no great fruity flavour; well made and in the modern manner it lures you in with its sappy smell and a combination of soft juiciness and a slight nip – the perfect recipe for quenching thirst.

It is worth remembering that Beaujolais' best wines are known simply by the names of their *crus* on the label.

THE APPELLATIONS OF BEAUJOLAIS

The most basic Beaujolais is from the southern half of the region, south of Villefranche, where the Gamay is encouraged to produce large quantities on heavy soil. (Although there is nothing to stop growers anywhere in Beaujolais using the appellation.) This is essentially now-or-never wine, originally destined to be sold on draught in local cafés and by the carafe in restaurants. It is best drunk as young as possible. The date after which it can be sold *en primeur* is the third Thursday in November. The term *nouveau*, while often used with the same intention, really only means the wine of the last harvest, until the next. The minimum alcoholic degree is 9, but this is regularly exceeded either naturally or by adding sugar. For this reason the appellation Beaujolais Supérieur, only different in requiring 10 degrees, is little used. 'Beaujolais' applies to red, white or rosé, but the great majority is red.

Total area is 24,000 acres; average production 6.6m. cases a year.

GROWERS
Raymond Alloin Montée du Château, 69480 Morancée, with 37 acres.
Jean-François Garlon Beauvallon, 69620 Theizé, with 7.5 acres.
René Marchand Les Meules, 69640 Cogny, with 15 acres.
Raymond Mathelin & Fils Domaine de Sandar, 69380 Chatillon d'Azergues, with 10 acres.
Marcelle Pein 69260 Theizé, with 30 acres.
Georges Subrin 69480 Morancé, with 25 acres.
Christian Vivier-Merle Les Verjouttes, 69620 Theizé, with 37 acres.
Member of the Eventail de Vignerons Producteurs: Jacques Montagne at Leynes.

CAVES COOPERATIVES

Cave Coop Beaujolaise 69620 St-Laurent-d'Oingt.
Les Vignerons de la Cave de Bully 69210 Bully. The largest coop in Beaujolais.
Beau Vallon Theizé, 69620 Le Bois d'Oingt, with 951 acres.

Beaujolais-Villages

The northern half of the region, or Haut-Beaujolais, has steeper hills, warmer (because lighter and more sandy) soil, and makes better wine. Beaujolais-Villages is the appellation that covers the whole of this area, 39 villages in all, but 10 small zones in the north, identified by combinations of slopes and soils that are peculiar to themselves, are singled out as the Beaujolais 'crus' – the aristocrats.

Beaujolais-Villages makes a better *vin de primeur* than plain Beaujolais, except in untypically hot vintages. It has a minimum of 10 degrees alcohol and more backing of fruit and body – more flavour, in fact – to complement the rasp of new fruit juice. It is almost always worth its fairly modest premium both *en primeur* and even more when it has been or will be kept. Good -Villages is at its best in the summer after the vintage, and can hold for another year. Besides the 'crus', the region as a whole has some producers whose wines are regularly up to 'cru' standards.

Total area is 14,250 acres; average production 3.6m. cases a year.

GROWERS

Jacky Gauthier Dom. de Colette, 69430 Lantigné, with 10 acres.
Bruno Jambon Le Charnay, 69430 Lantigné, with 30 acres.
Claude & Michelle Joubert 69430 Lantigné, with 20 acres.
Durieu de Lacarelle Dom. de Lacarelle, 69830 St-Etienne-des-Ouillières, with 345 acres.
Domaine Christian Miolane Le Cellier, 69830 Salles, with 34 acres.
Monternot 'Les Places', 69830 Blacé, with 20 acres.
Jean-Charles Pivot Quincié-en-Beaujolais, 69430 Beaujeu, with 30 acres.
Soc. Viticole Beaujolaise Liergues, 69400 Villefranche-sur-Saône, with 240 members and 1,161 acres.
Members of the Eventail de Vignerons Producteurs include: Jacques Montagne, Roger and Jean-Luc Tissier at Leynes and André Jaffre at Charentay.

THE CRUS OF BEAUJOLAIS

Between the railway along the Saône Valley and the 450-metre contour line in the Beaujolais mountains to the west, from just south of Belleville to the boundary with the Mâconnais, the vine has the landscape to itself. Sandy, stony or schistous granite-based soils without lime give the Gamay a roundness and depth of flavour it lacks elsewhere. Here it is pruned hard and the plants trimmed individually. Minimum strength of the wine is 10 degrees, but when it is sold with a vineyard name the required minimum is a degree higher.

Cru Beaujolais can be offered *en primeur*, but not until a month after Beaujolais and Villages, from 15 December. It would be a pity to prevent it being poured for Christmas. The best *crus* are never treated in this way; they are kept in barrel or vat until at least the March after the vintage. Their full individuality and sweet juicy smoothness take anything from six months to six years in bottle to develop. Three of the *crus*, Morgon, Chénas and above all Moulin-à-Vent, are looked on as *vins de garde*, at least by Beaujolais standards.

Brouilly

The southernmost and the largest of the *crus*, enveloping areas in 6 villages (Odenas, St-Lager, Cercié, Charentay, St-Etienne-la-Varenne and Quincié) grouped around the isolated Mont de Brouilly (*see* Côtes de Brouilly). The word 'typical' is most often used for Brouilly – not surprisingly for the biggest producer lying in the very heart of the region. This means the wine is full of grapey flavour and vigour but not aggressive in its first year.

Total area is 3,000 acres; average production 800,000 cases a year.

Château du Bluizard Jean de St-Charles, 69460 St Etienne-la-Varenne.
Château de la Chaize Marquise de Roussy de Salles, 69460 Odenas. The biggest estate in Beaujolais with 360 acres.
Dom. de la Fully P. & M. Vermorel, Chambon, 69460 Blacé.
Bernard Jomain Les Clous, La Chaize, 69460 Odenas.
Jean Lathuilière La Pisse Vieille, 69220 Cercié-en-Beaujolais.
Alain Michaud Dom. de Beauvoir, 69220 St-Lager.
Cave Coopérative de Bel-Air St-Jean d'Ardières, 69220 Belleville, with 300 members and 1,080 acres (*see* also Côtes de Brouilly).
Members of the Eventail de Vignerons Producteurs are Fabrice Ducroux at Charentay; André Large at Odenas.

Chénas

The smallest *cru*, sheltered from the west by a wooded hill (Chénas is derived from *chêne*, an oak) and including part of the commune of La Chapelle-de-Guinchay. Certain Chénas wines achieve formidable strengths, but its vineyard sites are too varied for the appellation to be readily identifiable or its style reliable.

Total area is 625 acres; average production 164,000 cases a year.

Domaine Champagnon Les Brureaux, Chénas, 69840 Chénas.
Fernand Charvet Le Bourg, Chénas, 69840 Juliénas.
Emile Robin Le Bois Retour, Chénas, 69840 Juliénas.
Domaine Georges Trichard 71570 La Chapelle-de-Guinchay.
Cave du Château Chénas (Coopérative) Chénas, 69840 Juliénas, with 278 members and a total of 674 acres.
Members of the Eventail de Vignerons Producteurs: Georges Rossi of La Chapelle de Guinchay and Château de Chénas.

Chiroubles

All southeast-facing on the higher slopes, making some of the best-balanced and most prized Beaujolais in limited quantities. This is the first *cru* to be 'supple and tender' for the eager Paris restaurateurs.

Total area is 875 acres; average production 220,000 cases a year.

Domaine Emile Cheysson Les Farges, 69115 Chiroubles, with 54 acres.
Château Javernand M. Fourneau, 69115 Chiroubles, with 47 acres.
Alain Passot Dom. de la Grosse Pierre, 69115 Chiroubles, with 20 acres.
Château de Raousset Héritiers de Raousset, 69115 Chiroubles, with 50 acres.
Cave Coopérative (Maison des Chiroubles) 69115 Chiroubles, with 63 members and 217 acres.
Cave Coopérative Vinicole 69115 Chiroubles.
Members of the Eventail de Vignerons Producteurs: René Savoye, Alain Passot at Dom. de la Grosse Pierre and Philippe Gobet.

Côte de Brouilly

The slopes of the Mont de Brouilly give a stronger, more concentrated wine than the surrounding appellation Brouilly, but in smaller quantities. The minimum degree here is 10.5 – the highest in Beaujolais. They are said to develop the high-toned scent of violets after 2–3 years in bottle. After warm vintages they benefit from keeping that long.

Total area is 860 acres; average production 198,000 cases a year.

Domaine de Chavanne 69460 Brouilly.
Château Delachanal M. Leffert, Odenas, 69830 St-Georges de Reneins.
Château Thivin Mme Geoffray, Odenas, 69830 St-Georges de Reneins.
Cave Coopérative de Bel-Air St-Jean d'Ardières, 69220 Belleville, with 300 members and 1,080 acres (AC Brouilly, Côte de Brouilly, Morgon, Beaujolais and -Villages).

Fleurie

The pretty name, a substantial supply and a singular freshness of flavour all contribute to making this the most memorable and popular Beaujolais *cru*. Fleurie is often irresistible in its first year, with the result that the full, sweet silkiness of its maturity at 3 or 4 years is little known.

Total area is 2,100 acres; average production 467,000 cases a year.

Domaine Berrod Les Roches du Vivier, 69820 Fleurie.
Michel Chignard Le Point du Jour, 69820 Fleurie.
M. Darroze Clos de Quatre Vents, 69820 Fleurie.
Robert Depardon et Michel Perrier Dom. des Chaffangeons, 69820 Fleurie.

Jean-Marc Desprès La Madone, 69820 Fleurie.
Château de Fleurie Mme Roclore, Mâcon 71000.
Société Civile du Château de Poncié 69820 Fleurie.
Cave Coopérative des Grands Vins de Fleurie 69820 Fleurie, 323 members, 983 acres.
Member of the Eventail de Vignerons Producteurs: Maurice Bruone at Montgenas. Produces about 1,000 cases a year.

Juliénas

With St-Amour, the northernmost *cru* (the *département* boundary of Rhône and Saône-et-Loire runs between them). Substance, strong colour and vigour, even tannin, mean that Juliénas needs two years or more to age. It is generally considered to be a mealtime Beaujolais rather than a thirst quencher.

Total area is 1,450 acres; average production 363,000 cases a year.

Château des Capitans Bernard Sarrau, 69840 Juliénas.
Château de Juliénas M. Condémine, 69840 Juliénas.
Domaine de la Maison de la Dime, M. Foillard, 69830 St-Georges-de-Reneins.
M. J. Perrachon Dom. Bottière, 69840 Juliénas.
Georges Rollet La Pouge, 69840 Juillé.
Domaine de la Vieille Eglise E. Loron et Fils, Pontanevaux, 71570 La Chapelle-de-Guinchay.
Cave des Producteurs Juliénas 69840 Juliénas.
Members of the Eventail de Vignerons Producteurs are the Domaine René Monnet and André Pelletier.

Morgon

The wide spread of vineyards around Villié-Morgon, between the *crus* Brouilly and Fleurie, are credited with a character so peculiar that '*morgonner*' has become a verb for a way that other wines sometimes (when they are lucky) behave. The soil here is schistous, and the peculiarity is described as a flavour of wild cherries. I have not found them so identifiable as this suggests, but they are among the bigger and longest-lasting wines of Beaujolais.

Total area is 2,750 acres; average production 675,000 cases a year.

Domaine Aucoeur 69910 Villié-Morgon.
Paul Collonge Domaine de Ruyère, 69910 Villié-Morgon.
Louis Claude Desvignes Le Bourg, 69910 Villié-Morgon, with 20 acres.
G.F.A. Domaine Lièven, Château de Bellevue 69910 Villié-Morgon, with 29 acres.
Dominique Piron Morgon, 69910 Villié-Morgon, with 30 acres.
Château de Pizay 69220 St-Jean-d'Ardières.
Domaine Savoye Pierre Savoye, Les Micouds, 69910 Villié-Morgon, with 33 acres.
Members of the Eventail de Vignerons Producteurs: Louis Genillon and Louis Desvignes at Villié-Morgon.

Moulin-à-Vent

There is no village of Moulin-à-Vent, but a sailless windmill among the hamlets between Romanèche-Thorins and Chénas gives its name to the most 'serious' and expensive Beaujolais appellation. Moulin-à-Vent *en primeur* is almost a contradiction in terms. It should be firm, meaty and savoury wine that has less of the surging scent of Beaujolais in its first year but builds up a bouquet resembling burgundy in bottle. Some growers age it briefly in small oak barrels to add to the structure that will preserve it. Moulin-à-Vent is always served last in a Beaujolais meal, often with the cheeses, which will dominate the lighter wines (and it, too, as often as not).

Total area is 1,650 acres; average production 412,000 cases a year.

Propriété Bourisset Fermier des Hospices de Romanèche, Romanèche-Thorins, 71570 La Chapelle-de-Guinchay.
Château des Jacques Dom. J. Thorin, Romanèche-Thorins, 71570 La Chapelle-de-Guinchay.
Domaine Jacky Janodet 71570 Romanèche-Thorins.
Propriété Labruyère Romanèche-Thorins, 71570 La Chapelle-de-Guinchay.
Château du Moulin-à-Vent The Bloud family, Romanèche-Thorins, 71570 La Chapelle Pontanevaux.
Domaine de la Tour du Bief Chénas, 69840 Juliénas.
Cave du Château de Chénas Chénas, 69840 Juliénas (appellations Chénas and Moulin-à-Vent), with 278 members and 674 acres.
Members of the Eventail de Vignerons Producteurs: Pierre Belicard at Lancié and Jean Brugne at Vivier and Fleurie.

Regnié

The newest Beaujolais *cru* to the west of Brouilly and Morgon from the commune of Regnié-Durette. While it shows a particular resemblance to Brouilly, it nonetheless has a personality of its own with its well-defined aroma of red fruits. The soils of Regnié are sandier than the other *crus*.

Total area is 18,000 acres; average production 390,000 cases a year.

Member of the Eventail de Vignerons Producteurs is Jean-Charles Braillon.

St-Amour

The one Beaujolais appellation in the Mâconnais – its white wine is entitled to the appellation St-Véran. The power of suggestion is strong, so its promising name may have some bearing on my predilection for this wine. I find it next to Fleurie and Chiroubles in delicacy and sweetness – pleading to be drunk young, yet tasting even better after 2 or 3 years in bottle. As one of the smallest areas it is, alas, not often seen.

Total area is 700 acres; average production 182,000 cases a year.

Denis et Hélène Barbelet Les Billards, 71570 St-Amour-Bellevue.
Domaine des Duc La Piat, 71570 St-Amour-Bellevue.
Madeleine et Jacques Janin Domaine des Darrèzes, 71570 St-Amour-Bellevue.
Jean-Guy Révillon Aux Poulets, 71570 St-Amour-Bellevue.
Château de St-Amour M. Siraudin, 71570 St-Amour-Bellevue.
Paul Spay Au Bourg, 71570 St-Amour-Bellevue.
Member of the Eventail de Vignerons Producteurs: Patissier.

Leading Merchants of Beaujolais and Mâcon

Aujoux & Cie

St-Georges de Reneins.
A Swiss-owned company which supplies a great deal of Beaujolais in bulk to Switzerland. Their own vineyards surround their cellars. The Aujoux label is seen particularly in Scandinavia.

Paul Beaudet

Pontanevaux, 71570 La Chapelle-de-Guinchay.
Fourth-generation family firm run by Paul's son Jean, well known in top restaurants and in the USA for its own Domaine Chénas and other good wines.

Chanut Frères *see* SVGC

Georges Duboeuf

71570 Romanèche-Thorin.
A young, dynamic and skilful company, leader in the café, hotel and restaurant (not supermarket) business. Duboeuf is widely regarded as 'Mr Beaujolais'.

Pierre Ferraud

31 rue Maréchal Foch, 69220 Belleville.
A small company with one of the highest reputations for quality.

Jacquemont Père & Fils

Romanèche-Thorins, 71570 La Chapelle-de-Guinchay.
Not a label you will see, but the biggest *commissionaires* or middlemen in Beaujolais.

Gobet *see* SVGC

Labouré-Roi

A small négociant firm which owns Domaine Roland Piquard, where they make Morgon and Domaine du Griffon, where they make Côtes du Brouilly.

Loron & Fils

Pontanevaux, 71570 La Chapelle-de-Guinchay.
A large, high-quality family business, formerly mainly dealing in bulk but now selling more and more in bottle, under several brand names. Offers some good domaine wines and good-value, non-appellation *vins de marque*.

Mommessin et Thorin S.A.

La Grange St-Pierre, 71850 Charnay-lès-Mâcon.
Until recently a very traditional family business, now diversifying into *vins de marque* as well as Beaujolais, where it has exclusive arrangements with several good domaines. The house also owns the Grand Cru Clos de Tart in the Côte de Nuits.

Piat

71570 La Chapelle-de-Guinchay.
Founded in Mâcon in 1849. Now one of the biggest firms, especially in export, belonging to International Distillers and Vintners. Uses a special 'Piat' bottle, based on the traditional 'pot' of Beaujolais, for a classic range of Beaujolais and Mâcon wines, including a good standard Beaujolais and Mâcon-Viré. Also red and white branded table wines 'Piat d'Or'.

Sarrau *see* SVGC

SVGC

Les Chers, 69840 Juliénas.
Recent organization regrouping some of the well-known merchant houses of Beaujolais: Chanut, Gobet, Dépargneux, Thorin and Sarrau.

Louis Tête

St-Didier sur Beaujeu, 69430 Beaujeu.
A specialist in the high-class restaurant trade, particularly well known in Switzerland.

Thorin *see* SVGC

Trenel Fils

Le Voisinet, 71870 Charnay-lès-Mâcon.
A small family affair with a very good local reputation. Their wines are particularly featured in Mâcon restaurants. They also produce delectable *crème de cassis* and *crème de framboise*.

Valette

77 route de Lyon, 71000 Mâcon.
A subsidiary of the Société des Vins de France, the same company as Lionel J. Bruck in Nuits St-Georges.

The Eventail de Vignerons Producteurs

This establishment at Corcelles-en-Beaujolais is a group of conscientious small producers from all parts of the region and the southern Mâconnais who make their own wine but collaborate in bottling and marketing it. Their average holdings are between 12 and 25 acres. Their central cellars offer a fascinating range of the products of the region. The names of the members of the Eventail (the word means 'fan') are given below those of other recommended producers under each appellation.

JURA

Connoisseurs of the French countryside each have their favourite corner. I hope never to be forced to make a final choice, but I have a shortlist ready, and the Jura is on it.

These limestone mountains (they give their name to a whole epoch of geology – the Jurassic) roll up towards Switzerland from the plain of the Saône in Burgundy. Halfway in a straight line from Beaune to Geneva you come to the delicious timbered and tiled little town of Arbois (where Pasteur lived), then Poligny, then Château-Chalon, the heart of a completely original wine country. The Jura vineyards are small (much smaller than they once were; currently 4,000 acres and growing). But their origins are as old as Burgundy's, their climate and soil singular and their grapes their own.

Jura producers are fond of making a wide range of wines, from *méthode traditionnelle* sparkling to *vin jaune*. The overall appellation is Côtes du Jura. This appellation covers a long strip of country from north of Arbois to south of Cousance. Arbois is another general AC with higher alcohol stipulated. L'Etoile covers whites and *vins de paille* from the valley around the village of L'Etoile to the south.

The vineyard sits on a band of heavy clay, rich in lime, exposed along the mountain slopes between 900 and 1,350 feet high. Woods, bovine pastures and limestone cliffs constantly interrupt the continuity of the vines. Unlike Alsace to the north, which lies in the rain shadow of the Vosges, the west-facing Jura is often deluged by summer rain. Hail is a frequent problem here. But September and October are usually sunny. Jura grapes have been selected because they thrive in deep damp soil, given a good sun-warmed slope. The most widespread is the Poulsard (confusingly referred to as Plousard in the Pupillin region) – a pale red which is the nearest thing to a rosé grape. Another obscure red, the Trousseau, is grown with it to stiffen its too 'supple' wine. Pinot Noir is increasingly added to give more colour and backbone to red wine – but red is in a minority here: most of the wine is rosé, fermented on its pale skins as though intended to be red.

Nowadays the Chardonnay is the standard grape for light white wines; it performs well (under the alias of Melon d'Arbois or Gamay Blanc) but certainly not spectacularly. Much of it is made into sparkling wine. But the real speciality is a local variant of the Traminer called the Savagnin or Nature. Savagnin is a late ripener and a small cropper, but its wine is powerful in alcohol and flavour. Used merely for topping up barrels of Chardonnay it gives them, as they age, a marvellously rustic style. Used alone it behaves in a most peculiar way that makes it comparable with *fino* sherry. The young wine is left in old barrels with a history of making *vin jaune*, not filled to the top but in the normally perilous state of 'ullage'. A flor yeast, presumably residing in the barrel wood, rapidly grows as a film on the surface of the wine, excluding direct contact with oxygen. The wine is left thus, for a statutory minimum of six years, without being topped up. At the end of six years, a miraculous stability has (or should have) come over it. A finished *vin jaune* is an impressive apéritif, intense in flavour, obviously slightly oxidized but long and fine and altogether worthwhile. The village (not château) of Château-Châlon and a few adjacent communes are famous for the best, although good *vins jaunes* are made all over the area.

Wine produced in such restricted quantities (and by no means every year), then aged for six years, is inevitably expensive. Like Tokay *vin jaune* comes in smaller than standard bottles that help to disguise the price. (The *clavelin* of the Jura, long-necked and hunch-shouldered, holds 64 centilitres.) I cannot pretend it is anything like as good value, as reliable, or even as delicious, as a first-class *fino* sherry. But it exists – and as wine lovers we should be grateful for variety and support it, especially in such time-honoured forms as this. Travellers to the region may even come across white wines labelled simply '*blanc typé*' – which means they are gently oxidized to be more or less 'jaune'.

Another time-honoured regional speciality, *vin de paille*, has virtually disappeared – at least in its authentic form. It was made by hanging bunches of grapes in the rafters (or laying them on straw – *paille* – mats) to dry and concentrate their sweetness in the manner of Italian Vin Santo. The modern method is to place the bunches in stacked boxes in well-ventilated areas.

The Jura vineyard was decimated by phylloxera and took many years to recover. Today it thrives – largely on the tourist trade and faithful private customers in France. There are 1,000 growers, but only 200 who make more than 330 cases a year, and only about a dozen with more than 30 acres. One of the biggest is merchant-grower Henri Maire who has been a significant force in achieving recognition for the region and its wines.

Leading Jura Producers

Château d'Arlay

Arlay, 39140 Bletterans.
The Jura's one lordly estate, descended in the same family since the 12th century, when it was a Hapsburg stronghold, and at various times in the hands of the Prince of Orange, William the Silent, the English King William III and almost but not quite Frederick the Great of Prussia. The present owners, the Count and Countess Renaud de Laguiche, can claim indirect descent not only from this galaxy of monarchs but also have family ties with the Marquis de Laguiche of Montrachet, the de Vogüés of Champagne and Chambolle-Musigny, and the Ladoucettes of Pouilly-Fumé.

Château d'Arlay uses traditional Jura varieties to produce an excellent range of wines, including an unusual, dark-coloured red blend of Poulsard, Trousseau and Pinot Noir, an excellent nut- and spice-filled *vin jaune* as well as the rare *vin de paille*. As négociants the estate trades under the names of Comte de Guichebourg (for non-vintage wines) and Baron de Proby.

Caves Jean Bourdy

Arlay, 39140 Bletterans.

A cornerstone of the Jura wine industry, dating back to the 16th century, with bottles of such famous vintages as 1820 and 1784 still in the cellars. Jean Bourdy retired in 1979 after 52 years to be succeeded by his son Christian. Their model Jura wines come from 1 acre of Savagnin in Château-Chalon and 12 in Arlay, where they make red, rosé and Chardonnay white as well as *vin jaune*. Like most Jura vignerons, Bourdy sales are mainly mainly to private clients in France.

Hubert Clavelin

Le Vernois, 39120 Voiteur.

The proprietor of 38 acres between Château-Châlon and L'Etoile, highly regarded by his neighbours for his Côtes du Jura red, white and 'yellow', and his *méthode traditionnelle* Brut. His name recalls the unique long-necked pint bottle used uniquely for *vin jaune*.

Château de l'Etoile

39570 L'Etoile.

The Château de l'Etoile exists no more, but the name is used by a large producer famous for its traditional-method sparkling wines. *Vin jaune* and red and rosé Côtes du Jura are also produced.

Château Gréa

Rotalier, 39190 Beaufort.

A mere 16 acres, but the pride of the Gréa family for nearly 300 years. Their descendants the de Boissieus have owned it since 1962 and made it the quality leader of the southern Côtes du Jura.

Their specialities are a *méthode traditionnelle brut*, Le Chanet, a blend of Chardonnay with Savagnin which gives a much more forceful *vin de garde*, a red called Sur La Roche and a *vin jaune* of pure Savagnin, En Cury.

Domaine Frédéric Lornet

39600 Montigny-lès-Arsures.

A 32-acre domaine, mainly planted with Savagnin and Trousseau with which Frédéric Lornet is reviving the name of the north of the Arbois appellation, principally with his reds. The Trousseau is richly coloured and concentrated, the tannins silk-soft. His Cuvée des Chamoz is a Côtes du Jura blend of Trousseau and Poulsard.

Henri Maire

Château-Montfort, 39600 Arbois.

Very much the biggest producer and marketer of Jura wines. M Maire is a tireless promoter of the region, and his imaginative and aggressive sales strategy has made Maire a household name. The very modern Maire domaines produce a vast range of wines under all the Jura appellations, plus many other wines. Sparkling Vin Fou is perhaps the best known; its name is on street corners all over France. One of my favourites is the pale dry rosé, or *vin gris*, called Cendré de Novembre. Some of the reds are distinctly sweet – not to my taste.

Domaine Désiré Petit

Pupillin, 39600 Arbois.

An old family property of nearly 30 acres, divided into 11 little parcels in the sheltered coomb of Pupillin, and neighbouring Arbois and Grozon. Stainless steel and old casks stand side by side. The investment in modern equipment means that the wines, red, white and rosé, can now be drunk young.

Domaine de la Pinte

39600 Arbois.

A large modern estate (now 74 acres) created by Roger Martin in 1955 on abandoned vineyard land of the chalky clay loved by the Savagnin, which occupies almost half the acreage. The domaine is now acknowledged to occupy some of the best *terroirs* in Arbois. All the wine is appellation Arbois if it reaches the necessary alcoholic degree (11.5° for rosé, 12° for white and 14° for *vin jaune* – which is the highlight of the domaine).

Domaine Xavier Reverchon

GAEC de Chantemerle, 39800 Poligny.

Xavier Reverchon has taken over the family's 15-acre domaine (appellation Côtes du Jura), producing a typically wide range of hand-made wines in small quantities – including intense *vins jaunes*, *méthode traditionnelle* and Macvin (red and white), as well as many small lots of red, white and rosé. His Les Boutasses is a *vieilles vignes* (predominantly Savagnin) blend with a characteristically nutty note. Dispatch is no problem: tourists take it all away with them.

Domaine Rolet

Montigny-lès-Arsures, 39600 Arbois.

One of the most important producers in Jura after Henri Maire (q.v.). Founded in 1968, they have now expanded to 143 acres. Now in streamlined modern premises, they concentrate on single-grape variety wines including Chardonnay, Poulsard and a Trousseau built to last. They also make a *vin jaune*. Experiments with a shorter vinification period for the Poulsard have produced a fresh fruity rosé, representing something of a departure from the traditional Jura style.

André and Mireille Tissot

Montigny-les-Arsures, 39600 Arbois.

Sixty-acre family domaine making good Arbois wines of all colours including *vin jaune*, a splendid blend of Poulsard, Trousseau, Chardonnay and Savagnin. The whites, including an Arbois Chardonnay, are exemplary.

Domaine Jacques Tissot

39 rue de Courcelles, 39600 Arbois.

Louis Pasteur made some of his fermentation experiments in the *chai* of this domaine in the centre of Arbois. All Jacques Tissot's wines are well made but his red-berry scented Trousseau is especially good. Rich full *vin jaune*, with an alluring aroma of mango is also to be sought out.

Caves Coopératives

Arbois

2 rue des Fossés, 39600 Arbois.
Founded 1906. 140 members; 518 acres; 99,000 cases. The oldest and biggest of the Jura coops, producing red, white and *jaune* wines, all AOC, both *tranquilles* and *mousseux*.

Fruitière Vinicole de Pupillin

Pupillin, 39600 Arbois.
Founded 1909. 35 members; 136 acres; 35,000 cases. A small coop producing especially interesting whites; also known for special barrels of spicy *vin jaune*. Pupillin is a perfect little example of a Jura country village, with some 200 inhabitants, all living by and for the vine.

Caveau des Jacobins

Rue Nicolas Appert, 39800 Poligny.
Founded 1907. 12 members; 86 acres; 20,000 cases. Côtes du Jura red, rosé and white as well as *mousseux* wines are produced by this little, long-established coop. Its traditional Poulsard has a good following. Also good Chardonnay aged in *barriques*.

Château-Châlon et Côtes du Jura

39210 Voiteur.
Founded 1958. 60 members; 160 acres; 33,300 cases AOC wines. The Côtes du Jura (white and rosé) is fresh and floral, made for drinking young. Also Château-Châlon Jaune and Côtes du Jura Jaune. The only cooperative producing Château-Châlon.

SAVOIE

The wine country of Savoie follows the River Rhône south from the Lake of Geneva, then lines the Lac du Bourget (the biggest lake in France) around Aix-les-Bains, then hugs the sides of the valley south of Chambéry and turns the corner eastwards into the Val d'Isère. The whole wine zone is affected by the proximity of the Alps. It exists more as opportunistic outbreaks occurring in four *départements* than as a cohesive vineyard. Its appellations are consequently complicated: more so than its simple, fresh and invigorating wine.

Three-quarters of Savoie wine is white, based on half a dozen different grapes. Along the south shore of the Lake of Geneva (Haute Savoie) it is the Chasselas, the grape the Swiss know as Fendant. Crépy is the best-known *cru*, with Marignan, Ripaille and Marin, all light and often sharp wines. Crépy is an all-white appellation which might have disappeared but for the efforts of Léon Mercier and his son Louis. The better wines are bottled *sur lie*, giving them a slight spritz. Ayze too has a name for its sharpish *pétillant*.

Seyssel is your chance to win a bet. Few people realize or remember that it is France's northernmost Rhône wine. The grapes here are Roussette (alias Altesse) for still wines and Molette for fizz. Roussette, the aristocrat, reaches a relatively high degree of sugar, body and flavour; Molette is a mild little thing. Seyssel has built an international reputation by developing its naturally fizzy tendency into fully fledged classic-method sparkling. The specialists are Varichon & Clerc, who produce a singularly delicate and delicious *cuvée* – quite one of France's best – but demand seems to have outrun supply; they have been forced to buy grapes outside the area and relabel it Blanc de Blancs Mousseux.

Still or *pétillant*, dry or sometimes slightly sweet Roussette wines with local reputations are made along the Rhône Valley and Lac du Bourget at Frangy, Marestel, Monterminod and Monthoux. Occasional super-vintages put them on a level with Vouvray.

The third principal white grape, and the commonest of the region, is the Jacquère. South of Seyssel, still on the Rhône, the district of Chautagne, centred on its cooperative at Ruffieux, makes Jacquère white and the grape dominates the vineyards south of Chambéry: Chignin, Apremont, Abymes and Montmélian. Chignin has the best southern hillside exposure. Its Jacquère fetches a franc or two more a bottle than its neighbours, Apremont and Les Abymes. Red Gamay, Pinot Noir and Mondeuse are also important.

Suburbia is invading these lovely vineyards fast. Montmélian, a little alpine village a few years ago, is now hideous with housing estates. So far the red-wine vineyards on the slopes of the Val d'Isère are almost intact, but for how long? Their centre is the cave coopérative at Cruet, serving Cruet, Arbin, Montmélian and St-Jean de la Porte. Much its best wine, to my mind, is its Mondeuse (especially that of Arbin). Gamay costs a little more, and Pinot Noir more again, but Mondeuse is the character: a dark, slightly tannic, smooth but intensely lively wine that reminds me a little of Chinon, the 'raspberry' red of the Loire.

There are other local specialities too: Roussette is the highest priced white of the Cruet cooperative; a yellow, full-bodied, slightly bitter wine you might take for an Italian. And Chignin grows the Bergeron, either a rare local grape or (say some) the Roussanne of the (lower) Rhône. This is the only Savoyard white wine that ages with distinction.

Savoie's AOCs are shadowed by the VDQS Bugey to the west on the way to Lyon, a mere 600 acres with an even more complex set of names, which is hard to justify in reality. The white VDQS is Roussette de Bugey, although the regulations only demand Roussette grapes if a village name is used (the '*crus*' are Anglefort, Arbignieu, Chanay, Langieu, Montagnieu and Virieu-Le-Grand). Plain Roussette de Bugey can contain Chardonnay as can Roussette du Savoie. Jacquère, Aligoté and Chardonnay are allowed in Vin de Bugey Blanc. VDQS Vin de Bugey is red, rosé or white and also has its *crus*: Virieu-Le-Grand, Montagnieu, Manicle, Machuraz and Cerdon. Cerdon, in turn, is also an individual VDQS for sparkling *mousseux*, including a rosé, and merely fizzy *pétillant*.

Savoie Districts and Producers

ABYMES
Cave Coopérative 'Le Vigneron Savoyard' 73190
Apremont (also for Apremont, Gamay, Mondeuse, Vin de
Pays de Grésivaudan).

APREMONT
Pierre Boniface 73800 Les Marches.
Gilbert Tardy 73190 Apremont.
and many others.

AYZE
Marcel Fert 74130 Marignier.

CHIGNIN AND CHIGNIN-BERGERON
J-F Girard-Madoux 73800 Chignin.
The Quénard family (five separate branches: André (and
son Michel), Claude, Jean-Pierre, Raymond, René) 73800
Chignin.

CHAUTAGNE
Cave Coopérative de Chautagne 73310 Ruffieux.

CREPY
L Mercier & Fils 74140 Douvaine.

CRUET
Cave Coopérative de Vente des Vins Fins 73800 Cruet
(also for Chignin, Roussette de Savoie, Gamay, Mondeuse,
Pinot, Arbin, *mousseux* and *pétillant*).

FRANGY
Domaine Dupasquier Aimavigne, 73170 Jongieux.
Michel et Jean-Paul Neyroud 74270 Designy.

MARESTEL
Henri Jeandet 73170 Jongieux.

MARIGNAN
Canelli-Suchet La Tour de Marignan, 74140 Sciez.

MARIN
Claude Delalex 74200 Marin.

MONTERMINOD
Château de Monterminod 73190 Challes-les-Eaux.

MONTHOUX
Michel Million Rousseau 73170 St-Jean-de-Chevelu.

MONTMELIAN
Cave Coopérative de Vente des Vins Fins 73800
Montmélian (also Abymes, Apremont, Chignin, Marestel,
Chignin-Bergeron, Gamay, Mondeuse, Arbin, Chautagne).
Louis Magnin 73800 Arbin (also red Arbin).
J Perrier & Fils 73800 Montmélian.

RIPAILLE
Fichard (négociant), Grands Chais Léman/Mont-Blanc,
74170 Chens-sur-Léman.
Château de Ripaille 74200 Thonon-les-Bains.

SEYSSEL
Etablissements Donati (J. Quénard) 73000 Barberaz.
Georges Mollex 01420 Corbonod.
Domaine de la Taconnière 01420 Seyssel.
Varichon & Clerc (négociants: producers of the best-
known sparkling Seyssel). General négociants for Savoie
wines. 01420 Seyssel.

THE LOIRE

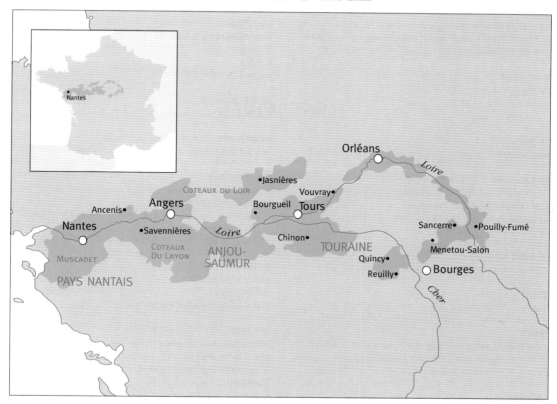

I t is marvellous with what felicity, what gastronomic *savoir-vivre*, the rivers Rhône and Loire counter-balance one another on their passage through France. For 100 miles or so they even run parallel, flowing in opposite directions 30 miles apart.

They decline the notion of rivalry: in every way they are complementary. The Rhône gives France its soothing, warming, satisfying, winter-weight wines. The Loire provides the summer drinking.

The Loire rises within 100 miles of the Mediterranean. Wine is made in earnest along some 250 miles of its course and on the banks of its lower tributaries. It is a big stretch of country, and one might expect a wide variety of wines. The long list of the appellations encourages the idea, but it is not difficult to simplify into half a dozen dominant styles based on the grape varieties.

The Loire has three principal white grapes and two red (but only one that gives fine wine). Among the whites, the centre stage is held by the Chenin Blanc (alias Pineau de la Loire). It dominates in Touraine and even more so in Anjou, its produce ranging from neutral/acidic base material for sparkling Saumur to toffee-rich, apparently immortal, dessert wines. It is so versatile because it has such subtle flavours (quince, citrus fruits, green apples): its qualities lie more in

balance and vitality. It keeps a high acid content even when it ripens (which it can do) to extremely high levels of sugar. Aromatically it is noncommittal – until it matures. Even then it has fruit salad and *crème brûlée* both within its repertoire.

Downstream from Anjou the dominant white grape is the Muscadet – again a low-profile variety. Early ripening and (in contrast) low acidity, rather than any great aroma, makes it ideal for instant drinking with *fruits de mer*.

Upstream in Touraine, east of Vouvray-Montlouis, and beyond to Pouilly and Sancerre is the country of the Sauvignon Blanc, in this climate one of the most intensely aromatic grapes in France.

The Cabernet Franc is the quality red grape of the Loire, at its very best at Chinon in Touraine and almost equally successful in parts of Anjou. It is shadowed everywhere by the Gamay, which is made into juicy, fresh, light-to-medium-bodied reds which can be delicious. Both, along with Grolleau, are responsible for very large quantities of more or less amiable rosé, one of the region's great money-spinners.

A number of grapes are named on Loire labels: the white Gros Plant of the Muscadet region (a sharp grape which might be described as its Aligoté); the Pinot Noir, grown to make red wine in Sancerre; Chardonnay in Haut-Poitou. A couple are traditional and accepted: a white variety called

Romorantin gives the thin wine of Cheverny; the red Grolleau gives café rosé everywhere. A great number of ignoble plants used to be grown, but in the last 30-odd years they have been slowly ousted from the vineyards in favour of the principal types and an understudy cast of Cabernet Sauvignon, Malbec (here called Cot), Pinot Meunier, and such local characters as Arbois and Pineau d'Aunis and even Furmint from Hungary and Verdelho from Madeira.

As with its grapes, so with its regions, the Loire is simply divisible into its upper waters, above Orléans, which together with their hinterland near Bourges are best known for producing whites from Sauvignon Blanc, its famous slow-moving centre, where it passes in infinite procession among the many châteaux of Touraine and Anjou, and its broad maritime reaches, where the wind carries the hint of shrimps far inland.

LOIRE WINES

All Loire AOC and VDQS wines are listed below. The production figures for each wine are given in cases. Most of these figures are an average of four crops, but in some cases only one year's total is available. Crops vary widely in the Loire and the figures should be considered approximate.

Coteaux d'Ancenis
(red and rosé) VDQS. Lower Loire. 176,000 cases. Light Gamay, occasionally Cabernet, reds and rosés from the north bank opposite Muscadet.

Coteaux d'Ancenis
(white) VDQS Lower Loire. 1,925 cases. Chenin Blanc and a miniscule quantity of Malvoisie (Pinot Gris).

Anjou
(red) AC. West central. 1.1m. cases. Light, mainly Cabernet Franc, reds from a wide area (an alternative to Saumur).

Anjou
(white) AC. West central, 770,000 cases. Mainly Chenin Blanc and often slightly sweet – no special quality.

Anjou Mousseux
(white and rosé) AC. West central. Rosés account for nearly 600 cases; whites, 34,400 cases. Made throughout the entire Anjou zone. Chenin Blanc is the base of the whites though Cabernet, Cot, Gamay, Grolleau and Pineau d'Aunis are permitted (to a maximum of 60%). Rosés are made from Cabernet, Cot, Gamay, Grolleau and Pineau d'Aunis.

Anjou Coteaux de la Loire
(white) AC. West central. 14,300 cases. A limited area along both banks of the river west of Angers. Chenin Blanc of variable quality, but often quite delicious normally off-dry or sweet wines.

Anjou Gamay
(red) AC. West central. 206,140 cases. Light yet tasty reds for first-year drinking which can often have more character than many a Beaujolais.

Anjou-Villages
(red) AC. West central. 152,440 cases. There are 48 communes entitled to this appellation for the production of Cabernet Franc and Cabernet Sauvignon. The wines cannot be sold before the September after the harvest.

Cabernet d'Anjou
(rosé) AC. West central. 1.3m. cases. The best-quality rosé, normally rather sweet; at its best from Martigné-Briand, Tigné and La Fosse-Tigné in the Coteaux du Layon.

Rosé d'Anjou
(rosé) AC. West central. 1.6m. cases. Pale sweet rosé mainly from Grolleau.

Coteaux de l'Aubance
(white) AC. West central. 30,240 cases. Chenin Blanc, in a range of styles from off-dry to *doux*, from the south bank opposite Angers, north of the (not automatically superior) Coteaux du Layon.

Côtes d'Auvergne
(red and rosé) VDQS. Extreme upper Loire. 220,000 cases. Near Clermont-Ferrand. Chanturgues, Châteaugay, Corent and Mandargues are considered *crus* and their names are used on the labels. Made principally from Gamay and Pinot Noir.

Côtes d'Auvergne
(white) VDQS. Extreme upper Loire. 4,250 cases. Very light Chardonnay, superseding the red.

Bonnezeaux
(white) AC. West central. 20,000 cases. 182-acre Grand Cru of Chenin Blanc in the Coteaux du Layon, Anjou. In fine years with noble rot, or super-ripe grapes, a great sweet wine; otherwise 'nervy' and fine.

Bourgueil
(red and rosé) AC. Central. 600,000 cases. Excellent red of Cabernet Franc from the north bank facing Chinon, Touraine. For drinking young and cool or maturing like Bordeaux.

Châteaumeillant
(red and rosé) VDQS. Upper Loire. Minor area of Gamay and Pinot Noir south of Bourges. Light reds or very pale *gris rosés*.

Cheverny
(red and rosé) AC. East central. 73,000 cases. Small but growing supply of light Gamay and Pinot Noir blends with up to 15% Cabernet or Cot for the red and pure or blended Gamay for the rosé.

Cheverny
(white) AC. East central. 55,000 cases. Sharp white mainly from Sauvignon south of Blois.

Chinon
(red and rosé) AC. Central. 865,000 cases. Fine Cabernet Franc red, sometimes superb and capable of ageing many years, but generally drunk young and cool. The most important Loire red.

Chinon
(white) AC. Central. 5,250 cases. Chenin Blanc, Rabelais' *vin de taffetas*, once practically extinct but production is now increasing, despite the effect on production of spring frosts in 1991 and 1994.

Cour-Cheverny

(white) AC. 6,200 cases. A pungently vinous wine made from the local Romorantin grape in the heart of the Cheverny zone.

Fiefs-Vendéens

(red and rosé) VDQS. West. 190,000 cases. Light reds and rosés made principally from Gamay, Pinot Noir and Cabernet.

Fiefs-Vendéens

(white) VDQS. West. 37,400 cases. Quaffable whites made chiefly from Chenin Blanc, Chardonnay and Sauvignon Blanc.

Côtes du Forez

(red) VDQS. Extreme Upper Loire. 110,000 cases. The southernmost Loire vineyards, south of Lyon: Gamay, Beaujolais-style.

Coteaux du Giennois

(red and rosé) VDQS. Upper Loire. 52,000 cases. Light to medium-bodied reds from just downstream of Pouilly/Sancerre towards Gien. Well-made, they can be delicious. A recent ruling means that they must be a blend of Pinot Noir and Gamay.

Coteaux du Giennois

(white) VDQS. Upper Loire. 29,500 cases. Sauvignon from the same area.

Haut-Poitou (Vin du)

(red and rosé) VDQS. South central. 140,000 cases. Flourishing vineyard south of Anjou mainly Gamay and Cabernet, with some Merlot, Pinot Noir, Cot and Grolleau.

Haut-Poitou (Vin du)

(white) VDQS. South central. 140,000 cases. Expanding production of Sauvignon, Chardonnay, Chenin Blanc and Pinot Blanc.

Jasnières

(white) AC. North central. 11,000 cases. Small Chenin Blanc area north of Tours. Wine like Vouvray, if less rich. Ages very well.

Coteaux du Layon

(white) AC. West central. 404,000 cases. The biggest area of quality Chenin Blanc, south of Angers, generally fully sweet, *moëlleux* or *liquoreux*; it includes the Grands Crus Quarts de Chaume and Bonnezeaux.

Coteaux du Layon Chaume

(white) AC. West central. 20,200 cases. A superior appellation for Coteaux du Layon with an extra degree of ripeness, comparable to a 'Villages' AC in the Rhône.

Coteaux du Layon-Villages

(white) AC. West Central. 70,000 cases. Layons with an extra degree of ripeness from one of the six communes. They are: Beaulieu-sur-Layon, Faye-d'Anjou, Rochefort-sur-Loire, Rabelais-sur-Layon, St-Aubin-de-Luigné and St-Lambert-du-Lattay.

Coteaux du Loir

(red and rosé) AC. North central. 11,000 cases. Small area of Pineau d'Aunis and Gamay with some Cot and Cabernet north of Tours on the Loir, a tributary of the Loire.

Coteaux du Loir

(white) AC. North central. 5,665 cases. Chenin Blanc from the Loir. The best is Jasnières.

Crémant de Loire

(rosé) AC. Anjou-Saumur-Touraine. 13,800 cases. Recent appellation for high-quality sparkling wine.

Crémant de Loire

(white) AC. Anjou-Saumur-Touraine. 305,000 cases. Recent appellation for high-quality sparkling wine.

Rosé de Loire

(rosé) AC. Anjou-Saumur-Touraine. 390,500 cases. An appellation for dry rosés with 30% Cabernet – not widely used, but can be good.

Menetou-Salon

(red and rosé) AC. Upper Loire. 47,300 cases. A rival to Sancerre with similar light Pinot Noir.

Menetou-Salon

(white) AC. Upper Loire. 70,400 cases. Like the red, a rival to Sancerre with Sauvignon Blanc.

Montlouis

(white) AC. East central. 99,000 cases. The reflected image of Vouvray across the Loire: dry, semi-sweet and occasionally sweet wines.

Montlouis Pétillant and Mousseux

(white) AC. East central. 91,000 cases. The sparkling version of Montlouis Blanc.

Muscadet

(white) AC. Lower Loire. 770,000 cases. A large area but a small part of Muscadet production (see Muscadet de Sèvre et Maine).

Muscadet des Coteaux de la Loire

(white) AC. Lower Loire. 275,000 cases. The smallest section of Muscadet, upstream of Muscadet de Sèvre et Maine.

Muscadet Côtes de Grand Lieu

(white) AC Lower Loire. 33,000 cases. The newest Muscadet subregion stretches west of Nantes airport.

Muscadet de Sèvre et Maine

(white) AC Lower Loire. 6.6m. cases. Much the biggest Loire AC: the best part of Muscadet, east and south of Nantes.

Gros Plant du Pays Nantais

(white) VDQS. Lower Loire. 2.4m. cases. Sharp white of Gros Plant (or Folle Blanche) from the Muscadet area.

Orléannais (Vin de l')

(red and rosé) VDQS. Upper Loire. 51,000 cases. Light reds of Pinot Meunier, Cabernet Franc and Pinot Noir.

Orléannais (Vin de l')

(white) VDQS. Upper Loire. 11,000 cases. Light Chardonnay.

Pouilly Fumé

(white) AC. Upper Loire. 528,000 cases. Powerful aromatic Sauvignon Blanc from opposite Sancerre.

Pouilly sur Loire

(white) AC. Upper Loire. 38,500 cases. Neutral white of Chasselas from the same vineyards as Pouilly Fumé – must be drunk young.

Quarts de Chaume

(white) AC. West central. 7,200 cases. 112-acre Grand Cru of the Coteaux du Layon. In certain years, glorious rich wines of Chenin Blanc.

Quincy

(white) AC. Upper Loire. 54,000 cases. Small source of attractive Sauvignon Blanc west of Bourges.

Reuilly
(red and rosé) AC. Upper Loire. 15,400 cases. Pinot Noir and Pinot Gris reds and rosés.

Reuilly
(white) AC. Upper Loire. 18,700 cases. Sauvignon Blanc.

Côtes Roannaises
(red and rosé) VDQS. Extreme upper Loire. 77,000 cases. Gamay region not far from Beaujolais, in distance or style.

St-Nicolas de Bourgueil
(red and rosé) AC. Central. 440,000 cases. Neighbour to Bourgueil with similar excellent Cabernet Franc.

St-Pourçain-sur-Sioule
(red and rosé) VDQS. Extreme upper Loire. 198,000 cases. The famous local wine of Vichy: Gamay and Pinot Noir from chalk soil – good café wine.

St-Pourçain-sur-Sioule
(white) VDQS. Extreme upper Loire. 66,000 cases. Vichy's equally famous white of Tresallier, Chardonnay, Sauvignon and Aligoté. Quite commendable country white.

Sancerre
(red and rosé) AC. Upper Loire. 334,400 cases. Light Pinot Noir red and rosé from chalky soil better known for white. Real progress is being made here: the best wines are (increasingly) richer and longer-lived.

Sancerre
(white) AC. Upper Loire. 1.3m. cases. Fresh, eminently fruity and aromatic Sauvignon Blanc.

Saumur
(red) AC. West central. 415,000 cases. Light Cabernet reds from south of Saumur – can also be sold as Anjou.

Saumur
(white) AC. West central. 340,000 cases. Crisp Chenin Blanc with up to 20% Chardonnay and/or Sauvignon. Most is made into sparkling wine.

Cabernet de Saumur
(rosé) AC. West central. 33,000 cases. The upstream slightly drier equivalent of Cabernet d'Anjou.

Saumur-Champigny
(red) AC. West central. 66,000 cases. Possibly the best Cabernet reds of Anjou, from the northern part of the Saumur area just east of the city.

Coteaux de Saumur
(white) AC. West central. 3,000 cases. Chenin Blanc, often off-dry, sometimes *moëlleux*, from a similar but slightly larger area than Saumur-Champigny.

Saumur Mousseux
(rosé) AC. West central. 26,600 cases. *Méthode traditionnelle* rosé of Cabernet, Gamay, Grolleau, Pinots Noir and d'Aunis.

Saumur Mousseux
(white) AC. West central. 863,500 cases. *Méthode traditionnelle* Chenin Blanc (though up to 60% can be Grolleau, Pinots Noir and d'Aunis). Increasingly popular and sometimes excellent.

Savennières
(white) AC. West central. 30,800 cases. Sometimes splendid, powerful, long-lived, dry Chenin Blanc from west of Angers. It includes the Grands Crus Roche aux Moines and Coulée de Serrant.

Thouarsais (Vins du)
(red and rosé) VDQS. South central. 5,750 cases. A tiny enclave of Gamay and Cabernet south of Saumur.

Thouarsais (Vins du)
(white) VDQS South central. 4,600 cases. The Chenin Blanc of Thouars, sometimes with Chardonnay.

Touraine
(red and rosé) AC. East central. 1.7m. cases. Principal grapes are Gamay, Cabernet and Cot (the label will name the grape). Gamays can outshine many a Beaujolais – at least in warm years. In west Touraine pure Cabernet is generally bottled; in the east the authorities are encouraging blends. For rosés Pineau d'Aunis and Grolleau may also be used.

Touraine
(white) AC. East central. 1.4m cases. The label names the grape, usually Sauvignon Blanc, in a tolerable imitation of Sancerre. Chenin Blanc, Menu Pineau (alias Arbois) and Chardonnay now play a supporting role.

Touraine-Amboise
(red and rosé) AC. East central. 82,500 cases. Light reds made from Gamay, Cabernet and Cot from just east of Vouvray. Increasingly popular is the red blend called François 1er.

Touraine-Amboise
(white) AC. East central. 27,500 cases. Chenin Blanc, sometimes capable of Vouvray-like quality.

Touraine-Azay-Le-Rideau
(rosé) AC. East central. 8,800 cases. A minor outpost of Grolleau with some Gamay, Cot or Cabernet made between Tours and Chinon.

Touraine-Azay-Le-Rideau
(white) AC. East central. 12,100 cases. Tiny Chenin Blanc vineyard renowned for its Cheillé and Saché, the latter occasionally as rich as Vouvray.

Touraine-Mesland
(white) AC. East central. 16,500 cases. Less important dry white chiefly of Chenin Blanc, sometimes blended with Chardonnay and Sauvignon.

Touraine-Mesland
(red and rosé) AC. East central. 82,500 cases. Rather good blends of Gamay, Cabernet Franc and Cot for the red, and 80% Gamay for the rosé, from the north bank of the Loire opposite Chaumont.

Touraine Mousseux
(white and rosé) AC. East central. 190,500 cases of white, 23,000 cases of rosé. Semi- and full-sparkling versions. Whites are based on Chenin Blanc with up to 30% black grapes, including Cabernet, Pinot Noir, Pinot Gris, Pinot Meunier, Pineau d'Aunis, Cot and Grolleau. Reds are made from Cabernet Franc; rosés from Cabernet Franc, Cot, Gamay and Grolleau.

Valençay
(white) VDQS. Upper Loire. 21,560 cases. An outpost of Gamay on the eastern border of Touraine.

Valençay
(red and rosé) VDQS. Upper Loire. 67,500 cases. Dry white of Chenin Blanc, Sauvignon and others.

Coteaux du Vendômois
(red and rosé) VDQS. North central. 91,500 cases. The wines, particularly the rosés, are made chiefly from Pineau d'Aunis supported by Gamay, Cabernet and Pinot Noir.
Coteaux du Vendômois
(white) VDQS. North central. 14,000 cases. Chenin Blanc, pure or blended with Chardonnay.

Vouvray
(white) AC. East central. 550,000 cases. Dry, semi-sweet or sweet Chenin Blanc of potentially superb quality, according to the vintage.
Vouvray Pétillant and Mousseux
(white) AC. East central. 726,000 cases. The sparkling versions of Vouvray.

MUSCADET

It is hard to resist the notion of Muscadet as Neptune's own vineyard: nowhere is the gastronomic equation quite so simple and clear cut – or appetizing. Britanny provides the *fruits de mer*, the vineyards clustering south and east of Nantes provide oceans of the ideal white wine.

Muscadet is both the grape and the wine – and the zone. The grape came from Burgundy (where it is still sometimes found as the Melon de Bourgogne) as an early ripener that was satisfied with thin stony soil. Early ripening (about 15 September) gets it in before the autumn rain in this often cloudy and windswept vineyard. The Muscadet (or Melon) has low natural acidity that makes it particularly vulnerable in contact with air. To avoid oxidation and to bottle the wine as fresh and tasty as possible, the local tradition is to leave the new wine in its tank or barrel at the end of fermentation, lying on its own yeasty sediment (*sur lie*) and to bottle it in March or April from the barrel – racking it, as it were, straight into bottles without fining or filtering. A certain amount of carbon dioxide is still dissolved in the wine and helps to make it fresh and sometimes faintly prickly to the tongue.

With modern quantities and economics such careful bottling barrel by barrel is becoming rare, but the aim is still the same – except among certain growers who look for a more fully developed wine for further ageing. The latest regulation changes effectively make bottling *sur lie* an appellation in itself: now there are generic Muscadets and generic Muscadets *sur lie*, Muscadets de Sèvre et Maine and Muscadets de Sèvre et Maine *sur lie* – and so forth. A specially engraved bottle is now used to denote *sur lie* wines. The key differences are in the yield and in the timing of bottling following the harvest. Yields for *sur lie* wines, for example cannot exceed 55 hl/ha (for generic Muscadets the yield can be up to 68 hl/ha). As from 1997 *sur lie* wine must be bottled off its lees in the cellar in which it was vinified.

Thus there are different styles of Muscadet, but it is hard to pin them down except by tasting each producer's wares. The extremes are a very light, fruity but essentially rather mild wine or, by contrast, one with a pungently vegetable and somehow 'wild' flavour, which can be very exciting with oysters or clams. The latter style can mature surprisingly well: I have had a five-year-old bottle (of 1976) which had achieved a sort of quintessential soft dryness I found delectable with turbot.

Much the greatest concentration of Muscadet vineyards is just east of Nantes and south of the Loire, in the area named for the rivers Sèvre and Maine. Eighty-five percent of the 32,500 acres of vineyards are Sèvre et Maine; the rest is divided between the Coteaux de la Loire with 1,500 acres scattered eastwards towards Anjou, Côtes de Grand Lieu with 600 acres and plain Muscadet with 2,500 acres dotted over a wide area south of Nantes.

All four appellations are interspersed with plantations (7,250 acres in all) of the secondary white grape of the area, the Gros Plant or Folle Blanche, which stands in relation to Muscadet as Aligoté does to Chardonnay: an acknowledged poor relation, but with a faithful following of its own. Gros Plant du Pays Nantais is a VDQS, not an appellation wine like Aligoté. It is always sharp, often 'green', sometimes coarse, but can be made by a sensitive hand into a very fresh if fragile wine. It would be a natural Breton progression to drink a bottle of Gros Plant with oysters, then Muscadet with a sole. Gros Plant has a maximum alcoholic degree of 11; Muscadet a maximum of 12. Controlling the maximum degree is unusual, but particularly necessary in a region where chaptalization is normal and natural acidity low. Oversugared Muscadet would be a graceless brute.

For red wine the region has little to offer: 700 acres among the Muscadet vineyards of the Coteaux de la Loire around the town of Ancenis grow Gamay and a little Cabernet for light red and rosé, sold as VDQS Coteaux d'Ancenis. There is also Malvoisie (Pinot Gris), an off-dry speciality of Ancenis. Blends of Cabernet, Gamay and Pinot Noir are used in the up-and-coming VDQS wines known as Fiefs Vendéens, from the Atlantic coast region La Vendée, just south of Muscadet.

The name Vin de Pays du Jardin de la France is increasingly used for wines such as Chardonnay and Gamay from a wide area which covers 13 *départements*. Other *vins de pays* may put the name of the region on the label, including Marches de Bretagne, Retz, or the *département* name, such as Vin de Pays de Loire Atlantique.

Leading Producers of the Nantes Region

Château d'Amour

La Grenaudière, 44690 Maisdon-sur-Sèvre.
A pretty place, a true castle beside the river, producing soft, earthy wine from 52 acres.

La Ferme des Ardilliers

85320 Mareuil-sur-Lay.
A progressive grower-négociant in the VDQS Fiefs Vendéens whose best wines are supple, easy-drinking Cabernets from his own vineyards.

Chateau de Briacé

Ecole d'Agriculture de Briacé, 44430 Le Landreau.

Briacé's students of viticulture and oenology work the school's 26 acres of vines. The Muscadet de Sèvre et Maine, Gros Plant and various *vins de pays* are invariably clean, correct and nicely made.

Chereau-Carré

Chasseloir, 44690 St Fiacre-sur-Maine.

The Chereau-Carré family is one of Muscadet's largest proprietors as well as an important négociant house specializing in Loire wine. It markets four million bottles yearly, half from purchased wines, half from one of six estates belonging to various family members. The domaines are:

Chateau de Chasseloir, which serves as Chereau-Carré's HQ. A 62-acre property on the banks of the River Maine, it includes a parcel of century-old vines vinified separately as Comte Leloup de Chasseloir.

Chateau du Coing, a 100-acre estate on the confluence of the Sèvre and the Maine. Chereau barrel-ferments selected batches from both Chateau du Coing and de Chasseloir in new oak barrels.

Domaine du Bois Bruley, a 50-acre vineyard in Basse Goulaine. This property supplies Chereau's Gros Plant du Pays Nantais as well as Muscadet de Sèvre et Maine *sur lie*.

Grand Fief de la Corneraie, a 12-acre vineyard in the commune of Monnière. Commandeur is the name of the old vines bottling.

Moulin de la Gravelle, a 32-acre vineyard in Gorges. Its two cuvées of Muscadet de Sèvre et Maine include an old vines bottling labelled Don Quichotte.

Chateau de l'Oiselinière de la Ramée, a 25-acre vineyard in Vertou. The old vines *cuvée* here is called L'Aigle d'Or.

Xavier Coirier

La Petite Groie, 85200 Pissote.

A dedicated grower with 45 acres of vines in the VDQS Fiefs Vendéens. Fresh, fragrant whites, rosés and reds for summer quaffing.

Donatien-Bahuaud & Cie

Château de la Cassemichère, La Loge, 44330 La Chapelle-Heulin.

A large négociant-grower, Donatien Bahuaud markets 10 million bottles of Loire wine a year, of which 25% is Muscadet. The firm's most famous Muscadet is 'Le Master de Donatien', which represents *cuvées* selected after blind tasting by juries of food and wine professionals. The selected *cuvées* are bottled at the property of the individual growers and are presented in seriographed bottles.

Donatien Bahuaud also produces Muscadet from its own vines at Château de la Cassemichère as well as eight other Muscadets, including the early-drinking Fringant. One of the first Nantais domaines to market Chardonnay, the firm offers two bottlings, Le Chouan, sold as Vin de Pays de Loire Atlantique, and Donatien Chardonnay, Vin de Pays du Jardin de la France. Chardonnay and Chenin Blanc form the blend for Donatien's Blanc de Mer, also a *vin de pays*.

Domaine des Dorices

44330 Vallet.

A fine sloping 92-acre vineyard run with great care by Léon Boullault and his sons Frédéric and François. The wines sell under the labels Domaine des Dorices or Chateau La Touche, depending on the market. Ther is no difference between them. The domaine distinguishes three *cuvées*, however. The first, Cuvée Choisie, which represents the major part of the production, is made for drinking young. The Hermine d'Or selection, and in great vintages, the Cuvée Grande Garde (which is kept as long as two years on its lees), benefit from three years or more of cellaring. Boullault also makes a *méthode traditionnelle* sparkling wine from Gros Plant called Le Conte.

Domaine de l'Ecu

La Bretonnière, 44430 Le Landreau.

Guy Brossard's 42-acre estate pioneered organic cultivation in the Sèvre et Maine in the 1970s. The richly textured, mineral Hermine d'Or *cuvée* shows the ability of his wines to develop in bottle. Bossard is also a nurseryman and makes organic grape juice as well as a range of other wines, including a very fine Gros Plant du Pays Nantais, a supple Cabernet Vin de Pays des Marches de Bretagne, and a nuanced *méthode traditionnelle* made chiefly from Gros Plant.

Domaine de la Fruitière

44690 Château-Thébaud.

A nurseryman as well as a grower, Jean-Joseph Douillard offers numerous *cuvées* of classic Muscadet de Sèvre et Maine *sur lie* from his 112 acres of vines. There are two excellent old vines bottlings, Première and Baron Noury. The Domaine de la Fruitière, Château de Belabord and a recent addition, Château de la Placière, are also well worth seeking out.

Marquis de Goulaine

Château de Goulaine, Haute-Goulaine, 44115 Basse-Goulaine.

The showplace of Muscadet; westernmost of the great Renaissance châteaux of the Loire. The Château de Goulaine is now an efficient example of the stately home trade with guided tours of Goulaine's rare butterfly collection, rooms available for functions, and its own wine as the inevitable choice. Grapes from 125 estate acres plus bought-in wine produce 25,000–30,000 cases a year, from a Chardonnay sold as Vin de Pays du Jardin de la France, to Gros Plant du Pays Nantais, to three different Muscadets, all bottled *sur lie*. The 'Cuvée du Millénaire', the domaine's best wine, is a Muscadet made from 50-year-old vines from Goulaine's 10-acre Clos La Tâche blended with wines from several growers.

Guilbaud Frères

Les Lilas, Mouzillon, 44330 Vallet.

Négociants producing above-average Muscadets under various names, including their own wines from Domaine de la Moutonnière and Domaine de la Pingossière. Each property produces two bottlings, a generic Muscadet de Sèvre et Maine *sur lie* and a deluxe *cuvée*, which is partially aged in old oak barrels. The Clos du Pont, from La Moutonnière, is Guilbaud's finest wine; Château de la Pingossière is also commendable. Le Soleil Nantais, Guildbaud's top of the range négociant wine, maintains a good standard.

Domaine Guindon

La Couleuverdière, St-Géréon, 44150 Ancenis.

A family of growers with 50 acres of vines who offer firm Muscadet des Coteaux de la Loire and the VDQS Gros Plant and Coteaux d'Ancenis (Gamay red and rosé) and unusual off-dry Malvoisie (Pinot Gris).

Domaine de la Haute Févrie

La Févrie, 44690 Maisdon-sur Sèvre.

A traditional grower with 37 acres of vines, Claude Branger produces elegant Muscadet de Sèvre et Maine *sur lie*. L'Excellence is the name of his old-vines bottling.

Domaine des Herbauges

Les Herbauges, 44830 Bouaye.

Luc Choblet makes superior Muscadet Côtes de Grand Lieu from over 100 acres of vines west of Nantes airport. Clos de la Senaigerie and Clos de la Fine are two notable single-vineyard bottlings. M Cholbet also produces pleasant Gros Plant du Pays Nantais.

Domaine Landon

Domaine de la Louvetrie, Les Brandières, 44690 La Haye-Fouassière.

Joseph Landron is an exciting young grower who bottles the Muscadet from his 64 acres by soil type. His lightest *cuvée*, Amphibolite, is named after its soils and is made to be drunk by the year. Landron's Hermine d'Or and Fief du Breil bottlings come from harder soils – silica-streaked orthogneiss – and benefit from a year or more of cellaring. The latter, the domaine's prestige bottling, issues from 35-year-old vines on a 12-acre slope which is well-exposed to the south.

Domaines Pierre Luneau-Papin

Domaine Pierre de la Grange, 44430 Le Landreau.

A skilled winemaker and dedicated grower, Pierre Luneau produces a range of Muscadet *sur lie* from 86 acres of vines; a lean, elegant Muscadet des Coteaux de la Loire and numerous Muscadets de Sèvre et Maine *sur lie*, including two single-vineyard bottlings. Les Allées and Les Pierres Blanches, the barrel-fermented Manoir la Grange and the prestige *cuvée* Le 'L' d'Or.

Château de la Mercredière

44330 Le Pallet.

The Futeul brothers produce 250,000 bottles of full, creamy Muscadet de Sèvre et Maine *sur lie* from their 100-acre plot. Château de la Mercredière formerly went under the name of Louis de Bruc.

Enjoying Loire wines

The wide range of Loire wines covers almost any gastronomic eventuality. For apéritifs there are excellent sparkling wines, and even better *crémants* (demi-sec or young *moëlleux* are also served by the locals as an apéritif) of Saumur and Vouvray, or the pungent dry Chenin Blanc wines of Savennières. Old *moëlleux* may be rich enough to match foie gras.

For seafood there is the incomparable match of Muscadet; for charcuterie Gros Plant du Pays Nantais, a young Pouilly Fumé, Chenin Blanc, a light cool red or a dry to off-dry rosé; for richer fish dishes with sauces either more and better Muscadet or a Sancerre or Pouilly Fumé 2 or 3 years old.

For entrées Chinon, Bourgueil and Saumur-Champigny provide either Beaujolais-style young wines, freshly fruity, or the weight of riper vintages with 5 or 6 years' maturity. Mature Savennières or Vouvray *sec* or *demi-sec* can make an interesting alternative to white burgundy for certain richly sauced creamy dishes.

Sancerre is the inevitable local choice with strong cheeses; with milder ones the sweet wines of the Coteaux du Layon can be excellent.

Light young Coteaux du Layon, appley sweet and very cold, can be a remarkable picnic wine. The nobly rotten sweet wines of Bonnezeaux and Quarts de Chaume are some of France's finest dessert wines. Like the great German sweet wines they are complete in themselves – perhaps better alone than with any food.

Louis Métaireau et ses Vignerons d'Art

La Févrie, 44690 Maisdon sur Sèvre.

A unique enterprise formed by eight producers led by Louis Métaireau, who sell selected *cuvées* of their wines under under his Vignerons d'Art label. The *cuvées* are chosen in a series of blind tastings in which all participate. Only those *cuvées* receiving higher than 15 out of 20 are selected. Then each grower bottles his own wine, *sur lie*, without filtering and brands the cork with his initials. All Métaireau wines are classic fresh Muscadets without exaggerated flavour. He insists on 'finesse'. The two deluxe bottlings, Cuvée LM and Number One, exemplify this style. The group has also purchased the 68-acre Domaine du Grand Mouton. Grapes from this property are picked slightly underripe; the wines are *très sauvage* for the first one or two years (when they go well with shellfish). At three or four years they mellow enough to partner sole. Métaireau bottles about 10% of Grand Mouton directly off its lees, without filtration. A tireless innovator, he has recently expanded his line with two Vins de Pays de Loire Atlantique, made from Melon, as well as two Muscadets de Sèvre et Maine *sur lie* – Premier Jour and 10,5. The first is made from grapes picked on the first day of harvest; the second is low in alcohol.

Château La Noë

44330 Vallet.

A lordly domaine, unusual in Muscadet, with a stately neoclassical mansion and the biggest single vineyard in the area, covering 172 acres, producing 150,000–200,000 bottles a year. The family of the Comte de Malestroit de Bruc has owned it since 1740. The present count (who is equally well known as an author) makes a full-bodied Muscadet with small crops. Some is bottled *sur lie*, some not, but both benefit from a year of bottle-ageing.

Henri Poiron et Fils

Les Quatre Routes, 44690 Maisdon-sur-Sèvre.

A grower with two properties producing three bottlings of meaty Muscadet de Sèvre et Maine *sur lie*, Domaine des Quatre Routes, Domaine du Manoir and Domaine des Grandes Noëlles. Gros Plant du Pays Nantais, Cabernet and Gamay Vins de Pays du Jardin de la France and a *méthode traditionnelle* complete the selection, amounting to 200,000 bottles annually.

Marcel Sautejeau

Domaine de l'Hyvernière, Le Pallet, 44330 Vallet.

One of the larger Loire-Atlantique négociants, family-run, with 222 acres of vines under its control. The 110-acre Domaine de L'Hyvernière is owned by Marcel Sautejeau and the 100-acre Château de la Botinière is owned by associate Jean Beauquin. The Muscadet is mechanically harvested and bottled *sur lie* to be drunk within 2 years. The Clos des Orfeuilles comes from a plot within L'Hyvernière. L'Exceptionnel is the firm's deluxe négociant bottling. Total turnover of wine from the whole of the Loire valley is more than 17 million bottles a year.

Sauvion & Fils

Château du Cléray, 44330 Vallet.

A flourishing family firm of growers and négociants. Their estate is the historic Château du Cléray, with 74 acres of Muscadet. The domaine wine *sur lie* is light and attractive though the firm's special bottlings often upstage it. Allégorie du Cléray is Muscadet fermented and aged in new oak barrels. Sauvion's Découvertes (Discoveries) are estate-bottled Muscadets from small domaines whose wines have been selected after a blind tasting by wine professionals. The Lauréat series represents wines which have won gold medals in local competitions. Cardinal Richard is the proprietary name Sauvion gives to a grower's wine which has been placed first after several juried tastings, the final panel composed of restaurateurs and sommeliers.

Les Vignerons de La Noëlle

44150 Ancenis.

Founded in 1955, this cooperative has 200 growers and approaching a thousand acres of vines spanning the Nantais and the western rim of Anjou. The majority of production is Muscadet, both Sèvre et Maine and Coteaux de la Loire, including an estate-bottling in each appellation: the Domaine des Hautes Noëlles in Sèvre et Maine and Château de la Varenne in the Coteaux de la Loire. It also produces Gros Plant du Pays Nantais, Gamay-Coteaux d'Ancenis (red and rosé), Anjou Coteaux de la Loire, Anjou Rouge and Villages and Crémant de Loire.

Daniel et Gérard Vinet

La Quilla, 44690 La Haie-Fouassière.

The Vinet brothers are ambitious young growers with 30 acres of prime Muscadet de Sèvre et Maine. All is bottled *sur lie*. Domaine la Quilla is their fine base Muscadet; Clos de la Houssaie comes from a small parcel, producing 5,000 bottles annually. The prestige *cuvée*, Le, is an assemblage of the Vinets' best *cuvées*, selected after numerous tastings.

ANJOU-SAUMUR

Muscadet is the most single-minded of all French vineyards. Anjou, its neighbour to the east, has a gamut of wines as complete as any region of France. Its biggest turnover used to be in rosé before spring frosts caused damage. However, Anjou's sparkling wine industry at Saumur is second only to Champagne in size, its best reds are considerable Cabernets, and its finest wines of all, sweet and dry Chenin Blanc whites, rank among the great apéritif and dessert wines of France. The wonderful 1989 vintage has brought them back squarely into the public eye.

Rosé d'Anjou is a sweetish light pink from which nobody expects very much – a blend of mainly Grolleau with Cabernet, Cot, Gamay and the local Pineau d'Aunis. It has not recovered its former hold on the export market. Cabernet d'Anjou, whose market is primarily national, is fighting back. It is also rosé (not red) but an appellation to treat with more respect: the Cabernet Franc (here often called the Breton) is the best red-wine grape of the Loire; its rosé is dry and can be full of its raspberry-evoking flavour, too. The best examples come from Martigné-Briand, Tigné, and La Fosse de Tigné in what is known as Haut-Layon – part of the Coteaux du Layon – which is also the most important district for Chenin Blanc white wines with an inclination to sweetness.

With one exception all the considerable vineyards of Anjou lie along the south bank of the Loire and astride its tributaries, the Layon, the Aubance and the Thouet. The exception is Savennières, the local vineyard of the city of Angers, which interprets the Chenin Blanc in its own way: as a forceful and intense dry wine. Savennières contains two small Grands Crus, La Roche aux Moines and La Coulée de Serrant. The wines of these, or of any of the top-quality Savennières growers, are awkward and angular at first with high acidity and biting concentration of flavour. They need age, sometimes up to 15 years, to develop their honey-scented potential. When they reach it they are excellent apéritifs. Drunk younger, they need accompanying food.

Savennières faces Rochefort-sur-Loire across the broad river, complicated with islands. Rochefort is the gateway to the long valley of the Layon, where the Chenin Blanc may be dry (and acid and pernicious) but where all the fine wines are at least crisply sweet like an apple, and the best deeply and creamily sweet with the succulence of Sauternes. The district contains two substantial Grands Crus, Quarts de Chaume and Bonnezeaux, where noble rot is a fairly frequent occurrence (less so than in Sauternes) and sheer concentration pushes the strength of the wine up to 13 or 14 degrees. Some great Layons are also made when the grapes are picked *passerillés* (shrivelled), or normally over-ripe. There is a return to harvesting grapes by *tri* and those from the Layon and the Aubance which meet certain specifications may carry the designation Sélection de Grains Nobles on their labels. Yet curiously almost none of these sweet wines are aged in barrels. They are in a sense the vintage port of white wines: like vintage port bottled young (in their case in their first spring) to undergo all their development with minimum possible access to oxygen. The eventual bouquet is consequently as clean, flowery and fresh-fruity as the grape itself, with the resonance and honeyed warmth of age. Great old Vouvray is so similar that it would be a brave man (or a native) who could claim to know them apart. Like German wines of fine vintages they perform a balancing-act between sweetness and sustaining acidity. But few German wines of modern times can hold their balance for half as long.

Trends in the sweet wine industry are being matched by progress in the production of the other styles of wine made in Anjou. The dry whites (Anjou Blanc) and the reds (both Anjou Rouge and Anjou-Villages) are similarly displaying a real improvement in quality. Anjou-Villages is the appellation which the top four dozen red-wine communes are entitled to use.

Saumur is the centre of eastern Anjou, with a set of appellations of its own, for dry or medium-dry white wines of Chenin Blanc (which is increasingly being bottled pure, though it can still be blended with up to 20% Chardonnay and/or Sauvignon), and for *mousseux* versions of the same. Saumur's sparkling wine industry is built upon Chenin Blanc, which has the acidity to produce successful *méthode traditionnelle* wines. The main producers, many of whom are also négociants dealing in a range of Loire wines, are listed on the following pages. Many grapes are permitted in *crémants*, including a number of black ones, but not Sauvignon Blanc. There are also appellations in Saumur for red and rosé wines of Cabernet Franc and Pineau d'Aunis. The red-wine vineyards are scattered to the south of the city. The appellation Saumur-Champigny (which covers almost 2,500 acres) has enjoyed a recent leap to fame and fashion, with its light, savoury, herby reds. The exceptional vintages of 1976 and 1989, when such wines as the Château de Chaintres took on deeper tones of real richness, were great boosts to their popularity. In normal years such concentration is hard to attain.

To the south of Saumur, the Thouet valley has its own VDQS for Gamay red and Chenin white, called Vins de Thouarsais after their country town.

Leading Anjou-Saumur Producers

Domaine de Bablut

49320 Brissac-Quincé.
Under the stewardship of Christophe Daviau this long-established family estate is taking exciting new directions, particularly in the production of Coteaux de l'Aubance. The deluxe bottling GN (for Grains Nobles) consists of botrytized grapes partially fermented and aged in new oak barrels. It is as delicious as it is nuanced. The domaine also produces the rest of the Anjou roster of wines and makes those of nearby Château de Brissas as well.

Domaine des Baumard

Logis de la Giraudière, 49190 Rochefort-sur-Loire.
Jean Baumard is a senior figure of the Loire, descended from a family who can trace their roots back to 1634 at Rochefort. He is a former professor of viticulture at Angers and president of the Union of Syndicats AOC de la Loire. His son, Florent, has now taken over the domaine, although Jean remains in an active role.

More than 85 acres of predominantly (80%) white grapes are in production in Quarts de Chaume, Savennières (including part of the Clos du Papillon) and Coteaux du Layon (Clos de Ste-Catherine). Twelve acres of Cabernet Franc and 5 of Cabernet Sauvignon produce Anjou Rouge Logis de la Giraudière. Five acres of Chardonnay are grown, along with Chenin, to make Crémant de Loire. M Baumard uses no wood 'to avoid oxidation'. He calls Savennières 'the Meursault of the Loire' and Quarts de Chaume its 'Yquem', preferring Savennières young and Chaume either before three years or after eight. Between three and eight years, he says, it goes through an eclipse. The Clos de Ste-Catherine is hard to classify: neither sweet nor dry but very lively – recommended with summer fruit or as an apéritif.

Domaine Beaujeau

Champ-sur-Leyon, 49380 Thouarcé.
A long-established family estate making award-winning Coteaux du Layon from 25 acres.

Château de Bellerive

49190 Rochefort-sur-Loire.
A major estate of the Grand Cru Quarts de Chaume with 25 acres surrounding the château. Jacques Lalanne recently sold the property to Serge and Michel Malinge, although he still tends the vines and makes the wines. Almost Yquem-like methods are adopted, which means accepting a tiny crop from old vines (no more than 22 hectolitres a hectare) and picking only nobly rotten grapes in successive *tris* around the vineyard. Fermentation, which takes place in barrels, requires most of the winter. The great difference between this and Sauternes (apart from the grapes) is that bottling is done at the end of April 'when the moon is waxing' and all maturation takes place in bottle rather than barrel. The wine can scarcely be appreciated for five, sometimes ten, years – and it lasts for fifty.

Domaine de Brizé

49540 Martigné-Briand.

A fine family winery with 74 acres of vines, currently run by the fifth generation. The spectrum of Anjou wines is made, among them sturdy Anjou-Villages called Clos Médecin, textbook Layon, dazzling Anjou-Gamay and award-winning Crémant de Loire.

Château du Breuil

Le Breuil, 49750 Beaulieu-sur-Layon.

A reliable family estate with 90 acres producing an annual 16,500 cases of the entire range of Anjou wines, including Vins de Pays du Jardin de la France, Anjou-Villages and several *cuvées* of Coteaux du Layon-Beaulieu, the deluxe bottling of which is the Vieilles Vignes which matures in new oak barrels.

Château de Chaintres

49400 Dampierre-sur-Loire.

Owner: Baron Gaël de Tigny. A charming old country house, once a priory, and notable producer of Saumur-Champigny from its 50 acres. The low underground barrel-cellars were used up to the 1978 vintage, and wood as well as stainless steel is still used. The '76 was a splendid wine. Baron de Tigny thinks highly of his '85.

Domaine du Closel

Savennières, 49170 St-Georges-sur-Loire.

A 37-acre estate producing classic white Savennières, concentrated wine fermented mostly in tank then aged in wood (excepting some *cuvées*, such as Clos du Papillon, which still ferment in barrel), and a little (7 acres) Cabernet (appellation Anjou or Anjou-Villages) also fermented in tank. Madame Michelle Bazin de Jessey is the great-granddaughter of Napoleon's aide-de-camp Emmanuel de Las Cases, who returned here in 1820 from St Helena to write his famous memoirs.

Clos de Coulaine

49170 Savennières.

A respected producer of good Savennières and silky Anjou rouge and -Villages. Since 1992 the domaine has been run by Claude Papin, one of the top producers of Coteaux du Layon (see Château de Pierre-Bise).

Château de la Coulée de Serrant

Château de la Roche-aux-Moines, 49170 Savennières.

A beautiful little estate in an outstanding situation, chosen by monks in the 12th century. The main vineyard is the 17-acre Clos de la Coulée de Serrant, run by Nicolas Joly, an ex-merchant banker, whose highly individual methods of growing vines and making wine are based around a theory of biodynamism. He uses no fertilizers or artificial pesticides and no modern technological equipment; the results are wines of unusual ageing qualities. M Joly also owns 12 acres of La Roche aux Moines called the Clos de la Bergerie and 5 acres of Cabernet for Château de la Roche. Another *cuvée* from 7 acres of Savennières, Becherelle, has recently been added to the Joly stable. Chenin Blanc here makes some of its most intense dry (or off-dry) wines of extraordinary savour and longevity. With a yield of only about 1,700 cases the wine is on allocation, at a suitably high price.

Daheuiller, Père et Fils

Domaine des Varinelles, Varrains, 49400 Saumur.

A long-established family of predominantly red-wine makers with 74 acres of Cabernet in Saumur-Champigny, now made with modern methods and winning medals in Paris. Their Vieilles Vignes selection spends more time in wood. The Daheuillers also make a little Crémant de Loire from Chenin Blanc grown on very chalky soil.

Domaine Philippe Delesvaux

'Les Essards', 49190 St-Aubin-de-Luigné.

A serious young grower with 36 acres (26 planted to Chenin Blanc, 6 to Cabernet Franc and 4 to Cabernet Sauvignon). Delesvaux produces pleasant Anjou Blanc *sec* and tasty Anjou Rouge, but pulls out all the stops with his Layon, particularly the *cuvées* from the *lieux-dits* La Moque and Clos du Pavillon and the luscious Sélection de Grains Nobles.

Domaine de l'Echalier

49750 Rablay-sur-Layon.

Isabelle Lorent and François Bureau, husband and wife oenologists, purchased 50 acres in the heart of Layon in 1990 and make classic Coteaux du Layon-Rablay, including a barrel-aged old vines Cuvée Jean Cesbrun, willowy Anjou-Villages and some of the pleasantest Cabernet d'Anjou and Rosé d'Anjou to be found.

Château d'Epiré

Epiré, 49170 St-Georges-sur-Loire.

Following the death of Armand Bizard in 1984 the estate has been run by his children, with son Luc now in charge. Family ownership of this 25-acre estate dates back to 1749. Stainless steel and barrels are used, picking is by hand. The aim is Savennières made for long ageing, full-bodied and dry – a *vin de garde*. In addition to Chenin the estate has a little Cabernet for Rosé d'Anjou and an Anjou-Villages, Clos de la Cerisaie. Rosé de la Loire is also made.

Château de Fesles

49380 Thouarcé.

An historic property, reputed for its remarkable Bonnezeaux, this 81-acre estate has undergone dramatic change in the recent past. In 1991 Gaston Lenôtre, the 'pastry king of Paris', purchased Fesles from the Boivin family which had, quite literally, created the appellation (Jacques Boivin lobbied for – and won – Bonnezeaux's status as a *grand cru* of Anjou). Lenôtre spent 30 million francs renovating the cellars, brought in a new winemaking team and bought two domaines in Coteaux du Layon-Chaume, as well as a 17-acre vineyard in Savennières. In 1996 he sold everything to Bernard Germanin, who has five properties in Bordeaux, including Château Yon-Figeac, and whose son recently bought the Domaine des Roches Neuves in Saumur-Champigny (q.v.).

Paul Filliatreau

Chaintres, 49400 Dampierre-sur-Loire.

One of the growers who has brought Saumur-Champigny to prominence. His 123 acres of Cabernet include some century-old vines; vinified separately as Vieilles Vignes. Cuvée Lena is a purchased wine. His own wines are designed to age. The 1983 was very good. Filliatreau has two new bottlings: La Grande Vignolle and Château Fouquet – an AC Saumur Rouge.

Domaine des Forges

49190 St-Aubin de Luigné.

Claude Branchereau makes the gamut of Anjou wines from his 74 acres but his heart is in his Coteaux du Layon of which he makes several marvellous *cuvées*, including an old-vines bottling from the *lieu-dit* Les Onnis (also spelled Aunis).

Jean-Louis & Bernard Foucault

49400 Chacé.

Two brothers run a century-old red wine estate with vintages in the cellars going back six decades. They buy their *barriques* from Château Margaux and other top Bordeaux châteaux, and some new, and age their wine in wood for up to two years. The wines are controversial but surely among the best and longest-lived of the appellation, if not of all Loire reds.

Château de la Genaiserie

49190 St-Aubin de Luigné.

Yves Soulez purchased a rambling old château with 104 acres of prime Layon vineyards after selling his share of the family domaine Château de Chamboureau in Savennières. Of his many *cuvées* of Layon, the richest, most concentrated and finest come from low-yielding old vines in the *lieux-dits* Les Petits Houx, Les Simonelles and La Roche.

Grosset-Château

49190 Rochefort-sur-Loire.

Oak-aged Cabernet Layons from the Grosset family. Their Rochefort-Layon and Layon-Chaume are, among other things, rustic, though not without charm.

Domaine de Haute Perche

St-Melaine-sur-Aubance, 49320 Brissec-Quincé.

The wines from Christian Papin's 72-acre estate are well represented on local restaurant lists. He keeps abreast of modern winemaking techniques and quality has improved steadily over the years. Papin makes the entire range of Anjou wines. His best, particularly in rich vintages, are his warm, supple Anjou-Villages, honeyed Coteaux de l'Aubance and delicious Anjou-Gamay.

Vignobles Laffourcade

Château Perray Jouannet, 49380 Chavagnes-les Eaux.

Once the principal proprietor of Quarts de Chaume, Pascal Laffourcade has diversified and in the process has been selling off bits of the Grand Cru. He still owns a large share of it, 40 acres at the last count, mostly at the Château de l'Echarderie.

His domaines also includes 5 acres of Bonnezeaux, 25 at the Château Perray Jouannet (where the winery is located) planted to Cabernet, Gamay and Chardonnay. Additionally, he rents 17 acres in Savennières and runs a négociant business, Anjou Viticole. Winemaking is modern. There are numerous *cuvées* of Quarts de Chaume and Savennières; the deluxe bottlings are Clos du Paradis and Clos la Royauté respectively.

Vignoble Lecointre

49380 Champ-sur-Layon.

A serious young producer with almost 100 acres of vines in the heart of Layon, Vincent Lecointre produces the range of Anjou wines. The Domaine de Pierre Blanche label covers his rosés, normal *cuvées* of Anjou Rouge and Blanc, Coteaux du Layon and *vin de pays* (Sauvignon Blanc and Chardonnay). Château la Tomaze is the label for his deluxe *cuvées*, the Coteaux du Layon-Rablay Cuvée des Lys and Anjou-Villages. The former features in a number of popular Paris restaurants.

Domaine Musset-Rouillier

Le Pelican, 49620 La Pommeraye.

Gilles Musset, a serious grower and president of the Syndicat d'Anjou Coteaux de la Loire, joined forces with Serge Rouillier, another good young producer, in 1994. On their combined 72 acres they produce exemplary Anjou Coteaux de la Loire, including a deluxe *cuvée* Tris Sélectionnés, as well as admirable Anjou Blanc *sec* and Anjou-Villages Clos de Rinières.

Rémy Pannier

St-Hilaire-St-Florent, 49400 Saumur.

The largest négociant of Loire wines, marketing more than 25 million bottles annually.

Château de Pierre-Bise

49750 Beaulieu-sur-Layon.

One of the top producers of Coteaux du Layon, Claude Papin owns 86 acres of vines. He bottles Layon by soil type, offering as many as a dozen different *cuvées*, including Layon-Chaume and Quarts de Chaume. Papin also produces excellent Anjou Blanc *sec*, Anjou-Villages and Anjou-Gamay. Since 1992 he has been making the wine at Clos du Coulaine in Savennières (q.v.).

Domaine Richou

Chauvigné, Mozé-sur-Louet, 49190 Rochefort-sur-Loire.

Didier Richou makes the full spectrum of Anjou wines on his 91 acres. He regularly wins awards for his supple Anjou-Villages and his impeccable Coteaux de l'Aubance, notably the oak-aged old vines *cuvée*, Les Trois Demoiselles.

Domaine des Rochelles

49320 St-Jean des Mauvrets.

Jean-Yves and Hubert Lebreton pioneered red winemaking in Anjou. Their Cabernets remain among the best and often win prizes. On their 110-acre estate they also produce exemplary Coteaux de l'Aubance and lively Chardonnay Vins de Pays du Jardin de la France.

Domaine des Roches Neuves

49400 Varrains.

Thierry Germain, a young Bordelais, purchased this 37-acre property in 1991 and ever since has been turning out flavoursome Saumur-Champigny, the two most concentrated being the Cuvée Vieilles Vignes Terre Chaude and the Cuvée Marginale.

Domaine du Sauveroy

49750 St-Lambert-du-Lattay.

Pascal Cailleau is winemaker at this family estate using modern winemaking techniques for Anjou reds which often win awards.

Château Soucherie

49750 Beaulieu-sur-Layon.

Tijou's parents bought this 75-acre domaine in 1952. Most is in Coteaux du Layon in Chenin Blanc, with Cabernet and Gamay for red and rosé. His best Layons are the Vieilles Vignes and the Layon-Chaume. Another top Coteaux du Layon, Beaulieu, is from 90-year-old vines. No wood is used for the white. An Anjou blanc sometimes has 20% Sauvignon added to Chenin Blanc for aroma. Tijou has recently purchased a small parcel in Savennières called Clos des Perrières.

Château de Targé

Parnay, 49730 Montsoreau.

A four-towered manoir, in the Pisani-Ferry family since 1655, with 50 acres of Cabernet (90% Franc, 10% Sauvignon) for Saumur-Champigny. Temperature-controlled stainless steel fermentation is usually followed by ageing in oak.

Château de Tigné

49770 Tigné.

Actor Gérard Depardieu purchased 124 acres of vines and a handsome château in a stately park in the Haut-Layon. He specializes in red wine, however, particularly Cabernet Franc, aged for at least a year in once-used barrels from Bordeaux or Burgundy. In good vintages there are two deluxe bottlings, Cuvée Mozart and Cuvée Cyrano. The winery, which is run by Tigné's mayor, Dominique Polleau, also produces a beefy Anjou Blanc, a vinous Cabernet d'Anjou and a charming Grolleau Rouge.

Les Vins Touchais and Les Vignobles Touchais

49700 Doué La Fontaine.

One of the biggest growers and négociants of the Loire. Les Vignobles Touchais own 355 acres, of which 66 are in Coteaux du Layon. Over 100 acres are Chenin Blanc, slightly more are Cabernet (mostly Franc). The Touchais family have been growers for centuries and have amassed astonishing stocks of fine old sweet Layon wines – the best, sold as Moulin Touchais, maturing almost indefinitely. Wines in stock include 1985, '84, '82, '81, '80, '79, '75 and '70. At 20 years the '59 was full of vigour and deep honeyed flavour – a very great dessert wine. The bulk of the négociant business of Les Vins Touchais (founded 1947) is in rosé and other popular regional wines to the tune of 2m. bottles of Loire wines a year. Cuisse de Bergère – Shepherdess's Thigh – is appropriately sweet and blushing.

Château de Villeneuve

49400 Souzay-Champigny.

Excellent family domaine with 62 acres of vines. the most powerful of the *cuvées* of Saumur-Champigny is the barrel-aged old vines bottling from the *lieu-dit* Le Grand Clos. There are two *cuvées* of singular Saumur Blanc, including Les Cormiers which ferments and ages in new oak barrels.

Caves Coopératives

Les Caves de la Loire

49320 Brissac.

A union of three cooperative cellars, at Brissac, Beaulieu-sur-Layon and Tigné. The cooperative has some 500 members and almost 5,000 acres, producing annually over 990,000 cases of the general Anjou appellations with modern equipment. As much as half of their production is exported.

Cave des Vignerons de Saumur

49260 St-Cyr-en-Bourg.

The growers' cooperative produces 30% of Saumur's wine, making the full spectrum of regional appellations. There are four *cuvées* of Saumur-Champigny, which represents more than 25% of the Cave's production, as well as Saumur blanc, Saumur rouge, Cabernet de Saumur and a range of *mousseux* and *crémant*. Production is 715,000 cases annually.

SPARKLING SAUMUR

The in-built acidity of Chenin Blanc is the cause and justification of the Saumur sparkling-wine industry, which is based in the chalk caves of St-Hilaire–St-Florent, just west of Saumur. It uses the classic method to produce cleanly fruity, usually very dry wines at half champagne prices, less characterful and complex but just as stimulating. However, an increasing number of producers are now making Crémant de Loire; and there is a corresponding number of deluxe *cuvées*. A few of these begin to approach champagne prices and, at times, champagne quality (relatively speaking).

Major Producers of Sparkling Saumur

Ackerman-Laurance

St-Hilaire-St-Florent, 49416 Saumur.

The original and probably still the biggest firm, founded in 1811 when Ackerman, a Belgian, introduced the *méthode traditionnelle* to the Loire. Still a leader with the new extra-quality Crémant de Loire. Its Crémant *cuvées* include Cuvée Privée, Cuvée Jean Baptiste and Cuvée Louis Ackerman. 292,000 cases.

Veuve Amiot

49400 Saumur.

Founded 1884, now owned by Martini & Rossi. 250,000 cases of sparkling Saumur, Anjou and Crémant de Loire). Its two bottlings are Cuvée Réserve and Haute Tradition.

Bouvet-Ladubay

St-Hilaire–St-Florent, 49416 Saumur.

The second oldest (1851) of the sparkling-wine houses, Bouvet-Ladubay became part of the Taittinger group in 1974. Excellent sparkling Saumurs include Bouvet Brut, Saphir (a vintage brut), Rubis (an off-dry red based on Cabernet) and three deluxe *cuvées*, each partially or entirely fermented in barrel: Trésor, Trésor Rosé and a *demi-sec* Grand Vin de Dessert. Overall, annual production is 2m. bottles, of which 100,000 is purchased Saumur-Champigny and 10,000 Anjou Blanc *sec*.

Gratien, Meyer, Seydoux & Cie

Château Gratien, 49401 Saumur.

A twin company to the Champagne house of Alfred Gratien. 40 acres of vineyards (Chenin Blanc and Cabernet) over the cellars. Products include Saumur Brut, Saumur Rosé Brut, Blanc de Noirs, Crémant de Loire Brut, Argent Extra Dry, a sweet sparkling Cabernet called Crémant Rouge and Cuvée Flamme – the top-drawer Saumur Brut.

Langlois-Château

St-Hilaire-St-Florent, 49416 Saumur.

This old house merged with Bollinger in 1973. Principally producers of fine sparkling Crémant de Loire (blanc, rosé and vintage) but also of still Loire wines from Muscadet to Sancerre. The best of these come from the firm's own vineyards, Château de Fontaine Audon in Sancerre, and Domaine Langlois-Château for Saumur red and white.

De Neuville

St-Hilaire-St-Florent, 49416 Saumur.

A family-run firm producing sparkling Saumur and Crémant de Loire. Their Château Midouin Crémant de Loire comes from the family's 74-acre vineyard.

Cave des Vignerons de Saumur

49260 St-Cyr-en-Bourg.

The Cave Cooperative makes the gamut of Saumur sparkling wines, including Saumur Brut (under a variety of labels), Saumur Rosé Brut, Crémant de Loire Cuvée de la Chevalerie Brut and Rosé, and a Rouge Mousseux *demi-sec*.

TOURAINE

It is hard to define Touraine more precisely than as the eastern half of the central Loire, with the city of Tours at its heart and a trio of goodly rivers, the Cher, the Indre and the Vienne, joining the majestic mainstream from the south.

Almost on its border with Anjou it produces the best red wines of the Loire. Chinon and Bourgueil lie on the latitude of the Côte de Beaune and the longitude of St-Emilion – a situation that produces a kind of claret capable of stunning vitality and charm. The Cabernet Franc, with very little if any Cabernet Sauvignon, achieves a sort of pastel sketch of a great Médoc, smelling of raspberries, begging to be drunk cellar-cool in its first summer, light and sometimes astringent, yet surprisingly solid in its construction: ripe vintages age almost like Bordeaux, at least to seven or eight years.

Much depends on the soil: sand and gravel near the river produce lighter, faster-maturing wine than clay over tuffeau limestone on the slopes (*coteaux*). These differences seem greater than those between Chinon and Bourgueil; certainly than any between Bourgueil and its immediate neighbour on the north bank, St-Nicolas de Bourgueil, although this has a separate appellation of its own.

Touraine's other famous wine is Vouvray, potentially the most luscious and longest lived of all the sweet Chenin Blanc whites, though, like German wines, depending more on the vintage than the site for the decisive degree of sugar that determines its character. The best vineyards are on the warm chalky tuffeau slopes near the river and in sheltered corners of side valleys. A warm dry autumn (1989 was optimal; one of the historic great years) can overripen the grapes here by sheer heat, or a warm misty one can bring on noble rot to shrivel them. In either case great sweet Vouvray will be possible, with or without the peculiar smell and taste of *Botrytis cinerea*. Cool years make wines of indeterminate (though often very smooth and pleasant) semi-sweetness, or dry wines – all with the built-in acidity that always keeps Chenin Blanc lively (if not always very easy to drink). The solution to overacid wines here, as in Saumur, is to make them sparkle by the *méthode traditionnelle*.

It is an odd coincidence that each of the great Loire wines comes with a pair across the river: Savennières with Coteaux du Layon, Bourgueil with Chinon, Sancerre with Pouilly and Vouvray with Montlouis. Montlouis, squeezed between the Loire's south bank and the Cher's north bank, is not regarded, except by those who make it, as having quite the authority and 'attack' of great Vouvray. Its sites are slightly less favoured, its wines softer and more tentative. They can sparkle just as briskly, though, and ripen almost as sweet.

Outside these four appellations Touraine, with its simple but all-purpose AC Touraine, has only a modest reputation although these wines continue to improve. I suggest that the future lies with the general (and self-explanatory) Sauvignon and Gamay de Touraine; some of the top *cuvées* of Sauvignon and Gamay can give – respectively – Sancerre and Beaujolais a run for their money. They are not as fine as either, but an awful lot cheaper. Increasingly, the wine authorities are encouraging (indeed, in the case of Touraine-Mesland mandating) blends of Gamay, Cabernet and Cot. Some producers now have a blend alongside their varietal reds, with proprietary names according to the subregion: Touraine Tradition and François 1er are two from Touraine-Amboise.

Leading Touraine Producers

Domaine Allias

Le Petit Mont, 37210 Vouvray.
Daniel Allias farms 25 acres of hilltop vines over the rock-cut cellars to produce concentrated, classic dry, *demi-sec* and *moëlleux* Vouvrays.

Claude Ammeux

Clos de la Contrie, St-Nicolas de Bourgueil, 37140 Bourgueil.
A charming 11-acre property at the foot of the *coteaux*, almost in Bourgueil. M. Ammeux feeds his very old vines on seaweed and looks for flavour and alcohol at the expense of big crops.

Domaine des Aubuisières

37210 Vouvray.
One of the best of the young crop of Vouvray producers, Bernard Fouquet produces sublime *secs, demi-secs* and *moëlleux* from three different vineyards, Le Marigny, Les Girardières and Le Bouchet. His sparkling Vouvray *méthode traditionnelle* is full-bodied and flavoursome.

Audebert & Fils

37140 Bourgueil.
One of the biggest négociant-growers in Bourgueil, St-Nicolas de Bourgueil, Chinon and Saumur-Champigny, with 82 acres and modern equipment. Domaine du Grand Clos and La Marquise are special *cuvées* from specific vineyards – easy wines for drinking cool in their youthful prime.

Le Clos Baudoin

Vallée de Nouy, 37210 Vouvray.
Maker of some immortal Vouvray from three Grand Cru vineyards, Le Clos Baudoin, Clos des Patys and Clos de l'Avenir. The fine vintages have what the owner, Prince Poniatowski, calls 'race' – breeding – that takes 25 or 30 years to reach its full flowering. The 1854 in the cellar is apparently excellent. The estate is 61 acres, most in Vouvray and a little in Touraine, used for *méthode traditionnelle* Brut de Brut. Half of some 12–13,000 cases a year is exported.

Marc Brédif

37210 Rochecorbon.
Négociant-grower with hospitable cellars in the rock caves below Rochecorbon. The firm belongs to the de Ladoucette concern of Pouilly. The wines are all Vouvrays, in both still and sparkling forms from the firm's 124 acres. Brédif invented Vouvray *pétillant* in the 1920s. The standards are commendably high.

Clos de la Briderie

41150 Monteaux.
On his 15 acres (cultivated according to biodynamic strictures) François Girault produces the best wines of the Touraine-Amboise appellation, including persuasive Chenins and succulent red blends of Gamay, Cabernet and Cot.

Caslot-Galbrun

La Hurolaie, 37140 Benais.
One of the oldest established families of growers in Bourgueil, whose 51 acres seem to produce some of the juiciest, deepest coloured, most age-worthy wine. The walled Clos de la Gaucherie at Restigné is theirs. Fermentation is in stainless steel, but methods and standards are unchanged.

Domaine de Cézin

La Chenetterie, 72340 Marçon.
The Fresnau family has nearly 2.5 acres of Jasnières and 22 acres in the Coteaux du Loir. The Jasnières and the Pineau d'Aunis Rouge are rustic and personalized and have immense charm.

Domaine de la Charmoise

41230 Soings en Sologne.
Henry Marionnet is a modern-minded grower with a new 124-acre vineyard of Gamay and Sauvignon Blanc. He uses *macération carbonique* to get a Beaujolais effect in his Gamay de Touraine, and strives for round and fruity Sauvignon. There are special *cuvées,* including M de Marionnet, a Sauvignon made from the late-harvested grapes of his old vines and Première Vendange, hand-harvested Gamay with no added sulphur, sugar or yeast.

Domaine de la Charrière

72340 La Chartre-sur-le-Loir.
Joël Gigou brought a whiff of modernity to the sleepy vineyards of Jasnières. From his 10 acres he produces among the best in that appellation, particularly his Cuvée Clos St Jacques, as well as some of the finest Coteaux du Loir, notably a pure Gamay, Cuvée Cénomane, which matures in barrel.

Domaine de la Chevalerie

37140 Restigné.
Paul Caslot farms 67 acres of old Cabernet vines on the hill and makes firm deep-toned Bourgueil, aged up to 18 months in wood and intended to age a further three, four or more years.

Château de Chenonceaux

37150 Chenonceaux.
The estate belonging to what must be the most beautiful of Loire showplace châteaux has 94 acres of vines, and a well-equipped little winery in a courtyard. A range of wines is made.

Domaine du Clos Naudin

37210 Vouvray.
The Foreau family own 30 acres of prime vineyards and aim to age their wine for as long as possible before selling it – an expensive procedure but essential to let its character develop. Ten years is a good age for a 'new' Vouvray. Their output is about 55,000 bottles of sweet, dry, *demi-sec* and sparkling.

Clos Neuf des Archambaults

37800 Ste-Maure de Touraine.

From 3.5 acres of vines Jean-François Dehelly prunes hard, thins clusters, hand-harvests and produces concentrated, barrique-aged Cabernets, red and rosé, to rival Chinon.

Couly-Dutheil

12 rue Diderot, 37500 Chinon.

A grower of Chinon and négociant for other Loire wines, founded in 1910 by B. Dutheil, developed by René Couly and now run by his sons Pierre and Jacques and Bertrand, son of Pierre. Their 185 acres of Chinon are divided between wines of plain and plateau, sold as Les Gravières d'Amador Abbé de Turpenay (the lightest) and Domaine René Couly, and the (better) wines of the *coteaux*, the Clos de l'Echo and Clos de l'Olive. La Diligence is a new bottling from 40 acres of recently purchased vineyard – for mid-term drinking. Equipment is modern, with temperature control and automatic turning of the skins in the stainless-steel vats. The object is wine drinkable by the following Easter but able, as Chinon is, to age in bottle for several years. Apart from Echo and Olive, another top wine is a selection labelled Baronnie Madeleine.

G & G Deletang

St-Martin-le-Beau, 37270 Montlouis-sur-Loire.

Good Montlouis from Chenin Blanc, and Touraine AC wines, from 50 well-placed acres.

Robert Denis

37190 La Chapelle-St-Blaise.

A dedicated grower who cossets his 10 acres of vines to produce full-bodied rosés and fine-boned dry and off-dry Chenin Blanc, all barrel-fermented, in AC Azay-le-Rideau.

Pierre-Jacques Druet

37140 Benais.

One of Bourgueil's finest producers, Druet has 44 acres of vines and offers 5 *cuvées* of Bourgueil and 2 of Chinon, including the Clos du Danzay. In Bourgueil he produces a meaty barrel-fermented rosé and, in order of age-worthiness, Les Cents Boissellées, Beauvais, Le Grand Mont and Vaumoreau.

Domaine Dubreuil

Le Breuil, 37400 Amboise.

A family estate, previously known by the name of its owner, Hubert Denay, with 231 acres, making classic Touraine Amboise, in particular the straight Cot.

Domaine Dutertre

37400, Limeray.

An 86-acre family property run by father (Jacques) and son (Gilles). Fifty-odd acres are Cabernet, Malbec and Gamay for red and rosé Touraine-Amboise, as well as François 1er, the name in Touraine-Amboise for the blend of Gamay, Cot and Cabernet. The Dutertres also make sparkling and still dry whites in their rock-cut cellar.

Domaine du Four à Chaux

Berger, 41100 Thoré la Rochette.

Dominique Norguet makes the best wine in VDQS Coteaux du Vendômois, particularly his *vin gris* of Pineau d'Aunis and his red blends, either of Gamay and Pineau d'Aunis or of Pinot Noir and Pineau d'Aunis.

Jean-Pierre Freslier

'La Caillerie', 37210 Vouvray.

Jean-Pierre has taken over from his father, André Freslier, and continues to make serious dry Vouvray from 22 acres, fermenting the wine in old 600-litre casks ('*demi-muids*'). He recommends 4–5 years ageing in bottle. In good years he makes tasty *moëlleux*; also dry and off-dry Vouvray *pétillant*.

Château Gaillard

41150 Mesland.

As serious a vintner as his father, François (see Clos de la Briderie), young Vincent Girault cultivates his 75 acres of vines according to the principles of biodynamics. His best wine is his Touraine-Mesland rouge Vieilles Vignes, a fleshy blend based on Gamay supported by Cot and Cabernet.

Le Haut-Lieu

37210 Vouvray.

Formerly known by the name of the owner, Gaston Huet, who is perhaps the most respected name in Vouvray. Huet, a former mayor of Vouvray, comes from a family of growers for three generations making wine of the highest quality from three vineyards, Le Haut-Lieu, Le Mont and Le Clos du Bourg, sweet or dry, still or sparkling according to the season. His son-in-law, Noël Pinguet, is the winemaker and has converted the domaine to biodynamic viticulture.

Domaine des Huards

41700 Cour-Cheverny.

The Gendrier family has 40 acres in AC Cheverny and a further 20 in AC Cour-Cheverny. In the former they produce estimable Sauvignon Blanc-based dry whites and Gamay- and Cabernet-based reds and rosés; in the latter they make some of the best examples of a unique dry white from the local Romorantin grape.

Vignoble de la Jarnoterie

La Jarnoterie, 37140 St-Nicolas de Bourgueil.

A grower with 33 acres, all beside his house. He makes as much as 2,000 cases of light red with the typical raspberry aroma, which he claims will keep for seven years even in 'medium' vintages, and up to 30 in great ones.

Charles Joguet

37220 Sazilly.

An artist-vigneron, painter and sculptor as well as farmer of 37 acres of Chinon and one of its best winemakers. Joguet's best old vines are in the Clos de la Dioterie. Clos du Chêne Vert is another noted vineyard. His up-to-date cellar has automated *pigeage* of juice and skins in stainless-steel vats then up to 18 months' ageing in used Bordeaux barrels.

Lamé-Delille-Boucard

Domaine des Chesnaies, 37140 Ingrandes de Touraine.
A considerable property totalling 74 acres, divided almost equally between four communes with the appellation Bourgueil: Ingrandes, St-Patrice, Restigné and Benais. The grouping is recent, although M Lamé comes from an old vigneron family. He uses wooden vats and describes his wines as ranging from succulent to fragile, depending on the vintage.

Domaine des Liards

37270 Montlouis-sur-Loire.
A third-generation property of 50 acres, 80% in Chenin Blanc for still, sparkling and *pétillant* Montlouis, the rest in Sauvignon for Touraine Blanc and Cabernet Franc for Touraine Rouge. The wine is all bottled in spring and aged in bottle – about 8,300 cases a year. The Bergers also put the bubbles into the still wines of many Montlouis growers.

Domaine Jacky Marteau

41110 Pouillé.
A reliable producer of superb Gamay de Touraine, Marteau also makes fine Sauvignon de Touraine, Cabernet and rosé of Pineau d'Aunis on his 50 acres.

Dominique Moyer

Husseau, 37270 Montlouis-sur-Loire.
A respected old family of growers (since 1830) with 30 acres of very old vines (30% are over 70 years old). The Moyers go to the length of successive pickings to crush nothing but ripe grapes, making *sec* and *demi-sec* as ripe and round as possible. A little sparkling wine now made.

François Pinon

Vallée de Cousse, 37210 Vernou-sur-Brenne.
A former child psychologist who took over the family's 27 acres, Pinon is scrupulous in both vineyard and cellar, producing high-quality *sec, demi-sec, moëlleux* and *liquoreux* as well as characterful *pétillant*.

Clos des Quarterons

37140 St-Nicolas de Bourgueil.
A property of 50 acres well distributed on the lighter soils of St-Nicolas which belongs to the Amirault family. 8,000 cases of lightly fruity wine are sold to restaurants and private clients.

Jean-Maurice Raffault

37420 Savigny-en-Véron.
In 25 years M. Raffault, whose family have been vignerons since 1693, has expanded his vineyards from 12 to 100 acres with parcels scattered over seven communes, all in the appellation Chinon. He makes the wines of different soils separately. Les Galluches, a light Chinon, comes from sandy soils; his longest-lived Chinons from the *lieux-dits* Les Picasses and Isoré. Raffault also makes Chinon Blanc, Eau de Vie de Poire Williams from his own pears and Marc des Coteaux de la Loire.

Olga Raffault

37420 Savigny-en-Véron.
One of several Raffaults in and around this village at the western end of the Chinon appellation. (Another, Raymond, owns Domaine du Raifault, *sic*). The estate is 50 acres, with fermentation in steel vats, then ageing in wooden ones, keeping the wine of different sites separate. Clients (who include the famous restaurant Barrier at Tours) can choose from a range of generally fruity and fairly full-bodied wines of which the longest-lived *cuvée* is Les Picasses Vieilles Vignes. Raffault also makes a tiny amount of Chinon Blanc.

Domaine des Raguenières

37140 Benais.
A 37-acre Bourgueil property making a little rosé as well as nearly 5,000 cases of clean, fairly tannic, marvellously scented red compared by owner Paul Maître to Bordeaux – especially in its keeping properties. They can, though, be rather rustic and often vegetal.

Rousseau Frères

37320 Esvres.
This family domaine annually produces 50,000 bottles, chiefly of an unusual wine called Touraine Noble-Joué, a lively rosé made from a blend of Pinots Meunier, Gris and Noir. The Rousseaus and other local vintners have applied for an official appellation for the wine, which is said to have existed in the area before the 15th century.

Domaine Joel Taluau

Chevrette, 37140 St-Nicolas de Bourgueil.
Forty acres of St-Nicolas and a handful of Bourgueil producing 1,500 cases of fragrant light red. Taluau ferments everything in stainless steel; and he doesn't believe in wood ageing. All but the old vines are harvested by machine and a severe pruning regime has been enforced. He has three *cuvées*: Jeunes Vignes, Domaine and Vieilles Vignes.

Caves Coopératives

Cave du Haut-Poitou

86170 Neuville de Poitou.
The VDQS zone of Haut-Poitou is well south of the Loire on the road to Poitiers, where 47 communes on the chalky soil of a plateau used to supply distilling wine to Cognac. In 1948, a cooperative was founded and succeeded in raising standards to the point where in 1970 the region was promoted to VDQS.

In September 1995 Georges Duboeuf of Beaujolais purchased 40% of the shares of the Cave. He ended its days as a cooperative but covered its considerable debts and bought himself a source of varietal wines – Sauvignon Blanc, Chardonnay, Gamay and Cabernet – in both the VDQS and *vin de pays* ranges. There are 449 growers in the current grouping, covering 2,100 acres in over 41 communes. Production in 1995 was 38,000 hectolitres; 2m. bottles were sold.

Cave Cooperative des Grands Vins de Bourgueil

37140 Restigné.

The cooperative cellars oversee some 865 acres. In return for grapes, growers receive allotted portions of bottled wine which they sell under their own labels. The Cave sells wine, too: the Cuvée Marie Dupin is a light Bourgueil from sandy soils; the Cuvée les Chevaliers is meant to age.

Cave des Producteurs la Vallée Coquette

37210 Vouvray.

Founded in 1953 this is one of Vouvray's two cooperative cellars. It controls 420 acres of vines and specializes in sound sparkling Vouvray, *pétillant* and *méthode traditionnelle*. Vouvray's other cooperative, Cave de Vaudenuits, has had similar success with the same type of product.

Confrèrie des Vignerons de Oisly et Thesée

41700 Oisly.

A young (1961) cooperative with 58 members, which is making great efforts to create a new style and image for the valley of the Cher in eastern Touraine. Their aim is to design a well-balanced light red and white using a blend of grapes. The white is Sauvignon, Chenin Blanc and Chardonnay, the red Cabernet Franc, Cot and Gamay. The cooperative's brand for their top *cuvée* of each is Baronnie d'Aignan; Prestige de la Vallée des Rois is the cheaper version. Château de Vallagon and Domaine de la Châtoire are estate-bottled wines; Excellence is a new *cuvée* of both Sauvignon and Gamay, each hand-harvested from old vines. Annual production of bottled wine is about 330,000 cases of which some 297,000 cases are in AC Touraine. All AOC wines.

THE UPPER LOIRE

It might well surprise the vignerons of Sancerre and Pouilly, the uppermost of the mainstream Loire vineyards, to learn what a profound influence their produce has had on forming modern tastes in white wine. It is an area of mainly small and unsophisticated properties – with one or two well-organized exceptions. But it has an easily recognizable style of wine, pungent and cutting, with the smell and acidity of Sauvignon Blanc grown in a cool climate.

Although Sauvignon is planted on a far larger scale in Bordeaux its wine never smelt and tasted so powerfully characteristic there as it does on the Loire. The Bordeaux tradition is to blend it with the smoother and more neutral Sémillon. But since Bordeaux has seen the world paying white burgundy prices for the assertive (some say obvious) Loire style, it is paying it the sincerest form of flattery. Californians, with vastly different growing conditions, have adopted the term Fumé to indicate that their Sauvignon Blanc aims at the Loire flavour (rather than the broader, riper, to some passé, style of Graves). One might say that the world discovered the Sauvignon Blanc and its singular flavour through the little vineyard of Sancerre and the even smaller one of Pouilly-sur-Loire.

What is the flavour? It starts with the powerful aroma, which needs no second sniff. 'Gunflint,' the smell of sparks when flint strikes metal, is one way to characterize it. In unripe vintages tasters talk of cats, and I am reminded of wet wool. Successful Sancerres and Pouilly Fumés have an attractive smell and taste of fresh blackcurrants, leaves and all, and a natural high acidity which makes them distinctly bracing. Sancerre normally has more body and 'drive' (and acidity) than Pouilly Fumé; consequently it can benefit from two or three years' ageing. Pouilly needs only a year or so.

For reasons of tradition the Pouilly vineyards also contain a proportion of the neutral Chasselas grape, which cannot be sold as 'Fumé', only as Pouilly-sur-Loire – a pale, adequate, rather pointless wine, which must be drunk very young. Sancerre, on the other hand, is almost as proud of its Pinot Noir red and rosé as its Sauvignon white. They never achieve the flavour and texture of great burgundy, although those being made by the best producers can match lighter red burgundies. More commonly they have the faintly watery style of German Spätburgunder (the same grape). Nor do they age so satisfactorily – at best for 5 to 10 years. But they are highly appreciated at source.

Leading Sancerre Producers

Bernard Bailly-Reverdy & Fils

La Croix St-Laurent, 18300 Bué.

A distinguished traditional grower with 50 acres in no fewer than 15 sites. Thirty-seven acres are Sauvignon, 13 Pinot Noir, the latter making good red Sancerre. The bottling from the famous Clos du Chêne Marchand is now called Caillottes. White from other vineyards is called Dom. de la Mercy Dieu; there is also a Chavignol bottling. He looks for (and finds) a balance of fruit and finesse, particularly in his whites.

Domaine Joseph Balland-Chapuis

Bué, 18300 Sancerre.

A descendant of a long line of growers with 74 acres, mostly in Sancerre with some in VDQS Giennois and a small parcel in Pouilly. Many *cuvées* of Sancerre, including two excellent whites, Chêne Marchand and Comte Thibault. The deluxe red, Comte Thibault Vieilles Vignes, matures in new oak. Cuvée Pierre and Cuvée Marguerite Marceau are late-harvest Sauvignons, off-dry or sweet, depending on the vintage.

Domaine Henri Bourgeois

18300 Bué.

One of the most important grower-négocians in Sancerre. The firm has 150 acres (10 in Pouilly-Fumé) and acts as a négociant in Sancerre, Pouilly, Reuilly, Menetou-Salon and Quincy. Bourgeois offers numerous high-end *cuvées*, including La Bourgeoise (red and white), MD de Bourgeois, Etienne Henri and Les Monts Damnés. The firm also sells the Sancerres of Domaine Laporte.

Francis, Paul & François Cotat

Chavignol, 18300 Sancerre.

A very small (1,000–1,500 cases), totally traditional and most prestigious grower. The Cotats do everything themselves, use an old wooden press, ferment in casks and never fine or filter: instead they bottle at the full moon in May when the wine is clear and still. Bottles from the 1930s in their cellar are still in good condition.

Domaine Lucien Crochet

Bué, 18300 Sancerre.

A family holding of 81 acres, three-quarters of it Sauvignon, the rest Pinot Noir. Crochet also buys in grapes for his modern, efficient cellars. Classic methods produce excellent wine, particularly his Clos du Chêne Marchand from his 17 acres there (although the Chêne Marchand designation is no longer used). bottlings include La Croix du Roy and the Cuvée Prestige (both red and white), an old-vines bottling often released several years after the vintage.

Domaine Vincent Delaporte & Fils

18300 Chavignol.

Delaporte and son Jean-Yves work 50 acres of vines, of which 10 are planted to Pinot Noir. All wines ferment in stainless steel tanks. The reds age in oak.

Gitton Père & Fils

18300 Ménétréol.

A family estate of 91 acres in Sancerre, Pouilly and Coteaux du Giennois, almost entirely Sauvignon, developed since 1945. The wines are made in many different batches according to different soils – at least 15 different Sancerre *cuvées* with different labels – Les Belles Dames, Le Gelinot, Les Romains and so on – and two Pouilly Fumés. The whites are fermented in barrels or tanks and aged eight months in *cuves*, the reds fermented in *cuves*, then aged two winters in barrels. Altogether an original house with a style of its own. M. Gitton *fils* has now taken over

Pascal Jolivet

18300 Sancerre.

A dynamic young grower and négociant with 20 acres in Sancerre and a further 20 in Pouilly (q.v.). Jolivet, who recently completed new wine facilities in Sancerre, still buys grapes and wine but puts out a number of domaine bottlings. In Sancerre these include Le Chêne Marchand and La Grande Cuvée, an old-vines bottling made only in good years.

Château de Maimbray

18300 Sury-en-Vaux.

The Roblins, a trustworthy family of growers, produce sturdy Sancerre (red, white and rosé) from their 37 acres.

Domaine Paul Millerioux

Champtin, 18300 Crézancy-en-Sancerre.

An old-style grower with brand-new cellars who turns out flavourful Sancerres (red, rosé and white) from his 40 acres of vines.

Domaine de la Moussière

18300 Sancerre.

Growers, négocians and propagandists for Sancerre with an important holding of 123 acres in good sites, mostly in La Moussière. The Mellot family, now headed by Alphonse, date back to the 16th century. Their deluxe bottling is Cuvée Edmond.

Domaine Roger Neveu

18300 Verdigny.

Neveu and sons Eric and Jean Philippe work 62 acres of vines, producing an average of 100,000 bottles annually of Sancerre (red, white and rosé). Reds age in new oak for up to a year and Neveu is experimenting with partial barrel-fermentation for his whites.

Pierre Prieur & Fils

Domaine Prieur, 18300 Verdigny.

A prominent family of growers for generations with 30 acres in several good sites, including Les Monts-Damnés (which is chalky clay) and the stonier Pichon, where an unusually high proportion (10 acres) of their property is Pinot Noir. Their white is made to age 2 or 3 years; the rosé of Pinot Noir mysteriously seems to share its quality – even its Sauvignon flavour. The red is made like very light burgundy. The deluxe Cuvée Maréchal Prieur is partially fermented and aged in new oak. Annually they produce some 100,000 bottles, half of which is sold to private clients, the other half to restaurants and shops.

Jean-Max Roger

18300 Bué.

An important grower-négociant with 70 acres of vines in Sancerre and Menetou-Salon. Of particular merit is his Sancerre Vieilles Vignes, from his own vines.

Jean Reverdy & Fils

Verdigny, 18300 Sancerre.

A succession of Reverdys since 1646 have farmed some 25 acres, now 15 Sauvignon and 10 Pinot Noir. They have installed modern equipment in the cellar but make fine classic wines, particularly their Clos de la Reine Blanche white, which can mature for 3 or 4 years.

Les Celliers St Romble

Chadoux, 18300 Verdigny.

André Dezat is an old-school grower, mayor of the village, who works, with his sons, in clogs and a beret and loves his red wines as they age – though I prefer them young. He has 52 acres in Sancerre and 30 in Pouilly. His whites are extremely fine, even elegant.

Domaine Vacheron

18300 Sancerre.

A particularly welcoming family of growers whose wines can be tasted in summer in the centre of Sancerre at Le Grenier à Sel. Jean Vacheron, who died in 1988, is succeeded by his sons Jean-Louis and Denis. They own 64 acres, 42 of them

Sauvignon, and offer white Le Paradis, red Les Cailleries and rosé Les Romains. Their equipment and ideas are modern, but the red ages a year in Burgundian casks. Another 25 acres are to be planted.

Cave Coopérative des Vins de Sancerre

18300 Sancerre.

Founded 1963. 155 members; 494 acres producing 176,000 cases annually. 100% AOC Sancerre. A serious producer of typical Sancerre under a variety of labels. The prestige bottling is Le Duc de Tarente.

Leading Pouilly Producers

Francis Blanchet

Les Berthiers, 58150 St-Andelain.

The fourth generation of Blanchets has 13 acres of vines and puts the bubbles into the still wines of his neighbours. His Cuvée Vieilles Vignes is a pungent, herbaceous Sancerre.

Jean-Claude Chatelain

Les Berthiers, 58150 St-Andelain.

A leading grower-négociant with 50 acres in Pouilly. Vinification is modern and there are numerous bottlings, including Les Charmes, St-Laurent-l'Abbaye and Cuvée Prestige Vieilles Vignes. Chatelain is also a shareholder in a new vineyard in La Charité-sur-Loire area south of Pouilly where he makes Chardonnay and Pinot Noir as *vins de pays*.

Didier Dagueneau

58150 St-Andelain.

The appellation's best winemaker, a maverick with 28 acres of vines, Dagueneau produces four decisive *cuvées* of Pouilly Fumé; En Chailloux, Buisson Ménard, Pur Sang and Silex. The last two ferment and age in new oak barrels.

Serge Dagueneau et Filles

Les Berthiers, 58150 St-Andelain.

A 37-acre family vineyard with a high reputation for typically fruity and full-flavoured Pouilly-Fumé and Pouilly-sur-Loire. His old-vines cuvée is Clos des Chaudoux.

Pascal Jolivert

18300 Sancerre.

Pascal Jolivet has 20 acres of his own vines in Pouilly from which he produces numerous bottlings, including Les Griottes and La Grande Cuvée, made from old vines in good vintages.

Domaine Masson-Blondelet

58150 Pouilly-sur-Loire.

The Masson and Blondelet families (united by marriage in 1974) work 40 acres of mainly Sauvignon and a small amount of Chasselas to produce 5,000 cases of Pouilly-Fumé and Sancerre and a little Pouilly-sur-Loire. Their best vines, in Bascoins and Criots, are vinified separately. 'Tradition Cullus' is their *cuvée prestige*. Great winners of medals.

Château du Nozet

58150 Pouilly-sur-Loire.

The major producer and promoter of the fine wines of Pouilly with a production of over 85,000 cases, largely from company-owned vineyards of 160 acres and the equivalent of a further 160 acres in purchased wine. The Baron Patrick de Ladoucette is the head of the family firm, which has 3 labels: Pouilly-Fumé de Ladoucette, Sancerre Comte Lafond (from bought-in grapes) and a prestige *cuvée* Pouilly-Fumé Baron de L. The Baron recently purchased Maison Cordier's vineyards on La Poussie in Sancerre. Half the total production is exported, the other half is sold in France exclusively to the grander restaurants.

Michel Redde & Fils

La Moynerie, 58150 Pouilly-sur-Loire.

One of the best-known producers of Pouilly-Fumé, from 86 acres in the heart of the appellation. A modern installation with stainless-steel vats, operated by the sixth generation of Reddes in succession. They have built modern *caves* and plan new vineyards. Cuvée Majorum is their top wine. Pouilly-sur-Loire is also produced.

Guy Saget

La Castille, 58150 Pouilly-sur-Loire.

A fifth-generation growers' family affair run by the brothers Saget, expanded since 1976 into a négociant business. They now sell 4 million bottles of Loire wines annually and control nearly 450 acres of vines, encompassing domaines in ACs Touraine-Mesland, Touraine-Amboise, Montlouis, Anjou and Coteaux du Layon. [not verified] Their technique is long cool fermentation with minimum disturbance of the wine and no malolactic fermentation to reduce the high natural fruity acidity.

Château de Tracy

58150 Pouilly-sur-Loire.

The family of the Comte d'Estutt d'Assay has owned the Château, on the Loire just downstream from Pouilly, since the 16th century. Sixty acres produce Pouilly-Fumé by traditional methods; a further 10 will come onstream in 1999.

Caves de Pouilly sur Loire

58150 Pouilly-sur-Loire.

The cooperative controls 370 acres of the Pouilly zone, vinifying more than 20% of the output of the two appellations. The wines are solid and respectable and the Pouilly-Fumé Vieilles Vignes Tinelum is a bit more than that. The cooperative also produces VDQS Coteaux du Giennois.

MINOR REGIONS

The success of Sancerre and Pouilly has encouraged what were dwindling outposts of vineyards in less favoured situations to the west of the Loire to expand their plantings. The names of Menetou-Salon, Quincy and Reuilly are now accepted as Sancerre substitutes at slightly lower prices (but longer odds against a fine ripe bottle). Three other regions of the upper Loire have now gained VDQS status: Coteaux du Giennois, the tiny Châteaumeillant (good for its rosé) and Vins de l'Orléannais.

Much higher up the river where it cuts through the Massif Central several scattered vineyard areas relate less to the Loire than to southern Burgundy and the Rhône. The most famous is St-Pourçain-sur-Sioule, once a monastic vineyard. Its wine is almost all consumed today to mitigate the effects of treatment at the spa of Vichy – but it is hard to see how it could ever have had more than a local following. Price remains the main thing in favour of the remaining areas of the heights of the Loire, but the quality is improving. The Côtes Roannaises (now AC) and the VDQS Côtes de Forez and the Côtes d'Auvergne grow the right grapes for quality – Gamay, Chardonnay, some Pinot Noir and Syrah.

REUILLY PRODUCERS

Claude Lafond Le Bois St-Denis, 36260 Reuilly. An energetic young grower, Lafond works 62 acres and makes some of the best wine in the appellation, including a dry white Clos des Messieurs, a dry rosé La Grande Pièce, and a light Pinot Noir called Les Grandes Vignes.

MENETOU-SALON PRODUCERS

Domaine de Chatenoy 18110 St-Martin d'Auxigny. The ancestors of Bernard Clément have owned this estate since 1560. 75 acres produce 37,500 cases of red, white and rosé Menetou-Salon. Despite their freshness, his wines sometimes reach 13° of alcohol. He recommends them as apéritifs as well as table wines.

Domaine Henry Pellé 18220 Morogues. A family winery with 74 acres of vines producing vigorous whites and pleasant light reds. The top white *cuvée* is Les Blanchais, made from old vines. Morogues, which abuts the Sancerre zone, is the only commune that may attach its name to that of Menetou-Salon on the label.

QUINCY PRODUCERS

Domaine Mardon 18120 Quincy. A good family winery with 32 acres producing brisk whites – among the best in the appellation.

COTEAUX DU GIENNOIS

Alain Paulat 58200 Villemoison St-Père. Alain Paulat is a passionate young grower with 12 acres of vines cultivated organically. He produces toothsome light reds from Gamay and Pinot Noir.

VIN DE L'ORLEANAIS

Clos Saint-Fiacre 45370 Mareau-aux-Près. A family winery with 42 acres of vines producing engaging light reds from Pinot Meunier and Pinot Noir as well as light Chardonnays and somewhat vegetal Cabernets.

CHÂTEAUMEILLANT

Maurice & Patrick Lanoix 18370 Châteaumeillant. Father (Maurice) and son (Patrick) work 47 acres, producing pleasant reds and rosés (predominantly Gamay) under two labels, Domaine du Feuillat (Maurice's wines) and Cellier du Chêne Combeau (Patrick's).

CÔTES D'AUVERGNE

Cave St Verny 68960 Veyre-Monton. Founded in 1950 as a cooperative, the Cave was purchased in 1991 by Limagrain, Europe's largest seed specialist. It produces nearly half the wine in the appellation in ultra-modern cellars, turning out clean whites, rosés (those from Corent are particularly noteworthy) and light reds based on Gamay. The deluxe bottling is called Première Cuvée.

CÔTES DU FOREZ

Les Vignerons Foreziens Trelins, 42130 Boen. The Cave controls 494 acres, produces 98% of VDQS Côtes du Forez and 60% of the Vins de Pays d'Urfe. The former is Gamay; the latter predominantly Chardonnay.

CÔTES ROANNAISES

Alain Demon 42820 Ambierle. From 10 acres on the steep slopes above the Loire, Demon produces silky characterful Gamays. His Réserve is made from 50- to 100-year-old vines.

Paul Lapandéry & Fils 42370 St-Haon-le-Vieux. A family winery with a 20-acre vineyard pitched at a vertiginous 72° angle. Lapandéry's highly personalized light reds are based on very low yields and very long barrel age.

ST-POURÇAIN

Union des Vignerons 03500 St-Pourçain-sur-Sioule. The cooperative (founded 1952) dominates this once famous 'central' vineyard, formerly a monastic stronghold. One hundred and sixty members farm 750 acres of Sauvignon, Sacy, Aligoté, Chardonnay and Tresallier whites and Pinot Noir and Gamay reds. It produces up to 65% of the appellation's wine or an annual 165,000 cases. The coop has a number of special bottlings, including its popular Ficelle, an easy-drinking Gamay, Réserve Spéciale (white and red), as well as reds and whites from two estates, Domaine de Chinière and Domaine de la Croix d'Or.

CHAMPAGNE

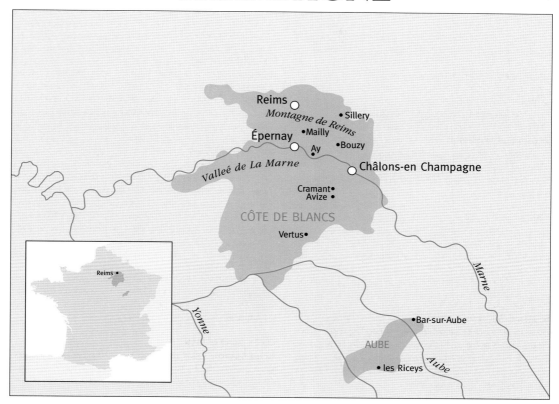

Champagne is the wine grown in the northernmost vineyards of France. The champagne method (or traditional method, as Brussels insists that we now call it) is something that is done to the wine to make it sparkle – and can be done to any wine. Other sparkling-winemakers would like us to believe that the method is all that matters. What really matters is the wine. It was one of the best in France long before the method was invented. The difference between the best champagne and the merely good is almost entirely a matter of the choice and treatment of grapes, their variety, their ripeness, their handling and the soil that bears them. Outside France, the champagne market is largely controlled by the *grandes marques*, the twenty or so great firms with the widest distribution. These great merchants actually own only about 14% of the vineyards and have to rely on 15,500 small farmers to provide them with grapes. Many growers in Champagne also sell their crop to cooperatives, though some – the *récoltants-manipulants* – make small amounts of champagne of their own. The best of these champagne growers are described on pages 171–74. Any merchant buying champagne can think up a name (a 'Buyer's Own Brand') and print a label. So there is no limit to the number of brands. In itself this lends strength to the *grandes marques* with the best-known names which are often bought simply as safe bets. But reputation and wealth also allow them to buy the best materials, employ the best staff and stock their wine longest. (Time is vital to develop the flavours.) The great houses push to the limit the polishing and perfecting of an agricultural product.

The 'method' began 200 years ago with the genius of a Benedictine monk, Dom Pérignon of Hautvillers, apparently the first man to 'design' a wine by blending the qualities of different grapes from different varieties and vineyards to make a whole greater, more subtle, more satisfying than any of its parts. This blend, the *cuvée*, is traditionally the secret patent of each maker, though during the 1990s in response to ever-growing consumer curiosity about the exact composition of individual champagne blends, the cellarmasters of Reims and Epernay have often invited the wine trade and press to observe the blending process first-hand. The best blends are astonishingly complex, with as many as 30 or 40 ingredient wines of different origins and ages, selected by nose and palate alone. Houses with their own vineyards tend to stress the character of the grapes they grow themselves: the heavier Pinot Noir of the Montagne de Reims or the lighter Chardonnay of the Côte des Blancs – each village is subtly different. Very few have enough to supply their own needs. Prices are fixed by a percentage system (*see* page 172).

It was not Dom Pérignon, but his contemporaries who discovered how to make their wine sparkling by a second fermentation in a tightly corked bottle – a process with dangers and complications that took another century to master completely. The principle of making champagne is outlined diagramatically on page 31. The sparkle is caused by the large amounts of carbon dioxide dissolved in the wine. The 'mousse' or froth in the glass is only part of it –

you swallow the greater part. Carbon dioxide is instantly absorbed by the stomach wall. Once in the bloodstream it accelerates the circulation, and with it the movement of the alcohol to the brain. This is where champagne gets its reputation as the wine of wit and the natural choice for celebration. Other sparkling wines made by the same method can justifiably claim to have the same effect. But not the same taste.

The Principal Champagne Houses

Besserat de Bellefon

51200 Epernay. Founded 1843. Owned by Marne et Champagne since 1992. Visits: appt. only. NV: Cuvée Blanc de Blancs, Brut, Cuvée des Moines Blanc and Rosé Vintage: Brut Intégral, Cuvée des Moines Blanc and Rosé.

A family business until 1959, the firm has had several corporate owners since then, the most recent being the anonymous giant, Marne et Champagne. The Besserat house style is for very fine light wines much appreciated in top French restaurants. The Chardonnay- led Cuvée des Moines Blanc with its gentle sparkle and creamy flavour makes a good apéritif, while the Cuvée des Moines Rosé has great finesse. France takes 80% of its total sales of 2.2m. bottles a year.

Billecart-Salmon

51160 Mareuil-sur-Ay. Founded 1818. Owners: the Roland-Billecart family. Visits: appt only. NV: Brut Réserve, Brut Rosé. Vintages: Cuvée Nicolas-françois Billecart, Blanc de Blancs, Cuvée Elisabeth Salmon Rosé Prestige: Grande Cuvée.

A small highly respected *grande marque*, this family firm is

currently producing exquisite champagnes of the highest class. Always respectful of the traditional composition of its *cuvées*, Billecart nonetheless uses very modern vinification techniques that involve 'cold settling' of the must (pressed grape juice) and long cool fermentations. the result is wine of floral aromas and delicate flavours that belie its ability to live a long distinguished life: a 1959 tasted in 1996 was still as fresh as a daisy. The Brut Réserve is quite exceptional; although dominated by the two Pinots, its Chardonnay content has been increased recently (35%) giving an extra dimension of finesse and elegance. The subtle pale-salmon coloured Rosé is Billecart's flagship wine in the United States. Outstanding vintage wines have a perfect balance of freshness and maturity, especially the late-disgorged Grande Cuvée.

J. Bollinger

51160 Aÿ. Founded 1829. Associated Companies: Langlois-Château (Loire), Joseph Drouhin (Burgundy), Petaluma (Australia). Visits: appt only. NV: Special Cuvée Brut Vintage: Grande Année Brut and Rosé, Traditional R., Vieilles Vignes Françaises. Still wines: Red, Aÿ, Côte aux Enfants.

Choosing champagne

The knowledge essential for buying champagne to your own taste is the style and standing of the house and the range of its wines. Other relevant points included in the entries on these pages are the ownership and date of foundation, whether you may visit the cellars, where most of the grapes come from, the annual sales and size of stock and the principal markets of the house. To some extent you may deduce style and quality from the sources of grapes and their standing in the percentage table on *page 172*, in conjunction with the average age of the wine (the stocks divided by the annual sales).

Most houses offer wines in the following categories:

Non-vintage (NV). A *cuvée* maintained, as near as possible, to exactly the same standard year after year: usually fairly young. The standard gauge of the 'house style'.

Vintage. Best-quality wine of a vintage whose intrinsic quality is considered too good to be hidden in a non-vintage *cuvée*. Normally aged longer on the yeast than non-vintage; more full-bodied and tasty, with the potential to improve for several more years.

Rosé. A small quantity of still red wine from one of the Pinot Noir villages (often Aÿ or Bouzy) is blended with still white wine, this blend undergoes a second fermentation, which creates the bubbles. In many cases entrancingly fruity and fine and one of the house's best *cuvées*.

Blanc de Blancs. A *cuvée* of white (Chardonnay) grapes only, with great grace and less 'weight' than traditional champagne.

Blanc de Noirs. A *cuvée* of black grapes only, sometimes faintly pink or 'gris' and invariably rich and flavoury.

Cuvée de Prestige (under many names). A super-champagne on the hang-the-expense principle. Moët's Dom Pérignon was the first; now most houses have one. Fabulously good though most of them are, there is a strong argument for two bottles of non-vintage for the price of one *cuvée* de prestige.

Crémant. The old name for a half-pressure champagne, preferred by some people who find a normal one too gassy – particularly with food. Since 1994 the houses have been forbidden to use the word on the front label.

Coteaux Champenois. Still white or red wine of the Champagne vineyards, made in limited quantities when supplies of grape allow. Naturally high in acidity but can be exquisitely fine.

Brut, Extra Dry, etc. What little consistency there is about these indications of sweetness or otherwise is shown on page *169*.

One of the 'greats' of Champagne, a traditionalist house making muscular wine with body, length, depth and every other dimension. Eighty percent of the harvest is barrel-fermented and wines are kept on their yeast as long as possible; in the case of RD about 10 years, giving extra breadth of flavour. A tiny patch of ungrafted pre-phylloxera Pinot Noir in Aÿ and Bouzy gives Vieilles Vignes Françaises: very rare, expensive 'combining the power of the New World with the elegance of the Old', in the words of Guy Bizot, great nephew of Madame Lily Bollinger. Sixty percent of grapes from Bollinger's own 346 acres, average rating 97% on the Echelle des Crus (q.v.). Remainder bought from Côte des Blancs and Verteuil, Marne Valley. Production: 1.5m. bottles. Exports, often by restricted quota, make up 80% of sales. The UK is the largest market. Ghislain de Mongolfier, the current head of the firm, is the great-great-grandson of the founder.

Deutz

51160 Aÿ. Founded 1838. Majority shareholding in company owned by Louis Roederer. Subsidiary and associated companies: Delas (Rhône), L'Aulée (Loire), Pressoir Deutz (California), Deutz (New Zealand). NV: Brut Classic, Kosher Brut Vintages: Brut, Blanc de Blancs, Rosé Prestige: Cuvée William Deutz Brut and Rosé.

Like many great Champagne firms, this house was founded by German immigrants. Although the Lallier-Deutz family are still involved in the business, a stake of 63% was acquired by Louis Roederer in 1993. The Roederer investment shows to good effect in the new Brut Classic, a first-rate non vintage *cuvée*, creamy, rich yet decidedly dry in the Deutz tradition. The vintage-dated *blanc de blancs* made from *grand cru* grapes is exquisite, so is the Cuvée William Deutz, a prestige blend of great vinous subtlety. A founder member of the *grandes marques* of Champagne.

Delamotte

51190 Le Mesnil-sur-Oger. Founded 1760. Owner: Laurent-Perrier. Visits: appt only. NV: Brut, Blanc de Blancs, Rosé Brut Vintage: Blanc de Blancs Prestige: Nicolas Louis Delamotte.

The sixth-oldest champagne house with close links to the Lanson and de Nonancourt families. Since Laurent-Perrier's purchase of Salon (q.v.) in 1989, the two firms, housed in adjacent 18th-century premises, have been managed by Bertrand de Fleurian. The firm owns 12 acres of grand cru Chardonnay in Le Mesnil which, though producing only about 25% of the company's needs, certainly shapes the Chardonnay-led style of the champagnes; fresh, aromatic, long-lived, they offer a very good quality to price ratio. The vintage-dated Blanc de Blancs is the most interesting: rich, peach-like and especially successful in the great 1990 vintage.

Drappier

10200 Urville. Founded 1802. Owners: the Drappier family. Visits: appt only. NV: Carte d'Or Brut, Extra Dry, Brut Zéro, Val des Demoiselles, Rosé, Signature Blanc de Blancs Vintage: Brut Millésimé Prestige: Grande Sendrée.

Vignerons in the Barsuraubois (Aube) since the time of Napoleon a dynamic merchant-grower house producing hedonistic champagne of great character which are now appreciated around the world from Tokyo to Tamworth. The heart of the business is the 86-acre domaine planted mainly with Pinot Noir on the southern limestone slopes of Urville. Meticulous winemaking in a pristine *cuverie* above cool 12th-century Cisterian cellars results in some memorable bottles; the Carte d'Or Brut suffused with aromas and flavours of red fruits (the Drappier style); the impressive Brut Zéro powerful, uncompromising, bone-dry but in no way astringent or bitter; the prestige Grande Sendrée mouthfilling, magnificent, very Pinot but with just the right amount of Chardonnay to add an extra touch of definition and refinement.

Duval-Leroy

51130 Vertus. Founded 1859. Owners: the Duval family. Visits: appt only. NV: Fleur de Champagne Vintage: Fleur de Champagne, Blanc de Blancs Prestige: Cuvée des Roys.

A quality-conscious but relatively little known family firm which saw a rapid expansion of turnover after 1945 and the acquisition of over 320 acres of choice Chardonnay vineyards mainly on the Côte des Blancs. Until recently much of the company's export business was in supplying 'Buyer's Own Brand' champagnes to merchants in Britain, Belgium and Germany. But in the late 1990s the marketing strategy is to establish the Duval-Leroy brand on world markets; and under the leadership of the current head of the company, Carol Duval, a formidably strong-willed widow, that ambition should become reality by the early years of the 21st century. The style of the champagne is subtle, fresh, aromatic and well illustrated by the Chardonnay-dominated Fleur de Champagne. The superb *blanc de blancs* is now a vintage wine, the classic 1990 a model of its kind. These champagnes are exceptional value for money.

Gosset

51160 Aÿ. Founded 1584. Owner: Frapin Cognac. Visits: appt only. NV: Excellence, Grande Réserve Vintage: Grand Millésime Brut, Grand Millésime Rosé Prestige: Gosset Celebris. Still wine: Coteaux Champenois Bouzy Rouge.

Gosset has good claim to being the oldest wine house in the Marne though Ruinart (q.v.) was the first to make sparkling champagne on a serious scale. After 410 years of Gosset ownership, control of the firm passed to the quality-conscious Cointreau family of Frapin Cognac in 1994. The new Brut Excellence is a brisk, racy wine dominated by Chardonnay (61%) and ideal as an apéritif. The real stars of the range are the floral, rich and complex Grande Réserve, a classic blend of Pinot and Chardonnay from three great years, and the lustrous vintage-dated Rosé, full, velvet-smooth, yet very elegant. Gosset champagnes are built to last, the malolactic fermentation deliberately avoided to ensure a long life.

Alfred Gratien

51201 Epernay. Founded 1867. Owners: the Seydoux family of Gratien & Meyer (Saumur). Visits: appt only. NV: Brut Vintage: Brut Prestige: Cuvée Paradis.

Small traditionalist house making excellent very dry wines

vinified in small barrels; the malolactic fermentation is entirely avoided to ensure maximum vitality and long life in the finished champagnes. The vintage wines have an unusually high Chardonnay content, though *chef de caves* Jean-Pierre Jaeger favours a significant amount of Pinot Meunier in the blends in order to add notes of spices and luxuriant fruit. The prestige Cuvée Paradis ranks among the very greatest champagnes, at once elegant and exotic. The Wine Society, Britain's most prestigious mail-order wine business, is Gratien's oldest and most important customer.

Charles Heidsieck

51100 Reims. Founded in 1851. Owner: Remy-Martin. Visits: appt only. NV: Brut Réserve Vintage: Brut Millésimé, Rosé Millésimé Prestige: Blanc des Millénaires.

The original Charles Heidsieck was the 'Champagne Charlie' of the song, who made a fortune in the USA but almost lost it in the Civil War. In 1985 the Rémy-Martin group, which already owned Krug (q.v.), bought the company. Under the new ownership, the quality of the wines has improved greatly, especially the Brut Réserve. The outstanding character of this flagship *cuvée* owes everything to natural vinification, technical treatments of the wine being kept to a minimum, and to the complexity of the blend which is composed of 300 components with at least 40% reserve wines. Honeyed, fleshy, yet with a discreet vinosity, this is a champagne par excellence to accompany fine cuisine. The prestige Blanc des Millénaires (great 1983 and 1989) is a magnificent Blanc de Blancs, a high wire-act of sharply defined mature Chardonnay flavours and exotic fruitiness.

Henriot

51066 Reims. Founded 1808. Once again in family ownership since 1994. Associated company: Bouchard Père et Fils. Visits: appt only. NV: Brut Souverain, Blanc de Blancs Vintage: Brut Millésimé, Rose Millésimé Prestige: Cuvée des Enchanteleurs.

Remois merchants and wine growers since the 17th century, the Henriots are as Champenois as the windmill of Verzenay. In 1994, Joseph Henriot took the firm back into family ownership. The price of independence from the LVMH group was the loss of title to the family's very fine 270-acre vineyards located mainly on the Côte des Blancs, though grapes are still sourced from these exceptional sites on a long-lease basis.

Henriot champagnes are very dry, pure-flavoured and based exclusively on Pinot Noir and Chardonnay, the latter seemingly if not actually dominant. The *blanc de blancs* is a model of incisive but persistent Chardonnay flavours. The Cuvée des Enchanteleurs is a prestige *cuvée* that ages beautifully; the remarkable 1985 will not reach its peak before the year 2000. In 1995 Joseph Henriot bought the Burgundy house of Bouchard Père et Fils (q.v.).

Jacquesson

51530 Dizy. Founded 1798. Owners: the Chiquet family. Visits: appt only. NV: Brut Perfection, Rosé Vintage: Blanc de Blancs Prestige: Signature Brut, Signature Rosé, Cuvée Dégorgement tardif.

Johann Joseph Krug, founder of the *nec plus ultra* of champagne houses, first learned the art of blending at Jacquesson and this low-key firm is still one of the best exponents of classic champagne-making. Subtly cask-aged reserve wines significantly contribute to the supple, rich yet structured housestyle of the finished champagnes. The Chiquet family's 76 acres of 95%-rated vineyards at Dizy, Aÿ, Hautvillers and Avize account for more than half their requirements. The Perfection Brut is a 70:30 mix of black grapes and Chardonnay, the wine of lovely Welsh gold colour, the flavour soft, creamy yet long in the mouth. The outstanding *blanc de blancs*, now a vintage wine, is a pure Avize from the family vineyards. the 100% wood-fermented Signature prestige *cuvées*, both white and rosé, are fascinating champagnes of multi-layered complexity.

Krug

5 rue Coquebert 51100 Reims. Founded 1843. Rémy Martin, Cognac, own majority of this private company. Visits: appt only. Multi-Vintage: Grande Cuvée, Rosé. The vintage is made in very small quantities and is not generally released until it is 9 years old. Single-vineyard vintage: Clos du Mesnil.

The house of Kurg sees itself as something apart from other champagnes, and indeed its wines are quite unlike any other. All are fermented in small oak barrels and then aged on the cork for an uncommonly long time before sale. The Grande Cuvée has a high proportion of Chardonnay brilliantly assembled with Pinot Noir and Pinot Meunier into a masterly blend composed of 7 to 10 vintages and 20 to 25 different growths; it has good claim to be among the finest of all champagnes, very dry, elusively fruity, gentle yet authoritative at the same time. The Krug Rosé, which was first introduced in 1983, is another masterpiece of fruit and savour and is intended to accompany the finest culinary creations. The vintage wines tend to be more powerful and need long ageing, sometimes 15, 20, even 25 years to reach their peak. This is especially true of the single-vineyard vintage Clos du Mesnil, a pure Chardonnay champagne, austere when young but with the potential to taste like a Corton Charlemagne with bubbles after a quarter of a century in bottle.

Lanson

12 boulevard Lundy 51100 Reims. Founded 1760. Owned since 1991 by consortium led by Marne et Champagne. Visits: appt only. NV: Black Label Brut, Demi-Sec, Rosé Vintage: Millésime Brut, Blanc de Blancs Prestige: Noble Cuvée.

Prospects looked bleak in 1991 when Lanson lost all 500-plus acres of its magnificent vineyards as part of the terms of sale to the present owners. Initial misgivings now seem to have been ill-founded, for Lanson's long-serving *chef de caves*, the meticulous Jean-Paul Gandon, still makes the extremely popular Black Label as he has always done: the vivid tingling style is shaped by a lot of Pinot Noir (50%) in the blend and the avoidance of any malolactic fermentation, thus increasing the fruity character of the wine. The well-aged Rosé is aromatic and fine-drawn, the *demi-sec* less cloying than many. Lanson vintage, dominated by Pinot Noir, is broad-shouldered, deep in flavour. Chardonnay

Moët & Chandon

Profile of a Great Champagne House

A bottle of Moët is uncorked somewhere in the world every two seconds. For such a vast champagne house, producing 21m. bottles a year, the quality of the wines is very high owing to the technical expertise of the cellar management and the house's financial muscle in having first call on the best grapes. Moët also owns the biggest vineyard holdings of any champagne firm, currently some 1,350 acres are in production. Yet these vineyards meet only about a fifth of the house's needs, so the remaining grapes for its *cuvées* come from a huge network of growers in all the Champagne regions. The provenances of the grapes are chosen less for their official rating on the *échelle des crus* but rather for the taste characteristics they can contribute to the Moët house style which is elegant, light, and easy to drink. The vintage wines have an extra dimension of creaminess, touched with a lingering vinosity.

From its early days, Moët has been a story of grit, courage, and high ambition. Jean-Rémy Moët, the grandson of the founder, seriously established the business in the early 19th century through his friendship with Napoleon: Jean-Rémy built the Trianon, twin white pavilions with an enchanting garden and orangery, as a guest house for Napoleon on his marches to and from the battlefields of eastern Europe. Nowadays, the Trianon is mainly used to entertain important customers and guests from the world of business, politics, the arts, or in fact anyone sufficiently influential to spread the word about the world's best-known champagne.

Jean-Rémy Moët personified the essential Champenois talent of turning disaster into a commercial opportunity. The story goes that when the murderous Russian Cossacks occupied Reims and Epernay at the time of Waterloo, he urged them to take the wine on the good commercial principle that they would be back. And this is what happened. Russia soon became one of the best export markets for Moët's champagnes.

Since 1832, the firm has been known as Moët & Chandon, thus incorporating the name of Jean Rémy's son-in-law, Pierre Gabriel Chandon de Briailles. The mid-19th century was a golden age for the house. The family became the most important vineyard owners in Champagne, sales boomed and by 1900 Moët & Chandon had a 16 percent share of the burgeoning export market. The firm then went into decline until it was revitalized by Comte Robert de Vogüé in the early 1930s.

Not a man to be daunted by the effects of the Great Depression, de Vogüé cajoled his fellow directors into relaunching a defunct *marque* called Dom Pérignon as a luxury brand for export markets. It was first released in England in 1935 and in New York the following year. Dom Pérignon has been the aspirational champagne in the United States ever since. After the Second World War, de Vogüé swiftly expanded the firm's sales. By 1962, Moët became the first Champagne house to be quoted on the French Bourse. A period of huge growth followed, with the firm's purchase of Ruinart (1963), Mercier (1970) and the Christian Dior perfume house (1971). Diversification into other sparking-wine ventures was marked by the acquisition of 1285 acres of vines in California in 1973 and nearly 200 in Brazil the following year. Most recently, excellent sparkling wine subsidiaries have been launched in Australia and Spain.

Since at least the mid-1980s, Moët has used its vast resources to lead research into the new techniques of improving champagne-making, generously sharing the results with the whole industry. An impressive research project at Moët has been the study of the bubbles (mousse) in champagne. Working in partnership with Heineken, the Dutch lager company, they have come up with a computerized camera, which, shot by shot, shows the process of the mousse, their aim being to make it more stable. Another impressive project has been the study of ageing champagne on the yeasts. Autolysis (the decomposing of the yeast sediments) is essential in developing the flavour style of champagne and makes it unique, adding extra complexity to the wine. Moët now knows that Pinot Noir and Chardonnay combine well with that autolytic character because these grape varieties are subtle enough to leave room for the complex yeast-aged taste to develop in the finished champagne.

The consumer should be very thankful that the world's largest champagne firm treats wine as wine and not as a commodity where the packaging is more important than the product.

(70%) is the motor of the Noble Cuvée, floral, supremely elegant but with a firm durable structure, making it one of the most long-lived champagnes.

Laurent-Perrier

51150 Tours-sur-Marne. Founded 1812. Majority shares owned by the de Nonancourt family. Close links with Antonin Rodet in Burgundy, and a joint venture in California. Visits: during working hours. NV: Brut, Ultra Brut, Rosé Brut Vintage: Brut Millésimé Prestige: Grand Siècle, Grand Siècle Exceptionnellement Millésimé, Grand Siècle Alexandra Brut Rosé. Still wines: Blanc de Blancs de Chardonnay, red Pinot Franc.

Laurent-Perrier non-vintage Brut is now a consistent champagne, fresh, racy, with a Chablis-like mineral character. Ultra Brut is a completely dry, sugarless wine but with no hint of the hairshirt as it is always made from grapes of a ripe year. The immensely successful Rosé is made the hard way – by putting the Pinot Noir grape skins in contact with the juice to obtain the right colour. The real triumph of the house, though, is the Cuvée Grand Siècle. Sumptuous, stylish and long-maturing, it is a blend of three vintages, though it is occasionally sold with a vintage label in exceptional years, for example the Exceptionnellement Millésimé 1985. Grapes come from nearly 2,000 acres, either owned or under long-term contract, in the best sites of the Montagne de Reims, the Côte des Blancs and the Marne Valley; the average rating is 96%. Under the direction of Bernard de Nonancourt, now semi-retired, the company rose from ninety-eighth position in 1948 to become one of the top four in the 1990s.

Mercier

75 avenue de Champagne, 51333 Epernay. Founded 1858, now owned by LVMH (Moët) group. Visits: at regular hours. NV: Brut, Rosé, Demi-Sec. Vintage: Brut Millésimé.

Mercier, like the rest of the Moët group, has the virtue of size: consistency of supply meaning reliability. The grapes come either from the firm's own 555 acres of vineyards, mainly in the Marne Valley, or under contracts with growers going back to 1945. The stress is on dry Brut champagne in a soft black grapes style. The Rosé Brut had a good balance of fruit and acidity; the excellent Demi-Sec is clean and incisive thanks to the dominant Chardonnay (55%). Sales totalled 5.7m. bottles in 1996, chiefly in the French market.

Eugène Mercier, the founder, was the pacesetter in bringing champagne to ordinary French people during the late 19th century. For the Universal Exhibition held in Paris in 1889, he built a huge wine barrel; it took a team of 24 oxen three weeks to tow the cask to the capital. But his most enduring memorial is the labyrinth of cellars beneath the crest of the hill on Epernay's Avenue de Champagne – 10 miles long and connected by miniature electric train.

Moët & Chandon

20 avenue de Champagne, 51333 Epernay. Founded 1743. Part of the LVMH group. Associated companies: Mercier, Ruinart, Domaine Chandon in California, Australia, Spain, Argentina and Brazil. Annual sales average 21m. bottles in 154 countries. Visits:

during regular hours. NV: Brut Impérial, Brut Premier Cru, Rosé (from 1998). Vintage: Brut Millésimé, Rosé Millésimé. Prestige: Dom Pérignon Blanc and Rosé.

Moët's various *cuvées* maintain a style that is elegant, light and easy to appreciate but also rounds out nicely with age. Very wide sources of supply ensure consistency of the huge quantities of Brut Impérial NV, which often scores high in competitive tastings for polish and balance. The Brut Premier Cru, launched in 1996, is sourced from better-class grapes, the bottle carrying a back label explaining how the wine is made. A Brut Imperial Moët, a true Champenois blend of the three principal grapes, is always a good representative of the character of each vintage yet with that supple creamy style that runs through the whole Moët range.

Exceptional winemaking by Richard Geoffroy, a former medical doctor, means that Dom Pérignon has been as fine as its reputation in such classic recent vintages as 1982, '85 and '88, distinctly luxurious and creamy. The Dom Pérignon Rosé, peach-coloured, subtle, nuancé, is outstanding.

The Moët group owns vineyards in 10 out of 17 Grand Cru vineyards. Total holding is 1351 acres, the largest of any champagne house. Grapes from these vineyards supply Ruinart (q.v.) as well as Moët. Annual sales average 21m. bottles in 154 countries. (*See* page 167.)

Mumm

29 rue du Champs de Mars, 51000 Reims. Founded 1827. Public company. Majority shareholder, Seagrams. Mumm owns Perrier-Jouët (q.v.) but sold Heidsieck Monopole to Vranken in 1996. Associated company: Dom. Mumm, Napa, California. Visits: at regular hours. NV: Première Cuvée, Chardonnay Réserve Privée, Rosé Première Cuvée, Cordon Rouge, Cordon Vert (*demi-sec*). Vintage: Cordon Rouge, Cordon Rosé, Mumm de Cramant, Blanc de Blancs. Prestige: René Lalou, Grand Cordon, Grand Cordon Rosé.

It is hard to be categoric about the overall quality and style of Mumm champagnes as the range is very diverse. The wines made from a preponderance of Pinot Noir are mainly solid and straightforward. Cordon Rouge non-vintage has recently been bland, lacking a little character. The vintage Rosé and lightly sparkling Mumm de Cramant, made from Chardonnay grapes of a single year from the village of Cramant, are excellent. René Lalou is a very presentable top *cuvée* in a full-bodied style, though the Chardonnay-led Grand Cordon, first introduced in the 1985 vintage, is the star: subtle, racy.

Grapes come from 800 acres of owned vineyards, producing 20% of the firm's needs, and on contract from 35–45 different vineyards according to the year. Mumm's own holdings are spread across the region, with the biggest concentrations in Mailly, Ambonnay, Bouzy, Vaudemanges, Avenay, Aÿ, Avize and Cramant. Annual production is about 9m. bottles. North America takes 36% of exports. Mumm is a leader of viticultural research in Champagne.

Bruno Paillard

Avenue de Champagne, 51100 Reims. Founded 1981. Privately owned by the Paillard family. Visits: appt. only. Associated company: Chanoine Frères. NV: Première Cuvée Brut, Chardonnay Réserve Privée, Rosé Première Cuvée. Vintage: Brut Millésimé.

The youngest classic champagne house, founded in 1981 by the perfectionist Monsieur Paillard, a broker with deep roots in the industry. His wines are consistent models of elegance and refinement, very dry, almost austere, and built to last. The first-rate Première Cuvée is now partially fermented in wood, the Chardonnay Réserve Privée made by the old method for *crémant* (lightly sparkling champagne). Paillard vintage wines are beautifully labelled, illustrated by prominent artists and always mention the date of disgorging. The wines are as exceptional as the packaging.

Sales are around 300,000 bottles a year, 80% going to the USA, Britain, Belgium and Switzerland.

Joseph Perrier

69 avenue de Paris, 51000 Châlons-en-Champagne. Founded 1825. Part family owned, the other shares now taken by Laurent-Perrier. Visits: appt. only. NV: Cuvée Royale, Brut Blanc de Blancs, Cuvée Royale Rosé. Vintage: Cuvée Royale Brut Millésimé. Prestige: Cuvée Joséphine.

With the injection of capital by Laurent-Perrier in 1995, the stylish fruit-laden wines of this family-owned Châlons house go from strength to strength. The Cuvée Royale non-vintage is a benchmark of succulent ripe Pinots (both Noir and Meunier) brilliantly blended with Chardonnay – this champagne offering one of the best ratios of quality to price available. The Chardonnay-led prestige Cuvée Joséphine is usually a memorable bottle.

One-third of grapes come from their 50 acres at Cumières, Damery, Hautvillers and Verneuil. Sales around 650,000 bottles a year with three years' stock for the NV. Vintage wines are not released until they are seven or eight years old. The main export markets are Belgium, Britain and Germany.

The house supplied Queen Victoria and Edward VII and today concentrates on restricted quantities, high quality, and a traditional approach.

Perrier-Jouët

26 avenue de Champagne, 51200 Epernay. Founded 1811. Owned by Mumm (qv). Visits: appt. only. NV: Grand Brut Vintage: Brut, Rosé Prestige: Blason de France Blanc & Rosé, Belle Epoque Blanc & Rosé.

Long respected for first-class, very fresh and crisp but by no means light non-vintage and luxury *cuvées* with plenty of flavour. Blason de France is their rarest wine, complex and age-worthy. The much better-known Belle Epoque, in its flower-painted bottle, is the flagship of the house: a prestige *cuvée* of consistently rich and harmonious style (the 1985 was one of the greatest wines of a very great year).

PJ (as it is fondly known) owns 266 acres of choice vineyards, with superb Chardonnay sites in Cramant and Avize. It is these that shape the hazelnut, creamy flavours of the excellent vintage wines. Grapes also come from 30 other *crus*. Sales average 2.85 m. bottles from stocks of at least 8m. 80% of the production is exported, 20% to the USA.

Piper-Heidsieck

51 boulevard Henry-Vasnier, 51100 Reims. Founded 1785. Owned since 1989 by Rémy Martin. Visits: open. NV: Brut Vintage: Brut Millésimé, Rosé Prestige: Brut Sauvage, Champagne Rare.

These well-regarded, very dry wines have changed a little in style since the firm was bought by Rémy Martin in 1989. Although still very fresh, they now have an extra dimension of floweriness on the nose and fruitiness on the palate; the Piper Rosé is an exuberant expression of youthful Pinot Noir

Serving and enjoying champagne

When. For celebrations any time, as an apéritif, very occasionally with light meals, with dessert (sweet 'demi-sec' only), in emergencies, as a tonic.

How. At 45°–50°F/7°–10°C, colder for inexpensive champagne, up to 54°F/13°C for very fine mature ones. In a tall, clear glass, not a broad, shallow one. To preserve the bubbles, pour slowly into a slightly tilted glass.

How much. Allow half a bottle (three glasses) per head for an all-champagne party. Allow half as much when it is served as an apéritif before another wine.

What to look for. Plenty of pressure behind the cork, total clarity, abundance of fine bubbles lasting indefinitely, powerful but clean flavour and finish, and balance – not mouth-puckeringly dry or acid, not cloyingly sweet. Above all it should be moreish. House styles will become apparent with experience.

Who makes champagne?

In 1970 there were 2,900 growers making their own champagne. By 1997 that figure had risen, after fluctuations, to 4,100.The proportion of sales represented by grower-producers and cooperatives rose from 25% in 1970 to 42%

in 1997. Most of this growth was within France, at first by direct sales and mail-order to private customers, more recently to high-quality fashionable restaurants. The *maisons* continue to dominate the export trade, though their share is being increasingly challenged by cooperatives and to a lesser extent by grower-producers, whose champagnes offer good value for money.

Dosage, dryness and sweetness

When champagne is disgorged the loss of the frozen plug of sediment needs making good to fill the bottle. At this stage the sweetness of the finished wine is adjusted by topping up (*dosage*) with a *'liqueur d'expédition'* of wine mixed with sugar and sometimes brandy. A few firms make a totally dry wine, topped up with wine only and known by names such as Brut Nature or Brut Intégral. The great majority have some sugar added. The following are the usual amounts (grams/litre) of sugar in the *dosage* for each style (although they vary from house to house): *Extra Brut*: 0g/l. bone dry. *Brut*: 1-15g/l. very dry. *Extra Dry*: 12-20g/l. dry. *Sec*: 17-35g/l. slightly sweet. *Demi-sec*: 33-50g/l. distinctly sweet. *Doux*: over 50g/l. very sweet.

yet it also ages well. Brut Sauvage is totally dry with no dosage, but there is no hint of asperity thanks to the ripeness of the grapes in the blend. The Chardonnay-led Champagne Rare is exceptional, with long citrus-like flavours and the potential to develop in bottle for up to 15 years.

A medium-sized *grande marque*, selling about 5m bottles a year, with 18m. bottles in stock. The United Kingdom, Italy and the USA are the main export markets. The firm used to own no vineyards but in 1994 bought 52 acres on the best slopes of the Montagne de Reims and Côte des Blancs as a start towards their vineyard strategy of greater control over the quality of the harvest. Piper-Heidsieck owns Piper-Sonoma in California and the linked consultancy Champagne Technologie has advised sparkling winemakers in India and the Americas.

Pol Roger

1 rue Henri Lelarge, 51206 Epernay. Founded 1849, still family-owned and run. Visits: appt. only. NV: White Foil, Sec, Demi-Sec. Vintage: Brut, Blanc de Chardonnay. Prestige: Sir Winston Churchill, Réserve Spéciale P.R.

Smallish *grande marque* consistently regarded among the best half-dozen and a personal favourite of mine for over 30 years. Outstandingly clean, floral and crisp NV; stylish long-lived vintage, one of the best roses and fragrant exquisite Blanc de Chardonnay. The Pinot-led Sir Winston Churchill is shamelessly sumptuous, exotically scented and satin-textured. The Réserve PR is supremely elegant.

Nearly half the grapes come from the firm's 200 acres, mainly in the Côte des Blancs and the Cubry Valley. Production is about 1.4m. bottles, stock 7m. bottles. 60% of sales are on export markets, the largest being Britain followed by Germany and Switzerland. The brand is particularly associated with Sir Winston Churchill who named one of his racing fillies after his friend, Odette Pol Roger.

Pommery

5 place du Général Gouraud, 51100 Reims. Founded 1836. Part of LVMH (Moët) group. Visits: at regular hours. NV: Brut Royal, Brut Rosé. Vintage: Brut, Rosé. Prestige: Louise Pommery, Flacons d'Exception.

The LVMH group acquired this well-known *grande marque* in 1990 and the firm's tradition for very fine and notably dry champagnes is now re-established with the Brut Royal, an elegant pure-flavoured wine of low *dosage*. Delicacy and refinement are the hall-mark of the vintage wines. Louise Pommery (since 1979) has been a revelation of Pommery quality: stylish, crisp, deeply winey and well structured.

Pommery's 758 acres of vineyards are magnificently sited in the best *crus* of the Montagne de Reims and the Côte des Blancs, with an average rating of over 99%. Pommery's cellars comprise 9 miles of Roman chalk-pits, some decorated with bas-reliefs. Production: 6.6m. bottles, with stocks of four years' supply. Exports take 73%, with Great Britain, Germany and Switzerland the largest markets.

Since 1996, mature vintage champagnes in magnums, the Flacons d'Exception, have been released in tiny quantities to connoisseurs. On receipt of the order, the wine is then disgorged of its deposit and delivered to the recipient's address within one month for optimal freshness in the finished champagne. (The 1979 is outstanding.)

Louis Roederer

21 boulevard Lundy, 51100 Reims. Founded 1776. Privately owned. Associated companies: Roederer Estate, California; Ramos Pinto, Portugal, Château de Pez (Bordeaux). Visits: appt. only. NV: Brut Premier, Rich, Demi-Sec, Carte Blanche (sweet). Vintage: Brut, Blanc de Blancs, Rosé. Prestige: Limited quantities of Cristal Brut, Cristal Rosé.

A very great family-owned Champagne house whose peerless reputation rests on its marvellous 444 acres of vineyards (supplying 70% of its needs), controlled sales (2.6m. bottles) and immaculate winemaking. The house style is notably smooth and mature, epitomized by the excellent full-bodied Brut Premier NV and the fabulous Cristal, one of the most luscious champagnes, racy but deeply flavoured. Recent vintages such as 1985, 1989 and 1990 are among the greatest Cristal ever released.

The firm's 1980s venture in Californian sparkling wine at Roederer Estate has been very successful, because of the chosen site in the cool Anderson Valley was a perfect one (the 1989 L'Ermitage *cuvée* is stunning). In the mid-1990s the company diversified into other winemaking ventures, acquiring both port-producers Ramos Pinto and Château de Pez in St-Estèphe.

Sales in France amount to 37%; the USA leads the export market with 20%. Stock: a high 12m. bottles, over four years' supply. Up to 1917 half the sales were in Russia, where Czar Alexander III demanded crystal (clear) bottles.

Ruinart

4 rue des Crayères, 51100 Reims. Founded 1729 – the oldest recorded champagne-making firm. Now owned by LVMH (Moët) group. Visits: appt. only. NV: R de Ruinart Brut, R de Ruinart Rosé. Vintage: R de Ruinart Brut Millésimé. Prestige: Dom Ruinart Blanc de Blancs, Dom Ruinart Rosé.

Extremely stylish among the lighter champagnes, both in non-vintage and vintage. The luxury Dom Ruinart is among the most notable *blanc de blancs*, uniquely fleshy and rounded owing to the Montagne de Reims Chardonnay grapes in the blend and on a winning streak in recent vintages (1982, 1983, 1985, 1988, 1989). Dom Ruinart Rosé is equally outstanding.

The firm owns 37 acres of Chardonnay vines in the Montagne Grands Crus of Sillery and Puissieulx, the grapes reserved for the Dom Ruinart *cuvées*. Sales 1.7m. bottles, 82% in France.

Napoleon's Josephine enjoyed Ruinart – but, alas, refused, after her divorce, to honour the bills she ran up as Empress.

Salon

Le Mesnil-sur-Oger, 51190 Avize. Founded 1920. Private company owned by Laurent-Perrier. Associated company: Delamotte Champagne (q.v.). The sole house to produce only vintage *blanc de blancs* champagne. Since 1920, vintages have been declared about 3 times a decade.

Salon pioneered *blanc de blancs* wines and still leads in quality if not quantity, with extremely delicate but subtly rich and very dry wines; really for connoisseurs. 15 years is a good age for them.

The firm owns 2.4 acres of vines in Le Mesnil which supply about one-fifth of its needs; the rest of the grapes are bought in from growers owning grand cru Mesnil plots in the village, the same ones since the early 20th century.

Production is only 50,000 bottles a year, yet stock is around 500,000 bottles (10 years' supply) – one of the biggest sales/stock ratios in Champagne. Sales to European and USA markets are rationed. Techniques are described as 'artisan' – everything done by hand. Marketing is entirely by personal recommendation.

Taittinger

9 place St. Nicaise, 51061 Reims. Founded 1734 as Forest Forneaux, name changed to Taittinger in 1931. Public company controlled by Taittinger family. Visits: appt. only. NV: Brut Réserve, Demi-Sec, Cuvée Prestige Rosé. Vintage: Brut, Prestige. Prestige: Comtes de Champagne (*blanc de blancs*), Comtes de Champagne Rosé.

An important force in the champagne world since 1945 and still family-controlled. The style of the brut wines derives from the dominance of Chardonnay in the blend; extra time in bottle has greatly improved the NV in the late 1990s. Comtes de Champagne is one of the most ageworthy, exquisitely luxurious prestige *cuvées* (the 1985 will make a superb bottle well into the 21st century).

Taittinger owns 640 acres and also buys from other growers, mostly on the Côte des Blancs. The principal sources of grapes are Avize, Chouilly, Cramant, Mesnil and

Champagne: a new beginning

The early 1990s was a time of trauma in Champagne. After a long bullish trading period, up until 1989, during which cycle sales and prices went way above the real demands of the market, the industry was stricken by the worst economic crisis since the 1930s. The sharp fall in sales led to a collapse in prices and a swelling of stocks, compounded by seven bumper crops between 1989 and 1996. All types of champagne producer – houses, coops, growers – have been hit hard and huge losses incurred.

Viewed from the late '90s, the worst is over. The Champagne economy is out of danger but it will need a period of convalescence to restore it to full health. Catastrophe has been avoided by draconian measures, initiated by the Champagne authorities in 1992, to reduce yields in the vineyard and improve procedures for the pressing of the harvest – a critical stage in champagne-making. Only two pressings of the grapes (the *cuvée* and the *taille*) are now allowed. A third pressing has been effectively abolished, and rightly so, for with each successive press the quality of the juice diminishes. The wines are now generally aged for longer on the yeasts (3–4 years for a non-vintage from a good house); the result is a leap in quality in the finished wines.

Oger. Annual sales are around 4m. bottles, stock 15m. bottles. France drinks about 40%; Italy leads the export market, followed by the USA, Belgium, Switzerland and the UK.

Alain Thiénot

14 rue des Moissons, 511000 Reims. Founded 1980. Privately owned. Associated wine companies: Château Rahoul, Graves; Château Ricaud, Loupiac. Annual production: 600,000 bottles. NV: Brut. Vintage: Brut, Rosé. Prestige: Grande Cuvée.

Formerly a broker from an old Champenois family, Alain Thiénot is a new champagne merchant to watch. The house style is for natural very dry wines, characteristically and deftly blended from all three principal grapes. The NV is fresh and sprightly yet with a good touch of maturity. The vintage Rosé is fine-drawn but firmly structured; the exceptional Grande Cuvée allies beautiful supple fruitiness with considerable complexity.

The firm owns 34 acres in excellent sites, notably at Aÿ and Le Mesnil-sur-Oger. Alain Thiénot also makes excellent Graves at Château Rahoul and lovely sweet Loupiac at Château Ricaud, his two splendid Bordeaux properties.

Veuve Clicquot-Ponsardin

12 rue du Temple, 51100 Reims. Founded 1772. Since 1989 part of the LVMH group. Visits: by appointment. NV: Yellow Label, White Label Rich. Vintage: Gold Label, Rosé. Prestige: La Grande Dame, La Grande Dame Rosé.

Large, prestigious and influential house making excellent classic champagnes in a firm, rich, full-flavoured style. Notwithstanding its respect for tradition, winemaking is thoroughly modern, no wood being used since 1961. The prestige La Grande Dame is a masterpiece of mouth-enveloping richness, and since its first release in 1996, La Grande Dame Rosé 1988 has quickly been lauded as one of the best pink champagnes.

700 acres of vineyards are very evenly spread across the classic districts, average 97%. Production 9.1m. bottles, stock 40m. bottles, over 4 years' supply. Exports dominate, especially to Italy, UK, Venezuela, Scandinavia, Australia.

The company's success was founded by 'The Widow' Clicquot, who took over the business in 1805 at the age of 27, when her husband died. She invented the now universal *remuage* system for clarifying the wine and produced the first rosé champagne.

OTHER KEY PRODUCERS

(Includes grower-champagne makers, the cooperatives and merchants houses)

Ayala, Aÿ Once highly fashionable, a traditionalist house making sound medium-bodied wines which are good value for money. The vintage *blanc de blancs* is the best wine. Montebello, another label, is now defunct.

Barancourt, Bouzy Bought by Champagne Vranken in 1994, a small house specializing in a densely structured vintage *blanc de noirs* and excellent still red Bouzy.

The percentage system

Each harvest, the price a grower gets for his grapes is determined by a committee made up of CIVC officials, growers, producers and a government representative. The CIVC – Comité Interprofessionel du Vin de Champagne – is the official body that controls, promotes and defends the industry. The vineyards of the region are rated on a percentage scale known as the *échelle des crus* (ladder of growths). Although this *échelle* is geographically based, it is essentially an index of price, graded on the reputed quality of grapes from particular wine villages. The 17 *grands crus* rate 100% (*see* chart below); *premiers crus* 90–99%; *deuxièmes crus* 80–89%. Like most vineyard classifications, the *échelle's* chief weakness is that it makes no qualitative distinction between individual vineyard sites within the same *cru*. The best cellar-masters do not slavishly follow the rating of grapes when selecting them for use in their champagne blends.

The leading vineyards, with their percentage ratings, are as follows:

MARNE VALLEY

Aÿ	100%	black grapes
Mareuil-sur-Aÿ	99%	ʺ
Bisseuil	95%	ʺ
Dizy-Magenta	95%	ʺ
Avenay	93%	ʺ
Champillon	93%	ʺ
Cumières	93%	ʺ
Hautvillers	93%	ʺ
Mutigny	93%	ʺ

COTE D'AMBONNAY

Ambonnay	100%	black grapes
Bouzy	100%	ʺ
Louvois	100%	ʺ
Tauxières-Mutry	99%	ʺ
Tours-sur-Marne	100%	ʺ
Tours-sur-Marne	90%	white grapes

COTE D'EPERNAY

Chouilly	100%	white grapes
Chouilly	95%	black grapes
Grauves	95%	white grapes
Pierry	90%	ʺ

COTE DES BLANCS

Avize	100%	white grapes
Cramant	100%	ʺ
Le Mesnil-sur-Oger	100%	ʺ
Oger	100%	ʺ
Oiry	100%	ʺ
Cuis	95%	ʺ
Cuis	90%	black grapes
Grauves	90%	ʺ

COTE DE VERTUS

Vertus	95%	black grapes
Bergères-Lès-Vertus	95%	white grapes
Bergères-Lès-Vertus	90%	black grapes

MONTAGNE DE REIMS

Beaumont-sur-Vesle	100%	black grapes
Mailly	100%	ʺ
Puisieulx	100%	white grapes
Sillery	100%	black grapes
Verzenay	100%	ʺ
Verzy	100%	ʺ
Trépail	95%	white grapes
Villers-Marmery	95%	ʺ
Chigny-Les-Roses	94%	black grapes
Ludes	94%	ʺ
Montbré	94%	white grapes
Rilly-La-Montagne	94%	black grapes
Villers-Allerand	90%	white grapes

Paul Bara, Bouzy Leading récoltant-manipulant in Bouzy making ample Pinot-led champagnes. The mouthfilling rosé is exceptional.

Beaumont des Crayères, Mardeuil Little coop just west of Epernay makes very good champagne at reasonable prices. Dominated by Pinot Meunier, the wines are fresh and fruity. 250,000 bottles annually.

Henri & Serge Billiot, Ambonnay Growers making tiny quantities of remarkable champagne culminating in the superb Cuvée Laetitia, a blend of many vintages.

Boizel, Epernay Family business founded 1834, the majority of shares now owned by Bruno Paillard and Chanoine Frères; also uses the name Camuset. Well-made fruity wines, kind prices. Production: 1m. bottles, half of which is exported.

Alexandre Bonnet, Les Riceys Champagne growers and makers of the rare Rosé des Riceys, the family became merchants in 1932. The grapes come from their own vineyards around Les Riceys and the best growths of the Marne, especially the Côte des Blancs. The vintage Cuvée Madrigal is a sumptuous wine.

Ferdinand Bonnet, Reims Now owned by Charles Heidsieck, the firm has 25 acres of excellent Chardonnay on the Côte des Blancs. Stylish vintage *blanc de blancs*.

Bricout, Avize Small champagne house making light racy champagnes. The Chardonnay-led Prestige is by far the best wine. Sales are mainly in France. Owned by Kupferberg of Mainz.

Canard-Duchêne, Ludes After a rough period during the early 1990s, when the wines did not live up to the firm's *grande marque* standing, there is now a reforming hand at work here. Improved Pinot-based NV, lively and fresh, and rich prestige Charles VII. Owned by Veuve Clicquot.

De Castellane, Epernay An old-established house with a grand past symbolized by its extravagant crenellated tower. Sound, rather light NV, more substantial vintage Cuvée Commodore. Part-owned by Laurent-Perrier.

Delbeck, Reims Fine small champagne house bought by Bruno Paillard in 1994. Grapes come from the firm's own 60 acres and from five other suppliers whose holdings rate on average 95%. Superb Pinot-led 1985 vintage Brut was one of the greatest wines of the year.

Demoiselle, Epernay Leading brand of the Vranken Champagne group which was created in 1976 by Paul-François Vranken, a Belgian marketing man. Light Chardonnay-dominant wines of fair quality. Veuve Monnier and Charles Lafitte are other labels. The group gained control of Heidsieck Monopole (q.v.), an under-performing *grande marque*, in 1996.

Jacques Defrance, Les Riceys Another excellent producer of the very rare and fine Rosé des Riceys (*see* also Alexandre Bonnet). The great 1990 vintage will live for 30 years.

Veuve A. Devaux, Bar-sur-Seine The flagship *marque* of the powerful Union Auboise cooperative. The brand is now established in key markets such as the UK and the USA. First-rate Grande Réserve, NV, mature, full-flavoured, spicy.

Daniel Dumont, Rilly-la-Montagne Growers and nursery-men cultivating 200,000 vines a year for sale to other producers. Their own champagnes are first-rate, especially the well-aged Grande Réserve and the very fine Demi-Sec.

De Venoge, Epernay Now owned by Charles Heidsieck group, sizeable house making pleasant, soft and supple champagnes. Very good vintage *blanc de blancs*.

Nicolas Feuillate, Chouilly This brand is the creation of the eponymous M. Feuillate, a globetrotting promoter, and the Centre Vinicole de la Champagne (CVC), the largest cooperative in the region. Very modern winemaking and 'correct' quality, with the occasional exceptional *cuvée* such as the vintage Palme d'Or Premier Cru. Eighty percent of the 1m. bottles annually produced is exported.

Georges Gardet, Chigny-les-Roses Rich, well-aged wines made mainly with highly rated Pinot Noir grapes from the Montagne de Reims. All the champagnes are marked with the date of disgorging. Second label: Boucheron. Popular in the UK.

Gatinois, Aÿ Small manipulant making concentrated Pinot Noir-based champagne and still red Coteaux Champenois wine in good years. High quality.

René Geoffroy, Cumières Vignerons in the Marne valley since the 16th century with fine Premier Cru holdings. The best sort of traditional producers using part-fermentation in wood and late-disgorging of vintage champagnes. Also an excellent Cumières rouge.

Pierre Gimmonet, Cuis Sizeable growers with enviably fine holdings on the Côte des Blancs, the Gimmonets are excellent winemakers too: brilliant bone-dry Maxi-Brut and the impressive Cuvée Gastronome, all finesse.

Emile Hamm, Aÿ Formerly Aÿ grower and a merchant house since 1930. Excellent very dry champagne (with less than 1% *dosage*): exemplary Premier Cru Réserve.

Rosé des Riceys

Within the borders of Champagne lies one of France's most esoteric little appellations, specifically for a Pinot Noir rosé. Les Riceys is in the extreme south of Champagne. Most of its production is champagne, but in good ripe vintages the best Pinot Noir grapes, with a minimum natural 10°, are selected. The floor of an open wooden vat is first covered with grapes trodden by foot. Then the vat is filled with whole unbroken bunches. Fermentation starts at the bottom and the fermenting juice is pumped over the whole grapes. At a skilfully judged moment the juice is run off, the grapes pressed and the results 'assembled' to make a dark rosé of a unique sunset tint and, as its makers describe it, a flavour of gooseberries. The principal practitioner used to be Alexandre Bonnet; his sons now continue this tradition. In the past 15 years they have made it only three times: in 1983, 1985 and 1990.

The postcode is 10340 Les Riceys.

Heidsieck Monopole One of the oldest champagne houses (founded 1777), this grande marque was sold by Mumm to the Vranken group in 1996. The quality of the Brut Dry Monopole NV slipped a little during the early 1990s; but the Diamant Bleu is still one of Champagne's real luxury cuvées: a powerful character to mature for years, illustrated in such concentrated vintages as 1976 (a collector's item) and 1985.

Jacquart, Reims Now the sixth-largest champagne firm, a cooperative turned merchant. The crisp, incisive Brut Sélection (mainly Chardonnay) is a bargain.

Le Brun de Neuville, Bethon The leading brand of the Bethon cooperative in the Côte Sézanne. High quality Chardonnay champagnes at low prices. The British supermarket chain, Sainsburys, has often bought here.

R & L Legras, Chouilly Growers since the 18th century and now a fashionable small house with a niche market among Michelin-starred restaurants in France. The lovely Grand Cru Blanc de Blancs is fairly priced.

Larmandier-Bernier, Vertus Excellent Chardonnay sites on the Côte des Blancs and Pierre Larmandier's own talent combine to create some of the most pure-flavoured Blanc de Blancs. Exceptional Cramant Grand Cru.

Leclerc-Briant, Epernay Family firm with 75 acres of fine mainly Pinot Noir vineyards and very original cuvées called 'Les Authentiques': these are three single-vineyard champagnes vinified separately, each with a particular taste reflecting each provenance.

Abel Lepitre, Mareuil-sur-Aÿ Part of the Marie-Brizard family drinks group which also owns Philipponnat (q.v.), a good smallish house with nicely mature wines, both NV and vintage. Annual production: about 400,000 bottles.

Mailly-Champagne, Mailly Small exclusive cooperative, each of its 70 member-growers own *grand cru* wines in Mailly on the Montagne de Reims. Full, muscular champagnes (with at least 75% Pinot Noir) which need at least 4 years on the cork to show their paces.

Serge Mathieu, Avirey-Ligney Top-flight grower of the Barséquenais (Aube) making champagnes which are rich yet superfine. Superb rosé and remarkably fresh and delicious Coteaux Champenois rouge from older vintages.

Philipponnat, Mareuil-sur-Aÿ Small traditionalist house making well-constituted wines built to last. Especially fine single-vineyard Clos des Goisses; the 1985 was a marvel of Pinot Noir concentration.

Alain Robert, Le Mesnil-sur-Oger Outstanding Mesnil grower and perfectionist champagne-maker. His Mesnil Sélection, never less than 12 years old, is a great *blanc de blancs*.

Christian Senez, Fontette Important Aube producer and talented winemaker producing champagnes of finesse and character. Older vintages and Coteaux Champenois Rouge a speciality.

Jacques Selosse, Avize Original grower fermenting all his wines in wood. A rich yet beautifully balanced range of top-class *blanc de blancs* includes a bone-dry Extra Sec and the Cuvée d'Origine vinified in new oak barrels.

Jean-Marie Tarlant, Oeuilly Top-flight grower who uses wood-fermentation of individual vineyard wines separately to give best expression to their respective soils. The Krug-like Cuvée Louis is outstanding.

Union Champagne, Avize The leader in quality of all the Champagne cooperatives, its member growers owning magnificent Chardonnay plots on the Côte des Blancs. The prestige Cuvée Orpale is a real bargain among the best *blanc de blancs*.

Vilmart, Rilly-la-Montagne Tiny firm making very high quality wines fermented in wood and aged for a long time in bottle. Vilmart believes in minimal use of chemicals in their vineyards.

Champagne and food

There is no single classic dish for accompanying champagne, but champagne makers like to encourage the idea that their wine goes with almost any dish (even game and cheese). Vintage champagne certainly has the fullness of flavour to go with most food – but many people find sparkling wine indigestible with food. Champagne is the apéritif wine par excellence, but can be marvellously refreshing after a rich meal. Meanwhile there is the less fizzy Crémant (meaning half-sparkling), and the non-sparkling Coteaux Champenois, white or red (notably Bouzy Rouge).

ALSACE

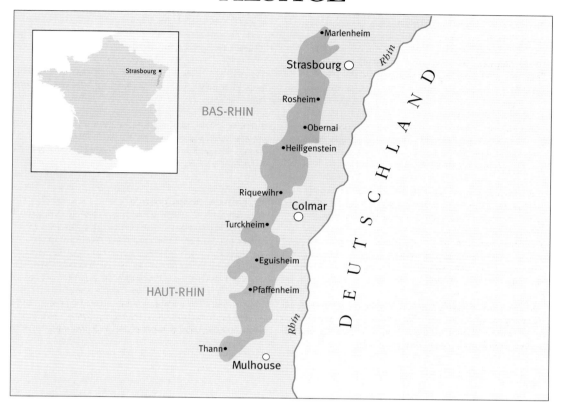

A fter all the regions of France whose appellation systems seem to have been devised by medieval theologians, Alsace is a simple fairy tale. A single appellation, Alsace, takes care of the whole region. Alsace Grand Cru is for chosen sites.

Nor are there Germanic complications of degrees of ripeness to worry about. Alsace labelling is as simple as Californian: maker's name and grape variety are the nub. The difference is that in Alsace a host of strictly enforced laws means that there are no surprises. The grapes must be 100 percent of the variety named, properly ripened and fermented dry with no sweetening added. The wines are correspondingly predictable and reliable. Their makers would like them to be considered more glamorous. In order to have their wines named among the 'greats' they place increasing emphasis on late picking, on wines from Grand Cru and selected sites – on 'Cuvées de Prestige' of various kinds. What matters more to most drinkers is that Alsace guarantees a certain quality and a style more surely than any other wine region. It makes brilliantly appetizing, clean-cut and aromatic wine to go with food, and at a reasonable price.

The region is 70 miles long by one or two miles wide: the eastern flank of the Vosges mountains in the *départements* of the Haut-Rhin and the Bas-Rhin where the foothills, between 600 and about 1,200 feet, provide well-drained southeast- and south-facing slopes under the protection of the peaks and forests of the Vosges. The whole region is in their rain-shadow, which gives it some of France's lowest rainfall and most sustained sunshine.

On the principle that watersheds are natural boundaries, Alsace should be in Germany. It has been, but since the Rhine became the frontier it has been French. Its language and architecture remain Germanic. Its grape varieties are Germanic, too – but handled in the French manner they produce a different drink.

What is the difference? The ideal German wine has a certain thrilling balance of fruity sweetness and acidity. It has relatively little alcohol and resulting 'vinosity', which allows the tension of this balance to stand out in sharp relief. The components in all their complexity (or lack of it) can clearly be tasted.

Most cheaper German wines are ingeniously, often excellently, made to reproduce this artificially. After fermentation the missing element is the sweet fruitiness. So it is supplied by adding grape juice. The wine is filtered to prevent further fermentation and the balance holds up in the bottle.

By contrast, an Alsace wine is given its extra or artificial ripeness in the form of sugar before fermentation. The natural ripeness must reach a level that in most parts of Germany would give it 'Qualitätswein' status. It can then be chaptalized with dry (not dissolved) sugar to give an extra 2.5 degrees of alcohol. The minimum permitted natural alcohol being 8.5 degrees, the resulting wine has 11 degrees, – the strength that the French are accustomed to in most of their white wines. All added sugar being totally fermented, the wine is completely dry. The aromatic (or otherwise) character of its grapes stand out cleanly and clearly.

Although many of the best Alsace wines are still fermented in oak the barrels are antiques, thickly lined with tartrate crystals that prevent any flavours of wood or oxidation. So the wines start very simple and straight. They are bottled as soon as possible in the spring (or latest in the autumn) after the vintage. Most are drunk young – which is a real pity. Bottle ageing introduces the elements of complexity which are otherwise lacking. A good Riesling or Gewürztraminer or Pinot Gris is worth keeping at least four years in bottle and often up to ten.

Late picking, Vendange Tardive, is the means by which Alsace growers are scaling the heights of prestige which Burgundy and Bordeaux have so far monopolized. A hot summer (1989, 1990 and 1994 are the latest famous examples) provides such high sugar readings in the grapes that fermentation can stop with considerable natural sweetness still remaining. The wines reach an alcohol level usually greater than that of a German Auslese. The resulting combination of strength, sweetness and concentrated fruity flavour is still peculiar to Alsace. The Hugels of Riquewihr were instrumental in creating what has become the Vendange Tardive legislation. Very ripe grapes with a high sugar concentration, usually sweetened by noble rot, produce wines of enormous power, which are classified as 'Sélection de Grains Nobles'. There has been increased interest in Alsace dessert wines recently, although quantities vary greatly from year to year as they are so much at the mercy of the weather.

The centre of the finest area lies in the Haut-Rhin, in the group of villages north and south of Colmar with Riquewihr an extravagantly half-timbered and flower-decked little town, as its natural wine capital; a sort of St-Emilion of the Vosges.

The climate is warmest and driest in the south, but scarcely different enough to justify the popular inference that Haut-Rhin is parallel to, let us say, Haut-Médoc. There is no suggestion of lower quality in the name Bas-Rhin; it is simply lower down the River Rhine. Even farther down, going directly north, are the German Palatinate vineyards, producing the richest and some of the greatest of all German Rieslings.

Human nature being what it is many truckloads of Bas-Rhin grapes are taken south at harvest time to go into blends with Haut-Rhin labels.

More important are the individual vineyard sites with the best soils and microclimates. Thirty or 40 Vosges hillsides have individual reputations, which in Burgundy would long ago have been enshrined in law but in Alsace have only just become so. After hovering on the brink of listing certain vineyards as 'Grands Crus' for many years, by the mid-1970s,

many growers felt that the time had come to make a proper classification of the great slopes of Alsace and a committee was formed to draft the appropriate AC regulations. A list of 94 lieux-dits or possible sites was drawn up, and from these, the first 25 received full Grand Cru status in 1983 followed by a further 23 in 1985 and finally two more in 1988. This total of fifty will probably not be exceeded for some time.

A few of the Grand Cru names are well established on labels. Schoenenbourg at Riquewihr is particularly noted for its Riesling; Kaysersberg's Schlossberg, Guebwiller's Kitterlé, Turckheim's Eichberg and Brand, Beblenheim's Sonnenglanz are other examples. Ownership of these vineyards is noted in the following list of producers.

Grand Cru wines must come from specifically delimited slopes and may only be single ('noble') variety wines of Riesling, Gewurztraminer, Pinot Gris and Muscat – now increasingly planted in the region. They have a lower permitted yield and a higher minimum alcoholic strength than other Alsace wines. Growers say that the Grand Cru legislation gives them the chance to demonstrate the terroir character of their best wines but not all the great houses agree with this.

Another great success story in Alsace has been the remarkable growth in popularity of Crémant d'Alsace, produced since the turn of the century but only recently seeing some success. Crémant is méthode traditionnelle sparkling wine from any Alsace grape – although in practice Muscat and Gewurztraminer are found to be too aromatic. Pinot Blanc is most used, and some Chardonnay may be added (although not permitted for the still wines). Crémant rosé is from 100% Pinot Noir.

The last ten years have also seen red wines reemerging. Careful selection of Pinot Noir clones combined with careful colour and flavour extraction are making fuller, more characterful reds.

GROWERS AND COOPERATIVES

The vineyards of Alsace are even more fragmented in ownership than those of the rest of France. With 7,000 growers sharing the total of 35,335 acres the average individual holding is just over five acres. (Although in truth, 80 percent of the vineyard area is accounted for by just 2,000 of the growers.)

The chances of history established a score or more leading families with larger estates – still rarely as much as 100 acres. With what seems improbable regularity they trace their roots back to the 17th century, when the Thirty Years' War tore the province apart. In the restructuring of the industry after the wars of this century these families have grouped smaller growers around them in a peculiar pattern consisting of their own domaine plus a wine-making and merchanting business. They contract to buy the small growers' grapes and make their wine – very often using their own domaine wines as their top-quality range. As the following details of these larger houses show, the pattern is repeated all over Alsace.

The small grower's alternative to a contract with a grower/négociant (or just a négociant) is the local cooperative. Alsace established the first in France, at the turn of the century, and now has one of the strongest cooperative movements. Their standards are extremely high and they often provide the best bargains in the region.

Leading Alsace Producers

Caves J Becker

Zellenberg, 68340 Riquewihr.

The Beckers have been growers at Riquewihr since 1618. Their 40 acres (10 of which are Grand Cru – Froehn at Zellenberg and Sonnenglanz at Beblenheim) are in the Zellenberg, Riquewihr, Beblenheim, Ribeauvillé and Hunnawihr vineyards. Oak barrels but modern controls make them a typical small firm of growers/merchants, buying grapes to make up a total of 20,000 cases a year (30% exports). Riesling is the major variety (23% of production) and there is also some unusual VT and SGN Muscat. They also own the brand Gaston Beck.

Léon Beyer

68420 Eguisheim.

A family firm founded in 1867, now directed by Léon Beyer and his son Marc. (The Beyers have been making wine in Alsace since 1580.) Their 50 acres of vines are in Eguisheim (Gewürztraminer, Riesling, Pinots Blanc, Gris and Noir and Muscat). Beyer's best wines are full-bodied and dry, clearly designed to go with food and often seen in top restaurants in France. I have seen some remarkably preserved 10- and even 20-year-old examples. Riesling Cuvée des Ecaillers and Gewürztraminer Cuvée des Comtes d'Eguisheim are their principal brands. Production is now 70,000 cases a year.

Domaine Paul Blanck & Fils

68240 Kientzheim.

Top-quality estate founded in 1922 and now producing some 35 wines each year (17 of which are Rieslings), entirely from its own 77 acres of vineyard. The holdings include part of the Kientzheim Grands Crus, Schlossberg and Furstentum – the Blancks have been registered Schlossberg owners since 1620 – and Grand Cru Mambourg. Fermentation is in stainless steel and temperature-controlled, with splendid results. All Blanck wines earn high praise, the most notable of late the sweet Riesling – the Blancks are proud of all their *vieilles vignes* wines, which also include Sylvaner, Auxerrois and Gewürztraminer. Total annual sales: 17,000 cases; 50% export.

E Boeckel

67140 Mittelbergheim.

Grower and négociant (founded 1853) with 50 acres in and around Mittelbergheim, regarded as a steady producer of traditional wines. His standard Sylvaner, Riesling and Gewürztraminer are labelled Zotzenberg; Brandluft and Wibelsberg are selected Rieslings; Château d'Isembourg his best Gewürztraminer. Recent emphasis has been on Grand Cru and *crémant* wines. Exports are 65% of a total of 42,000 cases.

Domaine Marcel Deiss

The Deiss family have been vignerons in Alsace since 1744 and founded the present domaine in 1949. It comprises 50 acres, including 6 acres of Grand Cru Altenbourg de Bergheim and 1.75 acres of Grand Cru Schoenenbourg. Annual production is about 12,500 cases. A reflection of *terroir* is the main objective of the Deiss family, using low yields and accurately-timed picking. The results include (unusually good) Pinot Noir, which was planted long before it became ubiquitously fashionable, and on chalky 'Burgundy-style' slopes.

Dopff 'Au Moulin'

68340 Riquewihr.

Another family firm of 17th-century origins, with the largest vineyard holdings of central Alsace. A total of 173 acres, principally in the Schoenenberg at Riquewihr for Riesling and Eichberg at Turckheim for Gewürztraminer, with Pinot Blanc in the Hardt vineyards near Colmar grown specifically for Crémant d'Alsace, which Dopff pioneered at the turn of the century. *Crémant* is an increasing part of their business, which is known for delicate and individual wines. Special Fruits de Mer is a good blend. Total sales 240,000 cases, 30% exported.

Dopff & Irion

Château de Riquewihr', 68340 Riquewihr.

One of the biggest grower/merchants of Alsace. The Dopff and Irion families whose forebears have made wine at Riquewihr for three centuries, combined in 1945 – they still have a strong influence on the company today. Dopff & Irion own 67 acres in Riquewihr, producing some 17,000 cases of their own Riesling Les Murailles (from the Schoenenbourg), Gewürztraminer Les Sorcières, the very attractive Muscat Les Amandiers and Pinot Gris Les Maquisards. They also have 12.5 acres in Rouffach, which includes Château d'Issembourg. In addition they produce 270,000 cases from the grapes of 300 small growers under contract, representing 500 acres. Brands include very dry Crustacés and the fuller Crystal; also a Crémant d'Alsace. 45% of sales are exports – of a total of 166,000 cases. Recent emphasis is on their 25 acres of Grand Cru.

Théo Faller

Domaine Weinbach, 68240 Kaysersberg.

A distinguished domaine of 54 acres of former monastic land, the Clos des Capucins, founded in 1898. Now run by the widow and daughters of the late Théo Faller, who is buried amongst his vines – Laurence Faller is in charge of the winemaking, Catherine the marketing. The family policy is to harvest as late as possible and use full maturity to give the wines maximum character, structure, length on the palate and the potential to age. Cuvée Théo is the standard label for Riesling and Gewürztraminer, with Vendanges Tardives in certain vintages (e.g. 1983). The Domaine Weinbach label is a superb piece of calligraphy: the best Alsace label. Total production is about 14,000 cases (35% exported) from 62 acres (22 of which are Riesling).

Rolly Gassmann

Founded in 1676, this 69-acre estate is mainly in Rorschwihr and partly in Bergheim and Rodern. Gassmann specializes in Muscat and Auxerrois, the latter growing particularly well in the *lieu-dit* Moenchreben. Balanced wines, rounded with residual sugar. Annual production: 16,000 cases; 20% export.

Maison Louis Gisselbrecht

67650 Dambach-la-Ville.

The Gisselbrechts formed two separate businesses in 1936. This is the smaller one, proprietors of 30 acres at Dambach-la-Ville and elsewhere, planted with Riesling,Gewürztraminer, Pinots Blanc and Noir, Sylvaner and Tokay. Riesling is the real speciality of the house; very clean, dry and balanced – especially from Grand Cru Frankstein vineyards. Pinot Blanc and Vendange Tardive are also important. Grapes are also bought to make a total of 70,000 cases. 85% is exported.

Willy Gisselbrecht & Fils

67650 Dambach-la-Ville.

The larger of the two Gisselbrecht houses, owning 37 acres in and near Dambach-la-Ville and buying grapes to make a total of 125,000 cases a year (41% exported). Regular exhibitors and medal winners at the Paris and Mâcon fairs, particularly with Gewürztraminer and also with Pinot Blanc.

Hugel & Fils

68340 Riquewihr.

The best-known Alsace label in the Anglo-Saxon world. A combination of grower and grape négociant, in the family since 1639, with 62 acres in Riquewihr producing their top wines. Of these 13 are in the Schoenenbourg and 21 in the Sporen vineyards. 42% is Gewürztraminer, 43% Riesling, 13% Pinot Gris and 2% is Pinot Noir. The house style is full, round and 'supple', fermented dry but less apparently so than some. The Hugels have pioneered late-gathered wines to the level of German Beerenausleses. The quality ladder for Riesling, Gewürztraminer, etc., goes Regular, Tradition, Jubilée Vendange Tardive (big wines with definite sweetness) and in certain years Sélection de Grains Nobles (very sweet). The Jubilée label is also used for top Riesling, Pinot Gris, Gewürztraminer and Pinot Noir. Other registered names made of purchased grapes are Fleur d'Alsace and Gentil d'Alsace (both 45% Sylvaner), Cuvée les Amours and (Pinot Blanc) Les Vignards. Gentil d'Alsace is a revival of 'Edelzwicker' using quality grapes. Sales about 100,000 cases a year, 80–85% export.

Jos Meyer & Fils

68920 Wintzenheim.

Growers and négociants since 1854, with 40 acres under vine at Wintzenheim and Turkheim (including Grands Crus Hengst and Brand), grapes are purchased from a further 50 acres. The full flavoured Gewürztraminers are particularly successful, but this house is most noted for its wide range of grapes. There is Chasselas from Grand Cru Hengst; Pinot Blanc features, and there are other less-used varieties too. 70% of the annual production of 33,000 cases is exported.

Domaines Klipfel

67140 Barr.

A leading family domaine combined with a négociant business (André Lorentz). Founded in 1824 by Martin Klipfel. 99 acres including the Grands Crus Kirchberg (Riesling), Kastelberg (Pinot Gris) and Wiebelsberg (Gewürztraminer) – all traditionally oak-fermented and matured, with occasional *vendanges tardives*. Bought-in grapes are vinified in tanks for the Lorentz label. Sales are largely to French restaurants and private customers. 30% is exported, mainly to Germany of 125,000 cases in total.

Domaine Marc Kreydenweiss

67140 Andlau.

From 32 organic acres including holdings in the Grands Crus Wiebelsberg, Kastelberg, and Moenchberg, Kreydenweiss produces beautifully made, concentrated wines. The Rieslings from 25- to 45-year-old vines in the steep Kastelberg site are made to last. Fermentation is temperature controlled and the wines stay on their lees until shortly before bottling. Unusually, the domaine produces a late-picked Pinot Blanc. As the law prevents it from being sold as Vendange Tardive, it is offered under the vineyard name *Kritt*, linked with the old Alsatian name for Pinot Blanc, *Klevner*. A little Chardonnay is grown, which is blended with Pinot Blanc, and there is also a blend 'Clos du Val d'Eleons' from 70% Riesling and 30% Pinot Gris. 5,000 cases are produced annually; 60% for export.

Kuentz-Bas

68420 Husseren-les-Châteaux.

A family firm of growers and négociants, owning 30 acres of Riesling, Muscat and Gewürztraminer, Pinots Blanc, Gris and Noir in Husseren, Eguisheim and Obermorschwihr. There are holdings in the Grands Crus Eichberg and Pfersigberg at Eguisheim. Grapes are also bought in from a further 75 acres. The house was founded in 1795 by Joseph Kuentz and became Kuentz-Bas in 1919. Regular prize winners with firm and dry, well-balanced and elegant wines. The wines have excellent acidity, and the *vendange tardive* wines are superb. 'K de Kuentz Bas' is a recently introduced non-vintage blend. 55% exported, of a 30,000-case production.

Maison Michel Laugel

67520 Marlenheim.

Perhaps the biggest of Alsace winemakers, with annual sales of 330,000 cases. Their popular brand is Pichet d'Alsace, a blend of 85% Pinot Blanc, 10% Riesling and 5% Gewürztraminer – an excellent Edelzwicker at a reasonable price. All their wines are well-made, quite light, for drinking fresh. The Laugels own a 12-acre vineyard of Pinot Noir in Marlenheim from which they make a well-known rosé.

Gustave Lorentz

68750 Bergheim.

160-year-old family firm (founded 1836) of growers and négociants, among the biggest producers and exporters with 150,000 cases a year, 40% exported. They own 80 acres with their best vines in the Grands Crus Altenberg (3.75 acres) and Kanzlerberg sites at Bergheim – other grapes are bought-in from nearby. Gewürztraminer and Riesling are the specialities. The house style is to produce wines with a fine and delicate nose that are quite round and rich on the palate with relatively high acidity. The best thus have good ageing potential.

Muré

68250 Rouffach.

A family of growers dating back to 1648. Owners since 1928 of a historic vineyard at Rouffach and 40 acres of Grand Cru Vorbourg bought in 1935 in the old monastic Clos St-Landelin – 52 acres in all. All the usual vines are planted in the Clos, which has warm, stony and limey soil and notably low rainfall. Its wines are full in character and round in style, intended (except the Sylvaner and Pinot Noir) as *vins de garde*. The Pinot Noir is some of the deepest and fullest in Alsace; Riesling and Gewürztraminer are not far behind. Muré also has a négociant business with a different label. Some 60,000 cases a year (12,000 of it Clos St-Landelin), exporting 40%.

Domaine Ostertag

67680 Epfig.

25-acre estate with a 5-acre holding in the Muenchberg Grand Cru vineyard (Riesling and Pinot Gris). An expressed desire to move from the technology to the 'poetry' of wine does not exclude Pinots Blanc, Gris and Noir aged in *barriques* (some of them new). Experimentation is key. Other specialities are Sylvaner Vieilles Vignes and Riesling. 60% of annual sales of 5,800 cases is exported.

Preiss-Zimmer

68340 Riquewihr.

300-year old firm of négociants producing consistently fine, ageable wines, particularly Gewürztraminer, Riesling and Pinot Noir, from vineyards around Riquewihr, including the Grands Crus Sporen and Schoenenbourg. Sold to CV Turckheim in 1988. 25 acres in total. Annual production is approximately 8,000 cases; 50% exported.

Domaines Schlumberger

68500 Guebwiller.

The biggest domaine in Alsace, family owned, with 346 acres at Guebwiller and Rouffach at the southern end of the region. Half of the estate is of Grand Cru vineyards. Guebwiller's warm climate, sandy soil and sheltered sites allied with old-style methods, relatively small crops and ageing in wood make Schlumberger wines some of the richest and roundest of Alsace, with sweet and earthy flavours of their own. The best are from the Kitterlé vineyard and repay several years' bottle-ageing. Total production is about 81,000 cases, 55% exported.

Albert Seltz & Fils

67140 Mittelbergheim.

A family of growers/négociants with 16th-century origins, particularly known for Sylvaner from 7 acres in the Grand Cru Zotzenberg (of 27 acres in total). Owner Pierre Seltz, who studied oenology in California, describes his wine-making as traditional Alsatian (he harvests as late as possible). Sylvaner is even produced to Sélection de Grains Nobles level. Annual production: 12,000 cases; 45% export.

Domaine Sick-Dreyer

68770 Ammerschwihr.

A 32-acre domain, with 6 acres in the top-quality, famously non-Grand Cru Kaefferkopf vineyard, specializing in Gewürztraminer. Sick-Dreyer produces fine, concentrated wines from grapes that are almost late-picked ('*semi-tardive*', e.g. Pinot Gris 'la Grappe des Oiseaux'), as well as the complete range of classic Alsace wines from the Côtes d'Ammerschwihr. Annual production is about 8,000 cases – all domaine bottled. 15% is exported.

Pierre Sparr & ses Fils

68240 Sigolsheim.

Another family firm of growers and merchants dating back to the 17th century. Their own vines cover 82 acres in 6 communes between Turckheim and Bennwihr, including Riesling in the Grand Cru Schlossberg (Kaysersberg, 2.8 acres) and Altenberg vineyards, and Gewürztraminer in Grand Cru Brand at Turckheim (6 acres) and Grand Cru Mambourg at Sigolsheim (7 acres). These are the company's top wines. The house style is to leave some residual sugar and produce rounded, supple wines. Specialities are the Kaefferkopff blend (75% Gewürz, 25% Pinot Gris), Klevener de Heiligenstein and their range of *crémants*. Total sales 140,000 cases, 55% of which is exported.

F E Trimbach

68150 Ribeauvillé.

A historic (1626) family domaine and négociant house with the highest reputation for particularly fine and delicate dry wines. They own 67 acres planted 30% in Riesling, 30% in Gewürztraminer. Vineyards also include 5 recently-acquired acres of Grand Cru Mandelberg. Their special pride is the Hunawihr Riesling Clos Ste-Hune, one of the most stylish Alsace wines. A fascinating tasting of old vintages showed it at its best after about 7 years. Each variety is made in the recently modernized cellar at three quality levels: standard (vintage), Réserve and Réserve Personnelle. The prestigious Riesling Cuvée Frédéric Emil, and Gewürztraminer Cuvée des Seigneurs de Ribeaupierre are considered Alsace's very best wines. 80% of some 80,000 cases is exported.

Alsace Willm

67140 Barr.

A very traditional firm with a high reputation, taken over in 1980 by Roger Bahl. Best known for its 18 acres of Gewürztraminer, Clos Gaensbroennel, and its 10 acres of Riesling in the Kirchberg. The Gewürztraminer is well ripened and fermented completely dry, making it a firm and impressive *vin de garde*. Its delicate Riesling and very clean, fresh Sylvaner (also Clos Gaensbroennel) are both very attractive. Total sales are about 40,000 cases, 90% exported.

Domaine Zind-Humbrecht

68920 Wintzenheim.

The domaines of the Humbrechts of Gueberschwihr (since 1620) and the Zinds of Wintzenheim united in 1959 and are now run by Léonard Zind and Olivier Humbrecht. The latter is a fanatic for the individuality of each vineyard, and a pioneer believer in low-temperature, slow fermentation. He makes highly individual wines from 4 Grand Cru vineyards: Brand at Turckheim (light and fruity wines, especially Ries.), Goldert at Gueberschwihr (full-bodied Gewürz.), Hengst at Wintzenheim (more full-bodied *vins de garde*) and Rangen at Thann, where his 10-acre Clos St-Urbain gives top-quality Rieslings. Thirty wines are made in order to capture the very best aspects of *terroir*. The whole domaine totals 104 acres. 75% of the 17,000-case (low average due to low yields) production is exported. Their new Turckheim winery winery relies on gravity instead of pumps.

Alsace Cooperatives

Andlau-Barr 67140 Barr. Founded 1959. 160 members with a total area of 588 acres including 3.2 acres Grand Cru. Speciality: Klevener de Heiligenstein. All wines bottled and sold by Obernai (q.v.). Like Obernai, this is now one of the Divinal group of coops.

Beblenheim 68980 Beblenheim. Founded 1952. 150 members with a total area of 618 acres including 45 acres Grand Cru. 220,000 cases (25% exports). Other labels: Caves de Hoen, Baron de Hoen.

Bennwihr 68630 Bennwihr-Mittelwihr. Founded 1946. 220 members sharing a total area of 914 acres including 64 acres of the Grand Cru Marckrain. 330,000 cases (40% of which is exported). The coop's specialities are Riesling (including

Alsace grapes

Area of grapes occupied is expressed as a percentage of the total Alsatian vineyard.

Chasselas (1.3%) (In German Gutedel, in Switzerland Fendant.) Formerly one of the commonest grapes, rarely if ever named on a label, but used for its mildness in everyday blends, including the so-called 'noble' Edelzwicker.
Clevner or Klevner A local name for the Pinot Blanc (q.v.).
Knipperlé Another anonymous common blending grape.
Gewürztraminer (17.6%) Much the most easily recognized of all one-wine grapes, whose special spicy aroma and bite epitomizes Alsace wine. Most Alsace Gewürztraminer is made completely dry but intensely fruity, even to the point of slight fierceness when young. With age remarkable citrus fruit smells and flavours, suggesting grapefruit, intensify. Gewürztraminer of a fine vintage, whether made dry or in the sweet *vendange tardive* style, is worth maturing almost as long as Riesling. The fault of a poor Gewürztraminer is sometimes softness and lack of definition, or alternatively a heady heaviness without elegance. In a range of Alsace wines Gewürztraminer should be served last, after Rieslings and Pinots.
Pinot Blanc (20.7%) An increasingly popular grape, giving the lightest of the 'noble' wines; simply fresh and appetizing without great complexity. Now seen as Alsace's answer to Chardonnay. This is the base wine for most Crémant d'Alsace.
Pinot Gris, formerly Tokay d'Alsace (8.5%) After Riesling and Gewürztraminer the third potentially great wine grape of the region. First-class Pinot Gris has a dense, stiff, intriguing smell and taste – the very opposite of the fresh and fruity Pinot Blanc. It is almost frustrating to taste, as though it were concealing a secret flavour you will never quite identify. Pinots Gris mature magnificently into broad, rich deep-bosomed wines whose only fault is that they are not refreshing. The name Tokay has been reclaimed by Hungary for its noble wine.
Pinot Noir (8.4%) A grape that is made into both red and rosé in Alsace, but it is sometimes necessary to read the label

to know which is which. The must is often heated to extract colour, but the result is rarely more than a light wine, without the classic Pinot flavour found in, for example, Bouzy Rouge from Champagne. Fuller-bodied examples are emerging.
Riesling (22.8%) The finest wine grape of Alsace, as it is of Germany, but here interpreted in a totally different way. Alsace Rieslings are fully ripened and usually fully fermented, their sugar all turned to alcohol, which gives them a firmer and more definite structure than German wines. Dryness and the intensity of their fruit flavour together make them seem rather harsh to some people. I have found a prejudice against Alsace Riesling in California. In fact, they range from light refreshment in certain years to some of the most aromatic, authoritative and longest-lasting of all white wines.
Muscat (2.3%) Until recently Alsace was the only wine region where Muscat grapes were made into dry wine. The aroma is still hothouse sweet but the flavour is crisp and very clean, sometimes with a suggestion of nut kernels. It is light enough to make an excellent apéritif.
Sylvaner (15.5%) Steadily being pushed out by Pinot Noir and Pinot Blanc but at its best (at Mittelbergheim, for example) a classy, slightly *'pétillant'*, flavoursome wine, which ages well.

Alsace appellations

One of the 'noble' grape names, or the term Edelzwicker, meaning a blend of grapes, is usually the most prominent word on Alsace labels – although with the trend towards quality, 'Edelzwicker' now appears less in favour of the noble names.
Appellation Alsace
Wine from any permitted grape variety with a maximum crop of 80 hl/ha and a minimum natural degree of 8.5 alcohol.
Appellation Alsace Grand Cru
Wine from one of the 'noble' grape varieties (Riesling, Gewürztraminer, Pinot Gris or Muscat), growing in a designated Grand Cru site, with a maximum crop of 60 hectolitres a hectare and a minimum natural degree of 10 for Riesling and Muscat, 12 for Gewürztraminer and Pinot Gris (Tokay).

100% Riesling *crémant*), Rebgarten, Gewürztraminer Côtes de Bennwihr and Bennwihr Brut Prestige. Brands are Poème d'Alsace and Rêve d'Alsace. Other labels: Victor Preiss, Lentz, Caves Klug.

Cleebourg Route des Vosges, Cleebourg, 67160 Wissembourg. Founded 1946. 180 members with a total area of 408 acres. 133,000 cases. This coop specializes in Pinots, especially Auxerrois. There are two *crémants* under the Clerostein label, one 100% Auxerrois; one 100% Pinot Gris.

Dambach-la-Ville 67650 Dambach-la-Ville. Founded 1902. 250 members with a total area of 1,112 acres including 25 acres Grand Cru. Approx. 420,000 cases. Wines mainly sold under the Wolfberger label.

Union Vinicole Divinal see Obernai, Andlau-Barr, Traenheim

Eguisheim 68420 Eguisheim. Founded 1902. 470 members with a total area of 1,655 acres including 124 acres Grand Cru. 1,250,000 cases (Eguisheim, Dambach and Soultz-Wuenheim). Over 20% exports. Specialities are top-quality varietals (Ries., P.G., Gewürz., and P.N.) called Armorie, sold in brown bottles embossed with a tiara as a reminder that Pope St-Léon IX was born in Eguisheim. All sold with the brand name Wolfberger. By far the biggest Alsace producer, though Wolfberger wines are not characteristic of a bulk producer. Much of the credit goes to their outstanding winemaker Roland Guth. Other labels: Domaine Jux (with its own presshouse), Alsace Willm, Clos de la Tourelle, Château Ollwiller.

Caves de Hoen see Beblenheim

Hunawihr 68150 Hunawihr. Founded 1954. 130 members with a total of 495 acres including 25 acres Grand Cru. 175,000 cases. Specialities: Riesling and Gewürztraminer from *lieu-dit* Muehlforst, of which they are particularly proud. Also *crémant* called Calixte.

Ingersheim 68040 Ingersheim. Founded 1926. 200 members. 670 acres including 32 acres Grand Cru. 250,000 cases (30% exports). Other labels are Jean Geiler, Weingartner, Kuehn and Albert Schoech.

Kientzheim-Kaysersberg 68240 Kientzheim. Founded 1955. 150 members with a total area of 420 acres including 50 acres Grand Cru. 140,000 cases (40% exports). Specialities include Riesling Kaefferkopf, Gewürztraminer Kaefferkopf, and Riesling Schlossberg.

Obernai 67210 Obernai. Founded 1964. 320 members with a total of 531 acres including 5 acres Grand Cru. 600,000 cases (28% of which is exported), including the production of the Andlau-Barr coop (q.v.) (all its wines are bottled and sold from here). Obernai is also the headquarters of the Divinal group of coops. Its own specialities are Clos Ste-Odile and Crémant Fritz Kobus.

Orschwiller 67600 Orschwiller. Founded 1957. 130 members with a total of 321 acres including 2.5 acres Grand Cru. 120,000 cases (20% exports).

Pfaffenheim-Gueberschwihr 68250 Rouffach. Founded 1957. 220 members, with a total area of 309 acres including 14 acres Grand Cru. 230,000 cases (40% exports). Specialities include Pinot Noir, Cuvée des Dominicains, Pinot Gris, Cuvée Rabelais, Chasselas, Cuvée Lafayette, and a Gewürztraminer from the Grand Cru Goldert. Other labels: Producteurs Réunis d'Alsace, Crémant Hartenberger, J. Hornstein and Ernest Wein.

Ribeauvillé et Environs 68150 Ribeauvillé. Founded 1895. 110 members with a total of 655 acres including 16 acres Grand Cru. 240,000 cases (60% export). The oldest growers' cooperative in France, making 13 different *grands crus*. Specialities are Le Clos du Zahnacker, a blend of Ries., Gewürz., and P.G. in equal proportions) and Andante (Gewürz. and Muscat Ottonel). Other labels: Les Producteurs Réunis de la Région de Ribeauvillé, Caves Martin Zahn, Caves Ph.-J. Spener, Caves de la Streng and Caves du Strengbach.

Sigolsheim 68240 Kaysersberg. Founded 1946. 130 members with a total of 346 acres including 69 acres Grand Cru. 330,000 cases (30% export). Specialities include Crémant Comte de Sigold, Gewürztraminer Vogelgarten and Pinot Gris Vogelgarten.

Soultz-Wuenheim 68360 Soultz-Wuenheim. Founded 1958. 130 members with a total of 371 acres including 49 acres Grand Cru. 145,000 cases. All wines are bottled and shipped by Eguisheim. This coop is also known as Vieil Armand. Other labels: Château Ollwiller (Riesling and Pinot Noir) and Clos de la Tourelle.

Traenheim 67310 Wasselonne. Founded 1952. 315 members with a total of 1,482 acres including 62 acres Grand Cru. 615,000 cases (10% exports). Brands used include Le Roi Dagobert and Cuvée St-Eloi.

Turckheim 68230 Turckheim. Founded 1955. 250 members with a total of 790 acres including 45 acres Grand Cru. 265,000 cases (25% exports). Specialities are Gewürztraminer Baron de Turckheim, Val St-Grégoire (50:50 Pinot Blanc and Auxerrois), Pinot Noir Cuvée à l'Ancienne (*en barrique*), and Crémant Meyerling. Other label: Preiss Zimmer.

Vieil-Armand see Soultz-Wuenheim

Westhalten 68250 Westhalten. Founded 1955. 180 members with a total of 495 acres including 17 acres Grand Cru. 250,000 cases. Specialities are the *crémants* Producteur (50:50 Pinot Blanc and Auxerrois), Maréchal Lefèvre (30% Auxerrois, 20% Pinot Gris, 50% Pinot Blanc), Madame Sans Gêne (100% Pinot Blanc). Other label: Heim.

Wolfberger *see* Eguisheim, Dambach-la-Ville and Soultz-Wuenheim.

RHONE

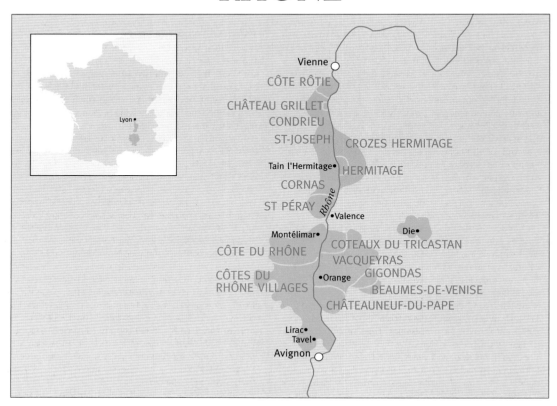

After many years of virtually ignoring the Rhône Valley and its wines, in the late 1980s the wine trade began to find in it all sorts of virtues. More perhaps than stood up to dispassionate examination.

Its finest wines, Côte Rôtie and Hermitage, were 'discovered', especially in the USA, and their prices forced up to hardly realistic levels, while great quantities of what is scarcely more than high-strength *vin de table* have climbed to the price of Bordeaux and beyond. (This has, though, facilitated some much-needed investment, especially in Northern Rhône.) It would be wrong to discount my personal taste in this. But prejudice aside, it seems to me that common grapes can never make better than common wine. Most of the red grapes of the Rhône, with the notable exceptions of Syrah and Mourvèdre, are either coarse or neutral in flavour. At their best they are grown in soil that exalts their qualities by men of taste who are aware of the flavours they are producing. More often, I have found, the well-worn eulogies of scents of truffles and woodlands, violets and raspberries are wishful thinking. Or (more charitably) that they only apply to wines far older than we are now accustomed to drinking. It is hard not to contrast the Rhône with California and the progress that has been made there in the last 20 years.

You will find that I wax more enthusiastic when talking about particular wines.

NORTHERN RHONE

The characteristic of the Northern Rhône is dogged single-mindedness: one grape, the noble Syrah, grown on rocky slopes that need terracing to hold the soil. The red wines made here are all Syrah (alias Sérine), a grape with concentrated fruity flavour but which is so darkly tannic that for long the custom was to add between 2 and 20% of white grapes to leaven it. Now, with the exception of Côte Rôtie, the northernmost appellation, producers with plantings of white varieties are more likely to use their grapes to make white wine.

Côte Rôtie used to be a mere 250 acres of terraced hill above the village of Ampuis. Somewhat controversially, the appellation has been enlarged to include up to 750 acres of plateau land behind the Côte proper. Côte Rôtie means 'roasted hill'; two sections of the hill, with paler (more chalky) and darker soil, are known respectively as the Côte Blonde and the Côte Brune. Their wines are normally blended by growers who have only a few acres in total. There is rather more wine labelled 'Côte' than can theoretically be produced – some growers appear to be using the terms Blonde and Brune as indicators of lighter or heavier styles. If no 'Côte' is credited, expect 'plateau' wine. The Syrah here is grown and mixed with up to 20% (but usually less – sometimes none) of Viognier. Partly from this aromatic component, but probably more from the singular soils or coolest microclimate of the hill, it draws a delicacy that makes Côte Rôtie eventually the finest, if not the most powerful, of all Rhône wines. Between 10 and 20 years of age it moves closer to great Bordeaux than any other French wine, with an open, soft-fruity, perhaps raspberry bouquet that recalls the Médoc, yet with a warmer texture. Recent developments include perhaps more stress on new-oak flavours than the wine will stand.

Condrieu, where the once rare Viognier makes white wine, is only three miles downstream from Ampuis on the same south-facing right bank. Cloning has much improved this difficult grape which is now far more reliable. It is therefore enjoying a mini-renaissance in the Rhône (and succeeding in the South of France, California and elsewhere). St-Joseph covers a 30-mile, 750-acre stretch of the same river bank and its immediate hinterland with some very good sites but no consistency. Legislation in 1992 has changed the territory covered by the appellation to force a move off the plateau and valley floor, back onto the slopes, although growers have until 2022 to make the move! A good example (such as Jaboulet's Grand Pompée) is clean, dark and sufficiently fruity Syrah without the grip or depth of Hermitage; wine to drink at four or five years.

The same in general is true of Crozes-Hermitage, the appellation for the east bank around Tain-L'Hermitage, without the advantage of the great upstanding mass of granite to help grill its grapes. It is the biggest AC of the Northern Rhône and the least expensive, so its wines are often the consumer's introduction to Rhône wines. Efforts have been made to improve the basic quality level of Crozes, and style differences are apparent between the traditional vinifiers and those who use *macération carbonique*.

Few famous vineyards are as consistent as Hermitage. Its whole 310-acre surface faces full south at an angle that maximizes the warmth of the sun. Four-fifths are planted with Syrah, the rest with two white grapes, Roussanne and Marsanne, that produce a wine as splendid in its way as the red. A century ago white Hermitage (then all Roussanne) was reckoned the best white wine in France, keeping 'much longer than the red, even to the extent of a century'. It is surprising to find white wine of apparently low acidity keeping well at all. Yet at ten years (a good age for it today) it has a haunting combination of foursquare breadth and depth with some delicate, intriguing, lemony zest.

St-Joseph and Crozes-Hermitage, incidentally, also make white wines of the same grapes which can be excellent. When they are aged they are best served cool, not chilled.

Red Hermitage has the frankest, most forthright, unfumbling 'attack' of any of the Rhône wines. Young, it is massively purple-black, frequently uncomplicated by smells of new oak (although Jaboulet's La Chapelle now has a whiff about it), powerfully fruity, almost sweet beneath a cloak of tannin and takes years to lose its opacity. Many people enjoy it in this state, or so it seems, because mature bottles are rare.

Cornas concludes the red-wine appellations of the Northern Rhône with a sort of country cousin to Hermitage – another dark Syrah wine of macho vigour which only becomes a drink for fastidious palates after years in bottle. The delimited area is large – nearly 1,360 acres – although not all is currently planted.

South of Cornas the appellation St-Péray is a surprising one – for a *méthode traditionnelle* sparkling wine made from Marsanne and Roussanne grapes which, providing you forget the finesse of champagne or the *crémants* of northern France, has much to be said for it. It is a heavy-duty sparkler of almost sticky texture, even when it is dry. With age it develops a very pleasant nutty flavour.

Leading Northern Rhône Producers

Gilles Barge

69420 Condrieu.
Forward-looking grower of fine Côte Rôtie and a little Condrieu from 11 acres. Gilles Barge is considered to be one of the 'young turks' by some traditionalists. He runs the Côte Rôtie Syndicat des Vignerons as well as his own domaine. Good, sometimes excellent wines, needing 10 years or so.

Guy de Barjac

07130 Cornas.
A 5-acre family vineyard going back to the 14th century. Two-thirds of the vines are now *en fermage* to J.-L. Colombo (q.v.) and S. Bernard. Old-fashioned 100% Syrah wine need 18 months in wood and several years in bottle. The label is La Barjasse. Annual production is some 350 cases.

Bernard Burgaud

69420 Ampuis.
Monsieur Burgaud believes in big, well-structured wines, discounting the current, lighter trend as mere fashion. He uses 20% new oak each year, producing 1,000 cases from his 10-acre domaine in Côte-Rôtie.

J. F. Chaboud

07130 St-Péray.
The fourth generation of the Chaboud family has 30 acres of Marsanne and Roussanne. 80% of production is classic-method St-Péray. The *sec* is pure Marsanne.

Emile Champet

Le Port, 69420 Ampuis.
The Champet family has an international reputation on the strength of a mere 6 acres of Côte Rôtie making up to 800 cases a year of sternly tannic red.

M. Chapoutier

26600 Tain L'Hermitage.
Founded in 1808, this is one of the most distinguished names of the Rhône both as growers and négociants. Their 176-acre domaine consists of 75 acres of Hermitage (red and white), 6.6 of Côte Rôtie, 12 of Crozes-Hermitages Les Meysonniers, 13.5 of St-Joseph Deschants (red and white) and 70 of Châteauneauf-du-Pape (red and white) La Bernardine. Methods are wholly traditional, even to treading the grapes. Their domaine wines are aged in small barrels of either oak or sweet chestnut. Everyone should taste their white Hermitage Chante Alouette at 10 or more years old – a revelation after most modern whites. Total sales 80,000 cases; 65% exported. 'Grandes Cuvées' (NV) are wonderful wines. A range of prestige *cuvées*, also non-vintage, are blended from Chapoutier's best wines.

Gérard Chave

Mauves, 07300 Tournon-sur-Rhône.
Gérard Chave in 1981 celebrated 500 years of direct succession in his 27 acres of Hermitage. His red and white are among the best and longest-lived wines in France. His tiny production – no more than 3,000 cases of Hermitage and 250 of St-Joseph – trails far behind his fame.

Auguste Clape

07130 St-Péray.
A grower with 10 acres of Cornas and 2.5 of St-Péray. His Cornas is dark purple, almost black, intensely tannic – the perfect wine for Roquefort, he says. Techniques are very traditional: no filters, no fining. Certainly it is the leader of the appellation.

Jean-Luc Colombo

07130 Cornas.
A consulting oenologist for many big names (Chapoutier, Château Fortia, qq.v.) Jean-Luc Colombo makes big 'plummy' Cornas built for long ageing (Les Ruchets is the top *cuvée*), well-made Côtes du Rhône and Vin de Pays des Collines Rhodaniennes from his 15-acre domaine.

Pierre Coursodon

Mauves, 07300 Tournon-sur-Rhône.
Family property of 47 acres of very old vines on the better slopes of St-Joseph. Both reds and whites demand to be aged.

Yves Cuilleron

Verlieu, 42410 Chavanay.
Since Yves took over the 40-acre domaine from his uncle, Antoine, in 1986 he has made spectacular improvements. Better vineyard practice, selective picking and careful winemaking have resulted in superb Condrieus – particularly his unusual Récolte Tardive.

Delas Frères

07300 Tournon-sur-Rhône.
Long-established growers and négociants now owned by Louis Roederer. They have 50 acres of vineyards, half in Hermitage (red and white), 12 in Cornas, 6 in Côte Rôtie and 5 in Condrieu. Delas wines are marginally cheaper than their rivals but seem to lack nothing in character and staying power. Delas Hermitage is notably good. Their Cornas is called Chante-Perdrix.

Pierre Dumazet

07340 Serrières.
A tiny trickle of Condrieu (from 3 acres of vines) to very smart restaurants and private clients. He has planted more Viognier at enormous expense. Thus, he explains, the price of his Condrieu.

Jules Fayolle & Ses Fils

Gervans, 26600 Tain L'Hermitage.
A family property of 17.5 acres in Crozes-Hermitage and 2.5 red Hermitage, founded in 1870. The reds are old-fashioned, 3 years aged in wood; the Marsanne white (from 6 acres) is bottled young and fresh. The red Hermitage is from a vineyard called Les Dionnières at the eastern end of the slope.

Domaine Ferraton & Fils

26600 Tain L'Hermitage.
Ten acres of Hermitage, plus vines in Croze, making solid, traditional wines. The red Hermitage spends at least 2 years in wood.

Domaine Alain Graillot

26600 La Roche de Glun.
A 53-acre domaine mostly in Crozes-Hermitage with 4 acres in St-Joseph and just over half an acre in Hermitage, producing red and white wines. Yields are deliberately low and the grapes picked when fully ripe to produce a very stylish white Crozes that repays time in bottle and an equally impressive red, La Guiraude.

Château Grillet

42410 Verin.
The smallest property in France with its own Appellation Contrôlée, owned by the Neyret-Gachet family since 1830. The vineyard is 7.5 acres of perilous terraces forming a suntrap 500 feet above the bank of the Rhône. 22,000 Viognier vines yield on average 600 to 800 cases a year of highly aromatic wine which is aged 18 months in oak. Opinions are divided about whether any sort of ageing improves Viognier wine. Recently Château Grillet's reputation has wobbled.

Bernard Gripa

Mauves, 07300 Tournon-sur-Rhône.
A traditionalist producer of St-Joseph. His 25 acres is 80% red, fermented with stems and aged a year in wood. His whites are 90% Marsanne, made crisp and deliciously refreshing.

Jean-Louis Grippat

La Sauva, 07300 Tournon-sur-Rhône.
The eighth generation of Grippats struggles with the terraces of St-Joseph (11 acres, mainly red) and Hermitage (4 acres,

mainly white) to produce a total 2,000 cases a year. Their St-Joseph red is a good 5-year wine, but their Hermitage white is worth 10 years.

E. et M. Guigal

69420 Condrieu.

The Guigal family are the leading producers of Côte Rôtie, which they grow themselves on 30 acres and buy as grapes from 40 other small growers. They ferment the whole bunches in a closed vat for up to 3 weeks, then age it in new oak barrels for 3 years, avoiding both fining and filtration if possible. The object is extremely long-lived wines. Their four labels are La Mouline, La Landonne, La Turque Côte Brune, and Côtes Brune et Blonde. La Landonne is a 3.5-acre plot in the Côte Brune. La Turque was only launched with the 1985 vintage. Whether Guigal's oak-scented style is true to the nature and traditions of Côte Rôtie is a question on which I feel differently from the majority. It certainly attracts extravagant praise, a worldwide demand and famine prices. In 1985 the Guigals bought the firm of Vidal-Fleury (q.v.). Guigal also produces Condrieu and Hermitage, Tavel and some of the very best Côtes du Rhône. Total production is 10,000 cases.

Paul Jaboulet Aîné

26600 Tain L'Hermitage.

Growers and négociants since 1834, now run by three members of the founding family with Gérard Jaboulet in charge. The house is a pacesetter for the whole Rhône both as grower and merchant. Their domaine of 200 acres is in Hermitage (46 acres red, 11 white) and Crozes-Hermitage (102 red, 17 white). All four are among the best each year; the red Hermitage La Chapelle in great vintages ('61, '78, '83, '85) is one of France's greatest wines, maturing over 25 years or more. The vines which produce La Chapelle are on average 35 years old. Each Jaboulet wine has a name as well as an appellation, as follows: Hermitage (red) La Chapelle; (white) Le Chevalier de Sterimberg. Crozes-Hermitage (red) Domaine de Thalabert (white) Mule Blanche. St-Joseph Le Grand Pompée. Côte Rôtie Les Jumelles. Tavel L'Espiègle. Châteauneuf-du-Pape Les Cèdres and a very full and fruity Côtes du Rhône Parallèle 45 (also rosé and white). There is also a Cornas. Another label is Jaboulet-Isnard. Total sales are about 125,000 cases, 55% exported.

Domaine Jamet

69420 Ampuis.

Brothers Jean-Paul and Jean-Luc have a 15-acre domaine comprising separate plots in the Côte-Rôtie. Their wine exhibits fine fruit and good structure, even in difficult years.

Robert Jasmin

69420 Ampuis.

A famous name, though a small property, with vines averaging 25–30 years old. Ten acres of Côte Rôtie. 1,000 cases produced per annum. Traditional vinification, adding 5–10% of white Viognier to the black Syrah and ageing in barrel for 18–24 months.

Marcel Juge

07130 Cornas.

A small grower of hearty red Cornas from 7.5 acres. Methods are traditional, the wine 'structured and fruity' – but not as fruity as his neighbour Clape's. Cuvée 'SC' is the top wine here.

Robert Michel

07130 Cornas.

A simple old-fashioned family holding of 17.5 acres, partly on the hills giving the typically tough red, partly from the foot of the slope for lighter wines. Neither is fined nor filtered before bottling. The former is at least a 10-year wine. 'La Geynale' is the top wine, from old vines on terraces facing due south.

Paul-Etienne Père & Fils

07130 St-Péray.

A family firm of négociants who have been producing sparkling St-Péray for 160 years. Wines of traditional style from all parts of the Rhône. Total production is 42,000 cases, 80% sells in France.

René Rostaing

69420 Ampuis.

A splendid 16-acre estate from some of the best vineyards in Côte-Rôtie (La Viallière, La Landonne). René Rostaing makes elegant, deeply coloured wines, as did his father-in-law (Albert Dervieux-Thaize) and uncle (Marius Gentaz-Dervieux) who left him 11 acres of prime vineyards *en fermage* on their retirement in 1990 and 1993.

Château du Rozay

69420 Condrieu.

Paul Multier was, until his death in 1984, among the few producers of Condrieu, with a reputation as high as any. His son Jean-Yves is now at the helm of the property which comprises 9 acres of precipitous terraces. Fermentation is in large, well-used casks, where the wine stays until its second fermentation is finished. Some Côtes du Rhône red is also produced.

Domaine Marc Sorrel

26600 Tain L'Hermitage.

Marc Sorrel has the largest (10 acres) of the two Sorrel estates (his brother Jean-Michel has 2.5 acres) created on the death of father Henri Sorrel in 1984. The top red Hermitage *cuvée* Le Gréal is always one of the best of the commune. The white Hermitage and Crozes-Hermitage are also very good

Domaine de Vallouit

07130 Châteaubourg.

Louis de Vallouit trained as a winemaker in Beaune and Dijon. He now runs this large (75-acre) domaine as well as a négociant business. The top label is Les Roziers, made from 25 acres in Côte-Rôtie, using traditional methods (fully ripe grapes, 15–20 days' *cuvaison* to extract maximum colour, and up to 40 months in wood). De Vallouit also has a range of impressive *cuvées spéciales* from St-Joseph, Cornas, Crozes-Hermitage and Hermitage, plus a very well-made Condrieu.

Georges Vernay

69420 Condrieu.
The leading figure in Condrieu with 17.5 acres of Viognier, mostly planted on reclaimed abandoned terraces. His wine is bottled in its first spring (or even winter) for freshness – and because demand outruns supply. A small amount spends longer in wood and becomes Coteaux de Vernon, a distinctly superior wine. He also has 4.5 acres of Côte Rôtie and small vineyards in St-Joseph and Côtes du Rhône.

J. Vidal-Fleury

69420 Ampuis.
The oldest (established 1781) and biggest domaine of Côte Rôtie terraces with a princely 25 acres, bought in 1985 by the Guigal family (q.v.). They make wines from the two Côtes,

Brune and Blonde, separately and also together. The total annual production of these is 2,500 cases. It takes 10 years for the real finesse of these wines to emerge. In addition, the firm has a full line of négoce wines of fair to fine quality.

Alain Voge

07130 Cornas.
The Voge family, in its fourth generation here, makes Cornas from 17.5acres by old methods and sparkling St-Péray, from 10 acres of Marsanne, by the classic method.

NORTHERN RHONE COOPERATIVES

Caves des Clairmonts Crozes-Hermitage. Small quality-conscious cooperative.

Caves de Tain-l'Hermitage 26600 Tain-l'Hermitage. A high-quality coop offering excellent Crozes-Hermitage, Hermitage (of which it is the largest producer), St-Joseph, Cornas and *vin de pays*. some Hermitage *cuvées* from this coop can match the best of the appellation.

SOUTHERN RHONE

The catch-all appellation for the huge spread of Southern Rhône vineyards is Côtes du Rhône. It is not a very exigent title – the equivalent of AC Bordeaux Rouge. Big crops of up to 55 hectolitres a hectare are eligible so long as they reach 10 degrees of alcohol. The area covers a total 99,000 acres of vineyards in more than 100 communes north of Avignon, describing a rough circle among the low hills surrounding the widening Rhône. It leaves out only the alluvial bottom land around the river itself. In an average year, it makes almost twice as much wine as the appellation Beaujolais – indeed not far short of the whole of Burgundy and nearly a third of the Bordeaux crop. Ninety-nine percent of it is red or rosé. In such an ocean of wine there are several estates that set standards of their own, and good négociants choose and blend well. The thing to bear in mind is that Côtes du Rhône is for drinking young, while it is reasonably fruity.

There used to be a tradition in the area of making a very light café wine known as *vin d'une nuit* – vatted for one night only. It has now been superseded by the adoption of Beaujolais tactics to make a Rhône *primeur* with some of the qualities of new Beaujolais – but not with the exciting smell of the new Gamay. It is the second biggest producer of *primeur*, but an annual average of 100,000 hectolitres puts the Rhône a long way behind Beaujolais. Regular red Côtes du Rhône is unpredictable, but compared with basic Bordeaux as a daily drink it is more warm and winey, less fresh and stimulating.

Côtes du Rhône-Villages is the inner circle. Forty years ago growers in two communes east of the valley, Gigondas and Cairanne, and two to the west, Chusclan and Laudun, raised their sights to making stronger, more concentrated *vin de garde*, modelling their wines on the *crus* of the Southern Rhône (Grenache base plus Syrah, Mourvèdre and Cinsaut).

Limiting their crop to 42 hectolitres a hectare (according to the vintage) and ripening their grapes to give 12.5 degrees alcohol they made better wine and got better prices. A number of their neighbours followed suit. In 1967, the appellation Côtes du Rhône-Villages was decreed for a group of what has now risen to 16 communes totalling 9,880 acres. (The list of the group of qualifying communes is given on page 188.) The village name is permitted on the label for this group but a total of 64 villages are still entitled to use 'Côtes du Rhône-Villages' where the wine is not exclusively from the named village. Gigondas and now Vacqueyras have appellation status, and this seems likely to happen to others in the group as they establish their identity and build their markets.

Certainly Vacqueyras deserved its promotion to AOC. As an example of the style of the area it might be compared with Gigondas. Tasted together the Gigondas is fuller and rounder, with more 'stuffing'; the Vacqueyras is more 'nervous', harsh at first but developing a very pleasant dusty, slightly spicy, bouquet. (The Gigondas has very little.) The wines from the best producers in both Vacqueyras and Gigondas are emphatically *vins de garde*: at five or six years they still need decanting a good 12 hours ahead – or keeping another three years.

There is a general and positive trend apparent in the Southern Rhône which places greater importance on the use of better varieties in the blend (Syrah and Mourvèdre in particular) – with correspondingly less reliance on the workhorse Grenache. Of the communes which are not -Villages, Uchaux and Châteauneuf-de-Gadagne are areas of apparent promise. On about the same quality level as Côtes du Rhône comes the appellation Coteaux du Tricastin, inaugurated in 1974, for vineyards higher up the east bank of the river.

Leading Southern Rhône Producers

Domaine des Anges

84570 Mormoiron.

Malcolm Swan, an English ex-advertising man, has 20 acres of Grenache, Syrah, Cinsaut and Carignan and makes 2,300 cases of full-flavoured 'Beaujolais-type' Côtes du Ventoux for drinking young.

Château d'Aqueria

30126 Tavel.

A 17th-century property owned by the Olivier family since 1919. 135 acres are in Tavel, a few in Lirac, producing up to 20,000 cases p.a. By ageing the Tavel in big casks for a few months they aim to stiffen it a little to survive longer in bottle.

Domaine Assémat

30150 Roquemaure.

The achievement, since 1963, of Jean-Claude Assémat, a young oenologist with modern ideas. He has created two properties: Domaine Les Garrigues of 40 acres (all Lirac) and Domaine des Causses et St-Eymes (85 acres in Lirac, 15 in Laudun). His wines range from Rouge d'Eté en primeur to a Syrah made by adding fresh Syrah to the pulp left after macerating his rosé – a double dose of skins, giving wine which will stand up, he says, 'even to thyme and rosemary'. They are lively wines made with flair and gastronomic awareness.

Domaine Brusset

Cairanne, 84290 St-Cécile-les-Vignes.

Daniel Brusset's Cuvée des Templiers, made from 104 acres, is a traditional Cavanne and one of the village's best.

Domaine de Castel Oualou

30150 Roquemaure.

An important Lirac property of 126 acres developed over the past 20 years by the Pons-Mure family. Splendid medal-winning Lirac Rouge, which contains Syrah and Mourvèdre. There is also a little pleasant white of Ugni Blanc, Clairette and Picpoul, and rosé containing Clairette on a basis of Cinsaut and Grenache. The domaine is now owned by J.-C. Assémat (q.v.).

Domaine du Cayron

84190 Gigondas.

Michel Faraud makes one of the finest Gigondas from 35 acres of 40-year-old vines scattered all over the appellation. Only one label, but well worth seeking out.

Didier Charavin

84110 Rasteau.

A family property going back to the years of the French Revolution; 37 acres making the classic sweet Rasteau, entirely from Grenache, and an old-style red from Grenache, Syrah and Carignan aged one year in oak barrels and bottled without filtering. Some of the barrels are 100 years old. Only his rosé is given modern treatment.

Domaine du Devoy

30126 St-Laurent-des-Arbes.

Owned by the Lombardo brothers. An excellent property of 100 acres, planted in Grenache, with Cinsaut, Mourvèdre and Syrah. Full-coloured, distinguished, even elegant reds with no wood-ageing. Also a little rosé.

Domaine Durban

84190 Beaumes de Venise.

Jacques Leydier is a reticent but excellent producer of both Muscat de Beaumes de Venise and red Côtes du Rhône-Villages from 86 acres.

Château de l'Estagnol

26130 St-Paul Trois Châteaux.

The Chambovet family have built up a vineyard of 200 acres, 16 miles north of Orange on sandy slopes that give Côtes du Rhône of warm piney and herbal character. The vines are Syrah, Grenache, Cinsaut and Mourvèdre in approximately equal proportions; the Syrah is fermented by macération carbonique. A special cuvée with extra Syrah, more colour and body is called La Serre du Prieur.

Domaine du Grand Montmirail

84190, Gigondas.

An 80-acre Gigondas estate owned by Denis Cheron (see Pascal SA). Low production from old Grenache vines has been adapted with more Syrah, white Mourvèdre and Cinsaut also used to make more assertive wines for longer life in a new winery. The 5,500-case production has three names: Domaine du Roucas de St Pierre, Domaine de St Gens and Domaine du Pradas.

Château du Grand Moulas

84550 Mornas.

Marc Ryckwaert owns 72 acres of vineyard in the Côte du Rhône and makes three reds (top label: Cuvée de l'Ecu) and a white, all very fine examples of the appellation. No wood.

Domaine Maby

30126 Tavel.

A family property of 250 acres, half in Tavel, where they make the wine as fresh as possible by the old method, a quarter in Lirac for 'big' reds and a quarter Côtes du Rhône for light red.

Etablissement Gabriel Meffre

84290 Gigondas.

A major modern domaine of 1,680 acres in Châteauneuf, Gigondas and the Côtes du Rhône. The Meffre family have 12 Rhône and Provence properties; including Château de Vaudieu, 173 acres of Châteauneuf-du-Pape making a vin de garde; the Domaines des Bosquets, Raspail and la Daysse in Gigondas (Bosquet fruitier, Raspail more powerful); the Domaine du Bois des Dames of 250 acres at Violes and the huge and historic Château de Ruth with 285 acres at Ste-Cécile des Vignes. The last two make good fruity Côtes du Rhône red, and Château de Ruth a light fresh white as well.

187

A. Ogier & Fils

84700 Sorgues.

The great-grandsons of the founder run this Avignon firm of négociants, dealing in most Southern Rhône appellations. They have exclusive rights in two Côtes du Rhône estates, Domaine Romarin at Domazan and Château St-Pierre d'Escarvaillac at Caumont, and with Domaine de la Gavotte at Puyloubier, Côtes de Provence. They also market several brands of table wine. Total sales exceed 150,000 cases a year.

Domaine les Palleroudias

La Beaumette, 84190 Gigondas.

The fourth generation of the Burles still have 60-year-old Grenache vines in their vineyards in Gigondas and Vacqueyras – about 40 acres in scattered parcels. Vinification is 'modernized traditional' with concrete vats and a hydraulic press. Gigondas Les Pallierondes is their *vin noble*, which Edmond Burle likes to deliver to clients personally.

Domaine Les Pallières

84190 Gigondas.

The Roux family has been making wine in the manner of Châteauneuf-du-Pape in Gigondas for 500 years. Low yields, long macerating of the bunches, three years oak-ageing make tannic wine for patient clients – 80% in France. 60 acres produce 6,500 cases.

Pascal SA

Vacqueyras, 84190 Beaumes de Venise.

A 60-year-old merchant house revitalized by its *recent* owner and winemaker, Denis Cheron. Pascal own 8 acres of Vacqueyras and buy grapes for a total of 85,000 cases of Vacqueyras, Gigondas, Côtes du Rhône and -Villages, Côtes du Ventoux and Vins de Pays de Vaucluse. Cheron looks for roundly fruity wines with depth and vitality, removing all stalks and fermenting 5-8 days. Good selection and technique make him a quality leader. 50% of production is exported, some under the name Augustin Peyrouse. Cheron also owns the Domaine du Grand Montmirail (q.v.).

Domaine Pelaquié

30290 Laudun.

The grandsons of Joseph Pelaquié, one of the vignerons who first promoted the Côtes de Rhône, run a small estate, principally in Laudun with a little Lirac (more to come). Very old vines make it a good example of the region.

Domaine Rabasse-Charavin

Cairanne, 84290 St-Cécile-les-Vignes.

A top producer of Cairanne, Corinne Couturier farms 160 acres to make several wines, including a straight Syrah and the Cuvée d'Estevenas from old vines.

Domaine Raspail-Ay

84190 Gigondas.

One of the best domaines in Gigondas. Dominique Ay produces a very well-structured and fruity wine from his 45-acre estate.

Les Fils de Gabriel Roudil

Le Vieux Moulin, 30126 Tavel.

This family property (since 1870) is run by three brothers, with 150 acres, 112 of them in Tavel with some in Lirac and some in Côtes du Rhône. Some 225,000 cases of Tavel Domaine du Vieux Moulin are their main product. The formula is 60% Grenache, 25% Cinsaut, 10% Picpoul, and 5% Carignan, macerated on the skins for between 12 and 24 hours, fermented dry and bottled at 6 months. Red Lirac has Syrah and Mourvèdre in addition for colour, macerates for 8-10 days and spends a year in wood. The same traditional method is used for red Côtes du Rhône. Another label for Roudil's Tavel is Réserve de Carvaillons.

Domaine Louis Rousseau

Les Charmettes, 30290 Laudun.

The Rousseaus have 60 acres in Lirac for red and 10 in Laudun for Côtes du Rhône-Villages red and rosé. Like many growers in the area they settled from Algeria in the early 1960s. Their winemaking is 'traditional', but without barrels. Several wines are named for notable Popes.

Château St-Estève

Uchaux, 84100 Orange.

The Français-Monier family have owned the 130-acre estate for 200 years. Uchaux lies on a sandy ridge north of Orange which gives ripe, warm wines with body and character. From 50% Grenache, 18% each Syrah and Cinsaut and a little Mourvèdre, Roussanne and even Viognier. The property produces seven wines including St-Estève Grande Réserve red *vin de garde*, St-Estève Tradition, a light Friand de St-Estève *en primeur*, a rosé, a Viognier white and a *méthode traditionnelle blanc de blancs*.

Domaine St-Gayan

Gigondas, 84190 Beaumes de Venise.

The Meffre family (Roger, father, and Jean-Pierre, son) claim to have 400 years of Gigondas vigneron forebears. They produce much-appreciated tannic Gigondas up to 14.5 degrees alcohol, reeking (they say) of truffles and crushed fruit, from ancient vines. Also big-scale Côtes du Rhône-Villages in Sablet and Rasteau.

Château St-Roch

30150 Roquemaure.

The 150-acre Lirac property of Antoine Verda, making good warming red Lirac intended to age in bottle, some 'supple' rosé and a trace of soft white. The top wine is the Cuvée Ancien Vigurie, which gets an extra year in wood. The same

Côtes du Rhône-Villages

The 16 communes entitled to this appellation are: Drôme: Rochegude, Rousset-lès-Vignes, St-Maurice-sur-Eygues, St-Pantaléon-lès-Vignes, Valréas, Visan, Vinsobres. Vaucluse: Cairanne, Rasteau, Roaix, Sablet, Séguret, Beaumes de Venise. Gard: Chusclan, Laudun, St-Gervais.

proprietor has started the new Domaine Cantegril-Verda, also at Roquemaure, with 45 acres of Côtes du Rhône red and a little white. The crop is 25% higher than in Lirac and the wine correspondingly lighter, for drinking young.

Domaine Ste-Anne

Les Celettes-St Gervais, 30200 Bagnols sur Cèze.

A 72 acre estate making Côtes du Rhône and -Villages red and white; the reds by *macération carbonique*. They also produce good Viognier.

Château de Ségriès

30126 Lirac.

The 50-acre estate is owned by Comte de Regis de Gatimel, whose family inherited it in 1804. He makes a tannic red *vin de garde*, fermenting stalks and all and ageing 2 years in concrete tanks. His rosé is also aged but his white, picked just before ripeness, is bottled as young as possible. Notwithstanding the whites apparently age well in bottle for up to 5 years.

Domaine de la Tour d'Elyssas

26290 Donzère.

Pierre Labeve is a dynamic pioneer of the Coteaux du Tricastin who arrived from the north of France in 1965, bulldozed 2 barren hilltops and planted 360 acres of Grenache (150 acres), Cinsaut (100), Syrah (75) and Carignan. The varieties are vinified separately in an ultramodern gravity-fed system. Production is 100,000 cases a year of three main types: Syrah (unblended) aged 2 years in vats, Cru de Meynas, one-third Syrah, a *vin de garde*, and Cru de Devoy, largely Grenache but no Syrah, for drinking young.

Château du Trignon

Gigondas, 84190 Beaumes de Venise.

An old (1898) family estate with modern ideas making excellent wine. Charles Roux uses *macération carbonique* to make rich and savoury Gigondas, more fruity and less tannic in youth than the old style, maturing up to, say, 8 years. His 120 acres are divided among Gigondas, Sablet and Rasteau.

Château de Trinquevedel

30126 Tavel.

François Demoulin, with 64 acres, is one of the leading growers of Tavel, with interesting ideas on adapting his methods to the state of the crop, using partly old techniques and partly new (chilling and *macération carbonique*). He believes a little bottle-age improves his Tavel.

La Vieille Ferme

84100 Orange.

The négociant brand of the Perrin family famous for their Châteauneuf-du-Pape Château de Beaucastel. La Vieille Ferme has become the world's most famous brand from the Southern Rhône. The excellent red is made as a *vin de garde* from the Côtes du Ventoux and the delicate fresh white from high vineyards on the Montagne de Luberon. Both are exceptional value.

OTHER SOUTHERN RHONE PRODUCERS

Domaine Georges Bernard 84190 Beaumes de Venise. The Bernards have two properties, Domaine de la Genestière in Tavel and Lirac and Domaine de Longval in Tavel.

Romain Bouchard Domaine du Val des Rois, 84600 Valréas. Not the same Bouchards as a family tree as tall, and wines they compare with Beaune. They make Côtes du Rhône-Villages from the named village of Valréas which is built to last.

Domaine du Gour de Chaulé 84190 Gigondas. Owner Mme Bonfils makes powerful yet elegant wines from 25 acres. 2,500 cases.

SOUTHERN RHONE COOPERATIVES

There are more than 60 coops producing Côtes du Rhône and the other wines of the region. Overall, they account for 64% of all Rhône wines. A few have gained a reputation equal to that of the best private growers and négociants. These include:

Les Vignerons Ardèchois 07120 Ruom. A grouping of 25 coops spread over 22,500 acres and offering a wide range of wines including Cabernet Sauvignon, Chardonnay and Viognier varietals, VDQS Côtes du Vivarais and AC Côtes du Rhône, Coteaux du Tricastin and St-Joseph. They produce 90% of the Vin de Pays de l'Ardèche.

Cairanne 84290 Cairanne. Founded 1929. 200 members; 2,950 acres (80% of the Cairanne appellation) producing Côtes du Rhône, Côtes du Rhône-Cairanne and Vins de Pays de la Principauté d'Orange. Réserve des Vocondes is their top wine, a solid mouthful that tops 14°. There is also a good oaked white *cuvée*, Antique.

Coteaux de Saint-Maurice 26110 Saint-Maurice-sur-Eyges. 2,000 acres. A reliable coop producing Côtes du Rhône-Saint-Maurice and Vinsobres from Grenache (70%) and Syrah (20%) (red) and Ugni blanc (35%), Clairette (70%) and Viognier (20%) (white).

Vacqueyras 84190 Vacqueyras. 123 members, 2,100 acres. This coop, founded in 1957, vinifies 60% of the Vacqueyras appellation. The top label is Cuvée des Seigneurs de Fontimple. There is also straight Côtes du Rhône and Gigondas.

Cave La Vinsobraise 26110 Vinsobres. Coop producing straight Côtes du Rhône and Côtes du Rhône-Villages Vinsobres. Top labels are Cuvée de Terroirs and Vinsobres *fût de chêne*.

Chusclan 30200 Bagnols-sur-Cèze. Founded 1939. 137 members with 1,850 acres producing 200,000 cases of Côtes du Rhône and -Villages (Chusclan). Painstaking methods include vinifying each variety (there are nine) separately by both traditional vatting and *macération carbonique*.

M. Rivier, the founder, was very specific about the attributes of his wines: reds 'scented with ripe plums and bay leaves', rosé 'perfumed with acacia and wild strawberries'. The white, merely described as 'young and fruity', is in fact a technical achievement; a well-balanced wine with plenty of flavour. Brand names are Seigneurie de Gicon, Les Abeilles, Cuvée des Monticaud, Prieuré St-Julien.

La Courtoise St-Didier, 84210 Pernes-Les-Fontaines. Founded 1924. 350 members. 2,500 acres producing 280,000 cases, of which 95,000 are AC Côtes dU Ventoux. More Syrah is being grown to stiffen the previously pale and light reds.

Gigondas Gigondas, 84190 Beaumes de Venise. Founded 1955. 120 members. 617 acres producing Gigondas and Côtes du Rhône. Three-quarters of the grapes are Grenache; Syrah and Mourvèdre add colour and grip. The wine is bottled after 18 months in wood.

De Orgnac-L'Aven 07150 Vallon-Pont-d'Arc. Founded 1924. 83 members. 1,100 acres producing 29,000 cases, of which half is VDQS Côtes du Vivarais. Syrah, Cinsaut, Grenache and Clairette make light but firm reds, rosés and whites, 'which perfectly reflect our wild and arid hills'. A year in bottle is enough.

Rasteau 84110 Rasteau. Founded 1925. 180 members. 1,850 acres producing sweet *vins doux naturel* (red and white), Côtes du Rhône-Villages, plain Côtes du Rhône and Vin de Table Festival du Crutat. By far the biggest producer of Rasteau.

Tavel 30126 Tavel. Founded 1937. 130 members; 1,000 acres producing 83,000 cases. They use the traditional local method of macerating the skin, cold fermentation to avoid tannins, then sell (and drink) as soon as possible.

Union des Vignerons de l'Enclave des Papes 84602 Valréas. Union of 800 growers marketing Côtes du Rhône and Coteaux du Tricastin from 9,000 acres under the Enclave des Papes label.

TAVEL AND LIRAC

A similar area to Châteauneuf-du-Pape a few miles west, on the other side of the Rhône, has traditionally been famous for its rosé, made with the same grapes. Tavel has a unique reputation for full-bodied dry rosé, made not by fermenting the wine briefly on its (red) grape skins, as most other rosés are made, but by a period of up to 2 days of maceration before fermentation starts. (The yeasts have to be inhibited by sulphur dioxide, or in modern cellars by cooling.) The wine is then pressed and fermented like white wine. I have never been attracted by this powerful, dry rather orange-pink wine, any more than by similar rosés from Provence. It is regarded, though, as one of the classics. Like Racine, it should be re-read from time to time.

Lirac, the northern neighbour to Tavel, has been specializing more recently in red wines, which at their best can be very pleasantly fruity and lively, and in other cases strong and dull.

VENTOUX AND LUBÉRON

Where the Rhône Valley merges with Provence to the east, the appellation Côtes du Ventoux has forged ahead in volume, now far out-producing the united Côtes du Rhône-Villages. Among some very reasonable reds the outstanding wine is La Vieille Ferme (q.v.) of Jean-Pierre Perrin, brother of the owner of Château de Beaucastel. He has also made a Chardonnay from Lubéron. The Côtes du Lubéron, the hills along the north of the Durance Valley (famous throughout France for its asparagus), also makes a substantial contribution to this great source of red wine. Lubéron has been promoted to AC and its reds and whites may appeal more for their crisp well-defined flavours than some of the more pedestrian efforts of the Rhône. There is some very adequate sparkling white Lubéron.

North of the Lubéron near Manosque, the VDQS Coteaux de Pierrevert is a further extension of these Rhône-style vineyards, making light wine.

Clairette de Die

Clairette de Die is like a sorbet between the substantial main dishes of the Northern and Southern Rhône. The energy of the local cooperative has revived a fading appellation. Clairette de Die is at its best when made sparkling, but one or two traditional growers make a satisfying nutty still wine.

Cave Coopérative de Clairette de Die

26150 Die. Three-quarters of the appellation is handled by the 500-plus members of this coop producing 273,000 cases of Brut, Tradition and still wines from 2,000 acres. The Brut is a dry sparkling wine of Clairette grapes 'with an aroma of lilac and lavender'. Tradition is a sweet fizz of Muscat de Frontignan. The method involves fermentation in bottle (but, unlike champagne, of the original grape-sugar), then filtering and decanting to another bottle under pressure. Other wines are Gamay red and Aligoté/Chardonnay white, for which they have their own AOC Châtillon en Diois.

CHATEAUNEUF-DU-PAPE

Châteauneuf-du-Pape is much the biggest and most important specific Rhône appellation. If its 8,150 acres of vines produced as plentifully as those of its neighbours there would be almost as much Châteauneuf-du-Pape as Côtes du Rhône-Villages. But small crops are mandatory: the yield of Châteauneuf-du-Pape is set at 35 hl/ha; for Côtes du Rhône-Villages it can be up to 42 hl/ha. Concentration is the very essence of this wine. Its vines grow in what looks like a shingle beach of big, smooth, oval stones that often cover the whole surface of the vineyard. Each vine is an individual low bush.

Where all other French appellations specify one or two, at most four, grape varieties of similar character, the tradition in Châteauneuf-du-Pape is to grow a dozen with widely different characteristics. It is not clear whether this is primarily an insurance policy, or simply accumulated tradition. Some growers assert that each of them, even the coarse or simply neutral ones, adds to the complexity of the wine. New plantations, however, are tending to cut down the number to four or five. The base, always in the majority and sometimes as much as 80%, is Grenache. The other essentials are Cinsaut, Syrah, Mourvèdre, and the other white Clairette or Picpoul, or both. Varieties that could be described as optional are (red) Cournoise, Muscardin, Vaccarèse and (white) Piccardan, Roussanne, Terret Noir and Bourboulenc. The white varieties were once used in the red wine as well as made into white Châteauneuf-du-Pape on their own; these days there is a new demand for the white version.

Grenache and Cinsaut are described as providing strength, 'warmth' and softness; Mourvèdre, Syrah, Muscardin and Vaccarèse as adding structure, colour, 'cut' and refreshment to the flavour, and the ability to live for long enough to develop a bouquet. Although the legal minimum is 12.5 degrees of alcohol, 13.5 degrees is considered the lowest acceptable by the best growers, who are happy to see 14.5 degrees.

And the result? We have all had great, dull, headachy wines called Châteauneuf-du-Pape. There is no distinct 'varietal' handle by which to grasp either the aroma or the flavour. Commercial examples are usually made to be very warm and 'giving' and slightly fruity. The best estates, however, make magnificient *vins de garde* that start to open up after five years and develop after ten or more. When a bouquet starts to develop it is still elusive. It is rather part of a glowing roast-chestnut warmth about the whole wine. Eventually, in the best examples, latent finesse and the essential sweetness of a great wine will emerge. Much the best I have ever drunk was a 1937, still in perfect condition in 1997.

White Châteauneuf-du-Pape, formerly a long-lived wine, rich and elusive, is today more often made for drinking within three years at most.

Leading Châteauneuf-du-Pape Producers

Père Anselme

84230 Châteauneuf-du-Pape.

The name recalls a wise old ancestor of the founder of this firm of négociants and wine makers, producing most of the Rhône appellations with a total sale of 170,000 cases a year. Brands include La Fiole du Pape, Marescal Côtes du Rhône-Villages and Petit Duc Côtes du Rhône; they also own Mule du Pape restaurant at Châteauneuf and a famous old nougat factory, Arnaud-Soubeyran, at Montélimar. Négociants Jean-Pierre Brotte are part of the same concern. Other ventures include a wine museum visited by 40,000 people a year and experimental winemaking from 20 acres.

Château de Beaucastel

84350 Courthézon.

Brothers Jean-Pierre and François, the fourth generation of the Perrin family, make one of the best wines of the region on this big property dating back to the 17th century. Their Châteauneuf vineyard is 173 acres, plus 125 of Côtes du Rhône. All 13 authorized grapes, with relatively high proportions of Syrah and Mourvèdre, a 25 hl/ha crop, 15-day fermentation in the traditional square stone vats and 2 years' ageing in oak give the wine depth and durability. Organic methods are used in the vineyards and the wine is bottled unfiltered leading to some glorious bottles but also too often to farmyard smells. A small amount of delicious white Châteauneuf is made of 80% Roussanne and 20% Grenache Blanc. Their Côtes du Rhône (a notable bargain for this quality) is called Cru de Coudoulet de Beaucastel. See also their Côtes du Ventoux La Vieille Ferme.

Domaine de Beaurenard

84230 Châteauneuf-du-Pape.

Paul Coulon represents the seventh generation on this family property of 75 acres. He also owns 110 acres of Côtes du Rhône at Rasteau. Both are planted with the same mixture of 70% Grenache and 10% each of Syrah, Cinsaut and Mourvèdre. He stresses careful, bunch-by-bunch selection in the vineyard and *cuvaison à l'ancienne* – long, carefully controlled vatting – in the cellar.

Caves Bessac

84230 Châteauneuf-du-Pape.

A century-old firm of négociants with a good name for traditional Châteauneuf-du-Pape, Tavel, Côtes du Rhône and -Villages. Also Côte Rôtie and Hermitage. Sales are 200,000 cases a year. Huge stocks or Châteauneuf-du-Pape are still kept in barrels.

Domaine Chante Cigale

84230 Châteauneuf-du-Pape.

The name means 'the song of the cicada' – if song is the appropriate word. Noël Sabon with his son-in-law Christian Favier is the third generation to own this 100-acre property, which is now considered among the top ten of Châteauneuf.

The vineyards are 80% Grenache, 10% Syrah and 5% each of Mourvèdre and Cinsaut – no white grapes and no white wine. Old-style vinification and at least 18 months in cask make serious *vin de garde*.

Domaine Font de Michelle

84230 Châteauneuf-du-Pape.
Both red and white Châteauneuf-du-Pape are made at this 75-acre domaine owned by the brothers Gonnet. The red is elegant rather than powerful; the white fresh and attractive.

Château Fortia

84230 Châteauneuf-du-Pape.
The family estate of the instigator of the system of Appellations Contrôlées, Baron Le Roy de Boiseaumarie, who in 1923 first defined the best vineyard land of the region in terms of the wild plants, thyme and lavender, growing together; an early ecologist. Today the best 7,000 cases from the 70 acres are château bottled; the rest sold in bulk but standards are far from what they were. 10% of the production is white Châteauneuf-du-Pape.

Château de la Gardine

84230 Châteauneuf-du-Pape.
A family property of 175 acres, half of them in Châteauneuf-du-Pape, the remainder in Côtes du Rhône and -Villages at Rasteau and Roaix. Both the Châteauneuf (red and white) and Côtes du Rhône-Villages carry the château name. The Brunels aim for a reasonably 'supple and elegant' wine rather than a pugilist, ageing their Châteauneuf three years in wood.

Domaine de La Janasse

84350 Courthézon.
Christophe Sabon produces Côtes du Rhône and Châteauneuf-du-Pape from his 75-acre domaine, mostly planted with old vines (some 80-100 years old in Châteauneuf). Low yields and a long *cuvaison* ensure very powerful wines, now among the best of the appellation. Top labels are Cuvée Chaupin (80% Grenache, 15% Syrah) and Vieilles Vignes (90% Grenache). Also exceptional white wine.

Clos Mont Olivet

84230 Châteauneuf-du-Pape.
The 3 sons of Joseph Sabon are the fourth generation to make wine they describe as 'well-structured, highly aromatic and long in the mouth' – traditional Châteauneuf – from 59 acres. The top *cuvée* is called Papet. Another 20 acres at Bollène (Vaucluse) produces Côtes du Rhône.

Domaine de Mont-Redon

84230 Châteauneuf-du-Pape.
The biggest single vineyard (235 acres) in Châteauneuf, with a long history ('Mourredon', part of the episcopal estate, had vines in 1334), bought in 1921 by Henri Plantin and now run by his grandsons M. Abeille and M. Fabre. Its immensely stony ground used to produce a benchmark Chateauneuf for endless ageing. Today it is a good middle-weight. The same wine is sold in some markets under the following names: Cuvées des Felibres, Vignoble Abeille, Vignoble Fabre and Les Busquières. Mont-Redon is the largest producer of white Châteauneuf. The estate also includes 50 acres of Côtes du Rhône at Roquemaure.

Société Louis Mousset

84230 Châteauneuf-du-Pape.
One of the biggest estates of the Rhône, built up by five generations of the Mousset family to a total of more than 600 acres, 260 in Châteauneuf-du-Pape including the Ch. des Fines Roches (112 acres), Dom. de la Font du Roi (62), Dom. du Clos St-Michel (25) and Dom. du Clos du Roi (62). There are four Côtes du Rhône estates, called Ch. du Bois de la Garde, Ch. du Prieuré, Dom. de Tout-Vent and Dom. du Grand Vaucroze. The Moussets also have three brandnames: Cigalière, Les Trois Couronnes and Tourbillon. The headquarters is the Ch. des Fines Roches, one of the great names of the area.

Société du Domaine de Nalys

84230 Châteauneuf-du-Pape.
Estate of 120 acres growing the classic 13 grapes to make one of the fresher examples of Châteauneuf, using carbonic maceration and aged only up to a year in wood before bottling. Also small amounts of notably good white for fairly early drinking.

Domaine de la Nerthe

84230 Châteauneuf-du-Pape.
One of the great names of Châteauneuf, quoted in the 19th century as being a separate and slightly better wine than Châteauneuf itself. The estate now boasts 225 acres with a rather simplified planting (Grenache, Mourvèdre, Cinsaut, Syrah and Clairette). Vintages of the '90s are showing new ideas: fruitier and untypically new oak-aged. The top *cuvées*, called Cadettes (red) and Beauvenir (white), have been outstanding.

Clos des Papes

84230 Châteauneuf-du-Pape.
A property in direct descent from father to son for more than 300 years. Paul Avril has 80 acres, 70% Grenache with Syrah, Mourvèdre, Muscardin and Vaccarèse. His aim is power and structure. He is not afraid of tannin and believes Châteauneuf needs years in bottle. 10% of his 9,000-case total is white.

Château Rayas

84230 Châteauneuf-du-Pape.
A small but outstanding property often cited as the best of Châteauneuf. The Reynaud family have 38 acres (5 are white grapes), planted with 90% Grenache, the balance Cinsaut and Syrah. They age the red for 2 or 3 years in wood depending on the vintage. Château Fonsalette (a top Côtes du Rhône) is also made at Rayas. Fonsalette Cuvée Syrah is heroic for its appellation.

Caves St-Pierre-Sefivin

84230 Châteauneuf-du-Pape.

A very large family company of proprietors and négociants with a stable of well-known names, including four Châteauneufs: St-Pierre, Ch. St-André, Dom. des Pontifs and Dom. Condorcet, and the Lirac Ch. de Ségriès. Their bottling company, the Société des Vins Fins de la Vallée du Rhône, handles an annual 500,000 cases.

Domaine du Vieux Télégraphe

84370 Bédarrides.

A long-established 180-acre estate taking its name from the old signal tower on the hill. The third and fourth generations of the Brunier family make 5,800 cases of conservative Châteauneuf; dark, peppery and intense. The vines are 80% Grenache, 10% Cinsaut and 5% each of Syrah and Mourvèdre. The stony soil, a yield of only 34 hl/ha and long fermentation of the whole bunches account for the concentration of the wine.

Cellier des Princes

84350 Courthézon.

The only coop in Châteauneuf was founded in 1962 and produces 82,000 cases of lighter than average Châteauneuf (but not light wine). The top *cuvée* here is Souleiado; there is also good-value Côtes du Rhône and Vin de Pays de la Principauté d'Orange.

OTHER CHATEAUNEUF-DU-PAPE PRODUCERS

Henri Bonneau An old family of growers producing Cuvée Marie Beurier and the Réserve des Célestins, a solid spicy, even massive red. The top *cuvée*, Boisrenard, is spectacular.

Bosquet des Papes Maurice Boiron. Traditional wine from 57 acres of very old vines.

Domaine les Cailloux André Brunel. 51 acres. One of the top domaines of Châteauneuf. A new silkier style of wine came with a change in vinification techniques (destemming and longer *cuvaisons)* in the late-'80s.

Domaine de Cabrières Louis and Guy Arnaud. 138 acres. Depending on the vintage, the wine here spends between one and five years in wood before bottling.

Les Cèdres The excellent brandname Châteauneuf of Paul Jaboulet (see Northern Rhône entries).

Domaine Chante-Perdrix. Remy and Guy Nicolet. A 47-acre property to the south of Châteauneuf, not far from the Rhône itself. Very concentrated high-strength wine which spends three years in wood.

Château de la Font du Loup J. R. Melia. A small (40-acre) estate with old vines and traditional methods making fine aromatic wine.

Domaine du Grand Tinel A traditionalist estate of 180 acres, the property of M. Elie Jeune, the former mayor of the commune.

Domaine Jean Trintignant 85 acres of Châteauneuf, plus Côtes du Rhône. Good red wine in the lighter style and sometimes admirable white.

Château de Vaudieu 180 acres, part of the large Gabriel Meffre properties based at Gigondas. Sound wines from an admirably situated vineyard near Ch. Rayas.

Université du Vin

The crenellated towers of the ancient château of Suze-La-Rousse house the Rhône's Université du Vin, founded in 1978. The first institution of its kind in the world, it is open to professionals – growers, négociants, restaurateurs – and amateurs.

From October to April, courses are run for growers; for the rest of the year others in the wine business and amateurs study tasting, the whole spectrum of viticulture and winemaking and 'the art and civilization of wine'.

Highly sophisticated laboratories and tasting rooms ('with the calm ambience that allows the necessary concentration') serve the University and the official bodies of the Rhône. The laboratories have the latest electronic equipment for wine, vine and soil analysis. Other amenities are an oenothèque and a museum.

Université du Vin, Château de Suze-La-Rousse, 26130 Suze-La-Rousse.

PROVENCE

Not so long ago it was just as well to approach Provence in an indolent frame of mind with serious judgement suspended. Most of its wine was passable at best; sun-glass rosé with too much alcohol and too little taste. There were a few reds of character, and careful winemakers even made white wine that was almost refreshing, but the quality rarely justified the price. Wines as good could be found in the Rhône, and even in the hills of the Midi, for less money.

Provence depended for too long on its captive audience of holiday makers. I have tried, but always failed, to enjoy traditional strong dry rosé made from the non-aromatic grapes of the region, the same Carignan, Cinsaut and Grenache as the Rhône, with an even smaller proportion of Syrah and Mourvèdre to give flavour. There are sometimes aromas of herbs and pines – the heady sunbaked smell of the land.

Times have changed. There are now some deliciously light rosés, a much greater number of serious reds and more well-made whites. Better grapes have been planted (there is growing emphasis on Syrah and Mourvèdre, and Tibouren for rosés) and modern controls implemented. 1977 was the year when Côtes de Provence was promoted from a VDQS to an AOC. For a few estates it was recognition of their real quality. For the majority it was more in anticipation and encouragement of the future progress, now apparent in the increased success of smaller estates. Individual growers have capitalized on the California-like climate and the wider availability of classic grape varieties. In Provence, the estate or growers' name is all. Appellations are now a much more reliable guide to quality too; Aix-en-Provence and especially Baux-de-Provence have become serious contenders in the quality stakes. Areas of Côtes de Provence, such as Mont Sainte-Victoire, now also have a number of good producers, especially of red wines.

Côtes de Provence was an alarmingly wide area for a single appellation, including the coast from St-Tropez to beyond Toulon to the west, and a great stretch of country inland, north of the Massif des Maures back to Draguignan and the first foothills of the Alps. Before all this became an AOC, however, there were already four little local appellations where the wine was considered consistently above average.

The biggest and unquestionably the best – indeed a wine that must be included among France's most splendid reds comes from Bandol, a ten-mile stretch of coast and its hinterland just west of Toulon. The production is some 200,000 cases, and good Bandol red has a quality that has traditionally been rare in Provence: tannic firmness that makes it a three-year wine at the very least, lasting without problems but maturing in splendour up to 10 years or more. The law requires Bandol vines to be at least 8 years old for the wine to qualify for appellation status, and the wine must spend 18 months in cask. The reason is a high proportion (the legal minimum is 50% but many of the best estates will now use 100%) of the 'aromatic' Mourvèdre, which appreciates the heat of rocky terraces. There is also Bandol rosé and white.

Farther west along the coast, almost in the outskirts of Marseille, the fishing port of Cassis is known for its (relatively) lively and aromatic white, for which the bouillabaisse restaurants of Marseille see fit to charge Grand Vin prices.

The wines of the district of Aix-en-Provence, north of Marseille, come under the AOC Coteaux d'Aix-en-Provence. The area was VDQS until 1985. The microscopic enclave of Palette, an appellation area just east of Aix, is dominated by Château Simone (q.v.). Aix-en-Provence includes one of the best red-wine estates in Provence, newly revived Château Vignelaure (q.v.). Others are probably only a little behind it. Since the 1994 vintage neighbouring Les Baux has achieved appellation status for its reds and rosés – Côtes des Baux de Provence (for the present, the whites remain under the more general Coteaux d'Aix-en-Provence appellation). Many of the top-quality producers in Les Baux are using some Cabernet Sauvignon and most adopt organic methods to grow their vines.

Behind Nice in the hills at the extreme other end of Provence the 100-acre appellation of Bellet is justified by wine that is considerably better than the generally dismal prevailing standard of its neighbours; the whites are better than the reds. The Côte d'Azur seems to disprove the theory that a sophisticated clientele spurs wine makers to make fine wine.

Some 20 estates in Provence use the title *cru classé*: this dates back to the 1950s and an attempt to raise local quality standards. It was originally used by producers who were the first to bottle their wines at the estate. The term should not be taken too seriously.

Leading Provence Producers

Jean Bagnis & Fils

83390 Cuers.
A family company of growers and négociants with 32 acres (making an annual 6,600 cases) at Château de Crémat in the tiny appellation Bellet above Nice in the hills. This is expensive wine but distinctly tastier than their standard Côtes de Provence, the ubiquitous brand L'Estandon served in all the cafés.

Domaine la Bernarde

83340 Le Luc.
M. and the late Mme Meulnart did a California-style switch from industry *par amour du vin* and took over this old farm north of the Maures. Meulnart Père et Fils now have 37 acres for red wine and 15 for white. Their special Cabernet Sauvignon/Syrah *cuvée*, Clos St-Germain – best vintages only, long fermentation, wood-aged then bottle-matured – has won a run of medals at Mâcon. Also good rosé; Clos la Bernarde, a lighter red, and a white. 14,500 cases.

Domaine de la Courtade

83400 Ile de Porquerolles.

An outpost of experimentation, west of Toulon, begun in 1983. Despite the youthful vines the '87 and '88 vintages, released in 1990, proved excellent. Reds are blends of Mourvèdre, Grenache and Syrah; whites of Sémillon and Rolle.

Commanderie Peyrassol

83340 Le Luc.

The Commanderie was founded by the Templars in 1204 and acquired by the Rigord family in 1890. 160 acres produce 33,000 cases of two ranges: Cuvée Eperon d'Or and Cuvée Marie Estelle from older vines. Both reds have substantial percentages of Cabernet Sauvignon and Syrah, and new oak is used for ageing. Their white wine includes Sémillon.

Château La Coste

13610 Le Puy-Ste-Réparade.

One of the largest estates in Provence. The Bordonado family owns Château La Coste and two associated estates: Domaine de la Grande Séouve and Domaine de la Boulangère. Winemaking techniques are modern for rosés and whites, but traditional for reds. Nearly half the production is of red, with 40 percent rosé and 15 percent white. For such large-scale production, the quality of the wines is very high – especially for the reds. The Bordonado family also own the 75-acre estate, Château de Costefriede, whose first vintage was the 1987.

Domaine de Curebeasse

83600 Fréjus.

Jean Paquette's 44 acres produce 7,700 cases of Côtes de Provence, half rosé. The best red is Roches Noires from wines grown on volcanic soil. M. Paquette is a partisan for his region's wines. The whites are especially well thought of.

Mas de la Dame

13520 Les Baux-de-Provence.

Mmes Poniatowski and Missoffe produce one of the best wines from the recent (1994) appellation Les Baux de Provence. Their Cuvée de l'Estelle, aged in oak, is the top label. Production is 20,000 cases from 137 acres.

Domaine des Féraud

83550 Vidauban.

Owned by the Laudon-Rival family for three generations. Paul Rival, the former owner of Château Guiraud, Sauternes, ran the property for 25 years until 1955 then handed over to his nephew Bernard Laudon, who is still in charge. 100 acres of AOC Côtes de Provence. Médoc-inspired Cabernet Sauvignon, Syrah and Grenache red, whites from Sémillon, also rosé. Production 14,700 cases.

Château de Fonscolombe

13610 Le-Puy-Ste-Réparade.

The Marquis de Saporta has two Coteaux d'Aix AOC properties north of Aix – this (410 acres) and the Domaine

de la Crémade (250 acres). Both have been in his family since 1720. A noble Renaissance château now notable for upgrading local wine quality, especially in whites. Modern techniques for whites and rosés and traditional oak vinification for reds. The Cuvée Spéciale red has 15–20% Cabernet.

Domaines Gavoty

83340 Le Luc

Some of the top Côtes de Provence are produced by Roselyne Gavoty from 75 acres, including the sumptuous Cuvée Clarendon.

Château Grand'Boise

13530 Trets.

A handsome and ambitious estate of 105 acres around a 17th-century château, belong to the Gruy family. The oak-aged red has won gold medals at the Mâcon fair.

Château Minuty

Gassin, 83990 St-Tropez.

François and Jean-Etienne Matton run this sizeable property near St-Tropez which has a fine house and a serious reputation for its oak-aged red. Production 62,000 cases from 250 acres.

Domaines Bunan

83740 La Cadière d'Azur.

The brothers Bunan, Paul and Pierre and Paul's son Laurent, have 168 acres of steep vineyards at La Cadière (Moulin des Costes) and at nearby Le Castellet (Mas de la Rouvière). Most is rosé AOC Bandol, but some excellent and increasingly important, long-lived red (70% Mourvèdre, 30% Grenache - no Cinsaut) is made and in exceptional years a special *cuvée* is produced under the Château de la Rouvière label. Varietal *vins de pays* (Mourvèdre and Cabernet Sauvignon) are also very good. The Bunans also have Domaine de Belouve *en fermage*.

Domaines Ott

06601 Antibes.

Founded in 1896 by a native of Alsace, now the owner of three properties producing good old-fashioned Provence wines by traditional, organic methods: limited yield, no sulphur, oak ageing. Ott rosés in particular are superb. Estates owned are Clos Mireille, Château Romasson, Château de Selle.

Domaine des Planes

83520 Roquebrune-sur-Argens.

Swiss Christopher Rieder, who with his oenologist wife Ilse farms 62 Côtes de Provence acres in the Argens valley, is a graduate of both Geisenheim and Montpellier and owns vineyards in Germany and Switzerland. 14,000 cases include unblended Muscat, Grenache, Mourvèdre and Cabernet Sauvignon wines, plus AOC Côtes de Provence red, white and two rosés, one from the Tibouren grape. The Mourvèdre is a conspicuous success.

Les Maitres Vignerons de la Presqu'île de St-Tropez

Gassin, 83990 St-Tropez.

This semicoop chooses *cuvées* made by member producers, from 1,700 acres, bottles the wine and markets it. Production 45,000 cases. Uses brands Ch. de Pampelonne and St-Martin-les-Roches, plus Cuvée du Chasseur and Carte Noire for the top reds and rosés.

Domaine Richeaume

13114 Puyloubier.

The German proprietor, M. Hoesch, ages his Cabernet-based reds in oak for 2 years. 3,300 cases from 61 organically farmed acres in the east of the Côtes de Provence. He makes a red from Cabernet Sauvignon and Syrah, which is aged for two years in wood, and maintains that even his rosé and white are wines for keeping. A *blanc de blancs* from Clairette is certainly well made in a traditional way. Hoesch also produces unblended Syrah and a *rosé de saignée* from Grenache. One of the best estates of Provence.

Domaine de St-André de Figuière

83250 La Londe-Les-Maures

Alain Combard has 40 acres between St-Tropez and Toulon, producing 8,500 cases of red and rosé, including a Vieilles Vignes Cuvée de Rosé. Grenache is predominant in the reds; Clairette in the whites.

Château Sainte-Anne

Ste-Anne d'Evenos, 83330 Le Beausset.

The Marquis François Dutheil de la Rochère owns two estates: the 49 acres and 16th-century building of Château Sainte-Anne, producing Bandol, and 12 acres producing Côtes de Provence. Winemaking methods are traditional and the use of chemicals for vinification is avoided. The red wines are wood-aged for up to 22 months. In 1989 a Vin de Collection (98% Mourvèdre, 2% Grenache) was introduced. Bandol wines also include a light rosé and some white. The Côtes de Provence is all rosé.

Château Simone

Palette, 13100 Aix-en-Provence.

One of two properties in the tiny AOC Palette and owned by the sixth generation of the Rougier family. 42 acres provide local restaurants with a very satisfactory speciality: wines that really taste of the herbs and pines of the countryside. On average the vines are 60 years old. The red ages well; the white could be considered an acquired taste.

Domaines et Châteaux Elie Sumeire

38 Grand'Rue, La Croix Rouge, 13013 Marseille.

The Sumeire family owns these three estates (Château Coussin Sainte-Victoire, Château des Anglades and Château l'Afrique), in different parts of the Côtes de Provence appellation, making it one of the appellation's largest landowners with 360 acres. All the vineyards are run without chemicals. Whites and rosés are sold young, but they make a practice of ageing reds for a period of between six months and two years.

Domaine Tempier

Le Plan du Castellet, 83330 Le Beausset.

Lucien Peyraud is regarded as the 'father of the Bandol appellation', for his part in rescuing it from decline. He and his two sons make the finest wines of Bandol, hence of Provence, superbly flavoury, and long-lived red and rosé from 70 acres. Many of the vines are up to 70 years old; the average age is 35 years. The red (two-thirds of production) used to be 60% Mourvèdre, the rest Grenache, Cinsaut and a little Carignan from very old vines. The Cuvée Cabasson is now 100% Mourvèdre.

Domaine des Terres-Blanches

13210 St-Rémy-de-Provence.

Quality red, white and rosé by M. Noël Michelin from a leading les Baux AOC estate with 100 acres. Special cuvées are Cuvée Aurélia with Cabernet Sauvignon made in exceptional vintages only (1990 and 1995).

Domaine de Trévallon

13150 St-Etienne-du-Grés.

The rich, intense half-Cabernet Sauvignon, half-Syrah blend from this 50-acre domaine has a name for the best wine in the village of Les Baux, but is not entitled to the appellation, as the INAO only allows 20% Cabernet Sauvignon. Monsieur Eloi Durrbach therefore produces 5,000 cases of red Vin de Pays des Bouches du Rhône, and a tiny amount (350 cases) of white from 60% Marsanne and 40% Roussanne.

Château Vannières

83740 La Cadière d'Azur.

A leading Bandol producer on an estate of 81 acres dating back to 1532. Total production is 13,000 cases of an excellent red made of 90% Mourvèdre and some rosé.

Château Vignelaure

Route de Jouques, 83560 Rians.

The first estate to show the world that Provence could produce very good wines of more than local interest. Georges Brunet had already restored Château La Lagune in the Médoc when he came here in the 1960s and planted Cabernet Sauvignon with the local vines. This estate was widely seen as making the best wine in Coteaux d'Aix-en-Provence. A decline in quality in the late 1980s and early '90s has now been arrested as new owners, the Irish O'Brien family, make use of the latest advice and technology from Bordeaux-based Michel Rolland and Hugh Ryman. The 1995 Château Vignelaure will be the first of these new wines when it is released, but lovers of the estate can buy the *vin de pays* Domaine de Vignelaure as a taste of what is to come.

OTHER PRODUCERS

Domaine du Bagnol 13260 Cassis. Mme Lefèvre's small estate produces good whites and an excellent rosé.

Domaine de la Bastide Neuve Le Cannet des Maures, 83340 Le Luc. 7,000 cases from 42 acres. Mr Wiestner makes his wines either in the traditional way with his Cuvée d'Antan – Syrah and Mourvèdre aged in oak – or uses *macération carbonique* for his Cuvée Beaux Sarments of Cinsaut and Cabernet Sauvignon.

Château de Beaulieu 13840 Rognes. A large (740-acre) estate in the Coteaux d'Aix-en-Provence AOC region. Reds contain 20% Cabernet Sauvignon, whites are half Sauvignon Blanc. Vinification in its new cellars is traditional. The proprietors, R. Touzet & Fils, produce 125,000 cases.

Château de Bellet St Romain de Bellet, 06200 Nice. M. Ghislain de Charnacé's 25-acre property is one of only two sizeable ones in the tiny AOC Bellet. The other is Ch. de Crémat (see Bagnis).

Château de Berne Route de Berne, 83510 Lorgues. Despite the initial appearance of Hollywood in the Provençal pine trees, this 120-acre estate is producing some good-quality, modern-style wines. Côtes de Provence white, red (which contains Syrah, Grenache and Cabernet) and rosé (made from Cinsaut) are made here. Two styles of red – a standard *cuvée* and a Cuvée Spéciale – are made. A Roman-style amphitheatre in the grounds is intended for plays – and presumably the audience will drink the wines.

Domaine de Bertaud-Belieu 83580 Gassin. The exotic *chai* close to Saint-Tropez in the Cotes de Provence – designed a little like a Roman temple or classical church – suggests, quite rightly, that this is an estate where money is no object. They make 40% red and 50% white, with the remainder rosé. The white, from Rolle with Sémillon and Ugni Blanc, is crisply perfumed. The red is a blend of Cabernet Sauvignon and Syrah, a rich wine, very elegant.

Domaine de Clastron 83920 La Motte. A new (1980) start for a large old farm in the Argens Valley making Côtes de Provence of all 3 colours and red and rosé Vin de Pays du Var. Traditional varieties plus Cabernet Sauvignon. Cool fermentation whites and rosés, traditional reds.

Vignobles Crocé-Spinelli Château des Clarettes, 83460 Les Arcs. Monsieur Crocé-Spinelli owns three estates in Cotes de Provence: Château des Clarettes near Les Arcs, Domaine du Saint-Esprit and Domaine de Fontselves near Draguignan. The wine from Saint-Esprit has a high percentage of Syrah, while the Clarettes relies more on Mourvèdre. At Fontselves some Cabernet Sauvignon is used. Rosé wines are also made.

Château de Gairoird 83390 Cuers. Philippe Deydier de Pierrefeu makes 6,500 cases, mostly red, some rosé, from 74 acres northeast of Toulon, using modern methods. Other label: Domaine St-Jean. The rosé leads his exports, especially to the US.

Château du Galoupet Saint-Nicolas, 83250 La Londe. This British-owned property aims to combine traditional grape varieties of the Côtes de Provence region with modern winemaking techniques. The estate has been modernized and new equipment installed since its current owners bought it in 1993. But, more traditionally, reds are aged in large 500 litre vats for up to 18 months, while the actual château dates back to Louis XIV, and the older part of the cellar is Roman. Wines made here include red, white and rosé Côtes de Provence, a special *cuvée* of rosé produced mainly from Tibouren. There are also two Vins de Pays des Maures, made from Chardonnay and Cabernet Sauvignon.

Domaines Walter Gilpin 3345 Montée du Château, 83330 Le Castellet. One of the leading lights in the Bandol appellation, Walter Gilpin makes robust wines in a traditional way. He owns 37 acres in Bandol, making red and rosé, and 17 acres of red, rosé and white Côtes de Provence.

Château La Gordonne Pierrefeu du Var, 83390 Cuers. A 284-acre estate owned by Domaines Viticoles des Salins du Midi (q.v. Bouches du Rhône) producing red, white and rosé Côtes de Provence from shale soil on the Maures foothills. Cabernet Sauvignon grown is 77,000 cases.

Domaine de la Jeanette 83400 Hyères. The Moutte family make classic reds from 15 acres.

Château de Mentone 83510 Lorgues. Traditional property west of Draguignan, 150 years in Mme Perrot de Gasquet's family. Côtes de Provence from 74 acres. Total production 2,900 cases.

Château Montaud Pierrefeu du Var, 83390 Cuers. Family company (Vignobles François Ravel) with 1,000 acres AOC Côtes de Provence and 150 of Vin de Pays des Maures (there is an unblended Cabernet Sauvignon Vin de Pays des Maures. Production 160,000 cases AOC, 40,000 *vin de pays*. Other labels: Ch. de Guiranne and Ch. Garamache.

Domaine de Nestuby Cares, 83570 Cotignac. Jean Roubaud's 100 acres in the upper Argens Valley yield up to 33,000 cases of well-built white and red Côtes de Provence.

Domaine de Peissonnel Route de la Garde Freiner, 83550 Vidauban. Unusually for Côtes de Provence, this estate produces only red wines. And, even more unusually, they make a wine from 80% Merlot with 15% Cabernet Franc: best in cooler years, when the wine's structure shows through. The Domaine de Peissonnel red *cuvée* is a blend of 50% Syrah and 50% Cabernet Sauvignon: a strongly tannic wine which needs at least four years before drinking.

Pradel 06270 Villeneuve Loubet. Merchant dealing in Côtes de Provence, Bellet and Bandol wines. Annual production 110,000 cases, 75% exported.

Domaine de Rimauresq 83790 Pignans. 50-acre property in the Maures, rated Cru Classé, which has been taken in hand by new owners. The wines are predominantly rosé and white Côtes de Provence.

Etablissements Bernard Camp Romain 83550 Vidauban. Leading négociant founded in 1910, today doing worldwide business in Provence wines, such as 'Bouquet de Provence'. Sales 290,000 cases.

Domaine de St-Antoine 83990 St-Tropez. 3,000 cases of red and rosé from 17 acres of very old vines.

Clos Ste-Magdeleine 13260 Cassis. 30 acres of vineyards right beside the Mediterranean, producing 3,300 cases of classic white Cassis and rosé. The property is now owned by GFA Lafiropoulo.

Château St-Martin Taradeau, 83460 Les Arcs. A handsome old house with deep cellars, in the Rohan Chabot family since the 17th century. The proprietor, Comtesse de Gasquet, makes 13,000 cases of Côtes de Provence Cru Classé from 99 acres.

Château Sainte-Roseline 83460 Les Arcs-sur-Argens. The red is the best wine made at this Côtes de Provence estate, based around an ancient monastery. It is made from 60% Mourvèdre, 30% Cabernet Sauvignon and 10% Syrah, a potent combination which gives considerable power, good structure and longevity.

Domaine de la Tour Campanets 13610 Le Puy Ste-Reparade. A 65-acre vineyard in the region north of Aix-en-Provence.

CAVES COOPERATIVES

Vinicole l'Ancienne 83490 Le Muy. Côtes du Provence and Vin de Pays du Var, all three colours, from a coop founded in 1913. 139,000 cases.

Vins de Bandol Moulin de la Roque. 83740 La Cadière-d'Azur. Founded 1950. 183 members with 667 acres of AOC Bandol – red, white and rosé. Production 104,000 cases. Vins de Bandol is a 'serious' cooperative, which ably competes with the private estates in the appellation, producing quality wines at sensible prices.

De Pierrefeu-du-Var 83390 Cuers. Founded 1922, 284 members farming 2,129 acres, production of AOC wines: 341,000 cases, producing AOC Côtes de Provence and *vins de pays*.

La Vidaubannaise 83550 Vidauban. The coop's 455 members farm 2,700 acres of AOC Côtes de Provence and 3,446 for *vins de pays* in the Argens Valley. Production 728,000 cases.

THE MIDI

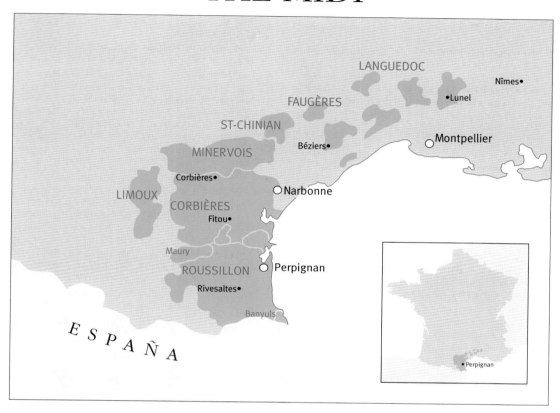

T he arc of country from the Spanish border to the mouth of the Rhône may well be France's oldest vineyard. It is certainly its biggest. Now it is where the experimentation is. Times have changed. Uncountable quantities of unwanted wine were once pumped from its plains to the despair of politicians all over Europe. Until ten years ago there was not a great deal more to say. Traditions of better wine-growing persisted in the hills, but at such economic disadvantage that there seemed little future for them. Such traditions are being grafted onto new techniques to produce – at last – some memorable Midi wines. Interest and investment from Australia has made the locals sit up and take notice. The region is now coming to life again – Corbières and Minervois and also Roussillon.

There was no demand and no premium for extra effort until the 1960s, when educated winemakers and merchants began to realize that it was only the grapes that were wrong: the soils and climates of hundreds of hill villages have enormous potential. The penny dropped at the same time as California rose from its slumber. In the Midi, low morale, bureaucracy, peasant conservatism and typically complicated land ownership have all been brakes on progress. Otherwise there would long before have been famous Cabernets from the Corbières. But California has

done it, so why not the South of France? The French way is to move cautiously along established lines. To improve wines, not to change them.

Upgrading started with the winemaking process and then spread to the marketing of its produce. The introduction of *macération carbonique* was the vital first step. It extracted from dull grapes juicy flavours that nobody knew were there. The process is now a long way down the road, and a handsome list has emerged of properties and cooperatives with good wine to offer, more of the 'aromatic' grapes that the public want. It is now the estates rather than the cooperatives that lead the way in quality.

The Midi of quality wine divides into four distinct regions. Following the right-hand curve of the coast north from the Spanish border, they are the Roussillon in the Pyrenean foothills, most famous for sweet apéritif and dessert wines; the Corbières, red-wine country; the smaller Minervois in the southernmost foothills of the Cévennes, also best known for red wine; and the scattered Coteaux du Languedoc, producing decent red, white and rosé as islands in an ocean of *vin ordinaire*.

Precisely what constitutes a quality area and which are the 'right' grapes for it is studied here with as much Gallic precision as on the slopes of Beaune. It is not long since

VDQS was the senior rank in these parts. Now many areas have been promoted to AOC (and others are about to matriculate). More detailed gradings will be needed, by which some areas will be 'villages' or 'supérieurs'. Layer upon layer of legislation is the French way.

This is also the country of the *vins de pays*. Pages 229–37 give details of the innumerable 'country wine' districts. But to sell your wine as a *vins de pays* is also an interesting alternative to growers who find the panoply of appellation too oppressive. There is a danger of the situation arising which Italy already knows, where the bright pioneer believes (and rightly) that his wine is more important than its label. Some of the best wines of the Midi are sold as *vins de pays* because Cabernet or Merlot is not cricket under the existing rules.

In most areas, cooperative cellars dominate. They vary widely in size, sophistication and quality. As the foundation dates show, most of the cooperatives were started between the wars as a response to depressed wine prices. The best produce wine as good as the best growers.

ROUSSILLON

Of all the endless vineyards of the Midi, Roussillon is most firmly planted in Frenchmen's minds as a place of promise. It has the prestige of an ancient and unique product, its *vin doux naturel*, practically unknown outside France but so proud of its origins that it looks on port (an approximate equivalent) as an imposter.

Wines from the smaller properties in Roussillon are on the improve. They are now developing a 'boutique' style: carefully using new wood for fermentation and maturation, and able to aim for quality because they can sell their best wines to a waiting market. There is a trickle-down effect of these estates to the coops – smaller properties being a model to work towards, particularly for prestige wines.

The sheltered seaside hills around Perpignan and inland up the valleys of the Agly and the Tet make some formidable red wines; the biggest and most highly coloured of the many based on the Carignan around the coast. The best examples, stiffened with superior 'aromatic' grapes, have some of the structure of, for example, Châteauneuf-du-Pape, though with more roundness and a softer texture. Many are best drunk young when their fruit flavour is at its peak, but more and more growers are deliberately ageing in oak and sometimes in bottle too, to add complexity to sheer beef. Better grapes are making headway: Syrah and Mouvèdre, taken together, make up 20 percent of the vineyard.

One small red-wine area at the seaside resort of Collioure on the Spanish border has had its own appellation since 1949 for a singular concentrated wine in which Carignan plays little part, a blend principally of Mourvèdre and Grenache Noir with intense flavours unlike anything else north of the Spanish border. Alas, it is a declining AOC as local development eats into the rocky vineyard area. Top producers include the Banyuls coop, using the name Guy de Berlande; Château de Jau, and Domaine du Mas Blanc. Two other villages 20 miles inland from Perpignan, Caramany and Latour-de-France, acquired their own AOCs in 1977 but as a part of Côtes du Roussillon-Villages. The activities of the extremely modern coop at Montalba-Le-Château in the same 'Villages' zone between the Agly and Tet valleys are creating more and more interest in this area.

The *vins doux naturels* apparently owe their origin to the revered figure of Arnaldo da Villanova, the 13th-century sage and doctor of Montpellier, who introduced the still from Moorish Spain. It was he who first added *eau de vie* to naturally very strong wine to stop the fermentation and maintain a high degree of natural sugar – hence the term 'doux naturels'. But whereas in port the *eau de vie* represents a quarter of the volume and more than half the alcoholic strength, in *vins doux naturels* it is limited to 10 percent of the volume, while the natural strength of the wine has by law to reach no less than 15 degrees. It is not for a foreigner, with the privilege of an education in port, to hold forth on the qualities of *vins doux naturels*. Aged, they acquire an oxidized flavour known by the Spanish term *rancio*. A few producers age them in 30-litre pear-shaped glass jars known as *bonbonnes* (again, from the Spanish: *bombonas*). *Vin doux naturel* is made in three styles; the best of which is solely from Muscat grapes and called Muscat de Rivesaltes. A major promotion campaign is at present underway, in an attempt to promote Rivesaltes abroad.

Leading Roussillon Producers

Mas Amiel

66460 Maury.
Owner: M. Dupuy. Wine consultant: M. Mayol. The appellation's best producer, offering a choice of ten vintages for sale. Improved grape selection and vinification techniques since 1990. 345 acres; 35,000 cases of Maury from Grenache Noir.

Château de Caladroy

Belesta, 66720 Latour-de-France.
Owner: The Arnold-Bobo family. A large estate, with a beautiful 12th-century castle. 296 acres; 38,500 cases of Muscat de Rivesaltes, Rivesaltes and Côtes du Roussillon.

Domaine de Canterrane

Trouillas, 66300 Thuir.
Owner: Maurice Conté. One of the finest estates in Roussillon, with stock of more than 1m. bottles. Vintages

back to1980 are very impressive. 395 acres; 80,000 cases of Rivesaltes. Muscat de Rivesaltes, Côtes du Roussillon and *vin de pays*. Eighty percent is exported.

Château Cap de Fouste

Villeneuve de la Raho, 66200 Elne
Bought in 1979 by the local growers' *mutualité agricole* and extensively replanted to good effect. 148 acres; 20,000 cases of Côtes du Roussillon, using the name St-Galderic for their best reds.

Domaine Força-Réal

Mas de la Garrigue, 66170 Millas.
In a spectacular mountain-side setting, J.-P. Henriques produces red and white Côtes du Roussillon and Rivesaltes from a vineyard which he is in the process of restoring and replanting. The second wine of the estate is Mas de la Garrigue, while the Domaine Força-Réal is a wood-aged Côtes du Roussillon. His pride is a caramel-and-coffee-flavoured Rivesaltes Hors d'Age.

Domaine Cazes

66600 Rivesaltes.
Modernized and replanted with Grenache, Syrah, Mourvèdre and Malvoisie. Cellar practices include *macération carbonique*, ageing in oak and bottle in air-conditioned cellars. 420 acres; 27,500 cases of Rivesaltes, Muscat de Rivesaltes, Côtes du Roussillon, Côtes du Roussillon-Villages and *vin nouveau*. *Vin de pays* accounts for two-thirds of their production; the best wine being Le Canon du Maréchal, the white a dry Muscat. In 1993 they produced Credo, a Cabernet Sauvignon and Merlot wine, designed, successfully, to show how well the Bordeaux grapes work in the region.

Domaine Gauby

Le Faradjal, 66600 Calce.
A small family-owned domaine where Gérard Gauby makes a fascinating collection of wines, including red and white Côtes du Roussillon in various blends, and *vins de pays*. The white Vin de Pays des Côtes Catalanes (a blend of Carignan Blanc, Grenache Blanc and Maccabeo) sells for more than the Côtes du Roussillon. Fifty-year-old vines produce Vieilles Vignes. Wood ageing is a serious consideration here.

Mas Chichet

Chemin de Charlemagne, 66200 Elne.
Owner: Paul Chichet. A pioneer with Cabernet and Merlot in association with Grenache and Syrah – and also remarkable pure Cabernet aged in oak. 74 acres; 15,500 cases of Vin de Pays Catalan red and rosé.

Château de Corneilla

66200 Corneilla-del-Vercol.
Owner: M. Philippe Jonquères d'Oriola. Wine consultant: M. Mayol. 148 acres producing AOC red. Grape varieties are Carignan, Grenache Noir, Merlot, Cabernet Sauvignon and Syrah. The property was built in 1150 and the Jonquères d'Oriola family have been there since 1485.

Château de l'Esparrou

Canet-Plage, St-Nazaire, 66140 Canet.
Owner: J.-L. Rendu. Replanted with stress on Mourvèdre and Syrah. Excellent Côtes du Roussillon by *macération carbonique* and barrel-ageing. 247 acres; 60,000 cases: Rivesaltes, Muscat de Rivesaltes, Côtes du Roussillon, *vins de pays*.

Château de Jau

Cases de Péné 66600 Rivesaltes.
Owners: the Dauré family. Improving vines and *macération carbonique* make some of the best Côtes du Roussillon on this 550-acre estate. Also outstanding Muscat and good whites of Malvoisie and Maccabeo. Grape varieties planted are Syrah, Mourvèdre, Grenache Noir and Carignan. Another estate under the same ownership, Le Clos des Paulilles, produces Collioure and quantities of *vin de pays*. A third property, producing Rivesaltes, is called Mas Cristine.

Jaubert et Noury

St-Jean Lasseille, 66300 Thuir.
Old Carignan vineyards replanted with Syrah and Mourvèdre, and Malvoisie for white, which are flourishing in the sea wind. Good Côtes du Roussillon Château Planères, also light *vin nouveau*, by *macération carbonique*. 173 acres; 38,500 cases of Rivesaltes, Muscat de Rivesaltes, Côtes du Roussillon.

Domaine du Mas Blanc

66650 Banyuls-sur-Mer.
Owners: Dr André and Jean-Michel Parcé. Leading producer of AOC Collioure. 10 acres of schist: 40% Mourvèdre, 40% Syrah, 20% Grenache. Long fermentation and 2 years in wood give remarkable wine. 25 acres of Banyuls *vins doux naturel* (90% Grenache Noir, 10% Carignan) aged either in wood or in bottle.

Le Moulin

66330 Cabestany.
Owner: Vidal Rossines. An old estate with a fine reputation, particularly for aged Banyuls. 118 acres; 26,500 cases of Rivesaltes, Muscat de Rivesaltes, Banyuls and Côtes du Roussillon.

Mas Péchot; Mas Balande

66600 Rivesaltes; 66000 Perpignan.
Owner: Henri Lacassagne. Mas Péchot is one of the best vineyards of Muscat 'petits grains' in the region. 370 acres; 66,500 cases of Muscat de Rivesaltes and Côtes du Roussillon-Villages.

Mas Rancoure

Laroque-des-Albères, 66740 St-Genis-des-Fontaines.
Owner: Dr Perdineille. A small (20-acre) red wine property producing a dramatic Cuvée Vincent.

Domaine Piquemal

1 Rue Pierre Lefranc, 66600 Espira de l'Agly.
In a series of cellars in the centre of Espira de l'Agly, Pierre Piquemal makes a wide range of wines, including a Merlot-

dominated red, rosé and a white from Muscat Sec. Recent vintages of Côtes du Roussillon have been vinified in wood and emphasize soft tannins and ripe fruit. Also Rivesaltes.

Château Planères

66300 St-Jean Lasseille.
Reliable Côtes du Roussillon are made at this 222-acre estate, of which the best is the Château Planères Prestige. Other wines include varietal Maccabeo and Vermentino whites. The cellars are housed in an 18th century, typically Catalan, *mas*. The property is owned by Jaubert et Noury (q.v.).

Château de Rey

St-Nazaire, 66140 Canet.
Owner: Mme Georges Sisqueille, 247 acres; 30,000 cases of Muscat de Rivesaltes, Rivesaltes and Côtes du Roussillon.

Domaine de Roquebrune

St-Nazaire, 66140 Canet.
Owner Marcellin Casenobe cherishes his old Carignan vines. Very sound *macération carbonique* reds. 64 acres; 16,500 cases of Rivesaltes and Côtes du Roussillon.

Domaine du Mas Rous

66740 Montesquieu.
Owner: José Pujol. 95 acres. 20,000 cases of well-made Côtes du Roussillon, Rivesaltes, Muscat de Rivesaltes and *vin de pays*.

Sarda-Malet

Mas St-Michel, 12 Chemin de Ste-Barbe, 66000 Perpignan.
The bulk of this 124-acre estate produces AOC Côtes du Roussillon and Rivesaltes Vin Doux Naturel. There are also two Côtes du Roussillon whites from a blend of Grenache, Roussanne, Marsanne, Malvoisie and Maccabeo grapes, one tank fermented, the other vinified in wood, and a range of red Côtes du Roussillon wines including a wood-aged Etiquette Noire which requires ageing for four or five years. The top wine is a Syrah–Mourvèdre blend, called Terroir Mailloles. The *vins doux naturels* include red Rivesaltes and Muscat de Rivesaltes. The Sarda-Malet estate also produces Vin de Pays Catalan.

Domaine St-Luc

Passa Llauro Torderes, 66300 Thuir.
Owner: M. Talut. 100 acres; 15,000 cases of Rivesaltes and Côtes du Roussillon.

Domaine de Sau

66300 Thuir.
Owner: Albert Passama. 222 acres; 50,000 cases of Côtes du Roussillon and *vins de pays*.

Tresserre

66300 Thuir.
Owner: M. Vaquer. Well-made red, rosé and white are fermented long and cold; reds are aged in bottle up to six years before being released. 86 acres; 12,000 cases of *vin de pays* rosé, red and white.

Caves Coopératives

L'Agly

66600 Rivesaltes.
Founded 1942. 103 members; 785 acres producing 46,600 cases of AOC Côtes du Roussillon and Villages, Rivesaltes Doré and Muscat de Rivesaltes; 53,900 cases *vins de table*.

Baixas

66390 Baixas.
Founded 1923. 380 members; 5,200 acres producing 935,000 cases of AOC Rivesaltes; Muscat de Rivesaltes; Côtes du Roussillon; Côtes du Roussillon Villages; plus Vin de Pays des Côtes Catalanes and *vins de table*. Dom Brial is their brand name, Château Les Pins their top label. By far the largest producer of Muscat de Rivesaltes.

Les Dominicains

66190 Collioure.
Despite the address, most of the land belonging to this cooperative produces Banyuls. Most of the wine is sold to négociants, but some is bottled under the Le Dominicain name, and there is an attractive Collioure Cuvée Matisse.

Banyuls L'Etoile

66650 Banyuls-sur-Mer.
Founded 1921. 60 members; 420 acres producing 36,500 cases of AOC Banyuls, Banyuls Grand Cru and Collioure; plus *vins de table*.

Caramany

66720 Latour-de-France.
Founded 1925. 106 members; 800 acres producing 109,600 cases of AOC Côtes du Roussillon Villages Caramany red and Côtes du Roussillon red, plus 55,200 cases *vins de pays* and *vins de table*.

Cellier des Capitelles Cassagnes

Cassagnes, 66720 Latour-de-France.
Founded 1924. 81 members; 988 acres producing 96,000 cases of AOC Côtes du Roussillon Villages, Rivesaltes and Muscat, plus 87,300 cases Vin de Pays des Vals d'Agly, Pyrénées-Orientales and *vins de table*.

Groupement Interproducteurs du Cru Banyuls

Route de Mas Reig, 66650 Banyuls-sur-Mer.
This is a large-scale operation, a grouping of three cooperatives which also acts as a négociant. It dominates the Collioure and Banyuls AOC areas (with 6,400 acres in Banyuls). There has been considerable investment in equipment and the general quality is good. Brand names used include Templiers and Cellier des Templiers.

Lesquerde

66220 Lesquerde.
Founded 1923. 62 members, 950 acres producing 165,000 cases of AOC Rivesaltes, Muscat de Rivesaltes, Côtes du Roussillon and -Villages.

Maury

66460 Maury.

Founded 1910. 300 members; 4,199 acres producing 85% of the Maury output. The top *cuvée*, Chabert de Barbera, is predominantly Grenache. Côtes du Roussillon and Villages, plus *vins de table* are also made

Montner

66720 Latour-de-France.

Founded 1919. 107 members; 1,111 acres producing 92,300 cases of Côtes du Roussillon-Villages, Rivesaltes red and white, Muscat de Rivesaltes white, plus 109,300 cases Vin de Pays des Vals d'Agly and *vins de table*.

Pezilla-La-Rivière

66370 Pezilla-La-Rivière.

475 members, 1,890 acres. Their Cuvée Blancs has been well received. One of the most go-ahead cooperatives in the region, producing a fascinating selection of *vins de pays* (including a Chardonnay) as well as Côtes du Roussillon wines from separate domaines (Château de Blanes is vinified in wood) and a range of Rivesaltes.

Rasiguères

66720 Rasiguères.

Founded 1919. 81 members 790 acres producing 137,600 cases of AOC Rivesaltes; Muscat de Rivesaltes; Côtes du Roussillon-Villages red, plus *vins de table*.

Tautavel Les Maîtres Vignerons

66720 Tautavel.

Founded 1927. 189 members producing 155,100 cases of AOC Rivesaltes; Muscat de Rivesaltes; Côtes du Roussillon and Villages red: plus 67,200 cases Vin de Pays des Côtes Catalanes and *vins de table*.

Terrats

66300 Terrats.

Founded 1932. 150 members, sharing 2,000 acres and producing 385,000 cases of AOC Muscat de Rivesaltes, Rivesaltes, Côtes du Roussillon (red and white), and Vin de Pays Catalan.

Terroir de Cerbère

66290 Cerbère.

Founded 1931. 100 members; 203 acres producing 15,800 cases of AOC Banyuls.

Les Vignerons de Rivesaltes

2 Rue de la Roussillonnaise, 66602 Rivesaltes.

The largest cooperative in the region with 540 members sharing 3,952 acres, and the largest producer of Côtes du Roussillon as well as Rivesaltes. Their top *cuvée* of Côtes du Roussillon is Arnaud de Villeneuve, which is aged in wood. They are also increasingly producing *vins de cépage* – Vins de Pays d'Oc made from single grape varieties such as Malvoisie, Cabernet Sauvignon, Sauvignon Blanc and Chardonnay. Total production: 3m. bottles

OTHER COOPERATIVES

Aglya 66310 Estagel

Bages 66670 Bages.

Banyuls-dels-Aspres 66300 Thuir.

Belesta 66720 Latour-de-France.

Le Boulou 66160 Le Boulou.

'La Cabestanyenca' 66330 Cabestany.

Elne 66200 Elne.

Feilluns 66220 St-Paul-de-Fenouillet.

Fourques 66300 Fourques.

Lamsac 66720 Latour-de-France.

CORBIERES

Justice has been slow in coming to the Corbières, until overdue promotion in 1985 the biggest VDQS area in France, now *appellation contrôlée*. It is a huge region, stretching from Narbonne inland almost to Carcassonne and the same distance south to the borders of the Roussillon. It rises and rolls in parched hills of pale limestone suddenly embroidered in bold patterns with the green stitches of vines. The neutral black grape the Carignan has long been dominant but must not now exceed 60 percent of the blend. Syrah, Mourvèdre and Grenache are blended with it.

A good site, restraint in cropping and careful winemaking made solid enough wines, but with little flavour and no future. Improvements are taking the form of winemaking with *macération carbonique*, to coax at least an illusion of fruitiness from the grapes, and more radically replanting with 'aromatic' (i.e. not neutral) varieties. There is also greater use of wood – for fermenting and maturing – to add an extra taste component in the wines, and greater

ability to finance superior production. A small but significant growth of white wine in the region is notable – some of it barrel-fermented and oak-aged.

There are some big properties as well as the thousands of growers who contribute to the cooperatives. Two areas in the southeast corner of Corbières, largely coop country, have long enjoyed the appellation Fitou for their reds, on the grounds that they are more age-worthy than the rest. Corbières Supérieurs is an AOC for 39 villages where the yield must be held down to 40 hl/ha. There has also been a more recent division of the Corbières appellation into different zones to highlight the varying *terroir* – the climate ranges from maritime to arid.

The following listing describes the currently best-performing properties, district by district, together with entries for some of the promising ones: names to look out for in the future.

The total production of the Corbières averages 5.5m. cases.

Leading Corbières Producers

Château Aiguilloux

M. and F. Lemarié, 11200 Thézan-des-Corbières.
François Lemarié runs this 81-acre estate, producing 6,600 cases of structured, tannic wine.

Château la Baronne

Dr André Lignières, 11700 Fontcouverte.
Carignan, Grenache and a little Syrah and Mourvèdre are hand-picked for *macération carbonique* in this vineyard outside the village of Fontcouverte. 74 acres of Corbières, 37 of *vin de pays*. Château des Lanes is the export label.

Château de Beauregard

Simone Mirouse, 11200 Bizanet.
High-quality Syrah rosé from one of the top Corbières properties. Also a Cabernet Sauvignon *vin de pays*. 107 acres; 28,500 cases.

Bringuier

Coustouge, 11200 Boutenac.
A small property on excellent soil that makes good wine even of the dominant Carignan. 39.5 acres; 13,500 cases.

Château de Cabriac

11600 Douzens.
Corbières red and white are made here at this estate which has a minority shareholding from Château Chasse-Spleen in Bordeaux. The wines are not aged in woo, and are designed for relatively early drinking. 204 acres; 43,000 cases.

Château de Caraguilhes

M. Faivre, 11220 St Laurent-de-la-Cabrerisse.
150 acres producing 9,000 cases of dark, warming *macération carbonique* wine from an organic vineyard.

Cassignol

11360 Villeneuve-les-Corbières.
One of the few private producers of AOC Fitou. 112 acres; 16,500 cases.

Domaine des Amouries

Alain Castex, 11330 Davejean.
Bought by the present owner in 1981, this estate produces floral, fruity elegant wines combining *macération carbonique* and traditional techniques.

Château du Grand Caumont

Mme Rigal, 11200 Lézignan-Corbières.
This old estate, close to the autoroute near the River Orbieu has been energetically modernized. 252 acres; 58,000 cases.

Château Etang des Colombes

H. Gualco, 11200 Lézignan-Corbières.
The average age of the vines here is 90 years. M. Gualco produces a variety of wines with a total production of 3,000 cases. Pretty painted bottles.

Domaine les Fenals

Mme Roustan, 11510 Fitou.
62 acres producing Fitou, Corbières, Muscat de Rivesaltes and *vin de pays* under the hand of Andrée Roustan-Fontanel.

Domaine de Fontsainte

Yves Laboucarie, 11200 Boutenac.
Some of the best land in the Corbières and very good winemaking. Maceration and wood-ageing for splendid reds, and a very pale rosé *gris de gris*. 104 acres; 41,000 cases.

Château Haut-Gléon

Villeseque-des-Corbières, 11360 Durban.
Modern cellars produce an especially attractive white Corbières at this estate. Both this wine and the red are aged in barrels, some of which are new, for eight to nine months. The buildings of the estate include a 12th-century chapel. 70 acres; 9,000 bottles.

Château de Lastours

J.M. Lignières, 11490 Portel-des-Corbières.
237 acres acres producing 37,500 cases a year. This château is a centre for the disabled of whom 60 are employed on the estate. The Cuvées Simone Descamps and Arnaud de Berre are serious, complex reds with ageing potential.

Château de Luc/Château Gasparets

11200 Luc-sur-Orbieu.
The Fabre family is a big landowner in Corbières. They run three estates: Château de Luc, Château Gasparets and Domaine de l'Ancien Courrier. They also make Vin de Pays des Coteaux d'Enserune from Merlot, Cabernet Sauvignon and Sauvignon Blanc, using the name Domaine de la Grande Courtade. Top wines from the Corbières estates are matured in *barriques*. Château Gasparets, a blend of Mourvèdre and Grenache is a particularly fine wine. 422 acres; 50,000 cases.

Château de Mandourelle

E. Latham, 11360 Villeseque, 11360 Durban.
103 acres; 6,000 cases. Eric Latham, who runs this château, has named one of the wines after his grandfather Henri de Monfreid. The red wine is complex and aromatic.

Château de Mattes

11130 Sigean.
Corbières and *vin de pays* are both produced on this estate. The Corbières comes in a number of different *cuvées*: Anne Laure, Bacchus and Anne Joséphine de Sabran. None has wood vinification, although top wines are aged in barrels for six months. The domaine has been in the Brouillat-Arnould family since 1731. 225 acres; 12,500 cases.

Domaine de Montjoie

M. Guiraud. St-André-de-la-Cabrerisse, 11220 Lagrasse.
Replanting and modern methods; stylish, full-flavoured wine. 83 acres deep in central Corbières.

Château de Nouvelles

Robert Daurat-Fortes, 11350 Tuchan.
One of the finest estates in the region. Part has the appellation Fitou. Also Rivesaltes VDN. 217 acres. 12,500 cases.

Château des Ollieux

Mme Surbezy-Cartier, 11200 Montséret.
A very good vineyard replanted with 'aromatic' varieties. Up-to-date maceration methods are making good wine. 106 acres; 26,500 cases.

Château Les Palais

M. de Volontat, St-Laurent-de-la-Cabrerisse, 11220 Lagrasse.
This estate made a name for itself when it pioneered the use of carbonic maceration for red wines in Corbières back in the 1960s. It continues to make soft, fresh, fruity wines, which have made it one of the most familiar Corbières names. 252 acres; 54,000 cases.

Château de Latt

Antoine André, 11220 Lagrasse.
A fine ex-monastery property with a wide range of red, rosé, white and VDNs. 250 acres; 43,000 cases.

Domaine des Pensées Sauvages

11360 Albas.
This estate, owned by the Bradfords, an English family, concentrates mostly on one wine: a red Corbières which is aged in *barriques* and larger wood. They have recently planted more Syrah in the vineyard, and also Viognier, to make a white wine. 168 acres; 2,000 cases.

Château de Quilhanet

Marie Terral. Bizanet, 11200 Lézignan-Corbières.
A Grenache and Carignan vineyard, sensibly undercropped. *Macération carbonique* and barrel-ageing. 270 acres; 41,500 cases.

Domaine du Révérend/Domaine du Trillol

Cucugnan, 11350 Tuchan.
Owned by Peter Sichel, the Bordeaux négociant and château-owner. Domaine du Révérend, the larger estate, is in Cucugnan, while Domaine du Trillol is in even more remote country at Rouffiac. The wines are made in the Bordeaux manner, with considerable wood ageing. Both estates make white and red Corbières, while Domaine du Révérend also makes small amounts of rosé. 146 acres; 22,500 bottles.

Roque Sestieres

Jean Berail, 11200 Ornaisons.
18 acre estate producing 1,600 cases a year. Jean and Isabel Bérail spend much time promoting the wines of Languedoc. Their white wine is 80% Maccabeo.

Prieuré de St-Amans

Mme Thomas. Bizanet, 11200 Lézignan-corbières
One of the best red Corbières, made by *macération carbonique* followed by ageing in oak barrels. 27.5 acres; 7,000 cases.

Château Saint-Auriol

Claude Vialade, 11220 Lagrasse.
Red Corbières is the principal wine from this highly regarded estate run by Claude Vialade and her husband Jean-Paul Salvagnac. They are great proponents of the different *terroirs* of Corbières, believing the region of Lagrasse gives a particularly mild climate for grape growing. Their wines certainly are generous, the reds aged for six month, the white for three months. They also make a red Vin de Pays de l'Aude. 96 acres; 20,000 cases.

Château de Vaugelas

M. Bouffet, 11200 Camplong.
A substantial estate with low yields producing good wine. 258 acres; 41,000 cases.

Domaine de Villemajou

Gérard Bertrand, 11200 Boutenac
One of the best technicians of the region with a fine vineyard. Reds (maceration and wood-ageing) and dry rosés are full of character. 124 acres; 32,000 cases.

Château la Voulte-Gasparets

P Reverdy, 11200 Boutenac
Ideal soil and first-class techniques of *macération carbonique* and wood-ageing. 125 acres; 27,000 cases.

CAVES COOPERATIVES

L'Avenir Villeseque des Corbières, 11360 Durban Corbières. Founded 1932.
Cap Leucate 11370 Leucate. Founded 1921.
Cascastel 11360 Durban Corbières. Founded 1926
Cave Coopérative 'La Corbière Bizanetoise' Bizanet, 11200 Lézignan Corbières. Founded 1935.
Les Vignerons de Cucugnan Chemin du Malpas, 11350 Cucugnan
Durban 11360 Durban Corbières. Founded 1913.
Embrès & Castelmaure 11360 Durban Corbières. Founded 1921.
Fitou 11510 Fitou. Founded 1933.
Fraisse Les Corbières 11360 Durban Corbières. Founded 1920.
Cave Coopérative Lagrasse 11220 Lagrasse. Founded 1952.
Cave Coopérative Montseret 11200 Lézignan Corbières. Founded 1949.
Cave Coopérative Mont Tauch 11350 Tuchan. Founded 1931.
Paziols 11530 Paziols. Founded 1913.
Pilote de Villeneuve Les Corbières Villeneuve Les Corbières, 11360 Durban Corbières. Founded 1948.
Portel 11490 Portel des Corbières. Founded 1924.
Chateau de Queribus Cucugnan, 11350 Tuchan. Founded 1928.
Château de Ribaute Cave de Ribaute, 11220 Ribaute.
Cellier St-Martin 11540 Roquefort des Corbières. Founded 1966.
Les Vignerons de St Roch Cave de Padern, 11350 Padern. Founded 1922

CREMANT DE LIMOUX

The most unexpected and original of all the wines of the Midi is the high-quality sparkling wine of Limoux, tucked away behind the Corbières on the upper reaches of the River Aude above Carcassonne. There is substantial evidence that this lonely area of hilly farms produced France's first sparkling wine, about 200 years before Champagne. The wine used to be called Blanquette de Limoux – 'Blanquette' coming not from the colour of the wine but from the white film that covers the underside of the leaves of the Mauzac (alias Blanquette) grape.

Mauzac is the white grape 'with a slight smell of cider' that is the base for the rustic bubbly of Gaillac. (Gaillac was a Roman wine town; its antiquity may be immense.) Whatever its origins, the traditional Limoux formula is Mauzac for sprightliness plus Clairette for mildness, originally just *pétillant*, but now made by the *méthode traditionnelle* to full pressure and extremely high standards of delicate blending. Chenin Blanc also plays a part. The latest development is the addition of Chardonnay in the best *cuvées* for fuller flavour; if Blanquette has a fault, it is a slightly pinched, lemony finesse which can benefit by plumping out. The rules now insist on at least 10 percent Chenin or Chardonnay. A pure Chardonnay *cuvée* is extraordinarily rich and creamy.

Sixty percent of the entire production of the 8,000 acres under vines is in the hands of the vast and ultra-modern cooperative. Founded in 1946, the coop now has some 550 members and produces around 425,000 cases of Blanquette a year.

A few *cooperateurs* take back their wine to 'finish' it themselves, but the remarkably high standards of the cooperative make it hard to improve on their product – and certainly not in value for money.

Crémant de Limoux is a gently sparkling version which must have 30 percent Chenin or Chardonnay.

Recently the coop has added to its repertoire a selection of the best red wine from its members' vineyards, which include a surprising proportion of Cabernet and Merlot. It offers a very pleasant full-bodied and soft brand called Sieur d'Arques, an excellent Vin de Pays de la Haute Vallée de l'Aude under the name Fécos, and an astonishingly Bordeaux-like *cuvée* called Anne des Joyeuses – one of the best non-appellation coop wines in France.

Another coop, at Gardie, near St-Hilaire, makes small quantities of Blanquette de Limoux from 250 acres.

There are also a number of good individual producers, such as the 200-acre Domaine de Martinolles near St-Hilaire, which sells some grapes to the coop as well as making its own wines.

Use of the term *méthode champenoise* has rightly been reclaimed by the Champenois for the sole use on labels of wines from their own region. The new labelling phrase used outside Champagne is *méthode traditionnelle* or the classic method.

MINERVOIS

The River Aude parts the last wrinkles of the Pyrenees from the first of the Massif Central, and the Corbières from the Minervois. The Minervois is a 40-mile stretch of its north bank, encompassing both the gravelly flats along the river and the very different hills behind, topped by a plateau at 600 feet. Rivers have cut deep ravines in its soft brown rock, in one place leaving a mid-river island for the tiny town of Minerve. The plateau is dry, treeless garrigue where the vine struggles and even the Carignan makes wine with nerves and sinews. Modern wine-making in the high Minervois has produced some deliciously vital, well-engineered wines with a structure not of old oak beams, as the word *charpente* seems to imply, but more like an airframe; delicately robust.

The commercial centre of the region is below, on the plain. A SICA, a group of ten cooperatives, produces large quantities of Vin de Pays de Peyriac to the specification of Chantovent, one of the biggest table-wine companies. Chantovent is also the owner of an estate at La Livinière in the foothills which produces some of the best Minervois, going to the length of ageing it in retired Médoc barriques, and the cooperative in the same village has followed suit. More recently, smaller estates have overtaken the cooperatives in importance. AOC status was granted to the Minervois in 1985 and a slow upgrading of the permitted grapes is taking place.

Total area: 85,000 acres (half is potential AOC but only 10,000 is fully qualified with the appropriate grape varieties). Annual production: 2.6m. cases of Minervois, 14,000 cases of the deliciously sweet Muscat de St-Jean-de-Minervois *vin doux naturel.*

The Minervois is semi-officially divided into five zones, distinguished by topography and weather conditions. These are listed below with their best producers.

ZONES AND PRODUCERS

Zone One

Around Ginestas in the east, on the plain with relatively high rainfall. Its light reds are for drinking young. There are also some clean modern white wines.

Christian Bonnel

Domaine de la Lecugne, Bize Minervois, 11120 Ginestas
22.5 acres; 4,500 cases of red.

Bernard Mazard

Château du Vergel, 11120 Ginestas
34 acres; 9,000 cases of red and white.

Château Canet

11800 Rustiques.

A Minervois vineyard owned since 1992 by the Alsace producer Dopff et Irion (q.v.). Red, made from Carignan, Syrah, Grenache and Cinsaut, is aged for six months in wood, white, from Roussanne, Bourboulenc and Terret, for three months. 96 acres; 20,000 cases.

Château La Grave

11800 Trèbes.

A new barrel-ageing cellar sets the scene for this estate, whose top red Minervois, Privilège, which is based on Syrah, Grenache, Carignan and Mourvèdre is aged for up to 12 months in wood. There is also a lighter style of red, Expression, which is matured in bottle before release. La Grave also makes a white *vin de pays*, which includes Chardonnay in the blend, makes the other half of their production. 192 acres. 17,000 cases.

Jacques Meyzonnier

Pouzols-Minervois, 11120 Ginestas.

Very good medal-winning *macération carbonique* wine with the label 'Domaine Meyzonnier'. 25 acres; 5,400 cases of red Minervois.

Château de Paraza

11200 Lézignan Corbières.

The two reds are 'Tradition' (classic) and 'Cuvée Speciale' (produced by carbonic maceration) and the rosés fresh and fruity. 427 acres; 37,000 cases of red and rosé.

Guy Rancoule

Domaine de l'Herbe Sainte, Mirepeisset, 11120 Ginestas

A good varied vineyard; the rosés and whites are fine and fruity. 99 acres; 5,000 cases of red, white and rosé.

Les Coteaux de Pouzols-Minervois

Pouzols-Minervois, 11120 Ginestas.

Pouzol coop, founded 1936. 136 members; 995 acres producing 320,000 cases, of which 55,000 are AOC.

Les Crus de Montouliers

Montouliers, 34310 Capestang.

Montouliers coop, founded 1937. 106 members; 768 acres producing 420,000 cases, of which 34,000 are AOC red and rosé.

Zone Two

The south-central area on the plain of the Aude is hottest and driest with richer reds, also for drinking young.

Jean Barthes

Château de St-Julia, 11800 Trebes.

33 acres. 7,500 cases of red and white.

Jean Baptiste Bonnet

Domaine de Gibalaux, 11800 Laure-Minervois.

Bernard de Crozals

Domaine de Homs, Rieux, Minervois, 11160 Caunes-Minervois.

Château de Fabas

11800 Laure-Minervois.

Already quite a high percentage of Syrah and Mourvèdre – and more is being planted in this vineyard. But Grenache still dominates the red Minervois, giving a typical southern taste and a warm, rounded finish. Jean-Pierre Ormières uses temperature-controlled fermentation and a long maceration, and his Cuvée Spéciale gets some wood-ageing. A rosé and a small amount of white wine are also made. 105 acres, 22,000 cases.

Christian Ferret

Château de Badens, Badens, 11800 Trèbes.

35 acres; 10,000 cases of red.

Alfred Keim

Domaine de Prat Majou, Laure-Minervois, 11800 Trèbes.

25 acres; 5,500 cases of red.

Soc. Mesnard Bellissen

Domaine de Millegrand, 11800 Trèbes.

101 acres. 22,500 cases of red.

Guy Panis

Château du Donjon, Bagnoles. 11600 Conques-sur-Orbiel.

42 acres; 10,500 cases of red.

Aymard de Soos

Château de Russol, Laure Minervois, 11800 Trèbes.

74 acres; 20,000 cases red.

Jean de Thelin

Château de Blomac, Blomac, 11700 Capendu.

Eighty acres of vines produce 18,000 cases of Minervois, traditional red wine, well made with 10% Syrah. There are also 175 acres of *vins de table* vineyard where experiments are being made with Cabernet, Merlot and the Spanish Tempranillo. Château de Blomac is one of the grandest cellars of the region.

CAVES COOPERATIVES

Les Coteaux du Minervois Pépieux, 11700 Capendu. Founded 1951. 265 members; 2,595 acres producing 800,000 cases, of which 53,000 are AOC red, white and rosé.

Laure-Minervois 11800 Trèbes. Founded 1929. 288 members; 3,088 acres producing 1m. cases, of which 181,000 are AOC red, white and rosé.

Peyriac Minervois 11160 Caunes-Minervois. Founded 1930. 250 members; 768 acres producing 494,000 cases, of which 34,000 are AOC red, white and rosé. Peyriac and its district have given their name to France's biggest-selling *vins de pays*, produced for Chantovent by a group of cooperatives.

Zone Three

The north-central area in the foothills; makes the best-structured reds for keeping.

Domaine de Ste-Eulalie

La Livinière, 34210 Olonzac.
30 acres; 7,000 cases red.

Mme Suzanne de Faucompret

Domaine de la Senche, La Livinière, 34210 Olonzac.
39 acres; 8,750 cases red.

Soc. Gourgazaud

Château de Gourgazaud, La Livinière, 34210 Olonzac.
Highly influential pioneering property of Chantovent. Success with *macération carbonique* encouraged investment in (e.g.) SICA Coteaux de Peyriac for *vins de pays* and the Dom. de Gourgazaud for experimental Vin de Pays de l'Hérault. 168 acres; 441,600 cases of red.

Marcel Julien

Château de Villerambert-Julien, 11160 Caunes-Minervois.
144 acres. 31,000 cases of red.

Paul Mandeville

Domaine de Vaissière, Azille, 11700 Capendu.
Pioneering property – Cabernet, Merlot, even Bleu Portugais.

Jacques Maris

Domaine Maris, 34210 La Livinière.
An expanding property (now 175 acres) in hand-picked sites around La Livinière. The Cuvée Spéciale is the best red.

Mme Moureau & Fils

Chx de Villerambert Noureau/ de Villegly, 11160 Caunes-Minervois.
288 acres; 25,000 cases of red and rosé.

Domaine du Pech d'André

Azillanet, 34210 Olonzac.
47 acres; 6,600 cases of red, rosé and white made by Marc Remaury at a 300-year-old estate.

CAVES COOPERATIVES
Les Vignerons du Haut-Minervois Azillanet, 34210 Olonzac. Founded 1922.
Les Costos Roussos Trausse, 11160 Caunes-Minervois. Founded 1937. Good Mourvèdre.
Coteaux du Haut Minervois La Livinière, 34210 Olonzac. Founded 1924. 180 members; 1,560 acres. The best red, Jean d'Alibert, is made by *macération carbonique* and aged in Bordeaux barrels.
Felines Minervois 34210 Olonzac. Founded 1922.
La Vigneronne 11160 Caunes-Minervois. Founded 1922.

Zone Four

The high plateau around Minerve has the harshest climate and makes the strongest, biggest wine. St-Jean-de-Minervois has its own appellation for Muscat *vin doux naturel*.

Mme Jacqueline Le Calvez

La Caunette, 34210 Olonzac.
Well sited on the sunny hillsides of La Caunette. Replanting has made a first-class vineyard. Very good vinification. 30 acres, 5,750 cases of red.

CAVES COOPERATIVES
Vinification d'Aigne 34210 Olonzac. Founded 1948.
St-Jean-de-Minervois 34360 St-Chinian. Founded 1955. Main cellar for the little appellation of St-Jean-de-Minervois.

Zone Five

The western zone, which has the highest rainfall and least distinguished wines.

CAVES COOPERATIVES
La Grappe Villeneuve Minervois, 11160 Caunes-Minervois. Founded 1925.
Malves Bagnoles Malves-en-Minervois, 11600 Conques-sur-Orbiel. Founded 1948.
Villalier 11600 Conques-sur-Orbiel. Founded 1934.

COTEAUX DU LANGUEDOC

The stress in this name is on the Coteaux. The plains of the Languedoc between Narbonne and Montpellier are the notorious source of calamitous quantities of low-strength blending wine. But certain of its hillsides have AOC status and hardly less potential for quality than Corbières and Roussillon. In general their wines are lighter and harsher – but not necessarily so. A dozen areas, confusingly scattered across the map, produce named and worthwhile wines. Yet only one domaine so far, has made a true international reputation for extraordinary quality: the highly individual Mas de Daumas Gassac at Aniane just north of Montpellier.

The concentration is to the north of Béziers, in the first foothills of the Cévennes where the River Hérault leaves its torrents to become placid and poplar-lined. Cabrières, Faugères, St-Saturnin are such foothill vineyards. The best known of them, are Faugères and St-Chinian, in the hills to the west towards the Minervois. Their reds can be full-bodied, distinctly savoury wines, admirably suited to vinification by *macération carbonique*. St-Chinian, partly on chalky clay and partly on dark purple schist full of manganese, is worth careful study. The variety of soils in these hills gives character to their wine. The Berlou Valley, on the purple schist, is outstanding for riper, rounder reds than the rest of the region.

The most individual, and an area with exciting potential, is

La Clape, the isolated limestone massif like a beached island at the mouth of the River Aude, between Narbonne and the sea. The soil and climate conditions on La Clape have shown that they can produce highly distinctive white wines. Cool sea breezes give the hills a microclimate of their own. Blanc de la Clape, made of standard southern grapes, or better from the Malvoisie (alias the Bourboulenc), is clean if unexciting when young. But real character comes with ageing: at five or six years it can have some of the style of a good Rhône white. Better grape varieties may make magnificent wines. Several domaines have planted Chardonnay. Coteaux du Languedoc-Saint-Saturnin also makes stylish wines, often with a significant proportion of Syrah.

Many growers in the Coteaux now make use of the *vins de pays* regulations to make such non-conforming wine as Merlots and Chardonnays which can be excellent: look for 'Domaine' names on labels otherwise identical to those of reputable châteaux. By law 'Château' must not appear on a *vin de pays* label.

Leading Coteaux du Languedoc Producers

Château La Condamine Bertrand

34230 Paulhan.

Stainless steel has been installed at this family-owned estate and whites and rosés are vinified at controlled temperatures. Reds – the bulk of production – go through carbonic maceration which brings out the fruit and colour. Red and rosé are made under the Coteaux du Languedoc AC, the white has the Clairette du Languedoc AC. A range of wines in the interesting Vin de Pays des Côtes de Thongue includes reds from Syrah, Mourvèdre, Merlot and Cabernet Sauvignon. 153 acres, 7,200 cases.

Château des Hospitaliers

Place Général-Chaffard, 34400 St-Christol.

Red and rosé Coteaux du Languedoc-St-Christol are produced at this small estate, using traditional methods. The red is a rich, smooth wine aged in wood. Some Syrah is used in the blends, including a Cuvée Spéciale. The estate also produces a white Vin de Pays de la Bénovie from Chardonnay, Grenache Blanc and Ugni Blanc. 49 acres, 6,000 cases.

Mas de Daumas Gassac

Aniane, 34150 Cignac.

The best, certainly the most famous, 'new' wine of the Languedoc. From a vineyard on eccentric volcanic soil high up in the hills behind Montpellier. The red is 85% Cabernet Sauvignon. The white is a blend of Chardonnay and Viognier; a fatly aromatic wine. The only begetter of this inspired estate, Aimé Guibert, can justly be said to have brought pride to the Languedoc for the first time. Professor Peynaud was the original consultant.

Château de Nizas

34320 Roujan.

Red Coteaux du Languedoc under the name Château Carrion-Nizas is produced at this property, using carbonic maceration and some wood ageing. The result is a typical southern taste which is improved with a touch of Syrah. Perhaps more interesting is the estate's Vin de Pays de Caux: the red is made from the usual local varieties plus 10% Cabernet Sauvignon and 15% Merlot. Small amounts of rosé and white *vins de pays* are also made. 103 acres. 15,000 cases.

Domaine du Poujol

34570 Vailhauques.

A newly acquired British-owned property which produces both Coteaux du Languedoc in red and rosé and *vin de pays*. Yields in the vineyard have been halved, and there has been investment in new plantings as well as in equipment in the cellars. The Coteaux du Languedoc wines red is aged for 10 months in wood. Vin de Pays de l'Hérault wines include a red which is a blend of Merlot, Cinsaut and Carignan. 39 acres. 8,333 cases.

Prieuré de St-Jean-de-Bébian

Owner: Alain Roux.

80 acres. Highly distinctive wine produced from all 13 Châteauneuf-du-Pape grape varieties. It is entitled only to *vin de pays* status, but deserves far better.

Château Saint-Jean d'Aumières

34150 Gignac.

While the bulk of Daniel Delclaud's production is of *vin de pays*, he also produces some Coteaux du Languedoc from Grenache, Cinsaut and Syrah. His range of wines include Vin de Pays de l'Hérault made from 50% Cabernet Sauvignon, with Grenache, Cinsaut and Syrah. Probably his most interesting wine is a 100% Cabernet Sauvignon Vin de Pays des Gorges de l'Hérault, which is matured in wood. 65 acres. 2,500 cases.

Skalli

278 Avenue du Mal-Juin, 34200 Sète.

Robert Skalli is the revolutionary producer of stylish Vins de Pays d'Oc from Cabernet, Merlot, Viognier and Chardonnay. (see Vins de Pays.) Fortant de France is his standard brand.

OTHER PRODUCERS

J M Bonnevialle St-Jean de La Balaquière, 34700 Lodève.
Daniel Delclaud Domaine de St-Jean d'Aumières, 34150 Gignac.
André Heulz St-André-de-Sangonis, 34150 Gignac.
Domaine du Parc 34120 Bézenas. Owner: M. Henri L'Epine. A 105-acre vineyard bounded by a 17th-century wall, producing Vin de Pays de l'Hérault from Carignan, Merlot and Cabernet Sauvignon.

CAVES COOPÉRATIVES

St-Félix de Lodez 34150 Gignac. Founded 1942.
St-Jean-de-la-Blaquière 34700 Lodève. Founded 1947.

COTEAUX DU LANGUEDOC DISTRICTS

Cabrières

In the Clermont l'Herault region of the Cévennes foothills. Best known for light *rosé de goutte*, made without pressing, but the schist soils are seen as suitable for producing quality wines, especially Syrah-spiced reds.

Cave Coopérative Les Coteaux de Cabrières

34800 Clermont-l'Hérault.
Founded 1937. AOC Coteaux du Languedoc Cabrières and Clairette du Languedoc. Brand names include L'Estable, and Cuvée Cabanon for a 90% Syrah red.

Coteaux de Vérargues

Near Lunel, between Montpellier and Nîmes. See Muscat de Lunel, page 216. Vérargues used to be famous for lightweight café wines but now produces soft gamey blends of Syrah and Mourvèdre. Useful reds from the Lunel-Viel coop, which has planted Merlot, and from estates including Château de Beaulieu.

Faugères

Westernmost of the Cévennes foothill districts with some very competent producers of red and instant rosé. An AOC in its own right since 1982, covering seven communes. Rules insist on at least 10% Syrah or Mourvèdre from 1990 vintage onwards. Wines may also be sold under the simple Coteaux du Languedoc appellation.

Domaine du Fraisse

34480 Autignac.
Jacques Pons created this 50-acre estate out of barren hillsides over the last 20 years. Growing in flavour as the vines mature.

Domaine de la Grange des Aires

Cabrerolles, 34480 Magalas.
Mme. Platelle's estate has classic red vine varieties for solid, long-lived wine.

Château La Liquière

La Liquière, Cabrerolles, 34480 Magalas.
Ideally situated with 150 acres of the best grape varieties for red, rosé and white with real finesse. Uses *macération carbonique*.

CAVES COOPERATIVES

Les Crus Faugères 34600 Bedarieux. Founded 1961.

Laurens 34480 Magalas. Founded 1938. Largest producers of AOC Faugères.

La Clape

Seaside area of limestone hills near Narbonne, best for white and rosé.

Soc. Aupècle

Domaine des Monges-Schaefer, Château de Capitoul, 11100 Narbonne.
A substantial estate in the centre of La Clape, using traditional methods.

J Boscary

Château de Rouquette-sur-Mer, 11100 Narbonne.
A remarkable 1,125-acre (130 under vine in 50 separate plots) site on the rocky slopes of La Clape near the sea. The most modern wine-making for high-quality red, white and rosé; perhaps the best of the area. The reds are aged in oak barrels.

Robert Bottero

11560 Fleury d'Aude.
Small but high-quality white-wine grower.

Combastet

Château de Ricardelle de la Clape, 11100 Narbonne.
Part of the estate is up on the limestone hills of La Clape and makes good traditional wines from a variety of grapes. The red is a blend of Carignan, Grenache, Syrah and Cinsaut. The rosé (or *gris*) omits the Syrah. Vins de Pays de l'Aude red and rosé, which include some Merlot, are also produced here.

Egretier

Château de Complazens, Armissan, 11110 Coursan.
Good grapes and useful situation on La Clape. Well-made wines, too.

Philippe Hue

Château de Salles, Salles d'Aude, 11110 Coursan.
Classic 'La Clape' reds made from Carignan, Grenache and Syrah come from part of the estate. M. Hue also makes an interesting *vin de pays* varietal from Merlot and a dry rosé with Cinsaut.

J B Jousseaume

Domaine de Ricardelle de la Clape, 11100 Narbonne.
Good quality white wines.

Yves Lignères

Domaine de Vires, 11100 Narbonne.
A property of 175 acres which shows signs of steadily improving both in choice of grape varieties and wine-making techniques. At present the best wines are maceration reds, including the superior Cuvée Saphir which mingles traditional and maceration.

Domaine de Pech-Redon

11100 Narbonne.
A restored old estate in a lovely situation high on the hills at

La Clape but near the sea. A wide variety of grapes from the 94-acre vineyards make good maceration red, white and excellent dry rosé.

de St-Exupéry

Château de Pech-Celeyran, Salles d'Aude, 11110 Coursan. 222 acres. A largely Cabernet and Merlot vineyard producing some good wine.

Jean Ségura

Domaine de Rivière La Haut, 11560 Fleury d'Aude. The 32-acre property of one of the leading protagonists in the area of high-quality white wine based on Bourboulenc grapes – the long-lived speciality of the La Clape region. A name to watch.

Vaille

Des Ruffes, Salleles du Bose, 11110 Coursan.

La Méjanelle

An obscure little gravel terraced region influenced by its proximity to the sea, east of Montpellier.

De Colbert

Château de Flaugergues, 34000 Montpellier. 131 acres. A family property for 300 years which has made a name for gentle, elegant reds. Henri de Colbert is also head of a group of local growers, 'La Domitienne', which aims squarely for quality.

Delbez

Mas de Calage, St-Aunès, 34130 Mauguio.

Teissier

Domaine de la Costière, 34000 Montpellier.

Montpeyroux

Northern district for full-bodied chewy reds from the foot-hills of the Larzac Mountains, near the famous Gorges de l'Hérault.

CAVE COOPERATIVE

Les Coteaux du Castellas 34150 Montpeyroux. Founded 1950. 285 members; 1,625 acres producing 410,000 cases of AOC Coteaux du Languedoc and typical full-bodied Montpeyroux.

Pic-St-Loup

2,000-foot peak due north of Montpellier. The AOC here limits Carignan to a maximum of 50% in red which can be light and refreshing. The best *terroirs* are: Hortus, Valflaunès, St-Mathieu and St-Jean-de-Cuculles.

Arlès Domaine de Lascours, Sauteyrargues, 34270 St-Mathieu de Tréviers.

Castries Château de Fontmagne. Baron Durand de Fontmagne. AOC and *vin de pays* reds and whites, including a Sauvignon Blanc.
Lauriol Domaine de la Roque, Fontanes, 34270 St-Mathieu-de-Tréviers.
Recouly Domaine de Cantaussels, Les Matelles, 34270 St-Mathieu-de-Tréviers.
Domaine de Villeneuve Claret, 34270 St-Mathieu-de-Tréviers.

CAVES COOPERATIVES

Les Coteaux de Montferrand 34270 St-Mathieu-de-Tréviers. Founded 1950.
Les Coteaux de St-Gely-du-Fesc 14980 St-Gely-du-Fesc. Founded 1939.
Les Coteaux de Valflaunes 34270 St-Mathieu-de-Tréviers. Founded 1939.

Picpoul de Pinet

The vines of Pinet overlooking the Etang de Thau produce the grapes for a pleasant dry white with 12% alcohol and a touch of freshness. In the Middle Ages the wine was called Picardan.

Cave Coopérative de Pinet 500 acres. Founded 1923. Largest producer of wine in the area.
C Gaujal Château de Pinet, 34850 Pinet.173 acres. Extremely carefully made Picpoul white and *vins de pays* from Merlot.

Quatourze

A neglected little zone near Narbonne which claims to be the oldest vineyard in Languedoc. Quartz and sandstone sites produced full-bodied reds and light, aromatic whites from the Maccabeo grape.

Georges et Yvon Ortola Château Notre Dame du Quatourze, Narbonne. 205 acres. Good Cinsaut-flavoured red.

St-Chinian

In the Cévennes foothills, to the west. The biggest and most important zone, now a cru of Coteaux du Languedoc since it became AOC in 1982. Potentially excellent solid and smooth reds. At least 10% of reds must be Syrah or Mourvèdre.

F Guy & S Peyre

Château de Coujan, 34490 Murviel-lès-Béziers. A 250-acre property making excellent Coteaux de Murviel (Merlot/Cabernet), classic St-Chinian (Cinsaut, Grenache and Syrah) by *macération carbonique*, and Cabernet rosé.

Domaine des Jougla

Prades-sur-Vernazobre, 34360 St-Chinian. A family estate since 1580 in the Cévennes foothills, now with modern equipment and new oak.

Libes-Cavaille

St-Nazaire de Ladarez, 34490 Murviel-lès-Béziers.

Miquel

Cazal-Viel, 34460 Cessenon.

Pierre Petit

Villespassans, 34360 St-Chinian.
A first-class St-Chinian property using *macération carbonique*.

CAVES COOPERATIVES

Causses & Veyran 34490 Murviel-Les-Beziers.
Founded 1946.
Les Couteaux de Cebazan 34360 St-Chinian.
Founded 1965.
Coteaux du Creissan 34370 Cazouls-Les-Beziers.
Founded 1951.
Les Coteaux du Rieu Berlou 34360 St-Chinian. Founded
1965. The best wine is produced under the brand name
Schisteil. Their Berloup Prestige cuvée is also noted.
Les Crus Cazedarnais 34460 Cessenon. Founded 1954.
Quarante 34310 Capestang. Founded 1934.
Les Vins de Roquebrun 34460 Cessenon. Founded 1967.

St-Christol

In a group with Verargues and St-Drézery north of Lunel.
The appellation area is limited to the commune of St-
Christol. Grenache is the dominant red grape, though Syrah
and Mourvèdre are also now making an appearance.

Domaine Martin Pierrat St-Christol, 34400 Lunel. 94 acres.
Medal-winning wines include a Syrah/Grenache red and a
Chardonnay *vin de pays*.
Cave coopérative Les Coteaux de St-Christol 34400 Lunel.
Founded 1940.

St-Drézery (see St-Christol)

Low-lying alluvial area. Lightweight reds best drunk chilled.

Spitaleri Mas de Carrat, St-Drézery, 34160 Castries. 114
acres, including some Merlot for *vins de pays*.
Cave Coopérative des Coteaux de St-Drézery 34160
Castries. Founded 1939. The top red carries the Carte Noire
label.

St-Georges-d'Orques

On the western outskirts of Montpellier, once fashionable
with English tourists interned by Napoleon. The author
Jullien once compared the wines favourably with those of
Burgundy. Full-bodied reds from Carignan, Cinsaut and
Grenache, with some Syrah.

Grill Château de l'Engarran, Laverune, 34430 St-Jean-de-
Vedas.150 acres. AOC reds and Sauvignon Blanc Vin de Pays
des Collines de La Moure white.

Caves Coopérative de St-Georges-d'Orques 34680 St-
Georges-d'Orques. Founded 1947. Château Bellevue is their
name for a *barrique*-aged red.

St-Saturnin

Active vineyards in the *garrigue* of the Cévennes foothills
with rather good lively reds and very light *vin d'une nuit*.

Cave Coopérative de St-Saturnin 34150 Gignac Founded
1951. Their 'Le Lucian' rosé displays its Syrah to effect.

THE MUSCATS OF LANGUEDOC

Three small zones along the central south coast, between
the wine port of Sète and the marshes of the Camargue,
have appellations (and an antique reputation) for sweet
Muscat *vins doux naturels*. Frontignan is the biggest and
best known. Its vineyards stretch along the coast through
Mireval (the second appellation) towards Montpellier.
The grape is the 'muscat à petits grains ronds'; its wine
powerfully aromatic, brown and sticky, but lacking (at
least as it is made today) the freshness and finesse of
Muscat de Beaumes de Venise. For the last 10 years an
independent producer, Yves Pastourel at Château de la
Peyrade has worked to improve this situation and
succeeded in producing a lighter and more refined wine.
The third area is Lunel, halfway between Montpellier and
Nîmes, just inland from the Carmargue.

The cooperatives of Frontignan and Lunel are the
major producers. One other big grower of Frontignan
and Mireval is M. Robiscau, who created Le Mas Neuf des
Aresquiers at Vic La Gardiole (34110 Frontignan) 20 years
ago, ripping up 200 acres of desultory vines from rocky
terrain to make a modern vineyard.

CAVES COOPERATIVES

Muscat de Frontignan 34110 Frontignan. Founded 1915.
340 members; 1,875 acres out of a total 2,000 for the AOC
producing 230,000 cases.
Muscat de Lunel Verargues, 34400 Lunel.
Founded 1956.
Muscat de Mireval – Cave de Rabelais 34840 Mireval.
Founded 1961.

CLAIRETTE DU LANGUEDOC

A scarcely merited AOC for a generally dull and dispiriting
dry white from Clairette grapes grown in several
communes along the Hérault. Much of it is fortified as a
cheap apéritif and sold under such names as 'Amber Dry'.

Domaine de la Condamine

34230 Paulhan.
M. Jany runs a very new property which has 84 acres of
Clairette of unusually good quality.

CAVES COOPÉRATIVES
Adissan 34230 Paulhan. Founded 1929.
La Clairette d'Aspiran 34800 Clermont-l'Hérault. Founded 1932.

La Fontesole 34320 Roujan. Founded 1930.
Peret 34800 Clermont-l'Hérault. Founded 1932.

THE GARD

This *département* of the Rhône delta was almost a vinous blank, a pause between the mass production of the Languedoc and the scattered vineyards of Provence, until modern technology stepped in. It has now been made a separate AOC. Only in one area south of Nîmes, the Costières de Nîmes, a deep deposit of pebbles from the former river bed provides good ripening conditions, officially recognized by a VDQS for Rhône-style reds and rosés in 1951 with the name Costières du Gard. This was changed in 1989 to the present name. For some strange reason a corner of this area even has an AOC for its white Clairette de Bellegarde.

Technology took an unexpected form. The massively wealthy Compagnie des Salins du Midi, producer of much of France's salt from the lagoons of this coast, experimented with vines in the sand flats along the shore. Their original wines were made with inferior varieties, but today the Vins des Sables du Golfe du Lion (under the trademark Listel) include such *améliorateurs* as Cabernet and Sauvignon Blanc.

Costières de Nîmes Producers

Château Roubaud

Gallician, 30600 Valivert.
Owner: Mme Annie Molinier. Founded 1902. 173 acres producing Costières de Nîmes. Total production 12,500 cases.

Mas St-Louis La Perdrix

30127 Bellegarde.
Owner: Mme Lamour. Run by the Lamour family for the past 35 years. 348 acres planted with Carignan, Cinsaut, Grenache, Cabernet, Syrah and Clairette de Bellegarde produce 44,500 cases. 80% of production is Costières de Nîmes. The rest is *vin de table*.

Cave Coopérative de Bellegarde

30127 Bellegarde.
President: M. Darboux. 260 members; 2,099 acres producing 797,800 cases a year, of which 32,700 are AOC.

Château de la Tuilerie

Route de St-Gilles, 30900 Nîmes.
An immaculately maintained estate owned by Mme Chantal Comte. The property, which she inherited from her husband, includes another 1,400 acres of fruit trees. She makes red, rosé and white Costières de Nîmes, the white with 100% Grenache Blanc, the red a blend of Grenache, Syrah and Cinsaut, and the rosé 100% Cinsaut. The red is the best of the three and ages well. 240 acres. 45,000 cases.

OTHER PRODUCERS
Domaine de l'Amarine 30127 Bellegarde. Nicolas Godepski.
Domaine de St-Benezey 30800 St-Giles du Gard. M. Pohe.
Château St-Vincent Jonquières St-Vincent, 30300 Beaucaire.

Vins des Sables du Golfe du Lion

Domaines Viticoles des Salins du Midi (Listel)

34063 Montpellier.
Founded 1856. Sales 1.6m. cases. The biggest wine estate in France, with 4,200 acres, largely in the sand dunes of the Gulf of Lions. Salins du Midi is a vast salt company. In the 19th century it started ploughing its profits into pioneering vineyards in the phylloxera-free sand. It has maintained the highest standards and made the Vins de Pays des Sables du Golfe du Lion a sort of appellation of its own, led by its Domaines de Villeroy, de Jarras and du Bosquet, under the management of Pierre-Louis Jullien who retired in 1986.

It uses sand as an almost neutral growing medium, excludes seawater with dykes of fresh water, fertilizes and fixes the sand with winter cereals and produces wines of remarkable clarity, simplicity and charm of flavour at moderate prices. As well as the sand vineyards 600 acres in the Var at Pierrefeu and Ollières produce Côtes de Provence and Vins de Pays des Maures and Coteaux Varois, a VDQS.

CORSICA: L'ILE DE BEAUTE

The importance of France's dramatically mountainous island of Corsica used to be almost entirely as a producer of bulk material for table-wine blends. When France lost Algeria, its wine growers flooded into the island to plant the plains of the east coast with the basic grapes of Algeria and the Midi – Carignan, Grenache and Cinsaut. In the period 1960–1973 the island's vineyards expanded from 20,000 to 77,000 acres. Then came a period of retrenchment, with 9,000 acres being pulled up again. So the vast majority of Corsica's vineyards are young, in common grapes and on relatively big properties formed for quantity rather than quality – with an average yield over the island of 76 hl/ha.

The appellation Vin de Corse was instituted in 1976 as an encouragement to limit crops. The specific interest of Corsican wine, such as it is, lies in crus of Vin de Corse and three more limited appellations (Patrimonio, Cap Corse and Ajaccio) relating to the best vineyards, which retain traditional grape varieties. These include the red Nielluccio (Italy's Sangiovese) and Sciacarello, which may be unique to Corsica, and the white Vermentino or Malvoisie de Corse and Trebbiano (Ugni Blanc). Most of the island's production is red wine, which is traditionally made as varietals, but

Syrah and Mourvèdre have now been planted for blending with Sciacarello.

Patrimonio in La Conca d'Oro in the north of the island is relatively long-established for rosé and red made primarily of Nielluccio and whites from Vermentino, with one degree higher minimum alcohol (12.5) than the rest of the island's wines.

Ajaccio, the capital, has Sciacarello red and rosé and Vermentino white. Calvi and the region of Balagne in the northwest have a relatively high proportion of AOC wine. Cap Corse specializes in dessert wines, including sweet Muscat.

Porto-Vecchio and Figari and the flat southeast have more vineyards, but using a good proportion of Nielluccio. Sartène, around Propriano in the southwest, is the area with the highest proportion of appellation wines (75 percent), of Corsican grapes – mainly Sciacarello – and of traditional-style small growers working on good hill slopes. On the whole, the south is the place to look for the most interesting wine. Plantings of Cabernet Sauvignon, Merlot, Chardonnay and Chenin Blanc on the eastern plain south of Bastia are included in increasingly interesting Vin de Pays de L'Ile de Beauté.

Principal Corsican Producers

Albertini Frères Clos d'Alzeto, 20151 Carri-d'Orcino.
Couvent d'Alzipratu 20214 Zilia
Clos Capitoro 20166 Porticcio
Dominique Gentile 20217 St-Florent
Clos Landry 20260 Calvi.
Clos Nicrosi 20247 Rogliano
Domaine Paviglia 2000 Ajaccio
Comte Peraldi 20167 Mezzavia
Domaine La Ruche Foncière, 20215 Arena-Vescovato
Domaine de Torraccia, 20137 Lecci de Porto Vecchio

Caves Coopératives

Agione 20255 Aghione
Aleria 20270 Aleria
Calenzana Coteaux de Balaone Suare, 20214 Calenzana
La Marana Ruisgnani 20290 Lucciana
Patrimonio 20253 Patrimonio
Sartène 20100 Sartène
SICA de Figari 20131 Pianottoli
Union des Vignerons Associés du Levant Rasignani, 20290 Borgo.

THE SOUTHWEST

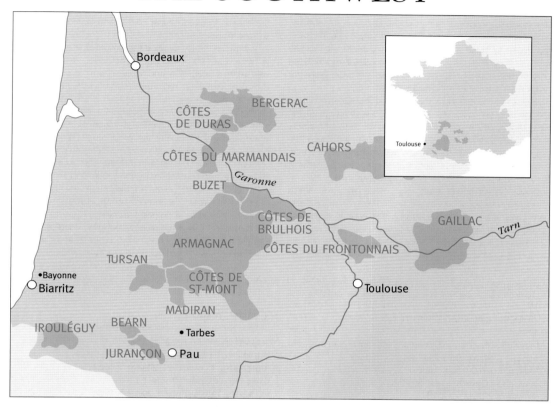

The southwest corner of France exists in calm self-sufficiency. Its rich food and notable wines seem, like its beauty and tranquillity, to be its private business. To the east lie the great vineyards of the Languedoc; to the north Bordeaux; Spain lies beyond the towering Pyrenees. In their foothills and the river valleys of the Tarn, the Garonne, the Lot, the Gers, the Adour and the Gave, a different race of wines is grown, bearing no relation to the Midi and remarkably distinct from Bordeaux. Historically some of these wines, notably Cahors and Gaillac, were exported via Bordeaux and known as the wines of the *haut-pays*, the high country. Some use the Bordeaux grapes. But all except those closest to the Gironde, such as Buzet, have real character of their own to offer. A variety of grapes with extraordinary local names, some of them Basque, gives a range of flavours found nowhere else. The world is beginning to discover them and encourage the expansion of a depleted vineyard. Happily, fashion is swinging towards the regional idiosyncrasies the southwest has to offer.

BERGERAC

The vineyards of Bergerac flank the Dordogne river, which joins the Garonne downstream from Bordeaux. The growers could thus escape the greedy clutches of the Bordeaux merchants who controlled the passage of wines from other *hauts-pays* such as Cahors and Gaillac. Bergerac had free access to overseas markets including the prosperous Dutch. The region's attachment to the Protestant religion caused many Huguenots to flee to Holland after the suppression of the reformed religion in 1698, and this reinforced Bergerac exports to that country. The Dutch taste was above all for sweet white wines which became and remained the pride of the Bergerac region. Monbazillac is its most famous name. But in the 20th century this style of wine has been hard to sell. So the Bergeracois tried red. Demand has switched to and fro between red and white with Bergerac tending to be a step behind. Recent plantings have been largely in the Bordeaux red grapes, which perform excellently here, with Merlot in the majority. With a current near-equilibrium between red and white grapes, Bergerac is at last well placed for the campaign it is waging to become better known.

It is not one simple appellation, but like Bordeaux an all-embracing one with subsections determined by slopes, soil and microclimates. Red Bergerac unqualified is light (minimum 10 degrees), unmistakably claret-like by nature; an indistinguishable substitute for many light Bordeaux reds, at a markedly lower price. Côtes de Bergerac are bigger, and more so still are the 12-degree wines from the chalky eastern part of the region with its own appellation Pécharmant which, like claret, improves with ageing.

The dry white is sold as Bergerac Sec. Several skilful and enterprising growers, not least at the cooperatives, have introduced a firm flavour of Sauvignon into wine that is still predominantly Sémillon and, to a lesser extent, Muscadelle. With cool, clean fermentation in stainless steel, they are making a Sancerre-style wine whose substance makes up for an occasional lack of finesse.

No fewer than five inner regions of Bergerac enjoy appellations for sweet and semi-sweet whites (which rely on Sémillon and hope for a degree of 'noble rot'). Just south of the town of Bergerac, Monbazillac, with its operatic château (the property of the local cooperative), is capable of truly luscious and powerful (15-degree) wines, after the style of Sauternes. The best now share the miraculous harmony of fruity acidity that makes a great Sauternes – and their lives are no shorter. I have lingered long over 40-year-old Monbazillac that had turned a fine tobacco colour.

Saussignac is a growing appellation for semi-sweet wines, but some producers are making wines as rich as those of Monbazillac. They are hoping one day for their own appellation, Côtes de Saussignac.

North of the Dordogne, Montravel is a usually superior Bergerac Sec – the names are interchangeable. The distinctions between the appellations Côtes de Montravel (*moëlleux*), and Haut-Montravel (fully sweet) complicate an already complicated situation for the Montravel growers, whose red wines cannot be called Montravel (they must be called Bergerac). The growers seek a review to simplify the rules, as well as the right to call their reds Montravel.

Rosette, an almost lost appellation, is having a mini-renaissance. It is another medium-sweet white, produced in the hills just north and west of Bergerac town.

Finally, Côtes de Bergerac, when applied to white wines, denotes a *moëlleux* style to which producers are not entitled or choose not to apply one of the inner appellations.

Leading Bergerac Producers

Basic red and dry white Bergerac is produced by most growers throughout the regions, even when they are entitled to use the name of an inner appellation.

Bergerac Rouge

Château Court-Les-Mûts

Razac de Saussignac, 24240 Sigoulès. Owner: Pierre-Jean Sadoux. 58 acres of white (Sém. 75%, Sauv. 25%) and red (Merlot 42%, Cab.Sauv. 33%, Cab.Fr. 25%).
A specialist in sweet white Saussignac, Sadoux produces a full range of Bergerac, notably one of the best of all Bergerac reds from the usual mix of grapes (half Merlot; a quarter each of the two Cabernets). Unwooded, straightforward and a worthy multi-medal-winner.

Domaine de Gouvat

24610 St Méard-de-Gurçon. Owners: Dubard frères et soeur.
A large property in the northwest corner of the Bergerac area, producing first-class red as well as dry and *moëlleux* Montravel and an oaked red, Château Laulerie. The family also has a small holding in Pécharmant from which they make excellent wine. They have also bought 45 acres in Lussac-St Emilion.

Château Grinou

24240 Monestier. Owner: Guy Cuisset.
Another all-rounder making good red Bergerac, as well as both dry and medium-sweet white.

OTHER PRODUCERS
Philippe Biau Château de la Mallavieille, 24120 Montfaucon.
M. Barde Château Le Raz, 24610 St Méard-de-Gurçon.

Pécharmant

Château Tiregand

24100 Creysse. Owner: Comtesse de St-Exupéry. 82 acres: 75 red (one half Merlot and a quarter each Cab.Sauv. and Cab.Fr.); 7 white (Sauv. 65%, Sém. 35%). 14,000 cases
The biggest Pécharmant property, replanted after the 1956 frosts replacing vines formerly produced by family cousins at Château d'Yquem. Iron in the soil gives a structure which called for ageing in bottle; only the best *cuvées* are lightly oaked. Wine from new vines is much lighter and sold as Clos de la Montalbanie.

La Métairie

24100 Bergerac. Owner: Guy-Jean Kreusch. 16 acres.
High-flying winemaker Daniel Hecquet uses up to 4 weeks *cuvaison*, followed by ageing in year-old oak. More Merlot has recently been planted and is due to come on stream. By common consent one of the best Pécharmants.

Domaine de Haut Pécharmant

24100 Bergerac. Owner: Michel Roches. 57 acres; Merlot 30%, Cab.Fr. 20%, Sauv. 40%, Malbec 10%. 21,000 cases.
The second-largest Pécharmant vineyard. Michel Roches likes experiments and has engaged Daniel Hecquet as consultant oenologist; try his Cuvée Veuve Roches, made from 70% Cabernet Franc. Another property for your Pécharmant shortlist.

OTHER PÉCHARMANT PRODUCERS
Guy Pécou Domaine de Bertranous, 24100 Creysse.
Arlette Best Château de Biran, 24100 St Saveur de Bergerac.
Françoise Bouché Châteaux Champarel, Pécharmant, 21400 Bergerac.

Bergerac Sec

La Tour des Gendres

24240 Ribagnac. Owner: Luc de Conti.

This vineyard is just to the south of Monbazillac. It makes a stylish and unusual dry wine from 100% Sémillon which is bottled on its lees to give it extra character. The wine has a distinct flavour of citrus fruits.

Domaine de la Jaubertie

Colombier 24560 Issigeac. Owner: Hugh Ryman. 114 acres, half red (Merlot 50%, Cabs 40%, Malbec 10%); half white (Sauv. 55%, Sém. 45%, a little Muscadelle). 28,000 cases.

Flying winemaker Hugh has taken over this important property, best-known for its dry white Bergerac, from his father Henry. Techniques learned in Australia enable him to produce a crisp 100% Sauvignon wine in stainless steel, which he bottles without delay. There are also wines from 70% Sémillon and 100% Muscadelle.

Château du Bloy

Bonneville, 24230 Vélines. Owners: Léopold and Jean Guillermier. 116 acres. Red: one quarter each Merlot, both Cabernets and Malbec; white, Sauv., Sém, Muscadelle and Muscadet.

A Montravel property which sometimes markets its wine under that name, sometimes as plain Bergerac. The pure Sauvignon wine is the one to go for here, bottled and marketed young.

OTHER PRODUCERS

J.-Louis Constant Domaine de Constant, 24680 Lamonzie-St Martin.

M.Becker Château de Panisseau, 24240 Thénac.

Monbazillac

Château de Theulet

Monbazillac, 24240 Sigoulès. Owner: Pierre Alard. 80 acres.

An estate which goes back to the time of the special relationship with Holland. The speciality is sweet Monbazillac from 80% Sémillon , 12% Muscadelle and only 8% Sauvignon. There are two *cuvées*: one matured entirely in stainless steel; the other partly in new wood. Both are luscious in the old-fashioned style, their sweetness redeemed by a lovely twist of acidity.

Château Le Fagé

Pomport, 24240 Sigoulès. Owner: François Gérardin. 100 acres: 25 red producing 6,500 cases, 65% Merlot and 15% each Cab.Sauv. and Cab.Franc; 75 white producing 1,500 cases dry Sauvignon, 1,500 Monbazillac, largely Sémillon with Sauvignon, Muscadelle and 1,000 rosé.

Although Gérardin likes to think of himself as an all-rounder, it is his Monbazillac which attracts the plaudits, from a high 90% Sémillon , with a fermentation of up to 10 weeks at low temperature and 30 months ageing in enamelled cement (no barrels).

Château La Borderie

Monbazillac, 24240 Sigoulès. Owner: Dominique Vidal. 150 acres. Monbazillac: Muscadelle, Sauvignon and Sémillon. Red: Merlot and the Cabernets.

Well over half of this vineyard is given over to Monbazillac of the highest quality, which can be aged for as long as four years in huge old vats soon due for replacement. The Vidals also own nearby Château Treuil de Nailhac, their older, smaller estate. Treuil de Nailhac has a distinct muscat taste, due to the high proportion of Muscadelle grapes.

Château Poulvère

Monbazillac, 24240 Sigoulès. Owner: Jean Borderie and his family. 212 acres.

The wines other than Monbazillac are marketed as Domaine des Barses, the name Poulvère being reserved for the flagship Monbazillac wine. Borderie also owns Château de la Haute-Brie et du Caillou, the two properties together covering over 200 acres. The Monbazillac is not as sweet as some, but makes up for that in elegance.

Clos Fondtindoule

Monbazillac, 24240 Sigoulès. Owner: Gilles Cros. 70% Sémillon, 20% Muscadelle, 10% Sauvignon.

Cros, the archetypal old-style vigneron, who, without the benefit of modern technology, is making some of the most astonishing wines of the areas. The only fertilizer is the manure from his own cows and the grapes have always been hand-picked, even before this became compulsory in Monbazillac in 1992. The wines are matured in huge old barrels and not bottled for at least six years, often longer.

OTHER PRODUCERS

Christian Roche L'Ancienne Cure, 24560 Colombier.

Comte Laurent de Bosredon Château de Belingard-Chayne, 24240 Pomport.

Jacques Blais Chateau Haut-bernasse, 24240 Monbazillac.

J.-P. Martrenchard Château le Mayne, 24240 Sigoulès.

Yves Feytout La Truffière-Tirecul, 24240 Monbazillac.

Saussignac

Château Les Miaudoux

24240 Saussignac. Owner: Gérard Cuisset.

One of the pioneers of the new-style ultra-sweet Saussignac white wines, taking their cue from neighbouring Monbazillacs. Cuisset's is every bit as good as the best of those. Pressed direct into new wood, it is fermented for about a month at low temperature. The tiny yield from over-ripe grapes means inevitably that wine like this is not cheap.

Domaine de Richard

La Croix-Blanche, 24240 Monestier. Owner: Richard Doughty.

Yes, an Englishman, also experimenting with extra-sweet Saussignac. Like Gérard Cuisset (Ch. Les Miaudoux), he relies on his dry white Bergerac for a living, but his heart is in the sweet wine.

Montravel

Château Calabre and Château Puy-Servain

3320 Port Ste-Foy-et-Ponchapt. Owner: Daniel Hecquet.
The whites here are the thing. Calabre wines are made without wood, while Puy-Servain is oaked. The dry white is very dry, the oaked version having plenty of body and fat. The Haut-Montravel sweet wines reflect the current styles in Monbazillac and Saussignac. Expertly made and long-lived.

Domaine de Krével

33220 Port Ste-Foy-et-Ponchapt. Owners: Guy-Jean Kreusch and Daniel Hecquet.
Adjoining Hecquet's own properties, this new vineyard is making highly fashionable oaked wines from 90% Sauvignon and 10% Muscadelle.

Domaine de Libarde

24230 Nastringues. Owner: Jean-Claude Banizette.
A fascinating example of the sweet Haut-Montravel style, from one of its leading exponents. Banizette was president of the Montravel Syndicat of growers for four years.

OTHER PRODUCERS

Jean Rebeyrolle Château la Ressaudie, 33220 Port Ste-Foy.
Mme Mahler-Besse Château de Montaigne, 24230 St Michel de Montaigne.
Pierre Sabloux Château Piquessègue, 33220 Ponchapt.
Itey de Peironnin Château la Raye, 24230 Vélines.

Rosette

Clos Romain

Les Côtes, 24100 Bergerac. Owner: Colette Bourgès.
One of only six growers currently declaring under this appellation, Mme Bourgès makes a distinctive half-sweet wine with real fruit and body, splendid as an apéritif or with mushroom dishes. A fascinating rarity. She makes good Pécharmant too.

OTHER PRODUCERS

Bernard Frères Domaine de Puypezat, Rosette, 24100 Bergerac

CAHORS

Cahors is certainly the most celebrated red wine of the scattered regions of the Southwest. The ancient town on the River Lot with its famous fortified bridge is linked in the public mind with dramatic-sounding 'black wine'. This was because so much of the wine made in Bordeaux was thin and travelled badly, and the merchants needed something to give strength and body to their exports. Their position at the commanding mouth of the Garonne enabled them to call the tune at Cahors, whose growers they encouraged to produce a thick dark brew by boiling some of their wine, even fortifying it. This was the famous 'black wine'.

Real Cahors wine has always been quite different, although the traditional methods of long fermentation and the universal use of the Malbec grape (called Auxerrois in Cahors) always produced a darker and more rustic wine than claret. Perhaps this explains why Cahors is still trying to live down the reputation it earned from its 'black wine'.

Cahors was destroyed by phylloxera in the 1880s and nearly a second time by the great frost of 1956. It struggled back very slowly, with little to raise it above the second class of VDQS until the 1960s and 1970s, when a business-like cooperative and a handful of old-time growers pulled the region together. It was promoted to appellation status in 1971, not for a revival of its 'black wine', but for well-balanced, vigorous and agreeable reds. The Auxerrois may now be blended with the softer Merlot as well as Tannat (the grape of Madiran). No other varieties are allowed today.

Most of the vines are now on the alluvial valley land, which is very gravelly in places, although there have recently been plantings on the *causses*, the limestone plateaux above the river. Despite the difference in the two *terroirs*, there is less distinction than might be imagined between the styles of *causse* and valley wines. The real contrast is between the traditional methods of vinification and those adopted by the newcomers, the négociants turned vignerons and the financial entrepreneurs who have spent fortunes in creating modern wineries. All too often these provide textbook examples of the law of diminishing returns. Some have even tried to create a Beaujolais look-alike by *macération carbonique*, overlooking the fact that the Auxerrois grape with its thick skin is not suited to this technique. The result is invariably a clean enough quaffable wine, but with no personality, let alone any resemblance to Cahors. For this reason the best Cahors today are still mostly produced by the long-established growers and a few younger ones from the region who, like their counterparts in Madiran, understand the importance of keeping the typicity of their own wine.

Leading Cahors Producers

Château La Caminade

46140 Parnac. Owners: the Resses family.
This 80-acre estate is worth a visit for the architecture alone; a fine example of a Quercynois presbytery, turrets and all, now given over to high-class viticulture. In addition to its mainstream wine, the Château La Caminade produces an oaked premium wine called Clos La Commendary as well as a lighter style called Château Peyrouse.

The Resses family are veterans of Cahors and their wines command a loyal following, particularly in the Netherlands.

Château du Cèdre

46700 Vire-sur-Lot. Owners: the Verhaeghe family.

Pascal and Jean-Marc Verhaeghe have taken over from their father, but had the bad luck to see nearly all their 1995 crop destroyed by a freak summer hailstorm. The Verhaeghes are among the most respected winemakers in the appellation. With more Auxerrois in their vineyards than most, the basic wine is finished with some Merlot, while in the special *cuvée* the Merlot is replaced by Tannat. They use long *cuvaisons* of up to four weeks. The Verhaeghes are experimenting with the possibility of a white Cahors, using the Rhône grape Viognier.

Clos La Coutale

46700 Vire. Owners: the Bernède family.

The Bernèdes have been making wine here since before the Revolution. Today it is noted for its round charm, and is often successful in difficult years like 1987 and 1992. Deeply coloured, the bouquet is often toasty, and there can be a hint of liquorice too.

Château Eugénie

46140 Albas. Owners: Jean and Claude Couture.

The Coutures make their premium wine (Réserve de l'Aïeul) exclusively from Auxerrois, while their other two wines, Etiquette Noire and Cuvée des Tsars, have only a little Merlot and Tannat respectively.

Clos de Gamot and Château de Cayrou

46220 Prayssac and 46700 Puy l'Evêque.

The colourful Jean Jouffreau, who died in 1996, will be a hard act to follow at these two properties, but his son-in-law, Yves Hermann-Jouffreau will doubtless manage it. The 25-acre Clos de Gamot vineyard has been in the family since 1610 and is planted exclusively with Auxerrois. Château de Cayrou was bought in 1971 and is planted with a more modern mix of 72% Auxerrois, 18% Merlot and 10% Tannat. The wines from both properties enjoy ultra-traditional production from modern plant. The Gamot can last as long as great claret in a good year. Cayrou is a little lighter in style, and has considerable elegance.

Château des Ifs

46220 Pescadoires. Owners: the Buris family.

The Buris' vineyards are located on rich alluvial soil close to the river, but not too rich to enable first-class wine to be made. Surprisingly full and generous, with the pronounced flavour of almonds and damsons so typical of the Auxerrois grape, these wines are good keepers.

Domaine de Paillas

46700 Floressas. Owner: M. Descombes.

Monsieur Descombes makes a *causse* wine which can be drunk younger than many of his neighbours', though the bouquet may remain closed for three years. Another property to suffer badly in the 1995 hail but sure to recover its former standing. The wines are stylish and attractive, rather than big and rustic.

Domaine du Pech de Jammes

46090 Flaujac-Poujols. Owners: Stephen and Sherry Schechter. 25 acres.

This American-owned vineyard produces the best of all the wines made by the négociant Georges Vigouroux. Its position on the causse lends it power to age and considerable body; the bouquet often suggests red fruits, and even a hint of the truffles growing nearby. Marketed in anglophone countries by the owners, elsewhere by Vigouroux.

Domaine Pineraie

46700 Puy l'Evêque. Owners: the Burc family.

The Burcs are neighbours of Teyssèdre-Vidal at La Reyne. Robert Burc is another lover of Auxerrois which represents 90% of his vineyard, the rest being Merlot. The best wine comes from the ground which rises up towards the *causse*. The wine from the lower ground is called Pierre Sèche.

Château La Reyne

46700 Puy l'Evêque. Owner: M. Teyssèdre-Vidal. 50 acres.

Monsieur Teyssèdre-Vidal comes from a long line of growers at this old-established estate, whose private cellars have, like the Jouffreaus', bottles going back to the 19th century. The vineyard is mostly Auxerrois, and some of the vines are 80 years old. A section of the vineyard is called Clos des Batuts.

Domaine des Savarines

46090 Trespoux-Rassiels. Owner: Danielle Biesbrouck. 10 acres.

Danielle Biesbrouck planted her few acres in 1970 in the middle of nowhere up on the *causse* just a few miles as the crow flies out of Cahors town. She has no Tannat and is able to reduce the *cuvaison* to twelve days. The wine still has good tannins and is attractively perfumed and soft in texture.

Clos Triguedina

46700 Puy l'Evêque. Owners: the Baldès family.

Dating back to 1830, this 140-acre estate makes wines which need some ageing. In addition to the mainstream wine, there is a special *cuvée* called Prince Probus, which is generously oaked, and a lighter wine sold as Domaine Labrande for earlier drinking.

OTHER GOOD GROWERS

Le Manoir du Rouergou, 46150 St Médard-Catus.
Michel Cassot Château La Coustarelle, 46220 Prayssac.
Gérard Decas Domaine de Decas, 46090 Trespoux-Rassiels.
Alex Denjean Château Lacapelle-Cabanac, 46700 Lacapelle-Cabanac.
Colin and Penelope Duns Château Latuc, 46700 Mauroux.
Durou et Fils Château de Gaudou,46700 Vire.
Gayraud et Fils Château Lamartine, 46700 Soturac.
Maradenne-Guitard Château de Nozières, 46700 Vire.
Jean-Pierre Raynal Domaine du Souleillou, 46140 Douelle.
Franck et Jacques Rigal Prieuré de Cénac, 46140 Albas; also **Château St. Didier-Parnac**, 46140 Parnac.
José Roucanières Domaine du Pic, 46140 Douelle.
Georges Vigouroux Château de Haute-Serre,46230 Cieurac; also Château de Mercuès, 46090 Mercuès.

AVEYRON AND THE UPPER LOT

Seventy miles upstream from Cahors, the *causses* give way to the foothills of the Massif Central, and the landscape starts to close in on the River Lot. Wine has been made here for centuries, from grapes grown on almost perpendicular slopes, terraced and walled with back-breaking effort. At Marcillac, the rich burghers of Rodez had their country homes where they employed resident winemakers to supply their needs; later, after the phylloxera epidemic the wine was made to slake the thirst of the coalminers of Decazeville. When the mines were closed down in the 1950s the Marcillac growers formed themselves into a cooperative to raise standards of production and to find a new market for their wine. It is highly original, made entirely from the Fer Servadou grape, called locally Mansois. It has a slight resemblance to Cabernet Franc, the same grassiness and flavour of soft red fruits, red- and black-currants and sometimes blackberries. There is only red and rosé Marcillac. They have enjoyed *appellation contrôlée* status since 1990.

The local white wine comes from further up the river at Entraygues, where the Lot is joined by the Truyère, and at Estaing. Here the Chenin Blanc grape is used to make a bone-dry, stylish and surprisingly modern-tasting wine; at Estaing some Mauzac is also used. The production is very small, but locally important; the wines are seen seldom outside the area, but are on the lists of all the local restaurants. Red wine too is made at both towns. Entraygues and Estaing both enjoy VDQS status, as do the wines grown in the upper valley of the Tarn in the vicinity of the town of Millau. Entraygues has no cooperative, and only seven or so producers, but Estaing and Millau both have small cooperatives in addition to a handful of private growers.

Leading Aveyron Producers

Entraygues

François Avallon 12140 Entraygues
Laurent Mousset (red wine only) 12140 Entraygues
Jean-Marc Viguier 12140 Entraygues

Estaing

Michel Alaux (for red wine) La Frayssinette, 12190 Estaing

Monique Fages (for white wine) La Ponsarderie, 12190 Estaing
Le Caveau de Viala 12190 Estaing

Marcillac

Cave des Vignerons du Vallon 12330 Valady
Jean-Luc Matha Le Vieux Roche, 12330 Bruéjols
Philippe Teulier Domaine du Cros, 12390 Goutrens

Millau

Cave des Vignerons des Gorges du Tarn 12520 Aguessac.

GAILLAC

Gaillac is one of the most productive and economically important of the scattered vineyards of the southwest. Historically it has supplied not only Albi, the capital of its département, the Tarn, but places much further away – its reds having a name for amazing transportability and longevity. It was established as a vineyard during the first century after Christ, during the Roman occupation of the Midi, and long before vines were planted at Bordeaux. Its unheard-of indigenous grape varieties, the bane of some modern producers but the pride and joy of others, encourage the idea of extreme antiquity. Its reds are the Duras (nothing to do with the wine area of that name), the Braucol, the local name for Fer Servadou and its whites are the Mauzac and the Loin de l'Oeil (or l'En de l'El), the other local variety, Ondenc, being almost extinct nowadays.

A century ago, just before the phylloxera, the production of Gaillac was almost entirely of red wine. The little white that was made was either sweet or sparkling or both, or else of a style not unlike that of a light sherry. The reds were big and sturdy, mostly sold down the river to Bordeaux for blending. When the vineyard was replanted the emphasis changed to white wine, because of the competition in reds from the Midi. The traditional white Gaillac grape, Mauzac, was exploited to produce sweet wines with an appley character. AOC-status was granted for the white wines in 1938. The red wines were not so recognized until 1970, largely because the growers had failed to replant post-phylloxera with good-quality varieties and had stuck to the old, rather commonplace stocks.

The modern reconstruction of the industry, sparked off by big cooperatives, has opted for more standardized production. A tradition of bottling white wine before its first fermentation was over was dropped in favour of the champagne method, despite the fact that the Gaillac process ante-dated the champagne technique by several centuries. Sauvignon, Merlot, Gamay and Syrah have been brought in, and where they are used the wines are lighter and more neutral than they used to be.

In addition to the three cooperatives there are today about 100 private producers, which is ten times as many as there were in 1970. Many of these are going back to the old Gaillac grapes in a search for typicity and distinctiveness. The modern range of Gaillac is thus bewildering; there are plain dry white wines, or dry with a slight prickle induced by keeping them on their lees; there are dry and *demi-sec* sparkling wines; and there are more or less sweet still wines. There are oaked and unoaked reds and a *vin de l'année* after the style of, and often much better than,

Beaujolais Nouveau. There are also rosé wines of course. In terms of quality, there are marked variations, and the situation is complicated by the fact that some growers excel in some styles of wine while succeeding less well in others. The list of producers therefore suggests some good all-rounders and then some specialists in the various styles.

Leading Gaillac Producers

Domaine de Labarthe

81150 Castanet.

Jean Albert disappoints nowhere throughout his complete range of Gaillac. Especially to be recommended are his white *perlé* from Mauzac, his sweet white from the same grape, his basic red wine and his rouge *primeur* made from Gamay. His top-of-the-range red, Cuvée Guillaume, is quite markedly oaked.

Mas d'Aurel

81170 Donnazac.

Monsieur Ribot has 35 acres seemingly on top of the world just south of Cordes. His red wines are always reliable, while his dry sparkler wins prizes regularly.

Mas Pignou

Laborie 81600 Gaillac.

A 50-acre property with a complete range of wine as well as the best view of Gaillac town and the valley of the Tarn. His dry white (half Sauvignon, half Len de l'El) is allowed a second fermentation before being matured a further year in barrel; unlike most dry Gaillac it ages well. The sweet wine is a stunner from Mauzac. The prestige red is Cuvée Mélanie, but the basic red is excellent too.

Domaine des Très Cantous

81140 Cahuzac-sur-Vere.

From his 44-acre vineyard, Robert Plageoles produces an astonishing range of varietal wines. Apart from his pure Sauvignon, all are from the traditional Gaillac varieties. A 100% Duras, a Gamay, dry and sweet whites exclusively from Mauzac, a dry sparkler made according to the old Gaillac method, sweet wines from 100% Ondenc and another from Muscadelle. The range is rounded off with the old sherry type of maderized white wine, also made from Mauzac.

Cave Coopérative de Técou

81600 Técou.

The best all-rounder of the three coops. The 220 members do not have the best terrain; most of the vineyards are on the south bank in the plain. But the quality of the winemaking is all the more remarkable for that. Their marketing is aimed very largely at the restaurant trade.

RECOMMENDED FOR PARTICULAR STYLES

White perlé:
Cave Cooperative de Labastide-de-Lévis 81150 Labastide-de-Lévis
Cave Cooperative de Rabastens 81800 Rabastens
Domaine de Salmes 81150 Bernac
Dry white:
Domaine de Long Pech 81310 Lisle-sur-Tarn
Domaine de la Ramaye Ste-Cécile d'Avès, 81600 Gaillac
Sweet white:
Mas de Bicary 81600 Broze
Château Mayragues 81140 Castelnau-Montmirail
Domaine de Vayssette Laborie ,81600 Gaillac
Red:
Domaine d'Escausses 81150 Ste-Croix.
Domaine du Moulin 81600 Brens.
Domaine de la Ramaye Ste-Cécile d'Avès, 81600 Gaillac.
Red primeur:
Domaine d'Escausses 81150 Ste-Croix.
Domaine de Moussens 81150 Cestayrols.
Rosé:
Château de Candastre 81600 Boissel.
Domaine de Gayssou 81600 Broze.
Domaine de Moussens 81150 Cestayrols.
Sparkling dry:
Domaine de Canto Perlic 81600 Gaillac.
Domaine René Rieux 81600 Boissel.
Domaine de la Tronque 81140 Castelnau-Montmirail.
Sparkling sweet:
Domaine René Rieux 81600 Boissel.
Domaine de Vayssette Laborie, 81600 Gaillac.

COTES DU FRONTONNAIS

The slopes around Fronton and Villaudric, 15 miles north of Toulouse and 20 west of Gaillac, achieved AOC status in 1975 for their ripely fruity red and rosé wines, which until then had been a secret kept by the people of Toulouse. The pink wines even today are billed as 'Le Rosé de la Ville Rose'. The local grape is called Négrette, brought back from Cyprus at the time of the Crusades by the Knights Templar, who owned much of the land covered by today's vineyards at Fronton. For those who cannot resist the complications of ampelography, I should add that the Négrette turns up in the Charente (of all places) as Le Petit Noir. Its only appellation appearance is however in the Frontonnais.

The Négrette, which by law must form between 50% and 70% of every Fronton vineyard, is, as its name implies, very dark-skinned and its juice is dark too. The grapes are small and the skins are thin, which has encouraged at least one good grower to vinify by *macération carbonique*. The bouquet of the Négrette is said to suggest violets, red fruits and/or liquorice; the flavour often brings to mind cherries and almonds.

The problem with the Négrette grape, though, is that it is liable to grey rot, but given that the climate of Toulouse is hot and dry during the growing season, it flourishes well there. It is a very adaptable grape; on its own it can make a light quaffing style of wine of some considerable character; and blended with the two Cabernets, Gamay and/or Syrah, it can also make a bigger wine, capable of four or five years' ageing.

Leading Frontonnais Producers

Château Bellevue-la-Forêt

31620 Fronton.
Patrick Germain has 280 acres under vine, which makes him the biggest producer in the Southwest. His wines include a virtually 100% light Négrette called 'Ce vin, une idée d'André Daguin', a traditional red which is his biggest selling line, as well as some oaked prestige wines. (Oak is controversial in Fronton, most growers believing that it does not suit the grape variety.) The rosé from this estate is popular and very good.

Domaine de Joliet

31620 Fronton.
Owners François and Marie-Claire Daubert specialize in an all-Négrette red, which is perhaps the best of its style in the region. There is no such thing as white Fronton, but Daubert makes a sweet *vin de pays* from the Mauzac grape, which is delicious.

Château le Roc

31620 Fronton.
The Ribes family make wines that are more structured than most, and need some cellarage. A fascinating contrast with Daubert's, highlighting the versatility of Négrette.

Château Plaisance

31340 Vacquiers.
Marc Penavayre and his father make three styles of Fronton, in addition to a good rosé; a so-called *vin de printemps*, whose style speaks for itself, an excellent mainstream red and an oaked prestige wine Thibault de Plaisance.

OTHER RECOMMENDED PRODUCERS
André Abart Château Devès, 31620 Castelnau-d'Estrefonds.
M. M. Bonhomme Château Bel Air, 31620 Fronton.
Baron François de Driesen Château la Colombière, 31620 Villaudric.
Louis Duplan Château la Bruyère, 82370 Campsas.
Jean Ethuin Château la Palme, 31340 Villemur-sur-Tarn.
Ferran Père et Fils Château Cahuzac, 82170 Fabas.
La Cave de Fronton 31620 Fronton.
Roger Kuntz Château Flotis, 31620 Castelnau d'Estrefonds.
Madame Linant de Bellefonds Château Peyreaux, 31340 Villematier.
F. Montels et G. Perez Domaine de Callory, 82370 Labastide-St Pierre.
Martine Rougevin-Baville Domaine Caze, 31620 Villaudric.
Claude Vigouroux Château Baudare, 82370 Labastide-St Pierre.

LAVILLEDIEU-DU-TEMPLE

A small cooperative to the northwest of Montauban was built in this small town in 1949 by the growers of vines on the low-lying ground at the confluence of the rivers Tarn and Garonne. They acquired VDQS status for their wines in 1952, but the name was not much used until recent years, members preferring to use the names of various local *vins de pays*. Today the VDQS may be claimed for wines from 13 communes; there is 25% each of Gamay, Syrah and Cabernet Franc, 15% Tannat and 10% Négrette. Such a cocktail does not add up to a distinctive wine, but it is usually agreeable, rounded and fruity; soft and easy to drink.

THE BORDEAUX SATELLITES

COTES DE DURAS

The Côtes de Duras has the misfortune, like Bergerac, to lie just over the departmental boundary from Bordeaux – more particularly from Entre-Deux-Mers. Its wine is in every way comparable; half of it dry white, made increasingly from Sauvignon, though the greater proportion of grapes are still Sémillon , Muscadelle and small amounts of Ugni Blanc and Colombard. The red wines have as much as 60% Cabernet Sauvignon, 30% Merlot and a little Cabernet Franc and Malbec. The Cave Coopérative Berticot, just outside the town of Duras, makes a red wine by macération carbonique, which produces a fleetingly fruity effect. A second coop called Les Peyrières lies over the border at Landerrouat in Entre-Deux-Mers, to cater for growers who have vines in both appellations. The best wines, both red and white, come from a handful among the 50 or so independent producers.

Leading Côtes de Duras Producers

Domaine de Laulan

47120 Duras.
Gilbert Geoffroy is a native of Chablis, and his white wines are outstanding. Made entirely from Sauvignon, they come both oaked and unoaked, they are deliciously fruity, thus demonstrating how different this grape can be at a southern latitude.

Château La Moulière

47120 Duras.

The brothers Blancheton cover the whole range of styles, taking particular pride in their *vin doux*. Although not botrytized, it is beautifully honeyed without cloying. Wonderful with foie gras, and nearly as expensive.

Château La Grave-Béchade

47120 Baleyssagues.

Daniel Amar's comfortable gentilhommière is the only wine-making property in the region aspiring to the status of a real château. Equipped with ultra-modern technology, his winemaker, Daniel Bensoussan, is making wines worthy of bourgeois château status in Bordeaux terms.

Domaine Amblard

47120 St Sernin.

Guy Pauvert has the biggest Duras vineyard – 160 acres, less densely planted than is nowadays fashionable. He uses no new wood because he said it is not popular with his clients, whom he tours personally as far away as Belgium during the winter. His dry white, based on Sauvignon is sometimes found under the name of Domaine la Croix-Haute.

Domaine de Durand

47120 St Jean de Duras.

Michel Fonvielhe's vineyard goes back hundreds of years; there are still some 100-year-old Sémillon vines. His dry white wine contains as much as 30% Muscadelle and 15% Ugni Blanc, while the red is high in Cabernet Franc and given two years' *élevage*. These are serious wines made for keeping.

OTHER PRODUCERS

Lucien et Philippe Salesse Domaine de Ferrant, 47120 Esclottes.
Bruno Rossetto Château Bellevue-Haut-Roc, 47120 Esclottes.
Bernard Bireaud Domaine du Vieux Bourg, 47120 Pardaillan.
Pascal Gitton Château Lafon, 47120 Loubès-Bernac.

COTES DU MARMANDAIS

The Côtes du Marmandais lies right on the fringes of Bordeaux. Its light red (its major product) could for many years come under the heading of 'claret', and its Sauvignon/Sémillon white is comparable to everyday Bordeaux. En route to AOC status, granted in 1990, growers were required, with a view to ensuring a distinctive quality for Marmandais as against Bordeaux wine, to grow whatever they might choose from a list of grapes specific to the Southwest, including Malbec, Fer Servadou and particularly a rare and local speciality called Abouriou. In this way Marmande wine has begun to acquire a character of its own, while retaining a fresh and fruity style. Two rival coops of roughly equal size make nearly all the wine, one to represent right-bank growers at Beaupuy, the other on the left bank at Cocumont.

Leading Marmandais Producers

Les Vignerons de Beaupuy

47200 Beaupuy.

The older (1948) of the two cooperatives has recently undergone a face-lift to meet the competition from its rival across the river. Right-bank wines are said to age more slowly than left-bank wines, so this coop ages some of its lines in new wood. More Abouriou is grown on the right bank than on the left. About 40% of the production at Beaupuy is of Vins de Pays d'Agenais or *vins de table*, sometimes made from old grape varieties such as Bouchalès.

Cave Coopérative de Cocumont

47250 Cocumont.

With the benefit of AOC status, this cooperative has invested in the latest state-of-the-art technology, so that there is virtually no handling of the wine at any stage by personnel. It is all done electronically and by remote control. The mainstream red wine called 'Tradition' is excellent in its class, better than the Bordeaux which the coop makes for those of its members who have vines over the border.

OTHER PRODUCERS

Vignobles Boissonneau (Domaine de Géais) at Château de la Vieille Tour, 33190 St Michel-de-Lapujade.
Robert Schulte Château de Beaulieu, 47250 Cocumont.

BUZET

When Bordeaux was firmly limited to the département of the Gironde, one of the up-country sources of claret to be hardest hit was the hills south of the Garonne to the north of the Armagnac country, the Buzet. Happily white wine for distillation was an alternative crop, but the gravel and chalky clay on good southeast slopes had long produced very satisfactory red wine. In the last 30 years they have been reconstituted and are doing better than ever.

The cooperative at Damazan near Buzet dominates the area, making red wine to good Bordeaux standards. It makes no secret of striving for a monopoly. There are though a handful of excellent private growers, continuing to contribute beneficial competition.

Leading Buzet Producers

Les Vignerons Réunis de Buzet

Buzet-sur-Baise, 47160 Damazan.

The overwhelming majority of Buzet comes from this model cooperative (with its own cooper), which has steadily expanded and improved the vineyards of the area since 1954, and can claim the credit for its promotion to appellation status in 1973. The red wines are aged in the home-made barrels, the new wood being given to the top range called Baron d'Ardeuil, and then passed on to the second in line, Carte d'Or, and finally to their least expensive range called Tradition. Small amounts of white and rosé wines complement the range. The coop also makes wines for a number of individual properties including Domaine Padère and Château de Gueyze (the best wine from this coop), and Châteaux Bouchet, Balesté, Larché, de Piis, Bougigues and Tauzia. There is tension between the coop and some of the private growers. The former make no secret of their aim to establish a monopoly, which is a pity, because the latter are making wines with often more local character.

OTHER PRODUCERS

Jean Ryckmann Domaine de Versailles, 47600 Montagnac-sur-Auvignon.

Bernard Thérasse Château de Sauvagnères, 47310 Ste-Colombe-en-Brulhois.

Daniel Tissot Domaine du Pech, 47310 Ste-Colombe-en-Brulhois.

Thierry Schellens Domaine de Tourné, 47600 Calignac.

Patrice Sterlin Château le Frandat, 47600 Nérac.

COTES DU BRULHOIS

This small VDQS area adjoins Buzet to the east, and makes more rustic wines than Buzet. Brulhois may for example contain Tannat, Malbec and Fer Servadou in addition to the two cabernets and Merlot. Some local growers have more rustic grapes still, but are not allowed to keep these and at the same time declare in a VDQS area, so many have given up altogether.

Production is almost entirely in the hands of two cooperatives, one in the Lot-et-Garonne, the other in neighbouring Tarn-et-Garonne. The *cave* at Goulens has eight members who have vines in Buzet, and a branch in the Buzet area to make it. The same *cave* also makes the Vin de Pays de Thézac-Perricard for the growers of that area (q.v.).

MADIRAN AND THE WINES OF GASCONY

Madiran and Pacherenc

Madiran is the wine that came back from the dead. Forty years ago the vineyard in the Vic Bilh hills on the southern edge of the Armagnac country, 25 miles north of Pau, had dwindled to a dozen acres. Today there are 2,000 and some would claim that Madiran is the best red of the southwest, Cahors included. If it lacked the advantages of Cahors, fame and accessibility, it also avoided the identity crisis which still bothers the better-known wine. The name of 'black wine' lingers, while the reality is merely a healthy red.

The peculiar quality of Madiran is to start life with a disconcerting bite, then to mellow quite rapidly into a wine with a most singular style and texture. The bouquet has the teasing qualities of a good Médoc or Graves. When I was looking for the right word for a nine-year-old 1973 from the main cooperative of the region, I was so struck by its silkiness

on the tongue that I hesitated over the rather lame 'liquid', then tried 'limpid'. Later I looked Madiran up in Paul de Cassagnac's *French Wines*, a little-known but extremely rewarding work of 1936. 'An infinitely fluid savour' were the first words that struck my eye. So Madiran is consistent, despite its near demise; across 55 years it still caresses the palate in a seductively swallowable way.

This is the more odd in that de Cassagnac fulminates against 'the inferior Tannat', a 'common grape' being introduced to replace the Cabernet in the region for the sake of its bigger crop. All real Madiran, he says, is Cabernet. Yet today its producers tell us the secret of its character is the grape that sounds like tannin, and gives all the harshness its name implies; a smaller-berried cousin of the Malbec, Cot or (in Cahors) Auxerrois. A high proportion of Tannat, they say, is essential. So do the wine authorities, because a Madiran vineyard must by law consist of 40–60% Tannat, and some growers make wines that are 100% Tannat. The best-known grower in the region, Alain Brumont, goes one stage further and believes that all other varieities should be banned from the appellation – and he should know. Personally, I should like to taste a wholly Cabernet Madiran to judge for myself.

The Vic Bilh hills, a sort of very piano rehearsal for the soaring Pyrenees, parallel to the south, give their name to the white wine called Pacherenc, a dialect equivalent of the French *piquets en rangs*, or 'stakes in rows'. Pacherenc sometimes lends itself as an alternative title to the Arrufiac grape, traditionally an important element in the wine. Gros and Petit Manseng and, to a lesser extent Sauvignon are other grapes used. Traditionally, like Vouvray, it was as sweet a wine as the autumn permitted, but most growers today try to make a dry and a sweet version by adopting different proportions of the grape varieties. Pacherenc was always a tiny local production, but nowadays most Madiran growers like to make some.

Leading Madiran and Pacherenc Producers

Château Montus and Domaine Bouscassé

32400 Maumusson.

Alain Brumont is the high priest of the Tannat grape. The premium wines from his two properties, which between them cover 150 acres, are both 100% Tannat, and they are vinified for five weeks. Not surprisingly they take several years to mature. At Montus the mainstream wine is 70% Tannat, 20% Cabernet Sauvignon and 10% Fer Servadou, while at Bouscassou 60% Tannat is complemented by 30% Cabernet Franc and 10% Cabernet Sauvignon, and even these wines are vinified for four weeks. The premium wines are given at least a year in new oak, which is then handed down to the mainstream wines the following year. A third wine, Domaine Meinjarre, is half Tannat, half Cabernet Franc and is priced at bargain level. There is a range of Pacherenc too, in varying degrees of sweetness depending on the date of harvesting. Brumont is not above making good *vins de pays* and has recently launched a range of varietal wines.

Château d'Aydie (Domaines Laplace)

64330 Garlin.

The Laplace family is one of the few who never gave up on Madiran, and there are still some pre-phylloxera vines to prove it. Château d'Aydie is where the family now lives, and it gives its name to their prestige wine, a mere 70% Tannat, complemented by Cabernet Sauvignon. The principal red is named after grandfather Frédéric Laplace and has 60% Tannat with equal quantities of the two Cabernets. François Laplace thinks highly of the future for the white Pacherenc, and his own version of the sweeter style is superb.

Château Laffitte-Teston

32400 Maumusson.

Jean-Marc Laffitte's red Madirans are among the best the region has to offer, and include a 100% Tannat prestige wine. Both his Pacherencs are consistently magnificent, winning prize after prize. They are good value too.

Domaine Berthoumieu

32400 Viella.

There is something immediately attractive about Didier Barré's Madirans. They are much less stern and forbidding than some and seem to come round more quickly than many, even though the prestige red Charles de Batz can be up to 90% Tannat in a good year. Barré goes over his white grapes no fewer than five times, and his sweet Pacherenc is made from the last three *triages*.

Domaine Mouréou

32400 Maumusson.

Patrick Ducournau is the think-tank of Madiran, much admired as one of the bright young hopes of the southwest. Although another devotee of 100% Tannat wines – his premium wine Chapelle Lenclos, for example – he is also keen to shorten the period of maturation, and has invented a system of oxygen-injection to reduce the need for frequent remontage and disturbance of the wine in *cuve*.

Les Vignerons du Vic-Bilh–Madiran

64350 Crouseilles.

A first-class coop whose top wine, Château de Crouseilles (a property which they own), is among the top wines of the region. It needs 8 years. The mainstream Madirans and Pacherencs are good too, and there is a large production of rosé and red Béarn, and vins de pays.

Domaine de Labranche-Laffont

32400 Maumusson.

Yvonne Dupuy and her daughter Martine are rapidly making a name for themselves in this male-dominated appellation. Their Madiran from their older vines took first prize at the important local show in 1995. Their Pacherenc too is among the best.

OTHER PRODUCERS

Jacques Achilli Château de Piarrine, 32400 Cannet.
André Beheity Domaine Damiens, 64330 Aydie.

François Bouby Domaine Taillerguet, 32400 Maumusson.
Denis Capmartin Château Barréjat, 32400 Maumusson.
Guy Capmartin Domaine Capmartin, 32400 Maumusson.
Roger Castets Château de Fitère, 32400 Cannet.
Richard Crouzet Château de Perron, 65700 Madiran.
Pierre Dabadie Domaine Laougué, 32400 Viella.
Vignobles du Domaine de Diusse 64330 Aydie.
Gilbert Dousseau Domaine Sergent, 32400 Maumusson.
André Dufau Domaine de Maouries, 32400 Labarthète.
Jacques Maumus Cru du Paradis, 65700 St-Lanne.
Alain Oulié Domaine de Crampilh, 64350 Auriions-Idernes.
Maurice Ponsolle Domaine de Lacave, 32400 Cannet.
René Tachouères Château Pichard, 65700 Soublecause.

COTES DE SAINT MONT

In 1974, André Dubosc created a cooperative of growers in the valley of the Adour, north of Madiran and south of Armagnac. There are three branches at Plaisance, St Aignan and St Mont. The coop is thus called Plaimont. The object was to find an alternative market for the dry white wine locally produced for distillation into Armagnac, because the demand for Armagnac had started to decline. Dubosc had hit on a winner, because it was not long (1981) before he had created almost single-handed his own VDQS under the name of Côtes de St Mont, for wines of all three colours. He was also to attract members from the Côtes de Gascogne, whom he persuaded to improve standards with the Colombard grape, which had been so successful in California. He attracted growers too from the northern part of the Madiran AC. Today therefore the coop produces Madiran and Pacherenc, both of excellent quality, St Mont reds and whites, basically from the same grapes as Madiran and Pacherenc, and a full range of *vins de pays* Côtes de Gascogne, mainly from Colombard.

Other St-Mont producers: Ch. de la Bergalasse 32400 Aurensan, André Dufau Dom. de Maouries, 32400 Labarthète.

The Gers: Armagnac country

Although a full range of wines is today made in the Armagnac area, it is the dry white wines largely from the Colombard grape which have attracted much popularity. There are typical inexpensive examples produced at coops such as Condom and Nogaro, as well as the Plaimont trio, though none to merit particular attention. Some independent growers are however producing wines of better class, of the sort which a buyer is likely to find in a good wine-bar.

Growers include:
The Grassa family, Ch. de Tariquet and Dom. de Rieux;. Dom. de Plantérie; Comte Laudet, Dom. de Laballe;
Albert Danzacq, Dom. de Pagny; Dom. Mesté-Duran;
Alain Lalanne, Dom. de Lahitte;
Dom. le Puts; Jean-Marc Sarran, Dom. de Bergerayre.

TURSAN

This is the leading vineyard of the *département* of Landes. Almost the entire production comes from the cooperative at Geaune, Les Vignerons de Tursan, which has 250 members owning about 875 acres of vines between them. The wines won VDQS status in 1958, although half of the production is still of Vin de Pays des Landes. The red wines are mostly Cabernet Franc with a little Tannat, while the whites are made principally from an obscure local variety called Barroque, with a little enlivening Sauvignon. There are Cabernet-based rosés too. The style of Tursan is aimed at the holiday-makers of the Atlantic coast; light, fruity and easy to drink; short *cuvaisons* at not too high a temperature for the reds, while the whites are given a cool fermentation under controlled temperatures. The red from Domaine de Castèle is made at the coop and is their flagship wine.

Other Tursan Producers

Domaine de Perchade-Pourrouchet

40320 Geaune.
Alain Dulucq claims to have started the cooperative, but left when he was forbidden to go on making wine at home, where he has 40 acres of vines. The white is 100% Barroque (with 10% Sauvignon added to the better *cuvée*), the rosé mostly from Cabernet Franc, and the red from a mixture of Tannat, Fer Servadou and the two Cabernets.

Château de Bachen

Duhort-Bachen 40800 Aire-sur-Adour.
The celebrated chef Michel Guérard has his elegant home here, and has built an architect-designed winery, a fifth of whose production is sold in his restaurants at Eugénie-les-Bains. He makes only white wine, of which the sweet version is still experimental. The vineyard is 50% Barroque, 12.5% each of Gros Manseng, Petit Manseng, Sauvignon and Sémillon. There are two grades of dry white, Château de Bachen and Baron de Bachen, the latter well-oaked. The wines are very high-class, but hardly typical of the Tursan appellation.

BEARN AND THE PYRENEES

BEARN

Country-style wines have been made in the Béarn district for centuries. In recent times they rose to prominence largely on account of their rosé which became fashionable throughout France in the middle of the 20th century. Today the red wines are overshadowed by Madiran and Irouléguy, and the whites by Jurançon, but good wines throughout the range are made at the cooperative at Bellocq near the pretty town of Salies-de-Béarn. Growers in Madiran sell their rosé as Béarn AOC, while those in Jurançon sell Béarn red. Just one independent estate in Béarn proper makes very good wine – the Domaine Guilhémas on the outskirts of Salies. They make two ranges, one sold under the name of the domaine, the other as Domaine Lapeyre.

JURANCON

All references to Jurançon start with the story of the infant King Henri IV, whose lips at birth were brushed with a clove of garlic and moistened with Jurançon wine – a custom said still to be followed in the Bourbon family, though without such spectacular results. The point is that Jurançon is strong, not just in alcohol but in character. Its highly aromatic grapes ripen on the Pyrenean foothills south of Pau in autumns warmed by the south winds from Spain. Its flavour is enhanced by small crops, in particular for the sweet wines. These are or should be made by harvesting very late, in November, when hot days and freezing nights have shrivelled the grapes (*passerillage*) and concentrated their juice.

The two principal grape varieties are the Gros and Petit Manseng, the latter not only smaller but with a much higher sugar content. Both give wines of high degree with a remarkably 'stiff' and positive structure in the mouth, almost fierce when young but maturing to scents and flavours variously likened to such exotic fruits and spices as mangoes, guavas and cinnamon. Some growers also use a little Petit Courbu in their dry wines to give them bite. Colette provided tasting notes I will not presume to rival: 'I was a girl when I met this prince; aroused, imperious, treacherous as all great seducers are – Jurançon.'

There are two appellations, Jurançon Sec and Jurançon, the latter applicable only to wines ranging from half-sweet to *liquoreux*. There is an important coop at Gan, and nearly 60 private producers. Generally they make three styles of wine, *sec*, *moëlleux* and ultra-sweet, sometimes oaked.

Leading Jurançon Producers

Cave des Producteurs de Jurançon

53 Avenue Henri IV, 64290 Gan.
The 275 members of this coop have only 1,350 acres between them. Most of the production is of dry wine, of which there are three grades – the highest called 'Peyre d'Or' being one of the best of the appellation. There are three *moëlleux* also, of which the top of the range, 'Prestige d'Automne', is also outstanding. A fourth *moëlleux* called Croix de Prince is aged

in new wood. The coop makes the wine for four private estates: Domaine des Terrasses, Château Navailles, Château Lasserre and Château Coute, and from its own Château des Astous.

Domaine Cauhapé

64360 Monein.

Henri Ramonteu is the best-known private grower, with the second largest vineyard of 62 acres. His basic *sec* accounts for three-quarters of his output of dry wine, and is widely known in the UK. He has another *sec* made from the oldest vines, and a third version which is oaked; a fourth is made unusually from Petit Manseng, the grape usually reserved for the sweet wine. Equally unusually his basic *moëlleux* is made exclusively from Gros Manseng; and a *vendanges tardives* from Petit Manseng. Finally there are two very small ultra-sweet and very expensive productions called respectively Noblesse and Quintessence du Petit Manseng.

Clos Uroulat

64360 Monein.

Charles Hours is President of the Syndicat of local growers and a producer of elegant and stylish, rather than fat and luscious wines. His *sec* is all the more crisp for the Petit Courbu that goes into it, and he uses some new wood for both his dry and sweet wines.

Domaine Bellegarde

64360 Monein.

Pascal Labasse is the prototype new-wave Jurançon grower, remaining open-minded on the use of new wood. He produces a bone-dry *sec* which ages well, a *moëlleux* called Cuvée Thibault, and an ultra-sweet *cuvée*, Sélection Petit Manseng, made entirely from that grape and modelled clearly on Henri Ramonteu's richest wines (see Domaine Cauhapé).

Domaine de Castéra

64360 Monein.

Christian Lihour scorns the use of new wood, but manages to make superb wines in all three styles. The *sec* is entirely from Gros Manseng, and the *moëlleux* almost so; the *liquoreux* is 100% Petit Manseng.

Domaine Bru-Baché

64360 Monein.

Claude Loustalot has taken over from his uncle Georges Bru-Baché and continues the same eccentric approach to Jurançon. Both dry and *moëlleux* wines are sold under the name of Cuvée des Casterasses.

Château Jolys

La Chapelle-de-Rousse, 64100 Jurançon.

With his 90 acres, Robert Latrille is the largest grower in Jurançon and one of the first to succeed as an independent. The vineyards of La Chapelle-de-Rousse are on much higher ground than those of Monein, usually built in amphitheatre-like folds of the hills called cirques. Latrille, however, has planted in vertical rows rather than on terraces. His wines are less eccentric than he, all good middle-of-the-road Jurançon, the *sec* from Gros Manseng, the *moëlleux* half Gros and half Petit, and his *liquoreux* all from the Petit.

Clos Lamouroux

La-Chapelle-de-Rousse, 64110 Jurançon.

Richard Ziemeck-Chigé now makes the wines at his former father-in-law's property, thoroughly traditionally and without regard to fashions like new oak which he abhors. He does not believe in Jurançon Sec, and makes wines only in varying degrees of sweetness as they always used to be hereabouts. The name of Clos Mirabel, an adjoining property recently purchased, is used for the red Béarn AOC using Cabernet Franc.

Clos Lapeyre

La Chapelle-de-Rousse, 64110 Jurançon.

Jean-Bernard Larrieu is another exciting young producer in a predominantly young appellation. As well as the usual *sec*, there is a special dry *cuvée* from old vines called Vitage Vielh, kept one year in wood and needing five years' ageing. A range of excellent sweet wines culminates in a superb 100% Petit Manseng *vendanges tardives* (the grapes were not picked until December in 1991).

Clos Guirouilh

64290 Lasseube.

Jean Guirouilh's 25-acre vineyard is tucked away at the southern end of the appellation, and has been in the family since 1670. His *sec* contains 10% Petit Courbu but otherwise is all Gros Manseng. It has tremendous style and elegance, the taste of apples and pears giving way to citrus fruits with age. The *moëlleux* is made of roughly equal parts of each of the Mansengs, some of the Petit being given some new oak. In good years he will make a *liquoreux* entirely from the Petit Manseng. Guirouilh is a master at managing new wood.

OTHER PRODUCERS

Casimir Capdevielle Domaine Capdevielle, 64360 Monein.
Francis Gaillot Domaine Gaillot, 64360 Monein.
Jean-Marc Grussaute Domaine Larrédya, La Chapelle-de-Rousse, 64110 Jurançon.
Jean Mondinat Domaine Mondinat, 64290 Gan.
Philippe de Nays Domaine de Nays, La Chapelle-de-Rousse, 64110 Jurançon.
Joseph Labat Château de Rousse, La Chapelle-de-Rousse, 64110 Jurançon.
Anne-Marie Barrère Clos de la Vierge (also Domaine Concaillaü), 64150 Mourenx.

IROULEGUY

The Basque growers make wines to match the taste of their fellow-countrymen for rugby and bull-fights; big sturdy wines, trying to outdo Madiran, and a perfect match for the local cuisine. Based, like Madiran, on the Tannat grape, most makers use also the two Cabernets. The vines are grown on steep terraces, so all picking is done by hand. Yields are small and the wines need time in bottle. The rosé wine is excellent, and there has been a small renaissance of the white wine, based on the Jurançon grape varieties. For many years the excellent cooperative had it all its own way but there are now some good independent producers making a name for themselves. This is an appellation to watch.

Leading Irouléguy Producers

Les Maîtres Vignerons d'Irouléguy

64430 St Etienne de Baïgorry.

The cooperative was founded in 1952 to exploit the grant of VDQS status, raised to AOC in 1970. The 230 members share 415 acres, so many holdings are tiny. Nearly half the production is of rosé, the basic version of which rejoices in the Basque name Argi d'Ansa; the better version, containing half each Tannat and Cabernet is called Terrasses d'Arradoy. The basic red is Gorri d'Ansa, but there are special *cuvées*: Domaine de Mignaberry, Domaine Iturritze (quicker maturing) and Domaine Mendisokoä. The small production of white wine is called Xuri d'Ansa.

Domaine Ilarria

64220 Irouléguy.

Peio (Pierre) Espil has but 15 acres of vines, but they are the benchmark for true Irouléguy. His two reds, made respectively from 80 and 100% Tannat, are serious propositions. The latter is called Cuvée Bixintzo (the Basque name for St Vincent). The *cuvaisons* are long (15 days for the Tannat, 20 for the Cabernet) and the wines are aged in a mixture of new and old wood for 18 months.

Domaine Brana

23 rue du 11 novembre, 64220 St Jean Pied-de-Port.

Jean and Martine's father, Etienne Brana, died tragically and suddenly just when the family, long-established négociants in the Southwest, had just planted their vines in 1985. Scenically magnificent – the splendid winery is hewn out of the mountainside – with breathtaking views to the mountains, the vines are planted in terraced rows on almost vertical slopes, which can only be worked by hand. Yields are tiny, and the wines as expensive as they are sought after. There is only 30% Tannat, the rest of the red vineyard being divided more or less equally between the two Cabernets. The *cuvaisons* are shorter than at Ilaria, and the wines mature earlier. There is no new wood.

OTHER PRODUCERS

Jean-Claude Errecart Domaine Abotia, 64220 Ispoure.
Michel Riouspeyrous Domaine Arretxea, 64220 Irouléguy.
M. Hillau 64430 St Etienne-de-Baïgorry.

VINS DE PAYS

Throughout 1981 and 1982 a stream of decrees flowed from Paris, signed by the Minister of Agriculture, setting out the regulations for newly coined *vins de pays*. The object was to give pride to local production that has hitherto had no identity. Since that time the junior rank of French country wines has undergone nothing short of a revolution. Wines that were previously used entirely for blending, or at best to go labelless to the local bars, are now made to minimum standards and in regulated quantities. The names of over 140 *vins de pays* names have come into active – sometimes hyperactive – use, with the south, the Midi, setting the pace. Outside interest, not least investment from New World wine countries, flying wine-makers and foreign supermarket winebuyers, has raised standards and broken the mould of generations of cautious vignerons. The results are many of the best value for money wines of France, including some real gems.

This list of *vins de pays* is still changing 15 years after the pioneers were promulgated. Some have been raised to VDQS and AOC status. New *vins de pays* have appeared. From vintage to vintage new ideas and new producers appear. This list sets out the ground rules for wines that will build reputations, for some that have earned their laurels – and no doubt also for others that nobody will ever hear of again. But in a sense it is a mark of the success of the idea that since 1995 the *départements* of the Gironde (Bordeaux), the Côte d'Or (Burgundy), the Marne (Champagne), Bas- and Haut-Rhin (Alsace) and the Rhône are no longer permitted to call any of their wines *vins de pays* – an attempt to protect the identity of the great wines of France from undercutting by their own growers.

The first essential information in this chapter is the area delimited. Some are as local as three or four parishes; some are departmental (Vins de Pays de Loire Atlantique, for instance); some as sweeping as the whole of the Midi (Vins de Pays d'Oc) or the Loire Valley (Vins de Pays du Jardin de la France). These last, of which there are four, were intended to give new life to traditional winemaking areas and be used as the vehicle for experimentation and new ideas – which

indeed they have done. It is the most precise, the *vins de pays de zone*, that usually have the highest standards.

The second important control is over the grape varieties to be grown. In some cases one or more classic grapes are prescribed as obligatory, while a number of others are tolerated up to a percentage. Some areas do not specify varieties at all. The most successful new *vins de pays* are single-grape productions – 85% of them from the Midi – and are generally seen as France's riposte to the varietals of the New World.

The last two controls are the minimum natural alcoholic strength required (of which you can broadly say the higher the strength the better the wine is likely to be) and the maximum crop allowed. Most *vins de pays* are allowed more than 80 hectolitres a hectare, which would be high in an appellation contrôlée area but low in the *vin de table* vineyards of Languedoc.

The entries are organized in the following way. The name of the *vin de pays* is followed by the *département* or region, whichever is more familiar. Next comes the date of establishment. Then the area delineated with, where possible, a central town and in some cases an indication of the type of terrain.

Maximum crop is only given when it differs from 80 hl/ha, and minimum alcohol when it differs from the almost universal 10.5 to 11 degrees. Grape varieties are listed where specified. Where the rules do not specify the grape varieties it can be assumed that the standard grapes of the region are used. The colour of wine is only given when all three colours are not made. Occasionally technical details such as planting density, pruning and training methods, sugar levels and minimum acidity are regulated, and this is noted in the entries. The producers whose names are given have been recommended by local experts. Most *vins de pays* production used to be the domaine of the *caves coopératives* although individual estates have now gained a hold, some expensively equipped and technically advanced – some far out ahead of their neighbours and playing the same card as the top *vini da tavola* of Italy.

RHONE AND PROVENCE

Most of the wine-growing areas of the Rhône and Provence are entitled to the wide-ranging appellations Côtes du Rhône or Provence. The *vins de pays* cover outlying, often interesting, districts and one or two zones within the AOC areas themselves. The wines, mostly red, are usually blends of the traditional grapes of the south, but increasingly the Bordeaux varieties are featuring.

Coteaux de l'Ardèche

Ardèche. 1981. Fourteen communes in the Ardèche and Chassezac valleys in the southern Ardèche, in the foothills of the Cévennes. 10°. Grapes, red: 70%, minimum of one or more of Cabernet Franc, Cabernet Sauvignon, Carignan, Cinsaut, Counoise, Gamay, Grenache, Merlot, Pinot Noir, Picpoul, Syrah. White: 70% minimum of one or more of Aligoté, Bourboulenc, Chardonnay, Marsanne, Roussanne, Sauvignon, Viognier, Picpoul Gris. Producers: M. Dupre, Lagorce, 07150 Vallon Pont d'Arc; GAEC Brunel, St-Remèze, 07700 Bourg St-Andéol. Six coops including Ruoms, 07120 Ruoms. Over 3m. cases.

d'Argens

Provence. 1981. Seventeen communes around Draguignan in the Argens Valley, mostly land also entitled to the AOC Provence. 126,000 cases.

Coteaux des Baronnies

Rhône. 1981. Area around Rémuzat and Rosans, north of Mont Ventoux in the Alpine foothills, especially for red wines (Cinsaut, Grenache, Gamay, Syrah, Pinot Noir plus up to 30% others). White: Rhône varieties plus Aligoté and Chardonnay. Three coops including Nyons (26110) and Puymeras (84110). 320,000 cases.

Bouches-du-Rhône

One of the largest *vin de pays*-producing areas in Provence. The wines come from three distinct zones: the Aix-en-Provence area, the main Côtes de Provence vineyards in the east of the département, and the Camargue. Seventy percent of the wines are red, made from the southern grape varieties, with some Cabernet.

Comté de Grignan

Rhône. 1981. Nine cantons around Vinsobres and Grignan in the lower Rhône. 10°. Grapes, red and rosé: Grenache, Syrah, Cinsaut, Mourvèdre, Gamay, Pinot Noir plus up to 30% others. White: normal Rhône varieties. Two coops at Suze La Rousse, 26130 and St-Marice-sur-Eygues, 26110 Nyons. 330,000 cases.

Comtés Rhodaniens

1989. One of the four regional *vins de pays* designations covering eight *départements* (the Ain, Ardèche, Drôme, Isère, Loire, Rhône, Savoie and the Haute Savoie). 155,000 cases.

Drôme

Wine production mainly from the south of the Drôme *département*, east of Montélimar. Over 80% is red, made from Carignan, Cinsaut and Syrah, supplemented by Gamay, Cabernet Sauvignon and Merlot. 475,000 cases.

Maures

Provence. 1982. In the Var *département*, east and southeast of the Maures mountain range extending east to the Estérel mountains. Grapes, red, rosé: Grenache, Cinsaut, Syrah, Mourvèdre, Cabernet Sauvignon, Merlot (two-thirds red, one-third rosé) and a little white. Producers: coopératives Gonfaron, Puget Ville, Le Luc, Pierrefeu, La Londe, Grimaud, Carnoules, Cogolin, Ramatuelle, Plan de la Tour, La Crau, Cannet des Maures, Pignans, Vidauban, Les Arcs, Collobrières, Le Muy, Fréjus-Roquebrune. 990,000 cases.

Mont-Caume

Provence. 1982. Twelve communes around Bandol. Top producers: Bunan, Vincent Racine, Hubert Jouve, La Cadière d'Azur (83740). Coop at St-Cyr-sur-Mer (83270). 282,300 cases.

Principauté d'Orange

Rhône. 1981. Cantons of Bollène, Orange, Vaison-La-Romaine and Valréas, east of the Rhône in the Côtes-du-Rhône Villages country: Min. alch: 10.8, max 11.8. Pruning methods specified. 535,500 cases.

Petite Crau

Bouches-du-Rhône. 1982. Four communes in the Petite Crau hills south of Avignon. Min. alch: 11°, no more than 12.5° for white and 13° for red and rosé. Pruning systems regulated. One coop at Noves (13550). 58,800 cases.

Collines Rhodaniennes

Central Rhône. 1981. Parts of four *départements* on both banks. 10°. Grapes, red and rosé: Syrah, Gamay, plus Pinot Noir, Merlot and Cabernet Franc in some districts, plus secondary grapes up to 30%. White: traditional Rhône varieties plus Chardonnay in some districts. Four coops including St-Désirat, 07340 Serrières. 116,000 cases.

Var

The most important *vin de pays* region in Provence, covering the whole of the Var *département*. Côtes de Provence AC is also produced in this region, although half the rosés made here are classified as *vins de pays*. 1.7m. cases of rosés are made from Grenache, Cinsaut and Syrah, with some Roussanne du Var. The reds (some 615,000 cases) are a blend of Carignan, Grenache, Cinsaut, Syrah, Mourvèdre and Cabernet Sauvignon. Less white (100,000 cases) is made.

Vaucluse

Another large *vin de pays* for wines from the Côtes du Rhône, Côtes du Ventoux and Côtes du Luberon regions, north and east of Avignon. The style of the red wines is that of Côtes du Rhône, although the blend includes Cabernet Sauvignon. There is also white Vin de Pays de Vaucluse, made from the Ugni Blanc. 1.7m. cases.

THE GARD

The *département* of the Gard stretches from the Rhône at Avignon west into the hills of the Cevennes. The chief town is Nîmes. Most of the *département* is wine-growing country, and there is a *vin de pays* for the whole area: Vin de Pays du Gard. Eleven other *vins de pays*, covering areas of varying size, are listed below. No specified grape varieties.

Mont Bouquet

Gard. 1982. Nineteen communes around Vézenobres, northwest of Nîmes. Two coops at Brouzet Les Alès, 30580 Lussan, and St-Maurice-de-Cazevieille, 30190 St-Chaptes. 222,000 cases.

Coteaux Cévennois

Gard. 1981. Twenty-four communes northeast of Alès in the Cévennes foothills. Producers: M. Silhol, St-Victor de Malcap, 30500 St-Ambroix. Four coops including Rochegude, 30430 Barjac. 56,000 cases.

Coteaux de Cèze

Gard. 1981. Forty-six communes on the west bank of the Rhône around Bagnols-sur-Cèze and Roquemaure. Four coops including Pont St-Esprit (30130) and Roquemaure (30150). 80,000 cases.

Coteaux Flaviens

Gard. 1981. Nine communes to the southwest of Nîmes. Top producers: Domaine de Campuget, 30129 Manduel. Domaine de Cassagnes, 30800 St-Gilles. Two coops at Beauvoisin (30640) and Bouillargues (30230). Up to 90,000 cases.

Coteaux du Pont du Gard

Gard. 1981. Nineteen communes around Remoulins, between Nîmes and Avignon. Eight coops including Vers-Pont-du-Gard, 30210 Remoulins. 367,000 cases.

Sables du Golfe du Lion

Gard. 1982. Sand dunes and coastal strips in parts of twelve communes to the west of the mouth of the Rhône. Grapes, red and rosé: Cabernet Sauvignon, Cabernet Franc, Carignan, Cinsault, Grenache, Lledoner Pelut, Merlot, Syrah and up to 30% others. White: Ugni, Clairette, Carignan, Muscats, Sauvignon and up to 30% others. Producers: Cave Coopérative d'Aigues Mortes, 30220 Aigues Mortes; Les Vignerons du Val d'Orbieu, 11000 Narbonne. 1.8m. cases.

Coteaux du Salavès

Gard. 1981. Twenty-eight communes centred around St-Hippolyte-du-Fort, in the west of the *département*. Producers include: M. Pieyte, Mandiargues, 30170. Four coops including Moulezan, 30350 Ledignan. Up to 22,000 cases.

Uzège

Gard. 1981. Twenty-six communes around Uzès, north of Nîmes. Producers: M. Reboul, Sagues, 30700 Uzès. Five coops including St-Quentin-La-Poterie, 30700. Up to 100,000 cases.

Vaunage

Gard. 1982. Fourteen communes to the west of Nîmes. Three coops including Clarensac (30870). 2,000 cases.

Vistrenque

Gard. 1982. Northeast of the Gard in the Plaine du Vistre. Up to 22,000 cases.

Côtes du Vidourle

Gard. 1982. Fifteen communes around Sommières, west of Nîmes. Producers: Marcel Granic, Aspères (30860). Three coops including Villevieille, 30250 Sommières. 37,000 cases.

HERAULT

This is France's biggest wine-producing *département*. Vin de Pays de l'Hérault covers the whole area. Twenty-seven local districts have their own sets of regulations. Some of the areas cover land in the St-Chinian and Minervois AOCs, others include communes entitled to the Coteaux du Languedoc AOC. The presence of one of the Midi's top estates – Mas de Daumas Gassac – proves that this is not only an area of inexpensive wines. *See* pages 203–217 on the Midi.

Ardailhou

Hérault. 1982. Southernmost part of the *département* at the mouths of the Hérault and Orb. Coops at Portiragnes, Vias, Villeneuve-les-Béziers, Sérignan. 275,000 cases red.

Vicomté d'Aumelas

Hérault. 1982. Fourteen communes south of Gignac in the Hérault Valley. Technical restrictions. Six coops, including Vendémian and Puilacher, 34230 Paulhan. 168,000 cases.

Mont Baudile

Hérault. 1981. Around St-Jean de la Blaquière at the foot of the Causses du Larzac and the Saint-Baudile Mountain. Two-thirds production red, rest rosé and some white. The leading coop is at St-Félix-de-Lodez. 88,000 cases.

Bénovie

Hérault. 1982. Fifteen communes in the extreme east of the *département*. Coop at Beaulieu, 34160 Castries. 33,000 cases.

Bérange

Hérault. 1982. Seven communes around Castries and Lunel in the southeast of the *département*. Producers: M. de Forton, Baillargues (34670). Two coops at Baillargues and Montaud, 34160 Montaud Castries. 88,000 cases.

Bessan

Hérault. 1981. Commune of Bessan, inland from Agde. Producers: René Fulcrand; Clarou L'Epine, both at Bessan (34550). Coop at Bessan. Up to 56,000 cases.

Côtes du Brian

Hérault. 1982. Thirteen communes around the centres of Minerve and Olonzac in the Minervois. Producers: Robert Caffort, Minerve; Aimé Fraisse, St-Jean de Minervois; Laurent Mari, Aignes; Luc Mondie, Aigues-Vives; M. Marcon, St-Jean de Minervois. Nine cooperatives including La Vigneronne Minervoise, 34210 Olonzac. 200,000 cases.

Cassan

Hérault. 1982. Four communes around Roujan in the central Hérault. Maximum yield 75hl/ha. Coopérative at Roujan, 34320. 99,000 cases.

Caux

Hérault. 1982. The commune of Caux, lying north of Pézanas. Top producers include: Henri Collet, Domaine de Daurion, Château de Nizas. Coopérative at Caux, 34720. 155,000 cases.

Côtes du Ceressou

Hérault. 1981. Fifteen communes near Clermont L'Hérault. Maximum yield: 70hl/ha. Producers: M. Servent, Domaine de Fabregues, Aspiran; GFA Pages Renouvier, Nizas; Bernard Jany, Domaine de la Condamine, Paulhan, 34230; SCA St-Pierre de Granonpiac, St-André de Sangonis. Eight coopératives including Aspiran, 34230 Pauhan. 123,000 cases.

Cessenon

Hérault. 1982. Commune of Cessenon, east of St-Chinian. Coop at Cessenon, 34460. 11,000 cases.

Coteaux d'Enserune

Hérault. 1981. Eleven communes west of Béziers. Top producers: Domaine d'Auveille et Montels, Capestang; Domaine de la Garrigue, Nissan Les Enserune; Domaine de la Grande Carmargue, Montady. Six coops including Nissan Les Enserune, 34440. 77,000 cases.

Coteaux de Fontcaude

Hérault. 1982. Six communes south of St-Chinian. Top producers include: Pierre Comps, Puisserguier, B. Farret d'Asties, Domaine de Cariètes, Quarante, 34310 Capestang. 143,000 cases.

Gorges de l'Hérault

Hérault. 1982. Three communes in the upper Hérault Valley around Gignac. Winemaking restrictions. White and rosé 11°, red 10.5°. Top producer: Château St-Jean d'Aumières. Two coops including Gignac (34150). 19,000 cases.

Coteaux du Libron

Hérault. 1982. Six communes around Béziers. Technical specifications. Best producers: G. Vidal, Béziers; Norbert Alker, Domaine Les Bergeries, Béziers; Georges Gaujal, Domaine de Libouriac, Béziers. Five coops including Béziers, 34500. 650,000 cases.

Val de Montferrand

Hérault. 1982. Parts of five cantons north of Montpellier. Technical specifications. Producers: M. Pagevy, Domaine du Viviers, 34170 Jacou; GAEC de Brunet, Causse de la Selle (34380). Nine coops including Assas, 34160 Castries. 120,000 cases.

Collines de la Moure

Hérault. 1982. Twenty-seven communes around Frontagnan and Mireval. Producers: P. Leenhard, Domaine de Lunac, Fabregues; H. Artignan, Vic La Gardiole; M. de Gaulard d'Allaines, Abbaye de Valmagne. Ten coops including Montarnaud, 34570 Pignan. 500,000 cases.

Coteaux de Murviel

Hérault. 1982. Nine communes in the Orb Valley. Producer: Château Coujan. Six coops including Murviel, 34490 Murviel des Béziers. 165,000 cases.

Haute Vallée de l'Orb

Hérault. 1982. Thirty-one communes in the northwest of the *département*. Maximum yield 70hl/ha. Two coops including Bousquet d'Orb (34260). 17,500 cases.

Pézenas

Hérault. 1982. Commune of Pézenas. Coop at Pézenas (34210). 66,000 cases.

Coteaux du Salagou

Hérault. 1981. Twenty communes around Lodève in the hills. Max. yield 70hl/ha. Technical specifications. Three coops including Octon, 34800 Clermont-l'Hérault. 3,850 cases.

Côtes de Thau

Hérault. 1981. Five communes around Florensac, near the coast at Agde. Technical specifications. Top producer: Claude Gaujal. Five coops including Pomérols, 34810. 500,000 cases.

Côtes de Thongue

Hérault. 1982. Red and white. Fourteen communes around Sevrain, north of Béziers. Eight coops, including Montblanc, 34290 Servian and Domaine de l'Arjolle in the village of Ponzolles. 385,000 cases.

AUDE

The entire *département* of the Aude, which stretches inland from Narbonne, is entitled to Vin de Pays de l'Aude. Top producers: Château de Ricardelle and Château St-Auriol.

Haute Vallée d'Aude

Aude. 1981. Fifty-five communes around Lomous. Min. 11°, max. 12°, max. yield 70hl/ha. Grapes, red and rosé: Cabernet Sauvignon, Cabernet Franc, Cot, Merlot. White: Chenin, Chardonnay, Semillon, Terret Blanc, Terret Gris. Pruning systems regulated. Two coops at Couiza, 11190 and Rouffiac-d'Aude, 11250 St-Hilaire. 630,000 cases.

Hautervie en Pays d'Aude

Aude. 1982. Eight communes in the Corbières and the Orbieu Valley. Grapes: wide range. Six coops. 62,500 cases.

Coteaux du Littoral Audois

Aude. 1981. Communes of Gruissan, Bages, Fitou, Lapalme, Leucate, Peyriac-de-Mer, Port-La-Nouvelle, Sigean, Caves, Feuilla, Portel and Treilles, on the coast east of the Corbières hills. Max. yield 100hl/ha. Four coops including Gruissan, (11430). 171,000 cases.

Hauts de Badens

Aude. 1982. Commune of Baden, south of the Minervois. Producers: Jean Poudou, Jacques Hortola, Gérald Branca, all at Baden, 11300 Trèbes. 19,500 cases.

Coteaux de la Cabrerisse

Aude. 1981. Three communes around Thézan in the Corbières. Grapes: only Carignan, Cinsaut, Grenache, Syrah, Mourvèdre, Terret, Clairette, Cabernet Franc, Cabernet Sauvignon, Merlot, Lladoner Pelut, Alicanté-Bouschet. Top producer: Les Aigletierres des Ollieux. Two coops at Thézan and St-Laurent, 11200 Lezignan. 121,000 cases.

Coteaux de la Cité de Carcassonne

Aude. 1982. Eleven communes around Carcassonne. 10.5°. Maximum yield 70hl/ha. Grapes, red and rosé: Carignan, Alicanté-Bouschet, Cinsaut and Grenache with minimum of 10% Cabernet Sauvignon, Cabernet Franc or Merlot. White: wide range. Producers: Pierre Castel, Pennautier; Louis Gobin, Cavanac; André Castel, Rustiques; Yves Barthez, Pennautier. 5 coops. 380,000 cases.

Cucugnan

Aude. 1982. Commune of Cucugnan in the Corbières. Coop at Cucugnan, 11350 Tuchan. 64,500 cases.

Val de Cesse

Aude. 1981. Canton of Ginestas, Minervois, northwest of Narbonne. Top producers: Domaine de l'Herbe Sainte, Ginestas, Jean Gleizes, Ouveillan; Pierre Calvet, Ouveillan; Pierre Fil, Mailhac; Jacques Mayzonnier, Pouzols. Four coops including St-Nazaire d'Aude, 11120 Ginestas. 792,000 cases.

Val de Dagne

Aude. 1981. Thirteen communes in the northern Corbières. 70hl/ha. Three coops at Montlaur, Monze and Servies-en-Val (11220). 167,000 to 222,000 cases.

Côtes de Lastours

Aude. 1981. Twenty-one communes in the Cabardès and the Fresquel Valley on the slopes of the Montagne Noir north of Caracassonne. Grapes: wide range. Producers: Mme Vve Cazaux, Villemoustaussou; M. Gianesini, Dom. Jouclary, Conques-sur-Orbiel; Antoine Maurel, Conques-sur-Orbiel. Coop at Salsigne, 11600 Conques-sur-Orbiel. 132,000 cases.

Coteaux de Lézignan

Aude. 1981. Ten communes around Lézignan north of the Corbières. Red wines only. Grapes: wide range. Four coops. 48,500 cases.

Coteaux de Miramont

Aude. 1981. Nine communes around Capendu east of Carcassone. Top producers: M. Lemaire, Capendu; Mme Yve Achille Marty, Douzens; Mme Alice Loyer, Fonties; Mme Hélène Gau, Barbaira, Château Pech-Redon, Narbonne. Five coops including Capendu, 11700. 222,000 cases.

Coteaux de Narbonne

Aude. 1982. Four communes near Narbonne. Three coops. 99,000 cases.

Val d'Orbieu

Aude. 1982. Twelve communes in the Orbieu Valley west of Narbonne. Grapes, red and rosé: Carignan, Cinsaut, Grenache, Alicante-Bouschet, Picpoul, Terret Noir. White: Clairette, Macabeu, Bourboulenc, Carignan Blanc, Grenache Blanc. Producers: Jacques Berges, Boutenac; M. Baille, Fabrezan; Armand Sournies, Camplong d'Aude; Honoré Deu, St-André Roquelonge; Mme Marie Rouanet, St-André Roquelonge; Mme Marie Huc, Fabrezan. Four coops. 330,000 cases.

Côte de Pérignan

Aude. 1981. Five communes in the area around La Clape at the mouth of the Aude. Top producers: Château Pech-Céleyran, Château de Salles, Coursan. Three coops including Fleury d'Aude, 11560. 82,500 cases.

Coteaux de Peyriac

Aude. 1982. Seventeen communes in the Minervois. Top producer: Château de Villerambert Moreau. Nine coops. 200,000 cases.

Côtes de Prouilhe

Aude. 1982. Thirty-nine communes around Razès, southwest of Carcassonne. Grapes: wide range. Producers: Château de Malviès, 11240 Belvèze du Razès. Two coops at Arzens, 11290 and Routier, 11240 Belvèze du Razès. 121,000 cases.

Coteaux de Termènes

Aude. 1982. Nine communes in the Corbières around Termènes. Grapes, red and rosé: Carignan, Cinsaut, Grenache, Syrah, Merlot, Cabernet, Cot, Terret, Alicante-Bouschet, Gamay. White: usual varieties. One coop at Villerouge Termènes, 11330 Mouthoumet. 111,000 cases.

Du Torgan

Aude. 1981. Ten communes around Tuchan. Grapes: wide range, red and rosé. Eight coops. 148,500 cases.

Vallée du Paradis

Aude. 1981. Eleven communes in the southern Corbières. Producers include: MM. Amiel, Mique, Bringuier and Navarro, all at Coustouge; M. Caziniol at Fraisse-Corbières. Seven coops including Cascatel, 11360 Durban Corbières. 242,000 cases.

ROUSSILLON AND THE CORBIERES

The Corbières hills, which the Pyrénées-Orientales *département* shares with the Aude to the north, have several interesting *vins de pays* that are listed here and under the Aude. Vins de Pays des Pyrénées-Orientales is the name used for the predominantly red wines produced in most areas of the *département*, except the southeast. The country to the south, consisting of plains and the foot-hills of the Pyrenees, uses the Catalan name for its two defined districts.

Val d'Agly

Corbières. 1982. Fifteen communes around St-Paul de Fenouillet. Eight coops including Belesta, 66720 La Tour de France. 99,000 cases.

Catalan

Roussillon. 1981. Area stretching inland from Perpignan and Argelès. Producers: Michel Cases, Ste-Colombe (66300); Domaine de Casinobe, Trouillas (66300). Twenty coops, SICA at Perpignan. 1.5m. cases.

Côtes Catalanes

Roussillon. 1981. North and west of Perpignan. Producers include: Cazes Frères, Rivesaltes, 66600; Maurice Puig, Claira, 66530. Mas Chichet, Perpignan. Ten coops. 550,000 cases.

Côteaux des Fenouillèdes

Corbières. 1982. Seventeen communes in the Corbières north of Prades. Eleven coops including Arboussols, 66320. 121,000 cases.

Côte Vermeille

1986. Roussillon. The area around Collioure on the coast. 7,150 cases.

THE SOUTHWEST

Nearly all of the Southwest is included in one or other of the many *vins de pays* now proliferating. Many of them overlap with or include the areas of AOC and VDQS production described on pages 216–218. The best tend to be produced by growers for whom they are their first and only wines, rather than a bolt-on to wines of superior appellation.

Agenais

Southwest. 1982. Covers the whole of Lot-et-Garonne from the Armagnac to Cahors boundaries. Cooperatives at Marmande (two),Duras (two), Buzet, Brulhois (two), all of which qq.v.; and at 47150 Monflanquin and 47170 Mézin (Gascon-type wines). Also Domaine de Campet 47170 Sos. 246,000 cases.

Aveyron

Little seen except as one of the lines of the coop at Aguessac, near Millau. The Millau VDQS is declassified if it contains too much Cabernet Sauvignon (!), and is sold as this *vin de pays*.

Bigorre

Hautes-Pyrénées. 1985. Certain communes in the region of Castelnau-Rivière-Bas in the Madiran district and Vic-de-Bigorre to the south. Produced by the coop at Castelnau 65700 from same grapes as Madiran and Pacherenc. Brumont at Madiran (q.v.) also uses Bigorre to describe some *vins de pays*.

Chalosse

Beef-growing country in the Landes west of Tursan and northeast of Dax. Lively cooperative at Mugron, making 200,000 cases a year, mostly sold in bulk. Mainly red wines, one from Cabernet Franc for quick drinking, the other from Tannat. Short *cuvaisons*. Some dry white from the rare Arriloba grape. Rosé contains another rarity, Egiodola.

Charentais

Charente and Charente-Maritime. 1981. Entire *départements*. Maximum yield 70hl/ha. 11° red, 11.5° white. Grapes, red; Cabernet Franc, Cabernet Sauvignon, Merlot, Tannat (on the Ile de Ré only) plus up to 20% others. White: Chenin Blanc, Colombard, Folle Blanche, Muscadelle, Sauvignon, Semillon and Ugni Blanc. Sugar and acidity regulated. 220,000 cases.

Condomois and Montestruc

Two theoretical *vins de pays* nowadays absorbed in practice by Gers or Côtes de Gascogne.

Corrèze

One cooperative at Branceilles between Brive and the Dordogne and one private grower at Voutézac to the N.W. of Brive (Domaine de la Mégénie) are pioneering this new *vin de pays*. Similar style to Glanes. 20,000 cases.

Dordogne

A designation mostly applied by cooperatives, e.g. Sigoulès, to sub-standard or declassified red wines of growers in the Bergerac appellation. 66,000 cases.

Côtes de Gascogne

Southwest. 1982. Almost the entire *département* of the Gers (the Armagnac country). Grapes: wide range of traditional and quality varieties. Producers: M. Esquiro, Domaine de la Higuère, Mirepoix (32540); M. Ribel, Pitre à Montestruc (32390). Seven coops including Lagrualet Gondrin, 32330 Gondrin. 460,000 cases.

Gers

Covers the whole *département*, overlapping Côtes de Gascogne. Much sold off *en négoce*. 6,050 cases.

Côteaux de Glanes

Southwest. 1981. A cooperative of eight growers is the sole producer (annual average 18,000 cases). Made in the hills to the east of Bretenoux (Lot) in the village of Glanes. Attractive wine, much drunk in local restaurants, from Merlot, Gamay and a blend of Jurançon Noir and Portugais Bleu called Ségalin.

Coteaux et Terrasses de Montauban

Southwest. 1981. Invented to designate wines of better than *vin de table* standard produced in the no-man's-land between Côteaux de Quercy, Fronton and Lavilledieu. Grape varieties include Gamay, Merlot, Syrah, Tannat and the two Cabernets, more rustic varieties being phased out gradually. Main producer: the cooperative at Lavilledieu (*see*

page 222), but also Philippe and Thierry Romain at Domaine de Montels (62 acres), 82350 Albias, are notable for excellent everyday red from 50% Syrah, 25% Gamay and 25% Cabernet Franc. 19,000 cases.

Coteaux du Quercy

Southwest. 1982. The area used to be called Bas-Quercy, the *causses* stretching south from Cahors. In the north the Cahors grapes, Malbec, Merlot and Tannat, dominate, but further south Cabernet Franc, Gamay and some Cabernet Sauvignon are also used. There is a lively cooperative at Monpezat-de-Quercy, whose best wine called Bessey de Boissy Tradition keeps well. The 20 private growers include Domaine d'Ariès (Pierre Belon 82240 Puylaroque) and Domaine de la Garde (Jean-Jacques Bousquet 46090 Labastide-Marnhac). Also made by cooperatives at Lavilledieu-du-Temple and Parnac. 126,000 cases.

Côtes du Tarn

Southwest. 1981. Covers the Gaillac AOC area and further land to the south as far as the River Agout. Large and important production of dry white, rosé and red wine. Sometimes declassified Gaillac, sometimes using grapes not permitted in AOC e.g. Jurançon Noir and Portugais Bleu. Mainstay of the cooperatives at Rabastens and Labastide-de-Lévis and featured by some independent Gaillac growers e.g. Jean Albert 81150 Castanet, and J.H.F. de Faramond at Château Lastours, 81310 Lisle-sur-Tarn. 1.5m. cases.

Thézac-Perricard

Adjoining and to the southwest of the Cahors AOC region, making red wines of similar but lighter style, as well as some rosé. The cooperative at Thézac is the only producer, and the wine is vinified at the cooperative at Donzac near Agen. 23,500 cases.

Comté Tolosan

Southwest France. 1982. Capable of designating most of the southwest, but in practice used for wines without appellation grown in the area of Toulouse, north to Montauban, and south towards Pamiers, e.g. white wines made by Fronton producers, the extraordinary varietals produced by Christian Gerber at Domaine de Ribonnet, 31870 Beaumont-sur-Lèze and the much more ordinary wines produced by country cooperatives south of Toulouse. 450,000 cases.

Montestruc *see* Condomois and Montestruc

Pyrénées-Atlantiques

Southwest. 1982. Covers the whole *département*, but mainly for wines grown in Béarn area which do not qualify for appellation. Cooperatives at Salies-de-Béarn and Madiran. Mostly red and rosé. 13,500 cases.

Saint Sardos

Southwest. 1982. The ambitious coop in garlic-growing area west of Montauban aspires to VDQS. About 82,000 cases (and increasing) produced from Syrah, Cabernet Franc and Tannat, with some Gamay and Abouriou. Rosé is *saigné* from the same grapes, with a separate *cuvée* from black Muscat. Wines made for two private estates, Domaine de Tucayne and Domaine de Cadis, both keepers.

Terroirs Landais

Landes. 1986. Covers the whole of the *département* of Landes. Used mostly for wines of the Gascon style (Colombard and Ugni Blanc for the whites, Tannat and Cabernets for the reds) produced over the border from the Gers; also smaller productions in the west of the *département*, especially *vins de sable*, mostly from Cabernet Franc, grown near the Atlantic coast. 66,000 cases.

LOIRE

Marches de Bretagne and Retz

Lower Loire. 1982. Area to the south of the Loire east of Nantes (Marches de Bretagne) and west of Nantes (Retz). Changes to the regional Vin de Pays du Jardin de la France have meant that with effect from the 1996 harvest the formerly separate Vins de Pays de Marches de Bretagne and de Retz are now subsumed. Top producers: Emmanuel Bodet, 44860 Saint-Aignan-de-Grandlieu; Domaine de l'Ecu, 44430 le Landreau; Domaine de Chêne, 44860 La Chevrolière; Domaine les Coins, 44650 Corcoué-sur-Logne; Joseph Hallereau 44430 Vallet; Joël Herissé, 44580 Bourgneuf-en-Retz; Domaine de la Houssais, 44430 Le Landreau; Domaine de la Senechalière, 44450 Saint-Julien-des-Concelles; Albert Forgeau et Fils, 44330 Mouzillon. Combined annual total: approx. 133,000 cases.

Coteaux Charitois

Nièvre. 1986. Area around La Charité-sur-Loire, south of Pouilly-sur-Loire. Caves des Hauts de Seyr, 58350 Chasnay. 16,000 cases.

Coteaux du Cher et de l'Arnon

Upper Loire. 1981. Ten communes around Quincy and Reuilly. Grapes, red and rosé: Gamay, Pinot Noir, Pinot Gris, plus 30% others. White: Chardonnay, Sauvignon, plus 30% others. 4,070 cases, sold mostly in local cafés.

Jardin de la France

Loire. 1981. Most of the lower and mid-Loire basin. The zone covers 13 *départements:* Vendée, Loire-Atlantique, Maine et Loire, Indre et Loire, Sarthe, Loir et Cher, Deux Sèvres, Vienne,

Indre, Nièvre, Allier and Loiret. Top producers: Domaines du Breuil, Château du Breuil, 49750 Beaulieu sur Layon; Donatien-Bahuaud, 44330 La Chapelle-Heulin; Domaines des Forges, 49190 Saint-Aubin-de-Luigné; Domaine de la Morinière, 44330 La Regrippière; Domaine des Hautes Noëlles, 44710 Saint-Léger-les-Vignes; Domaine de Pierre Blanche, 49380 Champ-sur-Layon; Château de Tigné, 49770 Tigné; Confrèrie des Vignerons de Oisly et Thésée, 41700 Oisly; Les Vignerons Réunis du Valencay, 36600 Valencay. Over 5.5m. cases a year, and growing.

Urfé

Upper Loire. 1982. A wide area in the *département* of Loire, in the upper Loire Valley. Grapes, red and rosé: at least 70% Gamay and Pinot Noir. White: Chardonnay, Aligoté, Pinot Gris, Viognier, Gamay. Top producers: Alain Demon, 42820 Ambierle; Domaines des Millets, 42820 Lentigny; Les Vignerons Foreziens, Trelins 42130 Boen. Under 10,000 cases.

CENTRAL FRANCE

Coteaux Charitois *see* Loire

Coteaux Coiffy *see* Jura

Gorges et Côtes de Millau

Aveyron. 1981. Twenty-five communes in the Tarn Valley. 60hl/ha. Four types of wine made: two reds based on Gamay and Syrah, rosé, 50% Gamay, and white from Chenin and Mauzac. Coop at Agnessac (12520). 33,000 cases.

MIDI AND CORSICA

Pays d'Oc

Midi and Provence. 1981. Covers the whole of Languedoc-Roussillon. This *vin de pays* is used for wines made from grape varieties which are not traditional to the region. There are thus Vin de Pays d'Oc made from Cabernet Sauvignon, Cabernet Franc, Merlot, Syrah and Mourvèdre, with whites from Chardonnay, Sauvignon Blanc, Chenin Blanc, Viognier and Vermentino. Seventy percent of production is of varietal wines. Many of the most interesting of the new wave of southern French wines are being made using this *vin de pays* name. Top producers: George Bonfils, Skalli Fortant de France; Domaine de la Baume; Domaine de l'Engarran. 800,000 to 1m. cases, 75% of it red; 20% rosé.

L'Ile de Beauté

Corsica. 1981. The entire island. Min. 10.5˚, max. 12˚. Grapes: many, with Carignan and Cinsaut not to exceed 25% and 50% respectively of planted area. Producers: M. René Touboul, Domaine de Pojale, 20270 Aléria. Domaine de San

Giovanni, 20270 Aléria. Mme Jeanne Salvat, Linguizetta, 20230 San Nicoloa. Mme Raymond Guidicelli, Domaine de Liccetto, 20270 Aléria. Seven coops. 1.1m. cases.

JURA AND SAVOIE

Allobrogie

Savoie. 1981. Communes in the two Savoie *départements*, around Grenoble, and in the Ain, around Seyssel. Grapes, red: Gamay, Mondeuse at least 5%. White: Chardonnay, Chasselas, Molette, Jacquère together 95%. 60,500 cases.

Balmes Dauphinoises

Savoie. 1982. Northern part of the *département* of the Isère, around Morestel and Crémieu. Min. alch: 9.5°. Grapes, red and rosé: at least 70% Gamay, Pinot Noir, Syrah, Merlot or Mondeuse. White: at least 70% Chardonnay or Jacquère. 14,000 cases.

Coteaux de Coiffy

Jura. 1989. A tiny zone, in the southeast of the Haute-Marne *département,* producing 6,000 cases of red and white wines annually.

Franche-Comté

Jura. 1982. *Départements* of Jura and Haute Saône. 9° for red and rosé, 9.5° for white. Grapes: only Chardonnay, Auxerrois, Pinot Noir, Pinot Gris and Gamay. 33,000 cases. Coop at Champlitte.

Coteaux du Grésivaudan

Savoie. The Isère Valley around Grenoble. 9.5°. Grapes, red and rosé: at least 70% Gamay, Pinot Noir or Etraire de la Dui. White: at least 70% Jacquère, Chardonnay or Verdesse. Two coops. 22,000 cases.

GERMANY

Hamburg

Bremen

Elbe

Hanover

Berlin

Leipzig

SAALE-UNSTRUT

Weser

Erfurt

SACHSEN

Dresden

Cologne

AHR   MITTELRHEIN

Koblenz

RHEINGAU

MOSEL-
SAAR-RUWER

Frankfurt

FRANKEN

RHEINHESSEN

Trier

Mannheim

Würzburg

NAHE

HESSISCHE-
BERGSTRASSE

Nürnberg

PFALZ

WÜRTTEMBERG

Main

Stuttgart

Baden Baden

Danube

BADEN

München

Freiburg

L. Bodensee

Rhine

It sometimes seems that in the past decade or so the international reputation or renown of every single wine-producing country has improved, with the exception of Germany. In the eyes of the outside work German wine has been a more or less unmitigated disaster-area.

A generation ago it was generally accepted that Germany made the world's finest white wines, with white burgundy as its only peer. No great dinner could begin without its Mosel or Rhine Spätlese. The Riesling was universally hailed as the queen of white grapes (while few people, believe it or not, had even heard of Chardonnay).

The slide began with the German Wine Law of 1971, ironically coinciding with a truly magnificent vintage. The law came down firmly on the side of the little man, the cooperative member – whose vote, one can be forgiven for thinking, the politicians were eager to attract.

The new law allowed him to label his wine with grand names that bore almost no relation to its origin. It permitted the use of the word 'quality' where it meant the opposite, while debasing such vital descriptive terms as Auslese to a mere matter of grams of sugar. It indirectly encouraged such colossal yields that wines tasted like sugar water (with the stress on the water) and consequently forced the price of German wine down to some of Europe's lowest levels. The country with the highest living standards and most expensive labour now makes some of western Europe's cheapest wine.

This sad recital is unfortunately a necessary prologue to understanding German wine today. The good news is that an ever-increasing number of proud producers are adopting an independent attitude, effectively bypassing legal minimum standards which they regard as dismally permissive. Some are even redesignating their wine to make their own names more prominent as brands than the famous names of the sites they farm.

Nowhere more than in parts of Germany is the precise vineyard site more crucial to quality. Think of the great loops of the River Mosel, where the sunshine on the vineyard varies with the shape and the exposure more than anywhere on earth. Free-draining slate or schist is vital for ripening Riesling here: the qualities of the best vineyards are known to everyone – and so is the impossibility of making fine wine on north slopes or flat alluvial land.

Compare the Côte d'Or of Burgundy. Over centuries it has been minutely divided into its Grands Crus, Premiers Crus and Villages sites. Its world fame rests on this classification; it simply works. The official German line is that such pinpointing of natural quality is 'elitist' and undemocratic.

Even more fundamentally, red burgundy is pure Pinot Noir, white burgundy pure Chardonnay. But wine sold as 'Bernkasteler' or 'Piesporter' need not be Riesling at all. It can legally be made from such inferior bulk-producers as Müller-Thurgau. If a region does not protect its own good name nobody else will do it. Hence the current débâcle.

On the other hand, what is true for the Mosel or the Rheingau, the regions where Riesling is the essential classic grape, is not necessarily true, or not true at all, for the Pfalz or Baden in the south, or Franconia where Silvaner comes into its own. Different soils and different traditions, not to mention longer growing seasons, offer other possibilities which thinking wine-growers must embrace.

Each region needs to work out its own best practice, just as the regions of other parts of Europe have done. When this happens Germany's awful problems will be solved. Meanwhile the wine-lover is faced with a system creaking at the joints.

In German thinking, and for good reasons, ripeness is all. All German quality criteria (at least the government-regulated ones) are based on the accumulated sugar in the grapes at harvest time. There is no official ranking of vineyards as in France; no specific recipes for varieties of grapes as in Italy. German labels, at least those of quality wines, make unequivocal statements. Despite the difficulties of Gothic type they can be the world's most consistent and informative – up to a carefully calculated point.

Since 1971 the wine laws have been subject to further revisions. But their strategy remains unaltered. They divide all German wine into three strata. The lowest, Tafelwein, subject to relatively few controls, is correspondingly barred from claiming any specific vineyard origin. It is assumed to be a blend of wines that have required additional sugar. The only technical point to remember is the difference between Deutscher Tafelwein, which must be German in origin, and Tafelwein without the qualification, which may contain wine from other European countries (formerly Italy, now more often eastern Europe). A low-strength neutral base wine is easily cleaned up and given some superficial German characteristics by using very aromatic 'sweet reserve'. The use of heavily Gothic labels is obviously intended to encourage the innocent to believe that the wine is indeed German. A new category of Tafelwein, called Landwein, with stricter rules, was introduced in 1982 as a sort of German *vin de pays*. But Landwein is far from matching its French counterparts in popularity or enterprise.

Much more significant is the rebellious use of the Tafelwein designation by proud growers who have despaired of official categories and consider their freedom to use their own judgement more important than official recognition.

The second category of German wine was christened Qualitätswein bestimmter Anbaugebiete: QbA for short. The term means 'quality wine from a designated region'. The use of the word 'quality' in this context is really meaningless. Nonetheless, to a German the difference between this and the top category of wine, Qualitätswein mit Prädikat, is doubtless clear and simple. Unfortunately the legislators did not take non-Germans into account. It must be stressed to them continually that the two classes of Qualitätswein are far apart, distinguished by a basic difference. The first is made with added sugar; the second is what used (before 1971) to be called, much more directly and succinctly, *natur* or *naturrein*. In other words the grapes had enough natural sugar to make wine. 'Mit Prädikat' is hard to translate. 'With special attributes' is the stilted official version. It certainly does not reflect the status of QmP wines as the top category in which, without exception, all the best wines of Germany are included.

Qualitätswein mit Prädikat carry a designation of maturity of their grapes as part of their full names, in the following order; simply ripe grapes of the normal harvest are Kabinett; late-gathered (therefore riper) are Spätlese; selected very ripe grapes are Auslese. The precise sugar content (or 'must weight') and therefore potential alcohol required for each category in each region is stipulated in the regulations (*see* the table opposite).

At this point most wines begin to retain distinct natural sweetness. If an Auslese is fermented fully dry it will be noticeably high in alcohol – often throwing it off-balance with headiness. Two levels of ripeness and selectivity beyond Auslese remain: Beerenauslese, in which the individual berries are selected for extreme ripeness and concentration, and Trockenbeerenauslese, in which only berries dried and shrivelled by noble rot (occasionally by unseasonal heat) are selected. Sugar levels in such wines are commonly so high that fermentation is seriously hampered and may be reluctant to take place at all. TBAs (to use the current American abbreviation) are usually a stable conjunction of very modest alcohol level (even as low as 5.5%) and startlingly high sugar. They are less than half as strong as Château d'Yquem, which is made in much the same way, and correspondingly twice as sweet (although great TBAs may be even more concentrated and intense than Yquem – but not necessarily better). It could, incidentally, be much less confusing for the consumer if the well-tried old term Edelbeerenauslese were used for this category of wine. 'Trocken' means dry, the word is used to describe wines with virtually no sugar. 'TBAs' are made from more-or-less dried-up grapes: a totally different proposition. Much confusion would be saved if 'Edel' – meaning 'noble' and referring to the 'noble rot' – were substituted for 'Trocken', making 'EBAs'.

One further category of QmP wine deserves to be considered separately because of the way it is made: Eiswein is made by crushing grapes that have frozen solid on the vine. Crushing before they thaw means that the almost pure water which constitutes the ice is separated from the sugar, acids and other constituents, which have a lower freezing point. The result, like a TBA, is intensely concentrated, but much less ripe and more acidic. It can be extraordinary, its high acid giving it the potential for almost limitless ageing.

The name and ranking of a QmP wine is conventionally set forth on its label in the same order. First is the town or village (Gemeinde) name; then the vineyard; then the grape (in some classic Riesling areas this is inferred and omitted); then the category of ripeness – Kabinett, Spätlese and so on.

One complicating factor, and the major fault in the 1971 German law, prevents this formula from being crystal clear. It is the concept of the Grosslage, or extended vineyard. Unfortunately labels do not, and are not allowed to, distinguish between a single vineyard site, known as an Einzellage, and a group of such sites with very much less specificity: a Grosslage. Grosslage groupings were made with the idea of simplifying the sales of wines from lesser-known Einzellagen. Notoriety comes more easily to bigger units. But their names are in no way distinguishable from Einzellage names and I have never met a person who claims to have memorized them. The consumer is therefore deprived of a vital piece of information. As a further confusing factor, in some areas Einzellagen are also groups of separate vineyards deemed to have a common personality. There is thus no truly clearcut distinction between the categories.

But far worse in confusing the public is the concept of the Bereich, a regional name by which, say, any Rheingau QbA wine can be sold as Johannisberg, or any Middle Mosel by the great name of Bernkastel. An exact French parallel would be that any Médoc could be sold as Margaux.

The often-quoted rule of thumb, based on the Kabinett-Spätlese-Auslese scale, is 'the sweeter the wine the higher the quality'. While it is still true to say that quality is directly related to ripeness, the question of sweetness is now very much at the discretion of the winemaker (and the consumer). Sweetness in modern commercial German wines is adjusted to suit the market, by adding (or not adding) unfermented grape juice to fully fermented, fully dry wine just before bottling. But the sweetness in wine from Germany's top estates is wholly natural – a result of the fermentation stopping itself or being stopped. The grower looks for a harmonious balance between acidity, alcohol and fruity sweetness in his wine.

The great change in German wine fashion over the past decade has been the demand for fully dry, unsweetened wines, to accompany food. To be so described, as 'trocken', on the label, these must contain less than 9 grams of sugar per litre. The taste for 'trocken' has grown with, and in turn boosted, the use of what are typically French grapes, mainly of the Pinot family, to make true 'table' or 'food' wines of a kind Germany has traditionally lacked. It has fundamentally shifted the emphasis southward from the northernmost vineyards, where Riesling reigns, to such regions as the Pfalz and Baden where the Pinots and similar grapes are fully at home. In tasting *trocken* wines of Riesling it soon becomes clear how much a little natural sweetness adds to the charm, balance and drinkability of most German wines: they have to have unusually good figures to survive such naked scrutiny. On the other hand, this is the area in which most progress has recently been made by the most ambitious producers. A halfway category, *halbtrocken*, with up to 18 grams of sugar per litre, more often achieves the right balance of fullness and bite to make satisfactory mealtime wine.

German growers produce astonishing quantities. France, Italy and other countries make low yields a pre-condition for their appellations. In Germany only 'must weight' counts. A big crop is simply taken as evidence of a healthy vineyard. Average crops have grown from 25 hectolitres a hectare in 1900 to 40 (about the French AOC level) in 1939, and in the 1970s were averaging over 100. 1982 hit a record: 173 hl/ha average, with a maximum close to 400. But this is the national average, including cooperatives, where anything goes.

A welcome move was made in 1989 by the government of Rheinland-Pfalz (which controls two-thirds of German wine production) to tighten the law and prevent excessive production. It set maximum permitted yields according to region, grape variety and quality classification. The Mosel-Saar-Ruwer was given an overall limit of 130 hl/ha for Müller-Thurgau; 120 hl/ha for Riesling. Other regions were given a sliding scale: in the Nahe, for example, growers can produce 120 hl/ha of table wine, 110 hl/ha of QbA wine but only 85 hl/ha of Prädikat wine.

On the other hand many have doubted the serious intent of a law that permits over-production in one vintage to be held over to the next. It appears that the political will to frustrate over-production is far from resolute. Meanwhile all serious growers attempting high-quality wines impose their own limits at a level well below the legal maximum. The average figure for Maximin Grünhaus and Robert Weil, for example, is 55hl/ha; Dr Loosen harvests at 50 hl/ha; and Egon Müller and Schlossgut Diel at 45 hl/ha.

Another serious concern is that the current law, in setting simple minimum ripeness standards for Ausleses and the other top categories, simply invites growers to achieve that minimum and no more. The old rules allowed eager winemakers to differentiate between their standard and better-than-standard Ausleses, such terms as 'Feine' or 'Feinste Auslese' carrying considerable premiums. If the terms were open to abuse, they also rewarded the patient and ambitious perfectionist. Today he will still signal to his clients which are his best casks of wine, but often in an obscure semaphore of gold capsules, no less open to abuse because it is closed to the uninitiated.

The official answer to any doubts about the standards or authenticity of quality QbA and QmP German wines is that each wine is both analysed and tasted officially before being issued with a unique Amtliche Prüfungs-nummer (A.P. number) which appears on every label. All official tastings employ a points scheme, which is also used for the awarding of the gold, silver and bronze medals at both national (D.L.G.) and regional levels. But here again it is the self-imposed criteria of top growers who really set the standard. It is here that the Verband Deutscher Prädikatsweinguter (VDP) has firmly taken the lead in setting far stricter quality criteria than the government. Membership of the VDP is open to growers (there are about 200 at present) who sign up for self-discipline. Its standards are well-policed and laggards lose their membership. The VDP and regional voluntary organizations ('Charta' in the Rheingau is the prototype) abide by maxima of production and minima of must-weight far stricter than those decreed by government. The VDP has also supported a long overdue, though still unofficial, classification of the German vineyards. The best are referred to here as 'First-Class'. It is on the VDP and the pride of its members that the future of Germany's high-quality wine industry depends.

German wine law: statutory sugar levels

Regions (in descending order of size)	Table wine	Quality wine	Kabinett	Spätlese	Auslese	Beerenauslese /Eiswein	Trockenbeeren-auslese
Rheinhessen	5°/44	7.5°/60	9.5°/73	11.4°/85	12.5°/92	16.5°/120	21.5°/150
Pfalz	5°/44	7.5°/60	9.5°/73	11.4°/85	12.5°/92	16.5°/120	21.5°/150
Baden zone B	5°/50	7.5°/60	9.8°/75	11.6°/86	14.1°/102	18.1°/128	21.5°/15
zone A	5°/50	7.5°/60	10°/76	11.4°/85	13.4°/98	17.5°/124	21.5°/150
Mosel-Saar-Ruwer	5°/44	6°/51	8.6°/66	10°/76	11.1°/83	15.3°/110	21.5°/150
Württemberg	5°/50	7°/57	9.3°/72	11.4°/85	13.0°/95	17.5°/124	21.5°/150
Franken	5°/50	7.5°/60	10°/76	11.4°/85	13.8°/100	17.7°/125	21.5°/150
Nahe	5°/44	6.5°/57	9.1°/70	10.3°/78	11.4°/85	16.5°/120	21.5°/150
Rheingau	5°/44	7°/57	9.5°/73	11.4°/85	13°/95	17.7°/125	21.5°/150
Mittel Rhein	5°/44	6°/51	8.6°/66	10°/80	13°/87	15.3°/110	21.5°/150
Ahr	5°/44	6°/51	8.6°/66	10°/76	11.1°/83	15.3°/110	21.5°/15
Hessische-Bergstrasse	5°/44	7°/57	9.5°/73	11.4°/85	13°/95	17.7°/125	21.5°/150
Saale-Unstrut	5°/50	7.0°/57	9.1°/70	10°/76	11.9°/88	15.3°/110	21.5°/150
Sachsen	5°/50	6.6°/54	9.1°/70	10°/76	11.1°/83	15.3°/110	21.5°/150

The first figure is potential degrees alcohol/ the second is degrees Oechsle (for Riesling)

GERMAN WINE REGIONS

Germany's finest wines come from hillside vineyards facing the southern half of the compass. In this northern climate the extra radiation on land tilted towards the sun is often essential for ripeness. Other factors also come into account: the climate-moderating presence of water; shelter from wind; fast-draining and heat-retentive soil.

Fine German wines, in fact, come from almost every type of soil from slate to limestone, clay to sand – given other optimal conditions. The effects of different soils on the character of wines from one grape, the Riesling, is a fascinating subplot of German oenology. But climate and microclimate, orientation and angle of hill come first.

Germany has 13 broadly designated wine regions (bestimmte Anbaugebiete) divided into 34 more narrowly defined Bereiche. The Bereiche are in turn divided into Gemeinden (villages) and the villages into Einzellagen (single sites, or vineyards). The latter are also grouped, several sites and often several villages at a time, as Grosslagen. In most cases a Grosslage name remains more or less permanently attached to the name of a single village, the best known within its radius, which is known as its Leitgemeinde. Niersteiner Gutes Domtal is the perfect example of a highly successful Leitgemeinde/Grosslage in the public eye and memory.

Top-quality wines are almost always pinpointed as narrowly as possible by their makers, and therefore come to market under their Einzellage names. There are some 2,600 Einzellagen (since the 1971 laws abolished a figure close to ten times this number). Even this rule, though, is changing rapidly as forward-looking producers rely more and more heavily on their own reputations. Brand-building, more confined to down-market wines, is seen today as the way forward for top estates too. In future we can expect something closer to the Bordeaux château-system where it is the regulation of the estate, rather than the Einzellage, that determines the price of the bottle.

The 13 principal wine regions fall into five broad divisions. The most important is the Rhine valley, including its lesser tributaries, from Pfalz (the Palatinate) in the south, past Rheinhessen, the Hessische Bergstrasse, the Rheingau and the Nahe, the Mittelrhein and finally to the little tributary Ahr near Bonn in the north. Second comes the Mosel, flowing north with its tributaries the Saar and the Ruwer to meet the Rhine at Koblenz. Third comes the vast but scattered region of Baden in the south, from Heidelberg all the way to the Swiss border. Fourth comes Franken (or Franconia), the vineyards of the Main Valley in northern Bavaria. Fifth, and rarely spoken of outside Germany, comes the disjointed and diverse region of Württemberg.

On the export market the first two are far and away the most important. The picture in Germany is rather different, with great loyalty (and high prices) for the wines of the last three. Foreigners tend to meet German wine either as a commercial blend ('Liebfraumilch') or as the produce of one of the many great historic estates of the Rhine or Mosel. Only rarely have the wines of the smaller local grower been offered abroad. Yet very often this small farmer-cum-innkeeper (for most of them sell their wine 'open' by the glass in their own cheerful little Weinstube) epitomizes the style and vitality of his region. His wines are generally less fine than those of sophisticated noble estates. But they have character, often charm, and sometimes brilliant dash and fire.

Germany in round figures

The total vineyard area of Germany is 256,980 acres, farmed by some 77,388 growers. Of this number, however, only 5,415 growers bottle and sell more than 90% of their wine themselves. Since the 1960s both the acreage and numbers of vintners have declined steadily, while modern methods have greatly increased productivity. The total harvest fluctuates widely with weather conditions; 1982 still the biggest to date, produced nearly double the modern (10-year) annual average of 8,500,000 hectolitres (94,440,000 cases).

The principal export markets for German wine (in hectolitres) in 1995 were:

Great Britain	912,958
The Netherlands	200,099
Japan	177,618
Sweden	143,587
Brazil	114,059
USA	111,368
Denmark	108,662
France	91,510
Italy	57,965
Canada	55,311
Total export quantity for1995 was	2,332,754 hl

Production in recent years with yield per hectare was as follows:

Year	hectolitres	hl/ha	no. of cases
1985	5,402,000	58.1	59.4m
1986	10,062,000	108.1	110.6m
1987	8,942,000	95.9	98.3m
1988	9,315,000	99.6	102.4m
1989	13,226,000	140.8	145.4m
1990	8,514,000	89.8	93.6m
1991	10,170,000	102.3	111.8m
1992	13,375,000	133.3	147.0m
1993	9,718,000	94.4	107.0m
1994	10,348,000	99.8	113.8m
1995	8,510,000	82.4	93.6m

GLOSSARY OF GERMAN WINE TERMS

For details of the main German white and red grape varieties, *see* pages 14–15.

Abfüllung bottling (*see* Erzeugerabfüllung).

Amtliche Prüfung certification of standard quality by chemical analysis and tasting. Compulsory since 1971 for all QbA and QmP wines (qq.v.). Each wine is given an A.P. number which must be displayed on the label.

Anbaugebiet the broadest category of wine region, of which (for 'quality' wines) there are 13 (e.g. Mosel-Saar-Ruwer, Baden).

Anreichern 'enriching' – adding sugar to the must to increase the alcohol, the equivalent of the French chaptalization. In Germany no sugar may be added to wines in the QmP categories (q.v.) but Tafelwein and QbA wine are usually 'enriched'.

Auslese literally 'selected': the third category of QmP wines, made only in ripe vintages and usually naturally sweet. Auslesen often have a slight degree of 'noble rot' which adds subtlety to their fruity sweetness. Good Auslesen deserve ageing in bottle for several years to allow their primary sweetness to mellow to more adult flavours.

Barriquewein Term for wines fermented and or matured in small new oak casks. Ageing in new oak is now standard practice for good red wines. White examples are more variable.

Beerenauslese literally 'selected berries': the category of QmP wine beyond Auslese in sweetness and price, and theoretically in quality. Only very overripe or 'nobly rotten' grapes are used to make intensely sweet, often deep-coloured wines which age admirably.

Blau 'blue'; when used of grapes, means 'red' or 'black'.

Bereich one of 34 districts or subregions (e.g. Bereich Bernkastel) within the 13 Gebieten. Bereich names are commonly used for middling to lower quality wines (they are legal for QbA as well as QmP) blended from the less-distinguished vineyards of the district.

Bundesweinprämierung a national wine award presented by the D.L.G. (q.v.) to wines selected from regional prize winners. The tastings are held at Heilbronn in Württemberg. 3.5 points out of 5 wins a bronze medal, 4 a silver medal and 4.5 a 'Grosser Preis'. Winners normally display their achievement on a neck label on bottles of the winning wine.

Deutsche(r) 'German'; distinguishes Tafelwein grown in Germany from inferior mixtures of the wines of 'various EU countries', often sold with pseudo-German labels.

Deutsches Weinsiegel a seal of quality awarded by the D.L.G. (q.v.) for wines that achieve a set level of points higher than the standard required to obtain an Amtliche Prüfungsnummer (q.v.). The standard seal is red, but there is a green seal for medium-dry wines and a yellow for dry wines that meet D.L.G. standards.

Diabetiker-Wein the driest category of German wines, with less than 4 grams of unfermented sugar per litre. It should be drunk by diabetics only after medical approval is given.

D.L.G. The German Agricultural Society (Deutsche Land-wirtschafts-gesellschaft), the body that judges and presents the national wine awards. *See* Bundesweinprämierung.

Domäne 'domain' – in Germany a term used mainly to describe the estates owned by Federal German States (e.g. in the Rheingau, Franken, Nahe).

Edelfäule 'noble rot'. For a full explanation *see* Château d'Yquem, page 69.

Eigene(m) 'own'. 'Aus eigenem Lesegut' means 'from his own harvest'.

Einzellage an individual vineyard site. There are some 2,600 Einzellagen in Germany. Officially the minimum size for an Einzellage is 5 hectares (12.3 acres) although there are a number much smaller than this. Not all Einzellagen are therefore in contiguous parcels, particularly in Baden and Württemberg. A Grosslage (q.v.) is a unit of several Einzellagen supposedly of the same quality and character. The Einzellage or Grosslage name follows the village (Gemeinde) name on the label.

Eiswein wine made by pressing grapes that have been left hanging on the vine into mid-winter (sometimes January) and are gathered and pressed in early morning, while frozen solid. Since it is the water content of the grape that freezes, the juice, separated from the ice, is concentrated sugar, acidity and flavour. The result is extraordinarily sweet and piquant wines with almost limitless ageing capacity, less rich but more penetrating than Beeren- or Trockenbeerenauslesen, often fetching spectacular prices.

Erzeugerabfüllung 'estate bottled'; the equivalent of the French *mis au domaine* or *mis au château*.

Erzeugergemeinschaft a producers' association, usually for sales purposes, as distinct from a cooperative for making wine.

Fass a barrel. 'Holzfässen' are oak barrels, the traditional containers in German cellars.

Flasche bottle – the same word as the English 'flask'.

Flurbereinigung the term for the Government-sponsored 'consolidation' of vineyard holdings by remodelling the landscape, a process that has revolutionized the old system of terracing in most parts of Germany, making the land workable by tractors and rationalizing scattered holdings.

Füder the Mosel barrel, an oak oval holding 1,000 litres or about 111 cases.

Gebiet region.

Gemeinde village, parish or commune. The village name always comes before the vineyard on German labels.

Grosslage a 'collective vineyard', consisting of a number of Einzellagen (q.v.) of similar character and quality. Unfortunately the wine law does not permit the label to distinguish between a Grosslage and an Einzellage name. Grosslage names are normally used for wines QbA, but also sometimes for such wines as Trockenbeerenauslesen when a single Einzellage cannot produce enough grapes to fill even a small barrel.

Jahrgang vintage (year).

Halbtrocken 'semi-dry' – wine with no more than 18 grams of unfermented sugar per litre, therefore drier than most modern German wines but sweeter than a *trocken* wine (q.v.).

Kabinett the first category of natural, unsugared, Qualitätswein mit Prädikat (*see* the table on page 241 for formal ripeness requirements). Fine Kabinett wines have qualities of lightness and delicacy which make them ideal refreshment, not inferior in the right context to heavier (and more expensive) Spätlese or Auslese wines.

Kellerei wine cellar; by inference a merchant's rather than a grower's establishment (which would be called a Weingut).

Landespreismünze regional wine prizes, which act as the 'heats' for the National Bundesweinprämierung (q.v.)

Landwein a category of *trocken* or *halbtrocken* Tafelwein introduced in 1982. *See* page 276.

Lesegut crop or grapes.

Liebfraumilch a much-abused name for a mild 'wine of pleasant character' officially originating in the Pfalz, Rheinhessen, Rheingau or Nahe. It must be in the QbA category and should be mainly of Riesling, Silvaner or Müller-Thurgau grapes. Since neither its character nor quality is remotely consistent, varying widely from shipper to shipper, its popularity can only be ascribed to its simple and memorable name.

Mostgewicht 'must weight'. The density or specific gravity of the grape juice, ascertained with a hydrometer, is the way of measuring its sugar content. The unit of measurement is the 'degree Oechsle' (q.v.).

Neuzüchtung new (grape) variety (*see* pages 14–15).

Oechsle the specific gravity, therefore sweetness, of German must is measured by the method invented by Ferdinand Oechsle (1774–1852). Each gram by which a litre of grape juice is heavier than a litre of water is one degree Oechsle. The number of degrees Oechsle divided by 8 is the potential alcoholic content of the wine. *See* page 241.

Offene Weine Wines served 'open' in a large glass in a café or Weinstube.

Ortsteil a suburb or part of a larger community with a standing independent from its Gemeinde or village. For example, Erbach in the Rheingau is an Ortsteil of the town of Eltville. Certain famous estates (e.g. Schloss Vollrads) are allowed to omit the names of their villages from their labels.

Perlwein slightly fizzy Tafelwein, often artificially carbonated under pressure. A small measure of acidic carbon dioxide freshens up dull wines.

Prädikat *see* QmP.

Prüfungsnummer the individual A.P. number given to each 'quality' wine after testing. *See* Amtliche Prüfung.

QbA Qualitätswein bestimmter Anbaugebiete: 'quality wine of a designated region'. The category of wine above Tafelwein and Landwein but below QmP (q.v.). QbA wine has usually had its alcohol enhanced with added sugar. It must be from one of the 13 Anbaugebiete (unblended), from approved grapes, reach a certain level of ripeness before sugaring and pass an analytical and tasting test to gain an A.P. number. In certain underripe vintages a high proportion of German wine comes into this category and can be very satisfactory, although never reaching the distinction of QmP wine.

QmP Qualitätswein mit Prädikat. 'Quality wine with special attributes' is the awkward official description of all the finest German wines, beginning with the Kabinett category and rising in sweetness, body and value to Trockenbeerenauslese. The ripeness requirements for each region are listed on page 241. QmP wines must originate in a single Bereich (q.v.) and are certified at each stage of their career from the vineyard on.

Rebe grape (Rebsorte: grape variety).

Restsüsse 'residual sugar': the sugar remaining unfermented in a wine at bottling, whether fermentation has stopped naturally or been stopped artificially. Some *trocken* (q.v.) German wines have less than 1 gram per litre. In a Trockenbeerenauslese it may reach astonishing figures of more than 200 grams a litre, with very little of the sugar converted to alcohol.

Roseewein, Roséwein pale pink wine from red grapes.

Rotling pale red wine from mixed red and white grapes.

Rotwein red wine.

Säure acidity (measured in units per 1,000 of tartaric acid). The essential balancing agent to the sweetness in German (or any) wine. As a rule of thumb a well-balanced wine has approximately one unit per 1,000 (ml.) of acid for each 10 degrees Oechsle (q.v.). Thus an 80° Oechsle wine needs an acidity of approximately 0.8.

Schaumwein sparkling wine – a general term for low-priced fizz. Quality sparkling wines are called Sekt.

Schillerwein a pale red (Rotling) of QbA or QmP status, produced only in Württemberg.

Schloss castle.

Schoppenweine another term for Offene Weine – wine served 'open' in a large glass.

Sekt Germany's quality sparkling wine, subject to similar controls to QbA wines. *See also* page 254.

Spätlese literally 'late-gathered'. The QmP category above Kabinett and below Auslese, with wines of a higher alcoholic degree and greater body and 'vinosity' than Kabinetts. Also often considerably sweeter but not necessarily so. A grower must notify the authorities of his intention to pick a Spätlese crop, and tasting panels establish a consensus of what constitutes proper Spätlese style in each vintage and region.

Spitzen 'top', a favourite German term, whether applied to a vineyard, a grower or a vintage.

Stück the standard traditional oak cask of the Rhine, holding 1,200 litres or about 133 cases. There are also Doppelstücke, Halbstücke and Viertel (quarter) stücke.

Süssreserve unfermented grape juice with all its natural sweetness, held in reserve for 'back-blending' with dry, fully fermented wines to arrive at the winemaker's ideal of a balanced wine. This sweetening (which also lowers the alcoholic content) is often overdone, but a judicious hint of extra sweetness can enhance fruity flavours and make an average wine more attractive.

Tafelwein 'table wine', the humblest category of German wine. (Without the prefix Deutsche it might not be German, however Gothic the label.) The origin, alcohol content and grape varieties are all controlled but Tafelwein is never more than a light wine for quenching thirst.

Trocken 'dry' – the official category for wines with less than 9 grams of unfermented sugar a litre. *Trocken* wines have become fashionable for drinking with food. Once frequently hollow and sour they have improved greatly in recent years.

Trockenbeerenauslese 'selected dried grapes' (frequently shortened to TBA). Ironically the precise opposite of the last entry, the 'dry' here referring to the state of the overripe grapes when picked in a shrivelled state from 'noble rot' and desiccation on the vine. Such is the concentration of sugar, acid and flavours that Oechsle readings of TBA must (never in more than minute quantities) can reach more than 300°. TBA wines are reluctant to ferment and rarely exceed 7° alcohol, the remaining intense sweetness acting as a natural preservative and slowing down maturation for many years.

VdP Verband Deutscher Prädikats-und Qualitätsweingüter, an association of premium growers.

Weingut wine estate. The term may only be used by growers who grow all their own grapes.

Weinprobe wine tasting.

Weinstein the deposit of potassium tartrate crystals forming a glittering rock-like lining to old barrels.

Weissherbst a rosé wine of QbA or QmP status made from red grapes of a single variety, the speciality of Baden, Württemberg and Pfalz, but also the fate of some sweet reds of other regions which fail to achieve a full red colour. ('Noble rot' attacks the pigments and often makes red Auslesen excessively pale.)

Winzer wine grower.

Winzergenossenschaft, Winzerverein cooperative.

MOSEL-SAAR-RUWER

The Mosel twists and turns its way more than 120 miles from the German–French–Luxembourg border to its confluence with the Rhine at Koblenz. It cuts deep into the hill country of the Eifel and Hunsrück; a huge mass of slate 400 million years of age that weathers to give the stony grey soil. On the steep sides of its narrow valley, and those of its tributaries the Saar and Ruwer, grow the brightest, briskest, most aromatic and hauntingly subtle of all German Rieslings. This is essentially Riesling country, and no soil or situation brings out the thrilling and fascinating personality of the finest of all white grapes to better effect.

The complex topography and the cool, northerly climate result in huge microclimatic variations between vineyards that lie only a stone's throw from one another. The steep, south-facing slopes in sheltered positions give noble Rieslings that are expressive and elegant, while the flat vineyards on heavy soil produce mean, watery wines from high-yielding grape varieties such as Müller-Thurgau and Kerner. Unfortunately, the German wine law does nothing to differentiate between these two worlds, indeed it confuses the two. Cheap generic wines are sold under plausible sounding 'Grosslage' names such as Piesporter Michelsberg and Ürziger Schwarzlay although little or none of the wine in the bottle originates from the towns named. These wines are a world away from Rieslings which grew in the great first-class Piesporter Goldtröpfchen and Ürziger Würzgarten sites.

The Mosel wears its first few tentative vineyards in France, flows through Luxembourg, then enters Germany near Trier, once the effective capital of the Roman Empire. On either side of the city it is joined by the rivers Saar and Ruwer. It is their side valleys, rather than the main stream, that have the first great Mosel vineyrads. Upper Mosel ('Obermosel' wine are at best light and refreshing. The ancient Elbling grape dominates here, giving appley, pleasantly tart dry wines. Riesling also has difficulty ripening on the Saar and Ruwer. But when it does, on the best slopes, the results are unsurpassed anywhere on earth; quinessential Riesling, clean as steel, with the evocative qualities of remembered scents or distant music. The Mosel Valley below Trier divides into two sub-regions, the Middle Mosel with its string of famous vineyards strung along the river's course like pearls on a necklace. Their wines are slightly fuller and more effusively aromatic than those of the Saar and Ruwer, but are equally long-living. The border between the Middle Mosel and the Terrassen Mosel ('Terraced Mosel') has long been disputed, but Zell is the logical dividing line. Below this point the vines tend to be planted on narrow terraces, rather than directly climbing the precipitous slopes as elswhere in the region. Here grow the fullest, most supple Mosel Rieslings.

SAAR

CLASSIFIED VINEYARDS

Great First-Class Sites

Scharzhofberg The greatest and most famous vineyard on the Saar, giving wines of the highest elegance and nobility in superior vintages. Their ageing potential is legendary, even Kabinett wines keeping for 25 years and more. This status was not ignored by the 197 law, which made the vineyard an Ortsteil (suburb) of Wiltingen, hence the village name does not appear on the label. Most important owners: Bischöfliche Weingüter (Hohe Domkirche), von Hövel, von Kesselstatt, Egon Müller-Scharzhof, Vereinigte Hospitien.

First-Class Sites

Ayler Kupp Some of the most charming and immediately appealing Saar wines. Most important owners: Bischöfliche Weingüter, Peter Lauer, Johann Peter Reinert, Dr Wagner.

Filzener Pulchen Sleek, steely wines with delicate apple and berry aromas. Most important owner: Piedmont.

Kanzemer Altenberg Very classic Saar Rieslings, subtlety and refinement married to racy acidity. Most important owners: von Kesselstatt, von Othegraven.

Obermmeler Hütte Monopoly site of the von Hövel estate. Elegant, long-living wines with pronounced floral aromas.

Ockfener Bockstein Sadly, substantially enlarged recently. Rieslings combining the forthright Mosel aromas with the steel of the Saar. Most important owners: Dr Fischer, Jordan & Jordan, von Kesselstatt, Sankt Urbanshof, Dr Wagner, Zilliken.

Saarburger Rausch Slow-developing, long-living wines with a pronounced citrus and mineral character. Most important owners: Dr Wagner, Zillkiken.

Serriger Schloss Saarstein Monopoly site of the Schloss Saarstein estate. Piercing acidity and a blackcurrant aroma make these very distinctive Saar wines.

Wiltinger Gottesfüß Small site yielding intense, succulent wines with a pineapple note in good vintages. Most important owners: Jordan & Jordan, von Kesselstatt.

Wiltinger Braune Kupp Monopoly site of the Le Gallais estate (*see* below) yielding substantial wines which often show a herbal character. Only QmP wines are sold as Braune Kupp; the Grosslage name Scharzberg is for QbA wine, some of which is from Egon Müller's own estate. Kabinetts are light; higher qualities aromatic and spicy. 100% Riesling.

Egon Müller
A Great Saar Estate

German winemaking at its highest level can best be described as wine for wine's sake. In a fine vintage the producer is almost passive, like a painter before a sunset. Rather than try to mould the vintage to his preconceived ideal he is dedicated to interpreting what nature provides. If one estate embodies this approach to wine it is that of Egon Müller-Scharzhof. Egon Müller IV's family has owned the Scharzhof Manor at Wiltingen on the Saar and 17.5 acres of the steep Scharzhofberg above it since 1797. His late-picked wines have frequently achieved world record prices at the annual auction of 'The Grosser Ring', or Great Ring, of leading Mosel-Saar-Ruwer growers at Trier. Egon Müller's great-great-grandfather bought the estate, formerly church land like so much of Germany's best, when it was secularized under Napoleon. It is very much the old family house, its hall lined with trophies of the chase and its library with leather-bound books. A tasting of the new vintage with Egon Müller takes place in the half-light of the hall, standing at a round table of black marble with a ring of green bottles and elegant tasting glasses.

The Riesling that he grows on the grey slate of the Scharzhofberg is Riesling in its naked purity. Only Kabinett and better wines are sold under the estate and vineyard names, and each is fermented apart in its own cask. The samples at the tasting are of different casks. As the end of the harvest approaches the differences between casks increase. The Kabinetts are often bottled as one wine, but Spätleses are usually kept in separate lots, and there may be five or six different Auslesen as each day's ripening intensifies the honeyed sweetness of the latest wines. It is very rare in the cool climate of the Saar to harvest grapes ripe enough for a Beerenauslese; Trockenbeerenauslesen are rarer still. But a 'Gold Cap' Auslese (a gold capsule replaces the words Feinste Auslese) from Egon Müller has as much penetrating perfume, vitality and 'breeding' as any wine in Germany. Its measured sweetness is matched with such racy acidity that the young wine may almost make you wince. Yet time harmonizes the extremes into a perfectly pitched unity, a teasing, tingling lusciousness that only Riesling, only the Saar, only the Scharzhofberg can achieve.

Egon Müller jointly owns (with Gerald Villanova) a second Saar estate, the 12-acre Le Gallais, which makes up the entire Wiltinger Braune Kupp site. Its wines, vinified in the Scharzhof cellars, are richer but less fine than the Scharzhofbergers.

RUWER

CLASSIFIED VINEYARDS

Great First-Class Sites

Eitelsbacher Karthäuserhofberg This monopoly site of the Tyrell family's Karthäuserhof estate gives explosively aromatic wines with a positively piquant interplay of fruit and acidity. Even the less favoured parts of this site are rated first-class.

Maximin Grünhäuser Abtsberg This site forms the heart of the famous Grünhaus estate's vineyards. Like the first-class Herrenberg it is a monopoly of the von Schubert family. The wines are exceptionally elegant and refined, possessing decades of ageing potential.

First-Class Sites

Kaseler Nies'chen Complex wines with pronounced blackcurrant aroma and more body than most Ruwer Rieslings. Most important owners: Bischöfliche Weingüter, Karlsmühle, von Kesselstatt.

Kaseler Kehrnagel Sleeker than the Nies'chen wines, but otherwise with similar character. Most important owners: Bischöfliche Weingüter, Karlsmühle, von Kesselstatt.

Maximin Grünhäuser Herrenberg The red slate soil of this famous site produces slightly leaner and more aromatic wines than those of its great neighbour, the Abtsberg. The names of the Grünhäuser sites recall the estate's monastic past: Herrenberg wines were for the monks; those of Abtsberg reserved for the abbot.

MIDDLE MOSEL

CLASSIFIED VINEYARDS

Great First-Class Sites

Bernkasteler Doctor Tiny, legendary site which towers above the roofs of old Bernkastel. Intense, sleek wines which are capable of great finesse. Many experts claim to detect a smoky aroma. Most important owners: Dr Thanisch, J. Wegeler (Deinhard).

Brauneberger Juffer-Sonnenuhr For centuries the combination of minerally power and racy elegance made the wines from Brauneberg's top site the most sought-after Mosel Rieslings. Their reputation is once again on the rise. Most important owners: Fritz Haag, Willi Haag, Paulinshof, Max Ferd. Richter.

Erdener Prälat Nestling between massive red slate cliffs and the bank of the river the tiny Prälat site enjoys the warmest microclimate in the entire Mosel-Saar-Ruwer. The result is rich wines with lavish almond, apricot and exotic fruit aromas and great ageing potential. Most important owners: Bischöfliche Weingüter, Christoffel-Berres, Dr Loosen, Vereinigte Hospitien.

Erdener Treppchen The Treppchen wines bear a family resemblance to those of the Prälat, but are more restrained and racy, many experts would say more classical. The eastern part of this site is rated first-class. Most important owners: Bischöfliche Weingüter, Joh. Jos. Christoffel, Dr Loosen, Merkelbach, Meulenhof, Peter Nicolay.

Piesporter Domherr This small site within the famous Goldtröpfchen produces more delicate, but equally great Rieslings which show their class both as young and mature wines. Most important owners: von Kesslestatt, Reinhold Haart, Kurt Hain, Weller Lehnert.

Piesporter Goldtröpfchen The extremely deep slate soils of this site yield the most baroque of all Mosel Rieslings. When young their explosive blackcurrant, citrus and peach aromas may be too much for some, but with ageing they acquire great elegance. In hot years such as '89 and '83 many of the best Mosel wines come from here. Most important owners: von Kesselstatt, Reinhold Haart, Kurt Hain, Lehnert-Veit, Reuscher-Haart, Vereinigte Hospitien, Weller-Lehnert.

Ürziger Würzgarten The red sandstone soil of this site results in astonishingly powerful, spicy Mosel Rieslings that need many years of ageing to reach their peak. Only the heart of this site is rated great first-class, the remainder is first-class or unclassified. Most important owners: Bischöfliche Weingüter, Joh. Jos. Christoffel, Joh. Christoffel Jr, Dr Loosen, Merkelbach, Mönchhof, Peter Nicolay.

Wehlener Sonnenuhr The stony slate soil of this, the most most famous of all Mosel vineyards, results in wines of almost supernatural grace and delicacy. Usually they are extremely charming from an early age, yet long-living. The highest lying parts of this large site are rated first-class. Most important owners: Dr Pauly-Bergweiler, Heribert Kerpen, Dr Loosen, Joh. Jos. Prüm, S.A. Prüm, Max Ferd. Richter, Studert-Prüm, J. Wegeler (Deinhard), Dr Weins-Prüm.

First-Class Sites

Bernkasteler Badtsube (Alte Badstube am Doctorberg, Bratenhöfchen, Graben, Lay, Matheisbildchen) Small Grosslage composed only of superior sites. Generally, sleek, racy wines that are the epitome of Mosel Riesling. In top vintages the Lay and Graben can give magnificent wines. Most important owners: Dr Pauly-Bergweiler, Dr Loosen, Dr Thanisch, Heribert Kerpen, Dr Loosen, Joh. Jos. Prüm, S.A. Prüm, Selbach-Oster, Studert-Prüm, J. Wegeler (Deinhard), Dr Wein-Prüm.

Brauneberger Juffer Large site surrounding the great Juffer-Sonnenuhr, giving slightly less refined wines with similar body and minerally character. Most important owners: Fritz Haag, Willi Haag, Max Ferd. Richter.

Dhroner Hofberg Little known site, the best part of which yields extremely juicy, appealing wines that show well from an early age. Most important owner: Bischöfliche Weingüter.

Graacher Domprobst The deep slate soil of Graach's finest vineyard gives firm, intensely minerally Riesling with a pronounced blackcurrant aroma. In hot years they are extremely long living. Most important owners: Freidrich-Wilhelm-Gymnasium, Kees-Kieren, Heribert Kerpen. Max Ferd. Richter, Willi Schaefer, Selbach-Oster, Dr Weins-Prüm.

Graacher Himmelreich Large site encompassing vineyards of variable quality. Generally more charming and supple wines than those from the Domprobst. Most important owners: Dr Pauly-Bergweiler, Friedrich-Wilhelm-Gymnasium, Kees-Kieren, Dr Loosen, Joh. Jos. Prüm, S.A. Prüm, Willi Schaefer, Studert-Prüm, Dr Weins-Prüm.

Josephshöfer Monopoly site of the von Kesselstatt estate yielding substantial Rieslings with a pronounced earthy note, and excellent ageing potential.

Leiwener Laurentiuslay With the quality renaissance in Leiwen this site's abilities to give Mosel Rieslings that are at once rich and refined has become more widely appreciated. Most important owners: Grans-Fassian, Carl Loewen, Sankt Urbanshof, Werner.

Lieserer Niederberg-Helden This once famous site gives wines with a strong family resemblance to those from the nearby Brauneberg. Most important owner: Schloss Lieser.

Pündericher Marienburg The steep slopes below the Marienburg castle give the finest and richest Rieslings in this stretch of the Mosel Valley. Most important owners: Clemens Busch, Herbert Dahm, Lenz-Dahm.

Thornischer Ritsch Little-known site with excellent exposure capable of yielding Rieslings with a Saar-like purity and steely intensity. Most important owner: Sankt Urbanshof.

Trittenheimer Apotheke Precipitously steep vineyard with stony slate soil giving wines with considerable elegance and subtelty. Most important owners: Ernst Clüsserth, Clüsserath-Weiler, Friedrich-Wilhelm-Gymnasium, Grans-Fassian, Milz.

Trittenheimer Leiterchen Tiny monopoly site of the Milz estate in the heart of the Apotheke. The very rocky soil often gives wines with a herbal note.

Zeltinger Sonnenuhr The best corners of this site are a match for the directly neighbouring and more famous Sonnenuhr vineyard of Wehlen. However, slightly richer soils result in more weighty, firmer wines. Most important owners: Molitor, Joh. Jos. Prüm, Selbach-Oster.

TERRASSEN MOSEL

CLASSIFIED VINEYARDS

First-Class Sites

Bremer Calmont This great amphitheatre of vines is the steepest vineyards in all of Europe. Its narrow terraces yield firmly structured Rieslings with pronounced minerally character. Most important owners: Reinhold Franzen, Freiherr von Landenberg.

Neefer Frauneberg Much more floral, charming wines than Calmont. Most important owners: Edouard Bremm, Reinhold Franzen.

Leading Mosel-Saar-Ruwer Producers

Weingut Joh. Jos. Christoffel Erben

Schanzstrasse 2, 54539 Ürzig. Owner: Hans-Leo Christoffel. 5.5 acres. Classified sites: Erdener Treppchen, Ürziger Würzgarten. Hans-Leo Christoffel produces some of the most polished, elegant Rieslings in this dramatic section of the Middle Mosel. Stars on the label (between one and five, the more indicating the better quality) are used to differentiate between the different bottlings of Würzgarten Auslese in fine vintages.

Weingut Forstmeister Geltz Zilliken (Forstmeister Gelz)

Heckingstrasse 20, 54439 Saarburg. Director: Hans-Joachim Zilliken. 25 acres. Classified sites: Saarburger-Rausch; Ockfener-Bockstein.

Winninger Röttgen The aromatic, silky wines from this site just downstream from the village of Winningen have been famous for centuries. Most important owners: von Heddesdorf, Heymann-Löwenstein, Knebel.

Winninger Uhlen The great soaring wall of narrow terraced vineyards which forms the Uhlen is one of the most imposing vineyards on the entire Mosel – an impressive sight from the Autobahn bridge where it crosses the river here. The firmly structured, minerally Rieslings produced from the Winninger Uhlen are arguably the finest of the Terrassen Mosel. Most important owners: Franz Dötsch, von Heddesdorf, Heymann-Löwenstein, Knebel, von Schleinitz.

The family estate of the much-respected Master Forester of the King of Prussia, Ferdinand Geltz (1851–1925), which is now run by his great-grandson, Hans-Joachim Zilliken. The wines are made very traditionally, in casks, and are designed for long age in bottle. The intensely minerally, racy wines from the Rausch are amongst the finest in the entire Saar.

Weingut Fritz Haag

Dusemonder Hof, 54472 Brauneberg. Owner: Wilhelm Haag. 13.6 acres. Classified sites: Brauneberger-Juffer-Sonnenuhr, Juffer. Distinguished estate whose history can be traced back to 1605. It is one of the top addresses for perfectly made, elegant, cask-matured Riesling wines. A century ago Braunebergers were the most sought-after of all Mosel Rieslings. Virtually single-handed Wilhelm Haag has rebuilt this reputation.

Weingut Reinhold Haart

Ausoniusufer 18, 54498 Piesport. Owner: Theo Haart. 11.5 acres.
Classified sites: Piesporter Domherr, Piesporter Goldtröpfchen.

The quietly determined Theo Haart runs Piesport's leading estate, producing wines that combine the extravagant personality of these top-site vineyards with charm and delicacy. International demand for the best Auslese and higher Prädikat wines mean that these masterpieces soon sell out. He also makes impressive wines from recently purchased vines in the unclassified Wintricher Ohligsberg.

Weingut Heymann-Löwenstein

Bahnhofstrasse 10, 56333 Winningen. Owner: Reinhard Löwenstein. 10 acres. Classified sites: Winninger Röttgen, Winninger Uhlen.

Reinhard Löwenstein's reputation as a rebel is well deserved, not least because of the fanaticism with which he has pursued top quality in an area where mediocrity is still largely the norm. His unusually full-bodied dry Rieslings are amongst the best examples of this style in the region. Since the vintages of the early 1990s he has also produced some imposing late-harvest wines. The 1994 Riesling TBA from the Uhlen was the most expensive, and one of the greatest wines ever made in the Terrassen Mosel.

Weingut von Hövel

Agritiusstrasse 5–6, 54329 Konz-Oberemmel. Owner: Eberhard von Kunow. 30.5 acres. Classified sites: Oberemmeler Hütte (solely owned), and Scharzhofberg.

Eherhard von Kunow makes some of the most immediately appealing Saar Rieslings. Rich and aromatic as young wines, they gain in elegance as they age. The Scharzhofberg wines are slightly more opulent than those from the estate's Hütte monopole, from which many superb Auslese and higher Prädikat wines are made. At Kabinett and Spätlese level the estate's wines offer excellent value for money.

Gutsverwaltung Karthäuserhof

(Formerly H. W. Rautenstrauch) Karthäuserhof 1, 54292 Trier-Eitelsbach. Owner: Christof Tyrell. 45 acres. Classified site: Eitelsbacher Karthäuserhofberg.

A beautiful old manor of the Carthusian monks in a side valley of the Ruwer, bought by the ancestor of the present owner when Napoleon secularized church land. Since Christof Tyrell took control of the estate in 1986 quality has improved in leaps and bounds. Today, the estate's dry and naturally sweet Rieslings are amongst the Mosel-Saar-Ruwer's finest. Intense blackcurrant and peach aromas and racy acidity are the hallmarks of the Karthäuserhof wines. The bottle is unmistakable with only a narrow label on the neck, none on the body. The vines are 90% Riesling.

Weingut Reichsgraf von Kesselstatt

Liebfrauenstrasse 9–10, 54290 Trier. Owners: the Reh family. 166 acres. Classified sites: Bernkasteler Doctor, Bernkasteler Lay, Graacher Josephshof (monopoly), Kaseler Kehrnagel, Kaseler Nies'chen, Piesporter Domherr, Piesporter Goldtröpfchen, Scharzhofberg, Trittenheimer, Apotheke, Wiltinger Gottesfuss.

This was the greatest private estate of the Mosel-Saar-Ruwer when it was bought in 1978 by Günther Reh. Today the estate is directed by his daughter, Annegret, who is Germany's leading woman winemaker. The entire estate is planted with 100% Riesling; between 60 and 70% of the wines are *trocken* or *halbtrocken*. Regardless of style, the wines are packed with fruit and have a vibrant, but never dominant acidity.

The headquarters are in the splendid baroque Kesselstatt palace in Trier, from which the Counts promulgated the planting of Riesling in the 18th century.

Weingut J.J. Prüm

54470 Wehlen. 35 acres. Owners: Dr Manfred and Wolfgang Prüm. Classified sites: Wehlener Sonnenuhr, Graacher Himmelreich; Zeltinger Sonnenuhr; Bernkasteler Lay.

The most famous estate of many belonging to the most famous family of growers of the Middle Mosel. The estate house, down by the river, looks across the water up to the great Sonnenuhr vineyard, of which it has one of the largest holdings. The huge sundials among the vines here and in Zeltingen were built by an earlier Prüm. The estate's signature is wine of glorious fruity ripeness, setting off the raciness of Riesling grown on slate with deep notes of spice and honey. As very young wines they often retain a yeasty aroma from fermentation, but this quickly dispenses. Their ageing potential is legendary, Spätlese and Auslese often needing 10 years and more to reach their peak.

Weingut Dr Loosen

St Johannishof, 54470 Bernkastel. Owner: Ernst Loosen. 25 acres. Classified sites: Bernkasteler Lay, Erdener Treppchen, Erdener Prälat, Graacher Himmelrech, Ürziger Würzgarten, Wehlener Sonnenuhr.

From old, ungrafted vines in great first-class vineyards Ernst Loosen produces some of the finest Rieslings made in the Mosel – and Germany – today. Their hallmarks are concentration, complex mineral, herbal and spice flavours and a distinctly drier balance than the norm for the region. The character of each site is extremely distinct, as one would expect for a leading campaigner in favour of a vineyard classification. The crowning glory of the peaks in the estate's wide range are the majesterial Auslese wines from the Erdener Prälat.

Weingut Schloss Saarstein

54455 Serrig. Owner: Christian Ebert. 23 acres. Classified sites: Serriger Schloss Saarstein (monopoly).

The charming and dedicated Christian and Andrea Ebert run one of the most consistent wine estates on the Saar. Absolute purity of flavour and steely intensity are the qualities which typify both the dry wines and those with natural sweetness. The BA, TBA and Eiswein are amongst the greatest in the entire Mosel-Saar-Ruwer with enormous ageing potential.

Weingut Willi Schaefer

Hauptstrasse 130, 54470 Graach. Owner: Willi Schaefer. 5 acres. Classified sites: Graacher Domprobst, Graacher Himmelreich.

This miniature estate in the Middle Mosel with a mere 5 acres of vineyards regularly produces the finest Rieslings from the excellent vineyards of Graach, and has consistently done so since at least the 1940s. The combination of very limited production and high demand means that Auslese and higher Prädikat wines sell out almost instantaneously. It would be difficult to find Mosels with better ageing potential than these beautifully crafted, sleek, racy wines.

C. von Schubert, Maximin Grünhaus

544318 Grünhaus/Trier. Owners: Andreas and Dr Carl von Schubert. 76.6 acres. Classified sites: Maximin Grünhäuser Herrenberg, Abtsberg (monopoly).

This is an outstanding estate of the Ruwer as well as one of Germany's finest, with a unique undivided hill of vines dominating the beautiful, formerly Benedictine-owned manor house, whose cellars go back to Roman times and whose records start in AD 966. The estate's three vineyards, Herrenberg, Abtsberg and the less well-exposed Bruderberg, produce distinctly different wines. It was bought by the von Schubert family in 1882. Since the beginning of the 20th century, the estate's miraculously delicate wines have been sold under an extravagant art nouveau label. In spite of their lightness of body even the 'simplest' Grünhaus Rieslings age magnificently – the epitome of great German Riesling. The naturally sweet Auslesen of good vintages are sublime: infinitely subtle but surprisingly spicy and powerful, ageing 20 years or more. The estate is also one of the most reliable producers of dry Rieslings in the Mosel-Saar-Ruwer.

Weingut Selbach-Oster

Uferallee 23, 54492 Zeltingen. Owners: Hans and Johannes Selbach. Classified sites: Bernkasteler Badstube, Graacher Domprobst, Wehlener Sonnenuhr, Zeltinger Sonnenuhr.

Father-and-son team Hans and Johannes Selbach make beautifully crafted Mosel Rieslings from 20 acres. Below Auslese level the wines have a distinctly dry finish. The finest wines almost invariably come from their many parcels in the Zeltinger Sonnenuhr site, which gives wines that combine richness with great subtlety and possess excellent ageing potential.

Weingut Dr Heinz Wagner

Bahnhofstrasse 3, 54439 Saarburg. Owner: Heinz Wagner. Classified sites: Ayler Kupp, Ockfener Bockstein, Saarburger Rausch.

In the cavernous cellars below his imposing 19th-century mansion close to Saarburg's railway station, Heinz Wagner produces unusually substantial Saar wines. The wines from the Bockstein are both subtle and seductive, while those from the Rausch are deep and long-living. One of the few reliable sources for dry wines in a region where they are seldom harmonious.

OTHER PRODUCERS

Weingut Bastgen 54518 Kesten. Owners: Mona Bastgen, Armin Vogel. Since Mona Bastgen and Armin Vogel took over this tiny estate it has begun to prove the true potential of sites such as the Kestener Paulinshofberg and Kueser Weissenstein; substantial wines, with plenty of fruit and character.

Verwaltung der Bischöflichen Weingüter Trier Gervasiusstrasse 1 (Ecke Rahnenstrasse), 54290 Trier. Director: Wolfgang Richter. About 260 acres in the Middle Mosel, Saar and Ruwer. The biggest estate under a single management in the Mosel-Saar-Ruwer was formed by the union in 1966 of three independent charitable properties: the Bishop's Seminary (Priesterseminar), the Trier Cathedral (Domkirche) estates and the Bishop's Hostel (Konvikt). It has now also leased four other small church estates. The vineyard management and the pressing are carried on independently of the three main charities' press houses; all the juice is then brought to the 400-year-old central cellar in Trier for fermentation and cask-ageing. Ninety-eight percent of the whole estate is Riesling. After a period of unexciting performance during the 1980s, quality has improved steadily during the early 1990s.

Weingut Eduard Bremm Moselferstrasse 4, Neef. Owner: Eduard Bremm. 7.4 acres. Classified sites: Neefer-Frauenberg and Rosenberg; Kinheimer-Rosenberg and Hubertuslay. A 400-year-old Mosel winemaking family, now well-known for its 100% Riesling wines from classic steep slate vineyards. All the wines are vinified and mature in *Füder* (1000-litre casks) and all are dry. They are delightfully old-fashioned in style.

Weingut Clemens Busch 56862. Clemens and Rita Busch. Busch is not only the Mosel's leading organic winemaker, but also makes the finest wines from the first-class Marienburg site. Highly individual dry Rieslings are the speciality, in which style the estate can challenge the best the Rheingau has to offer.

Jos. Christoffel Jr Moselufer 1–3, 54539 Urzig. Owners: Karl Jos. Christoffel and Annekatrin Christoffel-Prüm. A small family estate with holdings in excellent sites. (Christoffels have been vine growers for more than 300 years.) A list of some 120 wines includes examples of most vintages back to '71. The Christoffels are specialists in naturally sweet wines.

Weingut Ernst Clüsserath Moselweinstrasse 67, 54349 Trittenheim. Owner: Ernst Clüsserath. Tiny estate whose ever-improving wines have already won serious young owner/winemaker Ernst Clüsserath many tastings and awards.

Weingut Grans-Fassian Römerstrasse 28, 54340 Leiwen. Owner: Gerhard Grans. 24 acres. Classified sites: Leiwener Laurentiuslay; Piesporter Goldtröpfchen, Trittenheimer-

Apotheke and Apotheke. Gerhard Grans is one of the quality pioneers who have put Leiwen on the map during recent years. Even his basic Riesling QbA is of solid quality. Finest amongst his wide range of wines are the top Auslese, which are rich and very elegant. Eiswein is a speciality.

Weingüter Dr Fischer Bocksteinhof, Ockfen-Wawern. Owner: Hans-Henning Fischer. 60.5 acres. This is a large Saar estate with two centres: the Bocksteinhof in the vines at the foot of the great towering Bockstein and an 18th-century former monastic property in a meadow below the Herrenberg, the best site in Wawern. 98% is Riesling. Although quality here is mixed, the best wines are classic Saar Rieslings.

Stiftung Staatliches Friedrich-Wilhelm-Gymnasium Weberbachstrasse 75, 54290 Trier. Director: Helmut Kranichl. 86.5 acres. Another of the great institutions of Trier, this one a (formerly Jesuit) school, which was founded in 1561. The wines are clean, fresh and fruity but rarely more than that.

Weingut Willi Haag 54472 Brauneberg. Owner: Inge Haag. Inge Haag and her son Marcus make fine, traditional-style Brauneberg Rieslings from 7 acres of vineyards including large parcels in the Juffer and Juffer-Sonnenuhr. The best Spätlese and Auslese are impressive.

Weingut Kurt Hain 54498 Piesport. Owner: Gernot Hain. Gernot Hain is one of the most talented young winemakers in the Mosel. His expressive and beautifully crafted Rieslings with natural sweetness are amongst the best made from Piesport's great sites.

Carl Aug Immich-Batterieberg 56850 Enkirch. Owners: Gert and Sabine Basten. 15 acres. Einzellagen: Enkircher-Ellergrub, Zeppwingert, Sterffensberg and Batterieberg (solely owned). Since taking over this well-known estate self-taught winemaker Sabine Basten has demonstrated that she has a geniune talent. The best wines come from the Batterieberg site which was created by dynamiting the cliffs in 1844.

Weingut Karlsmühle 54318 Mertesdorf. Owner: Peter Geiben. Important 30-acre estate with vines in the first-class sites of Kasel (Nies'chen and Kehrnagel), plus the monopoly Lorenzhöfer vineyards. Geiben may strike many as a back woods philosopher, but his vibrant, super-clean wines are classic Ruwer Rieslings.

Weingut Kees-Kieren Hauptstrasse 22, 54470 Graach. Owner: Ernst-Josef and Werner Kees. 10 acres. Classified sites: Graacher-Himmelreich and Domprobst. The Kees family has been growing vines since the 17th century. The concentration today is on Rieslings which have won the highest awards at national competitions. Also dry and half-dry specialities.

Weingut Heribert Kerpen 54470 Wehlen. Owner: Martin Kerpen. In spite of having only 12 acres of vineyards this estate is one of the largest owners in the great Wehlener Sonnenuhr vineyard. In the dry style quality may be variable, but Martin Kerpen's elegant, floral Riesling Spätlese and Auslese with natural sweetness are consistently impressive.

Weingut Schloss Lieser 54470 Lieser. Owner: Wolfgang Reichel. Since being appointed director and winemaker in 1992 Thomas Haag (son of Wilhelm Haag, *see* Weingut Fritz Haag) has effected a miraculous transformation of this once famous estate. Today the concentrated, long-living wines are first-class Mosel Rieslings.

Weingut Carl Loewen Mathiasstrasse 30, 54340 Leiwen. Owner: Karl Josef Loewen. 15 acres. Classified site: Leiwener Laurentiuslay. Karl-Josef Loewen is one of the brightest rising stars amongst the many talented young winemakers in the Mosel-Saar-Ruwer. Both in the dry and naturally sweet styles he makes concentrated Rieslings of considerable sophistication. The Auslese wines from the Laurentiuslay possess real nobility.

Weingut Milz Laurentiushof 54349 Trittenheim. Owner: Karl Josef Milz. About 20 acres. Classified sites: Dhroner Hofberger; Trittenheimer, Apotheke, and Leiterchen (monopoly). A family house by the church, Milz property since the 17th century. All Riesling, the wines well-balanced towards dryness. The rising star of the Lower Mosel/ Terrassen Mosel.

Weinguzt Meulenhof 54492 Erden. Owner: Stefan Justen. Quality at Erden's number one estate is slightly erratic, but the best Riesling from the great Treppchen and Prälat sites of Erden are rich and complex.

Weingut Molitor 54470 Wehlen. Owner: Markus Molitor. From 37 acres of vineyards including a large share of the first-class Zeltinger Sonnenuhr, Markus Molitor makes a wide range of unusually full-bodied dry Mosel Rieslings and opulent dessert wines. A rising star of recent years that is worth following.

Rudolf Müller GmbH & Co. KG Postfach 20, Reil. Owners: Dr Richard Müller, Magrit Müller-Burggraef and Barbara Rundquist. 15 acres. Classified site: Ockfener-Bockstein. Best known for its brand of Bereich Bernkastel, 'The Bishop of Riesling'. Rudolf Müller also owns a fine estate. Although the wines are rather light they are very typical Saar and Mosel Rieslings.

Weingut Dr Pauly-Bergweiler and Weingut Peter Nicolay Gestade 15, 54470 Bernkastel-Kues. Owners: Dr Peter Pauly and Helga Pauly-Berres. 37 acres. Classified sites: Bernkasteler Alte, Badstube am Doctorberg, Bernkasteler Doctor, Bernkasteler Lay, Graachen Dampprobst, Graachen Himmelreich, Wehlener Sonnenuhr (Dr Pauly-Bergweiler), Erdener

Treppchen, Erdener Prälat, Urziger Goldwingent (monopoly), Urziger Würzgarten, Brauneberger Juffer-Sonnenuhr. Dr Peter and Helga Pauly own two estates which together have holdings in most of the classified sites of the Middle Mosel. The estate's wines are unashamedly *trocken* in style with vibrant fruit and crisp acidity; the wines with natural sweetness being significantly better than the often rather hard, dry wines. Best of the Pauly wines are those from the alte Badstube am Doctorberg site of Bernkastel, while the stars of the Nicolay range are usually the rich wines from the Urziger Goldwingent monopoly.

Weingut S.A. Prüm Erben, S.A. Prüm Uferallee 25–36, 54470 Bernkastel-Wehlen. Owner: Dr Renate Willkomm. 18 acres. Classified sites: Wehlener Sonnenuhr, Bernkasteler-Lay, Graben; Graacher-Himmelreich and Domprobst; Zeltinger and Sonnenuhr. Part of the great Prüm estate which became separate in 1911, was divided into six parts in 1964 but has since been partially reconstituted and enlarged. The wines are made with great emphasis on the character of each cask. The biggest holding (3.7 acres) is Wehlener Sonnenuhr. Winemaker Raimund Prüm's Rieslings are always fresh and elegant, a high standard being maintained from QbA upwards.

Ökonomierat Max-G. Piedmont Saartal 1, 54329 Konz-Filzen. Owner: Claus Piedmont. 15 acres. Classified sites: Filzeneu Pulchen. The Piedmont family has a long tradition of making light racy Saar Rieslings. Claus Piedmont continues this tradition, placing the main emphasis on dry wines.

Weingut Johann Peter Reinert 54441 Kanzem. Owner: Johann Peter Reinert. This one-man 9-acre estate makes delightfuly fruity, charming Saar wines. The finest of these come from the first-class Ayler Kupp.

Weingut Max Ferd. Richter Hauptstrasse 85, 54486 Mülheim. Owners: Horst and Dr Dirk Richter. 35 acres. Classified sites: Wehlener Sonnenuhr; Graacher Domprobst and Himmelreich; Brauneberger Juffer and Juffer-Sonnenuhr. This substantial estate with holdings scattered from Braundberg to Trarbach is an extremely consistent producer of classic Mosel Rieslings both in the dry and naturally sweet styles. His finest wines are the powerful, minerally Rieslings from the classified sites of Brauneberg, while the most charming are those from the Mülheimen Sonnenlay. Eiswein is a speciality produced almost every vintage.

St Nikolaus Hospital Cusanusstift, Cusanusstrasse 2, 54470 Bernkastel-Kues. 20 acres. Classified sites: Bernkasteler Graben, Bernkasteler Lay, Brauneberger Juffer-Sonnenuhr, Brauneberger Juffer, Graacher Domprobst, Graacher Himmelreich, Wehlener Sonnenuhr. This estate, the foundation of the 15th-century theologian Cardinal Nikolaus Cusanus, has wines in many of the Middle Mosel's top sites. Since Hermann Hochsheid became

director they have begun once again to make Rieslings worthy of these names. The St-Nikolaus Hospital still fulfills its original function, and houses the Middle Mosel wine museum.

Weingut Sankt-Urbanshof 54340 Leiwen. Owner: Hermann Weis. Best known for the 'Weis Clone' (B21) of Riesling selected by his vine nursery, Hermann Weis also directs the third largest privately owned wine estate in the Mosel-Saar-Ruwer. Best of the large range are the dry Rieslings from the first-class Leiwener Laurentiuslay and Ockfener Bockstein.

Bert Simon, Weingut Herrenberg 5512 Serrig-Saar. Owner: Bert Simon. 80 acres. A young estate started in 1968 with the purchase of the old von Schorlemer vineyards in Serrig. The estate's wines are fuller-bodied and less acidic than most Saar Rieslings, but rather variable in quality. The small percentage of Weissburgunder is made unblended as a dry wine.

Weingut Studert-Prüm/Maximinhof 54470 Wehlen. Owners: Stephan and Gerhard Studert. 13 acres. Classified sites: Bernkasteler Graben, Graacher Himmelreich, Wehlener Sonnenuhr. The Studert family, which has been growing vines since the 16th century, acquired the Wehlen vineyard holdings of the Benedictine St Maximin Abbey in Trier in 1805. Since the early 1990s quality has taken a significant jump up here. Classic Mosel Rieslings with a touch of natural sweetness make up the bulk of the production, the Wehlener Sonnenuhr wines often showing real class.

Weingut Wwe Dr H Thanisch 54470 Bernkastel-Kues. Owners: the Thanisch family. 16 acres. Einzellagen: Bern-kasteler-Doctor, Badstube, Graben and Lay; Brauneberger Juffer-Sonnenuhr. The family estate (with roots going back to 1650) that made the worldwide reputation of the famous Doctor vineyard at the turn of the century when King Edward VII, visiting Bad Homburg, took a fancy to the name. In recent years quality has been sadly erratic, even some of the most expensive Doctor wines disappointing.

Güterverwaltung der Vereinigten Hospitien Krahnenufer 19, 54290 Trier. Director: Dr Hans Pilgram. 130 acres. Classified sites: Scharzhofbergen (Saar), Bernkasteler Badstube, Graacher Domprobst, Graacher Himmelreich, Erdener Prälat, Urziger Würzgarten, Zeltingen Sonnenuhr (Mosel). One of the great charitable institutions of Trier, occupying Germany's oldest cellars, built as a Roman warehouse. Napoleon united ('Vereinigte') the numerous charities of Trier in the Benedictine abbey of St Irminen, which continues to be a free hospital like the Hospices de Beaune in Burgundy, financed by its vineyards and other considerable estates. It takes its label, a gold figure of Sanctus Jacobus (St James of Compostela) from the medieval hospital incorporated by Napoleon. The wines are made and mainly matured in cask and include some typical Mosels and Saars but some wines are dull and rustic.

Jordan & Jordan 5516 Wiltingen. Owner: Peter H. Jordan. 33 acres. Einzellagen: Wiltinger-Gottesfuss, Scharzhofberger, Ockfener Bockstein. Since taking over the run-down van Volxem estate in 1993, Peter Jordan has significantly expanded its holdings and completely changed the wine style. Today the majority of the production is full-bodied dry wine. From these Peter Jordan takes as his model the great Rieslings of the Wachau, but as yet he has not made anything which is up to this level.

Gutsverwaltung Wegeler-Deinhard Martertal 2, 54470 Bernkastel-Kues. Manager: Norbert Kreuzberger. Winemaker: Norbert Briet. 69 acres. Classified sites: Bernkasteler-Doctor, Graben, Lay, Bratenhöfchen; Graacher Himmelreich; Wehlener-Sonnenuhr; Kasteler-Nies'chen. The Mosel estate of the famous Koblenz wine merchants started in 1900 with the sensational purchase of part of the

Doctor vineyard for 100 gold marks a square metre. Further acquisitions totalled some 33 acres in 1981, when a long lease of vineyards in Wehlen from the Dr Zach. Bergweiler-Prüm estate more than doubled their Mosel holdings. The cellars, press house and a villa now occupied by the manager are in Kues. Always good, the quality of the Deinhard wines has taken a significant jump up since Norbert Breit (previously winemaker at Thanisch) was put in charge of the cellars.

Weingut Dr F Weins-Prüm (Selbach-Weins) Uferallee 20, 54470 Wehlen. Owner: Hubert Selbach. Classified sites: Bernkasteler Badstube, Erdener Prälat, Graacher Himmelreich, Graacher Domprobst, Urziger Würzgarten, Wehlener Sonnenuhr. This fine estate makes light but vivid Mosel Rieslings from a whole range of excellent vineyards. Those from the Erdener Prälat and Wehlener Sonnenuhr usually have most character.

AHR AND MITTELRHEIN

AHR

Perverse as it seems, Germany's northernmost wine region, specializes in red wine. The Ahr Valley is an appealing landscape of steeply terraced vineyards, wooded hills and rocky terrain. The Ahr is a western tributary of the Mittelrhein, not far south of Bonn, whose steep sides are clothed almost continuously in vines for ten miles: 1,000 acres, of which two-thirds are Spätburgunder (Pinot Noir), Portugieser and other red grapes. The remaining one-third is white grapes of which Riesling and Müller-Thurgau are the most important.

In the most sheltered corners of the Ahr temperatures soar when the sun shines, and in a good summer Spätburgunder grapes ripen fully. The pale, sweet-sour wines of the past were primarily the result of misconcieved winemaking. Since the late 1980s a handful of pioneers have proved that 'real' red wines can also be made here. Perfume and grace, rather than power and richness, are their strengths. The region's white wines are usually dry, but are seldom capable of competing with those of the Mittelrhein or the Mosel-Saar-Ruwer.

Leading Ahr Producers

Weingut Deutzerhof

53508 Mayschoss. Owners: Hella and Wolfgang Hehle. 17 acres. 5,000 cases. Classified sites: Altenahrer Eck.

At no other Ahr estate has the quality improved so dramatically during the last decade as here. Half the production is deep-coloured Spätburgunder red wine with a judicious touch of new oak (the best are sold as 'Selektion Caspar C'), but the white wines, the late-harvest Rieslings especially, are also remarkable. Weingut Deutzerhof is an estate to watch.

Staatliche Weinbaudomäne Kloster Marienthal Ahr

Klosterstrasse, 53507 Marienthal Ahr. 45.7 acres.
The Ahr State Domaine's deliberately old-fashioned winemaking without any ageing in new oak produces typical examples of Ahr red wines. Yields are kept low, resulting in wines that display good character and depth.

The domaine is experimenting with new oak, although to date with little success. However, the ex-Augustinian convent that houses the estate is worth a visit for the architecture alone.

Weingut Meyer-Näkel

Hadtbergstrasse 20, 53507 Dernau. Owner: Werner Näkel. 16 acres, 4,000 cases. Classified sites: Bad Neuenahr Sonnenberg, Dernauer Pfarrwingert

Ex-high school teacher and self-taught winemaker Werner Näkel was the dynamo of the red winemaking revolution of the 1980s. He makes the most elegant and sophisticated Spätburgunder red wines in the region, classifying these under an unusual personal system: 'G' for light, early-matureing wines, 'Blauschiefer' for the more sophisticated wines from slate soils, and 'S' for the most powerful, firmly-structured, slow developing wines. His subtle use of new oak is cautious and precisely judged. Werner Näkel's wines should lay to rest any remaining scepticism about the need to take the Ahr seriously.

MITTELRHEIN

Mention the Rhine to people of any nationality and images of its course through the narrow gorge between Bingen and Koblenz with its castles and vines clinging precariously to precipitous slopes will immediately be conjured up. This and the scattered vineyards between Koblenz and Bonn make up the little-known Mittelrhein region. In wine terms Lower Rhine might be a more appropriate name, since these are the last vineyards along the river's course.

Since 1980 the vineyard area has shrunk from 5,000 acres to a mere 1,600 acres. This is a sad development because the most favoured vineyards here give Rieslings which are quite a match for those of the western Rheingau, and it has often been good vineyards which have fallen out of cultivation. Fully 75 percent of the region's vineyards are planted with the noble Riesling grape. The elegant, medium-bodied dry and naturally sweet Rieslings made by the region's leading producers in recent years have resulted in a renaissance of interest in Mittelrhein wines. So far this has concentrated itself around Bacharach in the south, but competition is also beginning to hot up further north, around Boppard.

CLASSIFIED VINEYARDS

First-Class Sites

Bacharacher Hahn Arguably the best site in the southern Mittelrhein. Right on the bank of the Rhine its stony slate soil gives full-bodied Rieslings with rich peachy fruit. The Hahn is virtually a monopoly site of the Toni Jost estate.

Bacharacher Posten The Posten also enjoys the Rhine's warming influence. Its wines can show richness and refinement. Most important owners: Fritz Bastian, Mades, Ratzenberger.

Bacharacher Wolfshöhle Archetypal Bacharach Rieslings; sleek, racy wines with a strong minerally character from the slate soil. Most important owners: Fritz Bastian, Toni Jost, Randolf Kauer, Mades, Ratzenberger.

Bopparder Hamm This giant amphitheatre of vines divides into five sites. Of them the Feuerlay, Mandelstein and Ohlen-berg can all give magnificent Rieslings but few local vintners regularly realize this potential. Most important owners: Heinrich Müller, August Perll, Walter Perll, Adolf Weingart.

Oberdiebacher Fürstenberg Loamy quarzite soil here gives juicy, medium-bodied Rieslings with elegant acidity. Most important producer: Toni Jost.

Steeger St Jost This site yields steely Rieslings with the most intense bouquet of all Mittelrhein wines. Most important owners: Mades, Ratzenberger.

Leading Mittelrhein Producers

Weingut J.J. Adeneuer

Max-Planckstrasse 8, 53474 Ahrweiler. Owners: Marc and Frank Adeneuer. 20 acres. Classified site: Walporzheimer Gärkammer. The Adeneuer brothers make light but elegant Spätburgunder wines at this all-red estate.

Weingut Toni Jost

Oberstrasse 14, 55420 Bacharach. Owner: Peter and Linde Jost, 17 acres. Classified sites: Bacharacher Hahn, Bacharacher Wolfshöhle, Oberdiebacher Fürstenberg.

Peter and Linde Jost are not only one of the most likeable winemaking couples in Germany, but their richly fruity dry and naturally sweet Rieslings are also real charmers. Best are the concentrated late-harvest wines from the first-class Hahn site. They offer the finest Rheingau wines tough competition.

Weingut Dr Randolf Kauer

Mainzer Strasse 21, 55420 Bacharach. Owner: Randolph and Martina Kauer. 5 acres. Classified site: Bacharacher Wolfshöhle. Recently moved to more imposing surroundings, the Kauers' small estate makes racy, Mosel-like Rieslings which need time to show their best and are extremely long-living. Few Kauer vines are in classified sites yet the standard is very high.

Weingut Lanius-Knab

54430 Oberwesel. Owners: Jörg and Anne Lanius. 13.5 acres. Until the quality renaissance at this estate during the early 1990s Oberwesel's wines were completely overshadowed by those of neighbouring Bacharach. The Lanius's wines (dry and naturally sweet) are racy Mittelrhein Rieslings of crystalline purity. Their ambition surely gives this estate a great future.

Sekt

Germany has found a way of turning her awkward excess of under-ripe wine, the inevitable result of her northerly situation, into pleasure and profit. They are turned into her national sparkling wine, Sekt. Sekt may be either fermented in bottle or in tank, may be made from any grapes from any region and may even include imported wines.

All the better Sekts, however, fall, within the new (1986) German wine law as either Deutscher Sekt, which means that the wine must be from 100% German-grown grapes, or Deutscher Sekt bA, entirely from German grapes from one of the 11 designated wine-growing regions.

Many of the best specify that they are entirely Riesling wines and some specify their exact origins. There is, in fact, a huge range of qualities from the banal to the extremely fine. The best examples have nothing in common with champagne except bubbles: their flavour is essentially flowery and fruity with the inimitable Riesling aroma in place of champagne's mingled fruits and yeast and age. Leading specialists: Heymann-Löwenstein, Dr Loosen, Selbach-Oster, Dr Wagner (Mosel); Dr Randolf Kauer, Ratzenberger (Mittelrhein); Schlossgut Diel (Nahe); Hans Barth, Georg Breuer, Johannishof, Schloss Reinhartshausen (Rheingau); Bergdolt, Koehler-Ruprecht, Wilhelmshof (Pfalz); WG Königschaffhausen, Bernhard Huben, Schloss Neuweier.

Weingut Helmut Mades

Borbachstrasse 35–36, 55422 Bacharach. Owner: Helmut Mades. Although this estate is only 6 acres, it is one of the most reliable wine producers in the Mittelrhein. Year in year out Helmut Mades' Rieslings from the top vineyards of Bacharach are full of fruit, and well balanced. Excellent value for money.

Weingut Meyer-Näkel

Hardtbergstrasse 20, 5487 Dernau. Owners: Werner and Willibald Näkel. 13.6 acres. Einzellagen: Ahrweiler-Forstberg, Riegelfeld and Rosenthal; Neuenahrer Sonnenberg; Dernauer-Goldkaul, Hardtberg and Pfarrwingert; Marienthaler Trotzenberg. A small family estate that emerged in the 1980s, producing cask- and *barrique*-matured dry red wines, softened by malolactic fermentation. The vines are 80% Spätburgunder, 5% Portugieser, 5% Dornfelder, 5% Riesling. The average yield here is 50 hl/ha. In all, 80% is sold directly to the consumer, and the balance to top restaurants, including the well-known Ente vom Lehel in Wiesbaden and the Schiffchen in Dusseldorf.

Weingut Heinrich Müller

Mainzer Strasse 45, 56322 Spay. Owner: Matthias Müller. 15 acres. Classified sites: Bopparder Hamm (Feuerlay, Mandelstein, Ohlenberg). Young Matthias Müller has already proved that he can make wines that reflect the true class of the Bopparder Hamm vineyards. The emphasis here is always on ripe fruit and achieving harmonious acidity.

August Perll

Oberstrasse 81, 56154 Boppard. Mittelrhein. Owner: August Perll. 12 acres. Classified site: Bopparder Hamm.
A small grower of Riesling and Spätburgunder on the vertiginous slopes of the Boppard bend of the Rhine.

Weingut Ratzenberger

Blücherstrasse 167, 55422 Steeg. Owner: Jochen Ratzenberger. 17 acres. Classified sites: Bacharacher Posten, Bacharacher Wolfshöhle, Steeger Sankt Jost.
While Jochen Ratzenberger Jr still has something to learn before his wines reach the standards his father set, these are classic racy Mittelrhein Rieslings. His Sekt is excellent.

RHEINGAU

The Rheingau is not only the most famous of Germany's winegrowing regions, it is also the one which established the nation's reputation for world-class white wines at the beginning of the 19th century. This compact region, which lies on the right bank of the Rhine during the 20 miles it flows from east to west from Wiesbaden to Bingen, is not short of natural advantages. Most of its vineyards lie on gentle slopes with southerly exposure that are well protected from northerly air streams by the mass of the Taunus Mountains. Here on soils ranging from slate to loess and marl the Riesling vine can yield wines that are as aristocratic as the region's famous estates. It accounts for 81% of the vineyard area; next is Spätburgunder with 9%.

This unique combination of natural and human factors makes the recent problems of the region hard to understand. Since the mid-1980s a number of famous estates with glorious traditions have experienced difficulties, several changing hands and one closing its doors forever (Schloss Groenesteyn). Poor quality has been the main problem of the big estates, most of whom have been overtaken by a handful of ambitious young winemakers with small family-run estates. Thankfully, the combination of press criticism and competition from less famous neighbours has shaken most of the region's large estates out of their slumbers. Slowly but surely the Rheingau is begining to prove again that its white wines can be amongst the greatest anywhere in the world.

The region can be divided into several sub-areas. The first of these sub-areas is the island of vines at Hochheim on the River Main between Wiesbaden and Frankfurt, whose vineyards yield big, intense wines. The relatively fertile soils of the towns and villages that lie close to the bank of the Rhine between Walluf and Winkel give the most typical Rheingau wines; elegant and subtle to the point of a slight austerity. High up, close to the Taunus Forest, the wines are more racy, with a pronounced minerally character from the soil. The wines from Johannisberg and Rüdesheim in the west share this general character, but are fuller-bodied. Assmannshausen is famous for its Spätburgunder red wine.

CLASSIFIED VINEYARDS

First-Class Sites

Assmannshauser Höllenberg The stony slate soil of the Höllenberg gives light, elegant Spätburgunder reds with a delicate perfume. Most important owners: August Kesseler, Hotel Krone, Staatsweingut.
Eltville Sonnenberg Medium-bodied Rieslings with ample fruit and supple acidity that drink well from an early age, but also mature well. Most important owners: J.B. Becker, von Simmern.
Erbacher Hohenrain/Steinmorgen Racy Rieslings with firm acidity that need several years to unfold and reveal their class. Most important owners: Jakob Jung, von Knyphausen.
Erbacher Marcobrunn/Schlossberg/Siegelsberg The famous Marcobrunn gives the most powerful of all Rheingau Rieslings, its heavy marl soil giving them rich fruit, a firm structure and long ageing potential. The neighbouring sites yield slightly lighter wines with a similar character. Most

important owners: August Eser, Schloss Reinhartshausen (Schlossberg monopoly), Schloss Schönborn, von Simmern, Staatsweingüter.

Geisenheimer Fuchsberg/Kläuserweg With their heavy marl soils these two sites give substantial Rieslings with assertive acidity that need several years' ageing to reveal their full depths. Most important owner: H.H. Eser.

Geisenheimer Rothenberg A century ago one of the Rheingau's most renowned vineyards, the Rothenberg's red slate soil gives lavishly aromatic wines, often with exotic fruit aromas, with a beautiful fruit-acidity balance. Most important owners: Schloss Schönborn, J. Wegeler (Deinhard).

Hallgartener Schönhell The fullest and most harmonious of Hallgarten wines come from this site. Even so, the acidity can be pronounced in young wines. Most important owners: Fürst Löwenstein, Fred Prinz, Querbach.

Hattenheimer Nussbrunnen/Wisselbrunnen/Mannberg The famous Nussbrunnen gives full, aromatic wines whose ample fruit often masks their acidity, while the wines from the Wisselbrunnen are sleeker, more elegant and minerally. The Mannberg site gives lighter, racy wines. Most important owners: Augsut Eser, Schloss Reinhartshausen, Balthasar Ress, Schloss Schönborn, von Simmern.

Hattenheimer Pfaffenberg Monopoly of Schloss Schönborn whose light sandy soil and excellent micro-climate yield full, aromatic Rieslings with elegant acidity.

Hochheimer Domdechaney/Kirchenstück The two most famous vineyards of Hochheim yield dramatically contrasting wines; the Domdechaney's heavy marl gives powerful earthy wines, while the lighter soil of the Kirchenstück gives elegant, refined wines. Most important owners: Franz Künstler, Schloss Schönborn, Staatsweingüter, Domdechant Werner.

Hochheimer Hölle/Königin-Victoria-Berg Situated directly on the bank of the Main these sites have an exceptional micro-climate and deep marl-clay soils. This combination gives powerful, highly structured Rieslings for long ageing. Most important owners: Hupfeld (Königin-Victoria-Berg monopoly), Franz Künstler, Schloss Schönborn, Domdenchant Werner.

Johannisberger Hölle/Klaus The Hölle's deep stony soil gives firm, substantial wines with excellent ageing potential; those from the Klaus are more filigree and elegant. Most important owners: Prinz von Hessen, Johannishof, von Mumm.

Kiedricher Gräfenberg/Wasseros The stony phyllite slate soils of these steeply sloping sites give rich, aromatic wines with a very elegant acidity and enormous ageing potential. Most important owner: Robert Weil.

Martinsthaler Langenberg Siuated next to the great Rauenthaler Berg, this site has similar soil and exposition. Elegant, racy wines that drink well from an early age.

Mittelheimer St Nikolaus The light soil and riverbank situation of this site results in ripe juicy wines with plenty of charm. Most important owners: August Eser, Hupfeld, J. Wegeler (Deinhard).

Oestricher Doosberg/Lenchen The deep loess soils of Oestrich result in full-bodied, juicy wines with a firm acidity structure; the Lenchen wines are slightly lighter and more elegant, the Doosberg wines the more powerful. Most important owners: August Eser, Peter Jakob Kuhn, Querbach, Schloss Schönborn, J. Wegeler (Deinhard).

Rauenthaler Baiken/Gehrn/Nonnenberg/Rothenberg/Wulfen The Rieslings from the Rauenthaler 'Berg' are amongst the most sought after of all Rheingaus. The phyllite slate and excellent exposition high above the Rhine result in extremely elegant, racy wines with pronounced 'spice' and great ageing potential. The finest of all are those from the Baiken, the most vivacious those from the Rothenberg. Most important owners: Georg Breuer (Nonnenberg monopoly), August Eser, von Simmern, Staatsweingüter.

Rüdesheimer Berg-Rottland/Roseneck/Schlossberg The steep vineyards of the Rüdesheimer Berg climb dramatically from the bank of the Rhine where its course turns north again. Here the Riesling grape gives rich, supple wines which none the less need long ageing to show their best. Most important owners: Georg Breuer, Johannishof, Josef Leitz, Dr Nägler, Balthasar Ress, Schloss Schönborn, Staatsweingüter.

Schloss Johannisberg Monopoly site of the eponymous estate. One of the greatest vineyard sites on the entire course of the Rhine. Its wines may not be the richest, but at their best they possess a sublime elegance.

Schloss Vollrads Set well back from the Rhine, this monopoly of the eponymous estate has long been renowned for late-harvest Rieslings with a piquant interplay of fruit and acidity.

Steinberg Planted in the 12th century by the monks of Eberbach, this legendary walled vineyard is comparable to the Clos Vougeot of Burgundy. At their best its wines are racy, intense and refined. Today it is a monopoly of the Staatsweingüter.

Wallufer Walkenberg This little-known site gives powerful, firm wines that need many years of ageing to show their best. Most important owners: J.B. Becker.

Winkeler Hasensprung/Jesuitengarten Directly next to the vineyards of Schloss Johannisberg, the Hasensprung gives similar but rather more succulent wines that develop more quickly. The Jesuitengarten wines from vines close to the river bank are sleeker and more racy. Most important owners: Fritz Allendorf, Ausgust Eser, Johannishof, J. Wegler (Deinhard).

Leading Rheingau Producers

Weingut Georg Breuer

Grabenstrasse 8, 65385 Rüdesheim. Owners: Bernhard and Heinrich Breuer, 50 acres. Classified sites: Rauenthaler Nonnenberg (monopoly), Rauenthaler Rothenberg, Rüdesheimer Berg Roseneck, Rüdesheimer Berg Rottland, Rüdesheimer Berg Schlossberg.

During the early 1990s winemaker Hermann Schmoranz and director Bernhard Breuer have made this one of the top Rheingau wine producers. A founding member of the Charta association of Rheingau estates, Bernhard Breuer has become an outspoken promoter of a vineyard classification for the Rheingau. At his own estate an internal classification was introduced long ago: only the best dry and dessert wines sites from the very top sites are sold with a vineyard designation. 'Montosa' is the second tier in the range of dry Rieslings, followed by wines sold under the names of Rüdesheim and Rauenthal.

Weingut Prinz von Hessen

65366 Geisenheim am Rhein. Owner: Landgraf von Hessen. 121 acres. Classified sites: Rüdesheimer, Berg Rottland; Geisenheimer-Fuchsberg, and Kläuserweg; Johannisberger, Hölle, Klaus; Winkeler, Jesuitengarten, Hasensprung; Eltviller and Sonnenberg.

The Count (Landgraf) of Hessen bought this estate in 1958 from the family of Kommerzienrat Krayer. Here, 88% of the vines are Riesling, with a little Spätburgunder. After a period of underperformance during the late 1980s and early 1990s new director Klaus Herrmann has made good progress in improving the quality of the regular wines. The Auslese and higher Prädikat dessert wines have always been impressive.

Weingut August Kesseler

Lorcherstrasse 16, 65385 Assmannshausen. Owner: August Kesseler. 34.5 acres. Classified sites: Assmannshausen, Höllenberg; Rüdesheimer Berg Schlossberg, Berg Roseneck, Berg Rottland.

A remarkable young estate which is producing an outstandingly successful, deep-coloured Spätburgunder matured in *barriques* and sophisticated Riesling with natural sweetness. The prices are high but the wines have been taken up enthusiastically by top-quality restaurants and private customers. The vineyards are planted 50% Spätburgunder and 40% Riesling.

Weingut Freiherr zu Knyphausen

Klosterhof Drais, 65346 Erbach. Owner: Gerko Freiherr zu Knyphausen. 50 acres. Classified sites: Erbacher Marcobrunn, Siegelsberg, Hohenrain, Steinmorgen; Hattenheimer Wisselbrunnen.

A former monastic estate of the Cistercians of Kloster Eberbach, brought in 1818 by the Freiherr's (Baron's) forebears. 92% is Riesling, 4% Spätburgunder and 4% Ehrenfelser. The property is run on traditional and personal lines, making full-flavoured wines, 70% dry or medium-dry. The quality here is such that lesser vintages in difficult years are almost unknown.

Weingut Franz Künstler

Weingut Franz Künstler / Gutsverwaltung Geheimrat Aschrott. Kirchstrasse 38, 65239 Hochheim. Owner: Gunter Künstler. 57 acres. Classified sites: Hochheimer Domdechaney, Hochheimer Hölle, Hochheimer Kirschenstück

The son of a Sudentenland German refugee who founded the family estate in 1965, Gunter Künstler is one of the most talented young winemakers on the entire Rhine. His concentrated, minerally dry Rieslings catapulted him to fame during the late 1980s and continue to win blind tastings. However, his less well known Auslese and higher Prädikat dessert wines also deserve the highest praise. Recently Gunter Künstler has almost tripled the size of his holdings by purchasing the renowned Aschrott estate. The 15th-century estate house of Aschrott has now become the headquarters for both estates, which will continue to be marketed separately. With substantial holdings in virtually all of Hochheim's first-class sites at his disposal, Gunter Künstler is now in a position to prove what his full capabilities are.

Weingut Josef Leitz

Theodor-Heuss-Strasse 5, 65385 Rüdesheim. Owners: the Leitz family. 9.5 acres. Classified sites: Rüdesheimer Berg Rottland, Rüdesheimer Berg Roseneck, Rüdesheimer Berg Schlossberg.

Since Johannes Leitz began making the wines at this estate during the late 1980s it has shot into the first rank of Rheingau producers. His low yields and minimalist winemaking result in Rieslings of great individuality and elegance. Finest are the dry wines from the Berg Rottland and the late-harvested, naturally sweet wines from the Berg Schlossberg.

Schloss Reinhartshausen

65346 Erbach. Owners: the Leibbrand family. Director: August Kesseler. 165 acres. Classified sites: Hohenrain, Steinmorgen; Hattenheimer Wisselbrunnen and Nussbrunnen; Rauenthaler-Wülfen.

For more than a century, until its purchase by the grocery magnate Willi Leibbrand in 1988, this estate was the property of the Prussian royal family. Today it is one of the few large Rheingau estates to consistently produce high quality Rieslings that live up to the region's reputation. Best of all are the powerful, aristocratic wines from the Erbacher Marcobrun and the racy Mosel-like wines from the Hattenheimer Wisselbrunnen. They are amongst the region's most expensive wines, but even the simplest wines from the estate are well made and typical. Sekt is an important speciality and amongst the best produced in the Rheingau. In spite of these successes, director August Kesseler (whose own estate is in Assmannshausen – q.v.) is determined to push standards still higher; a fine estate with great ambitions.

Freiherrlich Langwerth von Simmern'sches Rentamt

Langwerther Hof, Kirchgasse, 65343 Eltville. The present Baron Friedrich owns a property held by his family since 1464, now amounting to 74 acres. Classified sites: Erbacher Marcobrun; Hattenheimer Nussbrunnen, Mannberg and Rauenthaler Baiken and Rothenberg; Eltviller Sonnenberg.

The Gutshaus is the beautiful Renaissance Langwerther Hof in the ancient riverside centre of Eltville – one of the loveliest spots in the Rheingau. The richly heraldic (if scarcely legible) red label was one of the most reliable in Germany for classic Riesling, whether dry or sweet, balanced to age for years. Sadly standards have dropped badly in recent years and the current production is a shadow of what it was until 1990.

Weingut Robert Weil

Muhlberg 5, 65399 Kiedrich. Owner: Suntory Limited. Classified sites: Kiedricher Gräfenberg, Kiedricher Wasseros.

The historic Weil estate has been owned since 1988 by Japanese drinks giant Suntory, which made huge investments including more than doubling the estate's vineyard area and building the most modern winemaking facility in the region. Important as these steps were, it is the work of director Wilhelm Weil which was decisive in pushing the estate back to the forefront of the region. Its late-harvested Riesling Auslese, BA and TBA and Eiswein from the Kiedricher Gräfenberg are amongst the greatest wines of this style made in Germany. While the dry wines are of good quality, they do not begin to scale these heights. More impressive are the *halbtrocken* and naturally sweet Kabinett and Spätlese wines. The neo-Gothic estate house is one of the most charming in the region.

OTHER PRODUCERS

Weingut Fritz Allendorf Winkel. Ownesr: the Allendorf family. A very old Winkel wine-growing family, more recently established as a substantial estate with 112 acres, planted with nearly two-thirds Riesling. The biggest holding is 17 acres of Winkeler Jesuitengarten. The wines are light and generally dry or medium-dry.

Weingut Hans Barth 65347 Hattenheim. Owner: Norbert Barth. 25-acre estate is best known for its Sekt, including the excellent 'Ultra'. The still, generally dry, Rieslings are more variable.

Weingut Weinhandel J B Becker Rheinstrasse 5–6, 65396 Walluf. Owners: the Becker family (Johann-Josef and Maria). The Becker family of Walluf are well-known as brokers as well as growers, with a wine garden by the river. Their vineyards now amount to 27 acres including substantial holdings in the first-class Wallufer-Walkenberg, Rauenthaler Wülfen and Eltviller Sonnenberg. 81% is Riesling, 17% Spätburgunder (made into powerful dry red wine in Wallufer-Walkenberg) and 2% Müller-Thurgau. Becker specialities are dry Rieslings that have great character with remarkable keeping powers.

Verwaltung der Staatsweingüter Kloster Erbach

Schwalbacherstrasse 56–62, 65343 Eltville. Director: Dr Karl-Heinz Zerbe. 350 acres. Classified sites: Assmannshäuser Höllenberg; Rüdesheimer-Berg Schlossberg, Berg Rottland, Berg Roseneck; Erbacher Marcobrunn, Siegelsberg; Steinberger (monopoly); Rauenthaler Baiken, Gehrn, Wülfen; Eltviller, Sonnenberg; Hochheimer Domdechaney, Kirchenstück, Hölle. The Rheingau State Domain at Eltville is based on monastic vineyards which were ceded to the Duke of Nassau under Napoleon, thence to the Kingdom of Prussia and now to the State of Hessen, whose capital is nearby Wiesbaden.

For its ceremonial HQ the Domain has the magnificent and perfectly preserved Cistercian abbey of Kloster Eberbach (1135), in a wooded valley behind Hattenheim, and the most famous of its vineyards, the Steinberg, a walled 'clos' comparable to the Clos Vougeot (but unlike Vougeot still in one ownership). Kloster Eberbach is the scene of annual auctions of the wines of the Domain and certain of its distinguished neighbours; also home to the German Wine Academy, which runs regular courses for amateurs and professionals. It was here that the word 'Cabinet' was first used (for the vintage of 1712) to designate reserve-quality wine – a meaning totally altered by modern laws.

The estates are planted with 88% Riesling, 10% Spätburgunder, 2% others. Winemaking methods are extremely modern; there is more stainless steel than oak and wines are bottled very young.

From the mid-1970s this great estate's performance underwent a steady decline until the arrival of Dr Karl-Heinz Zerbe as director. With his first vintage – 1995 – he has put the estate back on course to regain its rightful position amongst the region's elite.

Weingut Adam Nass-Engelmann Hallgartenerplatz 2, 65375 Hallgarten. Owner: Karl Josef Nass. Classified sites: Hallgartener-Schönhell. A small estate of only about 16 acres, but producing Hallgarten wines of classic quality.

Weingut August Eser Friedensplatz 19. 65375 Oestrich. Owner: Joachim Eser. A family estate since 1759, now consisting of 23 acres. Classified sites: Oestricher Doosberg, Lenchen; Winkeler-Hasensprung; Hallgartener Schönhell; Hattenheimer Engelmannsberg; Wisselbrunnen; Rauenthaler-Gehrn and Rothenberg. The vineyards are planted with 96% Riesling, 4% Spätburgunder. Joachim Eser makes a full range from dry to sweet. He maintains a generally high standard in all styles but the estate needs a top vintage to really shine.

Weingut Ökonomierat J. Fischer Erben 65343 Eltville. Owner: Frau Fischer. A small fourth-generation property founded in 1880. Vineyards are planted with 90% Riesling. The Fischers' wines are outstanding models of conservative Rheingau taste, weighty and rich in flavour and made to keep a decade.

Weingut Joachim Flick 65439 Wicke. Owner: Reiner Flick. Reiner Flick makes some of the best wines from the eastern end of the Rheingau although he owns no vines in the top sites (of Hochheim). The emphasis is on fresh, crisp dry Riesling.

Hessische Forschungsanstalt für Wein-, Obst- und Gartenbau 65366 Geisenheim. The horticultural and viticultural departments of the Hessen Technical School have a total of 54 acres of vineyards. Their holdings include substantial parcels in the first-class sites Geisenheimer-Rothenberg, Kläuserweg, Mäuerchen and Fuchsberg. Today standards are good if unremarkable. Riesling dominates the wide range which includes many grapes seldom found in the region such as Gewürztraminer and Chardonnay.

Weingut Hupfeld Erben and Weingut Königin Victoriaberg Rheingaustrasse 113, 65375 Oestrich-Winkel. Owners: the Hupfeld family. 30 acres. Classified sites: Hochheimer Königin-Victoria-Berg (monopoly); Oestricher-Lenchen; Winkeler-Jesuitengarten and Hasensprung; Johannisberger-Hölle. Planted with 94% Riesling; the rest consists of Spätburgunder. Wine growers since 1907 and merchants before that. Since the 1940s the Hupfelds have established themselves as a well-known small estate, aiming for medium-dry balance, and regularly winning medals.

The Hupfeld family also own the well-known Königin Victoriaberg estate at Hochheim, where Queen Victoria stopped to watch the vintage on the lower slopes in 1850. The then owners, the Pabstmann family, were not slow to commemorate the visit, getting the Queen's permission to rename the vineyard after her, erecting a Gothic monument and designing the most tinselly (now quite irresistible) label. Deinhards, who sell the wine abroad, go to great lengths to maximize its quality. It is not Hochheim's finest, but full, soft, flowery and just what Queen Victoria might well have enjoyed. The label is printed in black and white for QbA wines, yellow and gold for Trocken wines and glorious Technicolor for QmP wines. The wines from the Königin-Victoria-Berg monopoly are usually the most impressive of the wide range.

Weingut Johannishof, Eser 65366 Johannisberg. Owner: Hans Hermann Eser. 46 acres. Einzellagen: Johannisberger-Hölle, Klaus, Winkeler-Jesuitengarten, Hasensprung and Gutenberg; Geisenheimer-Kläuserweg; Rüdesheimer Berg Rottland, Rüdesheimer Berg Roseneck. This estate is conspicuous on the road up to Johannisberg for its huge 18th-century wine press by the door. Herr Eser comes from an old growers' family and has made a reputation for racy and full-flavoured wines including the finest Johannisberg Rieslings. The deep cellars, 30 feet under the hill, are traditional; cold and damp with dark oval casks for maturing wine of character. The recent addition of 11 acres in Rüdesheim opens a new chapter in this fine estate's long history.

Weingut Graf von Kanitz Rheinstrasse 49, 65391 Lorch. Owner: Count Carl Albrecht von Kanitz. 42 acres. Classified sites: Lorcher, Krone, Pfaffenwies. An ancient family property on steep slopes at the northeastern extremity of the region. The inheritance, dating from the 13th century, includes the earliest Renaissance building of the area, the Hilchenhaus in Lorch, now a fine Weinstube.

Weingut Jakob Jung 65346 Erbach Owner: Ludwig Jung. During recent years, the well-crafted, generally dry Rieslings from Ludwig Jung have attracted ever more attention. They offer rare value for money in an expensive region. Best are the elegant wines from the first-class Erbacher Hohenrain.

Weingut Robert König Landhaus Kenner, 65385 Rüdesheim-Assmannshausen. Owner: Robert König. 14 acres. Classified sites: Assmannshäuser-Höllenberg, Rüdesheimer

Berg Schlossberg. An estate that is 99% Spätburgunder, offering cask-matured wines that are traditional in style, but possess plenty of character.

Weingut Krone Rheinuferstrasse 10, 65385 Assmannshausen. Owner: Dr Irene Hufnagel-Ullrich. 11 acres. Einzellagen: Assmannshausener, Höllenberg; Rüdesheimer Berg Schlossberg. The estate of probably the most famous hotel on the Rhine, the 'Krone'. Since the arrival of young winemaker Peter Penaho in 1995, the Spätburgunder red wines have begun to challenge those of neighbour August Kesseler (q.v.).

Weingut Peter Jakob Kühn 65375 Oestrich. Owner: Peter and Angela Kühn. This dry wine specialist maintains a high standard. Full fruit and harmonious acidity are the qualities to be found right through the range. Recently, also impressive late-harvested wines.

Weingut Hans Lang Rheinallee 6, 65347 Hattenheim. 37 acres. Classified sites: Hattenheimer-Nussbrunnen, Wisselbrunnen, Hallgartener and Schönhell. A nurseryman, merchant and (since 1959) grower who has expanded rapidly. Hans Lang's style is robust with plenty of character and acidity. 75% of his wines are Rieslings and 9% Spätburgunders, matured in *barriques*. Best are the Charta Rieslings.

Weingut Dr Heinrich Nägler Friedrichstrasse 22, 65385 Rüdesheim. Owner: Dr Heinrich Nägler. A distinguished estate specializing in fine Rüdesheimer since the 19th century. 20 acres. Classified sites: Rüdesheimer-Berg Rottland, Berg Schlossberg, Berg Roseneck. Though this estate has a good reputation the quality has been less than spectacular in recent years. Dry Rieslings make up the majority of the production.

Weingut Prinz 65375 Hallgarten, Owner: Sabine Prinz. Fred Prinz has made some impressive dry and naturally sweet Rieslings at his wife's miniature wine estate during the 1990s; a star in the making.

Weingut Querbach 65375 Winkel. Owners: the Querbach family. The Querbachs maintain a solid standard right through their wide range of Rieslings from Oestrich, Winkel and Hallgarten.

Balthasar Ress 65346 Hattenheim 3. Owner: Stefan B. Ress. Some 74 acres. Classified sites: Rüdesheimer Berg Rottland, Berg Schlossberg; Geisenheimer Kläusweg; Hattenheimer-Wisselbrunnen, Nussbrunnen, Engelmannsberg. A century-old family firm of growers and merchants (under the name Stefan B. Ress). In 1978 Ress rented the 10-acre Schloss Reichartshausen, originally a Cistercian property but latterly rather neglected.

Each year a modern artist is commissioned to paint a label for a selected Auslese of top quality (e.g. Hattenheimer Wisselbrunnen, Oestricher Doosberg). This estate's wines are unashamedly modern in style, vinified in stainless steel and bottled early for maximum freshness. Quality is rather variable; most wines are best drunk young.

Weingut Jakob Riedel Taunusstrasse 1, 65375 Hallgarten. Owner: Wolfgang Riedel. 7.4 acres. Classified sites: Hallgartener, Hendelberg Schönhell. A 17th-century property making full-bodied dry wines with good acidity, bottled very young and intended for long maturing. 100% Riesling.

Schloss Johannisberg Fürst von Metternich-Winneburg'sche Domäne. 65366 Johannisberg. Owners: the Oetker family. 86.5 acres. The most famous estate of the Rhine, whose name is often used to designate the true Riesling vine. Its first planting is credited to Charlemagne; the first monastery was built on its hilltop commanding the Rhine in 1100; full flowering came in the 18th century under the Prince-Abbot of Fulda. Its vintage of 1775 was the first to be gathered overripe (the Abbot's messenger having arrived late with permission to pick): the term Spätlese and the appreciation of noble rot are said to have started with this incident.

The estate was secularized under Napoleon and presented in 1816, after the Treaty of Vienna, by the Austrian Emperor to his Chancellor, Prince Metternich, for his diplomatic services. In 1942 the Johannisberg monastery-castle (but not its cellar) was destroyed in an air raid. It is now totally rebuilt. The vineyard, in one block on the ideally sloping skirts of the castle hill, is planted entirely in Riesling and is one of the region's finest sites. Technically it is an Ortsteil – a local entity which needs no Einzellage name.

At their best the wine Schloss Johannisberg's are extraordinarily firm in structure, concentrated and long-lived, with every quality of classic Riesling grown on an exceptional site. I have drunk an 1870 which at a century old was still vigorous and bore traces of its original flavour. Recent wines, like those of several of the great lordly estates, have shown signs of commercialization.

Today only the late-harvested Auslese and higher Prädikat wines live up to the estate's great name.

Domänenweingut Schloss Schönborn Hauptstrasse 53, 65347 Hattenheim. Owner: Dr Karl Graf von Schönborn-Wiesentheid. 123.5 acres. Classified sites: Hattenheim–Pfaffenberg (sole owner), Nusbrunnen, Engelmannsberg, Erbacher Marcobrunn; Rauenthaler Baiken; Oestericher Doosberg; Winkeler Hasensprung; Johannisberger Klaus; Geisenheimer, Rothenberg and Kläuserweg; Rüdesheimer-Berg Schlossberg, Berg Rottland; Hochenheimer Domdechaney, Kirchenstück, Hölle.

The biggest privately owned estate in the Rheingau, since 1349 in the hands of a family of great political and cultural influence. The present owner lives in his Franconian castles of Pommersfelden and Wiesentheid.

Critics are divided over the recent performance of Schönborn wines. Some have described them as the 'Rubens of the Rheingau', while others have found them too heavy and clumsy. They come in vast variety from the central Marcobrunn to Lorch at the extreme west of the region and Hochheim at the extreme east. Since the arrival of director Günter Thies in 1995 signs of improvement have been in evidence, but there is still a long way to go before Schönborn matches its performance of the decades up to '71.

Schloss Vollrads 65375 Oestrich-Winkel. Owner: Count Matuschka-Greiffenclau. Also rents and manages Weingut Fürst Löwenstein. Director: Count Erwein Matuschka-Greiffenclau. 44.5 acres. Einzellagen: Hallgartener-Schönhell, Hendelberg and Jungfer.

Erwein Matuschka-Greiffenclau, who presides over this magnificent old estate in the hills a mile above Winkel, is the 27th in a line of Greiffenclaus who have owned estates in Winkel since at least 1100. Their original 'Grey House' in Winkel, the oldest stone-built dwelling in Germany, is now a wine-restaurant. In about 1300 the family built the castle, whose great tower symbolizes their estate, accepted as an Ortsteil, a separate entity which uses no commune or Einzellage name. 100% Riesling, of the old Rheingau strain that gives the 'raciest', relatively light but very long-lived wines. Schloss Vollrads specializes in dry wines with as little residual sugar as possible. On average about half the production of some cases is QmP wine, Kabinett or better.

Since 1979 the estate has rented the Weingut Fürst Löwenstein, a 42-acre neighbouring princely estate in Hallgarten, which produces relatively riper, mellower and more aromatic wines than the austere Vollrads style. After a difficult period during the late 1980s and early 1990s, the 1995 vintage saw signs of a return to form.

Weingut Troitzsch Haus Schöneck, Bächergrund 12, 65391 Lorch. Owner: The Troitzsch-Pusinelli family. 9 acres. Classified sites: Lorcher Kapellenberg, Krone, Pfaffenwies.

This estate, under the resolute hand of Otto Troitzsch, made fully fermented wines for over 40 years. To this day it remains true to his principles selling only bone-dry wines to loyal private customers.

Gutsverwaltung Geheimrat J Wegeler Friedenplatz 9, 65375 Oestrich-Winkel. 138 acres. Classified sites: Oestricher-Lenchen, Doosberg and Klosterberg, Winkeler Hasensprung and Jesuitengarten; Johannisberger Hölle; Geisenheimer-Rothenberg, Kläuserweg; Rüdesheimer, Berg Rottland, Berg Schlossberg and Berg Roseneck.

The substantial Rheingau estate of the Koblenz merchant house of Deinhard, assembled by Geheimer Rat (counsellor) Wegeler, a Deinhard partner and cousin, a century ago. 99% is Riesling. Almost a third of the estate is on very steep slopes. The average production is 40,000 cases.

Deinhards are known for their old-fashioned devotion to quality: Norbert Holderrieth is currently in charge. The Wegeler wines are true individuals; the best (especially from Oestricher Lenchen, Winkeler Hasensprung, Geisenheimer Rothenberg and the vineyards on the Rüdesheimer Berg) are often long-lived classics. Eisweins are a house speciality.

Altogether one of the biggest and most reliable Rheingau producers. The dry Spätlese wine, Geheimrat 'J', is much admired in Germany.

Domdechant Werner'sches Weingut Rathausstrasse 30, 65234 Hochheim. 30 acres. Classified sites: Hochheimer-Domdechaney, Kirchenstück, Hölle. The Werner family bought this superbly sited manor, overlooking the junction of the Rhine and Main, from the Duke of York in 1780. The buyer's son, Dr Franz Werner, was the famous Dean (Domdechant) of Mainz who saved the cathedral from destruction by the French. The same family (now called Michel) still owns and runs the estate, making some of the most serious, full-flavoured Hochheimers from the mingled soils of the old river terraces, sloping fully south.

Traditional barrel-ageing makes essentially dry but long-flavoured and long-lived wines. 97% are Riesling.

Weingut Freiherr von Zwierlein
Schloss Kosakenberg, Bahnstrasse 1, 65366 Geisenheim. Owner: Frau Gisela Wegeler. The Schloss, built by the Prince-Bishop of Mainz, took its name from a Cossack regiment in Napoleon's time. The present property is about 30 acres. After a period of poor performance during the late 1980s and early 1990s recent vintages have shown that winemaker Herr Decker-Horst is capable of making serious dry Rieslings.

NAHE

The River Nahe (the 'a' is long) is a tributary of the Rhine, with which it has its confluence at Bingen. The best Riesling wines from its 11,500 acres of vineyards have long been recognized by experts and connoisseurs as belonging to the finest which Germany has to offer. However, the boundaries of the region were finally fixed in 1971. As a result the name of the region is one known to rather few people either at home or abroad.

Since the Nahe's vineyards lie between those of the Mosel-Saar-Ruwer and the Rheingau the conventional way of describing Nahe wines is as being transitional between Mosel and Rhine; some say specificaly between Saar and Rheingau. This is true of the weight and balance, body and structure of the fine wines of the Middle Nahe; they do have the 'nerve', the backbone, of the Saar with some of the meat of the weightiest more densely flavoured Rheingau. The volcanic soil, however, adds something quite unique; to me the great Nahe wines often have a delicate hint of blackcurrant with delicious and fascinating mineral undertones. In their delicacy yet completeness they make hypnotic sipping, far into the night.

The greatest and most renowned vineyards of the Nahe lie in the rocky, winding strength of the valley upstream from Bad Kreuznach, particularly those of Niederhausen, Norheim, Traisen and Schlossböckelheim. Their wines frequently achieve that miraculous balancing act between ripeness and freshness of which only the Riesling grape is capable. Further upstream, where the valley is wider and more gently undulating Monzingen has the best sites. Bad Kreuznach's wines come from heavier, more fertile soils, and are consequently more generous and juicy. In years with hot summers they can be bombastic; in less extreme years the epitome of charm and harmony. Downstream towards the Nahe's confluence with the Rhine the landscape once again becomes punctuated with cliffs and steep slopes to which vines cling. Here the wines have similar minerally character to those of the Middle Nahe, but are fuller and more imposing.

CLASSIFIED VINEYARDS

First-Class Sites

Altenbamberger Rotenberg This steep site with reddish rhyolite soil yields juicy, aromatic Rieslings with supple acidity. Most important owners: Statliche Weinbaudomäne.
Dorsheimer Burgberg/Goldloch/Pittermännchen The red rotliegendes soil of the Goldloch and Burgberg gives full Rieslings with apricot fruit and a firm structure, while the grey slate of the Pittermännchen yields sleek, racy wines that possess an extraordinary resemblance to fine Mosel Rieslings. Most important owner: Schlossgut Diel.
Kreuznacher Brückes/Kahlenberg/Krotenpfühl Bad Kreuznach's finest vineyards all enjoy very sheltered positions in the outskirts of the town. The deep loam soils overlying rotliegendes sub-soil result in rich, fleshy wines. Most important owners: August Anheuser, Paul Anheuser, Anton Finkenauer, Carl Finkenauer, von Plettenberg.
Langenlonsheimer Rothenberg/Löhrer Berg The loam and rotliegendes soils here give medium-bodied Rieslings full of ripe fruit that drink well from an early age. Most important owners: Willi Schweinhardt, Wilhelm Sitzius, Tesch.
Monzinger Frühlingsplätzchen/Halenberg These steep sloping sites have contrasting soils. The Frühlingsplätzchen is rotliegendes giving more immediately appealing, supple wines, while the slate of the Halenberg gives very elegant, racy Rieslings. Most important owners: Paul Anhäuser, Emrich Schönleber.
Münsterer Dautenpflänzer / Kapellenberg / Pittersberg The graceful sweep of these excellent vineyards can be perfectly viewed from the A61 Autobahn as it crosses the Nahe. The mixture of slate and rotliegendes soils on these sites gives intensely aromatic, racy Rieslings, while those from the Dautenpflänzer posess the most power, and the Pittersberg wines are the most elegant. Most important owner: Kruger Rumpf.
Niederhäuser Felsensteyer/Kerz/Klamm/Rosenheck Though these are not the greatest of Niederhausen's vineyards, they none the less give sophisticated, racy Rieslings with a strong minerally character from the porphyry soil. Most important owners: Crusius, Mathern, Jakob Schneider, Staatliche Weinbaudomäne.

Niederhäuser Hermannsberg/Oberhäuser Brücke
These sites cover a single slope with southwesterly exposure and a stony porphyry-based soil. They are renowned for intense, minerally Rieslings. Most important owners: Dönnhoff (Brücke monopoly), Staatliche Weinbaudomäne (Hermmansberg monopoly).

Niederhäuser Hermannshöhle Since the Prussian classification of the Nahe vineyards (published in map form in 1901) the Hermannshöhle has been regarded as the greatest vineyard on the Nahe. Perfect exposure and an extremely stony soil composed of a complex mix of all the local soil types results in Riesling wines with the highest elegance and aromatic complexity. Most important owners: Dönnhoff, Jakob Schneider, Wilhelm Sitzius, Staatliche Weinbaudomäne.

Norheimer Delchen/Kafels/Kirscheck Extremely steep terraced vineyards, with stony porphyry soils, these are the least well known top sites of the Middle Nahe, yet they have the potential to challenge Niederhausen and Schlossböckelheim. Most important owners: Crusius, Dönnhoff, Lotzbeyer, Mathern, Jakob Schneider, Staatsweingut Bad Kreuznach.

Roxheimer Berg/Birkenberg/Höllenpfad/Hüttenberg / Mühlenberg To the northwest of Bad Kreuzheim the best sites of Roxheim in fact lie outside the Nahe Valley, but the combination of a southerly exposure and rotliegendes soil gives ripe, aromatic wines of elegant acidity. Most important owners: Paul Anheuser, Carl Finkenauer, Prinz zu Salm-Dalberg (Schloss Wallhausen).

Schlossböckelheimer Felsenberg/Kupfergrube The two great Schlossböckelheim sites stand side by side, but yield contrasting wines. The Felsenberg has been cultivated for centuries; its very stony melaphry soil gives richly aromatic Rieslings with a silky acidity. The Kupfergrube vineyard was created out of a former copper mine in 1902 and yields sleeker, intensely racy wines which have vast ageing potential. Most important owners: Crusius, Dönnhoff, Hehner-Kilz, Staatliche Weinbaudomäne.

Schlossböckelheimer In den Felsen/Königsfels The wines seldom match those of Schlossböckelheim's greatest sitess, they too give racy Rieslings with pronounced minerally character. Most important owners: Paul Anheuser, Hehner-Kilz.

Traiser Bastei/Rotenfels The famous Bastei vineyard lies between the bank of the Nahe and the 600-foot high mass of the Rotenfels cliffs. Extremely stony porphyry soil gives powerful, pungently minerally wines. The neighbouring Rotenfels site gives similar, but less extreme wines. Most important owners: Crusius, Staatliche Weinbaudomäne.

Wallhäuser Felseneck/Johannisberg/Pastorenberg Commanding a sheltered position high up the Gräfenbach Valley these steep vineyards with their slate-rich soils give remarkably Mosel-like Rieslings. Most important owner: Schloss Wallhausen.

Wintzenheimer Rosenheck/Bretzenheimer Pastorei These adjoining sites give similar, but slightly more elegant wines to the top vineyards of Bad Kreuznach. Most important owner: von Plettenberg.

Other Classified Vineyards

Ebernburger Schlossberg, Guldentaler Hipperich, Laubenheimer Karthäuser/St Remigiusberg, Münsterer Felseneck, Oberhäuser Leistenberg.

Leading Nahe Producers

Weingut Hans Crusius & Sohn

Hauptstrasse 2, 55595 Traisen. Owner: Dr Peter Crusius. 31 acres. Classified sites: Niederhauser Felsensteyer, Norheimer Kirscheck, Schlossböckelheimer Felsenberg, Traiser Bastei, Traiser Rotenfels. The Grand Seigneur of the Nahe wine industry, Hans Crusius, slowly handed over control of the family estate to his son, Dr Peter Crusius, from the late 1980s. Although the quality is not yet back at the high level maintained into the 1980s, the Rieslings are very clean and quite beautifully crafted.

Schlossgut Diel

55452 Burg Layen, Kreis Bad Kreuznach. Owner: Armin Diel. 37 acres. Einzellagen: Burg Layener-Schlossberg, Rothenberg, Hölle and Johannisberg; Dorsheimer-Goldloch, Honigberg, Pittermännchen and Klosterpfad. Classified sites: Dorsheimer Burgberg, Dorsheimer Goldloch, Dorsheimer Pittermännchen. Winegrower, wine journalist, restaurant critic and TV presenter, the multi-talented Armin Diel is one of the outstanding personalities on the German wine scene today. His substantial holdings in all three of Dorsheim's first-class vineyards makes this the leading estate of the Lower Nahe. Dry and late-harvested Rieslings with natural sweetness form the bulk of the production, although the new-oak-aged Weissburgunder, Grauburgunder and 'Victor' (a powerful blend of the two) also enjoy a high reputation. Schlossgut Diel's Eisweins hold the price record for young Nahe wines at more than DM 1,000. With the appointment of the talented young Martin Franzen as winemaker, the estate's wines have taken yet another step forward.

Weingut Hermann Dönnhof

Bahnhofstrasse 11, 55585 Oberhausen. Owner: Helmut Dönnhof. 25 acres. Einzellagen: Bad Kreuznacher Mollenbrunnen; Niederhausener Hermannshöhle; Oberhausener-Brücke (solely owned), Felsenberg, Kieselberg and Leistenberg; Schlossböckelheimer Felsenberg. Classified sites: Niederhäuser Hermannshöhle, Norheimer Dellchen, Norheimer Kirscheck, Oberhäuser Brücke (monopoly), Oberhäuser Leistenberg, Schlossböckelheimer Felsenberg. Today Helmut Dönnhof's Rieslings are the most perfect expressions of the great vineyards of the Middle Nahe. Behind his reserved manner lies a fanatical commitment to quality and a remarkable natural talent for winemaking. Virtually every barrel from this cellar (and wood is an article of faith for Dönnhoff) is bottled separately, resulting in a confusingly wide range. However, such is the consistency of high quality this hardly matters. It is difficult to pick out highlights from this embarassment of riches.

The most powerful wines are those from the Brücke, while those from the Hermannshöhle represent the ultimate in elegance and complexity. Dönnhoff's Eisweins are also amongst Germany's best.

Weingut Emreich-Schönleber

Naheweinstrasse 10a, 55569 Monzingen. Owner: Hannelore and Werner Schönleber. 30 acres. Classified sites: Monzinger Frühlingsplätzchen, Monzinger Halenberg.

Since the late 1980s the Schönlebers' estate has been the rising star producer of the Nahe region. Their Rieslings in both the dry and naturally sweet styles are very pure and expressive, with vibrant fruit and racy acidity. The wines from the Halenberg are the more refined, those from the Frühlingsplätzchen more generous. Also impressive dry Grauburgunder.

Weingut Mathern

Winzerstrasse 7, 55585 Niederhausen. Owner: Helmut Mathern. 21 acres. Classified sites: Niederhäuser Kerz, Niederhäuser Rosenheck, Norheimer Delchen.

Through a great deal of hard work and an almost obsessive attention to detail Helmut Mathern has succeeded in making his estate the number one in Niederhausen. The richly aromatic Rieslings, the majority of which are vinified with some natural sweetness, are of a consistently high standard. Excellent Niederhäusen Rieslings from the good vintages of the early 1990s. With the recent addition of vines in the Norheimer Delchen Mathern has the possibility to push quality even higher. This is an estate to watch.

Verwaltung der Staatlichen Weinbaudomänen

Niederhausen-Schlossböckelheim, 55585 Niederhausen. Director: Kurt Gabelmann. The vineyards total 89 acres. Classified sites: Schlossböckelheimer Kupfergrube and Felsenberg; Niederhäuser-Hermannshöhle, Kertz, Hermannsberg (solely owned), Steinberg; Traiser Bastei; Altenbamberger Rotenberg; Ebernburger Schlossberg.

The Nahe State Domain, which many consider to be the finest in Germany, was founded in 1902 by the Kaiser and King of Prussia, Wilhelm II. Its foundation pioneered viticulture on the steep slopes above the now-famous site of a former copper mine (the Kupfergrube) to grow Riesling. By 1920 its wines were acknowledged to be superlative. After a period of rather erratic performance at the beginning of the 1990s a radical restructuring was undertaken and Kurt Gabelmann was appointed director. Since then quality has improved steadily and the estate looks to be on course to regain its position amongst the top producers of the Nahe.

For a demonstration of the subtlety and finesse of great German wine, ranging from fine-drawn floweriness to sumptuous elegance, this estate's wines can rarely be beaten. Schlossböckelheimers are the most stylish and delicate: Niederhäusers fuller and more seductive; Traisers big, ripe and long-lived; the wines from the Lower Nahe full-bodied and spicy. The State Domain's label is the black eagle of Prussia.

OTHER PRODUCERS

Weingut Paul Anheuser Strombergerstrasse 15–19, 55545 Bad Kreuznach. Owner: Rudolf Peter Anheuser. The present estate consists of 150 acres. Classified sites: Kreuznacher-Brückes, Kahlenberg, Krötenpfuhl; Schlossböckelheimer-Felsenberg, In den Felsen, Königsfels; Niederhäuser-Felsensteyer; Norheimer-Dellchen and Kafels; Roxheimer-Berg and Höllenpfad; Mönzinger Halenberg. A family concern tracing its origins to 1627. Rudolf Anheuser, the occupier in the 1880s, was the first to introduce Riesling to the Nahe. His descendants stress variety and vineyard character in their wines, which mature in wood in deep, cool cellars. The aim is freshness and fruit. The vineyard is 73% Riesling, 11% Grauburgunder and Weissburgunder, 16% other varieties. In recent years the estate has failed to maintain the high standards set during the 1970s and 1980s.

Weingut Carl Finkenauer Salinenstrasse 60, 55543 Bad Kreuznach. Owners: Frau Elisabeth Finkenauer-Trummert and Hans-Georg Trummert-Finkenauer. 74 acres. Classified sites: Kreuznacher-Brückes; Winzenheimer Rosenheck; Roxheimer Mühlenberg. The sixth generation of the family runs this estate in the attractive spa area of Bad Kreuznach. The vineyards are 55% Riesling, 8% Müller-Thurgau, 7% Scheurebe, 5% Silvaner, 5% Weissburgunder, 5% Grauburgunder, 5% Spätburgunder, 10% other varieties. The quality is rather variable but the successful wines have plenty of character and vigour.

Weingut Hahnmühle 67822 Mannweiler-Cölln. Owners: Peter and Martina Linxweiler. 15 acres. The Linxweilers are best known for sleek, steely dry Rieslings from the rocky vineyards of the Alsenz Valley. A Riesling-Traminer from old vines in the Cöllner Rosenberg site is a speciality.

Weingut Hehner-Kilz 55596 Waldböckelheim. Owners: Georg and Helmut Hehner, 22.5 acres. As well as running one of the best country inns in the Nahe, the Hehners produce slightly erratic, but often good dry and naturally sweet Rieslings from the top sites of Schlossböckelheim.

Weingut Kruger-Rumpf Rheinstrasse 47, 55424 Münster-Sarmsheim. Owner: Stefan Rumpf. 35 acres. Classified sites: Dorsheimer-Burgberg and Goldloch; Münster-Sarmsheimer Dautenpflänzer, Kapellenberg, Pittersberg. This estate has become well-known in Germany for firm, dry wines of great style from top sites. 62% Riesling, 13% Silvaner, plus Müller-Thurgau, Weissburgunder and Spätburgunder and, as a sign of the owner's youthful exuberance, Chardonnay. All the wines can be tasted in the estate's excellent wine restaurant that offers some of the best regional cooking in the Nahe.

Weingut Adolf Lotzbeyer 67824 Feilbingert, Owner: Adolf Lotzbeyer. 15 acres. Lotzbeyer's impressive Riesling and Scheurebe dessert wines have attracted much praise. His Kabinett and Spätlese wines with natural sweetness can also impress, but the dry wines are rather rustic.

Weingut Bürgermeister Willi Schweinhardt Nachf
Heddesheimerstrasse 1–3, 55450 Langenlonsheim. Owner:
Wilhelm and Axel Schweinhardt. 59 acres. Classified sites:
Langenlonsheimer, Rothenberg, Löhrer Berg. A very old
family of growers, producing medium-sweet Rieslings and
Scheurebes as well as Weissburgunder and Grauburgunder
dry wines with up to 13% alcohol. The grapey, light and
charming wines are best drunk quite young.

Weingut Reichsgraf von Plettenberg Winzenheimerstrasse,
55545 Bad Kreuznach. Owner: Egbert von Plettenberg. 85
acres. Classified sites: Bretzenheimer, Pastorei; Winzenheimer-
Rosenheck; Kreuznacher-Brückes, Kahlenberg; Roxheimer,
Berg and Mühlenberg. A family domain since the 18th
century, known by this name since 1912. Now a modern
winery with little romantic appeal but well-placed vineyards,
and a wide selection of some of the best vineyards around
Kreuznach. The grapes are 67% Riesling, 20% Weissburgunder
and 13% others.

Prinz zu Salm-Dalberg'sches Weingut Schloss Wallhausen,
55595 Wallhausen. Owner: Prinz zu Salm-Salm. 23 acres.
Classified sites: Wallhauser-Johannisberg, Mühlenberg and
Felseneck and Roxheimer Berg. The estate of the VDP wine
estate association's national president Michael Prinz zu Salm-
Salm lies in a little-known idyllicly unspoilt corner of the
Nahe region. Today only the Rieslings (65% of the vineyard
area) from the best sites are sold with a vineyard
designation, the remainder being marketed under the

'Schloss Wallhausen' name. Dry Silvaner and Spätburgunder
rosé are important specialities. The wines are sleek and racy
with good ageing potential.

Staatsweingut Bad Kreuznach Rüdesheimerstrasse 68,
55545 Bad Kreuznach. 50 acres. Classified sites:
Kreuznacher, Kahlenberg; Norheimer, Kafels. Founded in
1900 as the provincial wine school; now owned by the State
of Rheinland-Pfalz and regarded as one of the best research
and educational stations in Germany. Its vineyards are
concentrated in Kreuznach and Norheim and have been
considerably restructured in recent years. The arrival of a
new team in charge of the viticulture, winemaking and
marketing has brought about a more dramatic improvement
in quality from the mid-1990s.

Weingut Schmidt 67823 Obermoschel, Owners: the Schmidt
family. 47 acres. The Schmidts run the largest estate in the
Alsenz Valley. Impressive Rieslings with natural sweetness.

Weingut Wilhelm Sitzius 55450 Langenlonsheim, Owners:
Sonja and Wilhelm Sitzius, 30 acres. Quality here is erratic,
but the best Rieslings from holdings in first-class sites that
include the Niederhäuser Hermannshöhle can be very good.

Weingut Steitz 55450 Langenlonsheim, Owners: Anni and
Hermann Steitz, 11 acres. The most southerly estate in the
Nahe produces, light, fruity Rieslings in both dry and
naturally sweet styles.

RHEINHESSEN

Anonymity behind the *nom de verre* of Liebfraumilch is
the fate of most Rheinhessen wine. In volume terms
production is dominated by soft, gently flowery Müller-
Thurgau, blunt rustic Silvaner and superficial, spicy wines
from new varieties. Only 9% of the 65,000-acre vineyard is
Riesling, concentrated in a few outstanding sites. The most
important of these lie around Nackenheim, Nierstein and
Oppenheim, just south of Mainz; the rather unluckily named
'Rhine Front'. The steep vineyards here give some of
Germany's richest Rieslings; wines with the body and spice
to take on the best of Alsace and Austria. In Bingen, at the

region's northwestern extremity, vineyards with a similar
quality potential yield more restrained classical Rieslings.

In the sea of vines covering the hill country that forms the
bulk of Rheinhessen are good vineyards which can yield
good dry Riesling, Weissburgunder, Grauburgunder and
traditional dry Silvaner. Efforts to give these wines more
profile and to distinguish them from the mass-produced
ones, especially the 'Rheinhessen Selektion' programme, are
being made. However, the success of a handful of dedicated
producers on the Rhine Front and in the 'Hinterland' is
doing just as much to change the region's image.

CLASSIFIED VINEYARDS

First-Class Sites

Binger Scharlachberg Elegant, refined Rieslings from the
Taunus quarzite soil of this terraced, south-facing site. Most
important owner: Villa Sachsen (Prinz zu Salm-Dalberg).

Nackenheimer Rothenberg The northern tip of the 'Roter
Hang', precipitously steep site with stony rotliegendes soil
and excellent exposure giving some of the most seductively

aromatic and longest-living Rieslings on the entire Rhine.
Virtually a monopoly of the Gunderloch estate.

Niersteiner Brudersberg Monopoly site of the Heyl zu
Herrnsheim estate. Steep slopes, rotliegendes soil and perfect
south exposition make for wines with richness and elegance.

Niersteiner Heiligenbaum Only a small part of this site is
classified due to the unremarkable loamy soil which
dominates here. The norm is charming, mid-weight wines
that drink well from an early age. Most important owners:
Heinrich Braun, Guntrum.

Niersteiner Hipping Arguments rage about the merit of this site. However, all are agreed that the ripe pineapple aroma typical of its wines make them extremely attractive from an early age. Most important owners: St Antony, Gunderloch, Heyl zu Herrnsheim, Georg Albrecht Schneider, Seebrich, J. u. H.A. Strub, Wehrheim.

Niersteiner Oelberg With the deepest soil of all Nierstein's top sites the Oelberg gives powerful wines that need a long time to reveal their depths, but are also very long living. Most important owners: St Antony, Heinrich Braun, Guntrum, Heyl zu Herrnsheim, WG Nierstein, Rappenhof, Georg Albrecht Schneider, Seebrich, Dr Alex Senfter, Georg Albrecht Schneider, J. u. H.A. Strub, Wehrheim.

Niersteiner Orbel This steeply sloping, stony vineyard to the west of Nierstein gives wines that combine mineral intensity with the raciest acidity of all Nierstein wines. Most important owners: St Antony, Heinrich Braun, Georg Albrecht Schneider, J.u.H.A. Strub.

Niersteiner Pettenthal Although enjoying identical exposition to the Nackenheimer Rothenberg the Pettenthal's shallow soil results in quicker developing Rieslings with a very pronounced minerally character. Most important owners: St Antony, Balbach, Heinrich Braun, Heyl zu Herrnsheim, Rappenhof, Georg Albrecht Schneider, J. u. H.A. Strub.

Oppenheimer Herrnberg/Kreuz/Sackträger The heavy marl soil of these sites gives completely different wines from Nierstein's top sites. Here even the Riesling gives weighty, corpulent wines with a firm underlying acidity. They tend to be heavy and charmless if not vinified expertly. Most important owners: Guntrum, Carl Koch, Kühling-Gillot, Domäne Oppenheim, Rappenhof, Dr Alex Senfter.

Leading Rheinhessen Producers

Weingut Gunderloch

Carl-Gunderloch Platz 1, 55299 Nackenheim. Owners: Agnes and Fritz Hasselbach. 60 acres. Classified sites: Nackenheimer Rothenberg (Gunderloch), Niersteiner Pettenthal (Balbach), Niersteiner Oelberg, Niersteiner Hipping.
Since the late-1980s the Hasselbachs' concentrated, explosively aromatic Rieslings from the great Nackenheimer Rothenberg vineyard have shot them to international fame. Their late-harvested Auslese and higher Prädikat wines are amongst the finest in the whole of Germany and the world knows it; demand far exceeds supply. Year in year out, the almost dry 'Jean Baptiste' Riesling Kabinett is a model example of this classic German wine style. In the dry style their 'basic' Gunderloch Riesling already sets a high standard, though. Both are excellent food wines. With the acquisition of the Balbach estate in 1996 the company doubled in size. Following restructuring the Balbach wines will continue to be vinified separately in Nierstein, but in the Gunderloch style.

Weingut Freiherr Heyl zu Herrnsheim

Mathildenhof, Langgasse 3, 55283 Nierstein. Owners: Isa von Weymarn, the Ahr family, Valckenberg. 50 acres. Classified sites: Niersteiner Hipping, Brudersberg (monopoly), Oelberg, Pettental. Ex-astrophysicist Peter von Weymarn has been one of the pioneers of organic viticulture in Germany since the 1970s. However, he has not brought a revolution to this great estate, rather, steered it back to its traditions. While colleagues and neighbours fell over themselves to enhance new winemaking technology he remained stubbornly true to modern casks and traditional vinification techniques. The result is wines of aristocratic reserve that frequently need several years' bottle age to show their best. The estate's Rieslings, Silvaners and Weissburgunders are amongst the region's finest wines.

Weingut Keller

Bahnhofstrasse 1, 67592 Flörsheim-Dalsheim. Owners: Klaus and Hedwig Keller. 30 acres. Classified sites: Kaseler Kehrnagel (Mosel-Saar-Ruwer), Rüdesheimer Berg Roseneck (Rheingau)
This estate stands out not just for owning vineyards in three different regions, but also for having set new quality standards in the hill country of Rheinhessen. Their Rieslings, Rieslaners, Huxelrebes and Weissburgunders are remarkable wines considering that Flörsheim-Dalsheim possesses no first-class vineyards. Clarity and effusive fruit and racy acidity are the hallmarks of the Keller wines regardless of whether dry, with a touch of natural sweetness or full-blown dessert wines. The vineyards in other regions are a hobby of Hedwig Keller's who comes from Trier on the Mosel. Although the wines are made by Klaus Keller, her influence is unmistakable.

Weingut St Antony

Wörrstadter Strasse 22, 55283 Nierstein. Owner: MAN. 47 acres. Classified sites: Niersteiner Hipping, Niersteiner Oelberg, Niersteiner Orbel, Niersteiner Pettental.
Dr Alex Michalsky has directed this important estate for its owners, the MAN truck and bus building company of Munich, since 1976 when he took over the post from his father. Long a specialist for dry Rieslings, during the 1990s the estate has continuously pushed forward the limits of what is possible in this style. The result of this quest has been extremely powerful, concentrated wines that have won high praise and blind tastings on the one hand, and been criticized for being untypical German Rieslings on the other. More recently great efforts have been invested in the harvesting of naturally sweet Auslese and higher Prädikat wines with considerable success. Unquestionably this is now one of the region's finest estates.

Weingut Georg Albrecht Schneider

Wilhelmstrasse 6, 55283 Nierstein. Owner: Albrecht Schneider. 32 acres. Classified sites: Niersteiner Hipping, Orbel, Oelberg, Pettental.
By his own admission, no self-publicist or salesman, Albrecht Schneider makes some of the most elegant, finely crafted Rieslings from the top sites of Nierstein. Although

Weissburgunder, Grauburgunder and Silvaner are minor specialities the estate's dry wines from these grapes can also be most impressive. Conscientious attention to detail in both the vineyard and cellar is the secret of the high standards set by this little-known estate.

OTHER PRODUCERS

Weingut Brüder Dr Becker 55278 Ludwigshöhe. Owner: Lotte Pfeffer-Müller. 23.5 acres. This organic estate rightly enjoys a good reputation for traditional style cask-matured dry Riesling and Silvaner and vibrantly fruity modern style Scheurebe with natural sweetness. The impressive 'Selektion Rheinhessen' bottlings, come from the calcareous loam of the Dienheimer Tafelstein site.

Brenner'sches Weingut Pfandturmstrasse 20, 67595 Bechtheim. Owner: Christian Brenner. About 20 acres. A family estate since 1877, which uses old methods: wooden casks in spacious cellars with an emphasis on substantial dry wines. 5% Silvaner, 15% Müller-Thurgau, 25% Riesling, 40% Weissburgunder, 15% Spätburgunder. Weissburgunder, Riesling and red wines are made absolutely dry – even Auslesen.

Weingut Jean Buscher 67595 Bechtheim. Owners: Michael Buscher, 37 acres. Best known for the challengingly contemporary modern artist's work which adorns the label of one wine each year, Jean Buscher's talents as a winemaker are sadly less widely appreciated. This is a good source for dry Riesling, Weissburgunder and Silvaner.

Bürgermeister Carl Koch Erben 55276 Oppenheim. Owner: Carl Hermann Stieh-Koch. 30 acres. Classified sites: Oppenheimer-Sackträger, Herrenberg. 35% Riesling, 10% Müller-Thurgau, 19% Silvaner, 5% Kerner, 6% Weissburgunder, 5% Gewürztraminer, etc.

Weingut Ökonomierat J Geil Erben 67595 Bechtheim. Owner: Karl Geil-Bierschenk. 62 acres. This little-known estate produces the full Rheinhessen gamut of wines, from dry Silvaner and Riesling to Huxelrebe dessert wines. Throughout the range the modest Karl Geil-Bierschenk maintains a standard which is far above the norm for Rheinhessen; wines to be enjoyed young for their fresh, clean fruit.

Weinkellerei Louis Guntrum Rheinallee 62, 55283 Nierstein. Director: Hanns Joachim Louis Guntrum. 120 acres. Classified sites: Nackenheimer Rothenberg; Niersteiner-Pettenthal. Olberg, Heiligenbaum, Orbel; Oppenheimer, Sackträger. The family business was started in 1824 in the present buildings, lying right on the Rhine. The estate wines can be ripe and lively with a wide range of flavours, each variety and site being bottled individually. The fifth Guntrum generation now directs the estate. In recent years quality has been erratic and some strange decisions have been made. A Riesling Kabinett wine with 14.5° alcohol can hardly be called typical.

Weingut Kühling-Gillot 55294 Bodenheim. Owners: Roland and Gabi Gillot, 21 acres. Roland Gillot is best known for his powerful, opulent dessert wines which can be amongst Rheinhessen's best. His dry Rieslings are rather less remarkable, often tending to be too plump.

Niersteiner Winzergenossenschaft 55283 Nierstein, 560 acres. This small cooperative has long maintained a good standard both with dry and sweet Rieslings. The Huxelrebe dessert wines can also be impressive.

Weingut Ohnacker Neustrasse 2, 67583 Guntersblum. Owner Walter Ohnacker. 33 acres in Guntersblum and Ludwigshöhe. The vines are 20% Müller-Thurgau, 25% Riesling, 20% Silvaner, 2% each of Scheurebe and Ruländer, 5% Spätburgunder and Portugieser, 3% Gewürztraminer. 150 years of family ownership; now one of the best specialists in the village, with wines ranging from dry Riesling (full-bodied and slow to develop) to light-drinking Müller-Thurgau.

Weingut Rappenhof Bachstrasse 47–49, 67577 Alsheim. Owner: Dr Reinhard Muth and Klaus Muth. 124 acres. Classified sites: Niersteiner Oelberg, Pettenthal, Oppen-heimer-Sackträger, Herrenberg. In recent years this very old family estate has grown substantially to become one of the region's largest. Although great energy has been invested in experiments with Chardonnay, nouveau-style red wines and *barrique* ageing, the quality has been frequently unremarkable.

Weingut Villa Sachsen Mainzerstrasse 184, 55411 Bingen. 67 acres. Classified sites: Bingener-Scharlachberg. After getting into trouble at the beginning of the 1990s, this renowned estate was purchased by Michael Prinz zu Salm-Salm of Wallhausen in the nearby Nahe. Hopefully his efforts will rebuild the fine reputation which this estate's rich, stylish Rieslings long enjoyed.

Weingut Schales 67592 Flörsheim-Dalsheim. Owners: the Schales family. 89 acres. A seventh-generation family, making the usual wide range of wines from the limestone soil of Dalsheim. The most impressive wines are the powerful dry Weissburgunders and the often magnificent Huxelrebe dessert wines. No Einzellage or Grosslage names are used. The estate has 30% Riesling, 18% Müller-Thurgau, 15% Weissburgunder, 5% Siegerrebe, 6% Kerner, 5% Silvaner, 5% Huxelrebe, 5% Scheurebe, 17% others.

Weingut Heinrich Seebrich 55283 Nierstein. Owner: Heinrich Seebrich. 22 acres. A specialist for sweet Rieslings, Heinrich Seebrich maintains a good standard in this style.

Weingut Dr Alex Senfter 55283 Nierstein. Owner: Jost Senfter. 25 acres. Young Jost Senfter is one of the brightest new winemaking talents on the Rheinhessen wine scene today. His dry and naturally sweet Rieslings display both depth and elegance.

Staatsweingut der Landes-Lehr- und Versuchsanstalt Zuckerberg 19, 55276 Oppenheim. Director: Dr Fuchss. 61.8 acres. Classified sites: Oppenheimer-Sackträger, Herrenberg; Niersteiner, Olberg, Glöck and Pettenthal. The regional wine school, founded in 1895 by the Duke of Hessen and now considered an exemplary college for winemakers, using the most modern methods. In 1980 the school opened a new German wine museum in the heart of Oppenheim. Some 40% of the estate is on steep slopes and half is Riesling. Among the many other varieties planted, a large number are experimental vines. Sadly, quality is erratic.

Weingut Stallmann-Hiestand 55278 Uelversheim. Owner: Werner Hiestand. 37 acres. A wide range of well-made dry wines. Rieslings, Weissburgunders and Grauburgunders stand head and shoulders above the average in this part of the region.

Weingut J & H A Strub Rheinstrasse 42, 55283 Nierstein. Owner: Walter Strub. 40 acres. Classified sites: Niersteiner Hipping, Oelberg, Orbel, Pettental. An old family estate wihich has a good name for producing gentle, mellow wines from some of Nierstein's top sites. The vineyards are planted in 63% Riesling, 15% Silvaner, 20% Müller-Thurgau, 2% other varieties.

Weingut Eugen Wehrheim Mühlgasse 30, 55283 Nierstein. Owner: Klaus Wehrheim. 25.5 acres. Classified sites: Niersteiner-Orbel, Olberg, Hipping, Pettenthal. Specialists in Nierstein since 1693. 50% Riesling, 20% Silvaner, 10% Müller-Thurgau, 20% other varieties. The Rieslings are light and sprightly; more serious wines are sweet, aromatic and heavy, for example Ruländer and Huxelrebe Beerenauslese.

PFALZ

No winegrowing region in Germany enjoys a more generous climate than the Pfalz. Nowhere in Germany is it warmer and drier than the band of vineyards which runs for 50 miles along the eastern flank of the Haardt Mountains from the southern border of Rheinhessen to the French fonrtier, where the Haardt become the Vosges. The combination of climatic advantage and generally light, sandy soils results in many of Germany's best dry wines and some remarkable dessert wines too. In spite of the proximity to Alsace they have a completely different style to those wines. Here the emphasis is firmly on fresh aromas and crisp acidity, rather than the savoury vinosity of Alsace.

With almost 59,000 acres of vineyards the Pfalz is second only to Rheinhessen in size, though it often produces a slightly more wine due to the intensive, highly mechanized viticulture practised in the flat vineyards down on the Rhine plain. Here it is possible to produce bulk wines more efficiently than anywhere else in Germany. However, it is with wines at the opposite end of the quality scale that the Pfalz has been attracting all the attention of late. Together with the Mosel-Saar-Ruwer the region boasts more ambitious young winemakers than any other region of Germany. Their rich, expressive wines have won countless tastings and prizes and been the subject of hundreds of enthusiastic articles in the domestic and international wine press.

Traditionally, quality-wine production was associated with the Mittelhaardt area of the Pfalz centred around the town of Bad Dürkheim. Here 'the 3 Bs' – the great estates of Dr von Bassermann-Jordan, Reichsrat von Buhl and Dr Bürklin-Wolf – and a clutch of smaller estates established the region's reputation for noble Rieslings during the 19th and early 20th centuries. At this time the rest of the region was seen as fit for producing nothing more than quaffing wines. The new generation has broken this mould, proving that the north and the south of the region can produce impressive white wines. Many of the most best examples are from varieties that are relatively recent introductions: the Riesling crossings Rieslaner and Scheurebe, the white Pinots (Weissburgunder and Grauburgunder) and the red Spätburgunder, St Laurent and Dornfelder. Thankfully the leading producers of the Mittelhaardt have responded to this challenge by redoubling their efforts, and quality competition is now intense.

The Pfalz may lack the dramatic scenery of the Mosel, Rheingau or Mittelrhein, but its gently undulating verdent country makes it one of the most charming of all Germany's winegrowing regions. The Pfälzer are renowned for their love of food and wine. This finds its fullest expression at Bad Dürkheim's famous Wurstmarkt ('Sausage fair'), in September where leading winemakers rub shoulders with local farmers while enjoying a 'Schoppen' (half litre glass) of wine.

CLASSIFIED PFALZ VINEYARDS

First-Class Vineyards

Birkweiler Kastanienbusch The only Pflaz site with stony rotliegendes soil gives subtly aromatic Rieslings with a silky acidity. Most important owners: Rebholz, Dr Wehrheim.

Burrweiler Schäwer The Schäwer is the only vineyard in the region with a slate soil like that of the Mosel. This results in exceptionally refined peachy Rieslings that are quite 'untypical' for the region. Most important owner: Herbert Messmer.

Deidesheimer Grainhübel/Hohenmorgen/Kalkofen/ Kieselberg/Langenmorgen/Leinhöhle/Maushöhle This cluster of small sites are responsible for Deidesheim's excellent reputation as a producer of rich, succulent Rieslings. Traditionally the Grainhübel is regarded as being the greatest of them. It, like the Kalkofen, has a limestone subsoil. The wines from these vineyards are slower developing and more long-living than the others. With its very light sandy soil the Leinhöhle is particularly sensitive to drought in hot years. Most important owners: Bassermann-Jordan, Josef Biffar, von Buhl, Bürklin-Wolf, Dr Deinhard, Kimmich, Georg Siben, Werlé, WG Deidesheim.

Dürkheimer Michelsberg/Spielberg/Ungsteiner Herrenberg These three fine vineyards occupy the southern, western and eastern side of a hill immediately to the north of Bad Dürkheim. The stony limestone soil and excellent exposition result in intense, beautifully balanced Rieslings that are particularly well suited to vinification in the dry style. Most important owners: Kurt Darting, Pfeffingen, Fitz-Ritter, Karl Schefer.

Forster Freundstück/Jesuitengarten/Kirchenstück/ Pechstein/Ungeheuer The great vineyards of Forst occupy one of the most sheltered positions in the entire Pfalz. This, together with a light quickly warmed top soil and a deep water-retentive subsoil, results in remarkable Riesling wines. Those from the Pechstein (so named because of the abundance of basalt in its top soil) are the raciest; those from the Ungeheur rich and fleshy; while the Jesuitengarten and Kirchenstück give wines with the highest elegance. They have been recognized as the greatest sites of the Pfalz since at least the first half of the 19th century. Most important owners: Bassermann-Jordan, von Buhl, Bürklin-Wolf, Lucashof, Georg Mosbacher, Mosbacherhof, Eugen Müller, Karl Schefer, J. Wegeler (Deinhard), WG Forst, J.L. Wolf.

Haardter Bürgergarten/Herrenletten/Herzog The best sites of Haardt close to Neustadt have unusually deep heavy soils for the Pfalz which yield powerful wines with a firm acidity structure and long ageing potential. At high levels of ripeness they can possess a ravishing apricot and pineapple bouquet. Most important owners: Müller-Catoir and Wegmüller.

Kallstadter Annaberg/Saumagen The limestone soil of the Saumagen and the southern exposition in the best part of this site makes for extremely powerful, highly structured wines that need years of ageing for the characteristic passion-fruit aroma to develop fully. The Annaberg wines are less expansive, but in hot years they can possess a marvellous elegance and their gunflint aroma is most distinctive. Most important owners: Henninger IV, Koehler-Ruprecht.

Königsbacher Idig Medium-bodied wines with a family resemblance to those of Ruppertsberg, but a slightly firmer structure. Most important owner: Christmann.

Mussbacher Eselshaut The very light sandy soil here gives full-bodied wines with extravagant aromas including exotic fruit notes. Most important owner: Müller-Catoir.

Ruppertsberger Gaisböhl/Hoheburg/Nussbien/ Reiterpfad The large area of good vineyards on the western side of Ruppertsberg generally yield Rieslings with pronounced

floral aromas that are charming from a very early age. Those from the Reiterpfad and Nussbien tend to be deeper and more complex. Most important owners: Bassermann-Jordan, Josef Biffar, von Buhl, Bürklin-Wolf, Christmann, J. Wegeler (Deinhard), Werlé.

Ungsteiner Weilberg This well exposed site gives extremely typical juicy, aromatic Pfalz Rieslings which show well from their early youth, but will also age well. Most important owner: Pfeffingen.

Wachenheimer Belz/Goldbächel/Germupel/Rechbächel The top vineyards of Wachenheim give Rieslings that combine the racy elegance of the Rheingau with the richness of the Pfalz. They can give dry wines which are every bit as impressive as the famous dessert wines. Most important owners: Josef Biffar, Bürklin-Wolf (including the Rechbächel monopoly), J.L. Wolf.

Leading Pfalz Producers

Weingut Josef Biffar

Niederkirchenerstrasse 13, 67146 Deidesheim. Owner: Gerhard Biffar. 27 acres. Classified sites: Deidesheimer, Kieselberg, Leinhöhle, Grainhübel and Kalkofen; Ruppertsberger-Nussbien and Reiterpfad; Wachenheimer, Gerümpel, Goldbächel.

With a string of concentrated, beautifully polished dry and naturally sweet Rieslings from the top vineyard sites of Deidesheim, Wachenheim and Ruppertsberg, this estate was catapulted into the first rank of Pfalz producers at the beginning of the 1990s. The estate and the family's candied-fruits company are jointly directed by Gerhard Biffar and his daughter Lilli.

Weingut Dr Bürklin-Wolf

Weinstrasse 65, 67157 Wachenheim. Owners: Bettina Bürklin-von Guradze, Christian von Guradze. Director: Christian von Guradze. 234 acres. Classified sites: Wachenheimer-Gerümpel, Goldbächel and Rechbächel (sole owner); Forster-Kirchenstück, Ungeheuer, Jesuitengarten, Pechstein, Deidesheimer-Hohenmorgen, Langenmorgen, Kalkofen, Ruppertsberger-Hoheburg, Reiterpfad, Nussbien, and Gaisböhl (sole owner).

With almost 250 acres of vineyards, this famous estate is one of the largest in Germany in private ownership. After taking over direction of Bürklin-Wolf in 1992 Christian von Guradze instituted a programme of radical changes which have already achieved their goal of placing the estate back in the first rank of Pflaz wine producers. Today only the wines from the first-class sites are sold with vineyard designations, and those from the lesser sites are marketed under the 'Villa Eckel' name.

Top of the wide range of dry wines are the 'Grosser Lagen' Rieslings, from vineyards with very low yields whose crop is selectively harvested and whole-cluster pressed (as in Champagne). The Auslese, BA, TBA and Eiswein dessert wines have always been amongst the greatest wines produced along the Rhine.

Weingut Knipser

Hauptstrasse 47, 67229 Laumersheim. Owners: Werner and Volker Knipser. 32 acres .

The Knipser brothers have been the leading figures in the Pfalz's red wine revolution. Since the late 1980s they have produced a string of impressively rich, tannic Spätburgunder, St Laurent and Dornfelder red wines from the little-known vineyards of Grosskarlbach and Laumersheim, recently adding Cabernet Sauvignon to this collection. Their powerful, oak-aged white wines divide critical opinion, but their dessert wines can also be magnificent.

Weingut Koehler-Ruprecht

Weinstrasse 84, 67169 Kallstadt. Owner: Bernd Philippi. 20 acres. Classified site: Kallstadter Saumagen.

Widely recognized as one of the Pfalz's leading estates Koehler-Ruprecht specializes in two dramatically contrasting styles of wine. The dry Rieslings sold under the Koehler-Ruprecht label are perhaps the most traditionally vinified wines in the region, spending one or two years in wooden casks. Those from the Saumagen possess extraordinary power and ageing potential, and are amongst the greatest dry wines made in Germany. The wines sold under the 'Philippi' label are all vinified in new oak *barriques* in a deliberately international style. Amongst them, the Spätburgunder reds and Weissburgunder/Grauburgunder whites are frequently impressively concentrated and very well made. The 'Elyssium' dessert wine is a dead-ringer for a top Sauternes.

Weingut Herbert Messmer

Gaisbergstrasse 132, 76835 Burrweiler. Owners: the Messmer family. 50 acres. Classified site: Burrweiler Schäwer.

Founded in 1960, this estate has long been one of the handful of dynamic estates which have changed the image of the Südliche Weinstrasse, or the southern Pfalz, from that of being only a bulk wine producer. Gregor Messmer is a talented young winemaker with some remarkable vineyards at his disposal, including the first-class Burrweiler Schäwer, the only vineyard in the Pfalz with a slate soil like that of the Mosel. The elegant dry and late-harvested Rieslings from this site are frequently amongst the finest wines made from this grape in the entire region. The dry Weissburgunder and Grauburgunder are much more typical Pfalz wines, but equally well crafted. Messmer's Spätburgunder, St Laurent and Dornfelder reds are also impressive wines

Weingut Georg Mosbacher

Weinstrasse 27, 67147 Forst. Owner: Richard Mosbacher. 26.5 acres. Classified sites: Forster Freundstück, Forster Ungeheuer.

This estate has long been the leading producer of Rieslings from the famous vineyards of Forst. Winemaker Richard Mosbacher is the very soul of modesty, but he sets the highest standards both for dry and dessert wines. Rich aromas, juicy fruit and bright acidity are the hallmarks of his wines. The modest prices mean that they sell out with great rapidity. His daughter Sabine Mosbacher-Düringer and her husband Jürgen Düringer are now in the process of taking control, but no major changes are planned.

Weingut Müller-Catoir

Mandelring 25, 67433 Neustadt-Haardt. Owner: Heinrich Catoir. 50 acres. Classified sites: Gimmeldinger Mandelgarten, Haardter Bürgergarten, Haardter Herrenletten, Haardter Herzog, Mussbacher Eselshaut. 55% Riesling, 10% Scheurebe, 8% Weissburgunder, 8% Rieslaner, 5% Muskateller, 4% Grauburgunder, 3% Gewürztraminer.

Two complex personalities, owner Heinrich Catoir and winemaker Hans-Günther Schwarz, have made this estate the undisputed number one in the Pfalz. The recently aquired walled vineyard which forms the original Haardter Bürgergarten site promises to add a new star to the estate's Riesling collection. (*See* Müller-Catoir: A Great Pfalz Estate, page 270.)

Weingut Pfeffingen

Weinstrasse, 67098 Bad Dürkheim-Pfeffingen. Owners: Karl Fuhrmann and Günter Eymael. 23.5 acres. Classified sites: Ungsteiner-Herrenberg and Weilberg.

A highly regarded consolidated estate which has capitalized on the reputation built up by Karl Fuhrmann from the 1905s to the 1970s. The influence of his son-in-law, Günter Eymael, is apparent, and of daughter Doris, who is now one of Germany's leading women winemakers. The vineyard is 62% Riesling, 9% Müller-Thurgau, 10% Scheurebe, plus Silvaner and Gewürztraminer. Pfeffingen wines have considerable finesse, the Rieslings often dry and the Scheurebes juicily rich. Even wines from 'off' vintages age long and gracefully.

Weingut Ökonomierat Rebholz

Weinstrasse 54, 76833 Seilbeldingen. Owner: Christine Rebholz. 24 acres. Classified site: Birkweiler Kastanienbusch.

The Rebholz family were the quality wine pioneers in the Südliche Weinstrasse, or the southern Pfalz, making the first BA and TBA wines in the area when such rarities were considered the exclusive preserve of the Mittelhaardt. Sleek, dry wines have been their speciality for decades and Hans-Jörg Rebholz continues the family tradition. Although Riesling is the most important grape in the estate's vineyards, Rebholz also has an excellent reputation for its Weissburgunder, Grauburgunder, Gewürztraminer and Muskateller white wines, and Spätburgunder reds (the latter both with and without new oak ageing). All of Hans-Jörg's wines are made with ageing in mind, and many of them can be quite tart and unyielding during the first year of their life. However, they gain enormously in elegance with one or two years' bottle maturation and all the Prädikat wines have excellent ageing potential.

Weingut Dr Wehrheim

Weinstrasse 8, 76831 Birkweiler. Owner: Karl-Heinz Wehrheim. 26 acres. Classified sites: Birkweiler Kastanienbusch.

Karl-Heinz Wehrheim makes some of the best dry Riesling, Weissburgunder and Grauburgunder wines in the southern Pfalz. Rich and elegant, the best wines come from the steep slopes and stony rotliegendes soil of the Birkweiler Kastanienbusch site. It is not only one of the finest vineyards in the region, situated high up close to the Haardt Forest with magnificent views over the Rhine plain, it is also one of the most beautiful.

Weingut Werlé Erben

Weinstrasse 84, 67147 Forst. Owners: the Werlé family. 31.5 acres. Classified sites: Deidesheimer Leinhöhle, Forster Jesuitengarten, Forster Kirchenstück, Forster Pechstein, Forster Ungeheuer.

It is perhaps not surprising that a family which has lived in one of the most beautiful houses of the Pfalz for more than two centuries should be commited unswervingly to its winemaking tradition. Claus and Hardy Werlé make Riesling wines with an aristocratic reserve that makes some modern-style Pfalz wines seem loud, even uncouth. All of their wines need time to show their true depth and class, being made with long ageing in mind. The most remarkable of them are those from the first-class Jesuitengarten and Kirchenstück vineyards of Forst: Rieslings which live up to the legendary reputation of these sites.

OTHER PRODUCERS

Weingut Dr von Bassermann-Jordan 67142 Deidesheim. Owners: Gabriele and Margrit von Bassermann-Jordan. 114 acres. Classified sites: Deidesheimer-Hohenmorgen, Grainhübel, Kieselberg, Kalkofen, Leinhöhle and Langenmorgen; Forster-Jesuitengarten, Kirchenstück, Ungeheuer, Pechstein, Freundstück; Ruppertsberger-Reiterpfad, Hoheburg, Nussbien. Following the death of Dr Ludwig von Basserman-Jordan in October 1995 this famous and historic estate has passed to his daughter and widow. Since the early 18th century when founder Andreas Jordan made the first vineyard-designated wines and the first Auslese in the region, this estate has been one of the most consistent producers of fine Pfalz Rieslings. After a difficult period during the last years of Dr von Basserman-Jordan's life the appointment of talented winemaker Ulrich Miell has effected a dramatic return to top form. Apart from the wine, the estate is worth a visit for the magnificent collection of Roman artefacts displayed in its cavernous cellars (by appointment only) amongst the wooden casks where the estate's wines continue to be made.

Müller-Catoir

A Great Pfalz Estate

The Pfalz's reputation as Germany's most dynamic winegrowing region would be unthinkable without the Müller-Catoir estate. It was founded in 1744 by the Huguenot Catoir family, but only in recent years has it written history.

The estate is in Haardt, a suburb of Neustadt an der Wienstrasse. None of the Haardt vineyard sites attracted attention until the arrival, in 1962, of the shy owner of Müller-Catoir, Heinrich Catoir (right), and ebullient winemaker, Hans-Günther Schwarz. Since then they have perfected a dramatic new style of German wine from a palate of grape varieties, making the estate the undisputed number one in the Pfalz. Their vivid, expressive wines have prompted writers around the world to reach for their most extravagant adjectives of praise. This is not surprising: every Müller-Catoir wine, dry or lusciously sweet, is a strong personality. The finest of them are unique expressions of the region's generous climate.

Riesling accounts for 60% of the estate's 50 acres of vineyards, and gives some of the richest and most aromatic dry wines made from this noble grape in all of Germany. It is, however, with rare grapes such as Rieslaner and unfashionable ones such as Scheurebe (both crossings of Silvaner and Riesling) that Catoir and Schwarz have made their name. In their hands Rieslaner gives Auslese and higher quality wines of scintillating freshness and unctuous richness, while their Scheurebes are lavish and exotic, yet silky and elegant. They each account for nearly 10% of the estate's vineyards.

In top vintages Grauburgunder (4%) and Weissburgunder (8%) give dry wines as bombastic as the stone façade with which the baroque estate house was fitted at the turn of the

century. Muskateller is a ravishingly perfumed dry wine, made only when nature smiles upon this fickle grape. Sometimes no Muskateller (4%) is harvested at all, a sacrifice typical of the uncompromising stance which Catoir and Schwarz share. With the 1993 vintage came their first successful Spätburgunder.

The Müller-Catoir wine style and commitment to quality have inspired an entire generation of young Pfalz winegrowers. Many of the region's leading young winemakers have worked at Müller-Catoir or are advised by Schwarz. Without him the region's quality renaissance of the past three decades would have been unthinkable.

Weingut Friedrich Becker 76889 Schwigen. Owner: Fritz Becker. 32 acres. Fritz Becker is best known for the high standard of his red wines, principally from the Spätburgunder grape and only usually made in neutral German oak rather than *barriques*. The whites are more variable, but the dry Weissburgunder, Grauburgunder and Gewürztraminer often have the same combination of heady richness and ripe fruit as the red wines.

Weingut Bergdolt Klostergut St-Lamprecht. 67435 Duttweiler. Owners: Rainer and Günther Bergdolt. 40 acres. The loess-loam soils of Rainer Bergdolt's vineyards may put a limit to what he can achieve with the Riesling grape, but his dry Weissburgunders are the finest wines made from this underrated grape in all Germany. In spite of up to 14° natural alcohol, they are always beautifully balanced. Most are vinified in the neutral German oak, but since the early-1990s the *barrique* (new-oak) aged examples have been no less impressive. Here too it is rich ripe fruit, nut and caramel aromas which stand in the foreground. In recent years Rainer Bergdolt's Spätburgunder red wines have made a big jump forward, and he must now be counted amongst Germany's top ten red-wine producers.

Weingut Reichsrat von Buhl Weinstrasse 16, 67146 Deidesheim. Owner: Georg Enoch, Reichsfreiherr von und zu Guttenberg. Director: Stefan Weber. 138 acres. Classified sites: Forster, Ungeheuer, Pechstein, Kirchenstück, Freundstück and Jesuitengarten; Deidesheimer, Kieselberg, Leinhöhle; Ruppertsberger, Reiterpfad. Since the end of the 1980s this substantial, renovated estate has been leased by a group of Japanese investors. While many good wines have been made since then, quality has not been consistent. Riesling continues to dominate the vineyard plantings (88%), but Grauburgunder, Spätburgunder and Scheurebe have been introduced as specialities.

Weingut Kurt Darting 67098 Bad Dürkheim. Owner: Kurt and Helmut Darting. 32.5 acres. In 1989 the Dartings left the local cooperative and established their own estate. Their wines are always fresh and vividly fruity, if rarely sophisticated. Best are the Rieslings from the first-class Ungsteiner Herrenberg.

Weingut K Fitz-Ritter Leistadterstrasse 1c, 6702 Bad Dürkheim. Owner: Konrad Fitz. 47 acres. Classified sites: Dürkheimer Michelsberg, Spielberg, Ungsteiner Herrenberg. A family estate with a fine classical 18th-century mansion (1785) whose park contains the largest maidenhair tree (*Ginkgo biloba*) in Germany, along with other noble trees. The Fitz family also started here (in 1837) one of the oldest Sekt businesses in Germany. The modern-style wines are always fresh and fruity. 65% of their vines are Riesling, 3% Gewürztraminer, 6% Spätburgunder, 26% others.

Weingut Rainer & Hermann Lingenfelder Hauptstrasse 27, 6711 Grosskarlbach. Owners: the Lingenfelder family. 25 acres. Einzellagen: Grosskarlbacher-Burgweg and Osterberg; Frienshiemer-Goldberg and Musikantenbuckel. This family estate produces wines high in extract, of considerable individuality and character. The vineyards are planted with 30% Riesling, 10% Scheurebe, 20% Spätburgunder, 10% Dornfelder and 12% Kerner. The Spätburgunder, made like a Burgundy, is matured in French oak. Rainer Karl Lingenfelder was the chief oenologist of the wine shippers H. Sichel Söhne.

Weingut Lucashof 67147 Forst. Owner: Klaus Lucas. 25 acres. This reliable estate makes clean, crisp Riesling with plenty of character. The emphasis is on dry wines, the best coming from the first-class Pechstein and Ungeheuer sites of Forst.

Weingut Eugen Müller 67147 Forst. Owner: Kurt Müller. 45 acres. This large estate owns the only old vines in Forst's first-class vineyards to survive the recent reorganization of the village's vineyards. The resulting wines are big, rich and muscular. The regular-quality wines can be plain, though.

Weingut Münzberg 76829 Godramstein. Owners: the Kesseler family. 27 acres. The Kessler family's estate close to Landau makes some of the best dry Weissburgunder and Grauburgunder in the Pfalz. Their red wines have also improved dramatically in recent years.

Weingut K Neckerauer Ritter von Geisslerstrasse 9, 67256 Weissenheim. Owners: Klaus and Arnd Neckerauer. 54.5 acres. An extremely erratic producer whose best wines are rich and expressive, but often simple and rustic. A wide range of traditional and modern grape varieties are cultivated, Riesling being the most important, comprising 40% of the total.

Weingut Karl Schaefer Weinstrasse Süd 30, 67098 Bad Dürkheim. Owner: Dr Wolf Fleischmann. 40 acres. Classified sites: Wachenheimer-Gerümpel; Dürkheimer-Michelsberg and Spielberg; Forster Pechstein; Ungsteiner Herrenberg. A family estate established in 1843, now in its fourth generation. With 86% of plantings Riesling dominates the vineyards. The estate is best known for rich, expressive dry Rieslings.

Weingut Thomas Siegrist 76829 Leinsweiler. Owner: Thomas Siegrist. 30 acres. Red-wine specialist Thomas Siegrist makes rich, substantial Dornfelder and Spätburgunder. The dry white wines were once rather severe, but have gained charm lately.

Weingut Heinrich Vollmer 67158 Ellerstadt. Owner: Heinrich Vollmer. Since 1969 native Badener, mountain climber and Argentinian winery-owner Heinrich Vollmer has built up an estate of more than 300 acres. While the wines (red and white) are rather less remarkable than their maker, many of them are none the less good and typical, and excellent value.

Gutsverwaltung Wegeler-Deinhard and Weingut Dr Deinhard Weinstrasse 10, 67146 Deidesheim. Wegeler-Deinhard owner: Deinhard & Co AG. 32.5 acres in Forst and Ungeheuer. Weingut Dr Deinhard owners: the Hoch family. Director: Heinz Bauer. 59 acres. Classified sites: Deidesheimer-Leinhöhle, Grainhübel, Kieselberg, Kalkofen; Ruppertsberger-Reiterpfad and Nussbien. A well-known estate built up in the 19th century by Dr Andreas Deinhard, a founder of the German Winegrowers' Association and an influential legislator. His handsome Gutshaus (built 1848) now houses both Weingut Dr Deinhard and the property rented to the Koblenz merchants Deinhard (Gutsverwaltung Wegeler-Deinhard) in 1973. 85% Riesling. The wines are richly aromatic, mainly *trocken* and *halbtrocken*. There are said to be old family connections and the two sections are run by the same director from the same fine sandstone Gutshaus in Deidesheim, but their wines are made apart and labelled differently. Wegeler-Deinhard wines, like those from their vineyards in the Rheingau and Mosel, are models of correct and characterful winemaking.

Weingut Wilhelmshof 769833 Siebeldingen. Owners: the Roth family. This estate particularly specializes in Sekt production, and makes some of the best sparkling wines in the Pfalz.

Weingut J. L. Wolf Erben Weinstrasse 1, 67157 Wachenheim. Owners: Christoph Hindenfeld, Ernst Loosen and Co. 40 acres. Classified sites: Wachenheimer-Belz (solely owned), Gerümpel, and Goldbächel; Forster-Ungeheuer, Jesuitengarten and Pechstein; Deidesheimer, Leinhöhle. In 1996 this estate was taken over by a consortium headed by local business-man Christoph Hindenfeld and winemaker Ernst Loosen of the Dr Loosen estate in Bernkastel/Mosel (q.v.). Their aim is to rebuild the estate's once excellent reputation.

COOPERATIVES

Winzerverein Forst Wienstrasse 57, 67147 Forst. Founded 1918. 158 acres. The highly regarded cooperative of Forst, with more than 100 acres of Riesling in fine sites. Half the sales are in bottle and half in cask.

Ruppertsberger Winzerverein 'Hoheburg' Hauptstrasse 74, 67152 Ruppertsberg. 504 acres. 50% of the vines are Riesling. Apart from the usual Silvaner and Müller-Thurgau, Kerner and Portugieser have an important share. The top Ruppertsberg Rieslings can be very good.

Winzergenossenschaft Vier Jahreszeiten 76098 Bad Dürkheim. 765 acres. A wide range of Pfalz wines. Particularly good are the Rieslings and dessert wines.

HESSISCHE BERGSTRASSE

Its 1,000 acres of vines clinging tenaciously to terraced hills to the north of Heidelberg, the Hessische Bergstrasse is one of the most beautiful winegrowing regions in Germany. However, since most of its produce is drunk within the region or sold to visitors, it is hardly known outside this area of Germany. This is a shame, because the best sites here are capable of giving elegant, sophisticated Rieslings which have no trouble standing next to the best from the better-known neighbouring regions.

The steep slopes of the Heppenheimer Steinkopf, the Bensheimer Kalkgasse and the Streichling are the three classified sites of Hessische Bergstrasse. The poor sandstone soil of the Steinkopf gives the most minerally and racy wines, the limestone of the Kalkgasse yielding more substantial rounder wines, while the Streichling is famed for producing a delicate bouquet and subtlety. On the loess-loam soils of the lower lying vineyards grow Weissburgunder and Grauburgunder grapes, producing medium-bodied dry wines that compare with those of northern Baden – not surprisingly, since in effect this region is a continuation of Baden's northernmost vineyards. Müller-Thurgau is the workhorse grape as in so many other regions of Germany.

Leading Hessische Bergstrasse Producers

Weingut der Stadt Bensheim

64625 Bensheim. Director: Axel Seiberth.
The town of Bensheim has a small estate of about 29.6 acres, mainly Riesling. The estate makes its own Sekt from Weissburgunder and Grauburgunder.

Domäne Bensheim

Grieselstrasse 34-36, 64625 Bensheim. Director: Heinrich Hillenbrand. 81 acres. Classified sites: Heppenheimer S teinkopf, Bensheimer Kalkgasse.
Heinrich Hillenbrand is the third generation of his family to direct this highly regarded estate since its foundation in 1904, following his uncle and grandfather. His many achievements include the production of the first TBAs in the region's history in 1971 and its first Eiswein the following year. Today it is dry-style Riesling, Weissburgunder and Grauburgunder that dominate the production. Technically the estate is part of the Rheingau Staatsweingüter, although in fact it functions as a virtually self-sufficient entity.

Weingut Simon-Bürkle

Wiesenpromenade 13, 64673 Zwingenberg.
Owners: Kurt Simon and Wilfried Bürkle.
This 45-acre estate was created by two ambitious young graduates of the Weinsberg wine school at the beginning of the 1990s. Although the quality is still a little erratic at this early stage, everything points to this producer becoming one of the quality leaders in the region.

FRANKEN

Fifty miles east of the Rheingau, beyond the city of Frankfurt, the River Main, flowing to join the Rhine at Hochheim, scribbles a huge drunken W through the irregular limestone and red marl hills of Franken (Franconia), the northern extremity of Bavaria.

The centre of the region is the baroque city of Würzburg. Its most famous vineyard, sloping down to the Main within the city itself, is Würzburger Stein. The name Stein has been traditionally borrowed by foreigners to describe Franconian wine generically (as the English shortened Hochheim to 'hock' for all Rhine wines). 'Steinwein' comes in fat flagons called Bocksbeutel, thus distinguishing itself from almost all other German wines, which come in elegant bottles. This is probably the extent of popular knowledge. Franken wine is a specialized subject, not least because its rarity value and local popularity keep the price higher than we are accustomed to pay for more famous names from the Rhine and Mosel. Most 'Frankenwein' is drunk in Bavaria, particularly in Munich, or in the wealthy cities of northern Germany. Besides, the area is exceptionally diffuse and hard to comprehend. Vineyards are only found on exceptional south slopes. The climate is harsh and serious frosts are common; the season is too short to achieve regular success with Riesling.

Traditionally Franken has made its best wine with the Silvaner. Only here and occasionally on the Rheinterrasse in Rheinhessen does this variety make wine of better-than-moderate quality. Silvaner grown in Franken can produce full-bodied dry wines (and more rarely sweet ones) with a noble breadth and substance; dense, even sticky in their intensity. They are regularly compared with white burgundy, not for their flavour but for their vinosity and ability to match rich food at table.

Unfortunately the Müller-Thurgau has now gained the upper hand. It works well, when not overproduced, and makes stylish, flavourful wines; although it rarely matches the remarkable low-key stylishness of Silvaner. Scheurebe and the new Perle can do better. Bacchus tends to be aggressively aromatic; somehow out of keeping for the region. Kerner is also too aromatic, although many people find it acceptable. In a ripe year Rieslaner is a good compromise, making excellent Auslesen with the breadth of a Silvaner and the depth of a Riesling. The 1976 harvest in the Steigerwald produced some extraordinary wines with a bouquet like salty honey.

The rambling region is divided into three Bereiche: Mainviereck for its lower reaches towards Frankfurt; Maindreieck for its heart, the district of Würzburg; and Steigerwald for its eastern extremities with the sternest climate of all. The Bereich names are frequently used, partly because a great number of the scattered vineyards are not included in any Grosslage.

A high percentage of wine, as in Baden, is made by cooperatives. Würzburg itself, however, boasts three of the oldest, biggest and best wine estates in Germany – the Bürgerspital, the Juliusspital and the Staatlicher Hofkeller.

CLASSIFIED FRANKEN VINEYARDS

Bürgstadter Centgrafenberg The most western first-class vineyard of Franken is also the warmest, lying on a sheltered south-facing slope in the small basin around the town of Miltenberg. This and the red sandstone soil combine to produce some unusually aromatic and racy Franken wines. Red wine from the Spätburgunder grape plays as important a role as Riesling.

Casteller Schlossberg This precipitously steep slope above the village of Castell is one of the top sites of the Steigerwald. The combination of excellent exposure and the heavy gypsum-marl soil results in powerful racy wines. Rieslaner scales the heights here in more senses than one.

Escherndorfer Lump The 'tramp' of Escherndorf is one of the most imposing vineyards in Franken; a great ampitheatre of vines in the crook of one of the River Main's most dramatic bends. It is particularly renowned for rich, succulent dry Silvaner.

Frickenhäuser Kapellenberg The finest vineyard of Frisckenhäusen is also one of the least-known top sites of Franken. The south-facing slope lies directly adjacent to the bank of the Main. While the wines it produces may not be the most powerful in the region they have ample fruit and lovely balance.

Homburger Kallmuth The towering wall of vines which forms the famous Kallmuth is one of very few top vineyard sites in Franken not to have been '*Flurbereinigt*' or reorganized by landscaping. The reddish sandstone soil gives richly fruity wines with a strong minerally character.

Iphöfer Julius-Echter-Berg/Kronsberg The vineyard named after the late-16th-century Prince-Bishop, Julius Echter of Mespelbrunn, is indisputably one of Franken's greatest. Situated at the southwestern tip of the Steigerwald it enjoys optimum exposure, which together with the gypsum-marl soil gives wines of enormous power with a strong earthy character. The wines from the neighbouring Kronsberg are hardly less imposing.

Randersackerer Marsberg/Pfülben/Sonnenstuhl/Teufelskeller The old town of Randersacker is blessed with more fine vineyards than any other in Franken. However much body and richness these wines have, they never show their muscles in the way some Franken wines can. Beautiful balance and a subtle spicy-smoky character are their hallmarks. The differences between these vineyards, all of which have limestone soils, are primarily of exposure. First amongst equals is the Pfülben.

Rödelseer Küchenmeister The town of Rödelseer lies just to the north of Iphofen and its finest site. The Küchemeister lies directly next to the top sites of its neighbour. The wines are similar in character, but a touch lighter.

Volkacher Ratsherr This imposing hillside vineyard lies only five miles to the north of the famous Escherndorfer Lump site and enjoys a similarly favoured location right next to the River Main. It gives rich, substantial wines with a good acidity structure.

Würzburger Abtsleite/Innere Leiste Though less famous than the Würzburger Stein vineyard, both these sites enjoy excellent locations and are capable of yielding top-class Riesling and Silvaner wines. Indeed, the Innere Leiste, situated immediately below the Marienburg fortress of Würzburg gives the town's most powerful wines. What the Abtsleite wines may lack in volume they more than make up for in racy elegance.

Würzburger Stein/Stein-Harfe The Stein and its sub-site the Stein-Harfe (solely owned by the Bürgerspital estate – q.v.) cover a slope that extends in length for more than five miles, directly to the northwest of Würzburg. For a long time the distinctive smoky note of these wines was explained by the proximity of the main railway line, but since electrification it has been obvious that this character comes in fact from the limestone soil. No wines in Franken can excel the finest Rieslings and Silvaners from this site in elegance or subtlety of fruit – the latter often distinctly citric, even slightly tropical.

Leading Franken Producers

Weingut Fürst

Hohenlindenweg 46, 63927 Bürgstadt. Owner: Paul Fürst. 28 acres. Classified site: Bürgstadter Centgrafenberg.

Paul Fürst is one of the most talented young winemakers in Germany. As well as producing impressive traditionally vinified dry Rieslings he also makes some of the best new oak-aged whites (Weissburgunders) and Spätburgunder reds in the country. Specialities include velvety rich Frühburgunder red wines, and superb naturally sweet Rieslaner and Scheurebe.

Juliusspital-Weingut

Klinikstrasse 5, 97070 Würzburg 1. Director: H. Kolesch. 287 acres. Classified sites: Würzburger-Stein, Innere Leiste and Abtsleite; Randersackerer-Teufelskeller and Pfülben; Escherndorfer Lump; Iphöfer-Julius-Echter-Berg; Rödelseer Küchenmeister.

A charitable foundation on a scale even grander than the Hospices de Beaune (in Burgundy), founded in 1576 by the Prince-Bishop Julius Echter von Mespelbrunn and now the third-largest wine estate in Germany, supporting a magnificent hospital for the people of Würzburg. Its low-vaulted cellar, 800 feet long, was built in 1699 under the great classical 'Fürstenbau' wing by Antonio Petrini. The vineyards are 35% Silvaner, 20% Müller-Thurgau, 18% Riesling. The remainder includes Gewürztraminer, Ruländer, Weissburgunder, Muskateller, Scheurebe, Spätburgunder (in Bürgstadt) and several new varieties. Today the estate is widely regarded as being the number one quality producer in Franken. Even Silvaner gives

vibrantly fruity, elegant wines while the dry Rieslings demonstrate what this grape is capable of in this region.

Weingut Johann Ruck

Marktplatz 19, 97346 Iphofen. Owner: Johann Ruck, 22.5 acres. Classified sites: Iphöfer Julius-Echter-Berg, Iphöfer Kalb.

Since the late 1980s Johann Ruck has been producing some splendid modern-style Franken wines. They marry beautifully the earthy and herbal qualities typical of the wines from Iphofen's famous vineyards with great freshness and racy acidity. In addition to fine dry Riesling and Silvaner, Herr Ruck also makes the most concentrated dry Grauburgunder in the region from old vines in Rödelsee. All his wines can be tasted at the historic estate house in the centre of Iphofen.

Weinbau Egon Schäffer

Astheimer Strasse 17, 97332 Escherndorf. Owner: Egon Schäffer. 7 acres. Classified site: Escherndorfer Lump.

This miniature estate makes perhaps the most seductively rich dry Silvaners in all of Franken. Egon Schäffer's vineyards are located on the slopes of the famous 'Lump' (or tramp) site. The Rieslings too are capable of achieving an imposing stature. The narrow cellars could not offer a more dramatic contrast to the grandeur of Würzburg itself, but there is no arguing with Egon Schäffer's commitment to quality or winemaking philosophy.

Weingut Robert Schmitt

Maingasse 13, 97236 Randersacker. Owner: Bruno Schmitt. 17 acres. Classified sites: Randersackerer-Pfülben, Randersackerer-Sonnenstuhl, Würzburger Abtsleite.

Bruno Schmitt, like his deceased uncle Robert before him, is wholeheartedly commited to uncompromising winemaking principles. Among these are that no wines should ever be chaptalized (i.e. have sugar added during fermentation to increase their alcoholic content) or de-acidified, and that every wine should fully ferment through to dryness. This philosophy might be too extreme were it not for the impressive concentration which the estate's Prädikat wines possess. Their ageing potential is legendary, and even Kabinett wines need two or three years' bottle ageing to show their best.

Weingut Schmitt's Kinder

Am Sonnenstuhl, 97236 Randersacker. Owner: Karl Schmitt. 32 acres. Classified sites: Randersackerer-Marsberg, Randersackerer-Pfülben, Randersackerer-Sonnenstuhl, Randersackerer-Teufelskeller.

With his self-consciously modern winery and the state-of-the-art cellar equipment Karl Schmitt is not afraid of being declared a progressive thinker amongst Franken's winemakers. The wines he produces are the epitome of modernism in the region; brimming with fruit and aroma, very clean and pure in flavour. While he is best known for his naturally sweet Rieslings and Rieslaners, in his hands even humbler grapes such as Bacchus and Müller-Thurgau give good wines.

Weingut Hans Wirsching

Ludwigstrasse 16, 97346 Iphofen. Owner: Dr Heinrich Wirsching.
137 acres. Classified sites: Iphofener-Julius-Etcher-Berg,
Kronsberg and Kalb; Rödelseer Küchenmeister.

A family firm since 1630 with its original Gutshaus and
cellars, as well as modern ones outside the village. Silvaner,
Müller-Thurgau and Riesling predominate; Kerner,
Scheurebe, Bacchus and Portugieser are also grown, with a
little Traminer. The generally dry wines are full, fruity and
aromatic with excellent balance. Those of Spätlese and
higher Prädikat age extremely well.

OTHER FRANKEN PRODUCERS

Weingut Josef Deppisch 97837 Erlenbach bei
Marktheidenfeld. Owner: Theo and Johannes Deppisch. 37
acres. Since the return of Johannes Deppisch to the family
estate in 1988 quality has improved steadily. Silvaner has
long been the grape with which the family name has been
most strongly associated. The red sandstone soils of the
Homburger Kallmuth give the wines from this grape
unusually pronounced fruit and elegance.

Weingut Michael Fröhlich 97332 Escherndorf. Owner:
Michael Fröhlich. 17 acres. It was only a decade ago that this
small estate became independent and began to sell bottled
wines. Michael Fröhlich's fresh, clean wines are amongst the
best in this part of the Main Valley, the Rieslings standing out
in a wide range.

Bürgerspital zum Heiligen Geist Theaterstrasse 19, 97070
Würzburg. Director: Rudolf Friess. 247 acres. Classified sites:
Würzburger-Stein, Abtsleite and Innere Leiste; Randersackerer-
Teufelskeller, Marsberg and Pfülben. A splendid charity
founded in 1319 for the old people of Würzburg by
Johannes von Steren, and although now somewhat
overshadowed by the even richer ecclesiastical upstart, the
Juliusspital (q.v.), still the fourth-biggest wine estate in
Germany, with the greatest share of Würzburg's famous
Stein and other good south slopes. The vineyards are 32%
Riesling, 21% each Silvaner and Müller-Thurgau, the rest
include Kerner, Scheurebe, Spätburgunder and several
new varieties.

Hearty, full-flavoured and dry Rieslings are the pride of
the house, though a tasting at the huge 500-seater Weinstube
in the venerable hospital buildings leaves an impression of
full-flavoured wines from almost any variety. Quality has
been mixed in recent years.

Weingut Fürst Löwenstein 97892 Kreuzwertheim. Owner:
Alois Konstantin Fürst zu Löwenstein-Wertheim-Rosenberg.
66 acres. After a period in the doldrums, this famous estate
has recently once again begun making impressive,
traditional-style Silvaners from the precipitous slopes of the
first-class Homburger Kallmuth site.

Fürstlich Castell'sches Domänenamt Schlossplatz 5,
97335 Castell. Owner: Prince Albrecht zu Castell-Castell. 148
acres. A princely estate with classic palace in a village on a
hill, the vineyards sloping up to perfectly kept oakwoods –
the prince's other pride. Müller-Thurgau accounts for 31%,
Silvaner 32% and there is a catholic range of newer varieties.
The most impressive wines of the estate's wide range are the
Rieslaner dessert wines, which are powerful, lush and
piquant. Silvaner and Müller-Thurgau tend to give savoury
wines with an earthiness that is often rustic. Visitors to this
remote spot can taste the wines in a beautiful tasting room
decorated with trompe l'oeil, or in the 'Weinstall', a stable-
turned-restaurant.

Weingut Sektkellerei Ernst Gebhardt Hauptstrasse 21–23,
97286 Sommerhausen. Owners: the Hügelschäffer family.
37 acres. Classified sites: Randersackerer-Teufelskeller and
Sonnenstuhl. An 18th-century family estate bought in 1888
by the Hügelschäffer family, who are also wine merchants.
They make somewhat fruitier and sweeter wines than the
old Franconian style with great skill, especially from their
best sites: Steinbach and the famous Teufelskeller. 26% is
Silvaner, 26% Müller-Thurgau, 20% Scheurebe (a favourite,
distinctly blackcurrant), 6% Bacchus and 6% Riesling. Their
Weinstube in the Flemish baroque style is a well-known
attraction, as is Gebhardt Sekt.

Weingut Martin Göbel 97236 Randersacker. Owner:
Hubert Göbel, 14.5 acres. Although this small estate divides
its energy too widely amongst a bewildering range of
classic and new grape varieties Hubert Göbel's best wines
are rich and expressive. His success rate is highest with
Rieslaner and Traminer, from which he makes superb
Auslese wines.

Staatlicher Hofkeller Residenzplatz 3, 97070 Würzburg.
Owner: the State of Bavaria. Director: Dr Rowald Hepp. 370
acres. Classified sites: Würzburger-Stein and Innere Leiste;
Randersackerer-Pfülben and Marsberg. The superlative vineyards of the lordly Prince-Bishops of Würzburg, orginating in
the 12th century, are now (since 1814) the Bavarian State
Domain, run by the Bayerische Landensanstalt für Weinbau
and Gartenbau. The great cellar under the baroque Residency
at Würzburg is one of the most stirring sights in the world of
wine. The vines, all on steep or sloping sites, on many
different soils, are 23% Müller-Thurgau, 23% Riesling, 15%
Silvaner, 7% Rieslaner, 6% Kerner and many others in smaller
quantities, including Spätburgunder. The object is wines of
true Franconian style, balancing high acidity with powerful
flavours, all either dry or semi-dry (except for Auslesen, etc.).
After achieving rather impressive results during the late '80s
and early '90s, new director Dr Hepp has rapidly put the estate
back on course.

Weinbau Ernst Popp 97343 Iphofen. Owner: Michael
Popp. 34.5 acres plus 49.5 on contract to Iphofen and
Rödelsee. Classified sites: Iphofener-Julius-Echter-Berg and
Rödelseer-Küchenmeister. A respected family firm since
1878 making dry, 'nutty' wines of character, typical of the
region. 51% Silvaner and 18% Müller-Thurgau and 10%
Riesling and others.

Weingut Gerhard Roth Büttnergasse 11, 97355 Wiesenbronn. Owner: Gerhard Roth. This small estate in the Steigerwald may be the best known for its new oak-aged reds, but its richly fruity, substantial dry Rieslings deserve to be taken equally seriously.

Weingut Horst Sauer 97332 Escherndorf. Owner: Horst Sauer. 16 acres. This small estate is a most reliable source for well-crafted dry Rieslings and Silvaners from the Escherndorfer Lump.

Weingut Schloss Sommerhausen 97286 Sommerhausen. Owners: the Steinmann family, 48 acres. Best known for their vine nursery, the largest privately owned business of its kind in Germany, the Steinmanns also own this fine estate. Dry Riesling, Silvaner and Müller-Thurgau make up the bulk of the production, but Sommerhausen is best known for its wines from the Pinot family of white grapes (Weissburgunder, Grauburgunder, Auxerrois) and Chardonnay.

Weingut Josef Störrlein 97236 Randersacker. Owner: Armin Störrlein. 17 acres. This small estate has enjoyed a rapid rise since it was created out of nothing by Armin Störrlein in 1970. Since the new cellars were constructed at the begining of the 1990s quality has taken another jump up. Modern Franken wines of considerable character, including very good dry Riesling, Silvaner and Müller-Thurgau.

Weingut Zehnthof 97320 Sulzfeld. Owners: the Luckert family. 30 acres. Young Wolfgang Luckert makes sleek, racy dry wines from a wide range of white grapes (most importantly Silvaner, Müller-Thurgau, Riesling and Weissburgunder) and superb dessert wines when conditions are right.

Landwein

This new (1982) category of German table wine was introduced as a response to the success of French *vins de pays* – as standard drinking but of some local character, with more style and flavour than the totally anonymous Tafelwein.

Fifteen designated regions with new names but roughly corresponding to the well-known basic regions of Germany have the right to christen a Landwein if the wine in question meets certain simple requirements. The alcohol content, for example, must be half a degree higher than that of Tafelwein. An important regulation is that the sugar content should not be more than 18 grams a litre (the upper limit for the *halbtrocken* or halfway category). Landwein is therefore intended as a relatively dry and briskly acidic wine suitable for mealtimes. The 15 Landwein areas are:

Ahrtaler Landwein Ahr
Starkenburger Landwein Hessiche Bergstrasse
Rheinburgen Landwein Mittelrhein
Landwein der Mosel Mosel and Ruwer
Landwein der Saar Saar
Nahegauer Landwein Nahe
Altrheingauer Landwein Rheingau
Rheinischer Landwein Rheinhessen
Pfälzer Landwein Pfalz
Fränkischer Landwein Franken
Regensburger Landwein a minuscule area on the Danube
Bayerischer Bodensee-Landwein a small area near Lindau on Lake Constance (Bodensee), which in QbA terms is part of Württemberg, although politically it belongs to Bavaria
Schwäbischer Landwein Württemberg
Unterbadischer Landwein northern part of Baden
Südbadischer Landwein southern part of Baden

WÜRTTEMBERG

With more than 110,000 acres of vineyards Württemberg was far and away Germany's largest winegrowing region three centuries ago. Today it may only boast a quarter of this area, but the large sprawling tract of vineyards around Heilbronn, Ludwigsburg, Stuttgart and Tübingen is difficult to make sense of at a glance. Experience Württemberg at first hand, though, and the distinctive identity of this region becomes immediately clear. This is the only part of Germany where wine plays a comparable role to that in France or Italy. Here the daily glass of Trollinger, a pale, light red wine, is a vital part of the Swabian diet. Württemberg accounts for fully 40% of Germany's red wine production, and noble red wine grapes such as Lemberger, Spätburgunder and Samtrot (a Pinot Noir mutation) play an important role next to the huge volumes of simple red wine from Trollinger and Schwarzriesling (Pinot Meunier). Riesling is the most important white wine grape, but gives completely different results compared to those of the Rhine or Mosel valleys to the west. The continental climate and gypsum-marl soils which are so well suited to the red grapes, give white wines that are full, broad and earthy. The challenge for winemakers is to give them at least a touch of elegance. The best of these come from steep, terraced vineyards in the Neckar Valley. Sadly, at present no winegrowing region in Germany has more unrealized potential than Württemberg. The ease with which wines of solid, everyday quality can be sold within the region seems to prevent more than a handful of winegrowers working for top quality – and recognition.

Bereich Remstal-Stuttgart Four thousand acres of vines are divided into five Grosslagen. Hohenneuffen is the uppermost of the river, round Neuffen, Frickenhausen and Metzingen. There is no Riesling grown here but light Silvaner, Müller-Thurgau and (for red) largely Schwarzriesling. Weinsteige is the Grosslage of Stuttgart, a city where the appearance of vineyards in its midst (or at least in its suburbs Bad Cannstatt, Mühlhausen and Zuffenhausen) is particularly surprising. The vines here are mainly Trollinger and Riesling, the best-known Einzellagen Berg, Steinhalde and Zuckerle, and in Fellbach, facing west over the Neckar towards Stuttgart, Wetzstein, Goldberg, Lämmler (entirely red wine) and Hinterer Berg.

The valley of the Rems (Remstal) has three Grosslagen: Kopf, centred round Schörndorf, with a good deal of Trollinger but also some fair sites for Riesling; Wartbühl, around Weinstadt and Korb, with Riesling and other white grapes in the majority; and Sonnenbühl, south of Weinstadt and the Rems, which specializes in robust Trollinger.

Bereich Württembergisches Unterland Much the biggest area, with 24,200 acres of Württemberg's vines. The Bereich, with nine Grosslagen, spreads across the Neckar Valley north of Stuttgart from Baden to the Bottwar Valley in the east.

Grosslage Schalkstein The first Grosslage, following the Neckar north, stretches from Ludwigsburg to Hessigheim, the wine centre, with red grapes in the majority, their best wines well-coloured and full-bodied.

Grosslage Stromberg A widely dispersed collection of Einzellagen along the tributary Enz Valley to the west, with Mühlhausen and Vaihingen as centres, stretching down the Neckar Valley to Kirchheim and Bönnigheim. Two-thirds are red vines, with considerable Lemberger.

Grosslage Heuchelberg A more intensive viniferous district just north of Stromberg to the west of the Neckar. The centres are Cleebronn and Schwaigem, responsible for some of the area's best Rieslings from lime-rich soil.

Grosslage Kirchenweinberg This is the real kernel of Württemberg's wine region. It includes the huge 1,140-acre Katzenbeisser at Lauffen. Talheim and Flein, on the outskirts of Heilbronn, are its other centres. Schwarzriesling is the most popular grape in a predominantly red-wine area.

Grosslage Wunnenstein A limited district east of the Neckar, including the town of Grossbottwar, mainly dedicated to red grapes.

Grosslage Schozachtal A small area just north of Wunnenstein, around Abstatt and Untergruppenbach. White wines are in the majority. Some good Riesling is grown here.

Grosslage Salzberg An important area east of Heilbronn, noted for some of Württemberg's best Rieslings. The 12 Einzellagen are spread between Eberstadt, Lehrensteinsfeld, Willsbach, Affaltrach, Eichelberg, Obersulm and Löwenstein.

Grosslage Lindelberg A more scattered region of mainly white wine, northeast of Heilbronn round the Brettach Valley between Bretzfeld and Untersteinbach.

Grosslage Staufenberg Heilbronn is an important wine centre with a first-class cooperative. Its vineyards and those of the Neckar downstream are in the Grosslage Staufenberg, which has Einzellagen divided almost equally between white grapes and red. The main centres are Gundelsheim, Erlenbach, Weinsberg and Heilbronn itself.

Bereich Kocher-Jagst-Tauber The northern Württemberg Bereich is much the smallest, with 1,000 acres, and the only one to specialize (90%) in white wine. It straddles the valleys of the Kocher and Jagst, Neckar tributaries from the east, and the Tauber.

Grosslage Kocherberg The southern half of the Bereich includes Ingelfingen and Niedernhall on the Kocher.

Grosslage Tauberberg The isolated Tauber Valley vineyards are centred on Bad Mergentheim, Weikersheim and Niederstetten. Both the limy soil and the use of Silvaner and Müller-Thurgau recall the fact that Franken is not far away.

Leading Württemberg Producers

Weingut Ernst Dautel

Lauerweg 55, 74357 Bönnigheim. Owner: Ernst Dautel. 21 acres. Classified sites: Besigheimer Wurmberg.

Known only to a few insiders a decade ago the young wine estate of Ernst Dautel is now widely recognized as one of Württemberg's small elite group of estates. This remarkable achievement is the result of hard work, intense study of other wine-growing countries and much experimentation. As one might expect for this region it is Dautel's red wines which have written the most headlines, although both the traditionally vinified dry Rieslings and (most unusually for Germany) the Chardonnay aged in new oak are also impressive wines.

Weingüter und Schlosskellerei Graf von Neipperg

74190 Schwaigern. Owner: Count Karl-Eugen zu Neipperg. 70 acres. Classified sites: Schwaigerner Ruthe; Neipperger Schlossberg. Documents prove the Neipperg family to have been making wine here since 1248, shortly after the building of Burg Neipperg, the original castle. There is now a Weinstube in Schloss Schwaigern, over the cellars. The Neippergs introduced the Lemberger to make red wine of colour and tannin; their other speciality is spicy Traminer, although their Riesling is highly thought of. Today, both for its red and white wines, the estate is considered to be one of Württemberg's top producers. Riesling accounts for 26% of plantings, Lemberger 25%, Schwarzriesling 18%, Gewürztraminer 4%, Muskateller 4%, Spätburgunder 4% and others 19%. Count zu Neipperg is also the owner of two properties in St-Emilion: Château Canon-La-Gaffelière and Château La Mondotte.

OTHER PRODUCERS

Weingut Graf Adelmann, 'Brüssele' Burg Schaubeck, 71711 Steinheim-Kleinbottwar. Owner: Graf Michael Adelmann. 40 acres. Classified sites: Kleinbottwaren, Süssmund. One of the best-known estates in Württemberg, instantly recognized by its pale-blue and red 'lacy' labels with the name 'Brüssele' (after a former owner). Burg Schaubeck is a small but towering and venerable stronghold, apparently with Roman origins, owned by the Adelmanns since 1914. The estate is best known for its red wines which, in the right vintage, can be amongst Germany's best. The most powerful of these are the Lembergers and the 'Cuvée Vignette', a blend of Lemberger and Pinot grapes. After some disappointing Rieslings during the early 1990s considerable changes have been made to the vinification of the white wines in favour of more fruit and freshness.

Schlosskellerei Affaltrach 74182 Obersulm. Owner: Thomas Baumann. 24.7 acres. Originally a 13th-century foundation, bought by the present owners in 1928 and now consisting of a small estate and an associated company buying grapes from some 200 small growers to make wine and Sekt. The estate wines are dry, intended for use at table and made to improve in bottle when possible. Eisweins and Trockenbeerenauslesen with some of the highest must weights in the country are produced here.

Weingut Gerhard Aldinger Schmerstrasse 25, 70734 Fellbach. Owner: Gert Aldinger. This 44-acre estate in the outskirts of Stuttgart is best known for its serious red wines, of which the blended 'C' is the most impressive.

Weingut Amalienhof 74074 Heilbronn. Owners: the Strecker family. 69 acres. Since taking over the Beilsteiner Steinberg site in a chaotic state in 1969 the Strecker family has built up a very successful estate. Best are the traditionally vinified Lemberger and Samtrot red wines.

Gräf von Bentzel-Sturmfeder-Horneck'sches 74360 Ilsfeld-Schozach. Owner: Count Benedikt von Bentzel-Sturmfeder-Horneck. 43.5 acres. Einzellage: Schozacher Roter Berg. This is an estate with 14th-century origins and 18th-century cellars. The vineyards include 30% Riesling, 25% Spätburgunder, 16% Samtrot and 7% Schwarzriesling, on clay and marl slopes which give body to the wines. The wines last well, even when the acidity is relatively low, with barrel-ageing giving them stability.

Weingut Drautz-Able 74076 Heilbronn. Owners: Christel Able and Richard Drautz. 34 acres. Although Riesling and Trollinger red wines account for more than half the production of this well-regarded estate it is the powerful, Lemberger reds aged in new oak which have rightly attracted the most attention. The white wines are good, but not spectacular.

Weingut Jürgen Ellwanger 73650 Winterbach. Owner: Jürgen Ellwanger, 30 acres. The Ellwangers cultivate a wide range of red grapes, including the Austrian Blauer Zweigelt, from which they make some impressively rich, fleshy wines. The estate's Riesling and Kerner white wines are rather less impressive.

Weingärtnergenossenschaft Grantschen 74189 Grantschen. 168 members, 285 acres. Fully two-thirds of the production of this small cooperative is red wine, and the top wines, particularly the 'Grandor', aged in new oak are amongst Württemberg's best red wines.

Weingut Karl Haidle 71394 Kernen im Remstal. Owner: Hans Haidle, 33 acres. If Hans Haidle's estate is not better known in Württemberg it is because he is a white-wine specialist in a region where red wines grab most of the limelight. His dry Rieslings are amongst the best in the region, and he makes unusually elegant wines from the Kerner grape.

Weingut Heinrich Riedstrasse 29, 74076 Heilbronn. Owner: Martin Heinrich. This 25-acre estate which looks back on 35 years of history has recently begun to attract attention with its new oak aged red wines. Top of the range is the Lemberger-based 'GA 1' *cuvée*.

Schlossgut Hohenbeilstein 71717 Beilstein. Owner: Hartmann Dippon. 22 acres. Young Hartmann Dippon recently took over the family estate, and has converted it to organic viticulture. Red wine remains the heart of the wide range, the best examples being made from the Spätburgunder grape.

Weingut Burg Hornberg 74865 Neckarzimmern. Owner: Baron Dajo von Gemmingen-Hornberg. 36 acres. An ancient steep vineyard site owned by this family since the 17th century, with 26% Riesling, 7% Spätburgunder, 12% Weissburgunder, 12% Müller-Thurgau as well as some Muskateller, Gewürztraminer and Ruländer. The wines are made by traditional methods, and the best are full-bodied and impressive. A restaurant provides a chance to taste a wide range.

Weingut Fürst zu Hohenlohe-Ohringen 74613 Ohringen, Schloss. Owner: Fürst Kraft zu Hohenlohe-Ohringen. 44 acres. Classified sites: Verrenberger Verrenberg (solely owned). A princely estate since the 14th century, with 17th-century cellars (and even a cask dated 1702). The Verrenberg is unusual in being a single sweep of vines, producing mostly dry whites. The vines are 50% Riesling (this much is unusual for Württemberg), 20% Limberger, 10% Spätburgunder and 20% others.

Weingut Albrecht Schwegeler 71404 Korb. Owner: Albrecht Schwegeler. 1.5 acres. It would be ridiculous to include an estate of such miniscule size in a work like this were it not for the fact that Albrecht Schwegeler's rich, concentrated 'Granat' is one of the finest red wines in Württemberg.

Staatsweingut Weinsberg Traubenplaz 5, 74189 Weinsberg. Director: Dr Günter Bäder. 84 acres. Founded in 1868 by Karl von Württemberg as the Royal Wine School, this estate is still part of one of Germany's leading wine schools. It is best known for its consistently good red wines, which are made both in the traditional and oak-aged styles. Riesling is the most important grape, though, with 22% of the vineyard area. It is followed by Lemberger and Trollinger, both with 11% and Spätburgunder, Schwarzriesling and Samtrot each with 9%.

Weingut Wöhrwag 70327 Untertürkheim. Owner: Hans-Peter Wöhrwag, 42 acres. With the entire first-class Untertürkheimer Herzogenberg vineyard site at his disposal Hans-Peter Wöhrwag has succeeded in making some of the finest Rieslings in Württemberg in recent years, making him the most important rising star winemaker of the region.

BADEN

Baden is the new force in German wine – at present only domestically, but soon no doubt on the world stage. Its vineyards have undergone no less than a revolution in recent years: they have been almost entirely rationalized and remodelled by *Flurbereinigung* (landscaping), have doubled in size and now lie fourth in yield in Germany, behind the Pfalz, Rheinhessen and the Mosel-Saar-Ruwer.

Baden faces Alsace across the Rhine. It is Germany's warmest (although not necessarily its sunniest) wine region, with correspondingly ripe, high-alcohol and lower in acid wines: the diametric opposite of Mosels in style and function. The best Mosel wines are for analytical sipping. Baden makes mealtime wines with a warm vinosity that approaches the French style. It is the choice of grape varieties and the taste for a trace of sweetness that distinguishes them from Alsace wines. The difference is reinforced by a slightly less favourable climate than the suntrap of the Vosges foothills.

Eighty percent of Baden's vineyards lie in an 80-mile strip running from northeast to southwest, from Baden Baden to Basel, in the foothills of the Black Forest where it meets the Rhine Valley. The balance is of purely local importance. The vineyards lie southeast on the banks of the Bodensee (alias Lake Constance), north of Baden in the minor regions of the Kraichgau and Badischer Bergstrasse, respectively south and north of Heidelberg (but now united in one Bereich with both names), and far north on the border of Franken, a little region known logically enough as Bereich Badlisches Frankenland. The main thrust of Baden viticulture is thus along the Rhine from where it leaves the Bodensee to where it enters the Pfalz.

Baden is, even more than the southern Pfalz, the land of the cooperative. More than 100 cooperatives process nearly 90 percent of the crop, and half of all their output finds its way to the huge Badischer Winzerkeller central cellars in Breisach on the Rhine. The cooperative, formerly called the ZBW (they've dropped the 'Zentrale') bottles some 400–500 different types of wine. Baden has no powerful preference for one grape variety. The Müller-Thurgau is the workhorse, with more than one-third of the acreage. Spätburgunder for red and light rosé (Weissherbst) comes second with one fifth. Then come Ruländer (Pinot Gris), Gutedel (Chasselas), Riesling, Silvaner, Weissburgunder and Gewürztraminer. Baden's taste is clearly not for the highly aromatic new varieties: the vast majority of its white wines are made from relatively 'neutral' grapes. Its best, however, are made from Riesling and Ruländer.

Ageing German wines

Good-quality German wines have a much longer lifespan, and benefit much more from being kept in bottle, than fashion suggests or most people suppose. The wine industry and trade have little to gain from older bottles and have tacitly agreed that German wines are ready to drink within months of being bottled. With the enormous crops (and hence the high water content) of standard-quality modern wines there is indeed no gain from keeping bottles more than 6 months or a year. But almost all the superior-grade (QmP) wines, delectable as they may taste in their flowery and fruity youth, have the potential to gain another dimension of flavour with maturity. When they are first offered for sale they are at their most brisk and lively, with acidity and fruitiness often tending to cancel each other out in a generally tingling and exciting effect. Some fine wines (particularly Rieslings) at this stage have remarkably little aroma. Sometimes after a year or two in bottle the first rapture goes without maturer flavours taking its place; the wine you bought with enthusiasm seems to be letting you down. Be patient. The subtle alchemy takes longer. It may be 4 or 5 years before the mingled savours of citrus and spice and oil emerge.

Each vintage has its own timespan, but as a generalization Kabinett wines from a first-rate grower need at least 3 years in bottle and may improve for 7 or 8, Spätleses will improve for anything from 4 to 10 years, and Auslesen and upwards will benefit from 5 or 6 years up to 20 or even more.

Liebfraumilch

For most foreigners the great stumbling block to the full enjoyment of German wines is the German language. It certainly takes dogged persistence for a non-German speaker to master the polysyllabic names and categories. It is little comfort to be told that they form a logical national system by which everything can be unravelled – and still less to discover that the vaunted logic often lapses into local exceptions. Small wonder then that most non-Germans shrug their shoulders and settle for the one name they know: Liebfraumilch – a name that guarantees nothing. The law requires only that Liebfraumilch wines should be 'of pleasant character', with more than 18 grams per litre of unfermented sugar, and be made of certain grapes in certain regions – those which in any case produce the greatest volumes of wine.

CLASSIFIED BADEN VINEYARDS

Achkarrer Schlossberg The steep slopes and stony volcanic tuff soil of this site result in dry Weissburgunder and Grauburgunder wines that perfectly marry power with elegance.

Durbacher Plauelrain/Kapellenberg/Olberg/Schlossberg/ Schloss Grohl/Steinberg The south-facing vineyards in the Durbach Valley are some of the steepest in all Baden, and their granitic soil is ideal for Riesling, Scheurebe and Gewürztraminer. The Plauelrain is the largest and best known of these excellent sites.

Ihringer Winklerberg The steep, terraced Winklerberg at the southwestern tip of the Kaiserstuhl is the warmest vineyard in all of Germany. The volcanic tuff soil results in full-bodied, minerally dry Grauburgunder and red Spätburgunder wines that belong to the finest which Baden has to offer.

Neuweier Mauerberg/Schlossberg Close to Baden-Baden at the northern end of the Ortenau lie the terraced hillsides which form these fine south-facing sites. The Rieslings from here are intense and elegant, needing several years of ageing to show their best.

Oberrotweiler Eichberg/Henkenberg/Kirchberg The town of Oberrotweil situated on the western flank of the Kaiserstuhl boasts three first-class sites, all of which give impressively rich, firmly structured dry Weissburgunder and Grauburgunder wines.

Ortenberger Schlossberg The narrow terraces of this small site with their poor granitic soil give perhaps the most intensely minerally Rieslings of the Ortenau. In the sole ownership of the Schloss Ortenberg estate.

Zell-Weierbacher Abtsberg The best of the vineyards to the east of the town of Offenburg, the Abtsberg gives some of the richest wines in the Ortenau. Riesling, Grauburgunder and Gewürztraminer give the best results.

Leading Baden Producers

Weingut Bercher

Mittelstadt 13, 79235 Burkheim. Owners: Eckhardt and Rainer Bercher. 47 acres.

The Bercher brothers run one of Baden's finest estates from an imposing 17th-century house in the beautifully preserved old town of Burkheim. Whether it is a simple Müller-Thurgau, sleek dry Riesling Kabinett or massively powerful Weissburgunder Auslese their white wines are of a uniformly high standard. Since the late 1980s they have also made superb oak-aged Spätburgunders which are amongst Germany's finest red wines. Although most of the estate's

wines are drunk shortly after release, everything of Spätlese or higher quality will benefit from at least five years of ageing. This is an estate where it is really possible to speak of a successful marriage of tradition and innovation.

Weingut Dr Heger

Bachenstrasse 19, 79241 Ihringen. Owner: Joachim Heger. 33.5 acres. Classified sites: Achkarrer Schlossberg, Ihringer Winklerberg.

Founded in 1935 by the country doctor Dr Max Heger, this estate has grown rapidly in extent and reputation during recent decades. Today, thanks to the efforts of its dynamic winemaker Joachim Heger, it is the best known in all of Baden. This fame is primarily due to the powerful, dry Weissburgunder and Grauburgunder whites, the best of which see just a whiff of new oak. During the 1990s the estate's Spätburgunders aged in new oak have also rightly attracted a good deal of attention. They may not be the silkiest or most elegant Pinot Noirs in Germany, but for concentration they are hard to beat.

Weingut Bernhard Huber

Heimbacher Weg 19, 79364 Malterdingen. Owner: Bernhard Huber. 31.5 acres.

Since leaving the local cooperative and becoming independent in 1987 Bernhard Huber has aquired an excellent reputation for his Spätburgunder red wines with astonishing rapidity. The best of these – the 'R' for Reserve bottlings – are arguably Germany's finest red wines offering Premier Cru red Burgundy a serious challenge. His aged in new oak 'Malterer' is an idiosyncratic dry white with considerable character, and his dry Rieslings from the Hecklinger Schlossberg are amongst Baden's best.

Weingut Karl H. Johner

Gartenstrasse 20, 79235 Bischoffingen. Owner: Karl H. Johner. 24.5 acres.

In ten years Karl Heinz Johner has not only built this estate up from scratch, but also made it one of Baden's most successful quality producers. The heart of his range, all of which are marketed as Tafelwein, are the new-oak-aged Weissburgunder dry whites and Spätburgunder reds. The best barrels are bottled sperately as 'SJ' or Selektion Johner. The California-style winery building with its circular barrel cellar is as distinctive as the estate's wines, and is a big leap forward compared to the garages in which Johner made the wines that made his reputation.

Weingut Andreas Laible

Am Bühl 6, 77770 Durbach. Owners: the Laible family. 10 acres. Classified site: Durbacher Plauelrain.

No self-publicist, Andreas Laible's winemaking talents only came to the attention of a wider public during the 1990s although he had been collecting medals at the regional wine competitions for years. His elegant, intensely fruity dry and naturally sweet Rieslings have almost Mosel-like character. Even more impressive are his powerful Scheurebe and Traminer Auslese and higher Prädikat dessert wines, which are amongst Baden's finest wines, in this or any other style.

Weingut Schloss Neuweier

Mauerbergstrasse 21, 76534 Baden-Baden. Owner: Gisela Joos. 20 acres. Classified sites: Neuweier Mauerberg, Neuweier Schlossberg.

Since purchasing the run-down Schloss Neuweier estate in 1992 Gisela Joos and her winemaker Alexander Spinner have put this estate back into the first rank of Baden's quality wine producers. The great majority of the production is dry Riesling of considerable sophistication and capable of long ageing.

Weingut Salwey

Hauptstrasse 2, 79235 Oberrotweil. Owner: Wolf-Dietrich Salwe. 48 acres. Classified site: Oberrotweiler Eichberg.

As well as producing some of the finest fruit brandies in the whole of Germany, multi-talented Wolf-Dietrich Salwey also makes some of the finest white wines in the Kaiserstuhl. Unlike so many of his colleagues he has resisted the temptation to experiment with ageing in new oak, and has remained true to the traditional vinification style. The result is rich but elegant dry Weissburgunder and Grauburgunder with excellent ageing potential. His dry Spätburgunder Weissherbst wines from the Glottertal are amongst the finest rosé wines in all Germany. The estate's occasional dessert wines are also impressive. Only the red wines do not yet measure up to the highest standards.

Gräflich Wolff-Metternich'sches Weingut

7770 Durbach. Owner: Count Paul Josef Wolff-Metternich. 79 acres. Under director Ottman Schilli, this noble estate has long stood at the forefront of quality wine production in the Ortenau. The dry Rieslings (32% of vineyard area) and dessert wines from the Scheurebe and Sauvignon Blanc (!) grapes are particularly impressive and sell out quickly.

OTHER PRODUCERS

Weingut Abril Talstrasse 9, 79235 Bischoffingen. Owner: Hans Friedrich Abril. This smallish estate is a reliable source for traditional style, full-bodied dry Weissburgunder and Grauburgunder wines. Some interesting red wines too.

Weingut Blankenhorn 79418 Schliengen. Owner: Rosemarie Blankenhorn. 41 acres. Since taking over the family estate in 1989 Rosemarie Blankenhorn has restructured it and switched to organic viticulture. Gutedel (30%), Grauburgunder, Weissburgunder and Müller-Thurgau (each 10%). Dry whites account for the majority of the production; they are light, fresh and crisp. Her red-wine ambitions have still to be realized.

Winzergenossenschaft Durbach Nachweide 2, 77770 Durbach. 320 members, with 765 acres. Arguably the best coop winery in Germany. The majority of the WG Durbach's production is dry Rieslings and Spätburgunder red wines.

Weingut Freiherr von und zu Franckenstein Weingartenstrasse 66, 77654 Offenburg. Owner: Freiherr von und zu Franckenstein. This estate's director/winemaker, Hubert Doll, produces juicy, elegant dry Rieslings,

Grauburgunders and Gewürztraminers from 30 acres of vines on the granitic slopes of Zell-Weierbach and Berghaupten in the Ortenau.

Weingut Reichsgraf & Marquis zu Hoensbroech 74198 Angelbachtal-Michelfeld. Owner: Rüdiger, Reichsgraf und Marquis zu Hoensbroech. 42 acres. A small lordly estate of the Kraichgau, south of Heidelberg in north Baden. Powerful dry wines are made from Weissburgunder (35%), Riesling (20%), Spatburgunder (20%), Grauburgunder (15%) and others.

Schlossgut Istein 79588 Istein. Owner: Albert Soder. 21 acres. This historic estate in the south of the Markgräflerland was first recorded in 1139. Today it produces modern-style dry white wines from a range of local grapes including Gutedel, Weissburgunder, Grauburgunder and Riesling. While not amongst Baden's finest they are very well made and of consistently good quality.

Weingut Franz Keller/Schwarzer Adler 79235 Vogtsburg-Oberbergen. Owner: Franz Keller. 32 acres. For many years Franz Keller has been a strong opponent of *süssreserve*, all his wines are allowed to ferment to dryness or come to a natural halt. His ideas on winemaking appear to be more French than German; the 'Schwarzer Adler' restaurant (owned by the Keller family), one of the best in Baden, with its magnificent list of French wines, bears witness to this. *Barrique*-ageing has also been a feature for some years, with a number of wines being sold (at a very high price) as Tafelwein.

Today Franz Keller's son Fritz runs the estate, has constructed expensive new subterranean cellars and given the wines a fresher more modern style.

Lämmlin-Schindler 79418 Machen. Owners: the Schindler family. 32 acres. This organic estate, founded only in 1962, is today the leading quality-wine producer of the Markgräflerland. Its elegant Weissburgunder and Grauburgunder Spätlese are amongst the most sophisticated dry white wines made in Baden, and even the simply dry Gutedel is well crafted. Only in the red-wine field do the Schindlers still have some ground to make up.

Weingut Gebrüder Müller Richard-Müller-Strasse 5, 79206 Breisach. Owner: Peter Bercher. This 17-acre estate boasts a sizeable holding in the first-class Ihringer Winklerberg at the southwestern tip of the Kaiserstuhl, but can claim to have made this site's reputation during the first half of the 19th century. Good as the dry white wines often are, it is the substantial Spätburgunder reds that rightly attract most of the attention.

Weinbauversuchsgut Schloss Ortenberg Burgweg 19a, 77799 Ortenberg. Director: Winifried Köninger. 17.5 acres. Classified sites: Ortenberger Schlossberg. The castle of Schloss Ortenberg belongs to the German youth hostel association, and its vineyards were purchased in 1950 by the regional council. Since Winifried Köninger was appointed director in 1991 standards have improved considerably. A wide range of grapes are cultivated, the best results coming from Riesling (25%) and Gewürztraminer (6%). Both give impressively powerful dry wines.

Schloss Salem 88682 Salem. Owner: Max, Markgraf von Baden. Holdings in three estates: Birnau, Schloss Kirchberg and Bermatingen, which all specialize in Müller-Thurgau and Spätburgunder Weissherbst. Schloss Salem is the Bodensee residence of the Margrave of Baden and the modern cellar of the widespread estate. Winemaker Herbert Senft maintains a good standard across the wide range. *See also* Markgräflich Badis'sches Weingut, Schloss Staufenberg.

Weingut Hartmut Schlumberger Weinstrasse 19, 79295 Laufen. Owner: Hartmut Schlumberger. 16 acres. An old family manor between Freiburg and Basel in the heart of the Markgräflerland, which is planted with 33% Gutedel, 20% Spätburgunder, 25% Weissburgunder, 5% Müller-Thurgau and 17% other varieties. Hartmut Schlumberger's wines, generally dry and refreshing, are 'made with love and developed in wood'.

Weingut Seeger 69181 Leimen. Owner: Helmut Seeger. 12.5 acres. Thomas Seeger's winemaking talents have developed with tremendous rapidity in recent years. Today his Spätburgunders, aged in new oak, belong to Baden's best, comparing favourably with the better-known wines of the Kaiserstuhl. The dry white wines have come on in leaps and bounds too, and the estate's Weissburgunder, Grauburgunder and Riesling deserve to be taken seriously. They can all be enjoyed in the Seegers' popular 'Jägerlust' wine bar.

Staatsweingut Meersburg Seminarstrasse 6, 88709 Meersburg. Director: Helmut Häussermann. 146 acres. Formerly the estate of the Prince-Bishops of Meersburg. In 1802 it became Germany's first state domain, its land largely in Meersburg on the banks of the Bodensee (Lake Constance). The vineyards at Hohentwiel bei Singen are 1700 feet above sea level – which makes them the highest in Germany. The specialities are Müller-Thurgau of the gentler kind and pinky-gold *spritzig* Spätburgunder. Despite the Meersburg estate's commercial success, quality is very mixed.

Markgräflich Badis'sches Weingut, Schloss Staufenberg 77770 Durbach. Owner: H.M. Max, Markgraf of Baden. 67 acres. Classified site: Durbacher Schloss Staufenberg. A homely old manor on a hill with skirting vineyards, 40% Riesling (alias Klingelberger), 30% Spätburgunder, 10% Müller-Thurgau, 5% Traminer (alias Clevner), some Weissburgunder, Ruländer, and Scheurebe. A place of great charm, with delicate and sometimes distinguished dry Rieslings. The Margrave also owns Schloss Salem (q.v.) and Schloss Eberstein-Murgtal (28 acres), whose Spätburgunder is made at Schloss Staufenberg.

Weingut Rudolf Stigler Bachenstrasse 29, 79241 Ihringen. Owner: Andreas Stigler. 19 acres. Classified sites: Ihringer Winklerberg. One of the best private estates in the Kaiserstuhl, known particularly for its Rieslings from the Winklerberg. Besides Riesling (24%), Spätburgunder (36%), Silvaner and Müller-Thurgau (both 9%), Traminer, Weissburgunder, and Grauburgunder are also grown. Andreas Stigler's style is deliberately traditional, if not old-fashioned, emphasizing body and extract rather than the fruit itself.

SAALE-UNSTRUT

A short distance to the south of Halle and to the west of Leipzig lie the 1,000 acres of vineyards which form the Saale-Unstrut region. The name comes from the two idyllic river valleys which offer shelter to some of Germany's most easterly and northerly vineyards. The region is centred around the historic town of Naumburg, whose cathedral is a Gothic-Romanesque masterpiece. It was the church that brought serious viticulture to the region with the foundation of the Cistercian monastry of Pforta in 1137. Today, the region still suffers from the hangover of the communist period. Fully two-thirds of the region's wines are made by the Freyburg cooperative with a further sixth in the hands of the Landsweingut Naumburg. Sadly, the region is best known in Germany for the Rottkäppchen Sekt company of Freyburg, most of whose cheap, commercial sparkling wine is made from imported base wines. A handful of independent growers are beginning to demonstrate that the limestone soils of the best sites are capable of producing subtly aromatic, mid-weight dry Weissburgunder, Riesling and Traminer though. Müller-Thurgau is the most widely planted grape, at best giving light, simple wines. As yet it is too early to classify individual sites.

Leading Saale-Unstrut Producer

Weingut Lützkendorf

Saalberge 31, 06628 Bad Kösen. Owner: Uwe Lützkendorf. 23.5 acres. After resigning as director of the Landesweingut Naumburg following German reunification in 1989, Udo Lützkendorf founded his own wine estate. It is now run by his son, Uwe, who is already setting exemplary standards: his dry Weissburgunder, Riesling and Traminer are clearly the best wines made in the region. Full of fruit, crisp acidity and enough vigour to improve with up to five years of bottle-ageing they prove what the beautiful Saale-Unstrut region is capable of producing.

SACHSEN

The 840 acres of vineyards dotted along the Elbe Valley around the historic cities of Dresden and Meissen form the smallest winegrowing region in Germany. During the reign of Sachsen's mighty ruler August the Strong in the first half of the 18th century the vineyard area was four times its present extent, and records indicate that the wines from Sachsen's top vineyard sites were regarded as being amongst Germany's finest. Since then, the phylloxera plague of the late 19th century, economic crises, war and dictatorship have all but eradicated the region's great wine culture. As in the Saale-Unstrut the structure of the wine industry is dominated by only two producers; the cooperative of Meissen which accounts for one-third of the region's production, and the Sächsisches Staatsweingut which makes up almost another third. However, over the last five years a dozen independent winegrowers have made increasingly sophisticated dry wines from a handful of grape varieties which prove that Sachsen is on the right road to making great wines once again. Traminer, Riesling, Weissburgunder and Grauburgunder have the most potential. The granite and ancient igneous rock soils result in wines that are more racy and minerally than those of the Saale-Unstrut. While it is too early to classify the region's vineyards, there are three obvious candidates, the Meissener Katzensprung, the Pillnitzer Königlicher Weinberg and the Raebeuler Goldener Wagen.

Leading Sachsen Producers

Weingut Schloss Proschwitz

01665 Proschwitz über Meissen. Owner: Dr Georg Prinz zur Lippe. 94 acres.

In 1991 Dr Georg Prinz zur Lippe bought back his family's Meissen vineyards to recreate the ancient Proschwitz estate. Much work remains to be done in the vineyards, but some good wines have already been made, particularly dry Weissburgunder and Grauburgunder, which are clean, fruity and polished.

Weingut Klaus Seifert

01445 Radebeul. Owner: Klaus Seifert. 0.5 acres.

It might seem ridiculous to include such a tiny property as this, but from the beginning of the 1970s Klaus Seifert showed himself to be the quality wine pioneer in Sachsen. His crystal clear, vibrantly fruity Müller-Thurgau and Kerner are fine examples of what these workhorse grapes can give in Sachsen when properly vinified. His dry Traminers from the granitic terraces of the Goldener Wagen are even more impressive.

Weingut Klaus Zimmerling

Bergweg 27, 01326 Pillnitz. Owner: Klaus Zimmerling. 8 acres.

Sachsen's leading wine estate came into existence in 1987 when Klaus Zimmerling, vintner, began clearing and replanting ancient vineyard terraces with the help of friends. Today his sophisticated dry Rieslings, Traminers and Grauburgunders from the Königlicher Weinberg are vinified in the cellars of nearby Schloss Pillnitz. Unusually for the region, a sizeable proportion of the crop is vinified in wood. Demand already far exceeds supply.

LUXEMBOURG

Luxembourg has some 3,285 acres of vines along the upper Mosel, above Trier. There are 1,200 small growers, but two-thirds of the country's wine is made in cooperatives. The industry is highly organized and controlled. All vines are graded in one of five qualities: *non admis* (not passed), Marque Nationale, Vin Classé, Premier Cru or Grand Premier Cru.

The grape varieties grown in Luxembourg are: Rivaner (Riesling x Silvaner) about 50 percent, Elbling about 25 percent, Riesling and Auxerrois about 10 per cent, with a little Gewürztraminer, Pinot Gris and Pinot Blanc. Elbling produces very weak juice but considerable quantities of light, often fizzy, and refreshing wine is made from a blend of Elbling and Rivaner. Rivaner is reliable, Auxerrois occasionally extremely tasty, Riesling always lean but sometimes classic.

The Domaine et Tradition estates association, founded in 1988, promotes quality from noble varieties. Major producers are Caves Bernard-Massard at Grevenmacher (good Cuvée de l'Ecusson classic method sparkling) and Vinsmoselles SC at Stadtbredimus (the organization of cooperatives). Others are M Bastian, Clos Mon Vieux Moulin, Aly Duhr et Fils, Caves Gales & Cie at Bech-Kleinmacher, Caves St Martin and Caves St Remy at Remich (also the HQ of the Government Viticultural Station), Caves Krier Frères at Remich, Feipel-Staar at Wellenstein, and Thill Frères at Schengen, also Château de Schengen and Sunnen-Hoffmann.

ITALY

VALLE
D'AOSTA

TRENTINO–
ALTO ADIGE

Bolzano

FRIULI–
VENEZIA
GIULIA

L Como

Trento

L Maggiore

VENETO

L Garda

Milano

Trieste

LOMBARDY

Verona

Venezia

Torino
PIEDMONTE

Po

EMILIA–
ROMAGNA

Genoa

Po

Bologna

LIGURIA

Firenze

Pisa

TOSCANA

Tevere

Siena

MARCHE

L Trasimeno

UMBRIA

L Bolsena

LATIUM

ABRUZZI

L Bracciano

Roma

MOLISE

CAMPANIA

Bari

Napoli

PUGLIA

Táranto

BASILICATA

SARDEGNA

CALABRIA

Cagliari

Palermo

Réggio di Calabria

SICILIA

In sheer quantity of wine made, Italy now regularly surpasses even France as the vine's own home. Every one of her 20 regions is in the wine business to a greater or lesser extent. Her geography, essentially a mountain range reaching south and east from the Alps towards the sub-tropics, offers as wide a range of vine-worthy sites and microclimates as nature has devised in any country.

It should come as no surprise that some of the world's best wines come from Italy. And yet it does. During the two and a half centuries when France was building the formidable structure and reputation of her quality-wine industry, and selecting and propagating her superlative vines, Italy was doing no such thing. Wine, like loyalty, remained very much a local, even a family, affair. Like bread, it was no less important for being taken for granted. But it was not measured even by national, let alone international, standards until well into this century. And when it was, Italy was inevitably judged simply as a source of low-priced wine, either for cheap and cheerful drinking or to be passed off as something else. To this day an almost incredible quantity, about half Italy's total wine exports, slinks anonymously out of the country in tankers to other parts of the EU – principally to France. High-quality wine depends entirely on demand, and nobody demanded it in Italy. It is still, to their own loss, the practice of many foreign wine merchants to list a token handful of the best-known Italian names rather than to investigate at first hand what Italy offers.

In the merchants' defence it must be said that the Italians seem to rejoice in giving their wines complicated labels. Access to them for non-Italians, even the most interested, is often blocked by a lilting litany of tuneful polysyllables in which not just the name of the wine and its maker but that of his property, and often an additional fantasy name for good measure all appear equally important. In writing tasting-notes on Italian wines it often takes me as long to identify them in my notebook as to taste and judge them.

Recent years have seen some dramatic changes in attitude and practice. The best winemakers are increasingly experimenting with untraditional ideas, grape varieties and techniques. They are offering distinctive wines with designer labels at high-fashion prices (which are not always justified by their quality). This producer-led revolution circumvents, or even ignores, the rules enshrined in the DOC system described below.

New developments at official level have proved equally important. New blood in the bureaucracy has seemingly meant an end to the scandal of deliberate wine surpluses; grapes grown to be distilled into unwanted industrial alcohol. Revisions of the law towards the French 'pyramid' concept of regional appellations, with smaller, higher-quality, zones within them are very slowly beginning to work. Those DOCs which are virtually unused have now been revoked.

It was the wine-law (called: '164') of 1992 that introduced a realization of the quality-pyramid philosophy. It peaks with Vigna zones (for example, parts of a DOCG-area, communes or parts of communes, estates), which – as in France – are subject to the strictest controls. The labelling of the vineyard is now also compulsory. DOCG and DOC follow. Half-way between the DOC-wines and the next level down, *vini da tavola*, is the new category of IGT-wines (*indicazione geografica tipica*): these are often wines with grape variety names, from a larger production-area and with more tolerant quality-requests than DOC-wines. The IGT classification provides clearer identity to much of what was the *vini-da-tavola* flood – and also enables greater control of this production. (In contrast to the *vini da tavola*, the IGT are subject to maximum crop limitations.)

The method of access to the essentials in the following pages tries to make the problems of identifying and judging Italy's wines as simple as possible. This is how it works.

The country is divided into 20 regions. Each is treated separately, in two parts: first the names and descriptions of the wines, then a wide selection of the better and bigger winemakers, with brief accounts of their standing, methods, size and a list of the wines they offer. If you know the name of the wine or the maker but not the region, the only place to start is the index. If you know the region, go straight to the wine or the maker. Cross-referencing goes from maker to wine but not (to avoid endless repetitive list) the other way round. The only list of producers, for example, of Chianti Classico is the list of winemakers in Tuscany, in which you will find that many Chianti makers also make other wines.

On the face of it, there is a radical division between officially controlled ('DOC') wines and others. The DOC (*Denominazione di Origine Controllata*) was instituted in 1963 as the very necessary regulatory system for Italian quality wines – an approximate equivalent to the French AC. At present approximately 16 percent of the country's total crop is thus regulated, depending on the harvest.

A DOC is a very detailed legal stipulation as to the precise character, origin, grapes, crop levels, strength, methods and ageing of a particular wine or group of wines agreed between the consortium of its producers and an expert committee in Rome. Since 1966, when the first DOC decree was signed by the President, approximately 300 have been declared. A summary of the DOC regulations for each of them is given in the following pages. It states the colour(s) of the wine(s), the province(s) within the region, the principal village(s) or a summary of the zone, the permitted grape varieties and their proportions, the maximum yield, the minimum alcohol level, the total annual production and any regulations concerning ageing – for example, when it may be sold as a *riserva*. The maximum crop is expressed in this book in hectolitres per hectare to make it comparable with those of other countries, although the DOC regulations stipulate both the number of quintals (100 kilograms) of grapes that may be picked and also what percentage of that weight may be processed into wine – the idea being to control the maker's urge to press every last drop out of his grapes. These listings do not include the stilted official descriptions of the style of the wine or the technical data on acidity, 'extract' and the rest.

In addition, an equal number of wines are listed that are not DOC and have no official delimitation. It is the great paradox of Italian wine today that a DOC freezes a type of wine in a historical moment. A DOC is essentially the definition of a tradition – at the very moment when wine technology has reached a pitch undreamed of before, when California (the outstanding example) is using its freedom to experiment to produce more exciting wine every year.

Not surprisingly, Italy's best winemakers are as eager to experiment with new ideas as anyone. They therefore either ignore DOC regulations or add to their traditional wares unconsecrated products representing their aspirations for the future. However good these have been – and they include almost all the great new wines of Italy – they have had to suffer the indignity of being officially classed as *vino da tavola* – table wine – the basic EU category for the blended wine of every day.

The reader of this book, therefore, should make no absolute distinction between DOC and other wines beyond the fact that a DOC is 'traditional' and subject to official regulation.

A further step in the regulation of certain DOCs has been instigated with an additional category: DOCG. The G stands for *Garantita*; the inference being that such wines are officially guaranteed as Italy's best. They are, indeed, the best geographically controlled wines. The first four DOCGs were Barbaresco, Barolo, Brunello di Montalcino and Vino Nobile di Montepulciano. Albana di Romagna was the next to be added to the list. Anyone who tastes it may be forgiven for asking how seriously the 'G' is to be taken. Candidates, Carmignano and Torgiano, go a long way to restoring faith. More recent DOCGs are Asti, Franciacorta (only the *spumante*), Gattinara, Taurasi, Vernaccia di San Gimignano and Brachetto d'Acqui. Amarone di Valpolicella is likely to be one of the next.

It is scarcely possible to summarize the state of Italian wine-making at present. Enormous recent investments in modern equipment and new ideas have already produced some wonderful results, but on the other hand some have stripped old friends of their character. So far the modern movement has succeeded in making both the most boring and the most brilliant of Italian wines. There is a balance to be found between tradition and technology (in grapes, in cellaring, in every aspect of winemaking). As the following pages show, Italy is very busy looking for it.

Italy in round figures

1 The production by region, average of years 1993–95 (in millions of litres)

2 Regional production as a percentage of national DOC total
3 Quantity of DOC wines as a percentage of regional total

	1	2	3		1	2	3
Piedmont	305.2	12.9	39.0	Abruzzi	397.8	6.6	15.2
Valle d'Aosta	3.0	0.0	11.8	Molise	40.5	0.2	3.7
Lombardy	147.8	6.5	44.8	Campania	223.5	0.7	2.8
Trentino-Südtirol	107.6	7.8	67.3	Apulia	1,037.0	1.8	1.8
Veneto	714.2	21.2	27.5	Basilicata	51.6	0.1	1.6
Friuli	117.5	6.4	53.1	Calabria	93.6	0.9	9.1
Liguria	22.7	0.2	6.5	Siciliy	998.4	1.6	1.7
Emilia Romagna	692.6	8.7	11.8	Sardinia	102.4	1.1	10.3
Tuscany	281.1	12.7	46.2	Italy	5,956.7	100.0	16.5*
Umbria	97.5	1.8	17.7				
Marches	189.9	3.7	18.1				
Latium	332.7	5.3	15.6				

* The figure 16.5 is DOC wines as total of Italian wine production

PIEDMONT

For uninhibited exploration of the varieties of grapes and what can be made from them, no part of Europe can compare with Piedmont. The vermouth of Turin witnesses that a good brew-up is part of local tradition. For ingredients the hills of Piedmont offer such an assortment of indigenous grapes that the accepted international varieties have scarcely been planted at all. Each of the local grapes is a character with something to offer. Each is made into wine unblended, often in several styles, and also mixed with others in brews which may be traditional or experimental, conventional or idiosyncratic. The former are frequently blessed with DOCs and DOCGs, the latter not – but this has no bearing on their respective qualities.

The emphasis is all on red wine. Only one Piedmont white has any history of other than local success before the last decade – and that is Asti Spumante. The Cortese is a good white grape now proving itself, but the catechism of important Piedmont wines must start with a list of the red grapes that enjoy the harsh climate of this sub-alpine area.

Nebbiolo comes first in quality. It takes its name from the

fog (*nebbia*) that characterizes autumn here, not only closing Milan airport regularly but creating quintessentially mellow fruitful pictures of gold-leaved vines tilting up to the grey hilltop villages.

The 1,600-foot Langhe Hills south of the town of Alba on the River Tanaro provide the slopes, shelter, soil, sunshine and humidity that bring Nebbiolo to perfection in Barolo (southwest of Alba) and Barbaresco (to its east). The style of Barolo, a wine of the maximum concentration, tannin and alcohol, has no very ancient history. But it has conviction, and its growers' palates are ready for as much power as their vines will give them. The inexperienced, the timid and the claret lovers should start with Nebbiolo in its less explosive manifestations.

Barbera comes first in quantity. But it too, unlike the common grapes of the south of France, carries conviction. It can be clumsy, but good Barbera is plummy and astringent in just the right measure.

Dolcetto is quite different. No other red grape succeeds in conveying such an impression of softness while being sometimes startlingly dry. It sounds odd, but with rich food it makes a tantalizing meal opener; it is a marvellous complement to antipasti, especially the cold meats. Dolcetto is not normally for ageing.

In complete contrast Freisa is inclined to be fizzy and sometimes even sweet, and again in contrast Grignolino tends to the pale, mild but teasingly bitter style of wine which is common in northwest Italy. Add the lively light Bonarda and the Croatina and Vespolina and the range of possible cocktails is almost limitless.

The following list reflects the complexity of the region with more DOCs and DOCGs than any other – and lots of unofficial 'table' wines besides. And Piedmont now has three new DOC designations: Langhe, Monferrato and Piemonte. These serve not only to give a legal home to huge quantities of not-yet-DOC wines, but also to catch existing DOC wines (like Barolos or Barbera d'Astis), before declassifying them to *vino da tavola* status.

Would that there were space for more than a low bow towards the best fare of Italy; the truffles, the *fonduta*, the game and all the simple but sensuous things that give these wines their proper context.

DOC and Other Wines

Arengo Made of excess Barbera and other red grapes, this wine was conceived by 18 producers acting in concert.

Barbaresco DOCG. Red wine. Province: Cuneo. Villages: Barbaresco, Neive, Treiso. Grape: Nebbiolo. Max. crop: 56 hl/ha. Min. alch: 12.5°. Aged for a minimum of 2 years, of which 1 is in wood, 3 years for *riserva*. Annual production: 178,000 cases.

The immediate neighbour of Barolo, sharing most of its qualities of power and depth, youthful harshness and eventual perfumed sweetness. Great Barbaresco has a style and polish it is hard to define; it is tempting, though inaccurate, to call it the Côte Rôtie to the Hermitage of Barolo. Neither lives as long or develops so sumptuously as the best Rhône wines; but recent bottlings (particularly the wines from Gaja) have added new superlatives to Italy's wine vocabulary: the most luxurious, the most vigorous, silky, incisive and memorable.

Barbera d'Alba DOC. Red wine. Province: Cuneo. Villages: many around Alba. Grape: Barbera. Max. crop: 70 hl/ha. Min. alch: 12° (12.5° for *superiore*). Aged for 1 year in oak for *superiore*. Annual production: 576,000 cases.

Barbera wines are ubiquitous in Piedmont, but the best of them fall into one of three DOCs. Alba is considered the best area for full-bodied Barbera apt for ageing – though the style is entirely at the producer's discretion.

Barbera d'Asti DOC. Red wine. Provinces: Asti and Alessandria. Villages: from Casale Monferrato to Acqui Terme. Grape: Barbera. Max. crop: 63 hl/ha. Min. alch: 12° (12.5° for *superiore*). Aged 1 year for *superiore* in oak or chestnut barrels. Annual production: 1.3m cases.

Critics disagree on whether this or Alba gives the best Barbera. This may be expected to be less of a 'character', with less bite. Many prefer it so.

Barbera del Monferrato DOC. Red wine. Provinces: Asti and Alessandria. Villages: a large number of the above provinces. Grapes: Barbera 85–90%, Freisa, Grignolino and Dolcetto 10–15%. Max. crop: 70 hl/ha. Min. alch: 11.5°. *Superiore* is aged for two years. Annual production: 910,000 cases.

The optional addition of other grapes allows this to be the most frivolous of the DOC Barberas – though none of them demands to be taken too seriously.

Barolo DOCG. Red wine. Province: Cuneo. Villages: Barolo, Castiglione Falletto, Serralunga d'Alba, La Morra, Monforte d'Alba, Verduno and parts of other communes. Grape: Nebbiolo. Max. crop: 56 hl/ha. Min. alch: 13°. Aged for at least 3 years, 2 of them in wood, 5 years for *riserva*. Annual production: 600,000 cases.

If Barolo gives the palate a wrestling match it makes its eventual yielding all the more satisfying. It takes practice to understand this powerful and astringent wine. For several years all flavour and most smell is masked and inaccessible. What is hidden is an extraordinary spectrum of scents (tar, truffles, violets, faded roses, incense, plums, raspberries have all been found).

Tasting notes on a 1974 Barolo in 1981 show just how slow the process can be: 'Still a deep blackish plum colour, smelling harsh and indistinct. Strong and hard to taste, full of glow but ill-defined. More study reveals sweetness and fruit flavours, if not depth; sweetness and a genial roast-chestnut warmth grow with acquaintance (and air). Still no real development.'

With such traditional Barolos maturity comes on quite suddenly at about 10 years and little is gained by keeping bottles beyond 15. The trend, though, is for more generous, though by no means easy, wines whose softer tannins make them more accessible sooner without shortening – indeed probably adding to – their long-term potential. In few areas anywhere has modern philosophy so successfully updated a natural classic.

The best vineyards are often signalled on the labels with the dialect words *sori* (meaning a steep sheltered slope) or *bricco* (a ridge). La Morra makes the earliest developing wines, Monforte and Serralunga the slowest.

Barolo Chinato A domestic tradition among Barolo growers is to brew apéritifs and cordials with their wine. This, the best-known *amaro*, is made bitter with an infusion of *china* bark. Another recipe includes green walnuts, tansy, garlic, cloves and cinnamon.

Boca DOC. Red wine. Province: Novara. Villages: Boca, part of Maggiora, Cavallirio, Prato Sesia, Grignasco. Grapes: Nebbiolo (Spanna) 45–70%, Vespolina 20–40%, Bonarda Novarese (Uva Rara) up to 20%. Max. crop: 63 hl/ha. Min. alch: 12°. Aged 3 years (2 in wood). Annual production: 1,445 cases.

One of several dry reds from the hills north of Novara where Nebbiolo is called Spanna. Blending with other grapes lightens this one.

Bonarda Piemontese Bonarda is a light red grape mostly grown in north Piedmont for blending. It can be fresh and pleasant on its own. Now has its own DOC (*see* Piedmont) as Piemonte Bonarda DOC.

Brachetto d'Acqui DOCG (in 1996). Red wine. Provinces: Asti, Alessandria. Villages: Acqui Terme, Nizza Monferrato and 24 others. Grape: Brachetto. Max. crop: 56 hl/ha. Min. alch: 11.5°. Annual production: 89,000 cases.

A light sweet fizzy red with more than a touch of Muscat in the aroma. That made by Villa Banfi is a marvel: one of the best examples of Italian tradition up-dated for modern times.

Bramaterra DOC. Red wine. Province: Vercelli. Villages: Massarano, Brusnengo, Cruino Roasio, Villa del Bosco, Sostegno and Lozzolo. Grapes: Nebbiolo (Spanna) 50–70%, Croatina 20–30%, Bonarda and/or Vespolina 10–20%. Max. crop: 49 hl/ha. Min. alch: 12°. Aged 2 years (18 months in wood); *riserva* 3 years (2 in wood). Annual production: 4,400 cases.

A 1979 DOC for a big solid blended red from the Vercelli Hills, increasing in production and evidently improving with age. Sold in Bordeaux-style bottles.

Bricco del Drago A Nebbiolo/Dolcetto blend from one grower near Alba.

Bricco Manzoni A Nebbiolo/Barbera blend; the excellent invention of one grower at Monforte d'Alba.

Bricco dell'Uccellone A single grower's highly successful interpretation of Barbera, aged in new oak casks.

Caramino A Spanna (Nebbiolo) blend from Dessilani's Cru vineyards in Fara DOC (q.v.). Well worth ageing for up to 10 years.

Carema DOC. Red wine. Province: Torino. Village: Carema. Grape: Nebbiolo (here called Picutener, Pugnet or Spanna). Max. crop: 56 hl/ha. Min. alch: 12°. Aged 4 years, of which 2 are in barrel. Annual production: 2,200 cases.

A wine from the borders of Piedmont and Valle d'Aosta; a relatively lightweight Nebbiolo which can gain in finesse what it loses in power. The terrain is steep and terraced, the climate cool, and prices (especially in ski resorts) can be excessive.

Colli Tortonesi DOC. Red and white wine. Province: Alessandria. Villages: Tortona and 29 others. Grapes: (red), Barbera 100%, or with up to 15% Freisa, Bonarda and Dolcetto; (white) Cortese. Max. crop: 63 hl/ha. Min. alch: 12° (red), 10.5° (white). Red aged 2 years (1 in oak or chestnut barrels) for *superiore*. Annual production: 167,000 cases.

A good-quality Barbera blend with ageing potential, and a very light dry Cortese white tending to sharpness and sometimes fizzy.

Cortese dell'Alto Monferrato DOC. White wine. Provinces: Asti and Alessandria. Villages: A large part of the above provinces. Grapes: Cortese 85%, other secondary white grapes – not aromatic ones – 15%. Max. crop: 70 hl/ha. Min. alch: 10°. Annual production: 278,000 cases.

An increasingly popular DOC for dry Cortese white, still or sparkling, at a humbler level than that of Gavi (q.v.).

Dolcetto d'Acqui DOC. Red wine. Province: Alessandria (vinification is also permitted in Asti). Villages: Acqui Terme and 24 others. Grape: Dolcetto. Max. crop: 56 hl/ha. Min. alch: 11.5°. Aged 1 year for *superiore*. Annual production: 133,000 cases.

Dolcetto from here can be expected to be light everyday red of good colour and certain character.

Dolcetto d'Alba DOC. Red wine. Province: Cuneo. Villages: Alba, Barolo, Barbaresco, La Morra and 30 others. Grape: Dolcetto. Max. crop: 63 hl/ha. Min. alch: 11.5°. Aged 1 year for *superiore*. Annual production: 670,000 cases.

Generally considered the best DOC of Dolcetto, partly because the most skilful growers are concentrated here. The style varies from the traditional soft but dust-dry to something more fruity and refreshing. In most cases youth is a virtue.

Dolcetto d'Asti DOC. Red wine. Province: Asti. Villages: Calamandrana, Canelli, Nizza Monferrato and 21 others. Grape: Dolcetto. Max. crop: 56 hl/ha. Min. alch: 11.5°. Aged 1 year for *superiore*. Annual production: 67,000 cases.

Less widely seen but not consistently different from Dolcetto d'Acqui.

Dolcetto delle Langhe Monregalesi DOC. Red wine. Province: Cuneo (vinification is also permitted in Imperia and Savona). Villages: Briaglia, Castellio Tanaro, Igliano, Marsaglia, Neilla Tanaro, part of Carru, Mondovi, Murazzano, Piozzo, S. Michele Mondovi and Vicoforte. Grape: Dolcetto. Max. crop: 49 hl/ha. Min. alch: 11°. Aged 1 year for *superiore*. Annual production: 4,400 cases.

A rarely used DOC established in 1974 for a lightweight Dolcetto said to have more aroma than most.

Dolcetto di Diano d'Alba or Diano d'Alba DOC. Red wine. Province: Cuneo. Village: Diano d'Alba. Grape: Dolcetto. Max. crop: 56 hl/ha. Min. alch: 12°. Aged 1 year for *superiore*. Annual production: 78,000 cases.

A premium Dolcetto, generally stronger, 'thicker' and less brisk than Dolcetto d'Alba.

Dolcetto di Dogliani DOC. Red wine. Province: Cuneo. Villages: Bastia, Belvedere, Langhe, Clavesana, Ciglie, Dogliani, Farigliano, Monchiero, Rocca de Ciglie and part of Roddino and Somano. Grape: Dolcetto. Max. crop: 56 hl/ha. Min. alch: 11.5°. Aged 1 year for *superiore*. Annual production: 167,000 cases.

Possibly the original Dolcetto; often a good one with more 'grip' (or less soft) than some.

Dolcetto di Ovada DOC. Red wine. Province: Alessandria (vinification is also permitted in Asti, Cuneo, Torino, Genoa and Savona). Villages: Ovada and 21 others. Grape: Dolcetto. Max. crop: 66 hl/ha. Min. alch: 11.5°. Aged 1 year for *superiore*. Annual production: 220,000 cases.

The best producers in this DOC make very lively wine, with as fruity an aroma as every Dolcetto and capable of developing in bottle like good Cru Beaujolais.

Erbaluce di Caluso, Caluso DOC. White wine. Provinces: Torino and Vercelli. Villages: Caluso and 35 others. Grapes: Erbaluce; *passito* with up to 5% Bonarda. Max. crop: 84 hl/ha. Min. alch: 11°; 13° for *passito*. *Passito* is aged at least 5 years. Annual production: 55,600 cases.

This is the northern Piedmont equivalent of the Ligurian Cinqueterre and Sciacchetrà: a pleasant dry white with a tendency to sharpness and a sweet *passito* made by half-drying the same grapes. The *passito* is sometimes boosted with alcohol and then called *liquoroso*.

Fara DOC. Red wine. Province: Novara. Villages: Fara and Briona. Grapes: Nebbiolo (Spanna) 30–50%, Vespolina 10–30% and Bonarda Novarese (Uva Rara) up to 40%. Max. crop: 77hl/ha. Min. alch: 12°. Aged 3 years with 2 in barrel. Annual production: 6,700 cases.

Fara, Boca and their neighbour Sizzano, similar reds of the same quality, were all early applicants for DOCs, recognized in 1969 (Boca and Sizzano) and 1976 (Fara) but still limited in production.

Favorita This white, dry wine from the grape variety of the same name grown in the Roero and Langhe Hills has recently made a comeback. Best drunk young. DOC has been requested.

Freisa d'Asti DOC. Red wine. Province: Asti. Area: the hills of Asti. Grape: Freisa. Max. crop: 56 hl/ha. Min. alch: 11°. Aged 1 year for *superiore*. Annual production: 67,000 cases.

A cheerful fruity sharpish red, sometimes sweet and often fizzy. It can be immensely appetizing, though the non-DOC Freisa d'Alba is often better made.

Freisa di Chieri DOC. Red wine. Province: Torino. Villages: Chieri and 11 others. Grape: Freisa. Max. crop: 56 hl/ha. Min. alch: 12°. Aged 1 year for *superiore*. Annual production: 7,800 cases.

Chieri on the outskirts of Turin specializes in the sweeter style of Freisa, often fizzy, which makes good café wine.

Gabiano DOC. Red wine. Province: Alessandria. Villages: Gabiano and Montecestino. Grapes: Barbera 90–95%, Freisa and/or Grignolino 5–10%. Max. crop: 56 hl/ha. Min. alch: 12°. (12.5° for *riserva*). *Riserva* aged 2 years. Annual production: 2,200 cases.

From the Gabiano village in the Monferrato Casalese Hills north of Asti. A very long-lived Barbera.

Gattinara DOCG. Red wine. Province: Vercelli. Village: Gattinara. Grapes: Nebbiolo (Spanna) with up to 10% Bonarda. Max. crop: 48 hl/ha. Min. alch: 12.5°. Aged 4 years (2 in wood). Annual production: 20,000 cases.

The best-known Spanna (Nebbiolo) of the hills north of Novara, a quite separate enclave from Barolo and the Langhe with a broader, juicier, less austere style of wine. Few if any Gattinaras reach top Barolo standards, but they are both

impressive and easy to like. The area is restricted. Prestige consequently often exceeds quality.

Gavi or Cortese di Gavi DOC. White wine. Province: Alessandria. Villages: Gavi, Carrosio, Bosio, Parodi S. Cristoforo. Grape: Cortese. Max. crop: 70 hl/ha. Min. alch: 10.5°. Annual production: 500,000 cases.

A recent international star, DOC'd in 1974 and led to distinction by the La Scolca estate under the name Gavi di Gavi. It does not quite reach the standards of mingled acidity and richness that say 'white burgundy'; several flavours castrated by too-cold fermentation. But this area can grow this grape superbly well.

Ghemme DOC. Red wine. Province: Novara. Villages: Ghemme and part of Romagnano Sesia. Grapes: Nebbiolo (Spanna) 65–85%, Vespolina 10–30%, Bonarda Novarese (Uva Rara) up to 15%. Max. crop: 70 hl/ha. Min. alch: 12°. Aged 4 years with 3 in barrel. Annual production: 6,700 cases.

A very similar wine to Gattinara, generally reckoned slightly inferior, though some (like me) may prefer the rather finer, less hearty style. The best bottles at 5 or 6 years incline towards a claret-like texture.

Grignolino d'Asti DOC. Red wine. Province: Asti. Villages: 35 communes in Asti. Grapes: Grignolino 100%, or with up to 10% Freisa. Max. crop: 52 hl/ha. Min. alch: 11°. Annual production: 167,000 cases.

Good Grignolino is refreshing and lively, slightly bitter, pale but not pallid.

Grignolino del Monferrato Casalese DOC. Red wine. Province: Alessandria. Villages: 35 communes (in the Monferrato Casalese). Grapes: Grignolino 100%, or with up to 10% Freisa. Annual production: 110,000 cases. Max. crop: 45 hl/ha. Min. alch: 11°.

An additional Grignolino area to the north gained DOC status a year after Grignolino d'Asti.

Lessona DOC. Red wine. Province: Vercelli. Village: Lessona. Grapes: Nebbiolo (Spanna) and up to 25% Vespolina and Bonarda. Max. crop: 56 hl/ha. Min. alch: 12°. Aged 2 years with 1 in wood. Annual production: 2,200 cases.

This remarkably fine claret-weight Nebbiolo blend is scarce. 6 years is a good age for it.

Langhe DOC. Red, white. Province: Cuneo. Grapes: almost all grapes grown in the province of Cuneo. Max. crop: 70 hl/ha for Nebbiolo and Freisa, 70 hl/ha for all others. Min. alch. between 10.5° for whites, 11.5° for Nebbiolo, 11° for the other reds.

Recently introduced DOC as a catchment for declassified or not yet DOC-classed Langhe-wines: Langhe Bianco, L Rosso, L Nebbiolo, L Freisa, L Dolcetto, L Arneis, L Favorita, L Chardonnay.

Loazzolo DOC. White. Province: Asti. Village: Loazzolo. Grape: Moscato. Max. crop: 27 hl/ha. Min. alch. 15.5° (at least 11° as alch. remaining as unfermented sugar: min: 50 g/lt.). Annual production: 560 cases.

A Moscato Passito, with a history. Can be a sinful sweet dream. Rediscovered in the 1980s by Giancarlo Scaglione and Giacomo Bologna, this is a dessert-wine produced only in small quantities by five producers. Forteto della Luja and Borgo Sambui are best.

Malvasia di Casorzo d'Asti DOC. Red to *rosato* wine. Provinces: Asti and Alessandria. Villages: Casorzo, Grazzano Badoglio, Altavilla Monferrato, Olivola, Ottiglio and Vignale Monferrato. Grapes: Malvasia Nera di Casorzo 100% or with up to 10% Freisa, Grignolino and Barbera. Max. crop: 77 hl/ha. Min. alch: 10.5˚, one-third of which is unfermented sugar. Annual production: 16,600 cases.

A rare sweet sparkling light red for café work. (The colour is generally clear red, almost pink.)

Malvasia di Castelnuovo Don Bosco DOC. Red wine. Province: Asti. Villages: Castelnuovo Don Bosco, Albugnano Passerano, Marmorito, Pino d'Asti, Berzano and Moncucco. Grapes: Malvasia di Schierano 100%, or with up to 15% Freisa. Max. crop: 77 hl/ha. Min. alch: 11˚ (fermented to 5.5–7˚, then sugar added). Annual production: 28,000 cases.

Similar to Malvasia di Casorzo d'Asti, either gently bubbly or fully sparkling.

Monferrato DOC. Red, white and *rosato*. Provinces: Alessandria and Asti. Grapes: almost all grapes grown in this region; max. crop varies between 63 and 77 hl/ha. Min. alch: between 10˚ and 11˚. No production figures available yet.

New DOC including a lot of the former table wines of the hills between the River Po and the Apennines: Monferrato Rosso, M Bianco, M Chiaretto, M Dolcetto, M Freisa, M Casalese (a white of Cortese-grapes).

Moscato d'Asti and Asti DOCG. White, usually sparkling (but can be still) wine. Provinces: Asti, Cuneo and Alessandria. Villages throughout the communes. Grape: Moscato Bianco. Max. crop: 75 hl/ha. Min. alch: (Moscato d'Asti) 11˚; (Asti) 12˚. Annual production: 6m. cases.

Moscato d'Asti and Asti are basically the same, but regulations allow Moscato d'Asti to be slightly sweeter and lower in alcohol. Generally Moscato d'Asti is better than Asti; the slightly fizzy Moscato is often made with great pains to be swooningly aromatic, sweet and swallowable. It *must* be drunk as young as you can get it. Asti itself is one of Italy's true and inimitable classics: sweet, buxomly fruity but girlishly giggly with its scented froth. It is a major industry dominated by big names in the vermouth field, normally produced in tanks, and hence moderate in price.

Möt Ziflon A Nebbiolo/Bonarda/Vespolina blend. Lighter than most of its area in the Gattinara country, developing bouquet after 3–4 years.

Nebbiolo or Nebbiolo del Piemonte An alternative title for any Nebbiolo wine. Not classified as DOC or DOCG. Ordinary to excellent wines.

Nebbiolo d'Alba DOC. Red wine. Province: Cuneo. Villages: Alba and 16 others (excluding Barolo and Barbaresco DOCGs). Grape: Nebbiolo. Max. crop: 63 hl/ha. Min. alch: 12˚. Annual production: 110,000 cases.

For those who can do without the stern majesty of Barolo but love the character of its grape this is the DOC to tie up in. 4 years is usually enough to develop a delicious bouquet of fruit ranging from plums to raspberries and, with luck, truffles.

Nebbiolo delle Langhe Name formerly used for *vino da tavola* by Barolo and Barbaresco for second selection wines, some of it good, some ordinary. DOCs Langhe and Langhe Nebbiolo have now (since 1995) replaced it.

Piemonte DOC. Red, white and *rosato* wines. Provinces: Alessandria, Asti, Cuneo. Grapes: Barbera, Bonarda, Grignolino, Brachetto, Cortese, Chardonnay, Moscato; Pinot Bianco, Pinot Grigio and Pinot Nero also for sparkling ('Piemonte DOC'); max. crop: varies between 63 and 82 hl/ha. Min. alch: 10.5–11°. No figures available yet.

New basket-DOC for whole region of Piedmont. Includes P Barbera, P Bonarda, P Brachetto, P Cortese, P Grignolino, P Chardonnay, P Spumante, P Moscato. Includes also new DOC for *spumante*, either *metodo tradizionale* or Charmat method.

Pinot Pinot Nero, Bianco and Grigio are all grown in parts of Piedmont. Fontanafredda (q.v.) makes top sparkling (Vigna Gattinera) Pinot Nero; there are also some interesting reds from Langhe- and from the Monferrato-region.

Roero-Arneis del Roero DOC. Red and white wine. Province: Cuneo. Villages: 19 in the province of Cuneo. Grapes: (red) Nebbiolo 95–98%, Arneis 2–5%, and a max. of 3% of other grape varieties recommended for Cuneo; (white) Arneis. Red aged 18 months, white *superiore* 1 year. Max. crop: 56 hl/ha. Min. alch: 11.5˚. Annual production: red (Roero) 53,000 cases; white (Roero Arneis) 222,000 cases.

A new category for red from Nebbiolo but growers may still opt to produce Nebbiolo d'Alba or Roero. This zone makes attractive red wines, good young but sometimes capable of ageing beyond 5–6 years. The white is a dry *vino da tavola* from the local Arneis grape grown in the Roero Hills north of Alba. Soft, richly textured and a bitter almond finish.

Rubino di Cantavenna DOC. Red wine. Province: Alessandria. Villages: Gabiano, Moncestino, Villamiroglio, Cantavenna, Camino. Grapes: Barbera 75–90%, Grignolino and/or Freisa up to 25%. Max. crop: 70 hl/ha. Min. alch: 11.5˚. Aged 1 year. Annual production: 4,400 cases.

A minor DOC for a respectable local dry red.

Ruchè de Castagnole Monferrato DOC. Red wine. Province: Asti. Villages: Castagnole Monferrato, Grana, Montemagno, Portacomaro, Refrancore, Scurzolengo, Viarigi. Grapes: Ruchè; with up to 10% Barbera Brachetto. Max. crop: 63 hl/ha. Min. alch: 12˚. Production: 6,600 cases.

A rare red grape found only in the sub-Alps above Castagnole Monferrato where it makes a tannic wine that ages to something perfumed and fine. Also known as Ruchè, Rouchè or Rouchet.

Sizzano DOC. Red wine. Province: Novara. Village: Sizzano. Grapes: Nebbiolo (Spanna) 40–60%, Vespolina 15–40%. Bonarda Novarese (Uva Rara) up to 25%. Max. crop: 70 hl/ha. Min. alch: 12˚. Aged 3 years with 2 in barrel. Annual production: 2,800 cases.

Considered by many the best of the north Piedmont Spanna (Nebbiolo) blends, to be compared with Boca and Fara. Potentially a 10-year wine.

Spanna The alias of the Nebbiolo grape in the Novara and Vercelli Hills of north Piedmont, also used as a wine name for Gattinara-style wines.

Vinòt The brandname of a pioneering Beaujolais-nouveau

style of instant red made from 100% Nebbiolo with *macération carbonique* by Angelo Gaja.

Leading Piedmont Producers

Elio Altare

La Morra, 12064 Cuneo.

DOC/DOCG: Barolo Vigneto Arborina, Dolcetto La Pria. Other: Barbera, Nebbiolo. Despite the small size (21 acres) of this vineyard, the wines have made international impact.

Antichi Vigneti di Cantalupo

Ghemme, 28074 Novara.

Owners: Alberto and Maurizio Arlunno. DOC/DOCG: Ghemme. Other: Agamium *vino da tavola*. One of northern Piedmont's best producers.

Antoniolo

Gattinara, 13045 Vercelli.

Owner: Rosanna Antoniolo. DOC/DOCG: Gattinara. Other: Spanna. A leading name in Gattinara, which has if anything improved in recent years.

Deciphering the label

The keys to deciphering Italian labels and wine lists are given below. For grape names, *see* pages 13–14. For DOC regulations *see* pages 285–86.

Abboccato slightly sweet.

Amabile a little sweeter than *abboccato*.

Amaro bitter.

Annata the year of the vintage.

Asciutto totally dry.

Azienda (on a wine label) a wine estate.

Bianco white.

Botte cask or barrel.

Bottiglia bottle.

Cantina wine cellar.

Cantina sociale or **cooperativa** a growers' cooperative cellar.

Casa vinicola a wine firm, usually making wine from grapes it has not grown on its own estate. *See also* Stabilimento and Tenementi.

Cascina northern term for a farm or estate.

Chiaretto 'claret' – usually meaning very light red, but it can also refer to rosé.

Classico the 'classic' heart of a DOC zone, by implication (and usually) the best part.

Consorzio a consortium of producers of a certain wine, who join forces to control and promote it.

Dolce fully sweet (technically, with between 5% and 10% residual sugar).

Enoteca 'wine library' – Italy has many establishments with wide national or regional reference collections of wine.

Etichetta label.

Fattoria Tuscan term for a farm or wine estate.

Fiasco (plural *fiaschi*) flask; the traditional straw-cased Chianti bottle.

Frizzante slightly fizzy, but with much less pressure than sparkling wine.

Gradazione alcoolica (**grad. alc.**) alcoholic degree in % by volume.

Imbottigliato (or **messo in bottiglia**) **nel'origine** (or **del produttore all'origine**) estate bottled.

Liquoroso strong, often but not necessarily fortified, wine, whether sweet or not.

Marchio depositato registered brand.

Metodo tradizionale or **classico** now the mandatory term for sparkling wines made using the champagne method.

Nero black or very dark red.

Passito wine made from grapes half-dried to concentrate them; strong and usually sweet.

Pastoso medium (not very) dry.

Podere a farm or wine estate.

Produttore producer.

Riserva, riserva speciale DOC wines that have been matured for a statutory number of years (the *speciale* is older). *See* DOC entries.

Rosato rosé.

Rosso red.

Secco dry.

Semisecco semi-dry (in reality, medium-sweet)

Spumante sparkling.

Stabilimento the company's premises.

Stravecchio very old (a term regulated under DOC rules, not permitted elsewhere).

Superiore superior in any one of a number of ways specifically designated by DOC rules. See DOC entries.

Tenementi or **tenuta** holding or estate.

Uva grape.

Vecchio old. See DOC entries for regulations.

Vendemmia the vintage. It can also be used in place of *annata* on labels.

Vigna, vigneto vineyard.

Vignaiolo, viticoltore grape grower.

Vin or **vino santo** wine made from grapes dried indoors over winter.

Vino da arrosto 'wine for a roast' implying a red of full body and maturity – 'Sunday best'.

Vino cotto cooked (concentrated) wine.

Vino novello the wine of the current year, now used in the same sense as Beaujolais 'Nouveau'.

Vino da pasto everyday wine.

Vino da taglio blending or 'cutting' wine, of high degree and concentration.

Vino da tavola the regulation term for non-DOC wines, the equivalent of French *vin de table* but not (such is the EU) of German *Tafelwein*.

Vite vine.

Vitigno grape variety.

Villa Banfi

Strevi, 15019 Alessandria.

Founded: 1960. Chief winemaker: Ezio Rivella. DOC/DOCG: Asti, Brachetto d'Acqui, Dolcetto d'Acqui, Gavi. Other: Moscato di Strevi, Banfi Brut *tradizionale*; Brut Pinot *Charmat*. The Gavi Principessa Gavia is a particularly good example of a cold-fermentation modern white. Banfi Brut is clean and correct Brachetto an exotic muscat mouthful.

Produttori del Barbaresco

Barbaresco, 12050 Cuneo.

Italy's most admired cooperative, with 65 growers, revived in 1958 by the families that founded the original winery in 1894. Director: Aldo Vacca. DOC/DOCG: Barbaresco. A remarkable array of cru Barbarescos vinified from individual plots. Some 42,000 cases of Nebbiolo *vino da tavola* are also made.

Marchesi di Barolo

Barolo, 12060 Cuneo.

One of the larger Barolo houses, founded in 1861, formerly owned by Marchesa Giulia Falletti, whose family originated Barolo wine. Now a corporation. DOC/DOCG: Asti, Barbaresco, Barbera d'Alba, Barolo, Cortese di Gavi, Dolcetto d'Alba, Freisa d'Asti, Nebbiolo d'Alba. The house owns 90 acres and buys from 400 more. Its collection of old vintages is probably unique.

Batasiolo

La Morra, 12060 Cuneo.

Formerly Kiola and Fratelli Dogliani, this winery is rapidly improving using nearly 300 acres of some of the best vineyard potential in Barolo. DOC/DOCG: Barolo, Moscato d'Asti. Other: Dolcetto, Chardonnay.

Bersano (Antica Podere Conti della Cremosina)

Nizza Monferrato, 14049 Asti.

Founded in 1896 by the Bersano family. The firm, bought by Seagrams in 1967, was recently resold. DOC/DOCG: Barbaresco, Barbera d'Alba, Barolo, Cortese di Gavi, Dolcetto d'Alba, Moscato d'Asti, Oltrepò Pavese Pinot Spumante. A large firm, its 100,000 cases come from its own land and other grapes bought in DOC zones. Some vineyards have been bought by Zonin. The wine museum created by the late Arturo Bersano is open five days a week. Its new, Italian, ownership is intent on restoring its former glory.

Braida-Giacomo Bologna

Rocchetta Tanaro, 14030 Asti.

Owners: the Bologna family (Anna, Raffaella and Beppe). Oenologist: Giuliano Noè. DOC: Brachetto d'Acqui, Grignolino d'Asti, Moscato d'Asti. Other: Bricco dell' Uccellone, Bricco della Bigotta. More than a talented winemaker, the late Giacomo Bologna was a prominent figure in Italian wine. The Barberas, Bricco dell'Uccellone and Bricco della Bigotta are outstanding.

Caudrina-Dogliotti

Castiglione Tinella, 12053 Cuneo.

Owners: Redento and Romano Dogliotti. DOC/DOCG: Dolcetto d'Alba, Moscato d'Asti. Other: Freisa. One of the best Moscato producers, with 62 acres.

Ceretto

Alba, 12051 Cuneo.

Founded: 1935. Owners: Bruno and Marcello Ceretto. DOC/DOCG: Barbaresco, Barbera d'Alba, Barolo, Dolcetto d'Alba, Nebbiolo d'Alba. The Ceretto brothers have expanded the family firm to include model estate wineries of *Bricco* Asili in Barbaresco, *Bricco* Rocche in Barolo and the Blangé estate in the Roero Hills where they make stylish Arneis. They are also part owners of I Vignaioli di Santo Stefano (for Asti and Moscato d'Asti) and the new Cornarea estate.

Pio Cesare

Alba, 12051 Cuneo.

A pillar of tradition in the Alba area, founded in 1881 by Pio Cesare, great-grandfather of Pio Boffa, who has given the winery a modern touch. DOC/DOCG: Barbaresco, Barbera d'Alba, Barolo, Dolcetto d'Alba, Gavi, Nebbiolo d'Alba. Other: Grignolino. Pio Cesare owns 20 acres in Barolo, 15 in Barbaresco and selects grapes from regular suppliers to make some of the best Piedmont wines.

Michele Chiarlo

Calamandrana, 14042 Asti.

Owner: Michele Chiarlo. Oenologist: Roberto Bezzato. DOC/DOCG: Barbaresco, Barbera d'Asti, Barbera del Monferrato, Barolo, Gavi, Grignolino del Monferrato Casalese. Other: Nebbiolo-Barbera *vino da tavola*, Granduca Brut *tradizionale*. The owner is currently developing key properties in Barolo and other zones.

Francesco Cinzano

10121 Torino.

Founded in the 18th century, now owned by Grand Metropolitan. Cinzano became a corporation in 1922. DOCG is Asti. Others are Cinzano Brut and Principe di Piemonte Blanc de Blancs *tradizionale*. The renowned vermouth firm, with affiliated bottling plants in other countries, also produces sparkling wines, *vini da tavola*, spirits and soft drinks. Cinzano controls the wine houses of Florio in Marsala and Col d'Orcia in Montalcino.

Tenuta Cisa Asinara dei Marchesi di Gresy

Barbaresco, 12050 Cuneo.

Founded in the last century on the site of a Roman villa. Owner: Alberto di Gresy. Winemaker: Piero Ballario. DOC/DOCG: Barbaresco, Dolcetto d'Alba. Other: Nebbiolo della Martinenga. From 67 acres of grapes planted in the prized Martinenga and Palazzina vineyards, di Gresy makes big, angular Barbaresco, lighter Nebbiolo and austere Dolcetto.

Le Colline (Monsecco)

Gattinara, 13045 Vercelli.

Founded in the early 1950s by Don Ugo Ravizza, who formed a corporation in 1974. Now run by Bruno Cervi. DOC/DOCG: Barbaresco, Gattinara, Ghemme, Moscato d'Asti. 45 acres in Gattinara, Ghemme and Treiso (for Barbaresco). The long-lived Monsecco shows just how good Gattinara could be.

Aldo Conterno

Monforte d'Alba, 12065 Cuneo.

DOC/DOCG: Barbera d'Alba, Barolo, Dolcetto d'Alba. Other: Freisa, Grignolino (Arneis and Chardonnay soon). Conterno's skills as grower and winemaker stem from 5 generations of forebears. He served in the US army before taking up the family tradition of making wine with passion and humour. His Dolcetto is soft, his Freisa brisk and his Barolo notably harmonious, despite its massive chassis of tannin.

Giacomo Conterno

Monforte d'Alba, 12065 Cuneo.

Founded: 1770. Owner: Giovanni Conterno. DOC/DOCG: Barbera d'Alba, Barolo, Dolcetto d'Alba. Brother of Aldo (*see* above), Conterno is particularly noted for his magnificent Barolo Monfortino, chosen from the best vintages and aged 8 years in casks.

Giuseppe Contratto

Canelli, 14053 Asti.

Founded in 1867, the firm is now owned by grappa-producer Bocchino. DOC/DOCG: Asti, Barbaresco, Barbera d'Asti, Barolo, Cortese dell'Alto Monferrato, Dolcetto d'Alba, Freisa d'Asti, Grignolino d'Asti, Nebbiolo d'Alba. Other: *metodo tradizionale* sparkling wines.

Coppo

Canelli, 14053 Asti.

Owners: Fratelli Coppo. DOC/DOCG: Asti, Barbera d'Asti, Gavi, Grignolino d'Asti. Other: Chardonnay, Brut Riserva

tradizionale. An established *spumante* house which is now earning new respect with its high quality DOC wines.

Luigi Einaudi

Dogliani, 12063 Cuneo.

Founded in 1907 by Luigi Einaudi, who later became president of Italy. Owners: Mario, Roberto and Giulio Einaudi. DOC/DOCG: Barolo, Dolcetto di Dogliani. Other: Barbera, Nebbiolo. From 60 acres, reliable though unadventurous wine with emphasis on Dolcetto and traditional-style Barolo.

Luigi Ferrando

Ivrea, 10015 Torino.

Oenologist: Gaspare Buscemi. DOC/DOCG: Carema, Erbaluce di Caluso. Other: Gamay-Pinot Nero della Valle d'Aosta; Nebbiolo. Quality Carema, bottled with a special black label for fine vintages; and small amounts of unclassified sweet wines, such as his *barrique*-aged Solativa, from 7.5 acres in the Caluso zone.

Fontanafredda (Tenimenti di Barolo e di Fontanafredda)

Serralunga d'Alba, 12050 Cuneo.

The most impressive wine estate of Piedmont, founded in 1878 by Conte Emanuele Guerrieri, son of King Victor Emmanuel II, and Contessa Rosa di Mirafiori; now owned by the Monte dei Paschi di Siena bank. Winemaker: Livio Testa. DOC/DOCG: Asti, Barbaresco, Barbera d'Alba, Barolo, Dolcetto d'Alba. Other: Nebbiolo, Contessa Rosa and Gattinara Spumante *tradizionale*, Noble Sec Spumante, Pinot Bianco. A major producer of Barolo and Asti. The winery has been perfecting production from 250 acres of estate and bought-in grapes. Admirable *vino da tavola* as well.

Gaja

Barbaresco, 12050 Cuneo.

Founded: 1859. Owner: Angelo Gaja (*see* feature, below). DOC/DOCG: Bar-baresco, Barbera d'Alba, Barolo, Dolcetto

ANGELO GAJA

Angelo Gaja of Barbaresco has the highest profile of any grower in Piedmont today, aggressively taking his own line on techniques, grape varieties, style and price. The 210 acres of Gaja vines produce 25,000 cases a year of Barbaresco and other Alba wines, as well as a Cabernet Sauvignon called Darmagi, a Chardonnay called Gaia & Rey, and a Sauvignon Blanc which Gaja promises will improve on the Napa Valley wines he openly admires. His exceptional array of Alba reds is epitomized by Barbaresco Sorì San Lorenzo and the massively ripe and rich Sorì Tildìn.

He has also created Vinòt (q.v.) as his answer to Beaujolais Nouveau. In 1988 Gaja bought the Marenca-Rivette estate at Serralunga where he has been making Barolo, which he aims to bring up to the level of his Barbaresco. He also controls the Brunello estate Pieve di Santa Restituta in Tuscany and has recently bought Marengo-Marenda, a Barolo-estate in La Morra, creating a new brand called Gromis for more commercial wines.

d'Alba, Nebbiolo d'Alba. Other: Chardonnay (Gaia & Rey), Cabernet Darmagi, Nebbiolo del Piemonte, Vinòt.

Fratelli Gancia

Canelli, 14053 Asti.
A family firm that pioneered the traditional (champagne) method in Italy. Founded in 1850 by Carlo Gancia, now headed by Piero and Vittorio Vallarino Gancia. DOC/DOCG: Asti, Barolo, Oltrepò Pavese Pinot and Riesling della Rocca. Other: Gran Riserva Carlo Gancia Brut *tradizionale*, Il Brut, Pinot di Pinot. Also a producer of vermouth and spirits, Gancia remains a leader in sparkling wine with more than 1.5 m cases a year. They have recently acquired vineyards in Piedmont and Apulia and are bottling wines under the Mirafiori brand and Barolo Chinato under Castello di Canelli.

Bruno Giacosa

Neive, 12057 Cuneo.
Founded: 1890. DOC/DOCG: Barbaresco, Barbera d'Alba, Barolo, Dolcetto d'Alba, Grignolino d'Asti, Nebbiolo d'Alba. Other: Arneis, Freisa, Spumante, Brut *tradizionale*. Bruno Giacosa is one of Piedmont's best winemakers, admired for powerful Alba reds that age with grace, and an excellent *tradizionale* made from Chardonnay and Pinot Nero. He buys all the grapes he needs from his pick of well-sited vineyards.

Cogno

Novello, 12060 Cuneo.
Owner: Elvio Cogno. DOC/DOCG: Barolo, Dolcetto d'Alba. Despite its small size (17 acres) Elvio Cogno's winery is a leading force in the area.

Martini & Rossi

10125 Torino.
Founded in 1863. Martini & Rossi IVLAS is now part of the international conglomerate General Beverage Corporation. DOC/DOCG: Asti. Other: Riserva Montelera Brut *tradizionale*. The world-famous (and world-leading) vermouth firm is a major producer (about 1.5m. cases) of sparkling wines.

Bartolo Mascarello

Barolo, 12060 Cuneo.
Founded in 1919 by Giulio Mascarello. The owner and winemaker is Bartolo Mascarello. DOC/DOCG: Barolo, Dolcetto d'Alba. Other: Nebbiolo delle Langhe. A tiny Barolo maker, steadfastly relying on traditional methods to produce his remarkable, polished wines.

Giuseppe Mascarello & Figlio

Monchiero, 12060 Cuneo.
Founded 1881. Owner/winemaker: Mauro Mascarello. DOC/DOCG: Barbaresco, Barbera d'Alba, Barolo, Dolcetto d'Alba, Nebbiolo d'Alba. The excellent Barolo Monprivato comes from a 6.8-acre family vineyard. Other grapes are bought from choice plots.

Monfalletto-Cordero Montezemolo

La Morra, 12064 Cuneo.
Owners: Giovanni and Enrico Cordero. DOC/DOCG: Barolo, Dolcetto d'Alba. The sons of the founder are carrying on the family tradition, building consistently on their father's reputation. With a total of about 40 acres of their own vineyard, they produce in particular a fine Barolo, Enrico VI, made for relatively young drinking, without losing depth and intensity.

Produttori Nebbiolo di Carema

Carema, 10010 Torino.
DOC: Carema. An admirable small cooperative founded in 1959. Run by Luciano Clerin, with 45 members. Their best wine is the barrel-aged Carema.

Castello di Neive

Neive, 12057 Cuneo.
Owner: Italo and Giulio Stopino. DOC/DOCG: Barbaresco, Barbera d'Alba, Dolcetto d'Alba, Moscato d'Asti. Other: Arneis. Small winery first made famous in 1862 when French oenologist Louis Oudart won a gold medal for his Neive wine at the London Exposition.

Luigi & Italo Nervi

Gattinara, 13045 Vercelli.
DOCG: Gattinara. Other: Nebbiolo. Respectable house run by Giorgio Aliata. There are two good single-vineyard bottlings: Molsino and Valferana, from 52 acres in all.

Alfredo Prunotto

Alba, 12051 Cuneo.
Founded in 1904 as a cooperative, acquired by Alfredo Prunotto in 1920 and then by oenologists Giuseppe Colla and Carlo Filiberti, who moved to a handsome new establishment on the edge of Alba. Now entirely owned by Piero Antinori. DOC/DOCG: Barbaresco, Barbera d'Alba, Barolo, Dolcetto d'Alba, Nebbiolo d'Alba. Very careful traditional winemaking produces benchmark Alba wines: gentle, plummy Nebbiolo and complex Barolo are first class. All wines are bottle-aged for a year before sale.

Renato Ratti (Abbazia dell'Annunziata)

La Morra, 12064 Cuneo.
Founded in 1962 in the cellars of the ancient abbey, dating from 1479. DOC/DOCG: Barbaresco, Barbera d'Alba, Barolo, Dolcetto d'Alba, Nebbiolo d'Alba. The founder, the late Renato Ratti, was president of the consortium of Asti, member of the national DOC committee, author, lecturer and curator of the wine museum in the abbey. His sons and nephew continue to make wines from 12 acres of own vineyard and grapes from committed friends. The family also owns the Villa Pattono near Asti.

Riccadonna

Canelli, 14053 Asti.
Founded in 1921, now headed by Ottavio Riccadonna. DOCG: Asti. Other: President Brut Riserva Privata and

President Extra Brut (both *tradizionale*), President Reserve Crystal Extra Secco, President Reserve Rosé. The large vermouth and marsala firm also markets the Valfieri line of Piedmont and Alto Adige wines in which it now has a controlling interest.

Rocche di Manzoni

Monforte d'Alba, 12065 Cuneo.

Founded: 1974. Owner: Valentino Migliorini. DOC/DOCG: Barbera d'Alba, Barolo, Dolcetto d'Alba. Other: Bricco Manzoni, Valentino Brut *tradizionale*. The innovative Migliorini makes Alba reds from 114 acres, including his original and excellent Bricco Manzoni Nebbiolo-Barbera blend aged in *barriques*.

Luciano Sandrone

Barolo, 12060 Cuneo.

DOC/DOCG: Barolo, Dolcetto d'Alba. The owner and his brother Luca produce slight quantities of top-ranked Barolo and Barbera and admired Dolcetto from a tiny (3-acre) vineyard.

Antica Casa Vinicola Scarpa

Nizza Monferrato, 14049 Asti.

One of the outstanding Piedmont firms founded in the mid-19th century; now directed by Mario Pesce. DOC/DOCG: Barbaresco, Barbera d'Asti, Barolo, Grignolino d'Asti, Nebbiolo d'Alba. Other: Brachetto, Dolcetto, Freisa, Rouchet. Scarpa's wines are all models of their genre, from Barolo to Barbera to his unique soft, rich red Rouchet or (a bargain) his smooth Nebbiolo.

Paolo Scavino

Castiglione Falletto, 12060 Cuneo.

DOC/DOCG: Barbera d'Alba, Barolo, Dolcetto d'Alba. A superb small grower. His Barolo Bric del Flasc gets top ratings.

La Scolca

Rovereto di Gavi, 15066 Alessandria.

Owner: Giorgio Soldati. DOC: Gavi. Other: Pados Spumante *tradizionale*. A 50-acre estate now run by the son of its founder, whose Gavi di Gavi made the world take the Cortese grape seriously.

Sella

Lessona, 13060 Vercelli.

Founded: 1671. Owners: the Sella family. DOC/DOCG: Bramaterra, Lessona. Other: Orbello, Piccone. The Lessona and Bramaterra estates (27 and 22 acres res-pectively) have recently combined under the Sella name. Lessona wine is light in style, for early drinking; Piccone is its younger brother.

La Spinetta-Rivetti

Castagnole Lanze, 14054 Asti.

Owners: the Rivetti family. DOC/DOCG: Barbera d'Asti, Moscato d'Asti. The family makes a fine Barbera, and the Moscato is often considered the finest in the zone.

Castello di Tassarolo

Castello di Tassarolo, 15060 Alessandria.

Owner: Marchesi Spinola. Winemaker: Giancarlo Scaglione. DOC: Gavi. The first quality is smooth, soft and excellent. A second pressing was rougher but full of character.

Vietti

Castiglione Falletto, 12060 Cuneo.

Owner/winemaker: Alfredo Currado (son-in-law of founder Mario Vietti) and son Luca Currado. DOC/DOCG: Barbaresco, Barbera d'Alba, Barolo, Dolcetto d'Alba, Nebbiolo d'Alba. Other: Arneis, Freisa, Grignolino, Moscato. Young wines are intensely vital and even fragrant; old vintages mellow and luxurious. For carefree zing their Freisa is hard to beat.

Roberto Voerzio

La Morra, 12064 Cuneo.

DOC/DOCG: Barbaresco, Barbera d'Alba, Barolo, Dolcetto d'Alba, Nebbiolo d'Alba. Other: Arneis, Dolcetto, Freisa. Owner Roberto Voerzio has split from the family winery (now run by Gianni Voerzio, his brother) to open his own operation, which is now one of the best Barolo estates.

OTHER PRODUCERS

Accademia Torregiorgi Neive, 12057 Cuneo. Owner: Mario Giorgi. DOC/DOCG: Barbaresco, Barolo, Barbera d'Alba, Dolcetto d'Alba.

Accomasso La Morra, 12064 Cuneo. DOC/DOCG: Barolo, Dolcetto d'Alba.

Azelia Castiglione Falletto, 12060 Cuneo. Owners: Luigi and Lorella Scavino. DOC/DOCG: Barolo, Dolcetto d'Alba. 17 acres.

Fratelli Barale Barolo, 12060 Cuneo. Founded: 1870. DOC: Barbera d'Alba, Barolo, Dolcetto d'Alba. A respected name in Barolo.

Cascina La Barbatella Nizza Monferrato, 14049 Asti. Owner: Angelo Sonvico. Barbera *vino da tavola*, Vigna del Sonvico (Barbera and Cabernet Sauvignon).

Terre del Barolo Castiglione Falletto, 12060 Cuneo. A big cooperative with high standards. DOC/DOCG: Barbera d'Alba, Barolo, Dolcetto d'Alba, Dolcetto di Diano d'Alba, Nebbiolo d'Alba. Members have holdings in some of Alba's best vineyards; the wines are reliable and often tasty.

La Battistina Novi Ligure, 15067 Alessandria. DOC: Gavi. A relatively new estate with 54 acres of Cortese vines.

Bava Cocconato d'Asti, 14023 Asti. Owners: the Bava family. DOC: Barbera d'Asti, Freisa d'Asti, Barolo. Other: Malvasia di Castelnuovo Don Bosco.

Bera-Cascina Palazzo Neviglie, 12050 Cuneo. Owners: Fratelli Bera. DOC/DOCG: Barbera d'Alba, Dolcetto d'Alba; a rising star with Moscato d'Asti and Asti.

Nicola Bergaglio Rovereto di Gavi, 15066 Alessandria. A widely admired maker of DOC Gavi.

A Bertelli Costigliole d'Asti, 14055 Asti. Owners: Fratelli Bertelli. DOC: Barbera d'Asti.

Alfiero Boffa San Marzano Oliveto, 12050 Asti. DOC: Barbera d'Asti. Emerging grower.

Carlo Boffa & Figli Barbaresco, 12050 Cuneo. DOC/DOCG: Barbaresco, Dolcetto d'Alba.

Vittorio Boratto Piverone, 10010 Torino. DOC: Caluso Passito. Excellent, rare, expensive.

Giacomo Borgogno & Figli Barolo, 12060 Cuneo. Owners: the Boschis family. DOC/DOCG: Barbera d'Alba, Barolo, Dolcetto d'Alba. A major Barolo firm, also owning the small and prestigious house of E Pira & Figli.

Serio & Battista Borgogno Barolo, 12060 Cuneo. DOCG: Barolo.

Bosca Canelli, 14053 Asti. Founded: 1831. Owners: the Bosca family. DOC/DOCG: Asti, Barbaresco, Barbera d'Asti, Barbera del Monferrato, Dolcetto d'Alba, Gavi, Grignolino d'Asti. Other: Chardonnay and *tradizionale* Brut Nature and Riserva del Nonno. With ample funds from the recent sale of Canei, the firm may emerge with some interesting wines. 370 acres are currently being devoted to quality wines.

Gianfranco Bovio La Morra, 12060 Cuneo. DOC/DOCG: Barolo, Dolcetto d'Alba.

Antiche Cantine Brema Incisa Scapaccino, 14045 Asti. DOC: Barbera d'Asti, Grignolino d'Asti. Carlo Brema's Barbera is outstanding.

Brezza Barolo, 12060 Cuneo. DOC/DOCG: Barbera d'Alba, Barolo, Dolcetto d'Alba. Other: Nebbiolo.

Poderi Bricco Mondalino Vignale Monferrato, 15049 Alessandria. Owner: Amilcare Gaudio. DOC: Barbera d'Asti, Barbera del Monferrato, Grignolino del Monferrato. A winery with high standards.

Luciano Brigatti Suno, 28019 Novara. Lone producer of Möt Ziflon *vino da tavola*. Also Bonarda.

Fratelli Brovia Castiglione Falletto, 12060 Cuneo. DOC/DOCG: Barbera d'Alba, Barolo, Dolcetto d'Alba.

G B Burlotto Verduno, 12060 Cuneo. DOC/DOCG: Barbera d'Alba, Barolo, Dolcetto d'Alba.

Piero Busso Neive, 12057 Cuneo. DOCG: Barbaresco.

Ca' Bianca Alice Bel Colle, 15010 Alessandria. DOC/DOCG: Barbera d'Asti, Bracchetto d'Asti, Moscato d'Asti. 50 acres.

Ca' Romé Barbaresco, 12050 Cuneo. Owner: Romano Marengo. DOCG: Barbaresco (highly praised Maria di Brun).

Luigi Calissano & Figli Alba, 12051 Cuneo. Founded in 1872, now part of Coltiva-Gruppo Italiano Vini complex. Produces and sells Piedmont DOC and other wines and vermouth.

Cantina Sociale di Canelli Canelli, 14053 Asti. Cooperative. DOCG: Asti, Moscato d'Asti.

Giorgio Carnevale Rocchetta Tanaro-Cerro, 14030 Asti. A distinguished family firm founded in 1880. DOC/DOCG: Barbaresco, Barbera d'Asti, Barolo, Brachetto d'Acqui, Freisa d'Asti, Grignolino d'Asti, Moscato d'Asti. Other: Cortese, Dolcetto, Nebbiolo. Carnevale selects, ages and bottles some of Asti's most impressive wines.

Tenuta Carretta Piobesi d'Alba, 12040 Cuneo. Owners: the Veglia family. DOC/DOCG: Barbera d'Alba, Barolo, Dolcetto d'Alba. Nebbiolo d'Alba. Other: Bianco dei Roero, Bonarda, Brachetto, Freisa. An interesting range of wines from four vineyards.

Castellari Bergaglio Roverato di Gavi, 15066 Alessandria. Owner: Wanda Castellari Bergaglio. DOC: Gavi. 17 acres. Some of the best Gavi wines.

Antica Contea di Castelvero Castel Boglione, 14040 Asti. Cooperative. DOC: Barbera d'Asti, Barbera del Monferrato, Dolcetto d'Asti, Freisa d'Asti.

Cascina Castlèt Costigliole d'Asti, 14055 Asti. Owner: Mario Borio. DOC: Barbera d'Asti. Other: Barbera Policalpo and Passum *vino da tavola*.

Fratelli Cavallotto Castiglione Falletto, 12060 Cuneo. Owners: Olivio and Gildo Cavallotto. DOC/DOCG: Barbera d'Alba, Barolo, Dolcetto d'Alba. Other: Favorita, Grignolino, Nebbiolo.

La Chiara Vallegge di Gavi, 15066 Alessandria. Owners: Ferdinando and Roberto Bergaglio. DOC: Gavi.

Quinto Chionetti & Figlio Dogliani, 12063 Cuneo. DOC: Dolcetto di Dogliani. Top Dolcetto producer.

Fratelli Cigliuti Neive, 12057 Cuneo. DOC/DOCG: Barbaresco, Barbera d'Alba, Dolcetto d'Alba. 11 acres.

Clerico Monforte d'Alba, 12065 Cuneo. Owner: Domenico Clerico. DOC/DOCG: Barbera d'Alba, Barolo, Dolcetto d'Alba. Other: Freisa, *barrique*-aged Arte di Nebbiolo. A rising star in Barolo: one to watch.

Colle Manora Quargnento, 15044 Alessandria. DOC: Barbera d'Asti. Other: Sauvignon Mimosa, Cabernet. On the ascendant.

Colué Diano d'Alba, 12055 Cuneo. Owner: Massimo Oddero. DOC/DOCG: Barbaresco, Barbera d'Alba, Barolo, Dolcetto d'Alba, Nebbiolo d'Alba.

Conterno-Fantino Monforte d'Alba, 12065 Cuneo. DOC/DOCG: Barolo, Dolcetto d'Alba. Other: Nebbiolo, Nebbiolo-Barbera *barrique* wine Monprà.

Cornarea Canale, 12043 Cuneo. Owner: Francesco Rapetti. DOC: Roero, Arneis di Roero. Other: *passito*.

Giuseppe Cortese Barbaresco, 12050 Cuneo. DOC/DOCG: Barbaresco, Dolcetto d'Alba.

De Forville Barbaresco, 12050 Cuneo. Owners: Paolo and Walter De Forville. DOC/DOCG: Barbaresco, Dolcetto d'Alba. Other: Chardonnay. 25 acres.

Luigi Dessilani & Figlio Fara, 23073 Novara. Founded: 1924. Winemaker: Enzo Lucca. DOC/DOCG: Fara, Gattinara. Other: Barbera, Bonarda, Caramino, Cornaggina, Spanna. Reliable, if coasting somewhat. The Caramino and Gattinara are the most admirable.

Poderi Colla San Rocco Seno d'Elvio, 12051 Cuneo. Founded: 1721. Owner: Tino and Federica Colla (brother and daughter of Beppe Colla, who used to own Prunotto). DOC: Dolcetto d'Alba. Other: Bricco del Drago (Dolcetto-Nebbiolo), Campo Romano (Freisa-Pinot Nero), Pinot Nero.

Eredi Virginia Ferrero Serralunga d'Alba, 12050 Cuneo. DOCG: Barolo.

Umberto Fiore Gattinara, 13045 Vercelli. DOC: Gattinara.

Forteto della Luja Loazzolo, 14050 Asti. Winemakers: Giancarlo Scaglione. Acclaimed sweet wine. The estate is leading the new Loazzolo DOC for Moscato *passito*.

Castello di Gabiano Gabiano Monferrato, 15020 Alessandria. Owner: Cattaneo Giustiniani. DOC: Barbera d'Asti, Gabiano, Grignolino d'Asti. Somewhat fading.

Gastaldi Neive, 12057 Cuneo. DOC/DOCG: Barbaresco, Dolcetto d'Alba.

Gatti Santo Stefano Belbo, 12058 Cuneo. DOCG: Moscato d'Asti.

Fratelli Giacosa Neive, 12057 Cuneo. Owners. Leone, Renzo and Valerio Giacosa. DOC/DOCG: Barbaresco, Barbera d'Alba, Barolo. Recently much improved.

Gillardi Farigliano, 12060 Cuneo. DOC: Dolcetto di Dogliani.

Cantina del Glicine Neive, 12057 Cuneo. Owner: Roberto Bruno. DOC/DOCG: Barbaresco, Barbera d'Alba, Dolcetto d'Alba. A minuscule wine house of consistent good quality.

La Giustiniana Rovereto di Gavi, 15066 Alessandria. DOC: Gavi.

Elio Grasso Monforte d'Alba, 12065 Cuneo. DOC/DOCG: Barbera d'Alba, Barolo, Dolcetto d'Alba, Nebbiolo d'Alba.

Domenico Ivaldi Strevi, 15019 Alessandria. DOC: Brachetto d'Acqui. Other: Moscato di Strevi, excellent Moscato *passito* Casarito.

Ermenegildo Leporati Casale Monferrato, 15040 Alessandria. DOC: Barbera del Monferrato, Grignolino del Monferrato.

Eredi Lodali Treiso, 12050 Cuneo. Owner: Rita Lodali. DOC/DOCG: Barbaresco, Dolcetto d'Alba.

Malabaila Canale, 12043 Cuneo. DOC: Arneis, Nebbiolo d'Alba, Roero. 19 acres.

Malvirà Canale, 12043 Canale. Owners: Roberto and Massimo Damonte. DOC: Arneis, Roero. Other: Favorita, *barrique*-aged San Guglielmo from Nebbiolo and Barbera.

Marenco Strevi, 15019 Alessandria. DOC/DOCG: Brachetto d'Acqui, Dolcetto d'Acqui, Moscato d'Asti.

La Meirana Gavi, 15066 Alessandria. Owner: Gian Piero Broglia. DOC: Gavi.

Moccagatta Barbaresco, 12050 Cuneo. Owners: Franco and Sergio Minuto. DOCG: Barbaresco. Other: Chardonnay and Barbera in *barriques*.

Moncucchetto Casorzo, 14032 Asti. DOC: Barbera d'Asti, Freisa d'Asti, Grignolino d'Asti. Other: Malvasia Nera.

Nuova Cappelletta Vignale Monferrato, 15049 Alessandria. Owners: the Arzani family. DOC: Barbera d'Asti, Barbera del Monferrato, Grignolino del Monferrato Casalese.

Fratelli Oddero La Morra, 12064 Cuneo. Founded: 1878. Owners: Giacomo and Luigi Oddero. DOC/DOCG: Barbaresco, Barbera d'Alba, Barolo, Dolcetto d'Alba, Nebbiolo d'Alba. Other: Freisa. Respected family winery with 57 acres. Recent single-vineyard bottlings show promise.

Orsolani San Giorgio Canavese, 10010 Torino. Owner: Francesco Orsolani. DOC: Erbaluce di Caluso, Caluso Spumante *tradizionale*.

I Paglieri Roagna Barbaresco, 12050 Cuneo. DOC: Barbaresco, Dolcetto d'Alba. Owner: Alfredo Roagna.

Armando Parusso Monforte d'Alba, 12050 Cuneo. Owner: Marco Parusso. DOC/DOCG: Barbera d'Alba, Barolo, Dolcetto d'Alba.

Secondo Pasquero-Elia Bricco di Neive, 12057 Cuneo. DOC/DOCG: Barbaresco, Dolcetto d'Alba, Moscato d'Asti. Other: Chardonnay. The Barbaresco of the Sori Paitin vineyard has Barolo-like depth and structure.

Luigi Pelissero Treiso, 12050 Cuneo. DOC/DOCG: Barbaresco, Barbera d'Alba, Dolcetto d'Alba.

Luigi Perazzi Roasio, 13060 Vercelli. DOC: Bramaterra.

I Vignaioli Elvio Pertinace Treiso, 12050 Cuneo. Cooperative. DOCG: Barbaresco.

Pianpolvere Soprano Monforte d'Alba, 12065 Cuneo. Owner: Ferruccio Fenocchio. DOC/DOCG: Barbera d'Alba, Barolo, Dolcetto d'Alba, Grignolino d'Alba.

Armando Piazzo San Rocco Seno d'Elvio, 12050 Cuneo. A range of Alba DOCs.

Castello del Poggio Portacomaro, 14037 Asti. Owner Zonin makes DOC/DOCG Barbera d'Asti, Grignolino d'Asti and Moscato d'Asti, and is developing the estate.

Cantina della Porta Rossa Diano d'Alba, 12055 Cuneo. Owners: Berzia and Rizzi. DOC/DOCG: Barbaresco, Barbera d'Alba, Barolo, Dolcetto di Diano d'Alba, Moscato d'Asti. Other: Nebbiolo. A noteworthy new house.

Punset Neive, 12057 Cuneo. Owners: Marina and Renzo Marcarini. DOC/DOCG: Barbaresco, Barbera d'Alba, Dolcetto d'Alba.

Renato Rabezzana San Desiderio d'Asti, 14031 Asti. DOC: Barbera d'Asti, Grignolino d'Asti.

Tenuta dei Re Castagnole Monferrato, 14030 Asti. Owners: the Re family. DOC: Grignolino d'Asti.

Francesco Rinaldi & Figli Barolo, 12060 Cuneo. Owners: Luciano and Michele Rinaldi. DOC/DOCG: Barbaresco, Barbera d'Alba, Barolo, Dolcetto d'Alba.

Rizzi Treiso, 12050 Cuneo. Owner: Ernesto Dellapiana. DOC/DOCG: Barbaresco, Barbera d'Alba, Dolcetto d'Alba.

Bruno Rocca-Cascina Rabajà Barbaresco, 12050 Cuneo. DOC/DOCG: Barbaresco, Dolcetto d'Alba. Other: Nebbiolo.

Rocche Costamagna La Morra, 12064 Cuneo. Owner: Claudia Ferreresi Locatelli. DOC: Barbera d'Alba, Barolo, Dolcetto d'Alba. Other: Nebbiolo.

Gigi Rosso Castiglione Falletto, 12060 Cuneo. Owner: Gigi Rosso. DOC/DOCG: Barolo, Dolcetto d'Alba, Dolcetto di Diano d'Alba.

Castello di Salabue Ponzano Monferrato, 15020 Alessandria. Owner: Carlo Cassinis. DOC: Barbera del Monferrato.

Tenuta San Pietro Gavi, 15066 Alessandria. Owner: Maria Rosa Gazzaniga. DOC: Gavi. 37 acres.

I Vignaioli di Santo Stefano Santo Stefano Belbo, 12058 Cuneo. Cooperative with 62 acres. DOCG: Moscato d'Asti.

Saracco Castiglione Tinella, 12053 Cuneo. DOCG: Moscato d'Asti. Top Moscato.

Cascina Scarsa Olivi San Lorenzo di Ovada, 15076 Alessandria. DOC: Dolcetto d'Ovada. A fanatical maker of lively Dolcetto, which he claims will keep for 10 years.

Giorgio Scarzello & Figli Barolo, 12060 Barolo. Owners: Giorgio and Gemma Scarzello. DOC/DOCG: Barolo, Dolcetto d'Alba.

Scrimaglio Nizza Monferrato, 14049 Asti. DOC: Barbera d'Asti, Barbera del Monferrato.

Sylla Sebaste Barolo, 12060 Barolo. Owner: Eleonora Limonci (also owns the Colle Manora estate). DOC/DOCG: Barolo, Dolcetto d'Alba. Other: Arneis, Freisa, Nebbiolo.

La Spinona Barbaresco, 12050 Cuneo. Owner/winemaker: Pietro Berutti. DOC/DOCG: Barbaresco, Barbera d'Alba,

Dolcetto d'Alba. Other: Freisa, Grignolino, Nebbiolo.

Castello di Tagliolo Tagliolo Monferrato, 15070 Alessandria. Owner: Olberto Pinelli Gentile. DOC: Barbera d'Alba, Dolcetto d'Alba, Cortese di Gavi.

Terre da Vino Moriondo, 10020 Torino. Owned by a group cooperatives and estates in a joint-venture operation with several Piedmontese DOCs. Average to top-quality wines.

Travaglini Gattinara, 13045 Vercelli. DOC: Gattinara. 42 acres.

Tre Castelli Montaldo Bormida, 15010 Alessandria. Cooperative. DOC wines include good Dolcetto di Ovada.

Renato Trinchero Agliano, 14041 Asti. DOC: Barbera d'Asti.

G D Vajra Barolo, 12060 Barolo. Owner: Aldo Vajra. DOC/DOCG: Barbera d'Alba, Barolo, Dolcetto d'Alba.

Antonio Vallana & Figlio Maggiora, 28014 Novara. Owner/winemaker: Bernardo Vallana. DOC: Boca. Other: Barbera, Bianco, Bonarda, Grignolino, Spanna. Producers of long-lived Spanna and reliable Boca.

Castello di Verduno Verduno, 12060 Cuneo. Owners: the Burlotto family. The former property of the Italian royal house. DOCG: Barolo and Barbaresco. Other: Pelaverga.

Gianni Voerzio La Morra, 12064 Cuneo. DOC: Barbera d'Alba, Barolo, Dolcetto d'Alba. Other: Arneis, Freisa. Split with more illustrious brother Roberto (q.v.), Gianni now runs the family winery.

Cantine Volpi Tortona, 15057 Alessandria. Specializing in Colli Tortonesi sparkling wines and Monferrato DOCs.

VALLE D'AOSTA

The Valle d'Aosta is France's umbilical cord to Italy (and vice versa). Its narrow confines lead to the Mont Blanc Tunnel and Saint Bernard Passes. Small vineyards perched in south-facing crannies along the valley manfully carry winemaking almost all the way from Piedmont to Savoie, with a corresponding meeting of their respective grapes: Nebbiolo and Barbera from the south join Gamay and Petit Rouge (which tastes suspiciously like Mondeuse) from the north, with Swiss Petite Arvine, some Moscato and Malvoisie (Pinot Gris) and two indigenous grapes, Blanc de Valdigne and red Vien de Nus.

Quantities are very small: the skiers of Courmayeur help the townsfolk of Aosta prevent exports from the region. In 1986 Italy's most comprehensive regionwide DOC was established. Valle d'Aosta or Vallée d'Aoste takes in 18 types of wine with their names in two languages. But even if classified, Aostan wines are interesting *sur place* but do not currently represent good value for money.

Leading Valle d'Aosta Producers

Caves Coopératives Donnaz

Donnaz, 11025 Aosta. Cooperative. DOC: Donnaz. 25 acres.

Costantino Charrère

Aymaville, 11010 Aosta. La Sabla is the fine red *vino da tavola* made here from Petit Rouge.

Co-Enfer Arvier

Arvier, 11011 Aosta. Cooperative. DOC: Enfer d'Arvier.

Les Cretes

Aymavilles, 11010 Aosta. Owner: Costantino Charrère. Various white and red Aosta-wines.

Delfino Grosjean

Quart, 11020 Aosta. Torrette and Pinot Noir in *barrique*, Blanc d'Ollignan *vino da tavola*.

Institut Agricole Régional

11100 Aosta. Experimental cellars of the regional agriculture school founded in 1969 and for many years directed by Joseph Vaudan, a priest. Malvoisie de Cossan, Petit Rouge, Riesling-Sylvaner, Sang des Salasses (Pinot Noir), Vin des Chanoines (Gamay), Vin du Conseil (Petite Arvine). Oenologist Grato Praz directs winemaking at the school, and some of the best wines of Aosta are consistently produced here.

La Cave du Vin Blanc de Morgex et de la Salle

Morgex, 11017 Aosta. Growers with 37 acres specializing in Blanc de Morgex and Blanc de la Salle. At 3,400 feet their vineyards are some of the highest in Europe. The wine has rarity value, but is light and can be sharp, though recent new cellars should mean an improvement in quality.

La Crotta de Vegneron

Chambave, 11023 Aosta. Cooperative directed by Yves Burgay. Impressive DOC: Chambave and Nus.

La Kiuva

Arnad, 11020 Aosta. Cooperative. DOC: Arnad-Montjovet.

Malga-Dayné

Villeneuve, 11018 Aosta. Owner: Marisa Dayné. Small vineyard making Torrette and Müller-Thurgau.

Alberto Vevey

Morgex, 11017 Aosta. Since Alberto Vevey's death his sons continue to make the most widely admired Blanc of this Aosta wine zone.

Ezio Voyat

Chambave, 11023 Aosta. Voyat's wines have an élite following in Italy. They are classic Chambave wines but he sells them as *vino da tavola* under non-DOC names: Rosso Le Muraglie (Chambave Rouge), La Gazzella (Moscato di Chambave) and Passito Le Muraglie (Moscato *passito*) – the latter superb.

LIGURIA

The crescent of the Ligurian coast, linking France and Tuscany, is scarcely regarded as a wine region and has never been an exporter. But in the centre of the crescent lies Italy's greatest port, and one of its most cosmopolitan cities, Genoa. Genoa demands, and gets, much better than ordinary whites for its fish and reds for its meat from the scattered vineyards of the hilly coast.

There are four DOC zones in Liguria: white Cinqueterre in the seaside vineyards to the east towards Tuscany; the red Rossese di Dolceacqua on the borders of France; the Riviera Ligure di Ponente (red: Ormeasco and Rossese; white: Pigato and Vermentino) grown on the western Riviera; and the new white Colli di Luni in the lower Magra and Vora valleys.

Liguria's wine list is a much longer one than its list of DOCs, but if the officially ranked wines are rarely exported, much less are the individualistic productions of its many small winemakers.

DOC and Other Wines

Cinqueterre DOC. White wine. Province: La Spezia. Villages: Riomaggiore, Vernazza, Monterosso, La Spezia. Grapes: Bosco min. 60%, Albarola and/or Vermentino up to 40%. Max. crop: 63 hl/ha. Min. alch: 11° for Cinqueterre, 17° for Cinqueterre Sciacchetrà. Aged 1 year for Sciacchetrà. Annual production: Cinqueterre 39,000 cases; Sciacchetrà 550 cases.

The largely legendary dry white of the beautiful Ligurian coast southeast of Genoa. It should be cleanly fruity. Sciacchetrà is made with the same grapes shrivelled in the sun to achieve concentration and sweetness. It is worth a detour, but not a journey.

Colli di Luni DOC. Red and white wines. Provinces: La Spezia, Massa e Carrara. Villages: 15 communes in La Spezia; Aulla, Fosdinovo and Podenzana in Massa e Carrara. Grapes: (red) Sangiovese 60–70%, Canaiolo/Polera Nera/Ciliegiolo min. 15%, other reds up to 25%; (white) Vermentino, Trebbiano Toscano. Max. crop: 70 hl/ha. Min. alch: (red) 11.5°; (white) 11°. Annual production: 39,000 cases.

Wine has been made in this area since Roman times, but it has only fairly recently (1989) been elevated to DOC status. Good reds are made from Sangiovese-based blends, whites that can almost rival those of Riviera di Ponente predominantly from Vermentino. Leading winemakers of the zone are investing heavily in new equipment and expertise, and look set to demand some respect in the future.

Riviera Ligure di Ponente DOC. Red and white wine. Province: Savona and Imperia. Villages: 67 communes in Imperia, 46 communes in Savona, plus 2 communes in Genoa. Grapes: (red) Rossese, Ormeasco; (white) Pigato, Vermentino. Max. crop: 63 hl/ha for Ormeasco, Rossese; 77 hl/ha for Pigato, Vermentino. Min. alch: 11°. Ormeasco aged 1 year for *superiore*. Annual production: 110,000 cases.

The red and white wines of this relatively new DOC are grown between Savona and Imperia. The whites are best drunk young, the reds gain with age.

Rossese di Dolceacqua or Dolceacqua DOC. Red wine. Province: Imperia. Villages: Dolceacqua, Ventimiglia and 13 others. Grape: Rossese. Aged 1 year for *superiore*. Max. crop: 63 hl/ha. Min. alch: 12°. Annual production: 14,000 cases.

The claret of the coast near the French frontier – a country wine with a good balance of fruit and bite, best after 2–5 years, when it can develop a real bouquet to linger over.

Vermentino The commonest white grape of the coast, grown particularly to the west of Savona (west of Genoa). Standards vary, but an example from Giuncheo was slightly green, yet with an almost oily softness. It should be faintly aromatic and dry: in fact a good fish wine. DOC in Riviera di Ponente, Colli di Luni and in Cinqueterre blend.

Leading Liguria Producers

Luigi Anfossi
Bastia d'Albenga, 17031 Savona. Good Pigato and Rossese.

Riccardo Bruna
Ranzo Borgo, 18028 Imperia. Some of the zone's finest Pigato, produced in small quantity.

Cane
Dolceacqua, 18035 Imperia. Owner: Giobatta Cane. Small production of admired Rossese.

Cascina du Feipù
Bastia d'Albenga, 17031 Savona. Owners: Pippo and Bice Parodi. Superb Pigato di Albenga and a fresh Rossese.

Colle dei Bardellini
Sant'Agata d'Imperia, 18100 Imperia. Fine DOC Vermentino; some Rossese.

Cooperativa Agricola di Cinqueterre
Riomaggiore, 19017 La Spezia. Oenologist: Nello Capris. Consistently good range of dry white DOC Cinqueterre, with Sciacchetrà being the top wine.

Conte Picedi Benettini
Baccano di Arcola, 19021 La Spezia. Good DOC Colli di Luni Vermentino del Chioso.

Enoteca Bisson
Chiavari, 16043 Genoa. Owners: Pier Luigi and Wally Lugano. Fine Vermentino di Verici.

Forlini Capellini
Manarola, 19017 La Spezia. A family vineyard producing a full-bodied, noteworthy DOC Cinqueterre.

Enzo Guglielmi

Soldano, 18030 Imperia. DOC Rossese di Dolceacqua, consistently good.

Michele Guglielmi

Soldano, 18030 Imperia. DOC Rossese di Dolceacqua. At 3 years 'Colli di Soldano' has a claret-like 'cut' and real style.

La Colombiera

Castelnuovo Magra, 19030 La Spezia. Owner: Francesco Ferro. A leading maker of fine DOC Colli di Luni and Vermentino; also *vino da tavola* Albachiara and Terizzo from Sangiovese and Cabernet respectively.

Ottaviano Lambruschi

Castelnuovo Magra, 19030 La Spezia. Good DOC Colli di Luni Vermentino.

Lupi

Pieve di Teco, 18026 Imperia. Owners: Tommaso and Angelo Lupi. Oenologist: Donato Lanati. Ormeasco di Pornassio, Pigato, Vermentino, Rossese di Dolceacqua. The region's top producer. Their Ormeasco di Pornassio made from grapes grown in mountain vineyards shows uncommon finesse for a Dolcetto and ages well, up to 6 years or more.

Mario Maccario

San Biagio della Cima, 18030 Imperia. His Dolceacqua has outstanding potential.

Podere Boiga

Finale Ligure, 17024 Savona. Owner: Domenico Boiga. Good DOC Vermentino and *vino da tavola* Lumassina.

Andrea Vercelli

Cisano sul Neva, 17035 Savona. Good Vermentino.

Pippo Viale

Soldano, 18030 Imperia. Consistently good Dolceacqua.

LOMBARDY

Lombardy has always kept a low profile in the world of wine. It has no world-famous names. Oltrepò Pavese, its productive and profitable viticultural heart, is scarcely a name to conjure with. Valtellina, the last alpine valley before Switzerland, commands more respect with its hard Nebbiolo reds. The lakeside wines of Garda have some romantic associations.

But a region needs a flag carrier which embodies its special qualities, and this Lombardy has only recently provided. An increasing number of DOCG Franciacorta *metodo tradizionale* sparkling wines are made, some of particularly high quality.

Prior to this, efforts to create a memorable name, particularly in the Oltrepò Pavese, have resulted in a confusion of faintly comic-sounding brands (Red Arrow, Spitfire, Judas' Blood). In contrast to Piedmont, with its proliferation of DOCs, Lombardy has a mere 13, but those of Oltrepò Pavese in particular, and Valtellina to a lesser degree, are umbrellas for a number of regulated brands or types of wine.

The grapes of Piedmont and the grapes of the north-east are all grown here, and frequently blended. It is inescapably a zone of transition with rich possibilities but no clear identity to bank on.

DOC and Other Wines

Barbacarlo An enclave of the Oltrepò Pavese (q.v.) near Broni well known for its unusual full-bodied *frizzante* red, which can be dry or semi-sweet but always finishes faintly bitter. Unlike other fizzy reds, Barbacarlo is often aged in bottle for one year.

Barbera One of the commonest red grapes of Lombardy, used both blended and alone. In Oltrepò Pavese it can be DOC.

Bonarda Another red grape with DOC rights in the Oltrepò Pavese. Dark, soft and bitter in the finish.

Botticino DOC. Red wine. Province: Brescia. Villages: Botticino, Brescia, Rezzato. Grapes: Barbera 30–40%, Schiava Gentile 20–30%, Marzamino 15–25%, Sangiovese 10–20%. Max. crop: 84 hl/ha. Min. alch: 12˚. Annual production: 11,000 cases.

A fairly powerful and sweetish red; the local red-meat wine, best with 3–4 years of maturity.

Buttafuoco A forceful concentrated red of blended Barbera, Uva Rara and Croatina produced near Castana (under the umbrella DOC Oltrepò Pavese).

Capriano del Colle DOC. Red and white wine. Province: Brescia. Villages: Capriano del Colle and Poncarale. Grapes: (red) Sangiovese 40–50%, Marzemino 35–45%, Barbera 3–10%; (white) Trebbiano. Max. crop: 87.5 hl/ha. Min. alch: 11˚. Capriano del Colle-Trebbiano is a white from Trebbiano di Soave grapes. Annual production: 22,000 cases.

A recent DOC for light local wines, unknown before.

Cellatica DOC. Red wine. Province: Brescia. Villages: Brescia, Gussago, Cellatica, Collebeato, Rodengo-Saiano. Grapes: Schiava Gentile 35–40%, Barbera 25–30%, Marzemino 20–30%, Incrocio Terzi n.l. (Barbera/Cabernet Franc) 10–15%. Max. crop: 84 hl/ha. Min. alch: 11.5˚. Annual production: 13,000 cases.

A respectable mild red, best within 2–4 years, which has been enjoyed in the area since the 16th century.

Colle del Calvario Potentially good Merlot/Cabernet red and Pinot white from Grumello, a town in the hills to the east of Bergamo.

Colli Morenici Mantovani del Garda DOC. Red, white and *rosato* wine. Province: Mantova. Villages: Castiglione delle Stiviere, Cavriana, Monzambano, Ponti sul Mincio, Solferino and Volta Mantovana. Grapes: (white) Garganega 20–25%, Trebbiano Giallo 20–25%, Trebbiano Nostrano 10–40%; (red and *rosato*) Rossanella 30–60%, Rondinella 20–50%, Negrara Trentina 10–30%. Max. crop: 65 hl/ha. Min. alch: 11˚. Annual production: 55,000 cases.

Lightweight local wines, though with a long history. Virgil mentioned them. The white could pass for Soave.

Terre di Franciacorta DOC. Red and white wine. Province: Brescia: 23 communes south of Lake Iseo. Grapes: (red) for Franciacorta Rosso: Cabernet (Sauvignon and/or Franc) more than 25%, Barbera more than 10%, Nebbiolo more than 10%, Merlot more than 10%, others up to 10%; (white) for Franciacorta Bianco: Chardonnay and/or Pinot Bianco and/or Pinot Nero. Max. crop: 78.5 hl/ha; min. alch. 11˚, when it is indicated a single-vineyard (Vigna …): 12˚. Annual production: 555,000 cases.

New DOC for the former 'Franciacorta' – Franciacorta DOCG is now for sparkling wines. Red Franciacorta is a very pleasant light wine of some character.

Franciacorta DOCG in 1995. Villages: as above. Grapes: Chardonnay and/or Pinot Bianco and/or Pinot Nero. Max. crop: 65 hl/ha. Annual production not yet known.

Classic-method Franciacorta sparkling that has obtained DOCG status. In white and *rosato* styles, from same province and villages as Terre di Franciacorta, above. This is Lombardy's best. Ca'del Bosco, Bellavista, Cavalleri, Ricci Curbastro, Faccoli are the top producers.

Groppello A local red grape of southwest Garda.

Grumello A sub-region of Valtellina Superiore (q.v.).

Inferno Another sub-region of Valtellina Superiore (q.v.).

Lambrusco Mantovano DOC. Red wine. Province: Mantova. Region: zones around the R. Po and the border of Emilia-Romagna. Grapes: Lambrusco Viadanese and other sub-varieties; Ancellotta/Fortana (Uva d'Oro) up to 15%. Annual production: 222,000 cases.

A fairly new DOC (1987) making Lambrusco from the local Viadanese sub-variety; robust in the west, lighter towards the east of the zone. Wines are dry or *frizzante*, and can hold their own with their counterparts from Emilia.

Lugana DOC. White wine. Provinces: Brescia and Verona. Region: the south end of Lake Garda between Desenzano and Peschiera. Grapes: Trebbiano di Lugano 100%, or with other light grapes up to 10% (but not aromatic types). Max. crop: 87.5 hl/ha. Min. alch: 11.5˚. Annual production: 356,000 cases.

Formerly a glamorous rarity to be sought out in such lovely spots as Sirmione. Now a very pleasant light dry white wine, scarcely distinguishable from an upper-class Soave.

Merlot Increasingly grown as a 'varietal' wine in Lombardy. Very satisfactory, though not included in a DOC. Part of blend in Franciacorta and Valcalepio.

Moscato di Scanzo A great rarity from Bergamo: an excellent tawny dessert Muscat.

Müller-Thurgau This German grape is successfully grown in the Oltrepò Pavese, though not admitted in its DOC.

Narbusto Made from the Oltrepò red grapes, this is a long-lived *vino da tavola* (aged at least 8 years).

Oltrepò Pavese DOC. Red and white wines. Province: Pavia. Area: Oltrepò Pavese. Grapes: (red) Barbera up to 65%, Croatina min. 25%, Uva Rara and/or Ughetta up to 45%; (white) Pinot Grigio or Riesling Renano, others up to 15%. Max. crop: between 65 and 84 hl/ha. Min. alch: 9.5–12˚ (varies with style). Annual production (total): 5m cases.

The DOC for general reds and whites from the Oltrepò Pavese. Most of the more distinctive wines of the area are either specifically named (e.g. Barbacarlo, Buttafuoco) or have a specified grape variety dominant (eg Barbera, Pinot, Chardonnay and Sauvignon).

Pinot Pinot Nero, Grigio and Bianco are all widely grown in Lombardy. The Oltrepò Pavese is a major supplier of base wines of Pinot for *spumante* made in Piedmont and elsewhere.

Riesling The Oltrepò DOC includes both Italian and Rhine Rieslings without distinguishing them. Both grow well here.

Riviera del Garda Bresciano DOC. Red and *rosato* wine. Province: Brescia. Villages: 30 communes on western and southwestern shore of Lake Garda. Grapes: Groppello 50–60%, Sangiovese 10–25%, Barbera 10–20%, Marzemino 5–30%. Max. crop: 85 hl/ha. Min. alch: 11˚. Aged for at least 1 year for *superiore*. Annual production: 222,000 cases.

The mirror image of Valpolicella and Bardolino from the other side of the lake. Commercial qualities at least are similar, although classic Valpolicella is much deeper in flavour. The village of Moniga del Garda makes a pale Chiaretto which is lively and good when very young.

San Colombano al Lambro or San Colombano DOC. Red wine. Provinces: Milan and Pavia. Villages: San Colombano al Lambro, Graffignana, S Angelo Lodigiano. Grapes: Croatina 30–45%, Barbera 25–40%, Uva Rara 5–15%; other reds up to 15%. Annual production: 33,000 cases.

Relatively recent DOC makes hearty reds on the slopes around San Colombano. Best for drinking after 2–4 years.

Sangue di Giuda A fizzy, often sweet red called 'Judas' Blood' is the sort of wine that makes 'serious' wine lovers turn their eyes to heaven. It should be tried without prejudice. There are good ones.

Sassella A sub-region of Valtellina Superiore (q.v.).

Sfursat or Sfurzat or Sforzato Valtellina's equivalent of the Recioto of Valpolicella in the Veneto; a strong (14.5˚) red made of semi-dried grapes, in this case Nebbiolo. Age certainly improves it as it turns tawny, but whether the final result pleases you is a personal matter.

San Martino della Battaglia DOC. White wine. Provinces: Brescia and Verona. Villages: Sirmione, Desanzano, Lonato, Pozzolengo, Peschiera. Grape: Tocai Friulano. Max. crop: 81 hl/ha. Min. alch: 11.5˚. Annual production: 39,000 cases.

A distinctive character among Garda wines; dry, yellow and tasty with something of the typical local bitterness in the finish. It is best drunk as young as possible. Also produces strong and sweet *liquoroso* wines.

Valcalepio DOC. Red and white wine. Province: Bergamo. Villages: 15 in the Calepio Valley. Grapes: (white) Pinot Bianco 55–75%, Pinot Grigio 25–45%; (red) Merlot 55–75%,

Cabernet Sauvignon 25–45%. Red aged 2 years. Max. crop: (white) 58 hl/ha; (red) 65 hl/ha. Min. alch: (white) 11.5˚; (red) 12˚. Annual production: 67,000 cases.

A small production, principally red, of light wines with an ancient name but modern grape varieties. The red is aged 2 years in wood, the white not at all.

Valgella A sub-region of Valtellina Superiore (q.v.).

Valtellina and Valtellina Superiore DOC. Red wine. Province: Sondrio. Subdistricts: Sassella, Grumello, Inferno and Valgella for *superiore*, 12 communes for Valtellina. Grapes: Nebbiolo (called Chiavennasca) 70%, plus Pinot Nero, Merlot, Rossola, Brugnola or Pignola Valtellinese max. 30%. Superiore is 95% Nebbiolo. Max. crop: 84 hl/ha; for V Superiore: 70 hl/ha. Min. alch: 11˚ for Valtellina, 12˚ for Valtellina Superiore. Aged for not less than 2 years, of which 1 is in wood, and 4 years for *riserva*. Annual production: 333,000 cases.

The most successful excursion of Nebbiolo outside its home region of Piedmont. Plain Valtellina can be expected to be a fairly 'hard' light red. The named *superiore*s develop considerable character as dry, claret-weight wines with hints of autumnal mellowness. It is hard to discern consistent differences between Sassella, Inferno, etc., but the first is generally considered the best. Switzerland (St-Moritz is just over the mountain) is a principal consumer. *See also* Sfursat.

Maurizio Zanella Cabernet Sauvignon and Franc with Merlot blended wine grown in Franciorta and named after its producer.

Leading Lombardy Producers

Guido Berlucchi

Borgonato di Cortefranca, 25040 Brescia.
President: Guido Berlucchi. Winemaker: Franco Ziliani. Cuvée Impériale Berlucchi. Brut, Grand Crémant, Max Rosé, Pas Dosé, all *tradizionale*. This firm is Italy's largest producer of classice-method wines – more than 400,000 cases. Berlucchi also owns Antica Cantine Fratta and produces *tradizionale* under that label.

Bellavista

Erbusco, 25030 Brescia.
Owner: Vittorio Moretti. Winemaker: Mattia Vezzola. DOC: Franciacorta red and white. Other: 5 types of *tradizionale*. The sparkling wines are stylish and very highly regarded, particularly the pure Chardonnay Gran Cuvée Crémant Millesimato and the still wines are elegant. This estate is Ca' del Bosco's closest competitor.

Ca' del Bosco

Erbusco, 25030 Brescia.
Founded: 1968. Owners: the Zanella family. Winemaker: Maurizio Zanella. DOC: Franciacorta Pinot, Rosso. Other: Ca' del Bosco, Chardonnay, Pinèro, Maurizio Zanella, Cabernet-Merlot. One of Italy's best sparkling-winemakers. Their production from 150 acres is dominated by Brut, Crémant and remarkably fine Dosage Zéro from Pinot and

Chardonnay plus the recently issued vintage 1980. Recent issues of Chardonnay, Pinèro and the highly acclaimed Maurizio Zanella confirm high standards in the still wines field as well.

Tenuta Castello/Perlage

Grumello del Monte, 26064 Bergamo.
Winemaker: Carlo Zadra. Valcalepio (labelled as Colle del Calvario), excellent wood-aged Chardonnay called Aurito, and 3 types of *spumante*, the most recent of which is a soft velvety *tradizionale*.

Cavalleri

Erbusco, 250030 Brescia.
Owner: Giovanni Cavalleri. DOC: Franciacorta. Other: *tradizionale* Brut, Pas Dosé and Rosé; barrel-fermented Chardonnay Seradina, and a French-style Cabernet-Merlot blend, Tajardino. This family estate, with 40 acres of vines, is continuing to make a name for itself with both its still and sparkling wines.

Fondazione Fojanini

23030 Sondrio.
DOC: Valtellina Superiore. The cellars and research centre are run by Alberto Baiocchi, a leader in Valtellina wine. He makes a fine Sassella sold under the label La Castellina.

Tenuta Mazzolino

Corvino San Quirico, 27043 Pavia.
Owner: Roberto Piaggi. Consultant: Giancarlo Scaglione. A fine range of DOC Oltrepò wines, as well as an excellent *barrique*-aged *vino da tavola* called Noir.

Nino Negri

Chiuro, 23030 Sondrio.
Founded: 1897. Now part of the Coltiva-Gruppo Italiano Vini complex. DOC: Valtellina, Valtellina Superiore. The zone's largest cellars, benefiting from advanced technology and under the direction of oenologist Casimiro Maule, remain a leading force. Their *riserva* is issued as 'Le Botti d'Oro'.

Premiovini

25100 Brescia.
Founded: 1825. This is the quality part of the Folonari operation (q.v.). The firm bottles or distributes numerous DOC wines from several regions under the trade or company names Anforio, Contessa Matilde, Della Staffa, Nozzole, Pegaso, Plauto, Poggetto, San Grato, Torre Sveva. Consistent, sometimes excellent, quality.

Cantina Sociale di Santa Maria della Versa

Santa Maria della Versa, 27047 Pavia.
A respected cooperative, founded in 1905, directed by Antonio Duca Denari. Its 700 members own nearly 5,000 acres of vines and produce nearly 80,000 cases. DOC: Oltrepò Pavese. It sells a fraction of the production under its own label, most notably Gran Spumante Brut *tradizionale*.

Visconti

Desenzano del Garda, 25015 Brescia.

A family firm founded in 1908; now headed by Franco Visconti. Oenologist: Gian Franco Tonon. DOC: Lugana, Oltrepò Pavese Moscato, Riviera del Garda Bresciano. Other: Merlot, Pinot Grigio, Riesling, Verduzzo. Visconti's skilled use of modern techniques makes him the quality leader in Lugana.

OTHER PRODUCERS

Giacomo Agnes Rovescala, 27040 Pavia. DOC: Oltrepò Pavese Rosso. Other: Gaggiarone from Bonarda and Barbera.

Anteo Rocca de'Giorgi, 27043 Pavia. Consultant: Beppe Bassi. *Tradizionale* Anteo Brut Rocca de'Giorgi and Nature from Chardonnay and Pinot Nero. 82 acres.

Franco Balgera Sondrio. Good DOC Valtellina Superiore.

Fratelli Berlucchi Borgonato di Cortefranca, 25040 Brescia. DOC: Franciacorta Pinot, Rosso. Other: Pinot Grigio. Still and sparkling wines.

Tenuta Il Bosco Zenevredo, 27049 Pavia. DOC: Oltrepò Pavese. Zonin property, along with San Zeno at Stradella, becoming the base of a major *spumante* operation.

Ca' dei Frati 25019 Lugana di Sirmione. DOC: Lugana. Other: Merlot Rosato, Rosso dei Frati.

Comincioli Puegnago, 25080 Brescia. DOC: Riviera del Garda.

Conti Sertoli Salis Tirano, 23037 Sondrio. Ancient house revived with the '89 vintage is aiming at the top in Valtellina.

Cornaleto Adro, 25030 Brescia. Owner: Luigi Lancini. DOC: Franciacorta Rosso. Also admired *tradizionale*. 45 acres.

Costaripa Moniga del Garda, 25080 Brescia. Owners: Bruno Vezzola and sons. DOC: Riviera del Garda. Other: Groppello red *vino da tavola*. 10 acres.

Doria Montalto Pavese, 27040 Pavia. Owners/winemakers: Adriano and Bruno Doria, Beppe Bassi. DOC: Oltrepò Pavese Pinot Nero (*barrique*-aged), Roncorosso, Bonarda, Riesling. Other: Charmat Querciolo.

Sandro Fay San Giacomo di Teglio, Sondrio. Good Valgella Ca' Morei.

Folonari Persico Dosimo, 26043 Cremona. Founded: 1825. Part of the Gruppo Italiano Vini complex. From a family firm this has grown to become one of Italy's largest *vino da tavola* producers, producing 4.5m. cases a year of DOC wine (mainly Verona) and *vino da tavola* of middling to economy class. Main cellars are near Cremona. *See also* Premiovini.

Fontanachiara Stradella, 27049 Pavia. Owner: Angelo Maggi. Winemakers: Marco Maggi, Beppe Bassi. Fine *tradizionale* Fontanachiara Brut and Riserva from Pinot Nero and Chardonnay.

Frecciarossa Casteggio, 27045 Pavia. A 50-acre estate founded in the early 1920s 'in imitation of Château Lafite' by the late Giorgio Odero, and now owned by his daughters, Anna and Margherita. DOC: Oltrepò Pavese. Odero had great influence in improving wine in Lombardy.

Faccoli Lorenzo Coccaglio, 25030 Brescia. White Franciacorta and outstanding Franciacorta DOCG.

Castello di Luzzano Rovescala, 27040 Pavia. Owners: Giovannella and Maria Giulia Fugazza. DOC: Oltrepò

Pavese Rosso. 150 acres. They also produce Colli Piacentini wines in Emilia.

Cascina Madonna Isabella Casteggio, 27045 Pavia. Owner: Giulio Venco. DOC: Oltrepò Pavese. Rosso della Madonna Isabella (800 cases) is one of the gems of the Oltrepò.

Lino Maga Broni, 27043 Pavia. Owner: Lino Maga. DOC: Oltrepò Pavese. Other: Montebuono. The estate originated Barbacarlo (now a proprietary wine), one of Italy's most praised and most durable bubbly reds.

Mairano Mairano di Casteggio, 27045 Pavia. Owner: Fernando Bussolera. DOC: Oltrepò Pavese.

Villa Mazzucchelli Ciliverghe, 25080 Brescia. Owner: Piero Giacomini. *Tradizionale* Brut, Pas Dosé and Riserva del Conte.

Monsupello Torricello Verzate, Pavia. Founded: 1893. Owner: Carlo Boatti. DOC: Oltrepò Pavese Rosso, Pinot Nero. 30 acres.

Cella di Montalto Montalto Pavese, 27040 Pavia. Owners: the Canegallo family. DOC: Oltrepò Pavese Riesling Italico.

Montelio Codevilla, 27050 Pavia. Founded: 1848. Owner: A Mazza Sesia. DOC: Oltrepò Pavese. Other: Merlot, Müller-Thurgau.

La Muiraghina Montù Beccaria, 27040 Pavia. Owner: Anna Gregorutti. Excellent *vino da tavola* of Riesling, Barbera and Malvasia.

Nera Chiuro, 23030 Sondrio. Founded: 1936; headed by Pietro Nera. DOC: Valtellina, Valtellina Superiore. 110,000 cases from 370 acres. The Valtellina Superiore Signorie is outstanding.

Tenuta di Oliva Oliva Gessi, 27050 Pavia. DOC: Oltrepò Pavese Riesling. 72 acres.

Pasini Produttori Raffa di Puegnago, 25080 Brescia. Owner: Diego Pasini. DOC: Riviera del Garda. Other: Groppello.

M Pasolini Mompiano, 25060 Brescia. Owner: Mario Pasolini. Ronco di Mompiano red.

Cascina La Pertica Picedo di Polpenazze, 25080 Brescia. Owner: Ruggero Brunori. DOC: Riviera del Garda. Other: barrel-aged Chardonnay. Labels: Il Colombaio and Le Sincette. Ambitious producer.

Ricci Curbastro Capriolo, 25031 Brescia. DOC: Franciacorta Rosso, Bianco and *tradizionale*.

Fratelli Triacca Madonna di Tirano, 23030 Sondrio. Winery run by Domenico and Gino Triacca. Heavy investment has produced much improved Valtellina Superiore.

Tronconero Casteggio, 27045 Pavia. DOC: Oltrepò Pavese led by a fine Bonarda. Other: Chardonnay.

Uberti Erbusco, 25030 Brescia. DOC: Franciacorta, including *tradizionale* Francesco 1 Brut and Pas Dosé. Other: Cabernet Sauvignon called Rosso dei Frati Priori.

Luigi Valenti Cigognola, 27045 Pavia. DOC: Oltrepò Pavese. The house specializes in *frizzante* Sangue di Giuda.

Enologica Valtellinese Sondrio. DOC: Valtellina Superiore. Other: Roccascissa (Nebbiolo white), Rossola (red).

Pietro Vercesi Rovescala, 27040 Pavia. Produces good Bonarda and *rosso*.

TRENTINO-ALTO ADIGE

The valley of the River Adige is Italy's corridor to the Germanic world and vice versa; a narrow, rock-walled but surprisingly flat-bottomed and untortuous trench among high peaks which has carried all the traffic of millennia over the Brenner Pass from the land of olives to the land of firs and vice versa.

So Germanic is its northern half, the Alto Adige, that its inhabitants know it as the Südtirol and think of Italy as a foreign country. A large proportion of its wine production is exported for sale north of the border with the bottles labelled in German.

The Trentino has a more southern culture, but even Trento feels only halfway to Italy. The region's wines are correspondingly cosmopolitan, using most of the well-known international grape varieties.

The Alto Adige has made more and more successful interpretations of the white classics. The shelter and warmth of its best slopes counterpoised by its altitude give excellent balance of ripeness and acidity.

Farther south in the Trentino the trend is also towards whites. But happily, local taste still maintains the survival of the native reds. The Schiava, Lagrein and Teroldego all seem to be mountain-bred versions of the grapes of Valpolicella. In slightly different ways they all share the smooth inviting start and the lingering bitter finish which you could call the *goût de terroir* of northeast Italy.

DOC and Other Wines

Alto Adige (Südtirol) DOC: Red, *rosato* and white wine. Province: Bolzano. Villages: 33 communes with vineyards up to 700 metres for red grapes and 1000 metres for white. Grapes: 95% of any of the following: Moscato Giallo (Goldenmuskateller), Pinot Bianco (Weissburgunder), Pinot Grigio (Ruländer), Riesling Italico (Welschriesling), Riesling-Sylvaner (Müller-Thurgau), Riesling Renano (Rheinriesling), Sylvaner, Sauvignon, Traminer Aromatico (Gewürztraminer), Cabernet, Lagrein Rosato (L. Kretzer), Lagrein Scuro (L. Dunkel), Malvasia (Malvasier), Merlot, Moscato Rosa (Rosenmuskateller), Pinot Nero (Blauburgunder), Schiava (Vernatsch), Chardonnay, plus 5% of any other; 85% Schiava and 15% of any other. Max. crop ranges from 98 hl/ha (for Schiava and Lagrein) down to 56 hl/ha (for Moscato Giallo). Min. alch: 11° for Moscato Giallo and Bianco, Riesling Italico, Riesling Renano, Riesling Sylvaner, Sylvaner, Merlot, Chardonnay; 11.5° for Pinot Grigio, Sauvignon, Traminer Aromatico, Cabernet, Lagrein Rosato, Lagrein Scuro, Malvasia, Pinot Nero; 12.5° for Moscato Rosa; 10.5° for Schiava. Annual production: 2.67 m cases. Alto Adige Lagrein Scuro, Merlot, Pinot Nero aged for a year is *riserva*; Cabernet aged for two years is *riserva*.

The general DOC for a large zone following the Adige and Isario valleys through the mountains, and including the Bolzano basin with altitudes ranging from 800 to over 3,000 feet. Red grapes are not grown over 2,300 feet. Of the 19 varieties allowed, the classic international grapes form the majority, several of them doing as well here as anywhere in Italy. Cabernet, Gewürztraminer, Pinot Bianco and Rheinriesling can all be outstanding. The local characters are the Lagrein, red or *rosato*, which makes a fruity, rich, smooth and flowing wine with a bitter twist, and the Schiava, which could be described as a jolly junior version of the same thing. The Traminer is also very much a local character, having its birthplace at Tramin (Termeno) just south of Bolzano.

The same geographic area has several more restrictive DOCs (Santa Maddalena, or St-Magdalener, for example) but they are not necessarily superior in quality. Alto Adige is one of Italy's biggest suppliers of export-quality wine.

Caldaro or Lago di Caldaro or Kalterersee DOC. Red wine. Provinces: Bolzano and Trento. Villages: 9 communes in Bolzano and 8 in Trento. Grapes: Schiava 85–100%, Pinot Nero and Lagrein 15%. Max. crop: 98 hl/ha. Min. alch: 10.5° (11° for Auslese or 'Scelto'). Annual production: 1.67m. cases.

The German name Kalterersee is more common than the Italian for this light and often sweetish red, originally grown around the lake southwest of Bolzano (now designated on labels as 'Classico'). The lake area has an exceptional microclimate for grape-growing. Like all Schiava it is an acquired taste with a bitter finish which helps to make it refreshing, though some of the bottles shipped to Germany are so revoltingly sweet and mawkish that putting them in the freezer is the only way of making them drinkable.

Castel San Michele One of the most highly regarded reds of the region, a Cabernet-Merlot blend from the regional agricultural college at San Michele, north of Trento. It needs 5–6 years or more bottle-age.

Casteller DOC. Red wine. Province: Trento. Villages: 27 communes, slopes no higher than 600 m. Grapes: Schiava at least 30%, Lambrusco up to 60% and Merlot Langrein, Teroldego 20%. Max. crop: 112 hl/ha. Min. alch: 10.5° (Casteller), 11.5° (Casteller Superiore). Annual production: 440,000 cases.

The light, dry, everyday red of the southern half of the region from Trento to Lake Garda but rarely seen outside.

Kolbenhofer A superior Schiava red made at Tramin by Hofstätter.

Adige Meranese di Collina or Südtiroler Meraner Hügel DOC. Red wine. Province: Bolzano, Villages: around Merano, on both sides of the Adige River. Grapes: Schiava (Grossa, Media, Piccolo, Gentile, Grigia, Tschaggele). Max. crop: 87.5 hl/ha. Min. alch: 10.5°. Annual production: 33,000 cases.

The local light red wine of Merano, for the young and hot to drink young and cool. Meraner Hügel is part of the Südtiroler DOC.

Nosiola DOC Trentino native white grape. The wine is fruity, dry and (surprise!) finishes with a bitter note; it has a distinctive hazelnut perfume (*nosiola* in Trentino-dialect means 'hazelnut'). It is also the base of Vin Santo.

San Leonardo One of the successful Cabernet-Merlot reds of the Trentino. *See* San Leonardo (Gonzaga) under Producers.

Santa Maddalena or St-Magdalener DOC. Red wine. Province: Bolzano. Villages: the hills to the north, above Bolzano (Classico is from Santa Maddalena itself). Grapes: Schiava (Grossa, Media, Grigia, Tschaggele); Lagrein, Pinot Nero up to 10%. Max. crop: 87 hl/ha. Min. alch: 11.5°. Annual production 189,000 cases.

An obvious relation to Caldaro but from better vineyards, more concentrated and stronger. Under Mussolini it was absurdly pronounced one of Italy's three greatest wines (Barolo and Barbaresco were the others). This and Lagrein Dunkel must be considered the first choice among the typical red wines of Bolzano.

Sorni DOC. Red and white wine. Province: Trento. Villages: Lavis, Giovo and S. Michele all'Adige, north of Trento. Grapes: (red) Schiava 70%, Teroldego 20–30% and Lagrein up to 10%, (white) Nosiola 70% and others 30%. Max. crop: 98 hl/ha. Min. alch: 10° white; 10.5° red, 11° is 'Scelto' or Auslese. Annual production: 22,000 cases.

DOC for reds and whites from around the village of Sorni. Both are light dry wines for summer drinking. The Sorni DOC is soon to become 'Trentino Sorni DOC' (as Sorni is part of the Trentino DOC).

Südtiroler Terlaner DOC. Was Terlano or Terlaner, since 1993 part of the Alto Adige/Südtiroler-DOC. White wine. Province: Bolzano. Villages: Terlano, Meltina, Nalles, Andriano, Appiano, Caldaro (Terlano and Nalles are 'Classico'). Grapes: Chardonnay, Müller-Thurgau, Pinot Bianco, Riesling Italico, Riesling Renano, Sauvignon, Sylvaner 90%, plus other DOC grapes of the same colour and the blend known as Terlano or Terlaner (Pinot Bianco 50%, Riesling Italico/Riesling Renano/Sauvignon/Sylvaner/ Müller-Thurgau up to 50%, other whites up to 5%). Max. crop: 91 hl/ha. Min. alch: 11.5° for Terlano, Riesling Renano and Sylvaner; 10.5° for Riesling Italico; 11° for Pinot Bianco and 12° for Sauvignon. Annual production: 122,000 cases.

The best whites of the Alto Adige are grown in this part of the valley, particularly just west of Bolzano where Terlano has excellent southwest slopes. Pinot Bianco, Riesling Renano, Sauvignon and sometimes Sylvaner can all make wines of real body and balance, occasionally in the international class. Terlano without a grape name will include at least 50 percent of either Pinot Bianco or Chardonnay, and may include both varieties; it is often a good buy.

Trento DOC. White and *rosato*. Province: Trento. Grapes: Chardonnay, and/or Pinot Bianco and/or Pinot Nero and/or Pinot Meunier. Max crop 105 hl/ha; min. alch. 11.5° (Riserva: 12°). Classic sparkling method and 15 months' ageing on yeasts in bottle (36 months for *riserva*) are obligatory.

Recent DOC for local traditional-method sparkling wine. One of Trentino's most successful wines.

Teroldego Rotaliano DOC. Red wine. Province: Trento. Villages: Mezzocorona, Mezzolombardo, S. Michel all'Adige (all on the Campo Rotaliano). Grape: Teroldego. Max crops: 119 hl/ha. Min. alch. 11.5° (12° aged 2 years is *superiore*). Annual production: 356,000 cases.

Pergola-trained Teroldego vines on the alluvial gravel deposited by the River Noce on the Campo Rotaliano give the best of the typical smooth, well-fleshed, finally bitter reds of the region. The wines are attractive when young but also have the potential to age well.

Trentino DOC. Red and white wine. Province: Trento. Villages: a long zone from Mezzocorona north of Trento to 15 miles north of Verona. Grapes: (red) 50–85% Cabernet and 15–50% Merlot; (white) 50–85% Chardonnay and 15–50% Pinot Bianco, Moscato (Giallo and Rosa), Müller-Thurgau, Nosiola, Pinot (Grigio and Nero), Riesling (Italico and Renano), Traminer Aromatico, Lagrein, Marzemino. Max. crop varies from 63 to 87 hl/ha. Trentino DOC means 25 different wine-types: Kretzer (p), Cabernet, Cabernet Franc, Cabernet Sauvignon, Chardonnay, Lagrein, Marzemino, Merlot, Moscato Giallo, Moscato Rosa, Rebo, Müller Thurgau, Nosiola, Pinot Bianco, Pinot Grigio, Pinot Nero, Riesling Italico, Riesling Renano, Sauvignon, Traminer Aromatico, Rosso, Bianco, Vin Santo, Sorni Bianco, Sorni Rosso. Min alch. lies between 10° (Kretzer, Müller Thurgau, Nosiola, Sorni Rosso) and 11° (Moscato Rosa, Pinot Nero, Traminer Aromatico), all others are 10.5°. Vin Santo is 10° + 6° (as unfermented sugar). Annual production: 2m cases. Aged 2 years (*riserva*) for Lagrein, Marzemino, Merlot, Pinot Nero, Cabernet; 3 for Vin Santo.

The southern counterpart of the DOC Alto Adige, with almost as great a range of wines but more emphasis on reds. Cabernet is well established here with excellent results; Lagrein gives some of the best examples of the regional style. Merlot is common – best in its blends with Cabernet. Pinot Bianco and Traminer are the best of the dry whites, while Moscato yields a potentially excellent dessert wine.

Valdadige or Etschtaler DOC. Red and white wine. Provinces: Trento, Bolzano and Verona. Villages: 38 communes in Trento, 33 in Bolzano and 4 in Verona. Grapes: (red) Schiava and/or Lambrusco 30% and the rest, Merlot, Pinot Nero, Lagrein, Teroldego and/or Negrara up to 70%; (white) Pinot Bianco, Pinot Grigio, Riesling Italico or Müller-Thurgau 20%; the rest, Bianchetta Trevigiana, Trebbiano Toscano, Nosiola, Vernaccia up to 80%. Max. crop: 98 hl/ha. Min. alch: white 10.5°, red 11°. Annual production: 1.56m cases.

The catch-all DOC for most of the Adige Valley from Merano to Verona. No high standards are imposed, but producers who add 'varietal' names self-impose them.

Südtiroler Eisacktaler DOC (Was Valle Isarco or Eisacktaler; since 1993 part of Alto Adige/Südtiroler-DOC). White wine. Province: Bolzano. Villages: parts of 12 communes in the Isarco Valley northeast of Bolzano to Bressanone (Brixen). Grapes: Traminer Aromatico, Pinot Grigio, Veltliner, Sylvaner or Müller-Thurgau. Max. crop: ranges from 70 to 91 hl/ha. Min. alch: 11° for Traminer Aromatico, Pinot Grigio; 10.5° for Veltliner, Sylvaner, Müller-Thurgau. Annual production: 100,000 cases.

The white wines of this alpine valley are all light and need drinking young in contrast to the 'stiffer' wines of Terlano to the west.

Leading Trentino-Alto Adige Producers

Abbazia di Novacella (Stiftskellerei Neustift)

Bressanone, 39042 Bolzano.
A lovely 12th-century monastery with 120 acres. DOC: Valle Isarco. Bottles Müller-Thurgau and Sylvaner entitled to the designation Brixner.

Ca'Vit (Cantina Viticoltori Trento)

38100 Trento.
Founded: 1957. A consortium of 15 cooperatives with no less than 4,500 growers, who produce about 75% of the wine of Trento province. Only a select part is issued under the Ca'Vit label. Chief winemaker: Giacinto Giacomini. DOC: Casteller, Teroldego Rotaliano, Trentino, Valdadige. Other: Chardonnay, Pinot Grigio, 4 Vicariati, Firmanto *tradizionale*, *vini da tavola*. This immense cooperative is unbeatable for quality at a reasonable price. Notable are Gran Spumante Ca'Vit Brut Brut (*charmat*) and 4 Vicariati (Cabernet-Merlot). A new project is a series of estate wines called Collezione di Ca'Vit.

Concilio

Volano, 38060 Trento.
Founded in 1972, a union of two older wineries. DOC: Teroldego Rotaliano, Trentino. Other: Chardonnay, Mori Vecio (Cabernet-Merlot), Moscato, Müller-Thurgau. A considerable establishment making each major type of wine, plus some Brut di Concilio *tradizionale*.

Conti Bossi Fedrigotti-Foianeghe

Rovereto, 38068 Trento.
A family firm founded about 1860. DOC: Trentino. Other: Foianeghe Bianco, Rosso, Schiava Rosato, Teroldego della Vallagarina. Best known for Foianeghe Rosso a blend of Cabernet and Merlot.

Ferrari

38040 Trento.
A family firm founded in 1902 in the heart of Trento; long the leading name in Italian classic-method wines. The firm is now run by Franco, Gino and winemaker Mauro Lunelli. Ferrari Brut, Brut de Brut Millesimato, Brut Rosé, Extra Dry, Giulio Ferrari Riserva del Fondatore has great finesse.

Gaierhof

Rovere della Luna, 38030 Trento.
Founded: 1976. Owner: Luigi Togn. DOC: Caldaro, Sorni, Teroldego Rotaliano, Trentino, Valadige. Togn is actively building production, here and at his Maso Poli estate.

Giorgio Gray

Appiano, 39100 Bolzano.
Owner/winemaker: Giorgio Gray. DOC: Alto Adige. The elusive Giorgio Gray (who designed a dozen or so wines in other regions) best demonstrates his gifts in some of Alto Adige's most convincing wines – red and white – now bottled under his own name rather than under the Bellendorf, Herrnhofer and Kehlburg labels of the past.

J Hofstätter

Tramin, 39040 Bolzano.
Founded: 1907. Now owned and operated by Paolo Foradori. DOC: Alto Adige, Cadaro. Other: de Vite, Kolbenhofer. An outstanding assortment of South Tyrolean wines partly from 86 acres of family vines. The Pinot Nero red from Barthenau is highly rated.

Instituto Agrario Provinciale San Michele all'Adige

San Michele all'Adige, 38010 Trento.
The agricultural college built around Castel San Michele is a national leader in viticultural research. There has been a revival in recent years under the guidance of winemaker Professor Salvatore Maule. From 100 acres of vines, the college makes several wines both for experiment and commerce, including the excellent Castel San Michele (a Cabernet-Merlot blend). There are single vineyard bottlings for Pinot Grigio, Chardonnay, Riesling Renano, Pinot Bianco and Sauvignon Blanc.

Kettmeir

Caldaro, 39052 Bolzano.
One of the biggest firms of the region. The controlling interest was recently sold to Santa Margherita of the Veneto. DOC: Alto Adige, Caldaro, Santa Maddalena, Terlano. Other: Chardonnay, Grande Cuvée Brut, Gran Spumante Rosé, Merlot Siebeneich, Moscato Atesino.

Alois Lageder

39100 Bolzano
Founded: 1855. DOC: Alto Adige, Caldaro, Santa Maddalena, Terlano. This well-known family winery owns 50 acres and buys from growers with another 1,000 acres to make some of the region's finest varietals. Lageder recently founded the Partico dei Leoni cellars to produce oak-aged Chardonnay and other *avant garde* wines.

Conti Martini

Mezzocorona, 38016 Trento.
Founded: 1977. Owners: the Martini family. Winemaker: Christina Martini. DOC: Teroldego Rotaliano, Trentino. Other: Müller-Thurgau, Pinot Grigio. A new 25-acre estate producing wines of exceptional class.

Pojer & Sandri

Faedo, 38010 Trento.
Founded: 1975. Owners: Mario Pojer (oenologist) and Fiorentino Sandri (viticulturist). Chardonnay, Müller-Thurgau, Nosiola, Pinot Nero, Schiava, Vin dei Molini and Trento DOC. The youthful producers, with 30 acres, use what they call 'technologically advanced artisan methods' to make about 2,000 cases each of Müller-Thurgau and Schiava, less of the others – all remarkable for a delicately floral scent and fruity crispness. The Schiava is pale and pretty.

Vinicola Santa Margherita

Caldora, Bolzano.
A new winery created next door to Kettmeir which this

Veneto company has recently taken over. There is a new prestige line of Alto Adige DOCs, Ca' d'Archi Chardonnay, Cabernet Sauvignon and Müller-Thurgau.

Armando Simoncelli

Navicello di Rovereto, 38060 Trento.
A leading estate with a fine Marzemino among the DOCs. Other: Simoncelli Brut Trento Classico and Navesel, a Cabernet-Merlot blend.

J Tiefenbrunner (Schloss Turmhoff)

Entiklar, 39040 Bolzano.
Owner and chief winemaker: Herbert Tiefenbrunner. DOC: Alto Adige, Caldaro. Other: Feldmarschall, *vini da tavola*. This established family winery produces some of the South Tirol's most exciting white wines. The Feldmarschall (a Müller-Thurgau) comes from vineyards 3,250 feet above sea level, the region's highest.

Zeni

Grumo di San Michele all'Adige, 38010 Trento.
Founded: 1882. Run by Roberto Zeni. DOC: Teroldego Rotaliano, Trentino. Other: Chardonnay, Rosé di Pinot. 800–1,200 cases of each type from 10 acres. Zeni is an excellent winemaker; his Chardonnay and Pinot Bianco are perfumed, his Teroldego harmonious and rounded.

OTHER PRODUCERS

Abate Nero Gardolo, 38100 Trento. Abate Nero Brut is first-rate classic method sparkling Trento DOC.

Bolognani Lavis, 38015 Trento. A quality producer of white Nosiola, Müller-Thurgau and Chardonnay.

La Cadalora Ala, 38061 Trento. A 10-acre estate producing Marzemino, Pinots and Chardonnay.

Maso Cantanghel Civvezzano, 38045 Trento. Fine, barrel-fermented Chardonnay Vigna Piccola and Pinot Nero from 5 acre vineyard.

Barone de Cles Mezzolombardo, 38017 Trento. Owners: Leonardo and Michele Cles. DOC: Teroldego Rotaliano, Trentino. Other: Chardonnay, Dama delle Rosé, Pinot Grigio.

Cantina Sociale Colterenzio (Kellereignossenschaft Schreckbichl) Cornaiano, 39050 Bolzano. A go-ahead group of 360 growers with a range of Alto Adige, Terlano, St-Magdalener and Kalterersee DOCs with some single vineyard bottlings. The Cornell label is used for selected wines aged in *barriques*.

Cantina Sociale Cornaiano (Kellereignossenschaft Girlan) Cornaiano, 39050 Bolzano. Winemaker: Hartmuth Spitaler. A specialist in Kalterersee plus good Riesling, Gewürztraminer and Pinot Nero under the Optimum label.

Anton Dissertori-Plattenhof Termino, 39040 Bolzano. Noted for Gewürztraminer.

Donati Mezzocorona, 38016 Trento. Owner: Pierfranco Donati. DOC: Teroldego, Trentino.

Fratelli Dorigati Mezzocorona, 38016 Trento. Owners: the Dorigati family. DOC: Teroldego, Trentino. Other: Rebo and Grener (from Teroldego with Cabernet).

Von Elzenbaum Tramin, 39040 Bolzano. Wine has been made on the estate since at least 1533. Owner: Anton von Elzenbaum. DOC: Alto Adige. Other: Edelweisser, Blauburgunder (Pinot Nero), Gewürztraminer and Rhein-riesling. The Gewürztraminer is Italy's most highly regarded – appropriately, since Tramin gave its name to the grape variety.

Endrizzi San Michele all'Adige, 38010 Trento. Founded: 1885. Owner: Paolo Endrizzi. DOC: Trentino, Valdadige. Other: Teroldego di San Michele, Trento DOC.

Foradori Mezzolombardo, 38017 Trento. DOC: Teroldego Rotaliano, Trentino. 30 acres. 12,000 cases. Important estate run by Elisabetta Foradori. Makes the best Teroldego; Teroldego 'Morei' is full of concentrated fruit, VDT Granatois is top level *barrique*-aged Teroldego. Also a fine Gewürztraminer from their Alto Adige Maso Foradori.

Alphons Giovanett Castelfeder
Egna, 39044 Bolzano. Alto Adige DOCs, most notably Gewürztraminer.

Anton Gojer-Glögglhof
39100 Bolzano. Good St Magdalener and *barrique*-aged red Lagrein Dunkel.

Haderburg Salorno, 39040 Bolzano. Owners: the Ochsenreiter

After DOC?

A monumental effort of organization and definition produced, within 20 years from 1962, 300-odd DOCs covering far over 1,000 styles of wine. It was precisely the discipline that Italy needed, both to concentrate her producers' minds on quality and to convince the rest of the world that she was in earnest, and that her labels were to be trusted.

The DOCs are accurate records of the regional practice of the time when they were promulgated. Whatever a consensus of growers agreed as normal and satisfactory within the traditions of their area was, after consultation with Rome, engraved on the tablets.

What is not often clearly understood is that the practices being followed and approved were in many, if not most, cases far from optimal. In the matter of grape varieties the DOC enshrined what the farmers had planted in their vineyards, not what they should, or might, have planted to produce the best wine. It allows for example, a proportion of white grapes in Chianti which can almost make it a *rosato*.

The growers in most cases allowed themselves crops far larger than could be consistent with fine wine. Since surplus is a perpetual headache in Italy this was short-sighted. They also set high minimum alcohol levels based on their old fear of unstable wine – whereas with modern techniques lower alcohol is both practicable and desirable.

Again, in their search for stability (and with their inherited taste for wines aged almost to exhaustion in oak) they set minimum ageing limits which run clean counter to the modern trends for clearly fruity and fragrant, or else bottle-aged and complex, wines. For the time being the only alternative, for producers who are unwilling to be bound by ideas they reject, is to label their wine *vino da tavola*.

family. Respected Haderburg Brut and Nature *tradizionale*. Work has begun on promising still wines.

Cantina Sociale di Isera Isera, 38060 Trento. Cooperative. DOC: Trentino. Other: Marzemino di Isera.

Graf Eberhard Kuenburg-Schloss Sallegg Caldaro, 29052 Bolzano. First-class late-harvest Rosenmuskateller and fine Kalterersee.

Cantina Sociale Lavis-Sorni-Salorno Lavis, 38015 Trento. Cooperative. DOC: Caldaro, Sorni, Casteller, Pinot Nero.

Le Brul Mezzocorona, 38016 Trento. Owner: Salvatore Maule. Trentino's leading consultant produces his own Gran Le Brul *tradizionale*.

Letrari Nogaredo, 38060 Trento. Founded: 1976. Owner: Leonello Letrari. DOC: Trentino, also sparkling Trento DOC. Other: Maso Lodron (Cabernet-Merlot).

Longariva Rovereto, 38068 Trento. Owner: Marco Manica. Admired DOCs plus Tre Cesure, a Cabernet-Merlot *vino da tavola* and a Ruländer (Pinot Grigio).

Madonna della Vittoria Arco, 38062 Trento. A promising new estate with a range of DOCs.

Conti Martini Mezzocorona, 38016 Trento. An old family estate making fine Teroldego and Lagrein and a perfumed, dry Moscato Bianco.

Karl Martini & Sohn Cornaiano, 39050 Bolzano. A range of DOCs including a good Kalterersee.

Cantina Mezzocorona Mezzocorona, 38016 Trento. DOC: Teroldego Rotaliano, Trentino, Valdadige. Other: Chardonnay, Pinot Grigio, Rotari Brut, Trento DOC.

Klosterkellerei Muri-Gries 39100 Bolzano DOC: Alto Adige, Santa Maddalena, Terlano. Other: Malvasier di Gries. The ancient cellars of the Benedictine monastery of Gries produce marvellously typical wines, eg Lagrein.

Fratelli Pisoni Pergolese Sarche, 38070 Trento. DOC: Trentino. Other: Gran Spumante Pisoni Brut Trento DOC, San Siro Bianco, Rosso.

Giovanni Poli Santa Massenza, 38070 Trento. Elegant, luscious Vino Santo though it is aged in stainless steel tanks and good Nosiola.

Maso Poli San Michele all'Adige, 38010 Trento. Owner: Luigi Togn. An old estate producing good Sorni Bianco and Pinot Nero.

Praeclarus San Paolo-Appiano, 39057 Bolzano. Owner: Johann Ebner. Noted *tradizionale* Praeclarus Brut and Extra Brut.

Castel Rametz Merano, 39012 Bolzano. DOC: Alto Adige, Meranese di Collina, Santa Maddalena.

Cantine Cooperativa Rotaliana Mezzolombardo, 38017

Trento. Admirable Teroldego along with Lagrein and Trentino DOCs.

Hans Rottensteiner 39100 Bolzano. A sound range of DOCs including good St-Magdalener.

Heinrich Rottensteiner 39100 Bolzano. A dedicated grower making excellent St-Magdalener.

Tenuta San Leonardo Avio, 38063 Trento. Owner Carlo Gonzaga is using *barriques* to bring new finesse to Cabernet Sauvignon and the Cabernet-Merlot blend of Campi Sarni.

Cantina Sociale San Michele (Kellereigenossenschaft St-Michael) San-Michele-Appiano, 39057 Bolzano. Emerging cooperative. A very good range of Alto Adige DOCs with *spumante* and Kalterersee. Top line is Sanct Valentin (includes classic sparkling, Sauvignon, Chardonnay, Pinot Nero, Pinot Bianco).

Schloss Schwanburg (Rudolf Carli Eredi) Nalles, 39010 Bolzano. Founded: 1884. DOC: Alto Adige, Caldaro, Santa Maddalena, Terlano. Other: *barrique*-aged Castel Schwanburg from Cabernet and Merlot.

Enrico Spagnolli Isera, 38060 Trento. A range of Trentino DOCs including a fine Marzemino and Müller-Thurgau.

Giuseppe Spagnolli Aldeno, 38060 Trento. Producer of the outstanding Trento DOC Spagnolli Brut – a blend of Chardonnay and Pinot Nero.

De Tarczal Marano d'Isera, Trento. An admirable range of Trentino DOCs with an exemplary Marzemino d'Isera.

Cantina Sociale Terlano (Kellereigenossenschaft Terlan) Terlano, 39018 Bolzano. DOC: Alto Adige, Terlano.

Cantina Sociale di Termeno (Kellereigenossenschaft Tramin) Tramin, 39040 Bolzano. DOC: Alto Adige, Caldaro. Other: Hexenbichler.

Vallarom Avio, 38063 Trento. Owners: the Scienza family. Good Marzemino, Pinot Nero, Merlot, Cabernet Sauvignon and an admired late-harvest Chardonnay.

Cantina Sociale Valle d'Isarco (Eisacktaler Kellerei-genossenschaft) Chiusa, 39043 Bolzano. DOC: Valle Isarco. A respected cooperative producing fine Isarco white wines.

Vivaldi Meltina, 39010 Bolzano. Owner: Josef Reiterer. Makes exemplary *tradizionale* Brut and Extra Brut and has acquired prized vineyards at Mazzon for still wines.

Elena Walch Tramin 39040 Bolzano. Small producer with beautiful vineyards overlooking the Lake Caldaro. Wines are from the Castel Ringberg and Kastelaz estates.

W Walch Tramin, 39040 Bolzano. Owners: the Walch family. DOC: Alto Adige, Caldaro, Santa Maddalena, Terlano.

VENETO

The hinterland of Venice is one-third mountain, two-thirds plain. Its northernmost boundary is with Austria, high in the Dolomites; in the south it is the flat valley of the River Po. All the important wines of the Veneto are grown in the faltering alpine foothills and occasional hilly outcrops in a line eastwards from Lake Garda to Conegliano. Verona, near Lake Garda, is the wine capital, with a greater production of DOC wine from its vineyards of Soave, Valpolicella and Bardolino than any other Italian region. So important are these three in the export market that Verona has a claim to being the international wine capital of the whole of Italy. The nation's biggest wine fair, Vinitaly, takes place in Verona every April. To the east, Conegliano has another claim: to be the nation's centre of viticultural technology and research.

The Verona and Conegliano areas have strong traditions of using grape varieties peculiar to themselves: Garganega, the Soave grape, the Corvina of Valpolicella and the Prosecco, which makes admirable sparkling wine at Conegliano, are unknown elsewhere. But less established and self-confident areas, such as the Berici and Euganean hills and the Piave, prolific flatland vineyards on the borders of Friuli-Venezia Giulia to the east, try their luck with a range of international varieties: Pinots, Cabernets and their kin. Merlot is the standby red of the region and is rapidly improving from acceptable to delicious.

DOC and Other Wines

Amarone *See* Valpolicella.

Bardolino DOC. Red and *rosato*. Province: Verona. Villages: Bardolino and 15 others. Grapes: Corvina Veronese 35–65%, Rondinella 10–40%, Molinara 10–20%, Negrara up to 10%, Rossignola, Barbera; Garganega and Sangiovese up to 15%. Max. crop: 91 hl/ha. Min. alch: 10.5°. Aged one year for *superiore*. Annual production: 2.22m. cases.

A pale red and even paler Chiaretto; a lighter version of Valpolicella with the same quality (in a good example) of liveliness. Bardolino is on glacial deposits which do not warm up as well as the limestone of Valpolicella. It is briskest and best in the year after the vintage.

Bianco di Custoza DOC. White wine. Province: Verona. Grapes: Trebbiano Toscano 35–45%, Garganega 20–40%, Tocai Friulano 5–30%, Cortese, Riesling Italico, Malvasia Toscano 20–30%. Max. crop: 97 hl/ha. Min. alch: 11°. Annual production 1.12m cases.

The southern neighbour of Soave, this white is increasingly seen, especially a *spumante* (usually Charmat).

Breganze DOC. Red and white wine. Province: Vicenza. Villages: Breganze and Maróstica, and parts of 13 other communes. Grapes: Breganze Bianco: Tocai, plus Pinot Bianco, Pinot Grigio, Riesling Italico, Sauvignon and Vespaiolo, max. 15%. Breganze Rosso: Merlot, plus Marzemino, Groppello, Cabernet Franc, Cabernet Sauvignon, Pinot Nero and Freisa, max. 15%. Breganze-Cabernet: Sauvignon or Franc. Breganze-Pinot Nero: Pinot Nero. Breganze-Pinot Bianco: Pinot Bianco and Pinot Grigio. Breganze-Pinot Grigio: Pinot Grigio. Breganze-Vespaiolo: Vespaiolo. Max. crop: 91 hl/ha. Min. alch: 11° for white, red, 11.5° for Cabernet, Pinot Nero, Pinot Bianco, Pinot Grigio and Vespaiolo. Annual production: 300,000 cases.

Light and agreeable 'varietal' wines from the birthplace of the great architect Palladio. Pinot Bianco and Cabernet are the best (*see* Maculan under Producers).

Cabernet di Pramaggiore *See under* Lison-Pramaggiore.

Campo Fiorin An unusually serious interpretation of Valpolicella by Masi (*see* Producers). The wine is macerated with the skins of Recioto Amarone (q.v.) after pressing. The prototype for *ripasso* wines.

Capitel San Rocco A similar serious red to Campo Fiorin from Tedeschi (*see* Producers). Also a clean, fairly pale-bodied dry white wine.

Colli Berici DOC. Red and white wine. Province: Vicenza. Villages: 28 communes south of Vicenza. Grapes: 7 varieties, with limited (10–15%) admixture of other local grapes. The range is Garganega (comparable with Soave), Tocai Bianco, Sauvignon, Pinot Bianco, Merlot, Tocai Rosso (sharp fruity young red), Cabernet. Cabernet is aged for three years for *riserva*. Max. crop: 78 hl/ha. Min. alch: 10.5° for Garganega, 11° for Tocai Bianco, Sauvignon, Pinot Bianco, Merlot and Tocai Rosso. Annual production: 890,000 cases.

These hills between Verona and Padua have clear potential for quality, best demonstrated by their Cabernet.

Colli Euganei DOC. Red and white wine. Province: Padua. Villages: 17 communes south of Padua. Grapes: (red) Merlot 60–80%, Cabernet Franc, Cabernet Sauvignon, Barbera and Raboso Veronese 20–40%; (white) Garganega 30–50%, Serprina 10–30% Tocai and/or Sauvignon 20–40%, Pinella, Pinot Bianco and Riesling Italico max. 20% (Moscato) Moscato Bianco. Max. crop: 98 hl/ha. Min. alch: 10.5° for white and Moscato, 11° for red, 11.5° for Cabernet. Annual production: 610,000 cases. Euganean wine, despite its long history, is generally rather dull.

Gambellara DOC. White wine. Province: Vicenza. Villages: Gambellara, Montebello Vicentino, Montorso and Zermeghedo. Grapes: Garganega 80–90%, Trebbiano di Soave up to 20%. Max. crop: 98 hl/ha (87 hl/ha for classico). Min. alch: 10.5° for Gambellara (11.5° for classico); 12° for Recioto di Gambellara; 14° for Vin Santo di Gambellara. Vin Santo di Gambellara aged for at least 2 years. Annual production 670,000 cases.

Soave's eastern neighbour, worth trying as an alternative. Its Recioto version is sweet (and sometimes fizzy). The Vin Santo is sweet and strong.

Lessini Durello DOC. White wine. Provinces: Verona and Vicenza. Area: 7 communes in Verona and 21 in Vicenza. Grape: Durello min. 85%, Garganega, Trebbiano di Soave, Chardonnay, Pinot Nero up to 15%. Max crop: 112 hl/ha. Min. alch: 10°, *spumante* 11°. 330,000 cases. DOC, making steely dry wines, both still and sparkling.

Lison-Pramaggiore DOC. Red and white wine. Provinces: Venice, Pordenone, Treviso. Area: 11 communes in Venice, 2 in Treviso and 5 in Pordenone. Grapes: Cabernet (Franc and Sauvignon), Chardonnay, Merlot, Pinot (Bianco and Grigio), Refosco del Peduncolo Rosso, Riesling Italico, Sauvignon, Tocai Italico and Verduzzo. Aged: (Cabernet) 3 years for *riserva*; (Merlot) 2 years for *riserva*. Max. crop: 91 hl/ha. Min. alch: 11°. Annual production 1m cases.

DOC comprising the areas of Tocai di Lison, Cabernet and Merlot di Pramaggiore. The wine list includes 12 types; the Pinot Bianco and Riesling Italico may also be *spumante*.

Merlot The major red grape of the eastern Veneto, included in the major DOC zones but often found as a '*vino da tavola*' which may be the sign of an individualist product of quality. (*See* Villa dal Ferro-Lazzarini under Producers.) Its best wines are dark and nicely fruity, often ending with an astringent note.

Merlot di Pramaggiore *See under* Lison-Pramaggiore.

Montello e Colli Asolani DOC. Red and white wine. Province: Treviso. Villages: 17 communes in the province. Grapes: Prosecco for white, Cabernet or Merlot for red (up to 15% blending allowed). Max. crop: 70 hl/ha. Min. alch: 10.5° for white; 11° for Merlot; 11.5° for Cabernet. Aged: (red) 2 years (1 in wood) for *superiore*. Annual production: 130,000 cases.

DOC with a small supply of Cabernet and more of Merlot and Prosecco, which is usually fizzy and often sweet. The hills around Asolo were a resort during the Renaissance, famous for Palladio's villas. The most famous wine estate of the area is Venegazzù (*see* Venegazzù-Conte Loredan-Gasparini under Producers).

Piave or Vini del Piave DOC. Red and white wine. Provinces: Venice, Treviso. Villages: from Conegliano to the Adriatic sea. 50 communes in Treviso, 12 in Venice. Grapes: Cabernet, Merlot, Pinot Bianco, Pinot Grigio, Pinot Nero, Raboso, Tocai or Verduzzo. Max. crop: 91 hl/ha. Min. alch: 11° for Merlot, Pinot Bianco, Tocai, Verduzzo, 11.5° for Cabernet, Pinot Grigio, Pinot Nero, Raboso. Aged: (Cabernet) three years for *riserva*; (Merlot) three years for *vecchio*; (Pinot Nero) two years for *riserva*. Annual production 2m. cases.

The River Piave flows through flat country to the sea north of Venice (at Jesolo). Cabernet and Merlot both thrive here, making rather dry wines that benefit from ageing. The whites need drinking young.

Pinot Bianco, Grigio, Nero All three Pinots are found in the Veneto; none achieves the quality found farther east in Friuli-Venezia Giulia. Some good Pinot *spumante* is made by Maculan and Chardonnay *spumante* by Venegazzù-Conte Loredan-Gasparini (*see* Producers).

Pramaggiore *See under* Lison-Pramaggiore.

Prosecco di Conegliano-Valdobbiadene DOC. White wine. Province: Treviso. Villages: Valdobbiadene, Conegliano, Vittorio Veneto plus 12 other communes. Grapes: Prosecco (85–100%), Verdiso, Pinot Bianco, Pinot Grigio, Chardonnay up to 15%, or Verdiso alone up to 10%. Max. crop: 84 hl/ha. Min. alch: 10.5° *frizzante*, 11° *spumante*. Annual production: 2.3m. cases

The native Prosecco grape gives a rather austere and charmless yellowish dry wine but responds well to being made fizzy, whether *frizzante* or *spumante*, particularly in its semi-sweet and sweet forms. Valdobbiadene is a restricted zone where the wines have a finer texture, greater length on the palate and the right to the title Superiore di Cartizze.

Raboso del Piave The local Raboso grape makes an astringent red wine which is worth meeting, especially with 4 or 5 years' bottle-age. *See* Piave.

Recioto *See under* Valpolicella.

Soave and Recioto di Soave DOC. White wine. Province: Verona. Villages: Soave and 12 others. Grapes: Garganega 70–90%, Trebbiano di Soave and Trebbiano Toscano up to 30%. Max. crop: 98 hl/ha. Min. alch: 10.5° for Soave, 11.5° for Soave Superiore. Aged 8 months for *superiore*. Annual production: 5.55m. cases.

The most popular of all Italian white wines. Its simple name seems to express its simple nature: it is smooth, light and easy to drink. When it is well made and above all fresh it is hugely tempting. The zone is immediately east of Valpolicella, making Verona a singularly well-watered city.

A central zone of Soave is entitled to the term Classico, which in this case is worth an extra thousand lire or two. To taste the wine at its best, look for Pieropan (*see* Producers), though Bolla and the colossal cooperative are reliable. Recioto di Soave is a concentrated, semi-sweet and rich-textured version made of semi-dried grapes.

Tocai di Lison *See under* Lison-Pramaggiore.

Valpolicella – Recioto della Valpolicella-Amarone DOC. Red wine. Province: Verona. Villages: 19 communes in the hills north of Verona, the westernmost 5 of which are the 'Classico' zone. Grapes: Corvina Veronese 40–70%, Rondinella 20–40%, Molinara 5–25%, Rossignola, Negrara, Barbera, Sangiovese up to 15%. Max. crop: 84 hl/ha. Min. alch: 11°. Recioto must have 14° potential alcohol of which at least 12° is actual. Aged one year for *superiore*. Annual production 3.67m. cases.

Valpolicella, like Chianti, has too wide a range of qualities to be easily summed up. At its best it is one of Italy's most tempting light reds, always reminding one of cherries, combining the smooth and the lively and ending with the bitter-almond hallmark of almost all northeast Italian reds. In commerce it can be a poor, pale, listless sort of wine. 'Classico' is better; the pick of the villa-dotted vineyards are in the hills skirted to the south and west by the River Adige, divided by the river from Bardolino. Soave lies at the opposite, eastern, end of the zone.

At any Veronese gathering the last bottle to be served is Recioto, either in its sweet form or its powerful, dry, velvety but astringent and bitter Amarone. Recioto is made by half drying selected grapes to concentrate their sugars, then giving them a long fermentation in the New Year. If the fermentation is allowed to go on to the bitter end the result is Amarone. Many critics find it one of Italy's greatest red wines. My advice is to keep a glass of young Valpolicella at hand to quench your thirst. Recioto is also made as a fizz.

Venegazzù della Casa The estate of Conte Loredan (*see* Producers) in the DOC Montello-Colli Asolani, but most famous for its non-DOC Cabernet-Merlot blend in the Bordeaux style, comparable perhaps to a powerful rustic St-Emilion, and its *metodo tradizionale spumante*.

Leading Veneto Producers

Allegrini

Fumane di Valpolicella, 37022 Verona.

Owners: the Allegrini family for three generations. DOC: Valpolicella, Recioto, Amarone. Other: Pelara. The late Giovanni Allegrini's three children, Walter, Marilisa and Franco, now run the estate which has about 50 acres of choice plots in Valpolicella Classico. Their increasingly admired wines include some of the most persuasive Valpolicella Classico Superiore and Amarone.

Anselmi

Monteforte d'Alpone, 37032 Verona.

Owner: Roberto Anselmi. DOC: Soave, Valpolicella. Other: Cabernet Sauvignon. With 62 acres of his own vineyard and 74 under contract, Anselmi has become a major force in the area, expressing the versatility of Soave. He also makes a widely admired *barrique*-seasoned Recioto.

Bertani

37121 Verona.

Founded: 1857; now headed by Gaetano and Giovanni Bertani. DOC: Soave, Valpolicella-Valpantena, Recioto, Amarone. Other: Bertarosé, *barrique*-aged Chardonnay, red *ripasso*. From 500 acres of family vines and 500–600 acres belonging to suppliers, this venerable house makes model wines, notably Secco-Bertani Valpolicella and aged Amarone. Always reliable, it is now beginning to reassert signs of leadership in Verona.

Bolla

37100 Verona.

Founded in Soave in 1883, the firm is now run by the Bolla brothers. DOC: Soave, Valpolicella, Recioto, Amarone. Other: Cabernet Sauvignon, Chardonnay. Grapes acquired from more than 400 growers are processed in ultra-modern plants in the Verona area to make nearly 2.5m. cases. Bolla, synonymous with Soave in the United States, is a leader in viticultural research through the Sergio Bolla Foundation. They also control the firm of Valdo, which makes sparkling wines at Valdobbiadene.

Carpenè Malvolti

Conegliano, 31015 Treviso.

A family firm, founded in 1868 by Etile Carpenè. His descendant Antonio Carpenè still directs and makes the wine. DOC: Prosecco di Conegliano. Other: Carpenè Malvolti Brut *tradizionale*. With production of 300,000 cases at two cellars, the firm is a leading name in Italian sparkling wine.

Guerrieri-Rizzardi

Bardolino, 37011 Verona.

A family estate going back to the 18th century, with a small but interesting museum. Owner: Cristina Guerrieri-Rizzardi. DOC: Bardolino, Soave, Valpolicella Amarone. Other: Bianco San Pietro red Castello Guerrieri, medium dry Moscato. From 370 acres in Bardolino, Valpolicella and Soave come splendid, gracious Verona wines. The Bardolino is admirably lively – one of the best of the pale breed.

Lamberti

Lazise sul Garda, 37017 Verona.

Part of the Gruppo Italiano Vini complex. DOC: Bardolino, Lugana, Riviera del Garda Bresciano, Soave, Valpolicella. From extensive company vineyards in Bardolino and purchases elsewhere, Lamberti produce red and white wines of good commercial quality. They are also a pioneer of Bardolino *novello*.

Maculan

Breganze, 36042 Vicenza.

Founded: 1937. Owners: Fausto and Franca Maculan. DOC: Breganze. Other: Costa d'Olio Rosato, Torcolato, Ferrata Chardonnay and Cabernet Sauvignon, Prado di Canzio, *charmat* Accademia Brut. From 75 acres, including family property, superb examples of each of 12 types of wine. The reputations of the Breganze Cabernet Fratta and sweet white Torcolato (a *barrique*-aged *recioto*) have combined to give this small winery a great reputation.

Masi

Gargagnago, 37020 Verona.

The firm is run by the Boscaini family, producers of wine for six generations. Winemaker: Lanfranco Paronetto. DOC: Bardolino, Soave, Valpolicella, Recioto, Amarone. Other: Campo Fiorin *ripasso*, red VDT Toar, white Masianco. Unerring selection (partly from their own vineyards) and ingenious techniques have made this medium-large winery a touchstone for Verona wines.

Pieropan

Soave, 37038 Verona.

Owner: Leonildo Pieropan (whose grandfather won a prize for Soave in 1906). DOC: Soave, Recioto di Soave. Other: Riesling Italico. Pieropan produces what is generally rated the best Soave Classico from his own and rented vines. His wines are colourful and flavoursome, partly due to his minimal use of filtering and other interventions.

Giuseppe Quintarelli

Cerè di Negrar, 37024 Verona.

Founded in 1924 by the current owner's father. DOC: Valpolicella, Recioto, Amarone. Other: Alzero red. Rich complex wines from 25 acres. Some consider his Amarone to be the finest.

Le Ragose

Arbizzano, 37020 Verona.

Founded: 1969. Owners-winemakers: Maria Marta Galli with her husband Arnaldo. DOC: Valpolicella, Recioto, Amarone. Other: Montericco. The Gallis meticulously select grapes from their 26 acres for some of Valpolicella's best wines.

Castello di Roncade

Roncade, 31056 Treviso.

Owner: Vicenzo Ciani Bassetti. DOC: Piave. Other: Villa Giustinian Riserva, *spumante*. An impressive fortress with a worthy Cabernet/Merlot blend.

Santa Margherita

Fossalta di Portogruaro, 30025 Venezia.

Owners: the Marzotto family. Director: Arrigo Marcer. Winemaker: Giorgio Mascarin. DOC: Alto Adige, Grave del Friuli, Piave, Pramaggiore, Prosecco de Conegliano, Tocai di Lison. Other: Chardonnay Atesino, Pinot Brut, Rosé Brut. Italy's leader in the Pinot Grigio field. Also owns Kettmeir in the Alto Adige and Cantine Torresella.

Serègo Alighieri

Garganego, 37020 Verona.

The owner, Pieralvise Serègo Alighieri (a descendant of Dante Alighieri), grows vines on 74 acres of ground surrounding his ancient villa. His grapes are bought by Masi (q.v.). His own DOC Valpolicella, Amarone and Recioto wines have considerable finesse, due partly to their ageing in cherry wood casks.

Cantina Sociale di Soave

Soave, 37038 Verona.

Among several claimants to be the largest cooperative in Europe, but certainly the biggest producer of Soave. Founded in 1930, it has 630 members with more than 6,000 acres of vines, 80% in the Soave DOC zone. DOC: Bardolino, Soave, Valpolicella. Production is more than 3m. cases, mostly of Soave, some under the Cantina's label, some to bottlers and shippers. It also makes Valpolicella, Bardolino and *spumante* wines.

Fratelli Tedeschi

Pedemonte, 37020 Verona.

Founded: 1884. Owners: Renzo Tedeschi and family. DOC: Bianco di Costoza, Soave, Valpolicella, Recioto, Amarone. Other: Capitel San Rocco Bianco, Rosso delle Lucchine, white Vin de la Fabriseria. From 20 acres of their own vines and discreet purchases the Tedeschi family makes some of the area's best wines.

Tommasi

Pedemonte, 37020 Verona.

Owner: Dario Tommasi. DOC: Bardolino, Bianco di Custoza, Soave, Valpolicella, Recioto, Amarone. Recently much improved, this estate of 87 acres makes an Amarone that can hold its own with the best.

Venegazzù-Conte Loredan-Gasparini

Venegazzù del Montello, 31040 Treviso.

The estate was founded in 1940 by Piero Loredan, descendant of Venetian doges, and bought by Giancarlo Palla in 1974. DOC: Prosecco del Montello e dei Colli Asolani. Other: Brut *tradizionale*, Pinot Bianco, Pinot Grigio, Venegazzù Della Casa, Venegazzù Etichetta Nera, Venegazzù Rosso. From 148 acres, wines include the famous reserve Della Casa, a Bordeaux-style blend of great character and class, like a big, not exactly genteel, St-Emilion. The estate seems to have been drifting lately.

Zonin

Gambellara, 36053 Vicenza.

The Zonin family firm, founded in 1821, claims to be Italy's largest private winery with production of nearly 3.2m. cases, of which about a third is exported. DOC: Bardolino, Gambellara, Recioto di Gambellara, Valpolicella. Other: *spumante* and *vini da tavola*. The firm bases its production on vineyards in the Veneto; it has a growing range of estates, including Pian d'Albola in Chianti Classico, Ca' Bolani in the Friuli; San Gimignano in Tuscany, Bersano in Piedmont and Il Giangio in Gambellara; and employs 16 oenologists. It also makes wine in Barboursville, Virginia, USA.

OTHER PRODUCERS

Adriano Adami Colbertaldo di Vidor, 31020 Treviso. DOC: Prosecco, Superiore di Cartizze.

Arvedi d'Emelei Cavalcaselle, 37066 Verona. DOC: Bardolino, Bianco di Custoza. Ancient family estate with 30 acres.

Astoria Vini Crocetta del Montello, 31035 Treviso. DOC: Prosecco, Cartizze. Other: Astoria Brut.

Desiderio Bisol & Figli Santo Stefano di Valdobbiadene, 31040 Treviso. DOC: Cartizze, Prosecco di Valdobbiadene. Other: *Tradizionale* Bisol Brut Riserva.

Paolo Boscaini & Figli Valgatara, 37020 Verona. DOC: Bardolino, Soave, Valpolicella, Recioto, Amarone. Other: Chardonnay, Pinot Grigio.

Brigaldara San Floriano, 37020 Verona. DOC: Val-policella, Amarone.

Brunelli S Pietro in Cariano, 37029, Verona. Owner: Giuseppe Brunelli. 25 acres. Makes top Valpolicella and Amarone.

Ca' Bruzzo San Germano dei Berici, 36040 Vicenza. Owners: Aldo Bruzzo and Sarah Wallace. DOC: Range of Colli Berici, particularly good Tocai Rosso. Other: Chardonnay and 'California Blush'.

Ca' del Monte Negrar, 37024 Verona. Owner: Luigi Zanconte. DOC: Valpolicella, Amarone.

Adamo Canel & Figli Col San Martino, 31010 Treviso. DOC: Cartizze, Prosecco di Valdobbiadene.

Canevel Valdobbiadene, 31049 Verona. DOC: Cartizze, Prosecco.

Cardinal Pieve di Soligo, 31053 Treviso. Winemaker: Gianni Bignucolo. DOC: Cartizze, Pinot Bianco *spumante*. Other: bright pink Cardinal Brut.

Le Case Bianche Pieve di Solido, 31053 Treviso. Owner: Alvise Orlandi. DOC: Sparkling Prosecco. Other: Wild-bacher, Camoi (Cabernet Sauvignon-Wildbacher).

Cavalchina-Piona Sommacampagna, Verona. DOC: Bardolino, Bianco di Custoza. Other: Pinot Bianco. Among the better whites of Verona.

Cecilia di Baone Terralba di Baone, 35030 Padova. DOC: Range of Colli Euganeis. Other: Moscato Fior d'Arancio (sweet, sparkling), Don Noè Spumante Brut.

Colle dei Cipressi Calmasino di Bardolino, 37010 Verona. DOC: Bardolino.

Cantina dei Colli Berici Lonigo and Barberana, 36045 Vicenza. Following 1989 merger of two cooperatives, now Europe's second largest wine production unit, producing over 8m. cases a year from nearly 10,000 acres. Mainly *vino da tavola*. DOC: Colli Berici.

Cantina Sociale Cooperative dei Colli Euganei Vò Euganei, 35030 Padova. DOC: Colli Euganei. Other: *vino da tavola, spumante*.

Corte Aleardi Gargagnago, 37020 Verona. Owner: Aleardo Ferrari. DOC: Valpolicella, Recioto, Amarone.

Corte Sant'Alda Mezzane di Sotto, 37030, Verona. Small estate (25 acres) belonging to Marinella Camerani. Makes very good red wines: Valpolicella, Amarone and Recioto.

Dal Forno Cellole d'Illasi, 37030, Verona. Romano Dal Forno produces small amounts of Valpolicella, Amarone and Recioto. His wines are even more concentrated than those of leader Giuseppe Quintarelli. Unique but very expensive. (18.5 acres.)

Villa dal Ferro-Lazzarini San Germano dei Berici, 36040 Vicenza. The vineyards and cellars of this 16th-century villa have been renewed in the last 20 years by Alfredo Lazzarini. DOC: Colli Berici. All varietals carry individual vineyard names.

Foss Marai Valdobbiadene, 31049 Treviso. DOC: Prosecco, Cartizze.

Fratelli Fraccaroli San Benedetto di Lugana, Verona. Owners-winemakers: Francesco and Giuseppe Fraccaroli. Good DOC Lugana.

Nino Franco Valdobbiadene, 31049 Treviso. Founded: 1919. Winemaker: Primo Franco. DOC: Cartizze, Prosecco di Valdobbiadene (sparkling and still). A leader in Prosecco production.

Cantina Sociale di Gambellara Gambellara, 36053 Vicenza. Cooperative. DOC: Colli Berici, Gambellara.

Villa Girardi San Pietro in Cariano, 37029 Verona. DOC: Bardolino, Soave, Valpolicella, Recioto, Amarone. Now owned by Tommasi (q.v.).

Girasole Lazise, 37017 Verona. Good DOC Bardolino and Valpolicella.

Gorgo Custoza, 37066 Verona. Owner: Roberto Bricolo. DOC: Bardolino, Bianco di Custoza. 74 acres.

Gregoletto Premaor di Miane, 31050 Treviso. DOC: Prosecco di Conegliono.

Liasora Ponte di Piave, 31047 Treviso. DOC: Piave. Other: Semi-sweet white Buschino. 99 acres.

Marcato Roncà, 37030 Verona. DOC: Lessini (still and *tradizionale*), Soave.

Maschio Visnà, 31050 Treviso. DOC: Prosecco. Other: *tradizionale* Maschio dei Cavalieri.

Il Maso Negrar di Valpolicella, Verona. Owner: Zonin (q.v.). DOC: Valpolicella, Amarone.

Merotto Col San Martino, 31049 Treviso. DOC: Cartizze, Prosecco. Other: Merotto Brut *tradizionale*.

La Montanella Monselice, 35043 Padova. DOC: Colli Euganei. Other: Moscato Fior d'Arancio. 32 acres.

Montecorno Sona, 37060 Verona. DOC: Bardolino, Bianco di Custoza. 57 acres.

Cantina Sociale La Montelliana e dei Colli Asolani Montebelluna, 31040 Treviso. Cooperative. DOC: Montello e Colli Asolani.

Montresor 37100 Verona. DOC: Bardolino, Bianco di Custoza, Soave, Valpolicella, Recioto, Amarone.

Abazia di Nervesa Nervesa della Battaglia, 31040 Treviso. DOC: Montello e Colli Asolani.

Opere Trevigiane Crocetta del Montello, 31035 Treviso. Owners: the Moretti family. Fine *spumante classico* and Prosecco DOC. Label is La Gioiosa.

Fratelli Pasqua 37100 Verona. DOC: Bardolino, Soave, Valpolicella, Recioto, Amarone. Other: Cabernet Morago.

Fratelli Poggi Affi, 37010 Verona. DOC: Bardolino. 99 acres.

Ponte (Cantina Sociale Cooperative di Ponte di Piave) Ponte di Piave, 31047 Treviso. Cooperative. DOC: Piave. Other: Pinot Bianco, Pinot Grigio, Riesling Italico, Raboso, Rosato, Sauvignon. A large supplier of Veneto wines.

Graziano Pra Monteforte d'Alpone, 37032 Verona. DOC: Soave Classico.

Rechsteiner Piavon di Oderzo, 31046 Treviso. Owner: Baroni Stepski-Doliwa. DOC: Piave. Other: Chardonnay. 110 acres.

Luigi Righetti Marano, 37020 Verona. DOC: Valpolicella, Amarone.

Castello di Roncade Roncade, 31056 Treviso. Owner: Vicenzo Ciani Bassetti. DOC: Piave. Other: Villa Giustinian Riserva, *spumante*. An impressive fortress with a worthy Cabernet/Merlot blend.

Russolo Pramaggiore, 30020 Venezia. Owner: I. Russolo. DOC: Lison-Pramaggiore. Other: Excellent Borgo di Peuma and Casali Bearzi *vini da tavola*.

Le Salette Fumane, 37022, Verona. Owners: the Scamperle family. 32 acres. Makes Valpolicella, Amarone and Recioto of outstanding quality.

Sanperetto Negrar, 37024 Verona. Owner: Roberto Mazzi. DOC: Valpolicella, Recioto, Amarone. 17 acres. Rising quality.

Le Vigne di San Pietro Sommacampagna, 37066 Verona. Owner: Carlo Nerozzi. DOC: Bardolino, Bianco di Custoza. Other: Good Cabernet Sauvignon Refolà. 12 acres.

Tenuta Sant'Anna Loncon di Annone Veneto, 30020 Venezia. Owner: Agricola Rus S.P.A. DOC: Grave del Friuli, Lison-Pramaggiore. Other: Pinot Grigio, Prosecco, *spumante*. The firm owns more than 600 acres of vines in the Veneto and some 250 acres in Grave del Friuli.

Santa Sofia Pedemonte, 37020 Verona. DOC: Bardolino, Bianco di Custoza, Soave, Valpolicella, Recioto, Amarone. Since the estate has been sold the name is used for a line of commercial wines.

Santi Illasi, 37031 Verona. Founded in 1843, the winery is now part of the Gruppo Italiano Vini complex. DOC: Bardolino, Soave, Valpolicella, Recioto, Amarone. Other: Carlo Santi Brut *tradizionale* Turà.

Sant'Osvaldo Loncon di Annone Veneto, 30020 Venezia. DOC: Lison-Pramaggiore. Other: Pinot Bianco, Pinot Grigio, Raboso, Refosco, Sauvignon.

Sartori Negrar, 37024 Verona. DOC: Bardolino, Soave, Valpolicella, Recioto, Amarone.

Scamperle Fumane di Valpolicella, 37022 Verona. Large bottler of Verona wines.

Scarpa Trevignano, 31040 Treviso. Corbulino Bianco (Pinot Bianco-Chardonnay) and Rosso (Pinot Nero blend).

Villa Sceriman Vò Euganei, 35030 Padova. Owners: the Soranzo family. DOC: Colli Euganei. Other: Moscato Fior d'Arancio. 62 acres.

Viticola Suavia Soave, 37038 Verona. Owner: Giovanni Tessari. DOC: Soave. A rising star with his single-vineyard Soave Monte Carbonare.

Cantine Torresella See Santa Margherita.

Tramanal Arbizzano di Negrar, 37024 Verona. Owner: Domenico Vantini. DOC: Valpolicella, Amarone, Recioto. A gem in Valpolicella.

Valdo Valdobbiadene, 31049 Treviso. DOC: Prosecco, Cartizze. *See* Bolla.
Cantina Sociale di Valdobbiadene San Giovanni di Bigolino, 31030 Treviso. Cooperative. DOC: Cartizze, Prosecco di Valdobbiadene.
Massimo Venturini San Floriano, 37020 Verona. DOC: Valpolicella, Amarone.

Zardetto Conegliano, 31015 Treviso. Founded in 1969 by oenologist Pino Zardetto. DOC: Cartizze, Prosecco di Conegliano.
Zenato San Benedetto di Lugana, Verona. DOC: Bardolino, Bianco di Custoza, Lugana, Riviera del Garda Bresciano, Tocai di San Martino della Battaglia, Valpolicella, Amarone. 40 acres.

FRIULI-VENEZIA GIULIA

There is a tidiness about the DOC arrangements in Friuli-Venezia Giulia which is due to their recent emergence as an important part of Italian viticulture. There was little folklore to get in the way of a simple carve-up into geographical zones whose wines are named for their grape varieties.

With six zones and some dozen varieties, as well as the brand names that some growers insist on adding, the combinations still reach a head-spinning number. It helps to distinguish between them if you are clear that there is one very big DOC that embraces most of the region, two superior hill zones with Colli in their names, and three smaller and newer DOCs of less significance in a row along the coastal plain.

The big zone is Grave del Friuli, DOC for the whole wine-growing hinterland from the Veneto border east to beyond Udine where the Alps reach down towards Trieste. The hills of Gorizia, right on the Slovenian border, are the oldest-established and best vineyards of the region. Today, this zone is generally known simply as Collio. To the north is the separate DOC of the Colli Orientali del Friuli ('the eastern hills of Friuli') with similar growing conditions.

The coastal DOCs from west to east are Aquileia, Latisana and Isonzo; the last, adjacent to the Gorizian hills, apparently having the greatest potential for quality. These coastal vineyards tend to stress red wine, whereas the reputation of the hills is mainly based on white – whether produced from such traditional grapes as Tocai Friulano, Malvasia, Picolit or Verduzzo, or more recent imports: the Pinot Bianco or Grigio, Sauvignon Blanc and Rhine Riesling.

DOC and Other Wines

Friuli Aquileia DOC. Red and white wine. Province: Udine. Villages: Aquileia and 17 others. Grapes: Merlot, Cabernet, Refosco, Tocai Friulano, Pinot Bianco, Pinot Grigio, Riesling Renano, Sauvignon, Traminer Aromatico, Verduzzo. Max. crop: 91 hl/ha. Min. alch: 10.5° for Merlot, Refosco, Tocai Friulano, Pinot Grigio, Riesling Renano, Rosato; 11° for Cabernet, Pinot Bianco, Sauvignon, Traminer Aromatico, Verduzzo. Annual production: 440,000 cases.

A DOC for the varied production of the cooperative at Cervignano, named after a Roman city. The land is flat, the climate temperate and efforts at quality production only recent, but signs are that it will come, particularly with Cabernet and Merlot.
Carso DOC. Red and white wine. Provinces: Trieste and Gorizia. Area: 6 communes in Gorizia and 6 in Trieste. Grapes: Terrano (85%), Pinot Nero, Piccola Nera up to 15%; Malvasia Istriana (85%), other authorized light grapes up to 15%. Max. crops: 70 hl/ha. Min. alch: 10.5%. Annual production: 14,000 cases.

Carso and Carso Terrano are virtually the same, both based on the Terrano (relative of Refosco) grape. Carso Malvasia is similar to other DOC Malvasia Istriana types.
Collio Goriziano or Collio DOC. White and red wine. Province: Gorizia. Villages: west of Gorizia. Grapes: Riesling Italico, Sauvignon, Tocai Friulano, Traminer Aromatico, Malvasia Istriana, Merlot, Pinot Bianco, Pinot Grigio, Pinot Nero, Cabernet Franc, Cabernet Sauvignon, Chardonnay, Müller-Thurgau, Picolit, Ribolla Gialla, Riesling Renano. Max.

crop: 77 hl/ha. Min. alch: Collio Bianco 11°; Malvasia 11.5°; Cabernet Franc, Merlot, Pinot Grigio, Riesling Italico, Tocai Friulano, Traminer 11.5°; Pinot Nero, Sauvignon 11.5°, Picolit 14°, Pinot Bianco 11°, Ribolla Gialla 11°. Annual production: 833,000 cases.

A DOC of such diversity of wines and styles that California comes to mind. Fruity early-developing reds of the Bordeaux varieties are less interesting than the white specialities, particularly the aromatic Tocai Friulano and Pinot Bianco and Grigio, which at their best balance Hungarian-style 'stiffness' and strength with real delicacy. Collio without a varietal name is a light dry white of Ribolla and other local grapes. 'Pinot Bianco' sometimes includes Chardonnay and can develop burgundian richness with barrel-age.
Colli Orientali del Friuli DOC. White and red wine. Province: Udine. Villages: 14 communes in the province. Grapes: Tocai Friulano, Verduzzo, Ribolla, Pinot Bianco, Pinot Grigio, Sauvignon, Riesling Renano, Picolit, Merlot, Cabernet, Pinot Nero, Refosco, Malvasia Istriana, Ramandolo (Classico), Rosato, Schioppettino. Max. crop: 77 hl/ha. Min. alch: mainly 11°; *superiore* 11.5°; Ramandolo 14°; Picolit 14°. Merlot, Cabernet, Pinot Nero, Refosco and Picolit are *riserva* after 2 years' ageing. Annual production: 890,000 cases.

The neighbouring DOC to Collio, with similar white wines, perhaps slightly less prestigious except in its native Verduzzo (q.v.) and its rare dessert white Picolit (q.v.). The splendid rustic red Refosco and Cabernet are better than the Collio red wines.
Friuli-Annia DOC. Red, white, *rosato*. Eight villages of the province of Udine on southern coast. Grapes: Cabernet

Franc, Cabernet Sauvignon, Refosco, Tocai, Pinot Bianco, Pinot Grigio, Verduzzo, Traminer, Sauvignon, Chardonnay, Malvasia. Max crop: 84 hl/ha. Min alch Bianco, Rosato and Rosso: 10.5°, variety-named wines 11°.

Recently introduced (1995) DOC. Not shining as brightly as Aquileia or Latisana. No figures available yet.

Friuli Grave DOC. Red and white wine. Provinces: Udine, Pordenone. Area: Udine and Pordenone. Grapes: Merlot, Cabernet, Refosco, Tocai, Pinot Bianco, Pinot Grigio, Verduzzo, Riesling Renano, Pinot Nero, Sauvignon, Traminer Aromatico, Chardonnay. Max. crop: 91 hl/ha. Min. alch: 10.5° for Chardonnay; 11° for Merlot, Refosco, Tocai, Pinot Grigio, Verduzzo, Cabernet, Pinot Nero, Pinot Bianco, Riesling Renano, Sauvignon, Traminer Aromatico. Annual production 3.3m. cases.

The largest DOC of the region: biggest source of Merlot, which accounts for half of its production. Grave Merlot is soft, dark and dry with a hint of grassiness; not as good as its Cabernet, which has more personality and life, nor as memorable as its fruity, bitter Refosco. Grave Pinot Bianco (sometimes Chardonnay) and Tocai can be good as the Collio equivalents.

Isonzo DOC. White and red wine. Province: Gorizia. Area: 20 communes around Gradisca d'Isonzo. Grapes: Tocai, Sauvignon, Malvasia Istriana, Pinot Bianco, Pinot Grigio, Verduzzo Friulano, Traminer Aromatico, Riesling Renano, Merlot, Cabernet, Chardonnay, Franconia, Pinot Nero, Refosco dal Peduncolo Rosso, plus a Bianco, Rosso and Pinot Spumante. Max. crop: 91 hl/ha. Min. alch. 10.5° for Tocai, Malvasia Istriana, Verduzzo Friulano and Merlot; 11° for Pinot (Bianco and Grigio), Sauvignon, Traminer Aromatico, Riesling Renano and Cabernet. Annual production: 780,000 cases.

The DOC zone between the Collio and the Gulf of Trieste also specializes in Merlot, which can be better than that of Grave del Friuli and Cabernet for drinking young. Its whites are light and pleasant, but they are rarely up to Collio standards.

Friuli Latisana DOC. Red and white wine. Province: Udine. Area: 12 communes in the province. Grapes: Merlot, Cabernet, Refosco, Tocai Friulano, Pinot Bianco, Pinot Grigio, Traminer Aromatico, Chardonnay and Verduzzo Friulano. Max. crop: 91 hl/ha. Min. alch: 11° for Latisana Merlot, Refosco, Tocai Friulano, Pinot Grigio and Verduzzo Friulano; 11.5° for Cabernet, Pinot Bianco. Annual production: 122,000 cases.

This DOC is dominated by Merlot, Cabernet and Tocai, but Refosco is more robust and durable.

Picolit A native grape of the Colli Orientali del Friuli and its dessert wine, the Picolit is one of the almost-lost legends of the 19th century, along with Romania's Cotnari and the (really lost) Constantia of the Cape. It yields a powerful, smooth, even dense-textured wine, not necessarily very sweet, and ending slightly bitter in the regional style. Bottles of the wine I have tasted have clearly been too young to have developed the glorious bouquet and flavour that others have reported. It is rare, extremely expensive and normally overpriced.

Schioppettino A native red grape of the Colli Orientali del Friuli, giving wine with some of the rasping fruitiness of a good Barbera from Piedmont.

Verduzzo A native white grape made either into a fresh dry white 'fish' wine or a sort of Recioto, an *amabile* of partly dried grapes – see Ramandolo, Colli Orientali. NB Verdiso is a different white grape, mainly grown in the Veneto.

Friuli-Venezia Giulia Producers

Abbazia di Rosazzo

Manzano, 33040 Udine.

The estate winery occupies an 11th-century abbey. Manager and winemaker: Walter Filiputti. DOC: Colli Orientali del Friuli. Other: Ronco dei Roseti, Ronco delle Acacie, Ronco di Corte, Pignolo. The reasonable range of Friuli varietals is enhanced by Ronco dei Roseti red from Tazzelenghe, Refosco, Cabernet and Merlot, and Ronco delle Acacie white from Tocai, Ribolla and Chardonnay.

Collavini

Corno di Rosazzo, 33040 Udine.

Manlio Collavini is the third generation of winemakers. DOC: Colli Orientali del Friuli, Collio, Grave del Friuli. Other: Conte di Cuccanea (a barrel-aged white wine), and sparkling wines Il Grigio, *Charmat lungo* Ribolla Gialla, *tradizionale* Applause Nature.

EnoFriulia-Puiatti

Capriva del Friuli, 34070 Gorizia.

Two establishments, both owned and run by winemaker Vittorio Puiatti and his son Giovanni. EnoFriulia (founded in 1967 as EnoJulia) makes a range of good quality Friuli wines, mainly *vino da tavola*. On the family estate at Farra d'Isonzo Puiatti makes prestigious Collio DOC. Also notable are the stylish white Nuvizial and Puiatti Bianco *vini da tavola*, as well as a *tradizionale*, Puiatti Extra Brut.

Livio Felluga

Brazzano di Cormons, 34070 Gorizia.

Livio Felluga's sons Maurizio and Andrea represent the fifth generation of winemakers. DOC: Colli Orientali del Friuli, Collio. From five estates with nearly 300 acres of vines, Felluga makes internationally-acclaimed wines. A Pinot *spumante tradizionale* is in preparation. The white *vino da tavola* Terre Alte is highly esteemed.

Marco Felluga-Russiz Superiore

Gradisca d'Isonzo, 34072 Gorizia.

Marco (brother of Livio) Felluga founded his wine house in 1956, the Russiz Superiore estate in 1967. DOC: Collio. The Marco Felluga label consists of the usual Collio varieties from grapes purchased from regular suppliers in Collio. Russiz Superiore, a model of its kind, consists of 170 acres of terraced vines. Two white *vini da tavola* are highly acclaimed: dry Roncuz and a light, subtly oaky Verduzzo. Felluga also bottles some wine under the Villa San Giovanni label.

Vie di Romans

Mariano del Friuli, 34070 Gorizia.

Now run by Stelio's son Gianfranco, who has turned the 12 acres of densely-planted, low-yielding vineyard into a model estate. His Isonzo DOC wines and *vino da tavola* Chardonnay are consistently among the region's top rated, and his Sauvignon is frequently outstanding.

Gravner

Oslavia, 34170 Gorizia.

DOC: Collio. A rising star in Collio. As well as superb DOC wines, Josko Gravner (whose 27 acres of vineyard stray in places over the border into Slovenia) makes interesting *vino da tavola*, including the red Rujno (Cabernet-Merlot) and the white Vinograd Breg. He ages most of his wines in wood, producing Chardonnay and Sauvignon Blanc of particular character.

Jermann

Villanova di Farr, 34070 Gorizia.

A family estate founded in 1880; now run by Silvio Jermann. Other: Engel Rosé, Picolit, Engelwhite, Vinnae, Vintage Tunina. Jermann makes first-rate now entirely non-DOC wines, including the very special Vintage Tunina (from Chardonnay, Sauvignon, Malvasia, Ribolla, Picolit) from 57 acres of vines. Taste Tunina if you are a sceptic about Italian whites. Jermann's most recent release is a formidably expensive, barrel-aged Chardonnay called 'Where the Dreams Have No End...'.

Mario Schiopetto

Capriva del Friuli, 34070 Gorizia.

Founded in 1969 by Mario Schiopetto on property belonging to the Archbishopric of Gorizia since 1859. DOC: Collio. Other: Cabernet, Merlot, Ribolla, Riesling Renano. Schiopetto is one of the most skilled and courageous winemakers of Italy. His whites (including Rhine Riesling) are perhaps the most exceptional.

Torre Rosazza

Poggiobello di Manzano, 33044 Udine.

DOC: Colli Orientali del Friuli. This historical 207-acre estate is being developed by the Generali insurance group under the supervision of winemaker Walter Filiputti. Both DOC and *vini da tavola* are promising, notably Ronco della Torre (Cabernet-Merlot). The *barrique*-aged Ronco delle Magnolie (Pinot Bianco-Chardonnay) and L'Altremerlot (a pure varietal) are also interesting.

Volpe Pasini

Togliano di Torreano, 33040 Udine.

A 74-acre estate owned by the Volpe Pasini family who make some of the zone's best wines. Tocai and Pinot Bianco are frequently the finest of their DOC (Colli Orientali) wines, which are labelled Žuc di Volpe. Of their *vini da tavola*, the white Le Roverelle (Tocai, Sauvignon, Pinot Bianco, Verduzzo) and the red Le Marne (Cabernet, Refosco, Pinot Nero) are noteworthy.

OTHER PRODUCERS

Angoris Cormons, 34071 Gorizia. Founded: 1648. Owners: the Locatelli family. Winemaker: Flavio Zuliani. DOC: Colli Orientali del Friuli, Isonzo. Other: Modolet Brut *tradizionale*, Spirfolét *spumante*. Angoris also owns Fattoria Casalino in Chianti Classico.

Conti Attems Lucinico, 34070 Gorizia. Owner: Douglas Attems Sigismondo, who carries on a centuries-old family tradition. DOC: Collio, Isonzo. Other: Rosato di Lucinico. Quality slipped badly, but recent collaboration with winemaker Collavini may restore class.

Fratelli Buzzinelli Cormons, 34071 Gorizia. An excellent family winery. The Buzzinelli brothers have been bottling wine since 1955. DOC: Collio. Other: Müller-Thurgau.

Ca' Bolani Cervignano del Friuli, 33052 Udine. Owner: Zonin (q.v.) of the Veneto, who also owns nearby Ca' Vescovo. The two estates together have 445 acres and mainly produce a stylish Aquileia DOC. Other wines include a Müller-Thurgau *vino da tavola*, Chardonnay *frizzante* and Conte Bolani Brut Riserva *tradizionale*.

Ca' Ronesca Dolegna del Collio, 34070 Gorizia. Owner: Sergio Comunello. Winemaker: Fabio Coser. DOC: Collio, Colli Orientali del Friuli. Other: Merlot-based Sariz. Decidedly on the rise.

Ca' Vescovo *See* Ca' Bolani.

La Castellada Oslavia, 34170 Gorizia. Owners: Giorgio and Nicolò Bensa. DOC: Collio.

Cantina Produttori Vini del Collio e dell'Isonzo Cormons, 34071 Gorizia. Cooperative. Cellarmaster: Luigi Soini. DOC: Collio, Isonzo. Other: *spumante* wines, Vino della Pace.

G B Comelli Nimis, 33045 Udine. Owner: G. B. (Filippon) Comelli. DOC: Colli Orientali del Friuli. A tiny estate renowned for Ramandolo Classico.

Borgo Conventi Farra d'Isonzo, 34070 Gorizia. The former walled convent, founded in 1876, is owned by Gianni Vescovo. DOC: Collio. Other: Tocai Italico. Good Sauvignon Blanc and Pinot Bianco.

Dario Coos Ramandolo, 33045 Udine. Noted for Ramandolo Classico.

Marina Danieli Buttrio, 33042 Udine. Stylish DOC Grave and Colli Orientali del Friuli. Other: Red Faralta (Cabernet-Tazzelenghe), Müller-Thurgau, Brut Mus *spumante*.

Girolamo Dorigo Vincale di Buttrio, 33042 Udine. DOC: Colli Orientali del Friuli. Other: Red Montsclapade, *tradizionale*, white and red Ronc di Juri.

Giovanni Dri Ramandolo di Nimis, 33045 Udine. DOC: Colli Orientali del Friuli. Dri's Ramandolo is a highly prized rarity; a lovely wine.

Le Due Terre Prepotto, 33040 Udine. DOC: Colli Orientali del Friuli. Recently much improved.

Fantinel Buttrio, 33042 Udine. DOC: Collio, Grave del Friuli. Gianfranco Fantinel also owns Santa Caterina where he makes impressive Collio DOC.

Conti Formentini San Floriano del Collio, 34070 Gorizia. The 16th-century castle and property have long belonged to the Formentini family, after whom the Furmint grape of Hungarian Tokaj is said to be named. Owner: Michele Formentini. DOC: Collio. Splendid Pinot

Grigio from 250 acres. The castle contains an *enoteca*, restaurant and wine museum.

Villa Frattina Ghirano, 33080 Pordenone. DOC: Grave del Friuli.

Viticoltori Friuliani-La Delizia Casarsa della Delizia, 33072 Pordenone. Cooperative. Director: Noè Bertolin. DOC: Aquileia, Grave del Friuli. Other: *spumante* wines. Annual production is more than a million cases from 3,700 acres.

Silvano Gallo Mariano del Friuli, 34070 Gorizia. DOC: Isonzo. 12 acres.

Gradnik Plessiva di Cormons, 34071 Gorizia. Wanda Gradnik maintains a century-old family tradition. DOC: Collio. A stalwart among Collio's small producers.

Isola Augusta Palazzolo della Stella, 33056 Udine. Owners: the Bassani family. DOC: Latisana reds and local. Other: *spumante* wines. A leading estate in Latisana.

Edi Kante San Pelagio, 34011 Trieste. DOC: Carso. Other: Sauvignon, white Vitovska. A new leader in Carso.

Vigneti Le Monde Prata, 33080 Pordenone. Owners: The Pistoni family. DOC: Grave del Friuli. Good Cabernet Sauvignon.

Livon Dolegano, 33048 Udine. A rising force in DOC Collio and Colli Orientali del Friuli. Also DOC Grave del Friuli. Other: *spumante*.

Borgo Magredo Tauriano, 33097 Pordenone. Owner: Generali insurance group. Winemaker: Walter Filiputti. DOC: Grave del Friuli.

Giovanni Marin Fornalis di Cividale, 33043 Udine. DOC: Colli Orientali del Friuli. Two outstanding small estates.

Nascig Corno di Rosazzo, 33040 Udine. DOC: Colli Orientali del Friuli. Other: Franconia, Vigna del Broili.

Lis-Neris-Pecorari San Lorenzo Isontino, 34070 Gorizia. DOC: Isonzo, Collio. Young Alvaro Pecorari makes *vino da tavola* Pinot Grigio, Chardonnay and Sauvignon to compare with the best in Collio.

Pierpaolo Pecorari S Lorenzo Isontino, 34070, Gorizia. Top Isonzo DOC wines and red VDT. Together with Gianfranco Gallo (Vie di Romans) and Alvaro Pecorari (Lis Neris), this is one of the rising stars of Isonzo.

Lina & Paolo Petrucco Buttrio, 33042 Udine. An emerging estate.

Fratelli Pighin Risano, 33050 Udine. Founded: 1963. Owners: the Pighin family. DOC: Collio, Grave del Friuli. Other: Gallorosé, Picolit, Pinot Nero, Soreli (Tocai, Pinot Bianco, Sauvignon), red Baredo.

Vigneti Pittaro Rivolto di Codroipo, 33033 Udine. Owner: Piero Pittaro, who heads Italy's oenologists and Friuli's wine development board. DOC: Grave del Friuli. Other: *tradizionale*, red Agresto, sweet, white, Chardonnay-based Apicio.

Plozner Spilimbergo, 33097 Pordenone. DOC: Grave del Friuli. Other: Chardonnay, Pinot Nero, Traminer. Plozner's Chardonnay is building an international reputation.

Prà di Pradis Pradis di Cormons, 34071 Gorizia. An emerging estate.

Doro Princic Pradis di Cormons, 34071 Gorizia. Owners: Doro and Sandro Princic. DOC: Collio. This tiny family winery makes gorgeous Tocai.

Radikon Oslavia, 34170 Gorizia. DOC: Collio. Other: Slatnik *vino da tavola* from Chardonnay, Tocai and Sauvignon.

Rocca Bernarda Ipplis, 33040 Udine. The old Perusini family estate, which recently became the property of the Sovrano Militare Ordine di Malta (Knights of Malta). DOC: Colli Orientali del Friuli.

Roncada Cormons, 34070 Gorizia. Owners: Silvia and Lina Mattioni. DOC: Collio. Other: Red Franconia.

Ronchi di Cialla Prepotto, 33040 Udine. Owners: Paolo and Dina Rapuzzi. DOC: Colli Orientali del Friuli. Other: Schioppettino. This small winery excels with obscure classics: Picolit, Schioppettino, Verduzzo.

Ronco del Gelso Cormons, 34071, Gorizia. Young winemaker Giorgio Badin makes top Isonzo DOC wines (Tocai, Merlot and others).

Ronco del Gnemiz San Giovanni al Natisone, 33048 Udine. Owner: Enzo Palazzolo. DOC: Colli Orientali del Friuli. Other: Müller-Thurgau, Chardonnay, Ronco del Gnemiz (Cabernets Sauvignon and Franc).

Rubini Spessa di Cividale, 33043 Udine. DOC: Colli Orientali del Friuli.

Villa Russiz Capriva del Friuli, 34070 Gorizia. Founded: 1869 by a French nobleman, La Tour. It now supports the A. Cerruti orphanage. Director and winemaker: Gianni Menotti. DOC: Collio. Other: Picolit.

San Cipriano Sacile, 33077 Pordenone. Owners: the Lot family. DOC: Grave del Friuli. Other: White Truola, red Fondreta.

Santa Caterina *See* Fantinel.

Specogna Rocca Bernarda, 33040 Udine. DOC: Colli Orientali del Friuli. Leonardo Specogna is rapidly on the rise. Especially good DOC Picolit.

Castello di Spessa Spessa di Capriva, 34070 Gorizia. Estate with potential to equal its neighbour Schioppetto (q.v.).

Subida di Monte Cormona, 34070 Gorizia. DOC: Collio.

Borgo del Tiglio Brazzano di Cormons, 34070 Gorizia. Owner: Nicola Manferrari. DOC: Colli Orientali del Friuli. Especially good Tocai and Malvasia. Fine *vino da tavola* Rosso della Centa (Merlot-Cabernet).

Vinicola Udinese 33100 Udine. DOC: Colli Orientali del Friuli, Collio, Grave del Friuli, Carso. Other wines include *spumante* as well as still *vini da tavola*.

Valle Buttrio, 33042 Udine. Owner: Luigi Valle. DOC: Colli Orientali del Friuli, Collio. Other: Franconia, Araldica range.

Redi Vazzoler Mossa, 34070 Gorizia. Owner: Redento Vazzoler. Winemaker: Walter Filiputti. DOC: Collio. Other: White Ghiaie Bianche (Tocai, Pinot Bianco, Müller-Thurgau).

Venica Dolegna del Collio, 34070 Gorizia. DOC: Collio.

La Viarte Novacuzzo, 33040 Udine. Owner: Giuseppe Ceschin. DOC: Colli Orientali del Friuli.

Vigne dal Leon Rocca Bernada, 33040 Udine. Owner: Tullio Zamò. DOC: White Colli Orientali del Friuli. Other: Schioppettino, Tacelenghe, Rosso di Vigne dal Leon (Merlot-Cabernet), oak-aged Pinot Bianco.

Tenuta Villanova Farra d'Isonzo, 34070 Gorizia. DOC: Isonzo, Collio.

EMILIA-ROMAGNA

It is ironic that Italy's greediest culinary region, by all accounts, should put the emphasis on quantity rather than quality in its wine. Any ambition to produce better than simple thirst quenchers is recent and limited to a select few.

Bologna, the cooks' capital, is the hub of the region and the meeting place of its two component parts. Most of the land is the flat Po Valley, following the river to the Adriatic between Ravenna and Venice. All the wine regions of interest lie in the foothills, however tentative, of the Apennines to the south, dividing the province from Tuscany.

DOC and Other Wines

Albana di Romagna DOCG. White wine. Provinces Ravenna, Forli and Bologna. Villages: 23 communes between Bologna and Rimini. Grape: Albana. Max. crop: 91 hl/ha (70 hl/ha for Passita). Min. alch: *secco* 11.5˚, *amabile* and *dolce* 12˚, *passito* 15.5˚. Annual production 333,000 cases.

The standard white of Bologna and east to the coast. The Albana is a mild, not to say neutral, grape whose dry wine tend to flatness, finishing bitter to satisfy local taste. It gains more character when made *amabile* and/or *spumante* but these may only be classed as DOC, not DOCG.

Barbarossa di Bertinoro A vine not found elsewhere, cultivated on a small scale at Bertinoro, the centre of the Romagna vineyards, for a good full-flavoured red with ageing potential.

Barbera The ubiquitous red grape is popular in the area of Piacenza and in the Colli Bolognesi, where it is given DOC dignity.

Bianco di Scandiano DOC. White wine. Province: Emilia-Romagna. Villages: commune of Scandiano plus five others southwest of Reggio. Grapes: Sauvignon (locally *Spergola* or *Spergolina*) up to 85%, Malvasia di Candia and Trebbiano Romagnolo up to 15%. Max. crop: 84.5hl/ha. Min. alch: *frizzante* 10.5˚, *spumante* 11˚. Annual production: 100,000 cases.

A white alternative to Lambrusco (q.v.) made either semi-dry or distinctly sweet, sometimes fizzy and sometimes fully frothy.

Bosco Eliceo DOC. Red and white wine. Provinces: Ferrara and Ravenna. Villages: six communes in the Bosco della Mésola and the Bertuzzi and Commacchio Lagoons. Grapes: Trebbiano Romagnolo; Sauvignon/Malvasia di Candia up to 30%. Fortana, Merlot and Sauvignon allow other varieties up to 15%. Max. crop: 105 hl/ha. Min. alch: 10.5˚ (Sauv. 11˚). Annual production: 78,000 cases.

The Fortana is a rustic red from this DOC from reclaimed marshland.

Cagnina di Romagna DOC. Red wine. Province: Forli and Ravenna. Villages: 16 communes in Forli, five in Ravenna. Grapes: Cagnina, other varieties up to 15%. Max. crop: 85.5 hl/ha. Min. alch. 11˚. Annual production: 28,000 cases.

A sweet red wine which was classified as DOC in 1989. It is enjoyed locally as an accompaniment to roast chestnuts.

Fizzy red Lambrusco leads, not just in Emilia but in the whole of Italy, for volume production of a distinct type of wine. It is an ingenious and profitable way of achieving notoriety in deep valley soils where more conventional quality is unlikely.

Romagna produces nothing so exceptional. Its best-known wine is the white Albana which has yet to distinguish itself. It is in the Colli Bolognesi and Piacentini, the hill areas nearest to Bologna and Piacenza, that progress is being made.

Chardonnay Strictly an outlaw in the region, but was planted with striking success by the late Enrico Vallania at Terre Rosse near Bologna.

Colli Bolognesi DOC: Red and white wine. Provinces: Bologna and Modena. Villages: 10 communes southwest of Bologna. Grapes: (white) Albana 60–80%, Trebbiano Romagnolo at least 20%, other whites up to 20%. For named varieties: Barbera, Merlot, Riesling Italico, Pinot Bianco, Cabernet Sauvignon, Sauvignon 85%, with 15% neutral grapes allowed. Max crop: 70–91 hl/ha. Min alch: 11.5˚ for Barbera, Merlot; 12˚ for Sauvignon, Cabernet Sauvignon, Pinot Blanc, Riesling Italico; 11˚ for Bianco. Barbera and Cabernet Sauvignon must be 3 years old, 1 in wood, for *riserva*. Annual production 280,000 cases.

An umbrella DOC for the everyday wines of Bologna. More remarkable wines are being made in the same vineyards by growers experimenting with better grapes, including Sauvignon, Cabernet Sauvignon and Chardonnay. Growing conditions are excellent.

Colli di Parma DOC. Red and white wine. Province: Parma. Villages: 14 communes in the Apennine foothills south and west of Parma. Grapes: (red) Barbera 60–75% with Bonarda or Croatina 25–40%, other dark varieties up to 15%; (Malvasia) Malvasia di Candia 85–100%, Moscato Bianco up to 15%; Sauvignon 100%. Max. crop: red 70 hl/ha, Malvasia 71.5 hl/ha, Sauvignon 49 hl/ha. Min. alch: red 11˚, Malvasia 10.5˚, Sauvignon 11.5˚. Annual production: 78,000 cases.

In this DOC, the red resembles Otrepò Pavese Rosso, the Malvasia may be either dry or *amabile*, usually *frizzante*; the Sauvignon usually still.

Colli Piacentini DOC. Red and white wine. Province: Piacenza. Villages: There are four sub-zones: Gutturnio (in three sectors and nine communes in the Tidone, Nure, Chero and Arda valleys); Monterosso Val d'Arda (in six communes in the Arda Valley); Trebbianino Val Trebbia (in five communes along the Trebbia); Val Nure (in three communes in the Nure Valley. Grapes: (white) 30–50% Malvasia di Candia, 20–35% Ortugo, 20–35% Trebbiano Romagnolo; Barbera, Bonarda, Malvasia, Ortugo, Pinot Grigio, Pinot Nero, Sauvignon. Max. crop: 63 to 84 hl/ha. Min. alch: white 11˚, Malvasia, Ortugo 10.5˚, Pinot Grigio, Pinot Nero, Sauvignon, Bonarda 11.5˚. Annual production: 2m. cases.

Three former DOCs – Gutturnio dei Colli Piacentini, Monterosso Val d'Arda and Trebbianino Val Trebbia with the newly approved Val Nure – plus seven others (mainly varietal wines) are included in this large zone.

Gutturnio dei Colli Piacentini *See under* Colli Piacentini.

Lambrusco Lambrusco from Emilia was the smash hit of the Italian wine industry in the 1970s, selling like Coca-Cola (in more senses than one) in the United States. It is simply a sweet, semi-sweet or occasionally dry fizzy red (or pink or occasionally white) wine such as any winemaker could produce who had the foresight to see the demand. The common qualities are scarcely drinkable by a discerning wine drinker, but this misses the point. The market is elsewhere. Some see it as the training ground for future connoisseurs. Such discerning palates will choose one from a named region, of which the best is Sorbara.

Lambrusco accounts for approximately five percent of all Italian wine: three million hectolitres in all. Roughly a tenth is of DOC quality and only a fraction of this is really worth drinking. A select few producers show true genius with this wine.

Lambrusco Grasparossa di Castelvetro DOC. Red wine. Province: Modena. Villages: 14 communes south of Modena. Grapes: Lambrusco Grasparossa 85%, other Lambrusco and Uva d'Oro 15% . Max. crop: 98 hl/ha. Min. alch: 10.5°. Annual production: 560,000 cases.

Dark-coloured, tannic, rather strong and always slightly sweet; comes from the hills southwest of Modena.

Lambrusco Reggiano DOC. Red and *rosato*. Province: Reggio Emilia. Area: 20 communes in the province. Grapes: Lambrusco Marani, Salamino, Montericco and Maestri either singly or together. 20% Ancellotta also allowed. Max. crop: 98 hl/ha. Min. alch: 10.5°. Annual production: 2m. cases.

Commonest, lightest and usually fizziest Lambrusco.

Lambrusco Salamino di Santa Croce DOC. Red wine. Province: Modena. Villages: Carpi and 10 other communes north of Modena. Grapes: Lambrusco Salamino 90%, other Lambrusco and Uva d'Oro 10%. Max. crop: 105 hl/ha. Min. alch: 11°. Annual production: 670,000 cases.

Salamino di S. Croce is a local sub-variety of the Lambrusco grape with a bunch said to resemble a little salami. Dark, soft, fruity and at their best when dry.

Lambrusco di Sorbara DOC. Red and *rosato*. Province: Modena. Villages: 10 communes north of Modena, including Sorbara. Grapes: Lambrusco di Sorbara 60%, Lambrusco Salamino max. 40%. Max. crop: 98 hl/ha. Min. alch: 11°. Annual production: 890,000 cases.

Good Lambrusco di Sorbara is a delight: juicy pink wine, racy, tingling and extraordinarily drinkable – a childish wine perhaps, but marvellously thirst-quenching with rich food. The pink froth is a pleasure in itself. Alas, offputting chemical flavours are all too common, even in this premium Lambrusco; do not store bottles of any of them.

Merlot Widely grown in Emilia-Romagna mostly for blending. In the Colli Bolognesi it is DOC.

Monterosso Val d'Arda *See under* Colli Piacentini.

Montuni del Reno DOC. White wine. Province: Bologna. Villages: five communes in Modena. Grapes: Montuni; other non-aromatic grapes up to 15%. Max. crop: 126 hl/ha. Min. alch: 10.5°.

Can be dry or semi-sweet and is usually *frizzante*.

Pagadebit di Romagna DOC. White wine. Provinces: Forli and Ravenna. Villages: 24 communes in Forli, five in Ravenna. Grapes: Pagadebit; other whites up to 15%. Max. crop: 98 hl/ha. Min. alch. 10.5° (11.5° for Bertinoro). Annual production: 33,000 cases.

A rare white vine enjoying revival and modernization around Bertinoro in Romagna. Gentle dry wine and an *amabile*. The commune of Bertinoro rates as a special sub-denomination.

Picòl Ross An esoteric, dry, *metodo tradizionale* Lambrusco of high quality from one grower, Moro of Sant'Ilario d'Enza near Reggio.

Pinot Bianco Widely grown in Emilia-Romagna; DOC in Colli Bolognesi.

Pinot Grigio Increasingly being grown, Pinot Grigio is DOC in Colli Piacentini. *See* Terre Rosse (Producers).

Sangiovese di Romagna DOC. Red wine. Provinces: Ravenna, Bologna, Forli. Villages: 42 communes in all three provinces. Grape: Sangiovese di Romagna. Max. crop: 71.5 hl/ha. Min. alch: 11.5°. Aged 2 years for *riserva*, 6 months for *superiore*. *Superiore* only from certain specified zones. Annual production 1.1m. cases.

Romagna has its own strain of the red Sangiovese, distinct from the Tuscan one which is the basis of Chianti. It makes pleasant light to medium-weight red, often with a slightly bitter aftertaste, produced in enormous quantities and enjoyed young as the Sunday wine of the region.

Sauvignon An up-and-coming white grape in this part of Italy, possibly the best of the DOC Colli Bolognesi and the major partner in the 1977 DOC Bianco di Scandiano.

Trebbianino Val Trebbia *See under* Colli Piacentini.

Trebbiano di Romagna DOC. White wine. Provinces: Bologna, Forli, Ravenna. Villages: 54 communes in all 3 provinces. Grape: Trebbiano di Romagna. Max. crop: 84 hl/ha. Min. alch: 11.5° Annual production: 1.1m cases.

Taking over the area as the everyday white. Its style is clean-tasting and unobtrusive.

Leading Emilia-Romagna Producers

Castelluccio

Modigliana, 47012 Forli.

Owner/winemaker: Gian Matteo Baldi. *Vini da tavola* known as Ronco Casone, Ronco dei Ciliegi and Ronco delle Ginestre from Sangiovese and Ronco del Re from Sauvignon Blanc are fashioned by young Baldi into some of Romagna's finest bottlings although there are doubts over the estate's future.

Cavicchioli

San Prospero, 41030 Modena.

Owners: Sandro Cavicchioli. DOC: Lambrusco di Sorbara, Lambrusco Grasparossa di Castelvetro, Lambrusco Salamino di Santa Croce. Other: Lambrusco Bianco. This medium-large winery is a quality leader for Lambrusco. The top Sorbara is called Vigna del Cristo.

Chiarli-1860

41100 Modena.

Founded in 1860 and still run by the Chiarli family. DOC: Lambrusco di Sorbara, Lambrusco Grasparossa di Castelvetro, Lambrusco Salamino di Santa Croce.

Corovin (Consorzio Romagnolo Vini Tipici)

47100 Forli.

A consortium of cooperatives founded in 1968. Corovin groups 12,000 growers in 23 wineries; they consign 235m. kilograms of grapes – enough for 155m. litres. DOC: Albana, Sangiovese and Trebbiano di Romagna. Other: Lambrusco and numerous *vini da tavola*.

Coltiva

41100 Modena.

Consortium owned by the cooperatives GIV & GIV (Emilia) and Cevico (Romagna): produces about 60 million bottles of Lambrusco (mainly) and DOC Romagna wines annually.

Fattoria Paradiso

Capocolle di Bertinoro, 47032 Forli.

A historic estate (founded in 1880) that has been shaped into a viticultural paradise by Mario Pezzi and his family. DOC: Albana, Sangiovese and Trebbiano di Romagna. Other: Barbarossa, Cagnina, Pagadebit. From 45 acres, Pezzi makes 13,300 cases of exemplary wine, including the unique red Barbarossa (of a vine only he grows) and white semi-sweet Pagadebit (literally 'debt payer'). There is also an *enoteca*, a museum and *tavernetta*, all open to the public.

Fattoria Zerbina

Marzeno Faenza, Ravenna.

A family winery, run by Vincenzo Geminiani and daughter Cristina with guidance from oenologist Vittorio Fiore, which has quickly become a top estate in Romagna. Their Scaccomatto is the best Albana DOCG. They also make Marzeno di Marzeno from Sangiovese with a little Cabernet, as well as a promising white called Vicchio, from Chardonnay with Trebbiano.

Giacobazzi

Nonantola, 41015 Modena.

DOC: Lambrusco di Sorbara, Lambrusco Grasparossa di Castelvetro, Lambrusco Salamino di Santa Croce. One of the largest producers, bottlers and shippers of Lambrusco but now moving more into light, fizzy wines.

Riunite

42100 Reggio Emilia.

Founded in 1950, Riunite is one of the world's largest winemaking operations, grouping 26 cooperatives, including 7 outside the province of Reggio, with 2 bottling plants. Corrado Casoli presides over the complex which includes 9,934 growers and 368 winery employees. DOC: Lambrusco Reggiano, Lambrusco di Sorbara and Bianco di Scandiano.

Other: White and *rosato vino da tavola* and *spumante* and a sulphur-free *vino da tavola* for the US market.

Spalletti-Tenuta di Savignano

Savignano sul Rubicone, 47039 Forli.

Conte G. Battista Spalletti's heirs own this winery housed in the 16th-century Castello di Ribano. Director-winemaker: Luigi Bonfiglioli. DOC: Sangiovese di Romagna. Rocca di Ribano *riserva* is often considered the best Sangiovese di Romagna.

La Stoppa

Anarano di Rivergaro, 29029 Piacenza.

A leader in Colli Piacentini owned by Raffaele Pantaleoni. There is La Stoppa, an impressive red *vino da tavola* and the *tradizionale* Pantaleoni Brut.

Terre Rosse (Vallania)

Zola Predosa, 40069 Bologna.

Founded in 1965 by the late Enrico Vallania, a physician, whose genius and tenacity charted new directions in Italian viticulture. DOC: Colli Bolognese. Other: Cabernet Sauvignon, Chardonnay, Malvasia, Pinot Grigio.

The Vallania family are still coming up with new creations including an impressive white from Viognier.

OTHER PRODUCERS

Tenuta Amalia Villa Verrucchio, 47040 Forli. Good Sangiovese Superiore.

Conte Otto Barattieri Vigolzone, 29010 Piacenza. Good Colli Piacentini DOC and *vino da tavola*.

Francesco Bellei Bomporto, 41030 Modena. Highly regarded Lambrusco di Sorbara DOC and Pinot-Chardonnay *tradizionale*.

Tenuta Bissera Bruno Negroni makes good Colli Bolognesi DOC and *spumante* wines.

Le Calbane Meldola, 47014 Forli. Good Sangiovese Superiore and Calbanesco, a red *vino da tavola* from a mystery variety found in the vineyards of this small estate.

Camarone Biancanigo di Castelbolognese, 48014 Ravenna. Good range of Romagna DOCs and *spumante* wines.

Cansetto dei Mandorli Predappio Alta, 47010 Forli. Good range of Romagna DOCs including Sangiovese and Cagnina.

Casali Scandiano, 42019 Reggio Emilia. Giuseppe Casali makes one of the best Lambrusco Reggianos at this estate. Also bottle-fermented sparkling wines.

Casetta dei Frati Modigliana, 47015 Forli. Good Sangiovese and the unique Rosso della Trafila from an unknown variety found in 25 acres of wines.

Cesari Castel San Pietro, 40024 Bologna. DOC: Albana, Sangiovese and Trebbiano di Romagna. The Sangiovese *riserva* is delicious, the Rèfolo *frizzante* is fun.

Colombini Castelvetro, 41014 Modena. Medium-large house respected for Lambrusco.

Comune di Faenza Faenza, 48018 Ravenna. DOC: Albana, Sangiovese and Trebbiano di Romagna.

Stephano Ferrucci Castelbolognese, 48014 Ravenna. Founded: 1931. Owner: Francesco Ferrucci. DOC: Albana, Sangiovese and Trebbiano di Romagna. A quality leader.

Fini Solara, Bomporto 41030 Modena. DOC: Lambrusco di Sorbara. The well-known family of restaurateurs have their own Lambrusco.

Cantina Sociale di Forli 47100 Forli. Good Sangiovese Superiore DOC.

Carla Foschi Cesena, 47023 Forli. Fine Sangiovese Superiore.

Fugazza Ziano Piacentino, 29010 Piacenza. Giovanna and Maria Fugazza also own Castello di Luzzano in Oltrepò Pavese, Lombardy. They make Gutturnio from vineyards in Colli Piacentini.

Guarini Matteucci San Tomé, 47100 Forli. Owner: Domenico Guarini Matteucci. DOC: Albana, Sangiovese and Trebbiano di Romagna.

Oreste Lini & Figli Correggio, 42015 Reggio Emilia. DOC: Lambrusco Reggiano.

Malaspina Bobbio, 29022 Piacenza. Owners: the Malaspina family. DOC: Trebbianino Val Trebbia. Other: Cabernet, Merlot.

Contessa Matilde 41100 Modena. An established Lambrusco house which is now part of the Premiovini group.

Giancarlo Molinelli Ziano, 29010 Piacenza. DOC: Gutturnio dei Colli Piacentini. Other: Barbera, Bonarda, Malvasia, Molinelli, Müller-Thurgau.

Tenuta del Monsignore San Giovanni in Marignano, 47048 Forli. Owner: Maria Sarti Bacchini. DOC: Sangiovese and Trebbiano di Romagna.

Moro Calerno di Sant'Illaio d'Enza, 42049 Reggio Emilia. Owner/winemaker: Rinaldini. DOC: Lambrusco Reggiano. Other: Picòl Ross, Sauvignon, Morone.

Mossi Ziano, 29010 Piacenza. Owner: Luigi Mossi. DOC: Gutturnio dei Colli Piacentini. Other: Müller-Thurgau.

Bruno Negroni (Tenuta Bissera) Monte San Pietro, 40050 Bologna. DOC: Colli Bolognesi. Other: Bruno Negroni Brut *tradizionale*.

Pasolini Dall'Onda Montericco di Imola, 44026 Bologna. Winemakers since the 16th century, the Pasolini Dall' Onda family owns properties in Romagna and Tuscany. DOC: Albana, Sangiovese and Trebbiano di Romagna, Chianti.

Al Pazz Monteveglio, 40050 Bologna. DOC: Colli Bolognese. Other: Rosso Montebudello.

Villa I Raggi Predappio Alta, 47010 Forli. Sangiovese Superiore.

Fratelli Rizzi Castell'Arquato, 29014 Piacenza. Good Monterosso Val d'Arda.

Cantine Romagnoli Villo di Vigolzone, 29010 Piacenza. A complete range of Colli Piacentini DOCs, plus *spumante*.

Cantina Sociale Ronco Ronco, 47010 Forli. Range of Romagna DOCs including single vineyard bottlings.

Samori Bertinoro, 47032 Forli. Promising new house producing Romagna DOCs.

San Patrignano Ospedaletto di Coriano, 47040 Forli. Good Sangiovese Superiore and Trebbiano as well as *vino da tavola* and *spumante*, made by young people at a drug rehabilitation centre.

La Tosa Vigolzone, 29010 Piacenza. An emerging estate making good Colli Piacentini wines.

Tre Monti Imola, 40026 Bologna. The Tarsallo label is used for good Albana.

Venturini & Baldini Roncolo di Quattro Castella, Modena. Fine, full-bodied Lambrusco Regiano and Cuvée di Pinot *tradizionale*.

Zerioli Ziano Piacentino, 29010 Piacenza. The Zerioli family make a complete range of Colli Piacentini DOCs plus *vini da tavola* and the *tradizionale* Zerioli Brut.

TUSCANY

To find a national identity in such a federation of disparities as Italy is not as difficult as it sounds. The answer is Tuscany. For foreigners at least, the old Tuscan countryside of villas and cypresses, woods and valleys where vine and olive mingle is Italy in a nutshell.

And so is its wine. Nine out of ten people asked to name one Italian wine would say 'Chianti'. They would have many different ideas (if they had any at all) of what it tastes like – for if ever any wine came in all styles and qualities from the sublime to the gorblimey it is Chianti – and this despite being the earliest of all regions, possibly in all Europe, to start trying to define and defend its wine. Certainly in modern times the Consorzio of its producers paved Italy's way to its DOC system.

Chianti started in the Middle Ages as a small region of constant wars and alarms between Florence and Siena. It is now the biggest and most complex DOCG in Italy. There is a real unity and identity, despite its varied soils, traditions and microclimates, because they all grow the same basic red grape, or versions of it. The Sangiovese is what holds Chianti together. On the other hand, Chianti is a blended wine, and individual inclinations can show up strongly in the balance of the blend, the type of fermentation, the use or neglect of the 'governo', the method and time of ageing.

Chianti has many departments and sub-regions. It also has several neighbours who claim superiority for their not-dissimilar wine: most notably Brunello di Montalcino and Vino Nobile di Montepulciano. Above all it is the firing range for the army of ambitious producers who believe that a dose of Cabernet, some new oak barrels and a designer bottle and label add up to The Great New Italian wine. Their Field Marshal, Piero Antinori, has successfully demonstrated that it can.

White wine is a relative stranger here. There is no white Chianti. But several small traditional supply points have been encouraged by the world's swing to white and others have been instigated recently. Of the former, Vernaccia di San Gimignano, Montecarlo and Elba are the most important; as are various excellent non-DOC brands.

DOC and Other Wines

Bianco dell'Empolese DOC. White wine. Province: Florence. Villages: communes of Empoli, Cerreto Guido, Fucecchio, Vinci, Capraia e Limite, and Montelupo Fiorentina. Grapes: Trebbiano Toscano min. 80%, other whites up to 20%, Malvasia del Chianti up to 8%. Max. crop: 84 hl/ha. Min. alch: 10.5°. Annual production: 89,000 cases.

Recent DOC, not well-known outside the hills of Empoli.

Bianco Pisano di San Torpé DOC. White wine. Provinces: Livorno and Pisa. Villages: 17 in Pisa and Collesalvetti. Grapes: Trebbiano Toscano 75%, other whites up to 25%. Max. crop: 84 hl/ha. Min. alch: 11°. Vin Santo aged 4 years in *caratelli*. Annual production: 122,000 cases.

DOC named after a (very) early martyr – who was beheaded in AD 68 at Pisa. A pale dry wine with some body and a touch of bitterness.

Bianco di Pitigliano DOC. White wine. Province: Grosseto. Villages: Pitigliano, Sorano, part of Scansano and Manciano. Grapes: Trebbiano Toscano 65–70%, Greco (Grechetto), Malvasia Bianca Toscana and Verdello 30–35% together but no more than 15% each. Max. crop: 87.5 hl/ha. Min. alch: 11.5°. Annual production: 222,000 cases.

Pitigliano is in the extreme south of Tuscany near Lake Bolsena, the home of Est! Est!! Est!!! (*see* Latium). Its soft, dry, slightly bitter white has no particular distinction.

Bianco della Valdinievole DOC. White wine. Province: Pistoia. Villages: communes of Buggiano, Montecatani Terme and Uzzano. Grapes: Trebbiano Toscano min. 70%, Malvasia del Chianti, Canaiolo Bianco, Vermentino max. 25%, other whites up to 5%. Max. crop: 75 hl/ha. Min. alch: 11°. 3 years is required for Vin Santo. Annual production: 13,000 cases.

A small production of plain dry, sometimes slightly fizzy, white from west of Florence. Production of Vin Santo is smaller still.

Bianco Vergine Valdichiana DOC. White wine. Provinces: Arezzo and Siena. Villages: 6 communes in Arezzo and 4 in Siena. Grapes: Trebbiano Toscano 70–85%, Malvasia del Chianti 10–20%, others 5–10%. Max. crop: 91 hl/ha. Min. alch: 11°. Annual production: 222,000 cases.

A satisfactory though pretty mild mid-dry white from eastern Tuscany often used as an apéritif in Chianti. A slightly bitter finish gives it some character. At least one producer (Avignonesi) makes it throughly crisp and tasty with additional Grechetto grapes.

Bolgheri DOC. Red, white and *rosato* wine. Province: Livorno. Villages: part of Castagneto, Carducci. Grapes: Bolgheri Bianco: Trebbiano Toscano 10–70%, Vermentino 10–70%, Sauvignon 10–70%, others up to 30%; Bolgheri Rosso: Cabernet Sauvignon 10–80%, Merlot up to 70%, Sangiovese up to 70%, others up to 30 %; Bolgheri Sassicaia: Cabernet Sauvignon 80%, others up to 20%. Max. crop: Bianco 65 hl/ha, Rosato and Rosso 63 hl/ha, Sassicaia 42 hl/ha. Min alch: 10.5°. Annual production: 67,000 cases.

Small region on the coast south of Livorno. Until 1994 DOC only for white and *rosato*, now also covers one of the most famous reds of Italy, Sassicaia – which was *vino da tavola*. Quality is improving rapidly, with exciting reds from both Lodovico and Piero Antinori. Angelo Gaja has also bought land in the region.

Brunello di Montalcino DOCG. Red wine. Province: Siena. Village: Montalcino. Grape: Brunello di Montalcino. Max. crop: 52 to 56 hl/ha. Min. alch: 12.5°. Aged for at least 4 years (3 in wood); 5 years for *riserva*. Annual production: 560,000 cases.

A big dry red produced for many years by the Biondi-Santi family on 'the Pétrus principle' – that nothing is too much trouble. But sold more in the spirit of Romanée-Conti – no price is too high. Made DOCG in 1980, the Brunello is a strain of Sangiovese which can be disciplined in this soil to give dark, deeply concentrated wines. Long (3-5 years) barrel-ageing and – the more vital – long bottle-age are used to coax a remarkable bouquet into its rich, brawny depths. Now it is made by about 150 growers, with inevitably varying standards.

Current leaders are Argiano, Campogiovanni, Caparzo, Casanova di Neri, Case Basse, Castelgiocondo, Cerbaiola-Salvioni, Cerbaiona-Molinari, Ciacci Piccolomini, Col d'Orcia, Costanti, Eredi Fuligni, Lisini, Pieve di Santa Restituta, Poggio Antico, Poggione, Siro Pacenti, Talenti.

Candia dei Colli Apuani DOC. White wine. Province: Massa-Carrara. Villages: communes of Carrara, Massa and Montignoso. Grapes: Vermentino Bianco 70–80%, Albarola 10–20%. Max. crop: 56 hl/ha. Min. alch: 11.5° Annual production: 8,900 cases.

A DOC whose white wine is rarely seen outside the marble-quarry coast.

Carmignano DOCG. Red wine. Province: Florence. Villages: Carmignano, Poggio a Caiano (10 miles northwest of Firenze). Grapes: Sangiovese 45–70%, Canaiolo Nero 10–20%, Cabernets Franc and Sauvignon 6–15%, Trebbiano Toscano, Canaiolo Bianco and Malvasia del Chianti up to 10%, other varieties up to 5%. Max. crop: 56 hl/ha. Min. alch: 12.5°. Aged 20 months for Carmignano, 3 years (2 in wood) for Carmignano Riserva. Annual production (DOC and DOCG): 33,000 cases.

Best described as Chianti with a just-tastable dollop of Cabernet, justified to the authorities by the fact that the Bonacossi family introduced it from Bordeaux generations ago. Carmignano is consistently well made and justifiably self-confident. Posterity may well thank it for the inspiration to aim all quality Chianti in this direction.

A younger, easier-drinking version of Carmignano is Barco Reale (DOC) – made from the same grapes, a maximum crop of 70 hl/ha and minimum alchohol of 11%. There are also a Carmignano Rosato DOC and a Carmignano Vin Santo DOC; the latter can be superb.

Chianti DOCG. Red wine. Provinces: Siena, Florence, Arezzo, Pistoia, Pisa. Villages: 103 communes: 19 in Arezzo, 34 in Florence, 16 in Pisa, 8 in Pistoia, 26 in Siena. Grapes: Sangiovese 75–90%, Canaiolo Nero 5–10%, Trebbiano Toscano, Malvasia del Chianti 5–10%. Max. crop: 75 hl/ha Chianti. Min. alch: 11.5° for Chianti, 12° for Chianti Rufina and Chianti Colli Fiorentini and superiore. 12.5° for *riserva*. Aged 6 months, 3 years for *riserva*. Annual production: 8.3m. cases.

There are two basic styles of Chianti: that made as fruity

and fresh as possible for local drinking in its youth (still often bottled in *fiaschi*, whether covered with straw or plastic) and drier, more tannic and serious wine aged in barrels or tanks and intended for bottle-ageing; therefore bottled in Bordeaux bottles which can be stacked. The traditional grape mixture is the same for both – basically Sangiovese but with variable additions of dark Canaiolo. White Trebbiano and Malvasia are added for quicker-drinking Chiantis. The *governo* is a local tradition of adding very sweet dried grape must (usually Colorino) to the wine after its fermentation to make it referment, boost its strength, smooth its astringency and promote an agreeable fizz which can make young *fiasco* Chianti delicious. Few producers now use the *governo* for wine that is to be aged before bottling.

Fine old Chianti Riserva has marked affinities with claret, particularly in its light texture and a definite gentle astringency which makes it feel very much alive in your mouth. Its smell and flavour are its own – sometimes reminding me faintly of mulled wine with orange and spices, faintly of chestnuts, faintly of rubber. I have also found a minty 'lift' in its flavour like young burgundy. Its mature colour is a distinct, even glowing garnet.

The future of Chianti is under constructive debate. Few serious producers now use any white grapes in their wine. Many have experimented with a little seasoning of Cabernet, and with new, rather than often reused, oak barrels. But most seem agreed that the ultimate Chianti will be made when the ultimate strain of Sangiovese has been identified (as it has in Montalcino), propagated and its use mastered. Chianti is betting its future on the qualities of its ancestral grape variety.

Chianti Classico DOCG. Red wine. Provinces: Florence and Siena. Villages: Radda, Gaiole, Greve, San Casciano, Castelnuovo Berardenga. Grapes: Sangiovese 75–100%, up to 10% Canaiolo Nero, up to 6% Trebbiano and Malvasia, up to 15% other red grapes. Max crop: 52.5 hl/ha. Min. alch: 12° (Riserva 12.5°). Aged 9 months, *riserva* 27 months. Annual production: 2.78m. cases.

Since 1966 separated from 'Chianti' and now an independent zone. The Classico area is the original zone between Florence and Siena. Most of its producers are members of the very active Consorzio del Marchio Storico, based near San Casciano, and seal their bottles with its badge, a black rooster. Chianti Classico's progress during the last 15 years has been some of the most impressive in all of Italy.

In 1930, when *vini tipici* were introduced, the original Chianti (which is today the Classico region) was not able to satisfy the enormous demand for Chianti wine. So the six neighbouring sub-zones that traditionally copied the Chianti style were officially granted the right to call their wines Chianti. In 1963, when the DOCs were introduced, almost half Tuscany, was consequently incorporated in a huge Chianti-zone. The original style was therefore blurred and huge differences in character and quality between the sub-regions and producers were lost. Since 1966, Chianti Classico, with independent status, has

usually been the best and most expensive wine, but very good Chiantis also come from the redefined sub-zones Rufina and Colli Fiorentini.

The six sub-zones are:

Chianti Colli Aretini The country to the east in the province of Arezzo; a good source of fresh young wines.

Chianti Colli Fiorentini The zone just north of Chianti Classico around Florence, especially east along the River Arno. Several estates here are at least on a level with the best Classicos.

Chianti Colli Pisane A detached area south of Pisa making lighter, generally less substantial wine.

Chianti Colli Senesi A fragmented and inconsistent zone including the western flank of the Classico area south from Poggibonsi, the southern fringes around Siena and the separate areas of Montepulciano and Montalcino to the south. A wide range of styles and qualities.

Chianti Montalbano The district west of Florence that includes the separate DOC of Carmignano. Also good Chiantis, though lesser known.

Chianti Rufina A small area 15 miles east of Florence. Rufina is a village on the River Sieve, a tributary of the Arno. The hills behind, where the magically named Vallombrosa is hidden, contain some of the best Chianti vineyards (*see* Frescobaldi under Producers).

Chianti Putto The name used for non-Classico Chiantis, made to drink young. Declining in importance.

Colline Lucchesi DOC. Red and white wine. Province: Lucca. Villages: Lucca, Capannori and Porcari. Grapes: (red) Sangiovese 45–60%. Canaiolo 8–15%, Ciliegiolo and Colorino 5–15%, Trebbiano Toscano 10-15%, Vermentino-Malvasia Toscana 5–10%; (white) Trebbiano. Max. crop: (red) 84 hl/ha; (white) 77 hl/ha. Min. alch: (red) 11.5°; (white) 11°. Annual production 56,000 cases.

A cousin of Chianti from nearer the coast, also made in both first-year and *riserva* styles. The white is as yet an unknown entity.

Elba DOC. White and red wine. Province: Island of Elba. Grapes: (white) Trebbiano Toscano (known as Procanico) 90%, other whites up to 10%; (red) Sangiovese at least 75%; Canaiolo, Trebbiano Toscano and Biancone 25%. Max. crop: (white) 67.5 hl/ha; (red) 63 hl/ha. Min. alch: 11° for white, 12° for red. Annual production: 61,000 cases.

The island off the south Tuscan coast, once a home for the exiled Napoleon, like a stepping stone to Corsica, has ideal dry white wines to wash down its fish and Chianti-style red wines from some highly competent producers.

Galestro An ultramodern white produced by a group of Chianti makers using cold fermentation to instil zip and fruity freshness into Trebbiano white (which often lacks these qualities). The name derives from a specific soil type. Galestro is the only Italian wine to have a ceiling on its alcoholic strength: 10.5°.

Montecarlo DOC. White and red wine. Province: Lucca. Villages: hills of Montecarlo. Grapes: (white) Trebbiano Toscano 60–70%, Sémillon, Pinot Gris, Pinot Bianco, Vermentino, Sauvignon and Roussanne 30–40%; (red) Sangiovese 50–75%, Canaiolo Nero 5–15%, Ciliegiolo,

Colorino, Malvasia Nera, Syrah 10–20%. Max. crop: 70 hl/ha. Min. alch: 11.5˚. Annual production: 89,000 cases.

A good example of the improvements possible to Tuscan wines by allowing some more aromatic grapes to elaborate the essentially neutral Trebbiano. Montecarlo's smooth, unaggressive but interesting white can develop a very pleasant bouquet with 2 or 3 years in bottle.

Montescudaio DOC. Red and white wine. Province: Pisa. Villages: Montescudaio and 6 other communes. Grapes: (red) Sangiovese at least 75%, Trebbiano Toscano and Malvasia 15–25%, other reds up to 10%. (white) Trebbiano Toscano 70–85%, Malvasia del Chianti and Vermentino 15–30%, other whites up to 10%. Max. crop: 84 hl/ha. Min. alch: 11.5˚ (17˚ for Vin Santo). Annual production: 67,000 cases.

Light red and white from near the coast west of Siena. The most distinguished is the strong white Vin Santo. *Vino da tavola* Cabernet and Merlot have had international success in the last few years.

Morellino di Scansano DOC. Red wine. Province: Grosseto. Villages: Scansano and 6 other communes in the very south of Tuscany. Grapes: Sangiovese plus up to 15% other red grapes. Max. crop: 84 hl/ha. Min. alch: 11.5˚ (12˚ with 2 years' ageing is *riserva*). Annual production: 156,000 cases.

DOC for an all-Sangiovese red increasingly seen in fashionable circles. The only other one is the famous Brunello di Montalcino. The intention is clearly to build up this burly wine into something notable. A couple of producers are already making extremely juicy wines and experimenting with *barriques* – not always with positive effects, however.

Moscadello di Montalcino DOC. White wine. Province: Siena. Village: Montalcino. Grapes: Moscato, plus max. 15% other white grapes. Max. crop: 65 hl/ha. Min. alch: 10.5˚. Aged 6 months from fortification for *liquoroso*. Annual production: 28,000 cases.

This sweet Moscato has been revived as a DOC due largely to Villa Banfi. There is also a still and sweeter *liquoroso* version, though rarely seen.

Parrina DOC. Red, white and *rosato*. Province: Grosseto. Village: the commune of Orbetello. Grapes: (red and *rosato*) Sangiovese 80%, Canaiolo Nero, Montepulciano, Colorino up to 20%; (white) Trebbiano 80%, Ansonica and/or Malvasia del Chianti up to 20%. Max. crop: (white) 84 hl/ha; (red and *rosato*) 77 hl/ha. Min. alch: 11.5˚ for white; 12˚ for red; 11˚ for *rosato*. Annual production: 33,300 cases.

Lively wines, both red and white, from near the Argentario peninsula in south Tuscany. Parrina Bianco caught young can be a good glass with seafood.

Pomino DOC. Red and white wine. Province: Firenze. Village: Pomino in the commune of Rufina. Grapes: (white) Pinot Bianco and/or Chardonnay (60–80%), Trebbiano max. 30%, other whites up to 15%; (red) Sangiovese 60–75%, Canaiolo and/or Cabernet Sauvignon and/or Cabernet Franc 15–25%, Merlot 10–20%; (Vin Santo) Sangiovese, Trebbiano and others. Max. crop: 73.5 hl/ha. Min. alch: Bianco 11˚, Rosso 12˚, Vin Santo 15.5˚. Red aged 1 year; 3 years (18 months in wood) for *riserva*; 3 years in *caratelli* for Vin Santo. Annual production: 50,000 cases.

The move for this DOC was led by Frescobaldis. It applies to Pomino Bianco which is based on Pinot Bianco and Chardonnay with Trebbiano. The zone was cited in 1716 by the Grand Duchy of Tuscany as one of the best wine areas.

Predicato A new category of wine from the hills of central Tuscany which does not qualify under DOC regulations but carries a certain prestige. There are four Predicato categories:

Predicato del Muschio: for white wine from Chardonnay or Pinot Bianco with up to 20% Riesling, Müller-Thurgau or Pinot Grigio.

Predicato del Selvante: for white wine from Sauvignon Blanc with up to 20% Riesling, Müller-Thurgau or Pinot Grigio.

Predicato di Biturica: for red wine from Cabernet with up to 30% Sangiovese and 10% other red grapes.

Predicato di Cardisco: for red wine from Sangiovese with up to 10% other red grapes.

Rosso di Cercatoia A handmade, barrel-aged red in the style of Chianti Riserva from Montecarlo, near Lucca, best known for its white. *See* Buonamico under Producers.

Rosso di Montalcino DOC. Red wine. Province: Siena. Village: Montalcino. Grape: Brunello di Montalcino. Max. crop: 70 hl/ha. Min. alch: 12˚. Aged for 1 year. Annual production: 22,000 cases.

A DOC made from Brunello grapes at Montalcino not qualifying as Brunello di Montalcino. Rosso can be rather average, but is often worth keeping for 3–4 years – then it is great value.

Rosso di Montepulciano DOC. Red wine. Province: Siena. Village: the commune of Montepulciano. Grapes: Sangio-vese (Prugnolo Gentile) 60–80%, Canaiolo Nero 10–20%, other varieties up to 20% though no more than 10% white. Max. crop: 70 hl/ha. Min. alch: 11˚. Aged for 6 months. Average production: 16,700 cases.

DOC which is enabling producers to make Vino Nobile better, by declassing some of it to Rosso. Always good value.

Sant'Antimo DOC. Red and white wine. Province: Siena. Village: Montalcino. Grapes: Chardonnay, Sauvignon, Pinot Grigio, Cabernet Sauvignon, Merlot, Pinot Nero. Max crop: 56 hl/ha for Cabernet, Merlot and Pinot Nero, 63 hl/ha for others. Min alch reds: 12˚, whites: 11.5˚. No figures available yet.

A new DOC (since 1996) that serves to avoid *vino da tavola*-status for the colourful quantity of innovative and experimental wines in the shadow of the big old Brunello di Montalcino estates.

Sassicaia An eccentric wine that has proved the most influential of all in the shaping of Tuscan wine-growing. The late Marchesi Incisa della Rocchetta grew pure Cabernet Sauvignon on the coast at Bolgheri, south of Livorno – outside any recognized wine zone. What started as a whim became a sensation. He aged it in *barriques* like Bordeaux. His cousin Antinori of Florence used to bottle and sell it but his son, Niccolò, has moved the bottling to Bolgheri, and sells about 16,700 cases a year. A bottle should be surreptitiously slipped into top-level Cabernet tastings. (The 1975 has beaten all Bordeaux of this vintage.) Since 1994 no longer has to be *vino da tavola*: now classified DOC Bolgheri.

Tignanello The firm of Antinori leads modern thinking about Chianti with this exceptional wine (and its Chiantis). Bordeaux-style winemaking and ageing using *barriques*. Tignanello, a Sangiovese-Cabernet,blend, is the obvious link between the eccentric Sassicaia and the traditional Chianti. It started the Tuscan revolution during the 1980s.

Val d'Arbia DOC. White wine. Province: Siena. Villages: 10 along the Arbia River between Radda in Chianti and Buonconvento. Grapes: Trebbiano Toscano 75–85%, Malvasia del Chianti 15–25%, a max. 15% other grapes also allowed (not Moscato Bianco). Max. crop: 84.5 hl/ha. Min. alch: 11˚. Annual production: 78,000 cases.

A DOC for a crisp, light, typically Tuscan white made in Chianti Classico country.

Val di Cornia DOC. Red, white and *rosato*. Provinces: Livorno and Pisa. Villages: Campiglia Marittima, San Vincenzo, Piombino and Suvereto in hills drained by the Cornia stream in southwestern Tuscany. Grapes: (for red and *rosato*) Sangiovese 70–100%, Canaiolo Nero, Ciliegiolo, Cabernet Sauvignon and/or Merlot at max. 30% but not more than 15% each; (white) Trebbiano Toscano 60–70%, Vermentino 15–30%, other white varieties up to 20%. Max. crop: 68 hl/ha for red and *rosato*, 82 hl/ha for white. Min. alch: 11.5˚ for red (12.5˚ for *riserva*, which must be aged 2 years), 10.5˚ for white, 11˚ for *rosato*. Annual production: 28,000 cases.

As in Bolgheri, Sangiovese gives only average results, some new estates are very successful with Cabernet and Merlot grapes.

Vernaccia di San Gimignano DOCG. White wine. Province: Siena. Villages: the communes of San Gimignano. Grape: Vernaccia di San Gimignano. Max. crop: 63hl/ha. Min. alch: 11˚ (11.5˚ and aged 1 year for *riserva*). Annual production: 444,000 cases.

Old-style Vernaccia was made as powerful as possible, fermented on its (golden) skins and aged in barrels for gently oxidized flavours to emerge. This was the wine Michelangelo loved. It can still be found like this, or in a modernized pale version which can be good but is hard to identify.

Vin Santo Wine of grapes dried in the loft until Christmas (to shrivel and sweeten them) is found all over Italy, but most of all at every farm in Tuscany where it is enjoying a resurgence. It can be red or white, but white is more common. Under several DOCs it is defined and regulated, but farmers make it regardless. It should be at least 3 years old, and may be sweet or dry. A few producers age it in small barrels under the roof tiles to produce a madeira-like effect. The results can be sensational.

Vino Nobile di Montepulciano DOCG. Red wine. Province: Siena. Village: the commune of Montepulciano. Grapes: Sangiovese (Prugnolo Gentile) 60–80%, Canaiolo 10–20%. Other varieties up to 20%, though no more than 10% white. Max. crop: 56 hl/ha. Min. alch: 12.5. Aged 2 years in wood; 3 years for *riserva*. Annual production: 333,000 cases.

Montepulciano would like to rival Montalcino, also in the south of the Chianti country. It is highly debatable whether it has anything as exceptional as Brunello to offer. This is essentially Chianti but professional winemakers have come to the fore and the DOCG is justified by an increasing number of excellent examples.

Leading Tuscany Producers

Castello d'Albola

Radda, 53017 Siena.

Zonin's base in Chianti Classico, a 10th-century castle with 128 acres. He also produces DOC Bianco Val d'Arbia, a *novello* called Sant'Ilario, and a new red *vino da tavola* called Acciaiolo.

Altesino

Montalcino, 53024 Siena.

Director: Claudio Basla. Winemakers: Angelo Solci and Pietro Rivella. DOC: Brunello di Montalcino, Rosso di Montalcino. Other: Bianco di Montosoli, Palazzo Altesi, Altedi Altesi (a Brunello-Cabernet Sauvignon mix), and Ambro d'Altesi (a Moscadello *passito*). Increasingly respected small producer. The *vino da tavola* Palazzo Allesi is *barrique*-aged, to produce an almost Burgundy-like suppleness and fruitness.

Fattoria di Ama

Ama in Chianti, 53010 Siena.

DOC: Chianti Classico. Other: Collino di Ama, Pinot Grigio, Sauvignon, Chardonnay. Former manager Sivano Formigli brought this estate into the front rank of Chianti Classico and winemaker Marco Pallanti maintains high quality with first-rate single-vineyard Chiantis, as well as Merlot and Pinot Noir.

Marchesi L & P Antinori

50123 Firenze.

Owner: Piero Antinori (succeeding Antinoris since 1385). DOC: Chianti Classico, Orvieto Classico. Other: Aleatico, Brut Nature *tradizionale*, Galestro, Rosé di Bolgheri, San Giocondo, Tignanello, Villa Antinori Bianco, Vin Santo. See page 327 and Barolo and Barbaresco.

Argiano

Montalcino, 53024 Siena.

The ancient estate of the Lovatelli family, now part of the stake of the Cinzano group in Brunello and reduced to 50 acres. Winemaker Maurizio Castelli makes noteworthy DOC Brunello di Montalcino and Rosso Argiano *vino da tavola*.

Avignonesi

Montepulciano, 54045 Siena.

The 16th-century Palazzo Avignonesi, over its 13th-century cellars in the heart of Montepulciano, houses the family's barrel-aged Vino Nobile. The firm is owned and run by the three Falvo brothers, whose experiments with Cabernet and

Chardonnay are showing great promise. A second estate near Cortona makes exceptional dry Bianco Vergine della Valdichiana, a good dry Malvasia *vino da tavola*, a Chardonnay called Il Marzocco and a Sauvignon Blanc called Il Vignola. A tiny amount of excellent Vin Santo is made, called Occhio del Pernice. At the recently acquired Sovana estate near Pitigliano they are making a fine sweet Aleatico.

Badia a Coltibuono

Gaiole, 53013 Siena.
DOC: Chianti Classico. Other: *bianco, rosato* and Vin Santo. The monks of this magical 11th-century abbey in the woods might have been the original growers of Chianti. The buildings, cellars and gardens (with an excellent restaurant) are perfectly preserved by the Stucchi-Prinetti family, owners since 1846. The hills are too high here for vines; the 150 acres of vineyards are at Monti, to the south, half-way to Siena. There are few more consistently first-class Chiantis, as *riserva*s back to 1958 prove.

Villa Banfi

Montalcino, 53024 Siena.
Founded in 1977 by the House of Banfi, the largest US importer of wine. DOC: Brunello di Montalcino, Moscadello di Montalcino, Rosso di Montalcino. Other: Tavernelle Cabernet Sauvignon, Fontanelle Chardonnay, San Angelo Pinot Grigio, Santa Costanza Vino Novello, Sauvignon Blanc Fumaio, and the unusual Castello Banfi from Brunello, Cabernet Sauvignon, Petite Syrah and Pinot Nero.

The firm, under the direction of Ezio Rivella and Pablo Härri, is developing vineyards and cellars on its vast Poggio all'Oro estate at Montalcino which has expanded through the purchase of the neighbouring Poggio alle Mura estate. From almost 2,000 acres, Banfi is producing growing quantities of premium red and white wines, as well as the sparkling and sweet Moscadello, plus Cabernet Sauvignon, Chardonnay and Rosso di Montalcino. In Piedmont, Banfi is producing Asti Spumante Brachetto d'Acqui, which makes a *spumante tradizionale* and Charmat Banfi Brut; also from Gavi, Principessa Gavia-Banfi. Rivella, Italy's foremost oenologist, is using Montalcino as his base for leading Italian wine into the future. *See* page 332.

Fattoria dei Barbi

Montalcino, 53024 Siena.
Owner: Francesca Colombini Cinelli. Winemaker: Luigi Casagrande. DOC: Brunello di Montalcino. Other: Bianco del Beato, Brusco dei Barbi, Moscatello, Vin Santo. The Barbi estate has an old reputation. It makes excellent Brunello, selected from good vintages.

Fattoria di Felsina

Castelnuovo Berardenga, 53019 Siena.
Under manager Giuseppe Mazzocolin and winemaker Franco Bernabei, this estate is emerging as a leader for Chianti, especially with its *riserva* Vigneto Rancia. The Sangiovese *vino da tavola* Fontalloro is first-rate, as is the barrel-fermented Chardonnay I Sistri.

Biondi Santi – Il Greppo

Montalcino, 53024 Siena.
Founded in 1840 by Clemente Santi, whose grandson, Ferruccio Biondi Santi, is credited with creating Brunello di Montalcino. DOC: Brunello di Montalcino. 4,000 cases of some of Italy's most expensive wine come from Il Greppo and its 30 acres of old vines. Sometimes described as 'Italy's first *grand cru*'.

Poderi Boscarelli

Cervognano di Montelpulciano, 53045 Siena.
Founded: 1963. Owner: Paola de Ferrari Corradi. DOC: Chianti Colli Senesi, Vino Nobile de Montepulciano. The little (22-acre) estate is considered the best in Montepulciano; its Vino Nobile has more depth, tone and muscle than its rivals. Fine *vino da tavola* Boscarelli is made with the aid of winemaker Maurizio Castelli.

Brolio Barone Ricasoli

50123 Firenze.
Owners: the estate has been in the Ricasoli family since 1141. DOC: Chianti, Chianti Classico, Orvieto. Other: Arbia, Brolio Bianco, Galestro, Rosé, Torricella, Vin Santo; Barone Ricasoli Brut *tradizionale*, Vernaccia di San Gimignano. The great grim brickbuilt stronghold is the site where the great grim Bettino Ricasoli, second Prime Minister of Italy in the 1850s, 'invented' Chianti – or at least the blend of grapes and method of production. The 620-acre Brolio estate is where the current Barone Ricasoli grows vines on some of Chianti's finest plots. Its former 'first-growth' reputation has been in eclipse as the pace becomes faster, but a new generation and chief oenologist Carlo Ferrini are working to restore it to its former position. The omens are good.

Fattoria del Buonamico

Montecarlo, 55015 Lucca.
Founded: 1954. Owner: Rina Berti Grassi. Winemaker: Vasco Grassi. DOC: Montecarlo Bianco and Rosso. Other: Superb Sangiovese blend Rosso di Cercatoia. A leading Montecarlo maker, started by the well-known Turin restaurant Al Gatto Nero.

Castello di Cacchiano

Monti, 53010 Siena.
A 12th-century estate near Gaiole, owned by Elisabetta Ricasoli Balbi Valier. DOC: Chianti Classico. A steady producer of good vintages, this is becoming one of Chianti's top estates. Also produce a fine new *vino da tavola*, called 'RF'.

Tenuta Caparzo

Montalcino, 53024 Siena.
Manager: Nuccio Turone. Winemaker: Vittorio Fiore. DOC: Brunello di Montalcino, Rosso di Montalcino. Other: Ca' del Pazzo, Le Grance Chardonnay. A Brunello of growing quality and importance; particularly fine single-vineyard Brunello La Casa.

Antinori

Charting Tuscany's Future

The Marchese Piero Antinori may well be to 21st-century Chianti what the Barone Ricasoli was to the Chianti of the 19th and 20th – the man who wrote the recipe. Antinori is persuasive with the eloquence of an aristocrat who does not have to raise his voice. He and his former winemaker Giacomo Tachis have made this ancient Florentine house – based in the Renaissance Palazzo Antinori, Piazza Antinori, Florence – the modern pacesetter, not only for exemplary Chianti but more prophetically for Tignanello, which is Sangiovese blended with Cabernet Sauvignon and aged, Bordeaux style, in new oak *barriques*. By replacing the formerly obligatory 10 percent of white grapes in Chianti with Cabernet he has set a precedent that others are now following in droves – whether or not they are permitted to call the result Chianti.

The Antinori family has almost 2,000 acres under vines in Tuscany (Santa Cristina, Peppoli, Badia a Passignano and Chianti Classico at Bolgheri) and Umbria (Castello della Sala). Extra grapes and extra wine are bought under contract. The ultramodern winery is at San Casciano (near Santa Cristina) and the Palazzo Antinori in Florence has tasting facilities. The splendid Villa Antinori, portrayed on labels of the vintage Chianti Classico (which is made by the rule book) was destroyed in World War II. Antinori and Tachis, then Renzo Cotarella who followed Tachis, are also in the forefront of white (including sparkling) winemaking in Italy, buying Pinot and Chardonnay grapes in Lombardy for their excellent sparkling Brut. Antinori has taken over Prunotto in Alba (Piedmont) and has recently bought vineyards at Barbera d'Asti (see Prunotto). The Marchese also owns an estate at Montepulciano (Siena), La Braccesca, for DOC Nobile and Rosso di Montepulciano.

Tenuta di Capezzana

Carmignano, 50042 Firenze.
Founded in the 15th century. Owned and run by Ugo Contini Bonacossi and his family. DOC: Carmignano, Chianti Montalbano. Other: Capezzana Bianco, Ghiaie della Furba, Vin Ruspo, Vin Santo. The ex-Medici villa of the Bonacossis, with its 260 acres of vines, may be the first place Cabernet Sauvignon was grown in Tuscany. The excellence of their Carmignano assured the establishment of what seemed an alien DOC in the heart of Chianti (the finest is selected and sold as Villa Capezzana and Villa di Trefiano; named after the two estates where it is made). Other innovations include the *rosato* Vin Ruspo and red Barco Reale, and a Cabernet-Merlot blend called Ghiaie della Furba. A still Chardonnay has been introduced, along with a blended *tradizionale* called Villa di Capezzana Brut.

Case Basse

Montalcino, 53024 Siena.
Owned by Milanese stockbroker Gianfranco Soldera, this 15-acre estate makes exceptional Brunello that often comes top in tastings. A *vino da tavola*, Intistieti, is also notable.

Castelgiocondo

Montalcino, 53024 Siena.
The estate with the largest tract of Brunello vines (395 acres of a total 543) is owned by the Frescobaldi family. DOC: Brunello di Montalcino, Rosso di Montalcino. Production, which began with the 1975 vintage, includes various *vini da tavola*, such as the oaky Sauvignon Blanc Vergena.

Castelgreve

Mercatale Val di Pesa, 50024 Firenze.
The Castelli del Grevepesa cooperative is the largest Chianti Classico producer: 335,000 cases from growers with more than 1,600 acres. DOC: Chianti Classico. Other: Coltifredi, Valgreve Bianco, Vin Santo. Some of the Chianti Classico is bottled under the Castelgreve label, the rest as Lamole, Monte Firidolfi, Panzano, Sant'Angelo Vico L'Abate, and Selezione Vigna Elisa.

Castellare

Castellina in Chianti, 53011 Siena.

Owners: Paolo and Fioretta Panerai. Winemaker Maurizio Castelli. DOC: Chianti Classico. Other: Castellare Bianco, I Sodi di San Niccolò in Santo, Canonico Chardonnay, Spartito Sauvignon Blanc. A fine Chianti in the *barrique*-aged I Sodi di San Niccolò. Maurizio Castelli has built a sterling reputation for this small estate. The *vini da tavola* are particularly successful, including a new pure Cabernet called Coniale.

Castell'in Villa

Castelnuovo Berardenga, 53053 Siena.

Founded in 1968 by Riccardo and Coralia Pignatelli della Leonessa (the winemaker). Excellent Chianti Classico, Bianco Val d'Arbia and good Vin Santo. Also an impressive Sangiovese *vino da tavola* called Balastrada.

Luigi Cecchi & Figli & Villa Cerna

Castellina in Chianti, 53011 Siena.

Owner: the merchant house of Luigi Cecchi & Figli. Founded: 1893. DOC: Chianti, Chianti Classico. Other: Bianco della Lega, Galestro, Sarmento, Spargolo. Annual production: 550,000 cases.

Agricoltori del Chianti Geografico

Gaiole in Chianti, 53013 Siena.

Cooperative. Winemaker: Vittorio Fiore. DOC: Chianti Classico. About 220,000 cases are selected and bottled with the respected Contessa di Radda and *riserva* Tenuta Montegiachi labels. Other DOC wines include Vernaccia di San Gimignano and Bianco Val d'Arbia; *vini da tavola* include Galestro and Sarmento.

Col d'Orcia

Montalcino, 53024 Siena.

A considerable estate bought by Cinzano in 1973 and managed by Edoardo Virano. DOC: Brunello di Montalcino, Chianti Colli Senesi, Moscadello di Montalcino. Other: Rosso Col d'Orcia, Novembrino *novello*, Vin Santo. One of the largest and best Brunello producers, progressing with Maurizio Castelli as winemaker.

Conti Costanti

Montalcino, 53024 Siena.

Owner: Andrea Costanti. Winemaker: Vittorio Fiore. DOC: Brunello di Montalcino, Rosso di Montalcino. A 17-acre property, whose 1,600 cases include some of the grandest and longest-lived Brunello.

Fattoria di Cusona

San Gimignano, 53037 Siena.

Owners: Girolamo Strozzi and Robert Guicciardini. DOC: Chianti, Vernaccia di San Gimignano. Other: Vin Santo, *spumante*, Sangiovese Sòdole. Leading producer of Vernaccia, dating back to the 16th century, which is now being revitalized with the aid of the winemaking skills of oenologist Vittorio Fiore.

Ricardo Falchini-Il Casale

San Gimignano, 53037 Siena.

Founded: 1965. Falchini makes some DOC Chianti, and is a principal producer of admired Vernaccia. He also makes good Vin Santo, a *tradizionale* called Falchini Brut, and a fine Sangiovese-Cabernet blend called Paretato. He has recently expanded the property to 79 acres and is making notable Cabernet and Chardonnay *vino da tavola*, including an outstanding pure Cabernet Sauvignon called Campora.

Castello di Fonterutoli

Castellina in Chianti, 53010 Siena.

Owners: the Mazzei family since 1435. DOC: Chianti Classico. Other: Bianco della Lega, red Concerto. Lapo Mazzei is president of the Classico Consortium, and a modest but wholly convincing champion of true Chianti. His sons Filippo and Francesco, with oenologist Carlo Ferrini, are excelling with the *riserva* Ser Lapo and the *vino da tavola* Concerto, a Cabernet-Sangiovese blend.

Fontodi

Panzano, 50020 Firenze.

Owners/winemakers: Domizano and Dino Manetti. DOC: Chianti Classico. Other: Flaccaniello della Pieve. Fine Chianti and outstanding *barrique*-aged Flaccaniello (which is pure Sangiovese) make this estate a quality leader in Tuscany.

Marchesi de' Frescobaldi

50125 Firenze.

Owners: the Frescobaldis since 1300, now three brothers: Vittorio (president), Ferdinando (manager for Italy), Leonardo (export manager). Winemaker: Luciano Boarino. DOC: Chianti Rufina, Pomino. Other: Frescobaldi Brut *tradizionale*, Galestro, Nuovo Fiore, Villa di Corte Rosé, Vin Santo. Like the Antinoris, an ancient noble house leading the way for Tuscany with wines of outstanding quality, reliability, value and originality. All Frescobaldi wines come from their eight estates east of Florence in Rufina, totalling 1,300 acres. Castello di Nipozzano is their most famous red (a superior selection is called Montesodi). Other estates are Pomino and Poggio a Remole. Pomino Bianco is an excellent white seasoned with Chardonnay. Frescobaldi also manages Castelgiocondo (q.v.) at Montalcino.

Grattamacco

Castagneto Carducci, 57022 Livorno.

Owner: Pier Mario Meletti Cavallari. DOC: Bolgheri. A small estate producing artisan wines, first making its name with Grattamacco Bianco from Trebbiano and Malvasia. The recent Grattamacco Rosso, made from Sangiovese and Merlot with Cabernet Sauvignon, is highly regarded in Italy and can hold its own with Sassicaia.

Isole e Olena

Barberino Val d'Elsa, 50021 Firenze.

Owned by the de Marchi family since 1954. DOC: Chianti Classico. On this increasingly admired 90-acre estate winemaker Paolo de Marchi makes a fine Sangiovese *vino da tavola* called Cepparello, excellent Vin Santo, Chardonnay and a recent Cabernet Sauvignon. 1989 was the first vintage of a unique Syrah.

Melini

Gaggiano di Poggibonsi, 53036 Siena.
Founded: 1705. Now part of the Gruppo Italiano Vini complex, and managed by Nunzio Capurso. In the 1860s, Laborel Melini devised the strengthened Chianti flask which enabled shipping the wine, thus Chianti becoming one of the best-known names abroad. DOC: Chianti, Chianti Classico, Orvieto, Vernaccia di San Gimignano, Vino Nobile di Montepulciano. Other: Lacrima d'Arno Bianco and Rosato, Spumante Brut, Vin Santo, red Coltri and Chardonnay Granio. Melini owns about 310 acres of vineyards.

Monsanto

Barberino Val d'Elsa, 50021 Firenze.
Founded: 1962. Owner: Fabrizio Bianchi. Distinguished DOC Chianti includes Il Poggio *riserva* and Sangioveto Grosso. As well as good Vin Santo the estate produces a Sangiovese-Cabernet *vino da tavola* called Tinscvil, and a pure Cabernet called Nemo.

Monte Vertine

Radda, 53017 Siena.
Owned and run by Sergio Manetti; with consultant Giulio Gambelli. A fastidiously tended little vineyard producing Chianti-like Sodaccio (no longer under the DOC) – and Le Pergole Torte, an oak-aged all-Sangiovese red wine of unusual quality, and also an interesting white wine and a first-rate Vin Santo.

Ornellaia

Bolgheri, 57020 Livorno.
Forward-looking estate developed by Lodovico Antinori, with cellars designed by California's André Tchelistcheff, and advisers including viticulturalist Mario Fregoni, Antinori, winemaker Giacomo Tachis and French oenologist Jacques Puisais. The resident winemaker is Federico Staderini, whose white Poggio alle Gazze (Sauvignon Blanc with Sémillon), first issued in 1988, is highly praised. The red Ornellaia *vino da tavola* (Cabernet Sauvignon, Merlot and Cabernet Franc) is set to rival (though not imitate) Sassicaia.

Tenuta Il Poggione

Montalcino, 53024 Siena.
Founded: 1890. Owners: Clemente and Roberto Francheschi. Winemaker: Fabrizio Bindocci. DOC: Brunello di Montalcino, Rosso di Montalcino. Other: Moscadello di Montalcino, Vin Santo. One of the biggest Montalcino estates of consistently good quality.

Poliziano

Montepulciano, 53045 Siena.
Owned by Federico Carletti who, with the help of Carlo Ferrini, makes admired Chianti, Bianco Vergine and Vin Santo. Carletti is turning this estate into a first-class Vino Nobile producer. Impressive *vini da tavola* include Elegia, a pure Sangiovese, and Cabernet-based Le Stanze. New vineyards are planned for Rosso di Montepulciano.

Castello dei Rampolla

Panzano in Chianti, 50020 Firenze.
Owners/winemakers: the Di Napoli family. DOC: Chianti Classico. Other: Sammarco and Trebbiano. Sammarco (a Cab./ Sangio blend) has become a major new *vino da tavola*.

Riecine

Gaiole, 53013 Siena.
Founded in 1971 by an Englishman, John Dunkley, and his wife Palmina Abbagnano. DOC: Chianti Classico. Other: Riecine Bianco, La Gioia di Riecine. Dunkley proved himself a perfectionist from his first vintage. His attitude and his excellent, truly typical, Chianti have helped to make the British more attentive.

Rocca delle Macìe

Castellina in Chianti, 53011 Siena.
Founded in 1974. A respected producer, with 543 acres in Chianti. Their top wines are the *riserva* Chianti Fizzano and the red *vino da tavola* Ser Gioveto. They also produce Orvieto Classico, Galestro, Rubizzo and Decembrino.

Rocca di Castagnoli

Castagnoli, 53013 Siena.
Owner: Calogero Calì. DOC: Chianti, Val d'Arbia. Other: Chardonnay, Sangiovese, Cabernet.

Ruffino

Pontassieve, 50065 Firenze.
Founded: 1877. Owners: the Folonari family. DOC: Chianti, Chianti Classico, Orvieto. Other: Galestro, Sarmento, Predicato, Rosatello. One of the largest Chianti houses with vast holdings in the Classico zones, Ruffino has been moving smartly to upgrade its already solid image with Predicato wines devised by Ambrogio Folonari. The Ducale is the classic among Chianti *riserva* and the Cabreo Sangiovese/ Cabernet blend and Chardonnay have rapidly become models of the new style Tuscan Predicato wines. A Pinot Nero, called Nero del Tondo, is also impressive. Their holdings in Chianti Classico are the source of the respected Riserva Ducale. They also own the Nozzole estate at Greve.

San Felice

San Gusmè, 53030 Siena.
Owner: Riunione Adriatica di Sicurtà. Manager: Giovanni Battista Gorio. Winemaker: Leonardo Bellacini. DOC: Chianti Classico, Val d'Arbia. Other: Galestro, Chardonnay, Vigilio, Vin Santo, Vigorello (pure Sangiovese), Predicato di Biturica. A steadily improving estate making fine Chianti, and a special red Vigilio from some 470 acres. They also own neighbouring La Pagliaia, Campogiovanni near Sant'Angelo, and the small Poggio Rosso estate, from which young winemaker Leonardo Bellacini styles some of the region's finest reds.

San Giusto a Rentennano

Monti, 53010 Siena.
Owner Francesco Martini di Cigala and family make Chianti, Percarlo (strong, pure, *barrique*-aged Sangioveto) and Vin Santo that are among the best.

Tenuta San Guido-Sassicaia

Bolgheri, 57020 Livorno.
Owner: Niccolò Incisa della Roccetta DOC: Bolgheri Sassicaia. The late Marchese Mario Incisa della Rocchetta planted Cabernet Sauvignon on his seaside estate near Bolgheri, Tenuta San Guido, in 1942. His Sassicaia emerged in the late 1960s as Italy's finest Cabernet. Since Mario Incisa's death in 1983 his son Niccolò has taken personal control of selling the 16,000 cases produced annually. *See also* Sassicaia, page 324.

Castello di San Polo in Rosso

Gaiole, 53013 Siena.
Cesare and Katrin Canessa, with oenologist Maurizio Castelli make some fine Chianti Classico, and a superb pure Sangioveto *vino da tavola* called Cetinaia, plus Bianco and Rosato d'Erta.

Selvapiana

Pontassieve, 50065 Firenze.
Founded: 1840. Owner: Francesco Giuntini. DOC: Chianti Rufina and Pomino. An old family property brought to the top ranks in Chianti with the help of winemaker Franco Bernabei.

Conti Serristori

Sant'Andrea in Percussina, 50026 Firenze.
Part of the Gruppo Italiano Vini complex. DOC: Chianti, Chianti Classico, Orvieto, Vernaccia di San Gimignano. Other: Bianco and Rosato Toscano, Galestro, Vin Santo. The property includes the country house where Machiavelli once lived in exile.

Teruzzi & Puthod – Ponte a Rondolino

San Gimignano, 53037 Siena.
Founded in 1975 by Enrico Teruzzi and Carmen Puthod. DOC: Chianti Colli Senesi, Vernaccia di San Gimignano. Other: Galestro, Terra Peperino, Sarpinello *tradizionale*. The estate is expanding; 84 acres provide exemplary Vernaccia and also a wood-aged *riserva*, known as Carmen and Terra di Tufi respectively.

Castello di Uzzano

Greve, 50022 Firenze.
Owner: Briano Castelbarco Alabani Masetti, whose family has owned the property since the 17th century. DOC: Chianti Classico. One of the greatest names of Chianti, whose 14th-century cellars (the walls are 27 feet thick) slowly mature wines of sweet harmony and long life. As well as Castello di Uzzano, Castelbarco and friend Marion de Jacobert make *vino da tavola* called Vigna Niccolò da Uzzano from more than 100 acres of vines.

Val di Suga

Montalcino, 53024 Siena.
DOC: Brunello di Montalcino, Rosso di Montalcino. Owner: the Angelini family; they also own Tenuta Trerose in Montepulciano and San Leonino in Chianti Classico, making the family a major force in Tuscan estate wines. From 57 acres they produce wines of good quality and their reputation is steadily improving.

Vecchie Terre di Montefili

Greve, 52022 Firenze.
Owner: Roccaldo Acuti. Winemaker: Vittorio Fiore. Fine DOC Chianti wines, and an interesting white *vino da tavola* called Vigna Regis, made from Chardonnay, Sauvignon Blanc and Traminer. With its red Bruno di Rocca, this estate is a rising star in Chianti.

Castello Vicchiomaggio

Greve, 50022 Firenze.
Owner: John Matta since 1968. DOC: Chianti Classico. Other: Ripa delle More, Ripa delle Mimose. A 9th-century castle in a super site with 54 acres of vines. Under the guidance of winemaker Vittorio Fiore the estate has seen a rapid improvement, and is now the scene of some excellent modern winemaking.

Vignamaggio

Greve, 50022 Firenze.
Owner: Gianni Nunziante. Winemaker: Franco Bernabei. DOC: Chianti Classico. Other: Sangiovese Gherardino. The beautiful 15th-century villa where Mona Lisa probably lived, home of Michelangelo's biographer and one of the most prestigious Chiantis, if rather light in style. The new owner aims to take this historical estate back to Chianti's front ranks.

Castello di Volpaia

Radda in Chianti, 53017 Siena.
Owners: Giovannella and Carlo Stianti Mascheroni. Winemaker: Maurizio Castelli. DOC: Chianti Classico, Bianco Val d'Arbia. Other: Balifico, Coltassala, Torniello, Vin Santo. The medieval castle and its hamlet were high on the list of 15th-century *crus*. Its refined wines include the new delicately sweet and fruity Coltassala of Sangioveto and Mammolo, and the revelatory oak-aged Torniello.

OTHER PRODUCERS

Aiola Vagliagli, 53010 Siena. Owner: Giovanni Malagodi. DOC: Chianti Classico, Bianco Val d'Arbia. Other: Logaiolo.
Fattoria Ambra Carmignano, 50040 Firenze. Owners: the Rigoli family. DOC: Carmignano. 15 acres.
Amorosa Sinalunga, 53046 Siena. Owners: Carlo Citterio. DOC: Chianti Colli Senesi. Other: Borgo Amorosa, Amorosa Bianca.
Artimino Artimino, 50040 Firenze. The 16th-century Medici villa, once encompassed by a 32-mile wall, is one of Tuscany's most impressive wine estates. DOC: Carmignano, Chianti. Other: La Ferdinanda da Bianco and Rosso, Vin Ruspo, Vin Santo.

Fattoria di Bacchereto Bacchereto, 50040 Firenze. Owner: Carlo Bencini Tesi. DOC: Carmignano, Chianti.

Baggiolino La Romola, 50020 Firenze. Owner: Ellen Fantoni Sellon. DOC: Chianti. Other: Poggio Brandi. 37 acres.

Erik Banti Montemerano, 59050 Grosseto. DOC: Morellino di Scansano called Ciabatta, Aquilaia and Piaggie. Other: Alicante. 26 acres.

Jacopo Banti Campiglia Marittima, 57021 Livorno. Leader of the new Val di Cornia DOC, with red Ciliegolo and white Corniello.

Bibbiani Capraia e Limite, 50050 Firenze. DOC: Chianti Montalbano.

Rudolf Bindella Montepulciano, 53045 Siena. Important Swiss importer makes fine Vino Nobile (Vallocaia estate) and has bought an estate in Chianti ('Borgo Scopeto').

Fattoria di Bossi-Marchese Gondi Pontassieve, 50056 Firenze. DOC: Chianti Rufina, Vin Santo. 41 acres.

La Brancaia Castellina, 53010 Siena. Owners: Bruno and Brigitte Widmer. DOC: Chianti. 12 acres.

Brugnano San Casciano Val di Pesa, 50026 Firenze. Owner: Conte Lodovico Guicciardini. DOC: Chianti.

Villa Cafaggio Panzano, 50020 Firenze. Owner/winemaker: Stefano Farkas. DOC: Chianti Classico. Other: Solatio Basilica, San Martino. Fine austere wine.

Caggiolo Castellina, 53010 Siena. Owners: Ezio and Pietro Rivella. Often excellent Chianti Classico.

Villa Calcinaia Greve, 50022 Firenze. Owned by the Caponi family since 1523. DOC: Chianti. 99 acres.

Le Calvane Montagnana Val di Pesa, 50025 Firenze. DOC: Chianti. Other: Sorbino (white). 35 acres.

Camigliano Montalcino, 53024 Siena. Owners: the Ghezzi family. DOC: Brunello di Montalcino. Other: Bianco, Rosso dei Vigneti di Brunello.

Campogiovanni *See* San Felice.

Candialle Panzano, 50020 Firenze. Owner: Gerd von Bentheim. DOC: Chianti. 7.5 acres.

Podere Capaccia Radda, 53017 Siena. Winemaker: Vittorio Fiore. DOC: Chianti. Other: Sangioveto Querciagrande. 7.5 acres.

Capannelle Gaiole, 53013 Siena. Owner: Raffaele Rossetti. A tiny 'boutique' winery, rare in Tuscany, making Capannelle Rosso, Bianco and Chardonnay *vini da tavola*, much prized but over-priced.

Caprili Montalcino, 53024 Siena. Owner: Alfo Bartolommei. Excellent DOC Brunello and Rosso di Montalcino. 17 acres.

Carmignani G 'Fuso' Montecarlo, 55015 Lucca. DOC: Montecarlo Bianco. Other: Red For Duke (from Sangiovese, Syrah and Malvasia Nera), white Pietrachiara. 10 acres.

Carpineto Dudda, 50020 Firenze. Owner: Giovanni Carlo Sacchet. Reliable Chianti, Orvieto and *vini da tavola*.

Fattoria Le Casalte Montepulciano, 53045 Siena. Owner: Paola Silvestri. DOC: Rosso di Montepulciano, Vino Nobile.

Casanova dei Neri Montalcino, 53024 Siena. Rising star in Montalcino with Brunello and Rosso. 30 acres.

Nittardi Castellina in Chianti, 53011 Siena. Owner: Peter Femfert. DOC: Chianti Classico. 5 acres.

Fattoria Casenuove Panzano, 50020 Firenze. Owner: Pietro Pandolfini. DOC: Chianti Classico. 59 acres.

Castiglion del Bosco Montalcino, 53042 Siena. Winemaker: Maurizio Castelli. DOC: Brunello and Rosso di Montalcino. 86 acres.

Cennatoio Panzano, 50020 Firenze. Owner: Leandro Alessi. Winemaker: Alfonso Garberoglio. DOC: Chianti. Second label: Luca della Robbia.

Fattoria del Cerro Montepulciano, 53045 Siena. Owner: SAI Agricola insurance company. DOC: Chianti, first-rate Vino Nobile. Second label: Cantine Baiocchi. 289 acres.

Le Chiantigiane Tavarnelle Val di Pesa, 50028 Firenze. DOC: Chianti (some Classico) and a range of others. Other: Galestro. 1.5m. cases.

Pieve di Santa Restituta Montalcino, 53024 Siena. Owners: Angelo Gaja and Roberto Bellini. Oenologist: Attilio Pagli. DOC: Brunello and Rosso di Montalcino. Among the best Brunello. 40 acres.

Chigi Saracini Castelnuovo Berardenga, 53033 Siena. DOC: Chianti Colli Senesi, Bianco Val d'Arbia. The ancient estate was bequeathed to the Chigiana Musical Academy of Siena by Conte Guido Chigi. 99 acres.

Tenuta La Chiusa Portoferraio-Elba, 57037 Livorno. Owner: Giuliana Foresi. DOC: Elba. Dignified wines from 12 acres.

Ciacci Piccolomini d'Aragona Montalcino, 53024 Siena. Old estate emerging with fine Brunello di Montalcino.

Villa Cilnia DOC: Chianti Colli Aretini. Other: Whites include Poggio Garbato, barrel-aged Campo del Sasso, sweet Sassolato, fizzy Le Bizze, and Predicato del Muschio; *rosato* Poggio Cicaleto; reds Vocato and Le Vignacce.

Colognole Rufina, 50068 Firenze. Owner: the Marchesa Spalletti (formerly of Poggio Reale). DOC: Chianti Rufina.

La Colonica Montepulciano, 53045 Siena. Owner: Fernando Cattani. Good Vino Nobile and Bianco Vergine. 74 acres.

Contucci Montepulciano, 53045 Siena. DOC: Vino Nobile di Montepulciano, Chianti, Vin Santo.

Fattoria Il Corno San Casciano Val di Pesa, 50026 Firenze. Owners: Antonio and Maria Teresa Frova. DOC: Chianti. *Barrique*-aged Sangiovese Fossespina. 148 acres.

Dievole Vagliagli, 53010 Siena. Great potential from 237 acres of vines being developed slowly.

Fanetti Montepulciano, 53045 Siena. DOC: Chianti Colli Senesi, Vino Nobile di Montepulciano.

Tenuta di Farneta Sinalunga, 53046 Siena. Good Chianti and a fine pure Sangiovese *vino da tavola* called Bongoverno.

Fassati Pieve di Sinalunga, 53046 Siena. Founded 1913. Owned since 1969 by Fazi-Battaglia (*see* Marches). DOC: Chianti, Chianti Classico, Vino Nobile di Montepulciano. A new property at Graccianello improves quality potential.

Le Filigare San Donato in Poggio, 50020 Firenze. Winemaker: Gabriella Tani. DOC: Chianti. Other: Stylish red Podere Le Rocce.

Fattoria di Fognano-Talosa Montepulciano, 53045 Siena. Manager: Ottorino De Angelis. DOC: Vino Nobile (single-vineyard Talosa), Chianti.

Castello di Gabbiano Mercatale Val di Pesa, 50024 Firenze. DOC: Chianti Classico. Other: Impressive pure Sangiovese Ania and Sangiovese/Cabernet/Merlot 'R&R' reds, and the white Chardonnay Ariella.

Il Greppone Mazzi The Folonari family make good Brunello from 20 acres.

Fattoria di Grignano Pontassieve, 50026 Firenze. Owner: the Marchesi Gondi. DOC: Chianti Rufina. 99 acres.

Carla Guarnieri Pozzolatico, 50023 Firenze. DOC: Chianti. Other: Highly praised Sangiovese Terricci.

Lamole di Lamole Owners: Santa Margherita. DOC: Chianti Classico. A small estate at Lamole near Greve, highly reputed for splendid old vintages.

Ezio Rivella

As the wine director and chief oenologist for Villa Banfi, the largest exporters of Italian wine to the United States, Ezio Rivella (Piedmont-born, a man of startling competence and vitality) has fabulous resources at his disposal. He is also president of the national committee for DOC in Rome. His chief preoccupation is the vast Banfi development at Montalcino in the south of Tuscany, where in the '70s the company acquired no less than 2,000 acres for planting. The principal goal is Brunello on a scale never contemplated before. Rivella has succeeded in making available to a world-wide public a fine example of one of Italy's rarest and most splendid wines. But his ambitions have gone much further: Cabernet, Chardonnay and Pinot Grigio have been striking successes, and he is experimenting with Sauvignon Blanc, Pinot Nero, Petite Syrah – and no doubt other varieties. Meanwhile the simple Rosso di Montalcino sold as Centine epitomizes Rivella's and Banfi's policy of offering value for money to everyone.

Lilliano Castellina in Chianti, 53011 Siena. Owners: the Ruspoli family. DOC: Chianti Classico. Distinguished wines from 120 acres.

Lisini Montalcino, 53024 Siena. Owners: the Lisini family. DOC: Brunello and Rosso di Montalcino. Winemaker: Franco Bernabei. Ranks with the best in some years.

Podere Lo Locco Carmignano, 50040 Firenze. Owners: the Pratesi family. DOC: Carmignano.

Tenuta di Lucciano-Spalletti Quarrata, 51039 Pistoia. Chianti Montalbano and *vini da tavola*. 110 acres.

Mantellassi Magliano in Toscana, 58051 Grosseto. DOC: Morellino di Scansano.

Fattoria di Manzano Manzano di Cortona, 52042 Arezzo. Owner: Massimo D'Alessandro. DOC: Bianco Vergine. Other: Vigna del Vescovo. Outstanding Syrah.

Le Masse di San Leolino Panzano, 50020 Firenze. Owner: Scotsman Norman Bain. Winemaker: Franco Bernabei. DOC: Highly praised Chianti Classico.

Mastroianni Montalcino, 53024 Siena. Owners: Gabriele and Antonio Mastroianni. Winemaker: Maurizio Castelli. DOC: Brunello and Rosso di Montalcino.

Fattoria Michi Montecarlo, 55015 Lucca. DOC: Montecarlo. Other: Roussanne white. 42 acres.

Montagliari Panzano, 50020 Firenze. Owner: Giovanni Capelli. DOC: Chianti. Other: Brunesco di San Lorenzo, Vin Santo.

Fattoria Montellori Fucecchio, 50054 Firenze. Owner: Giuseppe Nieri and son Alessandro. DOC: Chianti. Other: *barrique*-aged Castelrapiti Rosso, *tradizionale* Montellori Brut. 120-acre estate where ambition sometimes exceeds the results.

Montenidoli San Gimignano, 53037 Siena. Owner: Elisabetta Fagiuoli. DOC: Chianti Colli Senesi and Vernaccia. Other: white Vinbrusco, *rosato*.

Vecchia Cantina di Montepulciano Montepulciano, 53045 Siena. A cooperative founded in 1937, now with some 300 growers. DOC: Bianco Vergine della Valdichiana, Chianti, Vino Nobile di Montepulciano. The zone's largest producer of Montepulciano.

Pagliarese Castelnuovo Berardenga, 53033 Siena. Owner: Alma B. Sanguineti. DOC: Chianti, Bianco Val d'Arbia. Other: red Camerlengo, Vin Santo.

Fattoria Pagnana Rignano sull'Arno, 50067 Firenze. DOC: Chianti. Other: Bianco, Vin Santo.

Parri Montespertoli, 50025 Firenze. Owner: Luigi Parri. DOC: Chianti.

La Parrina Albinia di Orbetello, 58010 Grosseto. Owner: Franca Spinola. DOC: Parrina Bianco, Rosso. Other: Albinia Rosato. The principal producers of this dry white 'Vino Etrusco' from the coast near Orbetello.

Pasolini Dall'Onda-Enoagricola Barberino Val d'Elsa, 50021 Firenze. Owners: the Pasolini family. DOC: Chianti (noteworthy *riserva*, Montòli). 148 acres.

Peppoli Mercatale Val di Pesa, 50024 Firenze. Owner: Antinori. DOC: Excellent, traditional Chianti seasoned in large casks.

Fattoria di Petriolo Rignano sull'Arno, 50067 Firenze. Good Chianti and a fine Merlot.

Fattoria di Petroio Vagliagli, 53010 Siena. Owners: Pamela and Gian Luigi Lenzi. On the rise with their fine Chianti.

Le Pici San Gusmé, 53030 Siena. Owner: Gunnar Lüneburg. DOC: Chianti Classico. 22 acres.

Pietrafitta San Gimignano, 53037 Siena. Oenologist: Sergio Conforti. DOC: Chianti, Vernaccia di San Gimignano. 99 acres.

Pietraserena San Gimignano, 53037 Siena. DOC: Vernaccia (outstanding Vigna del Sole). 41 acres.

Cantina Cooperativa di Pitigliano Pitigliano, 58017 Grosseto. DOC; Bianco di Pitigliano. The cooperative (Tuscany's largest) includes most of Pitigliano's 1,000 registered growers.

Tenuta di Poggio Rufina, 50068 Firenze. Owner: Vittorio Spolveri. DOC: Chianti Rufina.

Poggio al Sole Sambuca Val di Pesa, 50020 Firenze. Owner/winemaker: Giovanni Davaz. DOC: Chianti Classico. Other: Vin Santo. 17 acres.

Il Poggiolino Sambuca Val di Pesa, 50020 Firenze. Owners: Carlo and Maria Grazia Pacini. DOC: Chianti. Other: Sangiovese Roncaia.

Il Poggiolo Poggiolo di Monteriggioni, 53035 Siena. Owners: the Bonfio family. DOC: Chianti Colli Senesi. 46 acres.

Fattoria Il Poggiolo Carmignano, 50042 Firenze. Owner: Giovanni Cianchi Baldazzi. DOC: Carmignano. Other: Vin Ruspo, Vin Santo.

Poggio Rosso *See* San Felice.

Castello di Poppiano Montespertoli, 50025 Firenze. Owner: Ferdinando Guicciardini. DOC: Chianti Colli Fiorentini.

Fattoria Le Pupille Magliano in Toscana, 58051 Grosseto. DOC: Morellino di Scansano.

Castello di Querceto Lucolena, 50020 Firenze. Manager-winemaker: Alessandro François. DOC: Chianti Classico. Other: Sangiovese La Corte, white Le Giuncaie, Vin Santo.

Fattoria Querciabella Greve, 50022 Firenze. DOC: Chianti. Other: Red Camartina.

Querciavalle Vagliagli, 53010 Siena. Owners: the Losi brothers. DOC: Chianti, Bianco Val d'Arbia.

Castello de Rencine Castellina in Chianti, 53011 Siena. DOC: Chianti Classico.

Rodano Castellina, 53010 Siena. Owner: Vittorio Pozzesi. DOC: Chianti. 45 acres.

Fattoria di Sammontana Montelupo, 50056 Firenze. Owners: Andrea and Michele Dzieduszycki, whose noble Polish ancestors acquired the estate in 1870. DOC: Chianti. 74 acres.

San Cosma San Gusmé, 53030 Siena. Owner: Bent Myhre. DOC: Chianti. 15 acres.

San Fabiano Calcinaia Poggiobonsi, 53036 Siena. Winemaker: Giuseppe Bassi. DOC: Chianti. Other: Cerviolo (red Cabernet, white Chardonnay-Sauvignon). This and nearby Cellole are being developed together, with great potential.

San Filippo dei Comunali Montalcino, 53024 Siena. Owner: Ermanno Rosi. DOC: Brunello and Rosso di Montalcino.

Fattoria San Leonino Castellina in Chianti, 53011 Siena. Owners: the Angelini family – one of their three Tuscan estates. 123 acres.

San Vito in Fior di Selva Montelupo Fiorentino, 50056 Firenze. Owners: Laura and Roberto Drighi. DOC: Chianti. White *vini da tavola*.

Villa La Selva Bucine, 52020 Arezzo. The ancient estate is owned by the Carpini family. Oenologist: Vittorio Fiore. DOC: Chianti, Vin Santo.

Fattoria di Selvole Vagliagli, 53010 Siena. DOC: Chianti Classico.

Soiana Terricciola, 56030 Pisa. Young Bruno Moos is leading a revival in Chianti Colline Pisane from his castle and handsome estate.

Sorbaiano Montecatini Val di Cecina, 56040 Pisa. Owner: Febo Picciolini. Winemaker: Vittorio Fiore. DOC: Montescudaio (single-vineyard Rosso del Miniere, barrel-fermented Lucestraia Bianco), Vin Santo.

La Suvera Pievescola, 53018 Siena. Owner: Marchesi Ricci Paracciani Bergamini. Winemaker: Vittorio Fiore. Oddly fascinating wines include the Chianti-like Rango Rosso and Bianco, sparkling Cuvée Italienne Brut.

Talenti-Pian di Conte Montalcino, 53024 Siena. Owner: Pierluigi Talenti (formerly winemaker at Il Poggione). First-rate DOC Brunello and Rosso di Montalcino. 6.5 acres.

Terrabianca Vagliagli, 53010 Siena. Owner: Swiss Roberto Guldener. Winemaker: Vittorio Fiore. DOC: Chianti Scassino and Vigna della Croce. Other: Campaccio (Cabernet-Sangiovese), Piano della Cappella (Chardonnay). A rapidly rising estate.

Torre a Cona San Donato in Collina, 50012 Firenze. Owners: the Rossi di Montelara family of Martini & Rossi. DOC: Chianti. 27 acres.

Torre a Decima Molino del Piano, 50065 Firenze. DOC: Chianti Colli Fiorentini. Other: Dolce Amore Bianco. A dramatic 13th-century castle built by the Pazzi family.

Travignoli Pelago, 50060 Firenze. Owners: Giampiero and Giovanni Busi. DOC: Chianti Rufina.

Fattoria dell'Ugo Tavarnelle Val di Pesa, 50028 Firenze. Owner: Franco Amici Grossi. DOC: Chianti. 94 acres.

Castello di Verrazzano Greve, 50022 Firenze. Owner: Luigi Cappellini. DOC: Chianti Classico. The castle where the explorer Giovanni da Verrazzano was born in 1485.

Villa Vetrice Rufina, 50068 Firenze. Owner: Fratelli Grati. DOC: Chianti Rufina, Vin Santo. 250 acres.

Vignavecchia Radda, 53017 Siena. Owner: Franco Beccari. DOC: Chianti Classico, including a small quantity of sought-after *riserva*. Other: Red Canvalle.

Vignole Panzano, 50020 Firenze. Fine, reasonably-priced Chianti Classico.

Vistarenni Gaiole, 53013 Siena. DOC: Chianti, Vin Santo and Bianco Val d'Arbia. Other: Red Codirosso. 99 acres.

Viticcio Greve, 50022 Firenze. DOC: Chianti. Other: Pure Sangiovese Prunaio. 37 acres.

UMBRIA

If Umbria figured on a discerning wine buyer's shopping list in the past it was purely for Orvieto, its golden, gently sweet and occasionally memorable speciality. Today it is more likely to be for Rubesco, the noble red of Torgiano near Perugia, one of the best wines and best bargains to be found in Italy.

If Torgiano can make such good wine, so surely can other hills in this inland region. New DOCs are appearing. Fifteen percent of the region is DOC, which is above the national average. They should allow for the maximum latitude in the choice of grapes, since those of the north and the south could both do well here, and there is no good reason for planting (say) Trebbiano if you could plant Sauvignon Blanc.

DOC and Other Wines

Colli Altotiberini DOC. Red, white and *rosato* wine. Province: Perugia. Villages: a wide sweep of country in northern Umbria, including Perugia and 8 other communes in the province. Grapes (red and *rosato*) Sangiovese 55–70%, Merlot 10–20%, Trebbiano and Malvasia 10%; (white) Trebbiano Toscano 75–90%, Malvasia up to 10%, others up

Dr Giorgio Lungarotti

The saturnine face of Dr Giorgio Lungarotti masks one of Italy's most original winemakers, a man of extraordinary energy and sagacity who has pursued his vision of great wine independent of any historic reputation. His creation is now the DOC Torgiano. The little hill-town across the River Tiber from Perugia is the Lungarotti republic, from its modern winery to its excellent wine museum and its beautifully restored and greatly enlarged hotel, the Tre Vasselle (where each October the Umbrian government holds an all-Italian wine competition).

Lungarotti's red, Rubesco di Torgiano, is like a first-rate, unusually concentrated Chianti. Its *riserva* from the Monticchio vineyard even more so, deserving ten years in bottle. In the 1970s he introduced Cabernet Sauvignon in a riserva called San Giorgio. His stylish, oak-aged, Torre di Giano is Trebbiano enlivened with Grechetto to be crisp and fragrant. In 1981 he introduced a Chardonnay, and also has Gewürztraminer in his 620 acres of vineyards. His Solleone is one of Italy's rare sherry-style dry apéritif wines made by *solera*. His daughter Teresa follows in her father's footsteps.

to 15%. Max. crop: 77 hl/ha. Min. alch: 10.5° for white; 11.5° for red and *rosato*. Annual production: 27,800 cases.

DOC from the hills of the upper Tiber. Production in the area is increasing. All its wines, including its dry red with Merlot, are intended for drinking young.

Colli Amerini DOC. Red, white, *rosato* and *novello* wine. Province: Terni. Villages: Amelia, Narni and 11 others along the Tiber and Nera valleys between Orvieto and Terni. Grapes: (red, *rosato* and *novello*) Sangiovese 65–80%, Montepulciano, Ciliegiolo, Canaiolo, Barbera and/or Merlot 20–35% (but no more than 10% Merlot); (white) Trebbiano Toscano 70–85%, Grechetto, Verdello, Garganega and/or Malvasia Toscana 15–30% (but no more than 10% Malvasia); (Malvasia) Malvasia Toscana 85–100%. Trebbiano Toscano and/or other white varieties up to 15%. Max. crop: 84 hl/ha. Min. alch. 11° for red, white, *rosato* and *novello*, 11.5° for Malvasia, 12° for *rosso superiore*. Annual production: 56,000 cases.

Production began only in 1990 and while all signs are promising, so far no reliable judgement can be made.

Colli Martani DOC. Red and white wine. Province: Perugia. Villages: From Bettona as far south as Spoleto; Gualdo Cattaneo, Giano dell'Umbria and parts of 12 other communes. Grapes: Grechetto; other whites up to 15%; Trebbiano

Toscano; Sangiovese; other reds up to 15%. Max. crop: Grechetto 77 hl/ha, Trebbiano and Sangiovese 84 hl/ha. Min. alch: 12° for Grechetto, 11° for Trebbiano, 11.5° for Sangiovese. Annual production: 67,000 cases.

This is the newest of Perugia's DOCs and the wines so far are promising. Of the three varietals, Grechetto seems to offer the brightest prospects.

Colli Perugini DOC. Red, white and *rosato* wine. Provinces: Perugia and Terni. Villages: 6 communes in Perugia province; San Vananzo in Terni province. Grapes: (red and *rosato*) Sangiovese 65–85%, Montepulciano, Ciliegiolo, Barbera and/or Merlot 15–35% (but no more than 10% Merlot); (white) Trebbiano Toscano 65–85%, Grechetto, Verdicchio, Garganega and/or Malvasia del Chianti 15–35% (but no more than 10% Malvasia). Max. crop: 84 hl/ha (72 hl/ha *rosato*). Min. alch: 11.5° for red and *rosato*, 11° for white. Annual production: 110,000 cases.

DOC wine from the area between Perugia and Todi.

Colli del Trasimeno DOC. White and red wine. Province: Perugia. Villages: 9 communes around Lake Trasimeno. Grapes: (white) Trebbiano Toscano 60–80%, Malvasia del Chianti, Verdicchio Bianco, Verdello and Grechetto up to 40%; (red) Sangiovese 60–80%, Gamay, Ciliegiolo up to 40%, Trebbiano Toscano; Malvasia di Chianti up to 20%. Max.

crop: 87 hl/ha. Min. alch: 11° for white, 11.5° for red. Annual production: 133,000 cases.

The red and white of this zone on the borders of Tuscany are both average. Gamay and Ciliegiolo give spirit to the red and Grechetto gives the white a slight edge of acidity essential for freshness.

Grechetto or Greco A 'Greek' white grape which plays an increasingly important role here and in DOC in Colli Martani farther south. Unblended its wine is somewhat more fruity, firm and interesting than Trebbiano.

Montefalco Sagrantino and Montefalco Rosso DOC/DOCG. Red and white wine. Province: Perugia. Villages: the commune of Montefalco and parts of 4 others. Montefalco Sagrantino DOCG: Grape: Sagrantino; max. crop: 52 hl/ha; min. alch. for *secco*: 13°, for *passito*: 14.5°. Montefalco Rosso DOC: Grape: Sangiovese 60–70%, Sagrantino 10–15%, other red grapes up to 30%; max crop: 77 hl/ha; min. alch: 12°. Montefalco Bianco DOC: Grechetto not less than 50%, Trebbiano Toscano 20–35%, other white grapes up to 30%; max. crop: 94 hl/ha; min. alch: 11°. Annual production: Sagrantino 22,000 cases; Rosso and Bianco 44,000 cases.

DOC for a small area south of Assisi where the local Sagrantino grape makes very dark red wine, described as tasting of blackberries. The true speciality is the sweet and strong *passito* version, a notable dessert wine which is aged for a year. Dry it is tough and tannic but may yet command respect. Plain Montefalco red uses Sagrantino as seasoning in a less original but still smooth and agreeable wine.

Orvieto DOC. White wine, Province: Orvieto, Terni and Latium. Villages: Orvieto and surrounding area; 11 communes in Terni province and 5 in Latium's province. 'Classico' is from Orvieto itself. Grapes: Trebbiano Toscano (Procanico) 40–65%, Verdello 15–25%, Grechetto, Drupeggio and other whites 20–30%, Malvasia Toscana up to 20%. Max. crop: 71 hl/ha. Min. alch: 12°. Annual production: 1.22m. cases.

The simple and memorable name that used to mean golden, more or less sweet wine now suffers from the same identity crisis as many Italian whites. The taste for highly charged, then gently oxidized wines has gone. Modern vinification answers the problem with pale, clean but almost neutered ones. Not long ago (perhaps still) you could see huge barrels in Orvieto with their glass fermentation airlocks still occasionally breaking wind after two years or more. The wine, laboriously fermented dry, was then re-sweetened with a dried-grape *passito* to be *abboccato*. If you found a good one it was memorably deep and velvety, but probably none too stable – like Frascati, a poor traveller.

Modern Orvieto is nearly all pale, but should still have a hint of honey to be true to type. Much is dry and frankly dull. Chianti shippers put their names to several, Antinori to one of the better ones.

Torgiano DOC. Red, white and *rosato* wine. Province: Perugia. Village: Torgiano. Grapes: (red) Sangiovese 50–70%. Canaiolo 15–30%, Trebbiano Toscano 10%, Ciliegiolo and/or Montepulciano 10%; (white) Trebbiano 50–70%, Grechetto 15–35%, Malvasia or Verdello up to 15%.

Max. crop: 81 hl/ha. Min. alch: 12° for red; 10.5° for white. Annual production: 144,000 cases.

Virtually a one-man DOC; local tradition reshaped in modern terms by Dr Giorgio Lungarotti (*see* opposite and Producers). This was Umbria's first DOC, its reputation built on the Lungarotti brands of Rubesco and Torre di Giano.

Bianco di Torgiano and Rosso di Torgiano both have DOC status; the Torgiano Rosso Riserva became DOCG in 1990: the wines almost have the same name, but production-rules differ (in the Italian way of creating transparency). For Torgiano Rosso Riserva grapes are the same as for Rosso di Torgiano, the maximum crop is 65hl/ha, with minimum alchohol of 12.5°. Ageing is for three years, with an annual production of 8,800 cases.

Leading Umbria Producers

Fratelli Adanti

Arquata di Bevagna, 06031 Perugia.
DOC: Montefalco Rosso, Sagrantino. Other: Rosso d'Arquata, Bianco d'Arquata, Rosato d'Arquata, Vin Santo. The Arquata estate is the quality leader for DOC Sagrantino di Montefalco. All wines, especially the non-DOC Bianco d'Arquata, the Sagrantino and the *vino da tavola* Rosso d'Arquata have been consistently improving but Alvaro, the talented winemaker responsible, has now left.

Barberani-Vallesanta

Baschi, 05018 Terni.
Owner: Luigi Barberani. Winemaker: Maurizio Castelli. DOC: Orvieto Classico. Other: Lago di Corbara. Castagnola, Pulicchio, and Calcaia (with impressive noble rot). One of the best old firms in Orvieto, modernized and maintaining high standards.

Luigi Bigi & Figlio

Ponte Giulio di Orvieto, 05018 Terni.
Founded: 1881. Part of the Gruppo Italiano Vini complex. DOC: Orvieto, Est! Est!! Est!!!, Vino Nobile di Montepulciano. Other: Rosso di Corbara. One of the best-known producers of several popular DOCs. Single vineyard Orvieto Torricella and Orzalume both notable. Annual production: over 3m. cases.

Val di Maggio-Arnaldo Caprai

Montefalco, 06036 Perugia.
Drawn from 62 acres, Montefalco DOCs include a consistently fine, dry Sagrantino. Grechetto dell'Umbria table and bubbly wines also produced.

Giorgio Lungarotti

Torgiano, 06089 Perugia.
Founded as a corporation in 1960. Owners: the Lungarotti family. DOC: Torgiano. Other: Cabernet Sauvignon di Miralduolo, Castel Grifone Rosato, Chardonnay, Rondo, Rosciano, Solleone. The creator of Torgiano as a DOC and one of Italy's greatest winemakers, though quality seems a

little less reliable of late. Giorgio's daughter Teresa and oenologist Corrado Cantarelli now share the credit for continuing innovation. About half the production is DOC Torgiano. The Rubesco Riserva Monticchio is the cream of this. Torre di Giano is the white. Cabernet (in a blend called San Giorgio) and Chardonnay are highly promising. Solleone is a sherry-style apéritif. Annual production: 270,000 cases, of which over half is exported. *See also* DOCG Torgiano and page 334.

Castello della Sala

Sala, 05016 Terni.

Antinori's Umbrian castle, run independently by Renzo Cottarella, has 74 acres of vines. 'Castello della Sala' are *vini da tavola*, the best being Cervaro della Sala and Borro della Sala 'Fumé'. Also a botrytized sweet wine, Muffato della Sala, and a sweet Gewürztraminer. Pinot Noir being considered.

OTHER PRODUCERS

Antonelli Montefalco, 06036 Perugia. DOC: Montefalco, including Sagrantino and Grechetto.

Castello di Ascagnano Pierantonio di Umbertide, 06015 Perugia. Colli Altotiberini DOC and *spumanti* – from 90 acres of vines. Not all of the 90 acres' produce is bottled, however.

Fattoria Belvedere Villastrada Umbria. Castiglione del Lago, 06060 Perugia. Owner: Angelo Illuminati. DOC: Colli del Trasimeno.

Domenico Benincasa Capro di Bevagna, 06031 Perugia. DOC: Sagrantino di Montefalco. Other: Capro/Bianco, Rosso, all from 18 acres.

Casole Otricoli, Terni. Elio and Alberto Carccarini, and Trentino's Salvatore Maule make Casole Bianco and Rosso *vini da tavola* here.

Cantina Colli Amerini 05022, Ternio Fornule di Amelia. DOC Orvieto Classico.

Colle del Sole-Polidori Pierantonio di Umbertide, 06015 Perugia. Owner: Carlo Polidori. DOC: Colli Altotiberini. Other: Rubino, Verdello.

CoVi P (Consorzio Vitivinicolo Perugia) Ponte Pattoli, 06080 Perugia. DOC: Colli del Trasimeno, Orvieto, Torgiano. Other: Bianco and Rosso d'Umbria. The consortium comprises 6 cooperatives and bottles wine from all 6 of the Perugia DOC zones.

Dubini-Locatelli Orvieto, 05019, Terni. In 1988, Giovanni Dubini began vinifying the entire production from 44 acres under the Palazzone label. The vineyards are at Rocca Ripesena and in Orvieto Classico.

La Fiorita Macchie di Castiglione del Lago, 06060 Perugia. 185 acres of vines for Colli del Trasimeno DOC (led by the red Sangue di Miura), *rosato vino da tavola* and *spumante*.

Conti Fiumi Petrangeli Orvieto, 05019 Terni. Orvieto Classico and red *vino da tavola*, both served at their restaurant La Badia.

Castello di Montoro Montoro di Narni. Montoro Umbro, 05020 Terni. DOC: none. Other: Castello di Montoro Bianco, Rosato, and Rosso. The outstanding red is blended from Sangiovese, Merlot, Barbera and Montepulciano. 370 acres.

Pieva del Vescovo Corciano, 06036 Perugia. DOC: Colli del Trasimeno.

La Querciolana Panicale, 06064 Perugia. Owner: Roberto Nesci. DOC: Colli del Trasimeno. The excellent red sold under the name Grifo di Boldrino.

Rocca di Fabri Montefalco, 06036 Perugia. DOC: Montefalco Sagrantino. *Vini da tavol,* include Grechetto dell'Umbria.

Sasso Rosso Capodacqua, 06082 Perugia. DOC: None. Other: *vino da tavola* Rosso di Assisi, a prizewinner which may well become one of the classic reds of central Italy.

Tenuta Le Velette Orvieto Stazione, 05019 Terni. DOC: Orvieto Classico. Other: Rosso Le Velette. A 16th-century estate restored and replanted in the 1960s.

Tili Capodacqua, 06082 Perugia. Assisi *vino da tavola* and a good Grechetto dell'Umbria from 32 acres. More consistent class than Sasso Rosso.

Cantina Sociale del Trasimeno Castiglione del Lago, 06061 Perugia. Cooperative. DOC: Colli del Trasimeno, and *vino da tavola*. From growers with over 2,200 acres.

Cantina Sociale Tudernum Todi, 06059 Perugia. Coop Grechetto di Todi and other *vini da tavola* from 1,600 acres.

Conti Vaselli Castiglione in Teverina, 01024 Viterbo. Orvieio Classico and *vino da tavola* red Santa Guilia have vastly improved.

Ruggero Veneri Spello, Perugia. Limited but very good production of Merlot and Gran Merlot di Spello *vini da tavola*.

Cantina Cooperativa Vitivinicola Orvieto, 05019 Terni. The best of this, the largest producer of Orvieto Classico, is bottled under the Cardeto trademark.

THE MARCHES

The central slice of the Adriatic coast, from the latitude of Florence to that of Orvieto, is probably even better known for its dry white Verdicchio than for the beaches and fishing boats that give the wine such a perfect context. The historic cities of Urbino in the north and Ascoli Piceno in the south of the region draw a proportion of its visitors inland, but the eastern flanks of the Apennines hardly rival the cultural crowd-pulling quality of Tuscany.

So the red wines of the Marches, potentially (sometimes actually) of good Chianti quality, are less well known than they should be. The Montepulciano grape gives them a quality missing in most of those in Romagna to the north.

DOC and Other Wines

Bianchello del Metauro DOC. White wine. Province: Pesaro. Villages: Eighteen communes in the valley of River Metauro. Grapes: Biancame (Bianchello) 95%, Malvasia 5%. Max. crop:

98 hl/ha. Min. alch: 11.5°. Annual production: 200,000 cases.

A pleasant sharp plain white from the north of the region, for drinking young with fish.

Colli Maceratesi DOC. White wine. Provinces: Macerata and Ancona. Villages: Loreto and all of Macerata. Grapes: Trebbiano Toscano 50–70%, with Maceratino; Malvasia Toscana and Verdicchio 15% Max. crop: 98 hl/ha. Min. alch: 11°. Annual production: 89,000 cases.

A minor DOC for another local dry seafood wine. Macerata is halfway from Ancona south to Ascoli Piceno.

Falerio dei Colli Ascolani DOC. White wine. Province: Ascoli. Villages: all of province of Ascoli Piceno. Grapes: Trebbiano Toscano 80%, Passerina, Verdicchio, Pinot Bianco, Pecorino up to 25%, Malvasia Toscana up to 7%. Max. crop: 98 hl/ha. Min. alch: 11.5° Annual production: 278,000 cases.

Another of the local dry whites associated with restaurants on the beach.

Lacrima di Morro d'Alba DOC. Red wine. Province: Ancona. Villages: Morro d'Alba, Monte San Vito, San Marcello, Belvedere Ostrense, Ostra and Senigallia. Grapes: Lacrima Montepulciano/Verdicchio up to 15%. Max. crop: 98 hl/ha. Min. alch: 11.5° (*riserva* 12.5° incl 2 yrs ageing). Annual production: 16,700 cases.

A DOC from around the ancient town of Morro d'Alba, south of Senigallia.

Montepulciano Important in the Marches as a constituent grape of the best red wines, also sometimes sold unblended.

Rosso Cònero DOC. Red wine. Province: Ancona. Villages: 5 communes in Ancona and part of 2 others. Grapes: Montepulciano over 85%, Sangiovese maximum 15%. Max. crop: 98 hl/ha. Min. alch: 11.5°. Annual production: 200,000 cases.

A full-strength, full-flavoured red from Monte Cònero, near the Adriatic just south of Ancona. One of the most flourishing of central and eastern Italy, with fruit to mellow and tannin to sustain it.

Rosso Piceno DOC. Red wine. Provinces: Ancona, Ascoli Piceno, Macerata. Villages: a large number in the above provinces. Grapes: Sangiovese over 60%, Montepulciano maximum 40%, Passerina/Trebbiano up to 15%. Max. crop: 96 hl/ha. Min. alch: 11.5°. Superiore, from a limited zone to the south, has 12°. Annual production: 500,000 cases.

The standard red of the southern half of the Marches, varying widely in quality from unremarkable to handmade and worth ageing, both in barrel and bottle. At its best it has Chianti-like weight and balance.

Colli Pesaresi DOC. Red and white wine. Province: Pesaro. Villages: 30 communes and part of 6 others in and around Pesaro. Grapes: (red) Sangiovese 85%, Montepulciano and/or Ciliegiolo; (white) up to 85% Trebbiano and 15% other grapes 15%. Max. crop: 77 hl/ha. Min. alch: 11.5°. Annual production: 133,000 cases.

A little-used DOC for a red of limited character. Sangiovese is frequently used for non-DOC reds.

Verdicchio dei Castelli di Jesi DOC. White wine. Provinces: Ancona. Villages: 17 communes and part of 5 others around the town of Jesi. Grapes: Verdicchio 85%, others up to 15%. Max. crop: 98 hl/ha; *riserva* and *superiore* 77 hl/ha. Min. alch: 10.5°, *riserva* and *superiore* 11.5°. Annual production: 2.1m. cases.

The great commercial success of the Marches. Straightforward, dry, well balanced and clean; one of the earliest Italian whites to taste both modern and international, thanks to the skill of its promoters, the firm of Fazi-Battaglia (*see* Producers). Their marketing flair produced the distinctive amphora-shaped bottle seen among the fishnets in practically every Italian restaurant abroad – although these are now for tourists only and better quality wines are sold in normal Bordeaux-style bottles. The Verdicchio is a tricky grape to grow but clearly has quality. The wine is short-lived, however, and bottles held too long in stock are often undrinkable. There is also a *tradizionale* sparkling version.

Verdicchio di Matelica DOC. White wine. Provinces: Macerata and Ancona. Villages: Matelica and 7 others. Grapes: Verdicchio 85%, Trebbiano Toscano and Malvasia up to 15%. Max. crop: 91 hl/ha. Min. alch: 11.5°. Annual production: 156,000 cases.

Verdicchio from higher ground farther inland, said to be superior, but hardly ever seen abroad. Another (non-DOC) with a similar reputation is Verdicchio di Montanello.

Vernaccia di Serrapetrona DOC. Red wine. Province: Macerata. Villages: Serrapetrona and part of Belforte del Chienti and San Severino Marche. Grapes: Vernaccia di Serrapetrona; Sangiovese, Montelpulciano, Ciliegiolo up to 15%. Max. crop: 70 hl/ha. Min. alch: 11.5°. Annual production 20,000 cases.

A locally popular, sweet, sparkling red which has been made since the 15th century.

Leading Marches Producers

Brunori
Jesi, 60035 Ancona.
Owners: Mario and Giorgio Brunori. DOC: Verdicchio dei Castelli di Jesi. A few hundred cases of splendid Verdicchio from the tiny San Nicolò vineyard, planted in 1972.

Fratelli Bucci
Ostra Vetere, 60010 Ancona.
Owned by Ampelio Bucci. DOC: Verdicchio dei Castelli di Jesi. Other: Tenuta di Pongelli.

Cocci Grifoni
San Savino di Ripatransone, 63030 Ascoli Piceno.
Owner: Guido Cocci Grifoni. An admirable producer whose Rosso Piceno is one of the best and whose Falerio has no rivals.

Colonnara
Cupramontana, 60035 Ancona.
Cantina Sociale di Cupramontana now goes under the name Colonnara and is making some of the best Verdicchio, still and sparkling, under winemaker Carlo Pigini.

Fazi-Battaglia

Castelplanio Stazione, 60032 Ancona.

Founded in 1949 by the Angelini family. DOC: Rosso Cònero, Rosso Piceno, Verdicchio dei Castelli di Jesi. Other: Rosato delle Marche, Sangiovese delle Marche. The house that devised the green amphora bottle that made Verdicchio famous. From 570 acres of company vines plus extra grapes bought in, Fazi-Battaglia makes about 400,000 cases of Verdicchio of which roughly 40% is exported.

Garofoli

Loreto, 60025 Ancona.

Founded: 1871. Now run by two generations of Garofoli. Winemaker: Carlo Garofoli. DOC: Rosso Cònero, Verdicchio dei Castelli di Jesi. A high-quality producer with the excellent single vineyard Verdicchio Macrina and oak-aged Serra Fioresa as well as sparkling versions by both tank and *tradizionale* methods.

Mecvini

Fabriano, 60044 Ancona.

Enzo Mecella is one of the region's most skilled and inspired winemakers with a good range of DOCs and innovative *vini da tavola*.

Monte Schiavo

Moie di Maiolati Spontini, 60032 Ancona.

A cooperative backed by the farm machinery manufacturers, Pieralisi, which competes in quality with top private wineries. From 35 growers with 360 acres come Verdicchio Classico and *spumante* as well as a Rosso Cònero.

Villa Pigna

Offida, 63035 Ascoli Piceno.

Founded about 1960. Owners: Constantino and Elio Rozzi. DOC: Falerio dei Colli Ascolani, Rosso Piceno. Other: Rosato, Villa Pigna Vellutato.

With 150,000 cases from more than 600 acres of vines, Villa Pigna quickly emerged as a model large-scale estate. A modern winery was built in 1979. Rosso Piceno Superiore is almost like claret. The Vellutato *vino da tavola* from Montepulciano is even better.

Umani Ronchi

Osimo Scalo, 60028 Ancona.

Founded in 1960 by Gino Ronchi, now managed by the Bernetti brothers. DOC: Rosso Cònero, Rosso Piceno, Verdicchio dei Castelli di Jesi. Other: Rosato delle Marche, Sangiovese delle Marche, Spumante Brut. One of the best-distributed brands of the Marches, producing 233,000 cases of good-quality estate-bottled wines from 320 acres of Verdicchio and Rosso Cònero. Other wines are made from bought-in grapes. Wines are exported under the trade name Bianchi.

Villamagna

Contrada Montanello, 62100 Macerata.

Founded in the 17th century. Owner/winemaker: Valeria Giacomini Compagnucci-Compagnoni. DOC: Bianco dei Colli Maceratesi, Rosso Piceno. Other: Mosanulus and Verdicchio di Montanello. The family company built new cellars in 1973 and has since made a name for some of the finest Rosso Piceno and Verdicchio on the market. About 2,200 cases of each wine are produced from 37 acres.

OTHER PRODUCERS

Anzillotti Solazzi Bonta di Saltara, 61030 Pesaro. Owners: Guglielmo Anzilotti and Giovanni Solazzi. DOC: Bianchello del Metauro, Sangiovese dei Colli Pesaresi.

Fratelli Bisci Matelica, 64024 Macerata. The Bisci brothers occasionally make magnificent Verdicchio di Matelica.

Bucci Ostra Vetere, 60010 Ancona. Makes 4,000 cases of singular Verdicchio dei Castelli di Jesi. Giorgio Grai is the winemaker.

Castellucci Montecarotto, 60036 Ancona. Owners: Armando and Corrado Castellucci. DOC: Verdicchio dei Castelli di Jesi.

Fattoria dei Cavalieri di Benedetti Matelica, 64024 Macerata. DOC: Verdicchio di Matelica.

Attilio Fabrini

Serrapetrona, 62020 Macerata. DOC: Bianco dei Colli Maceratesi, Vernaccia di Serrapetrona *tradizionale*. Other: Pian delle Mura Rosso, Verdicchio (still and *tradizionale*).

Marchetti 60125 Ancona. DOC: Rosso Cònero.

La Monacesca Civitanova-Marche, 62012 Macerata. Owner: Casimiro Cifola. DOC: Verdicchio di Matelica. Top wines.

Moncaro Montecarotto, 60036 Ancona. Very good working cooperative with 111,000 case annual production from 1,700 acres. Verdicchio dei Castelli di Jesi and Rosso Conero.

Fattoria di Montesecco Montesecco di Pergola, 61045 Pesaro. Owner/winemaker: Massimo Schiavi. No DOC. Other: Tristo di Montesecco. A unique, complex, dry, wood-aged white from a blend of Trebbiano, Malvasia, Riesling and Pinot Grigio.

Moroder Montacuto, 60029 Ancona. Alessandro Moroder produces a good Rosso Cònero from his small estate.

Picenum (Consorzio Agrario Ascoli Piceno) 63100 Ascoli Piceno. Cooperative. DOC: Falerio dei Colli Ascolani, Rosso Piceno.

Sartarelli Poggio San Marcello, 60036 Ancona. Small family-estate that makes one of the best Verdicchios, under trade name 'Tralivio'. Also makes a botrytized Verdicchio called 'Contrada Balciana'. Giancarlo Soverchia is the winemaker.

Serenelli 60125 Ancona. Alberto Serenelli makes typical Rosso Cònero, plus a special selection known as Varano aged in small oak barrels.

Tattà Porto San Giorgio, 63017 Ascoli Piceno. Good Rosso Piceno DOC and Montepulciano *vino da tavola*.

Le Terrazze Numana, 60026 Ancona. Paolo Terni makes good Rosso Cònero. The pink *tradizionale* Donna Giulia from Montepulciano grapes is a revelation.

Le Terrazze di Roncosambaccio-Giovanetti Fano, 61032 Pesaro. Good Bianchello and Sangiovese DOC.

La Torraccia Passo Sant'Angelo, 62020 Macerata. Owner: Piero Constantini. DOC: Bianco dei Colli Maceratesi, Rosso Piceno. Other: Bianco Anitori, Cabernet, and Villa Simone Frascati.

Vallerosa-Bonci Cupramontana, 60035 Ancona. Wines: Verdicchio dei Castelli di Jesi.

Cantina Cooperative tra Produttori del Verdicchio Montecarotto, 60036 Ancona. Sound Verdicchio Classico.

Vinimar (Associazione Cantine Cooperative Marche) Camerano, 60021 Ancona. A group of cooperatives bottling and selling all the region's DOC wines under the brandname of Vinimar.

Fratelli Zaccagnini Staffolo, 60039 Ancona. Verdicchio Classico, including the single-vineyard Salmagina.

LATIUM

Rome can be compared with Vienna, as a capital city with wine so much in its veins that such artificial obstructions as bottles and corks have traditionally been foreign to it. The winemakers' taverns of Rome are slightly farther out of town than the *heurigen* of Vienna, but are even more tempting as a summer outing, maybe to the cool of the wooded Alban Hills, or perhaps to the 'Castelli Romani' south of Rome.

Frascati, the hub of the hills and their wine, has the air of a holiday resort. The spectacular Villa Aldobrandini and its beautiful gardens in the heart of Frascati show that the taste is both patrician as well as popular.

Latium, both north and south of Rome, is pock-marked with volcanic craters which are now placid lakes. The rich, volcanic soil of the region is highly suited to the cultivation of vines. The choice of grape varieties, which is presumably based on the Roman taste for soft young wines, has determined that they should remain local. The low acidity of the Malvasia, the grape that gives character to Frascati, makes it prone to disastrous oxidation once removed from storage in its cold damp cellar, necessitating the introduction of such processes as pasteurization and, more recently cold treatments, which have restored the balance of modern wines.

DOC and Other Wines

Aleatico di Gradoli DOC. Red wine. Province: Viterbo. Villages: Gradoli, Grotte di Castro, San Lorenzo Nuovo, Latera (in the hills above Lake Bolsena). Grapes: Aleatico. Max. crop: 63 hl/ha. Min. alch: 12°. Annual production: 4,400 cases.

A limited production of a local speciality: sweet red wine with a faintly Muscat aroma made at both normal strength and *liquoroso* (fortified to 17.5° alcohol).

Aprilia DOC. Red, white and *rosato* wine. Provinces: Latina and Roma. Villages: Aprilia and Nettuno. Grapes: (red) Merlot, (*rosato*) Sangiovese, (white) Trebbiano. Max. crop: Merlot 91 hl/ha; Sangiovese 84 hl/ha; Trebbiano 90 hl/ha. Annual production 220,000 cases.

A vineyard area established by refugees from Tunisia after World War II. Merlot is reckoned its best product at 2 or 3 years of age. Although one of the first DOCs the wines scarcely merit the dignity; however recent experiments in vineyards and cellars are aimed at notable improvements.

Bianco Capena DOC. White wine. Province: Roma. Villages: Capena, Fiano Romano, Morlupo, Castelnuovo di Porto. Grapes: Malvasia di Candia, del Lazio and Toscana 55%, Trebbiano Toscano, Romagnolo and Giallo 25%, Bellone and Bombino up to 20%. Max. crop: 112 hl/ha. Min. alch: 11° (*superiore* 12°). Annual production: 22,200 cases.

Similar white wine to that of the Castelli Romani (e.g. Frascati) but from just north of Rome instead of south.

Castelli Romani An umbrella (non-DOC) name for the verdant region, otherwise known as the Colli Albani, where Frascati and its peers are grown.

Cerveteri DOC. Red and white wine. Province: Roma. Villages: Cerveteri, Ladispoli, Santa Marinella, Civitavecchia, part of Allumiere, Rome, Tolfa and Tarquinia. Grapes: (red) Sangiovese and Montepulciano 60%, Cesanese Comune 25%, Canaiolo Nero, Carignano and Barbera 30%; (white) Trebbiano (Toscano, Romagnolo and Giallo) 50%, Malvasia 35%, Verdicchio, Tocai, Bellone and Bombino 15%. Max. crop: 108 hl/ha for white, 95 hl/ha for red. Min. alch: 11° for white, 12° for red. Annual production: 330,000 cases.

Standard dry wines from the country near the coast northwest of Rome. A noteworthy *cantina* (cooperative).

Cesanese del Piglio DOC. Red wine. Province: Roma. Villages: Piglio and Serrone, Acuto, Anagni and Paliano. Grapes: Cesanese di Affile and/or Cesanese Comune min. 90%; Sangiovese, Montepulciano, Barbera, Trebbiano Toscano or Bombino Bianco 10%. Max. crop: 81 hl/ha. Min. alch: 12°. Annual production: 56,000 cases.

Dry or sweet, still or sparkling red from a zone just to the left of the Autostrada del Sole, heading southeast 40 miles out of Rome, where Anagni sits on its hilltop. Another two Cesanese DOCs exist, Cesanese del Piglio and Cesanese di Affile, both are similar to Cesanese del Piglio but scarcely used. All three were made DOCs in an excess of bureaucratic enthusiasm in 1973.

Colle Picchioni Surprisingly good dry red of blended Merlot, Cesanese, Sangiovese and Montepulciano grapes, made in the traditionally white (i.e. Marino) country of the Castelli Romani. The superior Vigna del Vassallo is a Cabernet-Merlot blend.

Colli Albani DOC. White wine. Province: Roma. Villages: Ariccia and Albano, part of Rome, Pomezia and Castelgandolfo. Grapes: Malvasia Rossa (or Bianca di Candia) 60%, Trebbiano Toscano, Romagnolo, di Soave and Giallo 25–50%, Malvasia del Lazio 5–45%, Bonvino and Cacchione up to 10%. Max. crop: 115 hl/ha. Min. alch: 10.5° (*superiore* 11.5°). Annual production: 1m. cases.

The local white of the Pope's summer villa (and that of the Emperor Domitian, too, on the same superb site with views west to the sea and east down to Lake Albano). Dry or sweet, still or fizzy.

Colli Lanuvini DOC. White wine. Province: Roma. Villages: Genzano and part of Lanuvio. Grapes: Malvasia Bianca di Candia and Puntinata max. 70%, Trebbiano Toscano, Verde and Giallo 30%, Bellone and Bonvino 10%. Max. crop: 101 hl/ha. Min. alch: 11.5˚. Annual production: 278,000 cases.

A lesser-known but recommended dry white of the Castelli Romani. Genzano is on Lake Nemi, to the south of Lake Albano.

Cori DOC. White and red wine. Province: Latina. Villages: Cisterna and Cori. Grapes (white) Malvasia di Candia up to 70%; Trebbiano Toscano up to 40%; Trebbiano Giallo, Bellone up to 30%; (red) Montepulciano 40-60%, Nero Buono di Cori 20–40%, Cesanese 10–30%. Max. crop: 112 hl/ha. Min. alch: 11˚ for white, 10.5˚ for red. Annual production: 110,000 cases.

Cori is south of the Castelli Romani where the country flattens towards the Pontine marshes. The red is soft and pleasant and, along with the white, is rarely seen.

Est! Est!! Est!!! di Montefiascone DOC. White wine. Province: Viterbo. Villages: Montefiascone, Bolsena, San Lorenzo Nuovo, Grotte di Castro, Gradoli, Capodimonte and Marta. Grapes: Trebbiano Toscano 65%, Malvasia Bianca Toscana 20%, Rossetto 15%. Max. crop: 91 hl/ha. Min. alch: 11˚. Annual production: 240,000 cases.

Large quantities of unpredictable wine take advantage of this the earliest example of what is now called a fantasy name. The emphatic 'It is' was the first 3-star rating in history, antedating the Michelin guide by some 800 years. More recent inspectors have had less luck, but now modernization of techniques and taste is producing an acceptable, usually dry, white.

Falerno or Falernum The most famous wine of ancient Rome, from the borders of Latium and Campania to the south. Then sweet and concentrated, now a good strong red of Aglianico and Barbera and a pleasant low-acid white. The red has a DOC in Campania.

Fiorano The best of Rome's own wines, from one producer (*see* next page) on the ancient Appian Way south of the city. The red is a blend of Cabernet and Merlot like Bordeaux, the whites Malvasia di Candia and Sémillon. The wines are aged in wood and set a standard far above the local DOCs.

Frascati DOC. White wine. Province: Roma. Villages: Frascati, Montecompatri, Monteporzio Catone and Grottaferrata. Grapes: Malvasia Bianca di Candia and Trebbiano Toscano min. 70%, Malvasia del Lazio and Greco max. 30%. Max. crop: 105 hl/ha. Min. alch: 11˚ (*superiore* 11.5˚). Annual production: 2.1m. cases.

In legend and occasionally in fact the most memorable Italian white wine, though possibly the one that originated the notion of wines that 'do not travel', even the 20 miles to Rome. Malvasia on volcanic soil gives a splendid sensation of whole-grape ripeness, a golden glow to the wine, encouraged by fermenting it like red on its skins. The dry variety should be soft but highly charged with flavour, faintly nutty and even faintly salty. Sweeter (*amabile*) and sweeter still (*cannellino*) versions can be honeyed, too, but I would not count on it.

These are tasting notes made in a cool damp Frascati cellar. Notes on the bottled wine vary from neutral and sterile with no character to flat and oxidized to (occasionally) an approximation to the real thing. The best way to learn the difference between old-style and new-style Italian whites is to go to a restaurant in Frascati and order a bottle of a good brand, and also a jug of the house wine. Sadly the luscious qualities of the latter are the ones that do not travel. The best producers manage a very satisfactory compromise.

Marino DOC. White wine. Province: Roma. Villages: Marino and part of Rome and Castelgandolfo. Grapes: Malvasia Rossa 60%, Trebbiano Toscano, Verde and Giallo 25–55%. Malvasia del Lazio 15–45%, Bonvino and Cacchione 10%. Max. crop: 115.5 hl/ha. Min. alch: 11.5˚ (*superiore* 12.5˚). Annual production: 778,000 cases.

First cousin to Frascati, preferred by many Romans who dine out at Marino to drink it fresh and unbottled.

Merlot di Aprilia *See* Aprilia.

Montecompatri-Colonna DOC. White wine. Province: Roma. Villages: Colonna, part of Montecompatri, Zagarolo and Rocca Priora. Grapes: Malvasia 70%, Trebbiano 30%, Bellone, Bonvino 10%. Max. crop: 108 hl/ha. Min. alch: 11.5˚ (*riserva* 12.5˚). Annual production: 33,000 cases.

Another alternative to Frascati in the Castelli Romani.

Sangiovese di Aprilia A strong dry *rosato. See* Aprilia.

Torre Ercolana The highly recherché speciality of one producer (*see* Colacicchi, page 341) at Anagni (*see* Cesanese del Piglio, page 339). A red of Cesanese with Cabernet and Merlot, powerful in personality and maturing to outstanding quality.

Trebbiano di Aprilia Rather strong dull wine *see* Aprilia.

Velletri DOC. White and red wine. Province: Latina and Roma. Villages: Velletri, Lariano and part of Cisterna di Latina. Grapes: (white) Malvasia 70%, Trebbiano 30%, Bellone and Bonvino 10%; (red) Sangiovese 20–45%, Montepulciano 30–35%, Cesanese Comune 15%, Bombino Nero, Merlot and Ciliegiolo 10%. Max. crop: 104 hl/ha. Min. alch: 11.5˚ for white, 12˚ for red. Aged 2 years for *riserva*. Annual production: 560,000 cases.

South of the Frascati zone of the Castelli Romani, Velletri has a DOC for both its pleasant white and its mild red.

Zagarolo DOC. White wine. Province: Roma. Villages: Zagarolo, Gallicano. Grapes: Malvasia 70%, Trebbiano 30%. Bellone and Bonvino up to 10%. Max. crop: 108 hl/ha. Min. alch: 11.5˚ (*superiore* 12.5˚). Annual production: 4,400 cases.

The smallest producer of the Frascati group, with similar white wine.

Leading Latium Producers

Colli di Catone

Monteporzio Catone, 00040 Roma.
Antonio Pucini makes good Frascati Superiore under the Colli di Catone, Villa Catone and Villa Porzina labels. His two special versions of Frascati are both made from pure Malvasia, one, the single vineyard Colle Gaio, is made only in good years from low-yielding vines.

Cantina Colacicchi

Anagni, 03012 Frosinone.

A family winery, made famous by the late Luigi Colacicchi, now run by his nephew Bruno. No DOC. Other: Romagnano (white), Torre Ercolana (red). The splendid red of Cabernet, Merlot and Cesanese, intense, long-lived and long on the palate, is one of Italy's rarest. Only about 700 cases are made from 8 acres.

Fiorano

Divino Amore, 00134 Roma.

Founded in 1946 by Alberico Boncompagni Ludovisi, Principe di Venosa. No DOC. Other: Fiorano Bianco, Rosso. A perfectionist 5-acre estate which has proved that exceptional wine can be made in Rome. Fiorano Bianco is made of Malvasia di Candia grapes and Fiorano Rosso of Cabernet Sauvignon and Merlot. There is also a little Fiorano Sémillon. All are splendid but rare.

Fontana Candida

Monteporzio Catone, 00040 Roma.

DOC: Frascati. Part of the Gruppa Italiano Vini complex owning extensive vineyards, cellars and bottling plants in the Frascati DOC zone. The production of more than 600,000 cases includes a choice parcel of Vigneti Santa Teresa, one of the best of all Frascatis.

Cantina Produttori Frascati (San Matteo)

Frascati, 00044 Roma.

The central Frascati cooperative. DOC: Frascati. San Matteo is the label of the cooperative's selected wine sold in bottle – a reliable brand in the modern style.

Cantina Sociale Cooperative di Marino (Gotto d'Oro)

Frattocchie di Marino, 00040 Roma.

Founded: 1945. A cooperative whose members have about 2,700 acres of vines. DOC: Frascati, Marino. Other: Rosata and Rosso *Rubino* dei Castelli Romani. Winemaker Manlio Erba produces consistent quality Frascati and Marino, sold under the Gotto d'Oro label.

Paola di Mauro (Colle Picchioni)

Marino, 00040 Roma.

This small estate is run by Paulo di Mauro and son Armando. DOC: Marino. Other: Colle Picchioni Rosso. From 10 acres they produce a remarkable traditional Marino and one of Rome's rare fine reds.

Villa Simone

Monteporzio Catone, 00040 Roma.

Piero Constantini selects from 15 acres of vines to make an impressive, full-scale Frascati Superiore, including the single vineyard Vigneto Filonardi, and the rare *cannellino*.

Conte Zandotti-Tenimento San Paolo

00132 Roma.

Founded in 1734 by the Zandotti family and now run by Enrico Massimo Zandotti. Modern methods are used in the cellars carved into the vaults of an ancient Roman water cistern beneath the San Paolo villa. There are 62 acres of vines used for a superb, dry Frascati Superiore.

OTHER PRODUCERS

Cantina Sociale Colli Albani (Fontana di Papa) Cecchina, 00040 Roma. Cooperative. DOC: Colli Albani and Marino. Other: Castelli Romani, Rosato, Rosso. Bottled wine is Fontana di Papa.

Casale del Giglio Borgo Montello, 04010 Latina. DOC: Aprilia. Good Trebbiano and Merlot made from 450 acres. New varieties and training methods are being studied on an experimental genetic engineering project.

Cantina Sociale Colli del Cavaliere Aprilia, 04010 Latina. Cooperative. DOC: Aprilia. Other: Colli del Cavaliere Bianco, Rosso.

F Cenatiempo & C Formia, 04023 Latina. No DOC. Other: Cècubo, Falerno, Falernum. The modern versions of the ancient wines.

Cantina Sociale Cooperative Cerveteri Cerveteri, 00052 Roma. Large production of Cerveteri DOC.

Cantina Sociale Cesanese del Piglio Piglio, 03010 Frosinone. Sound Cesanese del Piglio DOC.

Villa Clemens Velletri, 00049 Roma. A new winery founded by the oenologist Ivo-Straffi. Exemplary Velletri Bianco and Frascati DOC and a red *vino da tavola* called Zeus.

Collefiorito Rocca Sinibalda, 02026 Rieti. Englishman Colin Fraser is proving that good wines can be made in untried places. From 12 acres he produces light appealing *vino da tavola*. A Pinot Bianco called Rigogolo and the red Nibbio from Sangiovese and Montepulciano.

Cooperativa Enotria Aprilia, 04010 Latina. A huge cooperative, members have 2,200 acres of vines. DOC: Aprilia. Other: *vini da tavola*. Aprilia Merlot, Sangiovese and Trebbiano are sold with the Enotria label.

Falesco Montefiascone, 01027 Viterbo. Good Est! Est!! Est!!!

Cantina Sociale Cooperativa Feronia Capena, 00060 Roma. Good Bianco Capena DOC.

Cantina Sociale Cooperativa Gradoli Gradoli, 01010 Viterbo. Cooperative. DOC: Aleatico di Gradoli. Other: Greghetto.

Il Marchese Frascati, 00044 Roma. Good Frascati *Superiore* from 100 acres.

Massimi Berucci Piglio, 03010 Frosinone. DOC under Casal Cervino label.

Italo Mazziotti Bolsena, 01023 Viterbo. An old family winery. DOC: Est! Est!! Est!!! di Montefiascone. Other: Bolsena Rosso. Mazziotti is a keen oenologist and grower.

Conte Moncada-Monte Giove Cecchina, 00040 Roma. Owner: Raimondo Moncada. DOC: Colli Lanuvini. A good estate wine.

Cantina di Montefiascone Montefiascone, 01027 Viterbo. Cooperative. DOC: Est! Est!! Est!!! di Montefiascone. Other: Colli Etrusco Bianco, Rosso.

Principe Pallavincini Colonna, 00030, Roma. Good Frascati *Superiore* from 136 acres and *vino da tavola* under Marmorelle label.

Cantine Sociale Cooperative San Tommaso Genzano, 00045 Roma. Good Colli Lanuvini DOC.

Cooperative La Selva Genzano, 00045 Roma. Sound Colli Lanuvini DOC.

Colli di Tuscolo Frascati, 00044 Rome. Cooperative. DOC:

Frascati. Frascati *Superiore* under the De Sanctis and Vigneti Carlo Micara labels.

Consorzio Produttori Vini Velletri Velletri, 00049 Roma. Cooperative. DOC: Velletri Bianco, Rosso. Other: Castelli Romani Rosato.

ABRUZZI

The Apennines rise to their climax in the 9,000-foot Gran Sasso d'Italia, which towers over L'Aquila ('The Eagle'), the capital of the Abruzzi. Mountains only subside close to the sea, where Pescara is the principal town. Close as it is to Rome, the Abruzzi is a backward region with simple ideas about wine, but attachment to the red Montepulciano as chief grape, is a good one. Here and in the even more rural Molise to the south this grape makes wine of vigour and style, if not refinement. Whites at present are not remarkable, but only because the Trebbiano is the standard grape.

DOC Wines

Cerasuolo *see* Montepulciano d'Abruzzo.

Montepulciano d'Abruzzo DOC. Red wine. Provinces: Chieti, Aquilia, Pescara, Teramo. Villages: many communes in the 4 provinces. Grapes: Montepulciano, plus Sangiovese up to 15%. Max. crop: 98 hl/ha. Min. alch: 12°. V*ecchio* is aged for 2 or more years. Annual production: 4.4m. cases.

The production zone for this excellent red stretches along most of the coastal foothills and back into the mountains along the valley of the River Pescara, but the most complex Montepulciano comes from the Teramo Hills in the north. Standards in this large area vary widely, but Montepulciano at its best is as satisfying, if not as subtle, as any Italian red – full of colour, life and warmth. Cerasuolo is the name for its DOC *rosato* – a pretty wine with plenty of flavour.

A recently introduced DOC sub-zone, 'Montepulciano d'Abruzzo Colline Teramane' embraces the hills in the very north of Abruzzi, and produces wines under a little more discipline: maximum crop level is 77hl/ha, minimum alchohol 12.5° for the top wines.

Trebbiano d'Abruzzo DOC. White wine. Province: throughout the Abruzzi region. Villages: suitable vineyards (not exceeding 500–600 metres) in the whole region. Grapes: Trebbiano d'Abruzzo, and or Trebbiano Toscano; Malvasia Toscana, Coccociola and Passerina up to 15%. Max. crop: 122 hl/ha. Min. alch: 11.5°. Annual production: 2.2m cases.

A standard mild dry white, except in the case of Valentini (*see* Producers).

Leading Abruzzi Producers

Emidio Pepe

Torano Nuovo, 64010 Teramo.

DOC: Montepulciano and Trebbiano d'Abruzzo. Pepe runs his family winery with almost eccentric devotion. Grapes crushed only by foot and aged entirely in bottle.

Casal Thaulero

Roseto degli Abruzzi, 64026 Teramo.

Cooperative. DOC: Montepulciano and Trebbiano d'Abruzzo.

Sound quality Montepulciano including the special bottlings of Orisetto Oro. Abbazia di Propezzano is a pure Montepulciano aged in small barrels.

Cantina Sociale di Tollo

Tollo, 66010 Chieti.

DOC: Montepulciano and Trebbiano d'Abruzzo. This large cooperative is a top cellar for quality and price.

Edoardo Valentini

Loreto Aprutino, 65014 Pescara.

DOC: Montepulciano and Trebbiano d'Abruzzo. Valentini makes artisan wine of the highest order, including a singular aged Trebbiano and a sumptuous Montepulciano.

Ciccio Zaccagnani

Bolognano, 65020 Pescara.
A small but increasingly admired estate acclaimed for fine Montepulciano Castello di Salle.

OTHER PRODUCERS

Barone Cornacchia Torano Nuovo, 64010 Teramo. Owner: Piero Cornacchia. DOC: Montepulciano and Trebbiano d'Abruzzo.

Filomusi Guelfi Tocca da Causaria, 65028. A newly emerging estate with Montepulciano of power and grace.

Lucio di Giulio (Cantalupo) Tocco di Casuria, 65028 Pescara. DOC: Montepulciano d'Abruzzo.

Dino Illuminati (Fattoria Nicò) Controguerra, 64010 Teramo. DOC: Montepulciano and Trebbiano d'Abruzzo. Also *tradizionale* Diamante d'Abruzzo.

Elio Monti Controguerra, 64010 Teramo. Elio took over from his father Antonio in 1990. Good Montepulciano DOC.

Camillo Montori Controguerra, 64010 Teramo. DOC: Montepulciano, Trebbiano d'Abruzzo.

Bosco Nestore Nocciano, 65020 Pesaro; Montepulciano.

Masciarelli Marrucina, 66010 Chieti; Montepulciano.

Nicodemi Bruno Notaresco, 64024 Teramo. Concentrated and fine Montepulciano

Tenute del Priore Colle Corvino, 65010 Pesaro; Montepulciano.

Tenuta Sant'Agnese Città Sant'Angelo, 65013 Pescara. Owner: Nunzio Acciavatti. DOC: Montepulciano.

CAMPANIA

The region of Naples and the Sorrento peninsula may have been cynical about the taste of tourists in the past, and left some of its visitors with a nasty taste in their mouths, but in many ways it is superbly adapted for wine-growing. Volcanic soils, the temperate influence of the sea and the height of its mountains give a range of excellent sites. Its own grapes have character and perform well. The red Aglianico (the name comes from Hellenico) and white Greco both refer in their names to the Greeks who presumably imported or at least adopted them in pre-Roman times. Quality wines are made at Ravello on the Sorrento peninsula, on the island of Ischia, and above all in the Irpinian Hills north of Avellino, east of Naples, where the Mastroberardino winery has done more than anyone for the reputation of the region. Good wine is still very much in a minority, but it deserves recognition.

DOC and Other Wines

Aglianico del Taburno DOC. Red and *rosato*. Province: Benevento. Villages: Monte Taburno Torrecuso and ten other communes. Grapes: Aglianico min. 85%, Piedirosso/Sciascinoso/Sangiovese up to 15%. Annual production: 44,000 cases.

Recent DOC in an area where conditions are particularly suited to Aglianico. The wines are still rarely seen.

Asprino or Asprinio A welcome refresher; sharpish, fizzy white without pretensions: Naples' universal café wine.

Capri DOC. White and red wine. Province: Naples. Area: the island of Capri. Grapes: (white) Falanghina and Greco, plus Biancolella up to 20%; (red) Piedirosso, plus others up to 20%. Max. crop: 84 hl/ha. Min. alch: 11° for white, 11.5° for red. Annual production: 5,500 cases.

A small supply of adequate dry white and a minute supply of light red to drink young are lucky enough to have this romantic name.

Cilento DOC. Red, white and *rosato*. Province: Salerno. Villages: Agropoli and 60 other communes. Grapes: (Aglianico) Aglianico; other reds up to 15%; (red) Aglianico 60–75%, Piedirosso/Primitivo 15–20%, Barbera 10–20%, other reds up to 10%; (*rosato*) Sangiovese 70–80%, Aglianico 10–15%, Primitivo/Piedirosso 10–15%; (white) Fiano, 60–65%, Trebbiano Toscano 20–30%, Greco Bianco/Malvasia Bianco 10–15%; other whites up to 10%. Maxium crop: 70hl/ha. Min alch: Aglianico 12°, Rosso 11.5°, Rosado 11°, Bianco 11°. Annual production: 5,500 cases.

Approval has been granted for types of wine including a red from Aglianico.

Falerno del Massico DOC. Red and white wine. Province: Caserta. Villages: Mondragone, Sessa Aurunca and 3 other communes. Grapes: (red) Aglianico 60–80%, Piedirosso 20–40%, Primitivo, Barbera up to 20%; (white) Falanghina. Max crop 70hl/ha. Min alch white 11°, red 12.5°. Annual production 11,000 cases.

These wines, from a new DOC, show promise. Revived in their original area, they bear little similarity to their forbears but are worth watching.

Fiano di Avellino DOC. White wine. Province: Avellino. Villages: Avellino and 25 nearby communes. Grapes: Fiano min 85%, Greco, Coda di Volpe Bianco and Trebbiano Toscano up to 15%. Max. crop: 70 hl/ha. Min. alch: 11.5°. Annual production: 44,000 cases.

One of the best white wines of the south, light yellow and nutty in scent and flavour with liveliness and length. It is also known as Apianum, a Latin reference to bees, which apparently appreciated either its flowers or grapes – or juice.

Greco di Tufo DOC. White wine. Province: Avellino. Villages: Tufo and 7 other communes. Grapes: Greco di Tufo 80–100%, Coda di Volpe Bianco up to 15%. Max. crop 70 hl/ha. Min. alch: 11.5°. Annual production: 133,000 cases.

White wine of positive character, a little neutral to smell but mouth-filling with a good 'cut' in the flavour: highly satisfactory with flavoursome food. Some bouquet develops with 2–3 years in bottle. It leads all the Campania DOCs in volume. It can also be made *spumante* (rarely seen).

Ischia DOC. Red and white wine. Province: the island of Ischia. Villages: throughout the island. Grapes: (red) Guarnaccia 50%, Piedirosso (alias Per'e Palummo) 40%, Barbera 10%; (white) Forastera 65%, Biancolella 20%, others 15%; (Bianco Superiore) Forastera 50%, Biancolella 40%, San Lunardo 10%. Max. crop: 72 hl/ha. Min. alch: 10.5° for white, 11° for red. Annual production: 33,000 cases.

The standard red and white of this green island in the Bay of Naples are made to drink young and fresh. The white should be sharp enough to quench thirst. Bianco Superiore is sometimes fermented in the old way on its skins and becomes substantial, dry, golden and rather striking. Forastera, Biancolella and Per'e Palummo grapes now have their own DOCs.

Lacrimarosa d'Irpinia A very pale coppery *rosato* of good quality, aromatic to smell, faintly underripe to taste, made of Aglianico by Mastroberardino (*see* Producers).

Per'e Palummo The alternative name of the Piedirosso grape, meaning 'dove's foot', applied to one of Ischia's best reds, refreshingly tannic and a shade 'grassy' to smell. DOC as Ischia Per'e Palummo.

Ravello Red, white and *rosato*, each good of its kind, from the terraced vineyards leading up to the ravishing hilltop town of Ravello. Sea mists, I suspect, keep the wines fresh.

Solopaca DOC: Red and white wine. Province: Benevento. Villages: Solopaca and 10 neighbouring communes. Grapes: (red) Sangiovese 45–60%, Piedirosso 20–25%, Aglianico 10–20%, Sciascinoso 10%; (white) Trebbiano Toscano 50–70%, Malvasia di Candia 20%–40%, Malvasia Toscano and Coda di Volpe 10%. Max. crop: 105 hl/ha. Min. alch: 11.5° for red, 12° for white. Annual production: 222,000 cases.

A little-known DOC zone north of Naples with decent red but rather dreary white. There are also newer *rosato*, Falanghina and Aglianico wines as well as *spumante*.

Taurasi DOCG. Red wine. Province: Avellino. Villages: Taurasi and 16 other communes in the Irpinia Hills east of Naples. Grapes: Aglianico min 80%, Piedirosso, Sangiovese and Barbera max. 30%. Max. crop: 65 hl/ha. Min. alch: 12˚. Aged for not less than 3 years (1 in wood), 4 for *riserva* (18 months in wood). Annual production: 11,000 cases.

Possibly the best red of southern Italy, at least as made by Mastroberardino (*see* Producers). Aglianico ripens late in these lofty vineyards to make a firm wine of splendidly satisfying structure, still dark in colour even when mature at 5 years. It has a slightly roasted richness without being at all port-like. First class but impossible to pin down by comparisons.

Vesuvio (Lacryma Christi) DOC. White, red and *rosato*. Province: Naples. Villages: Boscotrecase, Trecase and San Sebastiano al Vesuvio, plus part of 12 other communes in Naples. Grapes: (white) Coda di Volpe and Verdeca; (red) Piedirosso; Sciascinoso up to 50%, Aglianico up to 20%. Max. crop: 70 hl/ha. Min. alch: 11˚ for white, 10.5˚ for red and *rosato*. Lacryma Christi: (white, *rosato* and red): 65hl/ha and 12˚ min alch. Annual production: 56,000 cases.

DOC, Vesuvio applies to the basic white, *rosato* and red while Lacryma Christi del Vesuvio applies to four superior versions which are capable of ageing 3–6 years or more. The white may also be sparkling.

Leading Campania Producers

D'Ambra Vini d'Ischia

Forio d'Ischia, 80070 Napoli.
Founded in the late 19th century by Francesco d'Ambra. DOC: Ischia. Other: Amber Drops, Biancolella, Forastera, Per'e Palummo. After a lapse in the firm's quality and prestige, the late Mario d'Ambra brought about a revival, introducing a new style to Ischia DOC and to the *vino da tavola* Sparkling Kalimera, created by Andrea d'Ambria. The Amber Drops and Forastera are both well made.

Mastroberardino

Atripalda, 83042 Avellino.
Founded in 1878 as a continuation of a long-standing business; now run by Antonio Mastroberardino and son Carlo. DOC: Fiano di Avellino, Greco di Tufo, Taurasi and Vesuvio Lacryma Christi. Other: Irpinia Bianco, Rosso, Lacrimarosa d'Irpinia. From 250 acres of family-owned vines and 370 acres of others under contract, Tonino the oenologist makes 75,000 cases. Cellars were renovated and expanded after being destroyed in the earthquakes of 1980. The subsequent installation of ultramodern equipment signalled a new approach to the style of their white Fiano and Greco, now made in temperature-controlled stainless steel tanks. The Mastroberardino firm split in two in 1994: Antonio keeps the winery in Atripalda, his brother Walter looks after the vineyards. The most recent Mastroberardino label (from Walter and his sons) is 'Vignadoria-Mastroberardino', located in Montefusco (Avellino province). So far Vignadoria seems superior to the Mastroberardino wines.

Molise

Molise, a slice of central Italy stretching from the Apennines to the Adriatic, is a newcomer to Italy's wine map. Bottles with labels on are a relative novelty in a land of bulk production.

The first Molise DOCs date from 1983. They are Biferno, for red and white wine from 42 communes in Campobasso province and Pentro, for red and white wines from 16 communes in the hills around Isernia. Both specify Montepulciano for red, in Biferno it is the dominant variety, in Pentro it is used half and half with Sangiovese. Both whites are based on Trebbiano Toscano. Both allow the addition of Bombino, in Biferno Malvasia Bianco may also be added.

One outstanding Molise winery, and one of the most modern in Italy, is:

Masseria di Majo Norante-Ramitello (Campomarino, 86023 Campobasso). Owned by Luigi di Majo, the property is managed by his son Alessio. His Montepulciano is as good as the best of Abruzzo, and Ramitello is a bargain in tasty everyday reds. He also makes Trebbiano del Molise, *rosato* and Frizzante.

Other Molise producers include:

Cantina Cooperativa Valbiferno Guglionesi, 86024 Campobasso. Biferno DOC and *vini da tavola* Bianco and Rosso di Molise, Valbiferno. The region's largest winery, processing some 8m. litres a year.

VI.TA-Viticoltori del Tappino Gambatesa, 86013 Campobasso. Biferno DOC with the Serra Meccaglia and Rocca del Falco brands, as well as Vernaccia di Serra Meccaglia white and other *vini da tavola* and *spumante*.

OTHER PRODUCERS

P Caruso Ravello, 84010 Sorrento. Founded: 1896; owned by the Caruso family. No DOC wine. Other: Gran Caruso Ravello Bianco, Rosato, Rosso. Well-made red and a 'fish' white of style.

CS del Cilento Rutino, 84070 Salerno. Cilento DOC.

Cantine Episcopio-Pasquale Vuilleumier Ravello, 84010 Salerno. Founded: 1860; owned by the Vuilleumier family. No DOC. Other: Episcopio Ravello Bianco, Rosato, Rosso.

D'Antiche Terre Vega Manocalzati, 83030 Avellino. Especially good Greco and Fiano.

Di Meo Salza Irpinia, 83050 Avellino. Improving Greco and Fiano wines.

La Guardiense Guardia Sanframondi, 82034 Benevento. Large producer of Solopaca DOC, *vini da tavola* and *spumante* from growers with almost 3,700 acres of vines.

Villa Matilde Cellole, 81030 Caserta. Very good Falerno del Massico DOC and *vino da tavola*.

Michele Moio Mondragone, 81034 Caserta. Substantial Primitivo will come under Falerno del Massico DOC.

Mustilli Sant'Agata dei Goti, 82019 Benevento. Good *vini da tavola* from typical Campania varieties. Aglianico matches Falanghina and Greco.

Perrazzo Vini d'Ischia Ischia Porto, 80077 Napoli. Founded in 1880 by Don Alfonso Perrazzo. DOC: Ischia. Other: Don Alfonso Bianco, Rosato, Rosso. The Ischia Bianco *Superiore* is noteworthy.

Giovanni Struzziero Venticano, 83030 Avellino. The Fiano, Greco and especially Taurasi DOC can be impressive from this emerging winemaker.

Antica Masseria Venditti Castelvenere, 82030 Benevento. The quality of Solopaca DOC and red and white *vini da*

tavola has improved in recent years and continues to do so.

Vignadoria-Mastroberardino Montefusco, 83030 Avellino. Recent label from Mastroberardino, producing some impressive Fiano and Greco and other DOC-wines from Avellino (*see* Producers, page 344).

APULIA

The heel and hamstrings of Italy are its most productive wine regions. Their historic role has been to supply strength and colour for more famous but frail wines in blending vats farther north. The reds are very red indeed, very strong and often inclined to portiness. The whites are the faceless background to vermouth. This is the one region where the best wines until recently were the rosés – or at least some of them.

The Salento Peninsula, the heel from Taranto south-eastwards, is the hottest region. A few producers here are learning to moderate the strength and density of their reds to make good-quality winter-warming wines – though a bottle still goes a long way. Their grapes are the Primitivo (possibly California's Zinfandel) and the Negroamaro – 'bitter black'.

North of Taranto the hills have well-established DOCs for dry whites, originally intended as vermouth base-wines, but with modern techniques increasingly drinkable as 'fish' wines in their own right. As elsewhere in Italy the existence of a DOC is better evidence of tradition than of quality. There is more interest in the fact that even in this intemperate region successful spots have recently been found to plant superior northern grapes – even Chardonnay (*see* under Apulia Producers).

Much the best-known DOC is Castel del Monte, and this is largely due to the crisp *rosato* of Rivera – which has been for many years one of Italy's best. The list of producers shows that things are changing: Apulian reds are no longer ashamed of their origin.

DOC and Other Wines

Aleatico di Puglia DOC. Red wine. Provinces: Bari, Brindisi, Foggia, Lecce, Taranto. Area: the whole of Apulia. Grapes: Aleatico 85%, Negroamaro, Malvasia Nera and Primitivo 15%. Max. crop: 52 hl/ha. Min. alch: 13° plus 2° of sugar for *dolce naturale*; 16° plus 2.5° of sugar for *liquoroso*. Aged 3 years for *riserva*. No production since 1992.

A dessert wine, approaching ruby port in its fortified (*liquoroso*) version. Small supply, and of local interest only.

Alezio DOC. Red and *rosato* wine. Province: Lecce. Villages: Alezio, Sannicola, plus parts of Gallipoli and Tuglie. Grapes: Negroamaro, plus Malvasia Nera di Lecce, Sangiovese and Montepulciano up to 20%. Max. crop: (red) 98 hl/ha; (*rosato*) 49 hl/ha. Min. alch: 12°. Annual production: 111,000 cases.

A DOC for the red and *rosato* of the tip of Italy's heel, made from Negroamaro and Malvasia Nera and every inch a southern red, dark and powerful. It is moot whether to try ageing it or to take it on the chin as it is. Like many Apulian *rosatos* the paler wine has more immediate appeal.

Brindisi DOC. Red and *rosato* wine. Province: Brindisi. Villages: Brindisi and Mesagna, just inland. Grapes: Negroamaro, others up to 30%. Max. crop: 105 hl/ha. Min. alch: 12° (12.5° and 2 years' ageing for *riserva*). Annual production 28,000 cases.

The local red of Brindisi can age for 5–10 years or more. Also makes a pleasant *rosato*. There is one outstanding example of Brindisi DOC: the 'Patriglione' from Cosimo Taurino (*see* producers).

Cacc'e Mmitte di Lucera DOC. Red wine. Province: Foggia. Villages: communes of Lucera, Troia and Biccari. Grapes: Uva di Troia 35–65%, Montepulciano, Sangiovese and Malvasia Nera 25–35%, others 15–30%. Max. crop: 91 hl/ha.

Min. alch: 11.5°. Annual production 38,900 cases.

Scholars tell us that the dialect name refers to a local form of '*governo*', in which fresh grapes are added to the fermenting must.

Castel del Monte DOC. Red, *rosato* and white wine. Province: Bari. Villages: Minervino Murge and parts of nine other communes. Grapes: Bianco (Pampanuto and/or Chardonnay and/or Bombino Bianco), Rosso (Uva di Troia and/or Aglianico and/or Montepulciano) Rosato (Bombino Nero and/or Aglianico and/or Uva di Troia), Chardonnay, Sauvignon, Pinot Bianco, Bianco da Pinot Nero, Aglianico Rosso and Aglianico Rosato. Max. crop: 95 hl/ha. Min. alch. varies between 10.5° for the whites and 12° for the reds. Annual production: 444,000 cases.

Castel del Monte, the octagonal fortress of the medieval Hohenstaufens, lies 30 miles west of Bari near Minervino Murge. The leading DOC of Apulia deserves its name for an outstanding red and famous *rosato*. The red has a fat, inviting smell and considerable depth and vitality, with a certain bite and long pruney finish. Rivera's Il Falcone is the best example. The pale *rosato* has long been popular all over Italy for balanced force and freshness.

Copertino DOC. Red wine. Province: Lecce. Villages: Copertino and five other communes. Grapes: Negroamaro, plus others up to 30%. Max. crop: 98 hl/ha. Min. alch: 12° (12.5° and 2 years' ageing for *riserva*). Annual production 77,800 cases.

A warmly recommended red made in some quantity south of Lecce on Italy's heel. The *riserva* is said to be smooth with plenty of flavour and a bitter touch.

Five Roses A powerful dry *rosato* from Leone de Castris (*see* Producers), so named by American soldiers who gave it one more rose than a famous Bourbon whiskey.

Gioia del Colle DOC. Red, white and *rosato* wine. Province: Bari. Villages: Gioia del Colle and 15 neighbouring communes. Grapes: Aleatico, Trebbiano Toscano, Primitivo, Montepulciano, Sangiovese and others. Annual production: 16,700 cases.

Gioia is halfway from Bari south to Taranto. The Primitivo gives a pretty brutal red in these hot hills. With age it becomes more politely overwhelming.

Gravina DOC. White wine. Province: Bari. Village: Commune of Gravina and parts of Altamura and Spinazzola. Grapes: Malvasia del Chianti 40–65%, Greco di Tufo and Bianco d'Alessano 35–60%. Max. crop: 105 hl/ha. Min. alch: 11°. Annual production: 22,000 cases.

Dry white from around Gravina. A *spumante* is also permitted.

Leverano DOC. Red, *rosato*, white wine. Province: Lecce. Villages: commune of Leverano. Grapes: (red and *rosato*) Negroamaro, plus others up to 35%; (white) Malvasia Bianco, plus others up to 35%. Max. crop: 67 hl/ha. Min. alch: white 11°, *rosato* 11.5°, red 12° (12.5° aged 2 years is *riserva*). Annual production: 50,000 cases.

One of the 1980 class of DOCs for Salento wines. The red and the *rosato* stand with Salento's finest.

Lizzano DOC. Red, white and *rosato* wine. Province: Taranto. Villages: communes of Lizzano, Faggiano and part of Taranto. Grapes: (red and *rosato*) Negroamaro 60–80%, Montepulciano, Sangiovese, Bombino Nero, Pinot Nero max. 40%, Malvasia Nera di Brindisi or Lecce max. 10%; (white) Trebbiano Toscano 40–60%, Chardonnay, Pinot Bianco min. 30%, Sauvignon, Bianco di Alessano max. 25%, Malvasia Bianca Lugna max. 10%. Max. crop: red 98 hl/ha, *rosato* 91 hl/ha, white 104 hl/ha. Min. alch: 10.5° for white, 11.5° for red and *rosato*. Malvasia Nera and Negroamara Rosso can also be *superiore* at 13°. Annual production: 22,000 cases.

Latest Salento DOC with six new, but as yet untried, wines.

Locorotondo DOC. White wine. Provinces: Bari and Brindisi. Villages: Locorotondo, Cisternino and part of Fasano. Grapes: Verdeca 50–65%; Bianco di Alessano 35–50%; Fiano, Bombino, Malvasia Toscana 5%. Max. crop: 91 hl/ha. Min. alch: 11°. Annual production: 278,000 cases.

Locorotondo is famous for its round stone dwellings. With Martina Franca it lies east of Bari at the neck of the Salento peninsula. Serious efforts are made to keep its white wine fresh and brisk.

Martina or Martina Franca

DOC. White wine. Provinces: Taranto, Bari and Brindisi. Villages: Martina Franca and Alberobello, and part of Ceglie, Messapico and Ostuni. Grapes: Verdeca 50–65%, Bianco di Alessano 35–50%, Fiano, Bombino and Malvasia Toscana 5%. Max. crop: 91 hl/ha. Min. alch: 11°. Annual production: 111,000 cases.

Grapes and wine amount to much the same thing as Locorotondo.

Matino DOC. *Rosato* and red wine. Province: Lecce. Villages: Matino and part of seven other communes in the Murge Salentino, at the tip of Italy's heel. Grapes:

Negroamaro 70%, Sangiovese and Malvasia Nera 30%. Max. crop: *rosato* 78 hl/ha, red 84 hl/ha. Min. alch: 11.5° for *rosato* and red. Annual production 16,700 cases.

An early (1971) DOC but still obscure.

Moscato di Trani DOC. White wine. Provinces: Bari and Foggia. Villages: Trani and 11 other communes. Grapes: Moscato di Trani (or 'Reale'), plus other Muscats up to 15%. Max. crop: 58 hl/ha. Min. alch: 13° plus 2° of sugar for *dolce naturale*, 16° plus 2° of sugar for *liquoroso*. Annual production: 2,780 cases.

Sweet golden dessert Muscats of good quality, fortified or not, from the north coast west of Bari. Other Apulian Muscats, particularly those of Salento, can also be very drinkable.

Nardò DOC. Red and *rosato* wine. Province: Lecce. Villages: Nardò and Porto Cesarco. Grapes: Negroamaro and Malvasia Nera. Annual production: 5,500 cases.

Recent DOC for red and *rosato* wines. The red is best after 3–6 years.

Orta Nova DOC. Red and *rosato* wine. Province: Foggia. Villages: Orta Nova, Ordona and parts of Ascoli Satriano, Carapelle, Foggia and Manfredonia. Max. crop: red 105 hl/ha, *rosato* 97.5 hl/ha. Min. alch: 12° for red, 11.5° for *rosato*. Annual production: 1,600 cases.

A DOC for red and *rosato* wines grown at Orta Nova.

Ostuni and Ottavianello di Ostuni DOC. White and red wine. Province: Brindisi. Villages: Ostuni, Carovigno, S. Vito dei Normanni, S. Michele Salentino and part of three other communes, including Brindisi. Grapes: (white) Impigno 50–85%, Francavilla 15–50%, Bianco di Alessano and Verdeca 10%; Ottavianello: four others up to 15%. Max. crop: 77 hl/ha. Min. alch: 11° for Ostuni, 11.5° for Ottavianello. Annual production: 33,300 3,300 cases.

The unusual white grapes give a very pale mild and dry 'fish' wine; Ottavianello is a cheerful cherry-red dry wine, pleasant to drink cool.

Primitivo di Manduria DOC. Red wine. Provinces: Taranto, Brindisi. Villages: Manduria and 15 other communes along the south Salento coast. Grape: Primitivo. Max. crop: 63 hl/ha. Min. alch: 14° for Primitivo di Manduria; 13° plus 3° of sugar for *dolce naturale*, 16° plus 1.5° of sugar for *liquoroso dolce naturale*; 15° plus 2.5° of sugar for *liquoroso secco*. Aged 2 years for *liquoroso* types. Annual production: 16,670 cases.

The Primitivo grape variety, which may well be the same as California's Zinfandel, makes blackstrap reds here, some sweet and some even fortified, as though 14° were not enough in the first place. You may age them or not, depending on whether you appreciate full-fruit flavour or just full flavour.

Rosato del Salento *Rosatos* are perhaps the best general produce of the Salento peninsula. It is not a DOC but this name is widely used.

Rosso Barletta DOC. Red wine. Province: Bari and Foggia. Villages: Barletta and four other communes. Grapes: Uva di Troia, plus others up to 30%. Max. crop: 105 hl/ha. Min. alch: 12°. 'Invecchiato' if aged for 2 years. Annual production: 5,500 cases.

Some drink this relatively light red young and cool – others age it moderately and treat it like claret.

Rosso Canosa DOC. Red wine. Province: Bari. Village: Canosa di Puglia. Grapes: Uva di Troia 65%, others 35%. Max. crop: 98 hl/ha. Min. alch: 12° (13° plus 2 years' ageing for *riserva*). Annual production: 3,300 cases.

Canosa, between Bari and Foggia, was the Roman Canusium (an alternative name for the wine). Its wine is in a similar style to Rosso Barletta.

Rosso di Cerignola DOC. Red wine. Province: Bari. Villages: Cerignola, Stornara, Stornarella, part of Ascoli Satriano (east of Foggia). Grapes: Uva di Troia 55%, Negroamaro 15–30%, Sangiovese, Barbera, Montepulciano, Malbec and Trebbiano Toscano 15%. Max. crop: 98 hl/ha. Min. alch: 12° (13° aged 2 years in wood is *riserva*). No longer producing.

A big dry heady red with faint bitterness.

Salice Salentino DOC. Red and *rosato* wine. Provinces: Brindisi and Lecce. Villages: Salice Salentino and six other communes in the centre of the Salento peninsula. Max crop: Salice Salentino Aleatico 70hl/ha, all others 84 hl/ha. Wines: red and *rosado*: up to 80% Negroamaro (min. alch. 12° for red, 11.5° *rosado*), Aleatico: min. 85% Aleatico (*dolce* 15°, *liquoroso* 18.5°), white: up to 70% Chardonnay (min. alch: 11°), Pinot Bianco: up to 85% Pinot Bianco (min. alch: 10.5%). Annual production: 167,000 cases.

Typically big-scale southern reds which have a porty undertone accompanied by a balancing measure of astringency. I have found this to be a rather clumsy wine, but I am prepared to believe I have been unlucky – other Salento reds are often nicely balanced with an attractively clean finish. The *rosatos* can be fresh and flowery and complex with time and are among the most distinctive of Italian rosés.

San Severo DOC. White, red and *rosato* wine. Province: Foggia. Villages: San Severo, Torremaggiore, San Paolo Civitate and part of five other communes north of Foggia. Grapes: (white) Bombino Bianco and Trebbiano Toscano 40–60%, Malvasia Bianca and Verdeca up to 20%; (red and *rosato*) Montepulciano di Abruzzo 70–100% plus Sangiovese up to 30%. Max. crop: white 98 hl/ha red and *rosato* 84 hl/ha. Min. alch: 11° for white, 11.5° for red and *rosato*. Annual production: 555,600 cases.

Inoffensive wines of no special qualities but offering good value for money.

Squinzano DOC. Red and *rosato* wine. Province: Lecce. Villages: Squinzano and eight others. Grapes: Negroamaro plus 30% others. Max. crop: red 98 hl/ha, *rosato* 42 hl/ha. Min. alch: 12.5° (13° aged 2 years is *riserva*). Annual production: 55,600 cases.

Salento wines of moderate quality. The *rosato* is much less tiring to drink than the red.

Torre Quarto A notable individual estate at Cerignola east of Foggia. It is setting itself high standards for a red wine produced from a blend of Malbec, Uva di Troia and Negroamaro, which is intended for long ageing. Its purchase by ERSAP, the regional development board, has left the estate's future uncertain.

Leading Apulia Producers

Leone de Castris

Salice Salentino, 73015 Lecce.

The ancient estate of the Leone de Castris family, which has a large ultramodern winery, is now directed by Salvatore Leone de Castris. DOC: Locorotondo, Salice Salentino. Other: Albino, Blhiss Frizzante, Five Roses, Il Medaglione, Negrino, Primofiore, Rosato and Rosso del Salento, Spumanti, Ursi, Vini Novelli. Since 1929 the estate of 1,000 acres has bottled some of its (and Apulia's) best wine; rich and heady but not gross reds and (among others) Italy's first bottled *rosato*, Five Roses. 80% of their grapes are estate-grown and potential production is more than 1m. cases.

Cantina Sociale Cooperativa di Locorotondo

Locorotondo, 70010 Bari.

Founded: 1932. A cooperative grouping of 1,300 growers producing 1.3m. cases. DOC: Locorotondo. Other: Rosso Rubino, Rose de Rosé. Locorotondo DOC is selected and aged briefly in barrels into an impressive, crisp, but by no means neutral, white wine.

Rivera

Andria, 70031 Bari.

Founded by the De Corato family in the locality of Rivera. Bottling began in the early 1950s. Gancia have acquired half-ownership. Winemaker: Carlo De Corato. DOC: Castel del Monte, Locorotondo, Moscato di Trani. Rivera makes about 90,000 cases of Castel del Monte from family vineyards and grapes from regular suppliers. The popularity of the lively *rosato* overshadows the quality of Il Falcone Riserva, one of Apulia's best-constructed reds. Since the collaboration with Gancia, De Corato has broken new ground with varietal *vini da tavola* from Pinot, Sauvignon and Aglianico under the Vigna al Monte trademark.

Rosa del Golfo

Alezio, 73011 Lecce.

The Calò family has been selling wine from its estate near Gallipoli since 1938. No DOC. Other: Portulano (Rosso del Salento), Rosa del Golfo (Rosato del Salento). Family and neighbouring vineyards produce wines of consistent class, two-thirds of it Rosa del Golfo, one of Italy's most limpid and lovely *rosatos*.

Cosimo Taurino

Guagnano, 73010 Lecce.

Cosimo Taurino is a skilled winemaker who with oenologist Severino Garofano, makes admirable Brindisi and Salice Salentino DOC. Other: Notarpanaro and Chardonnay.

Tenuta di Torrebianco

Andria, 70031 Bari.

A new estate owned by Gancia with Giorgio Grai as consultant winemaker. It has made its debut with Preludio No. 1, a Chardonnay *vino da tavola*. Sauvignon Blanc, Pinot Bianco, Pinot Nero and Aglianico have also been planted.

Agricole Vallone

72100 Brindisi.

A 350-acre estate owned by Vittoria and Maria Teresa Vallone. They produce fine Brindisi and Salice Salentino DOCs from the Vigna del Salento, and other *vini da tavola*.

OTHER PRODUCERS

Cantina Sociale Cooperativa Alberobello Alberobello, 70011 Bari. DOC; Martina Franca.

Barone Bacile di Castiglione 73100 Lecce. Owner: Fabio Bacile di Castiglione. DOC: Copertino.

Cantina Sociale di Barletta Barletta, 70051 Bari. Cooperative. DOC: Rosso Barletta.

Borgo Canale Selva di Fasano, 72015 Brindisi. Good Locorotondo and Martina Franca DOCs. Also *vini da tavola*.

Felice Botta Trani, 70059 Bari. DOC: Aleatico di Puglia, Castel del Monte, Moscato di Trani.

Michele Calo & Figli Tuglie, 73058 Lecce. Alezio DOC and Salento *vini da tavola*.

Francesco Candido Sandonaci, 72025 Brindisi. DOC: Aleatico di Puglia, Salice Salentino. Other: Bianco, Rosato and Rosso del Salento.

Chiddo Vini Bitonto, 70032 Bari. DOC: Castel del Monte.

Niccolò Coppola Alezio, 73011 Lecce. A family estate since 1460, now run by Carlo and Lucio Coppola. No DOC. Other: Alezio, *rosato*, red.

Cantina Sociale di Copertino Copertino, 73043 Lecce. The best coop of Salento with a huge production including good Copertino DOC.

Distante Vini Cisternino, 72014 Brindisi. DOC: Locorotondo. Other: Negroamaro, Rosato and Rosso del Salento.

Favonio Attilio Simonini 71100 Foggia. No DOC. Many attractive wines.

Lippolis Alberobello, 70011 Bari. DOC: Aleatico di Puglia, Martina Franca.

Gennaro Marasciuolo Trani, 70059 Bari. DOC: Castel del Monte, Moscato di Trani.

Miali Martina Franca, 74015 Taranto. DOC: Martina Franca. Other: Aglianico dei Colli Lucani, Apulia, Rosato.

Fratelli Nugnes Trani, 70059 Bari. Small production of refined Moscato di Trani Dolce Naturale.

Santa Lucia Corato, 70033 Bari. Emerging estate with Castel del Monte DOC.

Giovanni Soloperto Manduria, 74024 Taranto. DOC: Primitivo di Manduria. Other: Bianco, Rosato and Rosso del Salento.

Cantine D'Alfonso del Sordo San Severo, 71016 Foggia. DOC: San Severo.

Cantina Sociale Svevo Lucera, 71036 Foggia. DOC: Cacc'e Mmitte di Lucera.

Torre Quarto Cerignola, 71042 Foggia. DOC: Rosso di Cerignola. Other: Torre Quarto Bianco, Rosato, Rosso. Torre Quarto in central Apulia was once one of Italy's greatest estates.

Conti Zecca Leverano, 73043 Lecce. Owner: A. Zecca. DOC: Leverano. Other: Donna Marzia Bianco, Rosso. The rich red and agreeable white are among the most admired wines of Salento.

CALABRIA

The vast mountainous peninsula that forms the toe of Italy has no famous wines, unless Cirò, with its athletic reputation, can be so called. The local red grape is the Gaglioppo, a variety of deep colour and potentially very high alcohol, but the spots where it is grown to best effect are (with the exception of Cirò) high enough in the Calabrian Hills to cool its fiery temper.

The local grape for white wines is the Greco, which is used in the extreme south at Gerace to make a very good dessert wine which has the ability to age well and which goes for a high price.

With little established winemaking except of the most primitive kind, Calabria, like Sicily, is modernizing in a hurry. Its DOCs, though little known, represent wines that meet up-to-date criteria.

DOC and Other Wines

Cirò DOC. Red, white and *rosato* wine. Province: Catanzaro. Villages: Cirò, Cirò Marina, part of Melissa and Crucoli. Grapes: (red and *rosato*) Gaglioppo, plus 5% Trebbiano Toscano and Greco Bianco; (white) Greco Bianco and up to a maximum of 10% Trebbiano Toscano. Max. crop: (red and *rosato)* 80hl/ha (white) 97hl/ha. Min.

alch: 12.5° for red and *rosato*, 11° for white. Aged for three years for the *riserva* (which is red only). Annual production: 556,000 cases.

Bruno Roncarati, himself an athlete, tells us that the Italian Olympic team maintain a 2,500-year-old tradition by training on this blockbuster of a wine from the heel of the toe of Italy. Red Cirò is certainly a full diet, but a soporific rather than a stimulating one. Earlier picking and new cellar techniques have reduced its tendency to oxidize though only the *riserva* can be aged beyond 3–4 years. White Cirò, as modernized, is a decent standard dry white to drink young.

Donnici DOC. Red and *rosato* wine. Province: Cosenza. Villages: 10 around and including Cosenza. Grapes: Gaglioppo 60–90%, Greco Nero 10–20%, Malvasia Bianca, Montonico Bianco and Percorella 20%. Max. crop: 84 hl/ha. Min. alch: 12°. Annual production: 4,400 cases.

A relatively light and fruity red to drink young and fairly cool, from the central western coastal hills of Calabria.

Greco di Bianco DOC. White wine. Province: Reggio Calabria. Villages: Bianco and part of Casignana. Grapes: Greco plus other whites up to 5%. Max. crop: 45 hl/ha. Min. alch: 14° plus 3° of sugar. Aged 1 year. Annual production: 2,200 cases.

A smooth, juicy and intriguingly orange-scented sweet dessert wine made of Greco grapes at Bianco, where a few small vineyards make it their speciality. Bianco is on the south coast of the extreme toe of Italy. More vineyards are expanding production. Bianco also produces a drier, more lemony, barrel-aged dessert or apéritif white called (after its grapes) Mantonico.

Lamezia DOC. Red, white and *rosato* wine. Province: Catanzaro. Villages: Part of 10 communes around Lamezia Terme. Grapes: (red and *rosato*) Nerello Mascalese and Nerello Cappuccio (either separately or together) up to 30–50%, Gaglioppo (known locally as Magliocco) 25–35%, Greco Nero (locally called Marsigliana) 25–35%, other varieties up to 20%; Bianco: Greco up to 50%, Trebbiano Toscana up to 40%, Malvasia 20% and more, others up to 30%; Greco: Greco min. 85%, others up to 15%. Max. crop: 77hl/ha. Min. alch: 12° (*rosato* 11.5°). Annual production: 5,500 cases.

A straightforward, fairly pale dry red from around the gulf of St Eufemia on the west coast. Drink it young and cool. Lametina is the name of the local non-DOC sweet or dry white.

Melissa DOC. White and red wine. Province: Catanzaro. Villages: Melissa and 13 other communes. Grapes: (white) Greco Bianco 80–95%, Trebbiano Toscana and Malvasia Bianca 5–25%; (red) Gaglioppo 75–95%, Greco Nero, Greco Bianco, Trebbiano Toscana, Malvasia Bianca 5–25%. Max. crop: 84 hl/ha. Min. alch: 11.5° for white, 12.5° for red. Aged for two years for *superiore* (red only). Annual production 33,000 cases.

The light, yellow, dry seafood wine of the heel of the toe of Italy, around the port of Crotone. The wines resemble Cirò but don't match it for quality. Most of it is drunk locally where it represents good value.

Pellaro Powerful but light red or pink wines of imported Alicante vines grown on the Pellaro peninsula in the extreme south.

Pollino DOC. Red wine. Province: Cosenza. Villages: Castrovillari, St. Basile, Sarancena, Cassano Ionio, Civita and Frascineto. Grapes: Gaglioppo 60–80%. Greco Nero max. 40%, Malvasia Bianca, Montonico Bianco, Guarnaccia Bianco max. 20%. Max crop: 77 hl/ha. Min. alch: 12°. *superiore* must be aged for two years. Annual production: 8,800 cases.

Monte Pollino is a 7,000-foot peak that divides northern Calabria from Basilicata. Its slopes produce a pale but powerful red.

Sant'Anna di Isola Capo Rizzuto DOC. Red and *rosato* wine. Province: Catanzaro. Villages: Capo Rizzuto and parts of the communes of Crotone and Cutro. Grapes: Gaglioppo 40–60%, Nocera, Nerello Mascalese, Nerelo Cappuccio 40–60%, Malvasia, Bianca and Greco up to 35%. Max. crop: 84 hl/ha. Min. alch: 12°. No longer producing.

A pale red/*rosato* to drink young and cool, from the easternmost cape (not an island) of the Calabrian coast.

Savuto DOC. Red wine. Provinces: Cosenza and Catanzaro. Villages: 14 communes in Cosenza and 6 in Catanzaro.

Grapes: Gaglioppo 35–45%, Greco Nero, Nerello, Cappuccio, Maglicco Canino, Sangiovese max. 10%, and up to 25% Malvasia Bianca and Pecorino. Max. crop: 77 hl/ha. Min. alch: 12°. Aged for at least 2 years for *superiore*. Annual production: 1,670 cases.

A recommended red of moderate strength and some fragrance. Worth choosing the *superiore*.

Squillace A locally popular fresh medium-dry white of Greco Bianco and Malvasia. Squillace is south of Catanzaro.

Leading Calabria Producers

CACIB (Cooperativa Agricola Calabro Ionica Bianchese)

Bianco, 89032 Reggio Calabria.
DOC: Greco di Bianco. Other: Mantonico del Bianco.

Caparra & Siciliani

Cirò Marina, 88072 Catanzaro.
Founded: 1963. DOC: Cirò. A major Cirò producer. From 445 acres, potential production is 110,000 cases, but careful selection reduces the numbers.

Fratelli Caruso

88063 Catanzaro Lido.
DOC: Cirò. Other: Villa Santelia Bianco.

Umberto Ceratti

Caraffa del Bianco, 89030 Reggio Calabria.
DOC: Greco di Bianco. Other: Mantonico di Bianco. Minute production of the best dessert white of the south. (Mantonico is an apéritif.)

Enotria Produttori Agricoli Associati

Cirò Marina, 88072 Catanzaro.
Cooperative with 70 growers. DOC: Cirò.

Vincenzo Ippolito

Cirò Marina, 88072 Catanzaro.
Founded: 1845. Now run by Antonio and Salvatore Ippolito. DOC: Cirò. Potentially 60,000 cases, including a fine white Cirò, from 173 acres.

Cantine Lamezia Lento

Lamezia Terme, 88046 Catanzaro.
DOC: Lamezia. Also *Vini da tavola*.

Librandi

Cirò Marina, 88072 Catanzaro.
Founded in 1950 by Antonio Cataldo Librandi. DOC: Cirò. Under the supervision of winemaker Severino Garofano, Librandi makes traditional Cirò using modern techniques (Riserva Duca Sanfelice); the non-DOC blended wine called Gravello, made with Cabernet/Gaglioppo, is outstanding.

Ferdinando Messinò

Bianco, 89032 Reggio Calabria.

This is a tiny estate producing non-DOC Greco di Gerace, the finest wine in Bianco. Ferdinando Messionò also makes some Mantonico di Bianco.

Aloisio Nicodemo

Cirò Marina, 88072 Catanzaro.
DOC: Cirò.

Giovanni Battista Odoardi

Nocera Terinese, 88047 Cantanzaro.
Progressive winery with 150 acres of vines. DOC: Savuto. *Vini da tavola*: Scavigna red, white and *rosato*, interesting sweet Moscato called Valeo. Good potential.

Cantina Sociale Vini di Pollino

Castrovillari, 87012 Cosenza. Cooperative.
DOC: Pollino.

Fattoria San Francesco

Cirò, 88071 Catanzaro.
Owners: the Siciliani family are trying hard with their admired Cirò DOC red, white and *rosato*.

Cantina Sociale Vini del Savuto (Giambattista Longo)

Savuto di Cleto, 87030 Cosenza. Cooperative.
DOC: Savuto. Also *Vini da tavola*.

BASILICATA

This mountainous region of the central south, almost entirely landlocked and chronically poor, would not feature on the wine list at all were it not for its romantically named Aglianico del Vulture, a close relation of Taurasi and one of the best reds of southern Italy.

Aglianico dei Colli Lucani A worthwhile red, from the Apulia side of Basilicata. It is worth tasting any wine made from this grape.

Aglianico del Vulture DOC. Red wine. Province: Potenza. Villages: 15 communes north of Potenza. Grape: Aglianico.

Leading Basilicata Producers

Donato Botte

Barile, 85022 Potenza.
DOC: Aglianico. Other: Moscato.

Giuseppe Botte

Barile, 85022 Potenza.
DOC: Aglianico.

Fratelli d'Angelo

Rionero, 85028 Potenza.
Founded: 1944. Directors: Donato (oenologist) and Lucio d'Angelo. DOC: Aglianico del Vulture. Other: Malvasia and Moscato del Vulture (both sparkling). Basilicata's leading winery. The brothers make 13–15,000 cases a year of Aglianico from grapes bought in from high-altitude sites; they have also started developing an estate.

Armando Martino

Rionero, 85028 Potenza. DOC: Aglianico del Vulture. Other: Malvasia and Moscato del Vulture *spumante*.

Max. crop: 70 hl/ha. Min. alch: 11.5°. Average production: 111,000 cases. Aged 3 years, 2 in wood, is *vecchio*. Aged 5 years, 2 in wood, is *riserva*.

Monte Vulture, an extinct volcano, lies right in the extreme north of Basilicata, not far from the Iripinia Mountains where Campania's splendid Taurasi is made. The same grapes grown at high altitudes on volcanic soil give a well-balanced red wine of firm structure, which is sometimes offered as a young, sweet, sparkler, but more often as a matured red with real quality and character.

Fratelli Napolitano

Rionero, 85028 Potenza.
DOC: Aglianico del Vulture. Other: Malvasia and Moscato.

Paternoster

Barile, 85022 Potenza.
DOC: Aglianico del Vulture. Other: Malvasia and Moscato del Vulture and *spumante*.

Francesco Sasso

Rionero, 85028 Potenza.
DOC: Aglianico. Other: Malvasia.

Società Cooperativa Vinicola del Vulture

Rionero, 85028 Potenza.
DOC: Aglianico. Other: Malvasia and Moscato.

Consorzio Viticoltori Associati del Vulture

Barile, 85022 Potenza.
DOC: Aglianico. Also *Vini da tavola*.

SICILY

Of all the regions of Italy the island of Sicily has changed most in the past few decades. Thirty years ago it was an almost medieval land. The marriage of dignity and squalor was visible everywhere. Its unsurpassed Greek ruins lay apparently forgotten; Syracuse was still a small city commanding a bay of incredible beauty and purity where you could easily imagine the catastrophic defeat of the Athenian fleet 2,000 years before; Palermo was sleepy, violent, indigent but magnificent. As far as wine was concerned, there was Marsala, a name everyone knew but which nobody drank, and a few small aristocratic estates – the best-known on the ideal volcanic slopes of Mount Etna, and around Syracuse, from which there was a trickle of legendary sweet Moscato. But the general run of wine was almost undrinkable, and the best of it was exported northwards for blending.

An apparently well-directed regional development programme has changed all this. Palermo is now a great semi-modern city and Syracuse has been disfigured by industry. But the wine industry has become the biggest in Italy and one of the most modern. Enormous new vineyards supply automated cooperatives, which churn out 'correct', clean and properly balanced modern wines. Three-quarters of Sicily's wine is white. Eighty percent of the colossal total is made in the cooperatives. DOCs are almost irrelevant here; less than five percent qualifies. It is a table-wine industry, based not on local traditions but on choosing appropriate grapes, converting cornfields into mechanized vineyards, and making wine with cool efficiency. None of this could have been achieved without New World techniques – and huge government grants.

The wine industry has grown far faster than its market. Although fair quality, good reliability and modest prices have made one or two brands (above all Corvo) famous on the international stage, most Sicilian wine remains in bulk quantities looking for a blender to buy it and turn it into something else – be it Vermouth or even an apparently German wine.

DOC and Other Wines

Alcamo or Bianco Alcamo DOC. White wine. Provinces: Palermo and Trapani. Villages: around the town of Alcamo. Grapes: Catarratto Bianco Comune or Lucido plus 20% Damaschino, Grecanico and Trebbiano Toscano. Max. crop: 84 hl/ha. Min. alch: 11.5˚. Annual production: 277,000 cases.

A straightforward, fairly full-bodied dry white. Rapitalà is a far superior brand with some nuttiness and some astringency. Rincione Bianco is another similar brand.

Cerasuolo di Vittoria DOC. Red wine. Provinces: Ragusa, Caltanissetta and Catania. Villages: 11 communes in southeastern Sicily. Grapes: Frappato min. 40%, Calabrese up to 60%, Grosso Nero and Nerello Mascalese up to 10%. Max. crop: 65 hl/ha. Min. alch: 13˚. Annual production: 25,600 cases.

An unusual pale 'cherry' red of high strength which the critic Luigi Veronelli recommends keeping for as many as 30 years. Little is made, but its reputation is high.

Contessa Entellina DOC. White wine. Province Palermo. Commune: Contessa Entellina. Grapes: Catarratto, Grecanico, Chardonnay, Müller-Thurgau (maximum 5%), Sauvignon. Max crop 78 hl/ha. Min. alch: 11° to 11.5°. Production: 11,000 cases.

New DOC for selected whites of Palermo province. Main producer is Donnafugata.

Corvo Perhaps the best known of all Sicilian wines today, a highly successful brand from Duca di Salaparuta at Casteldaccia near Palermo (*see* Producers). A green-labelled white is reasonably full-bodied but not over-strong and nicely in balance, a yellow-labelled one is very pale and delicate. The red is a brilliant piece of modern wine design; clean, warm and satisfying without leaving any clear memory of scent or flavour. There are also *spumante* and dry fortified Stravecchio Corvo wines.

Etna DOC. White, red and *rosato* wine. Province: Catania. Villages: Milo and 20 other communes on the lower eastern slopes of Mt Etna. Grapes: (white) Carricante at least 60% with Catarratto Bianco 40%, Trebbiano, Minnella Bianca and other whites 15%; (red and *rosato*) Nerello Mascalese at least 80% with Nerello Mantellato making up the rest. Max. crop: 63 hl/ha. Min. alch: 11.5˚ for white; 12.5˚ for red and *rosato*. Annual production: 77,800 cases.

Until recently this was the only quality table-wine area in Sicily. The volcanic soil of the still-fiery volcano and the cool of its altitude allow both reds and whites of vigour and some refinement. The reds age well to a consistency not far from claret and the whites are brisk and tasty young. The leading estate is Villagrande (*see* Other Producers).

Faro DOC. Red wine. Province: Messina. Village: Messina. Grapes: Nerello Mascalese 45–60%, Nerello Cappuccio 15–30%, Nocera 5–10%, Calabrese, Gaglioppo, Sangiovese up to 15%. Max. crop: 70 hl/ha. Min. alch: 12˚. Annual production: 556 cases.

Limited production of a distinctly superior red, best aged 3 years or so.

Malvasia delle Lipari DOC. Dessert white wine. Province: Messina. Villages: islands of the Aeolian archipelago, especially Lipari. Grapes: Malvasia delle Lipari 95%, Corinto Nero 5–8%. Max. crop: 63 hl/ha. Min. alch: 11.5˚ (18˚ plus 6˚ of sugar for *passito*, which must be aged 9 months; 20˚ plus 6˚ of sugar for *liquoroso*). Annual production: 4,400 cases.

Well-known but scarcely exceptional wines (except in their lovely birthplace). There are many good dessert wines in Sicily; Moscato is much more interesting than Malvasia.

Marsala DOC. Apéritif/dessert wine. Provinces: Trapani, Palermo and Agrigento. Villages: throughout the provinces but above all at Marsala. Grapes: (*oro* and *ambra*) Catarratto and/or Grillo, plus Inzolia up to 15%; (*rubino*) Perricone, Calabrese, Nerello Mascalese, whites up to 30%. Max. crop:

75 hl/ha. for *oro* and *rosato*, 67.5 hl/ha. for *rubino*. Min. alch: 17° by volume for *fine* (or Italia Particolare); 18° aged two years for *superiore* (or London Particular, or Superior Old Marsala, or Garibaldi Dolce – or the appropriate initials); 18° by volume aged five years for *vergine*. Annual production: 1.1m. cases.

An Englishman, John Woodhouse, started the Marsala industry in 1773. Nelson stocked his fleet with it. In a sense it is Italy's sherry, though without sherry's brilliant finesse or limitless ageing capacity. Its manufacture usually involves concentrated and/or 'muted' (stopped with alcohol) musts, known as *cotto* and *sifone* – but the best, *vergine*, is made with neither, simply by an ageing system similar to the soleras of sherry. *Fine* is normally sweet and rather nasty, *superiore* can be sweet or dry, with a strong caramel flavour; *vergine* is dry, with more barrel-wood flavour. *Speciali* used to be a strange aberration – Marsala blended with eggs, or even coffee – but is now no longer permitted under DOC regulation. Other recent changes to the DOC are the descriptions *oro* (gold), *ambra* (amber) and *rubino* (ruby); the former two refer to the wines based on white grapes, while the latter refers to the darker varieties less often seen. A great deal of Marsala is used for making *zabaglione* (just as France buys volumes of Madeira for *sauce madère*).

Moscato di Noto DOC. White dessert wine. Province: Siracusa. Villages: Noto, Rosolini, Pachino and Avola. Grape: Moscato Bianco. Max. crop: 81 hl/ha. Min. alch: 11.5° (3.5° of sugar) for naturale; 13° (3.5° of sugar) for Spumante and 22° (6° of sugar) for *liquoroso*. Annual production: 11,000 cases.

Little of this delicious Moscato is made, but the *liquoroso* is a very good example of this sumptuous genre. The Greeks introduced the Muscat grape here 2,500 years ago.

Moscato and Passito di Pantelleria DOC. White wine. Province: Trapani. Villages: the island of Pantelleria. Grapes: Zibibbo. Max. crop: 49 hl/ha. Min. alch: 12.5° (4.5° of sugar) for *naturale*; 14° for *passito*. Annual production 55,600 cases.

The island of Pantelleria is closer to Tunisia than Sicily. Moscato from its Zibibbo grapes has singular perfume, whether made as *spumante*, *naturale* or best of all *passito* (which can also be fortified). The best quality is simply known as Extra.

Moscato di Siracusa DOC. White wine. Province: Siracusa. Village: Siracusa. Grape: Moscato Bianco. Max. crop: 49 hl/ha. Min. alch: 16.5° (min. 2.5° of sugar).

The celebrated old Moscato vineyard of Syracuse, once the greatest city of the Greek world, home of Plato, Theocritus and Archimedes, is apparently extinct, like the matchless beauty of its bay before Sicily began to modernize. The fact that it is no longer produced will not stop a bar selling you a glass of sticky aromatic wine at a high price as 'Siracusa'.

Regaleali The brand name of a good-quality range of wines, perhaps the island's best brand, from Conte Tasca d'Almerita (*see* Producers). The Riserva Rosso del Conte is as good as any Sicilian red; the white contains Sauvignon Blanc.

Settesoli The acceptable handiwork of a Cantina Sociale at Menfi on the western south coast. Red and white are both well made, if not memorable.

Leading Sicily Producers

Giuseppe Coria

Vittoria, 97019 Ragusa.

The ancient estate owned by Giuseppe Coria began bottling its own wine exclusively in 1968. DOC: Cerasuolo di Vittoria. Other: Moscato di Villa Fontane, Solicchiato Bianco, Cerasuolo Villa Fontane, Villa Fontane Perpetuo. Coria is a former army officer, a dedicated winemaker, lecturer and author of books on Sicilian and Italian wines. From 7.4 acres he makes extraordinary wine, including a Cerasuolo Invecchiato (formerly known as Stravecchio Siciliano) aged 40 years in barrel, and Perpetuo, of which bottles are filled annually from a large cask which is then topped up with new wine.

Donnafugata

Contessa Entellina, 90030 Palermo.

Owned by Gabriella Anca and Giacomo Rallo, who are making this into a much-noticed estate. With new cellars and 170 acres of vines, they produce stylish dry *vini da tavola*, including the award-winning Donnafugata Bianco and Rosso. They also make a single-vineyard white called Vigna di Gabri, a *rosato*, some Chardonnay and the interesting white Damaskino.

Florio

Marsala, 91025 Trapani.

Founded in 1883 by Vincenzo Florio. In 1929 the firm was incorporated along with Ingham, Whitaker and Woodhouse as S.A.V.I. Florio & Co., part of the Cinzano group. DOC: Marsala. Florio was known in his day as 'the king of the historic Marsala'; now this rather lack-lustre company has no vines but still makes Marsala, including the fine *superiore* ACI 1840 and Riserva Egadi. Ingham, Whitaker and Woodhouse are sold under separate labels.

Carlo Hauner

Salina, 98050 Leccena.

Owners/winemakers: the Hauner family. DOC: Malvasia delle Lipari. Other: Capo Salina. Milanese Carlo Hauner died recently, but his family are still adding new dimensions to the wines made by this widespread family; including a unique, acclaimed dessert wine.

Enopolio

Pantelleria, 91017 Trapani.

A cooperative of about 600 growers on the island of Pantelleria. Director: Vito Valenza. DOC: Moscato di Pantelleria. Other: *vini da tavola*. Besides much ordinary wine the cooperative bottles a notable dessert Moscato *passito* extra called Tanit and a growing amount of sparkling Solimano.

Carlo Pellegrino

Marsala, 91025 Trapani.

Founded 1880. DOC: Marsala. Other: Grecanico, Pignatello. Marsala Superiore ranks with the finest.

Nuova Rallo

Marsala, 91025 Trapani.

Founded in 1860 by Diego Rallo. The large family winery is run by his descendants. DOC: Alcamo, Etna, Marsala. Other: Normanno Bianco, Rosso, Royal Club Spumante. Rallo makes about 90,000 cases of Marsala and a significant amount of other wines from 295 acres of company vines, supplemented by farmers. The best wine of the distinguished range is Vergine 1860. Rallo also supplies *vini da tavola* to the US market.

Rapitalà

Camporale, 90043 Palermo.

Owned by the Adelkam corporation and run by the French Comte Hugues de la Gatinais. The winemaker is Gigi Lo Guzzo. DOC: Alcamo. Other: Rapitalà Rosso. An earthquake destroyed the winery in 1968. It was rebuilt in 1971. With 370 acres it produces 125,000 cases of Alcamo DOC and 40,000 cases of Rapitalà Rosso *vino da tavola*. Rapitalà adds unaccustomed lustre to the DOC with another dimension of balance and finesse.

Regaleali-Conte Tasca d'Almerita

Vallelunga 93010 Caltanissetta.

A family estate founded in 1835. Owner: Giuseppe Tasca d'Almerita. No DOC. Other: Regaleali Bianco, Rosato, Rosso, Rosso del Conte; Nozzo d'Oro. 741 acres of estate vineyards produce some of Sicily's finest dry wines, including the excellent Rosso del Conte and the first-rate Nozze d'Oro (a white from Sauvignon Blanc and Inzolia). Cabernet Sauvignon here is one of the best of southern Italy; Chardonnay is also particularly good.

Duca di Salaparuta (Corvo)

Casteldaccia, 90014 Palermo.

Founded in 1824 by Edoardo Alliata di Villafranca, Duca di Salaparuta. The modern winery is owned by the region. Chief winemaker: Franco Giacosa. No DOC. Other: Corvo Ala, Bianco, Colomba Platino, Rosso, Spumante, Stravecchio di Sicilia, Vino Fiore (red), Prima Goccia (white). Corvo is the most famous brand of Sicilian wine. Production is about 830,000 cases, prevalently in Corvo Bianco and Rosso and the white Colomba Platino, from grapes bought in the hills of central and western Sicily. New vines of interest are the red Duca Enrico, an aged, pure Nero d'Avola, one of the most successful new reds, not only of Sicily but of all the south, and Bianco Valquarnera from Inzolia and aged in small oak barrels.

Cantina Sociale Settesoli

Menfi, 92013 Agrigento.

A cooperative founded in 1958, which now claims to be Europe's largest winery, with 9,880 acres producing a staggering 8m. cases. No DOC. Other: Settesoli Bianco, Rosato, Rosso, Bonera, Feudo dei Fiori. California techniques are evident in the light, suprisingly high-acid wines sold under the Settesoli brand name. Some 20% of production is sold in bottle, the rest in bulk.

Vecchio Samperi-De Bartoli

Marsala, 91025 Trapani.

Owners: Marco de Bartoli. DOC: Marsala and Moscato di Pantelleria. De Bartoli selects grapes from 37 acres for a limited production of Vecchio Samperi, an outstanding apéritif wine, a superior virgin Marsala in all but not DOC. He also makes a Marsala Superiore Riserva, sweet white Inzolia di Samperi, dry Joséphine Doréo, and Bukkuram *passito*.

OTHER PRODUCERS

V. Giacalone Alloro Marsala, 91025 Trapani. DOC: Malvasia delle Lipari, Marsala.

Cooperativa Agricola Aurora Salemi, 91018 Trapani. DOC: Alcamo. Other: Castelvecchio Bianco, Rosso.

Bagni Santa Margherita, 98020 Messina. Owner: Giacomo Currò. Lone producer of Faro DOC. 5 acres.

Cantina Colosi 98020 Messina. DOC: Malvasia delle Lipari. Other: Salina Rosso, Bianco.

Vito Curatolo Arini Marsala, 91025 Trapani. Founded in 1875, the family firm is run by Roberto Curatolo. DOC: Marsala. Other: Marina Bianco, Rosso.

Fratelli De Vita Marsala, 91025 Trapani. DOC: Marsala.

Cantina Sociale Enocarboj Sciacca, 92019 Agrigento. Cooperative. No DOC. Other: Rosso di Sciacca, Trebbiano di Sicilia. Carboj: brand name for some very drinkable wines.

Fratelli Fici Marsala, 91025 Trapani. Oenologist Nicolò Fici runs the family firm. DOC: Marsala. Fine Marsala Vergine from a reliable range.

Fontanarossa Cerda, 90010 Palermo. Red, white and *rosato* Cerdese *vino da tavola*.

Cooperativa La Ginestra Malfa, 98050 Messina. Small group of growers on the island of Salina making DOC Malvasia delle Lipari.

Fratelli Lombardo Marsala, 91025 Trapani. DOC: Marsala (Superiore). Also *vini da tavola*. 1,050 acres.

Marino Grandi Vini Siciliani Marsala, 91025 Trapani. DOC: Marsala, Alcamo. Other: White Verdello Siciliano, red Nerello Siciliano.

Mirabella Marsala, 91025 Trapani. Admirable Marsala Vergine DOC from this dynamic firm, which also uses the Cudia brand.

Fratelli Montalto Marsala, 91025 Trapani. DOC: Alcamo, Marsala. Other: Grecanico, Malvasia, Moscato, Nerello, Zibibbo.

Salvatore Murana Pantelleria, 91017 Trapani. Small but admirable production of Moscato di Pantelleria DOC and *vino da tavola*.

Rincione Calatafimi, 91013 Trapani. Owner: Pietro Papè. DOC: Alcamo. Other: Rincione Bianco, Rosso, Rosato.

Cooperativa Agricoltori Saturnia (Draceno) Partanna, 91028 Trapani. Draceno Bianco, Rosato, Rosso.

Terre di Ginestra Sancipirello, 90040 Palermo. Maurizio Miccichè is developing this estate with good *vini da tavola*: white Terre di Ginestra and red Tenuta Casalbaio Rubilio.

Cantina Sociale Sambuca di Sicilia Sambuca di Sicilia, 92017 Agrigento. Large production of Cellaro red, white and *rosato vini da tavola*.

Cantina Sociale Torrepalino Solicchiata, 95030 Catania. Cooperative. DOC: Etna. Also *vini da tavola*. 400 acres.

Barone di Villagrande Milo, 95010 Catania. Owner: Carlo Nicolosi Asmundo, Barone di Villagrande, whose son, Carlo, a professor of oenology, makes the wine. DOC: Etna.

This is a dignified old estate which made Etna wine respectable when little else in Sicily was; but it is now standing still.

Cantina Sociale La Vite Partanna, 91028 Trapani. Cooperative. *Vini da tavola*: Donzelle Bianco, Rosso.

SARDINIA

Sardinia is a strange, timeless island adrift in the centre of things and yet remote, without Sicily's innate drama, without Corsica's majestic mountains or sour social history.

The modern world comes and camps on the coastline of Sardinia, the jet-set on the Costa Smeralda, the wine world on the opposite coast at Alghero, where one of Italy's most sophisticated and original wineries takes advantage of ideal natural conditions to break all the rules.

Sardinia's original wines are heroically strong, designed it seems by and for the supermen who built the round fortress houses of colossal stones that dot the island: the *nuraghe*. The most characteristic wine of the island is Cannonau, an indigenous red with a minimum alcoholic degree of 13.5 and often much more. The traditional practice is to prevent all the sugar from converting to alcohol; to balance strength with sweetness in something faintly reminiscent of port. The sweet red is actually best *liquoroso*, fortified with brandy,

when it goes all the way to a port-style dessert wine. The Anghelu Ruju of Sella & Mosca is the version of Cannonau most likely to appeal to untrained tastes. Two other grapes, Girò and Monica, make similar sweet and heady reds.

Nor are old-style Sardinian white wines any easier to cope with. Nasco, Malvasia and Vernaccia are three white grapes that all achieve formidable degrees, often tempered, like the reds, with unfermented sugar left to sweeten them.

Sweet Malvasia is a serious speciality that can reach very high quality. Vernaccia, on the other hand, is best fermented dry and aged in the same way as sherry. (It even develops the same flor yeast that allows it to oxidize very gently to a nicely nutty maturity.) Old dry Vernaccia needs no apology.

The modern movement in Sardinia consists largely of cooperatives, but is symbolized, and indeed led, by the Sella & Mosca winery at Alghero.

DOC and Other Wines

Alghero New DOC (1995). White, red, *rosato*. Area: seven comunes in the province of Sassari. Grapes: Torbato. Sauvignon, Chardonnay, Cabernets Sauvignon and Franc, Sangiovese, Cagnulari, Vermentino, others up to 15%. Max crop: between 91 and 112 hl/ha. No production figures yet.

This is a new and unproven DOC, but Sella & Mosca (*see* Leading Producers) are almost certain to prove its worth given time.

Arborea DOC. Red, white and *rosato* wine. Area: many communes in Oristano province. Grapes: (red and *rosato*) Sangiovese min. 85%; (white) Trebbiano Romagnolo or Toscano min. 85%. Max. crop: 126 hl/ha. Min. alch: (red) 11°; (white) 10.5°. Annual production: 4,400 cases.

New and unproven DOC, the white also possibly *frizzante* or *amabile*.

Campidano di Terralba DOC. Red wine. Provinces: Cagliari, Oristano. Villages: Terralba and 22 communes nearby (vineyards not exceeding 400 metres). Grapes: Bovale (others up to 20%). Max. crop: 105 hl/ha. Min. alch: 11.5°. Annual production 5,500 cases.

A lightish dry red, pleasantly soft, best young and cool.

Cannonau di Sardegna DOC. Red and *rosato* wine. Province: whole of Sardegna. Grapes: Cannonau, plus 10% Bovale Grande Carignano, Pascale di Cagliari, Monica and 5% Vernaccia di S. Gimignano. Max. crop: 77 hl/ha. Min. alch: 12.5° for Cannonau di Sardegna (1 year old: 3 years for *riserva*); 15° for *superiore naturale*; 18° for *liquoroso*. Annual production: 167,000 cases.

The complicated set of DOC rules means that much Cannonau is sold as *vino da tavola* (without the DOC qualification 'di Sardegna'), and is none the worse for a little less alcohol. It is the basic Sardinian red grape, traditionally both strong and sweet – in fact anything but refreshing, however rich (which it is) in flavour. The most famous old-style Cannonau is that of Oliena, near Nuoro in the eastern centre of the island, which can be called Nepente di Oliena.

Carignano del Sulcis DOC. Red and *rosato* wine. Province: Cagliari. Villages: the islands of S. Antioco and S. Pietro on the southwest coast. Grapes: Carignano and up to 15% Monica, Pascale and Alicante-Bouschet and other red varieties. Max. crop: (*rosso*) 71.5 hl/ha; (*rosato*) 66 hl/ha, Rosso Superiore 49 hl/ha. Min. alch: 12° Rosso, 11.5° Rosato, 13° Rosso Superiore. Annual production: 44,000 cases.

Both reasonable red and a quite smooth and fruity *rosato* are made from the French Carignan in this area of hilly islets and lagoons, known to the ancients as Sulcis. The red will take 1–2 years' ageing.

Girò di Cagliari DOC. Red wine. Province: Cagliari. Villages: 72 communes in Oristano. Grape: Girò. Max. crop: 72 hl/ha. Min. alch: 14.5° for *dolce naturale*, 14° for *secco*, 17.5° for *liquoroso* and *liquoroso secco*. Aged at least 2 years for *riserva*. Annual production: 556 cases.

Girò, like Cannonau, is a traditional red grape of formidable sugar content, most often seen as a sweet wine; impressive rather than attractive when it is made dry.

Malvasia di Bosa DOC. White wine. Provinces: Nuoro and Oristano. Villages: Bosa, Flussio, Magomadas, Modolo, Suni, Tinnura, Tresnuraghes – near the west coast south of

Alghero. Grape: Malvasia di Sardegna. Max. crop: 56 hl/ha. Min. alch: 14.5° plus 0.5° of sugar for *secco*; 13° plus 2° of sugar for *dolce naturale*; 15° plus 2.5° of sugar for *liquoroso dolce naturale*; 16.5° plus 1° of sugar for *liquoroso secco*. Annual production: 1,100 cases.

The most highly prized of several Sardinian amber whites that can best be compared with sherry – at least in function. They go through a shorter and simpler ageing process but acquire smoothness and some depth of flavour, ending in a characteristically Italian bitter-almond note. Dry versions, served chilled, are good apéritifs.

Malvasia di Cagliari DOC. White wine. Province: Cagliari. Villages: entire province and several in Oristano. Grape: Malvasia di Sardegna. Max. crop: 72 hl/ha. Min. alch: as for Malvasia di Bosa. Aged for 1 year in wood for *liquoroso dolce* and *liquoroso secco riserva*. Annual production: 4,400 cases.

Similar wines to the last but from less exclusively southern vineyards.

Mandrolisai DOC. Red and *rosato* wine. Province: Nuoro. Villages: Sorgono and six other communes. Grapes: Bovale Sardo 35%, Cannonau 20–35%, Monica 20–35%, max. 10% other grapes allowed. Max. crop: 84 hl/ha. Min. alch: 11.5°. Annual production: 8,900 cases.

A new DOC for less than full-power Cannonau and *rosato* from modernized cooperatives.

Monica di Sardegna DOC. Red wine. Province: the whole island. Grapes: Monica, other reds up to 15%. Max. crop: 105 hl/ha. Min. alch: 11°; 12.5° for *superiore*. Aged 6 months, *superiore* 1 year in wood. Annual production: 133,000 cases.

A standard dry red *vino da tavola* of acceptable quality, perhaps more enjoyable rather cool.

Moscato di Cagliari DOC. White wine. Province: Cagliari. Villages: throughout the province. Grape: Moscato Bianco. Max. crop: 72 hl/ha. Min. alch: 16° (3° of sugar) for *dolce naturale*; 17.5° (2.5° of sugar) for *liquoroso* (fortified). Aged for 1 year for *riserva*. Annual production: 8,800 cases.

The Muscat grape has a stronger tradition in Sicily than Sardinia. What is made here is reasonable local drinking. The fortified *liquoroso* is the most convincing.

Moscato di Sardegna DOC. White wine. Province: the whole island. Grapes: Moscato Bianco plus 10% others. Max. crop: 91 hl/ha. Min. alch: 11.5° (3.5° of sugar). Annual production: 20,000 cases.

A new DOC for low-strength sweet Muscat *spumante* – in fact the Asti of Sardinia. It can use the geographical term 'Tempo Pausania' or 'Tempio e Gallura' if the grapes are vinified at Gallura in the province of Sassari in the northwest.

Moscato di Sorso-Sennori DOC. White wine. Province: Sassari. Villages: Sorso and Sennori, north of Sassari. Grape: Moscato Bianco. Max. crop: 14 hl/ha. Min. alch: 13° plus 2° of sugar. It can also be fortified to make a *liquoroso dolce*. Annual production: 1,100 cases.

A local Muscat DOC for a strong sweet white, reputed better than that of Cagliari in the south.

Nasco di Cagliari DOC: White wine. Province: Cagliari. Villages: throughout the province. Grape: Nasco. Max. crop: 72 hl/ha. Min. alch: 14.5° (2.5° of sugar) for *dolce naturale*; 14.5° (0.5° of sugar) for secco; 14° for *liquoroso*; 17.5° (2.5° of

sugar) plus 2° of sugar for *liquoroso dolce naturale secco*. Aged at least 2 years in wood for *liquoroso dolce naturale* and *secco riserva*. Annual production: 4,400 cases.

Another rustic island white more appreciated sweet and strong by the locals, but in its modernized, lighter and drier versions by visitors. Sella & Mosca (*see* Producers) spurn the DOC to make the latter.

Nuragus di Cagliari DOC. White wine. Provinces: Nuoro (part) and Cagliari. Grapes: Nuragus 85–95%, Trebbiano Toscano and Romagnolo, Vermentino, Clairette and Semidano 5–15%. Max. crop: 140 hl/ha. Min. alch: 10.5°. Annual production: 222,000 cases.

A light and essentially neutral dry white wine, the standard resort of those who have been overwhelmed by Sardinia's more characteristic products.

Torbato di Alghero The fruit of modern technology and intelligent market planning applied to a number of Sardinian white grapes by Sella & Mosca (*see* Producers). Not exactly a thrilling wine, but an extremely well-designed dry white of just memorable personality, and just what is needed with the island's fish. In fact it is a bargain anywhere.

Vermentino di Gallura DOC. White wine. Provinces: Sassari and Nuoro. Villages: 19 communes in the north of the island. Grape: Vermentino, max. 5% other grapes allowed. Max. crop: 98 hl/ha. Min. alch: 12° (13.5° for *superiore*). Annual production: 311,000 cases.

By tradition the sort of strong dry white with low acidity that does the opposite of quenching your thirst – epitomized by the 14° *superiore*. One of the best Sardinian wines and a likely candidate for DOCG.

Vernaccia di Oristano DOC. White wine. Province: Cagliari. Villages: 15 communes in south and west, including Oristano. Grape: Vernaccia di Oristano. Max. crop: 52 hl/ha. Min. alch: 15° (and 2 years in wood). Aged for 3 years in wood for *superiore*, 4 for *riserva*. Annual production: 33,000 cases.

On first acquaintance I found this the most appealing of all Sardinian wines; a sort of natural first cousin to Spain's Montilla, or an unfortified sherry. The grapes are slightly shrivelled before fermentation, the natural strength slows down oxidation while subtle, distinct flavours develop – such as the characteristic Italian bitterness lingering in the finish.

Vermentino di Sardegna DOC. White wine. Province: the whole island. Grapes: Vermentino, plus other whites up to 15%. Max. crop: 130 hl/ha. Min. alch: 10.5°, *spumante* 11°. Annual production: 333,000 cases.

The wine is dry white and may also be *amabile* or *spumante*. Standards are improving but remain behind Vermentino di Gallura.

Leading Sardinia Producers

Attilio Contini

Cabgras, 09072 Oristano.
Founded in the late 19th century. Owners: the Contini brothers. DOC: Vernaccia di Oristano. Other: White Contina, *rosato*. The most respected of Vernaccia producers, whose *riserva*s are a high point for this type of wine.

Sella & Mosca

Alghero, 07041 Sassari.

Founded in 1899 by the Piedmontese Emilio Sella and Edgardo Mosca, now owned by the INVEST group. Chief winemaker: Mario Consorte. DOC: Vermentino di Sardegna. Other: Anghelu Ruju, Cannonau di Alghero, I Piani, Monica, Nasco, Rosé di Alghero, Torbato di Alghero, Vermentino di Alghero. One of Europe's largest wine estates and a model of contemporary viticulture. 1,235 acres of vines have a potential production of 420,000 cases. The principal lines are Vermentino, fine dry white Torbato, Cannonau and the port-like Anghelu Ruju.

OTHER PRODUCERS

Argiolas Serdiana, 09040, Cagliari. Good Cannonau and Vermentino, but really outstanding *vino da tavola* Turriga: a blend of Cannonau, Carignano, Bovale and Malvasia.

Giovanni Cherchi Usini, 07049 Sassari. *Vini da tavola.* Unique red Cagnulari, and a Vermentino di Usini which is considered top of category.

Cantina Sociale di Dorgali Dorgali, 08022 Nuoro. DOC: Cannonau di Sardegna. Other: Bianco, Rosato and Rosso di Dorgali. One of the biggest and best producers of Cannonau.

Gabbas Giuseppe Nuoro, 08100, Nuoro. Small producer (25 acres) making good DOC Cannonau di Sardegna Lillové, and very good *vino da tavola* Dule: a blend of mainly Cannonau, Cabernet, Dolcetto and Sangiovese.

Cantina Sociale Gallura Tempio Pausania, 07029 Sassari. DOC: Vermentino di Gallura, Moscato di Sardegna. Other: *Vini da tavola*, including rare Nebbiolo di Luras.

Cantina Sociale Marmilla Sanluri, 09055 Cagliari. A huge cooperative founded in the early 1950s. DOC: Cannonau di Sardegna, Monica di Sardegna, Nuragus di Cagliari. Other: Malvasia, Nasco, Rosato. Run by oenologist Enzo Biondo.

Meloni Vini Serlargins, 09047 Cagliari. DOC: various Cagliari, plus Cannonau and Vermentino di Sardegna.

Cantina Sociale Il Nuraghe Mogoro, Oristano. DOC: Nuragus di Cagliari and others. Rare white Semicano di Mogoro *vino da tavola* is their speciality.

Cantina Sociale Ogliastra Tortoli, 08048 Nuoro. Good Cannonau DOC and *vini da tavola*.

Perda Rubia Tortoli, 08048 Nuoro. Perda Rubia. A good sweet port-like Cannonau.

Produttori Riuniti Baratili San Pietro, 09070 Oristano. DOC: Vernaccia di Oristano. 120 acres.

Cantina Sociale Regione su Concali Jerzu, 08044 Nuoro. DOC: Cannonau (under the Jerzu trademark) and also *vini da tavola*.

Cantina Sociale della Riforma Agraria Alghero, 07041 Sassari. *Vini da tavola*: Aragosta, Le Bombarde. Aragosta is a good dry Vermentino.

Cantina Sociale di Samugheo Samugheo, 09020 Oristano. DOC: Mandrolisai, Campidano di Terralba, exquisite, amber Nasco di Ortneri *vino da tavola*.

Cantina Sociale di Sant'Antioco Sant'Antioco, 09017 Cagliari. DOC: Carignano del Sulcis, Monica di Sardegna. Sardus Pater is the trademark of a notable red Carignano from this cooperative.

Cantina Sociale di Santadi Santadi, 09010, Cagliari. DOC. Very good Carignano del Sulcis, Riserva Rocca di Rubbia is best. Other: Outstanding *vino da tavola* Terre Brune from Carignan grapes.

Cantina Sociale del Vermentino Monti, 07020 Sassario. Large output including DOC Vermentino di Gallura, red Abbaìa and *rosato* Thaòra *vini da tavola*.

Cantina Sociale della Vernaccia 09025 Oristano. Founded: 1953. DOC: Vernaccia di Oristano. The best Vernaccia produced by this large cooperative is the brand Sardinian Gold.

Italy's export trade

Italy's average exports of wine for the years 1993, 1994 and 1995 were 170 million cases, about 12% of the total production.

In 1995, some 198 million cases were exported, of which 43 million cases (21.7%) were DOC. The total value of exports for 1995 was just over 3,000 billion lire. The value of DOC wine exports was 1,300 billion lire, or not quite half the total.

Italian wine exports in 1995

	quantity (in million litres)	value (in billion Lire)	average value (Lire/litre)
Germany	585.4	1,081.9	1,848
France	463.4	387.9	837
United Kingdom	150.9	342.3	2,268
USA	135.8	477.3	3,515
Spain	135.3	108.3	800
Switzerland	56.3	176.2	3,130
Russia	51.3	91.1	1,776
Belgium/Luxembourg	30.1	63.3	2,103
Portugal	26.3	34.8	1,323
Austria	24.7	61.1	2,474
Canada	24.5	77.7	3,171
Netherlands	24.1	63.0	2,614
Denmark	17.8	54.4	3,056
Sweden	15.1	48.5	3,212
Japan	12.6	59.3	4,706
Finland	6.2	15.5	2,500
Australia	6.2	19.9	3,210
Ireland	3.1	8.0	2,581
Greece	1.8	4.4	2,444
Total	**1,770.9**	**3,174.9**	

SPAIN

Santiago de Compostela

Bilbao

Bierzo

RIAS
BAIXAS RIBEIRO

RIOJA Ebro NAVARRA
Logroño Somontano

Valdeorras

Ampurdán-
Costa Brava

CIGALES
Valladolid Campo de Borja

Conca de Barbera Costers
del Segre

Duero

Ribera del
Duero Calatayud

Cariñena Priorato Alella
Barcelona

Douro Toro Rueda

Terra
Alta Tarragona PENEDÈS

Madrid Vinos
de Madrid

Mentrida

Tagus UTIEL-
Requena VALENCIA

BINISSALEM

LA MANCHA Valencia

Palma

Guadiana Almansa Valencia

VALDEPEÑAS Jumilla Alicante

Yecla Alicante

Guadalquivir

Sevilla MONTILLA
MORILES

CONDADO
DE HUELVA

MÁLAGA

Jerez de la Frontera JEREZ

Cádiz Málaga

Even in the few years since the last edition of this book was published, Spain has continued to reinvent itself and redefine what it is trying to do in the world outside. Old attitudes have been changing, new ideas have been accepted – sometimes, admittedly, grudgingly – but the end result is that Spain produces more better-quality wines with more regional credibility even than it did five years ago.

Part of the reason for this has been the re-establishment of real regional feelings of identity through the country's 17 *autónomas* (autonomous communities): the Franco years put Spanish winemaking into something of a state-controlled strait-jacket, from which only the most well-established – notably Rioja and sherry – managed to manifest their individuality. Twenty years after the new constitution restored some level of self-government to the regions, Catalunya, the Basque Country and Galicia once again display their nationalist aspirations – in the bottle as well as in the ballot-box – and other regions are rediscovering a heritage which had been allowed to wither under the conformity and lack of investment which characterized the Franco era.

The last edition of this book listed 35 areas of Spain with the Denominación de Origen (DO). Today there are 51 regions with that status (and others pending), and each of them claims its own individuality and heritage, fuelled by a reinvigorated local pride and the pragmatic acceptance that the market is, after all, king, and producers who want to be in it have got to make the effort to win it.

This is not to say that all 51 DO zones produce wines of export quality or, indeed, that attitudes everywhere are as enlightened as they have been at the cutting edge of the Spanish wine business, but the fact remains that even the most stick-in-the-mud growers and *bodegueros* have noticed that their more enterprising peers are making something better, more easily saleable and (most important of all) for a better price than they themselves are getting. The Instituto Nacional de Denominaciónes de Origen (INDO) in Madrid has always had a programme of education and encouragement for regions which genuinely want to improve their wine... But all the lecturing and cajoling in the world, it seems, is worth less than a sight of your neighbour's balance-sheet.

Spain is Europe's second-biggest country (after France) and, with some four million acres under vine, Europe's biggest vineyard. However, the hotter climate brings the need for sparser planting patterns and lower yields, so that France and Italy still make far more wine. Spain's viticultural map is dominated by the two great rivers Ebro and Duero, both of which find their source in the mountainous Cordillera Cantábrica which divides the cool, wet northwest from the continental interior. The Ebro runs southeast into the Mediterranean in the province of Tarragona, while the Duero flows southwest, through Portugal (where it is known as the Douro) and into the Atlantic at Oporto. These two rivers and the mountain range in which they find their origins are responsible for most of the microclimates of northern Spain.

South of Madrid, the sun is king – wider plantations of hardier grape varieties are the norm, and water, when it comes, is gratefully received by the spongy subsoils of the most successful wine-producing districts. The principal rivers in south-central Spain are the Guadiana which waters the great central plains of La Mancha (with part of its course actually underground) and flows west then south into the Gulf of Cádiz, having formed the boundary between Spain and Portugal for its final stretch; the Tajo (or Tagus), which flows from the plateaux of Madrid west through Toledo and Extremadura into Portugal (where it is known as the Tejo) and thence into the Atlantic at Lisbon; the Júcar flows south and east from the mountains of Guadalajara through the winelands of the Levant, into the Mediterranean in the province of Valencia; and the Guadalquivír runs southwest from the central Meseta to skirt the sherry country. These, between them, are nearly all the irrigation seen by most of the vineyards in the south of the country.

From an information point of view, Spanish wines have been difficult to categorize and understand, partly because the excellent Spanish bureaucracy has always listed them in strict alphabetical order and partly because of the piecemeal growth of the DO system over the past 25 years. However, a pattern has begun to emerge – helped along by the resurgence of regional pride – which allows us to identify the styles of wine produced by each region of Spain, why they are as they are, and how they have come to be so.

SPANISH WINE REGIONS

For all the inevitable complications of the system of *denominaciónes de origen*, painstakingly worked out by the Spanish authorities over many years (and of which they can be proud), there is still a natural geographical logic to the different styles of wine of Spain. The entire country, mainland and offshore islands, divides into eight major wine-producing regions, each of which shares a common heritage, gastronomic culture and climate, and it is these factors, of course, which determine the way wine has evolved over the years anywhere in the 'old' world of wine. For each of the eight regions, production figures are average annual figures for the past five years or of whatever recent figures are available.

THE NORTHWEST

This is the slice of Spain in the top left-hand corner, above Portugal, and along the coast of the Bay of Biscay towards France. Its southern border is the Cordillera Cantábrica, which shelters the rest of Spain from the excesses of Atlantic weather. The climate is comparatively cool and wet, the landscape is lush and green and the original culture is non-Spanish. Celtic influences dominate in Galicia, Asturias was and is a separate principality under the Spanish Crown (exactly as is Wales in the United Kingdom) and the Basque Country has one of the oldest pre-Christian cultures in

Europe. Add to this the local gastronomic culture – fish, fish and more fish – and it is not surprising that the wines produced here have evolved to be mainly light, fresh, crisp, dry and, predominantly, white. The DOs and their average production figures are as follows.

Region	DO	Cases
Galicia:	Rías Baixas	240,800
	Ribeira Sacra	*
	Ribeiro	1,367,800
	Valdeorras	465,050
	Val do Monterrey	*
Basque Country (north):		
	Chacolí de Getaria	28,100
	Chacolí de Bizkaia	*

*these areas have yet to report on a full vintage season under DO regulations

THE UPPER EBRO

In the shelter of the Cordillera Cantábrica the climate is more continental, with only the very highest vineyards (Rioja Alavesa, Navarra Estella) gaining some benefit from the influences of the Bay of Biscay. Politically, the area is sandwiched between the Spanish heartland of Castilla-León and the resolutely non-Spanish region of Catalunya. In the 15th and 16th centuries the royal house switched capitals throughout the region as Castilian, Catalan and Aragonés monarchs married each other and merged their kingdoms, so there were always rich and powerful people with money available for good-quality wine. The main gastronomic influence here is meat – whether from herds and flocks or running wild in the forests – so it is no surprise that this is predominantly red-wine country. The final quality 'burnish' was provided towards the end of the last century when phylloxera devastated the French vineyards, and a vast but discerning export market opened up for this, the region closest to the French border. The DOs and their average annual production figures are as follows:

Region	DO	Cases
Basque Country (south):		
	Rioja DOCa	see below
La Rioja:	Rioja DOCa	16,062,300
Navarra:	Navarra	5,065,550
	Rioja DOCa	see above
Aragón:	Calatayud	225,600
	Campo de Borja	732,700
	Cariñena	2,966,000
	Somontano	143,700

THE DUERO VALLEY

With one exception, this area has most of the attributes of the Upper Ebro: a continental climate – although higher and rather cooler here – abundant food on the hoof, in the fields and forests, and a population of rich, influential people from Valladolid and Zamora, where Royal Courts once sat, to Salamanca, site of Spain's oldest university. So we may expect quality red wines to have been supplied to princes, bishops and professors. The difference in style between the Duero and the Upper Ebro is export influence: in the Upper Ebro they made wine to please the French market, as well as themselves; in the Duero they made wine to please themselves. The result, traditionally, was wines with less oak, more fruit and more alcohol, and it is still apparent today. The DOs and their average production figures are as follows:

Region	DO	Cases
Castilla-León:	Bierzo	396,750
	Cigales	264,000
	Ribera del Duero	920,200
	Rueda	491,450
	Toro	188,050

CATALONIA AND THE BALEARICS

The culture here has always been fiercely independent – Catalunya (along with the Balearic Islands and other territories) was a Mediterranean power in the Middle Ages and, in its thinking, traditionally looks to sea rather than inland towards Madrid. The style of cooking here is strongly Mediterranean in character – indeed, very similar to the neighbouring French region of Roussillon. Gastronomy is strong on fish, of course, and the wines which evolved naturally in the region were largely simple whites and rosados to suit the cookery. However, the independent spirit of the region encouraged early experimentation with non-Spanish grape varieties and today Catalunya is as strong on new-wave varietal wines as on its traditional styles. Most Cava – Spain's best sparkling wine, is also produced here. The DOs and their average production figures are as follows:

Region	DO	Cases
Catalunya:	Alella	57,000
	Ampurdán-Costa Brava	783,500
	Conca de Barberà	1,026,600
	Costers del Segre	1,131,200
	Penedès	5,686,050
	Priorato	70,850
	Tarragona	3,285,550
	Terra Alta	1,141,500
	Cava	14,672,000
Baleares:	Binissalem (Mallorca)	51,600

THE LEVANT

The export culture evident in Catalunya is even more well-developed in this region. The hot Mediterranean-maritime climate is ideal for the production of everyday wine, and local consumption of fish dishes (the paella was invented here) evolved a plentiful supply of adequate uncomplicated whites and rosados, but the region's main claim to fame is its resolutely 'out-to-sea' vision. With modern technology, the Levant has become the powerhouse of Spanish exports of low-cost wines. Valencia is the country's biggest wine port, from which wines are exported in road- rail- and sea-tankers as well as in bottle and cask, all over the world. The DOs and their average production figures are as follows:

Region	DO	Cases
Valencia:	Alicante	1,224,250
	Utiel-Requena	2,895,350
	Valencia	6,407,050
Murcia:	Bullas	*
	Jumilla	3,473,250
	Yecla	148,600

*these areas have yet to report on a full vintage season under DO regulations

THE MESETA

The winemaking culture here is based on survival. There was no market for the wines of Spain's great central plateau until Madrid was founded in 1561; there was no chance of shipping them to the Levantine coast and, in the south, the (nominally teetotal) Moors ruled until 1492. Although food was abundant, it was plain, and the climate is so searing in the summer and freezing in the winter that only the hardiest of vines would survive. So the wine was poor and rustic and made in the cheapest available material (earthenware jars) because there was only the local market to satisfy. The main contact with the outside world was the royal road from Madrid to Granada. One of the stopping-off places for official retinues was the town of Valdepeñas, and this ready market for better quality wines still shows today. This isolation and the resulting low land prices led to massive redevelopment in the 1970s and '80s, with the result that many of today's everyday wines will have a La Mancha DO. The DOs and their average production figures are as follows:

Region	DO	Cases
Madrid:	Vinos de Madrid	196,650
Castilla-La Mancha:		
	Almansa	1,172,100
	La Mancha	12,511,800
	Méntrida	1,179,250
	Valdepeñas	7,516,550

ANDALUCÍA

This is the crucible of winemaking for Spain and a good deal of Western Europe. The Greeks and other winemakers from the eastern Mediterranean settled here some 3,000 years ago and the wines they made were in the Levantine or Greek tradition; products of a fiercely hot climate with ameliorating influences around the coast to meet the demands of burgeoning export markets throughout the Mediterranean – especially during the Roman Empire – and the western European coast. The Greek taste was for powerful sweet wines with plenty of alcohol. Even at this distance, we can see this legacy in the fortified wines of Andalucía. By Shakespeare's time the wines of southern Spain, known then as 'sack' after the Spanish word *saca*, meaning 'withdrawal' (ie from the butt) were famous. Today they find their being in one of the world's greatest wines – sherry. The DOs and their average production figures are as follows:

Region	DO	Cases
Andalucía:		
	Condado de Huelva	1,681,400
	Jerez/Xérès/Sherry	11,263,700
	Málaga	377,700
	Montilla-Moriles	4,856,750

THE CANARY ISLANDS

The Canary Islands are in some ways a snapshot of what Spanish wine used to be like 500 years ago, when they were rediscovered and claimed for the Spanish Crown. Varieties are grown here which died out on the peninsula centuries ago, production is small, and 'Canary-Sack' of Shakespearean fame is still made. Most of the production, however, evolved for local consumption and has developed to supply the tourist trade. Those bodegas with serious ambitions are hampered by the sheer cost of shipping their wines to the mainland, let alone the markets of northern Europe. The DOs and their average production figures are as follows:

Region	DO	Cases
Canarias:	Abona (Tenerife)	*
	El Hierro	*
	Lanzarote	*
	La Palma	28,350
	Tacoronte-Acentejo	24,550
	Valle de Güimar	*
	Valle de la Orotava	*
	Ycoden-Daute-Isora	72,200

*these areas have yet to report on a full vintage season under DO regulations

NORTHWESTERN SPAIN

GALICIA

Galicia and the north coastal vineyards of the Bay of Biscay enjoy a wetter, cooler climate than the rest of Spain, and the wines are commensurately lighter and fresher. White wines predominate, although reds and rosados are widely made. In the ongoing search for the definitive white wine of Spain this area is one of the leading contenders.

RIAS BAIXAS

In the province of Pontevedra on the Atlantic coast between Santiago and the Portuguese border. The most excellent wines are whites made entirely from the Albariño grape, but planting on steep slopes and in small parcels means that they lack economy of scale and are likely to be expensive.

RIBEIRA SACRA

A beautiful area at the confluence of two rivers, the Sil and the Miño. Much of the winemaking is on a small and simple scale, but some winemakers have invested in new technology. The wines need a little more work, but there is some excellent Albariño and Godello and although most producers make red wine from a grape called the Mencía, very few do it well. One which does is Adegas Moure.

RIBEIRO

An old-established area in the province of Orense, lying just east of Rías Baixas. The vineyards are concentrated in the valleys of the Miño, Avía and Arnoya rivers. Ribeiro is famous for its light, fruity white wines. New development has provided it with some stars – mainly made from the Albariño but also from the more widely planted (and much lower-priced) Torrontés, Loureira and Treixadura.

VALDEORRAS

Both crisp fresh whites and light reds are made; the whites from the excellent Godello variety and the reds from the potentially good but usually under-achieving Mencía grape.

VAL DO MONTERREY

This is a very small region of white wines from the Godello and Doña Blanca grapes. Quality is potentially good but with only four bodegas affiliated to the Consejo Regulador it is difficult to give an overview. However, Bodegas Ladairo is worth watching.

BASQUE COUNTRY

Chacolí de Getaria (Getariako Txakolina) and Chacolí de Bizkaia (Bizkaiko Txakolina) are the two indigenous wines of the Basque Country. Most is white, made from the local Ondarrabi Zuri grape. At its best it is a very crisp, grapey, thirst-quenching wine, although the quantity is so small that exports are virtually non-existent.

Leading Northwestern Spain Producers

Albariño de Fefiñanes

Fefiñanes, Pontevedra, Galicia.
The aristocrat of Galician wine, made by the Marqués de Figueroa in a small modern bodega in his palace of Fefiñanes, near Cambados. It is 100% Albariño, the best white grape of the region (and of Portugal's Minho), aged for up to six years (for *reservas*) in oak. It bears no resemblance to *vinho verde* except in its remarkable freshness.

Albariño de Palacio

Fefiñanes, Pontevedra, Galicia.
The brother of the Marqués de Figueroa (see previous entry) makes this high-quality, typical fizzy young Albariño – but not in the palace.

Bodegas Chaves

Barrantes-Ribadumia Pontevedra, Galicia.
A small family-run bodega offering typical sharp and fizzy Albariño to a good standard.

Fernandez Cervera Hermanos

36770 O Rosal.
Bodega near the Portuguese border making crisp, appley tasting wines (labelled Lagar de Cervera) from 50 acres of their own Albariño vines. The bodega was recently bought by Bodegas La Rioja Alta (q.v.) which has invested large amounts of money updating the winery and vineyard.

Vinos Santiago Ruiz

36770 O Rosal.
Small producer of high quality white wines selling on the Spanish market and commanding a high price. Unusual blend of Albariño, Loureira and Troixadura grapes makes an especially aromatic, floral dry white.

Bodegas Vilariño-Cambados SA

06633 Cambados.

Eighty-five growers cultivating more than 200 acres of vines send their Albariño grapes to an up-to-date stainless steel winery in the Valle de Salnés north of Vigo. Good clean fragrant dry wines are bottled under the Martin Codax label.

Vinos Blancos de Castilla

Rueda, Valladolid.

A branch of the famous Rioja firm of Marqués de Riscal, founded in 1973 and built with advice from Professor Emile Peynaud. Riscal make three whites here, Marqués de Riscal blanco (Verdejo and Viura, no oak); Reserva Limousin (the same with a few months in oak); and a 100% Chardonnay.

Cooperativa Barco de Valdeorras

El Barco, Orense.

A substantial cooperative bottling very adequate plain still red and white (DO Valdeorras) with the name El Barco ('The Boat').

Cooperativa de Monterrey

Verin, Orense.

The only bottler of Monterrey wines. Red and white are both bubble-free; the best are labelled Castillo de Monterrey.

Cooperativa del Ribeiro

Ribadavia, Orense, Galicia.

Much the biggest cooperative in Galicia, with 800 members and very modern facilities, producing the equivalent of more than 750,000 cases a year. Its best white is crisp, clean and faintly fragrant, only slightly *pétillant*, like a Portuguese *vinho verde*. The red is fizzy, sharp and an acquired taste.

THE UPPER EBRO

This is the region of Spain which produces most (though not all) of the fine red wines for which the country is famous. Understandably, it tends to be dominated by Rioja, but recent developments in Navarra and, particularly, the Somontano region of Aragón have brought the whole region forcefully to the forefront of quality winemaking in Spain.

LA RIOJA

As a wine region, Rioja claims a longer history than Bordeaux. Some French historians believe that the Romans may even have found the ancestor of the Cabernet in this part of Spain. Certainly the Romans followed the River Ebro up from the Mediterranean much as they followed the Rhône, as a corridor of the climate and conditions they were accustomed to, into a colder and more hostile land. High in the headwaters of the Ebro, over 2,000 feet up, round its little tributary Rio Oja, they found ideal conditions for wine of good quality – and possibly even the necessary grapes.

The postclassical history of Rioja was similar to that of all the Roman wine regions. Rapid decline (accelerated in Spain by the Moorish invasion), the dominance of the Church, a slow renaissance in the 16th century, but no real changes until the 18th or early 19th centuries. Then it was the influence of Bordeaux that reached Rioja, the new idea of barrel-ageing the best wines. It was first tried in 1787, but was overruled by Luddite reaction, and finally introduced by reforming aristocratic landowners – in much the same way and at the same time as Chianti was 'invented' by the Barone Ricasoli.

The first commercial bodegas of the modern age of Rioja were founded in the 1860s, by the Marqués de Riscal and the Marqués de Murrieta, with the Bordeaux château system very much in mind. Both used (and still use) grapes from their immediate districts. They sold their wine in bottle and spread the reputation of the region at a most opportune moment. Phylloxera was invading Bordeaux, and French capital and technology were looking for a new region to develop. Before the end of the century a dozen much bigger new bodegas had been built, drawing on grapes from a much wider area – the three regions of Rioja all contributed to their blends.

The railhead at Haro formed the nucleus for this boom, and the bodegas round it remain both physically and spiritually the embodiment of the late-Victorian technology. The cluster of huge, rather raffish buildings almost recalls Epernay, the Champagne capital, that grew during the same lush decades.

Phylloxera reached Rioja in the early years of the 20th century. The disruption, followed by World War I, then the Spanish Civil War, prevented the bodegas from capitalizing on the foreign markets they had successfully opened, despite the fact that in 1926 Rioja became the first wine region of Spain to set up a Consejo Regulador to supervise its affairs. During this period the region was making and maturing some superlative vintages (examples can still occasionally be found). Yet Rioja remained the staple of connoisseurs only in Spain and Latin America until the international wine boom of the 1970s.

That decade saw the founding of a new wave of bodegas, a flurry of takeovers, and a vast increase in planting and production. It also saw modifications in winemaking techniques which have added new styles to the already wide range produced.

Rioja is in fact three regions, with a total vineyard area of more than 100,000 acres, following the valley of the Ebro from the Conchas de Haro, the rocky gorge where it bursts through the Sierra Cantabrica, to its much wider valley at Alfaro, 60 miles east and nearly 1,000 feet lower in altitude.

The highest region, La Rioja Alta, has the city of Logroño as its capital, although the much smaller Haro is its vinous heart. Cenicero, Fuenmayor and Navarrete are the other towns with bodegas. Haro has 14 out of a total of 40. There are 40,000 acres of vineyards. The soils are a mixture of chalky clay, iron-rich clay and alluvial silt. The climate is cool here and the rainfall relatively high. The minimum required strength for Rioja Alta wine is only 10 degrees. Rioja Alta wines have the highest acidity but also the finest flavour and structure, finesse and 'grip' that sometimes allows them to age almost indefinitely.

The Rioja Alavesa, north of the Ebro, in the Basque province of Alava, has more southern slopes and a more consistently clay soil. Its 18,000 acres of vines are largely Tempranillo, which here gives particularly fragrant, smooth, almost lush light wine, tending to be pale and quick-maturing. The minimum strength is 11–11.5 degrees. A dozen bodegas are based in four villages: Labastida, Elciego, Laguardia and Oyon.

The Rioja Baja ('Lower Rioja'), with 33,000 acres, has much the warmest and driest climate. Its soil is silt and iron-rich clay, its principal grape the Garnacha Tinta and its wine stronger, broader and less fine, with a required minimum strength of 12–12.5 degrees. There are only six bodegas for ageing in the region, but nearly all bodegas buy some of their wine here, and several have been planting the finer grapes in the highest parts of the region.

It is probably true to say that most red Riojas are blends of wines from all three regions, although the old-established bodegas draw most heavily on the areas in which they were founded, and a few in Rioja Alavesa make a particular point of the regional style of their wines.

RIOJA DOCa

From the 1991 vintage, Rioja was elevated to a new 'super-category' called Denominación de Origen Calificada which translates as 'Qualified Denomination of Origin'. The word 'qualified' in this context means 'quality-fied' rather than its normal English interpretation of 'with reservations' and is an attempt to offer an extra guarantee to the customer, exactly like the DOCG in Italy. And, exactly like the DOCG in Italy, its introduction was marked by anger, recriminations, argument, opprobrium and dismissal by the pundits as nothing more than a PR exercise. Certainly, it could have been done better, it could have been thought through more carefully, it could have changed the way Rioja is marketed... But it didn't. The main consequence that we see in the outside world is that bulk sales have been stopped and all Rioja is now bottled in the region. The result, at least in the short-term, seems to have been that there is a lot less poor-quality wine appearing under the Rioja label. For many of us, that's good enough for a start.

Long ageing in Bordeaux-type barrels is the hallmark of traditional Rioja. It gives the wines, whether red or white, an easily recognized fragrance and flavour related to vanilla. The best wines, with a concentrated flavour of ripe fruit, can support a surprising degree of this oaky overlay. Lesser wines become exhausted by it, losing their fruity sweetness and becoming dry and monotone. Spanish taste leans to emphasis on oak. International taste inclines to less oak-ageing for reds and little or none for whites. Many bodegas have therefore modified their old practice of bottling the wine at what they consider full maturity. By replacing time in barrel with time in bottle they reduce the impact of the oak in favour of the more subtle bouquet of bottle-age.

Red wines make up three-quarters of the total production of the region. The range offered by a typical Rioja bodega includes some or all of the following:

VINOS BLANCOS

White wines, either in Bordeaux-, burgundy- or German-shaped bottles. Normally very dry and gratifyingly low in alcohol (10–11°). Principally made of the Viura grape (alias Macabeo), with or without Malvasía and/or Garnacha Blanca. They have good acidity and resist oxidation well. Made in the old way they had little grape aroma but often very satisfying structure and balance.

Better whites were formerly all aged in old oak barrels for between about three and anything up to 12 years – the best longest. Outstanding examples of these *reservas* remain pale lemon-yellow and keep an astonishing freshness, roundness and vigour beneath a great canopy of oaky fragrance. They can be compared with the best old vintages of white Graves.

Many bodegas now make all or some of their whites by long, slow fermentation followed by almost immediate bottling, the object being to capture primary grape aromas in all their freshness. The Viura makes delicious wine in this style, possibly benefiting from some bottle-age (though Bodegas Olarra make a white 'Reciente', which they recommend be consumed within months of the vintage). Most bodegas also make a compromise, semi-modern white, cold-fermented and briefly oak-aged.

Sweet white Riojas are rarely a success. Noble rot is very rare in the dry upland atmosphere. Overripe grapes are simply half-raisined. But exceptional vintages have produced beautiful delicate and aromatic sweet wines of apparently limitless lasting power.

VINOS ROSADOS

Rosé wines, made in the customary way, normally dry and pale and not oak-aged.

VINOS TINTOS

Many bodegas now call all their red wines *tinto*. The former custom was to divide them into *clarete*, light-coloured red wine of fairly low strength (10–11.5%) bottled in Bordeaux bottles, and *tinto* (sometimes called Borgoña) sold in burgundy bottles. *Tinto* in this sense is much darker in colour, more fruity, fuller in body and higher in alcohol. Both are made of a mixture of Tempranillo, the dominant red grape, with the luscious and aromatic Graciano and the alcoholic Garnacha Tinta (the Rhône Grenache), often with some Mazuelo (or Cariñena), a cousin of the Carignan of the Midi. A little white Viura is also sometimes used in *claretes*.

Both types are equally made up to the level of *reservas* or *gran reservas*, but Rioja's ultimate glories tend to be of the *tinto* type, which resists barrel-ageing better without growing thin and (although less fragrant) can grow marvellously velvety in the bottle.

All wines can be sold either as *joven* ('young'), which means 'without oak ageing', or *con crianza*. A *vino de crianza* from Rioja is bottled at either three or four years old ('3°año' or '4°año'), of which at least one year must be in *barricas*, or 225-litre Bordeaux barrels. The rest will usually be in bigger oak containers. Wines of modest, medium and good quality are all handled like this. *Reservas* are specially selected wines at least three years old, of which one year was in *barricas*. Now, however, any of the statutory period can be substituted by twice as long in bottle. White *reservas* have a minimum of six months in oak.

Gran reservas are wines of at least five years old, with at least two years in *barricas*, or twice as long in bottle. These requirements for ageing are much less than they were only a few years ago. The reason given is a change in customers' tastes, although commercial necessity points in the same direction. Reputable bodegas will of course only select wines of fine quality to mature as *reservas* and top quality as *gran reservas* – although this is only implied, not required, by the regulations.

Leading Rioja Producers

AGE Bodegas Unidas

26360 Fuenmayor, Logroño, Rioja Alta.

A large modern bodega, but one with a long history. It was established in 1967 with the joining of Bodegas Romeral (founded in 1881 by Don Feliz Azpilicueta) and Las Veras (set up by Don Cruz Garcia Lafuente in 1926) and it is now owned by the American firm of Schenley and the Banco Español de Credito. Though they own vineyards, most grapes have to be bought in. The best of the reds are the traditional *reservas*, Marqués del Romeral, Fuentemayor and Siglo Saco, sold in a sacking wrapper. White wines, all in the new fruity style and bottled at five months old, include Romeral, Siglo Saco, Pedregal and Esmerado. The policy is to give the red wines less barrel-age and more bottle-age than formerly. Sales now amount to 1.66m. cases a year.

Bodegas Berberana

Ctra. Elciego, 26350 Cenicero, Rioja Alta.

Back in private hands after a period with Rumasa and then nationalization. Berberana was founded in Ollauri in 1877 and run by the same family until 1967. The huge new bodega in Cenicero (with no fewer than 34,000 barrels) dates from 1970. Grapes are from their own 130-acre vineyard, though some are still bought in. This impressive pioneering plantation is on high ground near Aldeanueva del Ebro. The classic Tempranillo of the Rioja Alta is thriving here. Preferido is their vigorous cheap *sin crianza* red, Carta de Plata is their big-selling 3° año, Carta de Oro the fuller-bodied 5° año. The *gran reservas* are big and velvety, while

the new Berberana white is young and fruity without barrel-age. Sales of 1.8m. cases a year are principally to Europe and the Americas.

In the early 1990s Berberana formed a joint-venture company with the Marqués de Griñon to market top-level Rioja wines which the company had formerly been unable to market singly for simple reasons of cost. The wines bearing the Marqués' name include jovenes made from grapes that might originally have been reserved for *crianza* or *reserva* wines, and *reservas* made from grapes that night formerly have been reserved for the finest *gran reservas*. They are amongst the best 'new-wave' wines that Rioja has to offer.

Bodegas Bilbainas

Particular del Norte 2, 48003 Bilbao, and at Haro.

The bodega was founded in 1901 and continues essentially as a family firm. 35% of their grapes are grown in their own 625 acres of vineyards in Haro (Rioja Alta) and Elciego, Leza and Laguardia in Alavesa. They sell nearly 300,000 cases of still and sparkling wines a year. Their aim is a wide choice of wines rather than a strong house style, but all the wines are conservative; rather austere by modern standards. Viña Paceta is a dry white, Cepa de Oro a sweeter white and Brillante a golden dessert wine. Viña Zaco is a high-quality *clarete*, while Viña Pomal is its more full-bodied *tinto* complement. Pomal *reservas* are the biggest and longest-lived wines. Royal Carlton is a *méthode traditionnelle* wine which they have been making since 1912. They also make a brandy, Imperator.

Bodegas Marqués de Cáceres

Union Viti-Vinicola, Carretera de Logroño, 26350 Cenicero, Rioja Alta.

Founded in 1970 by Enrique Forner (owner with his brother of Château de Camensac in Bordeaux), planned with the help of Professor Emile Peynaud, and recently modernized. Grapes come from 81 local growers, including the Cenicero cooperative. The red wines spend 15-18 months in wood and 15–18 months in bottle (though the Reserva and Gran Reserva spend 36 months in barrel and may be kept for 10 years in bottle). They emerge less oaky than traditional Rioja, but well balanced and fruity. The white Marqués de Cáceres, marketed young and without barrel-ageing, was the first of the new-style whites and, with its fruit and freshness without excess acidity, is still one of the best. The principal brand names is Marqués de Cáceres. 70% of the 500,000 cases sold annually is red wine, the rest being white or *rosado*. Forty-five percent of the production is for the export market.

Bodegas Campo Viejo

26006 Logroño, Rioja Alta.

One of the largest bodegas; owned by the Bodegas y Bebidas group and formed in 1963 by the amalgamation of two old firms. Capacity in the new premises, built in 1968 and extended in 1971, is now 50m. litres. 50% of production is from wine bought from cooperatives and 25% is from grapes bought in for vinification; 25% comes from their own vineyard of 1,200 acres, which include, in addition to the traditional grape varieties, experimental quantities of Cabernet Sauvignon, Pinot Noir, Gamay, Merlot, Chenin Blanc, Sémillon and Chardonnay.

Annual sales amount to 2m. cases. On the domestic market Campo Viejo, Almenar, Castillo de San Asensio and Foncalada are among the most familiar trademarks, accounting for 25–30% of all Rioja sold in Spain. Campo Viejo is consistently good value among the less ethereal red Riojas. San Asensio is a robust unaged red. Marqués de Villamagna is the bodega's top *gran reserva*.

In line with B y B's countrywide policy of developing varietal alternatives, the company has also recently introduced a single varietal Mazuelo (alias Carignan) wine.

CVNE (Compañia Vinicola del Norte de España)

Avda. Costa del Vino 21, 26200 Haro, Rioja Alta.

One of the top half-dozen Rioja houses, founded in 1879 by the Real de Asua brothers and still owned by this family. Though the home market is now their most important – accounting for 85% of annual sales of around 440,000 cases – for the first 60 years they exported all they produced. Their own 1,300 acres under vine provide 65% of the grapes needed for red wine. Other vineyards are under contract. The bodega has a capacity of 17m. litres of steel tanks, as well as 22,000 oak barrels for ageing. They make consistently good wines. Reds include the excellent, vigorous Cune, the velvety Imperial (a *reserva* from the Rioja Alta), and the notably full-bodied, spicy Viña Real from Alavesa (made at Elciego). For white wines, CVNE is best known for its traditional oak-flavoured white in a Moselle bottle, Monopole – a standard and reliable resource in most good Spanish restaurants.

In 1989 the company invested £12m. in a new state-of-the-art bodega incorporating stainless steel carousel technology, with grapes, musts and wines all moved by gravity and without pumping, and providing individual fermentation in more than 80 batches to ensure optimum quality-control. At the time, it was probably the most modern winery in the world.

Bodegas Domecq

Ctra. Villabuena, 9, Elciego, Alava.

Founded in the early 1970s by the sherry house of Pedro Domecq and the Canadian drinks giant, Seagram. When the two parted company in 1974, Domecq built a modern, vitrified-steel-equipped bodega (recently expanded by 25%) and began planting new vineyards and buying old ones in Alavesa. They now claim to be the biggest growers in Rioja, with 790 acres in production, but still have to buy in 60% of their grapes. White and red Marqués de Arienzo and the low-priced Viña Eguia are their main brands. Marqués de Arienzo is also made as *reserva* and *gran reserva*. Annual sales reach 300,000 cases. Thirty percent is exported.

Bodegas Faustino Martínez

Carretera de Logroño, 01320 Oyón, Alava.

Founded in 1860 and still family owned and run. All grapes come from around the Oyón area in Rioja Alavesa, 40% from their own 1,200 acres. Faustino I, the *gran reserva*, and Faustino V, an aromatic, lemony white in the new style, are made largely from their own grapes from first-class vineyards. The reds are given extra age in bottle rather than spending overlong in oak. Faustino V is the red *reserva;* Faustino I is the top wine. Total sales are 580,000 cases, with a high proportion of *reservas* and *gran reservas*. A recent development is the production of some *cava* using their own grapes.

R Lopez de Heredia Viña Tondonia

Avenida de Vizcaya 3, 26200 Haro, Rioja Alta.

One of the great bastions of Rioja tradition. A family-owned, family-run bodega founded by Don Raphael Lopez de Heredia y Landeta in 1877 and now headed by his grandson, Don Pedro. The premises, on a railway siding at Haro, are a marvel of Art Nouveau design; the underground tasting-room Wagnerian in its lofty cobwebbed splendour; the cellars damp and chilly. Approximately half the grapes come from their own vineyards in Rioja Alta and most of the rest from small local growers. All the wines are fermented and aged long in oak: the minimum is three years. Wines include Tondonia (fine red and white not less than 4˚ año), Bosconia (a bigger red, at best sumptuous) and Gravonia (an oaky white), and Cubillo, a red, and at 3˚ año their youngest wine. White wines are important, accounting for a quarter of their annual sales of 1.2m. litres. A 1964 Tondonia Blanco was still brilliantly fresh in 1996. The domestic and European markets are their biggest, with exports making up 30% of their sales.

Bodegas Muga

Barrio de la Estacion, 26200 Haro, Rioja Alta.

A small family firm founded in 1932 by Don Isaac Muga. His son, Don Isaac Muga Caño, took over on his father's death in 1969 and two years later moved to a new bodega by the famous Haro railway station.

Muga claim to be the only producer in Rioja to use American oak exclusively throughout fermentation and ageing. Their own 80 acres under vine provide 40% of their needs; the rest they buy from farmers in the Rioja Alta. Muga wines are almost alarmingly pale and ethereal but very fragrant. Much their best wine to my taste is the darker and richer Reserva Prado Enea, a wine with some of the velvet pungency of burgundy. They also make traditional white and a featherweight *méthode traditionnelle* with the name of Conde de Haro. Annual sales are 50,000 cases of which 20% is exported.

Marqués de Murrieta

Finca Ygay, Logroño, Ctra. de Zaragoza km 5, Rioja Alta.

With Marqués de Riscal, one of the two noble houses of Rioja, the first two bodegas to be founded, still with a special cachet, and remarkably unchanged by time. Don Luciano de Murrieta y Garcia-Lemoine founded this, the second oldest, in 1872. In 1983 control passed to Vicente Cebrian, Count of Creixel. Their own vineyards of 366 acres at Ygay near Logroño supply the majority of grapes and the new owner increased plantings to make the bodega self-sufficient.

Wines are made by wholly traditional methods and maintain a very high standard. The small range includes a fruity 4° año, Etiqueta Blanca, and their extremely rare and expensive Castillo Ygay – the 1934 vintage of which has recently been succeeded by the 1942. The current white Castillo Ygay vintage is 1968.

Bodegas Olarra

Polígono de Cantabria, Logroño, Rioja Alta.
Founded 1972. The most stylish bodega in Rioja, owned by a company founded by a Bilbao industrialist, Luis Olarra, and now controlled by the Guibert-Ucin family. The ultramodern winery, formed of three wings to symbolize Rioja's three regions, would look better in the Napa Valley than on an industrial estate outside Logroño. It owns no vines but has rapidly made a name for typical and stylish wines, red and white (the white very lightly oaked and ageing extremely well in bottle, viz. the '76 in 1982). Cerro Añon is the label of the fatter and darker *reservas*. Reciente is a new-wave white. Añares Crianza is their best-seller of recent years. Forty percent of their production of 500,000 cases is exported.

Bodegas Federico Paternina

Avda. Santo Domingo 11, 26200 Haro, Rioja Alta.
One of the largest bodegas, now owned by Marcos Equizabal, who also owns Lan and Franco-Españolas. It was founded in Ollauri in 1898 by Don Federico Paternina Josue. The extensive vineyards have been sold, and Paternina now buy in their grapes from cooperatives and growers. Wines include Banda Azul (a variable but popular young red), Viña Vial (full and fruity), a *gran reserva* and a *reserva especial* Conde de los Andes. Annual sales are 800,000 cases; 35% is exported.

La Rioja Alta

Avda. Vizcaya, 26200 Haro, Rioja Alta.
One of the group of top-quality firms round the station at Haro. Founded in 1890 and with descendants of the founders still on the board. They own 740 acres at various sites in Rioja, and also buy in a varying proportion of grapes from local producers. The reds are more distinguished than the whites. Viña Alberdi is the pleasant *crianza* red, Viña Arana is a fine light red (and a rather dull white) and Viña Ardanza a sumptuous full red worth laying down. The top wines are the Reservas 904 and 890, selected for depth of colour and flavour to withstand respectively six and eight years in American oak and emerge in perfect balance. They also own a Rías Baixas bodega in Galicia, Fernandez Cervera Hermanos, producing wine under its label Lagar de Cervera.

Bodegas Riojanas

Estacion 1-21, Cenicero, Rioja Alta.
A substantial and conservative bodega, conceived in 1890 as a sort of château in Spain, by families who still own and manage the company today. The original French staff stayed on until 1936. Some grapes are bought in, the rest come from their own 494-acre holding in Cenicero. Traditional methods are used to produce the *reservas*, Viña Albina, and Monte Real, a most pungent and admirable red. Albina is a semi-sweet white, Medieval a dry one and Canchales a young red. Puerta Vieja and Bori are other brands. Annual sales are 83,000 cases, with Italy among the export markets.

Herederos Marqués de Riscal

Torrea 1, Elciego, Alava.
The oldest existing Rioja bodega, founded in 1860 by Don Camilo Hurtado de Amezaga, Marqués de Riscal. The bodega was designed by a Bordeaux *vigneron,* and most of the wines continue to have a light, elegant, almost claret-like character – the epitome of the Rioja Alavesa.

Forty percent of the grapes come from their own vineyards, 49 acres of which are planted with Cabernet Sauvignon. Cabernet is used in a proportion of about 15% for all *reservas* and above, but occasionally much more. A 1970 *reserva* had 60% and an astonishing 1938, still vigorous in 1982, had 80%. The wines are aged in barrel for up to four years, then in bottle for a minimum of three, often ten – and no maximum. A recent launch, based on the Bodega's unique old plantations of Cabernet, is called Baron de Chirel. To save the blushes of the Consejo Regulador its grapes are listed as 25% Tempranillo, 35% Graciano and 40% 'others'. White Riscal wines are not Riojas, but come from Rueda. *See* Vinos Blancos de Castilla, page 362. Sales of 250,000 cases a year, including wines under the Riscalsa label, go to 82 countries.

OTHER RIOJA PRODUCERS

Bodegas Alavesas Laguardia, Rioja Alavesa. Founded 1972. Now owned by the group Alter. They own over 900 acres and also buy in some grapes from local growers. They make typically pale, light, fragrant Alavesa wines; *reservas* under the name Solar de Samaniego; other names include Solar de Iriarte and Solar de Berbete.

Bodegas Ramon Bilbao Avda. Santa Domingo, Haro, Rioja Alta. Founded in 1924; a family-owned company which buys in most of its wine and grapes from private vineyards. Wines under the bodega name include Turzaballa, Monte Blanco, Monte Llano and Monte Rojo.

Bodegas Martînez Bujanda Campo Viejo de Logroño, Oyón, Alava. A century-old family-owned bodega re-founded in 1988 and already making exceptional wines, especially its Valdemar Reservas, of which Centenario is the sumptuous best. Also fruity *joven* and very fruity *rosado.*

Bodegas Corral Carretera de Logroño km-10, Navarrete, Rioja Alta. Owned by Don Florencio Corral Daroca (grandson of the founder) and a group of Riojan friends. Their own 96-acre Rioja Alta vineyard provides 25% of their grape needs, the rest comes from growers in the same area. Traditional methods produce distinctly oaky wines under the Don Jacobo and Corral labels. Annual sales of 80,000 cases.

Bodegas El Coto Oyón, Alava, Rioja. A young bodega founded in 1970 and expanded in 1977 and 1988. The firm owns 300 acres of vineyards in Cenicero and Mendavia, providing 57% of the red and all the white grapes. Soft fruity reds, Coto de Imaz and El Coto, are made almost wholly from Tempranillo, while El Coto white is made in the new style almost entirely from Viura.

Bodegas Franco-Españolas Cabo Noval 2, Logroño, Rioja Alta. A big bodega in the city of Logroño, bought after Rumasa ownership by Marcos Equizàbel Ramiriz. Its French and Spanish founders (hence the name) included Monsieur Anglade, a fugitive from phylloxera-devastated France. The vineyards have been sold; they buy in grapes and wine from Rioja Alta and Alavesa. Traditional oak-aged whites, Viña Soledad and Vinã Sole, have been joined by a young no-oak white Diamante. Traditional reds include a dark and flavoury (if rather coarse) bargain, Rioja Bordon, the Royal *reservas* and Excelso *gran reservas*. Annual production 3,500 cases.

Bodegas Gurpegui Cuevas 38, Haro. One of the largest producers of wine to sell to other bodegas. Founded in 1872. Don Luis Gurpegui Muga is the third-generation proprietor. 10% of production comes from their own 250-acre vineyard, 90% from regular suppliers over many years. Two of the well-known brands of well-made classic Riojas from this stable are Dominio de la Plana and Berceo (and Gonzalo de Berceo). Annual sales of 208,000 cases.

Martinez Lacuesta Hnos Lda La Ventilla 71, 26200, Haro, Rioja Alta. A family firm founded in 1895 and now directed by Don Luis Martinez Lacuesta. All grapes, including an unusually high proportion of Garnacha, are bought in from cooperatives. Reds are a very pale and oaky *clarete* and a fuller, still oaky, Campeador. A white wine is called Viña De Lys. Average production is around 150,000 cases.

In 1995, 6.6 million cases of Rioja were exported (from an average annual production of 16.1 million cases). The top ten export customers were as follows:

Country	Cases	Population	Bottles per head (millions)
Sweden	1,289,341	8.6	1.80
Germany	1,235,822	79.8	0.19
UK	995,823	57.4	0.21
Denmark	771,091	5.1	1.81
Holland	509,342	15.0	0.41
Switzerland	476,927	6.7	0.85
USA	301,306	254.6	0.01
Norway	173,446	4.2	0.41
Belgium	125,195	9.9	0.15
France	113,002	6.6	0.02

Note: In Sweden the advertising of alcoholic products of all kinds is forbidden by law. This means that the choice is limited, but also that wine-lovers tend to vote with their palates, uncluttered by advertising messages. It is, perhaps, significant that in this advertising vacuum Rioja plays such a popular part.

Bodegas Lagunilla 26360 Fuenmayor, Rioja Alta. Next door to Lan (see next entry), a modern bodega but a century-old firm (founded in 1885), now owned by the Croft sherry group. Buys in wine to make fresh whites and reds to age, including a powerful *gran reserva*.

Bodegas Lan Paraje de Buicio, 26360 Fuenmayor, Rioja Alta. A large and very modern bodega founded in 1973. Tempranillo, Mazuelo and Viura from their own 270 acres in El Cortijo (Rioja Alta) provide some of their requirements. Most of the rest is bought from small growers, principally in Rioja Alavesa. The labels are Lan, Lander and Viña Lanciano (for *reservas*). Production is 150,000 cases and sales are to both national and international markets.

Bodegas Muerza Plaza Vera Magallon, San Adrian, Navarra. A small bodega founded in 1882. It has changed hands several times and now belongs to the Agronavarra group. Buys in all its grapes from both cooperatives and individual growers. Reds are made in the traditional way, whites and rosés in the no-oak style. There are two brand names: Rioja Vega and Señorial.

Bodegas Navajas Carnino de Balgoraiz 2, Navarrete. Founded in 1978. They have 12 acres but most of the grapes are bought in. There is one white made from 100% Viura but the reds are better, from 70% Tempranillo, 30% Garnacha. The aim is to unite the fresh and oaky styles of new and old Riojas.

Bodegas Palacio San Lazaro 1, Laguardia, Alava. Founded by Don Angel Palacio in 1894. Formerly famous for its splendid Glorioso, which is showing signs of regaining its reputation. Now owned by the Seagram group. They have small vineyards in Laguardia where they grow Tempranillo and Viura, but most grapes are bought in for their Glorioso, Portil and Castillo red, white and rosé Riojas.

Bodegas José Palacios Polígono de Calabria, PO Box 1.152, Logroño, Rioja Alta. Founded by Don José Palacios Remondo in 1947 and still in the family. All grapes are bought in, mostly from Alfaro (Rioja Baja). Brands are Eral, Utrero, Copa Remondo and Herencia. Reds are traditional; whites unaged.

Salceda Carretera de Cenicero km-3, 01340 Elciego, Alava. Founded in 1973. A red-wine-only bodega with 70 acres of its own vineyard, using modern methods to make good wine with a leaning to the soft Alavesa style. Recent expansion has enabled production to be increased. Viña Salceda is the 4-year-old quality; Conde de la Salceda the *reserva*.

Bodegas Carlos Serres
Avda. Santo Domingo 40, 26200 Haro, Rioja Alta. Founded in 1896 by Charles Serres, who arrived in Haro from phylloxera-infected France. Now a limited company. Grapes and wine are bought in from growers and cooperatives. Reds, whites and rosés are made by traditional methods with

very modern equipment. Red Carlos Serres *reservas* (the top wines) are good, usually rather light in style.

Cooperative Vinicola de Labastida Rioja Alavesa. Founded 1965. Its 160-odd members are all in Rioja Alavesa with admirable vineyards, and their cooperative competes

on equal terms with the best bodegas. The powerful reds range from the everyday Manuel Quintano and good-value Montebuena to very fine *reservas* and *gran reservas* called Gastrijo and Castillo Labastida (the top of the line). The white is unoaked, in the modern manner, and one of the best of its sort.

NAVARRA

Eastwards is the province of Navarra, which actually abuts onto Rioja and can lay claim to some of the vineyards of the Rioja Baja. Its limits are Catalonia in the east, the River Ebro in the south and the Pyrenees to the north. The province has some 60,000 acres (44,000 demarcated) of vines, and utilizes the same grapes as Rioja but with more emphasis on the heavy, alcoholic Garnacha. The best vineyards lie just south of the provincial capital, Pamplona, where the cooling influence of the Pyrenees can already be felt. The growers are being encouraged to replant with Tempranillo by increasing recognition of the best Navarra

estates. Some are also experimenting with small amounts of Cabernet Sauvignon.

Sterling work by the region's experimental laboratories at EVENA (Estación de Viticultura y Enología de Navarra) in the town of Olite has meant Navarra has become one of the leading research establishments in Spain, and experimental plantations of all major grape varieties are under evaluation all over the region. New thinking has included barrel-fermentation of white wines, Tempranillo/Cabernet mixes and a willingness to challenge even the mighty Rioja for quality red wines.

Leading Navarra Producers

Bodegas Julián Chivite

Cintruenigo, Navarra.
The largest private wine company in Navarra, founded in 1860. Its Gran Fuedo is a pleasant, full-bodied and oaky wine; the white Gran Fuedo too: able to age 3–4 years with benefit. Older *reservas*, Cibonero and the 10-year-old Parador, are fuller and more fruity in style. Chivite is a pleasant dry white.

Bodegas Magaña

31523 Barillas.
This family-owned property has gone further than any other in Navarra in uprooting Garnacha, replanting Cabernet Sauvignon and Merlot grapes. Magaña wines share more than a passing similarity with good Bordeaux.

Vinicola Navarra

Las Campanas, Navarra.
Century-old company with French origins; the biggest exporter of Navarra wine. No great refinement but reliable and increasingly tasty in the better qualities. Las Campanas Extra is a stout plain red; Castillo de Olite is a clean, pleasantly fruity, faintly sweet red and dry white. Castillo de Tiebas is the full-bodied *reserva* with Rioja-like oaky notes.

Bodegas Ochoa

Olite, Navarra.
A locally popular privately owned bodega in Olite, once the capital of the Kings of Navarra. The reds (including a 100%

Tempranillo) and rosés are soundly made, and now the white is excellent too.

Bodegas Principe de Viana

31001 Pamplona.
Set up with the support of the regional government, Principe de Viana selects wine from local growers and coops and bottles it under the Agramont label. Formerly traded under the name Cenalsa.

Bodega de Sarria

Puente de la Reina, Navarra.
The acknowledged finest wine estate in Navarra, unique in the region (almost in Spain) for its château-style approach and almost Bordeaux-like results. The ancient estate was bought by a wealthy builder, Señor Huarte, in 1952, and taken over by a bank in 1981 which has subsequently rebuilt, landscaped the vineyards, replanted vines and perfected cellarage. A total of 321 acres of the 2,500-acre estate are vineyard, with Rioja vines in appropriate proportions (60% Tempranillo) and a little Cabernet Sauvignon. Its best *reservas* are better than most Riojas; even the light Cosecha (non-*reserva*) wines are very well balanced, Bordeaux-like to smell with a nice plummy flavour. A three-year-old red is called Viña Ecoyen and a bigger, full-bodied red Viña del Perdon.

Cooperativa San Roque

Murchante, Navarra.
Widely held to be the best cooperative of southern Navarra, making powerful but clean reds typical of the warm and fertile region.

ARAGON

South and east of Navarra, astride the Ebro lies Aragón, whose climate tends more towards the Mediterranean. Aragón's once best-known *denominación*, Cariñena, is a byword for high-strength dark red wine with a rustic bite, though worth oak-ageing for two years to achieve a pleasantly smooth texture. The grape here is again largely Garnacha Tinta, despite the fact that the region gave its name to the great grape of France's Midi, the Carignan.

Cariñena lies in the south of the province of Zaragoza, with 54,000 acres of vineyard in all (50,000 demarcated). A small DO, Campo de Borja (with 23,000 acres, of which 21,000 are demarcated), lies halfway between Cariñena and the Rioja Baja. Borja (the origin of the Borgias) makes an even more rustic and alcoholic red, more in demand for blending than drinking. Calatayud, south of Borja, makes similar wines. Most interesting, however, is probably the DO Somontano in the Pyrenees, created in 1985 and updated in 1993. Incoming winemakers discovered that the sleepy local cooperative was actually turning out some excellent wines and that the soils and microclimates were perfect for serious viticulture. Today, the region grows white Macabeo, Garnacha Blanca, and Chardonnay alongside the local – and splendid – Alcañón; reds are Tempranillo, Garnacha and Cabernet Sauvignon alongside the indigenous Parreleta and Moristel (not the Monastrell in spite of many references to the contrary). The coop has modernized and new wineries are experimenting with everything from Pinot Noir to Gewürztraminer. Early results are extremely promising.

Leading Aragón Producers

Bodegas la Magallonera

Magallon, Zaragoza, Aragón.

A small family bodega in the DO Campo de Borja, founded in the 1950s by Andrés Ruberte, whose family are well-known winemakers. His wines are typically alcoholic and full-bodied; the red Pagos de Oruña is worth tasting.

Cooperativa Viticola San José de Aguaron

Aguaron – Cariñena (Zaragoza), Aragón.

A 500-member coop founded in 1948. Very sound wines aged in oak casks. Puente de Piedra is a typical Cariñena red.

Cooperativa San Valero

Cariñena, Zaragoza, Aragón.

A large coop (1,000 members) with a wide market in Spain for its 'Don Mendo' and Monte Ducay wines. Also produces a rather superior oak-aged 'Villalta' red and a cold-fermented 'Perçebal' rosé.

Bodegas Joaquin Soria

Cariñena, Zaragoza, Aragón.

A small family firm now over 150 years old, growing its own grapes for its benchmark Cariñena, Espigal *clarete*, made of Garnacha Tinta (Grenache Noir) and white Macabeo.

Vicente, Suso y Pérez

Cariñena, Zaragoza, Aragón.

This is biggest and best-known private bodega in Cariñena and the largest exporter. It buys in all its grapes from growers, and uses oak to age the wines. Don Ramon is the standard red and rosé; *reservas* include Comendador and Duque de Sevilla.

THE DUERO VALLEY

Surprisingly it is the very heart of the high plain of Old Castile, with some of the worst of Spain's savagely extreme climate, that is now producing wines of quality seriously to challenge Rioja. Big hot-country wines that they are, the red table wines of the Portuguese upper Douro and the Spanish Ribera del Duero seem to be kindred in their fine engineering. They have the structure, the cleanness and 'cut' of a massive Bordeaux – something not found (as far as I know) elsewhere in Spain, although well known as the hallmark of Portugal's best wine.

Some of Spain's greatest reds, including her most expensive by far, grow along the Duero banks, the Ribera del Duero, just east of Valladolid towards Peñafiel. This was the 'discovery' of the 1980s. There are 18,500 acres in the *denominación*. Vega Sicilia, aged 10 years in cask, is the crown jewel, but even the *reservas* of the cooperative at Peñafiel echo the underlying quality of the region.

Farther upstream at Aranda de Duero is the Ribera de Burgos, with 25,000 acres; not a DO but part of the Ribera del Duero. Its typical *claretes* lack the concentration and class of the Valladolid wines.

It is strange to find an up-and-coming white wine DO only 20 miles south of Valladolid, in the country that breeds such massive reds. Rueda made its name with a sort of sherry, a strong *flor*-growing yellow wine of Palomino, grown on chalky clay not unlike the *albariza* of Jerez. Modern white-wine technology has revolutionized Rueda. First the Marqués de Riscal from Rioja, then other investors, have seen enough potential here to call in the best advice from France and invent a new Rueda: a full-bodied, crisp, dry white of the kind Spain chronically needs.

Every other wine in Old Castile is red. Toro is Rueda's nearest neighbour: a massive wine for blending from the dusty Duero Valley, between Valladolid and Zamora. Cabreros, from over the mountains to the south between Avila and Madrid, makes powerful *claretes*. Cigales, just north of Valladolid, is another region of rough *clarete* – though pale in colour.

LEON

This sort of alcoholic dark rosé is met with all the way north to León, the capital of Castile's twin province. Benavente, with its castle-parador just south of León, is the centre for a bizarre sort of bodega burrowed in the ground. Among the vineyards of Los Oteros, along the shallow valley of the Tera River, and Valdevimbre nearer León, clusters of these extraordinary earthworks appear like ant cities. The city of León is now the commercial centre for the province. The region is dominated by the great VILE bodega which is turning

what are essentially peasant wine traditions to good account.

The last of the named wine areas of León, El Bierzo, lies west of the capital and over the mountains on the borders of cool Galicia. Vilafranca del Bierzo is the centre of a region of 24,000 acres, whose nearest wine-growing neighbour is the Galician *denominación* of Valdeorras. El Bierzo wines are correspondingly the lightest of León, with good acidity and not excessively strong. The Palacio de Arganza is perhaps the best producer of this region.

Leading Duero Valley Producers

Bodegas Alejandro Fernandez

47315 Pesquera del Duero.
Visits by appt. Grower with 150 acres of vineyard on the north side of the Duero. Alejandro Fernandez shot to stardom in the 1980s with Pesquera, a red wine made from Tinto Fino grapes, aged for two years in new American oak. American critics are particular admirers of his dense chewy style and powerful tannic structure. His reserve of reserves is called 'Janus'.

Bodegas Peñalba López

Aranda de Duero, Burgos.
A small family firm founded in 1903 with 500 acres of vineyard planted with Tinto Fino. It makes fruity and well-balanced Torremilanos wines, relatively light in style and among the best from this up-and-coming region. A big expansion programme, including a new winery and thousands of new *barricas*, is a testament to the Peñalba López family's confidence.

Bodegas Vega Sicilia

Valbuena de Duero, Valladolid.
The most prestigious wine estate in Spain: a legend for the quality (and the price) of its wines. It was founded in 1864 in limestone hills 2,400 feet above sea level on the south bank of the Duero. The founder imported Bordeaux grapes (Cabernet Sauvignon, Merlot and Malbec) to add to the local Tinto Aragonés (a form of Tempranillo) Garnacha Tinta and Albillo. Only 16,500 cases are made. There are plans to expand production to 25,000 cases – but slowly. Twenty years ago production was only 2,700 cases. The yield is very low and the winemaking completely traditional. Only the unpressed *vin de goutte* is used, fermented for 15 days and matured in Bordeaux *barricas* for no less than 10 years for the great *reserva* 'Unico' (Vega Sicilia itself) and three or five for its younger brother Valbuena. The result is a wine combining immense power (13.5° alcohol with formidable fruit) and unmistakable 'breeding'. The raciness of the flavour is astonishing and the perfume intoxicating. Vega Sicilia is one of Europe's noble eccentrics, but if proof were needed of the potential of the Ribera del Duero for fine reds of a more conventional kind Valbuena would be evidence enough.

VILE (Planta de Elaboracion y Embotellado de Vinos SA)

León.
A private consortium growing and buying León wines on a big scale (it owns 2,500 casks) and with modern ideas. Its young Coyanza red and white are well-made everyday wines. Older and *reserva* class include Palacio de Guzman, Catedral de León, Don Suero.

Cooperativa Ribera del Duero

Peñafiel, Valladolid.
A long-established cooperative (founded in 1927) with 230 members, producing red wines worthy of a more famous region, well above normal coop standards. Ribera Duero is their blackberryish red without oak ageing. Peñafiel is slightly oak-aged (they have 2,300 *barricas*) and Protos is a sensational *reserva*, deep in colour and in its oak and mulberry fragrance, at 10 years comparable to an excellent Rioja *tinto*; long, soft and delicious.

OTHER DUERO VALLEY PRODUCERS

Bodegas de Crianza de Castilla la Vieja Rueda, Valladolid. This began life in 1976 as a consortium of local growers seeking to upgrade their wine. Their speciality was a *solera*-aged, sherry-style white. In 1980 Professor Emile Peynaud of Bordeaux was engaged by new owners to make a small quantity of top-class modern white, carrying the name of the owner, Marqués de Griñon. The same nobleman has succeeded admirably with Bordeaux red grapes at Toledo. They also make a sparkling Brut wine called Palacio de Bornos.

Bodegas los Acros El Bierzo, León. A small family-owned bodega. Its Santo Rosado has a good reputation.

Bodegas Palacio de Arganza Villafranca del Bierzo, León. Since 1805 the bodega that occupies the 15th-century palace of the Dukes of Arganza has been the most important in Bierzo, the best wine area of León. It ages its potent *reservas* in oak casks.

Bodega Hnos Perez Pascuas 09314 Pedrosa de Duero. Visits by appt. Another rising star; the Pascuas brothers own 100 acres of vineyard north of the Duero and buy in grapes from other growers. Viña Pedrosa, made entirely from Tinto Fino, is full but round from short ageing in oak.

Bodegas Sanz Rueda, Valladolid. A small family-run bodega, founded in 1900. Its fresh young rosé is its best wine.

Agricola Castellana Sociedad Cooperativa La Seca Rueda, Valladolid. An important cooperative, founded in 1935, producing from huge stocks both traditional *solera*-aged Rueda whites (e.g. Camp Grande *fino* and Dorado 61) and a modern-style, unaged, fruity dry white, Verdejo Pallido.

CATALONIA & THE BALEARICS

Your Catalan is only half Spanish. He is proud of the autonomy of his privileged province. He basks in a temperate, mild-winter climate without the extremes of most of Spain. Catalonia lies on the same latitude as Tuscany, sheltered from the north by the Pyrenees, facing southeast into the Mediterranean. It can be considered as a southward extension of the best wine area of France's Midi: the Côtes de Roussillon. Both have the capacity to produce ponderous and potent reds and elaborate luscious dessert wines – and also to surprise with the quality of their white grapes.

Historically most important have been the dessert wines of Tarragona, the warmest part of the Catalan coast. From Priorato, an inland enclave in the same area, came red wines of legendary colour and strength (but also quality) for blending. A century ago the Raventós family of Penedès realized the potential of their native white grapes, naturally high in acid, for the champagne treatment. Today Penedès produces 90 percent of Spain's sparkling wine.

The latest development, but the most significant of all, has been the successful trial of the classic French and German grapes in the higher parts of Penedès. The Torres family, long-established winemakers of the region, have led the way with a judicious mixture of these exotics and the best of the well-tried Catalan varieties.

Among the native whites Parellada and Xarel-lo are crisply acidic with low alcoholic degrees, Malvasía is broadly fruity, with low acidity, and Macabeo (the Viura of Rioja) is admirably balanced and apt for maturing.

Catalonia shares the best red grapes of the rest of Spain, above all the Tempranillo (here called Ull de Llebre), the Garnacha Tinta and the deep and tannic Monastrell. The Cariñena (alias Carignan) is no more distinguished here than elsewhere.

Eight zones in Catalonia now have *Denominación de Origen* status and, of the Balearic islands, Mallorca now boasts a single DO. See below.

ALELLA

Coastal valley just north of Barcelona, now reduced to less than 1,000 acres of vines by urban sprawl. Almost all its many small growers take their grapes to the cooperative.

Its best wine is a mildly fruity semi-sweet white made from the fruit of the southern slopes. Also good are its dry whites, which are clean and acidic. The red is passable.

AMPURDAN–COSTA BRAVA

The northernmost DO centred round Perelada in the province of Gerona, behind the cliffs and beaches of the Costa Brava. The 6,500 acres produces mainly rosé, recently some *primeur*-style red called Vi Novell, and adequate whites, some made sparkling but without the quality of the best Penedès wines.

CONCA DE BARBERA

The newest Catalan DO (1989) covers some 21,000 acres inland from the DO Tarragona, adjoining that and Costers del Segre in the northwest. Much of the grape quantity grown here is for the cava industry, although new ideas are becoming well-established and there are large plantations of Chardonnay – indeed, this is where Miguel Torres grows the grapes for his flagship barrel-fermented Milmanda (which is then, confusingly enough, labelled Penedès). Bodegas Concavins at Montblanc has hit upon an excellent way to halve its infrastructure costs: Hugh Ryman turns out good, early-harvest 'price-point' wines for the supermarket trade under the brand name 'Santara', and then the winery is washed down just in time to be used a second time for the main harvest of Cabernet-Sauvignon, Merlot, et al. This is a region with promise.

COSTERS DEL SEGRE

This DO was ratified in 1988, really due to the influence of a single bodega, Finca Raimat (owned by Codorníu). The DO is in the rugged, fertile western region of Lleida (Lérida), and is made up of the four geographically disparate sub-zones of Raimat, Artesa, Valls de Riu Corb and Les Garrigues. Grape varieties are mainly traditional, but Cabernet Sauvignon, Merlot and Chardonnay are also found. Most of the vineyards are cooperative-owned and devoted to producing the white wine traditional to the area, though modern methods and technological innovations are being introduced. Wines are of varying quality, with Raimat far in the lead.

PENEDES

The biggest DO of Catalonia ranges from the coast at Sitges back into 2,000-foot limestone hills. Its centres are Vilafranca de Penedès, best known for its table-wine bodegas (among them Torres), and Sant Sadurni d'Anoia, 20 miles west of Barcelona, the capital of Spanish sparkling wine and headquarters of the vast firms of Codorníu and Freixenet.

The table wines of Penedès have been revolutionized in the last 20 years and now rival Rioja. The reds are generally darker in colour and fruitier than Riojas, lacking the delicacy and refinement of Rioja at its best, but adding a concentration that Rioja normally lacks. Exceptional wines, especially those with a proportion of Cabernet, reach the best international standards. Modern methods have brought the white wines under total control. There is now a benchmark dry fruity Catalan white, highly satisfactory if not exactly exciting. Unlike the best Rioja whites it does not (at least to my taste) take kindly to ageing in oak. Possibly less concentrated fruit, partly the result of bigger crops, is to blame.

PRIORATO

The long viticultural course of the River Ebro, starting near Haro in the Rioja Alta, might be said to end without shame in the western hills of Tarragona with this memorable wine. Priorato is a DO enclave, lying within the much greater *denominación* of Tarragona, applying to some 4,600 acres of steep volcanic hillside vines around the little tributary of the Ebro, the Montsant. The fame of Priorato is in the almost blackness of its red wine, a splendidly full-bodied brew of Garnacha and Cariñena that reaches 16 (sometimes even 18) degrees alcohol, with the colour of crushed blackberries and something of their flavour. Priorato is often used for blending, but at its unblended best it can be a triumph.

The most exciting work in Priorato is being done in the tiny hilltop village of Gratallops, beside the River Siurana. Here, half a dozen boutique wineries are making stunning wines from Garnacha, Cabernet-Sauvignon, Merlot and even Syrah grown in soil over the schistose bedrock which also provides the base for Ribera del Duero and the port vineyards of the Douro in Portugal. Their names are Clos Mogador, Clos l'Obac, Clos Dofi, Clos Martinet and the best of all (and which has just overtaken Vega Sicilia as the most expensive wine in Spain) Clos l'Ermita. This last is made from 90% Garnacha from 100-year-old vines, with 10% Cabernet Sauvignon added for aroma, and has a complexity which is astonishing.

There is also alcoholic amber-white Priorato deliberately oxidized to a rancio flavour.

TARRAGONA

The DO of Tarragona has almost the same vineyard area as Penedès spread over a wider region. The table wines are normally of blending quality without the extra distinction of Priorato. Its finest products are fortified dessert wines (*see* De Muller under Producers). But the great bulk of Tarragona's exports are of a more humble nature.

TERRA ALTA

A DO continuing south from that of Tarragona beyond the Ebro. Mora and Gandesa are the chief centres for the 22,000 acres of vines in the hills that rise to the mountainous province of Teruel. The wine is potent, vigorous and unpretentious, much used, like Tarragona, for blending.

CAVA

While technically a DO, this is not actually a geographical region. *Cava* is the official term for traditional method sparkling wine, and is produced predominantly in Penedès, though there are a few producers elsewhere in Spain.

It may have been characteristic leanness of Catalan white wine that inspired the creation of *cava*. The Xarel-lo, Parellada and Viura (locally called Macabeo) produce high-acid musts of only slight flavour – ideal base material: the flavour of champagne yeast comes through distinctly with its richness and softness. Wines that were stored in wooden vats (some still are) also picked up a very faint tarry taste which added character. Chardonnay is increasingly used both in blends and in premium 'varietal' *cavas*.

The *cavas* of Penedès today range from the extremely deft and delicate to the fat and clumsy. The best can certainly be counted among the world's finest sparkling wines. It is only in the inevitable comparison with champagne that they lose. Where champagne finally triumphs is in the vigour of the flavours that it assembles so harmoniously.

BINISSALEM

The Balearic Islands have a long vinous history, although Mallorca is the only one in the group which retains any vineyards at all. Binissalem, Spain's first offshore DO, was granted in 1991, largely the result of one bodega's campaign for recognition of the quality of its wines (see José L. Ferrer).

Leading Catalan Producers

Cavas del Ampurdán

4 Perelada, Gerona. DO Ampurdán-Costa Brava.
Founded in 1925, the sister company of Castillo de Perelada, makes very pleasant still red, white and rosé from bought-in grapes. The aged reds Tinto Cazador and Reserva Don Miguel are the top wines. 'Pescador' is a refreshing half-sparkling white. Sparkling wines are bulk produced by the *cuve close* method. The company was the defendant in a famous London court case in 1960 when the Champagne authorities succeeded in preventing it from using the term Spanish Champagne.

Masía Bach

Sant Esteve Sesrovires, Barcelona.
Masía means farm. Bach was the name of two bachelor brothers who in 1920 used a fortune made by clothing

soldiers to build a Florentine folly in Penedès, with garages for 40 cars and a winery which grew in reputation and size until its 1,000 yards of cellars held 8,500 oak casks. It was bought by Codorníu (q.v.) in 1975, but continues to make the house speciality, an oak-flavoured sweet white called Extrisimo Bach, but has added high-quality dry white and a fine light red to the range.

René Barbier

Ctra. S. Quintin km-5, San Sadurní d'Anoia 08770, Barcelona.
An old-established bodega now owned by Freixenet. Its wines are made in the cellars of Segura Viudas (q.v.). Kraliner is the fresh dry white. Reds are made fruity for everyday and oak-aged for Sundays. Sales are about 800,000 cases, almost half of which is exported.

Castell del Remei

Penelles, Lleida (Lérida).
A long-established firm on the inland fringes of Catalonia. Its vineyards include Cabernet Sauvignon and Sémillon and its wines have good reputation.

Bodegas José L Ferrer

C. Conquistador 75, 07350 Binisalem, Majorca.
The one distinguished bodega of the Balearic islands, founded by Señor Ferrer in 1931 and now owned by the firm Franco Roja SA. The 165 acres of vineyards are situated in the centre of the island. The local Manto Negro grape makes lively reds. Autentico is the young Ferrer wine. *Reservas* can be extremely good. There is also a dry Blanc de Blancs.

J Friexedas Bové

Avda. Barcelona 87–89, 08720 Vilafranca del Penedès, Barcelona.
A substantial bodega founded in 1897, owning 200 acres but buying the majority of its grapes for rather good sparkling wine and the Santa Marta range of Penedés table wines.

Jean León

Torrelavid, Barcelona.
A California transplant. León is the owner of La Scala Restaurant, Los Angeles. In 1964 he started to plant what is now 150 acres of Cabernet and Chardonnay in Penedès. The wines are first-rate, and excellent value. 60% of the 10,000 cases of Cabernet and 2,000 of Chardonnay are sold abroad.

Marqués de Monistrol

San Sadurní d'Anoia, Barcelona.
A family firm with 740 acres of vines making sparkling wines since 1882, recently bought by Martini & Rossi. Since 1974 they have added still wines, including an attractively lively 'Vin Nature Blanc de Blancs' and traditional-style red *reservas*, long-aged in oak and bottle.

De Muller

Real 38, 43004 Tarragona.
The great name in the classic tradition of sweet Tarragona wines. A family firm founded in 1851, now a limited company directed by the present Marqués de Muller y de

Abadal, still in its old bodegas by the harbour with a vast capacity of oak storage. The pride of the house are its altar wines, supplied to (among others) the Vatican, and its velvety *solera*-aged Moscatel, Pajarete and other dessert wines. The firm has a Priorato bodega at Scala Dei, producing both the massive red of the area and a *solera*-aged dry apéritif, Priorato Rancio Dom Juan Fort. Standard-quality table wines are called Solimar.

Raimat

Segrià, Lleida (Lérida).
The Raventós family of Codorníu has replanted the vine-yards of the Castle of Raimat, in the arid hill-region of Lérida, on a grand (1,700-acre) scale, and re-opened a magnificent bodega built early in the 20th century and subsequently abandoned. Cabernet Sauvignon, Merlot and Chardonnay are blended with native grapes and made 'straight'. The resulting wines are some of the most exciting in Spain.

Cellers de Scala Dei

43379 Scala Dei, Tarragona.
Scala Dei was a great Carthusian monastery, now in ruins. The small modern bodega is in an old stone building nearby, making high-quality oak-aged Priorato, deep, dark and strong (14.5°) but balanced with rich soft-fruit flavours. The labels include Cartoixa Scala Dei, a *gran reserva* made of 100% Garnacha Negra.

Viñedos Torres

Vilafranca de Penedès, Tarragona.
An old family company (founded 1870) which has changed the wine map of Spain in the last 20 years, putting Catalonia on a par with Rioja as a producer of top-quality wines. The family has 2,000 acres of vineyards, supplying half their needs, now planted with Chardonnay, Gewürztraminer, Riesling, Sauvignon Blanc, Cabernet Sauvignon, Merlot and Pinot Noir as well as the traditional Penedès varieties. White wines are cold-fermented, reds aged in oak for a mere 18 months, French style, then in bottle. Viña Sol is a fresh Parellada white; Gran Viña Sol a blend with Chardonnay. Green Label is Parellada and Sauvignon Blanc with a little oak age. Of the reds, Tres Torres is a full-bodied blend of Garnacha and Cariñena, Gran Sangre de Toro an older *reserva* of the same, Coronas either Monastrell or Ull de Llebra (Tempranillo), Gran Coronas Reserva, Tempranillo with some Cabernet Sauvignon. Gran Magdala is Pinot Noir, Viña Las Torres a Merlot. Mas la Plana, the top wine, is a Cabernet Sauvignon. Other wines include a semi-sweet Muscat/ Gewürztraminer blend, Esmeralda, a Chardonnay, Milmanda, and a successful Riesling, Waltraud. Total sales are well over a million cases per year, 40% of which are exported. (*See* page 374.)

Bodega Cooperativa Alella Vinícola

Rbla. Angel Guimerà 62, 08328 Alella, Barcelona.
The long-established (1906) cooperative of the dwindling Alella region, which is suffering building blight as Barcelona pushes north. There are some 150 members. Its

THE TORRES FAMILY

Such has been the contribution of this Catalan family to Spanish wine that their name has become as well-known in some quarters as Spain's most famous wine-producing regions. The reasons for this are two-fold.

First, in the 1950s, with the world recovering from war, the late Miguel Torres Carbó and his wife Doña Margarita travelled the world selling Torres wines and promoting the Torres name in countries as disparate as Belgium and Bali.

Second, their son Miguel A. Torres Riera studied chemistry at the University of Barcelona and went on to learn modern winemaking technology in Montpellier before taking over the role of winemaker in 1962.

This combination of worldwide market share and new-wave winemaking skill contributed to the famous occasion in 1979 on which Torres Mas la Plana beat all-comers (including Château Latour) in a tasting of wines made principally from Cabernet Sauvignon.

Today, Miguel Torres oversees an empire which includes vineyards in California's Sonoma Valley and Curicó, Chile, but his heart remains in his native Penedès, where he maintains a vineyard of more than a hundred Catalan vine varieties as well as the classic Cabernet, Merlot, Sauvignon and Chardonnay which have made the family's name in international markets. Miguel's sister Marimar runs the Torres operation in California, where the wines have achieved a renown all of their own, largely due to her marketing skills and knowledge of the US market. Their brother Juan-Maria looks after public relations throughout the world, from the company's head office in Vilafranca del Penedès. In the matters of investment, innovation and quality control, the Torres name has become an international brand, and the family's single-vineyard wines have established themselves to be amongst the best that Catalonia – or indeed Spain – has to offer.

wines, in hock bottles, are labelled Marfil ('Ivory'). The white *semisecco* is pleasant enough; the dry rather dull.

Cooperativa Agricola de Gandesa

Gandesa, Tarragona.
A old-established (1919) cooperative with 135 members now in the recent DO Terra Alta. Grandesa Blanc Gran Reserva is its most remarkable wine.

Cooperativa de Mollet de Perelada

Perelada, Gerona.
A considerable cooperative with a French-trained wine-maker specializing in *primeur* red, white and rosé called Vi Novell – the red modelled on Beaujolais Nouveau. Their Garnacha Blanca dessert white is also attractive and their sparkling wine worth trying.

Union Agraria Cooperativa

Reus, Tarragona.
A federation of all 180 cooperatives in Tarragona, founded in 1962. Tarragona Union and Yelmo are their popular labels but most wine is sold in bulk. The best are *reservas* from the Cooperativa de Gratallops.

OTHER CATALAN PRODUCERS

Alta Alella Alella, Barcelona. A newcomer causing comment with a good fruity dry white.

Aquila Rossa Vilafranca del Penedès, Barcelona. Century-old bodega good for Montgros Penedès table wine and vermouth.

José Lopez Bertran y Cia Tarragona. A long-established family business supplying such everyday wines as Vinate, Don Bertran and Corrida.

Bodegas Bosch-Guell Vilafranca de Penedès, Barcelona. A family company founded in 1886, using the name Rómulo for a range of sound Penedès wines.

La Vinicola Iberica Tarragona. A large old-established bodega in the bulk business.

Bodegas Pinord Vilafranca de Penedès, Barcelona. A family company with a range of labels: Chatel, Chateldon, Reynal and others.

Bodegas Robert Sitges, Barcelona. Small company making (now rare) sweet white Sitges, from Moscatel and Malvasía.

Pedro Rovira Mora la Nova, Tarragona. An old family firm producing *solera*-aged dessert Tarragona, 'Cream Solera' and 'Dry Solera', as well as everyday wines.

Vinos Jaime Serra Alella, Barcelona. A small private bodega: brand name 'Alellasol'.

Leading Cava Producers

Conde de Caralt

Ctra. S. Quintin km-5, San Sadurní d'Anoia 08770, Barcelona.
A famous old sparkling-wine bodega, now part of the Freixenet group and in the same cellars as Segura Viudas and René Barbier (qq.v.). The name now appears on a range of still wines, including delicate red *reservas*. About 200,000 cases are sold, mainly in the domestic market.

Castillo de Perelada

Perelada, Gerona.
A celebrated cava concern in a picturesque castle dating back to the 14th century, now housing a fine library, collections of glass and ceramics and a wine museum – and a casino. Half the grapes come from the firm's vineyards. The best wine, Gran Claustro, is one of Catalonia's most satisfying cavas. Others are less notable. A sister company, Cavas del Ampurdán, produces the cheap and cheerful *cuve close* sparkling Perelada.

Codorníu

San Sadurní d'Anoia, Barcelona.
The first Spanish firm to use the classic method and now the second biggest sparkling-wine house in the world. The Raventós family has made wine in Penedès since the 16th century. In 1872 Don José returned from Champagne to imitate its methods. The establishment is now monumental, its vast *fin-de-siècle* buildings and miles of cellars, lie in a green park with splendid cedars. They include a considerable wine museum and attract enormous numbers of visitors. A winery has recently been opened in Mexico.

Most of the grapes are bought from 350 local growers, for total sales of some 3m. cases. The wines range from simple and fruity to highly refined – the apogee being the vintage Non Plus Ultra and Gran Codorníu with longer age in bottle; and a 'straight' Chardonnay. Codorníu also owns the Raimat and Masía Bach bodegas (*see* Catalonia).

Freixenet

C. Jojan Sala, 2 San Sadurní d'Anoia 08770, Barcelona.
The biggest Spanish cava house and now the biggest sparkling-wine producer in the world, overtaking the giant Codorníu. Founded by the Bosch family in 1915. The top Freixenet wines are special vintage releases. Brut Barroco and Brut Nature are the best standard lines; Cordon Negro is the best seller. Carta Nevada is a cheaper brand, and a Brut Rosé is also made. Sales total almost 5m. cases, half being exports. Freixenet also owns 50% of the big *cuve close* sparkling-wine firm L'Aixertell. Its partner is Savin.

Cavas Mascaró

C. Casal 9, Vilafranca del Penedès, Barcelona.
An old family bodega with 170 acres, respected for its cava sparkling wines and fine brandy, and now owns the Compañia Vinicola del Penedès, dedicated to making still wines. Barrel-matured Cabernet Sauvignon is planned for the future.

Segura Viudas

Ctra. S. Quintin km-5, San Sadurní d'Anoia 08770, Barcelona.
The three cava companies owned by Freixenet all shelter in the same cellars. Segura Viudas is the prestige marque, made in a modern winery surrounded by a 556-acre vineyard that supplies part of its needs. Its best wine, Reserva Heredad, a very delicate production, comes in a rather vulgar bottle with a sort of built-in silvery coaster and other distractions. Half of its sales of 360,000 cases are to the export market.

OTHER CAVA PRODUCERS
Gonzalez y Dubosc The sparkling-wine subsidiary of Gonzalez Byass (*see* sherry) now with its own winery.
Cavas Hill Moja, Vilafranca del Penedès. The English Hill family arrived in Penedès in 1660. In 1884 Don José Hill Ros established this commercial bodega, recently expanded, which now produces both cava and still wines. Labels include Blanc Brut (dry white) and Gran Toc red *reserva*.
Juvé y Camps San Sadurní d'Anoia, Barcelona. Sizeable family firm making superior and expensive cava from grapes grown in its own 920 acres of vineyard and from free-run juice; 40% of its grapes are now bought in from carefully selected growers. Its *reserva*, Reserva de la Familia, and Gran Cru are available only in the best shops and restaurants – in the UK at Harrods. Some still wines are also produced.
Antonio Mestres Sagues San Sadurní d'Anoia, Barcelona. Particularly good small family-owned cava house founded in 1312.

See also:
Cavas del Ampurdán
J. Freixedas Bové
Marqués de Monistrol
Cooperativa de Mollet de Perelada

THE LEVANT & THE MESETA

By far the greatest concentration of vineyards in Spain lies south and southeast of Madrid in a great block that reaches the Mediterranean at Valencia in the north and Alicante in the south. This central band, with scattered outposts farther west towards Portugal in Extremadura, contained no great names, no lordly estates, no pockets of perfectionism. Its wines combined various degrees of strength with various degrees of dullness – but in the main a generous helping of body. The last ten years have seen changes. Spain's membership of the EU has exposed the traditional cooperative producers of the region to the realities of competition. Modern market forces – the ever-more-stringent quality demands of northern European customers – have prompted producers to invest in modern technology. Central Spain, like California's Central Valley, has a climate of extremes, but predictable extremes. This allows oenologists to 'design' wines by regulating picking dates and controlling fermentation.

While large-scale cooperatives still make much of the wine, estates and smaller bodegas are emerging. The Marqués de Griñon's Cabernet Sauvignon from Toledo has made a mark, as have wines from Bodegas Saviron and Vinícola de Castilla in La Mancha. Experimental plantings are introducing French grapes; unsuspected flavours being coaxed by skilled winemakers from local varieties.

Central Spain has a long road ahead of it, but it is no longer an unrelieved ocean of mediocrity.

Tierra de Barros, in the province Badajoz, though producing some of the best wine from Extremadura, was never confirmed as a DO. Its 100,000-odd acres are largely planted with a common white grape, the Cayetana, giving dry low-acid but high-strength wines – the curse of Spain, in fact. Its rarer red wines, however, have some merit; particularly those of Salvatierra de Barros on the Portuguese border, and the eccentric Montánchez, from the northern province of Cáceres, which grows a *flor* yeast like sherry. The same is true of the white of Cañamero.

Toledo province, southwest of Madrid, contains the DO of Méntrida, an 80,000-acre spread of Garnacha vines supplying strong red wine.

By far the biggest wine region in the whole of Spain, demarcated or not, is La Mancha, the dreary plain of Don Quixote. It has no less than 1.2 million acres under vine, almost all of a white variety called Airén. The best that could be said of most Airén wine was that it had no flavour beyond that of its 13–14° of alcohol, but some producers have been coaxing agreeable flavours from it by careful winemaking.

The one superior enclave of La Mancha is the DO Valdepeñas, 100 miles south of Madrid, where the tradition is to blend the Airén white with a small measure of dark red, made of Tempranillo (here called Cencibel) and Garnacha. So dark is the red that a mere 10 percent of it makes the wine – known as *aloque* – a *clarete* in colour, though it remains a soft rather spineless wine, low in acid and tannin. The old method is fermentation in the tall clay *tinajas*, obviously descended from Roman or earlier vessels. Modern methods have shown clearly how much better the wine can be. Such producers as Los Llanos and Felix Solin now cool-ferment and oak-age their wines with results worthy of the better parts of northern Spain.

The sorry tale continues with the DOP (provisional DO) of Manchuela, east of La Mancha and making both white and red wine on its 20,000 acres.

The smaller DO of Almansa around Albacete concludes the toll of the Castilian plain. Its 26,000 acres are planted in dark grapes.

The term Levant embraces six DOs of only very moderate interest at present, but some considerable potential as modern methods creep in. To the north on the coast is Valencia (and what was formerly called Cheste), liberal producers of alcoholic white wine and to a lesser degree red. Inland from Valencia lies Utiel-Requena, a hill region of black grapes (the principal one, the Bobal, as black as night) used expressly for colouring wine. The local technique is to ferment each batch of wine with a double ration of skins to extract the maximum colour and tannin: a brew called *vino de doble pasta*. Its by-product, the lightly crushed juice with barely any 'skin contact' or colour, surplus to the double brew, makes the second speciality of the region, a racy pale rosé more to the modern taste.

The DO Alicante covers both coastal vineyards producing sweet Moscatel and hill vineyards for red wines, *vino de doble pasta* and rosés. A little local white wine is (relatively) highly prized.

Behind Alicante in the province of Murcia there are three *denominaciónes*, Bullas, Yecla and Jumilla, whose respective cooperatives are struggling with their inky material to teach it modern manners. So far Jumilla seems to be marginally the more advanced of the three, with some wines showing surprising potential to age in bottle.

LEVANT AND MESETA PRODUCERS

Fermin Ayuso Roig Villarobleda, Albacete. A family concern based in Manchuela. Other labels are Armino and Estola.

Bodegas Bleda Jumilla (Murcia). The son of the founder (in 1935) still runs this pioneer house for Jumilla wine. He matures his powerful reds, Castillo de Jumilla and Oro de Ley, in oak casks.

Casa de Calderón Requena, Valencia. A small family vineyard and bodega making some of the best Requena. Their *generoso* has some of the flesh and grip of port.

Bodegas Delgado Camara
Valdepeñas. Traditional bodega praised for Marchante reds.

Bodegas Miguel Carrión
Alpera, Almansa. The best producer of the DO Almansa to

the east of La Mancha. A small company with a good soft strong Tinto Selecto, aged in oak.

Bodegas Cevisur Tierra de Barros, Almendralejo, Badajoz. A family concern bottling Tierra de Barros white, as Viña Extremeña.

Bodegas Galán Montánchez, Badajoz. A little family bodega in a village near Mérida. Of interest because it makes a red wine called Trampal, growing *flor* and tasting like sherry. It has a following in Madrid.

Industrias Vinícolas del Oeste Almendralejo, Badajoz. Best bodega of this region of *consumo* wines, making red and white Lar de Barros, though not from the typical grapes of the area.

Bodegas Los Llanos Valdepeñas, Cuidad Real. The first of the houses in Valdepeñas to bottle its wines. The oak-aged *reservas* and *gran reservas* are setting new standards for the region. Señorio de Los Llanos Gran Reserva is a fine, aromatic and silky wine by any standards, and the white Armonioso is clean and fruity. Both are bargains.

Marqués de Griñón Toledo. The recent enterprise of an ambitious landowner, advised by Emile Peynaud of Bordeaux. He is producing an excellent Cabernet Sauvignon here in Garnacha country.

Luis Megía Valdepeñas. A very modern mass-production wine factory.

Bodegas Murviedro Valencia. Long-established little bodega exporting above-average wines, with a reasonable white.

H L García Poveda Villena, Alicante. The two considerable bodegas of Alicante are both called Poveda. This one is in the hills behind the town, family run and making a range of strong red, white and rosé with the names Costa Blanca and Marquesado.

Bodegas Salvador Poveda Monovar, Alicante. Perhaps the best Alicante bodega, a family business known especially for its rich dessert Fondillón. Other labels for its strapping wines are Doble Capa and Viña Vermeta.

Bodegas Ruiz Cañamero, Cáceres. Unique bottlers of the roughish sherry-style Cañamero white, made of Palomino grapes and growing *flor*-like sherry. It is the house wine of the Parador at Cañamero.

Bodegas Schenk Valencia. The Spanish division of the biggest Swiss wine company, shipping from the Levant and La Mancha both blended (e.g. the well-known Don Cortez) and individual wines. Schenk's red Los Monteros, made entirely of the dark Monastrell (alias Mourvèdre), is one of the best of the region. Also a Valencian sweet Moscatel and a rosé from Utiel-Requena.

Bodegas Señorío del Condestable Jumilla, Murcia. A member of the big Savin group of wine companies, best known for its red Condestable, a well-made everyday wine, light in colour and flavour but with a fresh almost cherry-like smell and pleasant texture. The bodega has also recently released an excellent varietal Monastrell in the modern style which challenges most of the preconceptions about this under-rated grape variety.

Bodegas Félix Solís Valdepeñas. Large-scale maker of reds and *rosados* with a reputation for oak-aged reds, especially Viña Albali Reserva.

Vinival Valencia. A big bulk-wine shipping company founded in 1969. Its great vaulted brick bodega by the harbour handles the products of several producers under the label Torres de Serrano.

Visan Santa Cruz de Mudela, Valdepeñas, Ciudad Real. Producer of the agreeable Castillo de Mudela and Viña Tito.

Cooperativa del Campo La Daimieleña Daimieleña, Ciudad Real. One of the principal white-wine producers of La Mancha. The brand is Clavileño.

Cooperativa La Invencible Valdepeñas, Ciudad Real. The best cooperative of the region, making a clean *clarete*.

Cooperativa Nuestro Padre Jesus del Perdón Manzanares, Ciudad Real. A large cooperative known particularly for its dry white. The brand name is Yuntero. It is also sold in the UK under the brand name Casa la Teja.

Cooperativa La Purísima Yecla, Murcia. The major producer of Yecla wine. The huge bodega makes efforts to please the educated palate with wines of moderate strength (e.g. Viña Montana) but the result tends to mingle overripe and underripe flavours in rather thin wine.

Cooperativa de San Isidro Jumilla, Murcia. The major Jumilla coop, with 2,000 members. All its wines are strong and heavy. Rumor is the best known. Some *reservas* are aged in oak (without achieving distinction).

Cooperativa Santa Rita Fuenterobles, Valencia. A medium-sized modern cooperative turning out concentrated blending wine, *vino de doble pasta*, but also a remarkably fresh pale rosé, indicating what the region is capable of.

Cooperative Virgen de la Viñas Tomelloso, Ciudad Real. One of the bigger coops, known by its brand name Tomillar and its Reserva de Cencibel.

Bodegas Castaño, Yecla A family-run bodega in this smallest of DO zones producing excellent wines from mainly Monastrell under the names Castaño, Viña las Gruesas and (best of all) Pozuelo. These may be the best wines of Murcia.

ANDALUCIA

The great fame and success of sherry were achieved to some degree at the expense of the other regions of Andalusia. From their long-established trading base, the sherry makers were able to buy the best from their neighbours to add to their own stock. Sherry may be the best *vino generoso* of Andalucia, but it is not the only one. Montilla can compete with very similar wines, and Málaga with alternatives at the sweeter end of the range.

MALAGA

Málaga, on the Costa del Sol, is strictly an entrepôt rather than a vineyard centre. The grapes that make its sweet (occasionally dry) brown wines are grown either in the hills 25 miles to the east or the same distance to the north. East are the coastal vineyards of Axarquía, where the grape is the Moscatel. North around Mollina (in fact towards Montilla) it is the Pedro Ximénez. The rules require that all the grapes are brought to Málaga to mature in its bodegas. Various methods are used to sweeten and concentrate the wines, from sunning the grapes to boiling down the must to *arrope*, as in Jerez. The styles of the finished wine range from a dry white of Pedro Ximénez not unlike a Montilla *amontillado* to the common dark and sticky *dulce color*, thickly laced with *arrope*. The finest quality, comparable in its origins to the *essencia* of Tokay, is the *lagrima*, the 'tears' of uncrushed grapes. The difference is that noble rot concentrates Tokay; in Málaga it is the sun. Other Málagas are Pajarete, a dark semi-sweet apéritif style, the paler semi-*dulce* and the richly aromatic Moscatel. The finer wines are made in a *solera* system like sherry, with younger wine refreshing older. A great rarity, a century-old vintage Málaga from the Duke of Wellington's estate, bottled in 1875, was a superlative, delicate, aromatic and still-sweet dessert wine in 1995.

MONTILLA-MORILES

Montilla's wines are close enough to sherry to be easily confused with (or passed off as) its rivals. The soil is the same *albariza* but the climate is harsher and hotter and the Pedro Ximénez, grown here in preference to the Palomino, yields smaller crops, producing wines of a higher degree and slightly lower acidity. The wines are fermented in tall clay *tinajas*, like giant amphoras, and rapidly develop the same *flor* yeast as sherry. They fall into the same classifications: *fino*, *oloroso* or *palo cortado* – the *finos* from the first light pressing. With age *fino* becomes *amontillado*, 'in the style of Montilla'. Unfortunately, however, the sherry shippers have laid legal claim in Britain (the biggest export market for Montilla) to the classic terms. Instead of a Montilla *fino*, *amontillado* or *oloroso*, a true and fair description, the label must use 'dry', 'medium' or 'cream'.

Montilla has much to recommend it as an alternative to sherry. Its *finos* in particular have a distinctive dry softness of style, with less 'attack' but no less freshness. A cool bottle of Montilla disappears with gratifying speed as a partner to *hors d'oeuvre*.

Last of the Andalusian *denominaciones,* and most deeply in the shadow of Jerez, is the coastal region of Huelva near the Portugese border. Huelva (known in Chaucer's time as 'Lepe') has exported its strong white wines for 1,000 years. The commercial power of Jerez has effectively kept it in obscurity. Until the 1960s its wine was blended and shipped as sherry. Now that it has to compete with its old paymaster times are not easy and the region is increasingly making light white wines.

Leading Andalucia Producers

Alvear

Maria Auxiliadora 1, Montilla, Córdoba.
An independent firm founded by the Alvear family in 1729. Today it is jointly owned and managed by Alvaro de Alvear and his cousin Fernández. They have 308 acres under vine in Montilla-Moriles, much of it in the superior Sierra district, and 17,000 butts of maturing wine in their bodegas. Fermentation in *tinajas* and ageing through the *solera* system are carried out according to the traditions of Montilla, but bottling is done with very modern equipment, producing wines of high quality. Fino CB is their biggest seller, as is their No. 3 *fino* (behind two sherries) in volume terms in Spain. Festival is a slightly fuller *fino* and other names and styles include Marqués de la Sierra, Carlos VII, Pelayo, Asuncion and the *dulce* Pedro Ximénez 1830.

OTHER ANDALUCIAN PRODUCERS

Hijos de Antonio Barceló A family run firm founded in 1876, now a major exporter, also branching out into Rioja and Rueda in the north of Spain. The brand name is Bacarles, covering a wide range of typical Málaga styles, including old Moscatel and a very sweet Pedro Ximénez, Gran Málaga Solera Vieja.

Carbonell y Cia Córdoba. A substantial Montilla producer, equally well known for its olive oil. The Carbonell bodegas are in the Moorish city of Córdoba where some fine old *soleras* produce three *finos*, Moriles, Serranio and Monte Corto. Moriles Superior is a *fino amontillado* (the term is used for once in the literal sense). Flor de Montilla is an *amontillado pasado,* an older and nuttier wine. 'Nectar' is an appropriate description of both the *oloroso* and the dark Pedro Ximénez.

Gracia Hermanos Montilla, Córdoba. A family-run bodega with high standards. Their *fino*, Kiki, is a typically light and refreshing one.

López Hermanos Málaga. This is now the leading Málaga bodega (since the sad demise in 1996 of Scholtz) and is run by Don Rafael Burgos who is a leading light of the Consejo Regulador. He is said to have seen the writing on the wall before many other, now long-gone, producers and diversified, stepped up the marketing and made a real effort to re-interest the foreign wine-trade in Málaga wines as well as rekindling interest at home. As a result the firm makes wine in classic (*virgen*), modern (*pálido*) and dry styles and has cornered much of what little export market there is. Trajinero is probably the best dry Málaga; Cartojal is a 'pale-cream' *pálido* and the flagship is the straight Málaga Virgen. Only eight bodegas survive in the area, and this is the biggest of them.

Larios Málaga. Better known for its gin in Spain, but a Málaga bodega with an excellent sweet Moscatel, Colmenares.

Bodegas Monte Cristo Montilla, Córdoba. Large exporters of Montilla, now part of the Rumasa group. Sixty percent of Monte Cristo exports go to the United Kingdom, Montilla's biggest export market.

Bodegas Perez Barquero Montilla, Córdoba. Another Rumasa company. Brand name: Gran Barquero.

Perez Teixera Málaga. Málaga bodega making a true *lagrima* wine from the 'tears' of the uncrushed overripe grapes.

Bodegas Miguel Salas Acosta Bollullos del Condado, Huelva. A family-run company known for above-average sherry-style Huelva wines.

Hijos de Francisco Vallejo Bollulos del Condado, Huelva. A Huelvan family bodega with good sherry-style wines.

Bodega Cooperativa Vinícola del Condado Boilullos del Condado, Huelva. The main cooperative of Huelva, responsible for large quantities of brandy, some table wines and some good *solera*-aged sherry-style *generosos*.

SHERRY

Sherry, like many Mediterranean wines, was first appreciated and shipped to the countries of northern Europe for its strength, its sweetness and its durability – all qualities that made it a radically different commodity from medieval claret. By Shakespeare's day, while spirits were still unknown, sack (as it was then called) was hugely popular as the strongest drink available. The warming effect of a 'cup of sack', at perhaps 17 degrees alcohol, was the addiction not just of Sir John Falstaff but of every tavern-goer. 'Sack' came from Málaga, the Canary Islands, and even from Greece and Cyprus. But the prince of sacks was 'sherris', named after the Andalucian town of Jerez de la Frontera.

Jerez has had an international trading community since the Middle Ages. Until the rise of Rioja it was unique in Spain for its huge bodegas full of stock worth millions. The refinement of its wine from a coarse product, shipped without ageing, to the modern elaborate range of styles began in the 18th century. Like champagne (which it resembles in more ways than one) it flowered with the wealth and technology of the 19th.

What its makers have done is to push the natural adaptability of a strong but not otherwise extraordinary, indeed rather flat and neutral, white wine to the limit. They have exploited its potential for barrel-ageing in contact with oxygen – the potentially disastrous oxidation – to produce flavours as different in their way as a lemon and a date. And they have perfected the art of blending from the wide spectrum in their paintbox to produce every conceivable nuance in between – and to produce it unchanging year after year.

The making of sherry today, folklore apart, differs little from the making of any white wine. A fairly light wine is rapidly pressed and fermented. Its acidity is adjusted upwards, traditionally by adding gypsum or plaster. It is traditionally fermented in new oak barrels (with a violence in the early stages that sends fountains of froth high into the air). Eventually it reaches a natural strength of between 12 and 16 degrees. At this point it is fortified with spirit to adjust the strength to 15 or 18 degrees, depending on its quality and characteristics. This is where sherry's unique ageing process begins.

It is the wayward nature of sherry that different barrels (500-litre 'butts') of wine, even from the same vineyard, can develop in different ways. The essential distinction is between those that develop a vigorous growth of floating yeast, called *flor*, and those that do not. All the young wines are kept in the 'nursery' in butts filled four-fifths full. The finest and most delicate wines, only slightly fortified to maintain their finesse, rapidly develop a creamy scum on the surface, which thickens in spring to a layer several inches deep. This singular yeast has the property of protecting the wine from oxidation and at the same time reacting with it to impart subtle hints of maturity. These finest wines, or *finos*, are ready to drink sooner than heavier sherries. They remain pale because oxygen is excluded. They can be perfect at about five years old. But their precise age is irrelevant because, like all sherries, they are blended for continuity in a *solera* (*see* page 384).

Young wines of a heavier, clumsier and more pungent style grow less *flor*, or none at all. A stronger dose of fortifying spirit discourages any *flor* that may appear. This second broad category of sherry is known, if it shows potential quality, as *oloroso*, if not as *raya*. These wines are barrel-aged without benefit of *flor*, in full contact with the air. Their maturing is therefore an oxidative process, darkening their colour and intensifying their flavour.

A third, eccentric, class of sherry is also found in this early classifying of the crop – one that combines the breadth and depth of a first-class *oloroso* with the fragrance, finesse and 'edge' of a *fino*. This rarity is known as a *palo cortado*.

These three are the raw materials of the bodega – naturally different from birth. It is the bodega's business to rear them so as to accentuate these differences, and to use them in combinations to produce a far wider range of styles. A *fino* which is matured beyond the life span of its *flor* usually begins to deepen in colour and broaden in flavour, shading from straw to amber to (at great age) a rich blackish brown. Every bodega has one or more *soleras* of old *finos* which have been allowed to move through the scale from a fresh *fino*, to a richer, more concentrated *fino-amontillado*, to an intensely nutty and powerful old *amontillado*.

Commercially, however, such true unblended *amontillados* are very rare. In general usage the term has been more or less bastardized to mean any 'medium' sherry, between dry

Sherry glossary

Almacenista a wholesaler or stockholder of wines for ageing; also used for the individual old unblended wines he sells which are occasionally offered as collectors' items.

Amontillado literally 'a wine in the style of Montilla'. Not at all so in fact, but a well-aged *fino* that has developed a nutty flavour with maturity in oak. The term is also loosely used for any medium sherry.

Amoroso the name of a vineyard famous for *oloroso* sherry. Literally 'amorous': not a bad description of the sweet *oloroso* sold under the name.

Añada the wine of one year, kept as such in a butt until (or instead of) becoming part of a *solera*.

Arroba the working measure in a sherry bodega. The standard 500-litre butt holds 30 *arrobas*.

Arrope a *vino de color*: wine reduced by boiling it to one-fifth of its original volume. The result is an intensely sweet and treacly black brew, used only for colouring and sweetening blends. *Sancocho* is similar.

Bristol the historic centre of the sherry trade in Britain, a name much used on labels to imply quality, but not a reference to any particular style of wine.

Brown sherry sweet sherry blended from *olorosos* and *rayas* to be sweeter and darker than a 'cream'.

Cream sherry a blend of sweetened *olorosos*, with or without *vino de color*. Harvey's Bristol Cream was the original. Croft's successfully introduced the idea of a pale (uncoloured) 'cream' in the 1970s.

Dulce apagado intensely sweet wine made by stopping the fermentation of must by adding brandy. Used only for sweetening 'medium' sherries.

Dulce de almibar a mixture of young wine and invert sugar used for sweetening pale sherries without darkening them.

Dulce pasa dark sweetening wine made by leaving ordinary sherry grapes in the sun to concentrate the sugar, then stopping their fermenting must with brandy. Used for sweetening good quality 'cream'.

East India now a fanciful name for a sweet, usually Brown, sherry. It derives from the former custom of sending sherry (like madeira) to the Indies and back as ship's ballast to speed its maturity.

Entre fino the classification of a young wine which shows *fino* character but not the required quality for the finest *soleras*.

Fino the lightest, most delicate, and literally finest of sherries. It naturally develops a growth of *flor* yeast, which protects its pale colour and intensifies its fresh aroma.

Fino amontillado a *fino* on the way to maturing as an *amontillado*.

Fino viejo, viejissimo occasionally an old *fino* declines to enter middle age as an *amontillado* and simply intensifies its aristocratic finesse, growing formidably powerful, dusty dry and austere while remaining straw-pale.

Jerez quinado a cordial or apéritif made by mixing quinine with sherry.

Macharnudo the most famous of the *pagos*, vineyard districts, northwest of Jerez; sometimes mentioned on labels.

Manzanilla the speciality of Sanlúcar de Barrameda. Sherries matured in its bodegas by the sea take on a singular sharp and even salty tang that makes them the most appetizing of all. Removed to bodegas elsewhere they revert to normal wines. Most *manzanilla* is drunk as pale and unsweetened *fino*. With age it becomes *pasada*, darker and slightly nutty with an almost buttery richness. Eventually it becomes a deeply nutty *Manzanilla amontillado*; one of the most vivid and intense of all sherries.

Moscatel sweetening wine made of sun-dried Moscatel grapes for giving added sugar and fruity flavour to certain sweet blends.

Oloroso in its natural state, full-bodied dry sherry without the delicacy, fragrance or piquancy of *fino* but with extra richness and depth. It does not develop *flor* to the same extent but picks up colour and oak flavours in the butt. Old unblended *olorosos* are astonishingly dark, pungent and so concentrated that they almost seem to burn your mouth. In practice nearly all *oloroso* is used as the base for sweet sherries, particularly 'creams'.

Palma a classification for a particularly delicate and fragrant *fino*. Tres Palmas is the brand name of a very fine one.

Palo cortado an aberrant sherry which shows the good characters of both *amontillado* and *oloroso* at the same time. Palo cortado is a highly prized rarity nearly always kept apart and bottled as an unblended *solera* wine with only a little sweetening.

Pata de galina an *oloroso* which in its natural state shows signs of sweetness, derived from glycerine. Occasionally bottled as such, when it is incomparable.

Paxarete an alternative name for *vinos de color*.

Raya the classification for an *oloroso*-type wine of secondary quality; the makeweight in most middle-range blends.

Vino de color colouring wine, e.g. *arrope*.

Vino de pasto 'table wine' light medium-dry sherry of uncertain quality, now rarely seen.

fino and creamy old *oloroso* in style but rarely with the quality of either. All sherries in their natural state, maturing in their *soleras*, are bone dry. Unlike port, sherry is never fortified until fermentation is completely over – all sugar used up. Straight unblended sherry is therefore an ascetic, austere taste, a rarity in commerce. The only exception is *dulce* – concentrated wine used for sweetening blends.

As the sherry ages in the bodega, evaporation of water increases both the alcohol content and the proportion of flavouring elements. Very old sherries still on wood often become literally undrinkable in their own right – but priceless in the depth of flavour they can add to a blend. Classic sherry-blending is very much the art of the shipper, but anyone can try it for himself by acquiring, say, a bottle of a very old dry sherry such as Domecq's Rio Viejo or Gonzalez Byass's Duque, and simply adding one small glassful of it to a carafe of an ordinary 'medium' sherry. The immediate extra dimension of flavour in the everyday wine is a revelation.

The former custom was for every wine merchant to have his own range of blends made in Jerez to his own specification, and label them with brandnames from his own imagination. In practice this meant that there were far too many indistinguishable (and often undistinguished)

blended wines on the market. The more rational modern trend is for the shippers in Jerez to promote their own brands. The best of these will be the produce of a single prized *solera*, usually slightly sweetened with *arrope*, a special treacly sweetening wine. A touch of near-black but almost tasteless *vino de color* may be needed to adjust the colour. Possibly a little younger wine in the same style will be added to give it freshness.

A common commercial blend, on the other hand, will consist largely of low-value, minimally aged *rayas* or *entre finos* (the term for second-grade wine in the *fino* style). A small proportion of wine from a good *solera* will be added to improve the flavour, then a good deal of sweetening wine to mask the faults of the base material. It is, unfortunately, wines made to this sort of specification that have given sherry the image of a dowdy drink of no style.

The sad result is that the truly great wines of Jerez, wines that can stand comparison in their class with great white burgundy or champagne, are absurdly undervalued. There is no gastronomic justification for the price of Montrachet being five times that of the most brilliant *fino* – nor, at the other end of sherry's virtuoso repertoire, of the greatest *olorosos* selling at a fraction of the price of their equivalent in madeira.

THE SHERRY REGION

Jerez lies 10 miles inland from the bay of Cádiz in southwest Spain. Its vineyards surround it on all sides, but all the best of them are on outcrops of chalky soil in a series of dune-like waves to the north and west, between the rivers Guadalete and Guadalquivír. The Guadalquivír, famous as the river of Seville, from which Columbus set out to discover America and Pizarro to conquer Peru, forms the northern boundary of the sherry region. Its port, Sanlúcar de Barrameda, Jerez and Puerto are the three sherry towns. The land between them is the zone known as Jerez Superior, the heart of the best sherry country.

There are three soil types in the sherry region, but only the intensely white *albariza*, a clay consisting of up to 80 per cent pure chalk, makes the best wine. It has high water-retaining properties that resist summer drought and the desiccating wind, the 'Levante', that blows from Africa. It also reflects sunlight up into the low-trained bush vines, so that the grapes bask in a slow oven as they ripen.

Barro, a brown chalky clay, is more fertile but produces heavier, coarser wine. *Arena*, or sand, is little used now for vineyards at all.

Each distinct, low vineyard hill has a name: Carrascal, Macharnudo, Añina, Balbaina are the most famous of the *pagos*, as they are called, surrounding Jerez in an arc of *albariza* to the north and west. A separate outbreak of excellent soil gives rise to the *pagos* south and east of Sanlúcar, 14 miles from Jerez, of which the best-known name is Miraflores.

The regulations of the Consejo Regulador, the governing body of Jerez, stipulate that every bodega buys a certain

proportion of its wine from the Superior vineyards – a rule scarcely necessary today, since 85 percent of the whole region is Superior: the outlying low-quality vineyards have fallen out of use. Indeed, since the export market went into decline in 1979 there has been a massive reconversion in the sherry industry, with cash incentives to grub up excess vineyard land and a spate of takeovers and mergers in the business. Sherry had boomed – give or take the odd war – from the Middle Ages until 1979, and planting reflected everyone's expectation that it would continue to do so. In 1997 the job is completed, the vineyards are back at their 1970 area of around 28,500 acres, and the sherry market is on the move again.

Leading Sherry Producers

Manuel De Argueso

PO Box 6, Jerez de la Frontera.
Medium-sized company founded in 1822 by Don León de Argueso, from northern Spain. Good dry *amontillado* and *manzanilla* from a separate bodega in Sanlúcar.

Antonio Barbadillo

Calle Luis de Eguilaz 11, PO Box 25, Sanlúcar de Barrameda.
The biggest bodega in Sanlúcar with a big stake in the *manzanilla* business and some wonderful old wines. It was founded in 1821 by Don Benigno Barbadillo. Five generations later, the firm is run by Antonio Barbadillo y Ortiguelo, although Harvey's, which jointly run a vinification

centre in the vineyards, have a shareholding. Offices (in the former bishops' palace) and the original bodegas are in the town centre. In the surrounding *albariza* areas of Cádiz, Balbaina, San Julian, Carrascal and Gibaldin, they own 2,000 acres of vines, producing a wide range of *manzanillas* and other sherries: Solear, Eva, Pastora, Tío Río, Pedro Rodriguez, Principe, La Caridad, Ducado de Sanlúcar and Villareal. Recently they have pioneered with dry white table wines made from Palomino grapes called Castillo de San Diego and Gibalbino.

Hijos de Agustin Blázquez

PO Box 540, Carretera de la Cartuja.
A relatively small high-quality bodega founded in 1795 by the Paul family, now part of the Pedro Domecq group, operated independently under its own name, with three vineyards, two in the Balbaina district, one in Macharnudo. Stocks are 15,000 butts. Its best-known products are a well-aged *fino*, Carta Blanca, Carta Roja *oloroso* and Felipe II brandy. In smaller quantities, they make a *palo cortado* called Capuchino and a noble old *amontillado*, Carta Oro. They have recently introduced a new range in Spain under the name Balfour. Sales of sherry and brandy go to the Americas, Holland and Italy.

Bobadilla

Ctra Circunvalación, Apartado 217, Jerez de la Frontera.
This large company, which produces brandy as well as sherry, was founded in 1872. The original bodega was part of a monastery in Jerez, though the current premises are now modern. Wines include Victoria Fino, Alcázar Amontillado and Capitán Oloroso. Stocks are 15,000 butts. The Bobadilla house style is quite dry which makes the sherries more popular in Spain than in the export market. Manuel Fernández, the other half of the group, exports to Holland and Germany.

John William Burdon

PO Box 6, Puerto de Santa Maria.
Formerly an English-owned bodega founded by John William Burdon, an employee of Duff Gordon (q.v.) who subsequently set up on his own. It was one of the largest bodegas of the middle- to late-19th century and on Burdon's death passed to La Cuesta; it is now owned by Luis Caballero (q.v.). Wines are Burdon Fino, a Puerto style *fino*, Don Luís Amontillado and Heavenly Cream. Wines have improved in recent years.

Luis Caballero

San Francisci 32, Apartado 6, Puerto de Santa Maria.
Founded in the 1830s with a stock of wine from the dukes of Medina, this is now the sixth-largest firm in Jerez. Still family-run by Don Luis Caballero (the sixth generation), they also make an orange brandy liqueur called Ponche which is the leading brand in Spain. All wines are supplied from their own vineyards; major brands are Burdon and Troubadour of La Cuesta and a range called Benito. Stocks are 17,000 butts. Sound but not outstanding.

Croft Jerez

Rancho Croft, Carretera Madrid, Jerez de la Frontera.
The port shippers (founded 1768) gave their name to the sherry division (formerly Gilbeys) of International Distillers and Vintners in 1970. Rancho Croft is an ambitious development from Gilbeys' simple old bodegas; a huge complex of traditional-style buildings housing the most modern plant and 70,000 butts of sherry. Crofts have planted 865 acres of *albariza* land in Los Tercios and Cuartillos. Market research led them to launch the first pale cream sherry, Croft Original. Croft Particular is a pale *amontillado*, classic medium-dry and Delicado a true *fino*. They also make a *palo cortado* and a brandy called Gourmet. Exports (to 65 countries) are 1.5m. cases a year.

Diez-Merito

Ctra Nac IV Km 641.750, Jerez de la Frontera.
An amalgamation of bodegas specializing in supplying 'buyers' own brands'. It was founded in France in 1884 as Diez Hermanos and is now controlled by Marcos Eguizábal. The name was changed in 1979 when Diez took over the old house of Merito. Since 1972 expansion has been rapid. Stocks are now 72,000 butts. They have 430 acres of vines in the Jerez Superior area, with a huge new bodega in Jerez and one at Puerto de Santa Maria. Brands include Fino Imperial (a very old *amontillado*), a splendid *oloroso* Victoria Regina and the Diez Hermanos range. After the collapse of Rumasa, Diez-Merito took over Don Zoilo and Celstino Diez de Morales and now market the very fine 'Don Zoilo' *fino*, *amontillado* and cream.

Pedro Domecq

San Ildefonso 3, Jerez de la Frontera.
The oldest, largest and one of the most respected shipping houses, founded in 1730 by Irish and French families and including in its history (as English agent) John Ruskin's father. It owns 3,952 acres of vines and no fewer than 73 bodegas all over the region. Stocks are 92,000 butts. The late head of the firm, Don José Ignacio Domecq, was recognized world-wide both literally and figuratively as 'the nose' of sherry. The finest wines are the gentle Fino La Ina; Sibarita, an old amontillado/old *oloroso* cross, dating from 1792; Rio Viejo, a dark, rich but bone-dry *oloroso*, Celebration Cream and the luscious Double Century. Domecq also owns La Riva (q.v.).

Duff Gordon

Fernan Caballero 2, Puerto de Santa Maria.
Founded in 1768 by the British Consul in Cádiz, Sir James Duff, and his nephew Sir William Gordon. It remained in the family for more than a century, before being bought in 1872 by Thomas Osborne, who had been a partner in the firm since 1833. The Osborne company (owners of 618 acres of vines) continues to market the Duff Gordon sherries and brandies for export, but does not sell them in Spain. Their most popular brands are Fino Feria, El Cid *amontillado*, the dry Nina *oloroso*, the fuller Club Dry *oloroso* and Santa María cream.

Bodegas Jésus Ferris

Avenida San Fernando 118, Rota.

Small firm run from Rota but with a bodega in Puerto de Santa Maria. Owner Don Jésus Ferris Marhuenda has 86 acres and stocks of 8,000 butts. He exports to Europe and the US direct.

Garvey

Bodegas de San Patricio, Divina Pastora, 3, Apartado 12, Jerez de la Frontera.

One of the great bodegas, founded in 1780 in Sanlúcar de Barrameda by an Irishman, William Garvey, who built what for many years remained the grandest bodega in Spain: 558 feet long. A new winery and new maturing bodegas have recently been built on the outskirts of Jerez. Once part of the Rumasa empire, the firm was taken over by the German Coop group in 1985. Garvey's have 740 acres under vine in the *albariza* areas of Maribe, Balbaina, Macharnudo, Carrascal, Montegil and Campix, producing consistently good wines. San Patricio (named after the patron saint of Ireland), a full-flavoured *fino*, is their best-known sherry. Others include Tio Guillermo *amontillado*, Ochavico dry *oloroso*, Long Life medium-dry *oloroso*, La Lidia *manzanilla*, Lanza cream and Bicentenary pale cream. *Fino* accounts for 70 percent of all production.

Gonzalez Byass

Manuel M. Gonzalez 12, Jerez de la Frontera.

One of the greatest sherry houses, founded in 1835 by Don Antonio Gonzalez y Rodriguez, whose London agent, Robert Blake Byass, became a partner in 1863. The company is still directed entirely by descendants of these two men. They own nearly 15% of the vineyards in the Jerez area and have stocks of 132,000 butts. In addition to the world's biggest-selling *fino*, Tío Pepe, La Concha *amontillado*, Apostoles dry *oloroso*, San Domingo pale cream and Nectar cream are exported throughout the world. There is a range of glorious old sherries including Amontillado Del Duque. They also make very large amounts of brandy (mainly Soberano and Lepanto), and one of the greatest of all dessert sherries: Matúsalem. Other interests include Bodegas Beronia in Rioja and Gonzalez y Dubosc in Catalonia.

Harvey's of Bristol

John Harvey & Sons (España), Alvar Nuñez 53, Jerez de la Frontera.

The famous Bristol shippers were founded in 1796. In 1822 the first John Harvey joined the firm. In 1968 it was taken over by Allied Breweries, though John Harvey's great-grandson, Michael McWatters, is the present managing director. Another John Harvey, fifth of the name, heads the company's fine-wine business. The firm became famous as blenders of 'Bristol' sweet sherries, above all Bristol Cream, now the world's biggest-selling brand with a reported 20% of the British market and a huge export business. Not until 1970, when they bought McKenzie & Co., did Harvey's own bodegas or vineyards. Now they have 3,800 acres, all in fine *albariza* land, and stocks of 155,000 butts.

Bristol Cream, once the ultimate luxury sherry, is now merely good. Other brands are Bristol Milk (not sold in the UK), Club Amontillado, Bristol Dry (which is medium) and Luncheon Dry, a dry *fino*.

Bodegas Internacionales

PO Box 300, Carr M-Cádiz.

A public company founded in 1974 by Rumasa, but now under new ownership. It is said to be the largest bodegas in the world, covering 530,000 square feet and containing stocks of 68,000 butts. These house, in addition to their own Duke of Wellington and B.E.S.T. sherries as well as Primado, Solaron and Dickens brandies, the wines and *soleras* of the Varela, Bertola and Marqués de Misa companies which were taken over by Rumasa. Vineyards in the Añina district supply a proportion of the wines for Bodegas Internacionales.

Emilio Lustau

Plaza del Cubo 4, Jerez de la Frontera.

Founded in 1896, one of the largest independent family-owned producers (with 74 acres and stocks of 20,000 butts) making top-quality sherries under their own and customers' labels. Tomás Abad is a subsidiary company. Their best wines include Dry Lustau *oloroso*, Jerez Lustau *palo cortado* and a selection of rare *almacenista* reserve sherries from small private stockholders. Their newest introduction is a range of Landed Age Rare Sherries of which the Rare Dry *oloroso* and the *amoroso* are particularly fine. One of their two vineyards, Nuestra Señora de la Esperanza in the Carrascal district, was noted by Richard Ford in his travel journal in 1845, and they have recently built a new bodega here. The original bodegas, just outside the Jerez city walls, include one cellar with a high, vaulted dome, believed to have been the headquarters of the Guard during the Moorish occupation. Since the death of Don Rafael Balao the company has been sold and the principal shareholder is now the Luís Caballero company. However, Lustau continues to act independently and sell wonderful wines.

Osborne

Calle Fernan Caballero 3, Puerto de Santa Maria.

A large and expanding, entirely family-owned and -run bodega founded in 1772 by Thomas Osborne Mann from Exeter in Devon. The family today is totally Spanish and the title of Conde de Osborne was created by Pope Pius IX. In 1872 Osborne took over Duff Gordon (q.v.). Today, it is also co-owner of Jonas Torres y Cía (founded in 1980), Osborne de Portugal (founded in 1967) and Osborne de Mexico (founded in 1971), owner of Bodegas Montecillo in Rioja, Coivisa and Osborne Distribuidora. Osborne have 900 acres of vineyards and stocks of 60,000 butts. They are the biggest drinks company in Spain. Among their sherry brands are Quinta *fino*, IORF (or Reserva Familiale), Coquinero *amontillado*, Bailen *oloroso* and Osborne Cream. Their finest sherries are limited solera bottlings under the 'Rare' label. Their important brandy portfolio includes Veterano, Magno, Independencía and Conde de Osborne.

Palomino y Vergara

Colon 1–25, Jerez de la Frontera.

One of the oldest big bodegas in Jerez, founded in 1765, taken over by Rumasa in 1963, expropriated by the Government in 1983 and now resold to Harvey's. Its offices and bodegas (capacity 32,000 butts) in the centre of Jerez are housed in an extraordinary glass-domed building still equipped with the original mahogany and gilt counters. Palomino y Vergara is a name on the domestic market, but is less important in the export field. Brands include Buleria *amontillado*, Los Flamencos *oloroso* and 1865 Solera cream. Their brandies (Fabuloso and Eminencia) are also important.

Zoilo Ruiz-Mateos

PO Box 140 La Atalaya, Cervantes 3, Jerez de la Frontera.

Founded in 1857 by Zoilo Ruiz-Mateos and recently run by a descendant of the same name, who was also vice-president of his brother's company, Rumasa, the giant concern nationalized in 1983. Zoilo was bought by Diez-Merito after the demise of Rumasa. The Don Zoilo company has 556 acres of vineyards in the best *albariza* areas of Añina and produces an extremely high-quality (and expensive) Don Zoilo range of *fino*, *amontillado* and cream sherry, and one of Spain's best brandies, Gran Duque de Alba. The bodegas in Jerez contain 200,000 butts of 500 litres each.

Sandeman Hermanos y Cía

Calle Pizarro 10, Jerez de la Frontera.

One of the great port and sherry shippers, founded in London in 1790 by George Sandeman, a Scot from Perth. It now belongs to Seagrams, but a descendant, David Sandeman, is chairman. After shipping sherries for many years, Sandeman's founded their own bodega and now have 15 vineyards, totalling 1,600 acres, all on *albariza* soil. Traditional methods produce some fine sherries: Fino Apitiv, Dry Don Amontillado, Armada Cream and a *palo cortado*, Royal Ambrosante. Royal Corregidor and Imperial Corregidor are their rarest.

Williams & Humbert

Nuno de Canas 1, PO Box 23, Jerez de la Frontera.

Founded in 1877 by Alexander Williams. His partner was his brother-in-law, Arthur Humbert. Bought in 1972 by Rumasa, the firm quickly became one of the most important in Jerez and continues to be a major exporter, with markets in North and South America, Europe, Japan and the Far East. Vineyards on *albariza* soils in Carrascal, Balbaina and Los Tercios produce good wines. The best known is Dry Sack *amontillado*. Pando is an excellent fresh *fino-amontillado*; other brands are Canasta Cream, Walnut Brown, A Winter's Tale, As You Like It and Cedro.

OTHER SHERRY PRODUCERS

Tomás Abad Playa del Cubo 4, Jerez de la Frontera. Subsidiary of Emilio Lustau (q.v.), with stocks of 2,000 butts producing a first-rate *fino*.

Herederos de Manuel Baron Banda Playa 21, PO Box 39, Sanlúcar de Barrameda. A small family firm dating back over 300 years; now comprising Bodegas Tartaneros, Regina, Moninillo, Trabajadero and Carretería, and owning 346 acres of *albariza* vineyards at Viña Atalaya and Martin Miguel. A range of sherries under names such as Baron, Atalaya, Pinoviejo, Malva, Lider, Jorge III and Marqués de Casa Trevino.

Bertola Ca. M. Cádiz, 641–750 Apartado 33, Jerez de la Frontera. Founded in 1911 as the Jerez branch of the port firm of Kopke. It is now owned by Marcos Eguizábal and jointly run with Bodegas Internacionales. Best-known brand is Bertola Cream, and other wines include a *palo cortado*, an *oloroso* style and a heavy *fino*.

Cuvillo y Cia Puerto de Santa Maria. Founded 1783. A fine independent bodega of medium size with excellent wines to offer; notably its 'Fino C' Trabajadero dry *oloroso* and a model *palo cortado*.

Delgado Zuleta SA Carmen 32, Sanlúcar de Barrameda. Family firm founded in 1744 and still independent. Their best-known wine is La Goya, a *manzanilla pasada*. Other wines include a range under the Zuleta name, a *fino* called Don Tomás and also brandies under the Mateagudo label.

Francisco Garcia de Velasco Sebastian Elcano 2, Sanlúcar de Barrameda. A relatively small bodega, founded in 1803 by Francisco Garcia de Velasco, and now owned by Bodegas Barcena. Los 48 *manzanilla* is their most important product, but they make several other sherries under various labels, including El Padre, Los Angeles Diplomatico, Tia Anita and Tres Cañas.

The solera system

A *solera* is the bodega's way of achieving complete continuity in its essential stock-in-trade: a range of wines of distinctive character. It is a 'fractional blending' system, in which wine is drawn for use from the oldest of a series of butts, which is then topped up from the next oldest, and so on down to young wine in the youngest *criadera* in the series, which in turn is supplied with young sherry as close in character to its elders as possible. The effect of withdrawing and replacing a portion (normally about a third) of a butt at a time is that each addition rapidly takes on the character of the older wine to which it is added. An incalculable fraction of the oldest wine in the *solera* always remains in the final butt (or rather butts, for the operation is on a big scale, and each stage may involve 50 butts). At the same time, so long as the *solera* is operating, the average age of the wine at every stage (except the new input) is getting gradually greater; thus the individuality of the *solera* more pronounced. Certain famous *soleras* in Jerez, those that produce Tio Pepe, for instance, or San Patricio, were started over a century ago.

Here the word 'produce', however, is misleading. It is more accurate to say 'give character to'. For *solera* wine is rarely bottled 'straight'.

Luis G Gordon PO Box 48, Jerez de la Frontera. One of the oldest sherry companies, founded by a Scot, Arthur Gordon, in 1754. Brands include Alexander Gordon, Gordon & Rivero, Marqués de Irun, Doz y Cia. Specialities are Manola *fino* and Royal, an old brandy.

Emilio M Hidalgo Clavel 29, PO Box 221, Jerez de la Frontera. A family firm based in the old town of Jerez, now in the fourth generation of the Hidalgo family since it was founded in 1874. They have a total of 346 acres of *albariza* in Añina and Carrascal and have been vinifying their own grapes since 1926. Stocks stand at 8,000 butts. Their main brands, in addition to using the name of the bodega, are Rodil and Privilegio.

Vinicola Hidalgo y Cia Banda Playa 24, Sanlúcar de Barrameda. A small bodega founded in 1800 which is still owned and run by the Hidalgo family. They have 494 acres of *albariza* vineyards in Balbaina and Miraflores, a total stock of 6,000 butts and sell 30,000 cases a year on the domestic market. They have two principal brands – the fine La Gitana *manzanilla*, Jerez Cortado Hidalgo and Napolean *amontillado*.

Bodegas de los Infantes de Orleans-Borbon Sanlúcar de Barrameda. Torre Breva, the 543-acre vineyard owned by this company, was turned over to vines in 1886 by Don Antonio de Orleans, Duke of Montpensier, who had until then used it as a shooting estate. Bodegas Infantes was founded much later, in 1943. It now has stocks of 8,000 butts. Their principal sherries are Torre Breva and La Ballena *manzanillas*, Alvaro *fino*, Orleans cream and Fenicio *oloroso*.

Lacave & Cía Avda A. Alvaro Domecq 9, PO Box 519, Jerez de la Frontera. Founded in Cádiz in 1810 the firm was bought and moved to Jerez by Rumasa in 1972. They have 370 acres of *albariza* land in the Jerez Superior area and produce a range of three sherries and a brandy under the Lacave name.

B.M. Lagos Carretera de Sanlúcar, PO Box 440, Jerez de la Frontera. Founded in 1910. From stocks of 5,000 butts they sell 178,000 cases a year; 111,000 of these to Britain. (They have connections with Harvey's.) Their own brands include Señero and Tio Cani *finos*, Las Flores *manzanilla*, Gran Cartel *oloroso* and a range of brandies.

José Medina Banda Playa 46/50, Sanlúcar de Barrameda. A traditional family firm with 15,000 butts of sherry in its bodegas in Sanlúcar and vineyards in Carrascal.

Rafael O'Neale Jerez de la Frontera. Founded 1724. The earliest of the several houses founded by Irishmen and still independent. The present director is Señora Casilda O'Neale de la Quintana. Modest in size but fine in quality. Its labels are Wild Geese, Spanish Arch, Casilda Cream and a good *manzanilla*.

Luis Paez Jardinillo 2, PO Box 545, Jerez de la Frontera. Family firm with 6,000 butts of stock in Jerez and Sanlúcar, but no vineyards. Brandnames are Conqueror, Rey de Oro, Primavera, Verano, Otoño and Invierno.

Hijos de Rainera Pérez Marin, 'La Guita' Banda Playa 28, Sanlúcar de Barrameda. A small company known for its first-class *manzanillas*, especially La Guita, the name by which the bodega is often known. Other wines include Hermosilla *manzanilla* and Bandera *fino*.

Herederos del Marqués del Real Tesoro Ctra Nacional IV, km-640, Jerez de la Frontera. A respected small family firm founded towards the end of the 19th century by the Marqués del Real Tesoro. The company was taken over recently and moved to a purpose-built and very grand bodega on the outskirts of the town. The move also occasioned the purchase of the brand names and soleras of Tío Mateo *fino* from Palomino y Vergara.

La Riva SA Alvar Nuñez 44, Jerez de la Frontera. An old-established small bodega with some of the finest *soleras* in Jerez, taken over in the 1970s by Pedro Domecq but still operated independently for its lovely *fino* Tres Palmas, *amontillado* Guadalupe and old *olorosos* and *palo cortados* of superlative quality. Vineyards 130 acres and stocks 2,773 butts.

Felix Ruíz y Ruíz Calle Cristal 4, 6 & 8, Jerez de la Frontera. A small firm founded in 1809; now owning 3 bodegas and selling over 222,000 cases of sherry and brandy each year from stocks of 10,000 butts. They sell two ranges of sherries, Don Felix and Ruiz, each with three styles (dry, medium and cream) plus brandies of the same names.

Bodegas Sanchez de Alva Carretera de Arcos km-2, PO Box 26, Jerez de la Frontera. Founded in 1935 by Manuel Gil Luque and taken over by the Canterero group in 1978, since when turnover has increased considerably, particularly in export. Stocks are now over 10,000 butts, plus a wide range of brandies and liqueurs. Their main sherry names are Deportivo and Alba *finos*, Don Quijote *oloroso* and a range of five styles under the Sanchez de Alva label.

Sanchez Romate Lealas 26–30, 11404 Jerez de la Frontera. A respected small bodega, founded in 1781 by Juan Sanchez de la Torre, a well-known businessman and philanthropist. It remains an independent company owning 200 acres in four vineyards. One in Balbaina and two in Macharnudo are on *albariza* and the fourth, in the Cuartillo district, is on *barros* soil. Stocks are some 8,000 butts. Brands include Marismeño and Cristal *finos*; Viva la Pepa and Petenera *manzanillas*; NPU (Non Plus Ultra) *amontillado*; Iberia cream and Doña Juana *oloroso*. Cardinal Mendoza brandy (called Cardinal for the USA) is made in limited quantities.

José de Soto M. A. Jesus Tirado 6, Jerez de la Frontera. Founded towards the end of the 18th century by José de Soto, who acquired Viña Santa Isabel at the same time. They own six vineyards covering 370 acres of *albariza* in the finest districts of Balbaina and Macharnudo. Stocks of 10,000 butts go to make Soto and Camper *finos*, Don Jaime and La Uvita *amontillados* and La Espuela *oloroso*. Probably most famous for making the first *ponche* (a sherry-based liqueur) – and still one of the best.

Fernando A de Terry Sta. Trinidad 2, Puerto de Santa Maria. Founded 1883. Originally the foundation of an Irish family, now (after Rumasa control) owned by Harvey's. Better known for their Centenario brandy than their sherries. Ultramodern premises house over 50,000 butts. Camborio is their label in Spain. In the UK they supply Marks & Spencer's own-label sherries.

Valdespino SA Pozodel Olivar 16, PO Box 22, Jerez de la Frontera. Still the property of the Valdespino family. Their Ynocente, named from a single Macharnudo vineyard, is a classic *fino* and Tio Diego one of the driest dark and masculine *amontillados*.

Varela Ctra Madrid, Cádiz Km 641–750, Jerez de la Frontera. Founded in 1850 by Ramón Jiménez Varela and bought from his descendants by Rumasa in 1960 and since resold to Bodegas Internacionales. The *amontillado* and cream are the best known of the five Varela sherries.

Wisdom & Warter Ltd Pizarro 7, Jerez de la Frontera. Wisdom and Warter, although apparently a short-cut recipe for bargain sherry, are the names of the two Englishmen who founded the company in 1854. It currently owns a 173-acre *albariza* vineyard, La Bodogonera, in Los Tercios and has stocks totalling 20,000 butts. The main brands are Olivar *fino*, Royal Palace *amontillado*, Wisdom's Choice cream, Merecedor *oloroso* as well as a range under the Wisdom label.

CAYD Sanlúcar de Barrameda. The trading name of the important Sanlúcar cooperative, with 1,000 members and a stock of 50,000 butts. Its speciality is such *manzanillas* as Bajo de Guia and Sanluqueña.

THE CANARY ISLANDS

Wine production in the Canary Islands varies from a cottage industry turning out tiny quantities of excellent wine made from museum varieties which long ago died out on the peninsula, to quite large-scale wineries with real ambitions in the export department. However, even the largest winery in the largest DO (Bodegas Insulares in Tacoronte-Acentejo) is prepared to admit that the lack of economy of scale on the islands, the eternal thirst of the tourist trade and the sheer cost of shipping wine to mainland Europe are stacking the odds against them at the moment. However, the same used to be said of Australia and New Zealand, and there has been considerable development there.

There are seven main islands, and DO wine is produced on four of them, with country wines on some of the others. Three of the DOs are island-wide.

ABONA (TENERIFE)

This DO zone occupies the southwestern quarter of the island, planted in 70% Listán Blanco and 30% Listán Negro. Light wines in all three colours of no export significance.

EL HIERRO

The first vines on this island were planted by an Englishman, John Hill, in 1529. Today there are three subzones with vines planted on steep slopes up to 2,000 feet in altitude. As well as the staples Listán, Negramoll, Pedro Ximénez and Verdello they also grow the rare Bujariego, Bremajuelo, Gual, Baboso and Mulata. Some wines of exemplary quality, but the quantity is too small to be significant.

LANZAROTE

Beguiling black volcanic soils are the hallmark of this island, with vines planted in hollows scooped out of the ground to protect them from the prevailing winds. Most of the cultivation is of Malvasía and the sweet, semi-fortified style is an inheritor of the original 'Canary-Sack' which was famed in Shakespeare's day. There are also dry wines made from the same grape, as well as some small production of dry white from Listán and Diego, and a tiny amount of red and rosado.

LA PALMA

The 'Isla Bonita' is as famous for its banana plantations as for its wine, but there are three subzones, making anything from rustic artisanal wines in the north to some respectable examples in the south. Grapes are Malvasía, Listàn, Bujariego, Gual, Verdello, Bastardo, Sabro and Negramoll, and wines come in all three colours. There is some small amount of *crianza* aged in Tronçais oak.

TACORONTE-ACENTEJO (TENERIFE)

The Canary Islands' first and largest DO covers the northwest of Tenerife and, of all of them, has the best chance of achieving export markets. There are 30 bodegas in the area making good reds from Listàn Negro and pleasant whites mainly from Listàn Blanco and Malvasía. Development can be gauged by output since the DO was granted: 1991 – 5,767 cases; 1992 – 8,367 cases; 1993 – 24,567 cases.

VALLE DE GUIMAR (TENERIFE)

This is almost a continuation of the vineyards of Abona, running up the southeastern coast of the island, with mainly Listàn Blanco for mostly white wines of good, everyday quality. There is some small amount of rosado made from Listàn Negro.

VALLE DE LA OROTAVA (TENERIFE)

On the northwest coast between Tacoronte in the north and Ycod in the south, in a valley running down from the volcano to the sea. Pleasant, light white and red wines are made here in roughly similar quantities, with a small amount of rosado. Grape varieties: Listàn Blanco and Negro.

YCODEN-DAUTE-ISORA (TENERIFE)

This DO covers the extreme western portion of the island and takes its name from the town of Icod-de-los-Vinos, site of the famous 1,000-year-old 'dragon tree'. The area grows mainly Listàn Blanco and Negro and about two-thirds of production is white wine of good, clean, crisp style. There is also some light red and rosado. Total production in 1994 was around 68,000 cases.

Canary Islands Producers

El Grifo

Ctra de Masdache, 121, San Bartolomé de Lanzarote.
The oldest bodega on the island – founded in 1775, and re-established in 1980. Wines (mainly white – including an excellent sweet Malvasía) are sold under the El Grifo brand name.

Cooperativa Llanovid

Los Canarios, Fuencaliente, La Palma.
Founded in 1948, this coop produces good, sound wines, mainly white but some reds including experimental *crianza* wines and some made by *maceración carbónica*. The brand name is Teneguia.

Bodegas Insulares Tenerife

Vereda del Medio 8b, Tacoronte.
A spanking-new bodega with all the latest kit and plenty of built-in room for expansion. Their best wines are Viña Norte Tinto Maceración, made from Listàn Negro and Negramoll by *maceración carbónica*, and Viña Norte Tinto Madera made from the same grapes but aged for four months in oak. Very promising indeed.

Antonio Fernando Gonzàlez

Cueva del Rey, Icod.
A fascinating boutique winery which is run by an English teacher with a passion for white wines. He has a tiny bodega fitted with fibreglass tanks and regales visitors with excellent tapas as well as a look round his little museum of Icod past. His wines, both white and red, are currently amongst the best of the DO.

PORTUGAL

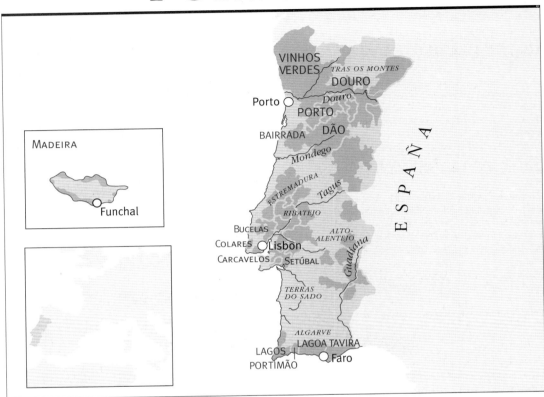

Portugal, conservative as she is, was the first country in modern times to invent a new style of wine for export, and to get it so spectacularly right that it became one of the biggest-selling brands on earth. The wine, of course, is Mateus Rosé. With its competitors it accounts for a large part of Portugal's wine exports – more than port, her traditional tribute to foreign taste – though it is now officially a 'stable' brand, and its principal producers are busily diversifying away from mono-brands.

Mateus is simply an imaginative development of peasant tradition: *vinho verde*, the sharp and fizzy 'green wine' of the country's northern province, the Minho. It is the measure of Portuguese conservatism that neither the Mateus style, nor even port, has ever caught on in a big way in their home country. With the rapid development of an urban middle class and a supermarket society outside Lisbon and Oporto, though, the Portuguese are gradually being weaned onto more international styles of wine, but still largely made from indigenous grapes – the nature and variety of which are justifiably Portugal's pride and strength on the international wine front (*see* pages 15-16).

Yet this is no little backwater. Portugal is firmly in the top ten in the league of wine-producing nations, although dramatically less wine is now consumed in the home market:

over the past ten years Portugal's position of third in the league of consumption per head has been dropping.

Conservative they may be, but the Portuguese were the first to establish the equivalent of a national system of *appellation contrôlée:* the first delimited area being the Douro in 1756. Then came a wave of demarcations, starting in 1908 with *vinho verde*. Portugal had legally defined boundaries, grapes, techniques and standards for all of what were then her better wines.

For many years, unfortunately, these have sat heavily on progress, leading to a distorted picture of where the best wines were really being grown. Happily, much of the confusion over regional boundaries has recently been resolved with the introduction of new legislation, more or less coinciding with Portugal's entry to the European Union.

The country now has a four-tier appellation system which parallels that of France. The best wines qualify for DOC (Denominacão de Origem Controlada) status, of which there are currently nineteen. Next are the twenty-eight IPRs (Indicaões de Proveniência Regulamentada), which are regions on a six-year probation for DOC status. In 1992, eight broader Vinhos Regionals were introduced. The fourth distinction is Vinhos de Mesa, which covers the rest: all the basic, unclassified table wines.

During the long period while the regional system was out of date, many of Portugal's better wine companies took to using brand names without any indication of origin. Now, however, all wines must have their region of origin indicated on the label, unless they are bottled as Vinho de Mesa, without a vintage date. Another Portuguese peculiarity was the ascendancy of merchant companies over primary producers. This situation has now been reversed, encouraged by the availability of EU grants, and primary producers are very much the rising stars.

There remain relatively few big wine estates outside the Douro, the port country in the north of Portugal, although the Alentejo now has some of the largest properties: Esporão is one property with over 1,200 acres of vineyards. The newer regions of the south also tend to have larger estates, but the production of the vast majority of Portugal's 180,000 growers is tiny. Forty per cent take their grapes to the country's cooperative cellars, of which there are over 100. Most of the rest who have wine to spare after supplying their families and friends sell it to merchants. Merchants and their brands rather than growers' names therefore remain the key to Portuguese wine. Most of the bigger and better merchants buy and bottle wine from each of the major areas: there is little regionality at this level either. The last 20 years have seen the rise of single *quintas* (estates): individual properties growing their own grapes and making their own wine and these are now making significant inroads, especially in Vinho Verde country, Bairrada, Dão and the Alentejo.

Traditionally, the Portuguese practice was to divide all wines into two categories: *verde* or *maduro,* and these names are still used on the wine lists of many restaurants. *Vinho verde* is unaged wine, and the use of the term is now legally limited to the northern province, the Minho. Sparkling rosés would, however, logically fit into this category. *Maduro* means mature. It implies long ageing in barrel (or, frequently in cement vat) and bottle. It is the natural, indeed essential, treatment for wines, red or white, made in the traditional manner of every part of Portugal except the Minho. But the *verde/maduro* division is becoming blurred as more young wines, red and white, are now reaching the market.

The very real virtue of Portuguese wine made in the time-honoured way is its structure: it is engineered to last for decades, evolving from gum-withering astringency to a most satisfying texture, when firmness is rounded out to velvet smoothness without losing the feel of the iron fist within. Its vice is lack of flavour, and often only the shyest fragrance for such a potent wine. Earlier picking, destemming bunches and cooler fermentation are among manoeuvres now being adopted. But in Portugal the old habits die hard.

A peculiar piece of terminology is used for selected, long-aged wines. The word *garrafeira* has much of the meaning of *reserva*, but with the added implication that it is the merchant's 'private' best wine, aged for some years in bottle and subsequently in barrel, to be ready for immediate drinking when sold. Alcohol levels for these wines should be at least 0.5% above the legal minimum.

PORTUGUESE WINE REGIONS

The wines of Portugal (excluding port) are described here in a progress as nearly as possible from north to south. The headings are the names of the officially recognized regions. For port *see* pages 395-400.

VINHO VERDE

This is the largest wine region, accounting for about twenty percent of the country's harvest, and which covers most of the northern province of the Minho from Oporto to the Spanish border. Its name is synonymous with the wines it produces; probably Portugal's most original and successful contribution to the world's cellar.

What is green about *vinho verde* is not its colour (55% is red and the white is like lemon-stained water). It is its salad-days freshness, which seems to spring straight from the verdant pergolas where it grows in promiscuous polyculture with maize and vegetables. Traditionally, the vines hang in garlands from tree to tree, or are trained on pergolas of granite post and chestnut lintel. Growing the grapes so high above the ground has several advantages: it slows their ripening and produces the desired sugar/acid balance; it counteracts the tendency to fungus diseases in a cool and rainy climate; it also allows for other cultivation below and between. However, modern vineyards are being trained on lower systems, making the operation easier to mechanize as well as producing wines with better acid balance.

The traditional method of making *vinho verde* is to encourage an active malolactic fermentation. The cool climate, the grapes cultivated (*see* page 16), and their elevated training result in very high levels of malic acid. The natural bacterial conversion of malic to lactic acid takes the rasp out of the acidity and adds the tingle of its by-product, carbon dioxide. In some country inns the jug wine from barrels is not unlike very dry, fizzy and rather cloudy cider.

Nowadays, however, only a few jug wines are made in the traditional way, and almost no *vinho verde* undergoes malolactic fermentation in bottle, as this creates a sediment. The vast majority of commercial wineries finish the wine to complete bacterial stability and then bottle it with an injection of carbon dioxide to arrive at approximately the same result. The last method also gives the winemaker the option of sweetening his wine (with unfermented must) without the danger of its refermenting. The total dryness and distinct sharpness of 'real' *vinho verde* is not to everyone's taste. In the red version, fermented stalks and all, it contrives with high tannin to make an alarmingly astringent drink which foreigners rarely brave a second time.

The merchants' brands of *vinho verde* do not normally specify which part of the wide region they come from. Of the eight sub-regions, Amarante and Peñafiel, just inland from Oporto, produce the the most white wine. Braga, the centre of the Minho, has good-quality fresh red and white.

Lima, along the river of the same name north of Braga, specializes in slightly more full-bodied reds. Monção, along the River Minho on the Spanish border in the north, is most famous for its single-variety white, its Alvarinho, much the most expensive (and most alcoholic) wine of the region but only by courtesy, if at all, a *vinho verde*. Alvarinho is smooth and still, aged in wood and softly fragrant of apricots or freesias, rather than brisk and tinglingly fruity. It is mostly bottled young but, unlike ordinary *vinho verde*, it can be aged for 2–3 years in bottle. Some of the best *vinhos verdes* are now being made by single vineyard properties – members of a self-styled group of grower producers called APEVV (Associacão dos Produtores-Engarrafadores de Vinho Verde).

DAO

The region of Dão, centred on the old cathedral city of Viseu, 50 miles south of the Douro, is much the biggest and the most established and prosperous producer of *vinhos maduros* under a seal of origin. It is pine-forested country along the valleys of three rivers, the Alva, the Mondego and the Dão, cut through hills of granite boulders and sandy soil. The vast majority of its 38,000 acres of vineyard is planted with black grapes (several of which it has in common with the Douro).

The profile of a red Dão remains, despite the care and skill of several of the merchants who mature it, a rather dry, hard wine reluctant to `give', excellent palate cleansing with rich food, smooth and inviting to swallow, yet strangely lacking in bouquet or lingering sweetness.

The reason is that until the 1990 vintage nobody except the 10 local cooperatives could make Dão except from his own grapes; the vineyards belong to small farmers, and there was for many years only one estate-grown Dão on the market – that of the Conde de Santar. It no longer has pole position, though, as a number of single *quintas* now make very good wine; the best two are Quinta dos Roques and Quinta de Saes. The merchant bottlers have had to make the best of what the farmers and cooperatives provide them with. Now that the cooperatives have lost their monopoly, a number of producers have been encouraged by the release of this stranglehold and are starting to buy in grapes and make their own wines. Sogrape, the makers of Mateus Rosé, are probably in the strongest position, having invested about £4 million in a new winery.

BAIRRADA

Although it remained undemarcated until 1979, some 70 years after the Dão region, Bairrada is a real rival in the quality of its wines. The name applies to an area between Dão and the Atlantic north of Coimbra and south of Oporto, with the towns of Mealhada and Anadia as its main centres. Its low hills of heavy lime-rich soil have a greater vineyard area than Dão, and the same preponderance of red grapes (90%) over white. But its climate is more temperate, its grape varieties different and its *adegas* more individual.

Two local grapes not found elsewhere have outstanding qualities. The red Baga is a late-ripening variety high in tannin and acid that gives real authority and 'cut' to a blend. As the dominant variety it needs 15 to 20 years' ageing, but eventually achieves the great fragrance of a fine claret.

The aromatic local white grape is the Bical, which seems to have an exceptional balance of acidity and extract, aromatic of apricots, brisk and long-flavoured. Another grape, called Maria Gomes, a more neutral variety, forms the basis of the sparkling-wine industry of Bairrada, which now has some very palatable products.

Garrafeira wines from almost any Portuguese merchant may contain or be based on Bairrada wines. The following firms are in the area and make good examples: Luis Pato (whose wines are from his own estate), Casa de Saima and Sogrape, who source much of the base wine for Mateus from Bairrada. Sogrape also makes a good dry rosé, Nobilis, entirely from the Baga grape.

THE DOURO

The mythology of the Douro reports that it was its terrible table wine that forced merchants to lace it with brandy and create port. It may have been so, but since 1991 the region has made great strides and today produces admirable wines, including Duas Quintas (from Ramos Pinto), Redoma (from Niepoort), Domingos Alves e Sousa (Quinta de Gaivosa and Quinta do Vale da Raposa), Quinta do Crasto and Quinta de la Rosa, It also provides a number of well-known merchants' *garrafeiras*, and, in the shape of Barca Velha (*see* the entry for A. A. Ferreira under Port Producers on page 397), a great red wine of international stature to put besides Spain's Vega Sicilia, from 100 miles farther up the same river.

Two of the new Vinhos Regionais, Trás-os-Montes, north of the Douro, and Beira Alta to its south, have well-balanced, not over-strong red wines to offer. (Beiras is the name for a catch-all Vinho Regional which includes Dão and Bairrada, as well as Portugal's entire centre.) Lafões is a recently regulated region in the wetter west of the Beira Alta, producing wine similar in style to *vinho verde*, called *verdasco*.

THE CENTRE AND SOUTH

Of the four historic wine regions demarcated with *selos de origem* clustering round the capital Lisbon two (Carcavelos and Colares) are reduced to relics, one (Bucelas) is still substantial but dwindling, and only the fourth, Setúbal, across the Tagus estuary, has escaped the attrition of housing development to prosper in modern times.

Estremadura

The biggest Lisbon area, immediately north of the city, is the Estremadura which includes three of the four historic wine regions. Carcavelos is nearest to extinction. The one remaining vineyard has almost 'given up the ghost'. Quinta dos Pesos was launched in 1990/91, but the sprawling resort of Estoril seems to have swallowed up the rest of wine-producing Carcavelos. The quality of the wine does repay a search. It is a light amber, velvety, not oversweet, slightly fortified dessert or apéritif wine like a soft, nutty and buttery Verdelho or Bual madeira.

More is heard of Bucelas, whose 450 acres of vineyards lie 10 miles due north of Lisbon. Despite its proximity to the capital, the region is enjoying a new lease of life. Until recently, there was only one producer turning out a rather old-fashioned oxidized style of white wine. Now there are four, the best of which is Quinta da Romeira (owned by Tate & Lyle), which produces Prova Regia, a distinctive, crisp and fragrant dry white from the aromatic Arinto grape.

· Still more is heard of Colares, not because there is any quantity but because it is a true original, and one of Portugal's most sought-after red wines. Its vineyards are an unplottable sprawl in the sand dunes of the Atlantic coast west of Lisbon, between Sintra and the sea. They grow the Ramisco, a tiny, bloomy dark-blue bullet of a grape whose thick skin would tan an ox-hide. Grown in pure sand (the plants have to be planted at the bottom of deep pits, which are then progressively filled in) it makes wine of quite unreasonable inkiness and astringency. Grafting is unnecessary: phylloxera is baffled by sand.

The Estremadura is home to some giant cooperatives, such as Torres Vedras, Arruda and São Mamede de Ventosa, as well as smaller, quality producers, including Quinta de Abrigada and Quinta de Pancas near Alenquer. Currently, it is also Portugal's most important wine region.

Terras do Sado

Across the Tagus, between the bridge and Setúbal on the far side of the Arrabida peninsula, lies a region with nearly 50,000 acres of vineyards, divided between good plain red wine and the sumptuously aromatic Muscat of Setúbal – a fortified wine with a minimum of 17% alcohol. It was apparently the creation of the firm of José Maria da Fonseca (q.v.) of Azeitão, in the middle of the region, who originally had a quasi-monopoly in the area (there are now other producers among whom J.P. Vinhos is leader). Setúbal in this form is a 'muted' wine, its fermentation stopped by the addition of spirit, in which the skins of more Muscat grapes, themselves highly aromatic, are steeped and macerated to give it the precise fragrance of a ripe dessert grape. The wine is barrel-aged and drunk, without further ageing in bottle, either at six years (when it is still amazingly fresh and grapey) or at 25 or more (when it has taken on more piquant notes of fragrance and developed the tobacco hue and satin texture of a fine tawny port).

RIBATEJO

The formerly undemarcated central coastal area, north of Lisbon, where Wellington held the famous lines of Torres Vedras, is now a Vinho Regional and has a series of IPRs.

From here eastwards to the far banks of the Tagus beyond Santarem, Ribatejo used to be bulk-wine country. For all that, it is a good source of wine and has attracted the interest of a new generation of young winemakers. It is also one of the few regions in Portugal to grow commercial quantities of international grapes, including Cabernet Sauvignon, Merlot, Chardonnay and Sauvignon Blanc. Traditional ways are not dead, though: the Quinta do Casal Branco (q.v.) is one that continues to make good wines, especially its Falcoaria.

ALENTEJO

The vast area south of the Tagus was 'discovered' in wine terms as recently as the beginning of the 1990s. Its brown hills are covered with the dark cork oaks that furnish the world with its best-quality corks. The Alentejo as a whole has seen a dramatic improvement over the past five years in the quality of its wines, while certain sub-areas are now recognized for making the best wines, notably the DOCs Reguengos (home to Esporão and José da Sousa), Redondo and Borba towards Elvas (of the famous preserved plums). Borba has a good coop and the Quinta do Carmo within its boundaries. There are good IPRs, too: Evora (Cartuxa is the leader) and Granja-Amareleja which has an extraordinary cooperative. Herdade do Mouchão and Tapada do Chaves at Portalegre are making wines which can be outstanding. Alentejo's potential has not been lost on the big merchants either: Caves Aliança have invested at Borba and Sogrape in Vidigueira, near Beja. These regions are almost neighbours of the Spanish Extremadura, and their wines are correspondingly high in alcohol.

ALGARVE

The wines of the demarcated Algarve on the south coast are likewise high in alcohol, but that is the only characteristic this region shares with the Alentejo. Only a coarse sherry-style white wine has any reputation at all – and that an appalling one! In fact, the four DOCs of the Algarve risk being demoted, given the poor quality of their wines.

ROSES

The fabulous success of Mateus and subsequent Portuguese semi-sweet, semi-sparkling rosés was achieved by applying the idea (not the traditional technique) of *vinho verde* to red grapes from a region where the wine had no particular reputation: the hills of north of the Douro round the town of Vila Real. It did not matter that this was not a demarcated region; rather the reverse: it meant that when the local grapes ran out supplies could be found in other areas. Today, rosés are made of grapes from almost anywhere in Portugal. The principal rosé winemaking areas are Bairrada and the Setúbal peninsula south of Lisbon. It is a process then, and not a regional identity that characterizes these wines. They are made in the usual rosé fashion, of red grapes with a very short period of skin contact after crushing to extract the required pink tinge, then fermented like white wine; the fermentation is stopped while about 18 grams per litre of original grape sugar remain intact. This is done by adding sulphur dioxide and then removing the remaining yeast with a centrifuge pump. The wine is then blended for consistency and bottled, with the addition of carbon dioxide under pressure.

Leading Wine Producers

Caves Aliança – Vinicola de Sangalhos

Sangalhos, 3783 Anadia. Founded 1920. Visits.

One of Portugal's principal still and sparkling wine producers. A public company controlled by the Neves family based in the Bairrada but offering *vinho verde* (the good dry Casal Mendes), Dão, and Douro rosé as well as its admirable Bairrada red Aliança Tinto Velho, and very passable *méthode traditionnelle* sparkling wine. The company has invested substantially at Borba in the Alentejo.

Quinta da Aveleda Lda

4650 Penafiel.

Makers of two of the most famous brands of *vinho verde*, Casal Garcia and Avelada, both of which are medium-dry. Quinta da Aveleda is a more traditional bone-dry wine and Grinalda is a fragrant, crisp dry wine from Loureiro and Trajadura, two of the best grapes in the region.

Fundação Eugenio de Almeida – Herdade de Cartuxa

Pateo S. Miguel, 7000 Evora.

This 17,300-acre property, managed as a charitable trust, has 500 acres of vines close to the city of Evora, capital of the Alentejo. Fairly rigorous selection means the foundation's main label, Cartuxa, is a firm, refined red, but the best Trincadeira and Aragonez grapes are held back for Pera Manca, which has quickly established itself as one of Portugal's leading wines. Reds are rather more successful than the whites. The remainder of the estate's production is bottled as *vinho regional*, or sold off to a local cooperative.

A. A. Ferreira S.A.

Rua da Carvalhosa, 19–103, 4400 Vila Nova de Gaia. Visits.

Barca Velha, launched by port producers Ferreira in the 1950s, has quickly earned itself the reputation as one of Portugal's most prestigious red wines. Grapes, mainly Tinta Roriz, are grown at Quinta do Vale do Meão and trodden in big, stone *lagares,* yielding about 4,000 cases of wine a year. Barca Velha is only released in the best vintages ('65, '66, '78, '83 and '85); lesser years are declassified to Ferreirinha Reserva Especial.

Finagra – Herdade do Esporão

7200 Reguengos de Monsaraz.

Finagra is the name of the holding company for the huge Esporão estate near Reguengos de Monsaraz in the Alentejo. Planted in the 1970s, the vineyards cover over 1,200 of the estate's 5,000 acres. Esporão suffered a chequered start to life, but under the shrewd ownership and management of business tycoon José Roquette the investment is now paying dividends. Sales of red and white wines bottled under the company's three labels, Alandra, Monte Velho and Esporão, are buoyant both at home and abroad. Much of the credit is due to Australian winemaker David Baverstock who has transformed Esporão into one of the most reliable wine producers in Portugal.

José Maria da Fonseca Succs.

The Old Winery, 2925 Azeitão. Founded 1834. Visits.

One of the leading wine companies of Portugal, famous as the largest producers of fortified 'Setúbal', though the quantities in commercial terms are not as significant as their range of quality red wines.

Periquita is the best known, made from a blend of local grapes of the same name; Quinta da Camarate is a ripe blackcurranty blend of Cabernet Sauvignon and Periquita and Tinto Velho from the José da Sousa *adega* in the Alentejo is a good peppery blend of local grapes fermented in large clay amphorae. The company also owns a winery in Dão which bottles the Terras Altas brand. Fonseca is run by two brothers, Antonio and Domingos Soares Franco, who are descendants of the founder.

J. M. da Fonseca Internacional

The New Winery, 2925 Azeitão. Visits.

This company was for a while owned by the American firm Heublein, part of Grand Met, but it has now been sold back to the Soares Franco family, who are also its managers. Apart from the enormous sales of Lancers Rosé, their semi-sweet, sparkling pink wine, Fonseca Internacional have recently invested in a plant producing sparkling wine by the continuous method first developed in Russia.

Luis Pato

Ois de Bairro, 3780 Anadia.

Luis Pato began making his own wines in 1980 and has subsequently established himself as one of the leading independent producers in Portugal. He farms around 150 acres of vineyard in the heart of the Bairrada region and relies heavily on the local Baga grape, continually monitoring its performance in a variety of different soils. This has resulted in two excellent single-vineyard wines, Vinha Pan and Vinha Barrosa, the latter made from very old, low-yielding vines.

Pato has spent many years experimenting in the vineyard and the winery with the result that there has been considerable variation in style from one vintage to the next. Since the early 1990s he seems to have found his feet, resulting in some particularly good 1995s, especially the Quinta de Ribeirinho Pe Franco, a limited production of excellent red made from incredibly low-yielding ungrafted Baga vines. Pato also makes attractive dry white wines from the local Arinto, Cerceal and Cercealinho varieties, and also has a small amount of Cabernet Sauvignon in his vineyards, which he usually blends with Baga grapes.

J.P. Vinhos

2955 Pinhal Novo.

Australian winemaker Peter Bright is consultant winemaker for J.P. Vinhos (formerly João Pires and Filhos). The delicious grapey dry Muscat João Pires, which was such a decisive hit both in Portugal and abroad, has now been sold to International Distillers and Vintners. Red wines from the J.P. Vinhos stable include Quinta da Bacalhoa; a minty Bordeaux-like blend of Cabernet and Merlot; Meia Pipa, a blend of Periquita and Cabernet grapes; and Tinto da Anfora, a warming spicy red from the Alentejo. Cova da Ursa, a barrel-fermented Chardonnay, has more than a hint of New World style about it.

Palace Hotel do Buçaco

3050 Mealhada

The cellars of this extravagant hotel mature one of Europe's most unusual wines. The hotel's 37-acre vineyards are near Luso on the fringes of the Bairrada region and grow its typical grapes. They are trodden (both black and white) in a 5,000-litre stone *lagar* and their wine made exactly in the manner of the last century; fermented in casks, then only racked and not filtered; the red wine is bottled at four to five years old, the white averages two to three years of age before bottling. Average production is 4,400 cases of red, 3,300 of white. Vintages available in the hotel go back to 1944 white and 1927 red, both still well preserved. The best vintages (e.g. white: 1985, '84, '66, '65, '56; red: 1982, '78, '70, '63, '60, '58, '53) have an exquisite hand-made quality, together with great fragrance and depth.

Caves São João

S. João de Anadia, 3780 Anadia.

Family-owned producer with 50 acres of vines in the heart of the Bairrada region. Two brothers, Alberto and Luis Costa, age, blend and bottle some of the most impressive red wines from Bairrada and the neighbouring Dão region. Bottled respectively under the Frei João and Porta dos Cavaleiros labels, the *Reservas*, sporting a cork label, have great depth and ageing potential. The company has recently launched a Cabernet-based wine called Quinta do Poço do Lobo from their own 86-acre vineyard.

Sogrape – Vinhos de Portugal SARL

Av. da Boavista, 1163, 4100 Porto. Visits.

Portugal's biggest winemakers and the producers of Mateus Rosé have annual sales of over 2.5 million cases and are the leading producers in terms of both quality and quantity in the north of the country. The founding Guedes family still control the firm, its subsidiary Vinícola do Vale do Dão and also now own Ferreira and Offley port (*see* page 397). They have made a big investment in Dão, at Quinta dos Carvalhais and at Vinha do Monte in the Alentejo. Mateus Rosé is made from grapes grown all over the north of Portugal, especially the Baga from Bairrada where Sogrape have a large winery. Other wines include Grão Vasco, a good Dão made at the company's own winery near Viseu; Vila Regia, a ripe Douro red; and Terra Franca, a soft, fruity Bairrada. The company also produces a deliciously oaky, dry white Reserva wine from grapes grown north of the Douro river around the town of Vila Real.

OTHER PRODUCERS

Domingos Alves e Sousa – Quinta da Gaivosa 5031 Santa Marta de Penagulão. Small producer with properties in the Baixo Corgo sub-region of the Douro now making some very good red wines from local (port) grapes. The oak-aged Quinta da Gaivosa is rich and concentrated for keeping; Quinta da Vale de Raposa is bottled early for drinking young.

Adega Cooperativa de Borba 7150 Borba. One of Portugal's most go-ahead cooperatives is to be found on the edge of the little Alentejo town of Borba. Balanced fruity red wines and crisp white wines bottled as Borba, with a second wine known as Convento da Vila.

Bright Bros Livramento, 2765 Estoril. Australian winemaker Peter Bright left J.P. Vinhos (of João Pires fame) to found his own company. He has now joined the flying winemaker set, making wines all over the world as well as in his adopted home, Portugal. He produces a broad range of Portuguese wines under the Bright Bros label from the Douro, Beiras, Ribatejo and Estremadura regions.

Quinta do Carmo 7150 Borba. Joint venture, in the Alentejo, between the Bastos family and the Rothschilds of Château Lafite-Rothschild, Bordeaux. Over 170 acres of vineyard produce firm red wines and steely whites; they also own cork forests. Some of the recent wines made under French management have been lighter and less satisfying than the solid examples of yesteryear.

Quinta do Casal Branco 2080 Almeirim. Ribatejo estate with over 250 acres of dry heathland vineyard bottling their own wines since 1990. Best red and white wines are under the Falcoaria label.

Caves do Casalinho Lda R. Duque de Saldanha 182, 4300 Porto. Family-owned company with several *quintas* in the *vinho verde* region. Casalinho is their principal *vinho verde* brand; others are Três Marias, and 5 Cidades. Casalinho Rosé is a Mateus lookalike rosé wine, without the same emphasis on quality control.

Adega Regional de Colares Colares, 2710 Sintra. The centre of Colares production, although most of its output is matured and bottled by several firms, including Real Companhia Vinícola and António B.P. da Silva, which labels its wines as Colares Chitas.

Quinta do Crasto Ferrão, 5060 Sabrosa. Well-situated, family-owned property in the Douro making some inspiring non-fortified Douro wines as well as port. David Baverstock as winemaker has managed to tame the hard tannins that mar so many Douro red wines and his success is noticeable in a fruity young wine and also a full, fleshy Reserva.

Fiuza-Bright Travessa do Vareta, 11, 2080 Almeirim. Partnership between the Fiuza family and Australian winemaker Peter Bright. Large property in the Ribatejo producing varietal wines with character mainly from international grapes.

Herdade do Mouchão Casa Branca, 7470 Sousel. Alentejo estate with over 2200 acres, over 50 of which are planted with vines. Huge red wines rely heavily on low-yielding Alicante Bouschet grapes for colour and structure. When Mouchão is on form, it is the Alentejo at its very best.

Vinhos Messias Apartado 1, 3050 Mealhada. Founded 1926. Growers and merchants with a wide range of different ports (*see* page 398) and wines. Quinta do Cachão is a full, spicy Douro red; Quinta do Valdoeiro a fresh-tasting, appley dry white from extensive Bairrada vineyards. Other wines bought in and blended at their cellars include the Santola brand of *vinho verde*, a solid, well-made red Dão, a Bairrada and good, sparkling *espumantes*.

Vinhos de Monção Lda 4950 Monção. Diminutive producers of the famous (and expensive) Alvarinho white, Cepa Velha, a potential *vinho verde* fermented and aged in wood to achieve a totally different result.

Niepoort Rua Infante D. Henrique 39, 4000 Porto. This Dutch family port shipper has gone from strength to strength under Dirk Niepoort. Redoma is the name given to their monumental Douro red, soon to be followed by an exciting dry white which resembles good Condrieu.

Quinta de Pancas Pancas, 2580 Alenquer. Splendid 16th-century *quinta* near the town of Alenquer, north of Lisbon. Delightful white wine made from the Arinto grape (Qta de Dom Carlos) and a soft, toasty Chardonnay. Successful reds made from a blend of Cabernet Sauvignon and the local Periquita.

Caves Primavera Agueda de Baixo, 3750 Agueda. Medium-sized Bairrada-based firm buying in and bottling wines from the north of Portugal. Reliable red wines from the Bairrada and Dão regions.

Palacio de Brejoeira 4950 Monção. Minho. The most prestigious producer of the rare Alvarinho white wine.

Ramos Pinto 380 avenida Ramos Pinto, 4401 Vila Nova da Gaia. Port producers Ramos Pinto have launched their own Douro wines under the Duas Quintas label. Blended from two quintas, Bom Retiro and Ervamoira, the wines (especially the Reservas) are solid and appealing. A wine from a single estate, Quinta dos Bons Ares, combines the local grape Touriga Nacional and Cabernet in an 80:20 blend.

Caves de Raposeira 5100 Lamego. The largest producers of Portuguese sparkling wine made by the classic method. Owned by the Canadian drinks multinational Seagram. Cool vineyards on the high land south of the Douro produce crisp, well balanced wines. Their Super Reserve includes a proportion of Pinot Noir and Chardonnay in the blend.

Real Companhia Vinícola do Norte de Portugal 4401 Vila Nova de Gaia. Visits. Royal Oporto, the old port monopoly company set up in the 18th century, is also known for its wide range of wines. These include a *vinho verde* called Lagosta; Dão, Colares, Evel reds from the Douro; and a sweet wine called Grandjó. The company was nationalized after the 1974 revolution but has returned to private hands.

Quinta dos Roques Abrunhoso do Mato, 3530 Mangualde. Family-owned estate with 100 acres in the Dão region which has broken away from the local cooperative. Serious reds from Touriga Nacional and Jean set the pace for the future of the Dão region. Also own Quinta das Maias.

Roqueval Apartado 210, 7003 Evora. Family-owned property with over 250 acres of vineyard at Herdade da Madeira near Redondo in the Alentejo. Traditional full-flavoured reds bottled under the Tinto de Talha and Terras do Xisto labels are better than the rather flat dry white wines.

Quinta de la Rosa 5085 Pinhão. The Bergqvist family broke their links with the port house Sandeman in 1988 to set up their own concern. The 100-acre property now produces a good range of estate-bottled ports and Douro wines, the latter under the auspices of winemaker David Baverstock.

Quinta de Sães Pinhancos, 6270 Seia. Small family property in the Dão region, close to the Serra de Estreia, Portugal's highest mountain range. Red and white wines from local grapes are refined and sophisticated. The family also owns another Dão property, Quinta de Pellada.

Casa de Saima Saima, 3782 Sangalhos. Diminutive property in Bairrada with winemaker Rui Moura Alves making outstanding red and white wines mainly from the local Baga and Bical respectively. Their red *Garrafeiras* age well.

Adega Cooperativa de São Mamede de Ventosa Arneiros, 2560 Torres Vedras. Huge coop in the Estremadura region: wines labelled as Alta Mesa, Ramada or Oria Maritima.

Caves Velhas – Companhia Portuguesa de Vinhos de Marca Lda Rua Fernão Lopes 9, Lisbon. Founded 1939. Visits. Trading name of Adegas Camilo Alves, one of the few producers of Bucelas wine. The firm owns nearly 200 of available 450 acres; Romeira is the name used for red and rosé wines from the Ribatejo; Caves Velhas for their Dãos.

PORT

What the English have long known as port, and the Portuguese and other nations as porto, belongs with champagne and sherry in the original trinity of great 'processed' wines. Each is an elaboration on the natural produce of its region to enhance its latent quality. Being capital intensive, requiring the holding of big stocks for long periods, their trade has become concentrated in the hands of shippers. Single-vineyard ports, and even single-vintage ports, are the exceptions in an industry which lives day to day on long-established, unchanging blends.

Unlike champagne and sherry, port was the child of political pressure. In the late seventeenth century the British were obliged by their government to find alternatives to the French red wines they preferred. They turned to Portugal, an old and useful ally, for a convenient substitute for claret. Finding nothing to their liking in the existing vineyards (which is surprising: Lisbon had good wine, if Oporto did not) the enterprising traders pushed inland from Oporto up the valley of the Douro into the rugged hinterland. What they tasted there that made them persevere is hard to imagine. They could hardly have chosen a more difficult and inaccessible place, with a more extreme climate, to develop as a major new wine area. They started around Regua, about 60 miles (or three mule-days) upstream from Oporto where the river Corgo joins the main stream. Gradually, finding that the higher they went the better the wine became, they built terraces up the almost impossible mountains surrounding the Douro and its tributaries: the Távora, the Torto, the Pinhão, the Tua. They dotted the mountainsides with white-walled quintas or farms, and demonstrated that once cultivated, the thin arid soil of granite and schist became extraordinarily fertile. Today not just the grapes but the nuts, oranges, almonds and even the vegetables of the Douro valley are famous.

The first port was apparently a strong dry red wine, made even stronger with 'a bucket or two' of brandy to stabilize it for shipping. It got a very cold reception from British claret lovers, who complained bitterly. The shippers tried harder, and at some time in the eighteenth century hit on the idea of stopping the fermentation with brandy while the wine was still sweet and fruity. History is unclear on when this became the standard practice, since as late as the 1840s the most influential British port shipper of all time, James Forrester (created a Portuguese Baron for his services), was urging a return to unfortified (therefore dry) wines. Modern ideas provide surprising justification for Forrester's notions: today the Douro is indeed providing some of Portugal's best dry red table wine. Sweet or dry, however, port was the most-drunk wine in Britain from the early eighteenth century to the early twentieth.

Today port is one of the most strictly controlled of all wines. A series of statutory authorities regulate and oversee every stage of its making. All 80,000 acres of vineyards are classified for quality on an eight-point scale by the register of each property (there are 30,000 growers), taking into account its situation, altitude, soil, inclination, grape varieties, standard of cultivation, fertility and the age of its vines. It is then given an annual quota. Only 40 per cent on average of the total Douro crop may be turned into port, the rest is just red wine. The maximum yield, allowed for vineyards classified as A on the eight-point scale, is 700 litres per 1,000 vines.

At harvest time, late September in the Douro, bureaucracy seems remote enough. The grinding labour of picking and carrying the crop from the steep terraces to the press-houses is carried on with amazingly cheerful, even tuneful, energy by gangs of villagers who often walk miles over the mountains for their annual 'holiday'. On remote little farms, and with the best-quality grapes at some of the largest quintas, the crop is still trodden barefoot by lamplight in open granite lagars, then fermented in the lagars until it is ready to be 'stopped' with brandy. In the case of most port shippers, however, much the greater proportion of the crop is machine crushed and fermented in stainless steel, which allows better temperature control than the closed concrete fermenting tanks of a kind introduced from Algeria, with a simple percolating system, operated by the natural build-up of carbon dioxide, to keep the juice constantly churning over the grape skins.

With either method the moment comes when about half the grape sugar is fermented into alcohol. This is when the half-made wine is run off into barrels one quarter full of brandy. Fermentation stops instantly.

The great majority of the port is moved, after its first racking off its gross lees, to the shippers' lodges to mature. The lodges are huddled together in the Oporto suburb of Vila Nova de Gaia, facing the steep streets of the city across the Douro and linked to it by a remarkable double-decker bridge. The down-river journey can no longer be made by the beautiful Viking-style barcos rabelos since the river was dammed for hydroelectric power. What was once a picturesque if perilous river highway is now a series of placid lakes, dotted with windsurfers and occasionally furrowed by water-skiers. It used to be obligatory for port to be shipped through the entreposto in Vila Nova da Gaia, but not any more. One important shipper, Noval, now moves its stock for maturation to air-conditioned warehouses upstream; while Sandeman and Cockburn keep substantial amounts of their port in the Douro.

Once in the shipper's lodge, port, like sherry, is classified by tasting and its destiny decided by its quality and potential for improvement. Most ports join a sort of perpetual blending system whose object is an unchanging product.

Simple, fruity and rather light wines without great concentration are destined to become ruby port, aged for up to about two years in wood and bottled while their bright red colour and full sweetness show no sign of maturity. This is the cheapest category.

Young wines with more aggressive characters and greater concentration, some outstandingly good, some of only moderate quality, are set aside to develop into tawnies – so-called from their faded colour after many years in wood.

Tawnies include some of the greatest of all ports, the shippers' own favourite blends, kept for up to 40 years in cask, then (usually) refreshed with a little younger wine of the highest quality. Tawnies also include some very ordinary mixtures with scarcely any of the character of barrel-age, made by blending young red and white ports (very popular in France as an apéritif). Their price varies accordingly. The best tawnies have an indication of age on the label. Twenty years is old enough for most of them – the high premium for a 30- or 40-year-old wine is seldom worth it. Styles among top tawnies vary from the intensely luscious (e.g. Ferreira's Duque de Bragança) to refinement and dry finish (e.g. Taylor's 20-year-old).

The great majority of port falls into one or other of the above categories, which together are known as 'wood ports'; their whole maturing process takes place in wood.

Vintage port, by contrast, is the product of one of the three or four vintages in a decade which come close to the shipper's idea of perfection – which have so much flavour and individuality that to make them anonymous as part of a continuing blend would be a waste of their potential. Whether or not a shipper 'declares' a vintage is entirely his own decision. It is very rare that all do so in the same year. The Douro is too varied in its topography and conditions.

Vintage ports are blended in the particular style the shipper has developed over many years, using the best lots of wine from his regular suppliers – including invariably his own best vineyards. They are matured for a minimum of 22 and a maximum of 31 months in cask for their components to 'marry', then bottled 'in Oporto' (i.e. in Vila Nova de Gaia) while they are still undrinkably tannic, aggressive and concentrated in flavour. Almost all their maturing therefore happens in the airless 'reductive' conditions of a black-glass bottle with a long cork, designed to protect the wine for decades while it slowly feeds on itself. Its tannins and pigments react to form a heavy skin-like 'crust' that sticks to the side of the bottle. Its colour slowly fades and its flavour evolves from violently sweet and harsh to gently sweet, perfumed and mellow. Yet however mellow, vintage port is designed to have 'grip', a vital ingredient in wine, which should never lose its final bite even in old age.

Between the clear-cut extremes of wood port and vintage port come a number of compromises intended to offer something closer to vintage port without the increasingly awkward need to cellar the wine for between 10 and 30 years. Vintage character (or vintage reserve) is effectively top-quality ruby port whose ingredient wines were almost up not up to true vintage standards, but kept for four or five years in cask. These potent and tasty wines are 'ready' when bottled, but will continue to develop, and may even form a slight 'crust' in bottle if they are kept too long. The term crusted or crusting port is sometimes used for the same style (though not officially recognized in Portugal).

Late-bottled vintage is similar, but is made of the wine of one 'vintage' year, kept twice as long as vintage port in barrel: i.e. from three and a half to six years. The label 'LBV' carries both the date of the vintage and the bottling, and the wine is lighter in colour and flavour than vintage port but should have some of its firmness. It may or may not form a deposit in bottle according to its maturity on bottling and the degree to which the shipper has chilled and filtered it for stability. Late-bottled vintage port which forms a deposit is usually labelled 'traditional'.

An increasingly popular compromise is to declare a single-*quinta* vintage port. Single-*quinta* family concerns, such as Quinta de la Rosa, and – exceptionally among the major shippers – Symington's Quinta do Vesuvio and Niepoort's Quinta do Passadouro, are declaring this category of port nearly every year. In years that are not generally up to vintage standard some wine of excellent quality is often made in the best sites. In several famous cases these belong to eminent shippers. In vintage years they are the backbone of the blend. In less-than-perfect years the shippers sometimes bottle them unblended, with the vintage date. They will mature sooner than classic vintages but often have distinct and charming character. Being bottle-matured these wines will of course form a crust and will need decanting. Some of the best-known single-*quinta* wines occasionally offered on the market are Taylor's Quinta de Vargellas, Graham's Quinta dos Malvedos, Croft's Quinta da Roêda and Cálem's Quinta da Foz.

White port is made in the same way as red port but of white grapes, usually fermented further towards dryness before being fortified with brandy. It is intended as an apéritif rather than a dessert wine, but never achieves the quality or finesse of, say, a fino sherry. Its underlying heaviness needs to be enlivened, and it can be far more enjoyable as a long drink with tonic water, ice and a slice of lemon.

Leading Port Producers

Borges E. Irmão

Avenida da Republica 796, 4401 Vila Nova de Gaia. Vintages: 1945, '55, '58, '60, '63, '70, '79, '80, '82, '83, '85 and '94. Founded 1884.

Founded by the Borges brothers, this port house has banking connections and a substantial interest in table wines; they have 2 vinification plants, for *vinho verde* and in Douro for port. Main exports are to Holland, Belgium and France. Best wines are Quinta do Junço, Soalheira and Roncão. Quick-maturing vintages but very average wines.

A. A. Cálem & Filho Lda

Rua de Reboleira 7, 4000 Porto. Stock: 15,500 pipes.
Vintages: 1935, '48, '55, '58, '60, '63, '66, '70, '75, '77, '80, '82, '83, '85, '91 and '94. Founded 1859. Visits.

Founded in 1859 by a family already long-established in the port trade, and who still own the firm. The Cálems own the excellent Quinta da Foz and three others, in total some hundred and twenty-five acres of vineyards, at Pinhão, where they still tread the grapes. They make other ports from bought grapes by 'autovinification'. Their Cálem and da Costa ports are well known in France, Germany, the Netherlands and the UK.

Churchill

Churchill Graham Lda, 63 Rua de Golgota, 4100 Porto. Vintages: 1982, '85, '91 and '94.

Founded in 1981 by John Graham and named after his wife, this is the first independent port shipper to be set up in the last fifty years. It has gone from strength to strength, making some splendidly concentrated wines from a number of well-situated *quintas* belonging to the Borges de Sousa family

Quinta de Agua Alta is bottled by Churchill as a single-*quinta* port. Churchill also make an excellent dry white port which has been aged for around ten years in wood, and are one of the few shippers to have good stocks of delicious mature crusted port.

Cockburn

Cockburn Smith & Cia, 13 Rua das Coradas, 4401 Vila Nova de Gaia. Stocks (including Martinez): 32,000 pipes. Vintages: 1900, '04, '08, '12, '27, '35, '45, '47, '50, '55, '60, '63, '67, '70, '75, '77, '83, '85, '91 and '94. Founded 1815. Visits by appt.

One of the greatest names in port, owned by Allied Breweries but still run by descendants of its Scottish founders. Cockburn vineyard properties are the Quintas do Tua (60 acres), da Santa Maria near Regua (40 acres), do Val do Coelho and do Atayde near Tua where they are planting 500 acres and Quinta dos Canais in the Upper Douro. 60 per cent of the *quinta* grapes are still trodden.

Cockburn's wines have a distinctive dry finish, or 'grip'. Their best tawny, Director's Reserve, with Special Reserve Tawny and Fine Old Ruby, make up 38% of port sales in the UK. Martinez Gassiot (q.v.) is an associated company.

Quinta do Cotto

Quinta do Cotto, Citadelha, Vila Real.

The Champalimaud family, who have owned their 271 acres near Regua since the 17th century, are now the best-known of the new breed of grower-bottlers; that is, their single-*quinta* vintage is made and matured in the Douro and not moved down to Vila Nova de Gaia for bottling. They also make one of the Douro's best red table wines.

Croft & Co.

Largo Joaquim Magalhães 23, Apartado 5, 4401 Vila Nova de Gaia. Stock: 30,000 pipes. Vintages: Croft – 1900, '04, '08, '12, '17, '20, '22, '24, '27, '35, '42, '45, '50, '55, '60, '63, '66, '70, '75, '77, '82, '85,'91 and '94. Quinta da Roêda – 1967, '70, '78, '80, '83 and '87. Morgan – 1900, , '04, '08, '12, '20, '22, '24, '27, '42, '45, '48, '55, '60, '63, '66, '70, '77, '82 and '85. Founded 1678. Visits by appt.

Perhaps the oldest port firm, founded in 1678, originally known as Phayre and Bradley, and now owned by International Distillers & Vintners (*see* also Sherry).

Croft are the owners of the superb Quinta da Roeda with 156 acres at Pinhão. Grapes from this quinta are responsible for the distinctive floweriness of their vintage wines, which are regularly among the finest of all vintage ports, early-maturing and well-balanced in style. Other wines from Croft & Co. include the excellent and popular Distinction Tawny, Distinction Finest Reserve, and their sister brands Delaforce (q.v.) and also Morgan.

Delaforce Sons & Co.

Apartado 6, 4401 Vila Nova de Gaia. Stock: 15,000 pipes. Vintages: 1908, '17, '20, '21, '22, '27, '35, '45, '47, '50, '55, '58, '60, '63, '66, '70, '75, '77, '82 and '85. Quinta da Corte: '78, '80, '84, '87, '92 and '94. Founded 1868. No visits.

Still family run by the Delaforces, although since 1968 it has been a subsidiary (like Croft, q.v.) of IDV. The firm's finest wines, which have great freshness and elegance, come from the contracted Quinta de Corte vineyard in the Rio Torto valley. His Eminence's Choice is a superbly succulent 10-year-old tawny port.

Dow's *see* Silva & Cosens Ltd.

A. A. Ferreira, S.A.

Rua da Carvalhosa 19–103, 4400 Vila Nova de Gaia. Stocks: 20,000 pipes. Vintages: 1945, '47, '50, '58, '60, '63, '66, '70, '75, '77, '78, '80, '82, '83, '85, '91 and '94. Founded 1751. Visits.

A historic Portuguese house, in the mid-19th century the richest in the Douro, then ruled over by the famous Dona Antónia, who built the magnificent Quintas do Vesuvio and do Vale de Meão, colossal establishments in the remotest high Douro. They still own, between the members of the family, many acres of vineyard although the company was sold in 1987 to Sogrape, who produce Mateus Rosé. Today Ferreira sells more bottled port in Portugal than any other house, and none in wood. Sales in 1982 were 3m. bottles. Their vintage wines are usually thought of as fairly light in style, and are less well known than their tawny ports. Superior, Dona Antónia and above all the superlative Duque de Bragança, are largely made of wines from the great Quinta do Roriz above Pinhão.

Hunt, Roope is a subsidiary company, which in turn ships Tuke, Holdsworth vintage ports. Another close link is with MacKenzie & Co. Ferreira also make, in the cavernous *lagars* at the Quinta do Vale de Meão, almost on the Spanish frontier, some 4,000 cases of one of the finest Portuguese wines, their Ferreirinha, in its best years (e.g. '65, '66, '78, '79, '80) christened Barca Velha.

Fonseca Guimaraens

Rua Barão de Forrester 404, 4400 Vila Nova de Gaia. Stock: 5,000 pipes. Vintages: 1904, '08, '12, '20, '22, '27, '34, '45, '48, '55, '60, '63, '66, '70, '75, '77, '80, '83, '85, '92 and '94. Founded 1822. Visits by appt.

Despite their name an English family business for over a century, now linked to Taylors. The firm started in the 18th century as Fonseca and was bought by Manuel Pedro Guimaraens in 1822. It was once known as Guimaraens Vinhos and the ports as Fonseca, but in 1988 the two names were merged.

Their vineyards of Quinta Cruizeiro (160 acres) and Quinta Santo António (100 acres), both in the Val de Mendiz near Alijo, are splendidly sited and they still make all their best wines by treading. Fonseca Guimaraens is regularly one of the finest and richest vintage ports and their Bin '27 an admirable premium ruby. They have an LBV and the single-*quinta* Quinta do Panascal.

Forrester & Co.

Apartado 61, Rua Guilherme Braga 38, 4401 Vila Nova de Gaia.
Vintages: 1945, '50, '54, '60, '62, '63, '66, '67, '70, '72, '75, '77,
'80, '82, '83, '85, '87 and '94. Founded 1737.

This firm was founded by William Offley and joined by
James Forrester in 1803. His nephew Baron Joseph James
Forrester was famous for mapping the Upper Douro and
saving the vineyards from a fungal disease in the 1850s. The
company was sold in 1929 and sold again in 1983 to Martini
& Rossi – who have since sold to Sogrape. Best wine is
Baron Forrester Tawny. Their style is generally considered to
be early-drinking, 'fat' and well-rounded.

Gould Campbell *see* Smith Woodhouse

W. & J. Graham & Co.

Rua Rei Ramiro 514, 4400 Vila Nova de Gaia. Stocks: 11,000
pipes. Vintages: 1904, '08, '12, '17, '20, '24, '27, '35, '42, '45,
'48, '55, '60, '63, '66, '70, '75, '77, '80, '83, '85, '91 and '94.
Founded 1820. Visits by appt.

A shipper renowned for some of the richest and sweetest
vintage ports, now part of the empire of the Symington family
(with Warre, Silva & Cosens etc, q.v.). Graham's Quinta dos
Malvedos on the Douro near Tua provides exceptionally ripe
fruit for vintage port of great colour, body and guts which
mellows to a singularly sumptuous wine. Part of the crop is
still trodden. Malvedos is also issued as a single-*quinta* wine.
Tawny and late-bottled vintage follow the full-bodied,
luscious style. Particularly good is the vintage Six Grapes
premium ruby port.

C.N. Kopke & Co.

P.O. Box 42, Rua Serpa Pinto 183–191, 4401 Vila Nova de Gaia.
Vintages: 1934, '35, '42, '45, '52, '55, '58, '60, '63, '66, '70, '74,
'75, '77, '78, '79, '80, '82, '83, '85, '87, '91 and '92. Founded
1638. Visits by appt.

In name at least the oldest of all the port firms, founded by a
German. It now belongs to Barros Almeida (q.v.). Kopke has
148 acres of vines and uses the names Quinta São Luiz for
vintages, Old World for tawny, Bridge for ruby.

dos Vinhos Messias SARL

Apartado 1, 3050 Mealhada, 4401 Vila Nova de Gaia. Stocks:
port 8,500 pipes; still and sparkling wines 200,000 cases.
Vintages: 1958, '60, '63, '66, '67, '70, '75, '77, '79, '80, '82,
'83, '84, '85 and '89. Founded 1926. Visits.

A Portuguese family-run company owning substantial port
vineyards, notably the Quinta do Cachão near San João da
Pesqueira (250 acres). The *quinta* crops are trodden for
vintage and vintage-style wines, which are reputed to have a
faint almond flavour. For still wines Messias have an *adega* at
Mealhada in the Bairrada in central Portugal.

Niepoort & Co. Ltd

Rua Infante D. Henrique 39, 4000 Porto. Vintages: 1945, '55, '60,
'63, '66, '70, '75, '77, '78, '80, '82, '83, '85, '87, '91, '92 and
'94. Founded 1842. Visits by appt.

A small Dutch family-owned company, currently being run
by the fifth generation of Niepoorts. Sales amount to some
50,000 cases of high-quality port a year, including a peculiar
category which is known as *garrafeira*.

Quinta do Noval

Rua Cândido dos Reis 575, Vila Nova de Gaia. Stock: 6,000 pipes.
Vintages: 1904, '08, '12, '17, '20, '24, '27, '31, '34, ('41 & '42),
'45, '50, '55, '58, '60, '63, '66, '67, '70, '78, '80, '82, '83, '85, '87,
'91 and '94. Founded 1813. Visits by appt.

Perhaps the most famous, and one of the most beautiful
quintas on the Douro, perched high above Pinhão. It
belonged to the van Zeller family, who also own the firm of A.
J. da Silva, until 1993, when it was sold to AXA-Millésimes. A
tragic fire in 1982 destroyed the historic records of the
company and part of the stock. Old Noval vintages were some
of the most magnificent of all ports. The '31 is legendary and
the '27 was even better. A small plot of ungrafted vines still
makes an astoundingly concentrated 'Nacional' vintage. Most
Noval wines have recently been in a lighter, more feminine,
very charming style. Noval late-bottled wines, tawnies and
white ports are good, though they are not single-*quinta*
wines. Quinta do Silval is another property.

Porto Poças Junior, Lda

Rua de Visconde das Devesas 186, 4401 Vila Nova de Gaia. Stock:
7,000 pipes. Vintages: 1960, '63, '70, '75, '85 and '91. Visits by
appt.

An independent family company founded in 1918, owning 2
Douro properties, the Quintas das Quartas and Santa
Barbara, run on traditional lines. Their brands Poças Junior,
Pousada, Terras, Almiro and Pintão have substantial sales in
Belgium and France.

Quarles Harris & Co. Lda

Tr. do Barão de Forrester, Apartado 26, 4401 Vila Nova de Gaia.
Stock: 4,000 pipes. Vintages 1908, '12, '20, '27, '34, '45, '47,
'50, '55, '58, '60, '63, '66, '70, '75, '77, '80, '83 and '85, '91
and '94. Founded 1680. Visits by appt.

Together with Warre, Graham, Dow, etc. (qq.v), now part of
the remarkable stable of the Symington family; there are no
vineyards, but only contacts with good growers along the
Rio Torto maintain a style of very intense full vintage port
with a powerful bouquet. Only a small proportion is still
trodden. Harris (not Quarles) is the brand for tawnies, ruby
and white ports.

Adriano Ramos Pinto Vinhos

380 Avenida Ramos Pinto, P.O. Box 65, 4401 Vila Nova de Gaia.
Stock: 8,000 pipes. Vintages: 1924, '27, '35, '45, '50, '52, '55,
'60, '61, '70, '75, '80, '82, '83, '85, '91 and '94. Visits.

Founded in 1880 and one of the most distinguished houses,
now owned by Louis Roederer. Their properties include the
famous Quinta Bom Retiro with 104 acres in the Rio Torto
valley, the 90-acre Quinta Santa Maria and the smaller San
Domingos. Tawnies (including a fine '1937') are their
specialities, but they also produce two highly successful
white ports. Brazil is their traditional market, although
France, Switzerland and Germany are now important.

Real Companhia Vinícola do Norte de Portugal

Rua Azevedo Magalhães 314, 4401 Vila Nova de Gaia. Vintages: 1908, '41, '43, '44, '45, '47, '54, '55, '58, '60, '62, '63, '67, '70, '77, '78, '79, '80, '85 and '87. Founded 1889. Visits.

Founded in 1756 by the Marquis de Pombal to control the port trade, the company is now part-owned by the Casa do Douro (set up as the controlling body for the port trade), the result of a now infamous business deal. Its interests are now half in port and half in other wines (of which half are sparkling). Its ports Quintas do Corval and do Sibio (near Tua) provide part of its needs for a stock of 8,000 pipes. See also under wine producers.

Robertson Bros

Rua António Granjo 207, 4401 Vila Nova de Gaia. Stocks: 3,100 pipes. Vintages: 1945, '47, '55, '63, '66, '67, '70, '72, '75, '77, '80, '83 and '85. Founded 1847. Visits.

Now a subsidiary of Sandeman. Shippers of Rebello Valente vintage ports, notably robust, tannic and fruity wines still trodden in *lagars*, largely at the Quinta de la Rosa at Pinhão. Robertsons also pioneered new-method vinification for their tawnies: Game Bird, Privateer, Pyramid, Izaak Walton and the splendid Imperial.

Sandeman & Co.

Apartado 2, Largo Miguel Bombarda 3, 4401 Vila Nova de Gaia. Stocks: 53,000 pipes. Vintages: 1904, '08, '11, '12, '17, '20, '27, '34, '35, '42, '45, '47, '50, '55, '60, '63, '66, '67, '70, '75, '77, '80, '82, '85 and '94. Founded 1790. Visits.

One of the biggest shippers of both port and sherry and the first company ever to advertise port, now a subsidiary of Seagrams but still chaired by George Sandeman, a direct descendant of the eponymous founder, a friend of the Duke of Wellington. The firm's vineyards are the Quintas de Confradeiro and Casal at Celeirós (118 acres on the Pinhão river). Quinta Laranjeira (528 acres at Moncorvo) is a big new development in the highest Douro near Spain. Another 60 acres at Vale de Mendiz near Pinhão are rented. Sandeman's view is that their vintage wines are on the dry side, which is not borne out by my experience. I find them fruity, if not as rich as (say) Graham. Their tawnies are nice and nutty, especially the 10-year-old Royal. Associated companies are Robertson, Forrester, Diez Hermanos and Rodriguez Pinho.

Silva & Cosens Ltd (Dow's Port)

Tr. do Barão de Forrester, Apartado 14, 4401 Vila Nova de Gaia. Stock: 15,000 pipes. Vintages: 1904, '08, '12, '20, '24, '27, '34, ('42 & '44), '45, '47, '50, '55, '60, '63, '66, '70, '72, '75, '77, '80, '83, '85, '91 and '94. Founded 1798. Visits by appt.

The proprietors of Dow's brand, named after a Victorian partner. Since 1912 a sister company of Warre, under the control of the ubiquitous Symingtons. The family Quinta do Bomfim at Pinhão is one of the finest on the Douro. Supported by the Quinta Santa Madelena nearby up the Rio Torto it gives mightily tannic and concentrated vintage port, recognized by its dry finish in maturity. Most is now made by 'autovinification'. Dow also sell 'Boardroom' and 30-year-old tawny, and ruby and white ports.

Smith Woodhouse & Co.

Apartado 19, 4401 Vila Nova de Gaia. Stock: 4,000 pipes. Vintages: 1904, '08, '12, '17, '20, '24, '27, '35, '45, '47, '50, '55, '60, '63, '66, '70, '75, '77, '80, '83, '85, '91 and '94. Founded 1784. Visits by appt.

Together with Dow, Warre, etc. (qq.v.), now part of the Symington family property (which altogether stocks some 40,000 pipes). Smith Woodhouse also ship Gould Campbell vintage ports. Both come largely from the Rio Torto (Vale Dona Maria). Gould Campbell vintages are big, dark, powerful and very long-lasting wines; the Smith Woodhouse style is more fragrant and fruity and their tawnies notably so. Part of the crop is still trodden and vintages reflect the quality of the year accurately.

Taylor, Fladgate & Yeatman

Rua do Choupelo 250, 4400 Vila Nova de Gaia. Stocks: 12,000 pipes. Vintages: 1904, '06, '08, '12, '17, '20, '24, '27, '35, '38, '40, '42, '45, '48, '55, '60, '63, '66, '70, '75, '77, '80, '83, '85, '92 and '94. Founded 1692. Visits.

One of the oldest and consistently one of the best shippers, still owned by descendants of the Yeatman family (Chairman, Alistair Robertson). The style of their tremendous vintage wines, of unrivalled ripeness, depth and every other dimension, is largely derived from their famous Quinta de Vargellas (551 acres), high on the Upper Douro above São João de Pesqueira. In 1973 they also bought the Quintas do Panascal (237 acres) at Tabuaço and de Terra Feita (247 acres) at Celeiros up the Pinhão valley. Their vintage ports are still trodden by foot, although they are experimenting with stainless steel fermenters at their vinification centre for ruby ports near Regua. In occasional second-quality vintages Vargellas wine is shipped unblended under its own label. Fonseca (q.v.) is an associate company. Taylor's LBV is the biggest selling one on the market. Their tawnies (particularly their 20-year-olds) are also exceptional.

Warre & Co.

Tr. do Barão de Forrester, Apartado 26, 4401 Vila Nova de Gaia. Stock: 13,000 pipes. Vintages: 1904, '08, '12, '20, '22, '24, '27, '34, ('42), '45, '47, '50, '55, '58, '60, '63, '66, '70, '75, '77, '80, '83, '85, '91 and '92. Founded 1670. Visits.

Possibly the oldest English port firm, now one of the largest firms in the group owned by the Symington family. The vintage wines are based on their Quinta da Cavadinha near Pinhão, produced by modern methods. The single-*quinta* Quinta da Cavadinha is a recent introduction. The style is extremely fruity with a fresh, almost herbal bouquet and a firm 'grip' at the finish. Some recent vintages have been beautifully balanced and lingering. Warrior is a good vintage-character wine and Nimrod a tawny. Warre's LBV is particularly good. Cintra is a label for France.

OTHER PRODUCERS

Barros Almeida Box 39, Ruada Leonor de Freitas 182, 4400 Vila Nova de Gaia. A family-owned substantial shipper of medium-quality ports, founded 1913. Also own Kopke, Feuerheerd and the Douro Wine Shippers Association.

J. W. Burmester & Co. Rua de Belomonte 39, 4000 Porto. Founded in 1750. Visits by appt. A small family-owned, now Portuguese, house, originally of English and German foundation. Grapes from their own vineyards and well-chosen wines from around Pinhão go to make their Tordiz tawny and vintages. Other names used are Jems and Southam's. Stocks: 4,500 pipes. Vintages: 1900, '10, '20, '22, '27, '29, '34, '35, '37, '40, '44, '48, '50, '55, '58, '60, '63, '70, '77, '80, '84 and '85.

Diez Hermanos Lda Rua Guilherme Baga 38, 4401 Vila Nova de Gaia. No visits. A small subsidiary of Forrester (q.v.). Stock: 6,000 pipes.

Feuerheerd Bros. & Co. PO Box 39, 4401 Vila Nova de Gaia. Founded 1815. The formerly British-owned company now belongs to Barros Almeida (q.v.).

Martinez Gassiot & Co. Ltd Rua das Coradas 13, Vila Nova de Gaia. Founded 1790. Visits. Bought by Harvey's in 1961, now a subsidiary of Allied Breweries; and allied to Cockburn (q.v.). Speciality is fine tawnies. Stocks: see Cockburn. Vintages: 1900, '04, '08, '11, '12, '19, '22, '27, '31, '34, '45, '48, '50, '55, '60, '63, '67, '70, '75, '82, '85, '87, '91 and 1994.

Rozés Lda Rua do Choupelo 250, 4400 Vila Nova de Gaia. Founded 1853. No visits. A shipper owned by LVMH, selling tawny, ruby and white ports, mainly in France. Stocks: 5,600 pipes. Vintages: 1963, '67, '77, '78, '82, '83 and '85.

Wiese & Krohn Sucrs. Ruade de Serpa Pinto 149, 4401 Vila Nova de Gaia. Founded 1866. No visits. A small independent company, originally German, without vineyards. Shipped the vintages of 1957, '58, '60, '61, '63, '65, '67, '70, '75, '78, '82, '84, '85 and '91.

MADEIRA

The very existence of madeira has been touch and go for a century and a half. No other famous wine region has suffered so much the combined onslaught of pests, diseases, disillusioned growers and public neglect. I doubt whether any other would have survived as more than a footnote.

What has kept madeira alive is the unique quality its old wines have of getting better and better. The remaining bottles of madeira from before its troubles began are proof that the island can make the longest-lived wines in the world. At a century old their flavours are concentrated into a pungency that would be overwhelming were it not so fresh. They leave the mouth so cleanly and gracefully as you swallow that water could not be more reviving. Harmony between sweetness and acidity can go no further.

Madeira is the largest of a cluster of islands 400 miles west of the coast of Morocco. In the 15th century the Portuguese who landed on the island set fire to the dense woodland that covered its slopes. The fire burned for years, the ashes from an entire forest enriching the already fertile volcanic soils.

Madeira flourished as a Portuguese colony. Prince Henry the Navigator ordered the sweet Malvasia grapes of Greece to be planted, as well as sugar cane from Sicily. Later, with the discovery of the West Indies, bananas became an important part of the island's harvest. The crops were, and still are, grown in a garden-like mixture on steep terraces that rise half-way up the 6,000-foot island-mountain. As in north Portugal the vines are trained on pergolas to allow other crops beneath. With its warm climate Madeira was a natural producer of 'sack', like Jerez and the Canaries. What settled its destiny was a piece of English legislation of 1665, forbidding the export of European wines to British colonies except through British ports and in British ships. Madeira was presumably deemed to be in Africa; at all events it became the regular supplier for American vessels heading

west. By the end of the 17th century the American and West Indian British colonists used madeira as their only wine.

Far from being spoilt by the long hot voyage across the mid-Atlantic, the wine proved better. Later, with growing British interests in the Far East, it was discovered to benefit even more from a voyage to India. So fine was their sea-matured madeira that casks were shipped as ballast to India and back to give connoisseurs in Europe a yet finer wine. It was during the 18th century that brandy was increasingly added, as it was to port, to sweeten and stabilize it.

In America the appreciation of old madeira became a cult – southern gentlemen would meet to dine simply on terrapin and canvas-back duck before 'discussing' several decanters of ancient wine, named sometimes for their grapes, or for the ship that carried them, or the families in whose cellars they had rested and become heirlooms. Thus a Bual might be followed by a Constitution, and that by a Francis, a Butler or a Burd. A popular pale blend, still sometimes seen, is known as Rainwater – because, apparently, of a similiarity of taste. Almost the same reverence was paid to its qualities in England – and still is, by the few who have tasted such wines.

Quantities became far too great to transport through the tropics as a matter of course. In the 1790s Napoleon's navy also put difficulties in the way of merchantmen. A practical substitute was found in warming the wines in hot stores (Portuguese *estufas*) for several months, depending on quality. The least good wine was heated the most, for the shortest period of time; the better for longer periods at more moderate temperatures. (Best of all received no artifical heat; rather, 3–5 years in cask in a sun-baked loft.) The rules today stiuplate 45˚C (113˚F) as the minimum temperature to which the wines must be heated.

Four principal grape varieties and three or four others were grown for different styles of wine. The original, the

Malvasia or Malmsey, made the richest: the Bual a less rich, more elegant but equally fragrant wine; Verdelho a soft, much drier wine with a faintly bitter finish, the Sercial (thought to be a clone of Riesling) a fine light wine with a distinct acid 'cut'. Tinta Negra Mole, reputedly an ancient forebear of Pinot Noir, was planted to make the red wine once known as 'Tent'. Bastardo, Terrantez and Moscatel were also grown in smaller quantities.

Madeira was at the peak of its prosperity when a double disaster struck. In the 1850s came oidium, the powdery mildew. In 1873 phylloxera arrived. Six thousand acres of vineyard were destroyed, and only 1,200 replaced with true madeira vines. To save grafting the remainder were replanted (if at all) with French-American hybrids whose wine no longer has claim to be called madeira at all.

Since then, Madeira has lived on its reputation, kept alive by memories, by a meagre trickle of high-quality wines, and by the convenient French convention of *sauce madère*, which is easily enough satisfied with any wine that has been cooked. Half the wine from the island today is destined for sauce-making with no questions asked. Unfortunately even the replanting of the original European vines, the four classics, was neglected in favour of the obliging Tinta Negra Mole. Today over 80 percent of the crop (hybrids apart) is Tinta Negra Mole. It has to do service for the Malmsey, Bual, Verdelho and Sercial (respectively 3.5, 2, 2 and 1.5 percent of the crop) in all except the most expensive brands. Tinta, in fact, is picked either earlier or later, fortified during or after

Vintages

The most famous madeira vintages up to 1900, bottles of which are still occasionally found, were 1789, 1795 (esp. Terrantez), 1806, 1808 (Malmsey), 1815 (esp. Bual), 1822, 1836, 1844, 1846 (esp. Terrantez and Verdelho), 1851, 1862, 1865, 1868, 1870 (Sercial), 1880 (esp. Malmsey).

Since 1900 over two dozen vintages have been shipped: 1900 (the last year Moscatel was made), 1902 (esp. Verdelho and Bual), 1905 (esp. Sercial), 1906 (esp. Malmsey), 1907 (esp. Verdelho and Bual), 1910, 1914 (Bual), 1915 (Bual, Sercial), 1916, 1920, 1926 (esp. Bual), 1934 (Verdelho), 1940, 1941 (esp. Bual), 1950, 1954 (esp. Bual), 1956, 1957, 1958, 1960 (Bual, Terrantez), 1965 (Bual), 1966 (Bual, Sercial), 1968 (Verdelho), 1969 (Terrantez), 1971, 1972 (Malmsey, Verdelho), 1973 (Verdelho) and 1974 (Terrantez).

Madeira Shippers

Barbeito 9000 Funchal. Founded 1947; now 52% owned by Japanese trading company. Impressive range of vintages in stock, some of which were purchased after the founding of the company. Stocks are 490,000 litres.

H. M. Borges Sucrs 9000 Funchal. Independent.

Henriques & Henriques Sítio de Belem 9300 Camara de Lobos. Founded 1850. The biggest independent (still family-run) and the only shippers to own vineyards (the largest on

fermentation, 'stoved' more or less, coloured and sweetened more or less, according to whether it is destined to be sold as Sercial, Verdelho, Bual or Malmsey.

Portugal's entry to the EU in 1986 has served notice on this practice. Its regulations require 85 percent of a wine to be of the grape variety named. 'Malmsey' can no longer be simply a style: it will have to be genuine Malvasia. Taking note of this, the islanders are busy regrafting vines, 100,000 of them a year, to the classic varieties. It is their only hope. They cannot thrive on cheapness and low quality. They have no cash crop of 'instant' wine; it all needs ageing. The estufas are expensive to run. The maintaining of dated solera (as in Jerez) used to be standard practice, but is no longer permitted. However, the Madeira shippers still occasionally declare a vintage – always a rarer occurrence with madeira than with port, and taking place not immediately after the vintage but some 30 years later.

Vintage madeira is kept in cask for a minimum of 20 years, then may spend a further period in glass 20-litre demijohns before bottling – when it is deemed ready to drink. In reality it is still only a young wine at this stage; it needs another 20 to 50 years in bottle to achieve sublimity.

The late Noël Cossart, the fifth generation of the old firm of madeira shippers Cossart Gordon, counselled 'never to buy a cheap Sercial or Malmsey; these grapes are shy growers and must consequently be expensive; whereas Bual and Verdelho are prolific and develop faster and may be both cheaper and good.'

the island). Now also the largest, most modern cellars. Wide range of well-structured rich, toothsome wines including very fine old reserves and vintages. Awards include the 1996 International Wine Challenge trophy.

Madeira Wine Company 9000 Funchal. In 1913 a number of shippers in the beleaguered trade formed the Madeira Wine Association to pool their resources and share facilities. Reconstituted in 1981 as the Madeira Wine Company, the group (now owned by port shippers Symington) controls 26 companies and accounts for about 40% of Madeira exports. The main winery is in an old army barracks – blends corresponding to its 120 different labels are made up in the Company's lotting rooms. One of its old lodges, next to the tourist office in Funchal, is open for visits and tasting. The wines are cellared together but preserve their house styles. The top two labels are:

Blandy's – most famous is the Duke of Clarence Rich Madeira. Glorious old vintages, mostly seen at auctions.

Cossart Gordon, once the leading Madeira shipper. Wines slightly less rich than Blandy's.

Leacock's and Miles (ex-Rutherford & Miles) are other brands.

Pereira D'Oliveira Vinhos 9000 Funchal. Founded 1820. Independent company making excellent wines, with a good stock of dated reserves.

Artur Barros e Sousa 9000 Funchal. Tiny producer but makes very good wines.

SWITZERLAND

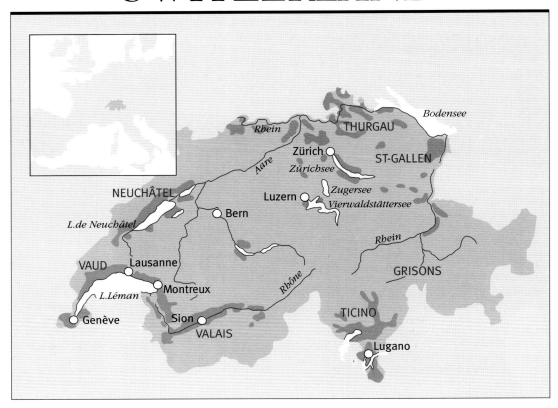

So rare are Swiss wines outside their own country that it is easy to assume that they fall short of international standards and remain the special taste of a blinkered culture.

The assumption is not wholly accurate. Many Swiss are critical and wine-conscious, most have money to spare – which is a good thing, for Swiss wines are expensive by almost any standards. Land prices and the cost of culture of their cliff-hanging vineyards are startlingly high. To justify inevitably high prices there should in principle be every pressure on growers to concentrate on high quality. In practice, growers were until very recently cushioned against market forces by subsidies and protectionist measures. Red wine is imported in large quantities, as not enough is made to meet demand, but white-wine production exceeds local demand, so stringently low import quotas were introduced to protect growers.

Now, however, the chill winds of competition are blowing through the vineyards, and white-wine import quotas have been relaxed. These allow more white wine into Switzerland each year; tankers queue at the border for admission on New Year's Day, so keen are importers to grab market share. The imported wines significantly undercut the home-grown version. Producers are belatedly waking up to the fact that they must export to survive, and have made tentative attempts to sell their wines abroad, but their excessively high prices render the wines uncompetitive. The future for many looks bleak.

One hundred and fifty years ago the emphasis was on red wines, the best of which came from Graubünden in the German-speaking east. The best whites came from the north shore of Lake Geneva between Lausanne and Montreux in Vaud canton, where the steep south slopes ripened the local Chasselas to perfection. Further up the Rhône Valley in the remote mountain area of the Valais there was a largely part-time winegrowing tradition. Vineyards were irregularly planted with obscure grapes chosen for their potentially dazzling sweetness and strength in the dry and sunny alpine climate.

The modern industry began to take shape when the Chasselas spread up the Rhône Valley, when pressure for the sunny lake slopes of Lake Geneva as building land drove half the wines out of the Vaud, and when selected forms of the Pinot Noir and Gamay began to penetrate from France, via Geneva and then eastwards. Meanwhile the Müller-Thurgau, bred by the eponymous Swiss scientist a century ago at Geisenheim, began to invade the eastern cantons. (Nowadays in Switzerland his name is forgotten and the variety is referred to as Riesling-Sylvaner.) In 1945 the Italian-speaking Ticino (or Tessin) adapted the Merlot of Bordeaux as its main red grape variety.

Although in the last 100 years the overall vineyard area has diminished considerably, selected areas such as German-speaking Switzerland, the Valais, Vaud and Geneva have increased their acreage. Plantings of red varieties are also increasing. Nevertheless, Switzerland remains a minnow in the grand scheme of wine, accounting for just 0.2 percent of global production.

The essential information given on the often rather taciturn, though frequently highly decorative, Swiss wine label is laid down by the federal government in the ODA (the Ordonnance sur les Denrées Alimentaires). Generally speaking, for white wines, if there is no other indication of grape variety, assume Chasselas. Red wines will in the main be Pinot Noir and/or Gamay. Some German-Swiss labels use terms with no international validity – but then they not only never travel abroad, they seldom leave the confines of the canton in which they were grown. Italian-Swiss wine labels

are simplicity itself as there are essentially only two types of wine: Merlot and the fast disappearing Nostrano, made from a clutch of hybrid grapes.

The maker's name seems to be considered of little importance to the consumer and is often tucked away down at the bottom in small print. Pride of place may be given to a brandname (Les Murailles), estate name (Château d'Allaman) or village name (St Saphorin). It is not always easy to tell which is which.

Although chaptalization is permitted, and quite commonly practised at the lower quality levels, all Swiss wines can be assumed to be dry unless a specific caution is included on the label: *mi-flétri* or *flétri* (literally 'shrivelled') in the French-speaking cantons, *Spätlese* where German is the lingua franca. (Switzerland's multilingual community copes well with the need to have at least two different names for most things.) The Swiss also make wide use of screw-tops instead of corks for wines designed to be drunk young – which includes most Chasselas.

THE FRENCH-SPEAKING CANTONS

All the principal vineyards of the French-speaking cantons (Suisse Romande) lie along the south-facing right bank of the Rhône, from its emergence into the Valais (a suntrap sheltered on both sides by towering Alps), round the shores of Lake Geneva – simply a widening of the Rhône – to its departure through the gently rolling farmlands of Geneva canton into France. Also included in this group are the three lakes of Neuchâtel, Biel/Bienne and Morat, each of which enjoys good, south-facing, lake-shore conditions. Three-quarters of all Swiss wine is grown in Suisse Romande, and most of it is white.

THE VALAIS (WALLIS)

The Valais (which begins, geographically, at the Grimselpass and ends at St Maurice on the right bank, and St Gingolph on the left) has Switzerland's driest and sunniest climate, frequently described as a cross between that of Spain and Provence. On its steeper vineyards, terraced on arid mountain slopes, irrigation by means of wooden channels known as *bisses* used to be common practice. Nowadays irrigation is limited to periods of severe drought and this only during the *période végétative*.

Wine-growing starts in earnest somewhere between Visp and Sierre, reaches a crescendo around Sion, the heart (and capital) of the Valais, and begins to wind gradually down after the Rhône has executed its sharp right turn at Martigny. At its upper extremes, the village of Visperterminen above Visp has what are reported to be Europe's highest vineyards at around 2,500 feet above sea level. In the upper Valais the principal wine-growing villages are Salquenen/Salgesch, Sierre and St Léonard; and in the lower Valais, Vétroz, Ardon, Leytron, Chamoson, Saillon and Fully are the most important centres.

Action has finally been taken in the Valais in response to an awareness of the urgent need for some notion of *crus*. For too long Fendant (i.e. Chasselas), which accounts for the largest quantity of wine produced in the Valais, was sold without mention of village or vineyard name. Since many were of poor quality (and the consumer had no way of differentiating), the result was that all Fendants, whether good, bad or indifferent, tended to be tarred with the same bottom-of-the-market brush. Nowadays there will often be a village or vineyard name appended; the appellation Fendant may even be omitted. Sylvaner, known here as Johannisberg (sometimes Rhin, either Petit or Gros), makes aromatic, fuller-bodied yet dry wines; when late harvested they can be impressive indeed.

Lakes of Chasselas are one thing; the so-called 'specialities' of the Valais, generally considered to be the great undiscovered potential of Swiss wines, are quite another. First comes the incomparable Arvine, its name said to come from the Latin meaning 'pale yellow'. Distinguished by its fine nose and characteristic salty finish, it is usually vinified dry; some growers harvest a small proportion of the crop late to make a *mi-flétri* or *flétri*. Humagne ('vigorous vine' in Latin), is a nervy, stimulating wine once prescribed as a post-partum tonic to young mothers. Its requires the best sites, performs rather irregularly and ripens late – all of which had contributed to a gradual decline over the years, but that decline is happily now in reverse. Amigne, whose favoured sites are concentrated in and around Vétroz, is made in extremely limited quantities into a rich, velvety wine, almost always with some residual sugar but sufficient acidity and backbone to give it good keeping qualities.

Rarer still are a clutch of very old, quaintly named varieties, found mainly in the upper Valais around Visp. In centuries past they were harvested early to give quite sharp, thirst-quenching wines designed for vineyard quaffing after a hard day's work. Of these, the finest is Heida (or Païen), thought to be a relation either of Savagnin (the same grape as used in *vin jaune*), or of Traminer. Himbertscha, whose name sounds vaguely raspberry-related, apparently means 'trellis-grown' in the upper Valais dialect, referring to the traditional method of training this particular grape, while Lafnetscha turns out to be the Blanchier of Savoie. Both give clean-tasting, rather acidic wines which need plenty of time to mature. Finally comes Gwäss (Gouais Blanc), another native of the Jura, sharply reminiscent of cider when young.

Of the non-indigenous but well-established varieties, the Marsanne grape thrives here under the name of Ermitage, giving (especially around Fully) a full-bodied wine with a striking nose and an elusively smoky flavour. Malvoisie (alias Pinot Gris) may be vinified dry (in which case it is often labelled Pinot Gris), or harvested late and made into a sweet wine – and often labelled Malvoisie. Muscat has been grown in the Valais since the 16th century, and is made here with all residual sugar fermented out, closer in style to a Muscat d'Alsace than to any other. Tiny quantities of Gewürztraminer, Riesling, Aligoté, Chardonnay, Chenin and Pinot Blanc are also to be found.

Over half of Valais wine is red and two-thirds of this is Pinot Noir, which acquits itself with some distinction, particularly around Sierre. The better growers are experimenting with Burgundy clones and varying proportions of new oak. Pinot Noir is also blended with Gamay and called Dôle, at its lower levels a good lunchtime wine quaffed throughout Switzerland in multiples of the decilitre to accompany uncomplicated meals. To qualify for the appellation, a Dôle must contain at least 51 percent Pinot Noir and reach a certain minimum Oechsle level prescribed by the cantonal wine commission; if it misses the mark it is labelled Goron. Gamay is also vinified alone, especially from the villages around Martigny.

Of antique red grapes there is Humagne Rouge (no relation of the white Humagne but reckoned by some to be Oriou, from the Valle d'Aosta). It makes robust, pleasantly tannic and appetizing country wine. Cornalin (alias Landroter or Rouge du Pays) is an extremely rare variety whose irregular yield and uneven performance makes it a tricky commercial proposition for most wine growers. Its deep colour, good tannins and superb fruit, however, make it an extremely interesting proposition for interested wine drinkers. Finally, in the upper Valais Eyholzer Roter (the Mondeuse of Haute Savoie) is to be found, which gives a tawny-reddish, rather rough country wine. Syrah, a fairly recent import, deserves special mention, particularly from around Chamoson; some Nebbiolo is also being grown.

THE VAUD

The canton of Vaud includes all the vineyards of the north shore of Lake Geneva and the Rhône, as high upstream as the border with the Valais at Bex: a 50-mile arc of southern slopes. It is divided into three main zones: Chablais, the right bank of the Rhône between Ollon and the lake; Lavaux, the central section between Montreux and Lausanne; and La Côte, from Lausanne round to Nyon at the border with Geneva. Further north, just short of Lake Neuchâtel, are the little enclaves of Côtes de l'Orbe and Bonvillars; half the villages in the Vully vineyard on Lake Morat also belong to Vaud. The canton has its own appellation systems, which control origin, grape varieties and Oechsle levels.

The appellations of Chablais include the villages of Villeneuve, Yvorne, Aigle, Ollon and Bex, all with good southwest slopes above the Rhône. Yvorne, with its minerally, gunflint character, real vigour, ripeness and length is generally considered to be the greatest of Chablais wines. At its best it is undoubtedly a match for (though subtly different from) the top wines from Lavaux.

Lavaux is certainly Switzerland's most scenic vineyard, piled high in toppling terraces above the lakeside villages. The view from among the vines is superb: the mountains of Savoie a great dark jagged-topped bulk against the sun opposite, the lake surface below gleaming grey, wrinkled by white paddle-steamers gliding from village pier to village pier. Erosion is a serious problem: a brown stain in the lake after a night's heavy rain is bad news for a wine grower.

Lavaux boasts the *crus* of Dézaley (for centuries considered the high point of Swiss white wine) and nearby Calamin, as well as six of Vaud's 26 appellations. Chasselas from the upper slopes takes on a liveliness and an almost aromatic quality which distinguishes it from the more austere dryness of the lower vineyards. Each village, however, has its committed supporters and the names of Epesses, St Saphorin, Rivaz, Cully, Villette, Lutry, Chardonne and others are writ correspondingly large on the label.

La Côte between Lausanne and Nyon has twelve appellations. The best-known are Féchy, Perroy, Mont-sur-Rolle, Tartegnin, Vinzel and Luins. This is a more gentle, often southeasterly sloping vineyard whose wines rarely have the vigour or flavour of those of Lavaux or Chablais, but make deliciously floral pre-prandial quaffing wines.

Chasselas dominates the Vaud vineyards; a very small part is made over to Pinot Gris, Pinot Blanc and Riesling-Sylvaner. Pinot Noir and Gamay are also found vinified singly, or blended and designated Salvagnin (a so-called 'label of quality' which has fallen somewhat into disrepute).

GENEVA

The canton is divided into three districts: the biggest – Mandement – to the north on the right bank of the Rhône, includes Dardagny, Russin and above all Satigny. South of the river (and of the city) is the region Arve-et-Rhône, centred around Lully-Bernex. The area which sets off round the other side of the lake is called Arve-et-Lac. Since the slopes are gentle and the vines well spaced out, mechanical harvesting is a possibility, which gives the wines a useful price advantage.

The area has increased its vineyards steadily and is now third in importance after the Valais and the Vaud. Chasselas (often, but not inevitably, known here as Perlan) accounts for about half the wine produced, a light, dry wine usually bottled with a slight prickle to make up for the character it frequently lacks. Some increasingly useful forms of Gamay have been introduced that suit both the conditions of the vineyard and the local taste, shaped by years of massive Beaujolais imports. Riesling-Sylvaner, Pinot Gris, Pinot Blanc, and Gewürztraminer are also to be found; impressive results are being achieved with Aligoté and Chardonnay.

LAKES NEUCHÂTEL, BIEL & MORAT

Vines grow all along the northern shores of all three lakes, sheltered by the Jura chain which forms the backbone of the route from Geneva up to Basle. The best-known villages on Lake Neuchâtel are Cortaillod, Auvernier, Boudry and St Blaise; on Lake Biel, the names of Schafis and Twann are famous, while on Lake Morat, the Fribourg villages of Praz, Nant and Môtier enjoy a certain renown.

Chasselas reigns here once more to give wines which are light, dry and given to a natural prickle (*l'étoile*) – a result of their being mainly bottled *sur lie*. There is no Gamay north of Geneva: Pinot Noir is the only permitted red variety. The limestone hills to the north and west of Lake Neuchâtel and the temperate climate seem to bring out some of the elusive finesse of the Pinot Noir grape. Neuchâtel Pinots from reputable growers may be expected to have some distinction; in a good year they may be considered the best Pinots Switzerland can produce. The pale rosé Oeil-de-Perdrix ('partridge's eye') – an appellation native to Neuchâtel, now widely used all over Switzerland – is an appealing Rosé de Pinot Noir.

Leading Valais Producers

Oscar Chanton AG

3930 Visp. Founded 1944. Owner: Josef-Marie Chanton. 17 acres.
Over 20 wines can be tasted in the venerable old Chanton cellar in Visp, including rarities from the upper Valais like Heida, Himbertscha, Lafnetscha and Gwäss, rescued from oblivion by Josef-Marie Chanton. The Arvine is superb, as are the late harvested Malvoisie and Gewürztraminer.

Gérald Clavien

3961 Miège/Sierre. Owner: Gérald Clavien. 11 acres.
The wines of this young, dynamic grower (who was a chef before taking over his father's vineyards) feature on the lists of all the top restaurants in Switzerland. Sierre is the hub of red wine-growing in the Valais: Clavien's straight Pinot Noir and Tête de Cuvée are notable, also the Dôle Blanche (a Rosé de Pinot Noir). Some Humagne Blanche is also made.

Michel Clavien

1962 Pont-de-la-Morge. Founded 1925. Owner: Michel Clavien. 62 acres (37 owned, 25 leased).
A prime mover in the *appellation d'origine* debate and a marketing man to his fingertips, Michel Clavien has worked tirelessly to raise the image of Valais wines both at home and abroad. The wines are elegant, the labels (especially of the Fin Bec line) eye-catching. Le Grand Sion is a blend of Chasselas from a number of *lieux-dits* around Sion; Dôle Fin Bec contains 85% Pinot Noir and 15% Gamay; Pinot Noir de la Follie comes from the eponymous vineyard.

Bon Père Germanier

1963 Vetroz. Founded 1907. Owner: Jean-René Germanier. 19 acres.
Perhaps more famous locally for fragrant eau-de-vie from Williams pears, Bon Père Germanier is a producer of a wide range of wines of good concentration and length. In addition to Chasselas they produce Chardonnay, Malvoisie, Dôle and Dôle Blanche, Pinot Noir and a very attractive Amigne de Vetroz. Wines from the highly rated Balavaud vineyard are worth seeking out.

Simon Maye

1956 St Pierre-de-Clages. Owners: the Maye family. 18.5 acres.
A small, top-quality grower making two highly prized Fendants (Le Fauconnier and La Mouette), Johannisberg, Dôle, Pinot Noir, Humagne Rouge, a richly spicy Syrah, plus some Chardonnay, Malvoisie and Arvine.

Domaine du Mont d'Or

1962 Pont de la Morge. Founded 1948. Owners: the shareholders (publicly quoted company). Director: Dominique Favre. 52 acres.
The most famous property of Sion, established in 1847 on a steep, dry, sheltered hill by a soldier from the Vaud, one Sergeant-Major Masson, who installed the irrigation system by *bisses* which is still in operation. The domaine is best known for its Johannisbergs: du Mont d'Or when vinified dry, or de la St Martin (and more rarely du 1er Décembre) when late harvested. Also produced are a magnificent Arvine, and strong tannic and alcoholic Dôle.

Provins Valais

Fédération des Caves des Producteurs du Vins du Valais. 1951 Sion. Founded 1930. Director: Jean-Marc Amez-Droz.
The enormous, highly regarded central cooperative of the Valais producing some 30% of all Valais wines – and this nearly 15% of all Swiss wine. Their Capsule Dorée range includes well-known brand names like Pierrafeu Fendant, Johannisberg Rhonegold, Oeil-de-Perdrix Perdrizel (a Rosé de Pinot Noir) and Pinot Noir St Guérin. To the usual vast Valaisan spectrum of grapes they add Pinot Blanc, Chardonnay and Cabernet Sauvignon. An exciting new development is their Chasselas St Léonard, made (exceptionally for Switzerland) without malolactic fermentation, and reserved for *la grande restauration*.

Marc Raymond et Fils

1913 Saillon. Founded 1948. Owners: Marc and Gérard Raymond. 9 acres.
Tiny family business producing top Fendant, Johannisberg, Arvine (the pride of the house), Muscat, Malvoisie and Dôle Blanche. Their reds are also noted, particularly Dôle and Pinot Noir. Marc Raymond is one of the few Valaisan growers to make Nebbiolo.

Eloi et Gérard Roduit

1926 Fully. Founded 1952. Owners: Eloi and Gérard Roduit. 15 acres.
A small family (uncle and nephew) business making the full range of Valais wines on some prime sites above the village of Fully. Of especial note are their Ermitage and Arvine (vinified dry and *flétri*), Gamay, Pinot Noir (of which a proportion is oak-aged), and Syrah.

Bernard Rouvinez

3960 Sierre. Founded 1945. Owners: Jean-Bernard and Dominique Rouvinez. 10 acres.
These brothers' estate lies next to a nunnery; they are the only men permitted to enter the nunnery grounds to tend the vines. On their own property, two-thirds of the grapes are red, predominantly Pinot Noir. They vinify excellent varietal Pinot Noir and Chasselas. However, their most notable creations are Le Tourmentin, a Pinot Noir-Syrah-Cornalin-Humagne Rouge blend, and Le Trémaille (Chardonnay and Petite Arvine). These elegant, attractively presented wines indicate fresh thinking and a willingness to innovate – a hopeful sign in a sometimes overly tradition-bound region.

Maurice Zufferey

3964 Muraz/Sierre. Founded 1963. Owner: Maurice Zufferey. 11 acres.
Sierre is red-wine country and M. Zufferey's are particularly notable (though he also produces many other specialities). Three Pinot Noirs are made (one oak-aged), Dôle, a deeply coloured Humagne Rouge and the tricky but infinitely rewarding Cornalin which M. Zufferey was among the first to revive in the Valais.

Leading Vaud Producers

Henri Badoux

1860 Aigle. Founded 1908. Owners: the Badoux family. 123 acres.
A substantial, second-generation family-owned business with vineyards in Yvorne, Aigle, Ollon, Villeneuve, St Saphorin, Féchy, Vinzel and Mont-sur-Rolle. The two wines considered *les moteurs de l'entreprise* are the famous Aigle les Murailles (with the classic lizard label) and Yvorne Petit Vignoble. Badoux's Aigle Pourpre Monseigneur, a Pinot Noir from the Chablais district, benefits from some ageing.

Jean-Michel Conne

1605 Chexbres. Owner: Jean-Michel Conne. 25 acres.
By dint of wise buying of vineyards outside Lavaux, and by inheritance of the family vineyards, a considerable holding of good sites around Lake Geneva has been built up. Especially famous is their Dézaley Plan Perdu, St Saphorin Le Sémillant and Ollon L'Oisement. Several Pinot Noirs (of which the oak-aged is labelled Cartige) are also produced.

Henri Delarze

1867 Verschiez/Ollon. Founded 1696. Owners: Henri Delarze and son. 8.5 acres.
Unusually for the area, this small estate specializes in (indeed, is particularly renowned for) its red wines which

are only commercialized between two and three years after bottling. Les Colondeys is a Pinot Noir produced from several different Pinot forms; La Pidance is made from Burgundy clones.

Grognuz Frères

1844 Villeneuve. Founded 1848. Owners: Marco and Frédéric Grognuz. 37 acres.
A medium-sized family firm in the heart of the Chablais, winemakers *de père en fils* for several generations with widely spread, excellently sited vineyards. From Villeneuve itself come some notable Chasselas and Pinot Noirs; further south, from Les Evouettes, come Chasselas, Pinot Noir and Oeil-de-Perdrix (rosé); from Lavaux an elegantly smoky St Saphorin. There are tiny quantities of Chardonnay and Gewürztraminer to complete the picture. Pride of the house, though, is Pinot Noir Selection Sang Bleu, which is made from selected Pinot Noir vines from Burgundy, aged in *petites pièces*.

Hammel

1180 Rolle. Founded 1920. Director: Gilbert Hammel Rolaz. 62 acres.
This is a leading domaine and merchant house of La Côte, producing Chasselas from various Vaudois vineyards: Domaine Les Pierrailles and La Bigaire (La Côte), Domaine de Riencourt (Bougy), Clos du Chatelard (Villeneuve) and Clos de la George (Yvorne).

Alain Neyroud

Chardonne. Owner: Alain Neyroud. 17 acres.
A fifth-generation business selling mainly to private clients in German-speaking Switzerland and to local restaurants. The Chasselas is labelled La Petite Combe, the Gamay La Perle Rouge, and the Pinot Noir Au Coin des Serpents. Unusually for a Vaud house, about 50% of their production is red.

Obrist

1800 Vevey. Founded 1854. Owners: the Schenk group. Director: Emile Saugy. 99 acres.
One of the largest growers of Vaudois white, with a particular reputation for their Yvornes: Clos du Rocher, Clos des Rennauds and Pré Roc. Also famous is their Cure d'Attalens and Salvagnin Domaine du Manoir. Owned by Schenk (q.v.).

Gérard Pinget

1812 Rivaz. Founded 1884. Administrator: C. Pinget. 25 acres.
A traditional estate whose top wines are Dézaley Renard (its label sports a fox), St Saphorin and Soleil de Lavaux.

Schenk

1180 Rolle. Founded 1893. Owner: André Schenk. 560 acres.
The giant Swiss wine firm (sometimes referred to as '*le Ciba-Geigy du vin*'), founded and based at Rolle. Its principal estates are in Yvorne, Mont-sur-Rolle, Vinzel and Féchy. Schenk has foreign subsidiaries and companies in Burgundy, the Midi, Spain, northern Italy, Belgium and the USA.

Jean & Pierre Testuz

1096 Treytorrens-Cully. Founded 1845. President: Jean Testuz. Administrator: Jean-Philippe Testuz. 486 acres.

The Testuz family (whose premises are actually in Dézaley) trace their wine growing roots back to the 16th century. In 1865 they sold the first bottled wine in Switzerland. Their Dézaley, L'Arbalète, is one of the finest of the area. Other Lavaux wines include the fine St Saphorin Roche Ronde and Epesses. Chablais wines include Aigle Les Cigales and Yvorne Haute-Combe. Lavaux and La Côte wines both include some from the vineyards of the city of Lausanne. The red label is Grand Croix.

Leading Geneva Producers

Pierre Dupraz

Lully/1233 Bernex. Founded 1909. Owner: Pierre Dupraz. 27 acres.

All Dupraz wines are labelled varietally (Chasselas, Aligoté, Chardonnay, Gamay and Pinot Noir) with the domaine's name (Domaine des Curiades) appended. Some Chardonnay is oak-aged.

Claude Ramu

1282 Dardagny.

A range of mythologically named (and artistically labelled) wines is produced in the district of Le Mandement, west of Geneva. Here the Pinot Gris, labelled Domaine du Centaure, stands out. Other whites include the Chasselas (known in the Geneva vineyards as Perlan), Aligoté, Pinot Blanc and Gewürztraminer. Reds are Gamay and Pinot Noir (some oak-aged) and a *crémant* labelled Les Compagnons de Vénus is also produced.

Vin-Union Genève

1242 Satigny. President: Jean Revaclier. Director: Fred Kummer. 365 members.

A federation of three coops whose members own some 2,400 acres, over 80% of the canton's vines. Members have vineyards in nine out of the recently designated *grands crus*, among them Rougemont (Gamay), La Feuillée (Chasselas) and Côtes de Russin – the favoured child of the house – where red and white are produced. Château du Crest from Jussy is mildly fruity, and better value for money than many Beaujolais. The label of their Chardonnay Le Bruant (showing a bunting) is even more appealing than the bottle's contents.

Leading Neuchâtel Producers

Samuel Chatenay

2017 Boudry. Founded 1796. Director: J. C. von Buren. 123 acres. Large quantities of white, rosé and red, the best of which come from the 4-acre Domaine de Château Vaumarcus.

Château d'Auvernier

2012 Auvernier. Founded 1603. Owner: Thierry Grosjean. 74 acres. One of Neuchâtel's oldest-established houses, making nervy Neuchâtel blanc, Oeil-de-Perdrix, Pinot Noir d'Auvernier, Pinot Gris and a little Chardonnay. High-quality winemaking

A. Porret

2016 Cortaillod. Founded 1858. Owner: Pierre-André Porret. Fourth generation making Chasselas labelled Domaine des Cèdres (after the 200 year-old cedars outside the family house). Also Chardonnay, an Oeil-de-Perdrix and a little Pinot Gris. Pinot Noir Cortaillod has a keen following.

THE GERMAN-SPEAKING CANTONS

Because the German-speaking cantons favour the same grape varieties and use broadly the same vinification techniques, they tend to be grouped together and called, for some obscure reason, eastern Switzerland. There are the usual concentrations around lakes (Constance, Zürich) and along rivers (Rhine, Aare, Limmat) with the odd microclimate thrown in for good measure (notably the four villages in Graubunden known as the Bundner Herrschaft). In eight of the Swiss-German cantons wine is grown: Graubunden, St Gallen, Thurgau, Schaffhausen, Zürich, Aargau, Baselland and Bern. The most productive cantons today are Zürich (scattered between Wädenswil, home of the Federal School of Oenology and Viticulture, Winterthur and the villages along the north shore of the lake); and Schaffhausen, whose Hallau vineyard is the largest in eastern Switzerland. Consumption of Swiss German-produced wines is almost exclusively local and entirely faithful: most growers are sold out by year's end.

Up here north of the Alps, the colour balance changes and red begins to predominate in the shape of Pinot Noir (alias Blauburgunder, or Clevner on Lake Zürich). Riesling-Sylvaner is the main white variety, which performs well in the right (i.e. secateur-wielding) hands to give suprisingly aromatic, lively wines – frequently of more interest than run-of-the-mill Chasselas from further south. Blauburgunder excels in the Bündner Herrschaft, whose warm autumn climate ripens it to real substance, with colour and a velvet touch. Elsewhere the Swiss Germans exhibit a mystifying fondness for pale, slightly fizzy Blauburgunders, a penchant not inevitably shared by others.

Besides these two (plus a little Gewürztraminer, Pinot Blanc and Pinot Gris) there are some specialities which are confined to the Swiss German cantons. Completer is an extremely rare, late-ripening, late-harvested speciality found in Graubünden, where it is long-matured and liquorous, and on the lakeshore of Zürich, where it is more austere. Its name is linked to the evening office of Compline, after which the monks were said to gratefully quaff a glass or two. Raüschling is an old-established Zürich variety which makes elegant, crisp white wines. Freisamer is a potentially promising cross between Sylvaner and Pinot Gris.

407

Leading Swiss German Producers

Schlossgut Bachtobel

8570 Weinfelden. Owner: Hans-Ulrich Kesselring. 14 acres.
Schlossgut Bachtobel producess 80% Blauburgunder, 15% Riesling-Sylvaner, and tiny amounts of Pinot Gris, Chardonnay and Riesling. An experimental classic method resulted in what Herr Kesselring once described as 'probably not the best, but certainly the dearest "champagne" ever made …'

Familie Donatsch

7208 Malans. Owner: Thomas Donatsch. 9 acres.
The beautiful old, wood-panelled Gasthof zum Ochsen in the patrician village of Malans has belonged to the family for over 150 years. Thomas Donatsch's superb Blauburgunders (Pinot Noir) and finely structured Chardonnays are found on the wine lists of most of the top Swiss restaurants. Also produced are Riesling-Sylvaner, Pinot Blanc, Pinot Gris, even some Cabernet.

Ruedi Honegger

8712 Stäf/Mutzmalen. Owner: Ruedi Honegger.
Herr Honegger, at the wonderfully-sited Itzikerhüsli, is one of the relatively small number of growers on Lake Zürich who bottles his own wine on the domaine. He makes fine Riesling-Sylvaner, Räuschling, Clevner (Pinot Noir) and rosé.

Hans Jörg Lauber

Gut Plandaditsch, 7208 Malans. Founded 1928. Owners: the Lauber family. 5 acres.
The lovely, onion-domed Gut Plandaditsch is a Malanser landmark. Especially notable is the Laubers' deep ruby Blauburgunder, powerfully aromatic Pinot Blanc, late-harvested Freisamer and Pinot Gris. Their mouth-filling Chardonnay, produced in tiny quantities, spends up to seven months in new oak.

Anton Meier

zum Sternen, 5303 Würenlingen. Founded: 1828. Owner: Anton Meier. 12 acres.
Anton Meier is a noted wine-grower, landlord of the village pub as well as the owner of one of Switzerland's foremost vine nurseries. He produces an extraordinarily fruity Riesling-Sylvaner, good Pinot Gris, a fine Gewürztraminer, some rosé (Pinot Noir) and, lately, a crisp *crémant*. His pride and joy, though, are the Blauburgunders, frequent winners of high-profile comparative (international) tastings of Pinot Noir.

Nussbaumer

4147 Aesch. Founded 1935. Owner: Kurt Nussbaumer. 12 acres.
A small firm producing Riesling-Sylvaner, Chasselas, Pinot Gris, Gewürztraminer and Blauburgunder in their Aesch (Kluser) and Arlesheim (Steinbrüchler and Schlossberg) vineyards, just a stone's throw from the border with Alsace. A more recent addition is Chrachmost, classic-method sparkling Chasselas.

Hans Schlatter

8215 Hallau. Founded 1931. Owner: Hans Schlatter. 25 acres.
A medium-sized grower and merchant of German Switzerland. The Hallauer Blauburgunder Spätlese, 16–Fahre Wy and Tokayer (Pinot Gris) are very popular locally.

Hermann Schwarzenbach

8706 Meilen. Founded: 1739. Owner: Hermann Schwarzenbach. 15 acres.
A small, old-established house with a range of wines, including Riesling-Sylvaner (some late harvested), Freisamer, the special Zürich-type Räuschling, Chardonnay, Pinot Gris and – the only grower still to make it on the lake – Completer. Clevner (Blauburgunder) is produced both straight and late harvested, fermented in oak vats and recommended as a keeper.

VOLG (Verband Ostschweizer Landwirtschaftliche Genossenschaften)

8400 Winterthur. Founded 1886. Director: F. Rottermann.
A major agricultural cooperative with a chain of stores. Vineyards are in Hallau, Winterthur and Graubünden, including an estate of 74 acres planted with 75% Blauburgunder, 20% Riesling-Sylvaner and 5% specialities. The wines are light, clean and well-made. Hallauer Blauburgunder has a reputation as a wine which has keeping qualities.

THE ITALIAN-SPEAKING CANTONS

The Ticino or Tessin divides into four main areas: north and south of Monte Céneri (Sopraceneri and Sottoceneri respectively), the shores of Lake Lugano (Luganese) and the districts of Mendrisiotto. It is a delightfully uncomplicated, area, producing mainly red wines, where Merlot holds sway over a bunch of miscellaneous black grapes (Bondola, Freisa, Barbera) blended into everyday table wine labelled Nostrano. The VITI 'label of quality' is awarded by a commission of experts to Merlot wines of one year's bottle age which pass chemical analysis and taste tests. A few growers are successfully ageing some Merlots in new oak (often calling the result Riserva). It gives them distinct character, no longer the typical, soft, one-dimensional Merlot del Ticino.

There is little white wine grown in Ticino: the soils are all wrong and the climate far too benevolent, though there is some Sémillon, Sauvignon, Pinot Gris and a little Chardonnay to be found. The foxy Americano hybrid is seldom vinified nowadays, but converted mainly into an excellent Grappa del Ticino.

Leading Ticino Producers

Angelo Delea

6616 Losone. Founded 1982. Owners: Angelo and Leopoldo Delea. 17 acres.

Restaurateur turned wine-grower, Angelo Delea produces some long-macerated, powerful Merlots. Each year he buys in 40% new barrels, into which goes his best Merlot (which is labelled Riserva); the remainder is aged in used *pièces*. He also produced a Chasselas del Ticino, Pinot Blanc and – for old times' sake – an Americano, cherry red and distinctly foxy.

Werner Stucky

6802 Rivera-Capidogno. Founded: 1982. Owners: Werner and Lilo Stucky. 7.5 acres.

One of the young Swiss German pioneers of the region, Werner Stucky produces tiny quantities of Merlot, straight and oak-aged, both of them sold out by year's end to private customers and a handful of top restaurants.

Fratelli Valsangiacomo fu Vittore

6830 Chiasso. Founded 1831. Director: Cesare Valsangiacomo. 55 acres.

Cesare Valsangiacomo is the fifth generation of this distinguished old Ticino house, and produces some of the most respected bottles of the regions: Roncobello, Dioniso, Merlot del Ticino Cuvée Spéciale, Riserva di Bacco, L'Ariete, Pedrinate del Piccolo Ronco (all Merlots), Cagliostro (a Merlot rosé) and two Merlot bubblies: Spumante Metodo Classico and Ronco Grande Extra Brut. A swashbuckling brigand (*un mattirolo*) adorns the label of Valsangiacomo's fruity blend of Chasselas, Sémillon and Sauvignon: Il Mattirolo.

Vinattieri Ticinesi

6853 Ligornetto. Founded: 1985. Owner: Signor Zanini. 62 acres.
Members of the Zanini family have long been known in the area as importers of fine Italian wines; now they have turned their hand to their own production and no expense has been spared in vineyard or cellar. Cocking a snook at the region's VITI 'quality' label, they are shortly to introduce their own DOC system. Bottles of the best Vinattieri Merlots bear vineyard names (sometimes complete with beautifully contoured sketch maps): Ligornetto, Tenuta ai Ronchi, Redegonda; all are oak-aged to some degree or other. With some good sites with chalky soils Vinattieri even manages to produce a creditable white, labelled simply Bianco Ticinese Vinattieri.

Eredi Carlo Tamborini SA

6814 Lamone. Founded 1944. Owner: Claudio Tamborini. 25 acres.

An important Ticino house whose Merlot is improving constantly. Vigna Vecchia is their best, oak-aged from vines between 30 and 60 years old. Collivo is also good, and the Castello di Morcote excellent.

AUSTRIA

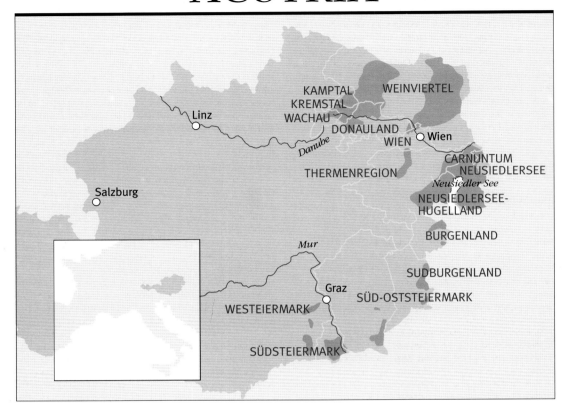

Austria's wine history goes back at least two millenniums – until shortly after the Roman conquered the Danubian provinces in 16 BC. It is an interesting question why modern wine culture arrived here far later than elsewhere in Western Europe. Even during the 1920s and '30s only the very finest Austrian wines were sold in bottle. Still today a significant proportion of Austrian wine is sold in wine inns run by vintners (called *Heurigen* or *Buschenschenken*). The 1985 diethylene glycol scandal put an end to the industry's commercial success with off-dry and sweet white wines in the German mould (regulated by a German-style wine law introduced in 1972). Diethylene glycol was added to such wines by a number of large commercial bottlers to make them taste fuller. Whilst there is no evidence of anyone's health having been damaged by this illegal practice – in contrast to the Italian methanol scandal of the following year – enormous damage was done to the good name of Austrian wine.

The Austrian authorities responded by rushing through legislation to control the wine industry further. The 1985 law (amended the following year) is complemented by a system of controls and monitoring which make the nation's wine industry the most strictly controlled in the world.

However, the scandal also had entirely unexpected consequences. Instead of turning domestic consumers off

their nation's wines, they switched from mass-produced wines to hand-crafted ones made by family-run estates. This coincided with a boom for light, dry white wines. The result was a renaissance for regions such as the Wachau and Kamptal whose vintners had previously made and sold good-quality dry white wines to loyal private customers in relative obscurity. In Styria an entire new wine culture was born during the late 1980s as a number of producers switched from wines for everyday drinking in 2-litre bottles (*Doppler*) to quality varietals.

In the early 1990s this was followed by a red-wine revolution during which dozens of a younger generation of Austrian vintners, particularly in Burgenland, mastered the making of international-style red wines. Much of their inspiration came from across the Alps in Italy, while France was the prime source of new grape varieties (and most importantly Cabernet Sauvignon). These are usually blended with indigenous grapes to create sophisticated *cuvées*; an adopted word in the vocabulary of many young Austrian winemakers. Unlike the majority of fine Austrian wines, which are sold under vineyard (or *Ried*) names, they tend to be sold under fantasy names such as 'Comondor', 'Bella Rex', or 'Perwolf' in the mould of Italian *vini da tavolas* such as 'Sassicaia' or 'Darmagi'.

Austria remains primarily a white-wine producer, and in this respect most producers are staunchly true to their nation's own winemaking traditions. Austria's wine industry is founded on light- to medium-bodied dry whites from the indigenous Grüner Veltliner grape. It accounts for a little over a third of Austria's 141,000 acres of vineyards, and gives wines with a distinctive aroma of white pepper. Lentils and other vegetal notes can be found in light Grüner Veltliners, but at high levels of ripeness they are replaced by smokey and even exotic fruit aromas. The grape's flexibility – it will yield dry wines with anything from 10° to 15° natural alcohol, and impressive dessert wines – is its greatest strength.

The white wines which have attracted most international praise of late have been the Rieslings. The noble white grape of Germany appears to have arrived in Austria towards the end of the 19th century, and there are still only 3,000 acres planted with it in Austria. However, on the primary rock soils of the Wachau, the ravishingly beautiful rocky gorge through which the River Danube flows between Melk and Krems it yields great dry wines that can match the finest of Alsace and Germany. Such is the strength of domestic demand for the top Wachau Rieslings that importers from other countries must beg for every bottle from the top producers. Names such as Franz Hirtzberger, Emmerich Knoll, F. X. Pichler and Prager are mentioned by Austrian wine lovers in tones of awe. Similarly fine dry Rieslings come from parts of other regions in Lower Austria, most importantly Senftenberg and Stein in the Kremstal, and Langenlois-Zöbing in the Kamptal. A comparable discrep-ancy between supply and demand exists with the best Sauvignon Blancs and Morillons from Styria (a synonym for Chardonnay, which arrived in the region during the 19th century) where producers such as Polz and Tement are almost perpetually sold out.

Although it was almost exclusively dessert wines which were affected by the 1985 scandal, in this field too recent years have seen dramatic developments. The Neusiedlersee-Hügelland region in the state of Burgenland has a recorded history of systematic dessert wine production which goes back to 1617. For much of its history it was part of Hungary. This tradition is centred upon the town of Rust on the eastern bank of the shallow Neusiedlersee lake, which is the source of autumnal mists that promote the development of noble rot. However, during the 1990s it has been the wines from Illmitz on the opposite bank of the lake which have attracted the most attention. The names of Illmitz wine-makers Alois Kracher and Willi Opitz are now known around the world. Most of Austria's lush, full-bodied dessert wines are sold under the Beerenauslese and Trocken-beerenauslese names borrowed from the Germans during the 1960s. Today some are vinified in new oak casks like top Sauternes, but fermentation and maturation in large barrels of neutral oak or acacia remains the norm today, as it was centuries ago. This is invariably the case for the most traditional of Austria's dessert wines: Ruster Ausbruch.

Sadly, the world-wide fashion for Chardonnay has not left Austria untouched. Although a handful of winemakers produce magnificent wines in the international style (most prominently Velich in the Neusiedlersee region), most results lag behind those achieved with traditional grapes such as Weissburgunder (Pinot Blanc), Grauburgunder (Pinot Gris) or aromatic grapes such as Muskateller and Traminer. The majority of Austria's fine dry white and dessert wines continue to be made from varieties such as these. Thankfully, the pendulum is begining to swing back in the direction of tradition. Even the style-conscious yuppies of Vienna enjoy an evening in a *Heurige* drinking unpretentious local wine out of chunky, old-fashioned glasses while listening to *Schrammelmusik*, Vienese folk music. The quality revolution of the late 1980s and 1990s has brought better and more diverse wines. There can be no doubt that Austria is a wine nation with a great future if it sticks to the quality path taken since 1985, and cultivates its wine traditions.

Leading Producers

COOPERATIVES

Winzergenossenschaft Dinstlgut Loiben 3601 Unterloiben, Wachau/Kremstal. Since Walter Kutscher took over the direction of this formerly famous cooperative, overall quality has improved significantly. The magnificent dessert wines he has produced have rightly attracted much praise, although to date the dry Riesling and Grüner Veltliner are no more than well made.

Winzergenossenschaft Wachau 3601 Durnstein. For long one of Europe's finest wine-making cooperatives. Quality at the Freie Weingärtner has taken another leap forward since the appointment of Fritz Miesbauer and Willi Klinger as co-directors with the 1995 vintage. Excellent Rieslings from the first-class Achleiten of Weissenkirchen and Singerriedel of Spitz and Grüner Veltliners from the Kellerberg of Dürnstein are the stars of the wide range produced from more than 1,500 acres. However, even the simplest wines are well made and full of character. The Baroque Kellerschlössel entrance house to the extensive cellars dates from 1715, but the Freie Weingärtner's roots go back to at least the 12th century.

Lower Austria

Weingut Bründlmayer

3550 Langenlois, Kamptal. Founded 1581. Family owned. 148 acres; 16,500 cases. Grapes: Ries., Chard., Weissburgunder, Grauburgunder, Spätburgunder, Grüner Veltliner, Merlot, Cab.Sauv.

The boyish, intellectual Willi Bründlmayer runs one of the largest and most modern wine estates in Austria. Although he is best known for his barrel-fermented Chardonnay and Burgundy-inspired Blauburgunder, most of his production is traditional-style dry whites. Right across the impressive Bründlmayer range the quality is excellent, the sublime Rieslings from old vines in the Heiligenstein site and magesterial Grüner Veltliner from the Lamm vineyard rank amongst Austria's greatest wines.

Weingut Franz Hirtzberger

3620 Spitz, Wachau. 27 acres. 6,000 cases. Grapes: Grüner Veltliner, Ries., Weissburgunder, Grauburgunder, Feinburgunder, Riesling-Sylvaner, Muskateller.

Franz Hirtzberger's natural optimism and talent for winning over opponents is in large measure responsible for the success of the 'Vinea Wachau' winegrowers association of which he is president. However, he is no less talented at making exceptionally elegant dry white wines. His Riesling from the great Singerriedel vineyard and his Grüner Veltliner from the first-class Honivogel site are amongst Austria's finest and most sought-after wines. The Hirtzberger's 13th-century estate house is one of the oldest and most beautiful in the Danube Valley.

Weingut Josef Högl

3620 Spitz-Viessling, Wachau. 11 acres. 2,500 cases. Grapes: Ries., Grüner Veltliner, Neuburger.

Modest, shy 'Sepp' Högl learnt quickly while he worked for the Prager and F. X. Pichler estates. Since going solo he has shot into the first rank of Wachau producers with dry whites that combine power with clarity and polish.

Weingut Emmerich Knoll

3601 Unterploiben, Wachau/Kremstal. 23 acres, 5,000 cases. Grapes: Grüner Veltliner, Ries., Feinburgunder, Muskateller.

Three generations of the Knoll family, all called Emmerich, are responsible for making this great estate's unique wines. The product of their teamwork are extremely long-living wines that need years of bottle-ageing for their full minerally character to emerge. The dry Rieslings from the Schütt, Loibenberg, and Kellerberg sites are amongst Austria's finest white wines. The love-it-or-loath-it neo-Baroque label featuring St Urban is the work of the local artist Soitzner.

Weingut Mantlerhof

3494 Brunn im Felde, Kremstal. Founded 1814. 30 acres. 5,500 cases. Grapes: Grüner Veltliner 50%, Roter Veltliner 20%, Rheinriesling 15%, Chard. 10%.

Garrulous Sepp Mantler's 40 acre estate is best known for the rare white Roter Veltliner (Malvasia) grape, from which he makes rich, supple dry wines. However, his Grüner Veltliners are also frequently first class.

Weingut Sepp Moser

3495 Rohrendorf, Kremstal/Neusiedlersee. 106 acres. 20,000 cases. Grapes: Chard., Ries., Grüner Veltliner, Sauv.Bl., Cab.Sauv., Zweigelt.

The roots of this estate go back to 1848, but in its present form it dates from the split up of the erstwhile Lenz Moser company in 1986. With the help of son Niki, Sepp Moser has rapidly made it not only one of the region's but also the nation's leading white-wine producers. The barrel-fermented Chardonnay is arguably Austria's best, but it is the lush, complex dry Riesling from the first-class Gebling site which is the real star. Increasingly good Burgenland reds too.

The Austrian wine law

Labels must show unfermented sugar content of the wine. *Trocken* is max. 4 grams/litre (g/l), *Halbtrocken* 9 g/l, *Halbsüss* or *Lieblich* 18 g/l. Higher levels are labelled *Süss*.

If vintage and/or grape variety are specified, the wine must be 85% from that vintage and variety. If a vineyard (Ried) is specified, the wine must be 100% from that site. Austria rates sugar content in degrees KMW (Klosterneuberger Mostwache).

Categories
Tafelwein Landwein: minimum 13° KMW (63 Oechsle). A Tafelwein must come from a single wine area, maximum alcohol 11.5%, max. unfermented sugar 6 g/l.
Qualitätswein: From a single wine area, minimum 15° KMW (73° Oechsle), enriched up to maximum 19° KMW (94° Oechsle), officially tested.
Kabinett: Minimum 17° KMW (83.5° Oechlse), maximum 19° KMW (94° Oechsle), maximum 9 g/l unfermented sugar, no enrichment.
Prädikatswein: Qualitätswein 'of exceptional maturity or vintage': no enrichment. The grades are:
Spätlese: late-picked grapes with minimum 19° KMW (94° Oechsle).
Auslese: selected late-picked grapes with minimum 21° KMW (105° Oechsle).
Eiswein: made from frozen grapes with minimum 25° KMW (127° Oechsle).
Beerenauslese: selected late-picked overripe grapes with noble rot, minimum 25° KMW (127° Oechsle).
Ausbruch: over-ripe, nobly-rotten grapes which have dried naturally. Minimum 27° KMW (138° Oechsle).
Trockenbeerenauslese: nobly-rotten, raisin-like grapes, minimum 30° KMW (150° Oechsle).

Weingut Familie Nigl

3541 Senftenberg-Priel, Kremstal. 21 acres. 4,000 cases. Grapes: Grüner Veltliner, Ries., Sauv.Bl., Chard.

In 1986 the Nigls left the local coop, giving son Martin full responsibility for their cellar. Since then his sleek, minerally dry Rieslings and Grüner Veltliners have made the estate the number one in the Kremstal region. Top of the range are the magnificent Rieslings from the first-class Hochäcker and Kremsleiten sites.

Weingut F X Pichler

3601 Oberloiben, Wachau. 18.5 acres. 4,500 cases. Grapes: Grüner Veltliner, Ries., Gelber Muskateller, Sauv.Bl.

Widely regarded as Austria's number one winemaker, Franz Xavier Pichler – frequently refered to simply as 'F X' – is a fanatical perfectionist with a sixth sense for wine. His great dry white wines are as concentrated as they are individual. The most spectacular Rieslings and Grüner Veltliners come from the great Kellerberg vineyard of Dürnstein, the wines simply labelled 'M' (for 'Monumental'). A decade ago the Pichlers' house was unremarkable, but it has slowly been transformed into a building worthy of the name 'Château'.

Weingut Franz Prager

3610 Weissenkirchen, Wachau. Founded 1715. 31 acres. 7,000 cases. Grapes: Ries., Grüner Veltliner, Feinburgunder, Sauv.Bl.
Since marrying Ilse Prager, renaissance man Toni Bodenstein has brought a revolution to the Wachau. His 1993 Riesling Trockenbeerenauslese was the first wine of this style made in the region's history, and has inspired many of the region's other winemakers to harvest dessert wines. However, he has not neglected the dry wines with which Franz Prager established the estate's reputation from the late 1950s. The estate's dry Rieslings from the first-class Achleiten and Klaus vineyards marry seductive ripe fruit with minerally depth.

OTHER LOWER AUSTRIA PRODUCERS

Weingut Leo Alzinger 3601 Unterloiben, Wachau. Extremely reliable producer of sleek, elegant dry Riesling and Grüner Veltliner from 13.5 acres of terraced vineyards including the first-class Steinertal and Höhereck sites.

Weingut Biegler 2352 Gumpoldskirchen, Thermenregion. Well-balanced sweet Spätlese and Auslese from 17 acres of the traditional local grapes, Rotgipfler and Zierfandler.

Weingut Ehn 3550 Langenlois, Kamptal. 27-acre estate specializing in sophisticated dry Riesling from the great Heiligenstein vineyard and rich, dry 'Alter Panzaun' from a mixed planting of ancient vines.

Weinberghof Fritsch 3470 Oberstockstall, Donauland. The leading producer of the Donauland region makes super-clean, vibrant dry Riesling, Grüner Veltliner and Weissburgunder from 17 acres of vines.

Weingut Peter Dolle Strass, Kamptal. 45-acre estate which does well with Weissburgunder and Rheinriesling.

Domäne Baron Geymüller 3506 Kremstal. A family property, founded 1811. 59 acres. 11,000 cases (Grüner Veltliner, Rheinriesling, Müller-Thurgau, etc). Traditional methods, dramatic labels and strict insistence on vineyard and variety origin make this a locally respected conservative house.

Schlossweingut Graf Hardegg 2062 Seefeld-Kadolz, Weinviertel. 100 acres; 28,000 cases. Grapes: Grüner Veltliner (40%), Rheinriesling, Weissburgunder, Müller-Thurgau. One of Austria's senior estates, in existence for 350 years, but with a very modern cellar. The stress is on dry wines.

Weingut Ludwig Hiedler 3550 Langenlois, Kamptal. Hiedler's white wines from 35 acres of vineyards are made for long-age rather than instant gratification. His dry Riesling from the great Heiligenstein and Weissburgunder from old vines are amongst the region's finest.

Weingut Josef Jamek 3610 Joching, Wachau. Josef Jamek pioneered dry, unchaptalized wines in the Wachau in the 1950s and remained one of the region's leading producers in the 1980s. Simultaneously his eponymous restaurant brought gastronomic culture to the region and became an institution. In 1996 his son-in-law Hans Altmann and daughter Jutta took over the estate and restaurant, and a new era began. The best wines from the 54-acre estate are the famous Riesling from the first-class Klaus vineyard of Weissenkirchen and the dry Weissburgunder. Elegance, rather than power, has always been the Jamek hallmark.

Weingut Jurtschitsch/Sonnhof 3550 Langenlois, Kamptal. Extremely reliable producer of super-clean, modern style whites from more than 80 acres of vineyards around Langenlois. Good Sauvignon Blanc and Chardonnay, but the Rieslings and Grüner Veltliner remain the stars.

Kelleramt Chorherrenstift Klosterneuburg 3400 Klosterneuburg. Founded 1108. 242 acres: Kloster-neuburg (83), Kahlenbergerdorf (83); Tattendorf (76). 63,000 cases. Grape var: various, 60:40 white:red. The Augustine monks of Klosterneuburg have made wine for nearly nine centuries, but the operation is now a commercial company wholly owned by the monastery. Grapes from the extensive vineyards are augmented by supplies from small producers in Burgenland and Niederösterreich. Weissburgunder and Rheinriesling are wood-aged, late-bottled, and can be distinguished, especially in QmP qualities. All wines use the characteristic squat bottle. Sekt – including a pink one – can be delicious. The enormous three-level cellars harbour 3m. bottles, including the Austrian State Wine Archive. Visitors are shown the tidemark three feet above the floor where wine flowed after Russian looters smashed all the casks in 1945. Klosterneuburg also controls the ancient Deutsch-Ordens-Schlosskellerei in Gumpoldskirchen.

Weingut Loimer 3550 Langenlois, Kamptal. 32-acre estate with a wide range of whites from traditional grapes. Fred Loimer's finest wine is the barrel-fermented old vine Grüner Veltliner from the Spiegel site.

Weingut Malat 3511 Furth-Palt, Kremstal. Gerald Malat is rightly best known for powerful, dry white wines from his nearly 75 acres of vineyards. Cabernet also shows promise.

Metternich'sche Weingüter Dominikanerplaz 11, 3500 Kremstal. 173 acres. 33,000 cases. An alliance of five princely estates, HQ at the Metternich estate in Krems. This 173-acre estate, at Schloss Grafenegg, is run on ecological principles. Other members are the estates of Prince Starhemberg in Krems (Starhemberg'sches Weingut), Count Abensperg-Traun in Maissau (Schloss Maisau), Prince Khevenhüller-Metsch in Pulkau (Schloss Riegersberg) and the Esterházy'sche Schlosskellerei (q.v.) in the Burgenland. The wines are made by each estate but marketed jointly under the name 'Erste Österreichische Weingüter-Kooperation'.

Lenz Moser 3495 Rohrendorf, Kremstal. Owner: GHG. Estates: Klosterkeller Siegndorf, Siegndorf, Neusiedlersee-Hügelland, 58 acres; Schlossweingut Malteser Ritterorden, Mailberg, Weinviertel, 119 acres. Dr Lenz Moser (d. 1978) was a leading figure in the Austrian wine industry, best remembered for the high trellis vine-training system named after him. Today the company is directed by his grandson the dynamic, cosmopolitan Lenz Moser IV. During the early 1990s it has grown to become the most important Austrian wine company. The basis of the huge range are the 'Servus' of dry white and red Burgenland wines, now Austria's biggest export wine brand. The varietal Lenz Moser 'selection' wines is the next step up, and, like Servus, these wines are made from grapes from contract growers rather than bought in wine. The estate-bottled wines form the pinnacle, of which the red *cuvée* 'Kommende Mailberg' (Cabernet-Merlot) enjoys a particularly good reputation.

Weingut Ludwig Neumayer 3130 Inzersdorf, Traisental. Ludwig Neumayer's sophisticated dry Rieslings and Grüner Veltliners from 17 acres of vines in the Traisental have put the region on the map.

Weingut Nikolaihof 3512 Mautern, Wachau/Kremstal. The recorded history of the Saahs family's 40-acre estate goes back more than a millennium, and the magnificent buildings stand on Roman foundations. Quality is somewhat mixed, but the best dry Rieslings are superb. The excellent *weinstube*/restaurant is rightly as famous as the wine estate.

Weingut Pfaffl 2100 Stetten, Weinviertel. Roman Pfaffl's dry Grüner Veltliner, Sauvignon Blanc, non-oaked Chardonnay and Riesling from 45 acres of vines just northeast of Vienna are the Weinviertel's finest.

Weingut Familie Rudolf Pichler 3610 Wösendorf, Wachau. Rudi Pichler Jr is rapidly gaining recognition as one of the Wachau's rising stars with lush, aromatic dry Rieslings from 13 acres of vineyards.

Weingut Familie Pittnauer 2464 Göttelbrunn, Carnuntum. From 21 acres of vineyards close to the Hungarian border Hans Pittnauer has proved this region's red wine potential. The powerful 'Franz Josef' blend is best.

Prinz Liechtenstein'sches Weingut 2193 Wilfersdorf, Weinviertal. Owners: E. and M. Müller. Growers/merchants. Founded 1813, bought by the Müllers in 1936. 13.5 acres in Riede Burgegg and Deutschlandsberg. Grape var: Blauer Wildbacher (for Schilcher), Welschriesling, Gewürz., Zweigelt, etc. Grapes are also bought in to make a total of 85,000 cases. The leading producers of the Schilcher rosé of Steiermark, plus whites and reds, all QbA standard.

Weingut Robert Schlumberger 2540 Bad Vöslau, Thermenregion. Founded 1842. Robert Schlumberger, son of a branch of the Alsace family, made Austria's first *méthode traditionnelle* Sekt in 1842 after learning his trade in Champagne (he rose to be manager of Ruinart) and marrying the daughter of a Vöslau grower. The large Sekt side of the business is now based in Vienna, its quality high as ever. Today the family firm makes respected reds from 22 acres. The Bad Vöslau reds are made from St Laurent, Cabernet Sauvignon, Merlot and Blauer Portugieser. Stress is on Bordeaux-style wines made by classic methods.

Weingut Schmelz 3610 Joching, Wachau. Reliable producer of juicy, substantial dry Riesling and Grüner Veltliner with 13 acres of vineyard.

Weingut Stadlmann 2514 Traiskirchen, Thermenregion. Johann Stadlmann makes the best wines of the Thermenregion from 30 acres of vineyards south of Gumpoldskirchen. Best are the dry Weissburgunder and Zierfandler.

Gräfl Stubenberg'sches Schlossweingut, Schloss Welkersdorf 3492 Schloss Walkersdorf/Kremstal. 25 acres, 5,500 cases. Grape var: Grüner Veltliner (60%), Ries., Sylv. The stress here is on wood-aged, traditional, dry Grüner Veltliner and Riesling. Another Vinobilities estate.

Weingut Salomon/Undhof 3504 Stein, Kremstal. Erich Salomon makes some of the best wines from the first-class vineyard of Krems' beautiful Gothic and Renaissance suburb, Stein. Most of his 50-acre production is dry Riesling and Grüner Veltliner Kabinett wines. The best, however, are naturally-sweet filigree Traminer and Riesling Auslese. The estate house dates back to 1792 and stands next to the Kloster Und wine centre which Erich Salomon founded.

Weingut & Sektkellerei R Zimmerman 3400 Klosterneuburg, Donauland. Founded 1920. 10 acres in Klosterneuburg (Reid Buchberg) plus grapes bought in, 2,000 cases. Grape var: Rheinriesling, Weissburgunder, Grüner Veltliner, Müller-Thurgau, St. Laurent. Grower, Sekt producer and owner of a popular *heurige* in the Vienna village of Grinzing. Quite good Riesling and red wines.

Burgenland

Weingut Feiler-Artinger

Rust, 7071 Neusiedlersee-Hügelland
Traditionalist with 42 high-class acres in Rust, making one of the best Ruster Ausbruchs and noted Trockenbeerenauslesen. In good years half the harvest can attain this quality. Production is 8,000 cases.

Weingut Familie Gesellmann

Deutschkreutz, Mittelburgenland. 47 acres. 7,500 cases. Grapes: Blaufränkisch, Cab.Sauv., Blauburgunder, Merlot, Chard., Grüner Veltliner, Welschriesling, Weissburgunder.
Engelbert Gesellmann has long had a good reputation for his red wines, but since son Albert returned from working tours to South Africa and California in 1991 this has been one of Austria's ground-breaking red-wine producers. Two powerful blends, 'Opus Eximum' (Blaufränkisch, Cabernet, St Laurent and Blauburgunder) and 'Bella Rex' (Cabernet and Merlot) are most impressive.

Alois Kracher/Weinlaubenhof

7142 Illmitz, Neusiedlersee. 18.5 acres. 2,000 cases. Grapes: Welschriesling, Weissburgunder, Scheurebe, Blaufränkisch, Bouvier, Chard., Muskat-Ottonel, Traminer.

A perfectionist with a cosmopolitan perspective who remains true to his roots in the sandy soil of Illmitz in spite of being ambitious, extrovert Alois Kracher is a phenomenon. During recent years his superbly-crafted dessert wines have picked up almost every concievable prize and accolade. They combine honeyed richness with perfect balance. The 'Zwischen den Seen' wines are made in old acacia casks in the traditional style, the 'Nouvelle Vague' wines in new oak like Sauternes, 'Grand Cuvée' is a super-elegant blend of the two styles.

Weingut Hans & Anita Nittnaus

7122 Gols, Neusiedlersee. 33 acres. 8,000 cases. Grapes: Cab.Sauv., Blaufränkisch, St. Laurent, Welschriesling, Chard., Sauv.Bl., Grauburgunder, Neuburger.

The ever more sophisticated red wines which Hans Nittnaus has made since the late '80s epitomize the red-wine revolution occurring in Burgenland. His rich, powerful 'Comondor', a Cabernet-Blaufränkisch blend from the first-class Ungerberg site is serious competition for classified Bordeaux.

Weingut Ernst Triebaumer

7074 Rust, Neusiedlersee-Hügelland. 30 acres. 5,000 cases. Grapes: Blaufränkisch, Cab.Sauv., Merlot, Welschriesling, Chard., Weissburgunder, Sauv.Bl.

Impish Ernst Triebaumer has singlehandedly proven that the Blaufränkisch grape can be made to produce great red wines if planted in the right place, in this case the first-class Mariental vineyard. This dark, rich, tannic wine is Austria's most sought-after red. Triebaumer's Ruseter Ausbruch dessert wines are also impressive, matching richness with harmony.

Weingut Umathum

7132 Frauenkirchen, Neusiedlersee. 37 acres. 7,000 cases. Grapes: Zweigelt, Blaufränkisch, St. Laurent, Cab. Sauv., Blauburgunder, Grauburgunder, Sauv.Bl.

It would be easy to mistake Josef Umathum's elegant reds for French wines, although he works almost exclusively with traditional Austrian grapes. The most impressive is the red *cuvée* from the Hallebühl vineyard, a powerful tannic blend of Zweigelt, Blaufränkisch and Cabernet. The Zweigelt-Merlot *cuvée* from the Haideboden is equally rich, but more supple.

Weingut Velich

7143 Apetlon, Neusiedlersee. 7.5 acres. 2,000 cases. Grapes: Chard., Neuburger, Welschriesling, Bouvier.

Within remarkably few years casino croupier Roland Velich and his brother Heinz, a full-time winemaker, have earned this tiny estate the reputation of being one of Austria's leading white-wine producers. Impressive as the entire range is, the seductively rich, barrel-fermented Chardonnay from old vines in the Tiglat vineyard has to be singled out as world-class.

OTHER BURGENLAND PRODUCERS

Weingut Paul Achs 7122 Gols, Neusiedlersee. 30-acre estate making richly fruity, modern style reds, particularly good Blauburgunder (Pinot Noir), and good dessert wines.

Esterházy'sche Schlosskellerei 700 Eisenstadt, Neusiedlersee-Hügelland. 106 acres, 75% white. 27,500 cases. Grapes: Welschriesling, Rheinriesling, Grüner Veltliner, Ruländer. The ancient princely family of Esterházy, patrons of Haydn and tamers of the Turks, have been making some of the best wine in the Burgenland since the 17th century. Vineyards include experimental plots run with Klosterneuberg college. Commercial vineyards in Rust, St Georgen, St Margaretten, Grosshöflein and Eisenstadt itself. 140 great casks line the cellars beneath the castle, their wines traditional, full and rich in extract. Some of the best dessert wines of the Burgenland carry the Esterházy label. The estate is part of the Metternich-led grouping of princely estates (*see* page 413).

Weingut Gernot Heinrich 7122 Gols, Neusiedlersee. Gernot Heinrich is one of the rising stars amongst the new generation of Burgenland winemakers. His 20 acres are split between white and red grapes, the latter giving impressively fleshy, supple wines, particularly 'Gabarinza'.

Weingut Hans Igler 7301 Deutschkreuz, Mittelburgenland. Hans' widow Waltraud and son Wolfgang cultivate 20 acres planted largely to red grapes. Best is the subtle, medium-bodied Blaufränkisch-Cabernet Sauvignon 'Cuvée Volcano'.

Weingut Krutzler 7474 Deutsch-Schützen, Südburgenland. Hermann Krutzler's rich, silky reds are Südburgenland's finest wines. Top of the range is the seductive 'Perwolff'.

Weingut Josef Lentsch 7141 Podersdorf, Neusiedlersee. 4-acre estate belonging to eponymous restaurant with fine class regional cooking. The region's best Blauburgunder (Pinot Noir) and Grauburgunder, and fine dessert wines.

Weinbau Willi Opitz 7142 Illmitz, Neusiedlersee. Born self-publicist Willi Opitz makes some remarkable dessert wines from 12 acres of vineyards, but his dry wines are often dull.

Weingut Helmut Renner 7122 Gols, Neusiedlersee. Red-wine specialist Helmut Renner is rapidly attracting attention with concentrated, elegant Blauburgunder (Pinot Noir) and 'Pannoibile' blend from 25 acres of vines.

Kollwentz/Weingut Römerhof 7051 Grosshöflein, Neusiedlersee-Hügelland. Andi Kollwentz is one of Austria's most talented young winemakers, and has played an important role in the country's recent red-wine revolution. The dry whites are clean and crisp, but rarely exceptional.

Georg Steigelmar/Weingut Juris 7122 Gols, Neusiedlersee. 27-acre estate run by the untiring Georg and Axel Steigelmar, who have won countless awards for Sauvignon Blanc and Chardonnay. Elegant reds, however, outclass the dry whites.

Wien (Vienna)

Johann Kattus Major Vienna merchant dating from 1857, now in the fourth generation, and specializing in Sekt under the Hochriegel brand. The founder was caviar merchant to both the Russian and Austro-Hungarian courts, and Austrian agent for Veuve Clicquot. Their *méthode traditionnelle* Alte Reserve, made from Riesling and Grüner Veltliner, is slightly fruity with a clean finish. Specialities include Gewürztraminer from Nussberg – in the Vienna suburbs.

Weingut Franz Mayer Founded 1683. 74 acres, yielding 44,000 cases in Nussberg, Grinzing and Alsegg. Grapes: Grüner Veltliner, Rheinriesling, Müller-Thurgau, Traminer, Weissburgunder, Chardonnay, and red varieties. Mayer is the largest grower in Vienna and owns the Beethovenhaus, probably the best known of all the *heurigen*. His modern, well-run cellar produces a range of wines, from Heuriger to Spätlese.

Weingut Wieninger Vienna's leading estate makes everything from traditional dry Riesling to barrel-fermented Chardonnay and deeply coloured Cabernet–Merlot from 32 acres of vines on the Bisamberg.

Styria

Weingut Erich & Walter Polz
(and Weingut Rebenhof)

8471 Spielfeld, Südsteiermark. 62 acres. 15,000 cases. Grapes: Morillon, Sauv.Bl., Welschriesling, Weissburgunder, Ries., Grauburgunder, Gewürztraminer.

Brothers Erich and Walter Polz are leading figures in the wine revolution which began in the Styria during the mid-1980s. They were pioneers in the move away from sweet wines and mass production in favour of quality dry wines. They produce two styles of wine, the lighter, very fresh 'steirische Klassik' wines and the richer, slower maturing vineyard designated wines. Best of the latter are the Weissburgunder, Morillon and Sauvignon Blanc from the first-class Hochgrassnitzberg vineyard direct on the Austrian-Slovenian border.

Weingut E & M Tement

8461 Berghausen, Südsteiermark. 33 acres. 6,500 cases. Grapes: Welschriesling, Sauv.Bl., Morillon, Weissburgunder, Grauburgunder, Traminer, Muskateller.

The interior of Manfred Tement's cellar may look like a Heath Robinson cartoon, but the dry white wines which come out of it are frequently Styria's finest. No other Austrian winemaker makes such judicious use of new oak casks for fermenting and maturing white wines than Manfred Tement. His Sauvignon Blanc and Morillon from the first-class Zierreg vineyard are masterpieces of this style, at once rich and refined. In contrast, the 'steirische Klassik' varietal wines are vividly fruity, very clean and crisp.

OTHER STYRIA PRODUCERS

Gräflich Stürgkh'sches Weingut Südoststeiermark. 30 acres. Grapes: Welschriesling, Traminer, Gewürz. and Rheinriesling. A leading Styrian estate, under the control of the Seyffertitz family, who strive for balanced, traditional wines.

Weingut Gross 8461 Ratsch, Südsteiermark. Alois Gross is one of the most consistent winemakers of the Steiermark, making elegant, aromatic wines from 24 acres planted with a wide range of grapes. Best are his Sauvignon Blanc and new oak aged Grauburgunder.

Weingut Lackner-Tinnacher 8462 Gamlitz/Steinbach, Südsteiermark. Husband-and wife-team making beautifully crafted traditional style Steiermark white wines from 30 acres of vineyards; superb dry Muskateller and rich Grauburgunder, but other wines all good.

Burgweinbau Riegersburg 8410 Wildon, Südoststeiermark. Once great estate returning to form under Andreas Tscheppe. Good Sauvignon Blanc and non-oaked Morillon (Chardonnay) from 10 acres of vines within fortifications of Medieval Riegersburg castle.

Weingut Sattlerhof 8462 Samlitz, Steiermark. Founded 1887. 12 acres. 3,000 cases. Grapes: Welschriesling, Muskat, Weissburgunder, Ruländer, Sauv.Bl., Kerner.

CENTRAL AND EASTERN EUROPE

Prague ○
CZECH REPUBLIC

SLOVAK REPUBLIC

Bratislava ○
Danube

Budapest ○
HUNGARY

Ljubljana ○
Drava
SLOVENIA
Zagreb ○
CROATIA
Sava

BOSNIA-
HERZEGOVINA

Split ○
Sarajevo ○

Dubrovnik ○

SERBIA

Belgrade ○

Timiisoara ○

ROMANIA

MOLDOVA

Kishinev ○

Olt

Prut

Bucharest ○

Danube

Danube

Varna ○

BULGARIA

Sofia ○

Plovdiv ○

Skopje ○
MACEDONIA

Tirana ○
ALBANIA

Thessaloniki ○

TURKEY

Evros

Istanbul ○

GREECE

TURKEY

Izmir ○

Patras ○

Athens ○

HUNGARY

The end of Communism in Eastern Europe had, and is still having, profound effects on wine industries that had been centrally directed for decades. Their markets had been almost exclusively the undemanding Soviet bloc. Existing sales channels disappeared almost literally overnight in 1989. For most of them (Bulgaria being the exception) trading links with western markets had eroded away. A fresh start was necessary.

Hungary, always the closest to the west, was the first to call in western aid and profit by flying-winemaker technology. But in any context, historical or cultural, Hungary is incontestably the regional leader. Indeed, in all of Europe only France and Germany have older and more evolved traditions of quality winemaking than Hungary's most famous vineyards. Whether the Hungarians can recapture their former standing in the world of wine depends in part on whether the world continues to prize the 'international' grape varieties above all others, or whether, as in Italy, there is a real place for authentic ethnic traditions. The Hungarian words of appreciation for the country's traditional wines sum up their character and appeal. Hungarians call a good white wine 'fiery' and 'stiff' – masculine terms which promise a proper partner for the paprika in their cooking.

Such wines can still be found in the historical sites of Hungarian viticulture, the hill regions which dot the country from the southwest northwards, skirt the long Lake Balaton, then run up the Slovak border from near Budapest to Tokaj. Use of the traditional Hungarian grapes ensures that the wines remain very much individuals.

Despite the grubbing-up of old vines and massive plantings of international varieties in the 1960s and early '70s Hungary remains rich in indigenous grapes of character that have the potential to contribute splendid wines to the world scene – grapes which often simply do not succeed elsewhere. Some of the older, tired or uneconomically low-yielding grapes have gone completely, replaced by newer fresh hybrids which are making their mark. The most notable of all is the vigorous Furmint, the dominant grape of Tokaj, which not only rots nobly but in its dry form gives strongly sappy and high-flavoured wine. The Hárslevelü or 'linden leaf' is scarcely less notable: an excellent dry-climate late ripener with abundant crops and good acid levels, resistant to fungus diseases – a model grape for South Africa, Australia or California.

Szürkebarát or 'grey friar' is more familiar than it sounds: it is a form of Pinot Gris (German Ruländer) grown to splendid effect on the volcanic Mt Badacsonyi. The Kéknyelü ('blue-stalk') of the same vineyards north of Lake Balaton is a modest producer of concentrated and complex golden-green wines for the fish course. More widespread are three other white Hungarians, Ezerjó ('thousand blessings'), which is a good bulk-producer on the Great Plain making fine wine only at Mór in the north, Leányka ('little girl') whose delicate dry white is probably the best wine of Eger, again in

the northern hills, and Mézesfehér ('white honey'), an archetypal description of the national view of a good glass of wine. The last is, regrettably, less grown now.

Most widespread of all is the international Olaszrizling (Italian Riesling). The Great Plain makes most of its white from it, and on Mt Badacsonyi it rises to its maximum flavour and concentration.

The great Hungarian red grape is the Kadarka, which flourishes equally on the Great Plain producing a firm wine with a slight but convincing 'cut', and at Eger and Szekszárd, producing a big stiff spicy red for ageing. Unfortunately, it is a late and unreliably ripening variety and its low yield has meant that the rather lighter Kékfrankos has been planted more and more as a substitute. The Austrian Zweigelt, on the other hand, is a newcomer with different virtues of softness, darkness and a pleasantly sweet scent. There is also a long tradition of growing Pinot Noir in southern Hungary around Villány and Merlot around Eger in the north.

Added to these are many grapes whose identification causes no problems: Szilváni, Cabernet (Sauvignon and Franc), Sauvignon Blanc, Pinot Blanc, Rajnairizling, Tramini, Muskat Ottonel or Muskotály.

Each of Hungary's notable wines is called by a simple combination of place and grape name. The place name has the suffix '-i'. Thus Ezerjó from Mor is Mori Ezerjó.

Hungary has around 275,000 acres of vines. Even under the former régime, even in Tokaj, the most important and famous area of all, many smallholders still owned land (a maximum of 25 acres) although their grapes had to be sold to the state farms for vinification. Today, although some vineyards remain in state ownership, the majority now have been wholly or partly privatized; substantial areas are owned by either major producers or cooperatives, but a very significant proportion is in the hands of small producers who, often with the assistance of foreign capital or partners, have invested in their own vinification and bottling facilities.

Currently there are 20 designated wine regions (although much very acceptable wine is produced outside them). Administration and appellation control is handling in each wine-producing 'commune' by a local French-style *comité interprofessionel* (*hegyközség*), through regional *hegyközségek* to a national appellations board. Quality control is undertaken by an independent national institute in Budapest.

Even in 1990 it was already possible for a would-be buyer from abroad to form a joint-enterprise company with a group of smallholders (the first was formed in the village of Mád, in Tokaj). Their wines could then be bottled individually, without the intervention of the state cellars.

There has been heavy foreign investment in major producers, particularly in the flagship region of Tokaj where stakes have been taken by French insurance companies (AXA and GAMA-Audy), the Spanish wine-producer Vega Sicilia, Japanese whisky firm Suntory and others.

THE GREAT PLAIN

The Danube divides Hungary almost down the middle. East of the river in southern Hungary lies the sandy Pannonian or Great Plain (Alföld), a vast expanse of steppe-like country which has a long tradition of winegrowing because vines help to bind the soil.

The Csongrád wine region embraces a total 14,250 acres, producing wines almost entirely for the domestic market. The most common varieties grown here are Rajnairizling, Zöldveltelini (the Grüner Veltliner) and Kékfrankos (the Austrian Blaufränkisch). The Hajós-Vaskút region, with more loess than sand, includes some 10,000 acres which give higher-quality wines, around half of which are exported. Principal grapes are Chardonnay, Cabernet Sauvignon and Kadarka. Hajósi Cabernet has a particularly good name.

By far the largest region of the Great Plain is Kiskunság, which totals 75,000 acres. Soil quality and water-table levels vary, the summers are dry, precipitation is low and winters frosty. A quarter of Hungary's total wine production comes from this region, the majority from the huge-scale winery, Kiskunhalas. Seventy percent of it is white, every-day wine, some of which is bound for Western Europe but most for Eastern Europe and the CIS. Both still and sparkling wines, the latter mainly reflecting the domestic market's preference for sweeter wines, are made from indigenous and international grapes, including Kadarka, Kövidinka, Ezerjó, Olaszrizling, Kékoportó, Kékfrankos, Cabernets Sauvignon and Franc, Zweigelt, Zöldveltelini and Ottonel Muskotály.

NORTHERN TRANSDANUBIA

This great area includes much of the traditional wine-growing districts on the slopes of the old volcanic hills which run up from Lake Balaton to the Danube/Slovakian border, but it also embraces newer wine districts.

The 5,000-acre Aszar-Neszmély region is dominated by a recently refurbished and re-equipped winery for white wine at Neszmély, owned by Interconsult. Its entire production is exported. The moderate climate and good soils produce white wines that are fragrant, rich in acids, full-bodied and keep well. Principal grape varieties of the region include Olaszrizling, Rizlingszilváni (alias Muller-Thürgau), Leányka, Sauvignon Blanc, Chardonnay and Tramini (alias Gewürztraminer).

Similar in size is the Badacsony region, a series of south-facing volcanic hills on the north shore of the 50-mile long Lake Balaton. After Tokaji, this region is second dearest to Hungarians and its basalt soils produce warming – sometimes fiery – full-flavoured and fruity white wines. The grapes are grown by cooperatives of small individual producers and the wines sold largely on the domestic market. Badacsony's best are reckoned to come from the Olaszrizling, Szürkebarát (Pinot Gris) and dryish Kéknyelü grapes, but Rizlingszilváni and Ottonel Muskotály are also widely planted.

Further east along the northern lake shore lies the Balatonfüred-Csopak region, some 7,000 acres of red sand soils, less hilly than Badacsony, but likewise farmed by coops and smaller individual producers. A slightly warmer microclimate gives wines with more roundness, less 'nerve'. Overall the style is softer than the Badacsony wines. They are exported to several West European countries. Here the Olaszrizling makes notable wines, but Rizlingszilváni, Rajnairizling, Chardonnay, Sauvignon Blanc, Tramini and Ottonel Muskotály are also widespread.

Almost behind the Badacsony region, on a second line of hills north of the lake, is the smaller (5,000 acres) Balaton-Mellék region. Here too the vines are on south-facing volcanic slopes, but lack the benefit of the sun's rays being reflected from the lake's surface. Mainly small growers produce excellent Olaszrizling, Pinot Gris and Rizlingszilváni, especially for the home market.

Twenty miles west of Budapest is the small (4,000 acres) Etyek region. A century ago the potential of its climate and loess and chernozem soils caught the eye of champagne-trained József Törley for growing Chardonnay to produce sparkling wines. Törley's successor in the region today is Hungarovin, joined by some small producers, growing Sauvignon Blanc, Zenit, Zefir, Pinot Blanc and Zengö, among other varieties.

Smaller still is the Mór region, a 3,000-acre stretch known principally for its robustly distinctive Móri Ezerjó wines, one of the country's best dry whites, although its quartz-rich soils over limestone also produce Sauvignon and a Rajnairizling which has acidity and 'fire'. Much of the total production of Mór is exported.

Further north and closer to the Austrian border is the 2,500-acre Pannonhalma-Sokoróalja region, lying at the foot of the Bakony hills. A quarter of its area is owned by a cooperative and virtually all of its production is consumed in the domestic market. The main grapes of the region are Olaszrizling, Rajnairizling, Chardonnay, Ottonel Muskotály, Rizlingszilváni and Tramini.

Hungary's smallest region is Somléo, just 1,250 acres on the slopes of a single volcanic plug. Wine-growing is largely in the hands of small producers, some with as little as 2.5 acres of vines, selling almost entirely to the domestic market. Characterful wines are made from Olaszrizling, Furmint, Tramini, Hárslevelú, Juhfark and Chardonnay.

The last of Northern Transdanubia's regions is Sopron, 4,500 acres that run up to the border with Austria's Burgenland. A milder climate than most of Hungary and diverse soils are more favourable to red-wine production. Here Kékfrankos is the principal grape, although Zweigelt, Merlot and Cabernet are also grown. There are whites too, made from Tramini, Leányka, Zöldveltelini and some Chardonnay.

SOUTHERN TRANSDANUBIA

The area south of Lake Balaton and west of the Danube houses four of Hungary's best-known wine regions. The most recent is Dél-Balaton (meaning 'south' Balaton), 7,500-acres of brown forest soils and sandy loess with a sub-Mediterranean climate, which means the springs are early, summers long and warm and frosts rare, although rain (and frequently hail) is plentiful. Red and white wines are produced, from Olaszrizling, Chardonnay, Sauvignon Blanc, Kiráylánky, Kékfrankos, Merlot and Cabernet Sauvignon. The majority of the vineyard area is under the control of the Balatonboglár Winery (owners of the Chapel Hill brand), the rest is in the hands of small growers. Balaton is generally reckoned to be a progressive area, the source of many sound wines. Some half of the production is exported.

To the south, around the town of Pécs, is the Mecsekalja, a region of 3,250 acres. It is the warmest of Hungary's wine regions and the wine produced here is almost all white, from local and imported varieties, much of it made sparkling, including very respectable off-dry Olaszrizling, good Pinot Blanc, Furmint, Cirfandli (a speciality), Chardonnay and Sauvignon.

One of Hungary's oldest and most renowned wine regions is Szekszárd in the south-central part of the country.

It produces some of Hungary's best reds on gentle slopes of sandy loess which follow the course of the Danube. It is the only region other than Eger permitted to produce Bikavér (Bull's Blood). It built its reputation for reds (likened to Bordeaux) on the Kadarka grape, some of which were made botrytized (Nemes Kadar), but Szekszárd now depends mainly on the international varieties of Merlot and the two Cabernets, and the native Kékfrankos. White wines are made from Chardonnay and Olaszrizling. Foreign investors are beginning to show interest in the region, among them Italy's Antinori.

Villány–Siklós is the combined name for two historic wine regions named after their principal towns. Red wines predominate in the Villány half where, on hills of stiff loess, the Kadarka has given way to the Kékoporto (probably the Blauer Portugieser) which takes full advantage of the mild winters and long hot summers to produce some splendidly concentrated and full-bodied wines which can take readily to oak. The two Cabernets, Merlot, Pinot Noir (producing some unmistakably Burgundian wines), Zweigelt and the native Kékfrankos are also grown in the Villány half. In the Siklós part of the region small producers concentrate predominantly on white grapes, notably Olaszrizling, Tramini, Chardonnay and Hárslevelü.

NORTHERN HUNGARY

The lower slopes of the Bükk Hills and the sheltering Mátra Mountains north of the vineyards produce some of Hungary's best-known wines. Between Eger and the industrial city of Miskolc the 6,750 acres of the Bükkalja (-*alja* means 'foothills') region benefit from a good microclimate and soils underlaid by tufa – perfect for vines. Cabernet Sauvignon, Leányka, Olaszrizling, Zweigelt and Kékfrankos are the principal grapes.

To the south of the baroque city of Eger is the Eger wine region itself. Eger is famous for its Egri Bikavér (Bull's Blood) on which its reputation as a potent red-wine producer was built. Bikavér is in fact a style of wine, not a brand, made from a blend of Kékfrankos, Merlot, Cabernets Sauvignon and Franc and Kékoporto. Kadarka is no longer the principal native grape in the blend. In fact today there is a range of Bikavérs as individual producers determine the exact blending proportions and amount of ageing. After a long spell in cellar some extraordinarily powerful wines can emerge, although inevitably, perhaps, some export versions are all too variable.

In addition to Bikavér, Eger produces some fine fresh white wines too, best of all from Leánkya which is a speciality of the region, but also using Chardonnay, Olaszrizling, Tramini and some Ottonel Muskotály. The underlying tufa may be the secret of Egri quality. The major producer, Egervin, now owns the impressive tufa-quarried cellars in the city, which are lined with vast red-hooped

casks. Here even the whites may be kept for up to five years without losing their freshness.

Further west, around the town of Gyöngyös, is the Mátraalja region, an almost exclusively white wine region of 17,500 acres. Today the region's biggest producers are two coops, Nagyréde and Danubiana, the latter German-owned. Danubiana bought and re-equipped the huge Gyöngyös winery, and brought in Hungary's first 'flying winemaker' Hugh Ryman. French and Australian investment has followed. There are several other coops in Mátraalja, including the modern Nagyréde Mátraalja, as well as small producers. Some half of its total output is exported. Principal grape varieties include Olaszrizling, Pinots Gris and Blanc, Rizlingszilváni, Zöldveltelini, Leányka, Tramini, Hárslevelü (most famously from the town of Debrö), Chardonnay, Sauvignon Blanc and the fragrant Ottonel Muskotály which produces the region's dry Muscat speciality.

The final region is Tokajhegyalja, usually shortened to Tokaj, in the far northeast of Hungary, adjoining the Slovakian border . Tokaji *aszú* is often thought to be the only wine of Tokaj (*see* page 421). There are in fact several table wines made from one or other of the four grape varieties permitted in the 'great' Tokaji wines: Furmint, Hárslevelü, Sargamuskotály (Yellow Muscat or Mucat Lunel) and Oremus, a hybrid cross between Furmint and the Bouvier grape which was only admitted to the Tokaji canon in 1994. A little Chardonnay also features.

TOKAJI

Tokaji stands head and shoulders above the other wine regions of central and eastern Europe as the producer of their one undisputed wine of luxury and legend. Late-harvested, unctuously rich Tokay (the western spelling of the name) was the choice of Russian Tsars, the Kings of Poland and Emperors of Austria – even of Louis XIV of France.

It was almost certainly the first wine to be made purposely of botrytis-shrivelled grapes. The mid-17th century is given as its known origin, at least a century before similar sweet wines were first made on the Rhine. Sweet Sauternes is also much more recent in origin, though its start date is obscure.

By 1700 the wines of Tokaji were so important that their overlord, the Prince of Transylvania (of the Rakoczi family) created the first recorded vineyard classification, grading the Tokaji vineyards into 'Primae', 'Secundae' and 'Tertiae' plots.

In some respects the Tokajihegyalya (Tokaji hills – the region's official name) compares with Burgundy's Côte d'Or. It occupies a similar area on the lower and mid-slopes, though of much higher, volcanic, hills. The best sites tend to be on the lower middle slopes, some on pure volcanic soil, some on warm light loess. Moreover the first-, second- and third-class growths correspond, up to a point, to the Grands and Premiers Crus and -Villages wines of Burgundy.

Like the Côte d'Or too, Tokaji has excellent cellars, but here they are narrow tunnels driven into the volcanic tufa, sometimes wandering for two miles or more, deeply lined with damp black fungus and sheltering single or double rows of little 136-litre casks, or gönci, usually black with age. As in Sauternes three grapes are grown: here the Furmint,

Hárslevelü and a little Yellow (or Lunel) Muscat. Vintage time is very late, delayed – ideally – until the hot sun, alternating with misty nights (the rivers Bodrog and Tisza skirt the hills) has induced a heavy infestation of botrytis. But unlike Sauternes, or any other wine, Tokaji Aszú is made in two stages: first a fully fermented 'base' wine; then the collection of dry (aszú) grapes, shrivelled either by botrytis or simple raisining, which are macerated with the base wine and re-fermented to absorb their sweetness and highly concentrated aromas.

The amount of aszú added to each barrel is conventionally measured in puttonyos – a puttonyo being a grape-carrying hod containing 20–25 kilograms. 3-, 4- and 5-puttonyos wines are the most usual; 6 is exceptional. Today the true measure is grams of sugar and 'extract' after fermentation. A 6-putt wine, for example, must have at least 150 grams of residual sugar and 45 grams per litre of extract.

Such wines, with their intense sweetness and concentrated dried-fruit flavours balanced by swingeing acidity, can be alarmingly penetrating when they are young, leaving the mouth with a whistle-clean sharpness despite their sugar content. With age they mellow to magical complexity and roundness, without losing their clean fresh finish. Apparently a century is not too great an age for them.

Eventually even more important than the degree of sweetness, though, will be the singular quality of the vineyard. A handful of great sites have been celebrated for centuries, and will presumably be so again when their wines, unblended, are seen on the world market once more.

The classes of the 'great' Tokaji wines

Tokaji szamorodni This is Tokaji 'as it comes' – i.e. the lesser 'great' wines, sweet (édes) or dry (száraz) according to the quantity of aszú grapes used.

Tokaji aszú Like Tokaji szamorodni, aszú wines can only be made in years when there are sufficient high-quality aszú grapes – i.e. grapes infected with noble rot (Botrytis cinerea). Destalked hand-picked aszú grapes are stored 6–8 days, then kneaded to a pulp which is added to a base Tokaji wine, or to must, by the puttony (a hod of 20–25 kilos). The eventual sweetness depends on the number of puttonyos added to the 136–140-litre barrels (called gönci) of one-year-old base wine – usually 3, 4 and 5 puttonyos. 6 is exceptional. The sequence then is:
- maceration and stirring for 24–48 hours
- settling and racking the must
- fermentation period depending on number of puttonyos
- racking, fining and filtering
- ageing in oak for not less than 3 years
- filtering prior to bottling
- if binned in Tokaji cellars, bottles are not laid on their sides but stood upright, and the corks changed every 15–20 years.

Tokaji aszú eszencia Only individually hand-selected aszú grapes. Only produced in exceptional years from the best vineyards. Method as for Tokaji aszú, but:

- quality cannot be measured by numbers of puttonyos as sugar content is higher than for 6 puttonyos
- fermentation takes several years (special yeast is used – Tokaj 22)
- minimum of 10 years' ageing in oak.

Tokaji eszencia Destalked hand-picked aszú grapes. While grapes are being stored (see Tokaji aszú) the pressure of their own weight produces a minute amount of highly concentrated juice at the bottom of the tub (one puttonyo yields only 142 millilitres of this essencia). The juice is then allowed to ferment extremely slowly for many years in oak casks. In practice it scarcely ferments at all; the sugar content is too high.

But Tokaji Aszús can no more be the only product of the region than can Ausleses in Germany. The regular drinking is dry, largely Furmint, table wine, which can be admirably lively and fiery. The less luxurious aperitif or dessert wine is Tokaji Szamarodni – literally 'as it comes'; which means the whole vineyard is harvested without any selection of *aszú* grapes. Szamarodni is edither *édes* (sweet) or *száraz* (dry) according to the proportion of *asúu* on the vines. At best it can be similar to sherry with its own distinctive 'cut'.

For those for whom the best is not good enough there remains a category richer even that a 6-putt wine: Tokaji Aszú Eszencia (or Essencia). Such sweet intensity is overwhelming; years of maturity are needed to tame it.

Leading Tokay Producers

Bodvin KTFT

3909 Mád.
16-acre property of the Bodnar family in Kiralydulo, Veres and Burja vineyards. Young Furmints and older Aszús from 3 to 6 years are exported (90% to the US).

The Royal Tokaji Wine Company

3909 Mád.
Anglo-Danish-Hungarian joint venture founded in 1990 (the first of the 'Tokay Renaissance') to specialize in Aszú wines. Parcels in two second-class and four first-class sites in Mád and Tarcal produce single-vineyard Bojta, Betsek, Birsalmás, Nyulászó, Szt Tamás and Mezés Mály. '90 and '91 wines are all 5-putt, '93 up to 6-putt. 'Blue Label' is vintage-dated Aszú. Cuvée 'Red Label' slightly lighter.

Tokaj Disznókö RT

3910 Tokaj.
One of the great old Tokay estates, 247 acres bought at privatization (1992) by the French insurance group AXA and directed by J.-M. Cazes of Bordeaux. Major investment in splendid volcanic clay vineyards and a new winery. Full range of wines includes Edes Szamorodni, Aszú 4-, 5- and 6-putt of Sauternes-like richness, Aszú Eszencia and also Tokaji Eszencia.

Tokaj Hétszölö

3910 Tokaj.
100-plus acres on the steep southern slope of the Tokaj mountain; an investment by Grands Millésimes de France. Modern methods and commitment are making fine single-variety wines for table, 4- and 5-putt Aszús and also Fordítas.

Tokaj-Oremus KFT

3950 Sárospatak.
The name, possibly the site, of the original 1630 Tokaj Aszú was bought at privatization by Vega Sicilia of Spain. Aszús have an extra year's bottle-age before release. Tokaji Eszencia in top vintages. Vines 70% Furmint, 30% Hárslevelü.

The legendary Tokaji 'Essence' goes even further: its sugar content is so high (up to 800 grams per litre) that yeasts can make no impression on it: an interminable snail's pace fermentation was traditionally ended by the discreet addition of a little brandy. Essenia is the free-run juice of a pile of *aszú* bunches, pressed by their own weight alone to produce egg-cup quantities. Since an egg-cup of the elixir was reputed enough to convert an Imperial deathbed into something much more lively, Essencia has for centuries been the most highly prized of all 'wines' – and virtually unobtainable.

The renaissance of the Tokaji region is now well under way, with over a dozen companies, including several major foreign investors, involved.

Megyer RT

3950 Sárospatak.
Major joint venture between GAN Avenir (French insurance company) and the Tokay Trading House. 200 acres.

Pajzos RT

3950 Sárospatak.
A French-Hungarian joint venture (the French investor is CFQVT) with 160 acres, based like Megyer, at Sárospatak.

Tokaj Kereskedöház RT/Tokaj Trading House Co.

3981 Sátoraljaújhely.
Former state-owned property with almost 180 acres in Szarvas, the famous first-growth of the village of Tarcal. It makes dry and sweet wines (Furmint, Hárslevelü, Yellow Muscat, Szamorodni, Aszú and 'museum' wines). 60% is sold at home, the rest in Germany, Japan, Sweden, Russia, Lithuania and Latvia. Also involved in joint ventures with French investors: Pajzos and Megyer (qq.v.).

Szepsy-Mád-Kirái y Szöleszft

3909 Mád.
6-putt Aszú and Aszú Essencia from 16 acres in Mád and Tarcal. Szepsys have been making Tokaj Aszú since the 16th century. 1993 was the first vintage to be released, and attracted much outside attention: so far production cannot meet the demand. Istvan Szepsy accounts for the quality by his vineyard practice: low-trained vines, hard pruning and rigorous selection of berries only at the peak of botrytis. Base wine added to the *aszú* grapes is must from the same vineyard. 3 years' maturation in new oak before bottling.

Lauder Láng Pincészet

1146 Budapest.
Two famous ex-pat Hungarians are aiming at traditional Tokays with modern methods. Vineyards in Mád. Also an investment in Eger making Bikavér, and in Gundel's celebrated restaurant in Budapest.

Dégenfeld

3915 Tarcal.
150-acre property selling Furmint, Hárslevelü (late harvest), Yellow Muscat, Fordítas and 5-putt Aszú under the Count Dégenfeld name. Small production so far but first-class land.

THE CZECH AND SLOVAK REPUBLICS

Unlike Hungary, the quality of whose top wines was world famous, these two republics have traditionally grown wine for their own use, rather than for export. Even with the advent of less repressive political regimes, they still do. The former capital of both countries, Prague, may account for much of the consumption, but the wine production capitals are Bratislava in Slovakia, and Brno in Moravia. Bratislava lies on the River Danube virtually on the Austro-Hungarian border; Brno is not far from the Czech border with Austria's Weinviertel.

Slovakia is the chief producer of the two republics, with some 90,000 acres. In the Czech system of classifying grape varieties 20% of this is planted with what are termed the First Class 'A' white varieties: Rhine Riesling, Pinot Blanc, Gewürztraminer, Sauvignon Blanc, Rülander and Muscat Ottonel. Half is planted with First Class 'B' whites of which Wälschriesling, Grüner Veltliner and Müller-Thurgau are much the most important. About a third is red, with Frankovka (Blauer Limberger) and Vavrinecke (St Laurent) the leading grapes. There are some 1,500 acres of Cabernet Sauvignon and a few rare plantings of Pinot Noir on the hills between Bratislava and Pezinok. The big old state bottling companies of Raca (in the outskirts of Bratislava), Pezinok, some 12 miles to the northeast, and Nitra, another 40 miles further on used to account for the vast majority of the entire state production.

Modra, just north of Pezinok has its own viticultural and oenology school as well as an independent bottling company. Nenince to the east along the Slovak-Hungarian border probably has a head start on quality production in the country. Kosice, far to the east is also surrounded by vineyard land. Names of breakaway cellars which may yet come to the fore include Topolčany, Hurbanovo, Gbelce, Hlohovec, Trnava all of which have some fine vineyards to draw on.

Slovakia's other special pride is in possessing a small corner of the Tokay vineyard on the Hungarian border, growing 65% Furmint, 25% Harslevelü and 10% Muscat de Frontignan to produce her own Tokay. Sadly, this cellar is in considerable disarray and rapidly falling behind the renascent Hungarian region which still produces around 90% of this wine.

Moravia's 35,000 acres of vineyards lie between Brno and the Austrian border and many of the grapes are similar to those of its neighbour. The industry is centred on the old state farms and cooperatives of Znojmo (perhaps the best), Blatnice, Hustopece, Saldorf and Velké Pavlovice, which are producing both still and sparkling wines. Although they grow more B varieties than As, their Müller-Thurgaus, Grüner Veltliners, Rülanders and Rieslings are the first choice in the *vinarnas*, the wine-bars of Prague, and have the spirit of Austria's *heurigen* when young. Moravia's wines score in terms of both value and variety.

Bohemia, the western province with Prague at its heart, has a mere 2,500 acres, including some Rhine Riesling of fair quality and some intriguing Pinot Noir based reds. But full ripeness does not come easily here and Moravian or Slovakian wine is the people's choice.

THE FORMER YUGOSLAVIA

Most of the countries that once made up Yugoslavia are in the wine business, some more traditionally and interestingly than others. Only land-locked and mountainous Bosnia-Herzegovina's production is negligible. Just two remain major exporters at present, both of them protected from the ravages of the last few years: Slovenia in the northwest and Macedonia in the southeast. Croatia and Serbia traditionally had the majority of the former nation's vineyards but it is too soon to take stock of what remains available from either country to come again to the export marketplace.

Yugoslavia came tenth among the world's wine countries and tenth among exporters: a respectable position for a country which had to build its wine industry almost from scratch after World War II. The industry's roots are as old as Italy's, but long occupation by the Turks in the easterly regions of the country removed the sense of continuity. The post-war reconstitution of the industry combined the Germanic Austro-Hungarian traditions of the north, the Italian influence down the coast and some truly Balkan traditions in the east and south. In particular Croatia's Dalmatian coast, and Madeconia likewise, have good indigenous grape varieties (*see* page 16), whose origins can be traced back to ancient times, although these are threatened by the general trend in all these countries to move towards adopting the tried and trusted international varieties as part of the concerted effort to regain a slice of the export market.

The old wine industry was state-controlled but always consisted almost half-and-half of small independent growers and state-owned farms. The small growers (the law allowed them to own up to 24 acres of land) took their crops to the local, giant-size, cooperatives. These in turn supplied the larger regional organizations, which acted as négociants, blenders and distributors. In the '90s many small, private producers are beginning to appear.

423

SLOVENIA

Slovenia, tucked into the Italian-Austrian-Hungarian north-west corner of the country, makes the best and most expensive wines of the countries that formerly made up Yugoslavia. Its principal grape is the Italian Riesling, called here Laski Rizling or Grasevina. The 51,000 acres of vineyards are divided by a no-man's land strip empty of vines from the alpine border, past the capital, Ljublijana, down to the border with Croatia. The most attractive of the northerly Germano-Austrian style wines come from around Maribor, Ptuj, Ljutomer (or Lutomer), and Ormoz, between the valleys of the Mura (which forms in places the border with Austria and Hungary), the Sava and the Drava tributaries to the Danube. The most exciting dry whites and reds produced in the Italian tradition come from the north of the Istrian peninsula and up into the mountains alongside the Friuli border region.

These days, Slovenia is taking a lot of care in the grading of her wines. Only the top 15–20% are deemed fit for 75cl glass bottles and these original, often exaggeratedly tall, slim presentations are the real bases on which the country should be judged. This is also rapidly becoming a very pleasant, civilised country for the tourist to visit .

The combined influences of the Adriatic, the Alps and the Hungarian plain make the climate moderate, while limestone subsoils favour white wine. The Adriatic influence gives more ripening potential for solid dry wines and the better reds; the long, cool autumns of the alpine Maribor region and the only slightly warmer hillsides south of Hungary give lighter, more aromatic and grapey styles the best of which are often sold under the familiar Kabinett, Spätlese, Auslese, Beeren- and TBA hierarchy. The hills between Ljutomer and Ormoz, only 50 miles from the west end of Lake Balaton, bear a vineyard almost as famous as Mt Badacsonyi, known by the name of Jerusalem from its crusader connections. The majority of the exports from this admirable region are unfortunately of Laski Rizling, although Pinots Blanc and Gris, Gewürztraminer, Sylvaner and Rhine Riesling are also grown. It seems a pity to waste a first-rate vineyard on what is essentially a second-rate grape, however satisfactory its performance – and some of the late-picked wines here are more than satisfactory.

South of the Drava the Haloze Hills produce a similar range of white wines. South again the Sava Valley, continuing into Croatia and on to its capital, Zagreb, makes light red Cvicek of local grapes.

At the western end of Slovenia on the Italian border four small viticultural regions with a total of 12,000 acres have a mild Mediterranean climate. Their best-known wine is a vigorous, crisp and tangy red called Kraski Teran. Teran is the Italian Refosco and Kraski signifies that it is grown on the rugged limestone *karst* that stretches up the coast. Merlot, both Cabernets and Barbera can be found but tend to be used to produce relatively high acid, Italian styles which crave the company of oily foods. However, the weight and quality of the best of the dry whites, from Sauvignon Blanc, Pinot Blanc and Pinot Gris to the earthy, slightly creamy yellow Ribolla or Rebula, another Italian export, deserve real international acclaim.

At this end of the country, names such as Vipava, especially for fresh, delicate young whites, Brda, which has some extraordinary private vineyards, and Koper, south of Trieste, hold promise for the future.

SERBIA

The republic of Serbia was formerly the whole of the eastern, landlocked, third of Yugoslavia from Hungary to Macedonia. Now its northern section, north of the River Danube, comprises the region of Vojvodina. It has two more enclaves to the south – Montenegro on the southeastern coast and Kosovo, squeezed into a circle of mountains between Albania, Macedonia and Serbia. It has, though, lost a significant southern slice, adjacent to Albania, cut away to become Macedonia.

Including Vojvodina, Montenegro and Kosovo, Serbia is still probably the major producer with some 222,000 acres of vines. It has been relatively conservative in its grape varieties, with the dark Prokupac as its chief red grape and Smederevka (Smederevo is near Belgrade) as its white. Its oldest and most famous vineyard is Zupa, 80 miles south of the capital between Svetozarevo and Kruževac. Zupsko Crno ('Zupa red') is a blend of Prokupac with the lighter Plovdina. Prokupac is also widely used for rosé ('Ruzica'). More and more Cabernet, Merlot and Gamay is now being planted. Some individual vats of Sauvignon Blanc, Gewürztraminer, Cabernet Sauvignon and Merlot, which rarely made it intact out of the country, suggest that, one day, this will be fine territory for all these varieties.

Vojvodina has a history of red-winemaking (Carlowitz was once a famous example). Today a wide range of mainly white grapes makes nicely aromatic and balanced wines, the best of them in the Fruska Gora Hills by the Danube north of Belgrade. Gewürztraminer and Sauvignon Blanc can be particularly tasty, though I fear they are less widely planted than Laski Rizling. Further north and east, Subotica and Banat are the areas bordering on Hungary and Romania, both with sandy Great Plain soils and light wines; Subotica growing the Hungarian red Kadarka and white Ezerjó.

Kosmet (or Kosovo) was extraordinarily successful for a relatively new exporter region. Its Pinot Noir-based pale red, made sweet for the German taste and labelled Amselfelder, regularly left Belgrade in train loads. Since war cut off supplies, this soft, empty style has been ruthlessly copied all over eastern Europe for this single market. Perhaps, when Kosovo becomes more accessible again and privatization maybe splits up the vineyard, this may prove a spur to make the best of Pinot Noir rather than the most of it.

The hearty red Vranac-based wines of Montenegro used to disappear to the Russian market. Since 1990, there have been some haphazard attempts to interest the West in them. They deserve to succeed as the wines can be balanced, ripe, quite intense and appear to take well to wood ageing.

This southerly end of the country counts an unusually good unknown white variety among its potential surprises: I have found a touch of the apricot smell of the Zilavka grape which makes me wonder whether its lightness is a clever piece of blending.

CROATIA AND DALMATIA

The old kingdom of Croatia musters the second-most vineyards among the republics with 130,000 acres. It falls into two distinct and very different parts: Slavonia, the continental north between Slovenia and Serbia, between the Drava and the Sava rivers, and the coast, from the Istrian peninsula in the north all the way south to Montenegro, including all Dalmatia and its lovely islands.

Slavonia has half the grape acreage, but its wines have neither the appeal of Slovenia's whites, close though they are, nor of some of the new wines of Vojvodina to the east. Wine shipped as Yugoslav Laski Rizling without further particulars often came from here.

Croatia's best wines come from the regions of Istria and Dalmatia. Istria grows the same grapes as western Slovenia: Merlot, Cabernet, Pinot Noir and Terran for reds – the Merlot is particularly good. The white wines include rich Muscats and Malvasias, and Pinot Blanc, the base of the local sparkling wine.

Dalmatia has Yugoslavia's richest array of original characters – mainly red. Plavac Mali (there seems to be no translation) is the principal grape, supported by Plavina, Vranac, Babic, Cabernet, Merlot and 'Modra Frankija' (Blau Frankisch). Plavac has its moments of glory. One is Postup, a concentrated sweet red, aged for years in oak, produced on the Peljesac peninsula north of Dubrovnik. A 15-year-old Postup is still bright red, a strange sort of half-port with more than a hint of retsina, a big (14.2°) well-balanced and structured wine that would appeal to those who like Recioto from Valpolicella. Dingac is very similar. Another is Faros from the island of Hvar, a degree lighter than Postup and softly dry rather than sweet; a full-bodied, warmly satisfying wine without coarseness. The regular quality of coastal red is simply called Plavac. Some find Babic, when aged three or four years, a better wine. The dry rosé of the coast, made from several grapes, is called Opol.

White Dalmatian wines are in a minority but in greater variety than red. The Marastina is the most widespread white variety and has its own appellation at Cara Smokvica. Grk is the oxidized, sherry-like speciality of the island of Korčula. Posip (which some equate with Sipon/Furmint) makes heavy but not flat wine. Bogdanusa, especially on the islands of Hvar and Brac, can be surprisingly light, crisp and aromatic. Vugava, grown on the remote island of Vis, is similar. Sometimes they are presented as separate varieties, sometimes in blends. It is hard to discover, in fact, whether some are different names for the same grape. But they certainly have old-style character to balance against the predictable correctness of Laski Rizling.

Dalmatia's dessert wines, whether of red or white grapes or both, are known as Prosek. The best Prosek tends to be a family matter, nursed in a little cask and given to guests in a thick tumbler with absolutely appropriate pride.

MACEDONIA

Seventy-four thousand acres of mostly red grapes, Vranac and Kratosija, which are mainly blended, set the scene. They are spiced up with more of the Cabernet and Merlot which seemed to have been coming on so well just prior to the latest round of upheavals. Prokupac is the best quality local red grape here, as in Serbia. Especially at the Povardarie winery, these reds are coming good and beginning to reconquer the export market. There seem to be one or two good whites in among the plethora of Smederevka whose only salvation lies in the soda water so ubiquitously added to it. Some leafy but quite balanced and intense Chardonnay has appeared and there are good reports of Zilavka.

ROMANIA

The long-established quality and individuality of Romanian wine has suffered badly in the socialist era. The country speaks a Latin-based tongue and has both cultural and climatic affinities with France. Once the wines of Moldavia were drunk in Paris. Today little Romanian wine is seen in the West but this is beginning to change. Much of the white wine from the western part of the country, especially the hilly enclave of Transylvania needed German terms on the labels to serve the needs of Romania's largest Western market. This has hardly helped the development or understanding of this still unnecessarily poor and secretive country. And yet Romania has well over 500,000 acres of vines. She makes in excess of 50m. cases of wine a year – and drinks most of it in very poor condition, often with soda water to drown the taste of oxidation. Now, better cellar hygiene and earlier bottling give the country the potential to rival the success of Bulgaria.

Since 1990, the most prosperous winemaking and bottling companies which led the export business have regrouped as shareholders of a private export marketing company with their major overseas agents. They have invited foreign winemakers in. Some individual batches of wine have resulted which show just what these beautifully sited vineyards can do.

Romania's wine-growing regions surround the central Carpathian Mountains. The main centres are Tirnăve, at 1,600 feet on the Transylvanian plateau to the north, Cotnari to the northeast in Moldavia, Vrancea (including the once-famous Panciu, Odobesti and Nicoresti) to the east, Dealul Mare to the southeast; Murfatlar in the extreme southeast by the Black Sea, and in the south Stefăneşti, Drăgăsani and Segarcea. In the west, part of the sandy Banat plain to the west of Timişoara (where the 1989 freedom movement began) carries on the viticultural region and traditions of the Great Hungarian Plain. Round Minis east of Arad and Recaş east of Timişoara some good red international grapes can be found including Pinot Noir. The remainder of the vineyards are stocked with a mixture of international varieties (Merlot and Sauvignon Blanc predominate) and Romania's own white grapes, the Fetească Albă and Regală, Grasă and Tamaioasă, and the red Babeaşcă and Fetească Neagră. Strangely, there is very little Chardonnay. Such as there is can mostly be found in Murfatlar where it has superb but rarely realized potential.

Cotnari produces the most individual wine. Despite its very northerly position near the Ukraine/Moldovan borders, long, fine misty autumn conditions permit white grapes to over-ripen, shrivel, even develop noble rot in some years. Native grapes, Tamăioasă Romanească, Grasă (akin to Furmint and probably the better of the two), Fetească Albă and Francusa are used to produce dessert wines aged in old oak casks.

Tirnave produces a reasonable white blend called Perla de Tirnave and 'varietal' Fetească and 'Riesling' (regrettably mostly Italian/Welsch/Laski rather than Rhein). Undoubtedly the best whites here are made from the rarer Pinot Gris and Gewürztraminer. Muscat Ottonel produces short-lived but highly scented styles which may be sweetened.

Among a sea of very dull whites and some often good (but make sure it is the less usual *brut*) sparkling wine from Panciu, Vrancea's most notable wine is the pale, acidic, brisk red Babească of Nicoresti.

The outstanding 40-mile stretch of south-facing hillslopes of the Dealul Mare overlooking the Bucharest plain specializes in Merlot, Cabernet Sauvignon and the scarcer but potentially fine Pinot Noir. The state experimental station at Valea Calugareasca has a 2,000-acre estate and lies next door to the plant which bottles much of the local production for export. Dionis is a label to look out for: there are some fine reds, especially Merlot, made in the state premises at Ceptura as a result of a joint venture with a French company. Urlat, Tohani, Sahateni are among other names behind which lies some great potential.

Murfatlar, just inland from Constanza on the Black Sea, is traditionally a white- and dessert-wine area. Yields are low, fruit quality is intense but, all too often, good white grapes are left to overripen and produce a clumsy sweetish dessert style wine from the likes of Chardonnay and Pinot Gris. There are, in fact, also excellent quality reds grapes in this area.

In the southern vineyards along the Danube tributaries such as the Olt, flowing down from the Carpathians to the river, Stefăneşti and Drăgăşani are better known for whites, including Sauvignon Blanc, and Segarcea and Sadova for reds including Cabernet Sauvignon. The vineyards of Samburesti are among the best managed and produce all the classics other than Chardonnay.

In all, Romania is a beautiful country except, unfortunately, for the very flat, dusty plains around the capital. It has enormous quality potential throughout its agricultural sector; it has coal, oil and natural gas. It has a steel industry and, indeed, many of its state wineries show the benefits of this as stainless steel is much more common here than elsewhere in Eastern Europe. Much of its infrastructure, especially in communications, is dramatically under-performing even seven years on from the overthrow of the Ceaucescus. Its agricultural output went down to a third of its pre-war total through the disincentive of collective farming and the loss of population to the cities. It would be tragic to lose any more of what could be some of Europe's greatest cool-climate vineyards for lack of a sense of direction.

BULGARIA

O f all the countries in Central and Eastern Europe, Bulgaria has always been most adept at re-programming its wine industry to earn Western currency. Since the late-1970s Bulgarian wine has not been an occasional exotic excursion, but standard fare in several Western markets. It is still the sixth largest world wide exporter behind France, Italy, Germany, Spain and Argentina. Today it offers some of the world's best value for money in familiar flavours – above all in rich Merlot and well-hyped Cabernet Sauvignon, which satisfies palates brought up on red Bordeaux.

Wine is a major preoccupation of the whole country. Over 320,000 acres is vineyard, marginally more planted in white varieties than red. Of the red vineyard the majority is Cabernet or Merlot. The rest is Pamid and such other traditional varieties as Gamza (the Hungarian Kadarka), Melnik and Mavrud, and a little Pinot Noir and Gamay.

The white vineyard caters much more for everyday local drinking and distillation: almost half is the lightly peachy Russian grape, Rkatziteli, backed up by Ugni Blanc, Rizling (here confusingly often referred to as Riesling), Red Misket, Dimiat (or Smederevka) and Muscat Ottonel with so far only nascent plantings of Chardonnay, Rhein Riesling, Sauvignon Blanc and Aligoté alongside small acreages of Tamianka and Gewürztraminer. Of late, progress in the control of the vinification process has conclusively demonstrated that the better white varieties are as much at home here as their red counterparts. Chardonnay is beginning to show its natural superiority with and without the use of new oak casks.

There are five main wine regions. The three major ones are grouped round the mountain range of the Stara Planina which forms the central backbone of the country from Serbia to the Black Sea. The fourth is perched in the high central valleys themselves. Fifth is a small region tucked away around Melnik on the southwest border. Conditions are cooler in the northern region but both north and south can produce good ripe raw material when political conditions permit.

Since 1978 there have been additions to the first 20 subregions officially recognised as appellations (Controliran Regions) for one or more grapes and the number will continue to increase as quality and consistency improve. The Controliran Region wines have to comply with regulations issued by the Government which cover grape varieties, cultivation techniques and vinification technology. Levels of alcohol, acidity and sugar are checked and the wines are approved by the National Tasting Committee. In 1985 a new classification was introduced, the Reserve category, for wines with ageing potential which have been matured in oak.

Wine production in Bulgaria has been industrialized and since 1971, enormous state-run agro-industrial complexes have evolved. Bulgaria's wine exports total up to 85 percent of its wine production (it is now the world's second largest exporter of bottled wines, after France). The land has been privatized and some big vineyards have been split up. As has frequently happened throughout the old Iron Curtain countries, there has been a breakdown of the tidy system of grape delivery which existed when vineyards were tied to a specific winery. There is now something of a free-for-all on the grape market each autumn. A great number of vineyards are in danger of falling out of production altogether. Many wineries, where they could afford it, have had to subsidize growers throughout the year in order to try to ensure that they would have a right to buy the resultant crop. Slowly, in this far from favourable climate, some wineries including Suhindol, Pavlikeni, Sliven and Iambol are managing to go private. The wonder is that the wines themselves are both good and improving; they still offer some of the world's most outstanding value.

EASTERN REGION

This region, between the mountains and the Black Sea, has 30% of Bulgaria's vineyards and specializes in white wines, sparkling wines and brandy. It includes many noted sub-regions, notably Varna, Schumen, Targovishte, and Razgad. The main grapes are Riesling, Rkatziteli, Aligoté, Chardonnay, Misket, Muscat Ottonel, Ugni Blanc, Dimiat and Fetiaska.

The Varna district on the Black Sea was recognized in 1986 as a Controliran Region for Chardonnay and the Schumen district, which is experimenting with fermenting Chardonnay in small oak barrels, has three Controliran Regions producing Chardonnay, Gewürztraminer and Sauvignon Blanc. Preslav, Khan Krum and Targovischte Chardonnays are probably showing the most real quality potential to date.

NORTHERN REGION

The northern region has the River Danube as its northern boundary. It is known for its quality red wines – the main varieties being Gamza (the Kadarka of Hungary), Cabernet Sauvignon and Merlot. The giant state winery of Russe on the Danube's banks controls a lot of potentially good red grapes from all over the region. Its satellite, Dve Mogili ('Twin Peaks') is particularly interesting. The wineries of Suhindol and Pavlikeni (now one private vineyard-owning cooperative) and Pleven in particular produce a lot of reliable Cabernets as well as good Merlots and silkily oak-aged Gamza. Sparkling wine is another speciality of the region, benefiting from its relatively high acid levels. The area has several Controliran Region wines – the best being the Gamza, Cabernet Sauvignon and Merlot of Suhindol and an Aligoté from Lyaskovets (which, like Targovischte, should probably be better known now for its Chardonnay).

SOUTHERN REGION

The southern region grows Cabernet and some Pinot Noir and Merlot but also makes some well-known traditional wines such as Mavrud, Bulgaria's pride, a substantial dark Rhône-like wine needing four years' ageing. The winery at Asenovgrad near Plovdiv has a reputation for Mavrud. Another traditional grape variety, Pamid, makes a rather pallid everyday wine. In fact, however, the region's greatest potential lies more in the richly ripe Merlots of Stambovolo, Liubimetz and the Sakar Mountain region.

SOUTHWEST REGION

A very small and distinct region on the Yugoslav border across the Rhodope Mountains in the southwest of the country. The Melnishki Controliran Region was designated in 1979 for the production of Melnik wine from Harsovo. Bulgarians have the greatest respect for Melnik, its red wine, which they say is so concentrated that you can carry it in a handkerchief. It needs five years' ageing and will last for 15. However, finding a sample of this mythical stuff presents certain difficulties.

SUB-BALKAN REGION

This is the narrow strip south of the Balkan range which includes the famous Sungurlare Valley where the Red Misket is grown, and the Valley of Roses (the source of attar of roses) which specializes in Muscats – Hemus is the brand name to look for. A fair proportion of Rhakziteli is also grown in this region where it can produce cool, delicate white peach aromas.

THE RUSSIAN EMPIRE

The former Soviet Union was the world's third-largest wine producer. It now has just under 2.2m. acres of vines. In late Communist times it was also a considerable net importer and continues to consume much of its own produce. This is despite two enormous hiccups in its progress. First came Gorbachev's reforms which caused nearly half the vineyard to be uprooted in 1985–86 in the drive to reduce alcoholism. (Sales of vodka rose in response.) Second came the post-Communist break-up of the Soviet Union. Ukraine became and remains independent but the remaining nations are more or less regrouped under the CIS banner.

Although a number of people and companies have tried to collaborate with wine producers in these countries, the Western world has seen few, if any, Soviet wines and is still in ignorance of their historical traditions and undoubted potential, mainly because there is no infrastructure to support economical, regular quality production and transport. It is gradually shaping up but is more likely to favour the home market first, because the locals see no reason to change their traditional styles to match the Western palate.

MOLDOVA

President Breznev would come to Moldova to while away a weekend among not only the long-lived local Cabernets but also some of the finest Bordeaux captured from the Germans during the last war. (Today sadly the condition of the old enamel-lined vats simply forces great quantities of the wine to deteriorate through metal contamination.) One look at the dark-soiled rolling vineyards over fine limestone subsoils and one taste of the immature wines is enough to show that this could be a first-class producer, as could its more easterly neighbours. Bottles of the fragrant Cabernet blend Negru de Purkar leave no one in doubt of Moldova's potential.

So far, the only successful Western-style wines have come out via the Hincesti winery with Hugh Ryman's involvement briefly helped by the Australian giant Penfolds. Visitors will find sparkling wines, made from Aligoté, Flor 'sherries' and other dessert wines which can be truly remarkable.

GEORGIA

Though tiny in relation to Russia, Georgia has a far more ancient and original wine culture, with at least 500 indigenous vine varieties. Its most famous wine region is

The vineyards can be found in a band stretching through the countries bordering first the Black Sea and then the Caspian. They are: Moldova (417,000 acres), Ukraine (400,000 acres), BieloRusse (254,000 acres), Georgia (320,000 acres) and on eastward into what might be thought of as more traditionally Muslim terrain, namely Azerbaidjan, Kazakhastan, Tadjikistan, Uzbekistan, Kyrgistan and Turkmenistan, which between them have a total of over 667,000 acres.

A glimpse of past glories appeared in London in 1990 at an auction by Sotheby's of dessert wines from the private estates of the Tsar's and other great families in the Crimea. The muscat wines of the Imperial Massandra estate were outstanding among a variety of very well-made old 'ports', 'sherries', 'madeiras' and even 'Cahorski'.

The Russian republic (including the Crimea) is very much the greatest producer of wines of all qualities, with sparkling wine as its great speciality. Russia's sweet tooth is well-known, but the technical competence displayed, especially in drier *cuvées*, is beyond denial.

Kakhetia, east of Tbilisi, where the climate is at its most continental. The princely estate of Tsinandali was developed in the 19th century to make the finest Kakhetian wines, famous for fragrance and bite – and preferred by the poet Pushkin to burgundy.

Today Tsinandali is the brand name of an adequate dry white; Gurdzhani and Mukuzani are others. Saperavi, Napareuli and Kindzmarauli make some of the best-known reds – although even in Georgia Cabernet Sauvignon is creeping into the repertoire. Of these indigenous grapes Saperavi is worth watching for as it gives a Syrah-like ripeness, with a solid peppery intensity.

To the west, towards the Black Sea coast, Imeretia has a more humid, less extreme climate and a winemaking tradition of its own, with scores of ancient indigenous grape varieties and a preponderance of white wines.

Throughout Georgia private farmers can still be found using methods of pre-classical antiquity. The *kvevri*, a clay fermenting jar buried in the ground, is still found in many properties. Its strongly tannic produce is not for fine palates.

Georgia is also the home of a flourishing sparkling wine industry. Most of the wine is sweet, which is the preferred national taste. The locals drink it in awe-inspiring quantities and its legend has spread to attract a number of major players from the West, including both Champagne and Cava companies, to invest in joint ventures.

GREECE

The ancient Greeks colonized the Mediterranean and the Black Sea with the vine, exporting their wines in exchange for Egyptian grain, Spanish silver and Caucasian timber. In the Middle Ages the Peloponnese and Crete were valued sources of Malmsey sack for northern Europe. The largely alkaline (in places, volcanic) soils and multifarious microclimates of Greece make her a natural country of the vine. With 403,000 acres of grapes (not all for wine) she is a major producer. In 1975, with entry into the EU imminent, there was a move towards varieties and systems of control that would lead to fine wine, and since then there has been very rapid progress.

Under the earlier primitive conditions, with hot fermentations, the best qualities that could be produced were all sweet wines. The Greek taste remained faithful to what appears to be an ancient tradition of adding pine-resin during fermentation to make retsina. It goes too well with Greek cooking to be ignored, but today demand for this wine is falling, except among tourists, as the national palate turns increasingly to the fine Greek wines.

At present Greek wine can usefully be divided into national brands (usually blends), retsina and other traditional and country wines for uncritical first-year drinking, and wines from defined areas now controlled by an appellation system in accordance with EU law. There are 27 such areas. In addition the past few years have seen the development of a number of small but high-quality wine estates experimenting with grape varieties, also often outside the delimited areas, whose wines can only be sold as *vins de table* or *vins de pays*.

The Peloponnese has more than half of Greece's vineyards and produces more than a third of her wine. Patras at the mouth of the Gulf of Corinth is the main wine centre, with four appellations: Muscat, Muscat of Rion, Mavrodaphne and plain Patras. Mavrodaphne can be the most notable of these: a sweet dark red wine of up to 16° alcohol, something in the style of Recioto of Valpolicella, much improved by long maturing. Plain Patras white is for drinking young. Two other appellations of the Peloponnese are interesting: the region of Nemea for strong red made of the Agiorgitiko (St George) grape and Mantinia for a delicate, spicy white. The main Nemea producer is the cooperative, which uses the name Hercules (the conqueror of the dreaded Nemean lion).

The 45,000 acres of vines in the north of Greece, from Thrace in the east through Macedonia to Epirus, appear to have most potential for quality. Its appellations are: Naoussa (west of Thessaloniki) for potent though balanced and nicely tannic red; Aminteion, at 2,000 feet in the mountains of Macedonia, producing lighter red; Zitsa (near Joannina in Epirus) for a light mountain white of Debina grape; and Metsovo in Epirus, which was replanted after phylloxera with Cabernet Sauvignon. The most important recent development was the planting of the Sithonian peninsula, the middle one of the three fingers of Halkidiki, with Cabernet and other grapes, by the firm of Carras.

The island of Crete is second to the Peloponnese in acreage, but only third in production (Attica has far more productive vineyards). Crete has four local appellations, all for dark and more or less heavy and sweet reds: Daphnes, Archanes, Sitia and Peza – Peza being the seat of the island's biggest producer, its cooperative. The grapes are Kotsifali, Mandilari and Liatico, old Cretan strains sometimes just called Mavro Romeiko.

Attica (including mainland Boetia and the island of Euboea) is Greece's most productive wine area, overwhelmingly for retsina, but there are now an increasing number of high-quality estates – Hatzimicheli, Semeli and Strofilia among them.

Next in importance for acreage and quality comes Cephalonia, which with the other Ionian (western) islands musters 25,000 acres. Cephalonia is known for its dry white Robola (exceptional from Gentilini), its red Mavrodaphne, and its Muscat. Zakinthos to the south makes a white Verdea.

The central mainland region of Thessaly also has 25,000 acres of vineyards, but only one appellation, Rapsani, a middle-weight red from Mt Olympus.

The wines of the Aegean islands, the Dodecanese and the Cyclades, have more renown, notably the pale gold Muscat of Samos, the luscious Vino Santo and dry white of the volcanic Santorini, the Muscat of Lemnos, and the sweet Malvasia and Muscat of Rhodes. (Rhodes' best wines are white Villare and red Cava Emery.)

Malvasia is grown on many islands and is often their best product. Other island wines with esoteric reputations are the very dark red Paros and the Santa Mavra of Levkas, whose grape, the Vertzani, is unknown elsewhere.

Leading Greek Producers

Achaia-Clauss

Patras.

Once the biggest and most famous Greek wine house, but now experiencing fierce competition from other expanding producers. Demestica is their best-known wine. Otherwise, a large variety of dry and sweet wines from vineyards in the Peloponnese and Crete, and a successful *vin de pays*, Peloponnesiakos – red and white.

J. Boutari & Son

Naoussa, Thessaloniki.

Long established producer who has grown rapidly in recent years, covering several appellations with new wineries at each locality. The main winery is in Naoussa specializing in Naoussa wines. Top red: Grande Reserve Boutari.

Andrew P. Cambas

Kantza, nr Athens.

Another long established producer who has wineries in

Kantza and Mantinia, and who produces a wide range of table and sparkling wines, as well as ouzo and brandy.

Domaine Carras

Sithonia, Halkidiki.
Developed primarily in the 1960s this now major estate, created by John Carras with advice from Professor Emile Peynaud of Bordeaux, produces the well-known Château Carras, a blend of the Cabernets Sauvignon and Franc with Merlot and Limnio, matured in French oak. There are several other labels under the appellation Côtes de Meliton. Carras also makes non-appellation wines, including Ambelos.

Gentilini

Minies, Cephalonia.
A small family estate, owned by Nicholas Cosmetatos, producing very fines wines mainly from the indigenous Robola. A cask-aged version (Fumé) is also produced.

Ktima Hatzimichali

Atlantes, Athens-Lamia.
75-acre private estate owned by Dimitri Hatzimichali, which prodes a range of wines from indigenous and international varieties.

D. Kourtakis

Athens.
A family merchant house. Brandname is Kouros. There are very successful red and white Vins de Crète and Mavrodaphne of Patras made here. They also produce large quantities of the international best-selling retsina from the Savatiano grape of Attica.

Chateau Lazaridi

Drama, N. Greece.
Private wine estate of one of two brothers producing fine wines in Drama. They use noble varieties, such as Cabernet Sauvignon, but have also brought home varieties from southern Italy which originated in Greece.

Ktima Kosta Lazaridi

Drama, N. Greece.
Main label is Amethystos, red, white and rosé. Also a high-class Tsiporou and interesting experimentation with oak, particularly with Sauvignon Blanc.

Ktima Mercouri

Nr Olympia, W. Peloponnese.
An old, private, family estate with an interesting wine museum. The main production is Domaine Mercouri, an outstanding red made from the Refosco grape, taken from Friuli in 1870.

Oenoforos

Selinous, nr Corinth.
A recently developed small estate producing fresh, long-lived, whites from amazingly high vineyards overlooking the Gulf of Corinth.

Chateau Pegasus

Naoussa.
The two Markovitis brothers use the native Xynomavro from their small estate to make a first-class oak-aged Naoussa red.

Semeli

Stamata, nr Athens.
Small family winery developed in the late 1970s. Produces quality wines both from traditional Greek grapes, like Savatiano and Agiorgitiko, as well as grapes from the estate's own Cabernet Sauvignon for the Château Semeli – winner of the Grand Prix d'Honneur in Bordeaux in 1995.

Skouras Winery

Argos.
Owned by George Skouras, a highly imaginative and talented winemaker producing magnificent Nemea, but also experimenting with Cabernet, Chardonnay and Viognier.

Strofilia

Anavisson, Attica.
Exciting red, white and rosé from a small estate near to Cape Sounion. The proprietors also run an excellent winebar, 'Strofilia', near the centre of Athens.

Tsantali

Aios Pavlos, Halkidiki.
Second-generation Macedonian merchant house which made its name with Olympic ouzo. A wide range of wines, some of which originate on Mt Athos and appear as *vins de pays* under the Agioritiko label; others from various appellation areas, such as the fine Rapsani and Cava Tsantalis.

Samos Union of Cooperatives

Samos.
With two wineries, this union of about 300 growers produces remarkable muscat wines which are either naturally sweet or fortified, and exported widely. Top of the range, the Samos Nectar, made from sun-dried grapes, is rich and golden, maturing continuously and darkening in bottle.

Union of Ioannina Cooperatives

Zitsa, Ioannina.
The growers from six mountainous villages in Epiros cultivate the grape Debina and produce Zitsa, both still and semi-sparkling.

Naoussa Wine Producers Cooperative

Naoussa.
Large cooperative in western Macedonia producing mainly strong, above-average red wines from the Xynomavro grape, under the labels of Naoussa and Vaeni.

Nemea Wine Producers Cooperative

Nemea.
Large cooperative in the Peloponnese producing mainly red wines from the Agiorgitiko grape, under the labels of Nemea and Hercules.

CYPRUS

Wine culture in Cyprus, most easterly of the Mediterranean islands, has had considerable changes in fortune over the centuries. Cypriot wines were famed throughout classical, Byzantine and early medieval times. Then came three centuries of Islamic rule, and production went into dramatic decline. British government from 1878 brought stability – and a market.

Modern Cyprus has no great range of wines to offer, but what she does she does well, producing low-cost 'sherries', both dry and sweet, modelled on the Spanish (the term Cyprus sherry can no longer appear on the labels of wines destined for sale in the EU), smooth dry red and white table wines and her own extremely luscious liqueur-wine, Commandaria, the modern successor to the classical wine Nama which was so highly prized over two and a half thousand years ago. Commandaria is to Cyprus what Constantia is to South Africa or Tokay is to Hungary.

Cyprus has until very recently been intensely conservative about grape varieties. Having never been afflicted with phylloxera, and intending to stay untainted, she spurned new-fangled introductions and planted only three grapes: Mavro the black, Xynisteri the white (which account for the vast majority of planting), and Muscat of Alexandria. Today there is a small but increasing volume of varietal wine made from international grapes, and wines from specific regions of the island. In 1990, after some 30 years of strictly controlled trials with non-native grapes, a few were made available for commerical cultivation. Among them Grenache, Carignan and a minute amount of Cabernet Sauvignon now produce varietal wines; Malvasia Grossa and Palomino (of Jerez) are usually used in blends with the indigenous white varieties. The quest for better wine has renewed interest in the island's less-planted native varieties, the black Maratheftico and Opthalmo. The former is difficult to cultivate but can produce outstanding wines. The traditional varieties can also produce good wines, Mavro particularly from high-altitude sites, provided its yield is restricted. Xynisteri has to be harvested most carefully as the grapes are prone to oxidization.

All the island's vineyards lie on the south, mainly limestone, slopes of the Troodos Mountains, between 800 and nearly 5,000 feet, the best located above 3,250 feet,

some on soils of igneous origin. Since 1990 total grape acreage has decreased from a peak of over 124,000 acres as the industry comes to terms with overproduction and a declining export market for its fortified and basic table wines. Most Cyprus wine is still made by a small number of very large wineries in the coastal towns of Limassol and Paphos (convenient for export) but as part of the quality drive the Cypriot government has supported the building of small modern wineries within the vineyard areas themselves. The wines from these locations are just becoming commercially available.

The island's most distinctive wine, Commandaria, was given full legal protection of origin and production in 1993. Its delimited region comprises 14 of the higher altitude wine-producing villages on the Troodos slopes. The most famous are Kalokhorio, Zoopiyi and Yerasa. The best Commandaria is made from pure Xynisteri – a light brown wine of considerable finesse which can be drunk young. Other commercially more important wines blend Xynisteri with Mavro to make a dark tawny wine, which can be superb after five or more years in barrel. The grapes are simply sun-dried for at least a week in the vineyard, then pressed and fermented. Long before all the grape sugars are turned into alcohol, fermentation stops naturally, giving a wine of at least 10° alcohol. Once fermentation is complete, the wine is fortified – usually to 15°, although the legal limit is 20°. Maturation takes place in oak casks in Limassol and Paphos for a minimum of two years.

Four concerns dominate the Cyprus trade. KEO produces the smooth red Othello and Commandaria 'St John', as well as one of the best dry Cyprus 'sherries', Keo Fino, and light table wines using the Laona label. Its slightly fizzy Bellapais is a refreshing white. ETKO makes the Emva range of fortified wines as well as a good white from Xynisteri called Nefeli and possibly the island's finest red, INO, a single-estate Cabernet, produced in tiny quantities. Loel has a sound red Hermes, Commandaria Alasia and a dry white made from the Palomino grape. Some of the best Cyprus brandies are also distilled by Loel. The cooperative SODAP (founded in 1844) has as its flagship wine the red Afames. It also makes dry white under the Arsinoe brand and Commandaria 'St Barnabas'.

TURKEY

I f Noah's vineyard on the slopes of Mount Ararat was really the first, Turkey can claim to be the original home of wine. Hittite art of 4000 BC is possibly better evidence that Anatolia (central Turkey) used wine in highly cultivated ways. In relation to such a time span the long night of Islam has been scarcely more of an interruption than Prohibition was in the United States. For since the 1920s Turkey has again been making good wines; much better than her lack of a reputation leads us to expect. One of the most surprising bottles of fine wine I have ever drunk was a 1929 Turkish red – at a friend's house in Bordeaux. I took it for a Bordeaux of that famous vintage.

Turkey has 1.5 million acres of vineyards but only 3 percent of their produce is made into wine – the rest are table grapes. Kemal Ataturk founded the 20th-century wine industry in his drive to modernize the country, although it is held back by lack of a domestic market: 99 percent of the population is Muslim. The state monopoly, Tekel, is much the biggest producer, with 21 wineries handling wines from all regions and dominating exports, particularly with popular bulk wines to Scandinavia. But there are over 100 private wineries, two at least with very high standards.

The main wine regions are Trakya, the Thrace–Marmara region on the European side of the Bosphorus, the Aegean coast around Izmir, central Anatolia around Ankara and eastern Anatolia. The majority of the grapes are local varieties (of which there are over a thousand) whose names are unknown in the West, except in Trakya, where Cinsaut, Gamay and Semillon (supported by Clairette) make the best-known red and white. A Gamay red called Hosbag (from Tekel) is not remarkable, but Trakya Kirmisi, made of the Turkish Papazharasi and Adakarasi varieties, is a good vigorous wine. *Kirmisi* is Turkish for red and *Beyaz* for white; *Sarap* for wine. Trakya Beyaz (a dry Semillon) is one of the most popular exports.

Of the private firms Doluca and Kavaklidere are the leaders. Doluca, at Mürefte on the Sea of Marmara, founded in 1926 (the first in modern Turkey), has well-made reds: Villa Neva and Villa Doluca of Gamay, Papazharasi and Cabernet. In my experience this is the best Turkish red. Doluca also makes oak-aged Semillon, unaged Semillon and some 'Johannisberg Riesling'. Kavaklidere, the largest independent firm, is based in Ankara but sources grapes from as far apart as Thrace and eastern Anatolia. It concentrates on Anatolia's indigenous grapes, producing Yakut and Dikmen, red blends of Bogazkere, Kalecik Karese and Oküzgözü (though Yakut may contain some Cabernet), and both sweet and dry whites from Narince, Emire, Sultanine (with a very fresh Primeur) and Cankaya. Eastern Anatolia is also the home of the best known of Turkish reds, the heavy and powerful Buzbag, made of Bogazkere near Elazig. This is the produce of Tekel, the state enterprise, and remains perhaps Turkey's most original and striking wine.

The Aegean region counts Cabernet and Merlot (known, I believe, as 'Bordo') among its reds, along with Carignan and Calkarasi. Most of the white is made of Sultanye, the seedless table grape with no real winemaking potential. Some Semillon and Muscat is grown – the Muscat probably the best.

THE LEVANT

LEBANON

What wine might be in the Levant, were it not for the followers of the Prophet, is a tantalizing topic. In 1840 Cyrus Redding had heard tell (he certainly had not been there) that 'Syria makes red and white wine of the quality of Bordeaux'. But there is current evidence that the eastern Mediterranean can make great wine. Noah's ancient land of Canaan, now the Bekaa Valley, emerged in the 1970s as a producer which compares with Bordeaux, just as Redding had reported.

In the early 19th century its reputation was for dry white '*vin d'or*'. In 1857 Jesuits founded a vast underground winery at Ksara, northeast of Beirut, with over a mile of barrel-filled natural tunnels. It is still the largest (and oldest) Lebanese winery, producing a very good fresh white. But the estate that fluttered the dovecots of the wine trade is Château Musar, at Ghazir, 16 miles north of Beirut. It was founded in the 1930s by Gaston Hochar, with vineyards in the Bekaa Valley. In 1959 his son Serge, after training in Bordeaux, became winemaker. Bottles started appearing in London. In 1982 he showed a range of vintages going back to the 1940s which proved beyond doubt that the region can make extra-ordinarily fine and long-lived reds based on Cabernet Sauvignon with some Cinsaut and Syrah, aged in *barriques* – not at all unlike big Bordeaux of ripe vintages. Whites include an oaked version from the indigenous Obaideh grape, similar to Chardonnay which is surprisingly capable of ageing a decade and more. During the civil war of the 1980s, Hochar, stoically carrying on making fine wine with Syrian tanks in his vineyards, became a figure of legend in the wine world.

Other Bekaa Valley producers include Kekfraya, which makes early-drinking wines, among them a Cinsaut-Carignan blend called Rouge de K (Château Kekfraya is reserved for the best years only) as well as rosé and white wines.

ISRAEL

Winemaking in Israel dates back to ancient times, although the modern industry was established at the end of the 19th century with a gift to the State from Baron Edmond de Rothschild – the founding of wineries at Rishon le Zion, south of Tel Aviv, and Zichron Ya'acov, south of Haifa. These two wineries, which remain the largest in Israel, controlling 60 percent of the business, are now part of the Société Cooperative Vigneronne des Grandes Caves, marketing wines under the Carmel brand.

In total Israel now has over 5,000 acres of vineyards. The first to be planted were concentrated in the hot coastal regions of Samson and Shomron (which is still the largest wine-growing region) with predominantly Carignan, Grenache and Semillon grapes to make sweet sacramental wine. Interest was primarily kosher.

In the mid-1970s the then principal of the University of California at Davis, Cornelius Ough, identified the cool-climate Golan Heights as an ideal location for wine grapes. The improvement in quality was considerable. There are now vineyards up to 3,600 feet, on a range of volcanic-basaltic soils in the Golan Heights and the Upper Galilee, producing the grapes for Israel's best wines.

The introduction of classic varieties, first Cabernet Sauvignon, then Merlot and Chardonnay, in the 1980s heralded the beginning of a quality-wine industry and a move to producing dry table and sparkling wines that could compete internationally. The Golan Heights Winery, in the small town of Katzrin high up in the Golan, leads the way, making oak-aged Chardonnay and Cabernet (Yarden is their premier label), classic-method sparkling wines and complex Merlot. Barkan, Israel's third biggest winery, makes promising Emerald Riesling, Sauvignon Blanc and Cabernet Sauvignon. Baron Wine Cellars in Binyamina is a small family estate winery which produces particularly good whites, including Sauvignon Blanc and dry Muscat, as well as brandy. There are now at least 21 wineries, many of them boutique-size, producing 25 million bottles annually, 60 percent of it white.

NORTH AFRICA

Nearly half a century ago North Africa's wine-producing countries, Tunisia, Algeria and Morocco, accounted for no less than two-thirds of the entire international wine trade. Algeria was by far the biggest producer of the three, with most of the vast quantity being exported to Europe (mainly to France) as blending wine. Independence from France resulted in an immediate decline, for there was practically no domestic market, and the trend has been either to pull up or neglect the vineyards. The drive, however, is towards improving wine quality from the best sites for export.

TUNISIA

The institution of an Office du Vin in 1970 marked the start of Tunisia's coordinated plan to make wines of export quality. Her vineyard area has been reduced from 124,000 in its heyday to some 22,000 acres, all in the vicinity of Tunis (and ancient Carthage) on the north coast. There are currently 13 state-owned, 13 cooperative and 10 private cellars offering a dozen wines for export. Muscats are the most characteristic wines of the country, as they are of the Sicilian islands lying not far off-shore. Reds, rosés and whites are made of French Midi-type grapes, in many cases using modern methods. As in Algeria the pale rosés are often the most attractive.

The biggest producer is the Union des Cooperatives Viticoles de Tunisie (route de Mornag, Djebel Djelloud). The union makes an unusual dry white Muscat, Muscat de Kelibia, from vineyards at the tip of Cap Bon to the northeast. It is highly aromatic, not overstrong at 11.8° but nonetheless a difficult wine to enjoy with a meal. Its best-quality red is Magon, from Tébourba in the valley of the Oued (River) Medjerdah, west of Tunis. The Cinsaut and Mourvèdre in this 12° wine give it both roundness and greater personality than the standard 11.5° Coteaux de Carthage. Other Union wines include Château Mornag (both red and rosé) from the Mornag hills east of Tunis, a pale dry Gris de Tunisie, a blend of Grenache and Cinsaut, from the same region, and a dry Muscat-scented rosé called Sidi Rais.

The most notable wines of the state-owned Office des Terres Domaniales are the red Château Thibar, from the hills 85 miles west of Tunis up the Medjerdah Valley, and Sidi Selem from Kanguet, near Mornag. Other noteworthy producers include the Société Lamblot for their 12° red Domaine Karim from the Coteaux d'Utique, near the sea north of Tunis, Château Feriani, which makes one of Tunisia's tastiest red wines from the same area, Héritiers René Lavau for their Koudiat, another strong red from Tébourba, and the Société des Vins Tardi at Aïn Ghellal, north of Tébourba, for their Royal Tardi, which contains a touch of Pinot Noir.

Perhaps better than any of these are the strong sweet dessert Muscats which come under the appellation Vin Muscat de Tunisie.

ALGERIA

The biggest and most intensely planted of France's former North African colonies has seen a reduction in her wine-grape vineyard from 900,000 acres, its total of the 1960s, to under 200,000 today (almost the equivalent of Germany's present total) – and her productivity has gone down by an even greater proportion. Most of this has been achieved by converting the fertile plains to cereals and concentrating efforts on the hill vineyards which produced superior wine in French days. A dozen 'Crus' were indeed given VDQS status before independence.

Seven regions are recognized by the Office Nationale de Commercialisation des Produits Viticoles as quality zones. They are all located in the hills about 50 miles inland in the two western provinces of Oran and Alger. Of the two, Oran has always been the bulk producer, with three-quarters of Algeria's vines. The ONCV has standard labels that reveal nothing about the origin of the wine except its region – and in the case of its prestige brand, Cuvée du Président, not even that. Le Président is a matured, faintly claret-like wine which, when last tasted, I did not find as good as the best regional offerings.

The western quality zone, the Coteaux de Tlemcen, lies close to the Moroccan border, covering north-facing sandstone hills at 2,500 feet. Red, rosé and white wines are well made: strong, very dry but soft in the style the Algerians have mastered. The rosés and whites in particular have improved enormously with cool fermentation.

The Monts du Tessala at Sidi-bel-Abbès to the northeast seem rather less distinguished; certainly less so than the Coteaux de Mascara, whose red wines in colonial days were frequently passed off as burgundy. Mascara reds are powerful and dark with real body, richness of texture and, wood-aged as they are sold today, a considerable aroma of oak and spice. A certain crudeness marks the finish. This I have not found in the Mascara white, dry though it is; it would be creditable in the South of France: pleasantly fruity, not aromatic but smooth and individual – probably as good as any white wine made in North Africa.

At Dahra the hills approach the sea. The former French VDQS Crus of Robert, Rabelais and Renault (now known as Taughrite, Aïn Merane and Mazouna) make smooth, dark and full-bodied reds and a remarkable rosé with a fresh almost cherry-like smell, light and refreshing to drink – a skilful piece of winemaking. Further east and further inland, in the province of Al-Jazair (Algiers), the capital, the Coteaux du Zaccar make slightly lighter, less fruity wines. Again the rosé, though less fruity than the Dahra, is well made. South of Zaccar and higher, at 4,000 feet, the Médéa hills are cooler, and finer varieties are grown along with the standard Cinsaut, Carignan and Grenache. Cabernet and Pinot Noir go into Médéa blends, which have less flesh and more finesse than Dahra or Mascara. Easternmost of the quality zones is Aïn Bessem Bouira, making relatively light (11.5°) reds and what some consider Algeria's best rosés.

MOROCCO

The vineyards of Morocco now cover only 35,000 acres. It has the tightest organization and the highest standards of the three North African wine countries. The few wines that are 'AOG' (Appellation d'Origine Garantie) have similar controls to French appellation wines, strictly applied. They are produced by a central organization, SODEVI, which includes the important cooperative union of Meknès, and are bottled and sold by a Moroccan company in Brussels, the Comptoir des Vins du Maroc (Avenue des Arts 20, 1040 Bruxelles).

Four regions of Morocco produce fair wines, but by far the best and biggest is the Fez/Meknès area at 1,500–2,000 feet in the northern foothills of the middle Atlas Mountains, where the regions of Sais, Beni Sadden, Zerkhoun, Beni M'Tir and Guerrouane are designated. The last two have achieved remarkable reds of Cinsaut, Carignan and Grenache, respectively sold abroad as Tarik and Chantebled (and in Morocco as Les Trois Domaines). Tarik is the bigger and more supple of the two, but both are smooth, long and impressive. Guerrouane also specializes in an AOG *vin*

gris, a very pale dry rosé of Cinsaut and Carignan, which substitutes well for the white wines Morocco lacks. SODEVI at Meknès makes sound non-AOG red and rosé under the name Aïn Souala.

A little wine, but none of consequence, is made in the Berkane/Oujda area to the east near the Algerian border. The other principal areas are around Rabat, on the coastal plain, in the regions of Gharb, Chellah, Zemmour and Zaer. The brand names Dar Bel Amri, Roumi and Sidi Larbi, formerly used for pleasant soft reds from these zones, have been abandoned in favour of the regional names.

Further south down the coast the Casablanca region has three wine zones: Zennata, Sahel and Doukkala. The first produces a solid 12° red marketed as Ourika. South of Casablanca the firm of Sincomar makes the standard drinking of every thirsty visitor, the Gris de Boulaouane. Boulaouane is the archetypal North African refresher: very pale, slightly orange, dry, faintly fruity, extremely clean and altogether suited to steamy Casablanca nights.

ASIA

The wine grape has been grown in the East for centuries. Chinese gardeners in the 2nd century knew how to make wine and did so. So did the Arabs, until they renounced alcohol in the 8th century – at least in theory. Afghan vineyards supplied the Indian Moghul court in the 16th century.

But wine never became part of daily life in these countries, unlike the West. The reason, perhaps, is the nature of their cuisine. Strongly seasoned dishes are best washed down by a simple refreshing liquid – even if each course is regaled by the local spirit. For all that, there are the beginnings of a modern industry in several Asian nations. Wines from Japan, India and China reach Western markets but Thailand, South Korea and Indonesia now have nascent industries, principally for local consumption. Even Nepal has 5 acres of *vinifera* – the world's highest vineyard – while the tiny Himalayan kingdom of Bhutan has ventured into wine-making under the patronage of its royal family.

CHINA

Vines were growing in China some 200 years before they reached the great regions of France. Wine, often sweet and fortified, has been consumed at Chinese banquets for centuries, but it is also used for medicinal purposes, infused with plants, herbs and, more exotically, animal organs, rodents and reptiles.

The practice of viticulture spread over the centuries throughout central and northwest China. The Autonomous Region of Xinjiang, in the far northwest, accounts for almost a quarter of the 350,000 acres of vines in China and for a third of the 1.5 million tonnes of grapes currently produced, but nearly all of the fruit is eaten fresh or as raisins. The major wine-producing regions are in the northeast – in Shandong, Hebei and Jiangsu provinces, and around Beijing and Tianjin.

The modern industry is largely the product of foreign intervention. Under its 'Four Modernizations' programme, beginning in the late 1970s, the Chinese government actively courted foreign interest in the modernization of its wine industry. The first was Rémy Martin. In 1980 Rémy teamed with a provincial farm bureau to establish a large-scale modern winery in Tianjin. Its Dynasty label quickly rivalled the longer-established Great Wall, now also with a foreign joint-venture partner. It has subsequently become the market leader among the Western-style domestic wines, with sales of 13 million bottles annually.

In the mid-1980s two further foreign joint ventures established large-scale plantings of premium European varieties. The Hua Dong (East China) winery at Qingdao on the northeast seaboard in Shandong Province was set up by Hong Kong-based investors. Hiram Walker is now the foreign partner. Dragon Seal Wines is a joint venture between Pernod Ricard and the Beijing Friendship Winery. Both Hua Dong and Dragon Seal are now leading brands. The Marco Polo Winery in Hangzhou (the origin of willow-pattern porcelain) is a joint venture between Italian interests and a local rice-winemaker, producing the Summer Palace range of wines. And in a significant move up-market, Rémy Martin launched a premium sparkling wine, Imperial Court, in 1992. It is made from the classic champagne varieties grown at Rémy's Shen Ma Winery near Shanghai.

China's wine-grape production is currently some 300,000 tonnes, and output is growing. Five large, long-established, wineries account for just under a quarter of the total. The Changu Yu Winery at Yantai in Shandong is the largest, producing almost 30,000 tonnes a year. The others – Beijing Yeguangbei, Lianyungang (Jiangsu), Great Wall and Tong Hua (Jilin) – make about the same volume combined. Their production is a mix of traditional style and more recently Western-style wines. Some now import bulk wine for blending purposes or for bottling locally. In all, there are at least 200 smaller wineries, possibly many more, but only a handful are known outside China, mostly those with foreign interests.

Native grape varieties are used to make most of China's wine. Best known is the Dragon's Eye, the grape used to make Great Wall. Beichun, a hybrid of the *Vitis amurensis* species native to north China, is suited to the harsh climate of its border region. Other varieties are being tried, especially Rkatsiteli, Muscat Hamburg (the backbone of the Dynasty operation) and Italian Riesling. Most impressionable of all are the wines being made from the more recently introduced classic varieties: Chardonnay, Riesling, Pinots Noir and Meunier, Cabernet Sauvignon and Gamay. Dragon Seal and Hua Dong have earned medals for their white wines against international competition. In the years ahead, the map of the world of classic wines may have to be considerably redrawn.

INDIA

India's first modern winemaking concern, the Andhra Winery and Distillery was established in 1966 at Malkajgiri, Hyderabad, in the state of Andhra Pradesh. It is still the country's largest.

What caused a stir, though, was the launch by a Franco-Indian firm in 1985 of Omar Khayyám, a sparkling wine based on Chardonnay, made at Náráyangoan near Poona in the Majarashtra Hills, southeast of Bombay. A sweeter Marquise de Pompadour followed and a slightly drier style, Princess Jaulke. There are plans to export up to 2 million bottles, and to add still Chardonnay and a Cabernet. Cabernet is already being grown in Grover Vineyards in the Dodballapur Hills near Bangalore.

INDONESIA

The solitary winemaking enterprise in Indonesia, Hatten Wines, is located on the tourist resort island of Bali. It relies on black Isabella (*Vitis labrusca*) grapes grown in vineyards a few miles from the city of Singaraja at the island's northern tip where the slopes provide some respite from the tropical heat and humidity. So far, small batches of a medium-dry rosé have been produced but Hatten's French winemaker is now experimenting with a sparkling wine.

JAPAN

The Daizenji Temple at Katsunuma, in the central Honshu prefecture of Yamanashi west of Tokyo, is the spiritual home of Japan's wine industry. Legend has it that the first vines were planted here in the 8th century by a holy man, although early interest in the grape, however, was probably for the medicinal value of the fruit itself. Winemaking came much later, in the 19th century, although Yamanashi remained at the centre and is home to the great majority of the modern 30-odd serious winemaking enterprises. Other significant wine-grape producing regions are Nagano, an adjacent prefecture to the west; Yamagate, further to the north on Honshu island; and Hokkaidò, the large island at the northern extremity of the country.

Growers must contend with unsuitable growing conditions – monsoonal weather patterns (central and southern regions), a long severe winter (the north), drainage problems and acid soils – and high costs. Overwhelmingly the focus of Japanese viticulture is on the growing of grapes for the table, rather than on providing top-grade raw materials for winemaking. This is reflected in the varieties grown and in viticultural practices.

Vitis labrusca varieties and hybrids, introduced over the course of the 19th century from North America, account for almost 80 percent of Japan's total of some 64,000 acres under vine. Kôshû, the local white and the *Vitis vinifera* descendant of the original vines planted at Katsunuma in the 8th century, provides the backbone of the industry's winemaking identity, if not the bulk of the wine produced. It is a heavy-bearing vine, producing big round pink-tinged berries with which winemakers habitually do battle to extract flavour and body in an almost colourless wine.

European varieties have been trialled since the 1960s. Seibel, a variety which looked promising in the experiments, was successfully crossed with the native vine to create a new variety called Kiyomi. It produces a more conventional though strongly acidic wine bearing some resemblance to Pinot Noir.

In more recent experimentation Kiyomi has been crossed back to the native vine to produce a new commercial hybrid, Kiyomai, which will not need to be buried in soil for protection during the severe winter, as is the case with other varieties, Kiyomi included. The northern European varieties such as Müller-Thurgau and Zweigelt may well prove to be suited to the harsh winter conditions in Hokkaidò.

The surprise is that there are some premium local wines (Sémillon, Chardonnay, Cabernet, Merlot and Kôshû) now being made in an attempt to keep pace with imports. Five huge, diversified beverage conglomerates, which together account for three-quarters of total output, dominate the industry. The brewer Suntory produces the most interesting (and costly) of all: Château Lion, a red Bordeaux-blend, and a very good Sémillon dessert wine. It vies for top position with soft-drinks giant Sanraku, which sells particularly good Merlot and Cabernet under the Mercian label. Manns Wine, a subsidiary of soy-saucemaker Kikkoman, is emphasizing the local varieties Kôshû, Dragon's Eye and local-Euro crosses which are adapted to Japan's rainy climate, as well as Chardonnay and a French-oaked Cabernet. Another brewer, Sapporo (Polaire label) and Kyowa Hakko Kogyo (Ste Neige label) are other big players. Smaller, family-owned wineries are likewise concentrated in Yamanashi, among them Marufuji (Rubiat label), Shirayuri (L'Orient), Maruki and Château Lumière. Such quality wines are, and are likely to remain, the exceptions: most wine labelled as 'Japanese' is blended with imports from South America and Eastern Europe.

SOUTH KOREA

South Korea has a wine industry of sorts. *Majuang* is the generic name for all local wine, mostly made from low-quality imported bulk wine with some locally grown Seibel and Muscat Hamburg grapes added for 'authenticity'.

THAILAND

The rapidly growing market for wine in Thailand has spawned one local winemaking venture so far. Château de Loei is a 300-acre vineyard and winery at Phurua in the cooler Loei River district in northern Thailand, close to the border with Laos. Château de Loei settled on Chenin Blanc as the base for its first commercial wine, released in 1995. Small quantities of red wine, made mainly from Shiraz, were available from the second vintage in 1996.

Total production at this stage is less than 4,000 cases per vintage, but substantial expansion is planned for the future. Prohibitive taxes and duties on imported wine provide a big incentive to meeting the challenge of growing wine grapes successfully in this part of the tropics.

UNITED STATES

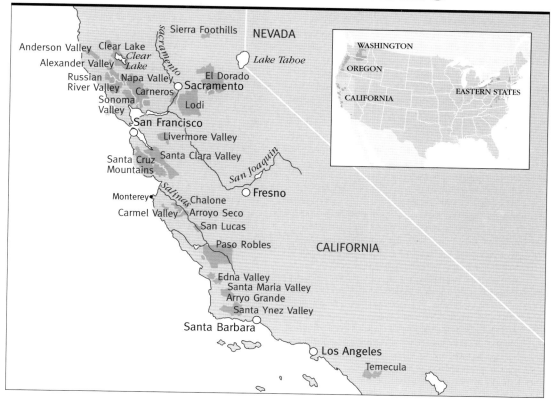

Anderson Valley
Clear Lake
Clear Lake
Alexander Valley
Russian River Valley
Napa Valley
Sonoma Valley
Carneros
Sacramento
Lodi
San Francisco
Livermore Valley
Santa Cruz Mountains
Santa Clara Valley
San Joaquin
Monterey
Chalone
Arroyo Seco
Carmel Valley
San Lucas
Paso Robles
Edna Valley
Santa Maria Valley
Arryo Grande
Santa Ynez Valley
Santa Barbara
Los Angeles
Temecula

Sierra Foothills
NEVADA
Lake Tahoe
El Dorado
Sacramento
Salinas
Fresno
CALIFORNIA

WASHINGTON
OREGON
CALIFORNIA
EASTERN STATES

Until the late 1960s it was true to say that wine-growing was an exotic activity that had only succeeded in gaining footholds on the fringes of North America. The distribution of all American wine was regulated (as it still is) by the Bureau of Alcohol, Tobacco and Firearms, as though it were an ignitable, if not explosive, substance. Wine-drinking was an infrequent, low-profile, even faintly suspect activity. Prohibition had almost snuffed out the promise of healthy Americans, free of neuroses, freely accepting the happy legacy of Mediterranean culture.

During the past forty years both the production and consumption of wine have vastly increased. In the world league of wine-producers the USA is now fifth, with California contributing 95% to its total, and regularly makes approximately a quarter as much wine as France or Italy, the

two giants of the wine world. Imports have soared. The per capita consumption has quadrupled from a mere two and a half bottles to steady at 11 a year.

The figure is still modest, and the neurosis has not entirely departed, but wine has finally permeated to America's soul as an essential part of the good life. Almost every state has aspiring winegrowers; a dozen have a wine industry. But it is the emphasis put on wine in restaurants and hotels, in publications and publicity, which proves that a great change has taken place. White wine is now a normal request as a 'cocktail'. America in fact has at last developed its own wine culture, with its own references, a budding appellation system, rating systems and indigenous ideas about the use of wine with food. What is more, it is successfully exporting aspects of this new thinking to the rest of the world.

CALIFORNIA

It now seems so natural to include California in the shortlist of the world's top winelands that it bears repetition that this status is relatively new. The 1970s was the decade when California decisively took up her position in the world of

wine. She had had what proved to be a false start, though a very promising one, a century earlier. An adolescent America was not ready for what she (and wine in general) had to offer. The generation of winemakers that followed the repeal of Prohibition did indispensable groundwork for an industry that appeared to be remarkably friendless. Hardly anyone was prepared for the impact when in the late 1960s Americans started to change their habits, to look outwards for new ideas, to start thinking about their environment, their diet and their health, and to discover that they had a well of the world's most satisfactory beverage in their own back yard.

From the early 1970s on, growth has been so rapid and change so breathless that one of the observers and critics closest to the scene in California, Bob Thompson, has compared an attempt to follow it to 'taking a census in a rabbit warren'. The figures hardly express the changes. In 1970 there were 220 wineries; in 1982, 591, in 1997, some 820. Wine-grape acreage has stabilized at around 300,000 acres, up from 170,000 in 1970. But beneath these figures, impressive as they are, everything was in ferment: grapes, men, priorities, areas, tanks and philosophy. They still are.

Predictably the other-drink businesses – brewers, distillers and soft-drink manufacturers – have moved in to control what they can of the mass-market production, though Gallo, the company that has done most for wine in America, is still run personally by the families of the brothers who started it.

At the other extreme, in what rapidly and rather unkindly became known as boutique wineries, fashion has rocketed about from one winery to another as drinkers even newer to wine than the winemakers tried to make up their minds what they liked, at the same time as discovering who made it – or if he made it again the following year. There are enduring landmarks, but they are few and far between. Essentially this is an industry with no structure and very few rules.

There are four approaches to finding what you want in California, and you need them all. There is no escaping the dominance of the brand or winery name. The grape variety is the only firm information available about what is in the bottle. The area of production is a good clue to the style of the wine, if not its quality. And the vintage date at least tells you how old it is – and often considerably more. Access to the essentials in this chapter is therefore organized into three alphabetical directories: of wineries and brands, of grapes (and wine types) and of areas.

How good are the wines, and where do they fit into an international comparison?

In the last 20-odd years the top class of handmade wines have proved that they can outshine in blind tastings the very European wines they emulate. The reason they do this with almost monotonous predictability is inherent in their nature. It is the fully ripe grape that makes California wines comparable with the great vintages and the best vineyards of Europe – the only places with those flavours.

There is also, however, the rate of ripening and the question of soil to consider. Both of these have more bearing on the long-term quality of wine than California is at present inclined to allow. The concomitant disadvantage of the super-ripe grape is the relentless force of flavour that it gives.

Heartiness suits Americans – at least the Americans of today. It suits many wine drinkers everywhere. The mood may waver, but only briefly. Not long ago the terms of highest praise were 'impressive fruit', 'heaps of varietal character', 'distinct notes of French oak'. There followed a time when 'delicacy', 'balance', 'harmony' and 'elegance' became the bywords. That moment turned out to be ephemeral. Within a very few years, 'heaps' and 'impressive' returned to fashion with greater vigour than before.

The proprietors of a great many California wineries are keen on their wines making a splash in society. Indeed, it is a rare thing to come across an owner whose aspirations lean in the direction of a solid Cru Bourgeois, but an everyday occurrence to find one who wants nothing less than First-Growth status. Being in the main first-generation men in wine, these entrepreneurs and their winemakers must respond to the latest sales reports rather than the voices of their fathers, or the voices of their often new vineyards. If society wants size, size it shall have, and California wine of late has become more top-heavy than ever with unabashed wines priced to appeal to princes.

Personal taste is the final arbiter – as I was reminded when I rashly asked a gathering in New York if they would really like all red Bordeaux to have the character of the great champion of modern vintages, 1961. 'Of course,' they said. What a fool I must be, not to want the most concentrated, the most overwhelmingly full-flavoured (but the least refreshing) of all wines with every meal. Perhaps they had a point. After all, the 1961 clarets are shy little things in the face of California's most outsized efforts.

THE CLIMATE

Since Prohibition ended or, more precisely, since the University of California became eminent in research, California has looked more to sun than soil for guidance as to where to plant which varieties. Between 1940 and 1960, scientists at the university developed a system of five climate regions that governed planting in California for several decades, but it is now substantially out of use. It was based on cumulative heat during an April 1–October 30 growing season. The measure is degree days (a day's average temperature minus 50).

The regions approximate roughly to: Burgundy (Region I, up to 2,500 degree days), Bordeaux (Region II, 2,500–3,000 degree days); the Rhône (Region III, 3,000–3,500 degree days); Sherry (Region IV, 3,500–4,000 degree days), and North Africa/Middle East (Region V, over 4,000 degree days).

The system worked well enough to steer growers to Monterey and the Santa Maria Valley in Santa Barbara in the 1970s, but mounting experience with climate regions has shown as many shortcomings as virtues. Chardonnay prospers in several locales where heat says it should not, and Cabernet refuses to ripen at sites where heat says it should.

THE SOILS

While, in California, the notion of climate regions rules, soil was thought to play a role only insofar as it drained well or poorly. Though a smattering of growers have begun to suspect a great role for it, soil has yet to be treasured in anything like the way it is in Europe.

Progress, give the devil his due, will be slow. In the coastal counties, where fine points matter most, soils are implausibly erratic because California's geologically young Coast Ranges are endlessly rearranging themselves. Two examples may suffice:

At the grandest scale, the San Andreas Fault marks two separate pieces of the North American Plate. Soils on opposite sides of California's most famous manufacturer of earthquakes can be completely unrelated within a distance of mere inches – most strikingly so in the Santa Cruz Mountains.

On a far smaller level, what is now called the Russian River drained through the Napa Valley into San Francisco Bay until geological acitivity caused Mount St. Helena to rise up, blocking its course, at which point it turned westward to flow into the Pacific Ocean, leaving the Alexander and Napa Valleys to evolve in different ways.

American Viticultural Areas (AVAs)

As climate was losing ground and soil was failing to gain it, American grapegrowers, led by Californians, persuaded the US federal government to establish a rudimentary system of appellations of origin, beginning in the early 1970s.

The regulations do nothing save draw boundaries around more or less homogeneous areas. They imply no degree of quality. They impose no limitations on varieties, nor planting practices, nor yields. Indeed, they permit a wine to carry the area name when up to 15 percent of it comes from grapes grown elsewhere.

In spite of all, the AVAs are proving useful at least up to a point. They are forcing growers to look to which varieties grow better than others, and to plant them. Carneros and Chardonnay are one case in point, the Russian River Valley and Pinot Noir another. As a result, the viticultural areas are the most useful framework for any *tour d'horizon* of contemporary California.

North Coast AVA This encompasses most of Lake County, Mendocino, Napa and Sonoma, the four major winegrowing counties north of San Francisco Bay. Together they form a rough rectangle lying entirely within the Coast Ranges, with sub-regions cooled in varying degree by sea air from the Pacific Ocean.

Napa County/Napa Valley AVA The most concentrated and prestigious region with 35,000 acres and nearly 300 wineries. The cooler southern tip (Carneros) of a 25-mile long valley opens onto San Francisco Bay, a warmer northern end (Calistoga) is sheltered by landmark Mt. St. Helena. The towns between, south to north, are Napa, Yountville, Oakville, Rutherford and St. Helena. Diverse soils and climates make it versatile but history old and new favours Cabernet Sauvignon above all other varieties. Recent acreage figures include: Cabernet Sauvignon (10,210), Merlot (4,565), Pinot Noir (2,200), Zinfandel (2,140), Chardonnay (10,150), Sauvignon Blanc (2,435). To watch: Sangiovese (307).

The Napa Valley's principal sub-AVAs are:

Atlas Peak AVA Small upland valley east of Stags Leap, recently developed with Sangiovese foremost in mind.

Carneros AVA At the southern end of the valley, the AVA shared with Sonoma County. Designed for Pinot Noir but Chardonnay is the gem and Merlot is coming up. Sparkling is a particular strength.

Howell Mountain AVA In the hills east of St. Helena; historic home of Zinfandel, now more planted to Chardonnay.

Mount Veeder AVA In hills west of Napa and Yountville; mostly Cabernet.

Rutherford AVA The heart of the valley, where Cabernet has grown longest and some would say best.

Oakville AVA Adjoins Rutherford on the south; extends Cabernet zone but grows every grape variety from Chardonnay to Zinfandel surprisingly well, no white better than Sauvignon Blanc.

St. Helena AVA Adjoins Rutherford on north; planted mainly to Cabernet Sauvignon.

Spring Mountain AVA The hills west of St. Helena grow Cabernet and Chardonnay, and should grow more Riesling

Stags Leap District AVA In the southeast quarter of the valley floor, devoted almost entirely to Cabernet Sauvignon, suppler here than elsewhere in Napa.

Other AVAs are pending, notably Calistoga. Two distinctive areas not established as AVAs are Chiles Valley (east of Howell Mountain, good for Cabernet) and Pope Valley (due north of Chiles, extending to the Lake County line, splendid for Sauvignon Blanc).

Sonoma County Napa's nearest rival both physically and in terms of prestige. Sonoma sits between the Pacific and Napa. It is much larger in area than Napa and more diverse, geologically and topographically. There is no blanket AVA covering its 36,000 acres of vines and 200-plus wineries. Nor is it synonymous with one grape variety. The major players by acreage are: Cabernet Sauvignon (7,000), Merlot (4,160), Pinot Noir (3,135), Zinfandel (4,070), Chardonnay (12,470), Sauvignon Blanc (1,585). To watch: Sangiovese (170).

Sonoma's AVAs and sub-AVAs are:

Alexander Valley AVA Reaches north from Healdsburg to Mendocino County line; a broad valley apparently at its best with Cabernet Sauvignon, Sauvignon Blanc and Zinfandel. Sangiovese is a prospect.

Carneros AVA Sonoma has more than half of the surface area in a region shared with Napa, less than half of the vineyards. *See* Napa.

Dry Creek Valley AVA Ever warmer as it runs northwest from Healdsburg, superbly suited to Zinfandel and Sauvignon Blanc, and showing promise with both red and white Rhône varieties.

Knights Valley AVA Due north of Calistoga in Napa; mostly Cabernet, most of which goes to wineries outside a sparsely populated region.

Russian River Valley AVA Fog-cooled broad expanse ranging from Healdsburg south to Santa Rosa, southwest to Forestville and Sebastopol; shows best with Pinot Noir, Chardonnay for both still and sparkling, yet does well with Sauvignon Blanc, Zinfandel too. Sonoma-Green Valley (Chard., sparkling wine) is the cooler sub-AVA of the Russian River Valley AVA; Chalk Hill (Chard., Sauv.Bl.) the warmer one.

Sonoma Valley AVA Stretches from Santa Rosa south through Kenwood and Glen Ellen to Sonoma town, where it opens to San Francisco Bay, without declaring a particular variety as premier. Cabernet-dominated Sonoma Mountain is a sub-AVA to Sonoma Valley; also, Sonoma Valley overlaps Sonoma's portion of Carneros.

Northern Sonoma AVA covers all of the Russian River drainage. **Sonoma Coast AVA** is another catchall.

Mendocino County/Mendocino AVA Directly north of Sonoma County, Mendocino – and the Mendocino AVA – are splendidly schizophrenic. The region from Redwood Valley south through Ukiah and Hopland is warmer and drier than any part of Sonoma, but over a markedly shorter season. The coastward Anderson Valley is as cool and rainy as California grape-growing areas can be. It has about 40 wineries and 13,000 acres under vine. Principal varieties are: Cabernet Sauvignon (7,000 acres), Zinfandel (1,830), Chardonnay (4,415), Sauvignon Blanc (685). Again, Sangiovese appears to be a comer (50). Despite a scant acreage (290), Gewürztraminer is important in the Anderson Valley.

Anderson Valley AVA Anchored on Boonville on the cool west side of the county, the short, swift drainage of the Navarro River has made some of California's most extraordinary dry Gewürztraminer, long-lived Chardonnay and champagne-like sparkling wines since its revival in the late 1960s.

McDowell Valley AVA A tiny, essentially one winery, area in the southeast corner of the county strives hardest with Rhône varieties, red and white.

Potter Valley AVA A sparsely settled upland valley east of Ukiah which sends most of its grapes elsewhere. Chardonnay currently appears to lead. The main drainage of the Russian River encompasses Redwood Valley, Ukiah, and – at Hopland – the Sanel Valley. No part of it is a more particular AVA than just Mendocino. Sunny and dry through a short summer, its Chardonnays have raised particular questions about the University of California's five-zone climate system, but Sauvignon and Zinfandel are its bankable varieties.

Lake County AVA North of Napa, east of Mendocino, Lake County is the smallest, warmest and driest grape-growing region in the North Coast. Primary plantings in its 3,330 acres of vineyard are: Cabernet Sauvignon (900), Chardonnay (640), and, most brilliant to date, Sauvignon Blanc (700).

Clear Lake AVA The majority of plantings are surrounding the lake that gives the county its name. From Lakeport to Middletown is where Sauvignon Blanc excels.

Guenoc Valley AVA A townless one-winery fiefdom bordering on Napa, where Cabernet is the prize, Chardonnay the surprise.

Central Coast Where the North Coast is a compact though woozy 2:1 rectangle, the Central Coast is a scaled-down imitation of Chile, a 350-mile-long snake-thin strip, running from southern San Francisco Bay all the way to Santa Barbara County. The principal wine-growing counties it includes are, north to south, Monterey, San Luis Obispo and Santa Barbara. Alameda County and San Benito counties add important bits.

Santa Barbara County Modern grape-growing dates only from the early 1970s, yet in this short career Santa Barbara has begun to emerge as a distinctive region in its own right. It still has fewer than 50 wineries, and not much more than 12,000 acres of vines, with Chardonnay (5,935) and Pinot Noir (875) primary among them. Santa Barbarans entertain the most extravagant hopes in California for Syrah (144), and also look for much from Merlot (335).

Santa Maria Valley AVA Seafog-cooled, true east–west valley running inland from the town of Santa Maria memorable above all for Pinot Noir.

Santa Ynez Valley AVA Pinot Noir excels in a fog-cooled stretch from Lompoc to Buellton; Cabernet, Sauvignon Blanc and (unaccountably) Riesling prevail in a sunnier and much warmer zone inland of Buellton, around Solvang and Los Olivos County.

San Luis Obispo County The county has a long history, but only with Zinfandel, a durable presence in hills west of Paso Robles. Diversity arrived with the wine boom of the 1970s in both the form of more varieties and more growing regions, especially down on the cool plain stretching south from San Luis Obispo town. The county has fewer than 40 wineries, more than 11,000 acres of vines. Cabernet Sauvignon (2,920 acres) and Zinfandel (1,375) dominate red plantings. Chardonnay is the white (3,980).

Arroyo Grande AVA Based in the eponymous town at the southernmost corner of the county, Arroyo Grande was planted for sparkling wine, but is showing a turn of speed with Pinot Noir in still wine too.

Edna Valley AVA Lies between the towns of San Luis Obispo and Arroyo Grande; planted almost entirely to Chardonnay.

Paso Robles AVA Mountain-sheltered, relentlessly sunny high inland valley; the hills west of Paso Robles town continue to produce heady Zinfandel, the rolling plain east of that town is newly famous for soft Cabernet. Muscat Blanc is an undiscovered treasure, Syrah a hope for the future.

Monterey County/Monterey AVA Monterey blossomed in the late 1960s as an easy answer to urban pressures on old vineyards in Alameda and Santa Clara counties, and then exploded in acreage in the early 1970s, to a peak of 37,000. Most of the vines are in the Salinas Valley from Gonzales down through Soledad and Greenfield to King City. For lack of local wineries, most of the grapes go elsewhere as the basis of 'Coastal' commodity wines. Leading grape varieties by acreage: Chardonnay (12,745), Cabernet Sauvignon (3,600). Also Merlot (2,055), Pinot Noir (1,370), Sauvignon Blanc (1,250).

Arroyo Seco AVA The floor of the Salinas Valley between Soledad and Greenfield grows whites well, especially lightsome Chardonnay. Sauvignon Blanc may do even better.

Carmel Valley AVA Monterey's only ocean-facing district, with only tiny acreage, grows some dark, intriguing Cabernet on high ground where seafog seldom reaches.

Chalone AVA High in the Gabilans above the east side of the Salinas Valley at Soledad is a virtual monopoly of Chalone Vineyards (q.v.).

Santa Lucia Highlands AVA The west hills of the Salinas Valley from Gonzales down to Greenfield, recently planted, newly defined, perhaps to become a superior source of Pinot Noir.

Alameda County Urban expansion has made the historic Livermore Valley virtually the last redoubt of grapes in the county. Lovermore is the main wine town, Pleasanton its satellite. Leading varieties among a total 1,500 acres: Chardonnay (700), Cabernet Sauvignon (250), Merlot (150), Sauvignon Blanc (100).

Livermore Valley AVA East of San Francisco Bay, anchored on the town of Livermore, Sauvignon Blanc and Semillon make inimitable wines in a historic district, but do not reign because Chardonnay rules the market.

Santa Clara–Santa Cruz counties In the 19th century, when Almaden and Paul Masson were powers, Santa Clara rivalled Napa, but those palmy times long since have given way to silicon in chips. Very little remains, but what does falls mostly within the well-regarded Santa Cruz Mountains AVA.

Santa Cruz Mountains AVA Encompasses parts of, from north to south, San Mateo, Santa Clara and Santa Cruz counties. Acreage here is tiny and, owing to vine diseases, dwindling in the mid-1990s.

San Ysidro AVA East of Gilroy, in essence a one-vineyard AVA has had brilliant success with a range of varieties, especially Chardonnay.

An old-line area called Hecker Pass, west of Gilroy, never has attained AVA status, and likely will not as housing supplants a scant acreage.

San Benito County In its heyday, Almaden planted several thousands of acres in San Benito, and wrought several AVAs to locate them before abandoning the region. Most of the AVAs (and some of the vineyards) have fallen into disuse, though some commodity producers have reached in during a time of scarcity. Only one AVA flourishes, Mt. Harlan.

Mt. Harlan AVA High in the Gabilans, the fiefdom of Calera Winery (q.v.) almost backs onto the similar fiefdom of Chalone (q.v.).

South Coast AVA Covers the sub-tropical to desertous counties south of the Techachapi Mountains, most notably riverside, where Temecula's 2,000 acres and dozen wineries dominate the region. Scattered small plantings are in Los Angeles, Orange and San Diego counties, larger ones in San Bernardino (where historic Cucamonga is fading towards extinction as a growing area, due to urban pressure from Los Angeles).

San Pasqual AVA A one-vineyard AVA near Escondido, east of San Diego, too often beset with Pierce's Disease to have declared itself.

Temecula AVA In the southwest corner of Riverside County, hard against San Diego County's north boundary. Pioneered in the late 1960s, versatile in a modest way, with several of its producers beginning to look beyond Chardonnay to Rhône and/or Italian red varieties for a new lift.

The Interior The huge San Joaquin Valley – modestly supplemented by the minnow Sacramento Valley – is California's Midi. Huge volume is generally the watchword in, from north to south, San Joaquin, Stanislaus, Madera, Fresno and Kern counties. A few particular areas give definition; quickly sketched, they are:

Lodi AVA A low-lying, rich-soiled, reliably sunny part of San Joaquin County, at the mouth of the San Joaquin Valley. Long famous for Zinfandel. More recently a source of large volumes of reliable Chardonnay, Cabernet Sauvignon and Merlot for – in particular – blending into commodity wines.

Clarksburg AVA In many ways a westward extension of Lodi into the Sacramento River Delta. It grows a Chenin Blanc of more character than most in California, but plantings there have turned toward Chardonnay in answer to a booming market for it.

Dunnigan Hills AVA Success by the pioneer R. H. Philips is drawing other growers into a nascent region just in the lee of the Coast Ranges, near the Sacramento County town of Woodside. Chardonnay is important by acreage, Sauvignon Blanc by result.

Sierra Foothills AVA The AVA covers nearly all of the vineyards in three counties, Amador, Calaveras and El Dorado. Amador, at the centre, has unbroken history going back to the Gold Rush. Calaveras on the south and El Dorado on the north are recent revivals. Acreage is modest (2,700), with Zinfandel (1,530) far in the forefront. Small wineries rule.

El Dorado AVA Covers all of the vineyards in the eponymous county. One centre is in the high hills north and east of Placerville; Merlot and Sauvignon Blanc were earlier hopes; Rhône and Italian varieties have since increasingly replaced them in the hearts of many growers.

Most of the other plantings in the region circling around Somerset, are virtual extensions of Amador's Shenandoah Valley by elevation, soil types, and favoured varieties.

Shenandoah Valley-California AVA The historic heart of Gold Country winegrowing stretches eastward from Plymouth to Fiddletown. It has made its fame with heady Zinfandels. Here too, Syrah and Sangiovese are the new challengers.

Fiddletown AVA Anchored on the eponymous village, Fiddletown is an eastward, more elevated extension of Shenandoah Valley.

Varietals and varieties

The useful word 'varietal' was coined in California as shorthand for a wine that is either made entirely from, or derives its character from, one named grape variety. Up to 1983 the law required that the named variety be 51% of the total. From 1983 the requirement is 75%. Most high-quality varietals have long been closer to 100%.

On a semantic note, varietal is an epithet that describes a wine. It is not a noun meaning a specific sort of grape. That noun is variety. The Chardonnay grape is a variety; its wine is a varietal wine.

Grapes and generic wine names

Angelica A fortified sweet wine traditional to California, usually made from the old Mission grape. Heitz has made the best-known samples.

Barbera High-acid variety planted mostly in hotter San Jaoquin Valley for blending; can be distinctive in warm Coast Ranges districts. 10,850 acres.

Burgundy A fading term for any red wine, with the vague implication that it should be dark and full-bodied (unlike real burgundy). California burgundy is usually slightly sweet. But it is not all low quality; some reputable firms use the term for good wine.

Cabernet Franc (Cab.Fr.) Plantings on the rise, especially in North Coast; mostly for blending with Cab.Sauv., Merlot, but increasingly for varietals. 1,900 acres.

Cabernet Sauvignon (Cab.Sauv.) Makes California's best red: fruity, fragrant, tannic, full-bodied. Needs maturing in oak, and at least 4 years in bottle. Also makes very pretty rosé or 'blush' wines. Highly recommended for region 1 and recommended for 2. Crop is 4 to 6 tons an acre. The best comes from the central Napa Valley, parts of Sonoma and of the Central Coast. 37,800 acres.

Carignane (Carig.) Recommended for warmer regions. 8,490 acres.

Carnelian (Carn.) Little seen as varietal. 1,040 acres.

Chablis Despite justified French protests that this is a part of France, it remains the uninformed American's term for (relatively) dry white wine from California, or anywhere else.

Champagne Until some imaginative new name for California sparkling wine appears, the name of the French region will continue to be used – although not by the French-owned producers.

Charbono Sometimes made as a varietal.

Chardonnay (Chard.) California's most successful white grape, capable of great wines in the Burgundian tradition with age, and sometimes fermentation, in oak. Nice judgement is needed not to produce over-intense, ponderous wines (especially in Napa). Parts of Sonoma and the Central Coast (Monterey) tend to have a lighter touch. The best examples age for 10 years or more in bottle. At pinnacle in Carneros, Anderson Valley; excels in Russian River Valley, cooler Napa Valley and (in a quirkier way) Edna Valley. Surprisingly good in Ukiah, even Lodi. Huge plantings – too many for use in commodity wines – have made it California's most-planted variety at 72,625 acres.

Chenin Blanc (Ch. Bl.) A surprisingly popular, usually rather dull white grape, appreciated for its high crop – 6 to 10 tons an acre – and clean, adaptable flavour, pleasant when semi-sweet (although best dry); good in blends; not needing age. Acreage peaked at 32,000 in 1990; now dropped to 23,315 acres.

Chianti The Italian name still occasionally used as a 'generic' for sweetish reds of moderate to poor quality.

Emerald Riesling (Em. Ries.) Virtually disappeared as a varietal. Acreage down to 675.

Flora Virtually disappeared as a varietal. Acreage diminished until no longer counted separately.

French Colombard (Fr. Col.) High-acid blending variety most planted in hotter regions of San Joaquin Valley. No longer the most widely planted variety, having dwindled from a peak of 62,000 down to 44,900 acres.

Fumé Blanc (Fumé Bl.) see Sauvignon Blanc.

Gamay Not Gamay at all, most probably Valdiguie.1,250 acres.

Gamay Beaujolais (Gamay Beauj.) Not the Beaujolais grape but a form of Pinot Noir, productive in cool regions but not recommended anywhere. 1,025 acres.

Gewürztraminer (Gewürz.) After a hesitant start, a great success in California, where its wine is oddly softer and less spicy than in Alsace. Crops 4 to 6 tons an acre. Most successful in Anderson Valley, nearly as good in Russian River Valley, parts of Salinas Valley. 1,610 acres.

Golden Chasselas An alias of the Palomino, the best sherry grape. Produces in hottest regions.

Gray Riesling (Gray Ries.) Not a Riesling but a minor French grape Chauché Gris, related to the Trousseau of the Jura. Acreage down to 240 and still declining.

Grenache (Gren.) A source of flavourful red or rosé in warmer Monterey areas near King City. Most plantings in San Joaquin, often for port-types. 11,460 acres.

Grignolino (Grig.) Non-recommended red grape, presumably from Italy, used by one or two wineries in cool regions to make off-beat red or rosé, which can sometimes be distinctly Muscat-flavoured.

Johannisberg Riesling (or White Riesling) (J.R. or W.R.) Much out of favour in US markets, acreage down to 3,000. Most delicate in Anderson Valley. Oddly successful as a rich wine from Napa Valley's Spring Mountain.

Malbec Most used in California for blending in Meritage types. Currently 140 acres.

Malvasia Bianca The common Italian grape, recommended for dessert wines in hotter regions but capable of pleasant, soft table wine in cooler areas. 2,825 acres.

Merlot The Pomerol grape has become a runaway success as a varietal, especially when made bland and priced moderately. 25,000 acres.

Mission The coarse old local grape of the Franciscan missionaries. Some 3,200 acres are left in the hottest regions. Crops 6 to 12 tons an acre and is used in dessert wines (see Angelica).

Muscat or **Moscato** The best is Muscat de Frontignan or Moscato Canelli, recommended for white table wines in cooler regions; for dessert wines in hotter areas. Crops 4 to 6 tons an acre. Its best production is a sweet, low-alcohol wine so unstable that it must be kept refrigerated. There are only 1,400 acres in the state. Muscat of Alexandria is a hot-climate grape grown mainly for eating.

Nebbiolo Piedmont's noble grape, now up to 130 acres in California. Fog is the very thing it likes best.

Petite Sirah (Pet. Sir.) California's name for a low-grade French grape, Durif. Can be intriguing, especially from Sonoma, sometimes Napa, but mostly useful for giving colour and tannin to Rhône-style blends. 2,375 acres.

Pinot Blanc (P.Bl.) Similar to a low-key Chardonnay, whether actually Melon (most of the total) or true Pinot Blanc. Some 1,045 acres.

Pinot Noir (P.N.) Burgundy's red grape is widely regarded as the last great hurdle for California's winemakers – early results were over-strong, heavy and dull. Recent years have seen intermittent but increasing success, especially in Russian River Valley, Santa Maria Valley, less often in Carneros, Santa Lucia Highlands. A major part of the annual crop goes to make classic-method sparklings. 9,075 acres.

Pinot St. George (P.St.Geo.) A minority speciality used by very few wineries. Most of the 700 acres are in Monterey. Never exciting wine.

Port A 'generic' name taken from the Old World for sweet dessert wine which rarely resembles the Portuguese original – although it may well have qualities of its own.

Ruby Cabernet (Ruby Cab.) Bred by H. P. Olmo at Davis to give balanced, Cabernet-like wines from warmest climates. Too-short trials did not disprove its fitness, but shy market caused its virtual disappearance as a varietal wine. Best performances in Monterey, Lodi, Madera. 6,420 acres.

Sangiovese (Sangioveto Grosso) (Sangio.) A new hope with the late 1980s, Tuscany's great red thus far has shown most brilliantly in Amador, almost as well in Mendocino (Ukiah-Hopland), Sonoma (Alexander Valley), Napa (Atlas Peak). 900 acres.

Sauvignon Blanc (Sauv.Bl.) Fashionable since the '70s, but always potentially excellent in California. Its best wine is closer to white Graves than Pouilly Fumé, although its frequent alias of Fumé Blanc suggests the Loire. It can be light and 'herbaceous' or oak-aged, solid and of Chardonnay quality. The single most reliable (and fascinating) variety for defining the differences between not just the North and Central Coasts, but divisions within each. 11,415 acres.

Semillon (Sem.) Bordeaux's sweet-wine and Australia's dry-wine grape, little exploited as yet in California. Recommended for cooler regions. Crops 4 to 6 tons an acre. Some 1,375 acres.

Sherry California 'sherry' has never achieved the standard of imitation of the Spanish original found in, for example, South Africa. There are, though, some tolerable sweet dessert wines under the name.

Souzão One of the Portuguese port grapes used for some of California's best sweet dessert wines.

Sylvaner (Sylv.) The decline of J.R. in the California market has nearly extinguished its lesser cousin; 96 acres remain.

Syrah Rhône rangers are busy searching for their very own Hermitage, but are not yet finding it if the diasporatic 1,330 acres are any clue.

Thompson Seedless A neutral white table, dessert and distilling wine grape which is never mentioned on the label, but frequently present in many jug whites and charmat sparklers. Grown mostly for raisins; about one-third of its crop is crushed for wine.

Viognier In the hands of Rhône Rangers, something of a fad in the early 1990s. All the coast counties share in 490 acres.

Zinfandel (Zin.) California's own red grape, possibly of Italian origin, immensely successful and popular for all levels of wine from cheap blends to fresh light versions and to galumphing sticky blackstrap. The best have excellent balance, a lively raspberry flavour and seem to mature indefinitely. 'White' (blush) Zinfandel is a commercial smash hit. Recommended for coolest region but grown everywhere – 44,000 acres of it. Crops 4 to 6 tons an acre.

CALIFORNIA WINERIES

It is a dull (and unusual) week in California when another new winery (or wineries) does not announce itself. The yeast of romance and experiment is so active that any list is out of date before it comes back from the printers.

Like the rest of this book, therefore, the following survey of the California wineries is a record of a moment in history: the winter of 1996–7, with as much hard fact as the wineries cared to make known about themselves and as much explanatory or critical comment as experience and space allows.

Specifically, each entry states (if the information was available) the location of the winery, its ownership (but not its winemaker, since in California it is impossible to keep tabs on them), date of foundation, vineyards owned (if any) and the principal wines produced. An asterisk indicates the best wine(s) in a range.

The most striking feature of the wine scene in California is the number of wineries founded since 1979. Clearly, any critical evaluation on the basis of a few vintages is extremely tentative: there simply has not been enough time for consistency – or lack of it – to make itself felt. So there are many entries which belong here as a matter of record, but where evaluation must wait.

Acacia

Las Amigas Road, Napa. Founded 1979. Owners: see Chalone. 50 acres in Carneros, Napa. 50,000 cases. Wines: Chard., P.N.
Acacia Pinot Noir has exciting qualities of freshness, the berry smell and soft texture of burgundy – clear indication, since reinforced, that the Carneros district is right for the variety, though wines assembled from several properties seem richer than single-vineyard models. Acacia once made four vineyard-designated Pinots per vintage, but now contents itself with a basic bottling and a barrel-selection Reserve. Fine as Acacia's Pinots are, its Chardonnays are still less to be overlooked. The founding partners sold to Chalone in 1986.

Ahern Winery

San Fernando, Los Angeles. Founded 1978. 6,200 cases. Wines: Chard. Sauv.Bl., Cab. Sauv. and Zin.

Ahlgren Vineyard

Boulder Creek, Santa Cruz. Founded 1976. 1,800 cases. Wines: Chard., Cab.Sauv. and Sem.
Ahlgren's first Cabernet was rapturously received by the critics. Since, minute amounts of hand-made wines have been released to more muted acclaim.

Alderbrook Vineyards

Healdsburg, Sonoma. Founded 1982. Owner: George Guillemot. 63 acres in Dry Creek Valley and Russian River Valley. 22,500 cases. Visits. Wines: *Chard., Gewürz., Sauv.Bl., Cab. Sauv., Merlot, P.N., Syrah, Zin.
Changes of owner and winemaker in 1994 occasioned switch from scintillatingly crisp whites to fatter style, plus the addition of reds.

Alder Fels

Santa Rosa, Sonoma. Founded 1980. Owners: David Coleman, Ayn Ryan. 26 acres. 10,000 cases. Wines: Chard., Gewürz., *Sauv.Bl., Sangio.
A hilltop winery buying in Sonoma grapes to make deeply flavoured whites, and Mendocino grapes to make a new (in 1994), promising Sangiovese.

Alexander Valley Vineyards

Healdsburg, Sonoma. Founded 1975. Owners: the Wetzel family. 130 acres in Alexander Valley, Sonoma. 50,000 cases. Wines: Chard., Ch. Bl., J.R., Gewürz., Cab. Sauv. Visits.
Dry Burgundian-style Chardonnay with life and length, accepted in England as one of California's best and an indication of the ideal climate of the Alexander Valley. Also good-value, well-made Cabernet.

Almadén Vineyards

Madera, Madera. Founded 1852, refounded 1941. Owners: Canandaigua. 1m+ cases. Wines: broad range. Visits.
A historic Central Coast name which now goes only on low-priced commodity wines, mostly made from San Joaquin Valley grapes.

Amador Foothill Winery

Plymouth, Amador. Founded 1980. Owners: Ben Zeitman and Katie Quinn.10.5 acres. 12,000 cases. Visits.
Small Shenandoah Valley vineyard. The winery is below ground for natural cooling. Zinfandel predominates.

S. Anderson Vineyard

Yountville, Napa. Vineyard founded 1971, winery 1979. Owners: Carole Anderson and family. 130 acres. 10,000 cases. Wines: Chard., Cab.Sauv., Brut, Blanc de Noirs, Tivoli. Visits.
Carole and the late Dr Stanley Anderson founded their vineyard and winery in one corner of the Stags Leap District to make nothing but estate Chardonnay and classic-method sparkling wines. Now the Chardonnay comes mostly from a newer vineyard in Carneros and Cabernet from a neighbour is a force in the line. but the sparklers go as planned, usually near the head of the class.

Arrowood

Kenwood,Sonoma. Founded 1985. Owner: Richard Arrowood. 20,000 cases. Wines: Chard., P.Bl., Cab. Sauv., Merlot, late harvest. Visits.
Long-time Chateau St. Jean winemaker has gone out on his own, to do better with Cabernet than his erstwhile staple, Chardonnay. All grapes are bought in.

Atlas Peak Vineyards

Foss Valley, Napa. Founded 1985. Owners: Piero Antinori, The Wine Alliance. 465 acres at Altas Park. 20,000 cases. Wines: Chard., Cab S., Sangio., 'Consenso'.
The first serious effort to make Napa Valley into Sangiovese as well as Cabernet country is truly more an alliance than a

partnership. Piero Antinori owns the vineyards and cellars. The Wine Alliance (Hiram Walker) owns the business, making and selling estate wines. Antinori selected the Sangiovese strain from Montalcino. Consenso is a Sangiovese–Cabernet blend.

Au Bon Climat

Santa Maria, Santa Barbara. Founded 1982. Owner: James Clendenen. 10,000 cases. Wines: Chard., P.Bl., *P.N.
Few have done better than irrepressible Jim Clendenen at capitalizing on the great discovery about Pinot Noir in California: the vines must be shrouded in seafog for the wine to attain delicacy or depth.

While Clendenen's single-vineyard Pinots from the Santa Maria and Santa Ynez Valleys often are superb, the whimsically named La Bauge au-Dessus sometimes stirs the soul more deeply.

Baldinelli Vineyards

Plymouth, Amador. Founded 1979. Owners: John Millar and estate of Edward Baldinelli. 70 acres. 16,000 cases. Wines: Zin., Cab.Sauv., Sauv.Bl.

Bandiera Winery

Cloverdale, Sonoma. Founded 1937. Owner: California Wine Corp. 90 acres. 175,000 cases. Wines: Cab. Sauv., Chard., Sauv.Bl., Zin., Wh. Zin.
When corporate owners took over (in 1975) from the founding Bandiera family, they created five different labels based on price and origin of the grapes. The scheme proved too much for the trade to sort out, so Bandiera again became the sole label for a broad range, the best of which is Cabernet Sauvignon from company-owned vines in Napa's Chiles Valley.

Bargetto's Santa Cruz Winery

Soquel, Santa Cruz. Founded 1933. Owners: the Bargetto family. 35,000 cases. Wines: Chard., Gewürz., P.N., Cab. Sauv., Ries., and Zin. Visits.
Grapes from Santa Barbara County are used for varietal whites, of which the Chardonnay and Gewürztraminer have been well received. Late-harvest botrytis Riesling is a speciality.

Beaucanon

St. Helena, Napa. Founded 1986. Owner: Jacques de Coninck. 250 acres. 25,000 cases. Wines: *Cab. Sauv., Chard., Merlot. Visits.
Promising Napa venture by co-owner of St-Emilion's Lebegue has anchored itself in four thoughtfully sited vineyards.

Beaulieu Vineyard

Rutherford, Napa. Founded 1900. Owners: Heublein, Inc. 1500 acres. 600,000 cases. Wines: *Cab.Sauv., Chard., *Sauv.Bl., P.N. Visits.
Founded by a French family, the de Latours, BV (as it is familiarly known) set the pace in the Napa Valley throughout the 1940s, 1950s and 1960s under a winemaker of genius, the late Russian-born André Tchelistcheff. At Beaulieu he pioneered small-barrel ageing and malolactic fermentation for reds, cold fermentations for whites, and was early to propound the virtues of the Carneros region south of Napa for cool-climate varieties.

After the founding family sold to Heublein, Inc. in 1969 and Tchelistcheff retired in 1973, Beaulieu went into a long period of drift. With new executives in place in the 1990s, Heublein now has BV poised to become a large business. There are four separate lines. At the top are the Reserves (including Carneros Chardonnay and Tchelistcheff's masterpiece, Georges de Latour Private Reserve Cabernet

André Tchelistcheff

Long before his death, at age 92, in 1994, the California wine world had silently and unanimously bestowed the title of its 'dean' on André Tchelistcheff. His career spanned the whole history of the industry from Prohibition to the current decade, for 36 years (1937-73) at Beaulieu and thereafter, from his home in Napa, as consultant to many of the best wineries all over California and beyond. Tchelistcheff was born in Russia and trained in Burgundy. He was chosen to make their wine by the French de Latour family, founders of Beaulieu and for many years the royal family of the Napa Valley. In the early 1940s he introduced the idea of ageing red wine in small oak barrels. His reserve Cabernet from the best Rutherford vineyards, named as a memorial to Georges de Latour, has served as a model for California winemakers ever since. Cold fermentation of white wine, malolactic fermentation … many of the house rules of California were written by Tchelistcheff and his knowledge continues to resonate today through the score and more of winemakers who learned much from him.

Among the many winemakers who owe at least part of

their training to him are such masters as Joe Heitz, Mike Grgich of Grgich Hills, Warren Winiarski of Stag's Leap, Richard Peterson of Folie à Deux and Judy Matulich-Weitz of Buena Vista.

Sauvignon). In the middle is an extensive grouping of Napa Valley varietals led by a vibrant Sauvignon Blanc. At the low end of the price scale is the Beautour line, from sources in and out of the Napa Valley. The fourth grouping, called Signet, covers experimental lots of such as Grenache, Sangiovese and Viognier; successes will be incorporated into one of the main lines.

Bellerose Vineyard

Healdsburg, Sonoma. Founded 1979. Owners: Jack and Ann Air. 52 acres in Dry Creek Valley. 6,000 cases. Wines: Cab.Sauv., Merlot, Sauv.Bl.

Belvedere Wine Co

Russian River Valley, Sonoma. Founded 1980. Owner: William Hambrecht. 80,000 cases. Wines: Cab.Sauv., Chard., Merlot, Zin. Most of the wines come from 250 acres of grapes which Hambrecht owns separately from the winery. Fittingly, the Zinfandel is in Dry Creek Valley, the Cabernet in Alexander. Hambrecht also owns the less expensive Grove Street label.

Benziger of Glen Ellen

Sonoma Valley, Sonoma. Founded 1981. Owners: Benziger family. 95 acres. 80,000 cases. Wines: broad range. Visits.
The late Bruno Benzinger (d. 1989) and five sons started out to build a small, Sonoma-based winery. Within a decade they found themselves selling well more than 1 million cases a year of commodity wines under the names Glen Ellen Proprietor's Reserve and M. G. Vallejo. Dismayed, they sold those labels to Heublein, Inc. in 1993, and returned to their original idea, this time under the family name. Already the business is growing like Topsy because genius marketers can't help marketing.

Beringer Vineyards

St. Helena, Napa. Founded 1876. Owners: Texas-Pacific Group, Silverado Partners 2,800 acres. 1.4 million cases. Wines: *Cab. Sauv., Chard., Ch. Bl., Merlot, Zin. and others. Visits.
One of the great old stone-built wineries of Napa, with coolie-cut tunnels into the hills as its original cellars. Under the Beringers it declined, was bought in 1969 by Nestlé, who fixed it on an upward course. The company now continues largely unchanged by the complicated group of partners who bought it in 1995. The late winemaker Myron Nightingale set a quiet, even reserved, style after 1969. His successor, Ed Sbragia, favours bold wines.

Beringer's owners also own Chateau Souverain, Chateau St. Jean, Meridian and Napa Ridge.

Boeger Winery

Placerville, El Dorado. Founded 1973. 35 acres owned, 20 leased. 10,000 cases plus. Wines: Cab. Sauv., Zin., Ch. Bl., Sauv.Bl., Merlot. Visits.

Bogle Vineyards Winery

Clarksburg, Yolo. Founded 1979. President: Warren V. Bogle. 650 acres in Clarksburg. Wines: Chard., Sem., Sauv.Bl., Ch. Bl., Cab. Sauv., Merlot, Zin. Visits by appt.

Bonny Doon Vineyard

Livermore Valley, Alameda. Founded 1981. Owner: Randall Grahm. 50,000 cases. Wines: broad range, often proprietary. Visits.
Grahm became the foremost of the Rhône Rangers while operating from a modest barn in the Santa Cruz Mountains. Failed vineyards (Pierce's Disease) and successful marketing led him to relocate to the historic but long-idle Ruby Hill winery in Livermore Valley in 1996. There he continues to pursue Rhône-like wines (a Mourvèdre called Old Telegram, a Grenache called Clos de Gilroy, a red blend called Le Cigare Volant, a Marsanne–Roussanne named Le Sophiste), and he is redoubling his recently begun efforts in the Italianate arena.

Bouchaine

Carneros, Napa. Founded 1981. Owner: Gerret Copeland. Vineyards 10 acres. 25,000 cases. Wines: *Chard., P.N. Visits.
Copeland was one of several partners who founded Bouchaine in an 1895 winery building in 1981. When the original group could not decide between a Bordelais versus a Burgundian model, Copeland seized the reins in 1986 and came down firmly on the side of Carneros Chardonnay and Pinot Noir. Under winemaker John Montero, the former is often a model for its peers, the latter always worthy.

The Brander Vineyard

Santa Ynez, Santa Barbara. Founded 1981. Owner: Frederic Brander. 40 acres. 8,000 cases. Visits.
Fred Brander makes outstanding Sauvignon Blanc, as well as Chardonnay, a Cabernet rosé and a Cabernet Franc/Merlot blend.

David Bruce Winery

Los Gatos, Santa Cruz Mountains. Founded 1964. Principal: David Bruce. 25 acres in the Santa Cruz Mountains. 32,000 cases. Wines: Chard., P.N., Cab. Sauv., Zin.
The owner believes in wine on a heroic scale from very ripe grapes. The results can impress or oppress, according to taste.

Buehler Vineyards

St. Helena, Napa. Founded 1978. Owner: John Buehler. 62 acres. 20,000 cases. Wines: Cab. Sauv., Zin., Musc. Bl., P.Bl.

Buena Vista Winery and Vineyards

Carneros, Sonoma. Founded 1857, refounded 1943. Owner: A. Racke. 1,100 acres. 125,000 cases. Wines: Cab. Sauv., *Chard., Gewürz, J.R., Merlot, P.N. Visits.
Historically important as the winery of Agoston Haraszthy, 'the father of California wine'. Restarted in 1943 by Frank Bartholomew, who was ahead of his time but never made great wine here. Things have much improved since German owners took over in 1979. First Jill Davis then Judy Matulich-Weitz have shown what potential lies in still-improving vineyards on Carneros' first slope. Matulich-Weitz shows the winemaker's hand more than Davis did, but vineyard character remains foremost. Cabernet Sauvignon can be a wonderful sleeper here.

Burgess Cellars

St. Helena, Napa. Founded 1972. Owner: Tom Burgess. 70 acres owned and 25 leased in Napa County. 30,000 cases. Wines: Zin., Cab.Sauv., Chard. Visits by appt.

This was the original little Souverain winery where Lee Stewart made great Cabernet Sauvignon in the 1960s. It was bought and rebuilt in the 1970s and is now best known for Cabernet Sauvignon partially barrel-fermented Chardonnay and heady Zinfandel. Bell Canyon Cellars is a second label.

Davis Bynum Winery

Healdsburg, Sonoma. Founded 1965. President: Davis Bynum. 28,000 cases. Wines: Chard., Cab. Sauv., P.N., Sauv.Bl., Zin. Visits. Producer of good Artist Series wines, especially Chardonnay and Pinot Noir, and a wide range of other varietals.

Byron Vineyards

Santa Maria, Santa Barbara. Founder 1984. Owner: Robert Mondavi Corp. 400 acres plus, 30,000 cases. Wines: Chard., P.Bl., *P.N. Visits.

Pioneer Santa Barbara winemaker Kenneth Brown sold the winery he founded to Robert Mondavi in 1990, but retains the help as Mondavi money expands vineyards and cellar from modest to major in the local landscape.

Cain Cellars

St. Helena, Napa. Founded 1981. Owners: the Meadlock family. 84 acres on Spring Mountain. 15,000 cases. Wines: proprietary reds, Sauv.Bl. Visits by appt.

'Cain Five' is an ambitious Bordeaux-style blend using estate and neighbouring Spring Mountain grapes. 'Cain Cuvée' is its declassified, good-value sibling. The Sauvignon is from Monterey plantings of the Musque strain.

Cakebread Cellars

Oakville, Napa. Founded 1973. Owner: Jack Cakebread. Winemaker: Bruce Cakebread. Vineyards: 75 acres. 60,000 cases. Wines: Cab. Sauv., Cab. Fr., Chard. and Sauv.Bl. Visits.

The Cakebreads are specialists in dry Sauvignon Blanc from their own vines. Two Chardonnays are produced, both from bought-in Napa grapes, as well as rich pungent reds including a Cabernet Sauvignon.

Calera Wine Company

Hollister, San Benito. Founded 1975. Owners: Josh and Jeanne Jensen. 24 acres of lime-rich hill in San Benito. 10,000 cases. Wines: P.N., Chard. Visits by appt.

Specialists in estate-bottled Pinot Noirs and Chardonnays from San Benito County.

Callaway Vineyards and Winery

Temecula, Riverside. Founded 1974. Owner: The Wine Alliance. 180 acres. 300,000 cases Wines: Cab. Sauv., *Chard., Ch. Bl., Sauv.Bl. Visits.

The most considerable pioneer of varietal table wine in Southern California. For most of the 1980s, it made only whites, but with the 1990s has returned to red winemaking as well. Callaway's Chardonnay, innocent of oak, is the redoubtable headliner. Pinot Gris, Viognier and Dolcetto are interesting experiments of the '90s.

Caparone

Paso Robles, San Luis Obispo. Founded 1980. 7 acres. 3,000 cases. Visits.

Nebbiolo and Brunello have been planted in an interesting attempt to fit these grapes into the California roster.

J. Carey Cellars *see* Curtis Cellars

Carmenet

Sonoma. Founded 1982. Owners: as Chalone (q.v.) Wines: Chard., Sauv.Blanc, Cab./Merlot, Fr.Col.

The Chalone team are aiming for Bordeaux here with Edna Valley Sauvignon and a Cabernet/Merlot blend from high above Sonoma town. The Chardonnay produced here comes from Carneros.

Carneros Creek Winery

Napa, Napa. Founded 1972. President: Balfour C. Gibson. 100 acres in Napa Valley, Carneros and Sonoma. 30,000 cases. Wines: P.N., Chard., Cab. Sauv., Sauv.Bl. Visits by appt.

Winery at the south end of the Napa Valley that caused a sensation with its first Pinot Noir. The '77 was the best I had tasted in California, with the combined velvet and carpentry of very good burgundy. The Chardonnay has the same conviction.

Caymus Vineyards

Rutherford, Napa. Founded 1971. President and winemaker: Charles F. Wagner. 73 acres. 30,000 cases.Wines: Cab. Sauv., P.N., Zin., Sauv.Bl., Chard. Visits by appt.

Charles Wagner's finest wine is his juicy, even flowery Cabernet, which, to many tastes, is the most harmonious and elegant in the Napa Valley. His white wine from Pinot Noir, the palest 'partridge eye', really tastes of the grape. The second label is Liberty School, which represents excellent value for money.

Chalk Hill

Chalk Hill, Sonoma. Founded 1974. Owner: Fredand Peggy Furth. 260 acres in Chalk Hill, near Windsor, Sonoma County. 60,000 cases. Visits by appt. Wines: Cab. Sauv., Chard., Merlot, Sauv.Bl.

Despite being an estate winery, it has been a medium in search of a message, or vice versa, for most of its career, changing names from Donna Maria to Chalk Hill in 1982 and changing styles to suit a succession of winemakers. The vineyards seem most suited to Sauvignon Blanc. Cabernet Sauvignon has prospects.

Chalone Vineyard

Soledad, Monterey. Chairman: Richard Graff. 174 acres. 15,000 cases. Wines: Chard., P.Bl., Ch. Bl., P.N.

For 50 years a lonely outpost of viticulture on a droughty limestone hilltop near the Pinnacles National Monument where all water had to be brought up by truck. Then the

Graffs stunned California with Pinot Noir successfully modelled on great Côte d'Or burgundies and Chardonnay maturing to the smoky fragrance of the great white wines of the northern Rhône. Pinot Blanc is also doing well on this elevated site. Now also owns Acacia and Carmenet (qq.v.). In 1989 Chalone traded shares with Domaines Baron de (Lafite) Rothschild.

Chappellet

St. Helena, Napa. Founded 1968. President: Donn Chappellet. 110 acres (with more leased) in Napa Valley. 30,000 cases. No visits. Wines: Cab. Sauv., Chard., Ch. Bl.

Donn Chappellet was the second man, behind Robert Mondavi, to build a new winery in the Napa for the new age of California wine. In 1968 he built a steel-clad, new-age pyramid, truly suggestive of its era, and put it to the most traditional use: to make wine from a single estate. Above all, to make a deep-flavoured, austere, built-to-last, think-Latour Cabernet Sauvignon from its topmost slopes.

In recent years there have been two Cabernets. One, subtitled Pritchard Hill, is approachable early, as the market demands. The other, Donn Chappellet Signature, upholds the original premise and fulfils the original promise.

There are other wines from Donn Chappellet's amphitheatrical vineyard in the hills east of St.Helena, a changing roster reflecting lessons he has learned from the iron-rich soils at his craggy site. Riesling has come and gone. A dry, firm, long-flavoured Chenin Blanc persists, though in diminished quantities. Sangiovese, meanwhile, is on the rise.

Château Chevre Winery

Yountville, Napa. Founded 1979. 4,000 cases. Visits by appt. Wines: Merlot, Sauv.Bl.

Château Montelena Winery

Calistoga, Napa. Founded 1881, refounded 1969. President: Jim Barrett. 100 acres (mainly Cab.Sauv.). 28,000 cases. Wines: Chard., Cab. Sauv., J.R., Zin. Visits.

Old stone winery north of Calistoga, at the foot of Mount St. Helena, which now has a 20-year record of some of the best California Chardonnays and Cabernets from the state vineyard and grapes bought in from Napa. The Napa wines tend to be richer – and so do their drinkers.

Two distinguished winemakers have set the style here: Mike Grgich up to 1974, followed by Jerry Luper up to 1981 – the first known for elegant discretion, the second for heaps of flavour.

Château Potelle

Mt. Veeder, Napa. Founded 1985. Owners: the Fourmeaux family. 45 acres. 20,000 cases. Visits by appt. Wines: *Cab. Sauv., Chard., Zin.

Jean-Noël and Marketta Fourmeaux du Sartel came to California as agents of the French government, to measure California's wine industry. They liked what they saw enough to join up, beginning as negociants, eventually buying vineyards and a winery.

Château Souverain (formerly Souverain Cellars)

Geyserville, Sonoma. Founded 1973. Owners: Texas Pacific Group, Silverado Partners. 400,000 cases. Wines: Sauv.Bl., Cab. Sauv., Chard., Zin. Visits.

Beringer (q.v.) took over this luxurious Alexander Valley winery in 1986.

Château St. Jean

Kenwood, Sonoma. Founded 1973. Owner: Texas Pacific Group, Silverado Partners 400,000 cases. 120 acres. Wines: Chard., Sauv.Bl., Gewürz., Ries, Cab. Sauv., Merlot, P.N. Visits.

A showplace winery specializing in white wines of the sort of subtropical ripeness more often associated with the Napa Valley. Robert Young Chardonnays are the biggest and lushest of all. I often prefer the more easily drinkable multi-vineyard regular bottling. Formidable sweet late-harvest Rieslings and Gewüztraminers are also to be watched.

Thus far in its short history, Château St. Jean has had more ownerships (three) than winemakers (two). The original owners sought to supplement Chardonnay via a major push in classic method sparklings in 1978. The second owners, Japan's Suntory, largely abandoned that programme in the mid-80s for a vigorous push into red wines.

Château Woltner

Howell Mountain, Napa. Founded 1985. Owners: the Woltner family. 60 acres. 10,000 cases. Wines: Chardonnay.

Françoise Woltner and Francis Dewavarin-Woltner sold their share of Haut-Brion in Bordeaux, and bought an old, long-idle Napa winery property called Nouveau Medoc in order to make… you guessed it, Chardonnay.

The Woltners divided their tumultous property east of St. Helena into four vineyards, three of them (Frederique, St. Thomas and Titus) bottled separately. Their standards are rigorously at the pinnacle, with prices to match.

Chimney Rock

Stags Leap District, Napa. Founded 1984. Owner: Sheldon (Hack) Wilson. 75 acres. 15,000 cases. Wines: *Cab. Sauv., Chard., Fumé Bl. Visits.

Winemaker Doug Fletcher's silky Cabernet epitomizes its region of origin. The winery's decision to go elsewhere for Chardonnay grapes recognizes how fully attuned to Cabernet the Stags Leap District is.

Christian Brothers Winery

Madera, Madera County. Napa. Founded 1888. Owner: Heublein, Inc. After a century under the ownership of a Catholic teaching order (the Order of LaSalle), the winery and brandy house passed to Heublein hands in 1989. Since then it has completely exited its historic home in the Napa Valley to become a San Joaquin Valley-based label, primarily for brandy.

Clos du Bois

Healdsburg, Sonoma. Founded 1974. Owner: Hiram-Walker Allied Vintners. President: Terrence Clancy. 200,000 cases. 690 acres in Dry Creek and Alexander Valley. Wines: Chard., Sauv.Bl., Gewürz., Cab. Sauv., P.N., Merlot. Visits.

Clos du Bois wines were well established before there was a winery. The best are boldly winey Gewürztraminer and an easily drinkable claret-style Cabernet. The Chardonnay is lively, long and dry, with a hint of green (in both colour and flavour) that seems to spell Alexander Valley. Marlstone Alexander Valley (Merlot-based blend), Briarcrest Alexander Valley Cabernet Sauvignon, Calcaire Alexander Valley Chardonnay and Flintwood Dry Creek Valley Chardonnay are named-vineyard wines of distinctive personality.

Clos du Val Wine Co.

Yountville, Napa. Founded 1972. Owner: John Goelet. 265 acres in Carneros and Stag's Leap. 60,000 cases. Wines: Cab. Sauv., P.N., Merlot, Zin., Chard., Sem.

Winemaker Bernard Portet was brought up at Château Lafite, where his father was manager. As in Bordeaux, he blends Merlot with Cabernet. His wines are reckoned soft and supple by Napa standards but they are still deep-coloured, juicy, and long on the palate. They can age beautifully. His Zinfandel is as strapping as they come. Like all good examples of this grape, they can be drunk young, sweet and heady or kept virtually for ever. Taltarni in Victoria, Australia, has the same owners.

Clos Pegase

Napa. Founded 1987. Owners: Jan and Mitsuko Shrem.

A major architectural competition was won by the American architect Michael Graves. The resulting winery is Napa's most striking post-modernist building to date. It produces steadily improving Chardonnay and Cabernet.

Codorníu Napa

Napa, Napa. Founded 1991. Owners: Codorníu S.A. 100 acres-plus. 30,000 cases. Wines: Brut, Carneros Cuvée. Visits.

The second major sparkling-wine producer established in Carneros by a Spanish cava house, Codorníu Napa is bold in architecture (glass house modern) but cautious in style.

Concannon Vineyard

Livermore, Alameda. Founded 1883. Owners: the Wente family. 180 acres. 40,000 cases. Wines: Cab. Sauv., Pet. Sir., Chard., proprietaries. Visits.

Founded by Col. Joseph Concannon to make altar wine in the same year as the other great Livermore Valley winery, Wente Vineyard, it has been owned since 1991 by members of the Wente family, but run separately. Under winemaker Tom Lane, there is renewed focus on estate Petite Sirah, Sauvignon Blanc and Assemblages – the latter paired red and white blends of the Bordeaux varieties. Grapes for Chardonnay and other varietals are largely bought-in from Central Coast sources.

Conn Creek

St. Helena, Napa. Founded 1979. Owners: Stimson Lane. 146 acres east of Yountville and north of St. Helena. 21,000 cases. Visits by appt. Wines: Cab. Sauv., Chard., Zin.

The first fame of the name was for Cabernet Sauvignon. That is now the sole product of a floating label chased out of its home by the other Stimson Lane-owned Napa winery, Villa Mt. Eden (q.v.).

Corbett Canyon Vineyards

Edna Valley, San Luis Obispo. Founded 1978. Owners: The Wine Group. Over 400,000 cases. Wines: Chard., Sauv.Bl., Cab. Sauv., Zin., P.N. Visits.

Purchased in 1988 from Glenmore Distillers by The Wine Group, who then added a 200-acre vineyard in Santa Barbara County. Over recent years, production has built up decent, well-made varietals. Good 'Reserve' wines in small lots.

Corison

St. Helena, Napa. Founded 1987. Owner: Cathy Corison. 4,000 cases. Wine: Cab. Sauv.

As winemaker at Chappellet from 1980 through 1989, Corison did much to solidify Chappellet Vineyard's reputation before launching out on her own. She makes nothing but Cabernet Sauvignon. After some years in leased space, the winery acquired a home of its own in 1996.

Cosentino Wine Co.

Yountville, Napa. Founded 1980. Owner: Mitchell Cosentino. 12,000 cases, rising to 20,000. Visits Mon–Fri. Wines: Cab. Sauv., Cab. Fr., Merlot, Chard., P.N., a lightly fortified Muscat-based wine and a sparkling wine.

Crichton Hall

Yountville, Napa. Founded 1985. Owners: the Crichton family. 17 acres. 8,000 cases. Wines: Chard., Merlot, P.N.

An expatriate Brit and reformed banker, David Crichton set out with a single-minded goal: to make estate Chardonnays competitive to the best of white Burgundies. However, caught in the French Paradox, he has added Merlot and Pinot Noir from Carneros.

Cronin Vineyards

Woodside, San Mateo. Founded 1980. Owner/winemaker: Duane Cronin. 1,200 cases. Visits by appt.

John Culbertson Winery *see* Thornton Winery

Curtis Cellars (formerly Carey Cellars)

Los Olivos, Santa Barbara. Founded 1978. Owner: Kate Firestone. 25 acres. 9,000 cases. Wines: Cab. Sauv, Chard., Merlot. Visits.

The Santa Ynez Valley winery and vineyard date from 1977, when the name was J. Carey Cellars. Firestone acquired the property in 1987, and renamed it after Kate Firestone's family in 1996. The estate La Cuesta Merlot has helped define its region. Winemaker John Kerr produces Syrah for his eponymous label under the same roof.

Cuvaison Vineyard

Calistoga, Napa. Founded 1970. Chairman: Schmidheiny family. 400 acres in Carneros. 80,000 cases. Wines: Chard., Cab. Sauv., Merlot, Zin. Visits.

The winery staggered through a succession of ownerships and styles before the Schmidheiny family, Swiss bankers, took over in 1979. They bought a 400-acre vineyard property in Carneros and installed John Thacher as winemaker, both shrewd moves. The vineyard yields superior Chardonnay and v.g. Merlot and Pinot Noir; Thacher shows just how fine is the fruit year after year. Calistoga Cellars is an occasional second label.

Deer Park Winery

Deer Park, Napa. Founded 1979. 5-acre vineyard east of St. Helena. 6,000 cases. Wines: Zin., Pet. Sir., Chard., Sauv.Bl.

Dehlinger Winery

Sebastopol, Sonoma. Founded 1976. Owner/winemaker: Tom Dehlinger. 31 acres in Sonoma County. 9,000 cases. Wines: Chard., P.N., Cab. Sauv., Zin.

Highly regarded little winery, offering wines that taste distinctly of the grape, not overstrong or overpriced.

De Loach Vineyards

Santa Rosa, Sonoma. Founded 1975 (winery built 1979). Owners: the De Loach family. 350 acres. 90,000 cases. Wines: *Chard., P.N., *Sauv.Bl., Zin. and others. Visits.

From tiny beginnings Cecil De Loach has built a substantial business by making wines that taste first and foremost of grape variety and vineyard. Chardonnay is by a wide margin the premier wine in his range. All of the grapes come from the Russian River Valley [in Sonoma], most of them from scattered winery-owned properties.

de Lorimier

Geyserville, Sonoma. Founded 1985. Owner: Albert de Lorimier. 64 acres 10,000 cases. Wines: Chard., Cab, Sauv.Bl. Visits by appt.

Deutz *see* Maison Deutz

Devlin Wine Cellars

Soquel, Santa Cruz. Founded 1978. Owner/winemaker: Charles Devlin. 10,000 cases. Wines: Cab.Sauv., Chard., Gewürz., Sauv.Bl., Mus., W.R., Zin., P.N.

Diamond Creek Vineyards

Calistoga, Napa. Founded 1972. Owner: Al Brounstein. 20 acres southwest of Calistoga, Napa. 3,000 cases. Wines: Cab. Sauv. only. Cabernet from 3 small vineyards, Volcanic Hill, Red Rock Terrace and Gravelly Meadow, reflects 3 different soils and situations – a subject little enough studied in California. They are all big, tough wines designed for long ageing. Cabernet Franc, Malbec and Merlot are added to the predominant Cabernet Sauvignon.

Domaine Carneros

Carneros, Napa. Founded 1986. Owners: Taittinger, Kobrand, P. Ordway. 140 acres. 40,000 cases. Wines: Brut, *Blanc de Blancs, Brut Rosé. Visits.

The winery, a maquette of la Marqueterie, makes a startling intrusion into the Carneros landscape; the wines, however, are a more graceful hybrid of Taittinger style and Carneros grapes.

Domaine Chandon

Yountville, Napa. Founded 1973; winery opened 1977. Owners: LVMH (Paris). 2,000 acres. 500,000 cases. Wines: Brut, Blanc de Noirs, Etoile, Reserve. Still Pinot Meunier 454-B2. Visits.

The spearhead of France's invasion of California, a characteristically stylish and successful outpost of champagne (but you must not use the word). A wine factory and an entertainment at the same time, with a first-class fashionable restaurant. All of the wines are excellent; the Reserve Cuvée is a showstopper. Out of context, in England, the sheer fruitiness of the Napa grapes make the wines taste rather sweet even though they are substantially drier than most Brut Champagnes (0.7 to 1.0% r.s. compared to 1.0 to 1.3%). The hefty, fruit-rich Blanc de Noirs is the particular example.

Domaine Laurier *see* Laurier

Domaine Michel *see* Michel-Schlumberger

Domaine Mumm *see* Mumm Cuvée Napa

Domaine St. George

Healdsburg, Sonoma. Founded in 1934 as Cambiaso. Owners: Four Seas Investment (Thailand). 300,000 cases.

Cambiaso was long associated with good cheap jug wines. Under a new name and new owners, it has much increased its output, producing a range of acceptable red and white wines from bought-in grapes.

Dominus

Yountville, Napa. Founded 1983. Owner: Christian Moueix. 124 acres. 8,000 cases. Wine: Cab-based proprietary

The maker of Pétrus found his ideal Napa vineyard (ex-Inglenook) in the early '80s. Applying Bordeaux techniques made his massive but unfriendly wines. Since '89 Dominus has relaxed enough to rank just below Napa's very best Cabernets.

Dry Creek Vineyard

Healdsburg, Sonoma. Founded 1972. President: David Stare. 105 acres in Dry Creek, Sonoma. 100,000 cases. Wines: Ch. Bl., Fumé Bl., Chard., Zin., Cab. Sauv., Merlot.

Maker of one of California's best dry Sauvignon Blancs (Fumé Blanc) with other whites in the same old-fashioned balanced, vital but not-too-emphatic dry style. Reserve Chardonnays are barrel-fermented and aged *sur lie*. The Cabernet Sauvignon was judged to be California's best in 1985.

Duckhorn Vineyards

St. Helena, Napa. Founded 1976. 105 acres. 45,000 cases. Wines: Napa Merlot, Cab. Sauv., Sauv.Bl.

One of the wineries provoking great interest in Merlot. Also Sauvignon Blanc.

Dunn Vineyards

Howell Mountain, Napa. Owner: Randall Dunn.

Ex-Caymus winemaker now makes small lots of dark, stern Cabernet at his own winery.

Durney Vineyard

Carmel, Monterey. Vineyards founded 1968, winery 1977.
Owners: the Durney family. 142 acres in hills above Carmel Valley.
15,000 cases. Visits by appt. Wines: Ch. Bl., J.R., Cab.Sauv.
Carmel's first vineyard, on steep slopes not far from the
ocean. The Cabernet is ripe, deep and impressive, the
Chenin Blanc equally well made.

Duxoup Wine Works

Healdsburg, Sonoma. Founded 1981. Owners: Deborah and
Andrew Cutter. 2,000 cases. Wines: Syrah, Napa Gamay.
Marx-inspired name (Groucho) but serious red wines with a
Syrah that has pleased local tasters. All grapes come from
Dry Creek Valley vineyards.

East Side Winery *see* Oakridge Vineyards

Eberle

Paso Robles, San Luis Obispo. Founded 1979. Owners: G. Eberle,
H. Steinbeck. 115 acres in Paso Robles. 14,000 cases. Visits.
Wines: Cab.Sauv., Chard., Zin., Muscat C., others.
An intense loyalist to Paso Robles, especially dedicated to
Cabernet Sauvignon.

Edmeades Inc

Philo, Mendocino. Founded 1968. Owner: Kendall-Jackson. 35
acres in Anderson Valley. 15,000 cases. Visits.
The Mendocino cog in K-J's Artisans and Estates wheel
specializes in named-vineyard wines, especially Pinot Noir and
Zinfandel. The name comes from founder Deron Edmeades.

Edna Valley Vineyard

San Luis Obispo. San Luis Obispo. Founded 1980. Owners:
Chalone Vineyard and Paragon Vineyards. 45,000 cases. Vineyards
in Edna Valley, San Luis Obispo County, planted with Chard., P.N.
Powerful barrel-aged Chardonnay from vineyards adjoining
the winery. Also Pinot Noir and Pinot Noir-based 'Vin Gris'.

Etude

Napa, Napa. Founded 1985. Owner/winemaker: Tony Soter.
8,000 cases. Wines: Cab. Sauv, P.N., P.M., P.G., P.Bl.
Consulting winemaker Soter started making wines under the
Etude label almost as much to showcase his technical ability
to potential clients as for commercial reasons. The latter
motivation prevails now, but the skills are dazzling as ever,
especially in the diverse Pinots from Carneros.

Evensen Vineyards & Winery

Oakville, Napa. Founded 1979. 7 acres between Rutherford and
Oakville.1,300 cases. Wine: Gewürz.
Specialist with an admirable Gewürztraminer.

Far Niente Winery

Oakville, Napa County. Founded 1979. Owner: Gil Nickel. 100
acres. 36,000 cases. Wines: Chard., Cab.Sauv.
A famous pre-Prohibition name reborn in its original stone
building with its old vineyard replanted and now bearing.
The Chardonnays are extravagantly full-flavoured.

Gary Farrell Wines

Forestville, Sonoma. Founded 1982. Owner: Gary Farrell. 10,000
cases. Wines: Chard., *P.N., Merlot, *Zin.
The adroit winemaker for Davis Bynum makes more
particular wines for his own label, many of them from
named vineyards in the Russian River Valley. Pinot Noir
'Allen Vineyard' is the memory-maker.

Fenestra Winery

Livermore, Alameda. Founded 1976. Owners: Lanny and Fran
Replogle. 3,000 cases. Wines: Chard., Sauv.Bl., Cab.Sauv., Zin.

Ferrari-Carano

Healdsburg, Sonoma. Founded 1981. Owners: Donald and
Rhonda Carano. Vineyards: 1,000 acres in Alexander Valley, Dry
Creek, Knights Valley and Carneros. 50,000 cases. Wines:
Cab.Sauv., Merlot, Chard. and Fumé Bl. Visits.
The winery is dramatic. So is the winemaking style. Reserves,
especially, exceed even Texas-sized expectations.

Gloria Ferrer

Carneros, Sonoma. Founded 1984. Owners: Freixenet S.A.
65,000 cases. Wines: méthode traditionnelle sparkling Brut, Blanc
de Noirs, Royal Cuvée. Visits.
Catalonia rather than Champagne is the parent of this
sparkling wine house, named after the wife of the president
of Freixenet. A capacious winery and 360-acre vineyard —
all Chardonnay and Pinot Noir — spell serious intent. Thus
far the vintage-dated Royal Cuvée exceeds the rest of the
range for depth and riches. Typical of its category, the n.v.
Blanc de Noirs is ebulliently fruity and fresh.

Fetzer Vineyards

Redwood Valley, Mendocino. Founded 1968. Owner: Brown-
Forman Distillers. 1,000-plus acres (Mendocino). 3m-plus cases.
Wines: Broad range under Fetzer, Bel Arbor labels. Visits.
Fetzer, operating from a base in Mendocino County but
reaching far beyond it, was among the first winery in
California to make good to outright excellent wines on a
large scale. It was also a pioneer in operating at several
different price levels by labelling wines clearly. In its case,
Reserve is at the top, Barrel Select in the middle (and the
most striking in value). Proprietary names such as Sun Dial
and Eagle Peak mark the lower tier. Bel Arbor is priced
lower yet. The late Bernard Fetzer founded the winery as a
retirement hobby. After his death in 1981, eight of his
staggeringly energetic children built the business to 3
million cases per year before selling it to Brown-Forman
in 1992.

Ficklin Vineyards

Madera, Madera. Founded 1946. President: Jean Ficklin.
Winemaker: Peter Ficklin. 10,000 cases. Visits by appt. Family
vineyards grow Portuguese port varieties.
California's most respected specialists in port-style wine,
neither vintage nor tawny in character but ages indefinitely
like vintage. It needs careful, often early, decanting. Recently
Ficklin has revived the issue of vintage-dated wines.

Field Stone Winery

Healdsburg, Sonoma. Founded 1976. Owner: the John Staton family. Vineyards in Alexander Valley, Sonoma. 12,000 cases. Wines: Gewürz, Pet.Sir., Cab.Sauv. Visits.

A gem of a winery, burrowed in the ground among the vineyards, designed by the late Wallace Johnson, who made picking machines. The grapes for white and rosé are crushed in the vineyard. They include a ravishingly pretty, pale pink 'Spring Cabernet', perhaps California's best picnic wine. Also good Petite Sirah.

Filsinger Vineyards & Winery

Temecula, Riverside. Founded 1980. 25 acres. 5,000 cases. Visits. Recently has added sparkling wines to a range of mainstream varietals.

Firestone Vineyard

Los Olivos, Santa Barbara. Founded 1974. Owner: the Leonard Firestone family. 275 acres in Santa Ynez Valley. 35,000 cases. Wines: Cab.Sauv., Merlot, Chard., Ries., Gewürz. Visits.

Firestone (of the tyres) pioneered the climatically quirky part of the Santa Ynez Valley around Los Olivos that does better by Cabernet and Merlot than it does by Pinot Noir, yet at the same time yields handsome Riesling and spicy Gewürztraminer. Among the reds, many prefer the Merlot to the Cabernet (though not me). The sweeter Rieslings appeal more than the drier ones. All of the wines are modestly priced for the quality, which over the range is as high as any to be found in California.

Fisher Vineyards

Santa Rosa, Sonoma. Founded 1979. Winemaker: Fred Fisher. 70 acres in Napa Valley and at the winery. 10,000 cases. Wines: Chard., Cab.Sauv.

Whitney's Vineyard is the 'home' Chardonnay.

Flora Springs Wine Co.

St. Helena, Napa. Founded 1978. Owners: the Komes and Garvey families. 500 acres in Napa Valley. 15,000 cases. Wines: Chard., Cab.Sauv., Sauv.Bl. Visits by appt.

After some years of courting delicacy, especially in the Sauvignons, Flora Springs has turned toward the gutsy in every wine on the list, nowhere moreso than the Cabernet-based Trilogy.

Thomas Fogarty

Woodside, Santa Clara. Founded 1981. Owner: Dr. Thomas Fogarty. 20 acres. 15,000 cases. Wines: Chard., Gewürz, Cab.Sauv., P.N.

Sparkling Gewürztraminer from Ventana (Monterey) is often stunning.

Folie à Deux

St. Helena, Napa. Founded 1981. Owners: Dr. Richard Peterson, Geo. Schofield & partners. 14 acres. 10,000 cases. Wines: Chard., Cab.Sauv., others. Visits.

The current owners took over in 1995, and are just now setting a course.

L. Foppiano Wine Co.

Healdsburg, Sonoma. Founded in 1896. Owner: Louis J. Foppiano. 200 acres in Sonoma County. 125,000 cases plus. Wines: *Cab.Sauv., Chard., Sauv.Bl., *Pet.Sir., Zin. Visits.

One of the oldest family-owned wineries, recently refurbished and raising its already respectable standards. Foppiano is the label for reds, Fox Mountain for whites, most of them from family vineyards. Riverside Vineyards is a second label.

Forman Winery

St. Helena, Napa. Founded 1980. Owner and winemaker: Ric Forman. 47 acres. 2,000 cases.

The former Sterling winemaker uses grapes from his own hill vineyards, and others down at Rutherford, to make classic 'French-style' Chardonnay and Cabernet.

Foxen Vineyards

Los Olivos, Santa Barbara. Founded 1988. Owners: Richard Dore, Bill Wathen. 10 acres. 3,000 cases. Wines: Chard., P.N.

Tiny winery, titanic Pinots.

Fortino Winery

Gilroy, Santa Clara. Founded 1970. Winemaker: Ernest Fortino. 75 acres. 30,000 cases. Wines: wide range. Visits.

Clear-cut, ripe-fruit wines in the Santa Clara Italian style.

Franciscan Vineyards

Rutherford, Napa. Founded 1973. Owners: Peter Eckes Co. and Agustin Huneeus. President: A. Huneeus. 250 acres at Oakville, Napa; 200 acres in Alexander Valley, Sonoma; 500 acres in Monterey. 100,000 cases. Wines: Cab.Sauv., Zin., Merlot., Chard. Visits.

Anchored in a brilliantly versatile vineyard called Oakville Estate, the winery is often at its peak with reds, most especially Cabernet Sauvignon. Zinfandel is another stellar performer.

Franciscan Vineyards is the Napa part of Franciscan Estates, which also includes Mount Veeder (q.v.), Estancia (Alexander Valley Cabernet and Sangiovese, Monterey Chardonnay and Sauvignon Blanc), and Pinnacles Estate (Monterey Chardonnay and Pinot Noir).

Franzia Brothers Winery

Ripon, San Joaquin. Founded 1906. Owners: The Wine Group. 5m. cases. Wines: Zin., Ch. Bl., Chablis.

Many generics and a few varietal wines under various names, all traceable by the Ripon address on the label. In recent years the winery has led the bag-in-box market under their Franzia and Summit labels.

Freemark Abbey Winery

St. Helena, Napa. Founded 1895, refounded 1967. Owners: partnership, Ted Edwards gen. mgr. 260 acres in Napa Valley. 30,000 cases. Wines: Cab.Sauv., Chard., Ries. (off-dry, L.H.), Merlot. Visits.

Perfectionist winery just north of St. Helena. Three of the owning families (Carpy, Jaeger and Wood) are leading Napa grape growers; other owners have smaller but important vineyards. One partner (Brad Webb) made history with barrels at Hanzel (q.v.) in the late 1950s. Their Chardonnay is often the best in the valley. My notes on the '79 read: 'generous and complex, round and silky but with good grip and sweet, clean finish.' Later vintages are much the same. Cabernet from a Rutherford grower called Bosché (and so labelled) is outstandingly concentrated and balanced, even better than their splendid regular bottling. Another, Sycamore Vineyard, threatens to replace it at the head of the list. In 1973 they pioneered sweet botrytis-rotten Riesling, labelled 'Edelwein'.

Frick Winery

Healdsburg, Sonoma. Founded 1976. Owners: Judith and William Frick. Winemaker: William Frick. 3,500 cases.

Fritz Cellars

Cloverdale, Sonoma. Founded 1979. Owner: Donald Fritz. 95 acres. 15,000 cases. Wines: Chard., Melon, Sauv.Bl., Zin. Visits. Once brilliantly age-worthy, individual whites turned so soft and oaky with 1995 as to fade into the pack. The change in style was deliberately undertaken.

Frog's Leap Wine Cellars

Rutherford, Napa. Founded 1981. Owners: the John Williams family. 18 acres (Napa). 40,000 cases. Wines: Cab.Sauv., Chard., *Sauv.Bl., *Zin. Visits.
Originally a partnership located on the site of the one-time frog farm that led to the name, it is now solely-owned and moved to drier land at Rutherford. But the wines remain everything they were when the winery was earning its reputation.

E. & J. Gallo Winery

Modesto, Stanislaus & Healdsburg, Sonoma. Founded 1933. Owners: Gallo families. 7,000-plus acres. 40–50 m. cases. Wines: long lists under many labels.
The world's biggest winemaker, still run by one of its founding brothers Ernest Gallo (the other, Julio, died in a road accident in 1994). Everything about Gallo is stupendous. They own the world's two biggest wineries to supply their incredible tank farm, which has a capacity of 265 m. gallons, including 1 m. gallon storage tank and a 25-acre warehouse. The bottling line starts with a glass factory.

For a long time, Gallo contented itself with raising commodity wines to previously unattainable levels of quality and consistency. Through the 1960s, its Hearty Burgundy and bizarre assortment of Chablis (Blanc, Pink, Golden, Ruby etc.) were patiently and thoroughly designed for their huge markets. So too were Gallo sparklings (Andre, Ballatore), dessert types (Livingston Cream) and brandies (E & J).

With the 1970s, Gallo foresaw the market for generic wines dwindling in favour of varietals, and began to move in the latter direction, hesitantly at first, then with the kind of power that created its size in the first place.

The company is now churning out new labels for varietal wines almost as fast as it churns out the wine. Anapauma, Gossamer Bay and Turning Leaf are but a few of the more recent. However, the programme that seems to be commanding the greatest attention of Gallos, especially the rising third generation, is Gallo-Sonoma. That programme, though nested within the biggest winery of all, is housed in its own buildings in Dry Creek Valley – and is bottling and selling 300 to 1,000 case-lots of single-vineyard varietals from various of the family's ever-expanding holdings in Sonoma County (2,500 acres and counting). And at prices to surpass such neighbours as Jordan, and rival the most regal of Napans.

It is also working on a much more Galloesque scale than the 1,000-case items.

Gan Eden

Sonoma. Founded 1985. 25,000 cases. Wines: Chard., Cab.Sauv., Gamay Beauj., Ch.Bl.
Kosher wines, using only bought-in Sonoma grapes, which win prizes and praise.

Geyser Peak Winery

Geyserville, Sonoma. Founded 1880. Owners: the Trione family. 1,100 acres in Sonoma County. 500,000 cases. Wines: broad range. Visits.
An old winery turned vinegar-works was bought in 1972 by Schlitz Brewery and sold a decade later to its current owners. The Triones briefly had Australia's Penfolds as a partner. Out of that deal, they kept sure-handed Aussie winemaker Daryl Groom. Fumé Blanc and Shiraz are the stars in a wide range, but others contend. A second label is Canyon Road.

Girard Winery

Oakville, Napa. Founded 1974. Owners: Leslie Rudd & partners. 80 acres in Napa Valley. 14,000 cases. Wines: Chard., Ch.Bl., Cab.Sauv. Visits.
Small winery founded by the Stephen Girard family changed hands in 1996.

Glen Ellen Vineyards & Winery

Sonoma, Sonoma. Founded 1980. Owners: Heublein, Inc. 100 acres, 20 acres leased. 4m. cases. Wines: Chard., Cab.Sauv. Merlot. Visits.
In 1993, Heublein bought the commodity wine end of a firm founded by the Bruno Benziger family (see Benziger of Glen Ellen). M.G. Vallejo is another line within the group.

Grand Cru Vineyards

Originally a Sonoma winery; now a commodity label for JFJ-Bronco (q.v.)

Green and Red Vineyard

St. Helena, Napa. Founded 1977. 17 acres. 2,000 cases.
Tiny Pope Valley winery. Freshly fruity Zin and a Chardonnay.

Greenwood Ridge Vineyards

Philo, Mendocino. Founded 1980. Owner: Allan Green. 4,000 cases. 8 acres in Anderson Valley. Wines: Chard., Ries., Sauv.Bl., Cab.Sauv., Merlot, P.N., Zin. Visits.
Splendid estate Anderson Valley Riesling. Bought-in Alexander Valley Zin. is the other star in a reliable line.

The Gallo Brothers

Ernest and the late Julio Gallo have done more to determine the direction and rate of growth of wine drinking in the USA than anybody else in history. By far the biggest wine producers in America, and probably the world, E. & J. Gallo is still privately owned and directed by Ernest Gallo and the second and third generations of his and his brother's families.

The sons of an Italian immigrant grape farmer, they were brought up in Modesto in the heart of the Central Valley. They started making wine in 1933, when Ernest was 24 and Julio 23. Julio made the wine and Ernest sold it.

They built their first winery in 1935 where the present vast plant now stands, and in 1940 started planting vineyards to experiment with better grapes. They realized the limitations of Central Valley grapes and bought from growers in Napa and Sonoma. They were prepared to outbid rivals. Today they are said to grow or buy one wine-grape in three in California.

In the 1950s the Gallos started a craze for flavoured 'pop' wines with the fortified Thunderbird, to be followed by a series of such enormously advertised and vastly popular gimmicks as fizzy Ripple and Boone's Farm apple wine. In 1964 they launched Hearty Burgundy which, with Chablis Blanc, set a new standard for California jug wines.

The Gallo trend has been slowly but steadily up-market, taking America with it. In 1974 they introduced their first varietal wines, which were much better than they were given credit for at the time. Their first generation of varietals, which included such compromises as Ruby Cabernet and Barbera, was replaced by a second, going all the way with wood-ageing for Chardonnay and Cabernet. In the process they made a two-acre cellar to house some two million gallons in oak.

When the day comes to inscribe a Gallo memorial, the word I would choose for it would be Consistency.

Grgich Hills Cellar

Rutherford, Napa. Founded 1977. Owners: Austin Hills and Mike Grgich. Winemaker: Mike Grgich. 360 acres in Napa Valley. 40,000 cases. Wines: Chard., J.R., Zin., Cab.Sauv. Visits by appt. Hills grows the grapes, Grgich (formerly at Chateau Montelena, q.v.) makes the wine, and of late has further enhanced his reputation for vigorous, balanced wines with more fruit than weight. Chardonnay and Riesling (especially late-harvest) have led the way with Cabernet since 1985.

Groth Vineyards & Winery

Oakville, Napa. Founded 1982. Owners: Dennis and Elizabeth Groth. 30,000 cases plus. Wines: Cab.Sauv., Chard., Sauv.Bl. Visits by appt.
Two vineyard sites totalling 163 acres provide grapes for some solid, oak-aged wines.

Grover Gulch Winery

Soquel, Santa Cruz. Founded 1979. Owners: Dennis Bassano and Rheinhold Banek. 1,000 cases. Wines: Cab.Sauv., Car., Pet.Sir., Zin.

Guenoc Vineyards

Middletown, Lake. Founded 1981. Owners: the Magoon family. 320 acres in Guenoc Valley. 80,000 cases. Wines: Chard., Sauv.Bl., white Meritage, *Cab.Sauv., red Meritage, Pet.Sir., Zin. Visits.
On a huge property straddling the Lake–Napa County Line, where Lily Langtry first planted vines in the 19th century. Her name goes on the top-of-the-line Meritages.

Emilio Guglielmo Winery

Morgan Hill, Santa Clara. Founded 1925. Winemaker: George E. Guglielmo. 115 acres. 50,000 cases. Wines: Cab.Sauv. Reserve, Pet.Sir., Chard., J.R., Sauv.Bl., Ch.Bl.

Gundlach-Bundschu Winery

Vineburg, Sonoma. Founded 1858, refounded 1973. President: Jim Bundschu. 375 acres in Sonoma Valley. 50,000 cases. Wines: Cab.Sauv., Merlot, P.N., Zin., Chard., Gewürz., J.R.
A famous San Francisco wine business destroyed by the 1906 earthquake. Grapes from the old vineyards were sold until 1973, when the winery reopened in a small way with Zinfandel. The range is excellent, especially Cabernet and Merlot and a crisp, refreshing Gewürztraminer like an Alsace wine. Chardonnay and Riesling are also admirable. Most grapes are from 130-year-old estate vineyards.

Hacienda Wine Cellars

Originally a Sonoma winery; now a commodity label for JFJ-Bronco (q.v.).

Hagafen

Napa, Napa. Founded 1980. Owner: Ernie Weir. 10,000 cases. Wines: Chard., Cab.Sauv., *Ries., proprietaries.
The original and still the leading producer of Kosher wines from classic *vinifera* varieties.

Handley Cellars

Anderson Valley, Mendocino. Founded 1980. Owner and winemaker: Milla Handley. 12,000 cases. Wines: Gewürz., Chard., Sauv.Bl., sparkling Brut.
Ex-Chateau St.Jean winemaker Handley is winning praise for Chardonnay, Gewürztraminer and classic method sparklers.

Hanna

Santa Rosa, Sonoma. Founded 1985. Owner: Dr Elias Hanna. 600 acres. 25,000 cases. Wines: Chard., *Sauv.Bl., Cab.Sauv., Merlot.
After a small and slow start the winery began hitting a stride in the 1990s, especially with its whites. Dr Hanna's vineyards are scattered among Sonoma's several climates.

Hanzell Vineyards

Sonoma, Sonoma. Founded 1957. Owner: Barbara de Brye. 32 acres. 3,000 cases. Wines: Chard., P.N., Cab.Sauv.
Scene of revolutionary winemaking in the late 1950s, when James D. Zellerbach set out to make burgundy-style wines in small French oak barrels. The steep south-facing vineyard gives high alcohol but the concentration and balance of both the Chardonnay and the Pinot Noir still makes them among California's most impressive, demanding long maturing. The winery is (vaguely) a miniature Château du Clos de Vougeot. An additional vineyard has been planted in Cabernet.

Harbor Winery

W. Sacramento, Sacramento. Founded 1972. Owner/winemaker: Charles H. Myers. 1,000 cases. Grapes from Napa and Amador County. Wines: Cab.Sauv., Zin., Chard., Mission del Sol. No visits.
A university professor's hobby and his friends' delight, especially Napa Valley Chardonnay and Amador Zinfandel.

Haywood Winery

Sonoma, Sonoma. Founded 1980. Owner: A. Racke. 84 acres in Sonoma Valley. 100,000 cases. Wines: Chard., Cab.Sauv., Zin. Visits.
Of two separate, mirror, lines, the limited production one uses grapes from original owner Peter Haywood's near-vertical Los Chamisal vineyard in Sonoma Valley. 'Vintner Select' offers attractive and attractively priced commodity wines introduced after Racke took ownership. Both are made at Buena Vista (q.v.).

Hecker Pass Winery

Gilroy, Santa Clara. Founded 1972. Owners: Mario and Frances Fortino (winemaker). 14 acres. 5,000 cases. Wines: Pet.Sir., Zin., Carig., Ruby Cab., Gren., Chablis., Fr.Col., sherry. Visits.
Stylish reds from southern Santa Clara County.

Heitz Wine Cellars

St. Helena, Napa. Founded 1961. Owners: Joe and Alice Heitz. Winemaker: David Heitz. 300 acres. 40,000 cases. Wines: Cab.Sauv., Chard., P.N., P.G. Visits.
Heitz is known worldwide for his Cabernet, more locally for his Chardonnay, and very locally for his surprisingly long list of other wines. Yet they all reflect the man; a sometimes gruff original whose palate has its own logic. The Heitz's white house and old stone barn in an eastern side-valley still have an early-settler feeling among far more sophisticated neighbours. Most of the grapes are bought from friends, one of whom, Martha May, has already passed into legend as the name on 'Martha's Vineyard', Heitz's flagship Cabernet – a dense and gutsy wine of spicy, cedary and gumtree flavours, somehow unmistakably the Mouton of the Napa Valley even at the teeth-staining stage. Bella Oaks vineyard is of similar stature. Young Heitz Chardonnay (his first was from Hanzell, q.v., in 1962) stands out in tastings as strong and dry, its fruit flavour held in check. Grignolino is a surprising Muscat-flavoured red. Angelica is a California tradition you would expect Joe Heitz to respect.

Hess Collection Winery

Napa, Napa. Founded 1982. Owner: Donald Hess. 630 acres (Napa & Mont.). 50,000 cases. Wines: Chard., *Cab.Sauv, Merlot. Visits.
Swiss businessman and art collector Hess (the winery is a museum) aims high with wines from 280 acres on Mt. Veeder. The Hess Select line, anchored in his 350 acre Monterey Vineyard, is more for everyday.

William Hill Winery

Napa, Napa. Founded 1976. Owner: The Wine Alliance. 250 acres. 100,000 cases. Wines: Chard., Sauv.Bl., Cab.Sauv., Merlot. Visits.
William Hill planted vineyards before launching a winery focused entirely on Chardonnay and Cabernet. The second owner narrowed the roster of vineyards, added to the list of wines, and is reshaping the style.

Hop Kiln Winery (at Griffin Vineyards)

Healdsburg, Sonoma. Founded 1975. Owner: Martin Griffin. 10,000 cases. 65 acres in Russian River Valley of Chard., Gewürz., J.R., Cab.Sauv., P.N., Zin. and Pet. Sir. Visits.
The Petite Sirah and Gewürztraminer are well spoken of. Reds are from Alexander Valley grapes.

Husch Vineyards

Philo, Mendocino. Founded 1971. Owner: Hugo Oswald. 164 acres. Grapes from Anderson and Ukiah valleys. Visits.

Inglenook – Napa Valley

Rutherford, Napa. Founded 1881. Owners: Canandaigua. 40,000 cases. Vineyards in Napa Valley and elsewhere.
One of the grandest names of Napa is now a homeless label, its wines made either at other Canandaigua properties or in leased space, using bought-in grapes. (The historic property is now Niebaum-Coppola, q.v.). Inglenook Navalle, also Canandaigua-owned, operates separately in the San Joaquin Valley.

455

Iron Horse Vineyard

Sebastopol, Sonoma. Founded 1979. Owners: the Sterling family. 192 acres in Sonoma–Green Valley and Alexander Valley. 25,000 cases. Wines: P.N., Cab.Sauv., Chard., Sauv.Bl. Visits by appt.

I took an instant liking to Iron Horse Cabernet, tannic to start, ripely sweet to finish, like good claret. Since then vibrant Chardonnay and even more lively sparkling Iron Horse have stolen the limelight.

Jade Mountain

Napa, Napa. Founded 1984. Owner: James Paris. 36 acres in Sonoma, 25 in Howell Mountain (Napa). 5,000 cases. Wines: Syrah, Rhône-style red blend.

Founded in Cloverdale (Sonoma) with other ideas in mind, Jade Mountain transformed itself into a specialist in Rhône-born varieties, especially Syrah, just before moving to Napa, where it leases space from White Rock (q.v.). The two now share the winery.

Jekel Vineyards

Greenfield, Monterey. Vineyard founded 1972, winery 1978. Owners: Brown-Forman Beverage Company. 330 acres in Arroyo Seco, Monterey. 50,000 cases. Wines: Chard., J.R., and Cab.Sauv. Visits.

The whites (especially Riesling and Chardonnay) produced by Jekel are among the best on offer in the region, ripe but not heavy. Cabernet Sauvignon – the excellent '83 Private Reserve in particular – has also been a huge critical success.

Johnson's of Alexander Valley

Owners: Tom and Gail Johnson. 45 acres in Alexander Valley, Sonoma. 5,000 cases. Wines: J.R., P.N., Zin., Cab.Sauv. Visits.

Johnson-Turnbull *see* Turnbull

Jordan Vineyard and Winery

Healdsburg, Sonoma. Vineyard founded 1972, winery 1976. Owner: Thomas N. Jordan. 275 acres in Alexander Valley, Sonoma. 70,000 cases. Wines: Cab.Sauv. (with Merlot), Chard. Visits by appt.

At least in folklore the most extravagant tycoon's château-in-California yet: a Bordeaux-style mansion and winery deliberately set on producing claret like the Médoc, in a setting of dark oaks and rolling golden grassland beautiful even by Sonoma standards. The first vintage, '76, made in barrels from Château Lafite, was light but very stylish. Now both Cabernet and Chardonnay are regularly among California's most stylish wines.

An affiliated company, J, produces one of California's most stylish classic method Bruts. In 1996 the firm acquired Piper-Sonoma's winery and vineyard as the basis for a rapid expansion of J.

Kalin Cellars

Novato, Marin. Founded 1977. 6,000 cases.

A scientist-winemaker produces five vineyard-denoted Chardonnays plus Semillon and reds.

Karly Wines

Plymouth, Amador. Founded 1980. 20 acres. 11,000 cases. Wines: Fumé Bl., Zin., Chard., Pet. Sir.

A subtle touch with Zinfandel and Sauvignon (called Fumé) Blanc plus Chardonnay and (occasionally) Petite Sirah from the Sierra Foothills.

Robert Keenan Winery

St. Helena, Napa. Founded 1977. Owner: Robert H. Keenan. 46 acres in Napa Valley. 9,000 cases. Wines: Chard., Cab.Sauv., Merlot.

High, cool vineyards on Spring Mountain Road produce Chardonnay, and Cabernet Sauvignon which is blended with Napa Merlot and oak-aged. Could be over-strong and tannic in early vintages; the recent style is more polite.

Kendall-Jackson Vineyard

Lakeport, Lake. Owner: Jess Jackson. 1m. plus cases. Wines: Chard., J.R., Sauv.Bl., Cab.Sauv., Zin.

K.J. for short, this is another whirlwind grown from small beginnings to industrial size in a short span by means of reliable and reliably attractive wines styled for the mass market (though everything seems to be called a Reserve).

The more fascinating part of the story is more recent. Owner Jackson has scooped up nearly a dozen existing small properties and invented a couple more for his Artisans and Estates division. As of 1996, the stable included: Cambria and Camelot (both Central Coast), La Crema (q.v.), Edmeades (q.v.), Hartford Court (specializing in single-vineyard Russian River Valley Pinot Noirs and off to a brilliant start), Robert Pepi (q.v.) and J. Stonestreet (q.v.)

Kathryn Kennedy Winery

Saratoga, Santa Clara. Founded 1979. 5 acres. 400–800 cases. Concentrates on solid Cabernet Sauvignon.

Kenwood Vineyards

Kenwood, Sonoma. Founded 1906 as Pagani Bros; renamed 1970. Owners: the Lee family. President: John Sheela. 185 acres. 100,000 cases. Wines: Cab.Sauv., P.N., Zin., Chard., Sauv.Bl., J.R., Gewürz., Ch. Bl.

Wide range of varietals from Sonoma grapes including Jack London Vineyard and Artist's Series Cabernet Sauvignons. Reds are increasingly stylish, and the Sauvignon Blanc is very good.

Kirigin Cellars

Gilroy, Santa Clara. Founded 1976. 48 acres. 3,000 cases of various varietals. Visits.

Kistler Vineyards

Glen Ellen, Sonoma. Founded 1978. President: Stephen Kistler. Winemakers: Stephen Kistler and Mark Bixler. 60 acres. 9,000 cases. Wines: Chard., P.N., Cab.Sauv.

Hilltop vineyards on the Napa/Sonoma watershed produce Chardonnay grapes for artisan-method wines. Subtlety of style is replacing headiness. Cabernet and Pinot Noir have been added, and more vineyards have joined the Chardonnay roster.

Konocti Cellars Winery

Kelseyville, Lake. Founded 1979. Owners: J. Parducci 50%, Lake County Vintners 50%. 500 acres (27 Lake County growers with 10 to 20 acres each). 40,000 cases.

Attractive, consistent Sauvignon Blanc, Cabernet and other wines from this remote northern district.

F. Korbel and Bros.

Guerneville, Sonoma. Founded 1882. President: Gary Heck. 400 acres owned, 200 leased in Russian River Valley, Sonoma County. 1.2 m. cases. Wines: sparkling, brandy and table. Visits.

Until Domaine Chandon came on the scene this was the first choice in widely available California 'Champagne'. It is still a reliable bargain, especially the extremely dry Natural. Additions are Blanc de Blancs and Blanc de Noirs and a tasty Sec. The winery is a lovely old place in coastal redwood country.

Hanns Kornell Champagne Cellars

St. Helena, Napa. Founded 1952. Owner: Rombauer Winery. 10,000 cases. No vineyards. Wines are all classic method sparkling: Sehr Trocken, Brut. Visits.

If Domaine Chandon is France's invasion of Napa, this is Germany's. The winery had wobbled before Hanns J. Kornell died in 1993. It closed not long after. The restoration under new owners was in its early days in 1996.

Charles Krug Winery

St. Helena, Napa. Founded 1861.President: Peter Mondavi Sr. 1,200 acres in Napa Valley. 200,000 cases (incl. jug 'C.K.'). visits. Wines: a wide range, including the second label, CK-Mondavi.

C. Mondavi & Sons is the company name at the oldest of Napa's historic wineries. The other son is Robert, who left in 1966 to start his own winery, with spectacular success. Krug led the field with Chenin Blanc as a semi-sweet varietal. Their Chardonnay is Napa at its least reticent – what Bob Thompson calls 'buttered asparagus'. Krug Cabernets also have a fine pedigree; the standard one is lightish and ready-matured but the Cesare Mondavi Selection is the typical deep-flavoured, ripe-fruit-and-dust sort from the Rutherford/Oakville foothills. New Chardonnays from Carneros vineyards, and a Pinot Noir, add depth to the range.

Kunde Estate

Kenwood, Sonoma. Founded 1990. Owners: the Kunde family. 650 acres. 40,000 cases. Wines: Cab.Sauv., Chard., Merlot, Sauv.Bl., Zin. Visits.

Long-time growers in the Sonoma Valley turned to wine-making late. Their most brilliant idea to date: blending small amounts of the Rhône variety Viognier with Sauvignon Blanc.

La Crema

Graton, Sonoma. Founded 1979. Owner: Kendall-Jackson. 60,000 cases. Visits by appt. Wines: Chard., *P.N

Largely from Russian River Valley grapes, wines are substantially less modest than their prices. Part of K-J's Artisans and Estates group.

Lakespring Winery

Napa, Napa. Founded 1980. Owner: Frederick Wildman. 30,000 cases. Wines: Chard., Sauv.Bl., Cab.Sauv., Merlot.

Once a winery, since 1995 a negociant label using Napa grapes.

Lambert Bridge

Dry Creek Valley, Sonoma. Founded 1975. Owners: private corp. President: Gary Moore. 119 acres in Dry Creek Valley. 25,000 cases. Wines: Chard., Cab.Sauv., Merlot. Visits.

Landmark Vineyards

Kenwood, Sonoma. Founded 1974. Owner: Damaris Ethridge. 77 acres in the Russian River, Alexander and Sonoma valleys. 20,000 cases. Wines: Chard. Visits.

Exaggerates the toasty-buttery school, most in the Damaris bottling, least in the Overlook.

Labels

Two pieces of information included on the label of many good California wines give a helpful indication of what to expect in the bottle.

Alcohol content is measured in degrees or percentage by volume (the two are the same). Traditional wines vary between about 11.5° and 14° enough to make a substantial difference to taste and effect. New-style 'soft' wines go down to 7.5°. But the law allows the labeller a remarkable latitude of 1.5° from the truth. As a practical tip, if you find a he-man Napa Chardonnay, for example, too powerful for you at 13.5°, there is no law against adding a drop of water. Perrier refreshes clumsy wines beautifully.

Residual sugar is most commonly reported on labels of Riesling and Gewürztraminer. It is the unfermented sugar left (or kept) in the wine at bottling. Below 0.5% by weight sugar is undetectable: the wine is fully dry. Above about 1.5% it would be described as 'medium sweet', above 3% as 'sweet' and above 6% as 'very sweet'. A 'selected late harvest' might have 14% and a 'selected berry late harvest' as much as 28%. Measurement in grams per 100 millilitres is the same as measurement in percentages.

California's range

One of the most impressive (and confusing) things about visiting a California winery is the range of products. To a European accustomed to the specialization of old wine areas, it is bewildering to be asked to sample the equivalent of claret, burgundy (red or white), German wines and Italian wines too, with possibly sparkling and dessert wines as well – all in the same tasting. And yet it is hard to tell a winemaker that you are only interested in his Cabernet, or his Riesling – at least on that occasion. Tasting at wineries can demand a prodigious effort of concentration.

Laurel Glen Vineyards

Santa Rosa, Sonoma. Founded 1980. 40 acres. 5000 cases of Cab.Sauv.

Sound Cabernet Sauvignon from mountain vineyards.

Laurier

Originally a Sonoma winery (as Domaine Laurier); now a negociant label for JFJ-Bronco in the noblest possible sense of the word. Star winemaker Merry Edwards draws upon a constant roster of four first-rank Sonoma vineyards for a Chardonnay of more than modest dimension. Pinot Noir of similar stature is a more recent project. The jewel in the JFJ-Bronco crown.

Lava Cap Winery

Placerville, El Dorado. Founded 1986. Owner: David Jones family. 23 acres in El Dorado. 5,000 cases. Wines: Cab.Sauv., Chard., *Sauv.Bl., *Zin. Visits.

One of the most consistently stylish of the Sierra Foothills producers.

Lazy Creek

Anderson Valley, Mendocino. Founded 1979. Owner: Hans Kobler. 20 acres. 2,000 cases. Wines: P.N., Chard. Gewürz.

The Gewürztraminer from this tiny Anderson Valley property is highly rated.

Leeward Winery

Oxnard, Ventura. Founded 1978. 18,000 cases of Chard., P.N., Cab.Sauv. Visits.

An ultra-toasty Ventura (Monterey) Chardonnay, plus other named-vineyard wines, has been promising for this coastal winery.

J. Lohr Winery

San Jose, Santa Clara. Founded 1974. Owner: Jerry Lohr. 1,000 acres in Mont. and S. Luis Obispo. 200,000 cases. Wines: Cab.Sauv., Chard., Ries., and others. Visits by appt.

Riesling and Chardonnay from Monterey. Cabernet from Paso Robles. Second line is Cypress.

The Lucas Winery

Lodi, San Joaquin. Founded 1978. Owner/winemaker: David Lucas. 30 acres. 1,200 cases of Zin., light dry and sweet late-harvest. Visits.

Lyeth Vineyard

San Francisco, San Francisco. Founded 1981. Owner: J.-C. Boisset. 30,000 cases. Wines: Chard., *red and white Meritages. The flagship of Burgundian Jean-Claude Boisset's extensive empire of negociant labels in California. Others include Christophe, Joliesse, Wm. Wheeler.

Lytton Springs Winery

One-time estate producer of heroic to homeric Sonoma Zinfandels was purchased by Ridge then closed down by that company, which has since taken the grapes for its Zin.-based proprietary, 'Lytton Springs'.

Maison Deutz

Arroyo Grande, San Luis Obispo. Founded 1983. Owner: Champagne Deutz. 300 acres. 25,000 cases. Wines: n.v. Brut, Brut Reserve, Blanc de Noirs, Brut Rosé. Visits.

The lone incursion into the Central Coast by a Champenois says that *terroir* is real in California. These wines range farther from the French parent's model than any other of the Californian arms, and are unlike their peers from North Coast vineyards as well.

Mark West Vineyards

Forestville, Sonoma. Founded 1974. Owner: Associated Vintners Group. 66 acres. 15,000 cases. Wines: Chard., *Gewürz., P.N. Visits.

The founding husband-and-wife team of Bob and Joan Ellis sold to Asssociated Vintners Group in 1995; for now the new owners are sticking with the Ellis' vineyard and roster of wines, but modifying the styles. The plan is to double production – at least.

Markham Winery

St. Helena, Napa. Founded 1978. Owners: Sanraku. 250 acres in Napa Valley. 20,000 cases. Wines: Chard., Sauv.Bl., Muscat Bl., Merlot. Visits.

Production based on three vineyards, near Calistoga, Yountville and Napa, gives a good range of wines.

Louis M. Martini

St. Helena, Napa. Founded 1922. President Louis P. Martini. Winemakers: Louis P. and Michael R. Martini. 235,000 cases. 800 acres in Napa and Sonoma. Wines: Cab.Sauv., P.N., Merlot, Zin., Barbera, Chard., J.R., Folle Bl., Gewürz., Moscato, Amabile. Visits.

Three generations of Martinis have their name on the short list of California's great individual winemakers. Martini Cabernets of the 1960s rank alongside Beaulieu in quality, but in a different style which, as Bob Thompson has noted, appeals strongly to Englishmen weaned on claret. Martini continues to go less for guts than good manners in his wine. His Special Selection Cabernets are best, but all are well-balanced. Pinot Noir (from Carneros) is only modestly fruity, but again hauntingly well-finished. Barbera and Zinfandel are true to type. Of white the best is dry and spicy Gewürztraminer. Chardonnays from Carneros and Russian River are the latest additions.

Masson Vineyards

Gonzales, Monterey. Founded 1852 (in Santa Clara). Owners: Canandaigua. 4m. cases. Wines: broad range.

The label was Paul Masson, after the 19th-century founder, until Canandaigua became the sixth owner in 1993, and dropped the 'Paul'. Masson remains the top label in a group also including Deer Valley and Taylor California Cellars.

Mastantuono

Paso Robles, San Luis Obispo. Founded 1977. President and winemaker: Pasquale Mastran. 15 acres. 15,000 cases. Wines: Zin., Fumé Bl., Wh. Zin., Mus. Canelli, Cab.Sauv. Visits.

The most concentrated of Zinfandels, from Templeton Vineyards, planted in 1925.

Matanzas Creek Winery

Santa Rosa, Sonoma. Founded 1977. Owner: Sandra P. MacIver. 50 acres in Bennett Valley. 30,000 cases. Visits by appt.

Having won acclaim with early vintages of Chardonnay, the proprietors now keep trying to outdo themselves. Recent luxury lots of Chardonnay and Merlot are called 'Journey', scaled to be mounted as trophies, and priced to shame the French. Regular bottlings of these and Sauvignon Blanc cost enough.

Maurice Car'rie

Temecula, Riverside. Owner: the Van Roekel family. 100 acres. 10,000 cases. Wines: Cab.Sauv., Chard., *Sauv.Bl. Visits.

Fictional family name covers some of the most telling wines from the Temecula AVA.

Mayacamas Vineyards

Miles up in the hills above Napa, Napa. Founded 1889. Refounded 1941. Owners: Bob and Nonie Travers. Winemaker: Robert Travers. 50 acres in Napa. Wines: Chard., Cab.Sauv., Sauv.Bl., P.N., Zin. 5,000 cases. Visits by appt.

Mayacamas is the name of the mountains between Napa and Sonoma counties. If it were the Indian word for 'white man's strongest medicine' it would not be far wrong. The Travers' predecessors, the Taylors, planted Chardonnay and Cabernet during the 1940s in a spectacular natural amphitheatre 1,000 feet up. The sun, the fogs, the winds, the cold and the rocks of the hills conspire to concentrate grape flavour into something you can chew. Hot autumns make the Chardonnay almost treacly. Travers' Cabernets are awe-inspiring in colour and bite for the first five years at least.

McDowell Valley Vineyards

Hopland, Mendocino. Founded 1978. Owners: Keehn family. 450 acres in McDowell Valley, Mendocino. 50,000 cases. Wines: Cab.Sauv., Chard., Grenache, *Syrah, Viognier. Visits.

The firm now is a tenant in the futuristic winery it built and later sold to Associated Vintners Group. But it remains true to the cause: make a statement about the tiny, once-forgotten McDowell Valley in south Mendocino as a source of wines from Rhône varieties, most especially Syrah. Also Grenache.

Meridian Vineyards

Paso Robles, San Luis Obispo. Founded 1984, relaunched 1989. Owners: Beringer Vineyards. 700 acres, 150,000 cases. Wines: Chard., Cab.Sauv.,*P.N., *Sauv.Bl., Syrah. Visits.

A Beringer-owned winery draws heavily upon 3,500 acres of Beringer-owned Central Coast vineyards (Paso Robles, Edna Valley in San Luis Obispo; Santa Maria Valley and Los Alamos in Santa Barbara). Tropical-ripe Chardonnays (Santa Barbara, Edna Valley bottlings) are the mainstays.

Merryvale Vineyards

St. Helena, Napa. Founded 1983. Owner: partnership. 20,000 cases. Wines: Cab.Sauv., Chard., Sauv.Bl., *white and red Meritages. Visits.

Michel–Schlumberger

Healdsburg, Sonoma. Founded 1984. Owners: Jean-Jacques Michel, Jacques Schlumberger. 53 acres. 25,000 cases. Visits by appt. Wines: *Cab.Sauv., Chard.

Formerly Domaine Michel.

Mill Creek Vineyards

Healdsburg, Sonoma. Founded 1976. President: Chas. W. Kreck. 65 acres in Russian River Valley, Sonoma. 15,000 cases. Wines: Chard., Cab.Sauv., Sauv.Bl., Merlot, Gewürz. Visits.

Soft and agreeable rather than competition wines, but the Chardonnay is underrated.

Mirassou Vineyards

San Jose, Santa Clara. Founded 1854. Owners: the Mirassou family. 1,100 acres in Monterey and Santa Clara. 350,000 cases. Wines: Wide range of table and sparkling. Visits.

Fifth-generation Mirassous run an enterprising company with panache. Being squeezed out of increasingly urban San Jose, most of their vines are now in the Salinas Valley where they pioneered field-crushing. Demand and problems for a time with the Salinas climate mean more grapes bought in. Their wines were more exciting 15 years ago.

Robert Mondavi Winery

Oakville, Napa. Founded 1966. Principal: Robert Mondavi. Winemaker: Tim Mondavi. 1,400 acres.1.5 m. cases plus. Wines: Cab.Sauv., P.N., Chard., Ch.Bl., Fumé Bl., J.R. Visits.

Mondavi's energy and his enquiring mind took less than 10 years to produce the most important development in the Napa Valley since Prohibition. He fits the standard definition of a genius better than anyone I know. His aim is top quality on an industrial scale. Inspiration and perspiration have taken him there (see page 460).

The winery is (in the local jargon) state-of-the-art. The art includes not only advanced analysis and every shiny gadget but a personal knowlege of every French barrel maker worth a hoop. Each vintage is like a frontier with the Mondavi family cheering each other on to reach it – and something new always develops.

Their best wine is their Cabernet Sauvignon Reserve; a gentle titan you can drink after dinner with relish but would do well to keep for 20 years. Their regular Cabernet is a model of balance between berries and barrels. Each vintage their Pinot Noir grows more velvetly satisfying. Among whites they are best known for Fumé Blanc, Sauvignon and Semillon with the body and structure (and barrel-age) of first-class Chardonnay. Their Chardonnay (notably the Reserve) compares with the best. The Riesling is rather sweet, but crisp and refreshing and ages well. Late-harvest, botrytized Riesling is golden treacle. Red and white table wines keep up the good work. Only the Chenin disappoints me.

The Mondavi empire reaches near and far beyond its Spanish mission-influenced building at Oakville. Opus One (q.v.) is right across the street, Vichon only a few miles up Napa's Highway 29. Byron (q.v.) is farthest afield, in Santa Barbara County. Mondavi-Woodbridge is the good-value, cut-price label, in Lodi.

Robert Mondavi

Only the brothers Gallo have rivalled Robert Mondavi as a force in California winemaking, and they did not altogether keep pace in recent years as the inexhaustible Mondavi has cast his nets wider than any other vintner in the state has dared to imagine.

When he left his family's Charles Krug winery to start his own company in 1966, Mondavi immediately established himself as a relentless experimenter on all fronts, and resolute champion of the Napa Valley as the New World's greatest wine region.

The mock-Franciscan mission winery buildings at Oakville still house endless experiments. Of the daunting quantities of Napa wine for sale under the Robert Mondavi name, the Cabernet Sauvignons trumpet his successes loudest, none more so than his gentle-but-gigantic Reserves. Fumé Blanc (his globally accepted coinage for Sauvignon Blanc) and Pinot Noir are no laggards on the world stage.

And yet these and other wines under his name are but the tip of the Mondavi iceberg, as an octogenarian Robert presses on in ever-multiplying directions. Except for a brief pause in his 76th year (1989) to replace his worn-out God-given knees with new, artificial ones, he has maintained to this day a pace that would fell a marathon-runner.

In 1979 he brought the prestige of a Bordeaux first-growth to Napa, when Baron Philippe de Rothschild became his partner in Opus One. In 1995, in a reverse gesture, he joined his own name with that of the Frescobaldis in Tuscany. In between, he turned Mondavi-Woodbridge into a formidable player in the low-priced field, acquired more than 1,000 acres of vineyard and the Byron Winery in Santa Barbara County, turned his company from private to a publicly owned corporation, bought Napa's Vichon winery and exported that whole business to the south of France, and became a partner in a Chilean winery. Who could know what else he might have accomplished were he not on the road so much of every year, promoting wine to the world as the beverage of civilization?

Monterey Peninsula Winery

Monterey, Monterey. Founded 1974. Owners: Rutherford Benchmarks. 12,000 cases. Wines: Chard., P.N., Zin. Visits.
Owners of Quail Ridge (q.v.) acquired the idle label and winery in 1995, and sent the first wines to market in 1996. Monterey is to be the sole source of grapes, mostly for vineyard-designated wines.

The Monterey Vineyard

Gonzales, Monterey. Founded 1973. Owner: Seagrams. 1,100 acres. 500,000 cases. Wines: *P.N., Zin., Chard., Sauv.Bl. Visits.
Early-on, strong-flavoured Riesling, Gewürztraminer and Sylvaner from north Salinas Valley vines stood out. Subsequently the vineyards have moved south into warmer climes, and the list has come to focus on sound if commercial Cab.Sauv., Chard. and Merlot.

Monteviña Wines

Plymouth, Amador. Founded 1973. Owners: Sutter Home. 50,000 cases. 250 acres. Wines: *Barbera, Sangiovese, Zin. Visits.
In the beginning the whole focus was Zinfandel. It still matters but the second owners – the Trincheros of Sutter Home – have turned the winery into an experimental station for 50-plus Italian varieties.

Monte Volpe

Ukiah, Mendocino. Founded 1988. Owner: Greg Graziano. 20 acres. 8,000 cases. Wines: Barbera, Sangiovese, P.B.
Old Mendocino hand Graziano is doing intelligent work with Italian varieties, especially Barbera. French varieties are labelled as Dom. St-Gregory.

Monticello Cellars

Big Ranch Road, Napa. Napa. Founded 1970. Managing partner: Jay Corley. 25,000 cases. 250 acres. Wines: *Cab.Sauv., Chard., P.N. Visits.
Monticello is the label for the basic production. Corley goes on reserve bottlings. The Reserve Pinot is the most intriguing in the range.

Mont St. John Cellars

Napa, Napa. Founded 1979. Owner: Louis Bartolucci. Winemaker: Andrea Bartolucci. 160 acres. 20,000 cases. Wines: Cab.Sauv., Chard., P.N. Visits.

Mosby Winery at Vega Vineyards

Buellton, Santa Barbara. Founded 1979. Owner: Bill Mosby. 45 acres in the Santa Ynez Valley. 8,000 cases. Wines: Chard. Gewürz., P.N. Visits.

Mount Eden Vineyards

Saratoga, Santa Clara. Founded 1975. 22 acres of vineyard in the Santa Cruz Mountains. 4,000 cases. Wines: Chard., P.N., Cab.Sauv. Visits by appt.

Merry Edwards set the style of these wines, and since her departure the tradition has been maintained. Mount Eden Chardonnay is a rich soft, spicy wine (in German terms, Pfalz-style). Pinot Noir deep and rich. Cabernet is tannic and gutsy.

Mount Palomar Winery

Temecula, Riverside. Founded 1975. Owner: John Poole. 125 acres. 13,000 cases. Visits.

Mt. Veeder Winery

Mt. Veeder, Napa. Founded 1973, vineyard since 1965. Owner: Franciscan Estates. 26 acres on Mt. Veeder. 5,000 cases. Wines: Cab.Sauv., Chard. Visits by appt.

Rocky vineyard known for concentrated, earthy, gummy, tannic Cabernets. Chardonnay was added in 1985.

Mumm Cuvée Napa

Rutherford, Napa. Founded 1985. Owner: Joseph Seagram & Sons. 105,000 cases. Wines: n.v. Brut Prestige, n.v. Blanc de Noirs, Reserve, Winery Lake, DVX, Sparkling Pinot Noir. Visits.

Project Lafayette while it was in secret development, Domaine Mumm when the first *cuvées* were laid down, the winery became Mumm Cuvée Napa just as its first classic method sparklers were disgorged. Their ebullient fruitiness has made them popular California originals in England and on their home turf. Blanc de Noirs is the archetype; luxury cuvée DVX reaches for the other end of the stylistic pole.

Murphy-Goode

Healdsburg, Sonoma. Founded 1985. Owners: the Murphy and Goode families. 325 acres. 45,000 cases. Wines: Cab.Sauv., Chard., Merlot, Sauv.Bl., Zin. Visits.

Nalle

Healdsburg, Sonoma. Founded 1984. Owner: Doug Nalle. 20 acres. 4,000 cases. Wine: Zin.

One of too few in California who pays more than lip service to *terroir*, Nalle has gone so far as to drop Cabernet the better to concentrate on Zinfandel. No other shows more clearly or seductively why Dry Creek Valley should be planted to more of the variety.

Château Napa-Beaucanon *see* Beaucanon

Napa Cellars

Yountville, Napa. Founded 1973. Owner: Rombauer Vineyards. Wines (only available at the cellar door): Cab.Sauv., Chard.

Napa Cellars to begin, it turned into DeMoor in 1983, then, in 1996, gained a new owner and regained its maiden name.

Navarro Vineyards

Philo, Mendocino. Founded 1975. Principal and winemaker: Edward T. Bennett. 12,000 cases. 50 acres of vineyards in Anderson Valley and Mendocino of Chard., Gewürz., J.R., Cab.Sauv., P.N.

A grower taking advantage of a relatively foggy area to make uncommonly long-lived wines, notably Chardonnay and Gewürztraminer.

Newton Vineyards

St. Helena, Napa. Founded 1979. Partners: Peter and Sue Hua Newton. 105 acres above St. Helena. 12,000 cases. Wines: Sauv.Bl., Cab.Sauv., Merlot, Chard.

Rich, enjoyable Chardonnay from bought-in grapes. The winery's own vineyards produce highly rated Cabernet, Merlot and Sauvignon Blanc in an opulent style.

Nichelini Vineyard

St. Helena, Napa. Founded 1890. Owner and winemaker: Jo-Ann Nichelini Meyer. 50 acres. 5,000 cases. Wines: Ch.Bl., Sauv.Vert, Cab.Sauv., Napa Gamay, Pet.Sir., Zin.

Niebaum Coppola Estate

Rutherford, Napa. Founded 1978. Owner: Francis Ford Coppola. 240 acres. 25,000 cases. Wines: Cab.Sauv., Cab.Franc, Chard., Rubicon. Visits.

Movie man Coppola has his winery poised in the mid-1990s to become a major force in the Napa Valley. He bought the hidden half of the historic Inglenook property in 1979, the showcase half in 1995. With the winemaking tuned up, Cabernet-based Rubicon at last begins to impress, as does a short list of varietals.

A. Nonini Winery

Fresno, Fresno. Founded 1936. Winemakers: Reno and Tom Nonini. 200 acres. 30,000 cases. Wines: Chab.Bl., Golden Chasselas, Wh. Zin., Barbera, Gren., Zin. Visits.

Oak Ridge Vineyards

Lodi, San Joaquin. Founded 1934. Owners: grower-cooperative. 150,000 cases. Wines: Cab.Sauv., Chard., Merlot, Sauv.Bl., Wh.Zin., *Zin.

In the long-ago, when this was East Side, Reg Gianelli showed how tasty Lodi Zin could be as a daily red. Now, as Oak Ridge, it is the place to get a global view of Lodi as an AVA, and still a resource for friendly Zin.

Obester Winery

Philo, Mendocino. Founded 1977. Owners: the Obester family. 10 acres. 8,000 cases. Wines: Gewürz, Chard., P.N.

Founded in Half Moon Bay south of San Francisco, the winery relocated to the Anderson Valley in 1989. The Obesters also own the Gemello label.

Opus One

Oakville, Napa. Founded 1979. Owners: Robert Mondavi, Philippine de Rothschild. 60 acres. 12,000 cases. Visits by appt. Wine: Opus One.

Cabernet-based red, originally a sort of Mondavi Reserve of Reserves, now has its own architecturally wondrous home at the centre of an estate vineyard planted at Bordeaux densities. In theory styled to be Franco-American, but ripe, rich Napa grapes rule.

Orleans Hill Vinicultural Association

Woodland, Yolo. Founded 1980. President/winemaker: Jim Lapsley. 22,000 cases. Visits (Sat.).

Page Mill Winery

Santa Cruz Mountain, Santa Clara. Founded 1976. Owner: Richard Stark. 2,500 cases of Chard., Cab.Sauv., Zin., Sauv.Bl., P.N.

Parducci Wine Cellars

Ukiah, Mendocino. Founded 1933. Owner: William Hill. 400-plus acres. 350,000 cases.

Long the heart and soul of Mendocino winemaking under the direction of the Parducci family, the winery was bought in 1996 by its current owners, who promise to head in new directions using several geographically-based labels.

Robert Pecota Winery

Calistoga, Napa. Founded 1978. Owners: Robert Pecota. 40 acres in Napa Valley. 18,000 cases. Wines: Cab.Sauv., Sauv.Bl., Gam.Beauj., Chard. Visits by appt.

Good Cabernet Sauvignon and an oak-aged Sauvignon Blanc. A Gamay from Napa grapes is made by *macération carbonique*.

Pedrizzetti Winery

Morgan Hill, Santa Clara. Founded 1919. Owners: the Pedrizzetti family. 100,000 cases. Wines: a wide range of varietals. Visits.

J. Pedroncelli Winery

Geyserville, Sonoma. Founded 1904. Owners: John and James Pedroncelli. Winemaker: John Pedroncelli. 135 acres in Dry Creek Valley. 125,000 cases. Wines: many generic and varietal table wines. Visits.

An old reliable for local country jug wines, now making Zinfandel, Gewürztraminer, Chardonnay and Cabernet Sauvignon to a higher and stylish standard, and at very reasonable prices.

Robert Pepi Winery

Napa. Founded 1981. Owner: Kendall-Jackson. 70 acres. 25,000 cases. Wines: Sangiovese, Sauv.Bl.

Specialist in Sangiovese got its name from the original owner. Now part of K-J's Artisans and Estates group, and looking far beyond original Napa vineyard for grapes.

Pesenti Winery

Templeton, San Luis Obispo. Founded 1934. 65 acres. 33,000 cases. Wines: Gray R., J.R., Gewürz., Zin. Rosé, Cab.Sauv. Rosé, Wh.Zin., Muscat, Carnelli, Cab.Sauv., Zin. Visits.

Joseph Phelps Vineyards

St. Helena, Napa. Founded 1972. Owner: Joseph Phelps. 340 acres in Napa Valley. 65,000 cases. Wines: Chard., Sauv.Bl., Cab.Sauv., Zin., Syrah., J.R.

An ex-builder with an unerring sense of style built his beautiful redwood barn in the choppy foothills east of St. Helena near the Heitz place. His achievement is like a scaled-down Robert Mondavi's; all his many wines are good and several are among the best. My favourites are distinctly Germanic late-harvest Riesling and beautiful with bottle-age; Syrah – real Rhône Syrah; Cabernets – far from obvious but inspiring confidence. The Insignia label is for a strongly tannic Cabernet/Merlot blend on Bordeaux lines not qualifying as 'varietal' by the rules. Phelps Chardonnay is also restrained at first, but secretly rich. The late-harvest Gewürztraminer ages beautifully.

R. H. Phillips Vineyard

Esparto, Yolo. Founded 1983. Owners: the Giguiere family. 475 acres. 175,000 cases. Wines: Ch. Bl., Sauv.Bl., Zin., etc. Visits by appt.

Once-lonely pioneer grower in Dunnigan Hills northwest of Sacramento now has company there. Consistently agreeable reds and whites from Rhône varieties enticed the rivals. Sauvignon is another success.

Pine Ridge Winery

Yountville, Napa. Founded 1978. Principal and winemaker: R. Gary Andrus. 147 acres. 41,200 cases. Wines: Cab.Sauv., Chard., Ch. Bl., Merlot. Visits.

Separately bottled Rutherford and Stags Leap Cabernets teach delicious lessons about internal divisions of climate and soil in Napa. The Chardonnay and Chenin Blanc are also attractive.

Piper-Sonoma

Windsor, Sonoma. Founded 1980. Owners: Piper Heidsieck. Consultant: Michel Lacroix. 20,000 cases. Wines: Brut, Blanc de Noirs. Visits.

Late in 1996 Piper sold its winery and vineyard to J, the sparkling wine half of Tom Jordan's Sonoma wine empire. In addition to J, the new owners are to make Piper-Sonoma wines under contract to the French founder.

Prager Winery & Port Works

St. Helena, Napa. Founded 1980. Winemaker: James Prager. 3,400 cases. Visits by appt.

Preston Vineyards

Healdsburg, Sonoma. Founded 1975. Owner: Louis D. Preston. 125 acres in Dry Creek Valley, Sonoma. 25,000 cases. Wines: Sauv.Bl., Marsanne, Viognier, Barbera, Syrah, Zin.

Grower first, vintner second, Lou Preston appropriately dotes on estate Sauvignon and Zinfandel from Dry Creek Valley – and turns increasingly towards Rhône and Italian varieties.

Quady Winery

Madera, Madera. Founded 1977. Principal and winemaker: Andrew Quady. 15,000 cases. Wines: vintage port, Essensia, Muscat dessert wine. Visits.

Quady uses Zinfandel from Amador County but has planted the classic Portuguese varieties for a range of dessert wines and 'port'. The vines produced their first crop in '82, under the name of Frank's Vineyard. The celebrated Essensia is from Orange Muscat; Elysium is a red version from Muscat Hamburg grapes.

Quail Ridge

Rutherford, Napa. Founded 1978. Owner: Rutherford Benchmarks, Inc. 15,000 cases. Wines: Chard., *Sauv.Bl., *Cab.Sauv., Merlot.

The name is in its third home, under its third owner. The wines are more consistent than that: rich Sauvignon and a toasty Chardonnay.

Quivira

Sonoma. Founded 1986. Owners: Henry and Holly Wendt. 90 acres. 12,000 cases.

Fine Sauvignon and Zinfandel from Dry Creek Valley estate. Recent vintages have been more oak insistent.

A. Rafanelli Winery

Dry Creek Valley, Sonoma. Founded 1974. Winemaker: Dave Rafanelli. 60 acres. 6,000 cases-plus. Wines: Zin. and Cab. Visits by appt.

Outstanding Zinfandel from Dry Creek and good intense Cabernet.

Rancho Sisquoc Winery

Santa Maria, Santa Barbara. Founded 1972, winery 1978. 211 acres in Santa Maria Valley. 8,000 cases. Visits.

Part of the 38,000-acre James Flood Ranch.

Ravenswood

San Francisco, San Francisco. Founded 1976. Owner and winemaker: Joel Peterson. 25,000 cases. Wines: Zin., Cab.Sauv. Visits by appt.

Relentlessly pushes California's considerable capacity for ripeness.

Raymond Vineyards

St. Helena, Napa. Founded 1974. Owners: the Raymond family, Kirin. 450 acres. 200,000 cases. Wines: Chard., Sauv.Bl, *Cab.Sauv., Merlot.

The Napa Valley Reserve line, especially, is high-quality, typically oaky. Long-time Napans, the Raymonds are pioneer growers in American Canyon (at extreme south end of Napa) for Pinot Noir, and venturing into Monterey for less expensive Amberhill range.

Renwood

Plymouth, Amador. Founded 1991. Owner: Robert Smerling. 30 acres. 25,000 cases. Wines: Barbera, Nebbiolo, Syrah, Zin.

A new name has set out to make Amador Zinfandel more famous by making it to a still more heroic scale than previously, and raising the prices in proportion. Smerling bought the old Santino winery to house Renwood, and made Santino a second label, mostly for White Zin.

Ridge Vineyards

Cupertino, Santa Clara. Founded 1959. Owner: Otsuka Co. (since 1987). 50 acres. Vineyards near the winery plus grapes bought elsewhere (see below) 40,000 cases. Wines: Cab.Sauv., Zin., Pet. Sir. Visits.

One of California's accepted first-growths, isolated on a mountain-top south of San Francisco in an atmospheric old stone building that is cooled by a natural spring. The adjacent vineyard produces Montebello Cabernet but Cabernet and Petite Sirah are also bought at York Creek, Napa, and Zinfandel from Geyserville, Sonoma, and Paso Robles.

All the wines have a reputation for darkness, intensity and needing long ageing. The York Creek Cabernet is heavier

What the jargon means

References to California wine in current literature, on labels and from winery tour guides are full of racy jargon. Some of the less self-explanatory terms are:

Botrytized (pronounced with the accent on the first syllable). Grapes or wine infected, naturally or artifically, with *Botrytis cinerea*, the 'noble rot' of Sauternes: hence normally very sweet.
Brix The American measure of sugar content in grapes, also known as Balling, approximately equal to double the potential alcohol of the wine if all the sugar is fermented. 19.3 Brix is equivalent to 10% alcohol by volume.
Cold stabilization A near-universal winery practice for preventing the formation of (harmless) tartaric acid crystals in the bottle. The offending tartaric acid is removed by storing wine near freezing point for about 15 days.
Crush A California term for the vintage; also the quantity of grapes crushed, measured in tons an acre.
Field-grafting A method much used recently for converting established vines from one variety to another – usually red to white. The old vine top is cut off near the ground and a bud of the new variety grafted on.
Free-run juice The juice that flows from the crushed grapes

'freely' before pressing. By implication, superior. Normally mixed with pressed juice.
Gas chromatograph An expensive gadget for analysing a compound (e.g. wine) into its chemical constituents.
Gondola A massive hopper for carrying grapes from vineyard to crusher, behind a tractor or on a truck.
Jug wines Originally, wines collected from the winery in a jug for immediate use – therefore of ordinary quality. Now standard wines sold in large bottles.
Ovals Barrels of any size with oval, rather than round, ends, kept permanently in one place and not moved around the cellar – the German rather than the French tradition.
Polish filtration A final filtration through a very fine-pored filter to 'polish' the wine to gleaming brilliance.
Pomace The solid matter – skins, pips and stems – left after pressing.
Skin contact Alas not that, but a reference to leaving the juice mixed with the skins before separating them. All red wines must have maximum skin contact. Some white wines gain good flavours from a few hours 'maceration' with their skins before fermentation. For the 'cleanest', most neutral wine, a winemaker would avoid any skin contact.

than the elegant, lingering Montebello. The Zinfandel from Geyserville can smell of honey, a beautiful wine. Ten years is a good age to allow for Montebello to reach maturity.

Ritchie Creek

St. Helena, Napa. Founded 1974. Owner and winemaker: Richard Minor. 1,000 cases from 10 acres of vineyard in Spring Mountains. Wines: Cab.Sauv.,Chard.

River Run Vintners

Watsonville, Santa Cruz. First harvest: 1979. Owner: Christine Arneson. 4 acres. 2,500 cases. Wines: Chard., W.R., Cab.Sauv., Zin., L.H. Zin.

J. Rochioli Vineyards

Healdsburg, Sonoma. Founded 1979. Owners: Joe and Tom Rochioli. 130 acres owned, 25 acres leased. 4,500 cases. Wines: Chard., Sauv.Bl., P.N. Visits.

Roederer Estate

Philo,Mendocino. Founded 1985. Owners: the Roederer family. 60,000 cases, rising to 90,000. Wines: classic method.

A large-scale venture owned by the Champagne house with 450 acres in the Anderson Valley. Impressive from the first vintage onwards.

Rombauer Vineyards

St. Helena, Napa. Founded 1982. Co-owners: Joan and Koerner Rombauer. 15,000 cases. Wines: Chard., Cab.Sauv.,Merlot. Visits. Well-made, classic Chardonnay and Cabernet. To watch. Merlot from 1986.

Rosenblum Cellars Winery

Emeryville, Alameda. Founded 1978. Winemaker: Kent Rosenblum. 5,000 cases. Visits by appt. Wines: J.R., Wh.Zin., Zin., Nouveau, Cab.Sauv., sparkling Gewürz.

Roudon-Smith Vineyards

Santa Cruz, Santa Cruz. Founded 1972. Owners: Bob and Annamaria Roudon, Jim and June Smith. Winemaker: Bob Roudon. 12 acres owned. 10,000 cases. Grapes from Santa Cruz, Monterey, Sonoma and Mendocino. Visits.

A two-family affair, children and all, producing a stylish Chardonnay, balanced between firm and smooth like a good Meursault. The Cabernet matches it well in style; the Zinfandel is more burly.

Round Hill Cellars

St. Helena, Napa. Founded 1978. Owners: Ernie van Asperen & partners. 300,000 cases. Wines: Chard., Sauv.Bl., Cab.Sauv., Merlot, Zin.

Not all new Napa wineries aim at Montrachet. Round Hill supplies a wider market with good-value versions of distinct variety-plus-region character, notably Napa Cabernet and Merlot under both the Round Hill and Rutherford Ranch labels. An excellent Round Hill Zinfandel is in lamentably short supply. Separate range of California-appellation Round Hill wines costs still less.

Rutherford Hill Winery

St. Helena, Napa. Founded 1976. Partners: Bill Jaeger and estate of Chuck Carpy. 150,000 cases. The partners own some 800 acres in the valley. Wines: Chard., Gewürz., Merlot., Cab.Sauv., Sauv.Bl. Visits.

Compare the partners with Freemark Abbey. Here they use their nicknames and relax. The winery was built for Souverain but sold to the present owners in 1976. Now the idea is true fruity varietals with a light touch for restaurant-drinking and the better class of picnic – which in California is saying a lot. Largest production is of Chardonnay, Merlot and Cabernet Sauvignon.

St. Clement Vineyards

St. Helena, Napa. Founded 1975. Owners: Sapporo USA. 20 acres. 10,000 cases. Wines: Cab.Sauv., Chard., Sauv.Bl., Merlot. Visits.

A small and specialized producer who sold to Sapporo in 1987; a great success with critics at the outset, though I found early Chardonnays too alcoholic for their fruit. The balance is apparently better now. The Sauvignon is well spoken of.

St. Francis Winery

Kenwood, Sonoma. Founded 1979. Owner: Kobrand. 34,000 cases from 90 acres of Chard., J.R., Gewürz., Merlot, Cab.Sauv. and Muscat Canelli. Visits.

Merlot is doing well, and Chardonnay and Cabernet also bring in praise.

St. Supery

Rutherford, Napa. Founded 1987. Owner: Robert Skalli. 300 acres. 50,000 cases. Wines: Cab.Sauv., Merlot, Chard., Sauv.Bl. Visits.

Cabernet and Sauvignon from Dollarhide Ranch show what Napa's easterly, upland Chiles Valley can do with Bordeaux varieties, red and white.

Saintsbury

Napa, Napa. Founded 1982. Partners: Richard Ward and David Graves. 40,000 cases. Wines: Chard., P.N. Visits by appt.

Burgundian inspiration here – Chardonnay and Pinot Noir are the only wines. Many consider them the leaders in their genre in America.

San Antonio Winery

Los Angeles. Founded 1917. Owners: the Riboli family. 400,000 cases. Wines: Chard., Cab.Sauv.,Ch. Bl., J.R., Wh. Zin. Visits.

Sanford Wines

Buellton, Santa Barbara. Founded 1981.Owners: the Sanford family. 140 acres. 50,000 cases. Wines: Chard., Sauv.Bl., P.N., vin gris of P.N. Visits by appt.

Sanford has earned a name for characterful Chardonnay and Pinot Noir. Now that the winery has gained a hold on the Sanford & Benedict Vineyard (in which Richard Sanford was an original partner), the resolute Pinot Noir from it is bottled separately as a Reserve. Sauvignon Blanc can be fascinating, especially with age.

Santa Barbara Winery

Santa Barbara, Santa Barbara. Founded 1962. Owner: Pierre Lafond. 75 acres. 28,000 cases. Wines: Chard., Sauv.Bl., P.N., J.R., Zin. Visits.

Santa Cruz Mountain Vineyard

Santa Cruz, Santa Cruz. Founded 1974. Principal and winemaker: Ken D. Burnap. 2,500 cases from 14 acres of vineyards in Santa Cruz Mountains of P.N., Cab.Sauv.
A locally respected specialist in powerful Pinot Noir, sometimes suffering from too much alcohol.

Santa Ynez Valley Winery

Santa Barbara, Santa Barbara. Founded 1976. Owner: Doug Scott. 20,000 cases. Grapes from 110 acres in Santa Ynez Valley, Santa Barbara, planted in Sauv.Bl., Chard., Ries., Gewürz., Cab.Sauv., Merlot. Visits.
A white-wine specialist celebrated from birth for marvellously confident and vital Sauvignon Blanc.

Santino Wines *see* Renwood

Sarah's Vineyard

Gilroy, Santa Clara. Founded 1978. 7 acres. 2,000 cases.
Sarah's Chardonnay has a high reputation. Merlot and Rhône-variety blends are recent ideas.

V. Sattui Winery

St. Helena, Napa. Founded 1885, refounded 1975 (by the same family). Owner and winemaker: Daryl Sattui. 69 acres. 35,000 cases, all sold at the winery. Wines: J.R., Cab.Sauv., Chard., Sauv.Bl., Gamay Rouge, Wh. Zin. Visits.
Good Cabernet and Riesling draw the customers. There is also a picnic ground and a deli at the winery.

Sausal Winery

Healdsburg, Sonoma. Founded 1973. Principal and winemaker: Dave Demostene. 14,000-plus cases. 125 acres in Alexander Valley, Sonoma. Wines: Zin., P.N., Chard., Cab., Sauv.Bl.
A former supplier of grapes and bulk wines launched (1979) with above-average Zinfandel and others.

Scharffenberger Cellars

Ukiah, Mendocino. Founded 1981. Owners: Veuve Clicquot Ponsardin. 25,000 cases. Visits by appt. Wines: Brut, Blanc de Blancs.
Champagne-owned pioneers of Mendocino sparklers, with grapes from Anderson Valley and other areas.

Schramsberg Vineyards

Calistoga, Napa. Founded 1862 by Jacob Schram, 1965 by Jack Davies. Owners: Jack and Jamie Davies. 40 acres in Napa Valley. 50,000 cases. Wine: bottle-fermented sparkling wines. Visits by appt.
Robert Louis Stevenson drank 'bottled poetry' at Schram's ornate white, verandahed house. So have I, many times, under the Davies regime. Jack has visited just about every sparkling-wine cellar on earth and learned something in all of them. He practises his mystery in shiny steel, in old coolie-driven rock tunnels, and in his forest-clearing vineyard.

Davies introduced a luxury *cuvée*, J. Schram, with a 1987, and instantly set new standards for California. His Blanc de Blancs is California's subtlest and driest, most age-worthy 'champagne', the Blanc de Noirs is outstanding, juicier and more generous, deserving 2–10 years' ageing, the Cuvée de Pinot a dry 'partridge-eye' pink and the Crémant a sweet, subtly Muscat, less fizzy party wine.

Schug Cellars

Sonoma, Sonoma. Founded 1981. Owner: the Walter Schug family. 30 acres. 15,000 cases. Wines: Cab.Sauv., Sauv.Bl., Chard., P.N, sparkling. Visits by appt.
Walter Schug focuses on understated yet indelible Chardonnay and Pinot Noir in his third, doubtless final, winery. The progression has been orderly, from Calistoga south to Yountville, then on to Carneros. The evolution of the German-born and trained Schug's commitment to Carneros grapes has been equally steady.

Sebastiani Vineyards

Sonoma, Sonoma. Founded 1904. Owners: the Sebastiani family. 300 acres in Sonoma Valley. 3.8 m. cases. Many wines. Visits.
A name intimately connected with the historic little city of Sonoma (which even has a turn-of-the-century Sebastiani Theatre). Sebastiani moved from being a bulk producer to high quality with smooth speed. Today their Cabernets are remarkable, their Barbera and Gewürztraminer robust and appetizing. Former president Sam Sebastiani left in 1986 to found his own winery.

Seghesio Winery

Healdsburg, Sonoma. Founded 1902. President: Eugene Seghesio. 350 acres. 85,000+ cases. Wines: Zin., Sangiovese, P.N.
A long-established concern that only began to bottle its own wines in 1980. Zinfandel has been the signature. Sangiovese from the family's Vitigno Toscano vineyard begins to be. The whole line offers notable value.

Sequoia Grove Vineyards

Napa, Napa. Founded 1980. 24 acres. 16,000 plus cases. Wines: Estate Chard., Cab.Sauv. Visits.

Shafer Vineyards

Napa, Napa. Founded 1979. Owner: John Shafer. 150 acres. 25,000 cases. Wines: Chard., Cab.Sauv., Merlot. Visits by appt.
Producer of immaculate Stags Leap Cabernet and Merlot and Carneros Chardonnay.

Shenandoah Vineyards

Plymouth, Amador. Founded 1977. 32 acres. 60,000 cases. Wines: Vintage Port, Zin. Port, Orange Muscat, Black Muscat, Zin., Cab.Sauv., Sauv.Bl., White Zin. Visits.
Sobon Estate is, in effect, the reserve label.

Sherrill Cellars

Woodside, Santa Clara. Founded 1973. Winemaker: Jan Sherrill. 2,500 cases from Central Coast; also called Skyline. Wines: Chard., Sauv.Bl., Gamay, Cab.Sauv., Pet. Sir., Zin. Visits.

Sierra Vista Winery

Placerville, El Dorado County. Founded 1977. Owner/winemaker: John MacCready. 6,000 cases from 28.5 acres owned and 8.5 acres leased. Wines: Chard., Fumé Bl., Viognier, Cab.Sauv., Zin., Syrah. Visits by appt.

Rhône blends plus Syrah have joined steady Cabernet, Zinfandel and other wines.

Silver Oak Cellars

Oakville, Napa. Founded 1972. Partners: Justin Meyer and Raymond Duncan. Winemaker: J. Meyer. 21 acres. 25,000 cases of Cab.Sauv. from Napa and Sonoma grapes.Visits.

Silver Oak makes separate Napa and Alexander Valley Cabernets in separate cellars, the Napa one at Oakville, its sibling at Cloverdale. The two wines are separated by their tannins (Napa is the tougher one), unified by prolonged and telling exposure to American oak, which is the cornerstone of Justin Meyer's style. Bonny's Vineyard, once kept separate, now goes into the Napa.

Silverado Vineyards

Napa, Napa. Founded 1981. Owner: Lillian Disney. 335 acres. 80,000 cases. Wines: Chard., Sauv.Bl., Cab.Sauv., Merlot.

Silverado's Chardonnay, Sauvignon Blanc and Cabernet Sauvignon are all ripe and sophisticated and share a growing reputation. Only estate grapes are used. 1986 saw the inauguration of reserve bottlings of Chardonnay and Cabernet Sauvignon.

Simi Winery

Healdsburg, Sonoma. Founded 1876. Owner: LVMH. 294 acres. 130,000 cases. Wines: Chard., Cab.Sauv., Cab.Rosé, Sauv.Bl. Visits.

Simi 1935 Zinfandel is one of the very few antique California wines to have survived in any quantity. It is marvellous. A 1974 begins to be its equal. Yet Simi dropped the variety by 1980 to focus more sharply on subtle Alexander Valley Cabernet and its barrel-fermented, barrel-aged Chardonnay, both regularly among the best in California. Its Sauvignon Blanc is splendid, its Cabernet Sauvignon Rosé irresistible. Owner LVMH undertook a major reorganization of Simi in 1996, the outcome of which I could not foretell.

Sky Vineyards

Mayacamas Mountains, Sonoma. Founded 1979. 12 acres. 1,600 cases. Wine: Zin.

Smith-Madrone

St. Helena, Napa. Founded 1977. Owners: Stuart and Charles Smith. 40 acres on Spring Mountain, Napa. 6,000 cases. Wines: J.R., Chard., Cab.Sauv. Visits by appt.

Vineyards at 1,700 feet and total hard-working dedication are making remarkable wines in a simple cellar. Sweet, lemony Riesling is easy to love, young or old. However an assertive Chardonnay can be the star of any vintage.

Sonoma-Cutrer Vineyards

Windsor, Sonoma. Founded 1981. President: Brice Jones. 600 acres. 75,000 cases plus. Wines: Chard., P.N.

For years the winery reigned as California's all-Chardonnay specialist, offering a range from named vineyards: Les Pierres, Cutrer and Russian River Ranches. So far, Les Pierres is the best. With 1994, owner Jones broke Chardonnay's hegemony, adding Pinot Noir.

Spottswoode Vineyard and Winery

St. Helena, Napa. Founded 1982. Owners: Mary Novak. 40 acres. 3,500 cases. Wines: Cab.Sauv., Sauv.Bl.

Stag's Leap Wine Cellars

Napa, Napa. Founded 1972. Owners: Warren and Barbara Winiarski. 200 acres in Napa Valley. 60,000 cases plus. Wines: Cab.Sauv., Chard., J.R., Merlot, Pet. Sir., Sauv.Bl. Visits.

Winiarski is a professor of Greek turned winemaker, whose Cabernets have startled the French with their resemblance to great Bordeaux. My notes are full of 'harmony, elegance, feminine, finesse'. Compared with Bordeaux they age relatively soon, offering, at 8 years, consistent sweetness from lips to throat. 'Cask 23' is a riper reserve Cabernet. Stag's Leap Merlot and Chardonnay get equally good reviews, although my favourite remains the Cabernet. These standards have been maintained for recent vintages. Hawk Crest, the second label, oftimes covers wines of substance.

Stags' Leap Winery

Napa, Napa. Founded 1972. President: Carl Doumani. 17,000 cases (planned 25,000) from 110 acres. Wines: Pet. Sir., Burg., Ch.Bl., Cab.Sauv., Merlot, Chard.

P. and M. Staiger

Boulder Creek, Santa Cruz. Founded 1973. Winemaker: Paul Staiger. 5 acres. 400 cases. Wines: Chard., Cab.Sauv., P.N. Visits by appt.

Steltzner Vineyard

Napa, Napa. Founded 1983. Owner and winemaker: Richard Steltzner. 78 acres. 7,500 cases. Wines: Cab.Sauv., Sauv.Bl., L.H. Gewürz. (when possible). Visits by appt.

Sterling Vineyards

Calistoga, Napa. Founded 1969. Owner: Jos Seagram. Visits. 150,000 cases. 1,100 acres in Napa Valley. Wines: Cab.Sauv., Merlot, Chard., Sauv.Bl., P.N.

The long white building like a Greek monastery hugs the top of a lump in the valley floor big enough to need cable cars to get up it. British money built it in the 1960s; Coca-Cola bought it in 1978, and Seagrams took over in '83. Ric Forman, now with his own winery, designed the Sterling style of original, serious wines. The Sterling speciality used to be an austere Cabernet with a daring level of volatile acidity, but recent vintages have been more conventional. The stress now is on single-vineyard wines, notably including a Merlot from Three Palms Vineyard and a Chardonnay from Winery Lake. The strong, dry Sauvignon Blanc can come as a relief after some of the more tropical-fruit flavours of the valley. Chardonnay follows the same lines.

Stevenot Winery

Murphys, Calaveras. Founded 1978. Principal: Barden Stevenot. 27 acres of estate vineyard. 50,000 cases. Wines: Ch. Bl., Zin., Fumé Bl., Muscat Canelli, Chard., Cab.Sauv. Visits.

Ambitious winery well-launched with Chenin Blanc and Zinfandel, followed up by Cabernet and Chardonnay.

Stonegate

Calistoga, Napa. Founded 1973. Owners: James and Barbara Spaulding. Winemaker: David Spaulding. 35 acres in Napa Valley. 12,000 cases. Wines: Cab.Sauv., Merlot, Chard., Sauv.Bl. Visits by appt.

Estate wines much improved recently, especially the Chardonnays and Sauvignon Blanc.

J. Stonestreet

Windsor, Sonoma. Founded 1990. Owner: Kendall-Jackson. 54 acres. 25,000 cases. Wines: Cab.Sauv, Merlot, Legacy (Cab.-based), P.N., Chard.

The first link in Kendall-Jackson's Artisans and Estates division has moved away from estate (the vineyard never has yielded an impressive Cabernet for the current or two previous owners) and towards artisan, with grapes brought in from ever-widening circles in coastal California.

Stony Hill Vineyard

St. Helena, Napa. Founded 1951. Owner: Peter McCrea. Winemaker: Michael Chelini. 42 acres in Napa Valley. 8,000 cases. Visits by appt. Wines: Chard., J.R., Gewürz.

Fred McCrea was the first of the flood of men from busy offices who realized that the Napa Valley offered something better. He planted white grapes in the 1940s and made 25 vintages of his own understated style of wine. Neither the variety nor the maturation grabs your attention; the point seems to be boundless vigour and depth without an obvious handle. At a 1980 tasting of all the Chardonnay vintages of the 1960s, the '62 was best, in fact fabulous, but not markedly older than the '69. 1980s vintages have perhaps been heavier and riper. Eleanor McCrea continued her husband's total integrity of purpose after his death. When she died, son Peter took up the reins with no compromise. A second label, SHV, uses non-estate grapes.

Storybook Mountain Vineyards

Calistoga, Napa. Founded 1979. Owner: Dr. J. Bernard Seps. 36 acres. 6,000 cases. Wine: Zinl. Visits by appt.

Rodney Strong Vineyards

Sonoma. Owner: Rodney Strong. 375,000 cases.
Single-vineyard Chardonnays and Cabernets are the mainstay.

Sullivan Vineyards Winery

Rutherford, Napa. Founded 1972. Winemaker: James Sullivan. 4,500 cases. Wines: Cab.Sauv., Merlot, Zin., Ch. Bl. Visits by appt.

Sunrise Winery

Cupertino, Santa Clara. Founded 1976. Owners: Ronald and Rolayne Stortz. 3 acres. 2,500 cases. Weekend visits.

Sutter Home Winery

St. Helena, Napa. Founded 1874, refounded 1946. President: Louis 'Bob' Trinchero. 2,200 acres. 3 m. cases. Wine: Chard., Cab.Sauv., Sauv.Bl., Wh.Zin., Zin. Visits.

A family operation (named after another, pre-Prohibition family) that once specialized in small lots of red Zinfandel, later in huge volumes of White Zinfandel, now offers the usual shortlist of varietals, most bearing California as an appellation, all at modest prices. One thing remains unchanged: a heady Amador Zinfandel Reserve is the flagship of the house.

Joseph Swan Vineyards

Forestville, Sonoma. Founded 1969. 10 acres in Russian River Valley, Sonoma. 1,200 cases. Wines: Zin., Chard., P.N., Cab.Sauv.

The late Joseph Swan's Zinfandel has always been a waiting-list wine for those whose cigar-scarred palates are looking for a perceptible flavour. His son-in-law carries on.

Swanson Vineyards

Rutherford, Napa. Founded 1987. Owner: W. Clarke Swanson. 200 acres. 25,000 cases. Wines: Chard., Cab.Sauv., Merlot, Sangio., Syrah.

In the increasingly common Napa practice, Swanson-owned vineyards range from Oakville to Carneros, to give a range of grape varieties proper homes. And still the style leans as heavily on new oak barrels as terroir. Banker Swanson also owns Avery's of Bristol.

Lane Tanner

Santa Maria, Santa Barbara. Founded 1986. Owner: Lane Tanner. 2,000 cases. Wines: P.N.

Tanner is emerging as a gifted interpreter of Santa Barbara Pinot Noirs, whether blended or from named vineyards.

Thornton Winery

Temecula, Riverside. Owner: John Thornton. Wines: Brut, Brut Reserve, Cuvée de Frontignan, Chard., Sauv.Bl., Nebbiolo.

Originally the Culbertson Winery, it was renamed after a takeover by its current owner (who began as a Culbertson partner). Labels are Culbertson for spakling wines and Brindiamo for still wines.

Philip Togni Vineyard

St. Helena, Napa. Founded: 1983. Owner: Philip Togni. 10 acres on Spring Mountain. 1,000 cases increasing to maximum 2,000. Wines: Sauv.Bl., Cab.Sauv., Ca' Togni (sweet). Visits by appt.

Topolos (Russian River Vineyards)

Forestville, Sonoma. Refounded 1980. Owners: Jerry and Michael Topolos. 110 acres, 8,000 cases. Wines: Zin., Pet.Sir., Alicante Bouschet, Chard., Sauv.Bl., 'Cab.Bl'. Visits.

Marimar Torres Estate

Sebastopol, Sonoma. Founded 1982. Owner: Marimar Torres. 47 acres. 12,000 cases. Wines: Chard., P.N. Visits by appt.

The emphatically individualistic Torres does all in her power to subdue California fruitiness in favour of bouquets from winemaking, above all in her Chardonnay.

Trefethen Vineyards

Napa, Napa. Founded 1886, refounded 1973. Owners: the Trefethen family. President: Gene Trefethen. 600 acres in Napa Valley. 70,000 cases. Wines: J.R., Chard., Cab.Sauv., 'Eshcol' (Cab.Sauv and Chard.). Visits.

The Trefethens bought the former 'Eshcol' vineyards, in mid-valley near Napa, in 1968, leased their grand old wooden barn to Moët-Hennessy for their first vintage of Domaine Chandon (for which they grew many of the grapes), then started using their best grapes to make their own wine. The whole line is highly polished and professional (and good value). Chardonnay attracted most notice at first, but the clean mid-weight Cabernet and the dry Riesling with no lush or melony touches make classy stable mates. Late-released 'Library' wines show remarkable ageing potential. The '83 Chardonnay was a noble wine in 1990 and still is. Blended 'Eshcol' table wines are some of the best value in the state. Eshcol was the valley where the monster grape cluster grew (Numbers XIII v. 23). So is this.

Trentadue Winery & Vineyards

Geyserville, Sonoma. Founded 1969. Owners: Leo and Evelyn Trentadue. 145 acres. 25,000 cases. Visits.

Tudal Winery

St. Helena, Napa. Founded 1979. Owner/winemaker: Arnold Tudal. 7 acres. 2,500 cases Wines: Cab.Sauv.

Tulocay Winery

Napa, Napa. Owner: W. C. Cadman. Founded 1975. 2,400 cases. Wines: Cab.Sauv., P.N., Chard., all from Napa grapes. Visits by appt. A small operation making full-flavoured reds designed for laying down.

Turnbull Vineyards (originally Johnson-Turnbull)

Oakville, Napa. Founded 1979. Owner: Patrick O'Dell. 150 acres. 7,500 cases. Wines: Cab.Sauv., Chard. Visits.

After purchasing the winery from its founders in 1993, O'Dell expanded the vineyard holdings and showed a willingness to think new thoughts, but thus far the Cabernet continues to out-mint, out-spice even Martha's Vineyard.

Ventana Vineyards Winery

Soledad, Monterey. Founded 1978. Owner: J. Douglas Meador. 400 acres. Many wines made.

Wines mostly as adverts for a superlative vineyard on the Salinas Valley's west side, oft-named on the labels of others.

Viader

St. Helena, Napa. Founded 1989. Owner: Delia Viader. 18 acres. 2,000 cases. Wine: proprietary Cabernet-based, estate-grown blend.

Vichon Winery

Oakville, Napa. Founded 1980. Owner: the Robert Mondavi family. Late in 1996 the Mondavis announced that Vichon will disappear from the Napa Valley, to reappear in the Languedoc – eventually with a new producing winery there. The Mondavis made 1995s in both regions.

Villa Mt. Eden

Oakville, Napa. Founded 1881, refounded 1970. Owners: Stimson Lane. 87 acres in Oakville, Napa. 50,000 cases. Visits. Wines: Chard., Cab.Sauv., P.N., Zin.

Founded on a historic vineyard by a family ownership, the winery moved to the former Conn Creek after Stimson Lane sold the original home property, and began buying grapes everywhere in California for wines that range from large-volume commodities (called 'Cellar Select') to tiny lots of named-vineyard varietals. A few of the latter still come from Napa.

Weibel Champagne Vineyards

Mission San Jose, Alameda/Mendocino. Founded 1945. Owners: the Weibel family. Many wines.

Under bankruptcy protection for several years, but still selling wine.

Wente Vineyard

Livermore, Alameda. Founded 1883. Owners: the Wente family (President: Carolyn Wente). 2,300 acres in Livermore Valley and Arroyo Seco, Monterey County. 300,000 cases. Wines: most varieties of table wine. Visits.

One of the greater wine dynasties of America. The founder, Carl, started with Charles Krug in the Napa Valley and moved to the stony Livermore Valley because land was cheaper. His sons Herman (winemaker and marketer, d. 1961), Ernest (grape grower, d. 1981) and Ernest's son Karl (d. 1977) are greatly respected names. Karl was a bold innovator, the first in California to build steel fermenting tanks outdoors and a pioneer of Monterey vineyards. The fourth generation bought 600 more potential vineyard acres (old Cresta Blanca and ranching land) in Livermore and planted in 1982–83. The name changed from Wente Bros to Wente Vineyard in 1996, shortly after Karl and Jean Wente's daughter, Carolyn, took the reins as winery president.

White wines made the Wente name. In the early 1960s their Sauvignon Blanc was my favourite; bold, sappy, old Bordeaux style. Since then, Riesling and Chardonnay have done brilliant turns as well, and reds have become firmly ensconced in a broad, sound range.

White Rock

Napa, Napa. Founded 1990. Owners: the Vandendriessche family. 35 acres. 3,000 cases.Wines: *Claret, Chard.

From a secluded vineyard not far from the Stags Leap District, in miles or flavour, Henri Vandendriessche makes a brilliant Cabernet-based estate red never to be seen in Europe because he insists Claret is the most honest name it might bear.

William Wheeler Winery

Healdsburg, Sonoma. Founded 1979. Owner:J.-C. Boisset. 25,000 cases. Wines: Chard., Cabernet, Merlot. Visits.

Once a winery, now a negociant label, which reached as far afield as the Languedoc to fill its bottles when California went short of grapes in the mid-1990s.

Whitehall Lane Winery

St. Helena, Napa. Founded 1980. Owner: Thos Leonardini. 55 acres. 25,000 cases. Wines: Chard., Cab.Sauv., Merlot, Zin. Visits.

White Oak Vineyards

Healdsburg, Sonoma. Founded 1980. Owner: Bill Myers. 6 acres. 11,000 cases. Wines: Chard., Cab.Sauv., Zin., Sauv.Bl., Ch. Bl. Private Reserve Chardonnay is rich and ripe, the Chenin and Sauvignon also win praise..

Wild Horse Winery

Paso Robles, San Luis Obispo. Founded 1983. Owner: Ken Volk. 38 acres. 15,000 cases. Wines: P.N., Cab.Sauv., Merlot, Chard. Another Pinot Noir specialist producing impressive results from mainly San Luis Obispo and Santa Barbara grapes.

Williams & Selyem

Healdsburg, Sonoma. Founded 1981. Owners: Burt Williams, Ed Selyem. 3,000 cases. Wines: P.N., Chard., Zin. Williams and Selyem make Russian River Pinot Noir for all it is worth, having taken DRC as their philosophical model. They produce as many as six named-vineyard wines per year, many of them able to out-duel their French tutors in the inevitable blind tastings.

York Mountain Winery

Templeton, San Luis Obispo. Founded 1882. 5,000 cases. Visits.

Zaca Mesa Winery

Los Olivos, Santa Barbara. Vineyards planted 1978. Owners: John and Lou Cushman. 240 acres near winery. 60,000 cases. Wines: Syrah, Marsanne, Cuvée Z, Chard.

With Firestone (q.v.) one of the first to plant in the Santa Ynez Valley. Pioneer vineyards on the 1,500-foot flat-topped 'mesa' (former cow country) are phylloxera-free and ungrafted. Chardonnay and Riesling were the first two successes. With Dan Gehrs as winemaker, it has shifted its focus to Rhône varieties in the 1990s. Syrah is the flagship, Marsanne the great white hope. Cuvée Z is a blend of estate-grown fruit.

ZD Wines

Napa, Napa. Founded 1969. Owners: the Norman de Leuze family. 3.5 acres of Cab.Sauv. with grapes bought in Napa, Sonoma, Santa Barbara and San Luis Obispo for Chard. and P.N. 18,000 cases. Visits.

Pinot Noir and Chardonnay (the latter with American oak) are the focus; the philosophy is to find the right grapes in any part of California.

THE PACIFIC NORTHWEST

If, in the early 1970s, America was waking up to superlative quality from Napa and Sonoma, by the end of the decade the *avant-garde* were heralding the Pacific Northwest as the coming wine region, with strong hints that the new area would make something closer to the European model: wines less overbearing than the California champions. Much of this potential has been fulfilled.

In the early 1960s, a young man from Salt Lake City, Utah, drove through the Donner Pass into Paradise – California's Napa Valley. Instead of enrolling in a dental school in San Francisco as he intended, he instead temporarily lost his mind and enrolled in a viticulture programme at the University of California at Davis. That man was David Lett. Lett became enamoured of Pinot Noir, but felt that in most cases California wasn't getting it right. He began studying climatological data from Oregon's Willamette Valley and became convinced that the valley was the best place outside Burgundy to grow Pinot Noir grapes. In 1965 he moved to Oregon and began planting a vineyard. The Eyrie Vineyards made its first wine in 1970.

About the same time, a group of University of Washington professors began a hobby winemaking project in a garage in Seattle. By 1967, they had made several very tasty wines from grapes grown in the Yakima Valley of central Washington. They invited the late André Tchelistcheff, then winemaker at Beaulieu Vineyard in Napa Valley, to taste their Gewürztraminer. Tchelistcheff not only loved the wine, but encouraged the men to produce more. Thus, Associated Vintners (now Columbia Winery) was born.

As early as 1979, Oregon Pinot Noir gained international accolades when David Lett's 1975 Pinot Noir was placed second in a competitive blind tasting in Paris organized by Robert Drouhin of Beaune: Drouhin's own 1959 Chambolle-Musigny won first place. Drouhin was so impressed that he visited Oregon several times, establishing a vineyard and winery near Lett's in 1988. Since the Paris tasting, many Northwest wineries have been in the international limelight for Chardonnay and Pinot Noir from Oregon and Cabernet Sauvignon and Merlot from Washington.

In less than 30 years, the Pacific Northwest wine industry has burgeoned from just a handful of wineries, many producing only fruit and berry wines, to approximately 200 ranging in production from a few hundred to millions of litres of premium *vinifera* wines yearly. Vineyard acreage has increased to nearly 25,000 acres, mostly planted to the classic European varieties. Viticulturalists have sought out the best microclimates for growing grapes, and winemakers throughout the Northwest have learned to work with the grapes to express their best potential. These focused efforts have created the true tastes of the Northwest.

The Pacific Northwest is not one grape-growing area, but two. North of the California border in western Oregon, the Coast Range asserts itself as a rain catcher, sheltering the Umpqua Valley to the south, then further north the Willamette Valley. Annual rainfall is a reasonable 30–40 inches, and the latitude the same as that of Bordeaux. For the most part, this is a gentle maritime climate, best suited to cool-climate grape varieties. Although the star to date has been Pinot Noir, with Chardonnay and Riesling also in abundance, recent years have seen increased plantings to Pinot Gris and Pinot Blanc. The quality of Gewürztraminer is generally high, and the area also produces some very good sparkling wines.

In complete contrast, the vineyards of Washington have been planted two ranges back from the Pacific Ocean, east of the much higher Cascade Mountains, in an area with a mere 10 inches of rain a year – the Columbia River Basin, and within it the more grape-specific Yakima Valley. Here, American Concord grapes first were grown for jelly making. But the region's deep sandy soil, long summer daylight hours and hot sunshine have proved ideal for wine grapes. The latitude – 100 miles further north than the Willamette – and the continental extremes of temperature (very cold in winter and surprisingly chilly even on a summer night) have proved particularly suited to the Bordeaux varieties – Semillon, Sauvignon Blanc, Cabernet Sauvignon, Cabernet Franc and Merlot. Chardonnay, Riesling and Gewürztraminer also fare extremely well in eastern Washington. Grapes ripen well while keeping remarkably high acidity, with consequent intensity of flavour.

Three regional designations are permitted on Oregon labels: Willamette Valley (AVA: nine counties from Portland 100 miles south to Eugene); Umpqua Valley (AVA: Douglas County, centred on Roseburg, another 50 miles south); and Rogue Valley (Jackson and Josephine counties, centred on Grant's Pass, 50 miles south again).

Washington's vineyards are concentrated in the Yakima Valley, but its established wineries are centred around Seattle. The three AVAs are Columbia Valley, Yakima Valley and Walla Walla Valley, south of the State line. Up to now the grapes have been transported the 150 miles over the Cascades to Seattle, but several companies have now built wineries near the vineyards, between the ridges of such unvinous-sounding ranges as the Rattlesnake and the Horse Heaven Hills. Watch out for such names as Ahtanum Ridge, Wahluke Slope, Canoe Ridge and Red Mountain.

The Oregon wine industry grew up in the Willamette, Umpqua and Rogue valleys near where grapes were grown. While vineyards in Oregon matured, many wineries purchased grapes from Washington vineyards. In Washington, most grapes are grown east of the Cascade Mountains, though the industry's first generation saw most of its winemaking in northwestern Washington, predominantly in the Woodinville-Kirkland area just north of Seattle. Today Woodinville is still the stronghold for many of Washington's largest and most prestigious wineries but more and more wineries, both large and small, are locating closer to the grape source. Neighbouring Idaho, whose vineyards are east of Oregon, along the Snake River, has 12 wineries and is making a name for itself with its Chardonnays.

OREGON

Leading Willamette Valley Producers

ACME Wineworks/John Thomas Winery

Carlton, OR 97111. Willamette Valley. Owner and winemaker: John Thomas.
Established in 1993, ACME produces small batches of hand-crafted Pinot Noir under two labels: the ACME label is better value, the John Thomas, sporting a traditional Burgundy-style label, the better wine.

Adelsheim Vineyard

Newberg, OR 97132. Willamette Valley. Owners: David and Virginia Adelsheim. Winemaker: Don Kautzner.
The winery first crushed in 1978, using mainly Washington grapes. Today, focus is on fine Pinot Noir from its own and neighbouring vineyards. Also produced are Chardonnay, Pinot Gris and a small amount of dry Riesling.

Airlie Winery

Monmouth, OR 97361, Willamette Valley. Owners: Larry and Alice Preedy. Winemaker: Larry Preedy.
Kansas transplants, the Preedys began growing grapes in Oregon in 1983. Their beautifully tended 35-acre vineyard yields Pinot Noir, Chardonnay, Müller Thurgau, Riesling, Gewürztraminer (the last often one of their best wines) and Marechal Foch. The winery produces approximately 5,000 cases of wine annually.

Amity Vineyards

Amity, OR 97101. Willamette Valley. Owners: Myron and Ione Redford, Janis Checchia. Winemaker: Myron Redford.
Amity, established in 1976, produces about 10,000 cases of wine a year. Its best efforts at present are dry Riesling, Gewürztraminer and Pinot Blanc. The quality of the Pinot Noir varies.

Archery Summit

Dayton, OR 97114, Willamette Valley. Owner and winemaker: Gary Andrus.
California-based Gary Andrus is owner of Pine Ridge Vineyards in Napa Valley. This new, state-of-the-art winery made its first wines (1993 and 1994 vintages) in California with Oregon fruit. The winery opened in May 1996. Primary focus is Pinot Noir, and the first releases indicate that these are competent wines.

Argyle/The Dundee Wine Company

Dundee, OR 97115. Willamette Valley. Owners: Brian Croser and Cal Knudsen. Winemaker: Rollin Soles.
A strange marriage of Australia (Croser), Washington (Knudsen – formerly a partner in Knudsen Erath Vineyards) and Texas (Soles) produces some of the best *méthode traditionnelle* sparkling wines in the United States. The 100,000-gallon capacity winery, founded in 1987, also produces very good Chardonnay, Pinot Noir, and a delicious dry Riesling.

Autumn Wind Vineyard

Newburg, OR 97132. Willamette Valley. Owners: Tom and Wendy Kreutner. Winemaker: Tom Kreutner.

A small, 5,000-case estate winery, a former cherry orchard in Yamhill County, Autumn Wind produces a rich and toasty Pinot Noir, plus Chardonnay, Müller-Thurgau, Sauvignon Blanc and Pinot Gris.

Beaux Frères

Newburg, OR 97132. Willamette Valley. Owners: Michael Etzel, Robert M Parker and Robert Roy. Winemaker: Michael Etzel.

Beaux Frères is currently the darling of the Oregon wine industry, devoted to small quantities of intense, oaky Pinot Noirs from its 16-acre vineyard. Co-owner Parker is the wine author and critic. First wine was from the 1991 vintage. A tiny amount of Chardonnay was also made in '94.

Bethel Heights Vineyard

Salem, OR 97304, Willamette Valley. Owners: Ted and Terry Casteel, Pat and Barbara Dudley and Marilyn Webb. Winemaker: Terry Casteel.

Since 1984, Bethel Heights has been one of Oregon's most consistent Pinot Noir producers and is widely known for its excellent 15-acre vineyard in the Eola Hills near Salem. Once a much-sought grape source, the winery now uses all its own grapes for a roster of fine wines that also include Chardonnay, Pinot Gris and Pinot Blanc. Grapes are picked as late as possible to give the wines intensity and a bold profile.

Chehalem

Newberg, OR 97132. Willamette Valley. Owners: Harry and Judy Peterson-Nedry, Bill and Cathy Stoller. Winemaker: Harry Peterson-Nedry.

From its first commercial crush in 1991, Chehalem has become known for deep, intense, estate-grown Pinot Noirs. The 1994 vintage saw the first collaboration between the Oregon winery and Burgundian winemaker Patrice Rion (Domaine Daniel Rion) for Rion Reserve Pinot Noir. 5,000 cases of wine yearly from 60 acres of vineyards. Chehalem also makes Pinot Gris, Chardonnay and Gamay Noir.

Cristom Vineyards

Salem OR 97304, Willamette Valley. Owners: Paul and Eileen Gerrie. Winemaker: Steve Doerner.

The Gerries established their winery in 1992 and hired one of California's brightest and best – Steve Doerner, formerly of Calera Vineyards – as their winemaker. Cristom annually produces some 5,000 cases of delicious Pinot Noir, Pinot Gris and Chardonnay. Most grapes come from neighbouring vineyards as the Gerries establish their own plantings.

Cuneo Cellars

Amity, OR 97101. *Willamette Valley*. Owners: Gino Cuneo and Martin Barrett. Winemaker: Gino Cuneo.

Formerly Hidden Springs Winery, Cuneo Cellars produces Pinot Noir from its estate grapes and Cabernet Sauvignon, Nebbiolo and Cana's Feast (a Bordelais blend) from Yakima Valley grapes. The Cana's Feast is particularly fine.

Domaine Drouhin

Dayton, OR 97114. Willamette Valley. Owner: Robert Drouhin. Winemaker: Véronique Jousset-Drouhin.

Dedicated to exceptionally stylish Pinot Noirs from its own and neighbouring vineyards, DDO has produced consistently fine wines since its first crush in 1988. The 200-acre estate, with its beautiful stucco winery partially buried in the hillside, is truly one of Oregon's showplaces.

Eola Hills Winery

Rickreall, OR 97371, Willamette Valley. Owners: Investor group headed by Tom Huggins. Winemaker: Kerry Norton.

Located near Salem, Eola Hills, established in 1986, has risen in stature due to its line-up of great tasting, reasonably priced varietals, including Pinot Noir, Chardonnay, Riesling and Sauvignon Blanc made from grapes grown on its own and neighbouring Eola Hills vineyards. Production is approximately 20,000 cases a year.

Elk Cove Vineyards

Gaston, OR 97119. Willamette Valley. Owners and winemakers: Joe and Pat Campbell.

The Elk Cove estate boasts more than 50 acres of vineyards, yielding nearly 20,000 cases of wine a year. In addition to Pinot Noir, well-oaked Chardonnay, Riesling and Pinot Gris, the winery produces a delicious line of ultra-sweet dessert wines – Riesling, Sauvignon Blanc, Pinot Gris and Gewürztraminer. The newest planting, La Bohème, has provided the winery's most delicious Chardonnays and Pinot Noirs to date.

Erath Vineyard and Winery

Dundee, OR 97115, Willamette Valley. Owners: Dick Erath and Rob Stuart.

With the addition of Rob Stuart, oenologist, and a change of name from Knudsen Erath to Erath Vineyard and Winery, this pioneer winery has gained new life. MOre delicious than ever are the dry Riesling and Gewürztraminer; Chardonnay has hit its stride with the new Dijon clones from Burgundy; Pinot Noir has stabilized and is beautiful; and new to the winery are Pinot Gris, Pinot Blanc and tiny bits of Arneis and Dolcetto (just for fun!). Stuart's presence has allowed Erath to oversee winemaking and spend more time in his beloved vineyards. Clear direction, excellent quality.

Evesham Wood Winery

Salem, OR 97304, Willamette Valley. Owners: Russell and Mary Raney. Winemaker: Russell Raney.

Small estate winery established in 1986, now producing approximately 3,000 cases of wine including a bold, intense Pinot Noir, Chardonnay, Pinot Gris and an exceptionally fine dry Gewürztraminer.

The Eyrie Vineyards

McMinnville, OR 97128. Willamette Valley. Owners: David and Diana Lett. Winemaker: David Lett.

Delicate, pretty Pinot Noirs, viscous, oaky Chardonnays and deliciously fruity Pinot Gris are this Oregon pioneer vintner's hallmarks. Since his first vintage in 1970, David Lett has been a maverick; he sticks to his style even though the industry around him has changed. His wines have proven remarkably and deliciously age-worthy. Also produces Pinot Meunier and dry Muscat.

Flynn Vineyards

Rickreall, OR 97371, Willamette Valley. Owners: Wayne, Mickey and Jeanne Flynn. Winemaker: Bob McRitchie.

With first vineyards planted in 1982 and first wines made in 1984, Flynn built a large new winery in 1990, and since then has devoted most of its efforts to sparkling wines, with Pinot Noir and Chardonnay too.

Hinman Vineyards

Eugene, Willamette Valley. Owner: Carolyn Chambers.

One of the largest and most advanced wineries in the state, with Gewürztraminer, Pinot Noir, Riesling and good Cabernet from Washington grapes.

King Estate

Eugene, OR 97405, Willamette Valley. Owners: the King family (Ed King is president). Winemakers: Brad Biehl and Will Bucklin.

This huge, new, well-financed operation is Oregon's largest winery with a capacity of 200,000 cases. Located on a 350-acre-plus estate, the château-style winery focuses on Pinot Gris, Pinot Noir and Chardonnay and has published two Pinot-devoted cookbooks. Pinot Gris is King's best wine to date. First vintage was in 1992.

Lange Winery

Dundee, OR 97115, Willamette Valley. Owners: Don and Wendy Lange. Winemaker: Don Lange.

Transplants from Santa Barbara (California), the Langes have established a lovely, family-run estate vineyard and winery in Yamhill County and since 1987 have produced some excellent wines, although the quality is not yet consistent. Top attention-getters are their Reserve Pinot Gris and Reserve Pinot Noir.

Montinore Vineyards

Forest Grove, OR 97116, Willamette Valley. Owners: Leo and Jane Graham. Winemaker: Jacques Tardy.

Magnificent 500-acre estate planted in the early 1980s with a dozen different vine varieties in 45 blocks. Today, under French winemaker Jacques Tardy's direction, production focuses on Pinot Noir, Chardonnay and Pinot Gris with smatterings of Riesling, Gewürztraminer and late-harvest wines rounding out the portfolio.

Oak Knoll Winery

Hillsboro, OR 97123, Willamette Valley. Owners: The Vuylsteke family. Winemaker: Ron Vuylsteke.

One of Oregon's most venerable wineries, Oak Knoll at first featured fruit and berry wines. These have given way to varietals, primarily Pinot Noir, Chardonnay and Riesling, all from purchased grapes. The 32,000-case facility has no vineyards.

Panther Creek Winery

McMinnville, OR 97128, Willamette Valley. Owner: Ron Kaplan; Winemaker: Mark Vlossak.

In 1994, Panther Creek changed hands and owner/winemaker Ken Wright moved on to another venture. Excellent, deeply flavoured Pinot Noir continues, along with Chardonnay and the little-known French variety, Melon.

Ponzi Vineyards

Beaverton, OR 97007. Willamette Valley. Owners: Richard and Nancy Ponzi. Winemaker: Luisa Ponzi.

This pioneer 12-acre Oregon winery has been passed on to the second generation now that its founders have retired. The three Ponzi children control operations. Still highly regarded for its dry Riesling, unctuous Chardonnay, lush Pinot Gris and hefty Pinot Noir, Ponzi is also experimenting with Arneis and Dolcetto at its new Aurora Vineyard site. Some 9,000 cases a year are produced.

Rex Hill

Newberg, OR 97132, Willamette Valley. Owners: Paul Hart and Jan Jacobsen. Winemaker: Lynn Penner-Ash.

From several vineyard sites throughout Yamhill County, winemaker Lynn Penner-Ash produces more than 30,000 cases of wine annually in a variety of price categories. Easy sippers are the Kings Ridge Pinot Gris, Chardonnay and Pinot Noir. More intense are the vineyard-designated Pinots and Chardonnays. Connoisseurs can revel in the Reserve Pinot Gris, Pinot Noir and Chardonnay and an occasional, intensely flavoured Cabernet Sauvignon.

Shafer

Forest Grove, OR 97116, Willamette Valley. Owner/winemaker: Harvey Schafer.

A firm belief that quality stems primarily from the vineyard motivates Shafer, whose Chardonnay and Riesling have been praised. Shafer is also a specialist in very good Pinot Noir, which produces both red and rosé, Sauvignon Blanc and Gewürtraminer. Quality tends to vary.

Sokol Blosser Winery

Dundee, OR 97115. Willamette Valley. Owners: Bill and Susan Sokol Blosser. Winemaker: John Haw.

One of Oregon's larger and more mature wineries, Sokol Blosser flagged briefly in the late 1890s with changes in winemaker and general confusion. Today, happily, it is back on its feet with John Haw producing excellent wines – particularly the Redland Chardonnay and Pinot Noir. Production is around 25,000 cases. Other varieties include Riesling and Muuller-Thurgau.

St. Innocent Winery

Salem, OR 97303, Willamette Valley. Owner: St-Innocent Ltd. Winemaker: Mark Vlossak.

Established in 1988, the winery is popular for its forward Pinot Noir and Chardonnay and a delightful sparkling wine. Production is 6,000 cases yearly; grapes are purchased from various Eola Hills vineyards.

Torri Mor Winery

McMinnville, OR 97128, Willamette Valley. Owners: Donald and Trisha Olson. Winemaker: Patricia M Green.

New, tiny and very promising. The first commercial wines were made in '93 from the Olsons' Dundee Hills vineyard.

Tualatin Vineyard

Forest Grove, OR 97116. Willamette Valley. Owners: Bill Malkmus and William Fuller. Winemaker: William Fuller.

All Tualatin wines come from grapes grown at the 85-acre estate vineyard established in 1973. Stellar achievements have been Riesling and Chardonnay, with Pinot Noir coming into its own recently. Bill Fuller did a stint with the Louis Martini winery in Napa. A very experienced winemaker and a great ambassador for Oregon wine.

Tyee Wine Cellars

Corvallis, OR 97333. Willamette Valley. Owners: Dave and Margy Buchanan, Barney Watson, Nola Mosier. Winemaker: Barney Watson.

A small gem of a winery, Tyee excels in Pinot Gris, Pinot Blanc and Gewürztraminer and also produces Pinot Noir and Chardonnay. Barney Watson, a Davis graduate, is research oenologist at nearby Oregon State University.

WillaKenzie Estate

Yamhill, OR 97148, Willamette Valley. Owners: Bernard and Ronni LaCroute. Winemaker: Laurent Montalieu.

Forty acres of young vines and a state-of-the-art, 25,000 case-capacity winery are big news for this farmstead-oriented estate in western Oregon. Add a brilliant young French winemaker (formerly from Bridgeview Winery in southern Oregon) and there looks to be a winning combination. First wines from WillaKenzie Estate were made in 1995. The Pinot Gris and Pinot Blanc are delicious; Chardonnay and Pinot Noir from barrel are promising.

Yamhill Valley Vineyards

McMinnville, OR 97128, Willamette Valley. Owner: Partnership managed by Denis Burger. Winemaker: Stephen Carey.

Established in 1983 and gained acclaim with their first Pinot Noir and are continuing to do so. Also produce Chardonnay and Pinot Gris.

Leading Rogue Valley Producers

Bridgeview Vineyards

Cave Junction, OR 97523, Rogue Valley. Owners: Robert and Lelo Kerivan. Winemaker: Bryan Wilson.

Bryan Wilson joined Bridgeview in 1995 replacing Laurent Montalieu who moved to WillaKenzie Estate in Willamette. Montalieu brought this large southern Oregon winery to prominence in the early 1990s with Pinot Gris, Pinot Noir, Chardonnay, Riesling and Gewürztraminer from the winery's 74-acre estate.

Foris Vineyards

Cave Junction, OR 97523, Rogue Valley. Est. 1973. Owners: Meri and Ted Gerber. Winemaker: Sarah Powell.

The Gerbers began producing wine commercially in 1987. Most delicious are the Merlot and Gewürztraminer, though all wines are well made. Production 7,000 cases yearly, also includes Pinot Noir and Chardonnay.

Valley View Vineyards

Jacksonville, OR 97530, Rogue Valley. Owners: the Wisnovsky family. Winemaker: John Guerrero.

This winery has recently made great strides with the Bordelais varieties, both reds and whites. The Anna Maria reserve line is particularly fine; also the big rich Chardonnay. Planting of the 26-acre vineyard began in 1978 on property rich in history: pioneer Peter Britt planted 200 varieties in experimental vineyards there in the 1850s.

Umpqua Valley

Henry Estate Winery

Umpqua. Owners: Scott and Sylvia Henry. Winemaker: Scott Henry III.

Scott Henry began in wine by designing oenological equipment. Now his estate, on the fertile valley floor, produces 10,000 cases annually from 31 acres: Chardonnay, Gewürztraminer and Pinot Noir. The Barrel Fermented and Select wines have pronounced American oak flavours. Gewürztraminer is probably Henry's best, but recently introduced Müller-Thurgau is generating interest.

WASHINGTON

Leading Columbia Valley Producers

Barnard Griffin

Kennewick, WA 99336, Columbia Valley. Owners: Deborah Barnard and Rob Griffin. Winemaker: Rob Griffin.

During his tenure at the Hogue, Rob Griffin began making his own wines – in fact, he did it in a corner of the Hogue. But he always had a hankering for his own small winery, and more experimental wines. His success with Cabernet Sauvignon, Merlot, Sauvignon (Fumé-style) Blanc and Chardonnay is legendary. Production small.

Columbia Crest Winery

Paterson, WA 98072. Owners: Stimson Lane Ltd. Winemaker: Doug Gore. Chard., Cab.Sauv., Sauv.Blanc., Merlot.

90% of the winery is underground making humidity and temperature control easier, and providing excellent storage conditions. Doug Gore takes the quality of his wines very seriously and makes a good cross-section of varietal wines, the best of which are the Merlot, the Cabernet Sauvignon, the Sauvignon Blanc and the Chardonnay. Now the State's largest single winery Doug Gore's deft touch with the Washington fruit and the Stimson Lane marketing machine have proved a winning combination.

Preston Premium Wines

Pasco, WA 99301, Columbia Valley. Est. 1976. Owners: the Preston family. Winemaker: Brent Preston.

Wide range from a quality-conscious operation. 80,000 cases from 181 acres. Fourteen varieties including Chardonnay, Cabernet Sauvignon, Fumé Blanc, Merlot, Riesling.

Leading Yakima Valley Producers

Chinook Winery

Prosser, WA 98350, Yakima Valley. Est. 1984. Owners: Kay Simon and Clay Mackey. Winemaker: Kay Simon.

Small winery producing excellent Merlot, Sauvignon Blanc and Chardonnay. Kay Simon was former winemaker at Château Ste-Michelle; husband and partner Clay Mackey was the Château's vineyard relations manager. 2,000 cases.

Covey Run

Zillah, Yakima Valley WA 98953. Owner: Associated Vintners (owners of Columbia Winery and Paul Thomas Winery). Winemaker: Dave Crippen.

Established 1982. An attractive winery making popular wines. Chardonnay stands out; there is also Riesling, Fumé Blanc, Cabernet Sauvignon and Merlot. Also produces 'Ice Wine' from berries harvested in January. Very sweet and intense. 40,000 cases from 180 acres.

Hedges Cellars

Benton City, WA 98320, Yakima Valley. Owners: Tom and Anne-Marie Hedges, Mats Hanzon. Winemaker: Pat Henderson.

Founded in 1990 by a potato farmer (Tom Hedges) with vision, Hedges Cellars found its niche exporting Washington wines to Europe and Scandinavia. While the corporate office is near Seattle, the Hedges vineyards on Red Mountain sport a beautiful new château-style winery. Cabernet-Merlot blend is the emphasis; the Sauvignon Blanc is also very fine.

Hinzerling

Prosser. Yakima Valley. Owner/winemaker: Mike Wallace. First vintage 1976. 6,000 cases. 30 acres. Ries., Gewürz., Cab.Sauv. Visits. A family affair capable of excellent wine (such as botrytis Gewürztraminer), but not consistent.

The Hogue Cellars

Zillah, WA 98953. Est. 1987. Owners: Leland and Lynda Hyatt. Winemaker: Ray Sandidge.

This 20,000 case-winery struck a chord from its earliest vintages. It now focuses on Merlot, Riesling and Black Muscat. Family-owned, family-operated and homey.

Kiona Vineyards and Winery

Benton City, WA 99320. Yakima Valley Owners: the Williams family. Winemaker: Scott Williams.

Established in 1979. Fermentation, lab work and storage began in family garages. The 10,000-case winery now specializes in deep, dark Cabernet Sauvignon and Merlot and delicious late-harvest Riesling and Gewürztraminer.

Paul Thomas Winery

Sunnyside, WA 98944, Yakima Valley. Owners: Associated Vintners Inc. Winemaker: Mark Cave.

The winery's tasting room is in the Seattle area; this new production facility was opened in 1995. Paul Thomas focuses on a full line of varietal wines; however, its dry rhubarb and dry Bartlett pear wines are also very popular.

Thurston Wolfe Winery

Prosser, WA 99350, Yakima Valley. Est. 1987. Owners: Wade Wolfe and Becky Yeaman. Winemaker: Wade Wolfe.

Consistently wonderful and eclectic wines including Zinfandel, Lemberger, fortified Muscat and two types of 'Port'. Production is small – less than 1,000 cases – as Wolfe is also vineyard manager at The Hogue Cellars.

Washington Hills Cellars

Sunnyside, WA 98944, Yakima Valley. Owners: Harry Alhadeff and Brian Carter. Winemaker: Brian Carter.

Brian Carter is one of Washington's most gifted winemakers. He began working with Alhadeff in 1990 and established the popularity of this premium brand. Carter also makes the ultra-premium Apex wines – Chardonnay, Cabernet, Sauvignon Blanc and late-harvest wines – under the auspices of Washington Hills. Total production: 100,000 cases.

Leading Walla Walla Producers

Canoe Ridge Vineyard

Walla Walla, WA 99362, Walla Walla Valley. Owners: the Chalone Group corporate partnership. Winemaker: John Abbott.

While the young 700-acre vineyard is located on the Columbia River (next to Château Ste. Michelle's Canoe Ridge Estate … yes, it does get confusing), the winery is 50 miles away in downtown Walla Walla. Canoe Ridge made its first wines – tantalizing Merlot and Chardonnay – in 1994. These remain the winery's focus.

Leonetti

Walla, Walla. WA 99362. Owners: Gary and Nancy Figgins. Winemaker Gary Figgins.

The outstanding Cabernet-maker of the Northwest, making deep-coloured, structured, aromatic, long-paced wines. Established in 1977; now 4,000-case turnover from 10 acres. Figgins concentrates on producing just three or four red wines each year. Selected grapes and new oak make for expensive but very worthwhile Merlot and Cabernet. Such success makes the wines difficult to obtain.

Waterbrook Winery

Lowden, WA 99360, Walla Walla Valley. Owners: Eric and Janet Rindal. Winemaker: Eric Rindal.

Stylistically distinct, with clean varietal flavours tempered with American oak, Waterbrook wines stand apart. They represent, for the most part, good value and excellent quality. Cabernet Sauvignon, Merlot, Sauvignon Blanc and Chardonnay are the focus.

Woodward Canyon Winery

Lowden, WA 99360, Walla Walla. Owners: Rick and Darcey Fugman-Small. Winemaker: Rick Small.

One of Washington's most popular brands. Noted for its toasty Cabernet and Merlot, and its ripe, rich, woody (either love it or hate it) Chardonnay. Annual 8,000 cases.

Other AVAs

Andrew Hill Winery

Vashon, WA 98070, Puget Sound. Owners: Chris and Annie Camarda. Winemaker: Chris Camarda.

Small, family-owned winery focusing on small quantities of Cabernet Sauvignon, Merlot and barrel-fermented Chenin Blanc (Cuvée Lulu).

Arbor Crest

Spokane. Owners: the Mielke family. Winemaker: Mikhail Brunshteyn.

Established in 1982. Good winemaking and ample capital have made this Washington's most prolific medal winner. Sauvignon Blanc, Merlot, Cabernet Sauvignon all arrive with perfect acids and sugars needing little or no correction.

Château Ste. Michelle

Woodinville, WA 98072. Owner: US Tobacco. Winemakers: Mike Januik and Charles Hoppes.

Much the biggest concern in the Northwest (1 million-case annual turnover), and with its top wines among the best. The large showpiece winery at Woodinville, 15 miles north-east of Seattle, has been outgrown and in 1983 a 26-million dollar River Ridge facility, three times as big, was built on the Columbia River near Paterson. The estate has also restored an old winery, at Grandview in the Yakima Valley.

Grapes are all planted on their own rootstock and come from two areas of the Columbia Basin: Cold Creek (especially good for Cabernet and Merlot) and Grandview, where whites do best. The wines produced cover the full spectrum: Chardonnay, Cabernet Sauvignon, Sauvignon Blanc Gewürztraminer, Chenin Blanc, Semillon, Merlot, Riesling and 'Port' – all notably well made, the whites being especially successful in the local market.

The new (1992) Canoe Ridge Vineyard houses the red-wine production: this huge area overlooks the Columbia River and is devoted to Chardonnay and Merlot. Special emphases in recent vintages have been laid on the winery's vineyard-designated Chardonnays, Cabernet Sauvignons and Merlots, which rank among the Northwest's finest.

Ste Michelle, by virtue of its size, its technical profession-alism and its marketing ability, stands as a worthy flagship for the whole winemaking industry in the Northwest. Oregon would benefit from something similar itself.

Columbia (formerly Associated Vintners)

Bellevue, WA 98004. A private corporation with 25 stockholders. Winemaker: David Lake, MW.

One of the pioneers of the Northwest, originally (1962) a group of professors at the University of Washington, and currently one of the best. Since 1976 it has been a fully commercial operation using Yakima Valley grapes and directed by a British Master of Wine, who worked with David Lett in Oregon. Now making a wide variety of excellent wines including Gewürztraminer, Cabernet Sauvignon, Merlot, Sémillon, Chardonnay and Riesling. The policy is to buy in grapes, at any rate until vineyards have established a track record. They have contracts with some of the best grape growers, particularly Otis Vineyards and Red Willow and Wyckoff in the Yakima Valley.

DeLille Cellars/Chaleur Estate

Woodinville, WA 98070, Seattle area. Owners: Charles and Greg Lill, Jay Soloff, Chris Upchurch. Winemaker: Chris Upchurch.

Up-and-coming winery focusing on producing 2,000 cases yearly of ultra-premium Bordeaux-style red blend from selected eastern Washington vineyards. First vintage 1992; a small amount of Sauvignon Blanc-Semillon was made with the 1995 harvest. Chaleur Estate is a complex and heady blend selected from the best barrels.

Latah Creek

Spokane, WA 99216. Winemaker and owner: Mike Conway.

Established in 1982. Emphasis has changed from light fruity white wines to meaty Merlot, Cabernet Sauvignon and robust Chardonnay. 15,000 cases. No vineyards.

Quilceda Creek

Snohomish, WA 98290. Owners: Alex and Jeanette Golitzin. Winemaker: Paul Golitzin.

Established in 1978; Alex Golitzin concentrates single-mindedly on making great Cabernet in the Médoc tradition, and he has already made some of the best in the Northwest. 2,000-case turnover.

Salishan

La Center, SW Washington. Owner/winemaker: Joan Wolverton.

Established in 1971. 2,000 cases from 12 acres of Pinot Noir, Riesling, Chardonnay and Cabernet Sauvignon.

SilverLake Winery/SilverLake Sparkling Cellars

Woodinville, WA 98070, Seattle area. Owners: Washington Wine and Beverage Co. Winemaker: Cheryl Barber-Jones.

Founded in 1989, SilverLake hit its stride with the hiring of former Château Ste-Michelle head winemaker Cheryl Barber-Jones. Approximately 14,000 cases of premium varietal wines are produced. Early 1997 saw the opening of the new sparkling wine facility.

Snoqualmie Winery

Snoqualmie, WA 98065. Owner: US Tobacco/Stimson Lane Wines & Spirits Inc. Winemaker: Joy Anderson.

Founded in 1983 by Joel Klein who had formerly worked for Château Ste-Michelle, where he helped to design the winery. 50,000 cases yearly of consistently made and reasonably priced varietal wines including Cabernet Sauvignon, Merlot, Sauvignon Blanc, Semillon, Chardonnay, Riesling, Gewürztraminer and Muscat Canelli.

IDAHO

Ste. Chapelle

Caldwell, ID 83605. Owners: the Symms family. Winemaker: Kevin Mott.

Founder Bill Broich, an excellent if restless winemaker, left in 1985 having established a fine track record with Riesling, Chardonnay, Gewürztraminer and sparkling wines made from Riesling, Chardonnay and Pinot Noir. Established in 1970 – the oldest and by far the largest of Idaho's dozen wineries, controlling over two-thirds of the state's 700 acres of vineyards. 130,000 cases from 260 acres. Also buys in Washington grapes to complete its roster of wines. The style is for crisp, elegant and slightly floral wines, dictated largely by the climate which does not reliably ripen the grapes.

Indian Creek Winery

Kuna, ID 83634. Owners: Bill Stowe and partners. Winemaker: Bill Stowe.

One of the half-dozen wineries grouped in the Caldwell area, southwest of Boise, and one of the State's most interesting properties. With some 20 acres of vineyards and production of about 6,000 cases of wine yearly, Bill Stowe devotes himself to better-than-average Pinot Noir, including a stylish dry White Pinot Noir, with smaller quantities of Riesling and Chardonnay. The winery's first vintage was in 1987.

Rose Creek Vineyards

Hagerman, ID 83332. Owner/winemaker: Jamie Martin.
Family-run winery established in 1984. 2,500 cases of wine produced annually from 35 acres of vineyard plus small lots from Idaho-grown grapes. Riesling and Chardonnay had to be discontinued when their own vineyard was frozen out.

OTHER PRODUCERS

Camas Winery Est. 1983. Northern Idaho's oldest premium winery.

Cana Vineyards Est. 1990 on the site of the former Lou Facelli winery.

Carmela Vineyards Some 48 acres in the Hagerman viticultural area.

Cocolalla Winery the state's northernmost winery, making an annual 400 cases of *brut* sparkling.

Hells Canyon Winery Est. 1980 and makes an annual 2500 cases of Chard and Cab.Sauv.

Petros Winery Est. in 1983 by Lou Facelli.

Pintler Cellar 13 acres planted to Ries., Sem., Chard., P.N. and Cab.Sauv.

South Hills Winery Family enterprise making an annual 1,000 cases of Ries and a blush blend of Ries. and P.N.

Weston Winery One of Idaho's oldest and highest wineries – at 2,750 feet.

OTHER REGIONS OF THE USA

For centuries the true wine-vine, *Vitis vinifera*, could not be successfully grown in the climate of most of North America. The problems are extremes of cold in the north and centre and of heat and humidity in the south. The cold simply kills the vines in winter. Humidity brings rampant mildew; the heat of southern summers, a general malfunction of the vine (instead of respiring at night and building up sugar the plant continues to grow; the sugar is used in excessive foliage and the grapes, despite months of broiling heat, are scarcely ripe). The south, moreover, is also troubled by a bacterial malady of the vine called Pierce's Disease, transmitted by leaf-hoppers.

Two regions, the northeast (led by New York State) and the southeast (led by Virginia), have strong wine traditions of their own and are now enjoying a great revival. Until very recently, their wine industry was based on native grapes, adapted to the local climate, but most wineries today concentrate on *vinifera*. In the south the grape is the Muscadine, or Scuppernong, a plant very different from the classic wine-vine (its berries are like clusters of marbles with tough skins that slip off the flesh). The powerful flavour of its sweet wine was once immensely popular in America in a famous brand called Virginia Dare. Scuppernong still flourishes but bears no relation to the wines of the rest of the world.

But now almost every state of the Union outside these areas has hopeful winemakers – hopeful of seeing their industry, fledgling or a century old, as some of them are, establish itself as part of the American wine boom.

A number of long-established wineries have distinct local markets. In the past, these tended to be a disincentive to experimenting with new grapes. When it was assumed for so long that *Vitis vinifera* could not be grown, it was a brave winemaker who did more than dip a toe in the water with an acre or two of experimental planting. With modern knowledge more and more dippers are reporting success. There are certainly quite large areas where the micro-climate appears to makes *vinifera* a practicable proposition after all. There are also new hybrid vines, crosses between *vinifera* and American natives, which show the hardiness of the natives without their peculiar flavours. These French-American hybrids have greatly improved over the past few years, but their overall importance in the eastern market has been overshadowed by recent successes with *vinifera*.

The wine boom is being led from the metropolitan areas of America, which have latched on to the varietal names of California. Riesling, Chardonnay, Cabernet Sauvignon are now household words. The best hybrids (Seyval Blanc, Vidal Blanc, Chambourcin) still have a long way to go. At present, in fact, wine growers in the eastern and central states are looking three ways at once: at the old American varieties of *Vitis labrusca*, the exciting but risky *viniferas*, and the hybrids between the two. In the east, hybrids and *labrusca* will probably always play a role, but the majority of wine growers are now betting on *vinifera*.

New York State and Virginia have the biggest and best-established wine industries, but there is no reason to think that they have overwhelming natural advantages. What the other regions lack is a bold entrepreneur to interpret their growing range of wines to the critical metropolitan public.

NEW YORK STATE

The New York State wine industry, long established around the Finger Lakes south of Lake Ontario, has up to now been considered a maverick backwater by most wine lovers. Originally based on varieties and chance hybrids of the native vine *Vitis labrusca*, its wines were characterized by the peculiar scent of *labrusca* known as 'foxiness'. Most also had high acidity, usually masked by considerable sweetness.

Non-foxy French-American hybrids replaced *labrusca* in all but the most conservative wineries for almost 40 years. Although it is usually acceptable and occasionally very good, little of the wine is exciting by European–Californian standards. Some companies in New York, as elsewhere in the east, still see *labrusca* as a reliable vine, well-adapted to the stresses of the eastern climate. These growers also believe that its wine's distinctive flavours might provide them with a unique niche in a crowded market. At present about 40% of New York wine is 'hybrid', 40% *labrusca* (mainly for less expensive 'jug' wines), while most premium wine companies use *vinifera*, with a smaller amount of hybrids. Twenty years ago *vinifera* accounted for only 2% of the total vineyard acreage; today the figure is 20%.

Since the mid-1950s, however, there has been a vocal minority, first led by Dr Konstantin Frank, dedicated to proving that *vinifera* vines can successfully be grown in the Finger Lake areas. Their successes, at least with white wines, convinced many. Most of the original vineyards have now planted at least some *vinifera*, and promising new vineyards are growing *vinifera* almost exclusively.

America's wine boom started to affect New York in the mid-1970s. In the late '80s there were shifts in the industry that would influence the direction of New York wine-growing. First Seagram and then Coca-Cola decided that the industry could be expanded. Seagram bought Gold Seal and Coca-Cola bought Taylors and Great Western, the largest and most important wineries in the region. All three wineries have since closed, and Seagram and Gold Seal have decided to get out of the Finger Lakes wine business altogether. Today a new generation of wine producers (many of them descendants of the original growers who supplied Taylors) is concentrating on the types of *vinifera* that do well in cool climates, especially Riesling, Chardonnay and Pinot Noir.

In 1976 the State law was changed to encourage 'farm wineries', lowering the licence fee for firms producing under 50,000 gallons (about 21,000 cases) a year and easing restrictions on their sales. The result was the rapid start-up of exactly the small, open-minded enterprises New York needed to improve its image. Three dozen small wineries were born or reborn, mainly in the Finger Lakes but also in the Hudson River Valley above New York City – which has a long history of nearly being a wine region – and on Long Island, where the maritime climate is kinder than upstate.

Of the State's four wine regions, it is Long Island that is booming, its wineries benefiting from two AVAs, the Hamptons and North Fork, created in 1985 and 1986. From small beginnings in 1973, when the Hargraves planted vines on North Fork, 17 wineries now dot the map. Of note are Pindar (one of the biggest), Palmer, Paumanok, Pellegrini, Peconic Bay Vineyards and Bedell Cellars The Hargraves began with Cabernet, Pinot Noir, Sauvignon and later, Chardonnay. This last and Merlot seem to be the consumers' preferred choice, but growers are also trying Riesling, Gewürztraminer, Chenin Blanc and Cabernet Franc.

Leading New York State Wineries

Benmarl Wine Company

Marlboro, N.Y. 12542. Founded 1957. Owners: Mark and Dene Miller. 10,000 cases. 75 acres of Verdelet, Vignoles, Chelois, Chard., Cab.Sauv., Seyval Bl., Baco Noir.
A historic vineyard in the Hudson River Valley where the hybrid Dutchess was raised in the 19th century, restored by Mark Miller who runs it as a cooperative of some 1,000 wine lovers, the Société des Vignerons, who help finance, pick and drink varietal Seyval, Baco Noir, Chelois and Maréchal Foch. Their wines are all highly regarded in New York.

Bully Hill Vineyards

Hammondsport, N.Y. 14840. Founded 1958. Owner: Walter S. Taylor. Winemaker: Gregg Learned. 220,000 cases. 130 acres. Visits. The only Taylor still making wine – on the original family property on Lake Keuka. Hybrid wines are some of the best of the old school, and 'champagne'. Splendid labels.

Canandaigua Wine Company, Inc.

Candaigua, N.Y. 14424. Founded 1945. Owner: Marvin Sands. Winemaker: Dominic Carisetti. 18m. cases. No vineyards. *Labrusca* wines under brand names Almaden, Dunwood, Inglenook, Paul Masson, Marcus James, Manischewitz, Richards (Wild Irish Rose) and J. Roget. Reputedly the nation's third-largest wine producer.

Dr. Frank's Vinifera Wine Cellars

Hammondsport, N.Y. 14840. Founded 1962. Owner: Willy Frank. Winemakers: Dana Keeler, Mark Veraguth. Visits by appt. 20,000 cases. 79 acres with 60 European varieties, most experimental, esp. J.R., Pinot Chard., Gewürz., P.N., Cab.Sauv., Rkatziteli and Merlot. The property of Dr. Konstantin Frank, now run by his son. Since 1965 Vinifera Wine Cellars has produced good, fine and sometimes brilliant white wine, including selected late-harvest Riesling, but less successful reds.

Fox Run Vineyards

Penn Yan, N.Y. 14840. Owners: Scott Osborne, Andy Hale. Winemaker: Peter Bell. Founded 1983. 40 acres planted.

The owners, who bought Fox Run in 1990, are convinced that European *vinifera* grapes can yield wine excellent enough to put the Finger Lakes in the ranks of the world's top wine producers. Their most recent Riesling, Chardonnay, Merlot do indeed show great promise. Pinot Noir, Cabernets Sauvignon and Franc are also coming along, and the company is also trying the little-known Lemberger grape.

Glenora Wine Cellars, Inc.

Glenora-on-Seneca, Dundee, N.Y. 14837. Founded 1977. Owners: Gene Pierce, John Potter, Ed Dalrymple. Winemaker: Jim Gifford. 30–35,000 cases. 15 acres of Chard., Ries., Seyval Bl., Cayuga, Ravat Bl. and buys from other growers. Visits.
One of the best-regarded smaller wineries of the Finger Lakes, specializing in sparkling wines. Early issues of Chardonnay are also successful, and Riesling very good.

Hargrave Vineyard

Cutchogue, Long Island, N.Y. 11935. Founded 1973. Owners: Alexander and Louisa Hargrave. 8,000–10,000 cases. 54 acres of Chard., Sauv.Blanc., P.N., Cab.Sauv., Pinot Bl., Cab.Franc, Merlot.
One of New York's great surprises. The pioneering Hargraves found ideal conditions for *vinifera* vines on the North Fork of Long Island, 70 miles east of New York City with the ocean close by on three sides. Their Chardonnay and Sauvignon Blanc can easily be confused with top-rank California or Oregon wines. Cabernet and Pinot Noir are aged for 3 and 2 years respectively in new American oak barrels without losing a fine flavour of ripe fruit. Not surprisingly, neighbours have planted too.

Lamoreaux Landing Winery

Lodi, N.Y. 14860. Owner: Mark Wagner. Winemaker: Rob Thomas. Founded 1950. 150 acres. 4,300 cases.
One of the best of the youngest generation of New York State wineries. Grows some hybrids, but mostly *vinifera*, including Chardonnay, Cabernet Franc, Pinot Noir and Cabernet Sauvignon.

Millbrook Vineyards & Winery

Millbrook, N.Y. 12545. Founded 1979. Owner: John Dyson. Winemaker: John Graziano. 50 acres *vinifera* only. 14,000 cases.
In addition to Chardonnay, Cabernet Sauvignon and Pinot Noir, Dyson is experimenting with Sangiovese, Merlot and other *viniferas*. Located in the Hudson Valley, he is one of today's trailblazing producers of European-style wines.

Standing Stone Vineyards

Valois, N.Y. 14888. Owners: Martha and Tom Macinski. Winemaker: David Whiting. 35 acres. 5,000 cases, 8,000 planned. Dry, well-balanced Riesling, Gewürztraminer and the hybrid Vidal Blanc are the particular strengths here, but the future of the Cabernet Franc and Merlot is also looking good.

Wagner Vineyards

Lodi, N.Y. 14860. Owner: Bill Wagner. Winemaker: Ann Raffeto. Visits. 40,000 cases. 135 acres of Cayuga, Ravat, Seyval, De Chaunac, Ries., Chard., Gewürz., P.N., Aurora and Vidal.

An attractive Finger Lakes winery. 85% of production is dry varietal table wines. The Chardonnay, including the barrel-fermented style is excellent, as are the Gewürztraminer and the Aurora. Medal-winners.

Hermann J. Weimer Vineyard

Dundee, N.Y. 14837. Founded 1979. Owner: Hermann J. Weimer. 12,000 cases. 35 acres (24 Riesling, 11 Chardonnay).
The Bernkastel-born ex-winemaker of Bully Hill has had striking success with Riesling (with a sparkling version and late-harvest) and now Chardonnay fermented in new French barrels. He credits Seneca, the biggest of the Finger Lakes, for the favourable microclimate. He is trying Pinot Noir, but Gewürztraminer suffers from bud injury in the cold.

Widmer's Wine Cellars, Inc.

Naples, N.Y. 14512. Founded 1888. Owner: Canandaigua Wine Company. Winemaker: Glenn Curtis. 250,000 cases. 250 acres of Niagara, Delaware, Cayuga Blanc, Elvira, Aurora, Foch. Visits.
Best known for wood-aged sherries, Lake Niagara sweetish *labrusca* wines and Widmer-brand hybrids, mostly with generic names. Now making dry *vinifera* wines (Cabernet, Chardonnay and Riesling) and has a list of Kosher wines.

OTHER NEW YORK STATE WINERIES

Cascade Mountain Vineyards Amenia, N.Y. 12501. Owners: the Wetmore family. Founded 1973. Winemakers: William Wetmore and Scott Kelsey. 4–6,000 cases. 12 acres of Léon Millot, Foch, Seyval and Vidal. Buys in from other growers in New York State. Careful producers of crisp dry whites as well as rosé and fresh young reds, described as 'Spring' wines. Also an aged Reserved Red.

Johnson Estate Westfield, N.Y. 14787. Founded 1962. Owners: the Johnson family. Winemaker: Mark Lancaster. 10,000 cases. 135 acres of Seyval Bl., Aurora, Vidal, Chancellor, Chelois, Cascade and Ives. Good-quality estate-bottled wines, which include a dry white Delaware. Their French-American hybrid whites are among the best of their kind.

Lenz Winery Suffolk County, Long Island, N.Y. 11058. Winemaker: Erik Fry. 8,500 cases. 25 acres of Gewürz., Chard., P.N., Merlot and Cab.Sauv. Close to the Hargrave Vineyard (q.v.). Very good Merlot.

North Salem Vineyard North Salem, N.Y. 10560. Founded 1965. Owner/winemaker: Dr George W. Naumburg. 3,500 cases. 18 acres of Seyval Bl., Foch., Chancellor, Chelois, De Chaunac. A Hudson River winery aiming to make fresh light whites and reds for drinking young.

Woodbury Vineyards Dunkirk, N.Y. 14048. Founded 1979. Owners: the Woodbury family. Winemaker: Andrew Dabrowski. 15,000 cases. 28 acres of Chard., J.R., De Chaunac, Seyval Bl. and Niagara. An old farming family who were the first (in 1970) to plant *vinifera* in Chautauqua County, on a gravel ridge overlooking Lake Erie.

NEW ENGLAND

Winemaking in New England is still on a small experimental scale. During the early years of the wine industry in the northeast, it was believed that the regional character should be asserted by developing the best of the hybrids alone. While opinion about the relative merits of hybrid and *vinifera* vines has shifted towards *vinifera* in recent years, hybrids will probably always play at least a minor role in New England because of the difficult growing conditions.

Off the Massachusetts coast the climate is sufficiently moderated by the ocean for *vinifera* to do well at Chicama on the aptly named island Martha's Vineyard.

The state of Rhode Island, deeply invaded by ocean inlets, has half a dozen small vineyards; the biggest, Sakonnet, growing both hybrid and *vinifera* vines. Sakonnet's Chardonnay, Gewürztraminer and Vidal Blanc have not only a loyal local following, but are also becoming known in other parts of the east, and even California. Prudence Island Vineyards, on that island in Narangansett Bay, has 16 acres of *vinifera* vines, the best being Chardonnay and Gewürztraminer.

Connecticut's first winery, Haight Vineyards at Litchfield, west of Hartford, managed to grow *vinifera* (Chardonnay) and the hybrid Seyval. Several other wineries have followed: the most promising are Chamard and Stonington Vineyards, both along the coast. Chamard, founded in 1980, grows only *vinifera* (Chardonnay, Cabernet Sauvignon, Pinot Noir and Merlot) on its 20-acre vineyard. Chamard wines are among the best in New England. Stonington Vineyards, produces both *vinifera* and hybrid wines, including Chardonnay, Pinot Noir and Seyval.

THE MID-ATLANTIC

There is growing conviction that Virginia may become the most promising wine-growing state in the east. The other mid-Atlantic states of Maryland, southern Pennsylvania and perhaps a belt stretching inland into West Virginia, Kentucky and Tennessee may have as much potential. It is a well-publicized fact that Thomas Jefferson had no luck, but modern vines, sprays and know-how have started to change the situation.

Maryland and Pennsylvania

In the 1940s Philip Wagner made history at Boordy Vineyards, near Ryderwood in Maryland, by planting the first French-American hybrids in America. These vines had been bred by the French to bring phylloxera-resistance to France, but ironically it was to be America that appreciated their virtues of hardiness and vigour. At Boordy winemaker Tom Burns continues to produce hybrid wines, although he has been influenced especially by Hamilton Mowbray at the erstwhile Montbray Wine Cellars at Westminster who, before his retirement, was a leader in *vinifera* plantings. Boordy has

now added Chardonnay (classic method sparkling) and Cabernet Sauvignon to its list, which includes the hybrids Seyval Blanc, Vidal Blanc and Chambourcin, and now makes 10,000 cases per year. From a rather casual undertaking, Maryland's wine industry has grown to producing some 400,000 bottles annually. Currently there are ten wineries in the state, making award-winning wines from both hybrids and *vinifera*. Basignani Winery has Cabernet, Chardonnay and Riesling along with Vidal and Seyval. Elk Run Vineyards boasts of its all-*vinifera* vineyard.

The southeast corner of Pennsylvania apparently has much in common with Maryland. Soils and climates are very variable; there are certainly good vineyard sites among them. Frank Mazza, of Mazza Vineyards, who abandoned *vinifera* trials at the other end of Pennsylvania on Lake Erie when 18 acres were wiped out, is happy with his south Pennsylvania Chardonnay and Riesling. He seems to be even happier with his white hybrids, which do exceptionally well. Twin Brook, east of Philadelphia, on the other hand, has done quite well with Pinot Gris, the 1995 showing layers of delicious fruit and hints of oak and vanilla. Eric Miller of neighbouring Chaddsford Winery makes excellent Chardonnay and Chambourcin, and is experimenting with Pinot Noir and Pinot Gris.

John Crouch of Allegro Vineyards has 12 acres of Chardonnay and Cabernet Sauvignon. Richard Naylor, at York near the Maryland border, is happy with Riesling and Cabernet Sauvignon but more at ease with Vidal, Seyval, De Chaunac, Chambourcin and a host of other hybrids.

Everybody believes hybrids are well suited to the region's natural conditions, but consumers' reactions are pulling wine growers increasingly towards Virginia.

Virginia

Lying between the cold weather extreme of the northeast and the intense heat and humidity of the south (where the deadly vine ailment Pierce's Disease thrives), Virginia is the rising star in the east. The state now has 46 wineries, a remarkable number considering that the first successful *vinifera* grape wines were made here less than 20 years ago. Contributing to this success is an unusually supportive legislation (Virginia has one of the most liberal farm winery laws in the Union) plus the affluent and educated customers in Washington D.C. who bolster the local wine industry.

Some Virginians are still wary of *vinifera*. Archie Smith of Meredyth Vineyards at Middleburg, who is one of the leaders, was initially entirely sceptical and planted only hybrids. He came round, first to Riesling and Chardonnay, and now the Cabernets. They need more maintenance, are less reliable and crop smaller, though Merdyth's results are encouraging, especially with Riesling. Much depends on the effectiveness of anti-rot treatments. Fungus infections develop immunity to one chemical and must be sprayed with another. Can the chemists produce enough alternatives?

Foreign investors were the first to show confidence. It made a great stir in 1976 when Zonin, a big wine company from the Veneto in Italy, bought 700 acres at Barboursville and started to plant *vinifera* vines, including Cabernets Sauvignon and Franc, Gewürztzraminer and Italian classics such as Pinot Grigio and Barbera. Like Barboursville, Montdomaine Cellars and Prince Michel are having success with Chardonnay, Riesling, Merlot, Cabernet Franc and Cabernet Sauvignon. Others who have shown that *vinifera* can do well in Virginia are Ingleside Plantation, Shenandoah, Oasis, Linde and Château Morrisette. Horton Vineyards, in Orange County, has Marsanne, Mourvèdre and the tricky Viognier. To illustrate the winemaker's talent, Horton also has a late-harvest from the hybrids Vidal and Norton.

Almost 80% of the Virginia vineyard – some 1,300 acres – is now *vinifera*. The ultimate deciding factors will be the health of the vines and the prices the public will pay.

THE MIDWEST

Lake Michigan and Lake Erie provide the heat storage to make life bearable for vines in the Midwest states of Ohio and Michigan. These large, relatively shallow bodies of water moderate temperatures to allow numerous families of grapes to be grown, including some of the more hardy *vinifera* varieties as well as hybrids such as Vidal Blanc, Seyval Blanc and Chambourcin. The Lake Erie Islands (known locally as the Wine Islands), lying in the shallow western basin of Lake Erie, are especially significant. For a dozen years several hundred acres of wine grapes, including Chardonnay, the two Cabernets, Riesling, Pinot Noir and Gewürztraminer have produced successfully on the lime-rich soils. Most of these grapes are used by Firelands Winery, located on the mainland in Sandusky, Ohio, and by Meier's Wine Cellars, south of Cincinnati. Lake Erie's central basin, just east of Cleveland, also provides important microclimates that are hospitable to wine grapes. Chalet Debonne Vineyards of Madison and Ferrante Winery of Geneva make wines from both *vinifera* and hybrid grapes. Further east, towards the Pennsylvania border, Markko Vineyards in Conneaut makes high-quality Chardonnay, Pinot Gris and a Mosel-style Riesling.

Michigan's vineyards and wineries are close to Chicago at the lake's southeast corner. Notable ones include Tabor Hill, Ferun Valley Vineyards and, biggest by far, St. Julian. These family-owned companies supplement their own production with grapes bought in from Washington and California to make good-quality *vinifera* and hybrid wines

There are wineries in the other northern Midwest states – in Indiana, Illinois, Wisconsin, even Minnesota, where small vineyards and dedicated growers often face sub-zero temperatures and other adverse growing conditions. Much of the production of Indiana and southern Ohio is located in the Ohio River Valley AVA which borders the river from West Virginia to its junction with the Mississippi.

Missouri and Arkansas would seem improbable places to plant vines, but both states have long-established vineyards. Missouri, indeed, enjoyed the distinction of having the first official appellation granted to a viticultural area in the United States, in 1980, when the Bureau of Alcohol, Tobacco and Firearms declared Augusta, just west of St. Louis, a designated region. Its first vines were planted in hills above the Missouri in the 1830s. Both states have strong research programmes at state-funded universities. Stone Hill, in Hermann, Missouri, is well known for its annual collection of gold and silver medals in national competitions. It is far too cold here for most *vinifera* vines, but wineries including Stone Hill and Mount Pleasant at Augusta grow excellent hybrids such as Seyval and Vidal for full-bodied wines somewhat different from the fruitier ones produced along the Great Lakes or in New York's Finger Lakes district.

Arkansas to the south has one unexpected outcrop of *vinifera* growing in the peculiar microclimate of a mountain plateau called Altus, settled in the 1870s by Swiss, Austrian and Bavarian immigrants who understood mountains. According to Al Wiederkehr, whose Swiss family founded its winery in 1880, thermal inversion currents produce a very tolerable climate in which Riesling, Chardonnay, Sauvignon Blanc, Muscat Ottonel, Cabernet, Pinot Noir and Gamay feel more or less at home. Most of his considerable acreage – 400 acres – is planted in these grapes, although he is not burning his boats with hybrids.

THE SOUTHWEST

Much of the Southwest is too humid, and subject, like the deep south, to Pierce's Disease, to make it a viable region for vines, although growing grapes and making wine began here before the business took hold in California. Southern New Mexico and west Texas have the oldest commercial wine-growing regions in America. Catholic priests founded a mission with vineyards in El Paso on the Rio Grande in Texas around 1600, producing sacramental wine from the Mission grape. Nevertheless, only over the past two decades has there been a serious move towards establishing a modern wine industry of some quality.

Of the Southwest wine-producing states, Texas is the clear leader with 26 wineries and over 450 growers. (New Mexico has 19 wineries, Colorado 16, Arizona 7, Oklahoma 2. Utah and Nevada have one apiece.) The Texas vineyards are widely spread out across the vast state, whose total area is larger than France. The wineries range in size from boutique to fairly large. Ste. Genevieve, near Fort Stockton, has links with the state university and Domaine Cordier, and the biggest vineyards of the region – 1,000 acres of *vinifera*, relying on drip irrigation and careful cultivation to survive the desert conditions. Its winery with a 1.2 million-gallon capacity.

Other promising Texan wineries include Sister Creek in the Texas Hill Country, where Danny Hernandez makes Pinot Noir, Chardonnay, Cabernets Sauvignon and Franc and Merlot; Grape Creek Vineyard, also in the Hill Country, produces medal-winning Chardonnay and commendable Cabernet; Fall Creek Vineyards, north of Austin; and Paul Bonarrigo's award-winning Messina Hof Wine Cellars. The cool dry climate of the high plateau area around Lubbock was the site of some of the first successful vineyards in Texas. Attention was drawn to the area by the premium wines from the Llano Estacado ranch, where the McPherson family and their partners pioneered *vinifera* vines. Kim McPherson, whose father was at Llano in the early days, is winemaker at the noteworthy Cap Rock.

Some small wineries still successfully grow hybrids in the more difficult areas, although almost everywhere the shift is to *vinifera*. In the 'dry' county of Springtown, La Buena Vida winery, led by winemaker Steve Smith, for long held out against the *vinifera* vogue but it too is now producing good Chardonnay and Cabernet as well as sparkling wine made from Vidal Blanc and Rayon d'Or, and surprisingly rich, red hybrid port-style dessert wines.

New Mexico now has 19 wineries, including La Chiripada Winery, north of Santa Fe, where Michael and Patrick Johnson produce award-winning wines from hybrids and *vinifera*, as does Madison Winery, a small family-run winery east of Santa Fe. Gruet represents the French influence in New Mexico (the winery is on the ouskirts of Albuquerque;

the vineyards are in southern New Mexico), with top award-winning sparkling wines from Chardonnay and Pinot Noir. Very good Chardonnay is also made by Ken Stark at La Viña, one of New Mexico's oldest wineries, in the south of the state.

Colorado's production capacity continues to rise. Its 410 acres of *Vitis vinifera* is predominantly Chardonnay, although Merlot, Cabernet Pinot Noir, Riesling and Sauvignon are doing well and one producer, Grande River Vineyards, is trying Viognier. Erik Bruner of Plum Creek Winery is well known for his Chardonnay, and has now planted Sangiovese.

Arizona's Callaghan Vineyards has widened the range to include Syrah, Mourvèdre, Grenache, Nebbiolo, Marsanne and Zinfandel, but the Cabernet still draws plaudits. The R. W. Webb Winery continues to offer easy-drinking wines.

Nevada's single winery, Pahrump Valley Vineyards near Las Vegas, currently imports grapes from California, but owner Jack Sanders has planted 4 acres of *vinifera*.

CANADA

Canada was discovered, in fine-wine terms, in the 1970s when old fears and prejudices about which vines could survive here were tossed aside. The formidable knowhow that had been accumulating in new wine districts around the world provided answers to problems that had seemed insuperable. A massive grubbing-up programme in 1988 in the two leading provinces, Ontario and British Columbia, encouraged growers to pull out their hybrids in favour of *vinifera*. Canada now has some 21,000 acres under vine.

ONTARIO

Ontario took its place at the high table of the world's cool-climate wine regions in the 1980s. In the south of the province, the Niagara Peninsula, lake-locked and escarpment-sheltered, is Canada's natural vineyard, lying on the same latitude as northern Oregon. It is one of the designated viticultural areas in the Vintner's Quality Alliance, Bitterly cold winters here produce conditions ideal for making one of the world's great icewines. As well as this luscious speciality Niagara produces Chardonnay, Riesling, Pinot Noir and Gamay. The 1990s are seeing Niagara fine-tune its style, identify its most privileged sites and build a world-class reputation. There are currently 35 wineries.

Leading Ontario Producers

Château des Charmes

St. David's. Est. 1978. Owner: Paul-Michel Bosc. 250 acres. 85,000 cases. Grapes: Chard., Ries., Auxerrois., Sauv.Bl., Viognier, Savagnin, Vidal., Gamay Noir, P.N., Cab.Sauv., Merlot., Cab. Fr.
Paul-Michel Bosc is a fifth-generation wine-grower who emigrated to Canada in the 1960s and became the first to plant a wholly *vinifera* vineyard. Award-winning VQA estate

wines include Icewine, late-harvest, an impressive range of both white and red varietals as well as *méthode traditionnelle* sparkling wines, made *sec* and *brut*.

Inniskillin

Niagara-on-the-Lake. Est. 1975. New winery 1978. Owners: Vincor International. Winemaker: Karl Kaiser. 120 acres (also buys in grapes). 130,000 cases. Grapes: Chard. Ries., P.Gr., P.N., Cab.Fr., Merlot, Vidal (for Icewine). Visits.
Founders Donald Ziraldo and Karl Kaiser spearheaded the birth of the modern wine industry in Ontario. Since its establishment, Inniskillin has concentrated on varietal wines from Niagara-grown grapes. The winery is now housed in a 1920s barn, possibly designed by Frank Lloyd Wright, on the Brae Burn Estate. All Inniskillin wines have VQA status and have earned strong national and international recognition, especially for Icewine and single-vineyard Chardonnays. Limited production of Reserve wines. Also select late-harvest Vidal. Alliance Chardonnay and Pinot Noir represent a joint venture with Jaffelin of Burgundy. Fleur d'Ontario is a white port-style dessert wine; L'Allemand is sparkling.

New ventures are Inniskillin Okanagan (BC) (q.v.) and Inniskillin Napa, Terra.

Henry of Pelham Family Estate

St. Catharines. Est. 1982. Owners: the Speck family. Winemaker: Ron Giesbrecht. 175 acres. 35,000 cases. Grapes: Chard., Ries., and Baco Noir especially; also Gamay Noir, Cab.Sauv., Merlot, Sauv.Bl., Gewürz.
Newish estate on land owned by the descendants of Henry Smith who was awarded crown land after the American Revolutionary War for being an Empire Loyalist. Dedicated to award-winning varietal wines from vineyards on the Niagara Bench. Founding member of the Vintners Quality Alliance. Flagship dessert wine is Riesling Icewine. Also a Cab.-Merlot blend and a Cab.-based rosé.

Hillebrand Estates

Niagara-on-the-Lake. Est. 1982. Owners: Andres. Winemaker: Jean-Laurent Groux. 35 acres plus grapes under contract. 300,000 cases. Grapes: Chard., Ries., Cab.Fr., Cab.Sauv., Sauv.Bl., Merlot, Gamay, Vidal (Icewine). Visits.

Canada's leading producer of VQA wines, bought by Andres in 1993. Varietals and blended wines under the Hillebrand label plus brand names Harvest, Trius (the red 1991 won the Pichon Longueville Comtesse de Lalande award in 1995) and Stone Road. Classic-method sparkling (Chard., P.N.).

Vincor International

T.G. Bright and Cartier & Inniskillin merged in 1993. Vincor International is now Canada's biggest producer of mass-market and premium wines from Canadian and imported grapes. 1996 production was 6.5 million cases. It uses the labels Jackson-Triggs and Sawmill Creek (for VQA wines), Entre-Lacs and L'Ambiance.

Vineland Estates

Vineland. Est. 1979. Owner: John Howard. Winemaker: Allan Schmidt. 75 acres. 18,000 cases. Grapes: Ries., Sey.Bl., Chard., P.N., Gewürz., Vidal, Cab.Sauv., Merlot, Gamay.

Hermann Weis planted vinifera and hybrid vines on the slopes of the Niagara Escarpment in 1979. The first bottling was in 1984. Vineland claims to have the best location for growing Riesling, but produces a wide range of red and white wines, dry, semi-dry and sweet. Much of the production is sold on site; the rest is exported to other provinces, the US, UK and the Far East. Weis sold out to local businessman John Howard in 1992.

BRITISH COLUMBIA

There are two distinct wine-growing regions in BC: the Okanagan and Similkameen valleys in the central-southern part of the province, and the coastal areas of the Fraser Valley and Vancouver Island. Almost all production comes from the 100-mile long Okanagan Valley, which has 3,750 acres of *vinifera*. The whole of the Okanagan is arid; its south end predominantly planted with classic red-wine grapes (Pinot Noir, Merlot and Cabernet Sauvignon); and the less arid north favouring white grape varieties (Riesling, Chardonnay, Pinot Blanc, Pinot Gris, Gewürztraminer and Semillon). The province currently has 35 wineries.

Leading British Columbia Producers

Gray Monk Estate Winery

Okanagan Centre, BC. Est. 1972. Owners: the Heiss family. Winemaker: George Heiss Jr. 32 acres. 31,000 cases. Wines: esp. P.Gr., P.Bl., Chard., and P.Auxerrois. Visits.

Gray Monk is a family-run winery overlooking Okanagan Lake. All their wines have attained VQA status – they concentrate on varietals only. Included in the range is a late-harvest Ehrenfelser and a Gewürztraminer Reserve.

Hawthorne Mountain Vineyards

Okanagan Falls. Est. 1987 (as Le Comte); 1996 under the present name. Owners: Limited partnership, managed by Harry McWatters and Bob Warham (Sumac Ridge). Winemaker: Eric von Krosigk. 170+ acres. 25,000 cases. Grapes: Gewürz., Ries., Merlot, P.N. Visits.

The Hawthorne brothers settled in Okanagan in the 1900s and planted vines, some of which remain in the present vineyard. *Vinifera* varieties are the focus of a current extensive planting programme. In addition to the award-winning varietals, there is *méthode traditionnelle* sparkling and Icewine.

Inniskillin Okanagan

Oliver. Est 1994. Owners: Vincor International. Winemaker: Karl Kaiser and Christine Leroux. 22 acres. 12,500 cases. Grapes: P.N., Merlot, Cab.Sauv., Cab.Fr., Chard., Chenin Bl.

The pioneers of Inniskillin Ontario (q.v.) continue the tradition in Okanagan, and have produced Canada's first Chenin Blanc icewine. Vineyards are located in the south of the valley, just north of the US border, in an area known as the Golden Mile. Currently the majority of the grapes are supplied by local quality growers, especially Inkarneep Vineyards.

Mission Hill Winery

Westbank. Est. 1965. Owner: Anthony von Mandl. Winemaker: John Simes. 70,000 cases. Wines: Chard., P.Bl., Ries., Cab.Sauv. Visits.

Mission-style winery in one of the loveliest settings in the province. John Simes was formerly winemaker at Montana Winery (New Zealand). His innovative techniques and increased use of fermentation and oak-ageing resulted in the launch of Mission Hill's Grand Reserve wines. Awarded the Avery Trophy for best Chardonnay at a recent International Wine & Spirit showing.

Quails' Gate Estate Winery

Kelowna. Vineyard est. 1961. Owners: Ben and Tony Stewart. Winemaker: Jeff Martin. 115 acres. 25,000 cases. Wines: Chasselas, Chard., P.N., Optima, Gamay, Gewürz., Ries. Visits.

One of the oldest producing vineyard sites in the Okanagan and the Stewarts were the first to introduce Chasselas, planting on the favour south slope of Okanagan Lake in 1961. First-class wines are being produced through careful vineyard management and a combination of New- and Old-world winemaking techniques.

Sumac Ridge Estate Winery

Summerland. Est. 1978 Owners: Harry McWatters and Bob Wareham. Winemakers: Mark Wendenburg and Harold Bates. 100 acres. 44,000 cases. Wines: P.N., Cab.Sauv., Merlot, Cab.Fr., Chard., Gewürz., J.R., Sauv.Bl., P.Bl. Visits.

Sumac Ridge Estate produced its first vintage in 1980, supplementing its own grapes with fruit from other vineyards in the Okanagan and Similkameen valleys. In addition to the *vinifera* varietals, Sumac Ridge also produces sparkling and 'port'-style wines.

AUSTRALIA

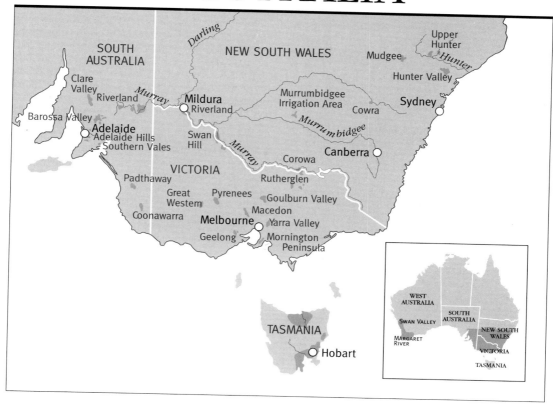

A ustralian wine swept into favour around the world in the mid-1980s with a suddenness that surprised almost everyone. The world was unprepared for such intensely fruity Chardonnays and Cabernet, lavishly seasoned with oak, at prices far below those for such wines in France or California. But then the world had resolutely ignored the quality of Australian wine for generations.

Until the revelation of the last ten years it used to come as a real surprise to visitors to discover how important wine is in the country's life; how knowledgeable and critical many Australians are; how many wineries, wine regions and 'styles' (the favourite Australian wine word) this country, with a total population only a quarter of that of California, can profitably support. Extraordinarily little of the buzz of Australian winemanship penetrated overseas largely because her best wines are made in vast variety but in small quantities, and partly because lack of any kind of central direction made Australian labels a pathless jungle.

By the early '80s open-minded critics overseas were acknowledging that Australia's best wines are excellent: different in flavour from California's but not a jot inferior, and presenting a far wider range of 'styles'. In Australia Shiraz (the Syrah of the Rhône), Sémillon and Riesling have been excellently grown for decades. First-class Chardonnay and

Cabernet joined them in the '70s. And the '90s have seen Australian winemakers succeed with Pinot Noir, and a surge of interest in Rhône-style wines based on Grenache, Shiraz and Mourvèdre (Mataro in Australia).

The whirlwind of change and innovation is no less strong in Australia than in California, but the establishment through which it blows is far older. Until recently an astonishing number of wineries still belonged to the families that founded them over a century ago. They still have powerful traditions. Although nearly all have now changed hands, and most of their turnover today is in bulk wines sold in 'cask', or 'bag-in-box', they continue to make small high-quality lots from their best grapes. Medium-sized and little boutique wineries have proliferated in direct competition with these established classics, adding to the alarming number of good wines there are to choose from.

Australia long ago lost any inhibitions (if she ever had any) about blending wines from different grapes and different regions – even as much as 1,000 miles apart. And within these regions, until the recent boom, Australia's four main wine-growing states had only half a dozen quality areas of any importance. New South Wales had the (then almost moribund) Hunter Valley, north of Sydney, Victoria had Rutherglen and its neighbourhood in the northeast, Great

Western in the west (and the lonely Château Tahbilk in the middle). South Australia, throughout the 20th century much the greatest producer, had the Barossa Valley, Southern Vales and Clare, grouped round Adelaide, and Coonawarra in the remote south. Western Australia had the Swan Valley at Perth In addition the Murray River, flowing between the three eastern states, irrigated large areas for low-quality wine, most of which was distilled.

Each of these areas had four grapes at most which it grew well for fine wines. And each was dominated by at most four or five considerable producers. Now new vineyards have sprung up in a score of districts which are either entirely new to the vine but promise cooler growing conditions, or which (like many parts of Victoria) flourished as vineyards a century ago. Southeastern Australia from Adelaide to Sydney is starting to look on the map like one great wine area. Soon, it seems, the same will be true of the southwest.

This explosion of new winegrowing areas has been accompanied by two significant developments: a passionate interest in regionalism, and the first stages in the formulation of an appellation system for Australia (the two being intimately related, of course).

Australian winemakers are increasingly realizing the benefits of connecting particular varieties or styles with particular regions – both from a marketing and wine quality point of view. Botrytis Sémillon from Griffith, Chardonnay from Margaret River, Riesling from Clare, Sémillon from the Hunter, Shiraz from the Barossa – all these combinations and more are reinforced constantly in the consumers' mind. And winemakers are now prepared to admit there may be something to the concept of *terroir* after all.

But it is not an acknowledgement of *terroir* that is the driving force behind Australia's appellation system; more an acceptance that, if it is to compete on a world stage and achieve its ambitious aim to become one of the world's leading wine exporting countries, the Australian industry has to conform in regards to accurate labelling.

A body called the Geographical Indications Committee has been set up to undertake the long, laborious process of defining Australia's disparate wine areas. Once the process is finished, the regional names that appear on Australian bottles will be set in stone, and will (hopefully) convey unambiguously to the consumer a clearer idea about what to expect once the cork is pulled.

Unfortunately, at the time of writing, the GIC was only half way through its deliberations. Consequently, the names of wine regions that follows is part authoritative fact and part educated guess. (Having said that, it is unlikely that what is finally decided will differ very much from what is here.)

In a departure from the last edition of this book, and in recognition of the increasing focus on regionalism, wineries are now grouped under regional headings. Where a producer has wineries or vineyards in more than one region, the most historically important site is listed. As much information as possible is given about the wineries and their wines, accompanied by tasting notes and commentaries.

AUSTRALIAN WINE REGIONS

NEW SOUTH WALES

Canberra Region of small newish wineries clustered around the Australian Capital Territory (ACT), many of them in decidedly cool spots at relatively high altitude.

Hunter Valley Australia's oldest wine region. The Lower Hunter, around Pokolbin, some 100 miles north of Sydney, is long-established as a producer of serious Shiraz and age-worthy Sémillon. Cloud cover mitigates the extreme summer heat but rain often dampens the vintage. Chardonnay and Cabernet have proved equally successful in the past 20 years. The Upper Hunter, developed since the 1960s, is predominantly a white wine area, particularly suited to Chardonnay.

Mudgee Small, long-established area 100 miles west of the Hunter Valley and 1,200 feet higher, with a sunnier but later season. Wines from Mudgee are usually full-flavoured, with Chardonnay often the best wine.

Riverina Fertile, flat, fruit-growing land around Griffith, 300 miles west of Sydney. Known predominantly for unexciting bulk wines until the mid-80s, when extraordinary Botrytis-affected Sémillon emerged as the area's speciality.

Other Areas A handful of exciting new wine regions have emerged across New South Wales in the last twenty years, including the warm Hastings Valley in the north and the cool regions of Cowra, Hilltops and Orange in the centre of the state.

VICTORIA

Central Victoria Diffuse region, spreading from around the old gold-mining towns of Bendigo and Ballarat and encompassing the area of Heathcote. All wineries are relatively new, and some excellent wines are produced, especially minty, intense, powerful Shiraz.

Geelong This cool area southwest of Melbourne was, in the last century, one of Victoria's most promising. It fell victim to phylloxera, but was re-established in the 1960s. Pinot Noir is very successful.

Goulburn Valley Important small, historic area 100 miles north of Melbourne, home to one of Victoria's oldest wineries, and one of its most successful. Marsanne is a regional speciality.

Grampians Region 140 miles west of Melbourne, with fairly new wineries jostling with very old at places like Great Western. Shiraz rich and flavoursome.

Macedon Ranges Small, cool, hilly region north of Melbourne, with a growing handful of wineries. Sparkling wine very good indeed. Sunbury to the south, slightly warmer and possibly more suited to red wines.

Mornington Peninsula Cool, still-fashionable, maritime-influenced region south of Melbourne with a surprisingly large number of small wineries.

Northeast Victoria Illustrious area, between Milawa and Rutherglen on the New South Wales border, famous for superb dessert wines, especially Muscat. More recent developments include large new vineyards in the King Valley, and smaller ones in the Ovens Valley, Beechworth and the Victorian Alps.

Northwest Victoria Long-established, mainly irrigated area along the Murray River, stretching from the huge vineyards at Mildura and Robinvale, through Swan Hill and down to Echuca. Source of much of Australia's good-value bulk wine.

Pyrenees Hilly region around the town of Avoca, 120 miles northwest of Melbourne. A handful of wineries turn out solid, rather earthy wines.

Yarra Valley A vine-growing region since the 19th century, 30 miles east of Melbourne, which is now re-established and realizing its full potential. Small wineries rub shoulders with some of the state's largest ones to produce exceptional cool-climate wines.

Other Areas Whether it is the scattered, disparate wineries of Gippsland, southeast of Melbourne, or the wineries strung along the Great Dividing Range which cuts a swathe through central Victoria and up into New South Wales, there are other regions that add to the state's viticultural colour.

SOUTH AUSTRALIA

Adelaide Hills Still one of Australia's most talked-about 'cool-climate' regions, around the Mount Lofty Ranges to the southeast of Adelaide. Some remarkable Sauvignon Blanc, Pinot Noir and Chardonnay are produced.

Adelaide Plains Formerly important vine-growing area, including recently restored Penfolds' Magill estate, now largely swallowed by the city suburbs.

Barossa Valley Oldest and most important region, 35 miles northeast of Adelaide, settled by Germans in the 1840s. Good all-round producer and home to many of Australia's largest wineries.

Clare Smaller area 40 miles north of Barossa with almost as long a history. 1,300-foot hills give it a cooler season in which Rhine Riesling does especially well, though Sémillon Shiraz and Cabernet can also be fine.

Coonawarra Remote area 250 miles southeast of Adelaide on an eccentric flat carpet of red earth over limestone with a high water table. Its latitude makes it relatively cool; its soil is absurdly fertile. The result is some of the best wines in Australia.

Eden Valley Cooler region to the south of the Barossa, home to a handful of high-quality wineries, and a useful source of premium grapes for others.

Langhorne Creek Tiny historic area 47 miles southeast of Adelaide on rich alluvial soil. Red wines are soft and wonderfully generous.

McLaren Vale Warm region immediately south of Adelaide. A combination of old, traditional wineries and younger, modern wineries, most producing particularly good wines.

Riverland The Murray continues its way across the border from Victoria and the region becomes known as the Riverland. The majority of Australia's bulk production comes from these huge vineyards and wineries, as do some good-value bottled wines.

Other Areas Coonawarra is not the only area suited to the vine in the vast tracts of land south of Adelaide. Padthaway has for a long time been an important source of good cooler climate grapes, and it is now joined by huge new vineyards in places such as Koppamurra, north of Coonawarra, and Mount Benson, over on the South Australian coast.

WESTERN AUSTRALIA

Great Southern Sprawling region of diverse topography and soil, including the regions of Mount Barker and Frankland River. A growing number of wineries are attracted to the cool, slow ripening conditions here.

Geographe New name for the long coastal plain between Perth and Margaret River, home to a handful of diverse wineries.

Margaret River Western Australia's top-quality wine region, 200 miles south of Perth on a promontory with markedly oceanic climate. The area does well with a wide variety of wines, especially sensational Cabernet and Chardonnay.

Pemberton New, much-hyped region with great potential. The cool-climate has provided some exceptional Pinot Noir and Chardonnay, and fruit from the region is already sought after by wineries in the eastern states.

Old, hot vine-growing area on the outskirts of Perth, traditionally known for jammy reds, dessert wines and the famous Houghton White Burgundy, but recently producing some surprisingly good wines.

QUEENSLAND

Minor wine-producing state. Most vines are grown in the Granite Belt region just across the border with New South Wales. Although Queensland well deserves its name as the Sunshine State, the best wineries here are at high altitude and a little cooler.

TASMANIA

Following the search for a cooler climate to its logical conclusion, a number of wineries have sprung up in Tasmania, near Launceston in the north of the island and Hobart in the south. Sparkling wine (as you would expect from the relatively chilly conditions) is very good, as are Pinot Noir and Chardonnay.

NORTHERN TERRITORY

The proud possessor of a single winery, Château Hornsby, at Alice Springs, obstinately irrigating in the fierce heat and producing passable wines too.

NEW SOUTH WALES PRODUCERS

Canberra

Clonakilla

Crisps Lane, Murrambateman, NSW. Est. 1971. 1,200 cases. Owners: the Kirk family. Winemakers: John and Tim Kirk. Vineyards: 6 acres of various varieties, including Shiraz, Ries., and Viognier. Visits.

One of the first and one of the best producers in the Canberra district. The Kirks' Riesling is good, experimental batches of Viognier are very exciting, but the best wine is the extraordinary, Côte-Rôtie-like, Shiraz.

Lark Hill

Gundaroo Road, Bungendore, NSW. Est 1978. 5,000 cases. Owners: the Carpenter family. Winemaker Sue Carpenter. Vineyards: 25 acres, producing Ries., Chard., Sauv.Bl, P.N., Merlot, Cab.Sauv. Visits.

The highest, and one of the best, wineries in the Canberra region. Wines include Chardonnay, Cabernet/Merlot and delicate Germanic Rieslings.

Principal Grape Varieties

Chardonnay Far and away Australia's most popular grape variety, planted almost everywhere, and produced in a variety of styles, from green-tinged, unwooded wines that are light and crisp to deep yellow barrel-fermented wines that are rich and creamy. Destined to be hugely popular until the end of time.

Shiraz The quintessential Australian red grape, currently enjoying massive interest, both at home and overseas. Styles rich, deep, chocolatey wines in warmer climates such as the Barossa Valley and McLaren Vale, through smooth, soft and relatively delicate in the Hunter Valley to dusty, peppery, elegant examples in cooler areas such as southern Victoria and Western Australia.

Cabernet Sauvignon Like Chardonnay, planted right across Australia, and relatively successful in most areas. At its best in fashionable regions such as Margaret River, Coonawarra and the Yarra Valley, usually when it is blended with varying proportions of Merlot and Cabernet Franc to produce 'Bordeaux blends' that bear little resemblance to Bordeaux.

Sémillon At its best, in the Lower Hunter, is a total (and thoroughly undervalued) triumph: a light, dry white wine, Chablis-green when young and lively, ageing superbly for up to 20 years. Also promisingly grassy in Margaret River, but most examples in the Barossa or Clare are masked by heavy-handed oak maturation. Also widely used for cheaper sparkling wines.

Riesling Despite a growing confidence on the producers' behalf – leading to the dropping of the 'Rhine' prefix – the much-touted revival of interest in Riesling among consumers has yet to fully take hold. This means some of Australia's best white wines – excitingly perfumed, crisply dry and full of the ability to age superbly – are also some of the best value .

Secondary Grape Varieties

Cabernet Franc Initially planted and mostly used to blend with Cabernet Sauvignon, but occasionally crops up as a brightly-flavoured, purple varietal.

Chenin Blanc Mainly used as a blending grape, but also occasionally appears on its own as a fresh white wine.

Doradillo Bulk white grape of the irrigation areas, used for distilling, sherry and 'cask' wines.

Durif A Shiraz-like grape used occasionally in northeast Victoria for interesting dark wine.

Gewürztraminer Mostly used to produce cheap, sweet, grapey white wine, blended with Riesling, but some makers treat it seriously and with great success.

Grenache Flavour-of-the-month in the early to mid-'90s, with fruit from old, dry-grown, low-yielding vines in great demand for Rhône-style reds.

Muscat Brown Muscat used in northeast Victoria for superbly luscious dessert wines; lesser variety, Muscat Gordo Blanco, or Lexia, used to make a fruity, sweet white in the irrigated areas.

Marsanne Once almost solely confined to the vineyards of Chateau Tahbilk, producing remarkably long-lived, aromatic whites, now another beneficiary of the interest in Rhône-style wines, and cropping up in all sorts of places.

Mourvèdre Yet another Rhône-style rediscovery, Mourvèdre (or Mataro, as it used to be known in its less trendy days) is often found in blends with Shiraz and Grenache.

Merlot On the verge of creeping onto the list of principal varieties, this red grape started life in Australia as a blender, but is increasingly beginning to prove itself on its own.

Muscadelle Occasionally used in dry white blends, but most impressive in its dark, luscious dessert form (known as Tokay) in northeast Victoria.

Pinot Gris Everybody seems to be planting this in the cooler areas, and it could be quite successful if small quantities produced thus far are anything to go by – especially if it is labelled far more appealingly as Pinot Grigio.

Pinot Meunier Important variety for sparkling winemakers, but not exactly widely planted.

Pinot Noir After years of promise and occasional brilliance, Pinot Noir producers finally began to consistently crack it in the early '90s. Another variety that probably deserves to be on the principal list, but more through its importance for sparkling winemakers.

Sauvignon Blanc Nowhere near as successful as in New Zealand, but in certain places such as the Adelaide Hills, central Victoria, Margaret River and Coonawarra, produces pungent, racy wines.

Trebbiano Also known as Ugni Blanc, and chiefly used as a blending variety in cheap bulk white wine.

Verdelho Surprisingly good, gently aromatic white variety that is often overlooked but can be delicious.

Other varieties currently produced on a very small scale (either by one or just a handful of winemakers) but nevertheless providing exciting glimpses of the future include: Barbera, Dolcetto, Nebbiolo, Roussanne, Petit Verdot, Sangiovese, Viognier and Zinfandel.

Hunter Valley

Allandale

Lovedale Road, Pokolbin, NSW. Est. 1978. Owner: Wally Attallah. Winemaker Bill Sneddon and Peter Orr. Vineyards: 15 acres of P.N., Sém. and Chard. 12,000 cases. Visits.

Good wines from a variety of sources: estate vineyards, other Hunter growers and the new, cooler region of Hilltops in central NSW.

Allanmere

Lovedale Road, Pokolbin, NSW. Est. 1985. Owners: Steve Allen, Craig Thomas, Garry Reed and Greg Silkman. Winemaker Greg Silkman. Vineyards: 12 acres of Chard. and Sém. 3,500 cases. Visits.

Small winery with good reputation, rescued from premature disappearance by a partnership of local vignerons.

Arrowfield

Jerry's Plains, Upper Hunter NSW. Est. 1969. Owners: Hokuriku, Coca-Cola Bottling Co (principal shareholders). Winemaker: Don Buchanan. Vineyards: 130 acres of Sém., Cab., Shiraz, Chard., Merlot. 80,000 cases. Visits.

The firm has now established a name for very good value. Best are a light spicy Cabernet Sauvignon, big California-style Chardonnay and powerful Show Reserve wines.

Brokenwood

McDonald's Road, Pokolbin, Hunter Valley, NSW. Est. 1970. Owners: a partnership, including, until 1984, wine author James Halliday. Winemakers: Iain Riggs and Matt Harrop. Vineyards: 40 acres, Graveyard and Cricket Pitch vineyards, Cab.Sauv., Shiraz, Sém., Sauv.Bl. 40,000 cases. Visits.

Originally set up by a partnership of Sydney wine-lovers that included wine author James Halliday, Brokenwood is now guided by the phlegmatic Iain Riggs. Multi-regional blends are produced here, but it is the estate wines – in particular superb, grassy Sémillon and (atypically sturdy for the region) Graveyard Vineyard Shiraz – that impress most.

Draytons Family Wines

Oakey Creek Road, Pokolbin, NSW. Est. 1853. Owners: the Drayton family. Winemaker: Trevor Drayton. Vineyards: 230 acres of Sém., Chard., Verdelho, Shiraz, Merlot, Cab. Sauv. 100,000 cases. Visits.

This old family company has been making wine for over a century. Traditional Hunter styles predominate, with the best Shiraz held back for five or more years to be released at its peak (and at a suitably inflated price).

Evans Family

Pokolbin, Hunter Valley, NSW. Est. 1980. Owners: Len Evans' family. Vineyards: 20 acres of Chard., P.N. and a little Gamay. 2,200 cases. Visits by appointment.

Australia's 'Mr Wine', Len Evans, produces 1,500 cases of well-received Chardonnay, 500 cases of Pinot Noir and 200 cases of Gamay at his small family vineyard. The wines are mostly exported.

Hungerford Hill

McDonalds Road, Pokolbin, NSW. Est. 1967. Owner: Southcorp Wines. Winemaker: Ian Walsh. Vineyards: 100 acres in the Hunter Valley and at Tumbarumba, and fruit also sourced from contract growers in up-and-coming new NSW regions. About 10,000 cases.

After years in the multi-regional wilderness, Hungerford Hill has been reborn with a clear purpose and direction. Smartly-packaged wines are now produced in the Hunter Valley only from fruit grown in newish wine areas in central and south New South Wales, with as-yet-unfamiliar names such as Young, Cowra and Tumbarumba accompanying varieties like Sémillon and Sauvignon Blanc on the label.

Lake's Folly

Broke Road, Pokolbin, NSW. Est. 1963. Owners: the Lake family. Winemaker: Stephen Lake. Vineyards: 30 acres of Cab.Sauv., Chard., Shiraz, some Petit Verdot. 4,000 cases. Visits.

First the hobby, then the passion of a distinguished surgeon from Sydney, Max Lake. He started the first new Hunter winery in 40 years, ignoring tradition to prove that Cabernet can be the same splendid thing under Hunter skies as elsewhere. Then he did the same with Chardonnay, making vibrantly lively wines. Both can be among Australia's best.

Lindemans

McDonalds Rd, Pokolbin, NSW. Est: 1870 as Ben Ean, bought by Lindemans in 1912. Owner: Southcorp Wines. Winemakers: Phillip John, Patrick Auld and Greg Clayfield. Vineyards: Hunter Valley, Sunraysia, Coonawarra and Padthaway.

One of Australia's great wine companies, now part of its largest, Southcorp Wines. Started in 1870 in the Hunter Valley, the wines produced under the Lindemans name now come in a range of guises, and from a variety of sources. At the base of the pyramid is Bin 65 Chardonnay, one of the world's most easily recognized white wines. Other wines include a solid range from Padthaway, the super-Coonawarra reds, Limestone Ridge, St George and Pyrus, and some traditional regional wines from the Hunter Valley.

Marsh Estate

Deasy's Road, Pokolbin, NSW. Est. 1971. 6,000 cases. Owners: Peter and Robyn Marsh. Winemaker: Peter Marsh. Vineyards: 60 acres of mixed varieties. Visits.

Small, traditional winery in the Hunter Valley producing a wide range of styles. Shiraz is the highlight, with various wines under different names made from different blocks in the vineyard.

McGuigan Brothers

Corner, Broke and McDonalds Road, Pokolbin, NSW. Est. 1992. Owner: A public company. Winemaker: Reid Bosward. Vineyards: 1,280 acres of mixed varieties in the Hunter, Cowra, Mudgee, Barossa, Adelaide Plains and Murray River. 400,000 cases. Visits.

After selling Wyndham Estate to Orlando, the McGuigan brothers set up on their own and started to build another empire. Neil left, but Brian is still there, larger than life and still the marketing supremo he always was. Wines are reliable and sometimes very good, with big Shiraz leading the pack.

Petersons

Mount View, Hunter Valley, NSW. Est. 1971. Owners: the Peterson family. Winemaker: Gary Reed. Vineyards: 50 acres of Chard., Sém., Cab.Sauv., Shiraz and P.N. 8,500 cases. Visits.

An accomplished, trophy-winning small winery whose first releases were in 1981. The range includes an exceptional Chardonnay, a good Sémillon, Cabernet, Shiraz as well as Pinot Noir.

Reynolds Yarraman

Yarraman Road, Wybong, Upper Hunter, NSW. Est. 1967. Owners: Jon and Jane Reynolds. Winemakers: Jon Reynolds and Stephen Phillips. Vineyards: 35 acres in the Upper Hunter, with fruit also sourced from other regions in NSW. 10,000 cases. Visits.

Former Wyndham Estate winemaker Jon Reynolds is now making good wine for himself in the Upper Hunter. Cleverly, he doesn't rely solely on the surrounding vineyards for his grapes, but sources fruit from as far afield as Mudgee and Orange.

Rosemount Estate

Denman, Upper Hunter, NSW. Est. 1969. Owners: the Oatley family. Winemaker: Philip Shaw. Vineyards: 2,500 acres Sém., Chard. in Upper Hunter; Shiraz Cab. in Mudgee; Cab. in Coonawarra; Shiraz in McLaren Vale and Langhorne Creek; Sauv.Bl. in Adelaide Hills, Chard. in Orange. Visits; restaurant.

One of the country's most confident wineries, with some of Australia's most popular wines in export markets. From the winery in the Upper Hunter (where the famous Roxburgh Chardonnay vineyard is situated) winemaker Philip Shaw draws fruit from across the country to produce a staggering array of good wines. Recent successes include a rich, oaky Chardonnay from the cool New South Wales region of Orange, and some delicious, heady Shiraz, especially the Balmoral (oddly labelled Syrah), from McLaren Vale.

Rothbury Estate

Broke Road, Pokolbin, NSW. Est. 1968. Owners: Mildara Blass. Winemaker: Alan Harris. Vineyards: 87 acres in the Lower Hunter Valley, 187 Upper Hunter and 105 Cowra of Chard., Sém., P.N., Shiraz. Also 27 acres of Sauv.Bl. at Marlborough in New Zealand. 100,000 cases. Visits.

Long-lived Sémillon in the true old Hunter style made the reputation of this impressive winery; Syrah backed it up. Production is now concentrated on barrel-fermented and matured Chardonnay. Shiraz is the main red wines. Top wines, including spicy, high-flavoured Chardonnays, bear the 'Reserve' label. The victim, in 1995, of an aggressive take-over by Mildara Blass.

Tulloch

De Beyers Road, Pokolbin, Hunter Valley, NSW. Est. 1895. Owners: Southcorp Wines. Winemaker: Jay Tulloch. Vineyards: 45 acres in Hunter of Sém., Chard., Shiraz, Verdelho.

Although owned by Southcorp, winemaking here is still carried out by a member of the Tulloch family. Wines range from newer, fresh white and red blends, to the staunchly traditional, earthy, Hector of Glen Elgin Shiraz.

Tyrrells

Broke Road, Pokolbin, Hunter Valley, NSW. Est. 1895. Owners: the Tyrrell family. Winemaker: Andrew Spinaze. Vineyard: 550 acres in the Hunter Valley and Upper Hunter, plus 40 acres at Heathcote; 40 acres at Coonawarra; 100 acres at McLaren Vale; 60 acres at Quirindi in central NSW. 580,000 cases.

Murray Tyrrell was one of the main architects of the Hunter revival of the 1970s, building on a traditional Sémillon and Shiraz base but startling Australia with his well-calculated Vat 47 Chardonnay, the wine that really led the way for the variety in Australia. Despite brief success with Pinot Noir, Tyrrells strength now lies in Shiraz (Vat 9), individual vineyard wines such as Fordwich Verdelho, and the reliable Old Winery and rather plain Long Flat commercial ranges.

Wyndham Estate

Dalwood, Branxton, NSW. Est. 1828. Owners: Orlando Wyndham. Winemaker: John Baruzzi. Vineyards: large vineyards in the Hunter and Mudgee. Many varieties are bought in. Visits.

One of Australia's oldest wineries, now one of the most popular. For a time, under the brash charge of Brian and Neil McGuigan, Wyndham's wines were seen everywhere. Now that the McGuigans are gone, and the winery is part of the huge Orlando Wyndham group, quality is just as reliable, but some of the spark has gone.

Mudgee

Botobolar

Botobolar Lane, Mudgee, NSW. Est. 1970. Owners: Kevin and Trina Karstrom. Vineyards: 66 acres. Wines: Cab.Sauv., Gewürz., Mataro, Shiraz, Crouchen, Chard., Rhine Ries., Trebbiano, Sém. 6,000 cases. Visits.

Although founder Gil Wahlquist is no longer involved with Botobolar, the winery continues to stick steadfastly to organic principles, and produces some of Mudgee's most engaging, characterful wines.

Craigmoor

Mudgee, NSW. Est. 1858. Owners: Orlando Wyndham. Winemaker: Robert Paul. Vineyards: 140 acres of Chard., Sém., Shiraz., Cab. 20,000 cases. Visits.

The oldest-established Mudgee vineyard, long owned by the Roth family; a pioneer of a dry blend of Sémillon and Chardonnay. The range of wines is wide, formerly made with a fairly heavy hand; recently more 'elegant'. Now part of the large Orlando Wyndham group.

Huntington Estate

Cassilis Road, Mudgee, NSW. Est. 1968. Owners: Bob and Wendy Roberts. Winemakers: Bob and Susie Roberts. Vineyards: 101 acres of Shiraz, Cab.Sauv., Chard., Sém., P.N., Merlot and Sauv.Bl. 24,000 cases. Visits.

One of Mudgee's most serious quality wineries. Winemaker Bob Roberts has been joined by daughter Susie, and together they are continuing to produce some lovely wines, especially refined but substantial Cabernet blends and Shiraz.

Miramar

Henry Lawson Drive, Mudgee, NSW. Est. 1974. Owners: Ian MacRae and partner. Vineyards: 60 acres of Shiraz, Cab.Sauv., Sém., Ries., Chard., Sauv.Bl. 12,500 cases. Visits.

One of the most competent wineries in Mudgee, bringing out powerful characteristics in each variety, especially Chardonnay, a Chardonnay/Sémillon blend, Cabernet and Shiraz. Also a clean rosé and 'vintage port'.

Riverina

De Bortoli Wines (Griffith)

De Bortoli Road, Bilbul, NSW. Est. 1928. Owners: the De Bortoli family. Production managers: Darren de Bortoli, Nick Guy. Fruit sourced from the region. 500,000 cases. Visits.

Mostly everyday wines, but remarkable botrytis Sémillon is too, as well as a Jean-Pierre *méthode traditionnelle* wine.

McWilliams

Anzac Street, Chullora, NSW. Est. 1877. Owners: the McWilliam family. Winemakers: Phil Ryan and Jim Brayne. Vineyards: in the Hunter Valley (Mount Pleasant) and near Griffith in the Riverina irrigated area (and 3 wineries: Hanwood, Yenda and Beelbangera), also a vineyard at Barwang in the Hilltops region of Central NSW. Visits.

A single-minded family business, with three centres of operation in New South Wales. The majority of production – bulk wines and occasional beauties such as botrytis Sémillon – is based at Hanwood in the Riverina, while flagship wines such as the extraordinary, long-lived Elizabeth and Lovedale Sémillons are made at the legendary Mount Pleasant winery in the Hunter Valley. A new vineyard, at Barwang, in the central part of the state, is producing encouragingly flavoursome, cooler-climate style wines.

Miranda Wines

Jondaryan Avenue, Griffith, NSW (and Rovalley winery in the Barossa Valley, SA). Est. 1939. Owners: the Miranda family. Visits. All fruit for production at Griffith bought in from all states, but also 100 acres at the Barossa. 1.5 million cases.

Majority of the production is bulk, but premium bottled wine such as an exceptional Griffith Botrytis Sémillon, Barossa Chardonnay and Victorian High Country Cabernet have recently shone at various wine shows.

Other Areas

Bloodwood Estate

Griffin Road, via Orange, NSW. Est. 1983. 2,500 cases. Owners: Stephen and Rhonda Doyle. Winemakers: Jon Reynolds and Stephen Doyle. Visits by appt. Vineyards: 20 acres of Chard., Cab. Sauv., Malbec, Ries., Cab.Fr.

The first and still among the best producers in the high region of Orange. Toasty Chardonnay, rich Cabernet, a ludicrously juicy Malbec rosé and occasional, brilliant Ice Wine made from Riesling.

Cassegrain

Fernbank Creek Rd, Port Macquarie, NSW. Est. 1980. Winemakers: Drew Noon and Karen Bishton. Vineyards: 420 acres. 50,000 cases. Visits.

A fascinating development in the warm region of the Hastings Valley, in the north of New South Wales. The vineyards are slowly moving over to being run on bio-dynamic principles, and wines can be very impressive – especially a softly spicy, generous Merlot and unusual, vibrant, purple-coloured Chambourcin.

VICTORIA PRODUCERS

Central Victoria

Balgownie

Hermitage Road, Maiden Gully, Victoria. Est. 1969. Owner: Mildara Blass. Winemaker: Lindsay Ross. Vineyards: 28 acres of Cab.Sauv., Shiraz, P.N. and Chard. 10,000 cases. Visits.

Established by Stuart Anderson, who sold the winery to Mildara (q.v.) in 1986. This modest ex-pharmacist studied French methods and built one of the best names in Australia for Cabernet Sauvignon built like Château Latour. In 1982 the '74 was ready, the '76 still very tannic. Under the present ownership, wines have been less impressive, with occasional surprises.

Jasper Hill

Drummonds Lane, Heathcote, Victoria. Est. 1975. Owners: Ron and Elva Laughton. Winemaker: Ron Laughton. Vineyards: 45 acres of Shiraz, Cab.Fr., and Ries., and 13 acres not yet bearing, including some Nebbiolo. 3,000 cases. Visits.

Remarkable wines from organically run vineyard in central Victoria. Riesling is as fragrant as you could wish, reds (Georgia's Paddock, a straight Shiraz, Emily's Paddock a Shiraz/Cabernet Franc blend) are massively structured but gorgeously approachable. Demand far outstrips supply.

Yellowglen

White's Road, Smythesdale, nr. Ballarat, Victoria. Est. 1971. Owner: Mildara Blass. Winemaker: Adam Eggins. Vineyards: 30 acres; grapes also bought in. 200,000 cases. Visits.

Established to make Australia's best sparkling, Yellowglen quickly became the provider of some of its best value – but not necessarily best quality – instead. Production has once more concentrated at the top end, and the results, especially in the biscuity, crisp Cuvée Victoria, have been encouraging.

Geelong

Bannockburn Vineyards

Midland Highway, Bannockburn, Victoria. Est. 1974 Owner: Stuart Hooper. Winemaker: Gary Farr. Vineyards: 60 acres. 8,000 cases. Gary Farr has worked in Burgundy during vintage for over a decade and this experience shines through in exceptional

Chardonnay and tight, long-lived Pinot. Recently, a change in winemaking (influenced by Alain Graillot at Crozes Hermitage) has also resulted in remarkably Rhône-like, dusty Shiraz.

Idyll Vineyard

Ballan Road, Moorabool, Geelong, Victoria. Est. 1966. Owners: Daryl and Nini Sefton. Vineyards: 35 acres, mainly of Shiraz, Cab.Sauv. and Gewürz. 4,000 cases.

The establishment of this winery in 1966 heralded the rebirth of Geelong's vineyards, wiped out by phylloxera and other factors at the end of the 19th century. Idyll's red wines range from an elegant oaky chunky Cabernet/Shiraz blend to Shiraz-based rosés. There is also a good Gewürztraminer made in individual style.

Scotchmans Hill

Scotchmans Road, Drysdale, Bellarine Peninsula, Victoria. Est. 1982. Owners: the Browne Family. Winemaker: Robin Brockett. Vineyards: 115 acres and still planting. 20,000 cases. Visits.

The winery is the leading light on the Bellarine Peninsula, south of Geelong, and is another favourite in trendy Melbourne bistros. The intense fruit flavours of Scotchmans Hill wines have ensured them a quick rise to the top.

Goulburn Valley

Château Tahbilk

Tabilk, Victoria. Est. 1860. Owners: the Purbrick family. Winemakers: Alister Purbrick, Neil Larson. Vineyards: 520 acres of Ries., Cab.Sauv., Chard., Shiraz, Merlot, Malbec, Cab.Fr., Marsanne, Sém., Sauv.Bl. and Ch.Bl, Roussanne, Viognier. 90,000 cases. Visits.

Victoria's most historic and attractive winery and one of Australia's best. The old farm with massive trees stands by the Goulburn River in lovely country, its barns and cellars like a film set of early Australia. Dry white Marsanne, starts life light but ages to subtle roundness; Riesling is crisp but full of flavour and also ages well. The Shiraz is consistently one of the best value in Australia, and 1860-vine Shiraz (from the remaining rows of original vineyard) remarkably Old World in style.

Mitchelton

Mitchelstown, Nagambie, Victoria. Est. 1969. Owner: Petaluma. Winemakers: Don Lewis and Alan George. Vineyards: 290 acres. Cab.Sauv., Ries., Chard., Marsanne, Shiraz, Sém. Grapes also come from other vineyards in Victoria. 150,000 cases. Visits.

An extraordinary edifice looking like a 1970s monastery on the banks of the lovely Goulburn River. A lookout tower, aviary and restaurant were built to attract tourists. But the wines are another matter. The Mitchelton label is used for estate wines: excellent Marsanne, aged in cask, and distinctly aromatic for this grape, well-made Riesling, hefty Chardonnay and excellent Shiraz. Other labels include Rhône-style white and red called Mitchelton III, and the lighter Chinaman's Bridge wines.

Grampians

Best's Wines

Great Western, Victoria. Est. 1866. Owners: the Thomson family. Winemakers: Viv Thompson and Simon Clayfield. Vineyards: 120 acres, at Great Western and Lake Boga. Wines include Shiraz, P.M., Ries., Chard., Gewürz., Mataro, Colomb., Ch.Bl., Cab.Sauv. 30,000 cases. Visits.

A famous old name in Victoria, highly picturesque in its original buildings at Great Western. The patchwork vineyard yields some fascinating wines, including an unusual, deep-tasting red Pinot Meunier and a cherry-like Dolcetto (until fairly recently wrongly identified as Malbec). Bin O Shiraz is reliably good and surprisingly elegant; Thomson Centenary Shiraz (exclusively from 130 year-old vines) is a much more serious affair: dark, chewy and glorious.

Mount Langi Ghiran

Buangor, Ararat, Victoria. Est 1964. Owners: Riquet Hess and Trevor Mast. Vineyards: 140 acres, predominantly Shiraz, and including P.G. and Sangiovese. 13,000 cases. Visits.

One of Australia's foremost exponents of rich peppery Rhône-like Shiraz, also producing fine Cabernet and Riesling. Expansion, winemaking ventures further afield and exciting experiments with Italian varieties bode well for the future.

Seppelt Great Western

Great Western, Victoria. Est: 1868 Owner: Southcorp Wines. Winemaker: Ian McKenzie. Vineyards: Great Western and Drumborg in Victoria, Tumbarumba and Barooga, NSW.

The historic old cellars at Great Western are now also home to a vast new development that handles all sparkling wine production for the Southcorp Wines group. Seppelt sparklings are still very much the focus here, from the great-value Great Western to the flagship Salinger. A revamped range of Seppelt table wines, all from Victorian fruit, have brightened this winery's image. Single-vineyard wines (such as Great Western Shiraz, Drumborg Cabernet and others from the company's South Australian vineyards) are released when mature and are excellent.

Macedon Ranges

Cope-Williams

Romsey, Macedon Ranges, Victoria. Est. 1977. Owners: the Cope-Williams family. Winemaker: Michael Cope-Williams. Vineyards: 50 acres of Chard., P.N., P.M., Cab.Sauv., Merlot. 7,000 cases. Visits, cricket pitch, Royal Tennis court.

In a setting that feels remarkably like a country garden in Sussex, the Cope-Williams family (originally from the old country) produce delicate cool-climate wines, the best of which is one of Australia's finest bubblies.

Craiglee

Sunbury Road, Sunbury, Victoria. Est. 1868, re-established 1976. Owners: the Carmody family. Winemaker: Pat Carmody.

Vineyards: 22 acres of Shiraz, Chard., Cab.Sauv., Sauv.Bl., and P.N. 2,500 cases. Visits.

The self-effacing manner of Pat Carmody hides a skilful grape grower and winemaker. His Chardonnay is tight and gently toasty, but it is the supremely elegant, enticingly peppery Shiraz that really shines from this historic winery.

Hanging Rock

Jim Road, Newham, Victoria. Est. 1987. Owners: the Ellis family and friends. Winemaker: John Ellis. Vineyards: 16 acres of P.N., Chard., Sauv.Bl., Sém., Gewürz. Also buy grapes from all over Victoria. 40,000 cases. Visits.

Reliable wines under the (cheap) Picnic or Victoria labels, but exceptional quality to be found in wines made from Estate fruit. Jim Jim Sauvignon Blanc can be almost searing in its grassy intensity, and *méthode traditionnelle* sparkling is one of the country's biggest and richest.

Virgin Hills

Kyneton, Macedon Ranges, Victoria. Est. 1968. Owner: Marcel Gilbert. Winemaker: Martin Williams (consultant). Vineyards: 30 acres of Cab.Sauv., Malbec, Shiraz, Merlot, P.N. 4,000 cases.

The dream of Melbourne restaurateur Tom Lazar, this cool-climate vineyard full of all sorts of red varieties has produced some of Australia's best but also most variable wine. All the varieties are blended together to produce one wine, and the result can be satisfyingly complex. Recent vintages have tended towards lightness, but age could fill them out.

Mornington Peninsula

Dromana Estate

Harrison's Road, Dromana, Mornington Peninsula, Victoria. Est 1982. Owner: Garry Crittenden. Winemakers: Garry Crittenden, Arthur O'Connor. Vineyards: 12 acres of mixed varieties, and a lot of bought-in fruit. 12,000 cases.

A leading estate in the up-and-coming Mornington Peninsula. Glorious Cabernet, Pinot Noir and Chardonnay are made. Other good wines, made from bought-in grapes, are sold under the Schinus label, joined recently by a range of Italian varietals (Dolcetto, Nebbiolo etc) under the 'I' label.

Elgee Park

Junction Road, Merricks North, Mornington Peninsula, Victoria. Owners: the Beaulieu Myer family. Winemaker: various contracted. Vineyards: 10 acres of Cab.Sauv., Cab.Fr., Merlot, Viognier and Chard. 1,000 cases.

Oldest winery in the region, producing very good wines in minute quantity. Viognier can be impressive.

Hickinbotham Winemakers

Dromana, Mornington Peninsula, Victoria. Est. 1981. Owners: the Hickinbotham family. Winemaker: Andrew Hickinbotham. Vineyards: 15 acres; most grapes are bought in. 7,000 cases. Visits.

A family of innovative winemakers closely associated with many of the most significant developments in Australian wine production, but scarred by the death of Bordeaux-trained Stephen Hickinbotham in an air crash. Brother Andrew took the reigns and wines are now produced from all over Victoria, with new vineyards planted in the Mornington Peninsula.

Paringa Estate

Paringa Road, Red Hill South, Mornington Peninsula, Victoria. Est. 1985. Owners: Lindsay and Margaret McCall. Winemaker: Lindsay McCall. Vineyards: 17 acres (some not yet bearing) of Chard., P.N., Shiraz and P.G. 2,500 cases. Visits.

The reputation and success of this tiny winery is out of all proportion to its size. Perfectly-sited, trellised vineyard produces exceptional fruit. Chardonnay is intense and lingering, Pinot is wild and spicy, Shiraz teeters on the edge of greenness, but pulls it off in dusty, peppery style.

Stoniers

Thompsons Lane, Merricks, Victoria. Est. 1982 Owners: the Stonier, Yuill, Hamson and Limb families. Winemaker: Tod Dexter. Vineyards: 50 acres at Merricks of Chard., P.N., Cab.Sauv., and fruit sourced from other Mornington Peninsula growers. 12,000 cases. Visits.

Now arguably the region's foremost winery, consistently successful with complex, extremely well-made Chardonnay, silky and berry-packed Pinot, and surprisingly ripe Cabernet. Not surprisingly, the Reserve range is substantially superior to the standard wines, which, nonetheless, are still good.

T'Gallant

Mornington-Flinders Road, Main Ridge, Mornington Peninsula, Victoria. Est. 1990 10,000 cases. Owners, winemakers: Kevin McCarthy and Kathleen Quealy. Visits. Vineyards: 20 acres of P.G., also fruit sourced from 6 other local growers.

Talented couple pioneering unusual, quirkily packaged wines such as hugely ripe and spicy Pinot Gris, yeasty, gently bronzed white Pinot Noir, crisp unwooded Chardonnay and Holystone, a good, dry rosé. Very successful with the trendy café set in Melbourne.

Northeast Victoria

All Saints

All Saints Road, Wahgunyah, Victoria. Owners: the Brown family. Winemaker: Peter Brown. Vineyards: 150 acres of mixed varieties. 20,000 cases. Visits, restaurant, wine museum.

Traditional old winery in north-east Victoria (established 1864), producing a full range of table, fortified and sparkling wines, recently bought and lavishly renovated by Brown Bros (q.v.)

Bailey's

Taminick Gap Road, Glenrowan, Victoria. Est. 1870. Owner: Mildara Blass. Winemaker: Colin Slater. Vineyards: 140 acres of Muscat, Tokay, Shiraz, Cab.Sauv., some whites. 30,000 cases.

The famous makers of heroic Shiraz, a caricature Aussie wine with a black and red label rather like a danger signal. A thickly fruity wine which ages 20 years to improbable subtlety. Even better (and amazing value, too) are their dessert Muscats and Tokays, profoundly fruity, intensely sweet and velvety.

Brown Brothers

Milawa, Victoria. Est. 1889. Owners: the Brown family. Vineyards: 400 acres at Milawa, Mystic Park, Hurdle Creek and Whitlands. Also grapes on contract from 300 acres in King Valley. 200,000 cases. Visits.

This old Victorian family winery seems to be continually expanding and innovating: new ideas are everywhere and growth is almost alarming. As well as a wide, reliable range of conventional wines, Brown Brothers also experiment with new varieties and styles (mostly sold cellar-door only), such as excellent ultra-cool climate Sauvignon Blanc and Italian varietals. A new Epicurean Centre restaurant and tasting facility has proved successful.

Bullers

Three Chain Road, Rutherglen, Victoria, and also at Beverford, Swan Hill, Victoria. Est. 1921. Owners: the Buller family. Winemakers: Andrew Buller (Rutherglen), Richard Buller (Beverford). Vineyards: 60 acres at Rutherglen, 70 at Swan Hill. 50,000 cases. Visits.

Old family firm producing superb, slippery fortified Muscat and Tokay at Rutherglen, and some enormously flavoursome – and highly alcoholic – red wines at Beverford.

Campbells

Murray Valley Highway, Rutherglen, Victoria. Est. 1870. Owners: the Campbell family. Winemaker: Colin Campbell. Grape grower: Malcolm Campbell. Vineyards: 140 acres. Wines: Muscat, Tokay, Ries., Shiraz, Malbec, P.X.; also Durif (The Barkly), Chardonnay and 'Port'. 50,000 cases. Visits.

This traditional Rutherglen winery has recently begun to smarten its image and modernize its approach. Muscat and Tokay (especially Merchant Prince and Isabella labels) are still the backbone, but wonderfully spicy Bobbie Burns Shiraz and a stout, impressive Durif called The Barkly are also very good.

Chambers Rosewood

Rutherglen, Victoria. Est. 1860. Owners: the Chambers family. Winemaker: Bill Chambers. Vineyards: 110 acres at Rosewood. Many varieties. Wines: various. 10,000 cases. Visits.

Bill Chambers is a veteran winemaker, respected most of all for his old Liqueur Muscat and Tokay. As always in Rutherglen the rich dry reds are better than the whites.

Morris Wines

Mia Mia Road, Rutherglen, Victoria. Est. 1859. Owner: Orlando Wyndham. Winemaker: David Morris. Vineyards: 200 acres of Muscat, Tokay, Sém., Chard., Durif, Shiraz, Cab.Sauv., Cinsaut, Touriga. 35,000 cases.

Morris's Liqueur Muscat is Australia's secret weapon: an aromatic silky treacle that draws gasps from sceptics. The old tin winery building is a treasure-house of ancient casks of Muscats and Tokays, so concentrated by evaporation that they need freshening with young wine before bottling. The

dark red Cabernet and Durif are impressive but hard wines; Sémillon and Chardonnay surprisingly good since Orlando's came under the same ownership.

Stanton & Killeen

Jack's Road, Rutherglen, Victoria. Est. 1875. Owners: the Stanton and Killeen families. Winemaker: Chris Killeen. 60 acres of Cab.Sauv., Shiraz, Muscat and Touriga, Durif and Chard. 11,000 cases. Visits.

A small old family winery revitalized since 1970. Its Moodemere reds, Cabernet, Shiraz and Durif are now among the best in northeast Victoria. Muscats, Tokays and ports are not luscious in the regional tradition, but light and elegant.

Northwest Victoria

Alambie Wine Company

Campbell Avenue, Irymple, Victoria. Est. 1975. Owner: Unlisted public company. Winemaker: Bob Shields. Vineyards: 100 acres at Koppamauura, SA, 385 acres at Loxton, SA, Shareholder-owned 1,000 acres at Nangiloc, Victoria. 1.6 million cases. Visits.

One of Australia's more successful bulk-producing, export-oriented companies, with a range of great value wines such as the Salisbury label at the tip of its iceberg that are very popular at home.

Deakin Estate

Kulkyne Way, via Red Cliffs, Murray Valley, Victoria. Est. 1979 (as Sunnycliff). Owner: Wingara Wine Group. Winemaker: Mark Zeppel. Vineyards: 1,600 acres of mixed varieties. 150,000 cases. Visits.

The rather plain (but successful) Sunnycliff brand was relaunched in 1995 as Deakin Estate with spanking new labels and a bright, breezy marketing approach. The change has done wonders, and wines under the Deakin label are now some of the most popular – and value for money – the country has on offer.

Trentham Estate

Sturt Highway, Trentham Cliffs, Mildura, NSW. Est. 1988. Owners: Anthony and Patrick Murphy. Winemaker: Tony Murphy. Vineyards: 42 acres of 16 different varieties. 50,000 cases. Visits.

A minnow compared to the very big company vineyards just across the river in Victoria, but a popular and reliable producer, nonetheless. Whites are clean and tasty, and reds - particularly good Merlot and Grenache - are characterized by soft, approachable, sweet fruit.

Woodley Wines

Edey Road, Karadoc, Victoria. Est. 1856. Owner: Southcorp Wines. Vineyards: Riverland SA; Sunraysia, Vic.

Woodley, once upon a time, was one of Australia's most highly-respected wine names, mostly for a series of remarkable red wines produced in Coonawarra in the '40s and '50s. Now, Woodley is merely the parent brand for Queen Adelaide, a budget range that includes Australia's largest selling domestic bottled Chardonnay.

Pyrenees

Blue Pyrenees

Vinoca Road, Avoca, Pyrenees, Victoria. Est. 1960. Owner: Rémy Martin. Winemaker Vincent Gere. Vineyards: 450 acres of Chard., Shiraz, Cab.Sauv. P.N, P.M., Cab.Fr., Merlot, Sémillon. 60,000 cases. Visits.

Originally established as Château Remy for brandy-making, this estate has slowly transformed into one of Victoria's most interesting wineries. Sparkling wines (especially Midnight Cuvée, made from grapes picked by hand under spotlights at night) have improved beyond all recognition; Blue Pyrenees red blend is remarkably European in style.

Dalwhinnie

Taltarni Road, Moonambel, Victoria. Est. 1976. Owners: David and Jenny Jones. Winemaker: David Jones. Vineyards: 35 acres of Chard., Shiraz and Cab. Sauv. 4,500 cases. Visits.

Possibly the best producer in the region, with powerful Chardonnay sensibly balanced by savoury, toasty oak; chunky, ripe, black Cabernet, and vibrant, resinous, lingering Shiraz.

Redbank

Redbank, Victoria. Est. 1973. Owners: the Robb family. Winemaker: Neill Robb. Vineyards: 40 acres of mixed varieties, with some fruit bought in. 46,000 cases. Visits.

Neill Robb's Redbank wines sometimes show the hard, unyielding quality that the Pyrenees region can bestow, but the top label, Sally's Paddock, a Cabernet Shiraz-based blend, is, in good years, one of the best red wines in the area: complex, spicy and satisfying.

Taltarni

Moonambel, Pyrenees, Victoria. Est. 1972. Owner: Red Earth Nominees (John Goelet). Winemakers: Dominique Portet and Greg Gallagher. Vineyards: 300 acres, of Ries., Chard., Sauv.Bl., Ch.Bl., Cab.Sauv., P.N., Merlot, Malbec, Shiraz. Also 50 acres at Clover Hill in Pipers Brook, Tasmania, for sparkling wine production. 60,000 cases. Visits.

The brother winery to Clos du Val in the Napa Valley: extremely modern and well equipped without extravagance. 1977 and '79 Special Reserve Cabernets were demonstrations of intent: enormous dark wines including pressings, built to last 20 years. More Merlot and Cabernet Franc have been added to recent vintages, bringing extra subtlety. Shiraz is made much lighter. Whites are less sure-footed, but Sauvignon Blanc is good.

Warrenmang Vineyard

Mountain Creek Road, Moonambel, Victoria. Est. 1974. Owners: the Bazzani family. Winemaker: Roland Kaval. Vineyards: 24 acres of Chard., Gewürz., Cab.Sauv., Cab.Fr., Merlot, Shiraz, Dolcetto. 7,000 cases. Visits, accommodation and restaurant.

The passionate venture of local Italian restaurateur, Luigi Bazzani, this attractive, inviting vineyard has produced some good weighty, earthy Shiraz over the years, as well as, more recently, lighter, more approachable, bistro-style wines under the Bazzani label.

Yarra Valley

Coldstream Hills

Maddens Lane, Coldstream, Yarra Valley, Victoria. Est. 1985. Owner: Southcorp Wines. Winemakers: James Halliday and Phil Dowell. Vineyards: 120 acres, mainly of Chard. and P.N., with some Cab.Sauv., Cab.Fr., Merlot. 50,000 cases.

Yarra winery founded by the country's leading wine critic, James Halliday, now owned by Southcorp, the country's largest company. Coldstream Hills makes some of Australia's best Pinot Noir and Chardonnay, as well as elegant Cabernet Sauvignon and Briarston, a Cabernet-Merlot blend.

De Bortoli (Yarra Valley)

Pinnacle Lane, Dixons Creek, Yarra Valley, Victoria. Est. 1987. Owners: the De Bortoli family. Winemakers: Steve Webber, David Slinsby-Smith and David Bicknell. Vineyards: 300 acres in the Yarra Valley. 100,000 cases. Visits.

This is the Victorian arm of the highly successful New South Wales wine family. Wines made from fruit grown across Victoria appear under the Windy Hill label and can be great value, wines from the Yarra Valley vineyards a great step up in quality, especially the citrus-tangy Chardonnay and the dark, berry-fruited Cabernet.

Diamond Valley

Kinglake Road, St Andrews, Yarra Valley, Victoria. Est. 1975. 4,500 cases. Owners: David and Cathy Lance. Winemaker: David Lance. Vineyards: 9 acres of Chard., Sauv.Bl., P.N., Merlot, Malbec, Cab.Fr., Cab.Sauv.

David Lance makes outstanding Pinot Noir, as well as Chardonnay and Cabernet. A second range, Blue Label, is made from bought-in fruit, and a new range, Black Label, accommodates small parcels of (great) experimental wines such as close-planted Pinot Noir.

Domaine Chandon

Maroondah Highway, Coldstream, Yarra Valley, Victoria. Est. 1985. Owners: Louis Vuitton Moët Hennessy (France). Visits. Winemakers: Dr Tony Jordan, Wayne Donaldson. 90,000 cases. Vineyards: 250 acres of Chard. and P.N., with a little P. M.

Exciting investment established with the foreign expertise of Moët and the local knowledge of Tony Jordan, one of Australia's foremost wine consultants. Wines are made from both home-grown and bought-in fruit. The first commercial classic method sparkler was released in 1989, and the name quickly rose to the top of Australia's competitive sparkling wine hierachy. Smaller production of *blanc de blancs* and *blanc de noirs* is exceptional. The brand name is Green Point.

Mount Mary

Coldstream West Road, Lilydale, Yarra Valley, Victoria. Est. 1971. Owners: Dr John and Marli Middleton. Winemakers: Mario Morson, Peter Draper. Vineyards: 28 acres of Cab.Sauv., Cab.Fr., Merlot, Chard., P.N., Malbec, Petit Verdot, Sém., Sauv.Bl. and Muscadelle. 3,000 cases.

A near-fanatical doctor's pastime which has become very serious indeed. His 'Quintet' Cabernet blend is like a classic

Bordeaux; mid-weight, complex and intensely fruity. Mount Mary Chardonnays are strong, rich and golden; new-oak fermented and, like the Cabernets, easily ten-year wines.

Oakridge Estate

Seville, Yarra Valley, Victoria. Est. 1982. Owners: Jim and Irene Zitzlaff. Winemaker: Michael Zitzlaff. Vineyards: 20 acres, of Cab.Sauv., Merlot, Chard. 4,000 cases. Visits.
High-quality family winery which makes small quantities of two reds: an excellent Cabernet Sauvignon and a Cabernet/ Merlot blend, and, more recently, a good Chardonnay.

St Huberts

St-Huberts Road, Coldstream, Yarra Valley, Victoria. Est. 1966. Owner: Mildara Blass. Winemakers: Rob Dolan, Adam Marks. Vineyards: 87 acres of Cab., Sauv.Bl. P.N., Chard., Merlot. 10,000 cases. Visits.
The modern re-incarnation of one of the Yarra's 19th-century showpieces. For a few years, only the Cabernet consistently performed well, but more recently quality has improved across the board, with a tingly Chardonnay and fascinating Roussanne. Now owned by Mildara Blass, who appear keen to ring in some changes.

Seville Estate

Linwood Road, Seville, Victoria. Est. 1972. 2,000 cases. Owners: P. G. and M. L. McMahon. Winemaker: Peter McMahon. Vineyards: 12 acres of Cab.Sauv., Cab.Fr., Merlot, P.N, Shiraz and Chard.
Tiny vineyard and winery in the southern Yarra Valley. Particularly elegant wines, with juicy Cabernet, spicy Shiraz and low-key, deeply flavoured Chardonnay. Alas, Riesling Beerenauslesen, Seville's trump card, is no longer made.

Tarrawarra Vineyards

Healesville Road, Yarra Glen, Yarra Valley, Victoria. Est. 1983. Owners: Marc and Eva Besen. Winemaker: Michael Kluczko. Vineyard: 62 acres of Chard. and P.N. 15,000 cases. Visits.
Single-mindedly striving to produce the region's best Chardonnay and Pinot Noir from a very impressive, expensive winery, and occasionally coming close to achieving that aim. A succession of winemakers has led to variations in style, but the quality of the vineyard's fruit always shines through.

Wantirna Estate

Wantirna South, Victoria. Est. 1963. Owners: Reg and Tina Egan. Winemaker: Reg Egan. Vineyards: 10 acres of Cab., Chard., P.N., Merlot, Cab.Fr., Petit Verdot. 1,000 cases. Visits by appt.
A tiny estate in the suburbs of Melbourne, producing a good Pinot Noir, a most gentlemanly Cabernet/Merlot blend and tiny quantities of other well-made wines.

Yarra Burn

Settlement Road, Yarra Junction, Victoria. Est 1969. Owners: BRL Hardy. Winemaker: David Fyffe. Vineyards: 25 acres, Yarra. Visits.
Good Yarra producer, now owned by BRL Hardy, and used by them as a production base for their steep, cool-climte Yarra vineyard, Hoddles Creek – a vineyard so steep in fact, that it has inspired a new range of wines called Bastard Hill.

Yarra Ridge

Glenview Road, Yarra Glen, Victoria. Est: 1982. Owner: Mildara Blass. Winemaker: Rob Dolan. Vineyards: 170 acres of Chard., P.N., Cab.Sauv., Merlot, Sauv.Bl. 60,000 cases. Visits.
Established by lawyer Louis Bialkower, Yarra Ridge became one of the great success stories of the region, enjoying popular and critical acclaim. It was bought by Mildara Blass in the mid-1990s, and after a dip in quality (with fruit being bought in from outside the region), the estate is now back on course.

Yarra Yering

Briarty Road, Coldstream, Yarra Valley, Victoria. Est. 1969. Owner/Winemaker Dr Bailey Carrodus. Vineyards: 50 acres of Cab.Sauv., Shiraz, P.N., Malbec, Merlot, Sém., Chard., Viognier, Marsanne and Petit Verdot. 6,000 cases. Visits.
An individualist who initiated the wine revival of the Yarra Valley, with a well-tended vineyard producing small yields of high-quality fruit. Carrodus is not keen on varietal labelling: a Bordeaux-type blend is called Dry Red No. 1, a Rhône-type, Dry Red No. 2. Both wines are widely admired for harmonious composition. Pinot Noir he makes straight, and recent vintages have been highly praised.

Yeringberg

Coldstream, Yarra Valley, Victoria. Est. 1862. Owner/winemaker: Guillaume de Pury. Vineyards: 5 acres of Cab., Merlot, Malbec, P.N., Chard., Marsanne and Roussanne. 1,000 cases. Visits only by appt.
The remnant of a wonderful old country estate near Melbourne, making some excellent wines. Pinot Noir, Chardonnay, Cabernet and Merlot are delicate and charming. The potential of the old estate shows, though production is tiny.

Yering Station

Melba Highway, Yarra Glen, Victoria. Est. 1838, re-established, 1988. 6,000 cases. Owners: the Rathbone family. Winemaker: Tom Carson. Visits. Vineyards: 20 acres plus 50 acres not yet bearing.
This historic old winery was one of Victoria's first, and its renaissance in the early 1990s was exciting, while wine quality was not always so. It is being expanded by new owners, and is also linked in a joint venture with Champagne Devaux to produce a sparkling wine called Yarrabank. Wines look set to improve beyond recognition.

OTHER AREAS

Bass Phillip

Hunts Road, Leongatha South, Victoria. Est. 1979 700 cases. Owner/winemaker: Phillip Jones. Visits by appt. Vineyards: 10 acres (plus 30 acres not yet bearing) in South Gippsland of P.N., Chard., Gamay.
This tiny Gippsland winery resembles a small domaine in Burgundy – in size, approach, passion, and more than occasionally in the glass. Few other Australian wineries even come close to making Pinot Noir as well as Phillip Jones. The three grades of quality are always eagerly sought.

Delatite

Stoney's Road, Mansfield, Victoria. Est. 1982. Owners: Robert and Vivienne Ritchie. Winemaker: Rosalind Ritchie. Vineyards: 60 acres of mixed varieties. 16,000 cases. Visits.

Successful family winery producing remarkable white wines and characteristically minty reds. Riesling and Gewürztraminer are among the best. Other wines include Pinot Noir, Cabernet/Merlot, Malbec, Sauvignon and a new sparkling wine.

Giaconda

McClay Road, Beechworth, Victoria. 1,000 cases. Owner/winemaker: Rick Kinzbrunner. Est 1982. 7 acres. P.N., Chard., Cab.Sauv. Visits by appt.

Small, fashionable winery in northeast Victoria producing good Pinot Noir and some of Australia's most reserved, stylish Chardonnay.

Tisdall

Cornelia Creek Road, Echuca, Victoria. Est. 1972. 45,000 cases. Owner: Mildara Blass. Winemaker: Toni Stockhausen. Vineyards: 200 acres at Mt Helen in the Strathbogie Ranges; 30 acres at Mt Ida in Heathcote; 120 acres at Rosbercon in Echuca.

Most of the production revolves around good commercial wines from Murray Valley grapes, but winemaker Toni Stockhausen also makes some extremely good smaller lots from vineyards further south in Victoria: Mount Helen (Merlot, Chardonnay) and Mount Ida (Shiraz), a vineyard just next to Jasper Hill (q.v.) in Heathcote.

SOUTH AUSTRALIA PRODUCERS

Adelaide Hills

Lenswood Vineyards

Crofts Road, Lenswood, SA. Est. 1981. Owners: Tim and Annie Knappstein. Winemaker: Tim Knappstein. Vineyards: 56 acres of Sauv.Bl., Chard., Sém., P.N., Merlot, Malbec and Cab.Sauv. 6,000 cases.

Now that Tim Knappstein has let go of his eponymous winery, he is concentrating on wines from his excellent cool-climate vineyards at Lenswood. Pinot Noir is deep, stone-fruity and gamey, Chardonnay is as rich as they come, and impossibly intense Sauvignon Blanc is possibly Australia's best.

Petaluma

Piccadilly, Adelaide, SA. Est. 1976. Owner: A public company. Vineyards: 180 acres in the Adelaide Hills, 120 acres in Coonawarra and 200 acres in Clare. 35,000 cases plus 30,000 classic method. Visits.

After some years involved in wine industry politics, Brian Croser is back where he likes to be: on the winery floor. Petaluma is still one of Australia's leading smaller wineries (considered small even though it also now owns Mitchelton and Tim Knappstein – q.v.), with wines such as the very

good sparkling, Croser, the brilliant Riesling from Clare and the constantly improving Chardonnay from the Piccadilly Valley in the Adelaide Hills continuing to shine. Coonawarra, a Cabernet blend, is clean, tight and slow to develop, and first releases of varietal Coonawarra Merlots are exciting: Croser believes this variety to be more suited to the region than Cabernet Sauvignon.

The second label, Bridgewater Mill, provides more immediate, approachable wines, and Croser's Sharefarmers Vineyard, just north of Coonawarra, produces a red and a white of impeccable quality.

Shaw & Smith

Main Road, Woodside, Adelaide Hills, SA. Est. 1989. Owners: Martin Shaw and Michael Hill Smith. Winemaker: Martin Shaw. Vineyards: 68 acres of Sauv.Bl., Chard., and some experimental Merlot. 18,000 cases.

The fortuitous pairing of winemaker Martin Shaw with restaurateur, Master of Wine and cousin Michael Hill Smith has resulted in one of the best wineries in the Adelaide Hills. Unwooded Chardonnay is one of the best in the country, all crisp apple fruit. Reserve Chardonnay is at the other end of the spectrum, with powerful, creamy oak treatment, and Sauvignon Blanc often rivals the best of Marlborough with its mouthwatering fruitiness.

Stafford Ridge

Stafford Road, Lenswood, SA. Est. 1982. Owners: Geoff and Judith Weaver. Winemaker: Geoff Weaver. Vineyards: 28 acres of various varieties. 5,000 cases.

Former Hardys winemaker Geoff Weaver is now ensconsed at his own Adelaide Hills winery and producing some wonderful, classy wines. Sauvignon Blanc can be pungently fruity, Chardonnay invariably brilliant and Cabernet Merlot uncommonly elegant.

Adelaide Plains

Barossa Valley Estates

Angle Vale, Adelaide, SA. Est. 1984. Owner: Valley Growers Cooperative. Vineyards: 65 growers across the Barossa Valley. 120,000 cases. Visits.

This winery produces and exports good-value wines under the Barossa Valley Estates labels and some more upmarket, extremely powerful wines under the E & E label.

Primo Estate

Old Port Wakefield Road, Virginia, Adelaide, SA. Est. 1978. Owners: Joe and Dina Grilli. Winemakers: Joe Grilli and Grant Harrison. Vineyards: 32 acres of Colomb., Ries., Sém., Shiraz, Cab.Sauv., Chard., some fruit bought in. 15,000 cases. Visits June–August.

Joe Grilli is deceptively softly spoken: his wines simply shout their flavours and quality. Deliciously fruity Colombard and intense Botrytis Riesling under the Primo label share the limelight with serious Amarone-style Cabernet and exotic Sparkling Red under the Joseph range (which also includes some of Australia's best extra virgin olive oil).

Barossa Valley

Basedows Wines

Murray Street, Tanunda, Barossa Valley, SA. Est. 1896. Owners: Terry and Jill Hill. Winemaker: Craig Stansborough. Vineyards: Contract growers across the Barossa Valley. 70,000 cases. Visits.

A sometimes excellent Barossa winery. In the late 1970s its Shiraz reached real heights of richness and complexity. Recently the Chardonnay and Sémillon ('White Burgundy') have been doing well. The vineyards were sold in 1982, and grapes are now bought locally.

Charles Melton

Krondorf Road, Tanunda, Barossa Valley, SA. Est. 1984. Owners: Charlie Melton and Virginia Weckert. Winemaker: Charlie Melton. Vineyards: 42 acres of Shiraz, Grenache, Cab.Sauv., and Mataro, also fruit bought from eight other growers. 8,000 cases. Visits.

One of the nicest men in the Barossa, Charlie Melton produces some of the region's best wines. Cabernet and Shiraz stuffed with ripe fruit, Rose of Virginia, an intriguing cross between a heavy rosé and a light red, and deep-flavoured Shiraz Grenache Mataro blend called Nine Popes, the catalyst for the revival in interest in Rhône styles.

Château Yaldara

Lyndoch, SA. Est. 1947. Owners: the Thumm family. Winemaker: Jim Irvine. Vineyards: 120 acres at Lyndoch of mixed varieties. 500,000 cases. Visits.

This winery covers a broad range of wines, from the very cheap Acacia Hill labels, through the medium-priced and good value Lakewood wines, to a very expensive and concentrated Merlot (Jim Irvine's particular passion) called The Farms.

Elderton

Tanunda Road, Nuriootpa, Barossa Valley, SA. Est. 1985. Owners: Neil and Lorraine Ashmead. Winemakers: Neil Ashmead, Jim Irvine (consultant). 72 acres of Shiraz, Cab.Sauv., Merlot, Ries. and fruit bought in from Barossa growers. Visits.

Neil Ashmead is a tireless self-publicist, but the quality of the wines usually matches the hype. Traditionally huge, chocolatey, alcoholic reds have amassed a clutch of awards at recent shows, among them the infamous Jimmy Watson trophy for a particularly liquorous Cabernet.

Grant Burge

Jacob Creek, Tanunda, Barossa Valley, SA. Est. 1988. Owners: Grant and Helen Burge. Winemakers: Grant Burge and Craig Stansborough. Vineyards: 700 acres of mixed varieties. 70,000 cases.

Grant Burge, yet another of the Barossa's 'characters', makes a range of varietals, including Chardonnay, wood-matured Sémillon and Merlot. Blockbuster Meshach Shiraz, a Grange pretender, is also worth seeking out.

Henschke

Keyneton, SA. Est. 1868. Owners: the Henschke family. Winemaker: Stephen Henschke. Vineyards: 250 acres at Keyneton and Eden Valley of Shiraz, Ries., Chard., Cab.Sauv., Sém., and Lenswood of Malbec, Cab.Fr., Sauv.Bl., Gewürz. 40,000 cases.

A fifth-generation family firm with two famous brands of Shiraz: Hill of Grace (deep wine from ancient vines) and Mount Edelstone (easier, more elegant red). Other wines include a crisp, dry and delicate Riesling and elegant Merlot blends and Pinot Noir from the Adelaide Hills. Fashion has swung back to their staunch traditional approach.

Krondorf

Krondorf Road, Tanunda, Barossa Valley, SA. Est. 1972. Owner: Mildara Blass. Winemaker: Nick Walker. Vineyards: Lyndoch in the Barossa, Eden Valley and McLaren Vale. 80,000 cases. Visits.

This old Barossa winery was revamped in the '70s by young winemaking whizz-kids, Grant Burge and Ian Wilson. Now owned by Mildara Blass, quality is still consistent, with generous-flavoured wines true to their region.

Leo Buring

Tanunda Road, Nuriootpa, Barossa Valley, SA. Est. 1945. Owner: Southcorp Wines. Winemaker: Geoff Henriks. Vineyards: 140 acres of Ries, Chard., Sauv.Bl., Cab.Sauv., predominantly at Clare but also in Eden Valley and Barossa.

Although the original Leo Buring winery in the Barossa Valley has now been transformed into Richmond Grove (q.v.), wines under the Leo Buring label continue to be produced at Penfolds, around the corner. Winemaker Geoff Henriks trained under legendary Buring winemaker John Vickery, and applies the same fastidious attention to detail. Reds are impressive, Chardonnay also, but it is the Rieslings, possibly Australia's best, that continue to shine the brightest.

Orlando

Rowland Flat, Barossa, SA. Est. 1847 by Johann Gramp. Owners: Orlando Wines and Pernod Ricard. Winemaker: Philip Laffer. Vineyards: at Barossa, Eden Valley, Riverland, Padthaway, Coonawarra, Langhorne Creek. Visits.

One of the biggest wine companies in Australia, and known world-wide for the phenomenally successful Jacob's Creek. Beyond that brand, however, lurk some far better wines. The Gramps wines are packed with succulent fruit; Russet Ridge Coonawarra red blend is warm and earthy; Carrington sparkler is good, (less cheap Trilogy is better); Steingarten Riesling, from an individual, rocky vineyard is beautifully steely and tight; and Coonawarra Cabernets such as St Hugo and Jacaranda Ridge, while very oaky, can be very enjoyable.

Penfolds

Tanunda Rd, Nuriootpa, Barossa, SA. Est: 1844. Owner: Southcorp Wines. Winemakers: John Duval and Dean Kraehenbuhl. Vineyards: Extensive own holdings and contract growers across South Australia.

While Grange may no longer be the only true first-growth of the Southern Hemisphere (arguably, Henschke's Hill of Grace has swelled the number to two) Penfolds remains Australia's most esteemed red-wine company (*see* opposite page). Classic Penfolds wines include Kalimna Shiraz, Magill Estate

Penfolds

Few wine companies anywhere else in the world could lay claim to being the undisputed number one in their particular country, but Penfolds undoubtedly occupies that enviable position in Australia.

Since 1844, when Christopher Rawson Penfold and his wife Mary established a vineyard at Magill, on the outskirts of Adelaide, the Penfold name has been synonymous with consistency and quality in wine. Initially, of course, and until the middle of the 20th century, after Penfolds had moved to its current huge winery in the Barossa Valley, most of that wine was fortified.

But from the 1950s on, when winemaker Max Schubert began to release his Grange Hermitage onto an unsuspecting market, the Penfolds banner was held aloft by rich oaky, quintessentially South Australian reds. More recently the white wines in the portfolio have begun to show the same kind of consistent quality, due in part to an ongoing commitment on behalf of the present-day winemakers to create a White Grange, but it is still the reds that most wine-lovers associate with the name.

The cornerstone of Penfold's success is the extraordinary range of choice vineyards – often old and low-yielding – that the company has amassed over the years. These vineyard resources allow almost unlimited flexibility when it comes to blending (the soul of Penfolds – indeed Australian – winemaking), and ensure remarkable consistency of style year after year. This consistency is enhanced by the characteristic Penfold's trademark: lavish, unrestrained use of new American oak.

Not surprisingly, Penfolds has been through a succession of owners over the years, moving from a strictly-run family empire through the hands of a couple of major brewers, and finally ending up as the flagship of Southcorp Wines, itself a part of the multi-billion dollar Southcorp Holdings. The Southcorp group, which also includes other great wine companies such as Seppelt, Lindemans and Wynns as well as such outstanding smaller wineries as Coldstream Hills, is Australia's largest wine producer (and one of the top ten biggest wine companies in the world), but it is the Penfolds name that is firmly at the top of the Southcorp hierarchy.

and Bin 707 Cabernet Sauvignon. 'Ports' are excellent, with Grandfather a legend, and white wines are slowly improving – mostly as a result of ongoing vineyard and winery trials to create a 'White Grange'.

Peter Lehmann Wines

Tanunda, Barossa Valley, SA. Est. 1980. Owner: A public company. Winemakers: Andrew Wigan, Peter Scholz, Leonie Lange. All grapes bought from the Barossa and Eden valleys. 200,000 cases.
Peter Lehmann is one of the great showmen and supporters of the Barossa. The wines that appear under his name are equally expressive, and bask in their sense of place. Rieslings, from both the Barossa and Eden valleys, can be wonderful, and Cabernet and Shiraz can be as rich and full as you'd wish. Clancy's is a good value red blend, while flagship wines The Mentor (a Cabernet blend) and Stonewell Shiraz are recent and worthy newcomers to the pantheon of Barossa legends.

Richmond Grove

Para Road, Tanunda, SA. Est. 1897 (as Château Leonay, by Leo Buring) Owner: Orlando Wyndham. Winemaker: John Vickery.

Vineyards: 25 acres at Tanunda, and fruit bought in. Visits.
Richmond Grove, formerly based in the Hunter Valley, now has its home in the heart of the Barossa, in the old Château Leonay winery established by Leo Buring at the end of the 19th century. Fittingly, John Vickery, the winemaker who made some remarkable, seemingly immortal Rieslings under the Leo Buring label during the 1960s, '70s and '80s, is back at Château Leonay, after a brief spell in retirement. Not surprisingly, the new Richmond Grove Rieslings are good, but so too are other wines from this revamped winery.

Rockford

Krondorf Road, Tanunda, Barossa Valley, SA. Est 1984. Owner: Tanunda Vintners. Winemakers: Robert (Rocky) O'Callaghan and Chris Ringland. Vineyards: grapes bought in from old Barossa vineyards. 25,000 cases. Visits.
Small Barossa winery with one of the region's true characters, the reticent Rocky O'Callaghan, at the helm. Styles are truly regional and thoroughly traditional: big, brawny Grenache and Shiraz are totally seductive, as is the exceedingly rare but worth searching for Sparkling Black Shiraz, which has almost achieved a cult following.

St Hallett Wines

St Hallett Road, Tanunda, SA. Est. 1944. Owner: Lindner McLean. Winemaker: Stuart Blackwell. Vineyards: 100 acres in the Barossa Valley. 15,000 cases. Visits.

Bob McLean, one of the owners of St Hallett, is about as good an ambassador for the Barossa as you could hope to find. He is also passionate about his wines – and with good reason. Across the board, the wide variety of styles are good, but the Old Block Shiraz (one of the first wines to exploit the marketing potential of the Barossa's ancient viticultural heritage) is consistently top of the tree.

Saltram

Angaston Road, Barossa Valley, SA. Est. 1859. Owner: Mildara Blass. Winemaker: Migel Dolan. Vineyards: 30 acres in Barossa; 12 acres in Clare. 120,000 cases. Visits.

For a while, in the '60s and '70s, when Peter Lehmann was winemaker, Saltram produced classic red wines such as Mamre Brook Cabernet and Metala Shiraz/Cabernet. During the '80s, under the ownership of Seagrams, quality was reliable but sluggish. The Rothbury Group took over wine-making in the '90s and the winery returned to form, with a much-improved Metala and new wines such as Saltram's Classic Range. Now the winery is owned by Mildara Blass, and the future is hard to predict.

Seppelt

Seppeltsfield, Barossa Valley, SA. Est: 1851. Owner: Southcorp Wines. Winemaker: James Godfrey. Vineyards: Barossa Valley, Adelaide Hills and Riverland.

The historic old home for the Seppelt company is now its base for fortified wine production. Winemaker James Godfrey is fanatical about fortifieds, a passion that translates to his wines. Tangy fino, complex amontillado and deeply nutty oloroso are complemented by luscious Rutherglen Muscat and Tokay and, arguably, Australia's very greatest tawny 'port', made from ancient, olive-brown, treacly reserve wines.

Tollana

Nuriootpa, Barossa Valley, SA. Est. 1888 as Tolley, Scott & Tolley. Owner: Southcorp Wines. Winemaker: Neville Falkenberg. Vineyards: 300 acres in the Eden Valley and fruit bought in from Adelaide Hills.

Although the winemaking for Tollana is based in the Barossa, most of the fruit is sourced from the Eden Valley and Adelaide Hills. Consequently, wines such as the Tollana Cabernet, Shiraz, Sauvignon Blanc and Botrytis Riesling all tend towards bright, fruity elegance and a refreshing lightness of touch.

Wolf Blass

Sturt Highway, Nuriootpa, Barossa Valley, SA. Est. 1966. Owner: Mildara Blass. Winemakers: John Glaetzer, Wendy Stuckey. Vineyards: 150 acres at Eden Valley of Shiraz, Ries., Cab.Sauv.; 200 acres at Clare of Shiraz, Ries., Cab.Sauv. 550,000 cases. Visits.

Wolf Blass arrived in Australia 30 years ago and immediately put his skills as a blender and marketer to good use, building one of Australia's most widely recognized wine empires. Although no longer involved in the day-to-day running of the company, the presence of Wolf Blass still makes itself felt in every bottle of wine that bears his name. The popularity of Wolf Blass continues unabated, with some wines – impressive Rieslings and richly oaky reds – even confounding the meanest critics.

Yalumba

Eden Valley Road, Angaston, Barossa Valley, SA. Est. 1849. Visits. Owners: the Hill Smith family. Vineyards: extensive vineyards at Coonawarra, Koppamurra and at Oxford Landing at Waikerie, on the Murray River. Also three other estate vineyards: Heggies, Pewsey Vale and Hill Smith Estate, all in the Eden Valley. 1.2 million cases.

The sixth generation of the Hill Smith family is active in this distinctively upper-crust winery with an air of the turf about it. Their finest wines in the past were 'ports', but since the planting of higher and cooler land in the 1960s, dry whites have been very good and hugely popular.

Yalumba wines range from the bargain bubbly, Angas Brut, through reliable stalwarts such as Galway Shiraz, to elegant Coonawarra Cabernet, The Menzies, and enormous flagship Shiraz, Octavius (aged in small American barrels called octaves). Wines from the Hill Smiths' cooler vineyard estates are very good. Hill Smith Sauvignon Blanc is crisp and grassy; Pewsey Vale Riesling is a classic wine, honeyed and long-lived; Heggies Cabernet and Merlot are brambly and fine, and Heggies Viognier is the best Australian example of this grape yet made.

Clare

Jim Barry

Main North Road, Clare, SA. Est. 1959. Owner: Jim Barry. Winemaker: Mark Barry. Vineyards: 300 acres of Clare vines bearing (200 not yet bearing). 75,000 cases.

One of the largest wineries in Clare, producing a wide range of wines. Whites include Chardonnay, Sauvignon and both dry and sweet Rieslings. Among the reds are Cabernet, a Cabernet/Merlot blend, port and a remarkable Shiraz called The Armagh.

Grosset Wines

Auburn, SA. Est. 1981. Owner and winemaker: Jeffrey Grosset. 7,500 cases. Vineyards: 5 acres and Clare grapes bought in from contract vineyards. Visits.

One of the region's (and Australia's) best small wineries. Jeffrey Grosset is a fastidious but open-minded winemaker, producing quite delicious Riesling and a Cabernet blend called Gaia from his and others' vineyards in the Clare Valley, as well as smaller quantities of intense Chardonnay and gamey Pinot from vineyards in the Adelaide Hills.

Mitchell Cellars

Hughes Park Road, Sevenhill, Clare, SA. Est. 1975. Owners: Andrew and Jane Mitchell. Winemaker: Andrew Mitchell.

Vineyards: 120 acres of Ries., Shiraz, Cab.Sauv., Merlot, Sém., Grenache. 20,000 cases. Visits.

Mitchell Cellars' wines include Watervale Riesling, Sémillon, Peppertree Shiraz and Cabernet. All are among Clare's best.

Leasingham

Dominic Street, Clare, SA. Est 1893. Owner: BRL Hardy. Winemaker: Richard Rowe. Vineyards: 345 acres in the Clare region. Visits.

New ownership (BRL Hardy) and a revamp for this famous old Clare winery has resulted in a great deal of new interest. Old labels such as the Bin 56 Cabernet Malbec and Bin 7 Riesling have been reintroduced, and a new premium range, Classic Clare, added. Riesling is excellent, and Shiraz – especially the resinous, thickly textured Classic Clare – is particularly good.

Pike's Polish Hill River

Sevenhill, Clare, SA. Est. 1984. Owners: the Pike family. Winemaker: Neil Pike. Vineyards: 45 acres at Polish Hill River, with a third of the grapes bought in. 20,000 cases. Visits.

The winery is no longer the part-time affair it formerly was, although one of the Pike brothers, Andrew, is still a senior viticulturalist for Southcorp. Neil, the winemaker, crafts particularly good Shiraz, and wonderfully zesty Riesling.

Tim Adams

Warenda Road, Clare, SA. Est. 1986. Owners: Tim Adams and Pam Goldsack. Winemaker: Tim Adams. Grapes sourced from 13 local growers. 15,000 cases. Visits.

All wines made by this talented winemaker display solid regional character. Riesling is crisp and limey, Sémillon lemony and balanced with good oak, Aberfeldy Shiraz full of big Clare red fruit flavours, and The Fergus Grenache suitably heroic.

Tim Knappstein

Pioneer Avenue, Clare, SA. Est. 1976, as Enterprise Wines. Owner: Petaluma. Winemaker: Andrew Hardy. Vineyards: 200 acres of Clare vines. 45,000 cases. Visits.

This well-known Clare winery is now owned by Petaluma, and winemaking is overseen by Andrew Hardy. Although Tim Knappstein is no longer involved (he's now wrapped up with his Lenswood Vineyards – q.v.) the reputation he established is in good hands. Riesling and Gewürztraminer are still fragrant and flowery, and Cabernet is as chunky and fruit-packed as it ever was.

Quelltaler

Watervale,Clare, SA. Est. 1865 by the Sobels family. Owner: Mildara Blass. Winemakers: David O'Leary, Wendy Stuckey. Vineyards: 400 acres in the Clare Valley. 50,000 cases. Visits.

This is a winery with an identity crisis. The estate was established more than a century ago, and made traditional wines until the 1970s, when it became the focus of innovation that was way ahead of its time. Bought by Wolf Blass in the late '80s, it became the Eaglehawk Estate, and now it is the home of two separate Mildara Blass brands,

the cheaper Black Opal range of reds and the new, more upmarket Annie's Lane range.

Sevenhill Cellars

College Road, Sevenhill, Clare Valley, SA. Est. 1851. Owner: the Manresa Society. Winemakers: Brother John May and John Monten. Vineyards: 145 acres of Ries., Muscadelle, Shiraz, Cab.Sauv., Merlot, Malbec, Verdelho, Ruby Cabernet. 24,000 cases. Visits.

This old Jesuit church and winery is one of the most attractive places in Clare, and the wines produced by brother John May are some of the region's best. Monumental in stature, with abundant fruit and spice, the reds, based on Shiraz, Cabernet, Malbec and Grenache, are surprisingly drinkable when young, but also capable of ageing for long periods. Whites, including an unusual dry Verdelho and a fragrant Riesling, are also good.

Taylors Wines

Auburn, Clare Valley, SA. Est. 1969. Owners: the Taylor family. Winemaker: Andrew Tolley. Vineyards: 1,200 acres of Cab.Sauv., Shiraz, P.N., Chard., Ries. 250,000 cases. Visits.

Taylors began with reds, and make pleasantly soft Cabernet. Whites were added in the mid-80s: the early-maturing, full Riesling is their best.

Wendouree

Clare, SA. Est. 1895. Owners: the Liberman family. Winemaker: Tony Brady. 25 acres of Shiraz, Cab.Sauv., Malbec, Mataro. 2,000 cases. Visits.

This small, old vineyard has produced some of Australia's most powerful, concentrated red wines for decades. Nothing is set to change, as Tony Brady sees himself merely as the guardian of a great tradition, preferring to interfere as little as possible during the fruit's passage from vineyard to bottle. Unfortunately, the Riesling, one of the region's most full-flavoured, is now no longer produced.

Coonawarra

Bowen Estate

Coonawarra, SA. Est. 1972. Owners: Doug and Joy Bowen. Winemaker: Doug Bowen. Vineyards: 60 acres, Cab. Sauv. and Shiraz, some Rhine Ries., Chard., Merlot and Cab.Fr. 12,000 cases. Visits.

An ex-Lindemans winemaker, Doug Bowen offers a near-model Coonawarra Cabernet which can age well. Riesling and Shiraz are also good examples of the area. He built a handsome new winery in 1982, and expanded again in 1995.

Brand's Laira

Naracoorte Road, Coonawarra, SA. Est. 1966. Owner: McWilliams Wines. Winemakers: Jim Brand, Bruce Gregory. Vineyards: 700 acres of Shiraz, Cab.Sauv., Merlot, P.N., Cab.Fr., Ries., Chard. 50,000 cases. Visits.

A reliable Coonawarra family winery, now owned by McWilliams. Reds appear quite austere in their youth, but blossom with age into some of the region's richest and most satisfying wines.

Hollick

Racecourse Road, Coonawarra, SA. Est. 1982. Owners: Ian and
Wendy Hollick. Winemaker: Pat Tocaciu and Ian Hollick.
Vineyards: 125 acres of Cab.Sauv., Cab.Fr., Merlot, P.N., Shiraz,
Ries., Chard., Sauv.Bl. and Petit Verdot. 20,000 cases. Visits.
Small Coonawarra producer making a successful range of
varietals: Cabernet, Pinot Noir and Shiraz for the reds;
Chardonnay and Riesling for the whites. Hollick's Cabernet
was a winner of the important Jimmy Watson Trophy,
Ravenswood is their flagship red, which has an important
following. The second label here is Terra.

Katnook Estate

Coonawarra, SA. Wines since 1979. Owner: Wingara Wine
Group. Winemaker: Wayne Stehbens. Vineyards: 360 acres of
Chard., Cab.Sauv., Ries., Sauv.Bl., Shiraz, Merlot, P.N., Cab.Fr.
12,000 cases.
The pinnacle of the large Wingara Wine Group (the bulk
being taken up by Deakin Estate – q.v.) Katnook Estate is
also one of Coonawarra's most unusual wineries, in that its
best wines are often not red but white. Certainly, Cabernet
and a varietal Merlot can be good, but the Katnook
Chardonnay, delicious Riesling and exceptional, long-lived
Sauvignon Blanc are often the best. Second label, Riddoch,
offers some great value for money (again, Sauvignon is often
best of the range).

Leconfield

Main Road, Coonawarra, SA. Est. 1974. Owners: the Hamilton
family. Winemaker: Ralph Fowler. Vineyards: 70 acres in
Coonawarra. 16,000 cases. Visits.
In the hands of experienced winemaker Ralph Fowler
(formerly at Tyrrell in the Hunter Valley) the quality at
Leconfield has improved dramatically. Chardonnay, both
crisply unwooded and splendidly oaked are good; Riesling,
unfortunately, has all but disappeared; but the reds
(Cabernet, Merlot, and some intriguing varietal releases of
Cabernet Franc and Petit Verdot) are the real strength: tight,
elegant and very stylish.

Mildara Wines

Main Road, Coonawarra, SA. Company originally founded in
1888; established in Coonawarra: 1955. Owner: Mildara Blass.
Winemaker: Gavin Hogg. Vineyards: Over 1,000 acres in
Coonawarra. 250,000 cases.
Although Mildara was founded in 1888 and the majority of its
production (bulk, table and fortified) is made at its Merbein
winery in northwest Victoria, it is Mildara's connection with
Coonawarra that has the highest profile. Jamieson's Run
continues to be a hugely popular brand, and has been joined
by the slightly more upmarket Cabernet blend, Robertson's
Well, but it is the top-of-the-range Alexanders and White
Label Coonawarra Cabernets, both with delicious blackcurrant fruit, that impress most. Mildara Blass has, over the
last few years, proved itself to be one of Australia's more
aggressive aquisitional wine companies, and a whole host of
other wineries – including those previously in the Rothbury
group – are now huddled under its umbrella.

Parker Estate

Main Road, Coonawarra, SA. Est. 1988. Owners: the Parker family
and interests associated with J.O. Fairfax. Winemaker: Chris
Cameron. Vineyards: 50 acres of Cab. Sauv., Merlot, Cab.Fr.,
Chard. 4,000 cases.
Until recently, only one Coonawarra wine was released
under the Parker Estate label: a Bordeaux blend called First
Growth (easily dismissed as arrogance until you try the
superb wine inside the bottle). Now also a Chardonnay, but
the homeless brand remains hard to pin down.

Penley Estate

Mcleans Road, Coonawarra, SA. Est. 1988. Owner/winemaker:
Kym Tolley. Vineyards: 170 acres of Cab. Sauv., Shiraz, Merlot,
Chard., P.N. 16,000 cases. Visits.
Born into a wine family, Kym Tolley did his apprenticeship
at Penfolds, before setting up on his own. He now produces
some seriously good wines in Coonawarra, especially a dark,
dense, multi-layered Cabernet.

Redman

Naracoorte Road, Coonawarra, SA. Est. 1966. Owners: the Redman
family. Winemakers: Bruce and Malcolm Redman. Vineyards: 80
acres, mainly of Shiraz, some Cab.Sauv. and a little Merlot. Visits.
Founded by the Redmans of Rouge Homme (q.v.) after
Lindemans took over the company in 1965, this winery
produces red wines from Coonawarra vines. The wines are
still staunchly old-fashioned: both the Shiraz and Cabernet
are refined, austere and rather subtle, when all around them
seems to be fruitiness and approachability.

Rouge Homme

Memorial Drive, Coonawarra, SA. Est. 1908. Owner: Southcorp
Wines. Winemaker: Paul Gordon. Vineyards: 222 acres of
Cab.Sauv., Shiraz, P.N., Chard., Merlot and Cab.Fr.
Old Coonawarra winery set up by the Redman family (hence
the terrible pun of a name), now owned by Southcorp and
producing some great value wines. Chardonnay and Pinot
Noir can be lovely, fruity wines, while the Cabernet blend,
Richardson's Red Block, is lithe, elegant and spicy.

Rymill Wines

Coonawarra, SA. Est. 1974. Owners: Peter and Judy Rymill.
Winemaker: John Innes. Vineyards: 300 acres at Coonawarra.
40,000 cases. Visits.
Quiet achiever, slowly building itself up into one of the most
impressive wineries in the region, and yet managing to
provide extremely good wines for comparatively low prices.
Showpiece winery building and elegant packaging complete
the picture.

Wynns

Memorial Drive, Coonawarra, SA. Est. 1891 as Riddoch Winery,
becoming Wynns in 1951. Owner: Southcorp Wines. Winemaker:
Peter Douglas. Vineyards: Coonawarra – 1,125 acres, of Chard.,
Ries., Cab.Sauv., Shiraz, Merlot.
The Wynns were an important Melbourne wine family who
ended up having greatest impact in South Australia. They took

over the old Riddoch winery in Coonawarra and promptly carved a name for the region with some spectacular Shiraz and Cabernet. Both remain reliably brilliant (with the former much better value), and have been joined by Chardonnay, Riesling and a Cabernet-Merlot-Shiraz blend. Two flagship wines, John Riddoch Cabernet and Michael Shiraz – hugely-structured, massively ripe, opulent wines – fill out the range.

Zema Estate

Main Road, Coonawarra, SA. Est. 1982. Owners: the Zema family. Winemakers: Matt and Nick Zema. Vineyards: 110 acres at three vineyards in Coonawarra. 12,000 cases. Visits.

The personable Zema family stoically continue to produce some of the region's richest, most powerful wines, while all around them things are increasingly dominated by the larger companies.

Eden Valley

Mountadam

High Eden Road, Eden Valley, SA. Est. 1972. Owner: Adam Wynn. Winemakers: Adam Wynn and Andrew Ewart. Vineyards: 100 acres, of Chard., Cab.Sauv., P.N., Shiraz and Merlot. 40,000 cases. Visits.

Adam Wynn, whose family founded the Coonawarra-based firm now owned by Southcorp, trained in Bordeaux and established this high-altitude winery with the help of his father David. The grapes grown here go into the Mountadam range of first-class varietals. A second label, called David Wynn, includes Chardonnay, Cabernet, Shiraz and Riesling, all made from bought-in Eden Valley grapes, and the Eden Ridge range of organic wines is also successful.

Langhorne Creek

Bleasdale Vineyards

Wellington Road, Langhorne Creek, SA. Est. 1850. Owners: the Potts family. Winemaker: Michael Potts. Vineyards: 130 acres of Verdelho, Chard., Ries., Cab.Sauv., Shiraz, Malbec, Merlot, Cab.Fr., Petit Verdot, Red Frontignac and Oeillade. 60,000 cases. Visits.

The fifth generation of the pioneering Potts family operates this working slice of Australian history (it still has the huge old red-gum beam press). In this arid area the vineyards are irrigated by flooding through sluices from the Bremer River. The wines are consistently good value.

McLaren Vale

Andrew Garrett

Kangarilla Road, McLaren Vale, SA. Est 1987. 140,000 cases. Owner: Mildara Blass. Winemaker: Phil Reschke. Vineyards: 500 acres in McLaren Vale and Padthaway; and fruit bought in.

Highly successful winery, recently taken over by Mildara Blass, making a best-selling range of varietals. The reds include Cabernet-Merlot and good-value Shiraz. A popular *méthode traditionnelle* wine is also made.

Chapel Hill

Chapel Hill Road, McLaren Vale, SA. Est. 1979. Owner: Gerard Industries. Winemaker: Pam Dunsford. Vineyards: 100 acres at McLaren Vale, with fruit also bought in from Eden Valley, Padthaway and Coonawarra. 45,000 cases. Visits.

Pam Dunsford fashions some of McLaren Vale's best wines at this modern winery, even though they are often multi-regional blends. Riesling is good, Chardonnay (wooded and unwooded) is very good, but the reds, especially the soft, concentrated Shiraz wines, are exceptional.

Château Reynella

Reynell Road, Reynella, SA. Est. 1838. Owner: BRL Hardy. Winemakers: Steve Parnell and Tom Newton. 25 acres at Reynella. 45,000 cases. Visits.

A famous old name, particularly for ports and red wines, with a historic cellar and vineyard just south of Adelaide. Bought by Thomas Hardy in 1982, and now the head-quarters of the huge company. The winery continues to make good wines – of which Cabernet, Cabernet-Merlot and 'Vintage Port' are best.

Clarendon Hills

Brookman Road, Blewitt Springs, McLaren Vale, SA. Est. 1989. Owner/winemaker: Roman Bratasiuk. Vineyards: 2.5 acres and fruit brought in from local growers. 6,000 cases. Visits by appt.

Pharmacist Roman Bratasiuk sources fruit from old, dry-grown low-yielding vineyards and uses 'traditional' techniques such as natural yeasts and minimal sulphur additions to produce huge, concentrated wines. Super-Premium Shiraz, Astralis, a conscious attempt to be more Côte-Rôtie than Côte-Rôtie.

Coriole

Chaffeys Road, McLaren Vale, SA. Est. 1918. Owners: the Lloyd family. Winemaker: Stephen Hall. Vineyards: 53 acres of Cab. Sauv., Shiraz, Ch.Bl., Rhine Ries., Grenache and P.N., Sangiovese, Merlot, Cabernet Fr., Sém., Chard. 24,000 cases. Visits.

Wonderfully ripe Shiraz is the main focus here, but Sémillon and Chenin Blanc can be refreshingly grassy. Pioneering work with Sangiovese (and olive oil) is most exciting.

D'Arenberg

Osborn Road, McLaren Vale, SA. Est. 1912. Owners: the Osborn family. Winemaker: Chester Osborn. Vineyards: 150 acres of Shiraz, Cab.Sauv., Gren., Chard., Viognier, Marsanne, Chambourcin and Ries. 120,000 cases. Visits.

Until recently one of McLaren Vale's most traditional producers, making good, rustic wines, and most famous for Grenache/Shiraz called d'Arry's Original Burgundy. With younger generation winemaker Chester Osborn at the helm, the family company has become a little more innovative, with forays into the world of obscure varietals (Chambourcin, Mourvèdre) and huge big reds such as the Dead Arm Shiraz particularly impressing.

Hardy's

Main Road, McLaren Vale, SA. Est. 1853. Owner: BRL Hardy. Winemakers: Peter Dawson, Tom Newton, Steve Parnell, Ed Carr. Vineyards: 1,000 acres at Padthaway, 700 acres at Coonawarra, 400 acres at Koppamurra, 200 acres at Elgin Valley, 245 acres at Langhorne Creek, 285 acres at Hoddler Creek (Yarra Valley). Visits.

One of the great old Adelaide wine dynasties, now merged with the Berri Renmano group and owner of some of Australia's most exciting wineries. The family's origins were in McLaren Vale, where rich and fruity reds are still made – including top-of-the-range labels such as Eileen Hardy Shiraz and Thomas Hardy Cabernet – but pioneering vineyard moves into Padthaway and, more recently, other new South Australian regions have resulted in fruit for a wide range of other well-known wines, such as the Nottage Hill varietals and the Bird Series. Quality is increasingly encouraging.

Hillstowe

Main Road, Hahndorf, SA. Est. 1980. Owners: the Laurie family. Winemaker: Chris Laurie. Vineyards: 35 acres at the Adelaide Hills, 42 acres at McLaren Vale. 12,500 cases. Visits.

As you would expect from a venture initiated by a seasoned and successful grape grower, the fruit quality in Hillstowe wines is more often than not exemplary: clean, full of freshness and life. Sauvignon Blanc particularly impresses, and represents good value.

Mount Hurtle

Pimpala Road, Reynella, SA. Est. 1897. Owner: Geoff Merrill. Winemakers: Geoff Merrill and Goe di Fabio. Vineyards: 54 acres of Cab.Sauv., Merlot, Chard. 80,000 cases. Visits.

Geoff Merrill is one of Australia's highest-profile wine-making characters. Serious, surprisingly understated and elegant wines are released under his eponymous label, while much more approachable, fruity wines come out as Mount Hurtle, and are blends of fruit from McLaren Vale and other regions.

Normans Wines

Grants Gully Road, Clarendon, SA. Est. 1853. Owner: A public company. Winemakers: Roger Harbord, Angela Meaney. Vineyards: 106 acres at Angle Vale of mixed varieties. 500,000 cases.

No longer family-owned, but still fertile with good ideas, and still producing the good value, cornily named sparkler, Norman's Conquest. Cheaper wines can be a little rough-and-ready, but wines such as those under the Chais Clarendon label – especially a particularly robust and deep Shiraz – can be great value.

Pirramimma

Johnston Road, McLaren Vale, SA. Est. 1892 Owners: the Johnston family. Winemaker: Geoff Johnston. Vineyard: 440 acres of Cab.Sauv., Shiraz, Ries., Petit Verdot, Grenache, Chard. and Sauv.Bl. . 20,000 cases.

Long-established estate, still making bulk wine but scoring high points for clean blackberryish Cabernet, aromatic Riesling, a soft light Shiraz and a bigger oak-aged one. Also gutsy vintage ports.

Richard Hamilton

Main Road, Willunga, McLaren Vale. SA. Est. 1972. Owners: the Hamilton family. Winemaker: Ralph Fowler. 86 acres in Willunga, including Cab.Sauv., Ch.Bl., Chard., Sém., Sauv.Bl. and 80 acres in Coonawarra with Cab.Sauv., Cab.Fr., Chard. 17,000 cases.

Producer of generous, rich wines from old vineyards in McLaren Vale and younger ones in Coonawarra. Whites include Chardonnay and Sémillon, while the reds are based on Cabernet, Shiraz and Grenache, with recent small and exciting releases of Merlot.

Seaview

Chaffey's Road, McLaren Vale, SA. Est 1855. Owner: Southcorp Wines. Winemaker: Mike Farmilo. Vineyards: 370 acres in McLaren Vale, with much fruit bought in. Visits.

Reliable producer of wines which theoretically have their basis in McLaren Vale. Standard Chardonnay, sparkling, Shiraz and Cabernet are often among the best value wines in Australia, while the same styles under the premium Edwards & Chaffey label, although markedly more expensive, are a significant step up in quality.

Wirra Wirra

McMurtrie Road, McLaren Vale, SA. Est. 1894, re-est. 1969. Owners: Greg and Roger Trott. Winemaker: Ben Riggs. Vineyards: 100 acres of Cab.Sauv., Shiraz, Grenache, Ries., P.N., Merlot, Chard., Sauv.Bl. 30,000 cases. Visits.

The resurrection (in 1969) of a fine old ironstone winery to make often more graceful wines than the macho style more usually emanating from McLaren Vale. The Rieslings are most remarkable. 'Church Block' is a Cabernet-Merlot-Shiraz blend. RSW Shiraz is dark and resinous, and late-harvest wines are bright and good.

Woodstock

Douglas Gully Road, McLaren Flat, SA. Est. 1974. Owners: the Collett family. Winemaker Scott Collett. 60 acres of Cab.Sauv., Shiraz, Chard., Ries., Grenache. 20,000 cases. Visits.

Woodstock began producing wines in 1982. It now makes a wide range of varietals, including Cabernet, Shiraz and Chardonnay, as well as an excellent sweet Botrytis white.

Riverland

Angoves

Bookmark Ave., Renmark, SA. Founded 1886. Owners: the Angove family. Vineyards: 1,185 acres of Rhine Ries., Sauv.Bl., Sylvaner, Traminer, Chard., Cab.Sauv., Shiraz, P.N. 800,000 cases. Visits.

A conservative old family company in the Riverland irrigated area well-known for producing good-value lines. In the '80s new-look whites changed the firm's image: all simple, fruity, lightweight, well made and cheap.

Renmano

Industry Road, Renmark, SA. Est. 1916. Owner: BRL Hardy. Winemakers: Glenn James, Anne-Marie Wasley. All fruit bought from local growers.

A huge coop, now part of BRL Hardy (see Hardy's). Production at Renmano concentrates mostly on bulk and cask wines, but the Chairman's Selection bottled wines – Chardonnay, Shiraz and Cabernet – can be particularly rich and flavoursome (not to say, in the case of the Chardonnay, truly voluptuous), and very good value.

WESTERN AUSTRALIA

Great Southern

Alkoomi

Wingeballup Road, Frankland, WA. Est. 1971. Owners: Mervyn and Judith Lange. Winemaker: Michael Staniford. Vineyards: 110 acres of Cab.Sauv., Ries., Shiraz, Malbec, Sauv.Bl., some Merlot and Sém.; also Chard., Cab.Fr., Verdelho. 40,000 cases. Visits.

The pace-setter for the new Frankland area, best in dense, full-flavoured Cabernet and clean tannic Shiraz. Riesling is light and sweetish in the finish, Malbec a good, although unpopular speciality.

Frankland Estate

Frankland-Rocky Gully Road, Frankland, WA. Est. 1988. Owners/winemakers: Judi Cullam and Barrie Smith. Vineyards: 50 acres at Frankland of Ries., Chard., Sauv.Bl., Shiraz, Cab.Sauv., Merlot, Cab. Fr., Malbec and Petit Verdot. 10,000 cases. Visits by appt.

A newcomer to the Great Southern region, but already there is an impressive line-up of wines. Riesling is typically full and fragrant, the evocatively named Isolation Ridge (Shiraz) and Olmo's Reward (Bordeaux blend) are tight and intriguingly austere.

Goundrey

Langton, Mount Barker, WA. Est. 1970. Owner: Jack Bendat. Winemaker: Brendon Smith. Vineyards: 290 acres of Cab.Sauv., Ries., Chard., Shiraz, Sauv.Bl., P.N., Cab.Fr. and fruit bought in. 120,000 cases. Visits.

Goundrey is one of the Great Southern region's most dramatically ambitious wineries which has expanded recently. Huge investment and rigorous winemaking have resulted in some superb wines, especially the brooding Reserve Shiraz.

Howard Park

Scotsdale Road, Denmark, WA. Est. 1986.Owners: Jeff and Amy Burch and John and Wendy Wade. Winemaker: John Wade. All grapes are sourced from contract growers in the Great Southern, Pemberton and Margaret River regions. 22,000 cases. Visits.

John Wade is one of the most influential winemakers in Western Australia. He makes very good wine under contract for many other people, but it is the Howard Park wines – fragrant, herbal Riesling and tight, long-lived Cabernet – that, one feels, get the most loving treatment.

Plantagenet Wines

Albany Highway, Mount Barker, WA. Est. 1968. Owners: Lionel Samson and son, and Tony Smith. Winemaker: Gavin Berry. Vineyards: 100 acres at Mt. Barker, of Chard., Ries., with Cab.Sauv., Shiraz, Sauv.Bl., Merlot, P.N., Cab.Fr. 30,000 cases. Visits.

The senior winery at Mount Barker. Chardonnay (either the excellent unwooded Omrah or spicy, wooded Plantagenet) is the white wine success here, and Shiraz, with dusty, edgy flavours, is remarkably Rhône-like.

Wignalls

Chester Pass Road, King River, Albany, WA. Est. 1982. Owners: the Wignall family. Winemaker: John Wade. Vineyards: 30 acres of Chard., Sauv.Bl., P.N., Cab.Sauv., Shiraz. 7,000 cases. Visits.

This vineyard is stuck out on its own near the remote West Australian town of Albany, but has managed to forge an impressive reputation with some of the state's best Chardonnay and Pinot Noir, made by the ubiquitous John Wade (see Howard Park). New plantings of Shiraz should prove interesting.

Geographe

Capel Vale

Mallokup Road, Capel, WA. Est 1973. Owners: Peter and Elizabeth Pratten. Winemaker: Rob Bowen. Vineyards: 250 acres of Shiraz, Cab.Sauv., Chard., Ries., 60 at Capel, 100 at Pemberton, 90 at Great Southern; also fruit bought in. 35,000 cases. Visits.

Successful winery, sourcing fruit from a number of regions for its wines. Those under the second, CV label can be good value; wines under the Capel Vale label – especially cedary, elegant Baudin Cabernet blend – can be very good indeed.

Peel Estate

Fletcher Road, Baldivis, nr. Mandurah, WA. Est. 1974. Owners: Will Nairn and a partnership. Vineyards: 40 acres of Cab.Sauv., Chard., Ch.Bl., Shiraz, Merlot, Verdelho and Zin. 6,000 cases.

Strong California influence shows in this blossoming estate. Chenin Blanc aged in oak is modelled on the lovely Chappellet Napa wine. Zinfandel is clean and aromatic, Shiraz with 15 months in French and American oak seems to be a wine for long ageing.

Margaret River

Amberley Estate

Thornton Road, Yallingup, WA. Est. 1986. Owner: A private company. Winemakers: Eddie Price, Greg Tilbrook. Vineyards: 80 acres of Sém., Sauv.Bl., Ch.Bl., Chard., Cab. Sauv., Merlot, Cab. Fr., Shiraz. 30,000 cases. Visits.

This small- to medium-sized company has established a good name for itself with clean, reliable, sometimes very good wines, including fruity, fresh, off-dry Chenin Blanc and medium-bodied, juicy Cabernet blends.

Ashbrook Estate

Willyabrup, Margaret River, WA. Est. 1975. Owners: the Devitt family. Winemakers: Brian and Tony Devitt. Vineyards: 30 acres of Chard., Sém., Cab.Sauv. and Verdelho, with small quantities of Ries., Sauv.Bl., Merlot and Cab.Fr. Visits.

Remote family-run winery in the middle of a red gum forest. Excellent and much sought-after white wines are produced, including Gold Label Rhine Riesling, well-made Sémillon, crisp Sauvignon Blanc and rich Chardonnay.

Brookland Valley

Caves Road, Willyabrup, WA. Est. 198. Owners: Malcolm and Deidre Jones. Winemaker: Gary Baldwin (consultant). Vineyards: 50 acres of Chard., Cab. Sauv., Sauv.Bl., Merlot, Cab. Fr. 48,000 cases. Visits, restaurant.

One of Margaret River's newer success stories, the Joneses manage to combine a popular approach to wine tourism at their Flutes restaurant, with some downright delicious wines. The Sauvignon-Sémillon is particularly good, with intense, grass and pea flavours.

Cape Clairault

Willyabrup, Margaret River, WA. Est. 1976. Owners: Ian and Ani Lewis. Winemaker Ian Lewis. Vineyards: 18 acres of Cab.Sauv., Sauv.Bl., Sém., Ries., Cab.Fr., Merlot. 9,000 cases. Visits and restaurant.

Small Margaret River Winery which has won many medals. Wines are not as obviously fruity as some of its neighbours', and include excellent Cabernet Sauvignon and Sémillon-Sauvignon, a style increasingly identified as particularly suited to this region.

Cape Mentelle

Wallcliffe Road, Margaret River, WA. Est. 1970. Founder and director: David Hohnen. Owners: Veuve Clicquot-Ponsardin. Winemaker: John Durham. Vineyards: 200 acres, Cab.Sauv., Sém., Merlot, Shiraz, Zin., Sauv.Bl., Ch. Bl., Chard. 55,000 cases. Visits.

One of the great success stories of the Margaret River. David Hohnen, Cape Mentelle's founder and original winemaker, trained in California, and that shows in his drive and dedication. Not content with making one of Margaret River's best Cabernets, Cape Mentelle also pioneered the Sémillon/Sauvignon blend in this area, and produce excellent Chardonnay, elegant, spicy Shiraz, and absurdly chunky, highly alcoholic and thoroughly idiosyncratic Zinfandel. Hohnen also established the remarkable Cloudy Bay in New Zealand.

Château Xanadu

Terry Road, Margaret River, WA. Est. 1977. 15,000 cases. Visits. Owners: Dr. Lagan and Sheridan. Winemaker: Jürg Muggli. Vineyards: 50 acres of Sém., Chard., Cab.Sauv., P.N., Cab.Fr., Merlot, Sauv.Bl.

Vastly improved Margaret River winery (whose name was, not surprisingly, inspired by Coleridge's poem), producing fine Sémillon in the whites, and some of the region's finest, earthiest Cabernets.

Cullen

Caves Road, Cowaramup, Margaret River, WA. Est. 1971. 12,000 cases. Visits. Owner: Diana Cullen. Winemaker: Vanya Cullen. Vineyards: 73 acres, mainly of Cab.Sauv., with Ries., Sauv.Bl., Chard. and some Merlot, P.N., Cab.Fr.

Cabernet made the Cullens' reputation, especially the quite brilliant Reserve, but this winery, one of Margaret River's first, is also producing quite excellent and incredibly flavoursome Chardonnay and (oak-aged) Sauvignon Blanc under the shrewd eye of winemaker Vanya Cullen.

Devil's Lair

Rocky Road, Margaret River, WA. Est. 1981.Owner: Southcorp Wines. Winemaker: Janice McDonald. Vineyards: 100 acres of Sauv.Bl., Sém., Chard., Cab.Sauv., P.N., Cab.Fr., Merlot. 18,000 cases. Visits.

Phil Sexton set up the enormously successful Matilda Bay Brewing Company in Perth, and applied the same entrepreneurial skills to this up-and-coming Margaret River winery before selling the business at the beginning of 1997. The dynamically packaged wines are quite excellent, with silky, spicy Pinot and generously flavoured Cabernet leading the way.

Leeuwin Estate

Stevens Road, Margaret River, WA. Est. 1974. Owners: the Horgan family. Winemakers: Bob Cartwright, Philip Tubb. Vineyards: about 270 acres of Cab.Sauv., Rhine Ries., Chard., plus some P.N., Malbec, Sauv.Bl., Petit Verdot. 35,000 cases.Visits.

A substantial, modern winery (built with advice from California's Robert Mondavi) in the green hills and woods of the Margaret River – although the ocean is only a jog away. The Chardonnays are sensational, with aromas, liveliness, richness and grip to outdo anything in Australia and most in California. Rieslings have varied from excitingly steely to melon-rich. Cabernets are rich but not overripe. After a period of uncertainty, Leeuwin's star is again shining as bright as ever.

Moss Wood

Metricup Road, Willyabrup, Margaret River, WA. Est. 1969. Owner/winemaker: Keith Mugford. Vineyards: 25 acres of Cab., Sém., P.N., Chard. 4,500 cases. Visits by appt.

The winery that put the Margaret River among Australia's top-quality areas. Moss Wood Cabernet seems to define the style of the region: sweetly clean, faintly grassy, intensely deep and compact – almost thick, in fact, but without the clumsiness that implies. Definitely for very long ageing. Good Chardonnay and Pinot Noir are also produced.

Pierro

Willyabrup, Margaret River, WA. Est. 1980. Owner/winemaker: Dr Michael Peterkin. Vineyards: 15 acres of Chard., P.N., Sauv.Bl. and other varieties. 3,000 cases. Visits.

Pierro is a high-quality (and high-price) winery producing small quantities of well-received wine, including what has come to be recognized as one of Margaret River's best barrel-fermented Chardonnays.

Vasse Felix

Cowaramup, Margaret River, WA. Est. 1967. Owners: the Holmes à Court family. Winemaker: Clive Otto. Vineyard: 40 acres at Vasse Felix and 60 acres at Forest Hill of mixed varieties. 40,000 cases. Visits.

One of the Margaret River pioneers, and still up there with the best. Cabernet can be dark, firm and undoubtedly long-lived, and late-picked whites can be refreshingly acid. Wines from the Forest Hill vineyard in Mount Barker are also made here.

Pemberton

Salitage

Vasse Highway, Pemberton, WA. Est. 1989. Owner: John Horgan. Winemaker: Patrick Coutts. Vineyards: 50 acres at Pemberton of Chard., P.N., Cab.Sauv., Cab. Fr., Merlot, Cauv. Bl., Petit Verdot. 20,000 cases. Visits.

What Dennis Horgan has done for Margaret River with the Leeuwin Estate, brother John hopes to do for the new, cool West Australian region of Pemberton with Salitage. Early signs are hopeful: complex, Burgundian Chardonnay and some hedonistically rich Pinot Noir have emanated from this state-of-the-art winery.

Swan Valley

Paul Conti

Wanneroo Road, Woodvale, WA. Est. 1948. Owners: the Conti family. Winemaker: Paul Conti. Vineyards: 42 acres of Cab.Sauv., Shiraz, Merlot, Grenache, P.N., Chard., Muscat, Ch.Bl. 6,500 cases. Visits.

A (stylistically) leading Swan Valley producer, with two well-placed vineyards at Marginiup and Yanchep. Elegant Shiraz and clean, balanced Chardonnay.

Evans & Tate

Swan St, Henly Brook, Swan Valley; Redbrook Vineyard, Willyabrup, Margaret River, WA. Est. 1972. Owners: the Tate family. Winemaker: Brian Fletcher. Vineyards: 110 acres at Redbrook (Margaret River) and 10 acres at Henley Brook. Shiraz, Cab.Sauv., Merlot, Cab.Franc, Chard., Sauv.Bl., Sém. 100,000 cases. Visits.

The old and new of Western Australia are combined in a winery that grows grapes in Swan Valley and at Margaret River. Under the recent guidance of winemaker Brian Fletcher the wines have improved from an already impressive level. Barrel-aged but restrained Sémillon is consistently excellent, as are Cabernet and the well-known and surprisingly (for the Swan Valley) elegant Gnangara Shiraz.

Houghton

Dale Road, Swan Valley, WA. Est. 1859. Owner: BRL Hardy. Winemakers: Paul Lapsley, John Griffiths. Vineyards: 109 acres at Swan Valley, 245 acres at Pemberton, 183 acres at Mt Barker, 221 acres at Frankland River. Also 230 acres at GinGin for the Moondah Brook label. 300,000 cases. Visits.

The most famous name in Western Australia, the wines at this Swan Valley winery were for 50 vintages made by the legendary Jack Mann. Now, as part of the BRL Hardy group, and benefitting from newer vineyards in cooler parts of the state such as Margaret River and Pemberton, Houghton's lustre has revived. The famous White Burgundy is a light, fresh, ageworthy wine, Cabernet very good and Chardonnay honest and good value.

Sandalford

Caversham, Swan Valley, WA. Est. 1840. Owners: Peter and Debra Prendeville. Winemaker: Bill Crappsley. Vineyards: 27 acres at Caversham; 300 acres at Margaret River; 130 acres at Mount Barker, fruit also sourced from Pemberton. 70,000 cases. Visits.

This old-established winery on the Swan River now relies almost entirely on fruit from its more southerly vineyards, and is producing some excellent wines. Chardonnay and Verdelho are best of the whites, and a spicy, elegant Shiraz best of the reds. The cheaper range, called 1840, provides good value.

Westfield

Baskerville, Swan Valley, WA. Est. 1922. Owners: John and Mary Kosovich. Winemaker: John Kosovich. Vineyard: 29 acres, 18 at Swan, 11 at Pemberton. 4,000 cases. Visits.

A Swan Valley miniature, notable for exceptional Sémillon, good Cabernet and Verdelho, and some exciting wines from the new vineyard at Pemberton.

QUEENSLAND

Ballandean Estate

Sundown Road, Ballandean, Granite Belt, Qld. Est. 1970. Owners: Angelo and Mary Puglisi. Winemaker: Adam Chapman. Vineyards: 45 acres at Ballandean of mixed varieties. 15,000 cases. Visits.

Angelo Puglisi is known as the Godfather of winemaking in Queensland, and Ballandean Estate, while the first, is still one of the best in the area. winemaker Andrew Chapman does particularly well with Shiraz and Merlot, and also produces an unusual sweet white from the rare (in Australia) Silvaner variety.

TASMANIA

Freycinet

Tasman Highway, East Coast, Tasmania. Est. 1980. Owners: G. and S. Bull. Winemaker: Claudio Rodenti. Vineyards: 12. 5 acres of Ries., Chard., P.N., Cab.Sauv., and a little Müller Thurgau. 4,000 cases. Visits.

One of Tasmania's top wineries, producing a delicious, refreshing, Germanic white by blending Riesling and Müller Thurgau, as well as superb, complex, beetroot-and-spice Pinot Noir.

Heemskerk

Pipers Brook, Tasmania. Est. 1868. Owner: Tamar Valley Wines. Winemaker: Garry Ford. Vineyards: 100 acres of Chard., P.N., P.M., P.G., Ries. 40,000 cases. Visits.

Heemskerk has suffered a chequered progression of owners, but now, as part of the Tamar Valley Wines group, its future looks a little more secure. Cabernet and Pinot Noir still tend towards greenness, but the sparkling wine, Jansz, initially developed in conjunction with Louis Roederer of France, is one of the small island's best: very crisp, very dry, but with plenty of tight, restrained, appley flavour.

Moorilla Estate

Main Road, Berriedale, Hobart, Tasmania. Est. 1958. Owners: a partnership. Winemaker: Alain Rousseau. Vineyards: 26 acres at Derwent River and 30 acres at Tamar. 6,000 cases. Visits.

One of the first bold souls to look for quality in Tasmania, and in a cool corner at that. Frost, birds and underripeness are persistent problems. Riesling does best to give Moselle-like flavours, Gewürztraminer can be as steely as Alsace, Pinot Noir as supple as those from the Côte d'Or. A distinctive label reveals the founder's background in textiles.

Piper's Brook

Piper's Brook via Lebrina, Tasmania. Est. 1974. Owner: Unlisted public company. Winemaker: Dr Andrew Pirie. Vineyards: 175 acres of Sém., Sauv.Bl, P.G., Cab., Chard., P.N., Ries., Gewürz., Merlot, Cab.Fr. 44,000 cases. Visits; also at the Strathlyan Wine Centre in West Tamar.

The bold enterprise of an eclectic mind in search of ideal conditions: cool but not too cool. Dr Pirie stresses that vines work most efficiently where evaporation is not too high – 'when the grass stays green'. His hill-top vineyard within sight of the island's north coast (and reach of sea winds) has made superb dry Riesling and austere Chardonnay, very characteristic Pinot Noir and Cabernet with lively and intense flavours. Ninth Island is the second label: wines with less intensity, but no less attractive.

Spring Vale

Tasman Highway, Cranbourne, East Coast, Tasmania. Est. 1986. Owners: Rodney and Lyn Lyne. Winemaker: Andrew Hood. Vineyards: 15 acres of P.N., Chard., Gewürz., P.G. 1,500 cases. Visits.

One of the wineries to confirm the East Coast of Tasmania as a great place to grow Pinot Noir. The Spring Vale Pinot is round, earthy and deliciously spicy.

NORTHERN TERRITORY

Château Hornsby

Petrick Road, Alice Springs, Northern Territory. Est. 1976. Owners: Denis and Miranda Hornsby. Winemaker: Gordon Cook. Vineyards: 7 acres of Cab.Sauv., Shiraz, Sém., Rhine Ries. Visits. Maverick winery, with heavily irrigated vines, in the searing heat of the outback. Reds are full and clean-flavoured.

NEW ZEALAND

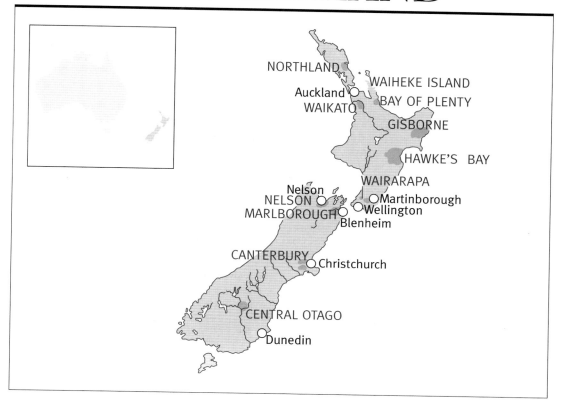

While almost every Australian settler, it seems, planted vines for wine, the new New Zealanders did much less to exploit the temperate climate and fertile soils of their islands. No real wine industry, beyond isolated missions and private estates, existed until Dalmatian Kauri-gum workers and Lebanese immigrants started to provide for their own needs in the Auckland area early in the 20th century. Their products were crude, from poor vines unsuited to the warm humidity of Auckland. Phylloxera forced them to plant hybrids. Most of the wine was fortified and probably deserved its unflattering title of 'Dally plonk'. And the small, strait-laced Anglo-Saxon community, frequently muttering about Prohibition, hardly provided an encouraging market-place.

Matters began to change quite briskly on a local basis in the late 1960s, as New Zealanders developed both a tentative export market to Australia and Great Britain – and also a taste for wine themselves. In 1960 almost half of the total 958 acres of vines was in the Auckland area, and most of the rest in Hawke's Bay on the central east coast of the North Island. The '60s saw a trebling of the Auckland acreage and the development of Waikato, 40 miles south. They saw the Hawke's Bay vineyards double in size and an important new area spring up at Poverty Bay near Gisborne, north of Hawke's Bay.

Results were encouraging, even if the first mass plantings were decidedly unambitious. The market's chief interest was in cheap fortified wines – made all the cheaper by the illegal addition of water. For table wines Müller-Thurgau was widely considered to be as high a mark as New Zealand could profitably reach. Early planters mistakenly took German advice that their climate was closer to that of Germany than of France.

Experiments with Sauvignon Blanc and then with Chardonnay in the '70s proved that the climate of the main fruit-growing region, the east coast of North Island, was not so much German as central French. These east-coast areas flourished in the 1970s, quintupling their acreage, while Auckland's shrank slightly. But the '70s also saw the vine move to the South Island: by 1980 Marlborough had nearly 2,000 acres and trial planting had moved as far south as Canterbury and Central Otago.

New Zealand's true potential as a producer of fine wine burst upon the world in the mid-80s: to be precise, in February 1985 when British wine critics, buyers and journalists attended a tasting (an annual event) held at New Zealand House in London. Those present are unlikely to forget the excitement of that morning, as it became apparent that a dozen different wineries had produced a

507

number of white wines of a racy vitality and tingling fruitiness that are only met with on rare occasions elsewhere in the world.

The best of the Sauvignon Blancs were the most memorable wines, giving an extra dimension to this essentially second-league variety. The verdict was unanimous: New Zealand had jumped straight into the first division of the world's white-wine producers.

Subsequent tastings confirmed the fact, adding Chardonnays of extremely sound quality, a few Rieslings, Chenin Blancs and Gewürztraminers of top quality by any standards, and some promising red wines. Any shortcomings in the early quality of the reds were more due to inexperience than to the quality of the grapes. Significant developments, especially with Pinot Noir which benefits from the cool climate from Martinborough southwards, and advances in vinification techniques, have proved their worth. Cabernet Sauvignon–Merlot blends, especially from Hawke's Bay, have also improved, again with better vinification techniques, better viticulture and improved site selection. In general there has been a considerable widening of the range of grape varieties planted. Several wineries now produce Syrah, and Zinfandel is out of quarantine. There is Viognier, great interest in Pinot Gris, Sangiovese and new clones of current varieties.

An enormous growth in vineyards has been witnessed. Existing wineries have planted new vineyards and there has also been a large increase in the number of winemaking facilities. New viticultural areas are being considered, with isolated wineries appearing in unexpected places.

Recent vintages suggest that the best makers have learned to temper the sometimes over-herbaceous or vegetal character of their wines, especially in the Cabernets and Merlots. 1989 was probably the first vintage to produce worthy reds, and they continue to improve. Pinot Noir in particular is a rising star, and a more individual one than some of the other New World versions of the grape. For the present, however, it is still with its white wines that New Zealand conquers.

New Zealand's natural gift is what the winemakers of Australia and California are constantly striving for: the growing conditions that give slowly ripened, highly aromatic fruit. The wines are developing the strength, structure and delicacy of those from (for example) the Loire, Alsace, possibly the Médoc, possibly Champagne – with a freshness and vigour that seem to be New Zealand's own. The country's considerable potential for sparking wines has been nurtured, using classic methods and nearly always with classic Pinot Noir and Chardonnay grapes. However a couple of sparkling wines also include Pinot Meunier.

THE NORTH ISLAND WINE REGIONS

AUCKLAND

Until the 1970s this was New Zealand's largest grape-growing region, but its almost subtropical climate, with considerable cloud cover and frequent autumn rain, was never suited to the vine. It is now eclipsed as a wine region (both in terms of quantity and quality) by Gisborne, Hawke's Bay and Marlborough to the south, though many important wine companies are still based here.

Wineries include: Babich, Collard Brothers, Cooks, Coopers Creek, Corbans, Delegat's, De Redcliffe, Goldwater, Kumeu River, Lincoln Vineyards, Matua Valley, Montana, Nobilo, St Nesbit, Selak's, Stonyridge Vineyard and Villa Maria.

GISBORNE

Gisborne was once the largest grape-growing region, but it has since been overtaken by Marlborough and Hawke's Bay. This fertile area on the east coast of the North Island is well-suited to white grape varieties, although it suffers from autumn rains which force the harvest forward, and from active phylloxera, which has resulted in almost total replanting. Wineries are few, as most grapes are sent for blending to the major producers in Auckland. Corbans and Montana dominate production, but some of the Auckland wineries have good sites, especially for Chardonnay.

Gisborne calls itself 'the Chardonnay capital of New Zealand', although Müller-Thurgau is currently the most widely planted variety.

Wineries include: Corbans, Matawhero, Millton and Montana.

HAWKE'S BAY

One of the top quality regions, situated on the east coast south of Gisborne, and in the rain shadow of the island's volcanic mountain centre. Its sunshine and its glorious mixture of soils – silt, shingle and clay – provide enormous potential for red and white grapes and the number of wineries is growing.

Wineries include: Brookfields, Esk Valley, Mission, Ngatarawa, C. J. Pask, Te Mata and Vidal.

NORTHLAND

This rainy, humid region in the extreme north of the island was the site of New Zealand's first vineyard, but it is ill-suited to grape-growing. A growing number of wineries are trying to prove its suitability, however, especially in the Matakana Valley. Now there are also a couple of isolated wineries even further north; Longview at Whangarei and Okahu Estate at Kaitaia.

Wineries include: The Antipodean.

WAIKATO

A small, rainy region, spreading eastwards from Waikato, about 45 miles south of Auckland, to the Bay of Plenty. There are scarcely 118 acres of vines now producing (with the acreage falling) and major wineries, such as Morton Estate, source their grapes from Hawke's Bay, Gisborne or elsewhere in New Zealand.

Wineries include: Cooks, Morton Estate.

WAIRARAPA

This is the region at the southern end of the North Island, just north of Wellington with the small town of Martinborough at its centre. Wairarapa's combination of good soil, low rainfall and autumn sunshine first prompted the planting of vineyards in 1978. Four wineries had their first vintage in 1984 and three of them, Martinborough Vineyards, Dry River and Ata Rangi, have since established a firm reputation for Pinot Noir. There have been dramatic developments in flavour complexity. Chardonnay is good too, and some winemakers are trying hard with Cabernet Sauvignon and Merlot.

WAIHEKE ISLAND

A small island in the Hauraki Gulf with a far drier climate than Auckland (30% less rainfall) and better soil (lighter and freer-draining). Vines were first planted by the Goldwaters in 1978, then by Stephen White at Stonyridge. Others followed suit, mainly planting Bordeaux varieties.

Wineries: Goldwater, Stonyridge and Waiheke Vineyards.

CANTERBURY

One of several newer wine regions in the South Island, around Christchurch on the mid-east coast. Its coldish climate and low rainfall lured an increasing number of small wineries into the area during the 1980s and resulted in some impressive Riesling and Pinot Noir. The plains around Christchurch, however, tend to be very prone to frost, which causes problems. There is, though, considerable potential in Waipara, a valley to the north of Christchurch, where the climate is distinctly warmer and the soil limestone-based, proving suitable for Pinot Noir and Chardonnay, and resulting in a growing number of wineries and vineyards.

Wineries include: Giesen Estate, St Helena, Pegasus Bay.

THE SOUTH ISLAND WINE REGIONS

CENTRAL OTAGO

The southernmost vineyards in the world on the 45th parallel, with dramatic scenery in the Gibbston Valley, close to Queenstown; on the shores of Lake Wanaka and around the town of Alexandra. Otago is currently the fastest growing vineyard area in New Zealand. The climate is more continental than the other regions and vintages can vary quite considerably. There is potential for Pinot Noir and there have been some good Chardonnays and Rieslings made here too.

Wineries include: Gibbston Valley, Rippon Vineyard.

MARLBOROUGH/BLENHEIM

Sunny, stony-soiled Marlborough, the region around the town of Blenheim at the northeastern tip of the South Island, has proved the making of New Zealand's wine industry. Since it was pioneered by Montana in 1973, it has produced some of the world's best Sauvignon Blanc, and is now the country's largest grape-growing region, pushing Hawke's Bay into second place.

Marlborough's excellent soil, low rainfall (irrigation is essential here, at least for young vines) and cool autumns, combined with its position in New Zealand's sunniest corner, make it ideal for growing well-flavoured fruit, especially for white wines: Sauvignon Blanc, Chardonnay

and Riesling have all proved successful. Wind is the only serious problem for Marlborough growers. The crowds are forming: from Australian giants such as Thomas Hardy to the Champagne house of Deutz.

Wineries include: Cellier Le Brun, Cloudy Bay, Corbans, Deutz, Highfield Estate, Hunters, Montana and Nautilus.

NELSON

Small, somewhat inaccessible region to the west of Marlborough, which shares some of that region's beneficial conditions, but suffers from autumn rainfall. The vineyards are hilly, not flat, and most of the growing number of wineries are boutique, rather than large concerns. The quality of the wines is excellent.

Wineries include: Seifried Estate.

Leading New Zealand Producers

Ata Rangi

Puruatanga Road, Martinborough. Est. 1980. Owners: Clive Paton and Phyll Pattie; Oliver Masters and Alison Paton. Winemakers: Clive Paton and Oliver Masters. 5,000 cases. 13 acres. Grapes: P.N., Cab.Sauv., Merlot, Syrah, Cab.Fr. and Chard. Visits by appt. Another brilliant Pinot Noir from Martinborough: Ata Rangi have just won the Bouchard–Finlayson award for it for the second year running. Clive Paton has had winemaking

509

experience in Burgundy, notably at Domaine Rion. Also produces good Chardonnay. The third wine is Celebre, a Cabernet– Merlot–Syrah blend in varying proportions, depending on the vintage.

Babich

Babich Road, Henderson, Auckland. Est. 1916. Owners: the Babich family. Winemaker: Neill Culley. 50 acres in Henderson and 123 in Hawke's Bay, plus contract vineyards in Gisborne, Hawke's Bay and Marlborough. Grapes: Chard., Cab.Sauv., Merlot, P.N., Syrah, Sauv.Bl., Ries., Gewürz. (coming into production in 1998, and ditto Ch.Bl.). Pinot Gris from Marlborough into production in 1997, from a contract grower; there is also a Sém.-Chard. blend for which the Sém. grapes are contracted. Average production: 80,000 cases. Visits.

A large old Auckland family winery, which is highly respected in New Zealand for consistent quality and value. The Babich reputation is largely based on Chardonnay, notably the Irongate Vineyard. There is also an Irongate Cabernet–Merlot blend. New vineyard Mara Estate is named after Peter and Joe Babich's mother, so far yielding Syrah and Merlot (1995).

Brookfields Vineyard

PO Box 7174, Taradale, Hawke's Bay. Est. 1937. 10,000 cases. Owner: Peter Robertson. Vineyards: 7+ acres planted with Chard. and Sauv.Bl.; grapes from 50 other acres are P.Gr., Gewürz., Riesling, Cab.Sauv., Merlot. Visits welcome.

Bought by Peter Robertson in 1977. Emphasis is on reds that will age in bottle: a pure Cabernet and a Cabernet–Merlot blend. One of the few wineries to make Pinot Gris. Sauvignon is oaked; Reserve Chardonnay is fermented and aged in French Allier oak for eight months, while the Estate Chardonnay is more accessible.

Cellier Le Brun

Terrace Road, Renwick, Marlborough. Est. 1980. Owner: Resene Paints Ltd. Winemaker: Graham McMorran. Vineyards: 65 acres of Chard., P.N. and P.Meunier on stony soil, also Merlot. 22,000 cases.

Daniel Le Brun's family were champagne makers in Epernay and here, with his wife Adèle, he is making *méthode traditionnelle* to the classic formula, plus still Chardonnay. This is one of two wineries concentrating on sparkling rather than still wine. There is a NV Brut, a vintage, Blanc de Blancs vintage, a rosé and a *tête de cuvée*, called Adèle – all from riper fruit than the French versions. The range of still wines, Terrace Road, is a new addition.

Chard Farm

Chard Road, Queenstown. Est.1987. Owners: Rob and Greg Hay. Winemakers: Rob Hay and Duncan Forsyth; Owen Bird for their sparkling wine. 30 acres. Grapes: Chard., P.N., Ries., Sauv.Bl., Gewürz. and P.Gr. Annual production: 7,000 cases. Visits.

Named after the Chard family who came out from the eponymous Somerset village – their NZ surroundings look more like Scotland. Best label is for Chardonnay – Judge and Jury – named after a nearby hill; also Closeburn Chardonnay,

with more obvious fruit. Their Pinot Noir, Bragato, is barrel-aged and they also made real icewine in 1992 from Riesling. Sparkling wine is a new development; as is Pinot Gris.

C. J. Pask

1133 Omahu Road, Hastings, Hawke's Bay. Est. 1985. Owner: Privately owned. Winemaker: Kate Radburnd. 115 acres. Grapes: Chard., Sauv.Bl., Ch.Bl., Cab.Sauv., Merlot, Cab.Fr., P.N. and Malbec. 26,000 cases. Visits.

Chris Pask, pilot-turned-viticulturist, was the first person to plant on what is now the highly rated Gimblett Road area – with silt over shingle in old river bed vineyards. He concentrates on Bordeaux varieties, plus Chardonnay; Pinot Noir is a more recent development.

Cloudy Bay

Jacksons Road, Blenheim, Marlborough. Est. 1985. Owner: Veuve Clicquot Ponsardin S.A. (since 1990) and David Hohnen.125 acres. 75,000 cases. Winemaker: Kevin Judd. Grapes: Sauv.Bl., Chard. and Sém. on own vineyards and Sauv.Bl., Chard., Ries., Sém., P.N., Cab.Sauv. and Merlot on growers' vineyards. Visits welcome.

Founded in 1985 by the Australian entrepreneur David Hohnen, whose Western Australian winery Cape Mentelle had already received great acclaim, Cloudy Bay rapidly became the spearhead of New Zealand's assault on the international wine market in the late 1980s. Its pungent, nettle-sharp Sauvignon Blanc, made from vines grown in Marlborough's stony soil and near-ideal climate for white wines, is regarded by some as the finest expression of this grape's varietal character to be found anywhere, and frequently sells out all around the world within weeks of its release – it includes some Sémillon and a small amount of oak. It does not come cheap, though, and nor do its two siblings, an excellent oaky Chardonnay and a relatively lean Cabernet–Merlot blend.

The range has recently extended to include Pelorus classic method sparkling wine – Kevin Judd initiated this idea before Veuve Clicquot bought Cloudy Bay – and also Pinot Noir (1994 was the first vintage) and Late Harvest Riesling.

Collard Brothers

303 Lincoln Road, Henderson, Auckland. Est. 1910. Owners: Lionel, Bruce, Geoffrey and Desma Collard. Winemaker: Bruce Collard. Vineyards: 40 acres – Chard., Sauv.Bl.,Cab. Sauv., Cab.Fr. in the Rothesay vineyard, Merlot, Cab.Fr., Rhine Ries. and Sém. in the home vineyard; Ch.Bl. from Hawke's Bay and P.N. from Marlborough. Visits welcome.

A well-established small company, very much a family concern: Geoffrey concentrates on the vineyards and Lionel runs the business. The wines are rather French in style. Rothesay Chardonnay is one of their best wines, disproving theories that Auckland is no good for vines. And more attention is paid to the Chenin Blanc than most. Riesling is stylish and elegant and Pinot Noir shows potential.

Cooks

PO Box 26-019 Epsom, Auckland. Est. 1969. Merged with McWilliams in 1984. Owner since 1987: Corbans. Winemaker: Kerry Hitchcock. Three wineries at Te Kauwhata and Napier.

Vineyards: 20 acres at Te Kauwhata, Sauv.Blanc., 215 at Hawke's Bay, Cab.Sauv., Cab.Fr., Merlot, Sauv.Blanc, Chard., Gewürz. Grapes are also bought in Gisborne and Hawke's Bay.

Cooks and McWilliams merged in 1984 leaving both names on the letterhead, and both labels are used, though since the takeover by Corbans in 1987 the McWilliams range has slowly been wound down. Cooks is an ultra-modern concern, active in exports. Top of the range is oak-aged Chardonnay of great charm, light but vividly fruity Cabernet, firm and lively Gewürztraminer with some sweetness and apple-sweet Chenin Blanc not unlike a Coteaux du Layon. Sauvignon Blanc 1989 from Hawke's Bay was long and tingling.

Coopers Creek

601 State Highway 16, Huapai, Auckland. Est. 1980. 50,000 cases. Owners: Andrew and Cynthia Hendry. Winemaker: Kim Crawford. Vineyards: 40 acres of Cab.Sauv., Merlot, P.N., Chard. Also Sauv.Bl., Sém. and Ries. from Marlborough and Gisborne grapes.

Successful small winery with high-quality varietals and popular blends from one of New Zealand's top winemakers. Coopers' best wines are the two Hawke's Bay Chardonnays, the finer of the two, called 'Swamp Road', demonstrates subtle use of oak. Other good wines include Fumé Blanc, Coopers Dry White (a blend of Chardonnay, Sémillon and Chenin Blanc) and Cabernet/Merlot. They are also particularly noted for Riesling, both Dry and Late Harvest, and have just released their first Pinot Noir and first sparkling wine.

Corbans

426–448 Great North Road, Henderson, Auckland. Est. 1902. 2m. cases, plus wine casks. Owner: D.B. Group. Winemakers: Gisborne: David Freschi; Hawke's Bay: Evan Ward; Marlborough: Alan McCorkindale (one of NZ's best winemakers). Vineyards: 550 acres of Sauv.Bl., Sém., Chard., Ries., Gewürz., Ch.Bl., Cab.Sauv., Cab.Fr., Merlot, P.N.; contract grown P.Gr., bulk varieties. Visits by appt.

Founded by a Lebanese family in the early 20th century and, since the takeover of Cooks McWilliams (q.v.) in 1987, the country's second-biggest wine company after Montana (q.v.) – the Cooks label is used on the export market. Of several ranges, the best are from Cottage block, notably Chardonnay: other varietals excel depending on what the winemakers consider the best each vintage. Stoneleigh is the name of the Marlborough winery; Longridge is used for Hawke's Bay grapes. Robard & Butler is a negoçiant label which includes some wonderful Amberley Riesling from just north of Christchurch. Amadeus is used for classic method sparkling; Liebestraum and Velluto are brands for the NZ market.

Delegat's

Hepburn Road, Henderson, Auckland. Est. 1947. Owners: Jim and Rosemari Delegat. Winemaker: Brent Marris. Vineyards: 315 acres: Chard., Cab.Sauv. and Merlot in Hawke's Bay and Chard. and Sauv.Bl. in Marlborough, under the Oyster Bay label. Visits.

Streamlining of production in the mid-1980s and good winemaking skills meant a significant improvement. This is a family winery and the only brother and sister team in New Zealand. Best wines are from Hawke's Bay sold under Proprietor's Reserve label.

De Redcliffe

Lyons Ropad, Mangatawhiri Valley, Auckland. Est. 1976. Owner: Japanese Otaka Holdings (NZ) Ltd. Winemaker: Mark Compton. Vineyards: 25 acres of gravel-based land with P.N., Chard. and Sém. 25,000 cases. Visits, with a smart hotel and restaurant 'Hotel du Vin'.

All wines are wood-aged; the Chardonnay undergoes barrel fementation too. Experiments with clonal selection and blending are under way with the aim of adding more substance to the light, elegant wines.

Streamlined winery in an attractive setting in the Mangatawhiri Valley. The Japanese have invested quite seriously. Sauvignon and Riesling come from Marlborough; Cabernet-Merlot from Hawke's Bay, and Mangatawhiri Chardonnay from the home vineyard.

Dry River

Puruatanga Road, Martinborough. Est. 1979. Owners: Dawn and Neil McCallum. Winemaker: Neil McCallum. Vineyards: 8 acres in the home vineyard; 8 acres in the Craighall vineyard (under long-term contract). Grapes: Gewürz., Chard., P.N., P.Gr., Sauv.Bl., Viognier (which is replacing some of the Sauvignon), Ries. from the Craighall Vineyard. 3,500 cases. Visits by appt.

Small estate with finely crafted wines, frequently described in superlatives. Complex Pinot Noir, made by blending different techniques and barrels, one of New Zealand's best Pinot Gris and lovely Rieslings, dry, Late Harvest and Botrytis Bunch selection.

Esk Valley

735 Main Road North, Napier, Hawke's Bay. Est. 1933 (as Glenvale), bought by Villa Maria 1987. Owner: Villa Maria. Winemaker: Gordon Russell. Vineyards: 4 acres, including the Terraces vineyard, planted with Merlot, Malbec, Cab.Sauv. and Cab.Fr., also grows Chard. (Terraces is virtually the only terraced vineyard in NZ). Also buys in grapes. 30,00 cases of Sauv.Bl., Ch.Bl., Chard. and Merlot-based blends. Visits.

Formerly a large family firm, now merged with Villa Maria/ Vidal, and producing some of the country's best reds. Esk Valley's Hawke's Bay grapes go into a wide range of wines, including Cabernet, Chardonnay, particularly crisp and fruity Chenin Blanc, and delicately oaky Merlot blends. Like other wineries in the Villa Maria group, it uses the 'Private Bin' and 'Reserve' labels. The 1994 Reserve Cabernet–Merlot and 1994 Terraces sold at a high NZ$49 – only 200 cases were made with yields of approximately one tonne per acre.

Gibbston Valley

Gibbston, RD1, Queenstown. Est. 1981. Owner: Gibbston Valley Wines Ltd. Winemaker: Grant Taylor. Vineyards: 8 acres plus 70 under contract. Grapes: P.N., Chard., Ries., Sauv.Bl., P.Gr. 11,500 cases. Visits.

Alan Brady, originally from Ulster, pioneered grape growing in Central Otago, the country's most southerly wine-growing region, on the 45th parallel. Brady is passionately committed to his cause. He is excited about the extension to his cellar, a cave excavated out of the hillside. The main winery was built in 1990, with vineyards first established in 1981. Two styles of Sauvignon are made, unoaked from Marlborough and wood-aged from Central Otago. Brady is particularly keen on Pinot Gris and Pinot Noir, and his dry Riesling has won accolades.

Giesen Estate

Burnham School Road, Christchurch. Est. 1981. 40,000 cases. Owners: Marcel, Alex and Theo Giesen. Winemaker: Rudi Bauer. Vineyards: 85 acres Sauv.Bl., Ries., Chard. and P.N., plus contract-grown fruit, and 20 acres of Sauv. in Marlborough. Visits by appt.

Giesen makes stylish dry Riesling, which develops with bottle-age, and in the right years has some lovely late harvest wines. It is also working hard on its Pinot Noir. The first sparkling wine was released in 1995, a Pinot Noir and Chardonnay blend.

The Giesen brothers came originally from the Palatinate, where their father just had two acres of vines as a hobby – they now have the largest winery in Canterbury.

Goldwater Estate

18 Causeway Road, Putiki Bay, Waiheke Island, Nr Auckland. Est. 1978. 15,000 cases. Owners: Kim and Jeanette Goldwater. Winemaker: Kim Goldwater. Vineyard: 15 acres of Bordeaux varieties – Cabernets and Merlot – on Waiheke, plus a 12-acre block being planted with Chard., plus 70 acres under contract in Marlborough for Sauv.Bl. and Chard.

The first vines on Waiheke – planted in 1978 on a beautiful island vineyard which benefits from a warm, dry micro-climate. The Goldwaters concentrate on three wines: a Bordeaux blend, Sauvignon and Chardonnay. Cabernet and Merlot are what Waiheke does best, with its much drier climate than the mainland.

Grove Mill

Waihopai Valley Road, Renwick, Blenheim. Est 1988. Owners: about 40 local investors. Winemaker: David Perce. 45 acres of own vineyards, planted with Chard., Sauvignon and Gewürztraminer, but also buy from contracted growers, Merlot, P.N., P'tage, Ries. and Pinot Gris. 50,000 cases.

The best wines from Grove Mill are the Gold label series, with vineyard names Lansdowne Chardonnay, Blackbirch Riesling and Drylands Sauvignon; also working hard on reds. There are some interesting Gewürztraminers and good Riesling. 1994 was the first vintage for Pinot Gris. Grove Mill has expanded from small beginnings as a boutique winery into 1,000-tonne capacity.

Heron's Flight

Sharp Road, Matakana, Warkworth. Owners: David Hoskins and Mary Evans. Winemaker: David Hoskins. Vineyard planted 1988, now 11 acres Cab.Sauv., Merlot, Cab.Fr., Chard. and Sangio. 1,500 cases. Visits.

David Hoskins is busy disproving the theory that Northland is too wet for vines. He follows renowned viticulturalist Richard Smart's principles of the 'big vine' (prolific grape yields are of good quality when balanced by prolific, sun-trapping foliage). Makes a Cabernet–Merlot blend and

Chardonnay. 1996 was the first vintage of Sangiovese: the plan is to release it as New Zealand's first straight Sangiovese varietal.

Hunters

Rapaura Road, Blenheim. Est. 1982. 25,000 cases. Owner: Jane Hunter O.B.E. Winemaker: Gary Duke. Vineyards: 40 acres own vineyards plus 130 acres with contract growers, planted with Sauv.Bl., Chard., Gewürz., Breidecker, Cab.Sauv., Merlot, P.N. and P.Meunier. 40,000 cases. Visits.

Expanding family winery producing some of the South Island's best wines. The varietal range includes good barrel-fermented Chardonnay and Sauvignon Blanc (and blended), Rhine Riesling, Cabernet and Pinot Noir. Excellent sparkling wines have recently been added.

Jackson Estate

Jacksons Road, Blenheim. Est 1988. Owners: John and Warwick Stichbury. Winemaker: Martin Shaw. Vineyards: 105 acres planted with Sauv.Bl., Chard., Ries. and P.N. 20,000 cases.

Jackson make Sauvignon Blanc, Chardonnay, Riesling called Marlborough Dry, Pinot Noir, sparkling wine and occasionally a reserve Chardonnay and a botrytis Riesling. Initially a vineyard, using Vintech's facilities, the Stichburys are now building their own winery. The range of wines has gradually developed, with Pinot Noir and sparkling wine the more recent introductions.

Kemblefield Estate Winery

Aorangi Road, RD1, Hastings, Hawke's Bay. Est. 1993. Owners: John Kemble and Kaar Field. Winemaker: John Kemble. 110 acres. Grapes: Merlot, Cab.Fr., Cab.Sauv., Chard. and Sauv.Bl.; also makes Gewürz. 15,000 cases. Visits.

John Kemble is still a shareholder of Ravenswood in Sonoma Valley; he takes credit for introducing Zinfandel to New Zealand; it has just come out of quarantine. Kemblefield have just harvested the first grapes from their own vines; earlier vintages were made from contracted grapes. Produces some interesting wines, adding to the diversity of Hawke's Bay, with vineyards away from the main area.

Kumeu River

550 State Highway 16, Kumeu, Auckland. Est. 1944 as San Marino Wines. 20,000 cases. Owners: the Brajkovich family. Winemaker: Michael Brajkovich (NZ's first MW). Vineyards: 60 acres of Chard., Sauv.Bl., Merlot, Cab.Fr., Malbec, P.N. and Sém.

A small Yugoslav family winery north of Auckland. Some serious Chardonnay is given the full Burgundian treatment here. Bordeaux blends that are predominantly Merlot, with Cabernet Franc and Malbec, and no longer any Cabernet Sauvignon – a reflection of the winemaker's St-Emilion experience (at Château Magdelaine); has also made a pure Cabernet Franc and also Sauvignon blended with a little Sémillon for more body.

Michael is a fervent exponent of the Auckland area for grape growing despite controversy. Brajkovich is the second label.

Lincoln Vineyards

130 Lincoln Road, Henderson, Auckland, North Island. Est. 1937. Owners: Peter and John Fredatovich. Winemaker: Ian Trembath. Vineyards: 10 acres in Henderson, the home vineyard, but mainly contract growers, in Auckland, Gisborne, Hawke's Bay and Marlborough. Grapes: Chard., Cabernet Merlot, Merlot, Sauvignon, Ries., Müller-Thurgau and Chenin Blanc. Visits.
Large family-owned winery, now in its third generation, producing a wide range of wines. Has successfully tranformed from port and sherry production to concentrate on table wines, in particular Chard., Cabernet and Merlot; also a partly barrel-fermented Sauvignon, Riesling and Chenin Blanc.

Martinborough Vineyards

Princess Street, Martinborough, Wairarapa. Est. 1980. 10,000 cases. Owners: Duncan and Derek Milne (brothers), Claire Campbell, Russell and Sue Schultz, Larry McKenna. Winemaker: Larry McKenna. Vineyards: 30 acres, plus managing another 15, planted with P.N., Chard., Sauv.Bl. and P.Gr.
One of the leading producers of Pinot Noir of Martinborough, and one of the four pioneers of the area in the early 1980s (the first vintage in 1984). Convinced of its suitability for Pinot Noir and Chardonnay (other wineries followed) Martinborough Vineyards now produces some of the best of each in New Zealand – as well as Sauvignon and Riesling. Larry McKenna became the winemaker in 1986, resulting in a considerable quality improvement which has been steadily maintained, with Pinot Noir of growing complexity. McKenna also makes good Chardonnay and Riesling. Gewürztraminer has recently been replaced with Pinot Gris, for which the first release is planned for 1997.

Matawhero

Riverpoint Road, Gisborne. Est. 1968. Owner and winemaker: Denis Irwin. Vineyards: 65 acres of river loam, Gewürz., Ch.Bl., Chard., Sauv.Bl., Sém., Cab.Sauv., Cab.Fr., Merlot, Malbec, Syrah. 8,000 cases.
A highly individual, small-scale family operation whose hand-made wines have attracted much critical attention. Their Gewürztraminer is notably dry, aromatic and lingering and Müller-Thurgau surprisingly flavoursome. Chardonnay is more European in style than some and the reds are generally better than would usually be expected from Gisborne, as a white wine area. Bordeaux varieties are grown in the Bridge Estate Vineyard, while Pinot Noir and Syrah are not yet much beyond the experimental stage. Performance can be erratic.

Matua Valley

Waikoukou Road, Waimauku, Kumeu, Auckland. Est. 1973. 140,000 cases. Owners: the Spence and Margan families. Winemakers: Ross Spence, Mark Robertson and Bill Hennessey. Vineyards: 68 acres in Auckland; 87 in Gisborne, 113 in Hawke's Bay; 70 in Marlborough, growing Sauv.Bl., Chard., P.N., Cabernet Sauvignon, Merlot, Cabernet Franc, Pinot Gris, Ries., Malbec, with contract grown Ries., Sauvignon, Chardonnay, P.N., Cab.Sauv. Visits and restaurant.

California-style winery just north of Auckland. Ross Spence is an uninhibited winemaker looking for original tastes. It was Ross who isolated and propagated the single clone of Sauvignon which has been planted in New Zealand for the past 20 years. Ararimu is the top label for Chardonnay and Cabernet Sauvignon. Marlborough wines are sold under the Shingle Peak label (Cabernet, Rhine Riesling, Chardonnay and Sauvignon). Since 1987 sparkling wine, with a high proportion of Pinot Noir, has become an important part of the portfolio. Pinot Gris is a new project.

Millton

Papatu Road, Manutuke, Gisborne. Est. 1984. 6,000 cases. Owners: James and Annie Millton. Winemaker: James Millton. Vineyards: 55 acres, in 4 vineyards (Chard., Ries., Ch.Bl., Malbec, Cabernet Sauvignon). Visits by appt.
Successful organic winery west of Gisborne (on a hillside vineyard – unusual in Gisborne). Produces an interesting range of styles which includes a fine botrytized Riesling. Clos Ste Anne is the best Chardonnay. Chenin Blanc of golden luscious character that could easily come from Anjou is occasionally made.

Mission

Church Road, Greenmeadows, Taradale, Hawke's Bay. Est. 1851 (the oldest winery in Hawke's Bay, still in existence and under the same ownership). Owner: the Catholic Society of Mary. Winemakers: Paul Mooney and Kel Dixon. Vineyards: 80 acres of vineyards, planted with Chard., P.Gr., Gewürz., Cab.Sauv., Cab.Fr., Merlot, Sauv.Bl. and Sém. 55,500 cases. Visits.
A historic and beautiful spot at the foot of grassy hills, seemingly old-fashioned. In recent years the wines have improved significantly, with the brothers investing in the winery. Top of the range under the Jewelstone label are Chardonnay, Cabernet-Merlot and Noble Riesling. New wines include a dry Pinot Gris from a new planting of an old clone and a botrytis Sémillon from 1995.

Montana Wines

171 Pilkington Road, Glen Innes, Auckland 6. Est. 1949. Owner: Corporate Investments Ltd. Chief winemaker: Jeff Clarke (with, at Gisborne, Steve Voysey, at Napier, Tony Pritchard and at Blenheim, Andy Frost). Vineyards: 2,180 acres (Gisborne 196, Napier 584, Blenheim 1,400). Grapes: Müller-Thurgau, Chard., Ries., Gewürz., Sauv.Bl., Dr. Hogg Muscat, Cab.Sauv., Pinotage, P.N., Merlot, Ch.Bl., Sém., Chasselas, Cabernet Franc, P'tage, Malbec, early white Muscat, Flora. 1.8m cases. Visits.
New Zealand's biggest wine company, begun by Dalmatian Ivan Yukich, was highly successful in expanding throughout the 1970s, when it pioneered the new Marlborough region, the source of most of its best varietals. During the 1980s it expanded further, taking over Penfolds (NZ) in 1986, and now has four wineries at Auckland, Gisborne, Marlborough and Hawke's Bay. Other proprietary names include Blenheimer, Ormond, Fairhall River and Lindauer sparkling (improving due to Deutz contact). Half the whites are semi-sweet. The Marlborough wines include a very dry Sauvignon Blanc, slightly spicy Riesling with good acidity, an excellent

Chardonnay, a Gewürztraminer and a rather pale but firm Cabernet, with a Médoc-like 'cut'. Newest is their work with Bordeaux varieties, the fruits of which are tasted in their Church Road wines and the joint venture with Champagne Deutz to produce Deutz Cuvée Marlborough. The best wines are sold under individual vineyard names, Brancott, Ormond, Renwick. Montana Sauvignon Blanc represents the great success story of NZ.

Morton Estate

Katikati, Bay of Plenty. Est. 1979. 42,000 cases. Owners: John and Alison Coney. Winemaker: Steve Bird. Vineyards: 400 acres of vines, in Marlborough and Hawke's Bay (they aim to be self-sufficient), with Chard., Sauv.Bl., Cab.Sauv., Merlot, P.N., Syrah. 100,000 cases. Visits.

This winery (its façade in an attractive Cape Dutch style) has benefited from the considerable talents of John Hancock, one of NZ's best winemakers (now doing his 'own thing' in Hawke's Bay). Morton's reputation stands on Chardonnay, with the Black Label the top of the range, closely followed by the White Label. Both are very good – Black Label has more oak, and probably more staying power. The sparkling wine is predominantly Pinot Noir, with some Chardonnay; the NV spends 12 months on the lees and the vintage wine four years. Work is also being done on Pinot Noir and Syrah as newer additions to the range. There are two styles of Sauvignon, unoaked and a Fumé Blanc. A new winery has been built in Hawke's Bay, at their Riverview Vineyard, which will be mainly a crushing plant – the juice going to Katikati for fermentation.

Neudorf

Neudorf Road, Upper Moutere. Planted 1978; first vintage 1982. Owners: Tim and Judy Finn. Winemaker: Tim Finn. Vineyards: 12 acres of vines planted with Chard., P.N., Sauv.Bl., Ries. 5,000 cases.

One of Nelson's leading wineries, owned by a friendly husband-and-wife-team. A 100-year-old clapboard building houses the winery. Chardonnay is the best wine, with considerable complexity, new oak, whole bunch pressing, about 8 months on the lees. The Riesling is good too, and the Pinot Noir improving all the time.

Ngatarawa

305 Ngatarawa Road, RD 5, Hastings, Hawke's Bay district. Est. 1980. Owners: Alwyn Corban and Penny Glazebrook Trust. Winemaker: Alwyn Corban. Vineyards: 50 acres Char., Sauv.Bl., Ries., Cab.Sauv. and Merlot.

An attractive winery building, around old racing stables (the Glazebrook family is involved with horseracing). Alwyn is the only member of the Corban family still to be actively involved in winemaking.

Top of the range is the Glazebrook label, which includes a Cabernet–Merlot blend, Chardonnay and a botrytis Riesling. The Stables range is more accessible in style with Cabernet–Merlot, Chardonnay, Sauvignon and late harvest Riesling. Corban's winemaking is very individual, with Chardonnay barrel-fermented in new oak and wines that develop with bottle age.

Nobilo

Station Road, Huapai Valley, Auckland. Est. 1943. Owners: 51% the Nobilo family; 49% Direct Capital Ltd. Winemaker: Greg Foster. Vineyards: 165 acres plus 1,257 acres with contract growers. Grapes: Cab.Sauv., P'tage, Müller-Thurgau, Chard., Sauv.Bl., Gewürz. and Ch.Bl. under contract. 400,000 cases. Visits by appt.

The Nobilos came from the Dalmatian island of Korcula. They have worked hard on red varieties that ripen well in the warm damp Auckland climate. Now best known for White Cloud (a blend of Müller-Thurgau with 15% Sauvignon and a hint of Muscat), a good range of Chardonnay (the unoaked Poverty Bay label, a Marlborough Chardonnay as well as from two vineyards in Gisborne; Tietjen and Dixon). They are unusual in making a New Zealand Pinotage and are pioneering the development of the new area of Mohaka, between Gisborne and Hawke's Bay.

Palliser Estate

Kitchener Street, Martinborough. Est. 1989. Owner: A public unlisted company. Winemaker: Allan Johnson. Vineyards: 75 acres, planted with P.N., Chard., Sauv.Bl. and Ries. Visits.

One of the leading Martinborough wineries, well run and focused, with a good export record. Commendable Riesling and Chardonnay, and Sauvignon that slips down a treat! Palliser was named after Cape Palliser, and in turn, a British Admiral, Sir Hugh Palliser.

Pegasus Bay

Stockgrove Road, Waipara, RD 2 Amberley. Est. 1986; first crush 1991. Owners: Ivan and Christine Donaldson. Winemakers: their son Matthew and Lynnette Hudston. Vineyards: 55 acres. Grapes: Chard., Sauv.Bl. and Sém. for a blend, Ries., P.N. and a Bordeaux blend of Cab.Sauv., Merlot and Cab.Fr., called Maestro. 16,500 cases. Visits (another son, Edward, is a trained chef and cooks for the winery restaurant).

Up and coming winery in Waipara at the eastern end of the valley. The only Canterbury winery to grow Sémillon. They also support the cause of Bordeaux blends, while others argue this area is too cool for reds (in the cooler vintages of 1992 and '93 they bought fruit from Marlborough and carefully renamed the wine 'Main Divide'). First-class Pinot Noir and Riesling.

Rippon Vineyard

Mount Aspiring Road, Wanaka. Est. 1986. Owners: Rolfe and Lois Mills. Winemaker: Axel Rothermel. Vineyards: 30 acres of P.N., Chard., Sauv.Bl., Gewürz., Ries., Merlot, Osteiner, Gamay. 4,500 cases. Visits.

One of the leading estates of Central Otago. Rolfe Mills planted the first vines in the region (apart from the 19th-century settlers) in 1976, after learning winemaking at the coop at Sigoulès in Bergerac. Rippon must rank as one of the world's most beautiful vineyards, on the shores of Lake Wanaka. French winemaking for three years (by *une champenoise*) did great things for the Pinot Noir (the '93 is stunning); Chardonnay and Sauvignon fare well too. Release of their first sparkling wine in 1997 is from the '93 vintage, after four years on yeast. This is a first for the Central Otago region and the only certified organic sparkling wine in New Zealand.

St Nesbit

Hingaia Road, Papakura, Auckland. Est. 1981. 1,000 cases. Owners: Anthony and Petra Molloy QC. Winemaker: Anthony Molloy. Vineyards: 11 acres of vines – Merlot, Cab.Fr., Petit Verdot and Malbec, but has just chainsawed the last of the Cabernet.

Growing boutique/hobby winery, currently with only one wine, a well-made *barrique-*aged blend of Cabernet Sauvignon, Merlot and Cabernet Franc (Bordeaux style, combined with NZ individuality). The '87 was well-made and delicate with a fine scent, if a little hollow and lacking richness. There is occasionally some rosé.

Seifried Estate

Redwood Road, Appleby, Nelson. Est. 1976. Owners: Hermann and Agnes Seifried. Winemakers: Hermann Seifried and Andrew Blake. Vineyards: 160 acres, planted with Chard., Ries., Gewürztraminer, Sauvignon, Cab.Sauv. and P.N. 65,000 cases. Visits.

A fast-growing enterprise; they have just built a new winery, not to mention restaurant and conference centre. Wines are sold under the Redwood Valley and Old Coach Road labels for the basic ranges. Some good dry and late-harvest Riesling; there is also a Gewürztraminer icewine made by artificial means. Good Chardonnay.

Selak's

15 Old North Road, Kumeu, Auckland. Est. 1934. 70,000 cases. Owners: the Selak family. Winemaker: Darryl Woolley. Vineyards: Auckland, Poverty Bay, Hawke's Bay and (mainly) Marlborough totalling 385 acres, planted with Chard., Sauvignon, Sém., Ries., Müller-Thurgau, Gewürz., Cab.Sauv., P. N. and Merlot. Visits.

An old concern founded by a Yugoslav pioneer family, now well equipped and modern in approach, with much wood fermenting of white wines. The best wines are sold under the Founder's Selection label, plus some vineyard names, Drylands, Brighams, Matador. Also makes sparkling wine, of which they were pioneers in NZ.

Stonecroft Wines

R.D. 5, Mere Road, Hastings. Owners: Alan and Glennice Limmer. Winemaker: Alan Limmer. Vineyards: 20 acres. Grapes: Cab. Sauv., Gewürz, Sauv.Fr., Chard., Syrah, Merlot. Experimenting with Cinsaut, Mourvèdre and Zin. 2,500 cases. Visits.

Worth visiting for lots of interesting opinions and insights into winemaking in Hawke's Bay. Alan Limmer pioneered Syrah in New Zealand. His first vintage, 1987, was released in 1990, and he has repeated its success in subsequent years. Limmer is very keen on trying different grape varieties, especially from the Rhône, and is also taking some Zinfandel from Kemblefield (q.v.). A penchant for tannin is revealed in the Cabernet–Merlot blend, and – new in 1996 – Ruhanui, which includes some Syrah with Cabernet and Merlot. Chardonnay and Gewürztraminer are commendable too.

Stonyridge

80 Onetangi Road, Waiheke Island, nr Auckland. Est. 1982. Owner and winemaker: Stephen White. Vineyards: 10 acres of vineyards. Grapes: Cab.Sauv., Cab.Fr., Merlot, Malbec and Petit Verdot, also Syrah, Gren. and Chard. Experimental Sangiovese. 900 cases. Visits.

The second winery to be founded on Waiheke Island after Goldwater Estate (q.v.) makes small quantities of two red wines – Airfield Cabernet Sauvignon and an excellent Cabernet blend called Larose. Larose is one of NZ's best Bordeaux blend labels and made very much in the Bordeaux manner (Stephen White has worked a vintage at Château d'Angludet in the Médoc, he is also the only producer in New Zealand to have all five red Bordeaux varieties). The second label is Airfield. Serious, perfectionist winemaking; attention to detail and passionately committed.

Te Kairanga

Martins Road, Martinborough. Est. 1984. Owner: A public unlisted company. Winemaker: Chris Buring (of the Australian wine family – Leo Buring was his great-uncle – Chris spent 23 years at Lindemans before arriving in New Zealand in 1990). Vineyards: 65 acres, planted with Chard., P.N., Cab.Sauv., Cab. Fr., Merlot, Sauv.Bl. 16,000 cases. Visits.

As well as the range of varietals, Te Kairanga make three blends; Castlepoint dry white, dry rosé and red. Chardonnay is their best wine.

Te Mata

Te Mata Road, Havelock North, Hawke's Bay. Est. 1896. Owners: John and Wendy Buck, Michael and June Morris, and Peter Cowley has a small share. Winemaker: Peter Cowley. Vineyards: 120 acres on north slopes with limestone and shingle subsoil, newly planted with Cab.Sauv., Cab.Franc, Merlot, Syrah, Chard., Sauv.Bl. 20,000 cases. Visits by appt.

One of the oldest wineries in New Zealand, recently restored and making one of the country's best Cabernet-Merlot blends; a fine wine. This and Chardonnay are wood-aged. (The restorations have resulted in an attractive winery complex, designed by New Zealand architect Ian Athfield, with a barrel cellar that would not be out of place in the Médoc, and also a high-tech fermentation hall). The owners see the conditions as similar to Sonoma, California, and aim to make long-lived wines with plenty of acid backbone. Great but compact range of wines, of which the best wines are Castle Hill Sauvignon, Coleraine Cabernet-Merlot and Elston Chardonnay. Bullnose Syrah is a more recent introduction.

A new estate is being developed, also in Hawke's Bay, called Woodthorpe Terraces. 50 acres are planted and 1996 was the first harvest – it will grow to 350 acres, with a separate winery planned for 1999.

Vavasour

Redwood Pass, Awatere Valley, Marlborough. Est. 1986. Owned by 27 private shareholders, including Peter Vavasour. Winemaker: Glenn Thomas. Vineyards: 35 acres, plus contracts for a further 160 acres – Sauv.Bl., Chard., Cab.Sauv., Merlot and P.N. 40,000 cases. Visits.

For the moment Vavasour is the only winery in the Awatere Valley (south of Blenheim and running parallel to the Wairau Valley). Other Marlborough wineries have now planted vines there. Vavasour's best wines are sold under the Vavasour label and are made only from fruit from the valley, while their second label, Dashwood, consists of Wairau fruit. As a winemaker, Glenn Thomas believes in minimal intervention in the winery, provided the fruit is good. The emphasis is on Sauvignon and Chardonnay and successfully too, and while they have made Syrah and Cabernet in the past, they are now turning their attention to Pinot Noir, considering it to have more potential in what is a fairly marginal climate for red wine.

Vidal

913 St Aubyn's Street East, Hastings, Hawke's Bay. Est. 1905. Visits and restaurant. Owner: Villa Maria Estate Ltd. Winemaker: Elise Montgomery. Vineyards: 70 acres owned (Cab.Sauv., Merlot, Cab.Fr. and Malbec), other grapes contract grown (Müller-Thurgau, Gewürz., Sauv.Bl., Chard., Sém., Ch.Bl., P.N.). 60,000 cases. Visits (there is a retail outlet and restaurant; tours by appt).
One of the oldest wineries in Hawke's Bay, atmospheric yet technically advanced. Vidal is now part of the Villa Maria group, offering aromatic Gewürztraminer, restrained Chardonnay, a promising Pinot Noir, and a Cabernet with beautifully sweet and lively flavours, from a grower with old vines on shingle at Takaupau to the south. They have established a serious reputation for their red wine, especially the Reserve Cabernet Sauvignon–Merlot. Recent is a botrytis Sémillon, of which the first vintage was 1994. Anthony Vidal was a Spaniard.

Villa Maria

5 Kirkbride Road, Mangere, Auckland. Est. 1961. Owner: George Fistonich. Winemaker: Michelle Richardson. Vineyards: 1,000 acres under contract. Grapes: Sauv.Bl., Cab.Sauv., P.N., Gewürz., Chard., Ries., Merlot, Malbec, Cab.Fr., Müller-Thurgau. 350,000 cases. Visits.
A modern winery. The best wines are Reserve, then Cellar Selection, and then Private Bin. Gisborne, Hawke's Bay (for good reds) and Marlborough are the main grape sources, and there is also some good Gewürztraminer from one of the few vineyards in South Auckland, near the airport, with new plantings in the Awatere Valley.

Waiheke Vineyards

76 Onetangi Rod, Onetangi. Waiheke Island. Est.1988; first vintage 1993. Owners: Terry Dunleavy and his sons Paul and John. Winemakers: Paul and John Dunleavy, with help from Mark

Robertson of Matua Valley. Vineyards: 10 acres of Cab.Sauv., Merlot and Cab.Fr. 1,400 cases and growing. Visits by appt.
The newcomer to Waiheke Island (there are many more vineyards in the pipeline, but none are producing much yet). Fermentation of the wines takes place here but it is then matured at Matua Valley – in Demptos American oak barrels and one-year-old French oak. The wines so far are encouraging.

Waimarama Estate

31 Waimarama Road, Havelock North, Hawke's Bay. Est. 1988. Owner and winemaker: Dr John Loughlin. Vineyards: 15 acres of Cab.Sauv., Cab.Fr., Merlot, Shiraz. 2,500 cases.
John Loughlin is an eye surgeon-turned-winemaker. Here the emphasis is on red wine, and, until 1997, Bordeaux style wines: serious Cabernet Sauvignon and a Cabernet-Merlot blend. He also makes a Dessert Cabernet, not unike ratafia. The first vintage was 1991. Waimarama means 'moonlight on the water' in Maori.

Waipara Springs

State Highway 1, Waipara, North Canterbury. Est.1990. Owners: Jill and Bruce Moore and the Grant family. Winemakers: Kym Rayner and Belinda Gould. Vineyards: 50 acres, planted with Chard., Ries., P.N., Sauv.Bl., Cab.Sauv. and Merlot. 7–8,000 cases. Visits.
Small winery, whose reputation was first made by Mark Rattray, who has now moved on to run his own even smaller winery. Waipara Springs is one of the pioneers of the Waipara area, concentrating on Pinot Noir, Chardonnay and Riesling. Its reputation is based on Chardonnay, with good Pinot Noir which is challenging that from Martinborough.

Wairau River

Giffords Road, Blenheim. Owners: Chris and Phil Rose. Winemaker: John Belsham. Est. 1977. Vineyards: 250 acres (three vineyards) planted with Sauv., Chard., Ries., P.Gr., P.N. 30,000 cases.
Phil Rose is a farmer turned grape-grower, initially for Montana. He wanted his own label and was one of Vintech's (now Rapaura Vintners) original clients for contract wine-making, employing John Belsham (who set up Vintech) as his winemaker. He now makes good Sauvignon and Chardonnay, and is adding Riesling, Pinot Noir and Pinot Gris to the range, including a 1996 botrytized Riesling. An important label on the export market.

SOUTH AFRICA

S outh Africa entered the New World fine-wine league in the mid-1970s – a decade later than California and Australia. She has not so far caught up with them, partly for self-imposed reasons. Government has purposely limited both the supply of good grapevines and the land to grow them on. Nonetheless there are those who argue that the natural conditions of the Cape for the vine are as good as any on earth. The essential grape varieties are now at last being planted and coming into bearing. Wines as good as Australia's are emerging, carrying the bizarre Dutch names of the lovely estates of Stellenbosch and Franschhoek.

The natural advantages of the Coastal Region of the Cape are impressive. Ideal slopes can be found facing every point of the compass. There is an eight-month growth period; never any frost, never any hail, no autumn rain, very few of the diseases that plague other vineyards. The soil is so fertile that the normal ration of fertilizer is one-tenth that needed by Europe's long-worked vineyards. An important quality factor is the wide range of temperatures: cool nights between hot days, the Cape pattern, reduce night-time respiration from the vine leaves. The plant, unable to consume sugars accumulated during the day, stores more of them. None of these conditions is a guarantee of good wine, but taken together, with intelligent handling, they encourage optimism.

On the down side, while most coastal region vineyards need soil pH adjustment – sometimes up to 40 tons of lime per hectare are added prior to re-planting – the major problems facing South Africa's growers in the past decade have related to the quality of planting material. It was only in the mid-'80s that the authorities liberalized the regulations governing the importation of vines. This followed the 'Chardonnay scandal' in which it became clear that the draconian agricultural legislation left the avant-garde farming community with no alternative but to smuggle in premium varieties that were not available at the nurseries. However, the vineyards established – particularly of Cabernet – were severely virus-infected, often revealing ripening problems. More recent plantings are all on virus-free material but nurseries in turn are not able to cope with the demand from growers. It will probably be the end of the 20th century before there are adequate plantings of appropriate clonal material.

Also lacking in Cape history has been a demand for fine table wines. The one historically famous wine was the dessert Muscat of Constantia (which in Napoleon's time fetched prices as high as any wine in the world). Britain, the principal export market, has been more interested in Cape sherry than Cape claret. South Africans were the world's thirstiest brandy drinkers. It is only with gradual liberalization (non-white prohibition ended in 1962; grocers could sell wine from 1979) and legislation aimed at quality control (Wines of Origin were implemented in 1973) that conditions have been created for a healthy domestic table-wine market: the essential spring-board for exports.

Another problem has been the apparently benevolent presence of the KWV (*see* page 525), an organization founded by the government in 1918 to protect grape farmers from low wine prices by fixing a minimum price and distilling the surplus. The KWV has been a bastion of protection and conservatism: the very thing a new wine industry can do without. Until 1992 the KWV controlled the issue of grape-growing quotas which were a prerequisite for anyone wishing to plant vines for producing wine. The organization still polices a minimum wine price system – which acts as a disincentive for low yield, high quality production and instead, in many cases, encourages the opposite. Wine certification still falls under the control of the Wine & Spirit Board, an organization which is separate from – but not wholly independent of – the KWV. While it ensures that all export wines meet with acceptable international quality standards, it is often not competent to judge the new varieties for the flavour expectations of international consumers.

The evidence that very fine wine is on the way is recent, but it is convincing. At present the finest wines of the Cape are the Cabernets and Pinotages made by producers with virus-free vineyards and extensive expertise in wood maturation. Merlot and, to a lesser extent, Cabernet Franc, have now replaced Cinsaut as the major blending variety for Cabernet Sauvignon while more recently Shiraz has seen a considerable renaissance. Sauvignon Blanc, which was only really introduced into the Cape in the early 1980s is now probably the country's most successful dry white variety. However, Chardonnay, particularly in the hands of those who have worked with it since the mid 1980s, is now showing real quality. And underpinning the whole industry, of inestimable value, there is South Africa's fortunate inheritance of the Steen, or Chenin Blanc, as its everyday white grape. It is a lucky country that will never go short of good cheap white wine.

REGIONS OF ORIGINS

Acreages are area under vine in 1996.

Benede-Orange The most northerly demarcated Ward of Origin. Irrigated vineyards along the Orange River producing mainly wine for distilling.

Boberg An appellation for fortified wines grown in the Paarl and Tulbagh districts (qq.v.). 579,083 acres.

Bonnievale *See* Robertson.

Breede River Valley The appellation for fortified wines grown in the Worcester, Robertson and Swellendam areas of origin districts (qq.v.), east of the Drakenstein Mountains. 1,731,302 acres.

Coastal Region An appellation that may be given to wines made from grapes grown in the Stellenbosch, Durbanville, Swartland, Paarl, Constantia and Tulbagh areas of origin districts (qq.v.). 1,935,189 acres.

Constantia Once the world's most famous Muscat wine, from the Cape. The ward in which it was produced is now a highly regarded cool climate area of origin. 10,951 acres.

Durbanville A small Wine of Origin district just north of Cape Town. 18,468 acres.

Klein (Little) Karoo The easternmost Wine of Origin district. Very little rainfall and all irrigated vineyards. Good only for dessert wine and brandy. Includes the wards of Koekenaap, Lutzville Valley, Spruitdrift, Vredendal. 4,224,808 acres.

Olifantsrivier Northerly Wine of Origin district, with a warm dry climate. Mostly wine for distilling from irrigated vineyards. Includes the wards of Koekenaap, Lutzville Valley, Spruitdrift, Vredendal. 1,750,314 acres.

Overberg Southern coastal Wine of Origin district. Contains the Walker Bay and Elgin wards, with some of the Cape's coolest vineyards. 1,113, 363 acres.

Paarl South Africa's wine capital, 50 miles northeast of Cape Town. It boasts some of the country's best vineyards. Includes the wards of Franschhoek (Franschhoek Valley) and Wellington. 383,427 acres.

Piketberg A small western Wine of Origin district north of Tulbagh, towards the Olifants River. A warm dry climate gives mainly dessert wine and wine for distilling. 1,125,821 acres.

Robertson A Wine of Origin district inland and east of Cape Town. Irrigated vineyards along the Kogmanskloof and Breede rivers provide some high-quality white and red table wines as well as fine fortified wines. Includes the wards of Agterkliphoogte, Bonnievale, Boesmansrivier, Eilandia, Hoopsrivier, Klaasvoogds, Le Chasseur, McGregor and Vinkrivier wards. 434,164 acres.

Stellenbosch The beautiful old Cape Dutch town and its demarcated region 30 miles east of Cape Town, extending south to the ocean at False Bay. Most of South Africa's best estates, especially for red wine, are in the mountain foothills of the region. Includes the wards of Bottelary, Devon Valley, Jonkershoek Valley, Papegaaiberg, Simonsberg-Stellenbosch. 107,108 acres.

Swartland A warm Wine of Origin district around Malmesbury, between Tulbagh and the west coast. Most growers supply cooperatives. 797,739 acres.

Swellendam One of the Wine of Origin districts of the Breede River Valley. 968,505 acres.

Tulbagh A demarcated district sheltered in the hills north of Paarl, best known for the white wines *See* also Boberg. 233,402 acres.

Walker Bay *See* Overberg.

Worcester Demarcated wine region round the Breede and Hex river valleys. Rainfall is high enough for good table wines, southeast to Swellendam irrigation is necessary. Many cooperative cellars make mainly dry white and dessert wines. Contains the wards of Aan-de-Doorns, Goudini, Nuy, Scherpenheuvel, Slanghoek. 1,004,823 acres.

South Africa in round figures

South Africa is the seventh largest wine producer, with 3.4% of total world production. The vineyard area of 225,313 acres, however, places the country in 20th position, with 1.3% of the world's vineyards. 82% of the grapes are white. Domestic wine consumption is 8.8 litres per head per year.

Wine production has risen from 395 million litres in 1960 to around 950 million today. Much of this crop is distilled and a significant percentage is used for grape juice concentrate. Fortified wines represent about 15% of the domestic market. There are 71 cooperatives, 78 estate wineries and 105 private cellars.

The Nederburg auction

The key social and commercial event in the Cape wine calendar is the Nederburg auction, held at vintage time in March since 1975. In 1975 six participants entered 12,500 cases of 15 different wines. In 1996 45 participants entered 10,000 cases comprising 112 different wines.

Leading Producers

Allesverloren

Riebeek West, Swartland. Founded 1972. Owners/winemakers: Danie and Fanie Malan. 395 acres. Wines: Cab.Sauv., 'port', Swartland Red, Tinta Barocca, Shiraz.

A specialist in port and dry red wines. Since the 1982 Shiraz became a trophy winner at Vinexpo in Bordeaux this variety has produced the estate's flagship wine.

Alto

Stellenbosch. Founded 1920. Owners: Distillers Corporation. Winemaker: Hempies du Toit. 247 acres. Wines: Cab.Sauv., Alto Rouge.

A superbly sited vineyard running straight up a mountainside near the sea for a mile and a half (in which it rises nearly 1,000 feet) yielding a Cabernet and a red blend.

Backsberg

Simondium, Paarl. Founded 1969. Owners: Michael Back. Visits. Winemaker: Hardy Laubser. 395 acres. Wines: Cab.Sauv., Chard., P'tage, Sauv.Bl., Shiraz, Special Late Harvest, Steen.

Backsberg was established by the late Sydney Back, one of the Cape's pioneering estate wine producers, and it has an enviable reputation for high-quality, value-for-money wines. The Chardonnay is a multiple award winner, the Estate Brandy recently took world honours at the International Wine & Spirit competition.

The Bergkelder

Stellenbosch. Founded 1972. Owners: Distillers Corporation. Chief Cellarmaster: Dr. Pierre Marais. Wines: Fleur du Cap, Grünberger, J.C. Leroux sparkling wine and Stellenryck ranges, plus many estate wines bottled by The Bergkelder.

The Cape's largest estate wine wholesale merchant, proprietor of several properties and a working partner with many others. An extensive barrel maturation cellar in Stellenbosch ages the country's largest stocks of wood -matured wines. The Bergkelder has also achieved considerable success for its classic-method sparkling wines.

Blaauwklippen

Stellenbosch. Founded 1972. Owner: Graham Boonzaier. Winemaker: Jacques Kruger. 35,000 cases. 247 acres. Wines: Cab.Sauv., Zin, P.N., Shiraz, Rh.Ries., Sauv.Bl., several blends. Visits.

Blaauwklippen specializes in softer easier drinking red and white wines, and is also the country's leading Zinfandel producer. Several vintages of the Cabernet, Shiraz and Pinot Noir have also made their mark.

Bon Courage

Robertson. Founded 1984. Owner: André Bruwer. Visits. 12,000 cases. 370 acres. Wines: Bouquet Bl., C.Ries., Rh.Ries., Sauv.Bl., Blanc Fumé (wood mat.), Blanc de Noirs, Cab.Sauv., Spec. Late Harv., Gewürz., Muscadel, Noble Late Harv.

A high average standard with full-bodied, richly flavoured dry whites, semi-sweet whites and fortified wines have earned André Bruwer several Estate Winemaker of the Year awards in young wine shows.

Le Bonheur

Muldersvlei, Stellenbosch. Founded 1973. Owners: Distillers Corporation. Winemaker: Sakkie Kotze. 114 acres. Wines: Cab.Sauv., Blanc Fumé.

Le Bonheur's vineyards, on the generally north-facing slopes of the Klapmutskop, have been extensively replanted over the last 20 years. Top Cabernet and good unwooded Sauvignon Blanc.

Boplaas

Klein Karoo. Owners: the Nel family. Winemaker: Carel Nel. First bottling 1982. 17,000 cases. 140 acres. Visits.

One of the Cape's leading port-type wine producers with several prize-winning vintage style wines.

Boschendal

Franschhoek. Owners: Anglo American Farms. Winemaker: Mike Graham. First bottling 1978. 963 acres. 250,000 cases. Wines: Chard., Sauv.Bl., Brut, Blanc de Noirs, Jean Le Long, and many others. Visits.

The Cape's largest single estate with substantial sales in the domestic and international market. Coolish vineyards stretching along the Simonsberg. Premium range wines are very good. The higher volume commercial wines sell out ahead of the next vintage.

Bouchard Finlayson

Hermanus. 9,000 cases. Owners: Klein Hemel-en-Aarde. Winemaker: Peter Finlayson. First bottling: 1992. Wines: P.N., Chard., Sauv.Bl. Visits.

One of the country's leading exponents of cool-climate winemaking and viticulture. Finlayson, formerly with Hamilton Russell Vineyards (q.v.), is now engaged in a joint venture with Paul Bouchard, formerly of Bouchard Aîné. Some grapes are bought in, but increasing volumes of own plantings are coming into production.

Buitenverwachting

Constantia. Re-founded 1985. Owners: Buitenverwachting Farm Trust. Winemaker: Herman Kirschbaum. 247 acres. 48,000 cases. Wines: Christine (Cabernet blend), Cab.Sauv., Sauv.Bl., Chard., Rh. Ries. and Buiten Blanc. Visits.

Originally part of Van der Stel's original Constantia farm, Buitenverwachting is a front-ranking Cape produce, with an excellent Cabernet–Merlot blend, regularly top-performing Sauvignon Blanc, good Chardonnay and Rhine Riesling.

Haute Cabrière

Franschhoek, Paarl. Founded 1984. Owner and winemaker: Achim von Arnim. 57 acres. 16,500 cases. Wines: Pierre Jourdan, P.N., sparkling wine. Visits.

Long recognized as one of the Cape's leading sources of *méthode traditionnelle* sparkling wine, Cabrière has more recently gained prominence for its new clone Pinot Noir.

Cape Independent Winemaker's Guild

Loose grouping of ambitious winemakers, encouraging developments of vineyard and cellar techniques and raising standard of quality. Annual auction of scrutinized young wines sold under common Guild label is well attended and brings high prices.

Delaire Vineyards

Stellenbosch. Owner: Masud Alikhani. Winemaker: Jan van Rooyen. First bottling 1985. 47 acres. 6000 cases. Visits.

Recently acquired by London-based international business-man Masud Alikhani, Delaire has well-established vineyards at the top of Helshoogte Pass between Stellenbosch and Franschhoek.

Delheim

Simonsberg, Stellenbosch. Founded 1941. Owners: the Hoheisen & Sperling families. Winemaker: Philip Costandius. 296 acres. 80,000 cases. Wines: Cab.Sauv., Heerenwijn, Grande Reserve (Cab. blend). Shiraz, and various others. Visits.

Stellenbosch property which manages its own vineyards and also buys in grapes, Delheim has been a leading private cellar since the establishment of the Stellenbosch Wine Route. Traditional Cape style reds have recently shown softer tannins and riper fruit. Flagship Grand Reserve made from new clone Cabernet grapes grown on the adjacent Vera Cruz vineyards has been one of the Cape's most sought-after reds.

Eikendal

Helderberg, Stellenbosch. Founded 1984. Owners: Eikendal Vineyards (Pty) Ltd. Winemaker: Josef Krammer. 148 acres. 30,000 cases. Wines: Classique (Cabernet blend), Merlot, Cab.Sauv., Chard., Duc de Berry range. Visits.

Consistently producers of good quality wines, some excellent Cabernet and Cabernet-based blends and a fine Chardonnay.

Fairview

Suider Paarl, Paarl. Founded 1974. Owner and winemaker: Charles Back. 457 acres. Visits. Wines: Cab.Sauv., Shiraz, P'tage, Merlot, Ch.Bl., Zin., Chard., Sém., and many others.

One of the country's best selling high-quality wine estates focusing on the New World style for fruit-driven wines, but still offering distinctive complexity with bottle-ageing potential. The Shiraz is highly regarded, as are several of the red blends.

Glen Carlou

Klapmuts, Paarl. Owners: the Hess & Finlayson families. Winemaker: David Finlayson. 86 acres. 8,000 cases. Wines: Grande Classique, Les Trois (both Cabernet blends), Cab.Sauv., P.N., Chard. Visits.

The recent acquisition of an interest in Glen Carlou by Donald Hess, proprietor of the Hess Collection in California, ensures that this leading Paarl producer will now have the capital and distribution network necessary to give its wines the access to the marketplace they deserve. Several Cabernet blends and one of the Cape's best Chardonnays are the stalwarts of the range.

Douglas Green Bellingham

Milnerton, Cape Town. Founded 1942. Part of the Rennie's group. Cellarmaster: Charles Hopkins. Wines: Douglas Green range, Côte de Rosé, Côte de Blanc, Fransteter, St. Augustine, St. Raphael, Valais Rouge.

One of the country's leading wholesale merchants recently acquired by the mining magnate and racehorse breeder Graham Beck. Properties include the original Bellingham farm in Franschhoek. The Sauvignon Blanc has been increasingly successful and some good Cabernet and Merlot blends have ensured the renaissance of the Bellingham range. The Douglas Green brands include St. Augustine and St. Raphael.

Graham Beck

Robertson. First bottling 1991. Owner: Graham Beck. Winemaker: Pieter Ferreira. 355 acres. 70,000 cases. Wines: Chard., Cap Classique, and others. Visits.

The Graham Beck/Madeba brands have obtained a significant share of the mid- to upper-end of the wine market. The bubbly is highly regarded.

Groot Constantia

Constantia, Cape Town. Founded 1685. Refounded 1975. Owners: Groot Constantia Trust. Winemaker: Martin Moore. 41,000 cases. 250 acres. Wines: Cab.Sauv., Ch.Bl., Heerenrood Gouverneurs Reserve. P'tage, Chard., Sauv.Bl., Shiraz, W.Ries. and others. Visits.

The original farm founded by the Cape's first Governor, Simon van der Stel in 1685 and the source of the legendary Constantia dessert wine of the 18th and 19th centuries. An extensive replanting programme and renovation of the cellar have contributed to a substantial overall improvement in the wines. The Chardonnay Reserve and Weisser Riesling are noteworthy.

Hamilton Russell Vineyards

Hemel-en-Aarde Valley, Walker Bay, Overberg. Founded 1974. Owners: Tim and Anthony Hamilton Russell. Winemaker: Kevin Grant. 138 acres. 22,000 cases. Wines: Chard., P.N., Southern Right Cellars range. Visits.

The first of the new generation of cool-climate producers focused on new clone Pinot Noir and Chardonnay. Recent replantings of Pinot Noir vineyards should ensure that Hamilton Russell holds its position in the front rank of the producers working with this variety.

Hartenberg

Koelenhof, Stellenbosch. Founded 1958. Owner: Kenneth McKenzie. Winemaker: Carl Schultz. 40,000 cases. 272 acres. Wines: Shiraz, Merlot, Zin., Shiraz, Cab.Sauv, Chard., W. Ries., Sauv.Bl. and others. Visits.

A substantial investment programme has contributed to noteworthy improvement in the estate's wines in the last five years. There is good Shiraz and Merlot and one of the Cape's best Weisser Rieslings.

Jacobsdal

Kuils River, Stellenbosch. Founded 1976. Owner/winemaker: Cornelis Dumas. 296 acres. Wines: P'tage.

Medium-bodied red with gentle fruit and long finish. One of the Cape's best examples of Pinotage.

Jordan

Vlottenburg, Stellenbosch. First bottling 1993. Owners/ winemakers: Gary and Kathy Jordan. 210 acres. 18,000 cases. Wines: Cab.Sauv., Chard., Sauv.Bl., and others. Visits.

After a stint at Iron Horse in California, the Jordans returned to the family farm and immediately established it as a quality avant-garde producer; healthy, virus-free vineyards and meticulous cellar practices have contributed to their success.

J. P. Bredell

Helderberg, Stellenbosch. First bottling 1991. Owners: the Bredell family. Winemaker: Anton Bredell. 573 acres. 1,000 cases. Wines: 'port', Jerepigo, P'tage.

Until recently the Bredell wines were sold in bulk to the KWV. Since the early '90s however some of the best ports and Jerepigos have been sold under the Bredell label, the former widely regarded as South Africa's top port-style wine.

Kanonkop

Muldersvlei, Stellenbosch. Founded 1973. Owners: the Krige family. Winemaker: Beyers Truter. 345 acres. 25,000 cases. Wines: Cab.Sauv., P'tage., Paul Sauer. Visits.

One of the Cape's best red-wine cellars. The Pinotage regularly wins major competitions and fetches high auction prices. Long-established vineyards and traditional vinifi-cation techniques ensure consistent quality.

Klein Constantia

Constantia. Founded 1986. Owners: the Jooste family. Winemaker: Ross Gower. 175 acres. 30,000 cases. Wines: Sauv.Bl., Cab.Sauv, Marlbrook blend, Chard., Vin de Constance and others. Visits.

Recently replanted historic property which was originally part of Van der Stel's original Constantia farm. Cool vineyards, state-of-the-art viticulture and a well-managed cellar ensure a high overall quality for all the estate wines.

La Motte

Franschhoek. First bottling 1985. Owner: Hannelie Neethling. Winemaker: Jacques Borman. 235 acres. 15,000 cases. Wines: Cab.Sauv., Shiraz, Red Blend (Millenium). Sauv.Bl., and others.

La Motte traces its origins back to the Huguenots. Under its present owner, Hannelie Neethling, daughter of Dr. Anton Rupert, the property has been fully restored and is now one of the country's leading producers of Shiraz. Winemaker Jacques Borman has also achieved great success with the Cabernet–Merlot blend which sells under the brandname of Millenium.

Laborie

Suider Paarl, Paarl. Founded 1972. Owner: KWV. Winemaker: Gideon Theron. 118 acres. 27,000 cases. Wines: Chard., Sauv.Bl., sparkling wines. Visits.

A very attractive estate on the northeast slopes of the Paarl Mountain, owned by the KWV and used as a guesthouse. Recent investments in an underground cellar and the launch of a new export range, Granite Creek, suggest that a major upgrade programme will see an overall improvement in all the wines.

Landskroon

Suider Paarl, Paarl. Founded 1974. Owners: the de Villiers family. Winemaker: Paul de Villiers. 674 acres. Wines: Cab.Sauv., Shiraz, P.N., Merlot, 'port' and others. Visits.

The eighth generation of a Huguenot family who have made wine at the Cape for three centuries. Long-established property with a reputation for full-bodied red wines and an excellent Cape port.

Lievland

Klapmuts, Stellenbosch. First bottling 1982. Owner: Paul Benade. Winemaker: Abe Beukes. 99 acres. 15,000 cases. Wines: DVB, Shiraz, Cab.Sauv., Sauv.Bl., Weisser Ries., Noble L.H. Visits.

A leading Shiraz producer with success in the Cabernet–Merlot blend (branded DVB), some interesting Weisser Riesling and several botrytis dessert wines.

L'Ormarins

Franschhoek. First bottling 1982. Owner: Dr Anton Rupert. Winemaker: Josef Minkowitsch. 494 acres. Visits.

Franschhoek property extensively replanted and restored in the past two decades. Good Cabernet based reds, fine Shiraz, and widely distributed Blanc Fumé.

Meerendal

Durbanville. First bottling 1969. Owner: the Starke family. Winemaker: Soon Potgieter. 309 acres. Wines: Shiraz, P'tage and some white wines.

One of the Cape's best-known Pinotage properties, old vineyards, traditional winemaking techniques.

Meerlust

Faure, Stellenbosch. First bottling 1975. Owner: Hans Myburgh (whose family bought Meerlust in 1776). Winemaker: Georgio Dalla Cia. 370 acres. 25,000 cases. Wines: Cab.Sauv., P.N., Rubicon (Cab.Sauv., Cab.Franc/Merlot blend).

One of the oldest farms in the Cape: a beautiful white manor house where vines have been grown for 290 years. A red-wine estate, which under Nico Myburgh's guidance, broke away from the hearty style of Cape reds and produced a blend aimed squarely at the Médoc. Myburgh started planting Cabernet Sauvignon in the 1960s with Merlot, Cabernet Franc and Pinot Noir following in the 1970s. Meerlust is one of the pioneer producers of Cabernet/Merlot blend in the Cape, and has recently added a selection of estate wine grappas to its range. It will shortly be launching a premium Chardonnay.

Middelvlei

Stellenbosch. First bottling 1973. Owners: the Momberg family. Winemaker: Tinnie Momberg. 345 acres.

An estate distributing wines through The Bergkelder (q.v.): long-established reputation for Pinotage and recently for Cabernet Sauvignon.

Morgenhof

Stellenbosch. First bottling 1984. Owners: Alain and Anne Huchon. Winemaker: Jean Daneel. 198 acres. 20,000 cases. Wines: Cab.Sauv., Merlot, Chard., Sauv.Bl. Visits.

Morgenhof was recently purchased by the Huchons, part of the Cointreau family, who have extensively renovated the homestead and vineyards and had a massive subterranean barrel maturation cellar constructed. The farm's position, dedication of the proprietors and the past success of winemaker Jean Daneel (winner of the Winemaker of the Year award) all suggest that Morgenhof will become a major player by the turn of the century.

Mulderbosch

Stellenbosch. First bottling:1991. Owner: Larry Jacobs. Winemaker: Mike Dobrovic. 50 acres. 10-13,000 cases. Wines: Sauv.Bl., Chard., Faithful Hound (Bordeaux-style blend).

Mulderbosch has the reputation of being the Cape's answer to NZ's Cloudy Bay: several highly successful Sauvignon Blanc vintages together with some excellent Chardonnay have contributed to this image, though winemaker Mike Dobrovic is too eclectic a personality to fit easily into so simplistic a comparison. A plummy style Merlot/Cabernet blend sold under the Faithful Hound brandname already shows a point of difference.

Nederburg

Paarl. First bottling 1937. Owners: the Stellenbosch Farmers' Winery. Winemaker: Newald Marais. 1,606 acres. 80,000 to 1 million cases. Wines: extensive range of auction, limited release and commercial wines. Visits.

Among the auction wines the Cabernet and Cabernet based blends as well as the Chenin Blanc botrytis wine sold under the proprietary name of Edelkeur are all excellent. The commercial range includes a very good Paarl Cabernet Sauvignon, a Cabernet/Shiraz blend sold as Baronne, Chardonnay, Rhine Riesling and Noble Late Harvest.

Neethlingshof

Vlottenburg, Stellenbosch. Founded 1974. Owner: Hans-Joachim Schreiber. Winemaker: Schalk van der Westhuizen. 80,000 cases. 395 acres. Wines: Chard., Gewürz., Cab.Sauv., Lord Neethling Reserve, Noble L.H. and others. Visits.

Hans-Joachim Schreiber, a retired German banker, bought Neethlingshof in the mid-1980s and it has since been extensively replanted. Substantial investments in the cellars have also contributed to a considerable improvement in wine quality. The Noble Late Harvest is a regular champion at the National Wine show. The Gewürztraminer is one of the Cape's best and the red wines are beginning to show marked improvement.

Neil Ellis

Stellenbosch. First bottling 1988. 10,000 cases. Owners: Neil Ellis and Hans Pieter Schroeder. Winemaker: Neil Ellis. Wines: Cab.Sauv., Chard., Sauv.Bl., and others including Inglewood. Visits.

In less than a decade Neil Ellis has set himself up as the leading winemaker/negociant at the top end of the Cape wine market. Working from the cellar attached to the Oude Nectar estate, he sources grapes from vastly different microclimates to produce a range of wines each with striking individuality. Several Sauvignon Blanc *cuvées* as well as some top Cabernets have established this reputation.

Overgaauw

Stellenbosch Kloof, Stellenbosch. Founded 1906, on a farm owned by the family since 1783. Owners: the van Velden family. 178 acres. 10,000 cases.Wines: Cab.Sauv., Chard., Merlot, Tria Corda (Cab.Sauv./Merlot), Sylvaner, Sauv.Bl., 'port'. Visits.

Long-established family-owned property producing one of the best Cape ports as well as an elegant Cabernet–Merlot blend and the Cape's only Sylvaner.

Paul Cluver

Elgin. Owner: Dr Paul Cluver. Winemaker: Newald Marais.

Recently established Elgin cool-climate vineyards on former orchards with production at Nederburg winery in Paarl. Very good Chardonnay and Weisser Riesling and credible Sauvignon Blanc.

Plaisir de Merle

Simonsberg, Simondium. First bottling 1993. Owner: Stellenbosch Farmers' Winery. Winemaker: Neil Bester. 10,000 cases. Wines: Cab.Sauv., Merlot. Chard., Sauv.Bl. Visits.

A supply farm for Nederburg, the country's largest premium winery, Plaisir de Merle has subsequently acquired a reputation as one of the Cape's 'first growth' properties. Outside consultant, Paul Pontallier – director of Château Margaux – working with winemaker Neil Bester and Nederburg management – has ensured that only the best wines reach the market under the Plaisir de Merle label. The Cabernet and Merlot are excellent.

Rust-en-Vrede

Helderberg, Stellenbosch. Founded 1979. Owner: Jannie Engelbrecht. Winemaker: Kevin Arnold. 11,000 cases. Wines: Cab.Sauv., Shiraz, Estate blend. Visits.

Historic Helderberg estate producing highly regarded Cape style reds that are tannic and often astringent in their youth. Shiraz and the Cabernet/Shiraz blends are the cellar's most sought-after wines.

Rustenberg

Simonsberg, Stellenbosch. First bottling: 1892. Owner: the Barlow family. Winemaker: Rod Easthorpe.160 acres. 20,000 cases. Wines: Cab. Sauv., Cab.-Merlot blend, Sauv. Bl., Chard. Visits.

Perhaps the most beautiful estate in the Cape; low white Dutch buildings shaded by enormous trees, and widely regarded as the Cape's longest established premium red-wine cellars, with extensive vineyards on south-facing slopes. Recent replanting, substantial cellar investment and a change of winemaker have all ensured that Rustenberg will regain its place in the front rank of South Africa's producers.

Saxenburg

Stellenbosch. First bottling 1986.Owners: Adrian and Birgit Buhrer. Winemaker: Nico van der Merwe. 198 acres. 20,000 cases. Wines: Cab.Sauv., P'tage, Shiraz. Merlot, Chard. Visits.

Another newcomer which has successfully moved to the front rankings, Saxenburg is widely regarded for its red wines, particularly those sold under the Private Collection (Reserve) label. The Shiraz and Cabernet Sauvignon have been particularly successful. Recent vintages of Pinot Noir and Sauvignon Blanc have also been noteworthy.

Simonsig

Koelenhof, Stellenbosch. Founded 1968. Owners: the Malan family. Winemaker: Johan Malan. 593 acres. 100,000 cases. Wines: Cab.Sauv., Gewürz, Chard., P'tage, Weisser Ries., Shiraz, Tiara (Cab.-Merlot blend), Noble L.H., Kaapse Vonkel (classic-method sparkling). Visits.

One of South Africa's best established wine estates, with extensive presence on the Stellenbosch Wine Route. After early emphasis on varietals, this innovative family, Frans Malan and his three sons, have had runaway successes with blended wood-matured whites and were the first in the Cape to make a true *méthode traditionnelle* wine. A full range of wines is offered but the reputation is firmly based on Pinotage, Kaapse Vonkel (*méthode traditionnelle*), and some excellent dry Weisser Riesling.

Stellenbosch Farmers' Winery

Stellenbosch. Founded 1935. Public listed company, controlled by the Rembrandt Group and the KWV. Man. Director: Frans Stroebel. Wines: Zonnebloem, Kellerprinz, Autumn Harvest, Virginia, Taskelder range, Château Libertas, Lanzherac, La Gratitude, Frand Mousseux, Monis dessert wines and other blends. Visits.

South Africa's largest wholesale winery with an extensive range of products reaching from the top to the popular end of the market. SFW buys grapes and wine from farms and co-operatives throughout the Cape and also processes fruit from the Group's own vineyards. It owns Nederburg and Plaisir de Merle. Brands like Château Libertas have been on the South African market for more than half a century and have played a key role in establishing a market for dry, unfortified red wines in South Africa.

Stellenzicht

Stellenbosch. First bottling 1987. Owner: Hans-Joachim Schreiber. Winemaker: Andre van Rensburg. 370 acres. 100,000 cases. Wines: Cab.Sauv., Shiraz, Sauv.Bl., red and white blends.

Following an extensive replanting programme undertaken in the 1980s, Stellenzicht has moved into the forefront of the country's private producers. It regularly features at the National Wine Show with Champion dry red and white wines as well as some remarkable Noble Late Harvests. Recent vintages of Shiraz have established Stellenzicht as the country's leading exponent of the variety.

Thelema

Stellenbosch. First bottling 1987. Owners: the Webb and McLean families. Winemaker: Gyles Webb. 84 acres. 22, 000 cases. Wines: Cab.Sauv., Cab./Merlot, Sauv.Bl., Chard., Rhine Ries. Visits.

The Cape's fastest rising star: in less than 10 years Thelema has established a worldwide reputation with several of its wines, notably its New World-style Cabernet Sauvignon, Cabernet/Merlot, Sauvignon Blanc and Chardonnay. Accountant turned winemaker Gyles Webb worked in California after he completed his oenology studies in Stellenbosch and now owns some of the best managed vineyards in Stellenbosch.

Twee Jonge Gezellen Estate

Tulbagh. Founded 1947, on a farm in the Krone family for 200 years. Owners: the Krone family. Winemaker: Nicky Krone. 677 acres. Wines: Krone Borealis Brut and several white blends. Visits.

Twee Jongegezellen ('TJ') was one of the pioneers of quality white wines in the Cape. It has recently moved into the focused production of classic method sparkling wine. Its leading brand is Krone Borealis, though the cellars also produce Cuvée Mumm for South Africa.

Uiterwyk

Stellenbosch Kloof, Stellenbosch. Founded 1946. Owner: the de Waal family. Winemaker: Chris and Daniel de Waal. 272 acres. 10,000 cases of estate-bottled wine. Wines: Cab.Sauv., P'tage, Merlot and Chard. Visits.

A beautiful estate (one of the less flamboyant) bottling a small quantity of its best wines in a traditional cellar. Consistently good red wines including a Cabernet/Merlot blend and Pinotage.

Uitkyk

Muldersvlei, Stellenbosch. First bottling:1943. Owner: Distillers Group. Winemaker: Theo Brink. 445 acres. Wines: Carlonet (Cabernet), Cab./Shiraz, Sauv.Bl., P.G.

One of the Cape's most impressive estates with a historic Georgian house in the grounds. Extensive replanting of vineyards has brought changes to the Uitkyk wines: more recent vintages of Carlonet-brand Cabernet show denser fruit, the Cabernet/Shiraz good accessibility. White wines, notably Sauvignon Blanc and Pinot Gris, also reflect new plantings.

Van Loveren

Robertson. First bottling: 1980. Owners: the Retief family. Winemakers: Wynand and Bussell Retief. 370 acres. 70,000 cases. Wines: Chard., Col., P.G., Sauv.Bl. and many others. Visits. One of the more important white wine producers in the Robertson area: easy-drinking wines, a good Chardonnay and an extensive range of interesting varieties such as Hárslevelü and Fernão Pires.

Veenwouden

Paarl. First bottling 1993. Owner: Deon van der Walt. Winemaker: Marcel van der Walt. 5000 cases. Wines: red blends – Merlot, Veenwouden, Vivat Bacchus. Visits. Veenwouden has made a remarkable debut. Both the Merlot and the Cabernet Sauvignon/Merlot blends have strong export sales. Veenwouden is owned by South Africa's most celebrated tenor, Deon van der Walt.

Vergelegen

Somerset West. First bottling 1992. Owner: Anglo American Corp. Winemaker: Martin Meinert. 252 acres of vineyards. 55,000 cases. Wines: red and white blends, Chard., Sauv.Bl. Visits. Vergelegen is one of the Cape's oldest properties (dating back to the turn of the 18th century). It has been extensively renovated since it was purchased by the Boschendal owners (Anglo American Corp,) in 1987. Winemaker Martin Meinert has produced high-quality wines from the young vineyards. This suggests that Vergelegen is destined to become one of the Cape's leading properties.

Vergenoegd

Faure, Stellenbosch. First bottling 1972. Owners: the Faure family. Winemaker: John Faure. 3,000 cases, 320 acres. Wines: Cab.Sauv., Merlot, 'port'. Visits. This 300-year-old estate has been a supplier of bulk grapes to wholesalers such as the KWV but still releases limited volumes of its own wines on the market. Vineyards are on level ground separated from False Bay by sand dunes and marshes. The sea lowers the temperature, though humidity is high except for the first 3 months of the growing season, when a southeast wind sweeps across the farm almost daily. Cabernet and Cabernet blends have achieved regular show success in the last 20 years, as has the Cape-style port.

Villiera

Koelenhof, Paarl. Founded 1975. Owners: the Grier family. Winemaker: Jeff Grier. 308 acres. 70,000 cases. Wines: Cab.Sauv., Cru Monro (Cab.Sauv. blend) Merlot, Sauv Bl., Ch. Bl., Tradition (range of sparkling wines) and others. Visits. This cooler-than-average Paarl estate is strongly focused on value-for-money, high quality wines. Villiera has been particularly successful with Merlot and Merlot/Cabernet blends and a complete range of classic-method sparkling wines sold under the brand name of Tradition.

Vriesenhof/ Talana Hill

Stellenbosch. Founded 1981. Owner: Syndicate led by Jan Boland Coetzee, who is also winemaker. 165 acres. 20,000 cases. Wines: Cab.Sauv, Kallista (Cab.Sauv. blend), Chard., Paradyskloof. Visits. One of the leading properties on the Helderberg side of Stellenbosch, the high mountain slopes cooled by the breeze coming off False Bay. A reputation for Cabernet and Cabernet-based blends sold either under the premium Talana Hill label or as Vriesenhof. The Kallista blend (50% Cabernet, 35% Merlot, 15% Cabernet Franc) is highly regarded.

Warwick Estate

Stellenbosch. First bottling 1984. Owners: the Ratcliffe family. Winemakers: Norma Ratcliffe and Marcus Milner. 37 acres. 10,000 cases. Wines: Cab.Sauv., Merlot, Trilogy (blend), P'tage. Visits. One of the Cape's leading boutique red wine properties with several excellent Cabernet and Cabernet blends and a recently released Pinotage made from traditional bush vines.

Welgemeend

Klapmuts, Paarl. First bottling 1979. Owners: the Hofmeyr family. 32 acres. Wines: Cab.Sauv., Merlot, Trilogy (blend), P'tage. Visits. A tiny estate by South African standards, but an influential pioneer of red wines. Billy Hofmeyr (a land surveyor, wine writer and now farmer) has demonstrated the merits of picking early, blending the two Cabernets with Merlot, Malbec and Petit Verdot, and maturing for up to 18 months in small, new oak barrels. The first Cape estate to produce traditional Bordeaux style blends, Welgemeend now offers several different combinations. The standard estate wine is predominantly Cabernet Sauvignon while the Douelle contains mainly Merlot and Malbec. Current vintages of the Amadé have Rhône varieties but with Pinotage in the blend.

Weltevrede

Bonnievale, Robertson. First bottling: 1975. Owner: Lourens Jonker. Winemaker: Simon Smith. 296 acres. Visits. Wines: Chard., Col., Gewürz. and several different Muscadels. An estate owned by the family of KWV Chairman, Lourens Jonker, for several generations, Weltevrede produces good value dry white wines and some of South Africa's best Muscat-based fortifieds.

De Wetshof

Robertson. First bottling 1973. Owner and winemaker: Danie de Wet. 345 acres. 35,000 cases. Wines: Chard., Rh.Ries, Noble L.H. and others. Visits. Danie de Wet was trained in Germany and brought back boundless enthusiasm for white wines of styles not then found in South Africa. His experimental work with Rhine Riesling, Sauvignon Blanc and Chardonnay, and with his noble-rot sweet wine, Edeloes, shook old ideas about the Robertson area, and about South African whites in general. He is one of the leading producers of Chardonnay in the Robertson region with several different cuvées ranging from Finesse (lightly wooded) to Chardonnay d'Honneur (barrel fermented). One of the most influential estates in the Cape.

Zandvliet

Ashton, Roberston. First bottling 1975. Owner: the de Wet family. Winemaker: Paul de Wet, jnr. 308 acres. Wines: Shiraz and Astonvale range. Visits.

Previously marketed by The Bergkelder (q.v.), Zandvliet wines are now handled exclusively by the De Wet family. The Shiraz was a pioneering red wine from the Robertson area, delicate and destined for early drinking. The Astonvale range is a recent addition to the cellar and focuses on value for money, varietal wines.

Zevenwacht

Kuils River, Stellenbosch. First bottling 1983. Owner: Harold Johnson. Winemaker: Hilko Hegewisch. 345 acres. 45,000 cases. Wines: Sauv.Bl., Gewürz., Rh.Ries., Cab.Sauv., and several others. Visits.

Zevenwacht's Kuils River vineyards are cooled by the breezes off False Bay. They yield easy drinking red wines with flavour rather than weight as well as several successful whites, notably Rhine Riesling and Gewürztraminer.

KWV (Kooperative Wijnbouwers Vereniging)

Paarl. Founded 1918.

The national wine cooperative was established in 1918 with statutory powers to govern the wine industry. Initially it was founded to protect grape growers in their price negotiations with wholesale merchants, but its role has changed and it now polices the entire wine industry. It fixes legally enforceable minimum prices for table wine and distilling wine and manages grape surplus and much of the distilling and grape-juice concentrate industries. The KWV is a shareholder in the country's two major wine wholesalers, Distillers and SFW, whose combined market share exceeds 70 percent of the total industry. It is, however, not permitted to trade with its own brands in the South African market. The cooperative also owns wineries, distilleries and grape concentrate facilities throughout the Cape and buys grapes as well as juice and wine from cooperatives and private producers.

The recent launch of the Cathedral Cellars range has introduced premium quality KWV red and white wines to the international markets. The Cabernet, Triptych (a Cabernet blend) and Chardonnay are all Reserve quality products, while the standard KWV wine range includes a popular-selling Chenin Blanc and the equally well known Roodeberg. The value-for-money range is usually marketed under the Springbok label. The KWV ports and sherries have likewise achieved a considerable amount of success in the export markets.

ZIMBABWE

Zimbabwe lies on the same line of latitude as much of Bolivia and southern Brazil and climate conditions are by no means perfectly conducive to growing quality grapes for making wine (heat and sunshine in abundance, but also frost during the growing season and summer rains which affect the harvest). An industry of sorts began in 1965. The first wines were of poor quality and dubious grapes – Jacques, Issor and Farrazza – which have since been replaced by the planting of noble varieties, imported from South Africa. The vineyards are mainly located some 4,000 feet above sea-level, north of Harare.

Since the early 1980s tremendous progress has been made. The use of irrigation, cold fermentation, modern equipment, winemakers trained in Germany, Australia and South Africa and consultation of 'flying winemakers' have brought about an upsurge in quality.

Currently there are just two Zimbabwean producers: Mukuyu at Marondera, 37 miles from the capital, has 250 acres under vine and currently produce 170,000 cases a year, including Merlot and Cabernet Sauvignon. African Distillers (Stapleford Wines), which is the bigger of the two, is based in Gweru, north of Harare, and produces some 555,000 cases (Sauvignon Blanc, Muscat, a Cabernet/Merlot blend and a very exciting Pinotage) from 450 acres of vineyards in Bulawayo, Gweru and Odzi. It also buys in grapes from private growers. The Private Cellar label is top of the Stapleford range.

Within a very short time Zimbabwe has surprised the established wine world and proved itself capable of producing quality wines which can be outstanding value – and even winning a string of international medals and awards to boot.

SOUTH &
CENTRAL AMERICA

Of all the New World wine producers, it is the countries of Latin America that are exciting most interest on the international scene. Chile and Argentina followed by Mexico may have had a head start, but there are promising signs of modern winemaking activity in Brazil, Peru and Uruguay with significant investment from some of the major players in the drinks industry. The rate of progress is rapid indeed, and from a mass of good wines – and plenty of poor – a few fine ones are beginning to show what the future could hold.

CHILE

At last Chile has rid itself of the 'unfulfilled potential' label. It is currently producing some of the most exciting wines in the New World. There was never any doubt about the quality of Chilean fruit, but for a long time, an uncritical domestic market and a rather naïve approach to modern winemaking prevented flavours getting from the vineyard into the bottle. Now, however, Chile is firmly on the international scene – and learning fast. Chilean winemakers are jumping from obscurity to become award-winners, and their portfolio of grape varieties and wine styles widens with every vintage.

Wine has been made in Chile since the missionaries introduced vines in the mid-16th century, but the first real quality developments only began when the copper-rich landowners of the 19th century decided to showcase their wealth with vineyards. A variety of French vine cuttings were shipped to Chile in 1851, just before phylloxera hit Europe, thus ensuring a store of unplagued rootstock and a unique marketing edge for future generations. The big leap came in the 1980s, when – prompted by the efforts of winemakers such as Miguel Torres – there was widespread investment in modern winemaking equipment.

Excluding the grapes grown for brandy production on the edge of the Atacarma Desert, the quality wine-growing region is spread across three main zones: the Aconcagua Valley, the Central Valley and the southern region. Aconcagua incorporates the main east-west valley to the north of Santiago, but also the cool coastal region of Casablanca, the source of Chile's best white wines. The Central Valley is where most wineries are based and is divided (moving north to south) into the four valleys of Maipo, Rapel, Curicó and Maule, each irrigated by rivers flowing off the Andes.

The climate is perfect, almost too perfect in that vines never have to struggle in the rich deep soils and hot dry conditions. Although rainfall increases as you move south, there is little difference between average temperatures in Maipo and Maule. The biggest variances are west to east, according to position relative to the Andean and Coastal ranges; and it is easier to find wine style differences within rather than between valleys.

With the isolationism of the Pinochet years long gone, the flow of knowledge, ideas and technology into the core of this 2,500-mile long nation has facilitated the harnessing of its viticultural resources. Winemakers are receiving better and better fruit as ampelographers get to the bottom of some very mixed-up vineyards. The mentality that wine of international standards is simply made with stainless steel and new oak has switched to a philosophy of 'vineyard first, winery second', bringing issues like canopy management, lower irrigation, and soil study to the top of the agenda. And many growers are no longer content to supply the big bodegas but are going it alone – and reaching export markets.

Among red varieties, Merlot now shares as much of the limelight as easy-drinking Cabernet Sauvignon, which has traditionally been the most successful Chilean signature in export markets. A few producers have managed to tame Pinot Noir, and Malbec shows great potential. In whites, Chardonnay and Sauvignon Blanc are the dominant pair, especially from Casablanca, Gewürztraminer and Chenin Blanc bringing scattered success. Other varieties may be hot on their heels: Syrah and Viognier are two that have now emerged from quarantine.

Leading Chile Producers

Viña Bisquertt

El Comendador 2264, Santiago. Family owned. 1,000 acres. 150,000 cases. Visits by appt.
Based in the Colchagua Valley, the Bisquertt family re-equipped their winery in 1993, with the aim to switch attention from bulk to premium bottled wine. Their reds (Merlot and Cabernet Sauvignon) are superior to whites but with consultant Doug Lehmann on board helping improve vineyard practices, expect better Chardonnay and Sauvignon Blanc soon.

Caliterra

Oficina 601, Bandera 206, Santiago. Founded 1989. Joint venture between Chadwick and Mondavi families. 455 acres.
One of Chile's newest and most dynamic wineries has been given an injection of capital from the recent Mondavi partnership. Vineyards are split between Maipo, Rapel, Curicó and Casablanca. The whites (particularly the green-tinged Chardonnay from Casablanca) have always been impressive. Maipo Cabernet Sauvignon and a simple, juicy Merlot are also released.

Viña José Canepa

Camino Lo Sierra 1500, Santiago. Founded 1930. Family owned. 1235 acres. Visits by appt.
A modern, highly progressive operation in Isla del Maipo that has carved a reputation by supplying vast amounts of the UK's supermarket own-label wines. Talented but shy winemaker Andreas Ilabaca is winning awards for Canepa-labelled wines like the oak-aged Magnificum Cabernet, a vastly improved Sauvignon Blanc, and oak-aged Semillon. This was the first winery to produce a Chilean Zinfandel.

Carmen Vineyards

Oficina 202, Hendaya 60, Santiago. Founded 1850. Private company. 790 acres. Visits by appt.
The oldest winery brand in Chile, but now boasting the most state-of-the-art winery in the Maipo Valley. It may be next door to its sister (Santa Rita), but in terms of technology and winemaking philosophy, the two are distant cousins. The winemaker here, Alvaro Espinoza, is a prodigious talent, who – despite the gleaming winery he works in – has a 'vineyard first' policy. The shortly-to-be-released Grande Vidure Cabernet will strengthen what is already a first-class range of reds. His oak-aged Merlot and Cabernet Sauvignon are consistently among Chile's finest. Espinoza is one of the few Chileans to experiment with organic viticulture.

Carta Vieja

Francisco Antonio Encina 231, Villa Alegra, Valle de Maule. Founded 1825. Owners: the del Pedregal family. 1480 acres.
One of the 'steady improvers' in an area (Talca) which is steadily gaining more respect for its fruit. A rigorous quality control programme and a drive towards grape self-sufficiency has lifted Carta Vieja out of the second division. Antigua Selection Chardonnay and Cabernet Sauvignon are both excellent. Unoaked Sauvignon Blanc, Chardonnay and Merlot are also produced.

Viña Casablanca

Owner: Santa Carolina (q.v.). 420 acres.
The pioneering label whose first vintage (in 1992) firmly put the cool-climate Casablance valley on the map. Winemaker Ignacio Recabarren has used the pungent Sauvignon Blanc and citrusy Chardonnay as his ticket to international acclaim, and quality should take a further jump up once a winery has been built alongside the vineyards. A white-label series is made using fruit sourced in Lontue, San Fernando and Maipo, but the best wines are those from Casablanca fruit,

including new, low-yield Cabernet and Merlot. Chardonnay, Gewürztraminer and Cabernet from the Santa Isabel estate are sold on an allocation-only basis.

Concha y Toro

Fernando Lazcano 1220, Casilla 212, Santiago. Founded 1883. Public company. 3,700 acres. Visits.

Chile's biggest winery and first to be listed on the New York stock exchange. A vast vineyard planting programme over the last five years enables access to enumerable different pockets of fruit. Reds continue to be led by the Casillero del Diablo Cabernet Sauvignon and Merlot. Recent releases include the Trio range of Chardonnay, Merlot and Cabernet Sauvignon and a new Zinfandel, Syrah and Aspiran Bouchet. Concha y Toro is also one of the largest vineyard owners in Casablanca, producing excellent Chardonnay and Sauvignon Blanc.

Cono Sur

Llano Subercaseaux 3355, Santiago. Owned by Concha y Toro. 890 acres.

Who would have thought a Chilean winery could forge its reputation on Pinot Noir? This Chimbarongo-based estate has, and it now delivers this varietal in four different guises: unoaked, special reserve, barrel select, and a reserve from Casablanca Valley. A red Cabernet blend and a Chardonnay are produced under the Isla Negra label. Newly acquired vineyards in Casablanca and Mulchen will strengthen their range of whites.

Cousiño Macul

Quilin con Canal San Carlos, Casilla 586, Santiago. Founded 1882. Family owned. Visits by appt.

Skirting precariously close to the suburbs and smog of Santiago, Cousiño Macul is one of the oldest and most beautiful wine estates in Chile. The Macul vineyard is also one of the closest to the Andes and is affected by large diurnal differences in temperature. A new Cabernet blend, Finnis Terra, reveals a more modern style of red to the renowned Antiguas Reservas, which itself has proved it has the ability to age many decades. Cousino's cellars contain one of the largest and oldest back catalogues of red wine in Chile.

Discover Wine

Av California 2521, Santiago. Founded 1988. 210 acres. Visits by appt.

The name behind the well-known Montes label. Aurelio Montes is one of Chile's most talented winemakers and his top range Montes Alpha Chardonnay and Cabernet Sauvignon have put Curicó (indeed Chile itself) on the viticultural map. The best wines come from old vines on the Nogales vineyard. Montes' range includes a crisp, aromatic Sauvignon Blanc, Merlot and a new highly promising Malbec.

Echeverria

Av Americo Vespucio Norte 568, Depto 201, Las Condes. Family owned. Visits by appt.

Since diverting attention from buik wine production to a premium range of varietals, Echeverria has been one of the leading boutique wineries. Self-sufficiency in grapes ensures control over quality. Cabernet Sauvignon is outstanding, particularly the family reserva. Whites (Chardonnay and Sauvignon Blanc) seem to improve with each vintage.

Luis Felipe Edwards Mery

Av Vitacura 4130, Santiago. Family owned. 500 acres.

Another of the emerging stars of the Colchagua Valley. This huge single estate of largely Chardonnay and Cabernet Sauvignon used to deliver fruit to Santa Rita, but the aid of winemaker Felipe Solminihac (Aquitania), it is now producing impressive wines itself.

Viña Errázuriz-Panquehue

Av Nueva Tajamar 481, Oficina 503, Vitacura, Santiago. Founded 1870. Owners: the Chadwick family. 900 acres. Visits by appt.

Out on its own in the Aconcagua Valley to the north of Santiago, Errazuriz is best known for the powerful and distinct Don Maximiano Cabernet Sauvignon. Their new (Californian) winemaker, Ed Flaherty, will take up the on-going projects, which include fermenting wines using wild yeasts to bring in local character, as well as specially selected oak barrels. Vineyards further south in the Central Valley provide Merlot, Chardonnay and Sauvignon Blanc grapes for the range.

La Fortuna

Av La Costa 901, Casilla 19, Lontue. Owners: the Guell family. 460 acres.

The first Chilean winery to export Malbec, and La Fortuna continues to show a red bias with simple, juicy Merlot and good Cabernet Sauvignon Reserve. The whites, though, are less impressive.

Viña La Rosa

Av Huerfanos 979, Oficina 819, Santiago. Owners: the Ossa family. 1,250 acres.

One of the oldest and least-known wineries in Chile, La Rosa has only recently switched from selling bulk to producing premium bottle wine. Extensive vineyards in the Cachapoal Valley, a new winery, and Ignacio Recabarren as consultant combine to produce an excellent range of four varietals. Unoaked Chardonnay and Merlot are particularly good and a new Cabernet Sauvignon from the Palmeria estate is beautifully structured.

Casa Lapostolle

Benjamin 2935, Oficina 801, Las Condes, Santiago. Founded 1994. Owners: Joint venture between the Rabat and Marnier-Lapostolle families. 320 acres. Visits by appt.

Under the direction of oenologist Michel Rolland from Pomerol, this new winery in the Rapel Valley received acclaim for its first vintage in 1994. As you would expect from Rolland, his signature wine is a Merlot (Cuvée Alexandre) which is macerated for 30 days and aged in new oak for 16 months. This is a first for Chile.

San Pedro

La Concepcion 351, Santiago. Founded 1851. Owners: Compania Cervecerias Unidas. 2,700 acres.

San Pedro was recently taken over by Chile's biggest brewer, leading to substantial investment in a state-of-the-art winery at Molina. The surrounding vineyards make up one of the largest single estates in the Central Valley. Renowned consultant Jacques Lurton heads the winemaking team, and has made enormous improvements in the Gato Negro and Castillo de Molina ranges.

Viña Porta

Av El Bosque Norte 140, Oficina 23, Las Condes, Santiago. Owners: the Gutierrez family. 160 acres.

A top boutique operation in the Cachapoal Valley that built a new winery in 1990, and which, with the help of French winemaker Yves Pouzet, has gained a strong reputation for top quality oak-aged Chardonnay and Cabernet Sauvignon. An excellent new Merlot has recently been released.

Santa Carolina

Rodrigo de Araya 1431, Castilla 1507, Santiago. Founded 1875. Private company. 432 acres. Visits by appt.

One of the easiest wineries for the traveller to visit as the old winery is in the heart of Santiago. Santa Carolina have planted extensively throughout all the main valleys, gaining a wide spectrum of fruit sources. From the Maipo, Chardonnay, Malbec and Cabernet Sauvignon come from close to the Cordillera. Excellent Merlot is grown in extensive vineyards near San Fernando, and 100 acres of Chardonnay has been planted in Casablanca.

Santa Mónica

Las Lilas 625, Rancagua. 230 acres.Owners: the Solminihac family. Visits by appt.

Santa Mónica switched from bulk production to bottled wine in 1981, but serious investment and drive towards premium export quality has only really happened in the last five years or so. All the grapes come from their own vineyard outside Rancagua. Riesling and Merlot are consistently good, as is the low-yield range under the Tierra del Sol label.

Santa Rita

Hendaya 60, Oficina 202, Santiago. Founded 1880. 560 acres. Visits by appt.

Erratic quality has seen this long-established Maipo Valley giant slip from its top league position, but expansion of their Buin estate to over 1,730 acres, and an extensive winery upgrade are having a huge effect. Other vineyards in Casablanca (Chardonnay and Sauvignon Blanc), Lontue and Palmilla add to a range that includes the best sellers on the export market: the 120 label, Medalla Real, Reserva and Casa Real.

Viña Tarapacá

Av Los Conquistadores 1700, Providencia, Santiago. Founded 1874. Owners: Compania Chilena de Fosforos. 1,500 acres.

Tarapacá has switched its activity from the western side of the Maipo Valley to the Isla del Maipo. The company now owns 3,500 acres of land, of which 1,500 acres have recently been planted with Chardonnay, Merlot and Cabernet Sauvignon. Tarapacá has also recently invested in a brand new winery which has storage capacity of over six million litres.

Torreon de Paredes

Av Apoquindo 5500, Las Condes, Santiago. Founded 1979. Owners: the Paredes family. 370 acres.

An independent, family-run estate with vineyards near to the town of Rengo in the Cachapoal Valley, south of Santiago. The reds (Merlot and Cabernet Sauvignon) are more impressive than the range of whites, although that includes a good oaked Sauvignon Blanc.

Miguel Torres

Panamericana Sur, KM 95, 163 Curicó. Established 1978. Owners: the Torres family. 620 acres. Visits by appt.

When Miguel Torres set up his winery in Curicó two decades ago, he ushered in a new era for the Chilean wine industry. The introduction of modern winemaking equipment – including stainless-steel fermentation tanks – allowed the white wines to be cold fermented, while imported oak barrels replaced old Rauli casks. The range is considerable: Sauvignon Blanc, Riesling, Gewürztraminer, Chardonnay, Pinot Noir, Syrah, Malbec, Cabernet Sauvignon and Merlot are among the varieties now planted on the estate. A sparkling wine is also produced.

Undurraga

Lota 2305, Providencia, Santiago. Founded 1885.Owners: the Underraga family. 840 acres. Visits by appt.

A traditional winery that is currently undergoing something of a renaissance, as signalled by its winning the gold medal for its Chardonnay Reserva in the 1996 International Wine Challenge. It has sizeable vineyards – split between the Maipo and Colchagua valleys – growing Sauvignon Blanc, Chardonnay, Merlot, Cabernet Sauvignon and Pinot Noir. Undurraga was the first Chilean winery to penetrate the American market and now exports are to more than 50 different countries.

Valdivieso

Juan Mitjans 200, Santiago. Founded 1876. Owner: the Mitjan Group. 1,000 acres. Visits by appt.

The biggest Chilean sparkling-wine producer has also made enormous strides with still wine in the last five years. Huge investment in their Lontué winery and the close involvement of California winemaker Paul Hobbs has lifted quality. Some of their best fruit comes from unirrigated vineyards located close to the coastal range of mountains. Oak-aged Pinot Noir, Merlot, Cabernet Franc and Cabernet Sauvignon make up a strong list of reds, topped by the new premium blend, Caballo Loco.

Los Vascos

Benjamin 2944, Las Condes, Santiago. Founded 1750. Re-established 1975. Owners: Partnership between the Eyzaguirre/

Echenique family and Domaines Barons de Rothschild (Lafite). 1,110 acres. Visits by appt.

Los Vacos is a French–Chilean collaboration which has attempted (with mixed success) to squeeze Chilean fruit into a Bordeaux mould. Flagship Cabernet Sauvignon Reserve has yet to reach the level that this sort of winemaking potential suggests.

Villard Fine Wines

Fernando Lazcano 1220, Santiago. Founded 1989. 200 acres. A partnership between Frenchman Thierry Villard and two Chilean growers. Sauvignon and Chardonnay come from Casablanca (where their new boutique winery is being built); Merlot and Cabernet are sourced from the Rapel Valley. So far all wines have been made at the Santa Emiliana winery.

ARGENTINA

Argentina, with its Hispano-Italian traditions, is the only country outside Europe with a natural wine culture, the fourth biggest producer and consumer of wine in the world.

During its 40-odd years of travail, first under Perón and then under assorted military authorities, Argentina was virtually a closed country. But the domestic market for wine was so enthusiastic (an annual 90-odd litres a head, more recently falling, as in Italy and France, to about half that level) that no one bothered about export – except in bulk to supply Japan's imaginary wine industry.

All this is changing. With a stable currency (the peso is pegged to the US dollar) Argentina is experiencing the sort of stability and prosperity it can scarcely remember. Its wine industry is chaning rapidly to keep pace.

Bodegas could, did, and I'm afraid in many cases still do offer their clients watery tired wines almost as a matter of course. Indeed many of their clients still insist on it. The wines of interest for export, therefore, are from a new generation, from bodegas gaining in competence and confidence with each vintage: especially from the overall success of 1996.

Argentina's principal grape-growing regions are (from north to south) Salta, Mendoza with several sub-regions), San Rafael and Rio Negro. The vineyards of Salta reach as high as 1700 metres in the Andean foothills, where the Cafayete Valley produces some notably aromatic, not over-heavy wine.

Mendoza City lies only a short distance from Santiago de Chile, but with the highest point of the Andes, Mount Aconcagua, in between. Its surrounding vineyards vary from the very warm plain of Guaymallen to the east, through the central long-established Lujan de Cujo region just south of the city where the principal bodegas are, up to a height of 1200 metres in the Tupungato foothills to the southwest, where cool conditions are making their impact.

Still in the province of Mendoza, but far south over the desert, the vineyards of San Rafael are irrigated by the Atuel and Diamante rivers. Further south, on the 39th parallel and equivalent to Hawkes Bay in New Zealand, is the fruit-growing region of the Rio Negro, where wine has until recently been a mere sideline, but were high quality is almost certainly possible.

Rainfall is rare in all these regions. The arid air cuts mildew and insect problems to a minimum. Hail, on the other hand, is a frequent scourge. Flood irrigation from the comprehensive canal network is the rule. Intelligently used it produces perfect grapes (it also rules out phylloxera), although some growers are now installing drip systems for greater control. Overused, I need hardly add, it makes the familiar watery wine.

Red wines are what Argentina does best – so far. The bulk of the planting is still in such primitive grapes as the Criolla, with huge plantings of Italian table-wine grapes: among them Bonarda, Barbera, Sangiovese and some Nebbiolo. The grapes that will make its name are Cabernet, Syrah, Merlot and most of all Malbec. Just why Malbec, relegated from Bordeaux in favour of the Cabernets during the 19th century, makes such satisfying juicy-textured wines here no one seems to know. Among the whites, Argentina's unique contribution is the Torrontes, an extremely aromatic variety vaguely related to Muscat, usually vinified dry but difficult to place at table.

The best bodegas, though, as well as Malbecs and Cabernet blends of exciting potential, are already turning in good Chardonnays. They are led, at a good distance, by Nicholas Catena. The other current front-runners are Nieto y Senetiner (aka Valle de Vistalba), Norton, Chandon, Trapiche (see Peñaflor), Luigi Bosca (first with very good Sauvignon Blanc and even Johannisberg Riesling), and Humberto Canale in Rio Negro.

Leading Argentina Producers

Arizu, Leoncio

An outstanding grape grower and the producer of Luigi Bosca wines: Malbec, Cabernet Sauvignon and Syrah from the small Mendoza (Maipu) bodega are all very good. Leonicio Arizu also has a name for interesting Chardonnay, Sauvignon Blanc, Pinot Noir and Riesling wines. To watch.

Balbi

San Rafael. Affiliate of Allied Domecq. Popular producer of Malbec, Cabernet, Chardonnay, etc.

Bianchi

San Rafael, Mendoza. Founded 1927. A subsidiary of Seagram and a well-known producer with 250 acres of vines. Their best wine is Cabernet Particular. Don Valentin is a good standard. Bianchi Borgogña (Barbera and Malbec) is the country's top-selling 'fine red'.

Humberto Canale

Rio Negro, Mendoza. The premier Rio Negro winery with very fair Semillon and better Pinot Noir. Both Merlot and Malbec wines are improving.

Bodegas Catena

Argentina's export pioneer, its best work coming from Bodega Esmeralda. Chardonnay and a Cabernet blend achieve flavours similar to fine Sonoma and Napa wines; a second label, Alamos Ridge, is also impressive. The Malbec is perhaps Argentina's best.

Etchart

Bodega in Mendoza and Salta with good Chardonnay and Chenin from both locations, and remarkable Cabernet Sauvignon from Salta – especially Bordeaux-style blend, Arnaldo B. Etchart – is among Argentina's very best wines.

Finca Flichman

5500 Mendoza. Good Merlot and Syrah and white and red 'Caballero de la Cepa'. More recent emphasis is on varietals, particularly good from the '96 vintage.

Goyenechea

A family-owned San Rafael estate of 740 acres. Aberdeen Angus is their heavy-duty label; Marqués del Nevado more modern.

Lagarde

An old bodega revived. Good Cabernets and Malbecs.

Bodegas Lavaque

A new quality leader in San Rafael, especially for Malbec. Michel Torino in Salta has the same address.

Bodegas Lopez

An old company with 2,500 acres, famous for its consistent Chateau Montchenot (exported as Don Federico). Merlot and Malbec are reckoned the best of their wood-aged reds. Cabernet Chateau Vieux is exported as Casona Lopez.

Bodegas Luigi Bosca

Small concern in Mendoza with a name for Malbec and Sauvignon Blanc.

M Chandon

Producers of Baron B and M Chandon sparkling wine under Moët & Chandon supervision. 1995 saw a quality leap with the first Chardonnay/Pinot Noir blend. Also still reds and whites for domestic sale including Castel Chandon, less exciting Kleinburg (whites), Comte de Valmont, Beltour and Clos du Moulin (reds). Chardonnay Renaud Poirier is the first of a range of varietals with higher aspirations. Paul Galard is more ambitious, with signs of distinct quality.

Martins

New estate. Recent Merlot and Malbec from Mendoza are the most notable.

Bodegas Nacari

Coop in La Rioja province. It has won medals in Bordeaux for its Torrontes white.

Navarro Correas

Three wineries, with particularly good Malbec, notable Syrah, and sparkling and Spätlese-style Riesling wines.

Norton

A classic Mendoza bodega with new Austrian owners, heading for the top. Already reds (especially Malbec) are notable: Chardonnay, etc. are coming up.

Orfila

San Martin, Mendoza. A family estate of 680 acres: Sauvignon, Chardonnay and Cabernet. Cautivo is their top label (the Cabernet is particularly good). Extra Dry Pinot Blanc is also worth watching. Orfila also make sparkling wine in France for sale in Argentina.

Peñaflor

Mendoza. The country's biggest wine company, with four modern bodegas and a huge range of wines, including the popular Andean export brand. A spearhead of technical advance now with French consultant Michel Rolland involved with premium label Trapiche whose wines (esp. Medalla) are the best. Varietals include Merlot, Malbec, Cabernet, Pinot Noir, Chardonnay and Torrontes. Also 'Oak Cask' selection, rosé Cabernet, native grapes and excellent Sauvignon from Tupungato Valley. Also good are Andean Vineyards and Fond de Cave Chardonnay and Cabernet.

H Piper

Sparkling wine made under licence from the Champagne house Piper-Heidsieck.

Proviar

Under Moët & Chandon supervision, producing Champaña (Baron B is the premium), a smooth light Castell Chandon white of Sauvignon, Semillon and Ugni Blanc, Valmont of Malbec and Cabernet Sauvignon and Valtour of Pinot Noir.

Bodegas La Rural

Maipú 5501, Mendoza. Historic bodega with 620 acres. Recently acquired by Nicholas Catena and a recipient of much-needed capital injection. Good Chardonnay, Merlot and Malbec. One to watch.

Viña Riojanas

Salta producer of some of the best Torrontes, wildly aromatic dry wines, especially Sta Florentina. Also a good Sta Florentina Malbec.

Santa Ana

Guymallen, Mendoza. An old established family property, now controlled by Chile's Santa Carolina (q.v.). Santa Ana makes a wide range, including good Syrah Val Semina, a Merlot-Malbec blend, Pinot Gris 'blush' and sparkling

(Chardonnay-Chenin blend) called 'Villeneuve'. Also prduces the commercial Casa de Campa wines.

Santa Julia

Mendoza. The label of Bodegas La Agricola for modest but pleasant Chardonnay, crisp Torrentes, etc.

San Telmo

A large modern concern making good varietal wines in the California manner. The Malbec is especially good.

Suter

San Rafael. A Swiss-founded Seagram subsidiary with 2,400 acres. Their Etiqueta Maron 'Pinot Blanc' is the brand leader in 'fine whites', 'JS' is the top red.

Michel Torino

Levaque's (q.v.) Salta bodega uses grapes from Cafayete at 4,200 feet. Don David Chardonnay/Torrontes blend is particularly good; reds, though, are less convincing.

MEXICO

Given the world-class produce of its northerly neighbour, it would be surprising if Mexico were not producing very creditable wines. The oldest American wine industry is being revived with investment from abroad, and technical advice from the University of California at Davis.

Vineyards have been part of the northern Baja California landscape since the 1880s when Bodegas de Santo Tomás first opened its doors. The Guadalupe Valley, north of Ensenada, now has extensive vineyards (85% of Mexico's total) with European varieties ousting the local Mission grape. Wente Vineyards of California and Santo Tomás recently joined forces to produce a Cabernet Sauvignon with equal amounts of wine from either side of the border used to make Duetto, a blend aimed at the American, European and Asian markets. 5,000 cases are planned.

Other pioneers of the modern wine industry are Bodegas Pinson, which uses the brandname Don Eugenio, and L. A. Cetto, making successful wines with Nebbiolo (Cetto is a native of Piemonte), Cabernet and Petite Syrah. But it was the investment of Pedro Domecq from Spain that set Mexican wine on a new course. Domecq now has about half of the 6,500 acres of vineyards in the Guadalupe Valley Its premium wine, Château Domecq, is a Cabernet blend. Freixenet is the other principal Spanish interest. Martell (of Cognac) has also invested. Two new notable wineries in the valley are Monte Xanic, founded in 1988, which has Napa-award-winning Cabernet and produced a very good 1995 Chenin-Colombard, and Château Camou, which, still under construction, has nonetheless managed to turn out prize-winning Fumé Blanc. The smallest winery in Mexico is a family operation, established on the outskirts of Ensenada in 1985: Cavas Valmar is also quality-driven. Their 1992 Cabernet Sauvignon was an international prize-winner.

Pascual Toso

San José, Mendoza. A small family concern best known for one of Argentina's finest Cabernets, Cabernet Toso. Also produces Riesling and sparkling wines, some of which are made by the classic method.

Trapiche

See Peñaflor.

Valle de Vistalba

The principal label of Nieto y Senetiner, one of Mendoza's most techically advanced bodegas. Chardonnay, Cabernet and Merlot are all well up to international standards, and Malbec is exciting.

Weinert

Mendoza. A small, modern winery currently producing classic reds which are led by a good Cabernet-Merlot-Malbec blend, 'Cavas de Weinert'. There is also promising Sauvignon 'Carrascal'.

Down south near Mexico City, Domecq has joined the pioneer, Caves de San Juan, in the mountains of Querétaro; Bodegas Pinson has gone further north, at Zacatecas. Undoubtedly Mexico has great potential, even if the local taste lags far behind the aspirations of her modern vineyards and wineries.

BRAZIL

The immense domestic market of South America's largest country has led some of the biggest names in drinks – Cinzano, Domecq, Heublein, Martini & Rossi, Moët & Chandon and National Distillers – to invest in Brazil.

By far the biggest and most important of Brazil's wine-growing regions is in the Rio Grande do Sul, high in the undulating hills around the towns of Bento Gonçalves and Garribaldi. Seven hundred feet above sea level, this sub-tropical region was settled by North Italians in the 19th century. Each family planted a small plot of vineyard on the steep slopes of land granted by the Brazilian government.

Most of vines are non-*vinifera* varieties (with better disease resistance) for wines for the domestic market. The best producers are now making acceptable wines from classic varieties, notably Chardonnay, Cabernet and Merlot, and experimenting with better clones and trellising systems.

The generally hot and sunny climate suits the vine, although rainfall is often in the form of torrential downpours. Early picking, to avoid the risk of disease under these conditions, often results in wine which is light in body and rather high in acidity.

The Brazilian wine industry is dominated by Vinicola Aurora, a huge cooperative in Bento Gonçalves which draws on 1,500 growers. About 1m. cases of *vinifera* wine is currently exported, principally to the United States and the UK. Other good producers are Martini and Moët & Chandon – which is producing quaffable sparkling wine.

PERU

One would be forgiven for not knowing that a Peruvian wine industry existed at all. Geographically (only 10° from the Equator) and socio-economically (political turmoil coupled with hyperinflation of the past), conditions in Peru would not seem conducive to the hedonistic world of grape-growing and winemaking.

Most of the country's grapes go for distillation into the ubiquitous Pisco to make the Pisco Sour that heals away the heat and dust of the day (despite its proximity to the Equator the wine region is arid). The parched lunar landscape results from being on the wrong side of the Andes, and vines need irrigation to thrive.

One hundred and eighty miles south of Lima along the Pan American Highway lies the town of Ica, at the heart of Peru's wine region. Of the half dozen wineries located here only one so far produces wines of quality. Viña Tacama is by far the biggest, best and most important winery in Peru. It is solely owned by the Olaechea family whose French winemaker, Robert Niederman, has been at the helm for every harvest since 1961, producing good Chenin Blanc, Sauvignon and Merlot. Professor Emile Peynaud has acted as consultant here. The recent political stability has encouraged the Olaecheas to update some of their outmoded equipment, and they have now found export markets in the UK and France.

Other regions, among them the Chincha, Moquegua and Tacha, are now also making progress.

URUGUAY

Uruguay is often called the Belgium of South America: small, flat, with a population of just 3 million it is dominated by its giant neighbours, Brazil and Argentina, both physically and oenologically.

Uruguay has been making wine since the 1700s, variously influenced by France, Spain, Germamy and Italy. Its Mediterranean-type climate suggest that it is eminently suited to producing quality-wine grapes. At present French grapes predominate. In addition to premium Chardonnay, Sauvignon Blanc, Cabernet Sauvignon and Merlot, the Tannat (the grape of Southwest France) is being widely planted – indeed in greater quantities than any other winegrowing country.

The country is principally divided into five wine zones, which are simply called the Southern, Southwestern, Central, Northwestern and Northern zones. The one showing most potential for quality is also the oldest and largest – the Southern zone, south of the capital Montevideo.

Urugay's biggest producer is Irurtia, which concentrates primarily on the bulk domestic market. The second largest, Castillo Viejo, currently produces mainly rosés in tetra bricks (some 2.1 million litres a year), but it is turning its attention to bottling quality varietal wines. Other premium wineries include Establecimiento Juanico and Castel Pujol.

Uruguay has the potential to make quality wines for export. Its first steps in this direction show much more promise than one might have thought.

ENGLAND & WALES

The fact that England and Wales are at the farthest northern limit of the zone where grapes will ripen has not discouraged some 1,000 landowners, farmers and gardeners from planting vineyards of between half an acre and 200 acres. The revival of English wine-growing (it was probably introduced by the Romans, and was widespread in the Middle Ages) started slowly in the 1950s and accelerated rapidly in the 1970s. The excellent summer of 1976 encouraged many to think that wine-growing could be more than a hobby and part-time job. In spite of a succession of dismal harvests in the late '70s, with vintage rain a regular occurrence, the little industry has consolidated its position, helped by a run of extremely successful harvests in the late '80s. There are now about 400 vineyards, many of them less than an acre, although in total almost 1,850 acres are in production. The properties are scattered across southern England and Wales, with concentrations in the traditional fruit-growing areas of Kent and Sussex, Essex and Suffolk, along the south coast through Hampshire as far as Cornwall and north through Berkshire, Wiltshire and Somerset as far as Hereford & Worcester. Total annual production is now averaging 18,000 hl – some 2.4 million bottles – almost all of it white.

It is too early to say that any regional styles have emerged. English wine is and presumably always will be a light, refreshing, often slightly tart summer drink. Its best qualities are floweriness, delicate fruitiness and a distinct crisp clean freshness. Its acidity should be noticeable and matched with fragrant, fruity flavours, whether dry or semi-sweet. A little *spritz* is often a good idea. Winemakers now successfully produce bottle-fermented sparkling wines which develop good lees character from 2–3 years'

ageing and still wines aged in oak. More complex flavours are evolving as the vines age and the winemakers grow more skilful. Good English wines clearly benefit from bottle-age – indeed that they need it, particularly in vintages of high acidity.

In the cool climate with uncertain summers and autumns, early ripening and resistance to rot are two of the major factors governing the choice of grapes. But some growers, especially the larger ones, are moving away from the typically German grapes such as Müller-Thurgau, Reichensteiner and Schönburger, and from varietal wines, in favour of blends. New German varieties designed to ripen well in cool weather and the (excellent) hybrid Seyval Blanc are still prominent, although classic French varieties are increasingly used, a change reflected in the bottles: Bordeaux and Burgundy shapes rather than those of Hock or Mosel. Nonetheless, the Liebfraumilch style remains popular on supermarket shelves. There are also some serious dessert wines now being made regularly, mainly from botrytis-infected Bacchus and Huxelrebe grapes.

The industry's regulatory body, founded in 1967, the English Vineyard Association (EVA), has been replaced by the United Kingdom Vineyards Association, an amalgamation of five of the six former regional associations. It can grant a 'Seal of Quality' to non-hybrid wines over 15% total potential alcohol, but the scheme is little used because it excludes the all important Seyval Blanc. More significantly, from 1996, the UK can produce regional wines – equivalent to the French *vins de pays* – which may be made from *vinifera* and non-*vinifera* grapes, and may include table wines, although they need no longer be labelled under this officially humiliating name.

Leading Producers

Barkham Manor

Piltdown, Uckfield, E. Sussex. Established 1985. 35 acres. Owners: Mark and Lynn Lambert. Winemaker: Ian Fuller. Wine Consultant: Karl Heinz Johner.

Good modern (stainless steel) winery making increasingly better range of wines, including sparkling. Kerner and Schönburger and Bacchus have taken a string of medals since 1989 including the South East Wine of the Year trophy. No oak.

Breaky Bottom

Rodmell, Lewes, E. Sussex. Established 1974. 6 acres. Owner/winemaker: Peter Hall. Visits.

Seyval Blanc and Müller-Thurgau planted on chalk downland. Wines made in individual style by Peter Hall and are much liked by afficionados. Since 1994 a very good classic-method sparkling has been made from Seyval Blanc, and is starting to be sought after. Also late Harvest 1995 from Müller-Thurgau.

Chapel Down Winery

Tenterden, Kent. Established 1992. Owners: private investors. Winemakers: David Cowderoy and Owen Elias.

Now one of the largest wineries in the UK handling grapes from all over the southeast (it has no vineyards of its own). Limited range of wines, but all of good quality, especially Epoch I red and Bacchus white.

Chiddingstone

Edenbridge, Kent. Established 66 acres. Owners: J. P. and M Quirk. Winemakers: D. Quirk and J. M. Payne.

Huge vineyard now starting to come on stream. Pinot can be good, favourably compared with French styles, and has been served at Her Majesty's banquets. Supplies several airlines.

Denbies

Dorking, Surrey. Established 1986. 265 acres. Owner: Adrian White. Consultant winemaker: Kit Lindlar. Visits.

The largest UK's vineyard planted with 18 varieties, mainly Müller-Thurgau. Teething problems led to a succession of winemakers. Comprehensive range of wines with some award-winning ones, especially Bacchus and dessert wine.

Halfpenny Green

Bobbington, Stourbridge, W. Midlands. Established 1983; new winery 1994. Owner: Go-Form Ltd. Grower: Martin Vickers. Winemaker: Clive Vickers. Visits.

20-acre vineyard producing a range of white and red wines in all styles now winning national and international awards. Labels are Black Country Gold and Staffordshire Silver. Single varieties include Huxelrebe and good Madeleine Angevine.

Hidden Spring

Horam, E. Sussex. Established 1987. 9 acres. Owners: Martyn Doubleday and Chris Cammell. Winemaker: John Worontschak. Visits.

Organic orchard/vineyard property with a range of varieties including Pinot Noir, Seyval Blanc, Ortega, Müller-Thurgau and Faber. Striking labels and good to very good wines – especially oak-aged and red.

Llanerch

Pendoylan, Vale of Glamorgan, Wales. Established 1986. 7 acres. Owners: Peter and Diana Andrews. Winemaker: Diana Andrews. Visits.

The largest and most commercial vineyard in Wales. Just under 7 acres of mixed varieties (including Reichensteiner, Bacchus, Kernling, Huxelrebe, Seyval Blanc and Triomphe d'Alsace) on south-facing slopes in the Ely Valley. Best quality and range of estate wines under Cariad label, including four white, one rosé and a sparkling, which have netted a number of international awards.

Northbrook Springs

Bishops Waltham, Hants. Established 1991. 15 acres. Owners: Brian and Sue Cable. Consultant winemaker: John Worontschak. Chalky downland location looks to be very promising. Wines good and improving, especially the '94 late harvest dessert wine. Now using new French oak for a Fumé-style blend of Reichensteiner and Bacchus grapes. The range also includes a classic-method sparkling, as well as dry and medium-dry whites.

Penshurst

Tunbridge Wells, Kent. Established: 1972. 12 acres. Owner/winemaker: David Westphal.

Well-established 12-acre vineyard and investment in modern winery (new press 1994). Good range of wines, especially Müller-Thurgau and Seyval Blanc. All wines are vegetarian (no fining) and are not released for at least two years. Labels used: Penshurst and Vine Cottage.

Pilton Manor

Shepton Mallet, Somerset. 10 acres. Established 1966. Owners: Jim and Anne Dowling. Winemaker: Jim Dowling.

Long-established vineyard, now totalling 10 acres. Produces a range of very good wines, especially late harvest sweet Westholme from Huxelrebe, which have won a clutch of awards. The Dowlings also make Harrod's English Wine, and an English brandy.

Sandhurst

Hoads Farm, Cranbrook, Kent. 15 acres. Vineyard established 1988–90. Owners: J. F. and C. A. Nicholas. Winemaker: Stephen Skelton at Tenterden. Visits.

Well-run vineyard producing prize-winning varietals and blends on a mixed Wealden farm. Good oak-aged Bacchus and Pinot sparkling. Trying Rondo and Dornfelder varieties.

Thames Valley Vineyard

Twyford, Berks. Established 1979. 25 acres. Owner: Jonathan Leighton. Winemaker: John Worontschak.

Serious wine producer making good to very good wines under Valley Vineyards, Clocktower and Thames Valley labels. Especially recommended are the oak-aged (white and red) and sparkling. Three times Gore Browne trophy-winner in five years for fumé, dessert and sparkling wine.

Three Choirs

Newent, Glos. Established 1973. 68 acres. Owner: limited company. Winemaker: Martin Fowke.

Probably largest producer in UK with New World styles. Also buys in grapes and makes wine under contract. Enviable record of consistent quality wine production. Vintage sparkling, white (including oaked), rosé, red and dessert.

OTHER GOOD PRODUCERS

Bearsted Maidstone, Kent. 4 acres. Good Bacchus and light reds improving.

Boze Down Whitchurch-on-Thames, Oxon. 4.5 acres of mixed varieties with interesting selection of high-quality reds.

Bruisyard Saxmundham, Suffolk. 10 acres of Müller-Thurgau established in 1974. Wines include oaked and sparkling.

Cane End Reading, Berks. 12 acres. Bacchus dessert wine can be good.

Carr Taylor Hastings, E Sussex. 35 acres established in 1973. Despite recent financial problems is still producing wide range of wines with sparkling and balanced grapey whites.

Chilford Hundred Linton, Cambs. Long-established. 18-acres.

Gifford's Hall Bury St Edmonds, Suffolk. Good wines from 12 acres, including East Anglian Wine of the Year 1996.

Lamberhurst Tunbridge Wells, Kent. 25 acres. Once UK's largest, since July 1995 under new ownership. Wines widely available and of fair to good quality.

Manstree Exeter, Devon. 3 acres. Good sparkling wine.

Nyetimber West Chiltington, W Sussex. 42 acres of Chardonnay, Pinots Noir and Meunier, solely for sparkling.

Plumpton College Lewes, E Sussex. 1.3-acre experimental vineyard at college which runs wine-growing/making courses.

Sedlescombe Robertsbridge, E Sussex. Organic vineyard makes a wide range of wines from 15 acres of mixed varieties.

Staple St James Canterbuy, Kent. 7 acres planted in 1974. Huxelrebe and Müller-Thurgau can be very good.

Tenterden Vineyards Tenterden, Kent. 15 acres of Müller-Thurgau and Seyval Blanc planted in 1979 now produce a range from very dry to sweet, a rose and sparkling. Award-winning oak-aged Seyval.

Wyken Bury St Edmunds, Suffolk. 7 acres of fairly young vines. Starting to make good wines. Prize-winning Bacchus.

ENJOYING WINE

It is the inquisitive who enjoy wine most. The essence of the game is variety; you could taste a different wine every day of your life and yet not learn it all. Each wine evolves with time. There will always be new wines to taste, and new combinations of wine with food to try. There will always be more to learn about yourself, your palate and its reactions, too.

No single attitude or set of rules can apply to a commodity that can be either a simple foodstuff as basic as bread and cheese, or one of the most recherché of luxuries, or anywhere in between. There are enamel-mug wines and Baccarat-crystal wines, and there is no point in pretending that one is the other.

This chapter is concerned with choosing, buying, storing, serving and appreciating wine that is above the *ordinaire* or jug level. Once a wine has a named origin (as opposed to being an anonymous blend) it reflects a particular soil, climate, culture and tradition. For better or worse it has some character.

The mastery of wine consists in recognizing, bringing out and making the most of that character. I cannot improve on the late André Simon's definition of a connoisseur: 'One who knows good wine from bad, and appreciates the distinctive merits of different wines.' Thank heaven all white wines are not Sauvignon Blancs, however fresh, flowery and fragrant, or all reds great thumping Cabernets.

It is a crucial (but also a common) misunderstanding of the nature and variety of wine to say that a Barolo, for example, is better than a Rioja, or a Pauillac than a Napa Cabernet. The secret is to learn to understand and enjoy each of them for what it is.

There is only one essential I would press on you, if you are going to spend more than a bare minimum and buy wines above the jug level: and that is to make a conscious act of tasting. Become aware of the messages your nose and mouth are sending you – not just about wine, but about all food and drink. Seek out new tastes and think about them.

By far the greater part of all fine wine, and even – perhaps especially – of the best, is thrown away by being used as a mere drink. A great bottle of wine is certainly wasted if nobody talks about it, or at least tries to pinpoint in his own consciousness the wonderful will-o'-the-wisp of fragrance and flavour.

BUYING WINE

To buy wine and get exactly what you expect is the exception rather than the rule. Wine is a moving target; a kaleidoscope of growers and vintages that never stands still. If this bothers you, there is a solution – stick to a brand. But you will be sacrificing the great fascination of wine; its infinite variety. Not to mention the fun of the chase: the satisfaction of finding a winner (and the chagrin of backing a dud).

There are few cardinal rules in such an open field, where one day you may be buying from the corner store, the next by mail-order and the third direct from the producer. But the first rule is absolute. Always buy ahead of your needs; never drink the bottle you have just bought. There are very good reasons for this rule. To start with, you need time to think. If you go shopping knowing that you must bring home some wine, the chances are that what you buy will be unsuitable and you will probably pay more than you really want to.

Nobody can take in all the offerings of a well-stocked store at a glance. Do your wine buying when you are in the mood and have time to browse, to compare prices, to make calculations, to use reference books. By far the best place to do this is at home, by comparing the price lists of alternative suppliers. Avoid traders who have no list and rely on you to fall for this week's 'special'.

Your wine needs time to rest. Although many modern white and light red wines are so stable that you could play skittles with them and do them no harm, all mature red wines need a settling period of at least several days after being moved. Your chances of serving a wine at its best are far greater if you can prepare it calmly at home.

Given time you can make an order that qualifies for a discount. Buying by the case is cheaper than buying by the bottle. Assuming you have a cupboard with a lock, and a reasonable resistance to temptation, you will use no more wine, and pay less.

An Investment in Pleasure

An investment in future pleasure is often one of the most profitable of all. Inflation aside, when you come to drink the wine, now better than when you bought it, the expenditure will be a thing of the past; the pleasure will seem a gift from the gods.

In fact, very little money is needed to convert you from a bottle-by-bottle buyer to the proud possessor of a 'cellar'. Calculate what you spend on wine in three months, or two months, or at a pinch only one month – and spend it all at once in a planned spree. Lock the wine away. Then continue to buy the same quantity as before but use it to replenish your stock, instead of for instant drinking. All you have done is to borrow three, two or one month's wine money and the interest on that is your only extra expenditure. Your reward is wine you have chosen carefully and kept well, ready when you want it, not when you can get to the shops.

Make an effort to be clear-headed about what you really need. Do not spend more than you can comfortably afford. Think twice before buying unknown wines as part of a package. Do not buy a quantity of wine you have never tasted and may not like. Consider whether home delivery is really practicable: will there be someone at home to answer the door? Can you easily lift the 40 or 50 pounds (20 or 25 kilos) that a case of wine weighs?

One of the wiliest ways of broadening your buying scope is to join with a small group of like-minded people to form a syndicate. A syndicate can save money by buying bigger lots of everyday wine. It can spread risks. It can also bring within reach extraordinary bottles at prices that would make you, on your own, feel guilty for months. Three or four friends who have never tasted Château Latour or Romanée-Conti will enjoy them more if they buy and open them together, sharing their opinions (and their guilt). While there may be laws that prevent an unlicensed citizen from selling wine, even to a friend, there is nothing to stop them sharing its cost.

The Wine Trade

The structure of the wine trade has changed radically in recent years from a fairly rigid pattern of brokers, shippers, agents, wholesalers and retailers to an intricate but fluid mixture of ingredients, some old and some new. It is not surprising that such a pleasant vocation has more volunteers than the army. The great growth areas have been in 'experts', writers and consultants, and in ingenious methods of selling with or without a shop.

In America the period has seen wine change from being a minority – even a faintly suspect minority – interest to a national pastime. The wine trade has recruited regiments of specialists at every level. Locally the retailers are the most prominent; nationally the marketing men. But what remains sovereign (and to the foreigner most bizarre) is the changing legislation from state to state. Scarcely two are alike. New York, California, Texas, Florida and a few more states are relatively free to benefit from all the rich possibilities; the remainder are more or less inhibited by local legislation. Even individual counties can stick their oar in and say what you may and may not drink. Seen from across the Atlantic it looks as though the Constitution is in mortal peril.

In Britain the changes started in the 1960s with the ponderous tread of the brewers, fearful that a growing taste for wine would erode their sales of beer, buying scores of traditional local wine shops and replacing them with chains tied to national brand-marketing ideas.

Whatever the merits of the old merchants (and many of them were excellent) the new shops were generally dismal, and the rising generation of vocational wine merchants – as opposed to accountants – wanted nothing to do with them. They found it easy to reinvent the old individualistic wine trade for the new generation of better travelled and more knowledgeable (if less wealthy) wine lovers. Some of them

specialized in particular areas or styles of wine. Gerald Asher in London was the first, shipping the 'lesser' wines of France – names like Touraine and Roussillon, which today are considered almost classic. The old trade, weaned on Bordeaux and burgundy, had never heard of them and the brewers (most of them) preferred a simple life with tank trucks of a Spanish blend. Today there is a specialist for almost every area of the wine-growing world and it must be said that the brewers now employ some of the best.

Other wine merchants offer the old virtues of personal service, delivery to your door and credit (at a price). Personal service consists largely of word-of-mouth recommendations based on a regular customer's known tastes and resources. A very few firms, including some of the oldest and one or two of the youngest, are prepared to become as involved as family solicitors, keeping track of what a customer has in his cellar and reminding him to drink it when it has reached its best. Such firms are skilful at offering the best wines of a new vintage early, while they are still in their makers' cellars and long before they are even bottled, at 'opening' prices that rarely fail to rise once the wines come on the general market.

At the opposite extreme, making wine available and tempting to every shopper, are the supermarkets, offering at first a rather simple and limited range, sometimes under their own brand names, and now a remarkable collection including fine wines and esoteric discoveries. These are nearly always the cheapest places to buy single bottles, which are usually good value for money, if rarely memorable. In their early days of selling wine most supermarkets left a lot to be desired, particularly by way of explanation and description, but today helpful labels and even in some cases trained staff have appeared and in certain stores the range is remarkable.

Learn While You Drink

Mail-order wine merchants prosper on the proposition that the calm customer, reference book and calculator to hand, is likely to aim true and be satisfied. Wine clubs and societies, often offering a great deal of information about the wines they sell, and usually setting up periodic tastings for members, feed the urge to learn while you drink.

Discount stores doing cash-and-carry business appeal to bargain hunters. Magazines can be highly persuasive about their mixed case of the month. There has even been a wine investment programme linked to a life insurance policy. All in all, the efforts of marketing men make a subject which is already confusing a great deal more so.

In the past twenty years or so auctions have come to epitomize both the scholarship and the showmanship of wine. At first Michael Broadbent at Christie's, then a succession of auctioneers at Sotheby's, have become wine's ringmasters and at the same time the repositories of esoteric vinous knowledge. Auctions are now regularly used in the United States, Germany, South Africa and many countries besides Britain to sell and publicize at the same time. But the London auction houses have another role, simply to turn over private cellars, surplus stocks and awkward small amounts of wine that complicate a wine merchant's life. There is a steady flow of mature wine, young wine and sometimes good but unfashionable wine at absurdly low prices. Anyone can buy, but the real bargains are often in lots larger than an individual may want. It is common practice to form syndicates to buy and divide such lots.

Speculating in Blue Chips

The auction houses established a flourishing market in old wines whose value had been unknown before. In their wake a new class of, so to speak, second-hand wine merchants or brokers has sprung up, led by Farr Vintners in London. Their business can be compared with antiquarian booksellers, finding rare wines on behalf of collectors – for collectors there certainly are today, as there never were in the spacious days when a gentleman filled his cellars with first-growth claret as a matter of course.

Those who buy such blue-chip wines in quantity these days are more likely to be engaged in the less gentlemanly game of speculation. Wine is a commodity susceptible to buying cheap and selling dear – but happily with no certainty of success.

The more expensive the wine the greater the chance of its appreciation. But other factors come into it, too: the vintage and its reputation (which will shift, not always predictably, as time goes on); the general financial climate; the popularity of the château or grower in question; perhaps most of all the proven ability of the wine to age. It is the classed growths of Bordeaux and vintage port that are known or presumed to have the longest potential life span; therefore the biggest spread of opportunity for reselling at a profit. Modern burgundies and German wines, even champagne, are considered relatively poor risks, with or without justification. The very best Italian wines, and such rarities as Tokay Essence, have a certain following. Some fine California wines are now gaining a considerable following, having proved their ability to age.

CHOOSING WINE

One of the many advantages of living in winemaking country is the way it simplifies your choice. You drink the local wine, preferably made by friends. You tend to suit your diet to it; if the wine is delicate you will go easy on the seasoning; if it is strapping you will make meals of garlic and peppers. All bets are off in California, where your friends and neighbours may make anything from a relatively fragile Sauvignon Blanc to a galumphing Zinfandel or Chardonnay, but most wine regions arrived at a balanced food and wine regime years ago.

In a country or region with no such traditions things are more complicated. In Britain, or the eastern United States, where the shops offer every wine there is, it is hardest of all to know where to start. Our wonderful variety makes a wonderfully difficult choice.

The realistic starting point, of course, is the price. The poorer you are the easier your choice will be. Together with the price goes the company and the occasion. If your companions are as interested in wine as you are you will want to seize the opportunity of discussing a good bottle with them. If they are indifferent, no matter how much you love them, remember that the wine itself is an occasion; it does not have to be fascinating too – unless to save you from death by boredom.

A Moment in the Limelight

In short, before you choose a wine, decide whether it is going to spend even a moment in the limelight – and who, besides yourself, will be drinking it. Test yourself with your reaction to the reported behaviour of Voltaire, who habitually gave his guests Beaujolais while he drank the finest burgundies himself.

Whether you give priority to the food or the wine is the next question. Ideally they should share the stage as harmonious equals – no more rivals than a hero and heroine. In a restaurant the menu and the wine list should be offered to you at the same time.

In practice the proposition is probably either 'what shall we drink with the lamb tonight?' or 'what shall we eat with this bottle of Pomerol? You need, in fact, a two-way frame of reference; a mental image of the flavours of both food and wine so that you can match them to bring out the best in both.

It is surprising how often I am asked 'You don't have to drink red wine with meat and white wine with fish, do you?', usually with a sort of indignation that implies that this simple piece of lore is a savage attack on liberty and the Constitution. Of course you don't have to. You may please yourself. But if you want to please yourself you could do worse than follow such sensible guidelines, based on sound reasons and centuries of practice.

The reasons are both chemical and aesthetic. The appetizing, refreshing quality of white wine is provided by acids that enhance the flavour of fish, while the saltiness of fish in turn emphasizes the fruity grape flavours of the wine. By contrast, the 'edge' of a red wine is not acidity but tannin, which can react disastrously with the salt, which makes it bitter, and the fishy oils, which leave a lasting metallic tang in your mouth.

Of course there are exceptions. Certain fish (and, best of all, lampreys) are cooked in red wine to make a dish that goes excellently with a full-flavoured red – not Beaujolais but St-Emilion. Pinot Noirs, low in tannin, are now becoming almost de rigueur with salmon or tuna, or indeed all except very oily fishes.

But on the aesthetic side the association of white wine with pale fish, and for that matter pale meat, is no accident either. Each foodstuff has its appropriate colour. The eye tells the brain what kind of flavour to expect. And the eye finds it natural to associate pale drink with pale food.

Some of the traditional associations have even simpler reasons. We drink dry white wine with goat cheese, for example, because the cheese's salty dryness makes us thirsty. Some associations are simply negative: we do not drink red wine with sweets because sugar, like salt, makes tannin taste bitter. Strong, savoury, protein-rich meat and game dishes are the natural partners of vigorous red wines; their tannin finds a match, and so does their colour. But light grapey reds ask for a less strenuous marriage with poultry or veal or pale lamb.

What the French so evocatively call 'la cuisine douce', such rich things of gentle savour as foie gras, sweetbreads, quenelles and cream cheeses, has a similar affinity for sweet, or at least fat and unctuous, white wines.

Clearly there are broad classes of wine that are more or less interchangeable. They can be matched with similar classes of dishes to achieve satisfactory harmonies, if not perfect ones. There are other dimensions of taste that have to be taken into account, too.

Intensity is one: a powerful flavour, however appropriate, will annihilate a bland or timid one. Unfortunately this is the effect many strong cheeses have, even on splendid full-scale red wines. Style is another: there are hearty rustic tastes and pronounced urbane ones; garlic, if you like, and truffles. The wine and the food should belong to the same culture. Peasant and aristocrat rarely show one another off to advantage; neither will bread and cheese and great claret.

The total context of the meal is important. Is it leisurely or hurried? Fine wine deserves time. Is the day hot or cold? Even air conditioning fails to make big red wines a good idea in tropical heat.

There are a few dishes that destroy the flavour of wine entirely. The commonest is salad dressed with vinegar. Surprisingly, even some of France's best restaurants serve violently acetic salads. Vinegar is best avoided altogether; lemon juice makes a better salad dressing in any case. Salad dressings with vinegar include the red 'cocktail sauce' of American restaurants, too.

Chocolate is another flavour that dominates and spoils the taste of most wines. In my view, most desserts are better served without wine; creamy highly perfumed concoctions fight wine rather than complement it. So do syrupy, fruity ones. Citrus fruit is particularly guilty. The one wine that challenges this rule is the newly revived classical Hungarian Tokay Aszú: the best examples are so richly penetrating that they handle desserts with aplomb. Where a very rich gâteau is on the menu I sometimes drink a glass of Madeira or even brandy with it. On the other hand raspberries and strawberries, and particularly wild strawberries, are a wonderful match for fine red wine. In Bordeaux they pour claret rather than cream over them.

There are times when no single wine will fill the bill. It happens in a restaurant where everyone is eating something different: one shellfish, another game, a third a dish with a creamy sauce. The cop-out answer is a neutral wine that will offend nobody. Liebfraumilch, 'blush' wines and Portuguese rosés made fortunes by offering themselves as the safe bet. A more swashbuckling (albeit less digestible) choice would be champagne. My suggestion is to start with a bottle of white wine that will match almost any hors d'oeuvre, and then (if it is a party of four or more) continue with both white and red. There is no good reason not to have both on the table at the same time.

The structure of a more formal meal with a succession of wines is the great opportunity of gastronomy. To achieve a graduated harmony of successive flavours it is worth taking pains. The ground rules are simple: follow lighter and more delicate with heavier and more pungent – both in wine and food. The fresh and hungry palate is susceptible to the subtlest flavours. Feeding fatigues it. It needs more powerful stimuli as the meal proceeds.

Occasionally the best way to bring out the singularity of a wine is to serve it concurrently with another which is similar and yet distinct; say either slightly younger or from a neighbouring property.

Wine divided into Ten Basic Styles

I have risked a rather arbitrary division of the infinite variety of wine into ten categories, and associated each category with a selection of dishes, as a guide to where to start to look, whether your starting point is the wine or the food.

No such generalization can be defended in every particular case, but it is true to say that certain criteria of flavour, age and quality can be applied across the board. Some wines could appear equally in two different categories, but for the sake of clarity I have put them firmly where, in my judgement, they most often belong.

Dry white wines of neutral, simply 'winey' flavour

Among the cheapest wines, generally useful but too plain to be exciting, or to be particularly pleasant as apéritifs without the addition of extra flavour (such as blackcurrant or grenadine syrup).

These wines are better with simple food, especially with strong-flavoured or highly seasoned dishes, e.g. hors d'oeuvres (antipasto), aïoli or fish stew, mussels, herrings and mackerel (which need a rather acid wine to cut their oil), salade niçoise, red mullet, grilled sardines, terrines and sausages, curry or Chinese food (both of these are better for a little sweetness in the wine, e.g. Australian Chardonnay). All should be served very well chilled (about 46°F/8°C).

Examples are: most branded 'jug' whites; Entre-Deux-Mers, Gaillac, Muscadet (Gros Plant du Pays Nantais or Aligoté for more acidity); many Swiss whites; most standard Italian whites (including Soave, Verdicchio, Orvieto Secco, Frascati, Pinot Bianco, Trebbiano, Sardinian and Sicilian wines); most standard Spanish and Portuguese whites; central and east European 'Welschrieslings' or Pinot Blancs (i.e. Hungarian, Yugoslav, Bulgarian, etc.); California jug whites and many Chenin Blancs; South African Sauvignon Blanc.

Light, fresh, grapey white wine with fruity and sometimes flowery aromas

This is the category of wine which has grown most in recent years, at the expense of the dry whites. Modern techniques, especially cold fermentation, capture whatever flavour the grape has (some have much more than others) and add as little as possible. The very aromatic German-style grapes are nearly always in this or the sweet white wine category.

All these wines make excellent apéritifs or refreshing between-meal or evening drinks, most of all in summer. Those with relatively high acidity are also good with many first courses, but are dominated by seriously savoury dishes and lack the substance to be satisfying throughout a meal. Suitable dishes to accompany them include: poached trout, crab salad, cold chicken. They need slightly less chilling than the previous category.

Wines include: German Tafelwein, Qualitätswein, most Kabinetts and some Spätleses; light French Sauvignons from the Dordogne and Touraine; Savoie whites (Crépy, Apremont); Portuguese Vinho Verde and Spanish Albariño; certain California Chenin Blancs and French Colombards; Australian Rieslings; some New Zealand Sauvignons and English Müller-Thurgaus and Seyval Blancs; and Austrian Grüner Veltliners.

White wines with body and character, aromatic from certain grapes or with the bouquet of maturity

The fine French dry whites all come into this category. High flavour often makes them taste rich even when they are fully dry.

Without food, these wines can be too assertive; they are best matched with a savoury dish which is also rich in flavour and pale in colour, e.g. oysters, clams, lobsters and prawns, smoked fish, frogs' legs, snails, onion or leek tart, ballotines, prosciutto, salmon, turbot and other rich fish in butter, hollandaise or other rich sauces, scallops, poultry, sweetbreads, hard Swiss cheeses. Wines should only be lightly chilled (50°–55°F/10°–13°C).

Examples are: all good mature Chardonnays (e.g. white burgundies after two or more years depending on their quality); their equivalents from California and Australia; Alsace Riesling, Gewürztraminer and Pinot Gris; Sancerre and Pouilly Fumé and Savennières from the Loire; fine white Graves; mature white Rhône wines (e.g. Hermitage Blanc) and young Condrieu; exceptional Italian whites (the best examples of Frascati, Soave Classico, Pinot Grigio, Cortese di Gavi, Pomino, or Chardonnay); best-quality mature Rioja, Rueda and Penedès whites from Spain, manzanilla sherry or montilla fino; Hungarian Szürkebarát, Kéknelyü and Furmint; Austrian Rotgipfler, and Ruländer from either Austria or Baden; Australian Sémillons and dry Barossa and Coonawarra Rieslings with three or four years in bottle; California Johannisberg Riesling.

Sweet white wines

Varying from delicately fruity and lightly sweet to overwhelmingly luscious, these wines are to be sipped slowly by themselves and are rarely improved by food.

Very rich and highly flavoured desserts, however delicious, tend to fight sweet wines. Chocolate and coffee ones are fatal. If you want anything at all, the best choice is a dessert such as French apple or raspberry tart, *crème brûlée*, plain sponge cake or such fruit as peaches or apples. Sweet white wines are usually drunk after meals, but in France often as apéritifs, too. They are normally served very well chilled.

The finest natural sweet wines are produced by the action of 'noble rot'. These include Sauternes and Barsac and the best qualities of Ste-Croix-du-Mont and Monbazillac, which are the most potent, Vouvray and Anjou whites of certain years, late-gathered wines of Alsace and Austria, and the rare and expensive very late-harvested wines of Germany, Beerenausleses and Trockenbeerenausleses (which have lately been imitated with real success in California). German wines offer every gradation between the light flowery whites and the intensely sweet ones with the same delicately acid flavour. None of them is really a mealtime wine. Tokay Aszú, on the other hand, the imperial 'botrytis' wine recently revived in Hungary (see page 420), finds matches at both the start of a banquet (with foie gras) and with fruity and/or creamy desserts at the end.

Sweet Muscats are found in most wine countries; the best 'natural' (not fortified) ones – *vins doux naturels* – are made in the south of France at Beaumes-de-Venise and at Asti in northern Italy, where the very low-strength base wine for Spumante is delicious. Heavier brown Muscats are made in Languedoc and Roussillon, parts of Italy (especially Sicily), on the east coast of Spain, at Setúbal in Portugal, in Greece and Russia and best of all) in northeast Victoria, Australia.

Rosé wines

Rosés are usually workhorse, compromise wines of adequate quality, made by fermenting the juice of red grapes very briefly with the skins, then separating it and making it like white wine. The great exception is pink champagne, which, although generally made in the same way as still rosé (before undergoing a second fermentation in the bottle), is very highly saught after. Few things are more delicious.

Rosés divide broadly into two camps: the light, pale purply pink, usually faintly sweet Loire style, and the drier, more orange-pink, stronger and more sunburnt Provençal variety. Portuguese carbonated fizzy rosés fit into the first category. Tavel from the Rhône and most rosés from Spain and Italy are stronger and drier. Some of Italy's best, called Chiaretto, are really very light reds. A third group that can be classed as rosé are *vins gris*, red-grape white wines merely shaded with colour, more grey than pink, and a fourth, *pelure d'oignon* ('onion skin'), which are very pale orange-brown. Both are usually made very dry; the *gris* more fruity and the onion skin more alcoholic. California 'blush' wines are a modern interpretation of the same tradition.

Rosés are best in summer with salads and on picnics, and the Provençal style with oily and garlicky or even oriental dishes. They have possibilities with such hors d'oeuvres as artichokes, crudités, salami or taramasalata. Pink wines need to be served really cold; colder than most whites. If this is difficult to arrange on a picnic choose a light red wine instead.

Grapey young reds with individuality, not intended to mature

Beaujolais is the archetype of a light red wine made to be drunk young while it is still lively with fresh grape flavour. Beaujolais-Villages is a better, stronger and tastier selection. Simple young Bordeaux, burgundy and Rhône reds, Cabernet from Anjou and Mondeuse from Savoie should have the same appeal. Similar wines are now made in the Midi (Corbières, Minervois, Roussillon, St-Chinian) by the Beaujolais technique of carbonic maceration and also of most of the popular red grape varieties; light wines to drink young.

Italy's Valpolicella and Bardolino, Barbera and Dolcetto and even Chianti can be freshly fruity if they are caught young enough. Fizzy red Lambrusco is a sort of caricature of the style. Spain provides few examples, although Valdepeñas has possibilities and no doubt will be made fresher in the future. Portugal's red *vinho verde* is an extreme example not to everyone's taste. California, Australia, South Africa and South America have been slow to master this style of wine. Light Zinfandels and Gamays from California sometimes achieve it.

In its liveliness and vigour this is perhaps the safest and best all-round class of red wine for mealtimes; appetizing with anything from pâté to fruit and often better than a more 'serious' or older wine with strong cheese, in mouthfuls rather than sips. For the same reason it is the easiest red wine to drink without food. It is always best served cool.

Ideal dishes include: pâtés and terrines (including those made from vegetables), quiches, salads, hamburgers, liver, ham, grilled meats, many cheeses, and soft fruits such as raspberries, plums, peaches or nectarines.

Plain everyday or 'jug' reds

These are unpretentious and anonymous blended wines with little body or flavour. French *ordinaires* in particular are often mere refreshment; dry, thin and frankly watery. Whether you prefer them or the usually softer and stronger Italian or Spanish style is a matter of taste. California's 'jug' reds have more body and are often rather sweet.

Most inexpensive imports from southern, central and eastern Europe, North Africa, Argentina, Chile, South Africa and Australia are in the classes that follow.

Like the 'neutral' cheap whites these are essentially wines for mealtimes, a healthy and stimulating accompaniment to almost any homely food. They are always best served rather cool. As drinks on their own they are improved by being iced in summer (as Sangria, with orange juice added) and 'mulled' on the stove with sugar and spices in winter.

The term 'table wine' has been adopted by the EU as denoting the lowest category of quality; wines without a specific origin (i.e. this group). The commissioners in their wisdom have ignored its English meaning, which is any wine you drink at table, including the best. They have also bracketed all wines that do not conform to national laws of appellation regardless of the reason. This produces total absurdity, for example, in Italy, where, until recently, several of the country's finest wines were non-traditional, therefore outside the DOC system, therefore *vino da tavola*, therefore officially relegated to jug-wine status.

Mature reds of light to medium strength and body

This category includes most of the world's finest red wines, epitomized by claret (red Bordeaux) and most of the typical wines of Burgundy and the Rhône, although some of the greatest fall into the next class, depending on the ripeness of the vintage. These wines need more care in serving than any others since they often throw a deposit in maturing.

They are wines for meat and game dishes with the best ingredients and moderate seasoning. Lamb, beef, veal (also sweetbreads and tongue), chicken, duck, partridge, grouse, pheasant are all ideal, although very gamey birds may need wines from the next category. Only mild cheeses should be served with these relatively delicate wines. They need to be served at a temperature of between 60° F and 65°F (15° and 18°C) to bring out their flavour.

Wines in this category (apart from French) include the best of Rioja and Penedès from Spain; Chianti Riservas, Tuscans such as Torgiano, Sassicaia and Tignanello, Carmignano, Venegazzú; Portuguese *garrafeiras* from Dão, Douro and Bairrada; top California, Oregon and Washington Cabernets and Pinot Noirs with the exception of a few mentioned in the next category; Coonawarra, Western Australian and some Hunter Valley reds; top South African estates; Chilean Cabernet; Château Musar from the Lebanon and Cabernet from New Zealand.

Exceptionally concentrated, full-flavoured and powerful reds, usually but not always needing to mature

In Europe this category depends more on the vintage than the producer. Wines that achieve this status fairly regularly include Pétrus in Pomerol, Chambertin and Corton in Burgundy, Hermitage and Châteauneuf-du-Pape (Côte Rôtie is more often in the previous category), exceptional Roussillons (not for maturing); Barolo and Barbaresco, Brunello di Montalcino, Recioto and Recioto Amarone from Valpolicella; Spanish Vega Sicilia and Pesquera (and on a humbler level Priorato); Portuguese Barca Velha; Dalmatian Posip and Postup; Bulgarian Cabernet. Occasional vintages produce many such wines: 1961 in Bordeaux, 1971 in Burgundy and more recently 1990 for both.

California, Australia and South Africa find it hard not to make such big reds. Most of their best wines are carefully restrained in ripeness, but in California a number of wines are made to be larger than life. Australia makes many such wines, especially in Victoria and Barossa and the Southern Vales in South Australia. Top Shiraz such as Penfold's Grange and Henschke's Hill of Grace are the supreme examples.

Well-hung game and strong flavoured cheeses are the obvious candidates for these wines, although those in the appropriate price bracket are also excellent with barbecues and on picnics, when someone else is driving.

Fortified wines

Wines whose natural strength is augmented with added alcohol, either during the fermentation to preserve the natural sweetness (as in port) or after they have fermented to dryness, as a preservative (as in sherry). Since the role of these wines is largely determined by their sweetness, which is at their makers' discretion, all that can usefully be said is that dry versions (whether of port, sherry, Madeira or their regional equivalents) are intended as apéritifs, while sweet ones are used either before or after meals according to local taste and custom. The French, for example, prefer sweet apéritifs, the Italians bitter ones and the British, who divide everything along class lines, some sweet and some dry. In all cases smaller glasses are needed because the alcoholic strength is higher than that of table wine.

They also have their uses with certain foods. Dry sherry is always drunk in Spain with tapas, which are infinitely various savoury snacks. It is one of the best wines for smoked eel. Old oloroso sherry, whether dry or with added sweetness, is very good with cake, nuts and raisins. Port, both vintage and tawny, is often drunk with cheese. Madeira has a cake especially designed for it.

Other wines in this category include Spanish Malaga and Tarragona, Sicilian Marsala, Cypriot Commandaria, French *vins doux naturels* (e.g. Banyuls) and a host of wines, usually with borrowed names, in the New World.

The alcohol in wine

The amount of alcohol in wine varies considerably. While alcohol provides much of the 'body' in many wines, it needs to be balanced by the flavouring elements: sugar, acidity, tannin and extract. These, combined with the alcohol, give richness of flavour. Alcohol alone makes a wine fierce and unpleasant. Typical alcoholic strengths, percent by volume, are:

German Kabinett	8.0	–	9.0	Beaune	11.0	–	14.0	Montrachet	12.6
German Tafelwein	8.0	–	11.0	California Cabernet	11.44	–	14.2	Châteauneuf-du-Pape	12.6+
French vin de table	9.0	–	12.0	Valpolicella			11.7	German Beerenauslese	12.8 – 14.0
German Auslese	10.0	–	10.5	Muscadet			12.0	Château Yquem	13.5 – 16.0
Beaujolais	10.0	–	13.5	Chianti	12.0	–	13.0	Australian Shiraz	13.8
Red Bordeaux	10.0	–	12.0	Barolo	12.0	–	14.0	Fino sherry	18.0 – 20.0
Alsace Riesling	10.5	–	11.5	Sauternes	12.0	–	15.0	Oloroso sherry	18.0 – 20.0
Chablis Premier Cru	10.5	–	12.7	California Zinfandel	12.0	–	16.0	Vintage port	19.0 – 20.0
California Chardonnay	10.5	–	14.0	Chambertin			12.4		
Bordeaux Cru Classé	10.5	–	12.5	Rioja Reserva			12.5		

STORING WINE

The greatest revolution in the history of wine was the discovery that if air could be excluded from wine its life span was increased enormously. And, even better, that it could take on an undreamed-of range of flavours and a different, less grapey and infinitely more subtle and interesting smell.

The invention that made airtight storage possible was the cork, which came into use some time in the 17th century. It is possible that the ancient Greeks knew the secret, but all through the Middle Ages and up to the 17th century the premium was on new wine, not old. The latest vintage often sold for twice as much as the remnants of the previous one, which stood a good chance of having become vinegar. The only exceptions were the class of high-strength and possibly sweet wines generally known as sack, products of hot sunshine in the eastern Mediterranean, southern Spain and later the Canary Islands. Their constitution allowed them to age in barrels in contact with air and take on the nuttiness and warmth of flavour we associate with sherry.

Ageing in bottles under cork is a totally different process. Instead of oxidizing, or taking in oxygen, the wine is in a state of 'reduction' – in other words what little oxygen it contains (absorbed in the cellars, while being 'racked' from one cask to another, and in being bottled) is being used up (reduced) by the life processes within it. So long as it lives (and wine is a living substance with a remarkable life span), it is the battleground of bacteria, the playground of pigments, tannins, enzymes … a host of jostling wildlife preying on each other. No air gets through a good cork as long as it is kept wet, in contact with the wine, so that there is no risk of the vinegar process starting.

Whether the reduction process is beneficial, and for how long, is the determining factor in deciding when a bottled wine will be at its best.

Which Wines to Store

The great majority of wines are made with the intention of being ready to drink as soon as possible. This is true of all bulk wines, most white wines except very sweet and particularly full-bodied ones, nearly all rosés and the whole class of red wines that can be compared with Beaujolais – whose character and charm lie in a direct flavour of the grape. Reduction spoils their simple fruitiness. The only table wines that benefit from storage are a minority of sweet or very concentrated, intensely flavoury whites and those reds specifically made, by long vatting with their skins and pips, to take up pigments and tannins as preservatives – which include, of course, all the world's best.

Precisely how much of these elements combines with the juice and how well they act as preservatives is only partly in the hands of the winemaker. The overriding decisive factor is the vintage. And no two vintages are exactly alike. The analysis of the grapes at harvest time may be similar, but each crop has stood out in the fields through a hundred different days since the vine flowers opened. The number and size of the grapes, the formation of the bunches, the thickness of the skins, the yeasts they gathered will always be subtly different. No two vintages develop in the same way or at precisely the same speed. But the better wines of each vintage will always last longer and mature further, to more delicious flavours, than the less good.

Thus laying down wines for maturing is always an exploratory business. Experts will give their opinion that the 1986 Bordeaux need from 5 to 15 years to reach their best, depending on their quality. Such a margin will be safe enough, although it is scarcely a very helpful guide. They will also tell you that, based on their assessment of the style of the 1985 vintage, which has less tannin and concentration (it was a record-size crop), its wines will be at their best well before the 1986s. (But they may be wrong.)

Merchants and Brokers

In the past, only the grandest producers were capable of maturing and bottling their wine satisfactorily, and marketing was an idea unknown to them. The key to what the consumer wanted was held by the merchants, who blended wine to the customers' tastes. Today, buying wine direct from the maker has largely changed the shape of the wine trade.

It is the broker's job to know his region in the finest detail, to be a sort of family doctor to the small grower's wine, to advise him on its condition, choose samples with him and take them to the right merchant. To the merchant the broker is a valued talent spotter who can gather and submit the right samples. The merchant's traditional function is to finance the wine while it is maturing, to make sure it suits the customers' tastes, then to bottle and ship it. In many cases he and his agents create both the wine and the market. His agents provide the link with the wholesalers, who are stockholders for retailers. The possible permutations of the system are endless. Its advantages are that each aspect of the chain from grower to table has its highly experienced expert, whether in knowing the right time to bottle or the turnover of a nightclub's refrigerator.

Is it Time to Try?

Happily there are always plenty of other people opening bottles of every vintage and adding to a general pool of information about it, transmitted through wine books and magazines and catalogues. You will never have to look very far for an indication of whether it is time to try the wine you are storing. You can even tell a certain amount about the maturity of red wine without opening the bottle by holding its neck up to a strong light: the depth and quality of colour are quite readable through the glass.

The more difficult decision, assuming you intend to lay down some wine, is how much of which vintages to buy. It is probably a mistake to plunge too heavily for one vintage – you never know whether the next one will be better. It is more sensible to buy regularly as good vintages turn up, which in Bordeaux in the 1980s was about two years out of three, but in the 1990s the success rate has been lower – one year in three, in Burgundy one out of three, in the Rhône two out of three and in California, for the sort of reds we are talking about, the same.

Since there is rarely enough space (and never enough money) it is worth making a calculation of how much dinner-party wine you are likely to use, which in turn depends on how many of your friends share your passion. Let us suppose that you give an average of one dinner party a month for eight people, and each time use four bottles of mature wine (in addition to such current items as young white wines and possibly champagne). Your annual consumption will be about 48 bottles. Perhaps you use another bottle a week on family occasions (or alone). That makes about eight dozens a year.

The theoretically ideal stock is arrived at by multiplying the annual consumption by the number of years it stays in the cellar. Since this number varies from perhaps two, for fine white wines, to ten or more for the best reds, a finer calculation is needed. Let us say that two of the eight dozens are two-year wines, four are five-year wines and two are ten-year wines. The total is 22 + 45 + 210 = 44 cases.

Storage systems
The commonest form of permanent wine rack is made of wooden bars joined with galvanized metal strips in a modular system which can be any shape or size. The wooden cases of the grander château wines are ideal storage. Another, more elaborate, idea is a modular spiral system building up into a flight of steps.

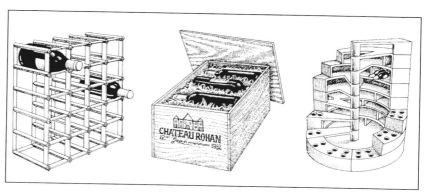

Besides table wines two other kinds of wine are worth laying down: champagne and vintage port. Champagne is a relatively short-term proposition. Vintage champagne almost invariably gains a noticeable extra depth of flavour over two or three years. Lovers of old champagne will want to keep it far longer, up to 10 or even 20 years, until its colour deepens and its bubbles quieten. In Britain it is worth keeping non-vintage champagne for a year or two as well, but I have found that in America it is usually mature (sometimes overmature) by the time it reaches the customer.

Vintage port is an entirely different matter. The way the wine goes through almost its whole life cycle in the bottle is explained in the section on port. It needs cellaring longer than any other wine – except the almost unobtainable vintage Madeira. All good vintages need 20 years or more to reach their hour of glory.

The practical arrangements for storing wine are a challenge to most householders. The ideal underground cellar is even more remote than its ideal contents. But the storage conditions that make an underground cellar ideal are relatively easy to reproduce upstairs (at least in temperate climates) if the space is available.

The conditions required are darkness, freedom from vibration, fairly high humidity and a reasonably even temperature. Darkness is needed because ultraviolet light penetrates even green glass bottles and hastens ageing prematurely. Vibration is presumed to be bad (on what evidence I am not sure; it would have to be pretty violent to keep any normal sediment in suspension). Humidity helps the corks to stay airtight; but much more important is that the wine remains in contact with the corks inside the bottle. It is essential to store all wine horizontally, even if you only expect to keep it for a month or two. Excess humidity is a serious nuisance: it rapidly rots cardboard boxes and soon makes labels unreadable. My own answer to the label problem is to give each one a squirt of scentless hair lacquer before storing it away.

Temperature and Time

Temperature is the most worrisome of these conditions. The ideal is anything between a steady 45°F and 65°F(7° and 18°C). A 50°F (10°C) cellar is best of all, because the white wines in it are permanently at or near the perfect drinking temperature. It is probable that wines in a cold cellar mature more slowly and keep longer than wines in a relatively warm one, but the excellent Mirabelle restaurant

Random storage

The best way to make use of a limited number of pigeonholes in a storage rack is to put new acquisitions into whatever holes are empty, regardless of order – even if it means scattering a dozen bottles in random ones and twos. All that is needed is a clear grid reference system and an entry in your cellar book or card index for each pigeonhole you have used. This is the only way to avoid wasting space.

Purpose-built private cellars are rare today, but they exist, in some cases with a degree of sophisticated planning undreamt of in the past. The cellar illustrated here is based on that of Tawfiq Khoury, a wine collector in San Diego, California. It has a total capacity of 40,000 bottles, with allowance for storage of every size up to 8-bottle Imperials. It is air-conditioned and is also used as a tasting room for small private parties, a wine book library and a museum of rare old bottles and glasses.

A roll-top desk for keeping accounts and writing notes. Records of the stock are kept in a card-index system. The volume and complexity actually justifies a small computer.

The whole cellar is air-conditioned to a constant 52°F (11°C) – perfect serving temperature for white wine and maturing temperature for reds. It is chilly for mere human beings: they have to wear an extra sweater.

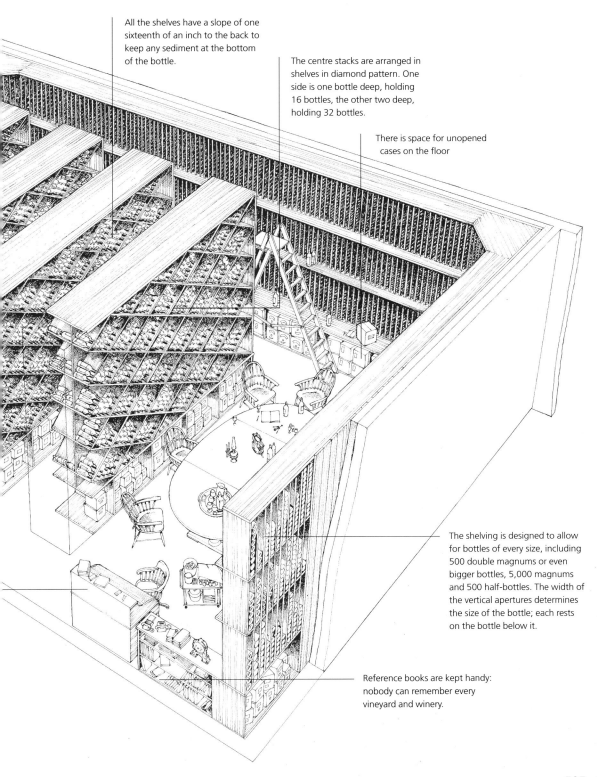

All the shelves have a slope of one sixteenth of an inch to the back to keep any sediment at the bottom of the bottle.

The centre stacks are arranged in shelves in diamond pattern. One side is one bottle deep, holding 16 bottles, the other two deep, holding 32 bottles.

There is space for unopened cases on the floor

The shelving is designed to allow for bottles of every size, including 500 double magnums or even bigger bottles, 5,000 magnums and 500 half-bottles. The width of the vertical apertures determines the size of the bottle; each rests on the bottle below it.

Reference books are kept handy: nobody can remember every vineyard and winery.

in London kept all its red wines – even the very old ones – permanently at serving temperature, about 18°C (65°F), and I have heard no complaints of premature ageing.

Chemists point out that chemical reaction rates double with each 18°F (10°C) increase in temperature. If the maturing of wine were simply a chemical reaction this would mean that a wine stored in a cellar at 68°F (19°C) would mature twice as fast as one in a 50°F (10°C) cellar. But it is not so simple; wine is alive. Its ageing is not just chemical but a whole life process.

One should not exaggerate the effects of fluctuation, either. My own (underground) cellar moves gradually from a winter temperature of about 48°F (8°C) to a summer one of over 60°F (15°C) without the wine suffering in any detectable way. The most common difficulty arises in finding a steadily cool place in a house or apartment heated to 70°F (21°C) or more in winter, when the outside temperature can range from 60°F (15°C) plus to well below freezing. The answer must be in insulating a small room or large cupboard near an outside wall. In practice fine wines are successfully stored in blocked-up fireplaces, in cupboards under the stairs, in the bottoms of wardrobes … ingenuity can always find somewhere satisfactory.

The same applies to racks and 'bins'. A bin is a large open shelf (or space on the floor) where a quantity of one wine is laid, bottle on bottle. In the days when households bought very few wines, but bought them a barrel at a time, the bin was ideal. For collections of relatively small quantities of many different wines racks are essential. They can either be divided into single-bottle apertures (either one or two bottles deep) or formed into a diamond pattern of apertures which are large enough to take several bottles – a half-dozen or a dozen depending on the quantities you usually buy. I find it convenient to have both single-bottle and dozen-bottle racks.

A much more complex problem, as a collection grows, is keeping track of the bottles. It is difficult not to waste space if you deplete your stock in blocks. Where space is limited you want to be able to use every slot as it becomes vacant. This is the advantage of the random storage system. But its efficaciousness depends entirely on dedicated book-keeping. If this is not your line you are likely to mislay bottles just when you want them.

Very fine wines – most classed-growth Bordeaux, for instance – are shipped in wooden packing cases, which are perfect storage while the wine matures. If you do buy

Maturity comparisons

Every bottle proceeds at its own pace towards maturity with almost incredible differences between the fastest and the slowest, between even similar types from the same regions, varieties and seasons.

It is interesting to plot the life span of a range of wines in a graphic form. In these diagrams I have assumed a notional (and unmeasurable) 'optimum' for each wine; the time when all its potential is realized. The better the wine the longer this 'plateau of perfection' is likely to be. The 'drinkability' of each wine up to the optimum is the vertical dimension of each diagram. For clarity it assumes that all wines are equally 'perfect' at some stage of their lives. The horizontal scale shows time measured from the vintage in years (or months, as indicated).

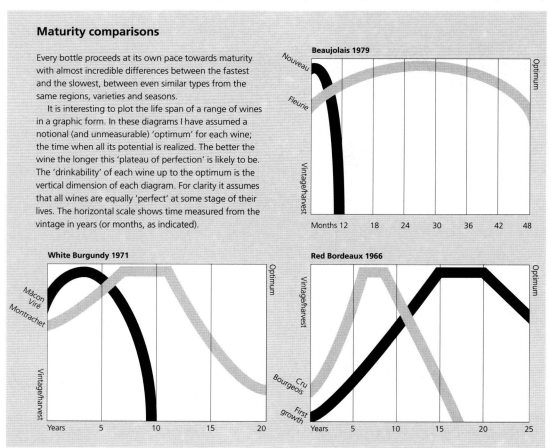

such wines by the complete case there is no point in unpacking it until you have reason to think the wine will be nearing maturity.

If possible make allowance in your storage arrangements for bigger-than-normal bottles. The 'standard' (75 centilitres before EU officials settled on 70 cl) bottle has been accepted by generations as the most convenient regular size – though whether it was originally conceived as being a portion for one person or two is hard to say. But bigger bottles keep wine even better. Length of life, speed of maturity and level of ultimate quality are all in direct proportion to bottle size. Half-bottles are occasionally convenient, particularly for such powerful and expensive sweet wines as great Sauternes, where a little goes a long way. Otherwise, bottles are better, and magnums better still. Double magnums begin to be difficult to handle (and how often can you assemble enough like-minded friends to do justice to one?). The counsel of perfection is to lay down 6 magnums to every 12 bottles of each wine on which you pin really high hopes.

It is not necessarily only expensive wines that are worth laying down. Many Australian reds, for example, will evolve from a muscle-bound youth into a most satisfying maturity. One of my greatest successes was a barrel of a three-year-old Chilean Cabernet which I bottled in my amateurish way in my own cellar. It reached its quite delectable peak ten years later.

Experiment, therefore, with powerful, deep-coloured and tannic reds from whatever source. Be much more circumspect with white wines. Most of those that have proved that cellaring improves them beyond a year or two are expensive already: the better white burgundies, the best Chardonnays, Sauternes of the best châteaux and outstanding German Ausleses – which probably provide the best value for money today.

The neglected areas to add to these are fine Chenins from the Loire (both sweet and dry), top-quality Alsace wines, and what was once considered the longest lived of all white wines, the rare white Hermitage of the Rhône.

Bottle size, shape and capacity

Each European wine region has a long-established traditional bottle shape which helps to preserve an identity in the public mind. In most cases the New World wines based on the same grape varieties are also sold in the appropriately shaped bottles to help identify the style of their wineries. Colour of glass is as important as shape. All Rhine wines are bottled in brown glass, all Mosels in green. White Bordeaux is in clear glass, red Bordeaux is in green.

For table wines whose origin is not important the 'cubitainer' or 'bag-in-box' is a plausible invention. The wine is in a plastic foil bag inside a cardboard box. As it is drawn off through a tap the bag collapses, theoretically protecting the remaining wine from harmful contact with air. But in practice, no wine is well served by such a device.

Red Bordeaux comes in several sizes. The bigger the bottle the longer the wine keeps, the slower it matures and the better it will become.

Champagne is the only other wine with the same range of bottle sizes – but in this case the various sizes available are for purely celebratory reasons.

GLASSES

Each wine region has its own ideas about the perfect wineglass. Most are based on sound gastronomic principles that make them just as suitable for the wines of other regions, too. Perhaps the most graceful and universally appropriate is the shape used in Bordeaux. A few are flamboyantly folkloric – amusing to use in their context but as subtle as a dirndl at a dinner party. The traditional *römer* of the Rhine, for instance, has a thick trunk of a stem in brown glass ornamented with ridges and excrescences. It dates from the days when Rhine wine was preferred old and oxidized, the colour of the glass, and presumably when Rhinelanders wanted something pretty substantial to thump the table with. The Mosel, by contrast, serves its wine in a pretty shallow-bowled glass with a diamond-cut pattern that seems designed to stress the wine's lightness and grace. Alsace glasses have very tall green stems which reflect a faint green hue into the wine.

Glasses like these are pleasant facets of a visit to the wine region, adding to the sense of place and occasion, but you do not need them at home.

The International Standards Organization has pre-empted further discussion by producing specifications for the perfect wine-tasting glass. Its narrowing-at-the-top shape is designed as a funnel to maximize the smell of the wine for the taster's nose. For ordinary table use this feature can be less pronounced. In all other respects it has the characteristics that any good glass should have: it is clear, unornamented, of rather thin glass with a stem long enough for an easy grip and an adequate capacity.

Capacity is important. A table wineglass should never be filled more than half full. A size which is filled to only one third by a normal portion (about 4 fl.oz/11 cl or an eighth of a bottle) is best of all. Anything larger is merely ostentatious – and more likely to get knocked over.

Types of glasses

You can argue that there is only one perfect wineglass, equally ideal for all table wines but there is also a case for enjoying the traditional, sometimes fanciful, shapes adopted by different regions to promote the identity of their products.

A 'tulip' glass has the rim turned in to concentrate the bouquet. This is the classic Bordeaux model.

A glass with an out-turned lip is conventional for top red burgundies. Some of these glasses are large enough to hold half a bottle comfortably.

Displaying the Bubbles

Sparkling wines are best served in a slightly smaller but relatively taller glass filled to about three-quarters of its capacity, giving the bubbles a good way to climb – one of the prettiest sights wine has to offer. They should never under any circumstances be served in the shallow 'coupes', now very rarely seen.

Dessert wines, being stronger, are served in smaller portions in smaller glasses, usually filled to between a half and two-thirds of their capacity. Their scents are more pungent than table wines; to plunge your nose into a wide bowl of port fumes would be almost overpowering.

When several wines are being served at the same meal it saves confusion if each has a slightly differing glass. In any case guests should be told that the order of pouring is from left to right (i.e. the first wine is poured into the left-hand glass and so on in order). I imagine this tradition is for the practical reason that a right-handed drinker is less likely to knock over this first glass in reaching for his second. As a further precaution against confusion (if two or more similar wines are being poured) it is a simple matter to slip a little rubber band around the stem of one of the glasses.

Wineglasses should be as clean as you can possibly make them – which is unfortunately beyond the capacity of any dishwasher. Detergents leave a coating which may or may not have a taste or smell, but is always detectable to the touch. It even affects the fizz of champagne. There is only one way to achieve a perfectly clean, polished, brilliant glass. After washing with soap or detergent to remove grease it should be thoroughly rinsed in clean hot water, then not drained but filled with hot water and only emptied immediately before it is dried. A clean linen or cotton cloth polishes a warm wet glass perfectly (and very quickly) whereas it leaves smears and fluff on a cold one.

The best place to keep glasses is in a closed cupboard, standing right way up. On an open shelf they collect dust. Upside down on a shelf they pick up odours of wood or paint. An alternative to a closed cupboard is a rack where they hang upside down, but dust on the outside of a glass is no better than dust on the inside.

White wines are served in smaller glasses than reds. A matching set is useful for dinners when more than one wine is being served.

A slender tulip glass is a good shape for displaying the bubbles in champagne or other sparkling wine.

A smaller version of the red burgundy glass for white wine served at table or as an apéritif. Good for 'aromatic' whites such as Chardonnay and Riesling.

Port, sherry or madeira are usually served in a glass with an inturned rim which concentrates the bouquet.

SERVING WINE

The no-nonsense approach to serving wine takes up very little space or time. The cork is out before discussion starts. There are times, and wine, for this can-of-beans attack which it would be pretentious to deny. But here I put the case for taking trouble to make the most of every bottle. On the basis that anticipation is a part of every great pleasure I argue that you should enjoy reading the label, be aroused by handling the bottle, relish removing the capsule, feel stirred by plunging in the corkscrew.

Sensuous enjoyment is the entire purpose of wine. The art of appreciating it is to maximize the pleasure of every manoeuvre, from choosing to swallowing. The art of serving wine is to make sure that it reaches the drinker with all its qualities at their peak.

No single factor is as important to success or failure as temperature. The characteristic scent and flavour of wine consists of infinitely subtle volatile compounds of different molecular weights, progressively heavier from 'light' white wines to 'heavy' reds. It is the temperature that controls their volatility – the point at which they vaporize and come to meet your sense of smell.

Each grape variety seems to behave differently in this respect. The Riesling scent is highly volatile: a Moselle sends out its flowery message even when it is too cold to drink with pleasure. Champagne's powerful fragrance of grapes and yeasts can hardly be suppressed by cold (although I have known people who seem to try). The Sauvignon Blanc is almost as redolent as the Riesling; the Chardonnay much less so – less so, in fact, than the Gamay; Beaujolais is highly volatile at low temperatures. The Pinot Noir vaporizes its ethereal sapidity even in a cool Burgundian cellar, whereas the Cabernets of Bordeaux hold back their aromas, particularly when they are young. In a Bordeaux *chai* it tends to be the oak you smell more than the wine. California and other warm-climate Cabernets are often more forthcoming.

Are Aromas Everything?

It will be seen that these observations tally more or less with the generally accepted norms of serving temperatures shown opposite. Not that aromas are everything. We expect white wines to be refreshingly cool; we expect red wines to awaken our palates with other qualities of vigour and completeness. It is fascinating to test how much your appreciation is affected by temperature. Taste, for instance, a good mature Meursault and a Volnay of the same quality (they are the white and red wines of neighbouring vineyards, made of grapes with much in common) at precisely the same fairly cool temperature and with your eyes shut. You will find they are almost interchangeable.

It is time to forget the misleading word 'chambré' to describe the right temperature for red wines. Whatever the temperature of dining-rooms in the days when it was coined (and it must have varied from frigid to a fire-and-candle-heated fug) the chances of arriving at the right temperature by simply standing the bottle in the room where it is to be drunk are slight. An American dining-room at 70˚F (21˚C) plus is much too warm for wine. At that temperature the alcohol becomes unpleasantly heady. Mine, at 60˚F (15˚C), is good for burgundy but too cold for Bordeaux.

Everybody has, in his refrigerator, a cold place at a constant temperature that can be used for cooling white wine. Nobody I have met has a 63˚F (16˚C) oven. On the other hand since an ice bucket is a perfectly acceptable (in fact by far the most efficient) way of chilling wine, why not a warm-water bucket for red? Water at 70˚F (21˚C) will raise the temperature of a bottle from 55˚F to 65˚F (15˚–18˚C) in about eight minutes, which is the same time as it would take to lower the temperature of a bottle of white wine from 65˚F to 55˚F (18˚–13˚C) in a bucket of icy water. (Ice without water is much less efficient in cooling.) In a fridge, incidentally, where air rather than water is the cooling medium, the same lowering of temperature would take about one hour.

Those who have accustomed themselves to microwave ovens will no doubt have experimented with them on red wine. I am told that the time it takes to warm a bottle from 55˚F to 65˚F is something under 20 seconds.

Bear in mind that the prevailing temperature affects the wine not only before it is poured out but while it is in your glass as well. Serve white wine on a hot day considerably colder than you want to drink it. Never leave a bottle or glass in the sun; improvise shade with a parasol, the menu, a book, under your chair … anywhere. At one sumptuous outdoor buffet in South Africa the white wine was admirably cold but the red wine was left on the table in the sun. Not only was it ruined beyond recognition but I nearly burnt my tongue on it. There are circumstances where the red wine needs an ice bucket too.

Do You Decant?

Wine lovers seem to find a consensus on most things to do with their subject, but decanting is a divisive issue. There is one school of thought, the traditional, that holds that wine needs to 'breathe' for anything from a few minutes to a few hours, or even days, to reach its best. Its opponents, armed with scientific evidence, proclaim that it makes no difference or (a third view) that it is deleterious. Each is right about certain wines, and about its own taste. But they are mistaken to be dogmatic.

There are three reasons for decanting. The most important is to clean the wine of sediment. A secondary one is the attraction of the plump, glittering, glowing-red decanter on the table. The third is to allow the wine to breathe. Nobody argues with the first two. The debate revolves around when the operation should take place.

The eminent Professor Peynaud, whose contribution to gastronomy in general and Bordeaux in particular should make us listen carefully, writes (in *Le Goût du Vin*), 'If it is necessary to decant [at all], one should always do it at the last possible moment, just before moving to the table or just before serving [the wine]; never in advance.' The only justification Peynaud sees for aeration, or letting the wine breathe, is to rid it of certain superficial faults that sometimes arise, such as the smell of slight refermentation in the bottle. Otherwise, he says, decanting in advance does nothing but harm; it softens the wine and dulls the brilliance of its carefully acquired bouquet.

Scientifically minded Americans have come to much the same conclusions, although their consensus seems to be that decanting makes no difference that can in any way be reliably detected.

My own experience is that almost all wines change perceptibly in a decanter, but whether that change is for the better or worse depends partly on the wine and partly on personal taste.

There are wine lovers who prefer their wine softened and dulled; vintage port in particular is often decanted early to soothe its fiery temper: its full 'attack' is too much for them. They equate mellowness with quality. Tradition in Spain equates the taste of oak (as in Rioja) with quality. Who can say they are wrong about their own taste?

The English have always had strong ideas about how their wines should taste. A hundred years ago they added Rhône or Spanish wine to claret; it was altogether too faint for them without it. There are surely some people who preferred the burgundies of the days before the strict application of the appellation laws to the authentic straight-from-the-grower burgundy we drink today. The Californians, too, have their own taste. They love direct, strong flavoured wines that often seem as though the transition from fruit juice was never fully completed. It is not surprising that ideas about decanting differ.

There are certain wines that seem to curl up when you open the bottle like woodlice when you turn over a log. The deeply tannic Barolo of Piedmont shows nothing but its carapace for an hour or sometimes several. If you drink it during that time you will have nothing to remember but an assault on your tongue and cheeks. But in due course hints of a bouquet start to emerge, growing stronger until eventually you are enveloped in raspberries and violets and truffles and autumn leaves.

The standard French restaurant practice is not to decant burgundy. If it is true that the Pinot Noir is more volatile than the Cabernet the practice makes sense: the contact with the air when pouring from bottle to carafe wakes the Bordeaux up; the burgundy does not need it.

Those who believe in decanting would give several hours' airing to a young wine, one or two to a mature wine (these terms being relative to the expected maturing time), and treat an old wine as an invalid who should be kept out of draughts. Yet strange to say it is an often repeated experience of those who have tasted very old and very great wines (Château Lafite 1803 was a case in point) that they can add layer upon layer of bouquet and flavour hour after hour – even, in some cases, tasting better than ever

the following day. I regularly finish the bottles the evening after opening them. The only general rule I have found is that the better the wine, taking both origin and vintage into account, the more it benefits from prolonged contact with the air. Sometimes a wine that is a distinct disappointment on opening changes its nature entirely. A bottle of Château Pontet-Canet 1961 (in 1982) had a poor, hard, loose-fitting cork and, on first tasting, a miserable timid smell and very little flavour at all (although the colour was good). Twenty-four hours later it seemed to have recharged its batteries; it opened up into the full-blooded, high-flavoured wine I had expected. The moral must be to experiment and keep an open mind.

The pros and cons of decanting are much more long winded than the process itself. The aim is simply to pour the wine, but not its sediment, into another receptacle (which can be a decanter, plain or fancy, or another bottle, well rinsed).

If there is enough advance warning take the bottle gently from its rack at least two days before you need it and stand it upright. Two days (or one at a pinch) should be long enough for the sediment to slide to the bottom. If you must decant from a bottle that has been horizontal until the last minute you need a basket or cradle to hold the bottle as near its original position as possible but with the wine just below cork level (*see* page 552).

Cut the capsule right away. Remove the cork gently with a counter-pressure corkscrew. Then, holding the decanter in the left hand, pour in the wine in one smooth movement until you see the sediment advancing as a dark arrow towards the neck of the bottle. When it reaches the shoulder, stop pouring.

It makes it easier to see where the sediment is if you hold the neck of the bottle over a candle-flame or a torch, or (I find best) a sheet of white paper or a napkin with a fairly strong light on it. Vintage port bottles are made of very dark glass (and moreover are usually dirty), which makes it harder to see the sediment. If the port has been lying in one place for years its sediment is so thick and coherent that you can hardly go wrong. If it has been moved recently it can be troublesome, and may even need filtering. Clean damp muslin is the best material; I have found that coffee filter papers can give wine a detectable taste.

The French way with burgundy

Serving burgundy, if you follow the French practice and do not decant it, presents more of a problem. Restaurants often serve it from a cradle; the worst possible system because each time the bottle is tipped to pour and then tipped back the sediment is stirred into the remaining wine. The Burgundian answer to this is the splendid engine that tips the bottle continuously, as in the motion of decanting, but straight into the guests' glasses. Without such a machine I decant burgundies at the last minute – but only when they have sediment. Unless they are very old they are often clear to the last drop.

Decanting

There is much debate about whether and when to decant wine; whether 'breathing' is a good thing or not. Modern 'scientific' opinion tends to be against it. Certainly its effects are hard to predict, but if a rule of thumb is called for I suggest that: Vigorous young ('young' in this context relates to the vintage – a great vintage is young at 10 years, a poor one up to 4 or 5) red Bordeaux, Cabernets, Rhône reds, Barolo and Barbaresco, heavy Zinfandels, Australian Shiraz, Portuguese reds and other similar tannic wines: decant at least 1 hour before drinking, and experiment with periods of up to 6 hours.

'Young' red burgundy, Pinot Noirs and Spanish wines: decant just before serving.

Wine for decanting needs to be held in a position as near to horizontal as possible. The purpose of a wine basket is to hold a bottle in this position while it is being opened prior to decanting. It should never be used for pouring wine at table.

The corkscrew being used here is the Screwpull, which draws the cork up into itself with almost infallible ease. The worm is Teflon-coated, which means the cork can be drawn with a smooth, single, screwing action.

Pour the wine into the decanter in one continuous movement, holding the bottle neck over a light so that you can watch the sediment. As soon as it approaches the neck, stop pouring.

A special silver funnel has been devised which has a perforated strainer in the base and a spout curved sideways to prevent the wine from splashing down the neck of the decanter.

The Temperature for Serving Wine

Nothing makes or mars any wine so much as its temperature. The following chart serves to show the ideal temperatures for each category of wine. It is wrong, however, to be too dogmatic. Some people enjoy red wines several degrees warmer than the refreshing temperature I suggest for them here, and some like their white wines considerably colder than the moderate chill I advocate for the best appreciation of scent and flavour.

Also remember that on a hot day 'room temperature' may be considerably higher than that listed below and red wines may need to be immersed briefly in an ice bucket.

DOMESTIC FRIDGE TEMP.		CELLAR TEMPERATURE ▼ THE IDEAL CELLAR		ROOM TEMP. ▶
SWEET WHITES	DRY WHITES	LIGHT REDS		FULL SCALE REDS

Temperature scale: C° 4 · 5 · 6 · 7 · 8 · 9 · 10 · 11 · 12 · 13 · 14 · 15 · 16 · 17 · 18
F° 39 · 41 · 43 · 45 · 46 · 48 · 50 · 52 · 54 · 55 · 57 · 59 · 61 · 63 · 64

Wine entries (approximate position by temperature):

- MUSCADET
- CHABLIS
- MACON
- CHINON
- BEST WHITE BURGUNDIES & GRAVES
- RED BURGUNDY
- BORDEAUX BLANC
- SAUTERNES
- BEAUJOLAIS
- BEAUJOLAIS CRU
- GEWURZTRAMINER
- NOUVEAU
- COTES-DU-RHONE (RED)
- TOP RED RHONE
- SANCERRE/POUILLY
- GROS PLANT
- ALSACE/RIESLING
- MIDI REDS
- VINTAGE PORT
- MUSCATS
- CORBIERES, ETC.
- ALIGOTE
- SYLVANER
- FINO SHERRY
- TAWNY PORT
- CREAM SHERRY
- ORDINARY RED BORDEAUX
- TOKAY
- NON-VINTAGE CHAMPAGNE
- AMONTILLADO
- MADEIRA
- CAHORS
- FINE RED BORDEAUX
- MONTILLA
- MADIRAN
- SPARKLING WINE
- VIN JAUNE
- BANDOL
- SEKT, CAVA, ETC.
- BEST CHAMPAGNE
- EISWEIN
- GOOD GERMAN & AUSTRIAN WINES
- BEST DRY GERMAN WINES
- BEST SWEET GERMAN WINES
- LIEBFRAUMILCH
- SWEET LOIRE CHENIN BLANCS
- FRASCATI
- VALPOLICELLA
- ORVIETO
- SOAVE
- FIASCO CHIANTI
- VERDICCHIO
- HUNGARIAN WHITES
- SICILIAN REDS
- 'BULLS' BLOOD
- VINHO VERDE
- BARBERA
- FENDANT
- VALDEPENAS
- DOLE
- LIGHT ZINFANDELS
- RETSINA
- LAMBRUSCO
- YUGOSLAV RIESLING
- S.AFR. CHENIN BLANC
- CALIFORNIA/AUSTRALIAN/OREGON PINOT NOIR
- LIGHT MUSCATS
- CHARDONNAY
- N.Z. SAUVIGNON
- TOP CALIFORNIA/AUSTRALIAN CHARDONNAYS
- BEST CALIFORNIA CABERNETS & ZINFANDALS
- JOHANNISBERG RIESLING
- CALIFORNIA SAUVIGNON BLANC
- BAROSSA RIESLING
- LIQUEUR MUSCATS
- OLD HUNTER VALLEY WHITES
- VIN ROSE
- TOP AUSTRALIAN CABERNET/SHIRAZ

Cooling vessels

Failing the ideal arrangement of storing white wine permanently at the perfect drinking temperature – that of a cool cellar – the most efficient way to chill it rapidly is by immersing the entire bottle in ice-cold water. A refrigerator takes up to ten times as long as an ice-bath to achieve the same effect. Ice-cubes or crushed ice alone are inefficient. Ice must be mixed with cold water for rapid conduction of heat from the bottle. The perfect ice bucket is deep enough to immerse the whole bottle, neck and all: otherwise you have to put the bottle in upside down to start with to cool the neck.

Insulated cooler sleeves, which are kept in the freezer and placed around the bottle when needed, are also effective. On the left of the photograph is another idea: a sort of open-ended Thermos flask which keeps an already chilled bottle cool by maintaining a wall of cold air around it.

Opening Sparkling Wine

1 Tear off the foil hiding the wire 'muzzle' to uncover the 'ring'. Tilt the bottle and untwist the ring, being careful not to point the bottle at anyone.

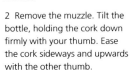

2 Remove the muzzle. Tilt the bottle, holding the cork down firmly with your thumb. Ease the cork sideways and upwards with the other thumb.

3 When the cork feels loose, grasp it firmly and twist, keeping the bottle tilted, with a glass beside you to take the first foam.

4 Specially made pliers are sometimes used when a champagne cork is very stiff, or when opening a number of bottles.

5 Butlers in the great champagne houses pour champagne by holding the bottle with a thumb in the indentation known as the 'punt'.

Retaining the sparkle

Sparkling wines should be spur-of-the-moment celebratory drinks. When opening expensive bottles, it is a good idea to have a stopper that will keep the fizz intact if the celebration should be short-lived.

Opening Vintage Port

Bottles of vintage port older than about 20 years often present a special problem: the cork becomes soft and crumbly and disintegrates in the grip of a corkscrew. Spongy corks are almost impossible to remove. The answer is to cut the top off the bottle, which can be done in either of two ways.

Port tongs are specially made for the job. Heat them until red hot over an open flame, than clamp the tongs around the upper neck of the bottle for a minute. Wipe quickly around the hot neck with a wet rag – it will crack cleanly all round and the top with the cork will come away easily.

An equally effective and more spectacular way of opening an old bottle of port is to grasp it firmly in one hand and take a heavy carving knife in the other. Run the back of the knife blade up the neck of the bottle to give a really sharp blow to the 'collar'. The neck will crack cleanly. Practise before making your début at a dinner party. Confidence is all.

If a port cork crumbles into the bottle it is possible to filter the wine through a clean muslin-lined glass or plastic funnel, or to use one of the handsome old-fashioned silver funnels which has a built-in strainer.

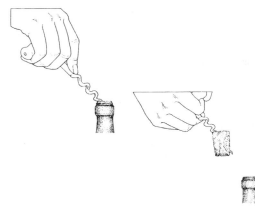

If a cork shows signs of weakness, or breaks in half when you pull it, the situation can sometimes be retrieved by inserting the corkscrew into the remainder of the cork diagonally, and pushing towards the opposite side of the neck.

CORKS AND CORKSCREWS

The first corks must have been like stoppers, driven only halfway home. There is no known illustration of a corkscrew until 100 years after corks came into use.

Although screw-caps, crown closures and synthetic corks now offer cheaper and simpler ways of keeping the wine in and the air out, cork remains the way fine wine is sealed.

What makes cork so ideal as a wine plug? Certainly its lightness, its cleanness, and the simple fact that it is available in vast quantities. It is almost impermeable. It is smooth, yet it stays put in the neck of the bottle. It is unaffected by temperature. It very rarely rots. It is extremely hard to burn. Most important of all it is uniquely elastic, returning, after compression, to almost exactly its original form. Corking machines are based on this simple principle: you can squeeze a cork enough to slip it easily into the neck of a bottle and it will immediately spring out to fill the neck without a cranny to spare.

As for its life span, it very slowly goes brittle and crumbly, over a period of between 20 and 50 years. Immaculately run cellars (some of the great Bordeaux châteaux, for example) recork their stocks of old vintages approximately every 25 years, and one or two send experts to recork the château's old wines in customers' cellars. But many corks stay sound for half a century.

The only thing that occasionally goes wrong with a cork is a musty smell that develops. Corks are carefully sterilized in manufacture, but sometimes one or two of the many cells that make up the cork (there are 20 to 30 in a square millimetre) are infected with fungus. When these cells are in contact with wine the wine picks up the smell and becomes 'corky' or 'corked'. The problem is fairly rare but when it happens it is instantly noticeable – and naturally disappointing. There is nothing to be done but to open another bottle.

Producing cork

Cork is the thick outer bark of the cork oak, *Quercus suber*, a slow-growing evergreen tree which has evolved this spongy substance for protection and insulation, particularly against fire. The world supply of cork is concentrated in the western Mediterranean area and the neighbouring-Atlantic coasts. Portugal, above all, furnishes half of the total, and almost all of the top-grade cork for use with wine.

The bark is cut into sheets from mature trees every 9 or 10 years between the months of June and August. (Each tree has a productive life of 165 years.) The sheets are stacked to dry for 3 months, then boiled in vats with fungicides. After several more months' storage in a dark, cold cellar, the corks are cut as plugs from the thickness of the bark.

The longest (up to 57 mm) and best-quality corks are graded for the best wine. Dust and scraps from the process are agglomerated to make cheap corks. For specialized use by champagne makers extra large corks are made of three layers glued together. A normal wine cork is 24 mm in diameter, compressed into an 18 mm neck. For champagne a 31 mm cork is compressed into a 17.5 mm neck, with the upper third protruding in the characteristic bulging mushroom shape.

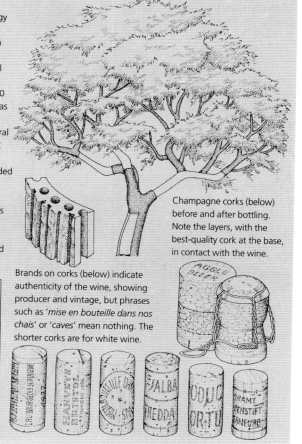

Champagne corks (below) before and after bottling. Note the layers, with the best-quality cork at the base, in contact with the wine.

Brands on corks (below) indicate authenticity of the wine, showing producer and vintage, but phrases such as 'mise en bouteille dans nos chais' or 'caves' mean nothing. The shorter corks are for white wine.

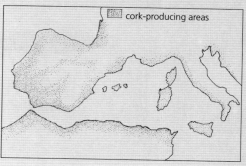

cork-producing areas

Good-quality corks produce no other problems. Poor ones do. Many Italian wine bottles have very hard, small, low-grade corks in necks that are narrower than the norm. They make it extremely tough going for the corkscrew, which sometimes pushes the cork in instead of pulling it out. If you have wiped the top of the cork clean with a damp cloth before starting to open the bottle, no harm is done. A gadget made of three parallel lengths of thick wire with a wooden handle is made for fishing for lost corks. It is reasonably effective, but a simpler answer is to leave the cork in and pour the wine out, holding the cork down with a knife or a skewer until it floats clear of the neck.

The quality of the corkscrew is extremly important. Enormous ingenuity has been expended on the engineering of corkscrews. The simple screw-with-a-handle has long since been improved on by designs that use counter-pressure against the bottle. The straight pull is strictly for the young and fit: it can take the equivalent of lifting 80 pounds to get a cork out.

Various dodges are used to provide leverage, but the most important factor of all is the blade – the screw – that pierces and grips the cork. At all costs avoid narrow gimlets on the one hand and open spirals of bent wire on the other. The gimlet will merely pull out the centre of a well-installed cork; the bent wire will simply straighten if it meets with resistance. A good corkscrew blade is a spiral open enough to leave a distinct chimney up the middle, and made like a flattened blade with a sharp point and two cutting edges on its horizontal sides. The points of corkscrew design are illustrated below.

Types of corkscrew

Endless ingenuity has been applied to the mechanical problem of grasping a cork in a bottle and pulling it out without exertion. A straight pull with the bottle between your knees is neither dignified nor necessary; all you need is some sort of leverage against the rim of the bottle. A foil cutter (shown centre bottom) cleanly removes the top of the foil capsule before the corkscrew is inserted into the exposed cork. Out of a catalogue of thousands of devices, these are some of the most popular and effective in current use.

TASTING WINE

There are wine tastings on every level of earnestness and levity, but to taste wine thoroughly, to be in a position to give a considered opinion, demands wholehearted concentration. A wine taster, properly speaking, is one who has gone through a professional apprenticeship and learned to do much more than simply enjoy what he tastes. He is trained to examine every wine methodically and analytically until it becomes second nature. Although I am by no means a qualified professional taster I often find myself, ridiculously, putting a glass of tap water through its paces as though I were judging it for condition and value. If I do not actually hold it up to the light I certainly sniff it and hold it in my mouth for a moment while I see how it measures up to some notional yardstick of a good glass of water. Then naturally I spit it out.

Whether or not you have any desire to train your palate (it has its disadvantages too; it makes you less tolerant of faulty or boring wines) it makes no sense to pay the premium for wines of character and then simply swallow them. It is one of the commonest misunderstandings about wine that if it is 'better' it will automatically give more pleasure. To appreciate degrees of quality you need conscious, deliberate awareness. You need to know what sort of quality you are looking for. And you need a method to set about finding it.

Pierre Poupon, one of the most eloquent of Burgundians, has written: 'When you taste don't look at the bottle, nor the label, nor your surroundings, but look directly inwards to yourself, to observe sensations at their birth and develop impressions to remember.' He even suggests shutting your eyes to concentrate on the messages of your nose and mouth.

Before dinner parties become like prayer meetings let me say that there is a time and place for this sort of concentration. But if you apply it at appropriate moments it will provide you with points of reference for a more sociable approach.

What, to start with, are you tasting for? A very basic wine tasting for beginners might consist of five wines to show the enormous variety that exists: a dry white and a sweet one; a light young red and a fine mature one, and a glass of sherry or port. The point here is that the wines have nothing in common at all. Another very effective elementary tasting is to compare typical examples of the half-dozen grape varieties that have very marked and easily recognized characters.

Most tastings are intended to compare wines with an important common factor, either of origin, age or grape variety. A tasting of Rieslings from a dozen different countries is an excellent way of learning to identify the common strand, the Riesling taste, and judge its relative success in widely different soils and climates. A variant of this, more closely focused, would be to take Rieslings of the same category of quality (Kabinett or Spätlese) from the four principal wine regions of Germany.

Vertical and Horizontal Tastings

Tastings of the same wine from different vintages are known in the jargon as 'vertical'; those of different wines (of the same type) in a single vintage are known as 'horizontal'.

Professional tastings concerned with buying are nearly always horizontal. The important thing here is that they should be comparing like with like. It is of no professional

Tasting table

A formal wine tasting need not be an elaborate affair. The arrangement below is all you need for a small group to taste and compare six similar wines.

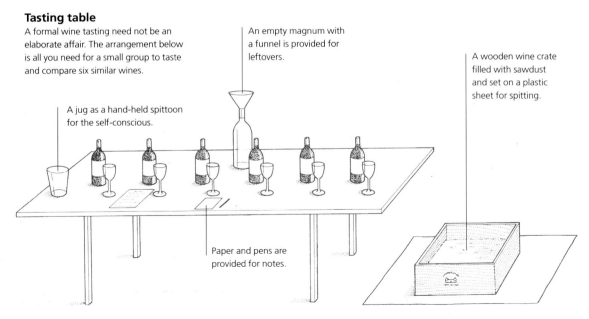

An empty magnum with a funnel is provided for leftovers.

A wooden wine crate filled with sawdust and set on a plastic sheet for spitting.

A jug as a hand-held spittoon for the self-conscious.

Paper and pens are provided for notes.

interest to compare Bordeaux with burgundy, or even Chablis with Meursault; if the Chablis is a good Meursault it is a bad (because untypical) Chablis. A Médoc that tasted like a Napa Valley wine would be a poor Médoc – although it might be hard to convince a Napa grower that the converse was true.

Most of us, of course, drink most of our wine with meals. We judge it, therefore, partly by how well it goes with the sort of food we like. Professional and competitive tasters always judge wine either by itself or in company with other wines, which gives them a different, and clearer, point of view. It is clearest of all when you are hungry and not tired; the end of the morning is the time most professionals prefer to attend a tasting.

The ideal conditions, in fact, are rather unattractively clinical; a clean well-lit place without the suggestive power of atmosphere, without the pervasive smell of wine barrels, without the distraction of friendly chatter – and above all without the chunks of cheese, the grilled sausages and home-made bread that have sold most of the world's second-rate wine since time immemorial.

Whether you should know what you are tasting, or taste 'blind' and find out afterwards, is a topic for endless debate. The power of suggestion is strong. It is very difficult to be entirely honest with yourself if you have seen the label; your impressions are likely to reflect, consciously or otherwise, what you think you should find rather than simply what your senses tell you – like a child's picture of both sides of a house at once.

If I am given the choice I like to taste everything blind first. It is the surest method of summoning up concentration, forcing you to ask yourself the right questions, to be analytical and clear minded. I write a note of my opinion, then ask what the wine is or look at the label. If I have guessed it right I am delighted; I know that my mental image of the wine (or memory, if I have tasted it before) was pretty close to reality. If (which is much more frequent) I guess wrong, or simply do not know, this is my chance to get to know the wine, to taste it again carefully and try to understand why that grape, in that vineyard, in that year, produced that result. This is the time to share impressions with other tasters.

It is always interesting to find out how much common ground there is between several people tasting the same wine. So little is measurable, and nothing is reproducible, about the senses of smell and taste. Language serves them only lamely, leaning on simile and metaphor for almost everything illuminating that can be said.

The convenient answer, normally used at competitive tastings, is the law of averages. Ask a group of tasters to quantify their enjoyment, and reduce their judgement to scores, and the wine with the highest average score must be the 'best'. The disadvantage of averaging is that it hides the points of disagreement, the high and low scores given to the same wine by different tasters who appreciate or dislike its individual style, or one of whom, indeed, is a better judge than another. At a well-conducted tasting the chairman will therefore consider an appeal against an

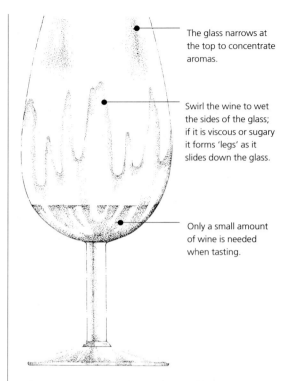

The glass narrows at the top to concentrate aromas.

Swirl the wine to wet the sides of the glass; if it is viscous or sugary it forms 'legs' as it slides down the glass.

Only a small amount of wine is needed when tasting.

An ideal tasting glass, to the specifications of the International Standards Organization, is about 6 inches (152 mm) high and would hold 7 fl. oz (215 ml). For tasting purposes it is usually only filled to about one-fifth of capacity. The tall funnel shape is designed to capture the aroma, or bouquet, for the taster's nose. It needs a long enough stem to keep the hand away from the bowl. (Professional tasters often hold their glass by its foot.) The thinner the glass, within reason, the better. Wine is tasted more vividly from thin glass.

averaged score and encourage a verbal consensus as well, especially where gold medals hang on the result.

This is as close to a final judgement on wine quality as fallible beings can get. But at best it represents the rating by one group of one bottle among the wines they tasted that day. It takes no account of other wines that were not tasted on the same occasion. All one can say about medal winners is that they are good of their sort.

For competitive tastings, taster against taster, 'blindness' is the whole point of the exercise. The individual (or team) with the widest experience and the best memory for tastes should win. For competitive tastings, wine against wine, it is the only fair method. But it can nonetheless produce misleading results. It tends to favour impact at the expense of less obvious but ultimately more important qualities. When California Cabernets are matched against red Bordeaux of similar age the Californians almost always dominate. They are like tennis players who win by serving ace after ace.

The Grand Tour

The act of tasting has been anatomized by many specialists. To me there are five aspects of wine that convey information and help me gauge its quality, origin, age, the grape varieties involved, and how long it will keep (and whether it will improve). They constitute the grand tour of its pleasures, the uplift excepted. To take them in order they are its appearance, smell, the first impression the wine makes in your mouth, its total flavour as you hold it there, and the taste it leaves behind.

I take each of these into account, note each separately (writing a note is not only an aide-mémoire, it forces you to make up your mind) and then draw a general conclusion. Tasting is a demanding discipline, quite distinct from the mere act of drinking. It sometimes has to be a quick and private little ceremony at a party where wine is not an accepted priority. Yet to contract the habit and apply a method of one kind or another is the only way to get full value out of your wine.

There is more to appearance than simply colour. Fine wine is brilliantly clear. Decanting should make sure that even old wine with sediment has the clarity of a jewel, capturing and reflecting light with an intensity that is a pleasure in itself.

Wine is more or less viscous, at one extreme forming heavy, slow-moving 'legs' on the walls of the glass, at the other instantly finding its own level like water. The more dense it is the more flavour-giving 'extract' and/or sugar it contains – which of course is neither good nor bad in itself; it must be appropriate to the kind of wine. On the other hand a deposit of crystals in white wine is (if anything) an indication of good quality; it is certainly not under any circumstances a fault.

'Colour [I quote Professor Peynaud] is like a wine's face. From it you can tell age, and something of character.' That is, you can if you have certain other information about the wine, which the smell will soon provide.

The best way to see its colour clearly is to hold the glass against a white surface – a piece of paper will do – and to tip it slightly away from yourself so that you are looking through the rim of the liquid. Shallow silver tasting-cups are common in parts of France – particularly Burgundy – where wine is kept in dark cellars. It is easier to judge the colour of red wine in a shallow layer over the brightly reflecting silver than in a glass, where it is in a greater mass. The 'tastevin' worn on a ribbon around the neck has become the ceremonial symbol of Burgundy.

White wines grow darker as they age; reds go through a slow fading process from purplish through red to a brickish reddy brown (which can be seen even through the green glass of the bottle by looking at the neck against a light). In young wines the colour in the glass is almost uniform from edge to edge (making allowance, that is, for greater density where you are looking through more wine). In older wines the rim is usually decidedly paler. A browning rim is a sure sign of maturity in red wines.

Sheer redness is an indicator of quality rather than a virtue in its own right. The famous 1961 Bordeaux vintage can often be recognized from right across the room by its extraordinary glowing darkness – even in maturity a colour of pregnancy and promise. A Priorato from Spain might well manage to be even darker still, without being fit to be on the same table.

Red burgundy rarely has the same deep tints, and never precisely the same hue as Bordeaux. Chianti is rarely deep red because of the proportion of white grapes it contains. Rioja is also generally rather pale, but this is because it has been aged for so long in cask, while Beaujolais is light coloured in a different way; it has more the translucent purple of grape juice. In general hot-country wines of good grape varieties, the Cabernets, for example, from Australia, California and South Africa, have more intensity of colour than their cool-country equivalents. Vintage port is deep purple-red, ruby port a much lighter, more watery colour, and tawny port, aged in wood for many years, can be anything from the brown red of old claret to a clear light amber when it is very old – the most extreme example of a red wine fading.

White wine has scarcely less variety than red. Chablis has a green light in its pale gold which is uncommon in other white burgundies. Mosels also have a touch of green, with less of the gold, while Rhine wines tend to a straw colour, deepening almost to orange in old sweet examples. Sherry is coloured by oxidation; young *finos* only very slightly, old olorosos to a mahogany brown. When great sweet Sauternes ages, it goes through all the tints of gold to arrive at a deep golden brown.

Hold Your Nose

You have only to hold your nose while you sip to realize that it is the organ that does most of the serious work of tasting. Unfortunately our sense of smell is our least cooperative, least stable faculty. While taste, like hearing and sight, is constantly awake, the sense of smell rapidly wearies. This is apparent if you sniff more than half a dozen times in rapid succession at the same glass (or the same rose): its message becomes dimmed. Your nose needs a different stimulus.

For this reason wine tasters place a great deal of faith in their first impression. They swirl the wine once or twice to wet the sides of the glass and volatize as much of the smell as possible. Then they exclude all other thoughts and sniff. The nerves of smell have instant access to the memory (their immediate neighbour in the brain). The first sniff should trigger recognition; possibly the memory of the identical wine tasted before. If the smell is unfamiliar it will at least transmit this piece of negative information, and suggest where in the memory-bank partially similar smells are to be found.

The smell will also be the first warning sign if there is something wrong with the wine: perhaps a slight taint of vinegar, the burning sensation of too much sulphur, or a mouldy smell from an unsound cork or an unclean barrel. Nowadays, with improved cellar hygiene, obvious faults like these are relatively rare. Most wines have a more or

Tasting wine

The secret of getting the maximum pleasure out of wine is to remember that we smell tastes: it is our noses and the nerves high in the brain behind the nasal cavity that distinguish nuances of flavour – not our tongues, lips or palates. The mouth detects what is sweet, sour, salt, bitter, burning, smooth, oily, astringent.

But the colour and character of a flavour lie in its volatile compounds, which need the nose to apprehend them. Thus the procedure for tasting wine pivots around the moment of inhalation: the first sniff is crucial, since the sense of smell rapidly wearies.

First look carefully at the precise colour, clarity and visual texture of the wine. Using a piece of white paper can help.

Swirl the wine to volatize its aroma while you concentrate. The glass should only be filled to about a fifth of its capacity.

Try to exclude all other thoughts and sniff. First impressions are crucial and should trigger recognition.

Take a generous sip, a third of a mouthful, and 'chew' it so that reaches all parts of your mouth.

The final judgement comes when the volatile compounds rise into the upper nasal cavity.

At a professional tasting you must spit out all the wine: it is essential to keep a clear head.

A tasting scorecard

Name of Wine *Ch. Giscours*	Vintage *1966*	
District/type *Margaux*	Date purchased *1969*	
Merchant/bottler *J. Morgan Furze / C.B*	Price *£2.00 ?*	DATE OF TASTING *15 · 1 · 82*

SIGHT Score (Maximum 4) 4		Comments
CLARITY: cloudy, bitty, dull, clear, brilliant DEPTH OF COLOUR: watery, pale, medium, deep, dark COLOUR: (White wines) green tinge, pale yellow, yellow, gold, brown (Red wines) purple/red, red, red/brown VISCOSITY: slight sparkle, watery, normal, heavy, oily		*Col. still deep & strong with sl. whitening at edge.*

SMELL   Score (Maximum 4)   3
GENERAL APPEAL: neutral, clean, attractive, outstanding, off (e.g. yeasty, acetic, oxidized, woody, etc)
FRUIT AROMA: none, slight, positive, identifiable (e.g. Riesling)
BOUQUET: none, pleasant, complex, powerful
Starts earthy / mineral stones, wood – hessian? Develops to sweetness, growing more high-pitched, neat violets but with undercurrent of ripe fruit

TASTE   Score (Maximum 9)   7
SWEETNESS: (White wines) bone dry, dry, medium dry, medium sweet, very sweet
TANNIN: (Red wines) astringent, hard, dry, soft
ACIDITY: flat, refreshing, marked, tart
BODY: very light and thin, light, medium, full bodied, heavy
LENGTH: short, acceptable, extended, lingering
BALANCE: unbalanced, good, very well balanced, perfect
Still, powerful and warm; excellently crisp & clear (typical Margaux). Essentially dry, a shade astringent long firm finish. V.V.G.

OVERALL QUALITY   Score (Maximum 3)   2½

Coarse, poor, acceptable, fine, outstanding

HOW TO USE THIS CHART
Wine appeals to three senses: sight, smell and taste. This card is a guide to analysing its appeal and an *aide-mémoire* on each wine you taste. Tick one word for each factor in the left-hand column and any of the descriptive terms that fit your impressions. Then award points according to the pleasure the wine gives you.

SCORING   Total Score (out of 20)   16½

A tasting scorecard produced by Michael Broadbent and myself – but never a great success, because it tried to embody both descriptive and qualitative terms, and a scoring system. Many scorecard systems have been elaborated, most notably in California, where the Davis campus is the world headquarters of what it pleases them to call organoleptic evaluation. The high priests of the discipline have a long list of proscribed descriptive words which should be avoided because they are not sufficiently accurate, or are positively misleading. Unfortunately it includes most of my vinous vocabulary. The virtues of this card are that it helps you to analyse a wine methodically, reminding you of each aspect to think about in turn.

less agreeable but simple compound smell of grapes and fermentation, and in some cases barrel-wood; the smell we recognize as 'winey'. At its simplest, the better the wine, the more distinctive and characteristic this smell, and the more it attracts you to sniff again.

At this stage certain grape varieties declare themselves. The eight 'classics' all set a recognizable stamp on the smell of their wine. Age transmutes it from the primary smell tasters call the 'aroma' to a more complex, less definable and more rewarding smell. This scent of maturity is known, by analogy with the mixed scents of a posy of flowers, as the 'bouquet'.

The essence of a fine bouquet is that you can never put your finger on it. It seems to shift, perhaps from cedarwood to wax to honey to wildflowers to mushrooms. Mature Riesling, for example, can smell like lemons and petrol, Gewürztraminer like grapefruit, Chardonnay like butter – or rather, they can fleetingly remind you of these among many other things.

By the time the glass reaches your lips, then, you have already had answers, or at least clues, to most of the questions about wine: its overall quality, its age, perhaps its grape (and by deduction possibly its origin).

If all is well the taste will confirm the smell like the orchestra repeating the theme introduced by a soloist, adding the body of sound, the tonal colours that were missing. Only at this stage can you judge the balance of sweetness and acidity, the strength of the alcohol and whether it is counterpoised by the intensity of fruity flavours, and the quantity and quality of tannin.

Each wine has an appropriate combination of these elements; its quality is judged on whether they harmonize in a way that is both pleasant in itself and typical of its class. In fact, typical comes before pleasant. A young red wine may be disagreeably tannic and astringent; the taster's job is to judge it for the latent fruitiness that in time will combine with the tannins.

Different parts of your mouth pick up different facets of flavour. It is the tip of your tongue that recognizes sweetness, so sweetness is the first taste you become aware of. Acidity and saltiness are perceived by taste buds along the sides of your tongue and palate, bitterness by the soft back part of your tongue.

The tastes switch off in the same order: sugar after a mere two seconds or so; salt and acid after rather longer. Bitterness, which you notice last, lingers – a quality the Italians appreciate; many of their red wines (Valpolicella is an example) have a slightly bitter aftertaste.

Science can measure many (not all) of the chemical constituents that provide these sensations. It has identified more than 400 in wine up to now. But our perception of them is entirely personal. A few tasters, like a few musicians, may have 'perfect pitch', but most people probably have slight blind spots. Someone who takes three spoonfuls of sugar in coffee must have a high threshold of perception for sweetness. If you need to smother your food with salt you will hardly pick up the subtle touches of saltiness in wine.

Sweet, sour, salt and bitter in any case hardly start to express the variety of sensations that evolve in your mouth between sipping and swallowing. The moment of maximum flavour is when the wine reaches the soft palate and you start to swallow. Its vapour mounts directly to the olfactory nerves through the channels that link mouth and nose. At a serious tasting, where it is essential to spit the wine out to keep a clear head and stay the course, this moment can be maximized by holding a small quantity in the very back of the mouth and breathing in through it between slightly parted lips. The grimace and the gurgling are a small price to pay for the redoubled concentration of flavour achieved.

Red wines contain more or less tannin, the substance that turns hide to leather. Very tannic wine is so astringent (like walnut or broad-bean skins) that your mouth can begin to feel leathery and further tasting can be difficult. Tannin varies in taste and quality, too, from fully ripe, agreeable astringency, or the mouth-drying astringency of oak, to unripe green harshness.

Acids vary from harsh to delicately stimulating – not just in their concentration, or their power (measured in units of pH), but in their flavours. Of the wine acids malic is green-appley, citric is fresh and lemony, tartaric is harsh. Acetic is vinegary, lactic is mild, and succinic is a chemical cousin of glutamic acid. We owe much of the lipsmacking, appetizing taste of wine to tiny traces of succinic acid generated as a by-product of fermentation.

As for the alcohol itself, in low concentrations it merely has a faintly sweet taste, but at about 11% by volume it begins to give the mouth the characteristic feeling of winey warmth known as 'vinosity'. (Lighter wines, such as many German ones at 8–9%, lack this feeling.)

Add the ability of your tongue to differentiate between (more or less) fluid or viscous, to pronounce that one liquid feels like satin, and another like velvet, and the permutations begin to be impressive.

Finally, add the all-important element of persistence – how long the final flavour lasts. Really great wines have more to offer at the beginning, in the beauty of the bouquet, and at the end, in the way they haunt your breath for minutes after they have gone. Logical in all things, French scholars have even invented a measure of persistence; one second of flavour after swallowing is known as a 'caudalie'. According to one theory the hierarchy of the wines of Burgundy is in direct proportion to their caudalie-count.

Order of Tasting

In tasting wine, as in serving it at a dinner party, take care to organize a crescendo of flavour. Powerful strong-flavoured wines followed by lighter ones, however good, make the latter appear as pygmies. The conventions are to follow younger with older, lighter with heavier, drier with sweeter, and to put red after white. Bordeaux professionals, however, will often taste red before white. It is worth trying both methods.

BORDEAUX CHATEAUX INDEX

GENERAL INDEX

Indexer's Note: Wines and wine properties which share the same names are indexed together. Bordeaux châteaux are indexed separately: *see* pages 562–3.

ACKNOWLEDGEMENTS

Listed below are the names of the many people whose
assistance has been invaluable in writing this book, whether
their contribution was written, spoken or in their printed work,
and to whom I offer my special thanks. First among these I
count my tireless colleagues at Mitchell Beazley.

For their contribution to the preparation of the fourth edition:
Max Allen, Gregory Bowden, Christine Coletta, John Cossart,
Helen Dean, Michael Edwards, Jacqueline Friedrich, Monty
Friendship, Michael Fridjhon, Denis Gastin, Rosemary George
MW, Shirley Jones, Maxwell Laurie, Gareth Lawrence, Andreas
März, Richard Mayson, Maggie McNie MW, Adam Montefiore,
Jasper Morris MW, Angela Muir MW, Richard Neill, Sebastian
Payne MW, Judy Peterson-Nedry, Stuart Pigott, John Radford,
Howard Sherry, Stephen Skelton, Paul Strang, Marguerite
Thomas, Bob Thompson, Roger Voss, John Worontschak, Hilary
Wright, David Wrigley MW and Donald Ziraldo.

For their contribution to previous editions:
John Adams, Miranda Alexander, Richard Allen, Roddy Alvarado,
Dr. Hans Ambrosi, Burton Anderson, Colin Anderson MW,
Marquis d'Angerville, Marchese Dot. Piero Antinori, Gerald
Asher, Rafael Balào, David Balls, the late Martin Bamford MW,
Jean Barbet, Mr & Mrs Graham Barrett, Antony Barton, Lillian
Barton, the late Professor Dr. Becker, Diana Beevers, Christine
Behey Molines, Katie Benjce, Professor Harold Berg, Jean-
Claude Berrouet, Alexis Bespaloff, the late Tim Bleach, Jean-
Eugène Borie, Professor Roger Boulton, Gerald D. Boyd, the late
Gordon Brown, Ross Brown, Brigitte Brugnon, Donn Chappelet,
Tim Clarke, the late Michael Cliffe MW, Bruce Coleman, Deeta
Colvin, Professor James E. Cook, David Cossart MW, Alain de
Courseulles, Henry Damant, Jean Demolombe, Professor A.
Dinsmoor Webb, Beltran Domecq, Sarah Drake, Georges
Duboeuf, Jean-Henri Dubernet, Hubrecht Duijker, Terry
Dunleavy, Diana Durant, Evelyn Ellis, The English Vineyards
Association, Jorge Erasodis, Len Evans, Charles Eve MW, Pat Eve,
Food and Wine from France, Derrick Foster, Geoffrey Francom,
Fromm and Sichell Inc., Diane Furness, Janet Furze, André
Gagey, Rosemary George MW, the late Anthony Goldthorpe,
Claudie Gomme, Richard Goodman, Dick Graff, Marie Christine
Machard de Grammont, James Halliday, Robert Hardy, Peter
Hasslacher, John Hawes, Serge Hochar, Denis Horgan, Russel
Hone, the late Dr. G. Horney, Stephanie Horner, Jean Hugel, V.
Ishpekov, Gérard Jaboulet, Fiona Jamieson, Ian Jamieson, Alan
Johnson-Hill, Andrew Jones, A.N. Kasimatis, Tawfiq Khoury,
Mark Kliewer, Graham Knox, Matt Kramer, Professor Ralph E.
Kunkee, Anthony Lacey, Tony Laithwaite, Daniel Lawson, Scott
Levy, John Lipitch, Nina Lobanov, Catherine Manac'h, Tim
Marshall, Sarah Matthews, Pierre Maufoux, Richard Mayson,
Malcolm McIntyre, Jean Miailhe, Dr. Franz Werner Michel, Dr.
Eric Minaric, Janel Minore, Robert Mondavi, Christian Moueix,
Alain Mozés, Mario B. Neves, Professor Ann Noble, Barbara
Onderka, Richard O'Quinn, John Parkinson, David Peppercorn
MW, Mr J. Petridus, Professor Emile Peynaud, Andrew Pirie,
Q.E.D. Publishing, Jean Quénard, Alain and Sheila Querre,
David Rayment, Jan and Maite Read, Mrs. Belle Rhodes, Dr.
Bernard Rhodes, M. Jean Riére, Bertrand de Rivoyre, the late
Geoffrey Roberts, Michael Rothwell, Eric de Rothschild, André
Roux, Hamilton Russell, David Rutherford, Henry Ryman, Brian
St. Pierre, Jean-Pierre Saboye, Raymond le Sauvage, Mark
Savage, Walter Schug, Debbie Scott, Peter Sichel, Joanna Simon,
Professor Vernon L. Singleton, Cornelia Smith-Bauer, Kerry Brady
Stewart, Sue Style, Serena Sutcliffe MW, Michael Symington,
Michel Tesserson, David Thomas, M. Thomas, Bob and Harolyn
Thompson, Helen Thompson, Miguel and Marimar Torres, Dip.
Ing. Traxler, John and Janet Trefethen, Ugurlu Tunali, Michael
Vaughan, Michel Villedey, Peter Vinding-Diers, Richard Vine,
Jeremy Watson, Tony Willis, Grant Willoughby, James Earl
Wilson, Wines from Spain, Robin Yapp.